Amnestic Disorders
Amnestic Disorder Due to a General Medical
Condition
Substance-Induced Persisting Amnestic
Disorder
Amnestic Disorder NOS

Other Cognitive Disorders
Cognitive Disorder NOS

**Mental Disorders Due to a General Medical
Condition Not Elsewhere Classified**

Catatonic Disorder Due to a General Medical
Condition
Personality Change Due to a General Medical
Condition
Mental Disorder NOS Due to a General Medical
Condition

Substance-Related Disorders

Alcohol-Related Disorders
Alcohol Use Disorders
Alcohol-Induced Disorders

**Amphetamine (or Amphetamine-Like)–Related
Disorders**
Amphetamine Use Disorders
Amphetamine-Induced Disorders

Caffeine-Related Disorders
Caffeine-Induced Disorders

Cannabis-Related Disorders
Cannabis Use Disorders
Cannabis-Induced Disorders

Cocaine-Related Disorders
Cocaine Use Disorders
Cocaine-Induced Disorders

Hallucinogen-Related Disorders
Hallucinogen Use Disorders
Hallucinogen-Induced Disorders

Inhalant-Related Disorders
Inhalant Use Disorders
Inhalant-Induced Disorders

Nicotine-Related Disorders
Nicotine Use Disorder
Nicotine-Induced Disorder

Opioid-Related Disorders
Opioid Use Disorders
Opioid-Induced Disorders

**Phencyclidine (or Phencyclidine-Like)–Related
Disorders**
Phencyclidine Use Disorders
Phencyclidine-Induced Disorders

**Sedative-, Hypnotic-, or Anxiolytic-Related
Disorders**
Sedative, Hypnotic, or Anxiolytic Use
Disorders
Sedative-, Hypnotic-, or Anxiolytic-Induced
Disorders

**Other (or Unknown) Substance-Related
Disorders**
Other (or Unknown) Substance Use
Disorders
Other (or Unknown) Substance-Induced
Disorders

Schizophrenia and Other Psychotic Disorders

Schizophrenia
Paranoid Type
Disorganized Type
Catatonic Type
Undifferentiated Type
Residual Type
Schizophreniform Disorder
Schizoaffective Disorder
Delusional Disorder
Brief Psychotic Disorder
Shared Psychotic Disorder
Psychotic Disorder Due to a General Medical
Condition
Substance-Induced Psychotic Disorder
Psychotic Disorder NOS

Mood Disorders

Depressive Disorders
Major Depressive Disorder
Dysthymic Disorder
Depressive Disorder NOS

Bipolar Disorders
Bipolar I Disorder
Bipolar II Disorder
Cyclothymic Disorder
Bipolar Disorder NOS

Other Mood Disorders
Mood Disorder Due to a General Medical
Condition
Substance-Induced Mood Disorder
Mood Disorder NOS

(Continued on inside back cover)

ABNORMAL PSYCHOLOGY

EIGHT EDITION

ABNORMAL PSYCHOLOGY
CURRENT PERSPECTIVES

LAUREN B. ALLOY
Temple University

NEIL S. JACOBSON
University of Washington

JOAN ACOCELLA

McGraw-Hill
College

Boston   Burr Ridge, IL   Dubuque, IA   Madison, WI   New York   San Francisco   St. Louis
Bangkok   Bogotá   Caracas   Lisbon   London   Madrid
Mexico City   Milan   New Delhi   Seoul   Singapore   Sydney   Taipei   Toronto

McGraw-Hill College

A Division of The **McGraw-Hill** Companies

ABNORMAL PSYCHOLOGY: CURRENT PERSPECTIVES, EIGHTH EDITION

 This book is printed on acid-free paper.

1 2 3 4 5 6 7 8 9 0 VNH/VNH 9 3 2 1 0 9 8

ISBN 0–07–292838–7

Editorial director: *Jane E. Vaicunas*
Senior sponsoring editor: *Joseph Terry*
Senior developmental editor: *Meera Dash*
Editorial assistant: *Kristen Mellitt*
Senior marketing manager: *James Rozsa*
Senior project manager: *Gloria G. Schiesl*
Senior production supervisor: *Mary E. Haas*
Coordinator of freelance design: *Michelle D. Whitaker*
Photo research coordinator: *John C. Leland*
Supplement coordinator: *Rita Hingtgen*
Compositor: *GTS Graphics, Inc.*
Typeface: *10/12 Sabon*
Printer: *Von Hoffmann Press, Inc.*

Freelance interior/cover designer: *Maureen McCutcheon*
Cover image: *Dream Motion (Traumerisch Regung), 1923 Vasily Kandinsky; Photograph by David Heald. © The Solomon R. Gugenheim Foundation, NY (FN 38.258); © 1998 Artists Rights Society (ARS), New York/ADAGP, Paris*

The credits section for this book begins on page 637 and is considered an extension of the copyright page.

Library of Congress Cataloging-in-Publication Data

Alloy, Lauren B.
   Abnormal psychology : current perspectives / Lauren B. Alloy, Neil
S. Jacobson, Joan Acocella. — 8th ed.
      p. cm.
   Includes bibliographical references and index.
   ISBN 0–07–292838–7. — ISBN 0–07–115653–4 (ISE)
   1. Psychology, Pathological.   I. Jacobson, Neil S., 1949– .
   II. Acocella, Joan Ross.   III. Title.
   RC454.B577   1999
   6 16.89—dc21   98–4014
                                      CIP

www.mhhe.com

About the Authors

LAUREN B. ALLOY

Lauren B. Alloy is an internationally recognized researcher in the area of mood disorders. Her work on depression has had a major impact on the fields of clinical, personality, social, and cognitive psychology. She is currently Professor of Psychology at Temple University. Previously, at Northwestern University, she became the youngest professor in the university's history and the first woman to become professor in the Northwestern Psychology department. She received both her B.A. and Ph.D. in psychology from the University of Pennsylvania. Dr. Alloy was awarded the American Psychological Association's Young Psychologist Award at the XXIII International Congress of Psychology in 1984 and the Northwestern University College of Arts & Sciences Great Teacher Award in 1988 for her classroom teaching and mentoring of students. She is a Fellow of the American Psychological Association and American Psychological Society. Dr. Alloy is the author of more than 85 scholarly publications, including her 1988 book *Cognitive Processes in Depression*. She has served on the editorial boards of the *Journal of Abnormal Psychology, Journal of Personality and Social Psychology,* and *Cognitive Therapy and Research;* she is the editor of the *Springer-Verlag Series on Psychopathology;* and she has served as guest editor for *Cognitive Therapy and Research* and the *Journal of Abnormal Psychology.* She regularly teaches courses on psychopathology.

Dr. Alloy's research focuses on cognitive, interpersonal, and psychosocial processes in the onset and maintenance of depression and bipolar disorder. Along with her colleagues, Lyn Abramson and Gerald Metalsky, she is the author of the hopelessness theory of depression, and she discovered, with Lyn Abramson, the "sadder but wiser," or "depressive realism," effect. In her leisure time, she enjoys sports, the theater, and good restaurants, and she is a movie fanatic. But, most of all, she loves being with her husband, Daniel, and daughter, Adrienne.

NEIL S. JACOBSON

Neil S. Jacobson has published more than 200 books and articles on marital and couple therapy, domestic violence, depression, and related topics, including *Clinical Handbook of Couple Therapy* and *Marital Therapy.* His more recent books include *Integrative Couple Therapy,* with Andrew Christensen, and *When Men Batter Women: New Insights into Ending Abusive Relationships,* with John Gottman. Dr. Jacobson received his Ph.D. in psychology from the University of North Carolina. He is currently a professor at the University of Washington. Dr. Jacobson has received numerous grants and research awards, including the MERIT Award and the Research Scientist Award from the National Institute of Health. The American Association for Marriage and Family Therapy and the American Family Therapy Academy have also honored him for his distinguished lifetime contributions to family therapy research. Dr. Jacobson is past president of the Association for the Advancement of Behavior Therapy and the American Psychological Association's Society for a Scientific Clinical Psychology.

JOAN ACOCELLA

Joan Acocella is a New York–based writer. A co-author of *Abnormal Psychology: Current Perspectives* since its second edition in 1977, she has contributed to a number of textbooks in the social sciences. Dr. Acocella received her Ph.D. from Rutgers, The State University. She has served as an editor for psychiatric writings and currently writes on the arts. She is a regular contributor to *The New Yorker* magazine and other publications.

Contents in Brief

Contents

Part One   INTRODUCTION TO ABNORMAL PSYCHOLOGY

Part Two   THEORETICAL PERSPECTIVES

List of Boxes

Preface

Abnormal is a relative term, the meaning of which has changed over the centuries. We hope that the eighth edition of *Abnormal Psychology: Current Perspectives* will make students of the abnormal psychology course not only more knowledgeable but also more understanding. In describing what we know so far about why people act as they do, we have attempted to present this complex subject from a human perspective. We offer a balanced approach to the standards by which *abnormality* is defined and the causal theories of the disorders. We intend for this approach to impress on the student the dynamic character of the field: its openness to dispute, to movement, and to change.

The theme of the eighth edition is *integration*. We have completely integrated the therapies into the discussions of the disorders in their chapters. All other changes flow from this integration and build on the strengths of the textbook.

Highlights of the Revision

To make the book more manageable for the course, we have reduced the number of chapters from 22 to 19. We have consolidated 3 chapters on the theoretical perspectives into 2, because we felt that we could provide the theoretical grounding more succinctly. We have reorganized these chapters by the orientation of the perspectives to the self. (Though these are somewhat simplified categories, biological, psychodynamic, and cognitive perspectives can be said to deal with issues "inside the self," while behavioral, family systems, and sociocultural perspectives address issues "outside the self.") Within this framework we discuss the diathesis-stress model, which reflects the current thinking of most researchers. We've chosen not to discuss the humanistic perspective, which is less used in psychopathology research today. More attention has been given to the biological, cognitive, behavioral, and family systems perspectives. We have combined what were two chapters on schizophrenia. We have also kept pace with developments in the field by devoting new chapters to "antisocial

and violent behavior" and "prevention and social change."

Every chapter is significantly updated. The integration of therapies into every disorders chapter has resulted in a more cogent discussion of the disorders, their causes, and their therapies. The therapies are presented within the context of the theoretical perspectives, under the heading "Theory and Therapy." Each disorder chapter also includes new "Groups at Risk" sections, which discuss differences in prevalence by gender, race, socioeconomic status, and other forms of diversity. And we've doubled the number of cases and added several new boxes. Other significant changes include, but are not limited to, the following:

Chapter 1: Abnormal Behavior: Historical Perspectives

- A new section on relating abnormal behavior to groups deals with cultural, ethnic, and gender diversity and establishes a groups-at-risk framework for the rest of the book.

- A new section discusses the community mental health movement.

- A new section on non-Western approaches discusses African and Asian views of abnormal behavior.

Chapter 2: Diagnosis and Assessment

- This chapter appears earlier in the table of contents, in direct response to reviewers' comments.

- A new case, including actual psychological assessment, is featured in eight boxes using the tools of diagnosis and assessment discussed in the chapter.

- New material has been added on the mental status exam and psychophysiological assessment.

- More evaluation of *DSM-IV* has been added, including a new section on cultural bias in assessment.

Chapter 3: Research Methods in Abnormal Psychology

- This chapter appears earlier, in response to reviewers' comments.
- A new section discusses hypothesis generation.
- New boxes highlight treatment development, the correlation coefficient, and the case study.

Chapter 4: The Biological, Psychodynamic, and Cognitive Perspectives

- Regrouping of theoretical perspectives focuses on "inside the self" orientation to theory and therapy.
- New material on biological theories and therapies includes genetic studies—including family, twin, and molecular genetics advances—as well as neurotransmitter receptor up and down regulation, and drug treatment.
- A new section on the attachment theories of Ainsworth and Bowlby highlights recent research on the importance of disturbed parent-child bonds to psychodynamic theory.

Chapter 5: The Behavioral, Family Systems, and Sociocultural Perspectives

- Regrouping of perspectives focuses on "outside the self" orientation to theory and therapy.
- New material on family and couples therapy has been added, and the family systems perspective replaces the interpersonal perspective.
- A new section on integrating the perspectives uses the diathesis-stress model to provide a current way of synthesizing the traditional theories.

Chapter 6: Anxiety Disorders

- The discussion of cued vs. uncued panic attacks has been revised.
- New material has been added on acute stress disorder; attributions, social support, and posttraumatic stress disorder (PTSD); attachment theory and cognitive theory of panic disorder; biochemical theory of panic disorder, including the "suffocation false alarm hypothesis"; and neurotransmitter research on social phobia and PTSD.
- New genetic research for anxiety disorders is included.

- Coverage of therapies includes the role of social support in PTSD, psychodynamic treatment and cognitive therapy for panic disorder, drug treatments, and combined drug therapy and psychotherapy.

Chapter 7: Dissociative and Somatoform Disorders

- More distinction is made between organic and dissociative amnesia.
- A new section discusses somatoform pain disorder.
- New material has been added on problems in diagnosing dissociative identity disorder; serotonin functioning in depersonalization and body dysmorphic disorders; and body dysmorphic disorder, including developmental risk factors and the relationship with depression and obsessive-compulsive disorder.
- A new biological hypothesis of dissociative amnesia featuring the role of the hippocampus and stress-induced changes in neurotransmitters is presented.
- Coverage of therapy has been expanded, with psychodynamic treatments for dissociative disorders, drug treatment for dissociative and somatoform disorders, and behavioral and cognitive therapies for body dysmorphic disorder and pain disorder.

Chapter 8: Psychological Stress and Physical Disorders

- A new section on coronary heart disease has been added.
- New research has been added on the roles of marital status, health benefits, and cognitive-behavioral stress-management intervention in disease and rehabilitation.
- New material includes the effects of stress on risk-preventing behaviors; Type A behavior, hostility, and heart disease; stress and hypertension; and emotional inhibition and stress-related disorders.

Chapter 9: Mood Disorders

- More distinction is made between bipolar and unipolar disorder.
- New material has been added on the course of major depression, the continuity hypothesis, early vs. late onset of depression, life stress and bipolar disorder, the role of the family in

teenage suicide, behavioral and cognitive therapies and genetic research for depression, and drug treatment for depression and mania.

- Statistics on suicide have been updated.

- New research updates the presentation of the hopelessness theory, Beck's theory of depression, and seasonal affective disorder.

- The biological perspective includes a new biochemical theory of depression involving a gene that affects neuronal growth and atrophy in the hippocampus.

Chapter 10: Personality Disorders

- For greater clarity, disorders are grouped by *DSM-IV* clusters.

- Antisocial personality disorder has been moved to Chapter 17, allowing for fuller coverage of every personality disorder.

- New information has been added on estimated prevalence rates and the dispute over gender bias.

Chapter 11: Substance-Use Disorders

- New research has been added on relapse prevention and the matching programs of Alcoholics Anonymous.

- The section on nicotine dependence has been expanded to include recent legal action against the tobacco industry.

- Coverage of therapy includes new information on such areas as self-care, behavioral couples therapy, and family systems therapy.

Chapter 12: Sexual Dysfunction, Paraphilias, and Gender Identity Disorders

- Regrouping of disorders distinguishes sexual dysfunctions, paraphilias, and gender identity disorders more clearly.

- Discussion of therapies for sexual dysfunction now includes cognitive-behavioral direct treatment and experimental medications such as sildenifil and apomorphine for sexual dysfunctions.

- The section on gender identity disorders has been completely rewritten to reflect a more current view of gender dysphoria and gender reassignment.

Chapter 13: Schizophrenia and Delusional Disorder

- Two previous chapters have been combined into one.

- New material has been added on loosening of associations, schizophrenics' inability to process context information, the relationship between hallucinations and difficulty with reality monitoring, suicide in schizophrenia, and disorganized-nondisorganized dimension.

- New information has been added on the genetics of schizophrenia, brain-imaging studies, prenatal brain injury, the viral hypothesis, the role of neurotransmitters and the dopamine hypothesis, and attention and memory deficits in schizophrenia.

- Discussion of therapies includes new sections on pharmacotherapy, cognitive therapy, and assertive community therapy, as well as new material on family therapy and social-skills training for schizophrenia.

Chapter 14: Neuropsychological Disorders

- The "Problems in Diagnosis" section has been reorganized to clarify the distinctions among delirium, specific cognitive disorders, and dementias, as described in *DSM-IV*.

- A new section on specific cognitive disorders identifies the common symptoms of brain injury.

- New sections discuss current research on mad cow disease and Lewy body disease.

- New material emphasizes the impact of HIV on brain infection.

- The terminology and therapies have been thoroughly revised and updated, especially in the areas of brain trauma and infection.

Chapter 15: Disorders of Childhood and Adolescence

- Discussion of eating disorders has been expanded to include childhood obesity and groups at risk for anorexia and bulimia.

- Sleep disorders and communication and learning disorders have been regrouped for clearer presentation.

- New therapies include cognitive strategies such as the STOP technique for childhood anxiety.

Chapter 16: Mental Retardation and Autism

- The section on the prenatal environment has been expanded and updated.
- New research has been added on the relationship between mental retardation and risk for other disorders.
- Statistics have been updated on levels of mental retardation and the prevalence of Down syndrome, phenylketonuria, fetal alcohol syndrome, and autism.
- The section on neurological research and the cognitive perspective on autism has been expanded.
- New sections on community integration and quality of life broaden the discussion of social programs aimed at mental retardation.

Chapter 17: Antisocial and Violent Behavior

- This new chapter covers rape, domestic violence, and antisocial personality disorder.
- An entirely new section on domestic violence explores the types of batterers, emotional abuse, the role of alcohol abuse, and the impact on relationships.
- A new box discusses the behaviors of serial killers.

Chapter 18: Legal Issues in Abnormal Psychology

- Information on the definition of *legal insanity* has been updated.
- New material has been added on the standards of dangerous behavior.
- New information has been added on the role of the courts in backing mental health professionals.

Chapter 19: Prevention and Social Change

- This new chapter highlights the history of and issues in prevention.
- Prevention is analyzed in the context of social change.
- Specific programs, such as FAST Track and the Penn Optimism Project, are evaluated.

Pedagogy

In addition to a well-developed internal structure, each chapter has several features that help students to master the material:

- A chapter outline offers a concise overview of the chapter.
- Case studies help to illustrate and humanize the disorders. Because of the importance of cases in mastering the material, we've doubled the number of cases in this edition and presented most of the new ones in the disorders chapters. The cases are drawn from various contemporary and historical sources and are easily identifiable at the start of a chapter or in salmon-colored boxes within the chapters.
- Boxes highlight high-interest topics and unresolved issues. From 1 to 4 boxes appear in every chapter. This edition includes 14 new boxes, plus 8 special boxes that illustrate psychological assessment in a particular case study in Chapter 2 on diagnosis and assessment. Any boxes that are not new have been updated or revised for this edition. Examples of the boxes include "Western and Non-Western Culture-Bound Syndromes," in Chapter 1 (new); "Persian Gulf War Syndrome," in Chapter 6 (new); "Recovered Memory of Child Abuse: A Modern Dilemma," in Chapter 7; "Recognizing Learning Disorders: Some Signs," in Chapter 15 (new); "Serial Killers," in Chapter 17 (new); and "Evolution, Misfortune, and Criminal Responsibility," in Chapter 18 (new).
- Key terms appear in boldface type in the text, in a list at the end of each chapter, and in an end-of-book glossary.
- A chapter summary is organized around the main sections in each chapter.

Supplements

The supplements listed here can accompany *Abnormal Psychology: Current Perspectives*, eighth edition. Please contact your local McGraw-Hill representative for details concerning policies, prices, and availability, as some restrictions may apply.

Casebook in Abnormal Psychology (0-07-303473-8) was written by John Vitkus of Medical College of Ohio. The casebook features 14 case studies from various mental health professionals. The cases cover a broad range of disorders and therapies. This casebook is shrinkwrapped with the textbook and sold separately.

The *Student Study Guide* (0-07-303469-X) was prepared by Gary Bothe and Susan Jones Bothe of

Pensacola Junior College. Each chapter of the study guide begins with a list of learning objectives, followed by key terms and important names. A guided self-study helps students to learn the information in the chapter, and multiple-choice practice tests enable them to assess their understanding of the material. A "Helpful Hints" section provides general studying tips and assists students with the chapter's most difficult concepts. An answer key, complete with feedback for all multiple-choice items, is also included.

The *Instructor's Manual* (0-07-303462-2) was prepared by Gregory Cutler of Bay de Noc Community College. Each chapter of the manual provides many ideas for lectures, demonstrations, activities, and classroom assessment techniques, as well as a "Talking Points" feature intended to stimulate class discussion. Learning objectives that correspond with the study guide and the test bank, as well as lists of relevant films and videos, are also included.

The *Test Bank* (0-07-303463-0) was prepared by Gary Bothe and Susan Jones Bothe of Pensacola Junior College, who also prepared the study guide. The consistency between the test bank and study guide has been improved for this edition. The test bank contains nearly 2,000 multiple-choice items and essay questions, classified by cognitive type and level of difficulty. Items that test knowledge of material in the textbook's boxes are indicated for easy reference as well.

Computerized Test Banks, available in Windows (0-07-303468-1) and Macintosh (0-07-303467-3) formats, make the items from the test bank easily available to instructors. MicroTest III, a powerful but easy-to-use test-generating program by Chariot Software Group, facilitates the selection of questions from the test bank and the printing of tests and answer keys. Instructors can customize questions, headings, and instructions and add or import their own questions.

Overhead Transparencies (0-07-303470-3) include full-color art from the book on overhead transparency acetates, to facilitate classroom presentation.

PowerPoint Slides (0-07-365921-5) enhance lectures and classroom presentation of material using bulleted text and art from the book.

Presentation Manager CD (0-07-365920-7) consolidates teaching and visual resources that support the book. Instructors can use this CD to enhance lectures and classroom presentation of material in the book for their abnormal psychology course.

Videos that can support the textbook in class include *DSM-IV Clinical Vignettes*, *The World of Abnormal Psychology*, and *The Brain*. Consult your McGraw-Hill sales representative for details.

Movies and Mental Illness (0-07-068990-3) was written by Danny Wedding, of the Missouri Institute of Mental Health, and Mary Ann Boyd, of Southern Illinois University at Edwardsville. *Movies and Mental Illness* discusses films that depict characters with various mental disorders, mental health professionals, and methods of treatment. The book portrays movies both as tools to help students understand abnormal behavior and as barriers to educating students accurately about mental illness. It is sold separately from the textbook. Each chapter of the instructor's manual of *Abnormal Psychology: Current Perspectives* helps instructors to integrate *Movies and Mental Illness* into their abnormal psychology course.

Acknowledgments

We have consulted several experts to ensure that *Abnormal Psychology: Current Perspectives* continues to represent the most current scholarship, coverage, and thinking in the field. The following people provided in-depth guidance early in the development of the chapters in their specialties.

Richard Carroll, Assistant Professor of Psychiatry and Psychology at Northwestern University Medical School, is a specialist in sexual disorders. He assisted with the chapter on sexual dysfunctions, paraphilias, and gender identity disorders.

Andrew R. Eisen, Associate Professor of Psychology at Fairleigh Dickinson University, is a specialist in child and adolescent anxiety disorders. He assisted with the chapter on disorders of childhood and adolescence.

Jennifer Haythornthwaite, Associate Professor of Psychiatry and Behavioral Sciences at The Johns Hopkins School of Medicine, is a specialist in behavioral medicine. She assisted with the chapter on psychological stress and physical disorders.

Christopher Kearney, Associate Professor of Psychology at the University of Nevada–Las Vegas, is a specialist in child behavior disorders and developmental disabilities. He assisted with the chapter on mental retardation and autism.

Howard Ulan, an attorney for the Pennsylvania Department of Public Welfare who also holds a Ph.D. in psychology, is a specialist in mental health and disability law. He assisted with the chapter on legal issues in abnormal psychology.

Thomas Widiger, Professor of Psychology at the University of Kentucky, is a specialist in diagnosis and the personality disorders. He assisted with the chapter on personality disorders.

We also express our thanks for the many useful comments and suggestions provided by the following reviewers: **Sheree Barron,** Georgia College; **JoAnne Brewster,** James Madison University; **Rolf W. Daniel,** St. Francis College; **Mary Dozier,** University of Delaware; and **Christopher Kilmartin,** Mary Washington College. **David Dunner,** University of Washington Medical Center, provided additional expertise in advising us on the sections describing biological theories and therapies.

We thank the staff of McGraw Hill—Joseph Terry, Kristen Mellitt, Gloria Schiesl, and above all our editor, Meera Dash—for their help. We appreciate the additional attention of Richard Mickey, Betty Morgan, Meg Muckenhoupt, and Debbie Sosin. Lauren Alloy also thanks her research assistants Allison Enke, Scott Safford, Robert Wheeler, and Lin Zhu for their invaluable help.

Lauren B. Alloy
Neil S. Jacobson
Joan Acocella

Part One | INTRODUCTION TO ABNORMAL PSYCHOLOGY

Chapter 1

Before we can begin a study of abnormal psychology, we need to think about what kind of behavior deserves to be called "abnormal." Consider the following examples:

1. A woman becomes seriously depressed after her husband's death. She has difficulty sleeping and loses her appetite. Does she have a psychological disorder or is this just a case of normal grieving?

2. A young man tries to force his date to have sexual intercourse, even though she says no and resists him physically. Is this evidence of psychological disturbance, or is it just a crime?

3. A man will not use airplanes for long-distance travel. He insists that his family take trains on vacations. Should we call this abnormal or just unusual and inconvenient?

4. A young woman occasionally indulges in binge eating, after which she forces herself to vomit. Does she have a psychological disorder, or is she just responding to the society's unreasonable standards for body weight?

5. A teenaged girl in Africa makes cuts in her arms and face in order to produce decorative scars. Is this pathological self-mutilation, or is it a normal practice of the girl's culture?

Abnormal Behavior and Society

Defining Abnormal Behavior

When we ask how a society defines psychological abnormality, we are asking, first, where that society draws the line between acceptable and unacceptable behavior and, second, which unacceptable behaviors the society views as evidence of "disorder" rather than simply as undesirable characteristics. The most common standard for answering these questions is the society's norms.

Norm Violation   Every human group lives by a set of norms—rules that tell us what it is "right" and "wrong" to do and when, where, and with whom. Such rules circumscribe every aspect of our existence.

Consider, for example, the matter of "personal space," the distance people like to maintain between themselves and those around them. This is something that is taken for granted by people within a culture, but it differs widely between cultures. In North America, when two people who do not know one another well are conversing, they stand about 3 feet apart, but in South America they stand much closer, and in Asia much farther apart. In one study, Japanese, American, and Venezuelan students were asked to

From culture to culture, definitions of normal and abnormal behavior vary. While this Kikuyu woman's dress is traditional in Kenya, a woman dressed in this fashion in the United States might be considered to be violating societal norms.

have a 5-minute conversation with a stranger of the same nationality. The Japanese sat about 40 inches apart; the Americans, 35 inches; the Venezuelans, 32 inches (Sussman & Rosenfeld, 1982). Arabs come even closer. According to Edward Hall (1976), the primary investigator of personal space,

> When standing on a street corner, an Arab may shove you aside if he wants to be where you are. . . . Years ago, American women in Beirut had to give up using streetcars. Their bodies were the property of all men within reach. What was happening is even reflected in the language. The Arabs have no word for trespass. (p. 66)

We judge others according to how well they conform to our norms. People who stand too close to us may seem pushy; people who stand too far away may seem cold. While we may shrug off such social oddities, psychological professionals do not. (In marriage counseling, the therapist pays careful attention to how close the couple sits to one another). In other words, norm violation tends to be viewed, in varying degrees, as abnormal. In the examples given at the beginning of this chapter, numbers 2 and 3 involve norm violation. In our culture, men are not supposed to force women to have sex, and we expect people traveling long distances to take planes. Example 5 involves conformity to the norms of an African culture, but, if someone in the United States were to engage in this behavior, it would probably be viewed as norm violation.

In small, highly integrated cultures, disagreement over norms is rare. In a large, complex society, on the other hand, there may be serious conflicts over norms. For example, the gay liberation movement can be conceptualized as the effort of one group to persuade the society as a whole to adjust its norms so that homosexuality will fall inside rather than outside the limits of acceptability.

Because norms are so variable, norm violation may seem a weak basis for judging mental health. It can also seem an oppressive standard, one that enthrones conformity as the ideal pattern of behavior. Nevertheless, norms remain a very important criterion for defining abnormality. Though they may be relative, they are so deeply ingrained that they seem absolute; therefore, anyone who violates them seems abnormal.

Norms, however, are not the only standard for defining abnormal behavior. Other criteria are statistical rarity, personal discomfort, and maladaptive behavior.

Statistical Rarity   From a statistical point of view, abnormality is any substantial deviation from a statistically calculated average. Those who fall within the "golden mean"—those who do what most other people do—are normal, while those whose behavior differs from that of the majority are abnormal. This criterion is used in some evaluations of psychological abnormality. The diagnosis of mental retardation, for instance, is based in large part on statistical accounting. Those whose tested intelligence falls below an average range for the population, and who also have problems coping with life, are labeled "mentally retarded" (see Figure 1.1).

The statistical-rarity approach makes defining abnormality a simple task. One has only to measure a person's performance against the average performance. If it falls outside the average range, it is abnormal. There are obvious difficulties with this approach, however. As we saw earlier, the norm-violation approach can be criticized for exalting the shifting values of social groups, yet the major weakness of the statistical-rarity approach is that it has *no* values—it makes no distinction between desirable and undesirable rarities. Such a point of view is potentially dangerous. For example, not only mentally retarded people but also geniuses—and particularly geniuses with new ideas—might be considered candidates for psychological treatment.

Personal Discomfort   Another criterion for defining abnormality is personal discomfort: if people are content with their lives, then they are of no concern to the mental health establishment. If, on the other hand, people are distressed over their thoughts or behavior—as the grieving widow mentioned at the beginning of this chapter might be—then they require treatment.

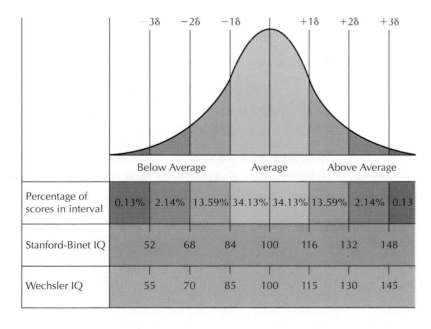

FIGURE 1.1   The distribution of IQ scores in the United States. More than 68 percent of the population scores between 84 and 116 points. Using the statistical approach to abnormality, diagnosticians designate as mentally retarded those falling below approximately 68 points. As the figure indicates, this group is statistically rare, representing only about 2 percent of the population.

	-3δ	-2δ	-1δ		$+1\delta$	$+2\delta$	$+3\delta$
		Below Average		Average		Above Average	
Percentage of scores in interval	0.13%	2.14%	13.59%	34.13%	34.13%	13.59%	2.14%	0.13
Stanford-Binet IQ		52	68	84	100	116	132	148
Wechsler IQ		55	70	85	100	115	130	145

This is a more liberal approach than the two we just discussed, in that it makes people the judges of their own normality, rather than subjecting them to the judgment of the society or diagnostician. And this is the approach that is probably the most widely used in the case of the less severe psychological disorders. Most people in psychotherapy are there not because anyone has declared their behavior abnormal but because they themselves are unhappy.

Reasonable as it may be in such cases, the personal-discomfort criterion has an obvious weakness in that it gives us no standard for evaluating the behavior itself. This is especially problematic in the case of behaviors that cause harm. Is teenage drug addiction to be classified as abnormal only if the teenager is unhappy with the addiction? Furthermore, even if a behavior pattern is not harmful, it may still seem to require psychological attention. People who believe that their brains are receiving messages from outer space may inflict no pain on others, yet most mental health professionals would consider them in need of treatment.

Maladaptive Behavior   A fourth criterion for defining a behavior as abnormal is whether it is maladaptive. Here the question is whether a person, given that behavior pattern, is able to meet the demands of his or her life—hold down a job, deal with friends and family, pay the bills on time, and the like. If not, the pattern is abnormal. This standard overlaps somewhat with that of norm violation. After all, many norms are rules for adapting our behavior to our society's requirements. (To arrive for work drunk is to violate a norm; it is also maladaptive, in that it may get you fired.) At the same time, the maladaptiveness standard is unique in that it concentrates on the practical matter of getting through life successfully. If the man with the fear of flying has a job that requires long-distance travel, his behavior (avoiding air travel) could be considered maladaptive.

This practicality makes the maladaptiveness standard a useful one. Also, many professionals favor the maladaptiveness standard for its elasticity: because it focuses on behavior *relative to life circumstances*, it can accommodate many different styles of living. But, as with the personal-discomfort criterion, this liberalism is purchased at the cost of values. Are there not certain circumstances to which people should *not* adapt? Of course, any responsible professional using the maladaptiveness standard would also assess the situation to which the person is failing to adapt. If a child whose parents leave her alone in the house at night is brought to a therapist with sleeping problems, the therapist is likely to direct treatment at the parents rather than at the child. Nevertheless, the

Whether a behavior is maladaptive is one of the criteria for defining abnormality. Many people, like those pictured here, gamble occasionally for fun. However, if someone's gambling leads to unmanageable debt and neglect of family and friends, it could be viewed as maladaptive.

maladaptiveness standard, like the norm-violation standard, raises the possibility of bias in favor of "fitting in."

A Combined Standard   The questions raised by these criteria for defining abnormality can be summarized as one question: should our standard be *facts*, such as statistical rarity or a clearly dysfunctional behavior (e.g., failure to eat), or should it be *values*, such as adaptation or adherence to norms? Many professionals feel that the question cannot be decided one way or the other but that the definition of *mental disorder* must rest on both facts and values. Jerome Wakefield (1992), for example, has proposed that mental disorder

lies on the boundary between the given natural world and the constructed social world; a disorder exists when the failure of a person's internal mechanisms to perform their functions as designed by nature impinges harmfully on the person's well-being as defined by social values. (p. 373)

People diagnosed as schizophrenic, for example, often cannot think or speak coherently. To use Wakefield's terms, their "internal mechanisms" are failing to perform "their functions as designed by nature." And these disabilities in turn impinge on their "well-being as defined by social values"—for instance, their ability to hold down a job or raise children. As we shall see, the current edition of the *Diagnostic and Statistical Manual of Mental Disorders,* the American Psychiatric Association's guidebook to identifying mental disorders, also rests on a combined standard of facts and values.

However much dispute surrounds the definition of abnormal behavior, it should be kept in mind that most societies identify the same *categories* of behavior as indicative of mental disorder. As Maher and Maher (1985) point out, there are four basic categories:

1. Behavior that is harmful to the self or that is harmful to others without serving the interests of the self
2. Poor reality contact—for example, beliefs that most people do not hold or sensory perceptions of things that most people do not perceive
3. Emotional reactions inappropriate to the person's situation
4. Erratic behavior—that is, behavior that shifts unpredictably

Relating Abnormal Behavior to Groups

The process of defining abnormality becomes more complex when we factor in differences among groups. Even in one small neighborhood—in Los Angeles, say—psychological disturbance affects the men and the women, the teenagers and the old people, the Korean Americans, the African Americans, and the European Americans in different ways. First, as revealed by epidemiology (to be discussed in Chapter 3), the study of the distribution of disorders within populations, various groups are at greater and lesser risk for specific disorders. Second, groups differ in how they experience and express psychological disorders. Finally, because groups vary in their norms, behavior that seems unremarkable to one group may appear bizarre to another, and this can affect diagnosis, the process by which abnormal behavior is identified and classified.

In the chapters that deal with specific disorders, we will discuss these matters under the heading "Groups at Risk." As you will see, there are many

TABLE 1.1	Lifetime Prevalence Rates per 100 for Major Depression, Based on Community Surveys
Place	**Rate**
United States	4.4
Edmonton, Canada	8.6
Puerto Rico	4.6
Seoul, Korea	3.4
Taiwan	
Urban areas	0.9
Small towns	1.7
Rural villages	1.0
New Zealand	12.6

Adapted from Smith & Weissman, 1992, p. 118.

kinds of groups—defined by gender, age, cultural and ethnic origin, social class, religion, place of residence (urban or rural), and other factors—that are differently affected. For the moment, we will focus on groups defined by ethnicity and gender.

Cultural and Ethnic Group Differences Depression offers a good illustration of the fact that psychological disorders strike different cultures at different rates. Look at Table 1.1. In the United States, the lifetime prevalence rate for major depression is more than four times the rate in Taiwanese villages. In turn, the rate in New Zealand is almost triple the U.S. rate. Within a society, as well, risk varies according to ethnic origin. In the United States, suicide, which is often the outcome of major depression, is almost twice as common among whites as among blacks (U.S. Bureau of the Census, 1990).

Different cultural groups also have their own ways of experiencing and managing psychological distress. Richard Castillo, in his book *Culture and Mental Illness,* offers this case of an American-style depression:

During his medical training, Bill experienced a four-month depression following the death of his father. He saw a psychiatrist, was put on antidepressant medication, and recovered. He graduated from medical school with honors, married, and soon became a successful pediatrician. Then, when he was 35, his wife was diagnosed with liver cancer. Watching her die, and wondering how he would raise their two daughters (aged 2 and 4) without her, he again succumbed to depression and had to be hospitalized for a month. Later he remarried and was happy for a while, until his new wife demanded an "open marriage." A divorce followed, but his ex-wife went on living in the same town as Bill. One night, after seeing her with another man at a restaurant, Bill got drunk, drove to her apartment, and banged on the door, demanding to speak to her. She called the police, and he was arrested. This scandal plunged him into another depression. He was hospitalized and given drugs and electroshock treatment. Upon his release, he was informed that the state medical board had decided to suspend his license because of his mental illness. When he appealed the board's decision, the story was picked up by the local newspapers and television, so that all his personal troubles were broadcast to the community. Bill won his appeal, but, two weeks later, at age 45, he committed suicide. (Adapted from Castillo, 1997, pp. 25–26.)

By way of contrast, Castillo tells the story of a man he interviewed in India, a clothing merchant named Mr. Sinha. Mr. Sinha had a disorder that in India is known as "dhat syndrome" and that is said to be caused by excessive loss of semen. Its symptoms are fatigue, body aches, sadness, anxiety, loss of appetite, insomnia, and suicidal feelings. That pattern is what we in the West call major depression. But Mr. Sinha, like other Indians, called it dhat syndrome, and he believed it was due to his having masturbated too much as a teenager. He explained this to Castillo:

During my high school days I was—well—I will put all the facts very open before you. I was in the acute habit of masturbation. . . . All the time I used to be indulged in sexual feelings—thinking about that. Always, you can say, daydreaming—doing masturbation. *Extremely.* So all this made me very weak, much more weak mentally than physically. And I connect the causes of the mental illness with that. (Castillo, 1997, p. 29)

In Bill and Mr. Sinha, both of whom probably had the same disorder, we can see how culture shapes psychological disturbance. To begin with, the two men had different subjective experiences of their symptoms. Bill, as an American and a doctor, saw his disorder as biologically based. Mr. Sinha, as an Indian, viewed his illness as a moral and religious problem. The two men also responded differently. Every culture has what is called its "idiom of distress," the pattern of behavior by which people in that culture signify that they are ill. Bill, using the American idiom, went to a medical doctor to get medical treatments: drugs and shock therapy. Mr. Sinha went to a Hindu religious healer, and he tried to avoid having sex with his wife, though he often slipped and felt guilty about this. Interestingly, neither treatment succeeded.

Culture impinges on abnormal psychology also in that the norms of different cultures can produce behavior that, while appropriate for people of that cul-

ture, may seem pathological to people of other cultures. If Mr. Sinha had emigrated to the United States and had tried to explain the sexual cause of his disorder to an American psychiatrist, the psychiatrist might have decided that this man was suffering from delusions (irrational beliefs) and, therefore, he was not just depressed but psychotic, or very drastically impaired. Likewise, many people from non–European American cultures report perceptual experiences, such as seeing the Virgin Mary or hearing the voice of God. An American diagnostician may view these reports as evidence of hallucinations (false sensory perceptions)—again, a symptom of psychosis. Meanwhile, for the person in question, such perceptions are a normal part of religious experience (American Psychiatric Association, 1994). Norm clashes of this kind have been a persistent problem in the psychological treatment of immigrant populations. The *Diagnostic and Statistical Manual of Mental Disorders* now specifically requires that mental health professionals take the patient's cultural background into account before deciding which psychological disorder, if any, he or she has. See the box on page 9.

Gender Differences Gender, like culture, affects the expression of psychological disorders. Depressed men are more likely to be withdrawn; depressed women are more likely to be dependent. Gender also affects susceptibility to a disorder. Depression, eating disorders, and anxiety disorders are more common in women; substance abuse, antisocial behavior, and paranoia are more common in men.

Specific disorders aside, many studies have found that psychological disturbance in general is more common in women than in men (Dohrenwend & Dohrenwend, 1974), though a number of researchers feel that the difference lies not in the rate of disturbance but in the rate of *reported* disturbance. Women, it is argued, are socialized to vent their problems, while men are told to keep their troubles to themselves. Women are taught to seek help; men, to be self-reliant. Consequently, women are more likely to go to a mental health professional, complaining of symptoms that will lead to a diagnosis of mental disorder (Gallagher, 1987), while men are more likely to go to a bar. Many of the missing cases of male psychological disturbance may be concealed under undiagnosed alcoholism.

Explaining Abnormal Behavior

Since antiquity, people have developed theories as to the causes of abnormal behavior. These theories have a common base in that they are all naturalistic. That is, they seek to account for abnormal behavior in terms of natural events—disturbances in the body or

Does every culture have the same psychopathologies? It is becoming increasingly clear that, although many types of psychopathology occur across cultures, a number of syndromes appear to be unique to certain cultures and societies. These culture-bound syndromes often entail dramatic symptoms and occur within a brief time period. Although these syndromes may seem bizarre to someone from a different culture, they are clearly recognized within their culture as the troubled reactions of people in distress, who need the help of others (Littlewood & Lipsedge, 1986).

Culture-bound syndromes occur in both Western and non—Western cultures. Indeed, the fourth edition of the *Diagnostic and Statistical Manual of Mental Disorders (DSM-IV)* recognizes the need to consider non—Western syndromes when evaluating the behavior of people from other cultures. Some examples of these syndromes, as recognized in *DSM-IV* (American Psychiatric Association, 1994), include the following:

- *Amok:* A predominantly male reaction characterized by brooding and sudden outbursts of aggressive or violent behavior. The episode often seems to be a reaction to an insult or a slight and is accompanied by feelings of persecution. It is often followed by withdrawal and fatigue. The syndrome is found in people from Southeast Asia and the Caribbean and in some Native American cultures (e.g., the Navajo).

- *Koro:* A sudden and intense fear that sex organs (the penis or nipples) will recede into the body and cause death. It is reported in South and East Asia, as well as in China. In some cases, there have been reports of local epidemics of the syndrome.

- *Nervios:* A very broad expression of distress that includes headaches, upset stomach, nervousness, dizziness, and inability to sleep. It is found in many cultures but is common in Hispanic communities. It tends to persist over time following periods of stress.

- *Pibloktoq:* An attacklike syndrome that can last up to 30 minutes, involving behavior such as tearing off clothing, shouting, becoming violent, and fleeing. It is often followed by convulsive seizures and a period of coma. Upon recovery, the afflicted individual seldom recalls the episode. The syndrome is primarily found in Eskimo communities, but it also has regional variations.

- *Susto:* A fright reaction that can last for days or years, often occurring in Latin America and in Hispanic communities, although variations of the syndrome have been observed in many other cultures. The reaction is often attributed to the soul leaving the body (*susto* means soul-less), with severe consequences for the person. In some cases, death is attributed to the condition. Many of the symptoms resemble major depressive disorders.

These examples illustrate some forms of psychopathology that are unusual in Western cultures. However, it is important to recognize that many forms of illness displayed in the West are also unique to our experience. Many of them are also more likely to occur only in one gender. The following are some examples of these Western culture-bound syndromes (Castillo, 1997; Littlewood & Lipsedge, 1986):

- *Agoraphobia:* An intense anxiety reaction upon leaving the home or entering a public space that is experienced primarily by women. It can be extremely debilitating in that the person is unable to carry on normal activities outside the home.

- *Anorexia nervosa:* A syndrome of intense dieting to achieve weight loss, primarily displayed by adolescent girls concerned about their physical appearance. First noticed in the 1800s in Europe, the syndrome has reached epidemic proportions in many industrialized countries.

- *Shoplifting:* A primarily female syndrome of stealing goods from stores that the person could otherwise afford to purchase. It is seen as an obvious attempt to gain attention.

- *Flashing:* A primarily male syndrome of brief but dramatic display (exhibitionism) of the naked body to a female onlooker.

---

disturbances in human relationships. Beyond this, however, they differ greatly. Because they will figure importantly in the later chapters of this book, it is worth examining them briefly at this point.

The Medical Model According to what is loosely called the **medical model** (or *disease model*), abnormal behavior is comparable to disease: each kind of abnormal behavior, like each disease, has specific *causes* and a specific *set of symptoms*. In its strictest sense, the medical model also implies that the abnormal behavior is biogenic—that is, it results from a malfunction within the body. However, even those who do not think that all abnormal behavior is biologically based are still thinking in medical terms when they speak of overt "symptoms" and underlying causes.

Biogenic theories of abnormal behavior have been with us since ancient times. In the Middle Ages and the Renaissance, biogenic theories coexisted with

During the Middle Ages and the Renaissance, abnormal behavior was often believed to be caused by the devil. In this late fifteenth-century painting, St. Catherine of Siena is casting the devil out of a possessed woman. It can be seen as a tiny imp flying out of the woman's mouth.

supernatural theory, the belief that abnormal behavior was caused by God or, more often, the devil. But, in the eighteenth and early nineteenth centuries, religious explanations were gradually eclipsed by biological explanations. This newly dominant medical approach was soon rewarded by a series of important breakthroughs. Several previously unexplained behavior patterns were found to result from brain pathologies—infection, poisoning, and the like. Such discoveries brought immense prestige to the biogenic theory of abnormal behavior. Medicine, it was assumed, would ultimately conquer madness. On this assumption, madness was increasingly turned over to the medical profession.

There remained many patterns of abnormal behavior—indeed, the majority—for which no medical cause had been discovered, yet, because researchers were confident that such causes would eventually be found and because abnormal behavior was by then the province of medicine, these patterns were treated *as if* they were biologically based. In other words, they were treated according to a medical "model." (In scientific terms, a *model* is an analogy.) This meant not only that abnormal behavior was best handled by physicians, in hospitals, and by means of medical treatments such as drugs but also that the entire problem of deviant behavior should be conceptualized in medical terms such as *symptom, syndrome, pathology, mental illness, patient, diagnosis, therapy, treatment,* and *cure* (Price, 1978). Although this book is not based on the medical model, such terms will occur here repeatedly. They are part of the language of abnormal psychology.

Not everyone accepted the medical model, however. Indeed, it was sharply criticized. As many psychological writers pointed out, biological causes had *not* been found for most patterns of abnormal behavior; therefore, it was wrong to think of such patterns as illnesses. Perhaps the most prominent critic of the

medical model was American psychiatrist Thomas Szasz. In a book called *The Myth of Mental Illness* (1961), Szasz claimed that most of what the medical model called mental illnesses were not illnesses at all but, rather, "problems in living," expressed as violations of moral, legal, and social norms. To label these deviations "sick" was, according to Szasz, not only a falsification of the conflict between the person and the society but also a dangerous sanctification of the society's norms. As others showed, the "sick" label also deprives people of responsibility for their behavior (they can't help it—they're sick) and relegates them to a passive role that makes it hard for them to return to normal behavior. In other words, the medical model can foster serious abuses.

This controversy is not as heated today as it was in the sixties and seventies, but it is still very much alive. In response to it, many psychological professionals now take a neutral position as to the ultimate causes of abnormal behavior. But biological research in abnormal psychology has made great strides in the past three decades, and as a result biogenic theories are viewed more respectfully.

In the chapters that follow, we will discuss some of this research, which we have grouped together as the **biological perspective** within abnormal psychology. Like the medical model, the biological perspective focuses on the physical components of abnormal behavior. Unlike the medical model, however, it does not suggest that all or even most abnormal behavior patterns are merely symptoms of biological abnormalities, or even that such patterns are best treated in a medical setting. Rather, the biological perspective simply concentrates on the physical aspects of a disorder in an effort to understand its characteristics. Consider sadness, for example. Sadness can be studied at many different levels of analysis. One can analyze the thoughts that accompany it, and that is what cognitive psychologists do (see Chapter 4). Another approach is to use brain imaging techniques to study the changes in brain cell activity that accompany reported states of sadness, and that is what biological researchers do. Both the thoughts and the brain changes are part of sadness and may, at various levels, cause it. Biological researchers do not claim that organic changes are the root cause, only that they constitute an important level of analysis. The biological perspective has thus retained the medical model's organic focus without expanding it into an all-embracing medical approach to abnormal behavior.

Psychological Approaches   In contrast to the medical model are the psychological theories of abnormal behavior. Such theories attribute disturbed behavior patterns not to biological malfunction but to psychological processes resulting from the person's interaction with the environment. Thus, disturbed behavior may be explained by negligent upbringing, by traumatic experiences, by inaccurate social perceptions, or by too much stress.

There are dozens of competing psychological theories of abnormal behavior. Still, it is possible to identify a few fairly unified *perspectives*—broad schools of thought based on the same fundamental assumptions. In this book, we will refer repeatedly to the following psychological perspectives:

1. *The psychodynamic perspective,* which assumes that abnormal behavior issues from unconscious psychological conflicts originating in childhood
2. *The behavioral perspective,* which holds that a primary cause of abnormal behavior is inappropriate learning, whereby maladaptive behaviors are rewarded and adaptive behaviors are not rewarded
3. *The cognitive perspective,* which maintains that abnormal behavior is an outgrowth of maladaptive ways of perceiving and thinking about oneself and the environment
4. *The family systems perspective,* which views abnormal behavior as the product of disordered relationships
5. *The sociocultural perspective,* which views abnormal behavior as the product of broad social and cultural forces. It also examines the biases that can influence diagnosis

In addition to considering these psychological viewpoints, we will pay close attention to the biological approach just described:

6. *The biological perspective,* which analyzes abnormal behavior in terms of its biological components

Each of these perspectives has made substantial contributions to the study of abnormal psychology, and each has shortcomings as a comprehensive approach to human behavior. The six perspectives will be discussed in detail in Chapters 4 and 5.

Another perspective that commanded much attention for many decades is the humanistic-existential perspective—not a single perspective but a collection of the belief systems of well-known thinkers as diverse as Carl Rogers, Abraham Maslow, Rollo May, Viktor Frankl, and R.D. Laing. Although some key premises of both the humanists and the existentialists overlap principles of the aforementioned psychological theories, the humanistic and existential schools are not strictly based on the methods of natural science; therefore, we will not discuss them in this book.

Treating Abnormal Behavior

However they explain abnormal behavior, most societies feel that something must be *done* about it. How do human groups arrive at a way of treating the deviant in their midst?

This depends on many factors. One is the nature of the society. In a small, traditional community, deviant persons are likely to remain at home. Typically, they are prayed over, relieved of responsibilities, and treated with mixed kindness and ridicule. A large, technological society, on the other hand, tends to isolate deviants so as to prevent them from disrupting the functioning of the family and the community.

A second factor influencing the society's treatment of abnormal behavior is its explanation of such behavior. If the deviant is seen as possessed by evil spirits, then the logical treatment is to draw out such spirits—by means of prayer, potions, or whatever. If, in keeping with the medical model, abnormal behavior is assumed to be the result of biological pathology, then it is handled by medical treatments: drugs, hospitalization, perhaps even surgery. If abnormal behavior is interpreted according to psychological theories, it is treated via psychological therapies. As we have seen, many psychological professionals today feel that, whatever its ultimate cause—if, indeed, ultimate causes can be found—abnormal behavior has psychological *and* biological components. Accordingly, in recent years there has been increased interest in *multimodal treatments,* the combining of two or more kinds of therapy—for example, "talk" psychotherapy and drugs. In the accompanying box on page 12, we describe the kinds of therapists who provide these treatments.

Our modern approaches are not new, however. They are the result of centuries of trial and error.

Psychotherapy is a relatively formal relationship between a trained professional and a person (or family) who seeks help with psychological problems.

There are four main types of mental health professionals. A **psychiatrist** is an M.D. who specializes in diagnosing and treating mental disorders. Because of their medical degree, psychiatrists can also prescribe psychoactive drugs, medications that can improve the functioning of people with mental disorders. Some psychiatrists, called *psychopharmacologists,* specialize in medical treatments. A **clinical psychologist** is a Ph.D. or Psy.D. who has spent four to six years in graduate school and has completed a one-year clinical internship. Clinical psychology programs train people to do diagnosis, therapy, and research. A **psychiatric social worker** has earned an M.S.W. (master of social work), with special training in psychological counseling. A **psychoanalyst** has had postgraduate training at a psychoanalytic institute and has undergone psychoanalysis. Most psychoanalysts are psychiatrists, but other mental health professionals may undertake this training.

There are as many as 1,000 distinct forms of psychotherapy. Which approach a therapist takes depends on his or her theoretical perspective, though there are growing trends toward eclecticism, or combining techniques from different schools, and toward combining medication with therapy sessions.

Accordingly, in the next section of this chapter, we will present a brief history of our ancestors' handling of abnormal behavior.

Conceptions of Abnormal Behavior: A Short History

Ancient Societies: Deviance and the Supernatural

We know little about the treatment of deviant behavior in prehistoric and ancient societies. What we do know suggests that our early forebears regarded deviant behavior, like most other things they did not understand, as the product of remote or supernatural forces—the movements of the stars, the vengeance of God, the operation of evil spirits. This idea seems to have endured for many centuries. References to possession can be found in the ancient records of the Chinese, the Egyptians, the Hebrews, and the Greeks. In the New Testament, Jesus is reported to have drawn out devils from the possessed.

The cure for possession was to coax or force the evil spirits out of their victim—a practice called **exorcism.** Many exorcisms were confined to prayer, noise-making, and the drinking of special potions. In more difficult cases, the possessed person might be submerged in water, whipped, or starved in order to make the body a less comfortable habitation for the devil. Not surprisingly, some people died in the course of exorcism. But most treatments were probably far less dramatic. For example, the person might simply be sent home to rest and given special mention in the community's prayers. Such remedies are common in small, traditional societies today, and they were probably common in ancient societies as well.

The Greeks and the Rise of Science

In ancient Greece and China began the evolution of a naturalistic approach to abnormal behavior. The earliest surviving evidence of this trend is found in the writings attributed to Greek physician Hippocrates (c. 460–c. 360 B.C.). In opposition to current supernatural theories, Hippocrates set about to prove that all illness, including mental illness, was due to natural causes. For example, in his treatise on epilepsy, known at the time as the "sacred disease," Hippocrates curtly observed: "If you cut open the head, you will find the brain humid, full of sweat and smelling badly. And in this way you may see that it is not a god which injured the body, but disease" (cited in Zilboorg & Henry, 1941, p.44).

Hippocrates undertook a number of reforms. First, he set himself the novel task of actually *observing* cases of mental disturbance and of recording his observations as objectively as possible. Consequently, his writings are the first in Western scientific literature to contain empirical descriptions (descriptions based on observation) of mental disorders such as phobia and epilepsy.

Second, Hippocrates developed several of the earliest biogenic theories of abnormal behavior. For example, he believed that many disorders were due to an imbalance among four **humors,** or vital fluids, in the body: phlegm, blood, black bile, and yellow bile. An excess of phlegm rendered people phlegmatic—indifferent and sluggish. An excess of blood gave rise to rapid shifts in mood. Too much black bile made people melancholic, and too much yellow bile made them choleric—irritable and aggressive. Primitive as this theory may seem, it foreshadowed today's biochemical research in abnormal psychology.

Greek physician Hippocrates rejected the supernatural theories of abnormal behavior that were prevalent in his time. Asserting that mental illness was due to natural causes, he developed the influential biogenic theory of the four humors.

Hippocrates made no important advances in the cure of mental disorder. However, his treatment methods were gentle and dignified, and this in itself was an advance. His treatment for melancholy, for example, involved rest, exercise, a bland diet, and abstinence from sex and alcohol. Because this regimen could be most easily followed under supervision, he often moved patients into his home, where he could observe them. In later Greek civilization, such thinking led to the establishment of retreats for the mentally ill. In Alexandria, for example, special temples dedicated to the god Saturn were set aside as asylums, where the mentally ill could recover with the help of rest, exercise, music, and other therapeutic measures.

The Middle Ages and the Renaissance: Natural and Supernatural

With the decline of Greek civilization and the rise of the Roman Empire, the enlightened Hippocratic approach to mental disorder survived for a few more centuries. In the first century B.C., Asclepiades, a Greek physician practicing in Rome, was the first to differentiate between chronic and acute mental illness.* In the second century A.D., Galen, another Greek physician who practiced in Rome, showed that the body's arteries contained blood—not air, as was commonly thought. This discovery led to the practice of bleeding the mentally disturbed, in the hope of restoring the proper balance among the humors of the body. (Bleeding persisted as a treatment for emotional and physical disorders into the nineteenth century.) But, with the fall of Rome in the fifth century, the study of mental illness, together with other branches of learning, shut down, not to be reborn until later, during the Middle Ages.

Medieval Theory and Treatment The Middle Ages was a period of ardent religiosity. Insanity, like all other things, was thought to be controlled by supernatural forces, and many of the insane were handled accordingly. Some were taken to shrines, prayed over, and sprinkled with holy water. Others were starved and flogged, to harass the devil within. Barbarous as the latter treatments may seem to us now, they were regarded as quite proper by most people, including the humane and the educated, and not only in the Middle Ages but well into the Renaissance. The wise and mild-mannered Sir Thomas More, later sainted, wrote to a friend about his handling of a lunatic: "I caused him to be taken by the constables and bound to a tree in the street before the whole town, and there striped [whipped] him until he waxed weary. Verily, God be thanked, I hear no more of him now" (cited in Deutsch, 1949, p. 13).

However, English legal records show that, when medieval officials examined deranged people, they often recorded natural, commonsense explanations for the derangement. One man, examined in 1291, was said to have lapsed into insanity after a "blow received on the head." The uncontrollable violence of another man, examined in 1366, was reportedly "induced by fear of his father" (Neugebauer, 1978). These are the kinds of causes that might be cited today.

Furthermore, whether insanity was attributed to natural or supernatural forces, it was often treated as

---

*In *chronic* mental illness, symptoms are long-standing and relatively unchanging. In *acute* mental illness, symptoms appear suddenly and dramatically. See Chapter 13.

a form of illness (Kemp, 1990). Windows of medieval churches show the saints curing the insane alongside the lame and the blind. Many of the insane were admitted to the same hospitals as other sufferers. For example, the deed of Trinity Hospital, founded in Salisbury, England, in the fourteenth century, provides for an institution in which, alongside patients with physical illnesses, "the mad are kept safe until they are restored to reason" (Alldderidge, 1979, p. 322).

The Witch Hunts   The Renaissance, stretching from the fifteenth to the seventeenth century, has long been regarded as a glorious chapter in the history of Western culture, yet it is during this period that occurred one of the ugliest episodes in European history: the witch hunts. Since the eleventh century, the church had been beleaguered by heresies, demands for economic and religious reform, and other types of insurrection. The church went on the counterattack, with increasing ferocity. Women (and a few men) whose behavior gave offense to church authorities were accused not just of being in league with the devil but of committing heinous acts—eating children, staging orgies, and the like. The charges soon spread, creating a climate of fear and hysteria, in which anyone who behaved strangely, or who behaved in a way that someone in power did not like, stood in danger of being executed for witchcraft.

The witch hunts soon received full endorsement from the church hierarchy in Rome. In 1484, Pope Innocent VIII issued a papal bull, declaring the church's intention of rooting out the offenders. Soon afterward, he appointed church officials, called inquisitors, to seek out witches and see that they were punished. Witch hunting was embraced by the new Protestant churches as well. It is estimated that, from the middle of the fifteenth century to the end of the seventeenth, 100,000 people were executed as witches (Deutsch, 1949). The hunting down of witches became a social and religious duty. Neighbors reported neighbors. Priests turned in their own parishioners. Everyone was suspect.

Renaissance Theory and Treatment   It has been argued (e.g., Spanos, 1978) that the witch hunts may have had little connection with the history of mental illness, as most of the accused were probably not mentally ill. In large communities, witch hunting apparently had less to do with bizarre behavior than with political and economic interests. That is, the trials were used to confiscate property and to eliminate political troublemakers. (Recall that Joan of Arc, who helped the French expel the English invaders in the early fifteenth century, was burned as a witch.) In smaller communities, however, the accused were often poor, old, socially marginal women or simply socially disreputable types—"fornicators, blasphemers, thieves, ill-tempered persons, and the like" (Spanos, 1978, p. 423)—and some of the mentally ill no doubt fell into this group.

The fact that the mentally ill suffered from the witch hunts is also clear from the writings of those who protested against the craze. In 1563, for example, German physician Johann Weyer, the first medical practitioner to develop a special interest in mental illness, published a treatise, declaring that those who were being burned as witches were actually mentally unbalanced and not responsible for their actions. Weyer was soon followed by an Englishman named Reginald Scot, who in 1584 published his *Discovery of Witchcraft,* a scholarly work pointing out, among other things, the evidence of mental illness in those being persecuted by the witch hunters.

It seems likely, then, that some of the "witches" were psychologically disturbed. At the same time, the evidence suggests that in the Renaissance most of the mentally ill were of little interest to the witch hunters. Instead, as in the Middle Ages, they were seen as sick people whose problems could be explained in natural terms (Neugebauer, 1978) and whose care, in any case, had to be seen to by the community. Some were apparently kept in almshouses (institutions for the poor), others in general hospitals. Indeed, London's Bethlem Hospital, founded in 1247, was given over almost exclusively to the insane by the fifteenth century. It is also in the Renaissance that we see the first major efforts to institutionalize the practice of community care (Alldderidge, 1979)—that is, supervision of the mentally ill within the community but outside the hospital. The "poor laws" of seventeenth-century England required that "lunaticks," along with the aged, the blind, and other unfortunates, be provided for by their local government or parish. Some patients were kept at home, while money for their maintenance was paid out of parish funds. Homeless patients might be boarded with families in the community. The legal records of a seventeenth-century English county include an order for the care of such a person:

> Daniell Hancox a poore Ideott who was borne in Weston . . . and is now in the care and custody of William Mulliner gent[lemen] on[e] of the Inhabitants there shalbe forthwith Clothed by and out of the stock of money given to the Inhabitants there to that purpose. And it is further ordered that the said Daniell shalbe forthwith removed from the said Mr. Mulliner and be kept and provided for by the Inh[ab]itants of the said parish from house to house as heretofore hee hath beene there mainteyned and kept. (Alldderidge, 1979, p. 327)

As we shall see, the practice of housing the psychologically disabled with willing families is being experimented with in the United States today.

The Eighteenth Century and After: The Asylums

The Early Asylums The practice of hospitalizing the psychologically disturbed is an old one. In Arab countries, general hospitals provided wards for the mentally ill as early as the eighth century (Mora, 1980). The first hospital exclusively for the insane opened in Spain in the early fifteenth century. This example was eventually followed in London, Paris, Vienna, Moscow, Philadelphia, and other major cities. More and more, the insane were removed to institutions.

Most of the early mental asylums opened with the best of intentions, but the conditions in which their patients lived were often terrible. London's Bethlem Hospital, mentioned earlier, became so notorious for the misery within its walls that it gave rise to the word *bedlam*, meaning "uproar." A writer in the seventeenth century described Bethlem as follows:

> It seems strange that any should recover here, the cryings, screechings, roarings, brawlings, shaking of chains, swarings, frettings, chaffing, are so many, so hideous, so great, that they are more able to drive a man that hath his wits, rather out of them, than to help one that never had them, or hath lost them, to finde them againe. (Allderidge, 1985)

Historians have produced many chilling descriptions of the early mental hospitals (Foucault, 1965; Scull, 1993), often with the suggestion that these institutions did not aim to cure, but only to isolate and humiliate the insane. Other writers have taken a more balanced view. In a study of the archives of Bethlem, for example, Allderidge (1985) has pointed out that the bedlam therein was almost certainly due to the difficulty of handling violent patients in the days before psychiatric medication. The hospital had rules against beating patients, and the archives show that some patients enjoyed privileges that would not be commonly found today in a public charity, which is what Bethlem was. Indictments of Bethlem, for example, often cite the case of James Norris, who was kept in chains there for 9 years in the early nineteenth century. But the records on Norris show that he was an extremely violent patient who had attacked a number of attendants and fellow patients before the staff resorted to chaining him. The records mention, furthermore, that while chained Norris occupied himself mainly by reading books and newspapers and by playing with his pet cat. Obviously, though he was in chains, someone on the staff remembered that he was a human being, with human needs.

The Reform of the Asylums The first serious efforts to improve treatment in the large hospitals began in the late eighteenth century. The reforms were begun by Vincenzo Chiarugi, superintendent of an asylum called the Ospedale di Bonifazio in Florence and by Jean-Baptiste Pussin, who directed the "incurables" ward at La Bicêtre, a large hospital in Paris. Pussin, for example, forbade his staff to beat the patients—an innovation that caused a near-revolt among the attendants. He also gave orders to unchain a group of patients who, having been declared "furious," had lain in shackles for years—in some cases, for decades. Without their chains, these patients could move about on the grounds, take the fresh air, and feel some sense of personal liberty. As Pussin had hoped, many of them became more manageable.

This painting shows Father Juan Gilabert Jofré protecting a mentally disturbed man from stones thrown by a crowd. It was reportedly this incident that inspired Father Jofré to found the world's first hospital for the insane, in Valencia, Spain, in 1410.

These woodcuts from 1875 show male patients (left) let out of their rooms to "take the air" in the corridor and female patients (right) eating a meal in Philadelphia's Blockley Hospital.

Pussin's reforms were extended by Philippe Pinel, who became chief physician of La Bicêtre's ward for the mentally ill in 1793. Pinel's position was that the mentally ill were simply ordinary human beings who had been deprived of their reason by severe personal problems. To treat them like animals was not only inhumane; it impeded recovery. Pinel replaced the dungeons in which the patients had been kept with airy, sunny rooms and did away with violent treatments such as bleeding and cupping (blistering the skin with small hot cups). He also spent long hours talking with the patients, listening to their problems, and giving them comfort and advice. He kept records of these conversations and began to develop a case history for each patient. This practice of recordkeeping, introduced by Pinel, was an extremely important innovation, for it allowed practitioners to chart the *patterns* that emerge in the course of various disorders—when and how the disorder first appears, which symptoms develop in which order, and so on. Knowledge of these patterns became the basis for the classification of disorders, for research into their causes, and for treatment. After Pinel's retirement, his student and successor, Jean Esquirol, founded 10 new mental hospitals in various parts of France, all based on the humane treatment developed by Pussin and Pinel.

At the same time that Pussin and Pinel were working in Paris, a Quaker named William Tuke was attempting similar reforms in northern England. Convinced that the most therapeutic environment for the mentally ill would be a quiet and supportive religious

Philippe Pinel supervises the unchaining of inmates at La Salpêtrière, the hospital he directed after his work at La Bicêtre. The reforms of Pussin, Pinel, and Tuke led to the movement called moral therapy, which was widespread in the eighteenth and nineteenth centuries.

setting, Tuke in 1796 moved a group of mental patients to a rural estate, which he called York Retreat. There they talked out their problems, worked, prayed, rested, and took walks in the countryside.

Though vigorously resisted by Pinel's and Tuke's contemporaries, these new techniques eventually became widespread, under the name of **moral therapy.** Based on the idea that the mentally ill were simply ordinary people with extraordinary problems, moral therapy aimed at restoring their "morale" by providing an environment in which they could discuss their difficulties, live in peace, and do some useful work. Apparently, this approach was extremely successful. Records show that, during the first half of the nineteenth century, when moral therapy was the only treatment provided by mental hospitals in Europe and America, at least 70 percent of those hospitalized either improved or actually recovered (Bockoven, 1963).

The Reform Movement in America The leader in the development of the American mental health establishment was Benjamin Rush (1745–1813), known as the "father of American psychiatry." A remarkable man—he was a signer of the Declaration of Independence, a member of the Continental Congress, the surgeon general to the Continental Army, the treasurer of the United States Mint, and the founder of both the first free medical dispensary and the first antislavery society in America—Rush advanced the cause of mental health by writing the first American treatise on mental illness, by organizing the first medical course in psychiatry, and by devoting his attention, as the foremost physician at Pennsylvania Hospital, exclusively to mental problems.

Today, some of Rush's thinking seems primitive: he believed that mental illness was due to an excess of blood in the vessels of the brain. To relieve the pressure in the blood vessels, he relied heavily on bleeding. He also had patients dropped suddenly into ice-cold baths or strapped into a device called the "tranquilizer." These procedures, however, were accompanied by a number of humane practices. Rush recommended that doctors regularly bring little presents, such as fruit or cake, to their patients. He also insisted that Pennsylvania Hospital hire kind and intelligent attendants—people who could read to patients, talk to them, and share in their activities. In sum, Rush guided American psychiatry in the direction of a humane therapy.

The task of extending these reforms fell to a Boston schoolteacher named Dorothea Dix (1802–1887). At the age of 40, Dix took a job teaching Sunday school in a prison. There she had her first exposure to the gruesome conditions suffered by the mentally ill. Later she went abroad, visiting York Retreat, as well as other moral therapy institutions, and became convinced of the need to reform mental health care (Rosenblatt, 1984). Soon she was traveling across the country, examining the squalid jails and poorhouses in which the mentally ill were confined and lecturing state legislators on their duty to these people. To the Massachusetts legislature, Dix spoke as follows:

> I come to place before the Legislature of Massachusetts the condition of the miserable, the desolate, the outcast. I come as the advocate of helpless, forgotten, insane and idiotic men and women . . . of beings wretched in our prisons, and more wretched in our Alms-Houses.
>
> I proceed, Gentlemen, briefly to call your attention to the state of Insane Persons confined within this Commonwealth, in *cages, closets, cellars, stalls, pens: Chained, naked, beaten with rods,* and lashed into obedience. (Deutsch, 1949, p. 165)

Dix called for the mentally ill to be removed to separate, humane facilities geared to their special needs. Carrying her campaign across the United States and eventually to Canada and Scotland as well, she was responsible for the founding and funding of 32 mental hospitals.

Dorothea Dix worked to expose the maltreatment of the mentally ill and to establish mental hospitals devoted to their care.

Hospitalization and the Decline of Moral Therapy Dix's reforms had one unfortunate result that she could not have anticipated: they contributed to the decline of moral therapy (Foucault, 1965). As hospital after hospital opened, there were simply not enough advocates of moral therapy to staff them. Indeed, there were not enough staff of any kind, for, though the state governments were willing to build mental hospitals, they still did not consider mental health as important as physical health. This meant less money for mental hospitals, and less money meant fewer employees. At the same time, the patient populations of these institutions grew year by year. With many patients and few attendants, the hospitals could not provide the sort of tranquil atmosphere and individual care essential to moral therapy. The new mental hospitals also helped the public to unlearn the lesson that Pinel and Tuke had worked so hard to teach: that the mentally ill were simply ordinary people. Walled off in somber isolation in rural areas, these large asylums seemed to the public to conceal some dark horror, and the mentally disturbed were once again seen as freakish and dangerous.

There were other reasons for the decline of moral therapy (Bockoven, 1963). To begin with its first-generation advocates—people such as Pussin, Pinel, and Tuke—were not succeeded by an equally powerful second generation. Second, by the turn of the century, many of the indigent patients who filled the mental hospitals were Irish Catholic immigrants, against whom there was considerable prejudice. The Protestant establishment might be willing to pay for these patients' hospitalization but not for the luxury of moral therapy. Finally, the growth of the state mental hospital system occurred at the same time as the rise of the medical model. The early successes of the medical model convinced psychiatric professionals that their efforts should be directed toward biological treatments rather than toward the psychological attentions of moral therapy.

Thus during the second half of the nineteenth century, moral therapy was increasingly replaced by custodial care. Throughout this period, communities showed less and less willingness to tolerate mentally ill people in their midst (Luchins, 1993). Therefore, many people whose behavior was merely eccentric, but not seriously disruptive, were sent off to the institutions. There they were no longer pressured to act normal, as they had been in the community. Meanwhile, all the effects of hospitalization—the social stigma, the damage to self-esteem, the loss of moorings in reality, the temptation of the "sick" role—pushed them toward permanent patient status. Recovery rates dropped (Bockoven, 1963; Dain, 1964). Care was custodial, not remedial.

This situation continued into the middle of the present century, often with dreadful consequences, particularly in the area of patient control. In the 1940s and 1950s, for example, thousands of mental patients who were considered uncontrollable in one way or another were subjected to a crude form of brain surgery called **prefrontal lobotomy**. In this procedure, an instrument is inserted into the brain's frontal lobe, immediately behind the forehead, and rotated, thus destroying a substantial amount of brain tissue. Many people emerged from their lobotomies in a permanent vegetative state; others died (Redlich & Freedman, 1966). It was thus with considerable relief that mental health professionals greeted the introduction, in the 1950s, of the phenothiazines, a new class of drugs that was highly effective in calming the severely disturbed.

The Exodus from the Hospitals In the 1950s and 1960s, evidence of the damage that hospitalization did to patients was mounting fast (Goffman, 1961; Scheff, 1966). Around the same time came the phenothiazines, calming patients to the point where, it seemed, they could be released from the hospital. The state legislatures were willing; hospitalization was expensive. Thus began the **deinstitutionalization** movement. Starting in the late 1950s, hundreds of thousands of mental patients, some of whom had been in the hospital for 20 or 30 years, were given bottles of pills and discharged.

Clearly, they still needed some sort of care, and so did new patients, if they were not going to be hospitalized. In 1963, Congress passed the Community Mental Health Centers Act, providing for the establishment, across the country, of mental health services that people could use without being uprooted from their normal lives. The new **community mental health centers** offered several kinds of care. One was **outpatient** (outside-the-hospital) psychological counseling. In the 20 years from 1955 to 1975, the rate of outpatient counseling in the United States increased twelvefold (Kiesler, 1982a). Another service was **inpatient** (in-the-hospital) care, but modified. There were *day hospital* programs, in which patients stayed in the hospital only from nine to five, returning home at night; there were also *night hospital* programs, in which patients went to work or school during the day and then came back to the hospital at night. Some community mental health centers also offered improved emergency services—for example, 24-hour storefronts where people in crisis could go to have a talk (and possibly a tranquilizer) and to make an appointment for outpatient counseling. Outside the community mental health centers, some patients were placed in *halfway houses,* or residences for people who, no longer requiring hospitalization, still needed help in readjusting to community life. In a halfway house, residents live together, talk out their problems, and relearn social skills. Indeed, there is now considerable evidence that hospitalization, where necessary, should be brief (Braun, Kochansky, Shapiro, et al., 1981; Caton, 1982; Straw, 1982)—perhaps two to three weeks—and that alternatives such as halfway houses are preferable.

Many of these community services are still in operation today, and some are excellent, but they are the rare ones. In 1981, a system of block grants to the states replaced the Community Mental Health Centers Act, shifting the responsibility for funding to state legislatures. In most cases, the state legislatures have not provided sufficient funds for the community mental health centers to give mental patients the support they need. Some community services offer nothing more than custodial care under a new name. For example, halfway houses, to be effective, have to be small and carefully run. A number of the so-called halfway houses, however, are merely seedy hotels, where patients see a social worker for a few minutes per week and spend the rest of their time in front of the television. Those patients are luckier than others, however. Many of the people returned to the community via deinstitutionalization are receiving no services at all. Of the million or so homeless people nationwide, about one-third are estimated to be mentally disturbed (Rossi, 1990). By day, they walk the streets; by night, they sleep in doorways. Many might be better off in the hospital, with a clean bed. (See the box on page 20.)

Some do go back to the hospital. It is still true that the population of the state mental hospitals is low compared with pre-1960s figures, for patients are now discharged quickly. Even in settings where, in earlier decades, people often stayed for life (e.g., public hospitals, Veterans Administration psychiatric hospitals), the current length of stay is less than three months (Kiesler, 1982b). On the other hand, a number of patients are no sooner discharged than they are readmitted—a situation called "revolving door syndrome"—because of the lack of services outside the hospital. While the inpatient population has decreased, the number of admissions has actually increased (Kiesler, 1982b).

The Foundations of Modern Abnormal Psychology

In the late nineteenth century, as the new mental hospitals were opening throughout the United States, the study of abnormal psychology was rapidly expanding in both Europe and America. New theories were being introduced and tested, while opposing theories arose to challenge them.

The Experimental Study of Abnormal Behavior In 1879, Wilhelm Wundt, a professor of physiology at the University of Leipzig, Germany, established a laboratory for the scientific study of psychology—that is, the application of scientific experimentation, with precise methods of measurement and control, to human thought and behavior. The opening of Wundt's laboratory is often cited as the beginning of modern psychology. Among Wundt's students was Emil Kraepelin (1856–1926), who eventually established his own psychological laboratory, devoted primarily to the study of **psychopathology**, or abnormal psychology. There Kraepelin and his students investigated how psychopathology was related to movement, to fatigue, to emotion, to speech, and to memory (Maher & Maher, 1979).

Kraepelin's approach was copied elsewhere. In 1904, the first American laboratory for experimental work with mental patients opened at the McLean Hospital in Massachusetts, and other hospitals soon followed McLean's example. In 1906, Morton Prince, an American physician specializing in mental disorders, founded the first journal specializing in experimental psychopathology, the *Journal of Abnormal Psychology*. (It remains the foremost journal on this subject today.) In all, experimental abnormal psychology made substantial strides in the first two decades of the century.

Kraepelin and Biogenic Theory Biogenic theory, as we have seen, originated in ancient times and persisted, though sometimes obscured by supernaturalism, through the Middle Ages and Renaissance. Then, in the late eighteenth and early nineteenth centuries, when medical research was making rapid advances, it again became dominant. Kraepelin, the founder of experimental abnormal psychology, was the person who first placed biogenic theory in the forefront of European psychiatry. In his *Textbook of Psychiatry* (1883/1923), Kraepelin not only argued for the central role of brain pathology in mental disturbance but furnished psychiatry with its first comprehensive classification system, based on the biogenic viewpoint. He claimed that mental illness, like physical illness, could be classified into separate pathologies, each of which had a different organic cause and could be recognized by a distinct cluster of symptoms, called a syndrome. Once the symptoms appeared, the mental disturbance could be diagnosed according to the classification system. And, once it was diagnosed, its course and outcome could be expected to resemble those seen in other cases of the same illness, just as

Shifting the care of chronic mental patients from state hospitals to the community is called deinstitutionalization, but many city dwellers call it "dumping." In cities across the country, hundreds of thousands of patients considered capable of functioning on medication outside the institution have been released. Of the million or so homeless people nationwide, approximately one-third are thought to be suffering from mental disorders, usually schizophrenia (Goleman, 1986a, 1986b; Rossi, 1990). In a study of homeless men recruited from the lines of a southwestern city soup kitchen, half showed evidence of either severe alcoholism or severe psychopathology (or psychological abnormality; Kahn, Hannah, Hinkin, et al., 1987). Community services in every city are insufficiently staffed and funded to see that the mentally ill are housed, put to work, or looked after.

Where do they live? Some are placed in inexpensive single-room-occupancy (SRO) "hotels"—often warrens of tiny, filthy rooms. Community services for the chronic mentally ill may consist of a welfare check and occasional visits by a social worker dispensing tranquilizers. Otherwise, they are typically on their own, sitting in their rooms or drifting through the streets. When they die, they are rarely missed.

Still worse, some of the mentally ill have no housing at all, since they lack the money even for the cheapest flophouse. Many have essentially no income and are dependent on city shelters and soup kitchens. Some spend their days wandering from neighborhood to neighborhood; others travel around one or a few blocks. They sleep where they can—if not in shelters, then in doorways, in parks, and in subways and train stations. They carry their belongings in shopping bags or roll grocery carts along the sidewalks.

For people with homes and jobs, it can be difficult to understand that the mentally ill "street person," ragged and dirty, once had a normal life. In 1991, composer and writer Elizabeth Swados told such a story, describing the descent of her brother Lincoln Swados into schizophrenia and eventually life on the street. The Swados family was privileged, and Lincoln grew up intelligent and talented. But he was eccentric, and he often misbehaved at school. When he went away to college, he broke down. As Swados (1991) describes it:

He never made it through his freshman year at Syracuse. . . . Lincoln promised to write, but he never did. Several months later, my father received an almost booklength letter from my brother describing himself as in a helplessly disoriented state. He was unable to go to classes, unable to leave his room. The voices in his head were directing him to do too many different things. My father showed the letter to several psychiatrists, who recommended that Lincoln be hospitalized immediately. (p. 18)

Released from the hospital after lengthy treatment, Lincoln again deteriorated. In a suicidal period, he tried to kill himself by jumping in front of a subway train. This resulted in the amputation of his right arm

---

one case of measles could be expected to turn out like other cases of measles.

Kraepelin's biogenic theory and his classification system received widespread publicity and generated high hopes that the mysteries of mental illness would be solved in commonsensical, natural ways. At the same time, the neurological and genetic components of psychopathology were gaining attention through the writings of another German physician, Richard von Krafft-Ebing (1840–1902), who emphasized organic and hereditary causation in his *Textbook of Psychiatry* (1879/1900) and in his pioneering encyclopedia of sexual disorders, *Psychopathia Sexualis* (1886/1965). It was from the work of these theorists that the modern medical model of psychological disturbance evolved.

As noted earlier, the medical model produced brilliant results in its early days. The senile psychoses, the toxic psychoses, cerebral arteriosclerosis, mental retardation—one mental syndrome after another was linked to a specific brain pathology. The most stunning success of all, however, was the discovery that **general paresis,** a mysterious syndrome involving the gradual and irreversible breakdown of physical and mental functioning was actually an advanced case of syphilis. This breakthrough had an immense impact on the mental health profession and helped to establish the medical model in the lofty position it still occupies today.

However, at the same time that neurological research was nourishing biogenic theory, other findings were laying the foundation for a comprehensive psychogenic **theory,** the theory that psychological disturbance is due primarily not to organic dysfunction but to emotional stress.

Mesmer and Hypnosis The history of modern psychogenic theory begins with a colorful figure, Franz Anton Mesmer (1733–1815). In the late eighteenth century, exciting discoveries were being made about magnetism and electricity. Mesmer, an Austrian physician, tried to apply this new knowledge to the

and leg. Then, disabled physically as well as mentally, Lincoln Swados went to live on the Lower East Side of New York, a poor and dangerous neighborhood. Repeatedly rejecting the efforts of family and friends to help him—he refused to answer the door when they came to see him—Swados sank further into mental and physical illness. His sister eventually found him dead in the middle of a shabby apartment. He was 46.

Compared with many schizophrenics, Lincoln Swados was fortunate—he had financial resources and a family that tried to help him. Given his fate, it is easier to understand how others with serious disorders end up on the street, penniless and in desperate need of care.

The deinstitutionalization movement of the past quarter-century has sought to release many mentally ill people from hospitals. Often, however, government funding has not followed the released patients into the community. As a result, adequate programs do not exist for the treatment and supervision of the thousands of homeless mentally ill people who now roam the streets of American cities.

study of mental states. His theory was that the movement of the planets controlled the distribution of a universal magnetic fluid and that the shiftings of this magnetic fluid were responsible for the health of mind and body. Furthermore, he was convinced that this principle of "animal magnetism" could be used in the treatment of **hysteria,** a disorder involving the impairment of normal function—for example, the person suddenly became blind or paralyzed—with no apparent organic cause. Hysteria was a common complaint at the time, especially in women.

Mesmer's treatment for hysteria was rather exotic. The patients sat around a huge vat containing bottles of fluids from which iron rods protruded. The lights were dimmed and soft music was played. Then Mesmer appeared, "magnetic" wand in hand, and went from patient to patient, touching various parts of their bodies with his hands, with his wand, and with the rods protruding from the vat, in order to readjust the distribution of their magnetic fluids. The most striking aspect of this treatment is that in many cases it worked.

Mesmer's theory of animal magnetism was later investigated and declared invalid, yet, even if his theory was wrong, his treatment was somehow right. What Mesmer had discovered, accidentally, was the power of suggestion to cure mental disorder. He is now regarded as the first practitioner of **hypnosis** (originally known as "mesmerism"), an artificially induced trance in which the subject is highly susceptible to suggestion.

The Nancy School Some years after Mesmer's death, his findings were reexamined by two enterprising French physicians, Ambrose-Auguste Liébeault (1823–1904) and Hippolyte-Marie Bernheim (1840–1919), both practicing in Nancy, in eastern France. For four years Bernheim had been treating a patient, with no success. Finally, after hearing that a certain Dr. Liébeault was having considerable success with unconventional methods, Bernheim sent the patient to him. When the patient returned completely cured, Bernheim called on Liébeault to ask what he had done. What

Liébeault had done was simple: he had hypnotized the patient and told him that, when he awakened, his symptoms would be gone (Selling, 1940).

Bernheim was persuaded, and thereafter the two physicians worked as a team. Together they discovered that hysteria could be not only cured but also induced by hypnosis. For example, if a hypnotized person were told that she had no feeling in her hand, the hand could then be pricked with a needle without producing any response. On the basis of such findings, Liébeault and Bernheim evolved the theory that hysteria was actually a form of self-hypnosis and that other mental disorders might also be due to psychological causes.

This view won a number of adherents, and the group became known as the "Nancy school." The Nancy school soon came under attack by a formidable challenger, Jean-Martin Charcot (1825–1893), a famous neurologist who at that time was director of La Salpêtrière Hospital in Paris. Charcot had also experimented with hypnosis, but he had abandoned it, concluding that hysteria was due to biogenic causes after all. The debate between the Paris school, consisting of Charcot and his supporters, and the Nancy school was one of the earliest major academic debates in the history of modern psychology. Eventually, the insurgent Nancy school triumphed, and Charcot himself was later won over to the psychogenic theory of hysteria. But this debate extended far beyond the specific problem of hysteria, for it raised the possibility that any number of psychological disorders might be due to emotional states rather than (or as well as) to biogenic causes.

Breuer and Freud: The Beginnings of Psychoanalysis   One of the many people affected by the debate over hysteria was a young Viennese physician named Sigmund Freud (1856–1939). Early in his career, Freud worked with Josef Breuer, a physician who was experimenting with hypnosis. A few years earlier, Breuer had treated a woman, later known to medical history as "Anna O.," who had various hysterical symptoms—partial paralysis, inability to swallow, and so on. Somewhat by chance, Breuer discovered that under hypnosis Anna O. was able to discuss her feelings uninhibitedly and that, after doing so, she obtained some relief from her symptoms. Anna O. called this the "talking cure."

Together Breuer and Freud experimented with talking cures. They soon became convinced that hysteria and other disorders were caused by "unconscious" conflicts; once aired via hypnosis, the conflicts lost their power to maintain the symptoms. In 1895, Breuer and Freud published their findings in a volume titled *Studies in Hysteria*. This book, in which the authors put forth their theory of the unconscious, was a milestone in the history of psychology.

Later, working independently, Freud abandoned hypnosis in favor of a technique he called free association: he asked patients to relax on a couch and simply to pour out whatever came to mind. Freud also encouraged his patients to talk about their dreams and their childhoods. He then interpreted this material to the patients according to the theories he was constructing about the unconscious. To this form of therapy, in which patients are cured through the gradual understanding of unconscious conflicts, Freud gave the name **psychoanalysis.** Freud's theories were very controversial at first. Eventually, however, they became the basis for the psychodynamic perspective (Chapter 4) and have exerted a profound influence on twentieth-century thought.

The French neurologist, Jean-Martin Charcot is shown here, with a patient on his arm, giving one of his famous lectures on hysteria. Charcot was at the center of the late nineteenth-century debate between psychogenic and biogenic theories of hysteria.

Non-Western Approaches to Abnormal Behavior

The history just outlined describes only one tradition, that of the West—of Europe and America. Asia and Africa have their own ways of handling abnormal behavior. Their traditions, thousands of years old, are impossible to summarize briefly, but they do share certain principles that distinguish them from Western abnormal psychology. First, Asians and Africans do not separate psychology from spiritual matters. In the West, psychology is part of science, or it tries to be. In Africa, psychology is part of religion. Second, in psychology, as in other areas of life, Asians and Africans do not prize individualism as much as Westerners do. Rather, they see human beings as part of a network of relationships, and those relationships are often the focus of psychological treatment.

Africa In Africa, a person who lives alone is likely to be considered odd. People lead their lives within large, extended families, and it is the family that is expected to handle psychological crises. When that fails, the troubled person goes to a psychological healer, who may well be the community's healer of physical problems as well. Generally, the healer attributes the problem to a disruption in the person's relationship with the spirit world—a situation that may be due to sorcery, the evil eye, the breaking of a taboo, or the failure to perform required rituals. Physical causes are also taken into account, and many healers recommend physical treatments such as herbs. But often the treatment, like the presumed cause, is spiritual: rituals, animal sacrifices, incantations, the wearing of amulets, and the use of special objects.

Such treatments may be very pragmatic. T. Asuni offers the following example:

> An African woman from a polygamous tribe went to a healer, complaining that her husband was threatening to send her back to her family because she was constantly having violent arguments with one of her co-wives, whom the husband seemed to favor. The healer gave her a small object and told her that it embodied the spirit of the other wife. Whenever she began to quarrel with the other wife, she was to put this object in her mouth and bite it. This, he said, would solve her problem. The woman returned several weeks later to thank the healer, saying that not she, but the other wife, had been sent away. (Adapted from Asuni, 1986, p. 313.)

Asuni speculates that the healer felt it was unrealistic to tell the woman not to quarrel with the co-wife. Instead, he gave her a less direct way of getting back at her rival, by biting the object. At the same time, the object-biting kept the patient from quarreling—she couldn't bite and argue at the same time—so the cause of her husband's anger with her was removed.

Here we see many of the same principles used in Western psychological treatment: suggestion, reassurance, and manipulation of the environment. Other techniques shared by Western and African psychotherapy are emotional venting and group treatment. (The previous case is unusual in that the woman went to the healer alone. Most African patients arrive with a large delegation of family members, and the prescribed rituals are performed by the whole group, with the healer as a sort of master of ceremonies.) What is not shared is Western psychotherapy's goal of insight. African patients are not asked to analyze themselves. This would be considered a distraction from the main goal of treatment, correcting the person's relationship to family and to ancestral spirits.

Asia Asian religious philosophies, such as Hinduism and Buddhism, emphasize self-awareness: people are taught to pay close attention to their inner states and thereby, in some measure, separate themselves from their own thought processes. The most common method of achieving this is meditation. Meditation is now widely used in the West for stress reduction. In Asia, where it has been practiced for thousands of years, it is used to relieve a wide variety of psychological problems—for example, phobias, substance abuse, and insomnia—and medical problems such as asthma and heart irregularities (Walsh & Shapiro, 1980).

Like meditation, other Asian psychotherapies tend to be "quiet therapies," in which patients deal mainly with themselves, though under the guidance of a professional. An example is Naikan therapy, a popular Japanese treatment that was developed in the 1950s. The fundamental principle of Naikan therapy is that many psychological problems are due to self-centeredness. Patients, therefore, are taught to engage in long periods of "self-observation"—16 hours a day, in the hospital, for the first week of treatment; and a few hours a day thereafter—during which they examine their relationships with others (especially their parents), asking themselves what they received from these people, what troubles they caused them, and what they gave back to them (Reynolds, 1993). The aim is to make patients more accepting and appreciative of those around them.

Another treatment widely used in Japan, particularly for anxiety disorders, is Morita therapy. Here again, patients are hospitalized, this time for four to five weeks, and required to engage in prolonged reflection. At first they remain inactive; then, gradually, they are allowed to take up tasks and mix with people again. The object is to clear the mind of anxiety-producing perfectionism and to make the patient yearn again for practical activity.

Though used for psychological purposes, these Asian therapies are all rooted in religion, in the Zen Buddhist goal of freeing oneself of thoughts that disrupt the harmony between the self and the universe. In all three, one detaches oneself from the world in order to return to it—to practical activity and social responsibility (Sharf, 1996).

A Multiperspective Approach

This book rests on three basic assumptions. The first is that *human behavior can be studied scientifically.* That is, scientists can observe objectively both behavior and the environment in which it occurs. From these observations, they can draw conclusions about the causes of behavior; knowing these causes, they can predict and influence behavior.

Second, this book assumes that *most abnormal behavior is the product of both psychological and biological processes.* The unobservable events of the mind, such as attitudes, memories, and desires, are unquestionably involved in most forms of psychopathology. Psychopathology, in turn, is connected to biological events: the secretion of hormones by the glands, the movement of electrical impulses across the brain, and so forth. How these two kinds of events hook together in the web of causation is, as we shall see, a maddeningly complex question.

The third assumption of this book is that *each human being is unique.* Human behavior may be discussed in general terms, but it still issues from individuals, each of whom has a unique set of memories, desires, and expectations, and each of whom has some ability to control his or her behavior.

In the following chapters, we will stress the perspectives on abnormal behavior described earlier: the psychodynamic, behavioral, cognitive, family systems, sociocultural, and biological perspectives. Each of these viewpoints is narrower and more specific than the broad approach just defined, and more often than not they disagree with one another. But, taken together, they provide a comprehensive view of modern abnormal psychology.

KEY TERMS

biogenic, 9	free association, 22	moral therapy, 17	psychoanalysis, 22
biological perspective, 10	general paresis, 20	norms, 4	psychoanalyst, 12
clinical psychologist, 12	humors, 12	outpatient, 18	psychogenic theory, 20
community mental health	hypnosis, 21	prefrontal lobotomy, 18	psychopathology, 19
centers, 18	hysteria, 21	psychiatric social worker,	syndrome, 19
deinstitutionalization, 18	inpatient, 18	12	
exorcism, 12	medical model, 9	psychiatrist, 12	

SUMMARY

- Definitions of abnormal behavior vary from century to century and from society to society. A common basis for defining behavior as abnormal is violation of the society's norms, or rules for correct behavior. Behavior that is statistically rare, causes personal discomfort to the person who exhibits it, or is maladaptive, may also be considered abnormal.

- Psychological disturbance has different effects on different social groups, defined by cultural and ethnic origin, gender, age, and other factors. Such groups are at differing risk for various disorders, and they experience and express the disorders differently. They may also embrace different norms, which affects diagnosis.

- Just as there are many definitions of abnormal behavior, so are there many explanations. According to the medical model, abnormal behavior is *like* a disease: even if the condition is not the result of organic dysfunction, it should be diagnosed and treated as an illness. A refinement of the medical model, the modern biological perspective seeks to identify the organic components of mental disorders but does not insist on an exclusively biological cause.

- Psychological theories trace abnormal behavior to a person's interactions with the environment. The most prominent psychological theories include the psychodynamic approach, which emphasizes unconscious conflicts originating in childhood; the behavioral perspective, which stresses inappropriate conditioning; the cognitive perspective, which focuses on maladaptive ways of perceiving the self and the environment; and the family systems perspective, which views abnormal behavior as the product of disordered relationships. The sociocultural perspective examines the influence of social forces on behavior and diagnosis.

- The treatment of abnormal behavior depends on the nature of the society, the criteria used to identify abnormality, and the society's explanation of abnormal behavior.

- Prehistoric and ancient societies apparently viewed abnormal behavior as a product of supernatural forces. Treatment consisted of various forms of exorcism.

- The naturalistic approach to abnormal behavior in Western culture dates from ancient Greece. Hippocrates observed and recorded cases of mental disturbance and developed an organic theory of abnormal behavior.

- In the Middle Ages, supernatural explanations of abnormal behavior were again dominant, though naturalistic theories also persisted.

- During the Renaissance, despite a growing trend toward regarding abnormal behavior as an illness, thousands of people, mostly women, were burned in witch hunts. Some of these people were probably psychologically disturbed.

- In the eighteenth and nineteenth centuries, hospitalization of the mentally disturbed became increasingly common. Conditions in the asylums were typically cruel and degrading. In the late eighteenth century, people such as Philippe Pinel and William Tuke began the reform of institutional care. The new approach, stressing a peaceful environment, useful work, and dignified treatment, came to be known as moral therapy.

- With the efforts of Dorothea Dix and others, many mental hospitals were built in the nineteenth century, but these institutions did not live up to the reformers' hopes. Moral therapy was replaced with custodial care. Mentally disturbed people were isolated in prisonlike institutions, sometimes for life—a pattern that continued into the mid-twentieth century.

- In the 1950s, with the introduction of a new class of tranquilizers, the phenothiazines, the deinstitutionalization movement began. But, because of lack of funding, this was not accompanied by sufficient growth in community services. Today, hospital stays are brief, but rates of admission remain high.

- In the late nineteenth century, experimental psychology, initiated by Wilhelm Wundt, was extended to the study of psychological disturbance. Emil Kraepelin's biogenic theory, together with breakthroughs in biological research, pushed the medical model to the forefront.

- With Franz Anton Mesmer's discovery of hypnosis in the eighteenth century, it became clear that some mental disorders could be cured by suggestion. This laid the groundwork for psychogenic theory. At the end of the nineteenth century, Sigmund Freud began developing his pioneering theory, psychoanalysis, which argued that psychological disorders were caused by unconscious conflicts.

- In contrast to the modern Western tradition, African and Asian approaches to psychological disturbance tend to be more closely connected to religion. They also place less emphasis on individualism and greater emphasis on social relationships.

- This book is based on three assumptions: human behavior can be studied scientifically; most abnormal behavior is the product of *both* psychological and biological processes; and each human being is unique. To present a comprehensive view of abnormal psychology, we will draw on all the theoretical perspectives described earlier.

Chapter 2

Most of this book is devoted to the common categories of abnormal behavior. As categories, such disorders are easy to discuss. We chart the symptoms, weigh the possible causes, and review the suggested treatments. It is only in the vocabulary of psychology, however, that abnormal behaviors exist as categories. In reality, they are the complex and ambiguous things that people do and say. And the first job of the mental health profession is to look at what people say and do and to make some sense out of it. This process is called **psychological assessment**, which may be defined as the collection, organization, and interpretation of information about a person and his or her situation.

Psychological assessment is not a recent invention. Throughout history, people have been developing systems for sorting people into categories so as to predict how they will behave. The first assessment system was probably astrology, developed by the ancient Babylonians and later disseminated to Egypt, Greece, India, and China (McReynolds, 1975). Initially, the stars were read only for clues about matters of public concern—wars, floods, crop failure. By the fifth century B.C., however, astrology was also being used as the basis of personal horoscopes, revelations of individual character and destiny.

Ancient societies also practiced psychiatric classification. By 2600 B.C., the Egyptians and the Sumerians had recognized what would later be called melancholia, hysteria, and senile dementia. By 1400 B.C., India had developed a psychiatric classification system in which seven kinds of demonic possession produced corresponding types of abnormal behavior. As mentioned in Chapter 1, Hippocrates, in fifth-century B.C. Athens, insisted on natural causes, as opposed to possession. In addition to his four humors, he and his followers devised a six-part system for classifying mental disorders: phrenitis (mental disturbance with fever), mania, melancholia, epilepsy, hysteria, and "Scythian disease," similar to what we call transvestism (Mack, Forman, Brown, et al., 1994).

An important thing to note about these assessment systems is that each is based on a theory of human behavior. To the astrologists, behavior was determined by the positions of the stars at one's birth. To the ancient Indians, it was controlled by spirits. Modern assessment procedures, in turn, are based on psychological theories, biogenic and psychogenic. These theories, too, will change. With assessment, as with the definition of abnormal behavior, we are looking at something that is the product of each generation's and each culture's efforts to make sense of the way people act.

In this chapter, we will first discuss the issues surrounding assessment: what it aims to do, how well it

Astrology represents the first method of psychological assessment, developed by the ancient Babylonians. Although personal horoscopes continue to be popular, astrology is generally not considered a viable means of assessment today.

succeeds, and what can cause it to fail. Then we will describe the most commonly used assessment techniques and their relation to the major psychological perspectives.

Diagnosis and Assessment: The Issues

Why do people undergo psychological assessment? In what cases, and why, does such assessment involve diagnostic labeling? How useful are diagnostic labels? How can we tell a good assessment technique from a bad one? These questions have no easy answers. The entire enterprise of diagnosis and assessment is surrounded by controversy.

Why Assessment?

All psychological assessment has two goals. The first is **description**, the rendering of an accurate portrait of personality, cognitive functioning, mood, and behavior. This goal would be important even if there were no such thing as abnormal psychology. Science aims to describe, and psychology, the science of human personality and behavior, aims to describe personality and behavior, simply for the sake of increasing our understanding of reality.

However, such descriptions may also be needed for decision-making purposes. This brings us to the second goal of psychological assessment: **prediction**. Again, prediction need serve no practical purpose. The mere desire to advance human knowledge could motivate a psychologist to try to predict, for example, whether children of divorced parents are likely to become divorced themselves. Within abnormal psychology, however, assessment often has important practical applications. Should this child be put in a special education program? Is this person psychologically fit to stand trial? Would that patient benefit from drugs? Should he be hospitalized—even against his will? These are the questions that clinical assessment addresses. The answers may determine the direction of the person's entire future.

Patients must also be reassessed to see if they are improving. Today, in the cost-conscious atmosphere of managed health care, insurers are asking for evidence that the treatments they are paying for are actually working. Because this evidence can be provided only by assessing the patients, psychological assessment is likely to be even more important in the coming years (Beutler, Kim, Davison, et al., 1996).

In this chapter, we will be tracking the psychological assessment of a patient named Joe, who is 23 years old. Joe has mild mental retardation and many related problems, such as impulsiveness and fits of anger. He had been placed in a "group home," a fairly nonrestrictive setting with professional counselors present only during the day, but because of his disruptive behavior he had been asked to leave the group home. He is now in the hospital, and the purpose of the assessment is to decide where he should be placed. Does he need to stay in the hospital longer? Could he go back to the group home? Or should he be placed in an intermediate setting, a "residential home," with 24-hour staff? Joe's assessment will be described in the text and in boxes throughout the chapter.

The Diagnosis of Mental Disorders

In nonclinical contexts, assessment may involve no labeling. When job applicants take psychological tests, one person is chosen for the job, while the others are not, and that is the end of it. Clinical assessment, however, often includes **diagnosis**, in which the person's problem is classified within one of a set of recognized categories of abnormal behavior and is labeled accordingly.

The Classification of Abnormal Behavior All sciences classify—that is, they order the objects of their study by identifying crucial similarities among them and sorting them into groups according to those similarities. Astronomers classify heavenly bodies according to color, size, and temperature. Physicians classify diseases according to the organ or system affected. And mental health professionals classify mental disorders according to patterns of behavior, thought, and emotion.

As we saw in Chapter 1, the first truly comprehensive classification system for severe mental disorders was developed by Kraepelin in the late nineteenth century. All later systems were influenced by Kraepelin's. Eventually, in 1952, the American Psychiatric Association (APA) published its own version of the system, under the title *Diagnostic and Statistical Manual of Mental Disorders,* or *DSM.* Since that time, the *DSM* has undergone several revisions. There was a *DSM-II,* followed in turn by *DSM-III, DSM-III-R* (revised), and, most recently, **DSM-IV,** which was published in 1994. *DSM-IV*'s listing of diagnostic categories may be seen inside the cover of this book.

Another classification system that should be noted is the mental disorders section of the *International Classification of Diseases (ICD),* published by the World Health Organization (WHO). All members of the WHO, including the United States, use the *ICD,* though each member can revise the *ICD* criteria for disorders to reflect diagnostic practices within that country. Most revisions of the *DSM* have been coordinated with revisions of the *ICD. DSM-IV* is consistent with the *ICD*'s current, tenth edition, *ICD-10* (Sartorius, Üstün, Korten, et al., 1995).

The Practice of Diagnosis It is the *DSM* that provides the foundation for diagnosing mental disorders. Each of the *DSM* categories is accompanied by a description of the disorder in question, together with a set of specific criteria for diagnosis. Faced with a patient, the assessor decides which diagnosis seems most likely, consults the criteria for that disorder, and then determines which criteria the patient actually meets. If the patient satisfies the minimum number of criteria specified by the *DSM* for that disorder, and if other choices have been eliminated, that is the patient's diagnosis. The purpose is to supply a description of the patient's problem, along with a **prognosis,** or prediction of its future course.

As the term *diagnosis* suggests, this procedure is analogous to medical evaluation, and, in the minds of some, it implies the medical model, the practice of treating abnormal behaviors as if they were symptoms of biological dysfunction (Follette & Houts, 1996). However, mental health professionals of all persuasions, including those who strongly object to the medical model, use diagnosis, and for good reasons.

To begin with, research depends on diagnosis. For example, in order to find out the causes of schizophrenia, researchers need to have groups of schizophrenics to study, and it is only through diagnosis—that is, labeling certain people schizophrenic—that they can gather such groups. Even apart from research requirements, mental health professionals, like other professionals, need a vocabulary in order to discuss their subject. If they did not establish a common vocabulary, such as that provided by the *DSM,* they would develop their own, idiosyncratic terms and definitions, with much resulting confusion. Finally, psychology is tied in with many other institutions in our society, and all of these institutions require the use of diagnostic labels. To get funding for its special education program, a school system has to say how many mentally retarded or autistic children it is handling. When hospitals apply for funds, they have to list the number of schizophrenics, alcoholics, and so on that they are treating. Insurance companies require a diagnosis before they will pay the bills. Thus, diagnosis is practiced, and its vocabulary—that of the *DSM*—has become our society's primary means of communicating about abnormal behavior.

Criticisms of Diagnosis   The major criticism of diagnosis has to do with what some perceive as its tie to the medical model. As noted in Chapter 1, Szasz (1961) and many other writers have vigorously attacked the medical model, and they have attacked the diagnosis of mental disorders on the same grounds—namely, that its purpose is to give psychiatrists control over other people's lives. In addition to this argument, four other criticisms of diagnosis merit consideration.

The first is that diagnosis falsifies reality by implying that most abnormal behavior is qualitatively different from normal behavior. *DSM-IV,* for example, lists a condition called "nightmare disorder," with, as usual, specific criteria for diagnosis: the person's nightmares must be "extended and extremely frightening" and they must occur repeatedly. One person with nightmares will meet these criteria, while another will not. But the application of the diagnosis to one and not the other suggests that there is a difference in kind between their two conditions, whereas, to all appearances, the difference is simply one of degree. Likewise, most forms of psychopathology are at the far end of a long continuum from normal to abnormal, with many gradations in between (Achenbach & McConaughy, 1996).

If diagnosis discounts the gradations between normal and abnormal, it is even more likely to discount the gradations between different forms of abnormality—a second major criticism. Many people with "depression" suffer the same problems as people

This woman is filing for unemployment. One criticism of diagnostic labeling is that it stigmatizes people, making it difficult for them to get jobs or establish personal relationships.

with "schizophrenia"; others have much in common with "anxiety disorder" patients. In other words, behavior is far less clear-cut than the diagnostic system, and, in imposing this artificial clarity, critics claim, diagnosis distorts human truth.

A third criticism is that diagnosis gives the illusion of explanation (Carson, 1996). For example, the statement "She is hallucinating because she is schizophrenic" *seems* to have explanatory value. In fact, it has none. "Schizophrenic" is simply a term that was made up to describe a certain behavior pattern involving hallucinations—a behavior pattern of which the cause is still largely unknown. Likewise, "depression," "phobia," "paranoia," and other diagnostic labels are not explanations but terms used so that researchers can do the work necessary to find explanations. This fact is often forgotten.

A fourth criticism is that diagnostic labeling can be harmful to people. As some theorists have argued, the label obscures the person's individuality, inviting mental health professionals to attend to the "phobia" or "depression" rather than the human being—or, for that matter, the family or the society, which may be the true source of the disorder. In addition, diagnostic labels can do concrete harm, damaging people's personal relationships, making it hard for them to get jobs, and in some cases depriving them of their civil rights. Furthermore, sociocultural theorists such as Scheff (1975) claim that diagnostic labels encourage people to settle back into the "sick" role and become permanent mental patients.

According to some writers, the shortcomings of *DSM*-based diagnosis are so serious that the system should be abandoned altogether. In a much-discussed

Can the sane be distinguished from the insane via *DSM*-based diagnosis? In the early 1970s, D. L. Rosenhan (1973) set up an experiment whereby eight psychologically stable people, with no history of mental disorder, tried to get themselves admitted to mental hospitals. The eight "pseudopatients"—three psychologists, a psychiatrist, a graduate student in psychology, a pediatrician, a painter, and a homemaker—presented themselves at separate hospitals in five states. They all went under assumed names, and those involved in mental health lied about their professions. Otherwise, they gave completely accurate histories, adding only one false detail: each of them claimed that he or she had been hearing voices that seemed to say something like "hollow," "empty," or "thud."

The pseudopatients' greatest fear in embarking on their experiment was that they would be unmasked as frauds and thrown out of the hospital. As it happened, they were diagnosed as schizophrenic and were all admitted as mental patients.

Once admitted, the pseudopatients made no further reference to the voices. They behaved completely normally, except that they made special efforts to be courteous and cooperative, yet none of them was ever exposed as a fraud. In Rosenhan's opinion, the staff simply assumed that, because these people were in a mental hospital, they were disturbed. This assumption persisted, despite the fact that all the pseudopatients spent a good part of the day taking notes on what went on in the ward. The staff either ignored the note taking or interpreted it as an indication of pathology. On one pseudopatient's hospital record, the nurse, day after day, noted this symptom: "Patient engages in writing behavior" (Rosenhan, 1973, p. 253). The genuine mental patients were apparently not so easy to fool. According to Rosenhan, they regularly accused the pseudopatients of being sane and speculated out loud that they were journalists sent in to check up on the hospital.

All the pseudopatients were eventually discharged. Their stays ranged from 7 to 52 days, with an average of 19 days. Upon discharge, they were classified not as being "cured" or as showing no behavior to support the original diagnosis but, rather, as having psychosis "in remission." In other words, their "insanity" was still in them and might reappear.

The evidence of this study led Rosenhan to conclude that, while there might in fact be a genuine difference between sanity and insanity, those whose business it was to distinguish between them were unable to do so with any accuracy. The focus of his criticism was the fact that, once the pseudopatients were admitted and began behaving normally, their normality was not detected. In his view, the reason for this was that in diagnosis the initial evaluation—which, as in this case, may be based on a single symptom—distorts all future evaluations of the patient, making it impossible for diagnosticians to see the person otherwise than in the role of "schizophrenic" or whatever he or she has been labeled. As a result, the sane cannot be distinguished from the insane.

Rosenhan's conclusion has been contested by a number of other investigators. Spitzer (1976), for example, argued that the fact that the pseudopatients were able to lie their way into the hospital was no proof that the diagnostic system was invalid. (If a person swallows a cup of blood and then goes to an emergency room and spits it up, and, if the physician on duty diagnoses the person's condition as a bleeding ulcer, does this mean that the diagnostic criteria for bleeding ulcer are invalid?) As for the hospital staff's failure to detect the pseudopatients' normality once they were in the hospital, Spitzer again argued that this was no reflection on the diagnostic system. People are not diagnosed solely on the basis of how they are behaving at the moment but also on the basis of their past behavior. If a person reports having repeated hallucinations and then reports no further hallucinations for 2 weeks, this does not necessarily—or even probably— mean that no psychiatric abnormality exists, much less that none ever existed. In the absence of alcoholism or other drug abuse, hallucination is ordinarily a sign of severe psychological disturbance; for a diagnostician to discount this symptom simply because it had not appeared for a few weeks would be extremely careless. Indeed, as Spitzer pointed out, the fact that the hospitals released the pseudopatients in an average of 19 days actually shows a rather rapid response to their failure to produce any further symptoms. And the fact that they were released as being "in remission," an extremely rare diagnosis, suggests that the hospital staff recognized that they were atypical, if not faked, cases; in any case, they were not just lumped together with all other diagnosed schizophrenics.

Rosenhan's study was widely debated in the 1970s. Whatever the validity of its conclusions, it added to the general dissatisfaction with *DSM-II*, which led to the continuing tightening of the diagnostic criteria and the effort to base those criteria on empirical evidence.

1975 paper, for example, Rosenhan argued that a diagnostic system must demonstrate that its benefits (in indicating appropriate treatments, for instance, or in leading researchers to causes) outweigh its liabilities in order to justify its use. As causes and effective treatments had not yet been discovered for so many of the *DSM* categories, there was no justification, as Rosenhan saw it, for continuing to use these labels. (For further discussion of Rosenhan's position, see the box above.)

Categorical vs. Dimensional Classification One proposed solution is that categorical classification—the sorting of patients into diagnostic categories, as per the *DSM*—be replaced by dimensional classification. In this method, the diagnostician would not try to pinpoint the person's "defining" pathology; instead, he or she would be scored on different *dimensions* of pathology. Essentially, the difference is between a qualitative and a quantitative analysis. In categorical classification, a patient might be given the diagnosis "major depressive episode." In dimensional classification, there would be no such diagnosis but, rather, a series of scores on depression, anxiety, sleep disturbance, and so forth.

Dimensional classification is not as simple as categorical classification, but, as its defenders point out, simplicity is not a virtue if it distorts reality. The *DSM* categories, they say, are based on arbitrary cut-off points. For example, to be diagnosed with schizophrenia, a person must have had the characteristic symptoms for at least six months. If the six-month requirement is not met, the person is said to have "schizophreniform disorder." These rules have resulted in a proliferation of mini-categories that may, in the end, tell us little about the patients. In the words of Widiger and Trull, "Rather than wrestle with the arbitrary distinctions between schizophrenia, simple schizophrenia, schizophreniform, schizoaffective, schizotypal, and schizoid . . . it might be preferable to assess patients along the dimensions that underlie these distinctions (e.g., severity, course, content, and pattern of schizophrenic symptomatology" (1991, p. 124).

Other writers have pointed out how much more information dimensional classification could offer. As we saw in Chapter 1, many disorders take different forms depending on gender and age. In dimensional classification, males and females, children and adults, could be graded within their own groups—on the curve, so to speak. Dimensional classification could also specify differences in information between different sources: what the child's teachers say about his disruptiveness, as opposed to what his parents say (Achenbach & McConaughy, 1996). According to some defenders of dimensional classification (Widiger & Trull, 1991), the only things standing in the way of conversion to this system are tradition and professional vanity. (Rendering a diagnosis, saying, "This patient has schizophrenia," implies a kind of authority that totaling up dimensional scores would not.) Adherents of categorical classification answer that the dimensional system is too complicated. At the same time, many of the *DSM* categories have been revised in order to allow for dimensional distinctions. In a number of categories, such as conduct disorder and substance abuse, diagnosticians are now asked to give severity ratings.

Defending Diagnosis Experienced diagnosticians harbor no hopes that *DSM-IV* is foolproof, yet most mental health professionals today would not side with the arguments that Rosenhan mounted against the *DSM* system in the seventies. The crucial point is, again, that research depends on diagnosis. As Spitzer (1976) wrote in response to Rosenhan's challenge:

> Is Rosenhan suggesting that prior to the development of effective treatments for syphilis and cancer, he would have decried the use of these diagnostic labels? Should we eliminate the diagnoses of antisocial personality, drug abuse, and alcoholism until we have treatments for these conditions whose benefits exceed the potential liabilities associated with the diagnosis? How do we study the effectiveness of treatments for these conditions if we are enjoined from using the diagnostic categories until we have effective treatments for them? (p. 469)

Such arguments have had their effect. Since the seventies, *DSM*-based diagnosis has become more widely used and, with successive improvements in the manual, less controversial.

In order to aid research, however, diagnosis must be consistent and meaningful. It must *mean* something—and it must mean the same thing to everyone—that a patient is labeled "schizophrenic" or "phobic." In this respect, diagnosis made a poor showing in the past. Earlier editions of the *DSM* offered relatively brief and vague descriptions of the disorders listed. As a result, there was a good deal of inconsistency in diagnosis, with the further result that diagnostic groups were disappointingly heterogeneous. That is, the symptoms of the patients assigned to many of the categories were not similar enough to make the label truly useful. Furthermore, the early editions of the manual explicitly or implicitly ascribed numerous disorders to causes that had not been definitely established, thus further complicating diagnosis and impeding research.

DSM-IV Beginning with *DSM-III* in 1980, the recent revisions of the manual have been, in large part, an effort to remedy these problems. In *DSM-IV* the major innovation was a concerted effort to base the manual on research. The revision team did a systematic study of the research findings on each disorder and in some cases even had research data reanalyzed. The team also conducted field trials, comparing the usefulness of the new diagnostic criteria with those in previous editions. Let us look at the changes that have been made in the manual over the past 20 years, as reflected in *DSM-IV*.

Specific Diagnostic Criteria First, the criteria for diagnosis are highly detailed and specific, including the following:

1. *Essential features* of the disorder: those that "define" it
2. *Associated features:* those that are usually present
3. *Diagnostic criteria:* a list of symptoms (taken from the lists of essential and associated features) that *must* be present for the patient to be given this diagnostic label
4. Information on *differential diagnosis:* data that explain how to distinguish this disorder from other, similar disorders

In addition, the descriptions offer information on the course of the disorder, age at onset, degree of impairment, complications, predisposing factors, prevalence, family pattern (that is, whether the disorder tends to run in families), laboratory and physical exam findings, and relationship of the disorder to gender, age, and culture. The most important feature of the descriptions, however, is the highly specific quality of the diagnostic criteria.

Five Axes of Diagnosis A second important feature of *DSM-IV* is that it requires the diagnostician to give a substantial amount of information about patients, evaluating them on five "axes," or areas of functioning:

Axis I—Clinical syndrome: the diagnostic label for the patient's most serious psychological problem, the problem for which he or she is being diagnosed

Axis II—Personality disorders or mental retardation: any accompanying long-term disorder not covered by the Axis I label.*

Axis III—General medical disorders: any medical problem that may be relevant to the psychological problem

Axis IV—Psychosocial and environmental problems: current social, occupational, environmental, or other problems that may have contributed to or are resulting from the psychological problem

Axis V—Global assessment of functioning: a rating, on a scale of 1 to 100, of the patient's current adjustment (work performance, social

relationships, use of leisure time) and of his or her adjustment during the past year**

To return to our case of Joe, his diagnosis was as follows:

Axis I: Adjustment disorder with mixed disturbance of emotions and conduct

Axis II: Mild mental retardation (principal diagnosis)

Axis III: No medical problems

Axis IV: Dismissed from group home

Axis V: Current—major impairment (40), in past year—moderate difficulty (60)

Thus, instead of simply writing down "depression," today's diagnostician must create a little portrait, the features of which may then be useful in devising a treatment program. Furthermore, it is hoped that this five-part diagnosis will help researchers in their exploration of connections between psychological disorders and other factors, such as stress and physical illness.

Unspecified Cause A final important feature of *DSM-IV* is that it avoids any suggestion as to the cause of a disorder unless the cause has been definitely established. This feature, introduced with *DSM-III* in 1980, necessitated substantial changes in the classification system. The term *neurosis*, for example, was dropped altogether, as it implies a Freudian theory of causation (i.e., that the disorder is due to unconscious conflict). Since 1980, the manual has simply named the disorders and described them as clearly and specifically as possible. Their causes, if they are not known, are not speculated upon. This change was not without cost, however. All successful classification systems in other sciences have been based on theory, and theory is the motor of research: it specifies what questions need answering (Follette & Houts, 1996). But only by removing causal assumptions was it possible to produce a manual that could be used by all diagnosticians, regardless of what theories they hold.

The major goal of the 1980 revision was to improve the reliability and validity of psychiatric diagnosis. Reliability and validity will be discussed as general scientific concepts in Chapter 3. Here we will see how they apply to the diagnosis of mental disorders.

Assessing the Assessment: Reliability and Validity

Reliability The reliability of any measurement device is the degree to which its findings can stand the test of repeated measurements. Thus, in its simplest

*Axis II is confined to disorders that generally date from childhood. They are separated from the Axis I "clinical syndromes" to give the diagnostician a chance to note not just the primary problem (Axis I) but also any other, chronic condition (Axis II) that accompanies the primary problem and perhaps contributes to it. In some instances, a chronic condition *is* the patient's primary problem, in which case it is still listed on Axis II but is marked "principal diagnosis."

**Reprinted with permission from the *Diagnostic and Statistical Manual of Mental Disorders,* Fourth Edition. Copyright © 1994 American Psychiatric Association.

sense, reliability is a measure of the consistency of such a device under varying conditions. A 12-inch ruler is expected to produce the same measurements whether it is used today or tomorrow, in Salt Lake City or New Orleans, by you or by me. Likewise, a psychological assessment technique, to be considered reliable, must produce the same results under a variety of circumstances.

There are three criteria for reliability in psychological assessment:

1. Internal consistency. Do different parts of the test yield the same results?
2. Test-retest reliability. Does the test yield the same results when administered to the same person at different times?
3. Interjudge reliability. Does the test yield the same results when scored or interpreted by different judges?

Each of these three criteria applies with particular force to certain kinds of tests. Test-retest reliability is most important in assessments of stable individual difference characteristics—for example, IQ tests. Internal consistency is most important in tests that use many items to measure a single characteristic—for example, a 60-item test for anxiety. In the diagnosis of mental disorders the most crucial criterion is interjudge reliability, the degree of agreement among different diagnosticians as to what specific disorder any given patient has.

As indicated earlier, the rate of agreement has been very low in the past. Indeed, Spitzer and Fleiss (1974), in a review of research on the reliability of psychiatric diagnosis, found that interjudge reliability was satisfactory in only *three* diagnostic categories: mental retardation, organic brain syndrome, and alcoholism. And these are broad categories. In one study, a number of psychologists and psychiatrists were asked to evaluate a series of simulated patient profiles and to assign each "patient" to a subtype of schizophrenia. The resulting rate of agreement between any two judges was a dismally low 25 percent (Blashfield, 1973).

When detailed, specific diagnostic criteria were introduced in *DSM-III*, this problem was solved to some degree (Leckliter & Matarazzo, 1994). In one study, with diagnosticians trained beforehand in the use of *DSM-III*, the rate of overall agreement was 74 percent, a comparatively good score (Webb, Gold, Johnstone, et al., 1981), yet, for certain *DSM-III* categories, notably the personality disorders, interjudge reliability was still poor (Drake & Vaillant, 1985; Mellsop, Varghere, Joshua, et al., 1982). This is one area of weakness that later editions of the *DSM* have

tried to address. As we shall see when we examine the personality disorders, the criteria for these diagnoses are now highly specific.

Increased interjudge reliability is not achieved without costs, however. As Blashfield and Draguns (1976) have pointed out, reliability is not the only consideration in creating a diagnostic system. Ideally, the system should also have high "coverage"—that is, most cases of abnormal behavior should qualify for one of its categories. Earlier editions of the *DSM* achieved high coverage by having loose diagnostic criteria; because the behavioral descriptions were so broad, almost any patient could be made to fit somewhere. The later editions, with their stricter criteria, have lower coverage, with the result that more patients are swept into residual categories—some writers call them "wastebasket diagnoses"—such as "psychotic disorder not otherwise specified." This problem, in turn, has been addressed by adding new categories. The number of categories has more than tripled since the introduction of the diagnostic manual. (See Figure 2.1.) Even so, the diagnostic criteria are so strict that many patients still end up with "not otherwise specified" (NOS) diagnoses. In certain categories, such as the dissociative disorders (Chapter 7), the *majority* of patients are given NOS diagnoses (Mezzich, Fabrega, Coffman, et al., 1989; Saxena & Prasad, 1989). Thus, as diagnostic groups have become purer, they have become smaller, leaving researchers less to work with.

Validity   Whereas *reliability* refers to the consistency of a measuring instrument under varying conditions, **validity** refers to the extent to which the test measures what it is supposed to measure. Do people who score high on a typing test really type better than people who score low? If so, the test is valid.

As with reliability, there are several kinds of validity. Because the major purpose of any assessment system is to describe and predict behavior, we will discuss the two kinds of validity that are most relevant to the diagnosis of mental disorders: descriptive validity and predictive validity.

Descriptive Validity   The **descriptive validity** of an assessment device is the degree to which it provides significant information about the current behavior of the people being assessed. A frequent criticism of the diagnosis of mental disorders is that it has little descriptive validity—that it does not tell us much about the people diagnosed. Proponents of this view point to the fact, mentioned earlier, that people assigned to the same diagnostic group may actually behave quite differently, while people assigned to different diagnostic groups may show many of the same behavioral oddi-

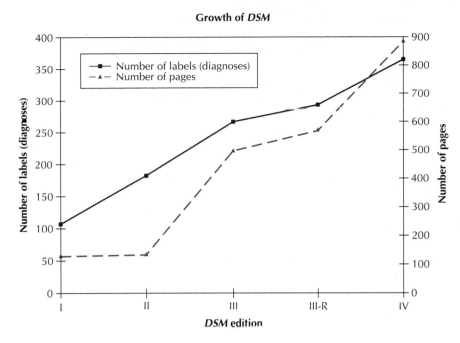

Growth of *DSM*

FIGURE 2.1 The growth of successive editions of the *DSM*. Versions I, II, III, III-R, and IV are the first, second, third, revised third, and fourth editions, respectively. (Adapted from Follette & Houts, 1996, p. 1125.)

ties—a problem that was not solved by *DSM-IV* (Frances, First, & Pincus, 1995; Follette & Houts, 1996). But diagnosis does not claim to produce groups that are completely homogeneous; this would be impossible, for no two people, normal or abnormal, behave exactly alike. Nor does it claim that a symptom typical of one diagnostic group will not be found in other groups. In all of abnormal psychology, there are very few *pathognomic symptoms,* symptoms that accompany all cases of a given disorder and that never accompany any other disorder. Like any other scientific classification system, diagnosis groups cases not according to individual characteristics but according to *patterns* of characteristics—patterns in which there is invariably some duplication of individual characteristics. Three people may have high fevers, yet, if their symptom pictures differ in other ways—one having a runny nose, another being covered with red spots, another having swollen cheeks—they will be diagnosed as having different diseases. Likewise, three people may have hallucinations, yet, if they differ in other important respects—one having a long history of alcohol abuse, the second showing severe depression, and the third believing that her thoughts are being broadcast so that everyone in the room can hear them—then they are likely to be given three different diagnoses: alcoholism, depression, and schizophrenia, respectively. In other words, research would have to show that the *pattern* of symptoms—not just individual symptoms—is substantially different within categories and substantially similar between categories before the diagnosis of mental disorders could be said to have poor descriptive validity.

A more serious challenge to the descriptive validity of diagnosis is the fact that most patients (Kessler, McGonagle, Zhao, et al., 1994) show comorbidity. That is, they meet the diagnostic criteria for more than one Axis I disorder. In such cases, the person is usually given more than one diagnosis, but such multiple diagnoses, implying that the person has two (or more) independent disorders, may not be accurate descriptions of the case. Comorbid conditions generally have a more chronic course, a poorer response to treatment, and a poorer prognosis than single disorders. In other words, they may represent a different, unrecognized disorder, rather than a combination of recognized disorders. (See the box on page 36.) Recent editions of the *DSM* have struggled with the question of comorbidity—some of the new categories cover what, earlier, would have been called comorbid conditions—but this problem will remain an issue for those revising the manual.

Predictive Validity   An assessment tool with high descriptive validity is one that helps us describe the person's current behavior. An assessment method with high predictive validity is one that helps us answer important questions about that behavior. In abnormal psychology, the most important questions involve determining cause, prognosis, and treatment. The extent to which a diagnosis answers those questions is the extent of its predictive validity.

Some diagnostic labels have high predictive validity in some respects. We know, for example, that people diagnosed as manic or schizophrenic are likely to respond to certain drugs. Likewise, we know that

Comorbidity: Disturbance as a Package

One of every two people in this country has had or will have a serious psychological disorder, and one of three has had to cope with such a disorder within the past year. These sobering figures were the product of a recent survey of over 8,000 people, ages 15 to 54—the first survey ever to administer a structured face-to-face mental health interview to a representative sample of the population of the United States (Kessler, McGonagle, Zhao, et al., 1994).

The subjects were questioned as to whether they had suffered any 1 of 14 major disorders described in the *DSM* and, if so, what treatment they had received. Leading the list were major depression, alcohol dependence, and phobias. (Remember that the prevalence rate of 50 percent was for only 14 disorders. What would the rate have been if the researchers had inquired about all the *DSM* disorders?) As surprising as the prevalence was the rate of treatment. Less than 40 percent of those who reported having had a disorder had ever sought or received treatment.

The primary focus of this study was comorbidity—two or more disorders occurring simultaneously—and the results were eye-opening. The National Comorbidity Survey (NCS) discovered that having two or more psychological disorders at the same time is more common than having just one. Almost 80 percent of the disorders reported to the NCS coexisted with at least one other disorder. Interestingly, these comorbid disorders tended to be concentrated in a relatively small sector of the population. More than 50 percent of all the reported disorders occurred in the 14 percent of the subjects who had a history of three or more comorbid disorders. This group—which also tended to have the most serious disorders—tended to be urban, low-income, poorly educated, white, female, and aged 20 to 40. (In general, the more years, the more money, and the more education a subject had, the less likely he or she was to report a current disorder.) If nothing else, we now know which segment of the population is most in need of psychological services.

Only recently has comorbidity come to be a pressing issue in abnormal psychology. Now, in view of the NCS findings, it will surely be more discussed. Perhaps the most important question about cases of comorbidity is whether, in fact, they represent comorbidity. When a person shows symptoms of two different disorders, does he or she really have two disorders—or just one complex disorder that our diagnostic system is wrongly separating into two?

Consider the relationship between antisocial personality disorder (a long-standing pattern of violating the rights of others—see Chapter 17) and substance dependence. These two disorders often turn up in the same person—so often, indeed, that each is mentioned in the *DSM*'s description of the other. But *are* they two different disorders? Sometimes it is possible, from the person's history, to see how one seemed to give rise to the other—how, for example, a heroin addiction eventually led the person into antisocial acts (theft, betrayal of friends, abandonment of children) or, conversely, how a long-standing pattern of antisocial behavior eventually came to include heroin addiction. But very often the two patterns develop simultaneously. Furthermore, even if one precedes the other, this does not prove that it caused the other. Possibly, both were caused by something else altogether.

The comorbidity question, then, has to do with more than terminology. How we define a disorder affects our theories of causation. It also affects treatment decisions. Consider, for example, a person whose heroin dependence developed as part of a long-standing pattern of antisocial behavior. If he is diagnosed as having two comorbid disorders—substance dependence and antisocial personality disorder—this may obscure the fact that what he really needs to be treated for is antisocial personality disorder and that, without such treatment, any therapy for the drug problem is likely to be a waste of time.

On the other hand, it might still be useful to provide both diagnoses; whether or not each represents a separate disorder, each may require separate treatment. In the above case, the fact that the drug dependence seemed to develop as a consequence of the antisocial personality disorder does not mean that it will automatically clear up if the person is treated for antisocial personality disorder. By that point, the drug habit may have developed a life of its own, creating the conditions for its continuance. Furthermore, any drug problem will seriously affect the person's chances of responding to treatment for antisocial personality disorder (just as, conversely, antisocial tendencies will undermine drug treatment).

Antisocial personality disorder and drug dependence are not the only pair of disorders involved in the comorbidity question. There are a number of such pairings, and the list will no doubt lengthen as research continues. In light of the NCS finding that most cases of psychological disorder are actually cases of more than one disorder, our current way of viewing psychological abnormality—as a matter of discrete syndromes—may have to be revised. Even if the syndromes remain separate, we will need to study them not in isolation but in interaction.

---

many people diagnosed as either manic or depressive will probably recover within a short time—and that they will probably have further episodes of mood disturbance. Diagnostic labels offer less information, however, as to the course of milder disturbances or the treatment they will respond to.

It is possible that the limited predictive validity of diagnosis is due primarily to its limited reliability.

Assessment techniques must be geared to the capabilities of the subject. Some children will not respond well to a formal interview. The assessor may find it more effective to let the child's concerns emerge through play in an informal setting.

While an assessment technique that has high reliability may have low validity,* the reverse is not true. To have high validity, a system must have high reliability. The improved reliability of the recent editions of the *DSM* may result in improved validity. In one study, for example, the records of 134 patients, all potential candidates for a diagnosis of schizophrenia, were examined. The patients were diagnosed according to four sets of criteria, one of which was *DSM-III*. Follow-up records were also available, in which the patients were interviewed on an average of 6½ years after the initial interview. Of the four sets of criteria, *DSM-III* was the most accurate in predicting which of the patients continued to show poor adjustment (Helzer, Brockington, & Kendell, 1981).

Problems in Assessment

The reliability and validity of any assessment tool can be affected by a number of problems, some having to do with the administration of the measure, others with its interpretation. One such problem is the assessor—his or her personal manner and how it affects the person being assessed (Leckliter & Matarazzo, 1994). If a diagnostician tends to be very formal and businesslike during a diagnostic interview, the subject—particularly a child or a troubled adult—may respond in a

guarded way. If the diagnostician interprets this behavior as a reflection of paranoid or depressive leanings and diagnoses accordingly, how are the people who later treat the patient to know that the "paranoia" or "depression" was, in part, a response to the diagnostician? Even attributes that the examiner cannot control, such as physical appearance, race, and gender, may affect the subject's performance.

Assessors affect examination results more directly through their interpretation of the evidence. Subjects present many different sorts of information; diagnosticians must filter all of it through their own minds, selecting what seems most important. In the process, they are bound to be influenced by their own biases. For example, some diagnosticians favor certain diagnoses over others. Indeed, there have often been marked differences in diagnosis between hospitals, between communities, and between countries. For years, what was called depression in England was often called schizophrenia in the United States (Cooper, Kendell, Gurland, et al., 1972). Likewise, one hospital may have long experience treating manic episodes, while a neighboring hospital has equally long experience with paranoid schizophrenia—largely because those are the diagnostic labels favored by their respective staffs. On a more comprehensive level, many critics feel that diagnosticians in general have a "pathological bias"—a tendency to see sickness instead of health. Diagnosticians often have neither the tools nor the training to assess areas of strength, whereas they are carefully trained to spot signs of weakness and deviance (Hartlage, Howard, & Ostrow, 1984). Consequently, it is weakness and deviance that they tend to find. (See the box on page 31.)

---

*For example, astrology has high reliability. People can be grouped according to birth date with great consistency and accuracy. But, in order to have high validity as well, these groupings would have to reflect what the astrologers claim they reflect—namely, individual personality traits. Because there is no evidence that they do, the system has low validity.

Finally, pragmatic considerations may interfere with accurate evaluation. When psychological treatment is paid for through company insurance, word of the patient's "condition" may reach the ears of his or her co-workers. Anticipating such gossip, diagnosticians may apply a label that indicates a milder disturbance than they feel the patient actually has. In other instances, they may exaggerate a patient's disturbance—again, for practical reasons. The Veterans Administration, for example, pays higher benefits to veterans diagnosed as psychotic than to those with less severe diagnoses. Thus, when a patient's financial circumstances are particularly bad, psychiatrists may favor the evidence for psychosis.

Recent editions of the *DSM* have tried to minimize these interferences in various ways, principally by making the criteria for a diagnosis very specific and by establishing for each disorder a fixed "decision rule," or minimum number of symptoms that must be present for a patient to receive that diagnosis. Under "major depressive episode," for example, the manual lists nine symptoms (Chapter 9) and then specifies that, for that diagnosis to be given, the person must have shown five of the symptoms during the same two-week period. Such a rule is harder to interpret freely than the vaguer descriptions in earlier editions of the manual.

Another suggestion that has been offered for minimizing assessment interferences is that diagnosticians should rely more on statistical relationships, or *actuarial judgment,* than on their own clinical judgment. Insurance companies, for example, use actuarial judgment to calculate risks. Given an applicant who is male, 50 years old, married, and the survivor of one heart attack, they use tables based on the histories of other such people to calculate what this person's life expectancy is and what his medical expenses are likely to be. Because research has shown that actuarial judgment is superior to clinical judgment (Dawes, Faust, & Meehl, 1989; Marchese, 1992), it has been proposed that particularly in making treatment decisions—whether a patient should be given psychotherapy, put on drugs, or hospitalized—diagnosticians should turn to the actuarial method. One problem with the actuarial approach is that diagnosticians sometimes confront rare situations for which statistical data are not available—for example, in deciding whether a particular type of person is likely to commit random acts of unprovoked violence.

Even if the diagnostic system were flawless, however, there would still be a problem, because a certain percentage of diagnosticians simply do not follow the rules. A study of *DSM-III* diagnoses made by psychiatrists and graduating psychiatric residents found that 48 percent of the psychiatrists' patients and 36 percent of the residents' patients did not satisfy the diagnostic criteria for the disorders ascribed to them (Jampala, Sierles, & Taylor, 1986). Many therapists whose patients tend to have the normal run of middle-class sorrows fall back repeatedly on certain diagnoses (anxiety disorder and adjustment disorder are particular favorites) that they feel are specific enough to satisfy the insurance company but "harmless" and vague enough not to invade the patient's privacy. Consequently, they seldom even open the diagnostic manual.

Methods of Assessment

Assessment techniques fall into four general categories: the interview, psychological tests, laboratory tests, and observation in natural settings.

The Interview

Of all the methods of assessment, the **interview,** consisting of a face-to-face conversation between subject and examiner, is the oldest, the most commonly used, and the most versatile. It may be highly structured, with the subject answering a prearranged sequence of questions, or it may be unstructured, giving subjects the chance to describe their problem in their own way. The evaluation method also varies from structured to unstructured. Even after a highly structured question-and-answer session, examiners may rely primarily on their own subjective impressions in evaluating subjects. Alternatively, they may follow a detailed manual to score subjects' responses, giving 1 point for one type of response, 2 points for another type of response, and so forth.

The degree of structure in the interview and the questions asked depend on the interviewer's purpose. If the aim is simply to put the client at ease, in an effort to promote trust and candor, then the structure will be loose. This is usually the case, for example, with the intake interview at the beginning of psychotherapy. However, interviewers often have a clear idea of what kind of information they need and cannot waste too much time obtaining it. Therefore, most interviews have a definable structure.

The major pitfall of assessment by interview is that it can give uncontrolled play to interviewers' subjectivity and biases. Interviewers, like most of the rest of us, have feelings about blacks and whites, women and men, handsome people and plain people, even short people and tall people, and such feelings, not to speak of more specific biases, can influence the results of the interview.

A Sample SCID Interview

In this section of the SCID interview, the diagnostician is evaluating the subject for major depressive disorder. Note how structured the interview is. The questions are specified, and they deal with six symptoms of the disorder. (See the sentences in italics.) Depending on the answers, the diagnostician will give the person a score of 1 (symptom absent), 2 (symptom mild), or 3 (symptom pronounced) for each of the six items.

Now I am going to ask you some more questions about your mood.

- In the last month . . .

  Has there been a period of time when you were feeling depressed or down most of the day nearly every day? (What was that like?)

  IF YES: How long did it last? (As long as two weeks?)

- *What about losing interest or pleasure in things you usually enjoyed?*

  IF YES: Was it nearly every day? How long did it last? (As long as two weeks?)

- During the worst two weeks of last month . . .

  Did you lose or gain any weight? (How much?) (Were you trying to lose weight?)

  IF NO: How was your appetite? (What about compared to your usual appetite?) (Did you have to force yourself to eat?) (Eat [less/ more] than usual?) (Was that nearly every day?)

- *How were you sleeping? (Trouble falling asleep, waking frequently, trouble staying asleep, waking too early, OR sleeping too much?*

  How many hours a night compared to usual? Was that nearly every night?)

- *Were you so fidgety or restless that you were unable to sit still? (Was it so bad that other people noticed it? What did they notice? Was that nearly every day?)*

  IF NO: What about the opposite—talking or moving more slowly than is normal for you? (Was it so bad that other people noticed it? What did they notice? Was that nearly every day?)

- *What was your energy like? (Tired all the time? Nearly every day?)*

Adapted from *SCID Newsletter*, vol. 1, issue 1.

For this reason, a fairly structured interview and scoring system are often recommended, even though the subject's responses and the interviewer's intuitive powers are thereby restricted. When the purpose of the interview is diagnosis, and particularly when the diagnosis is to be used in research—for example, to assemble a study group—researchers use highly structured interviews. One such interview is the Schedule for Affective Disorders and Schizophrenia, or SADS (Endicott & Spitzer, 1978), which, with its own, special scoring system, has proved highly reliable (Andreasen, McDonald-Scott, Grove, et al., 1982). Another is the Structured Clinical Interview for *DSM-IV*, or SCID, widely used by clinicians to help in providing *DSM*-based diagnoses. (See the box above.) A third is the Diagnostic Interview Schedule, or DIS, of the National Institute of Mental Health (Robins, Helzer, Croughan, et al., 1981), which yields diagnoses by computer. Such diagnostic tools do not have high coverage, but that is not their purpose. Their goal is to give diagnoses as precisely as possible, so that, when a team of researchers says that a new drug worked or didn't work with a group of schizophrenics, they can be fairly certain that it was, in fact, tested on a group of schizophrenics. A number of researchers (e.g., Blashfield & Livesley, 1991) have shown that structured diagnostic interviews do greatly improve the reliability of diagnosis.

A very widely used form of interview is the mental status exam, or MSE. The MSE is to mental problems what a physical checkup is to medical problems—that is, a very broad examination aimed at turning up any sign of disorder. Through observation and questioning, the diagnostician rates the patient on appearance, speech, mood, perception, thought content, and cognitive processes (Ginsberg, 1985). The purpose is not just to detect disorders but, above all, to spot dementia (severe mental deterioration) and other organic brain disorders. A shorter form of the MSE is the mini mental status exam, or MMS. (See the sample questions in the box on p. 40.) The MMS is the world's most widely used screening method for dementia (Mohs, 1995). Our sample patient, Joe, was given a clinical interview and a mental status exam. See the box on page 40 for the examiner's "behavioral observations."

Psychological Tests

More structured than the normal interview, the psychological test is a standard procedure in which persons are presented with a series of stimuli to which they are asked to respond. Such a test, like the highly structured interview, gives the subject little freedom in responding, but, because of its restrictive quality, the psychological test can be scored more easily and more objectively. In fact, many psychological tests are scored by computer.

The Mini Mental Status Exam

Orientation:
- What is the year?
- What is the season?
- What is the day of the week?
- What is the month?
- Can you tell me where we are? (residence or street name required)
- What city/town are we in?

Registration:
- I am going to name three objects. After I have said them, I want you to repeat them. Remember what they are because I am going to ask you to name them again in a few minutes. "Apple ... Table ... Penny."

Attention and calculation:
- Can you subtract 7 from 100, and then subtract 7 from the answer you get and keep subtracting 7 until I tell you to stop?
- Now I am going to spell a word forwards and I want you to spell it backwards (in reverse order). The word is WORLD. W-O-R-L-D.

Recall:
- Now what were the three objects I asked you to remember?

Language:
- What is this called? (Show watch.)
- What is this called? (Show pencil.)
- Now I would like you to repeat a phrase after me: "No ifs, ands, or buts."

- Take this paper in your right hand, fold the paper in half using both hands, and put the paper down, using your left hand.
- Pick the paper up and write a short sentence on it for me. (Sentence must have subject and verb and make sense.)
- Please turn to page 8 in your booklet. Now copy the design that you see printed on the page. (Design is interlocking pentagons. The result must have five-sided figures, with intersection forming a four-sided figure.)

Adapted from Holzer, Tischler, Leaf, et al., 1984, p. 6.

EVALUATION OF JOE: Behavioral Observations

Joe was a 23-year-old white male, heavy set. He was dressed in a T-shirt, shorts, and basketball shoes without laces. His movement was rather sluggish. He had a constant hand tremor, and his legs shook vigorously when he was nervous. His speech, though coherent, was hesitant and poorly articulated. He seemed proud and at ease when he was responding correctly; when confronted with failure, he became uncomfortable and embarrassed. His comprehension of the instructions was adequate, and he asked for clarification when he needed it. His concentration was satisfactory in general, but his attention wandered when he was having a hard time with a question. He was quick to establish rapport with the examiner and was cooperative throughout the examination.

For decades, the dominant method of psychological testing has been the **psychometric approach.** The aim of this method is to locate stable underlying characteristics, or **traits** (e.g., anxiety, passivity, aggression, intelligence), that presumably exist in differing degrees in everyone. Because it assumes the existence of stable traits and aims to measure them, the psychometric method considers response variability due to situational influences to be simply a source of error and makes every effort to screen out such influences. For example, instead of leaving it to examiners to give the test instructions in their own words—words that might vary in substance and tone from one examiner to the next—most psychological tests now

provide extremely precise directions that the examiner reads aloud to the subjects, just as with the Scholastic Assessment Test (SAT).

There are many kinds of psychological tests. We will discuss intelligence tests, projective personality tests, self-report personality inventories, and tests for organic impairment.

Intelligence Tests **Intelligence tests** were the first of the psychological assessment techniques to be widely used. Modern intelligence tests are based on the work of Alfred Binet, the French psychologist who in 1905 introduced the first intelligence test into the French school system to help teachers determine which children would require special education. Later revised by Lewis Terman of Stanford University and now known as the Stanford-Binet Intelligence Scale, the test measures a child's ability to recognize objects in a picture, to remember a series of digits, to define simple words, to complete sentences in a logical fashion, and so forth. There is also an adult version of the test, with comparable tasks scaled to adult abilities. The subject's final score on the test is rendered as an **intelligence quotient,** or **IQ.**

Another widely used series of intelligence tests is the Wechsler Intelligence Scales. Developed by American psychologist David Wechsler, these tests, unlike the Stanford-Binet tests, yield not only a general IQ but also a Verbal IQ, measuring verbal ability, knowledge, and comprehension, and a Performance IQ, measuring problem solving and intelligence in a way that does not depend upon verbal

The Wechsler Intelligence Scales measure a number of dimensions of intelligence, including Performance IQ. In the segment of that test shown here, the subject is being timed as he tries to reproduce a pattern of blocks.

■ EVALUATION OF JOE: Intellectual Functioning

Joe is functioning at a level of mild mental retardation (full scale IQ: 59; verbal scale IQ: 61; performance scale IQ: 56). His results on a school achievement test placed him at a third-grade level. His performance on a picture vocabulary test was equivalent to that of a 10-year-old. His main cognitive difficulties seem to be in perceptual accuracy, visual-motor-spatial integration, and information processing. This is probably due to an organic brain impairment.

Such cognitive problems are obviously an important factor in his current poor adjustment. His thinking is simple and concrete; therefore, he is at a loss, and becomes disorganized, in complex or ambiguous situations. In particular, he has difficulty understanding cause-and-effect relationships. He acknowledges, for example, that his temper and his drug use were the reasons for his dismissal from the group home, but he doesn't see why. His ability to distinguish right from wrong is at a very superficial level.

ability (see Figure 2.2). When Verbal IQ is being assessed, adults might be asked how many days there are in a year or how many state capitals there are in the United States. When Performance IQ is being assessed, they might be asked to transcribe a code or to reproduce a design with colored blocks. There are three Wechsler tests, each geared to a different age group: the Wechsler Adult Intelligence Scale–Revised (WAIS-R), the Wechsler Intelligence Scale for Children (WISC-III), and the Wechsler Preschool and Primary Scale of Intelligence–Revised (WPPSI-R). Joe was given the WAIS-R, together with two other intelligence tests. His results are summarized in the box in the next column.

The potential influence of intelligence tests is very great. Not only do they play an important part in the diagnosis of mental retardation and brain damage, but, unlike all other psychological tests, they are routinely given to schoolchildren across the country, often with serious consequences. Ability tests can determine whether students are placed in special education or "gifted" classes, what high schools and colleges they will attend, and in turn what kind of education they will receive.

Because of their importance, intelligence tests are very carefully designed. They have been shown to have high internal consistency: a person will do approximately the same on different items measuring the same kind of ability. They also have high test-retest reliability: a person who takes the same IQ test twice, several years apart, will score approximately the same both times (Lindemann & Matarazzo, 1990; Parker, Hanson, & Hunsley, 1988). Finally, the validity of the major IQ tests has been shown to be relatively high in that there is a strong correlation between children's IQ scores and their later performance in school (Anastasi, 1982; Parker, Hanson, & Hunsley, 1988).

But is the ability to do well in our school systems the most important measure of intelligence? As Wechsler (1958) pointed out, intelligence is not an existing *thing*, such as heart rate or blood pressure, that can be objectively quantified. Rather, it is an inferred construct. We infer what we call intelligence from what we consider correct behavior in response to various problems. For a number of years, it has been charged that both our schools and our IQ tests are culturally biased—that they interpret as intelligence what is actually just familiarity with middle-class culture (Armour-Thomas, 1992; Puente, 1990). A test question that asks whether a cup goes with a bowl, a spoon, or a saucer will not be easy for a lower-income child who has never seen a saucer.

Paraphrased Wechslerlike Questions

General Information
1. How many wings does a bird have?
2. How many nickels make a dime?
3. What is steam made of?
4. Who wrote "Paradise Lost"?
5. What is pepper?

General Comprehension
1. What should you do if you see someone forget his book when he leaves his seat in a restaurant?
2. What is the advantage of keeping money in a bank?
3. Why is copper often used in electrical wires?

Arithmetic
1. Sam had three pieces of candy and Joe gave him four more. How many pieces of candy did Sam have altogether?
2. Three men divided eighteen golf balls equally among themselves, How many golf balls did each man receive?
3. If two apples cost 15c, what will be the cost of a dozen apples?

Similarities
1. In what way are a lion and a tiger alike?
2. In what way are a saw and hammer alike?
3. In what way are an hour and a week alike?
4. In what way are a circle and a triangle alike?

Vocabulary
This test consists simply of asking, "What is a _____ ?" or "What does _____ mean?" The words cover a wide range of difficulty or familiarity.

Block Design

FIGURE 2.2   These test items are similar to those included in the various Wechsler Intelligence Scales. *(Left)* A sampling of questions from five of the verbal subtests. *(Right)* A problem in block design—the subject is asked to arrange a set of blocks to match a pattern like the one shown.

In recent years, efforts have been made to remove inadvertent cultural bias from the major IQ tests.

A more general challenge to IQ testing is whether it reflects too narrow a view of mental ability. Psychologist Howard Gardner (Gardner & Hatch, 1989) has argued that traditional IQ tests measure only three components of intelligence: verbal ability, mathematical-logical reasoning, and spatial-perceptual skills. In Gardner's view, there are at least four other important kinds of intelligence: musical ability, physical skill, interpersonal ability (the capacity to understand others), and intrapersonal ability (the capacity to understand oneself). The empathy of a friend, the skills of Michelle Kwan or Michael Jordan—in our culture these are not considered components of "intelligence," and they are not what IQ tests aim to measure. According to Gardner, they should be, for they are controlled by the brain and help to determine people's success in life.

One criticism of IQ testing is that it fails to measure all components of intelligence. For example, traditional IQ tests would not account for the musical talent demonstrated by this violinist. Howard Gardner proposed a broader view of mental ability, naming seven important kinds of intelligence, of which musical ability is one.

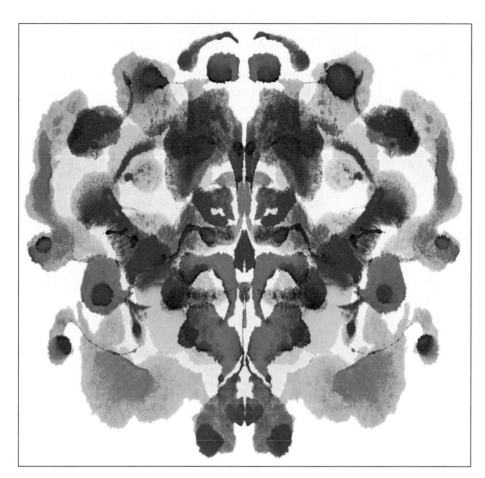

FIGURE 2.3 An inkblot card similar to those used in the Rorschach test. In this test, the subject is asked to describe what he or she "sees" in the design, and why.

Projective Personality Tests Projective personality tests are based on the psychodynamic assumption that people's true motives, because they are largely unconscious, must be drawn out indirectly. Accordingly, projective tests expose subjects to ambiguous stimuli into which they must "read" meaning. Whatever meaning they give to the stimulus is thought to contain clues to their unconscious processes—clues that the interviewer must interpret.

The Rorschach Most famous of the projective tests is the Rorschach Psychodiagnostic Inkblot Test (Rorschach, 1942), in which subjects are asked to respond to 10 cards, each showing a symmetrical inkblot design. The designs vary in complexity and coloring. The test is administered in 2 phases. In the first phase, the *free-association* phase, subjects are asked to describe as specifically as possible what each card reminds them of. In the second phase, called the *inquiry* phase, subjects are asked which characteristics of each inkblot contributed to the formation of their impression of that inkblot.

As we pointed out earlier, highly unstructured interviewing methods may be combined with highly structured scoring methods. This is the case with the Rorschach. The subjective material elicited by the inkblots is generally evaluated according to a detailed manual, indicating how specific responses are to be interpreted (Beck, 1961; Exner, 1978, 1982, 1986). For example, an important aspect of the evaluation depends on the extent to which the subject's responses represent what is called "good form"—that is, how plausible the subject's interpretation of a picture is in view of the shapes contained in it. Consider, for example, the inkblot in Figure 2.3, which might reasonably be interpreted as an elaborate flower or insect. Many other readings are plausible as well, but if a subject claimed that what he or she saw in this picture was a small boy crouching in a corner—something that actually contradicts the form of the inkblot—then the interviewer might conclude that the response reflected an inner conflict and distortion of reality (or that the subject was not taking the test seriously). See the box on page 44 for Joe's response to a Rorschach card.

The examiner also weighs the content of the subject's responses. If a certain theme keeps reappearing in the subject's interpretations, then, depending on the nature of the theme, the examiner may take it as

EVALUATION OF JOE: The Rorschach Test

The assessor (A) showed Joe (J) a card and asked him what it looked like:

J: A forest and a fire around it.
A: [Repeats Joe's response.]
J: Here is the fire.
A: What makes it look like a fire?
J: How the flames are up in the air.
A: What makes it look like flames?
J: Because it's burning the tree.
A: What makes it look like it's burning the tree?
J: Someone started it. You can tell by the bushes in flames.
A: What makes it look like flames to you?
J: How it's colored, because fire is yellow.
A: What makes it look like bushes to you?
J: Because you got the tree standing.
A: What makes it look like a tree to you?
J: Because it's big, and it has leaves on it.
A: What makes it look like leaves to you?
J: The way how it's shaded.

a clue to underlying conflicts. Water, for example, may be interpreted as a sign of alcoholism; eyes as indicative of paranoid suspicion; and so forth.

The TAT   A second popular projective technique is the Thematic Apperception Test, or TAT. In this test, the subject is presented with a series of pictures. Unlike the abstract Rorschach inkblots, most of the TAT pictures show a person, or possibly two or three people, doing something. The scenes are ambiguous enough to allow for a variety of interpretations, yet they nudge the subject in the direction of certain kinds of associations. For example, the picture at the far left in Figure 2.4, showing a man in a business suit coming through a door, might tap the subject's feelings about his or her father. Some researchers (e.g., Rapaport, Gill, & Shaefer, 1968) claim that certain cards are particularly useful in eliciting specific kinds of information, such as the presence of underlying depression, suicidal thoughts, and strong aggressive impulses. A sample of Joe's responses to the TAT test can be found in the first box on page 45.

As with the Rorschach, subjects go through the cards one by one. With each card, they are asked to describe what has led up to the scene presented in the picture, what is going on in the picture, what the characters are thinking and feeling, and what the outcome will be. Like the Rorschach, the TAT includes an inquiry phase to clarify ambiguous responses. Then, through a complex scoring system, the subject's responses are converted into an interpretation of his or her unconscious conflicts and motivations. A children's version of this test, the *Children's Apperception Test,* or *CAT* (Bellak, 1954), follows

FIGURE 2.4   Pictures similar to those used in the Thematic Apperception Test (TAT). In this test, the subject is asked to tell a story about what is being shown in the pictures.

EVALUATION OF JOE: The TAT Test

Following are Joe's responses to three of the TAT cards. Most of his responses contained themes of violence.

Card 1 This is a boy who is looking at a gun. Don't know if it's loaded or not. He's thinking about using it on himself, like killing himself. He tries to find some bullets for the gun in his dad's room, and he will find the bullets and will shoot himself three times in the head.

Card 14 This is a man who looks like he's escaping from prison because of a murder that he committed. So he asks his friend to go with him, and the friend goes with him, and they will run into the forest. The guards are chasing them with their dogs, and they get caught.

Card 13 This is John and his wife, Mary. John has been married to Mary for about 6 years. One day John came home from work and found Mary in bed dead. He was shocked, terrified. Police came to their home and questioned John, and he said he didn't do it. He was framed for murder, so then John had to go to jail because he was framed, and his lawyer talked to him. Then they went to court, and the jury decided that he was not guilty.

EVALUATION OF JOE: Sentence Completion Test

This is a sampling of Joe's responses to the Sentence Completion Test. His words are in italics.

He felt held back by *his anger.*
Because of his mother, *he ran away.*
Most women should *realize that they love their children.*
His family treats him as *dirt.*
Most of all he wants *another home.*
He got sore when *he started drinking.*
He would be happy if *he was more smarter.*
Most men act as though *they are rich.*
Ever since he got sick, *he got better.*
When others have to rely on him he *gets upset.*
When they turned him down for the job he *got mad.*
He is afraid of *himself.* [Interviewer asks why.] *Sometimes I feel like I'm in a different world.*
He is ashamed of *himself.* [Interviewer asks why.] *Because he can't get the attention that he needs.*
Whenever he was with his mother he felt *nervous.*
He thinks of himself as *mature.*
The main thing in his marriage is *money.*
His first sexual experience *was when I was about 16. I didn't get her pregnant.*
In the company of women he feels *happier.*
What he really thought would help him *is going for help, getting some help.*
When they left him flat, *he got an attorney.*
It makes him nervous when *he has to talk about different things that upset him.*
Following the sexual act he usually feels *embarrassed.*
He felt to blame when *it was his own fault.*
Taking orders, *couldn't take them good.*
When he saw that he was not getting ahead *he worked on it.*
Compared to most men he *hurts.*
The main thing in his life *is that he will get his life back together.*
Anybody would be angry if *I tried to kill myself.*

the same principles as the TAT, except that the scenes focus on situations particularly relevant to children, such as feeding, toileting, and rivalry.

There are other projective tests as well, including the *Sentence Completion Test*, in which the interviewer reads the first part of a sentence and the subject supplies the rest. The box in the next column shows Joe's responses to the Sentence Completion Test.

Evaluation of Projective Tests Of all the forms of psychological testing, the projective techniques allow subjects the greatest freedom in expressing themselves. However, these tests also allow the interviewer the greatest freedom in interpreting the responses, and herein lies their major problem. Opponents of the projective tests claim that the chain of inference leading from the subject's response to the interviewer's report is simply too long, too complex, and too subjective, with the result that the report may tell more about the interviewer than about the subject. This argument has been supported by numerous studies (e.g., Datel & Gengerelli, 1955; Howard, 1962; Little & Shneidman, 1959) showing poor interjudge reliability for the projective tests. And, as may be expected when a method lends itself to many different clinical interpretations, many researchers have found the validity of the projective tests to be disturbingly low (Dawes, 1994; Nunnally, 1978). It was partly in response to such findings that empirically based scoring systems were developed for the projective tests. The Exner scoring system for the Rorschach is a highly detailed procedure in which the subject's responses are reduced to a numerical pattern, which is then compared with patterns derived from a variety of normative groups. This system has led to improved validity of the Rorschach for several purposes (Parker, Hanson, & Hunsley, 1988; Weiner, 1996).

Whatever the scientific standing of projective testing, its supporters claim that this is the only assessment method open and flexible enough to provide information about the subject's unconscious processes. Furthermore, on a projective test it is hard for subjects to "fake" their responses (Ganellen, 1994). (As we shall see in the next section, falsification is a problem with the more objective self-report tests.) Because of these advantages, the Rorschach and the TAT are among the most frequently used psychological tests (Lubin, Larsen, & Matarazzo, 1984; Piotrowski, Keller, & Ogawa, 1993). It was on the basis of projective tests, together with the clinical interview and the mental status exam, that Joe's assessor drew up the personality profile in the box in the next column.

Self-Report Personality Inventories   Unlike projective tests, **self-report personality inventories** ask the subjects direct questions about themselves. Such a test may instruct subjects to rate a long list of descriptive statements—such as "I am afraid of the dark" or "I prefer to be alone most of the time"—according to their applicability to themselves. Or the test may consist of a list of things or situations that subjects are asked to rate according to whether they are appealing or frightening. In any case, in the self-report inventory, as the name indicates, subjects assess themselves. This self-assessment may not be taken at face value by the testers, but it is given some weight.

The MMPI-2   The most widely used self-report personality inventory is the **Minnesota Multiphasic Personality Inventory-2**, or **MMPI-2** (Hathaway & McKinley, 1943, 1989). The purpose of the MMPI-2 is to simplify differential diagnosis by comparing self-descriptive statements endorsed by new patients to those endorsed by groups of people already diagnosed as schizophrenic, depressive, and so forth. Thus, it is important to note that an evaluation produced by the MMPI-2 is not derived directly from the subject's self-description. A person who answers yes to such statements as "Someone is pouring dirty thoughts into my head" is not automatically judged to be schizophrenic. Rather, the evaluation depends on whether responses to these and other statements show a *pattern* similar to that seen in the MMPI-2 responses of already diagnosed schizophrenics.

The test items range from statements of ordinary vocational and recreational preferences to descriptions of bizarre thoughts and behaviors. We have already given one example of the latter. Other items similar to those on the MMPI-2 checklist are

"I go to a party every week."

"I am afraid of picking up germs when I shake hands."

EVALUATION OF JOE: Personality Profile

Joe's stress tolerance is far lower than the average. At the same time, he is faced with extraordinary stress in the form of neglect by his family, who essentially abandoned him four years ago. (See his sentence completion: "His family treats him as *dirt*.") He has a hard time controlling his emotions and tends to respond in an intense and impulsive manner. This causes him to be rejected by others, which makes him even more desperate and uncontrolled, which in turn provokes further rejection—a vicious cycle.

His poor perception of reality, due to his intellectual handicap, makes it even harder for him to respond appropriately. When frustrated, he becomes overtly aggressive. He seems to have a considerable amount of anger. Nearly all his TAT stories had to do with violence. His obsession with injury to himself and others should be taken seriously. He has been injured in the past. By his account, he was sexually molested by his stepfather on numerous occasions.

His self-image is both positive and negative. He sees himself as kind and generous, and on the Sentence Completion Test he describes himself as mature. He says that he wants to join the police force. On the other hand, he is aware of his intellectual shortcomings (see sentence completion: "He would be happy if *he was more smarter*"), and much of the time he feels inadequate, insecure, and confused. ("Sometimes I feel like I'm in a different world.")

"I forgive people easily."

"I sometimes enjoy breaking the law."

The test items were originally compiled from a variety of sources—psychiatry textbooks, directions for psychiatric and medical interviews, and previously published personality tests (Hathaway & McKinley, 1940). These items were tried out on groups of patients hospitalized for schizophrenia, depression, and so on, and then given to normal subjects. Only those items on which the pathological groups substantially diverged from the normal groups were retained. In the end, the test was made up of over 500 statements, yielding a rating of the subject on 10 clinical scales. The following are the 10 scales, along with the characteristics that might be inferred from a high score on any one of them:

Hypochondriasis: anxious over bodily functioning

Depression: hopeless

Hysteria: immature, suggestible, demanding

Psychopathic deviate: amoral, unscrupulous, rebellious

Masculinity-femininity: characterized by traits and interests typically associated with the opposite sex

Paranoia: suspicious, jealous

Psychasthenia: fearful, unconfident

Schizophrenia: withdrawn, disorganized in thought processes

Hypomania: impulsive, distractible

Social introversion: shy, self-effacing

In addition to the clinical scales, the MMPI-2 uses a number of control scales designed to measure the validity of the subject's responses. The *L (Lie) scale* indicates the degree to which the subject appears to be falsifying responses in a naive way in order to "look good." For example, if the subject checks "false" next to a statement such as "I do not always tell the truth," this will boost his or her score on the L scale. The *K (Subtle Defensiveness) scale* measures less obvious kinds of defensiveness. Most educated people would know better than to claim on a psychological test that they never told a lie, but if, for example, they were involved in a child-custody case, they might be motivated to distort the truth about their moral character in subtler ways. This is what the K scale is designed to detect. Roughly the opposite of the L and K scales is the *F (Infrequency) scale,* which measures the subject's tendency to *exaggerate* his or her psychological problems. Included on the MMPI-2 are a number of statements (e.g., "Someone has been trying to rob me," "Evil spirits possess me at times") that are very infrequently endorsed by normal subjects and that people with mental disorders endorse only selectively, in a manner consistent with their symptoms. Subjects who frequently and unselectively endorse these statements receive a high F-scale score, which may mean that they are trying to fake mental illness—for example, for the sake of a lawsuit claiming psychological injury—or that they are very distressed and trying to get help. (Alternatively, it may mean that they have reading problems or are responding randomly.) When the MMPI was revised in 1989, several additional control scales were added (Butcher, 1990).

The usual procedure for evaluating an MMPI-2 is to arrange the subject's scores on the various scales in numerical order, from the highest to the lowest score, and then to interpret the pattern of scores by comparison with patterns seen in normal and pathological groups, rather than to interpret any one scale separately. Some clinicians do draw diagnostic conclusions from scores on individual scales. A clinician may assume, for example, that a person who scores high on the depression scale is a good candidate for the psychiatric diagnosis of depression—that is, that he or she will show not only sadness but also guilt, lack of motivation, sleeping and eating problems, and other symptoms of depression. Such one-scale diagnoses are apparently not very meaningful, however. In a review of several studies on the relationship between specific symptoms and individual MMPI scales, Hedlund (1977) found that, although many of the scales were related to the expected symptoms, these symptoms were usually related to several (in some cases, almost all) of the other scales as well. Thus, scores on individual scales cannot, in general, yield sound diagnoses. Indeed, there is some doubt as to whether even the pattern of scores is a valid source of diagnostic information. The major value of the MMPI-2 is probably in communicating the degree of overall disturbance (mildly troubled, deeply troubled, etc.) rather than in pinpointing the exact nature of the disturbance.

Even as a measure of the degree of disturbance, the MMPI-2 is not an infallible instrument. A concern about the original edition of the test was the narrowness of the group of normal subjects on whom it was standardized. All were white, and most were young married people living in small towns or rural areas near Minneapolis, where the test was being devised. With the revision, the test was standardized on a much more representative sample (Graham, 1990) and modernized in other ways as well. Sexist language was removed, as were test items that seemed aimed at identifying people's religious beliefs.

However updated, the test still has many of its original shortcomings (Helmes & Reddon, 1993). Most important, it is still a self-report test and is thus faced with the problem that many people do not give accurate reports about themselves. Some will lie; others will fall into what are called **response sets**, test-taking attitudes that lead them to shade their responses one way or another, often unconsciously. One such response set is the *social desirability set,* the tendency to try to make oneself look good; another is the *acquiescence set,* the tendency to agree with statements whether they apply to oneself or not (Jackson & Messick, 1961). The control scales, as we saw, were designed to detect such distortions, but no one pretends that they eliminate all inaccuracy. In clinical settings, where people are usually taking the MMPI-2 because they have problems and want help, deliberate falsification is less likely, but it can easily occur in other situations, such as the screening of job applicants. As for unconscious falsification, it is probably common in all settings. The differences between the MMPI-2 and the Rorschach are summarized in Table 2.1.

The major argument in support of the MMPI-2 is that, because it can be scored by computer, it enables examiners to measure a given subject against

TABLE 2.1   Differences Between the Self-Report (MMPI-2) and the Rorschach Method of Personality Assessment

Characteristics of the Self-Report Method	Characteristics of the Rorschach Method
1. Expectations are well defined.	1. Expectations are minimally defined.
2. Stimuli are familiar.	2. Stimuli are novel.
3. It has a narrow range of response options.	3. It has a wide range of response options.
4. Task requires patient to consider self, decide if traits are characteristic, decide how to present self, and then indicate decisions on paper.	4. Task requires patient to formulate perceptions, decide which perceptions to articulate to the examiner, and then respond to further questions.
5. Administration and scoring require minimal skill.	5. Administration and scoring require considerable skill.
6. Patients are assumed to use a similar benchmark for deciding if trait is characteristic of themselves.	6. Examiner provides stable benchmark for classifying patient characteristics.
7. Measure is completed alone.	7. Measure is completed with an examiner.
8. It requires an in vitro description of personal characteristics.	8. It requires an in vivo demonstration of personal characteristics.
9. At best, raw data are dependent on conscious awareness and complexity of self-representations.	9. At best, raw data are dependent on engagement with the task and ability to articulate perceptions and their determinants.
10. Dissimulation and impression management affect reported symptoms.	10. Dissimulation and impression management affect engagement with task.
11. It is a better tool for obtaining information about specific overt symptoms, events, and experiences.	11. It is a better tool for assessing personality predilections which may or may not be evident in overt behavior or consciousness.

Source: Meyer, 1997, p. 299.

previously tested subjects with great precision (Butcher, 1978)—and with great speed. The computers that now analyze the answer sheets and make up the profiles can do so in less than 1½ seconds. Furthermore, although the test is not immune to error, it has been found to agree moderately with personality ratings by parents, spouses, and clinicians (Meyer, 1996).

The MCMI-III   While the MMPI-2 is used in a wide variety of contexts, another self-report test, the *Millon Clinical Multiaxial Inventory,* or *MCMI-III* (Millon, 1994), is intended specifically to aid in the diagnosis of disorders in the *DSM,* particularly the personality disorders. The personality disorders (Chapter 10) are long-standing patterns of maladaptive thought and behavior. Unlike most other disorders, they do not disrupt the person's life; they are part of that life—and, as such, they are hard to diagnose. The MCMI-III is an effort to solve this problem. The test is a 175-item true-false inventory that yields ratings on 20 clinical scales, all of which correspond to *DSM* categories, including the personality disorders. The correspondence between the *DSM* criteria and the MCMI-III is not exact. Millon has relied on his own theories, especially with regard to the personality disorders, as well as on the diagnostic man-

ual. But, as intended, the MCMI-III does a better job than other self-report inventories in identifying the patterns described in the *DSM* (Millon, 1994).

Psychological Tests for Organic Impairment   Psychological disturbance may be due to neurological problems rather than, or as well as, "life" problems. Thus, a major task of psychological assessment is to distinguish biogenic from psychogenic cases and, in biogenic cases, to determine what the neurological problem is.

In addition to the mental status exam, described earlier, certain pencil-and-paper tests have proved valid measures of neurological damage. One device that is widely used to screen patients for "organicity" (i.e., neurological malfunction) is the *Bender Visual-Motor Gestalt Test* (Bender, 1938). The subject is shown 9 simple designs, each printed on a separate card, and is asked to reproduce the designs on a piece of paper. If certain errors, such as rotation of the figures or rounding of the corners, consistently appear in the subject's drawings, the examiner is likely to suspect neurological impairment. (See Figure 2.5 for Joe's drawings.) In some cases, the test involves a second phase, in which the examiner asks the subject to reproduce the designs from memory. Failure to reproduce more than two designs is generally viewed as further evidence of impairment.

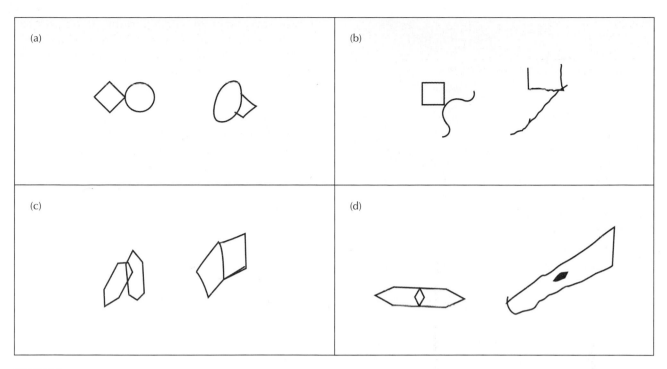

FIGURE 2.5   Joe's responses to the Bender Visual-Motor Gestalt Test. In each box, the design to be copied is at the left, and Joe's attempted copy is at the right. Brain impairment is indicated by certain characteristics of Joe's drawings: rotation, or turning a figure around *(a)*; "impotence," or inability to complete the figure *(b)*; difficulty in overlapping *(c)*; and simplification *(d)*.

More helpful in providing specific information is a coordinated group of tests called the *Halstead-Reitan Neuropsychological Battery.* These tests are based on our (still imperfect) knowledge of which areas of the brain control which intellectual and motor functions. The subject is confronted with a variety of tasks— several performance measures, including those of the Wechsler Adult Intelligence Scale, along with tests of perception and rhythm, a test measuring the subject's ability to fit various wooden forms into receptacles of the same shapes while blindfolded, and so forth. (The test takes two to eight hours to administer.) Each of these tasks was originally designed to assess the functioning of a specific area of the brain, so failure at any one task can presumably help the diagnostician pinpoint the site of the neurological damage. However, given the complex crisscrossings of the neural pathways—together with the equally complex interaction between the brain and behavior—such decisions are still not easily made (Milberg, 1996).

Laboratory Tests

While psychological measures can be of help in diagnosing brain dysfunction, the primary means of detecting such problems is direct testing of the structure and function of the nervous system through laboratory methods. A standard test is the electroencephalogram (EEG), in which the electrical activity in the brain cells is picked up by electrodes attached to the skull and recorded in oscillating patterns called *brain waves.* The EEG can detect tumors and injuries in the brain. Researchers have recently developed more sophisticated means of testing for brain dysfunction, such as *computerized tomography (CT),* which is essentially a series of computer-enhanced X rays of the brain, and *positron emission tomography (PET),* which involves tracing the progress of radioactive particles through the brain. Both techniques have already produced new findings about schizophrenia and other disorders. An even newer method is *magnetic resonance imaging (MRI).* Through the use of magnetic fields, MRI yields a highly precise picture of the brain from more vantage points than other methods.

Laboratory tests can also be used to identify psychogenic disorders. There is an intimate relationship between emotion and physiological functioning. When a person's anger level rises, so may the blood pressure. When a person's anxiety level rises, so may the activation level of the sweat glands. Such changes can be monitored by physiological recording devices such as the **polygraph**, a machine equipped with a number of sensors, which, when attached to the

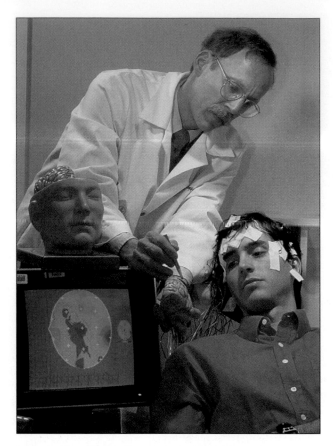

Here, a doctor uses an EEG to measure this patient's brain waves. The EEG, one of the laboratory methods used to test the structure and function of the nervous system, can detect tumors and injuries in the brain.

body, can pick up subtle physiological changes. These fluctuations, in the form of electrical impulses, are amplified within the polygraph and activate pens that then record the changes on a continuously moving roll of paper. When sensors are attached to the scalp, the result is an EEG. When the sensor measures changes in the electrical resistance of the skin—an indication of sweat gland activity—the result is a reading of **galvanic skin response (GSR)**. When the sensor is used to pick up subtle changes in the electrical activity of muscles, the result is an **electromyogram (EMG)**. The polygraph can also measure a number of other physiological responses, such as heart rate, blood volume, and blood pressure. (The polygraph is the standard lie-detector test, the assumption being that in people who are lying, anxiety over being discovered will produce the kinds of autonomic arousal that the machine records.)

Either the polygraph as a whole or its separate measures can be used as indicators of emotional responses to specific stimuli and, thus, can aid in assessment. For example, patients with high blood pressure may be fitted with a portable blood-pressure recorder so that they can take their own blood pressure at regular intervals during the day, at the same time recording in a notebook what they are doing at the time of each reading. When the two records are compared and elevations in blood pressure correlate consistently with a specific environmental stimulus, such as the family dinner hour, then the diagnostician has at least some preliminary clue as to the source of the patient's stress.

In other cases, physiological measures may be required to pinpoint the actual *nature* of the patient's problem. **Polysomnography**, the all-night employment of a variety of measures, including EEG, EMG, and respiration, can be invaluable in determining whether patients who complain of insomnia do, in fact, have what psychologists and physicians call insomnia or whether they are suffering from another sleep disorder. For example, people who complain of insomnia may actually have *sleep apnea*, a respiratory disorder in which breathing repeatedly stops for 10 seconds or more during the night. Because sleep apnea causes extreme daytime tiredness, both patient and doctor may assume that the problem is insomnia. Often it is only by means of polysomnography that sleep apnea can be detected.

Psychophysiological tests have a number of advantages. First, they tap into processes that the person is usually unaware of and therefore cannot report on. Second, they are often more precise than other measures. Many of them show reasonably good internal consistency and test-retest reliability. The only problem with them is in interpreting the psychological significance of the results (Tomarken, 1995). For example, the polygraph may be a good test of anxiety, but it is not a reliable test of whether a person is lying. (Many liars have passed, and many truth-tellers have failed, the polygraph.) For this reason, attempts to use polygraph test results in law courts as an index of truthfulness have always been surrounded by controversy.

Observation in Natural Settings

As noted earlier, the psychometric approach aims to measure what are presumed to be the person's stable personality characteristics. Supporters of this approach would not deny that behavior is influenced by **situational variables,** the environmental stimuli that precede and follow any given action. No one disputes, for example, that children who are coddled by their parents after temper tantrums are likely to have more temper tantrums. Nevertheless, adherents of the psychometric approach assume that behavior issues primarily from **person variables,** the person's stable traits.

A one-way window can be useful in assessing behavior in natural settings. Subjects are usually informed that they are being watched, but they are less aware of being observed and thus behave more naturally, because they cannot see the assessor.

In the past few decades, this theory has been challenged by a number of behavioral psychologists, who take essentially the reverse position. They acknowledge that human actions are determined in part by person variables (which they see as learned patterns of thought and behavior rather than as "traits"). But they claim that the major determinants of behavior are the situational variables—the physical and social settings in which the behavior takes place. From this point of view, it follows that abnormal behavior cannot be accurately assessed in a clinician's office. People must be observed in their natural settings—the classroom, the home, wherever the diagnostician can unobtrusively follow them—so that the connections between behavior and situation will be revealed.

Actually, a diagnostician need not subscribe to behavioral theory in order to value this method of assessment. It has been used for a long time by clinicians of many persuasions, especially in treating children. Its value is that it allows the diagnostician to pinpoint circumstances that elicit the problem behavior—information that is useful no matter what the behavior is ultimately ascribed to. Consider, for example, a child who is having discipline problems in school. An observer may be sent into the classroom to analyze precisely what environmental conditions provoke her outbursts—teasing by other children, difficult academic tasks, or whatever. Once this information is collected, the diagnostician is in a better position to determine what the child's problem actually is.

Direct observation has a number of advantages over other assessment techniques. For one thing, it does not depend on self-report, which, as we have

seen, may be inaccurate. While the parents of an aggressive boy may state that he is *always* making trouble, and, while the child may report that he makes trouble only when someone hits him or takes his things, the observer has a better chance of finding out where the truth lies. Second, observation cuts down on assessment errors caused by the subject's response to the examiner or by the examiner's overly subjective interpretations. Finally, observation tends to provide *workable* answers to behavioral problems. Whereas a projective test may show that a child's aggressive behavior is due to unconscious conflicts, situational observation may reveal that his aggression surfaces only during certain kinds of interaction with his parents—a variable that is much easier to deal with than unconscious conflict. Furthermore, if an underlying conflict does exist, it is possible that adjustment of the parent-child interaction will help resolve it.

Observation is not without its problems, however. In the first place, it requires a great investment of time. Second, the presence of observers may be "reactive." That is, the person being observed may act differently because he or she is being observed. "Problem" children (and "problem" parents and teachers) often show speedy improvement once they realize they are being watched by a person with a clipboard. Sometimes this problem can be solved through surreptitious observation. Either the assessor can watch through a one-way mirror, or, in the case of a classroom, he or she can be introduced as the "teacher's helper" for the day. However, such teacher's helpers often fool nobody, and surreptitious observation is ethically questionable in any case. An alternative, though it also presents ethical problems, is to use recording equipment rather than human beings to do the observing. Unlike a human observer, a video camera can be set up to operate continuously, with the result that the people being observed eventually forget its presence and resume their accustomed behavior.

Cultural Bias in Assessment

A major concern in diagnosis and assessment is the problem of cultural bias. We have already considered this matter in relation to IQ testing. Various studies have also revealed bias in diagnosis. For example, when diagnosticians are shown case studies identical in every respect except for race, blacks are more likely to be labeled alcoholic or schizophrenic, while whites tend to receive the less stigmatizing diagnosis of depression.

These, however, are only the most blatant examples of cultural bias in assessment. Researchers have revealed subtler distortions as well (Okazaki & Sue, 1995). For instance, several studies have shown that diagnoses bilingual patients receive can vary drastically, depending on whether the interview is conducted in the patient's first or second language. De Castillo (1970), the first researcher to raise this problem, and a Spanish speaker, described the following case:

> R. A. was a 28-year-old Cuban patient charged with murder. During his rather lengthy hospitalization he was under the care of a Spanish-speaking physician who found him to be psychotic, suffering from terrifying imaginary experiences. Occasionally he was interviewed by an English-speaking psychiatrist, in whose judgment the patient was coherent, factual, and free from overt psychotic manifestations. I was asked to evaluate his mental status on a few different occasions and encountered exactly what the other Spanish-speaking physician had found. (p. 161)

Later researchers (Price & Cuellar, 1981) have likewise shown that diagnosticians find less pathology in patients speaking a second language, and they explain the phenomenon as De Castillo did: using the second language requires patients to organize their thinking better, with the result that their thoughts seem less disturbed. Curiously, other researchers have found the opposite effect, that diagnosticians find *more* pathology in patients speaking a second language (Marcos, Alpert, Urcuyo, et al., 1973). (They explain this as the diagnostician's response to the patient's language problems—misunderstood questions, misused words, speech hesitations, etc.) How can we evaluate such contradictory evidence? For Lopez (1988), the opposing findings suggest that several kinds of

distortion can affect the assessment of bilingual patients. If you consider that most diagnostic interviews with nonnative English speakers are conducted in English, this could be a serious problem.

The broader matter of cultural bias was acknowledged in the latest revision of the *DSM*. Earlier editions of the manual contained very little information on how behaviors thought normal in one ethnic group, age group, or gender might be misinterpreted as abnormal by a diagnostician of a different gender, age, or ethnic background. Now, in *DSM-IV*, most of the diagnostic categories include such information. For example, the diagnostic criteria for "conduct disorder" (a pattern of antisocial behavior—aggression, destructiveness, deceitfulness—beginning in adolescence) are accompanied by a warning that this diagnosis may be "misapplied to individuals in settings where patterns of undesirable behavior are sometimes viewed as protective (e.g., threatening, impoverished, high-crime)" (American Psychiatric Association, 1994, p. 88). In other words, gang members in ghetto neighborhoods may have social, more than psychological, reasons for delinquency. Likewise, under "schizophrenia," the manual cautions that "in some cultures, visual or auditory hallucinations with a religious content may be a normal part of religious experience (e.g., seeing the Virgin Mary or hearing God's voice)" (p. 281) and therefore should not automatically be taken as symptoms of psychosis. As we saw in Chapter 1, the manual also has a new "Glossary of Culture-Bound Syndromes," including conditions such as "ghost sickness" ("a preoccupation with death . . . observed among members of many American Indian tribes"

Individuals living in poor and crime-ridden neighborhoods may have social, rather than psychological, reasons for delinquency. Unlike prior editions of the manual, the DSM-IV advises diagnosticians to take culture, ethnicity, age group, and gender into account to avoid misapplying diagnoses.

[p. 846]) and the "evil eye" ("a concept widely found in Mediterranean cultures" [p. 847]) that may or may not warrant diagnosis.

Such cautionary information may help people from various subgroups to receive less biased diagnoses. Or, ironically, it may not. Remember that the best diagnosis is not the mildest diagnosis but the most accurate diagnosis, which will presumably lead to the most appropriate treatment. In a large-scale study of California clinicians, Lopez and Hernandez (1986) found that some of these therapists, in an attempt to be sensitive to "cultural diversity," underestimated the seriousness of their patients' symptoms. One clinician, for example, had a patient who was hallucinating, but he did not consider the diagnosis of schizophrenia because the patient was black, and

black people, he reasoned, were culturally more prone to hallucinations than white people. His conclusion was not inconsistent with *DSM-IV*'s warning that hallucinations are a normal part of religious experience in "some cultures." Nevertheless, as the researchers point out, the woman may indeed have been schizophrenic—and deprived of appropriate treatment as a result of her therapist's scruples regarding cultural bias.

Still, as with the conflicting evidence about assessments in a second language, this does not mean that diagnosticians should give up trying to correct bias. Fifty years ago, many diagnostic practices were patently racist. If, today, the effort to solve that problem involves some error and overcompensation, the effort is still necessary.

KEY TERMS

categorical classification, 32
comorbidity, 35
description, 28
descriptive validity, 34
diagnosis, 29
dimensional classification, 32
DSM-IV, 29
electroencephalogram (EEG), 49
electromyogram (EMG), 50
galvanic skin response (GSR), 50

intelligence quotient (IQ), 40
intelligence tests, 40
interjudge reliability, 34
internal consistency, 34
interview, 38
mental status exam (MSE), 39
mini mental status exam (MMS), 39
Minnesota Multiphasic Personality Inventory-2 (MMPI-2), 46

person variables, 50
polygraph, 49
polysomnography, 50
prediction, 29
predictive validity, 35
prognosis, 29
projective personality tests, 43
psychological assessment, 28
psychological test, 39
psychometric approach, 40
reliability, 33

response sets, 47
Rorschach Psychodiagnostic Inkblot Test, 43
self-report personality inventories, 46
situational variables, 50
test-retest reliability, 34
Thematic Apperception Test (TAT), 44
traits, 40
validity, 34

SUMMARY

- Psychological assessment has two goals. The first is to describe the personality and behavior of the person being assessed. The second is to predict that person's psychological functioning in the future. Psychological assessment is used for such practical purposes as school placement and job screening. In the clinical context, it helps clinicians determine the most effective treatment; reassessment helps practitioners determine whether treatment is working.

- Clinical assessment is a form of diagnosis, in which mental health professionals label an individual's problems according to criteria specified in the *DSM* and suggest his or her prognosis. This classification provides an essential common vocabulary for researchers, practitioners, and public health officials. Critics argue that psychiatric diagnosis falsely implies that abnormal behavior is qualitatively different from normal behavior; that there are clear-cut differences between different diagnostic cate-

gories; that diagnostic labels may be mistaken for explanations; and that the person may be stigmatized. Some have proposed dimensional classification as a replacement for categorical classification, with the goal of making diagnosis more qualitative than quantitative.

- *DSM-IV* attempts to remedy these problems by offering detailed, specific criteria for a diagnosis and by requiring data on five dimensions or axes: the specific clinical syndrome being diagnosed; long-standing personality disorders (or, for children, mental retardation); relevant medical problems; psychosocial and environmental problems; and a numerical assessment of the patient's recent levels of adjustment and of the current degree of impairment. *DSM-IV* deliberately avoids reference to the causes of a disorder. Ideally, the result of assessment is a portrait, not a label.

- The usefulness of an assessment depends on reliability, or the consistency of measurement under varying conditions, and validity, or whether the assessment tool measures what it is supposed to measure. Diagnoses based on early editions of the *DSM* have shown low interjudge reliability and, perhaps for this reason, poor predictive validity. The more detailed, specific criteria and categories of recent editions of the *DSM* have corrected these problems to some degree. But growing recognition of comorbidity (in which one person exhibits symptoms of more than one disorder) has presented a challenge to the descriptive validity of diagnosis according to *DSM*.

■ Other problems relate to the assessor. The influence of the clinician's behavior and appearance on the subject's behavior and responses, the assessor's personal and professional biases, and pragmatic considerations all may interfere with accurate psychological assessment. The stricter criteria of recent editions of the *DSM* correct some problems but may also encourage clinicians to overuse residual diagnoses (such as anxiety disorder).

■ There are four common methods of assessment. The first is the interview, which may be structured or unstructured. Highly structured interviews—such as the SCID, the DIS, and the MSE—are called for when an unambiguous diagnosis is required.

■ A second method is psychological testing. Intelligence tests (e.g., the Stanford-Binet and Wechsler scales) have high internal consistency and reliably predict performance in school, but they may be culturally biased and measure too narrow a range of mental abilities. Projective personality tests (e.g., the Rorschach, the TAT, and the sentence completion test) allow subjects freedom of expression but also permit variable interpretations, which led to the development of empirical scoring. Self-report personality inventories such as the MMPI-2, likewise, are scored against norms (how people with known disorders responded). Despite controls against false answers, these tests are not foolproof. The MCMI-III, created to identify personality disorders, is one of the most accurate.

■ A third type of assessment is designed to detect neurological impairment. Today paper-and-pencil tests are supplemented by sophisticated laboratory tests which produce detailed pictures of the brain at work and physiological measures of emotional arousal (the polygraph) and sleeping patterns. Psychophysiological tests tend to yield superior consistency of results, but the significance of the results is often difficult to interpret.

■ A fourth method of assessment is observation of subjects in natural settings, either directly or surreptitiously, with one-way mirrors or video cameras.

■ Biases based on language, race, and culture have long been known to compromise the accuracy of psychological assessment and diagnosis. Such biases have been a subject of much research in recent decades, although some error still persists. A more recent hazard is error based on overcompensation to avoid possible bias.

Chapter 3

Though it is doubtful that Isaac Newton really stumbled on the law of gravitation by being hit on the head by a falling apple, the principle behind the story is sound. Scientific discovery sometimes occurs in a very unmethodical way, through accidents, hunches, and intuition. The earliest antipsychotic drug, for example, was developed by accident. Called chlorpromazine, it was first introduced as a treatment for surgical shock. Actually, it did little to reduce surgical patients' risk of going into shock, but, strange to say, it made them calm. The drug was then tested, quite successfully, with schizophrenics. It reduced these patients' hallucinations and thought disorders. Chlorpromazine is still used today, and its discovery has led to the development of other, more effective treatments for schizophrenia.

Thus, scientific discovery involves chance. But any discovery, in order to be confirmed, must be tested via meticulous, systematic research, often over long periods of time. This chapter describes the general principles of scientific research. First, we will examine the characteristics of the scientific method. Then we will look at the research designs that scientists use in the study of abnormal behavior.

Characteristics of the Scientific Method

Skeptical Attitude

More than anything else, scientists are skeptical. Not only do they want to see it before they believe it; they want to see it again and again, under conditions of their own choosing. Scientists are skeptical because they recognize two important facts. First, they know that behavior is complex: that many factors are often needed to explain any psychological phenomenon. They also know that it is usually quite difficult to identify those factors. Explanations are often premature or incomplete; not enough factors may have been considered. While it may seem that a child's asthma attacks always follow an emotional upset, for example, it is possible that cat hair, pollen levels, and the child's history of respiratory infection are also involved. Single-cause explanations, because they are simple, are appealing, but in the study of behavior they are rarely accurate.

The second reason for skepticism is that science is a human endeavor. Scientists are not simply passive observers of the phenomena they study. It is they who decide how to define the thing they are measuring, which questions to ask about it, and how to collect, analyze, and interpret the data. These decisions are subjective; reasonable minds may disagree about them. Therefore, scientists have to be skeptical about new discoveries, even after they are tested. In the field of abnormal psychology, findings often raise as many questions as they answer.

Objectives

Ideally, the scientific method is intended to meet four objectives: description, prediction, control, and understanding (Figure 3.1). *Description* is the defining and classifying of events and their relationships. To be

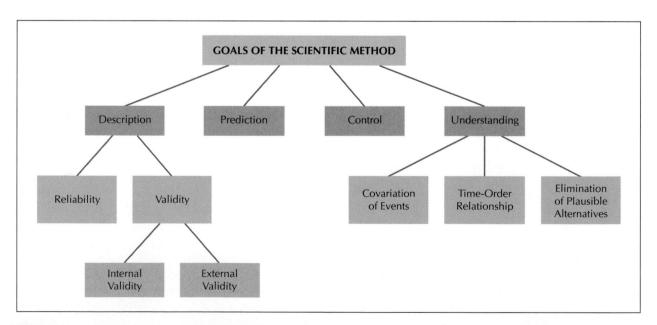

FIGURE 3.1 The four objectives of the scientific method, together with their individual requirements.

useful, a description must have reliability (Chapter 2) —that is, it must be stable over time and under different conditions. Suppose, for example, that a person is given an IQ test and scores very high; then he is given the same IQ test two days later and scores very low. Because intelligence is unlikely to change in the course of two days, we would assume that the test was unreliable. A useful description must also have validity (Chapter 2)—that is, it must measure what it claims to measure. If that IQ test actually measured social skills rather than intelligence, then it would not be valid. Assessment techniques have been developed to provide reliable and valid descriptions of a wide range of concepts, from extroversion to depression.

A description of events and their relationships often serves as a basis for *prediction*. If a description of schizophrenia notes that children of schizophrenic parents are 10 times more likely to become schizophrenic than are children of nonschizophrenic parents, it can reasonably be inferred that one cause of schizophrenia is having schizophrenic parents.

Successful prediction doesn't always pinpoint a cause, however. In the case of schizophrenia, for example, the fact that children of schizophrenic parents are at risk for schizophrenia does not tell us whether this relationship is due to genes or the stresses of growing up with schizophrenic parents—or to another factor. Still, it is useful to know that these children are at risk, for such knowledge can guide research into causes and can help in treatment and prevention.

Indeed, it is the development of treatment and preventive strategies that forms the basis of the third goal of science—*control*. When scientists can control behavior, they may be able to change it for the better. For example, there is a body of research showing that certain types of poor communication are highly predictive of relapse in adolescent and adult schizophrenics who are recovering from a psychotic episode. Guided by that research, psychologists have tried to teach parents of schizophrenics better communication skills, in order to prevent relapses.

If we ever find out how much responsibility can be assigned to each of the factors thought to lead to schizophrenia, we will have achieved the fourth goal of the scientific method: *understanding*, the identification of the cause or causes of a phenomenon. Before causality can be demonstrated, three conditions must be met. First is the covariation of events: if one event is to be accepted as a cause of another, the two events must vary together—that is, when one changes, the other must also change. Second is a time-order relationship: the presumed cause must occur *before* the presumed effect. The final condition is the elimination of plausible alternative causes: the proposed causal relationship can be accepted only after other likely causes have been ruled out. For most types of abnormal behavior, we will probably never be able to isolate one factor as *the* cause. As we shall see in later chapters, complex behaviors, normal and abnormal, are usually the product of many causes.

Internal and External Validity Scientists are often faced with a problem called confounding. **Confounding** occurs when two or more causal factors are exerting an effect on the same thing at the same time, thus interfering with accurate measurement of the causal role of either one. A good example is the infamous "executive monkey" study of vulnerability to ulcers (Brady, 1958). In this study, 4 pairs of monkeys were wired to receive electric shocks every 20 seconds. In each pair, however, 1 monkey, the so-called executive monkey, could turn off the coming shock if at any time in the intervening 20 seconds it pressed a lever near its hand. The second monkey in each pair, called the "yoked" monkey, had no such control. It simply received whatever shocks the executive received. The results of this study were dramatic. All 4 executive monkeys developed ulcers and died, while the yoked monkeys showed no signs of ulcer. The conclusion seemed clear: being in charge is stressful and can be hazardous to health.

However, after several researchers redid the experiment and got different results, people began to look more closely at the procedures followed in the original experiment. Rather than being chosen at random, the four executive monkeys had been selected because, on a preliminary test, they had shown higher rates of responding than their yoked partners. Subsequent research (Weiss, 1977) has shown that animals with higher response rates have an increased likelihood of developing ulcers (In fact, the more recent research findings suggest that being in charge *decreases* the likelihood of developing ulcers.) Thus, in the original study, the difference in response rates confounded the relationship between having control and developing ulcers. Studies that are free of confounding are said to have **internal validity**.

The internal validity of a study can be distinguished from its external validity. **External validity** is the extent to which research results can be generalized. **Generalizability**—a finding's ability to be applied to different populations, settings, and conditions—in turn depends on the **representativeness** of the sample from which the finding was gathered: the degree to which this sample's essential characteristics match those of the population we want to generalize about. An internally valid study may show, for example, that depressed women are more likely than nondepressed women to have suffered recent declines in

Most natural populations show demographic differences—variations in age, gender, race, and so on. Random sampling is the best technique for ensuring that variation within a population is adequately reflected in a research sample. This representativeness, in turn, helps ensure a study's external validity.

social support. Their marriages may have become strained, or their relationships with friends or family may have deteriorated. But, if the research sample is not representative of men as well as women, the finding is not generalizable to men. It is possible that in men the precursors of depression have more to do with failures at work than with social relationships. As pointed out in Chapter 1, gender differences turn up in many disorders.

The representativeness of a sample depends on how carefully the subjects, settings, and conditions of the study have been selected. The best way to achieve a representative sample is to use random sampling. In a **random sample**, every element of the population has an equal likelihood of being included. Given that the sample is large enough, random sampling makes it likely that the characteristics of the sample will generally match the characteristics of the population.

A common problem in studies of abnormal behavior is that they tend to rely on *samples of convenience*—for example, all the depressed women in the hospital where the researcher works or all the test-anxious students in a certain university clinic—rather than on more representative samples. In order to generalize the findings of such studies to the population as a whole (for instance, all depressed women, all test-anxious college students), we must repeatedly **replicate** them. That is, the study must be redone, producing similar findings, with another sample.

Scientific Procedures

Scientific methods should be put to use every time researchers perform a study. In any well-conducted study, the key elements are the generation of hypotheses, the formulation of operational definitions, and the establishment of methods of control.

The Hypothesis   A hypothesis is a tentative explanation for behavior; it attempts to answer the questions "How?" and "Why?" The object of research is to test hypotheses; however, before a hypothesis can be tested, it must be generated. Intuition often plays an important role here. Psychologist Neal Miller (1972) describes his state of mind during exploratory work and hypothesis generation:

> During this phase I am quite freewheeling and intuitive—follow hunches, vary procedures, try out wild ideas, and take shortcuts. During it, I am usually not interested in elaborate controls; in fact, I have learned to my sorrow that one can waste a lot of time on designing and executing elaborate controls for something that is not there. (p. 348)

A hypothesis often begins as a hunch, which in turn can come from various sources. Sometimes, in the course of an experiment, researchers notice something that they didn't expect, and this leads them down a new path, toward a new hypothesis. Recently, for example, two researchers, Jacobson and Gottman (Gottman, Jacobson, Rushe, et al., 1995; Jacobson, Gottman, & Shortt, 1995), were studying the physiological processes of men who beat their partners. As they analyzed their findings, they noticed something curious: some of the violent men tended to show internal calm the more outwardly aggressive they became. For example, although it is natural for heart rate to go up during an argument, for these unusual men it went down. The researchers hypothesized that such internal calm constituted a "marker" for the most severe types of wife-beaters.

For researchers who are also **clinicians**, or providers of treatment, hypotheses often arise from watching patients' reactions to treatment. That was the case, for example, with the development of chlorpromazine. As noted at the opening of this chapter, chlorpromazine was introduced as an aid to surgery. It took a sharp-eyed clinician to notice that the drug had the effect of calming patients and, thus, to hypothesize that it could be an effective tranquilizer. The same rules operate in psychotherapy. In responding to the patient, the therapist may say something that has an unexpectedly helpful effect. Suddenly, the patient is able to register for school, get a full night's sleep, or talk about a problem that she was unable to discuss before. The alert therapist notices this, and tries that response again, perhaps with other patients.

The Case Study

A **case study** is a detailed account of the treatment of a single patient. In its classic form, the case study begins with a description of the subject, including test results, interview impressions, and physical and psychological history. Then it describes the treatment of that person and the treatment outcome. Such studies have been instrumental in encouraging therapists to try new treatments. The vividness of the case study is itself inviting—clinicians can imagine themselves implementing the same procedure—and the amount of detail instructs clinicians as to exactly how the treatment is applied. Freud's famous case studies—of Little Hans (1909/1962), a child with a phobia; of Anna O. (1895/1962), a woman with hysteria (Chapter 1); of the Rat-Man (1909/1962), a patient with obsessional thoughts—did as much as his general writings to gain followers for his new psychoanalytic method. The same has been true of behavioral treatment. One of the crucial factors in the spread of behavioral therapy in the sixties and seventies was the publication, in 1965, of Leonard Ullmann and Leonard Krasner's *Case Studies in Behavior Modification.*

The case study is also a good way to describe rare phenomena. Tourette's disorder, for example, is a very rare condition involving motor and vocal tics. "Touretters" jerk their bodies this way and that; they also make involuntary sounds—clicks, grunts, barks, and snorts. To their embarrassment, they may shout insults or obscenities. Because the disorder strikes only 4 or 5 people out of 10,000, most clinicians will never see a patient with Tourette's disorder. Therefore, the case study included in neurologist Oliver Sacks' *An Anthropologist on Mars* is a useful contribution to the literature of abnormal psychology.

The limitations of the case study method are quite obvious. Because many variables are not controlled, cause-and-effect conclusions can rarely be drawn. Furthermore, it is impossible to generalize safely from one person. Who can say that the progress of a dog phobia in patient X is representative of phobics in general? However, case studies do have the unique advantage of immediacy. In reading a case study, one can actually feel what it is like to live with that disorder. In view of these strengths and weaknesses, case studies are regarded as most valuable when they are used to *complement* experimental research. That is how they will be used in this book.

If it goes on working, the therapist can use it to generate a new hypothesis about treatment. Such hypotheses can also originate from accounts of other clinicians' patients. Case studies (see the box above) have given many therapists good ideas. Today researchers are paying more and more attention to the development of effective treatments, an area in which hypothesis generation plays a major role. (See the box on page 62). That effort, in turn, may result in the development of an actual methodology, or systematic procedure, for generating hypotheses.

Operational Definitions   For a hypothesis to be testable, it must be *falsifiable.* That is, it must be stated in such a way that it can be proven untrue. To this end, the concepts in the hypothesis must be "operationalized," or given **operational definitions**—that is, they must be defined in terms of operations that can be observed and measured. "Depression," for example, could be operationalized by defining it in terms of the Beck Depression Inventory, a test in which subjects circle, as applicable or inapplicable to themselves, statements about sadness, discouragement, sleeping problems, and so forth. Their endorsement of these statements is an observable operation. It is also measurable. Subjects receive a score based on which statements they circle. A very low score indicates no depression, and a very high score means severe depression. The score serves as the operational definition of depression. Thus, in a study of nondepressed versus severely depressed people, the researchers might operationally define these two conditions as Beck Inventory 5-or-below (no depression) and Beck Inventory 28-or-above (severe depression), respectively. In doing so, they would be ensuring that everyone involved in that research, and everyone reading about it, understood these concepts in the same way.

Methods of Control   In setting up experiments to test their hypotheses, researchers need to control events that might influence the behavior they are studying. An experiment usually involves the *manipulation* (deliberate changing) of one or more factors and the *measurement* of the effects of that manipulation on behavior.

Independent and Dependent Variables   The **independent variable** is the factor that is manipulated by the experimenters in an effort to measure its effects. The **dependent variable** is the factor (or, in psychological research, the behavior) that will presumably be affected by the manipulation of the independent variable and whose changes the experiment aims to measure. If a hypothesis is to receive a fair trial, the experiment must be internally valid; that is, the cause of any obtained outcome must be the independent variable. The internal validity of a study is ensured if **control techniques** are used properly. The three methods of control are manipulating, holding conditions

One area of mental health in which hypothesis generation is receiving increasing attention is treatment development. In fact, beginning in 1992, the National Institute of Mental Health (NIMH), the federal agency that provides funding for mental health research, initiated a program to help recognize treatment development as a legitimate type of research investigation, one that could be funded as a separate phase of scientific inquiry. This is the first example of official recognition that hypothesis generation constitutes a legitimate phase of research design.

There is no universally recognized methodology for treatment development. However, as an example of how treatment development methodology can be applied, Kohlenberg (1997) has been funded to develop a treatment to enhance the effectiveness of a new variant of cognitive behavior therapy (CBT) for depression. The purpose of this treatment development study is to (1) show that the new version of CBT is promising, (2) demonstrate that it is clearly distinguishable from traditional CBT, and

(3) develop a treatment manual that can be used for hypothesis testing once the treatment is developed.

CBT for depression is described in Chapter 9. It was developed by Beck and his associates to treat depression by changing the way depressed people think. The cognitive theory underlying CBT is that depression is at least partly caused by faulty thinking and that, by correcting this faulty thinking, depressed people not only recover but leave therapy with permanent changes in their thinking such that they are inoculated against subsequent relapse. Research suggests that CBT is moderately effective. The purpose of Kohlenberg's research is to enhance both the short- and long-term effectiveness of CBT.

The NIMH treatment development project is designed to integrate CBT with a treatment developed by Kohlenberg and Tsai (1992), functional analysis psychotherapy (FAP). Standard CBT uses incidents primarily from the natural environment as "material" to examine and work on in therapy, whereas FAP focuses on correcting the abnormal behavior that takes place right in the therapy session, drawing on the intense relationship between therapist and client.

According to the theoretical rationale for FAP-enhanced CBT (or FECT), if depressed clients engage in behavior that makes them depressed in the therapy session and the therapist notices it, avoids reinforcing it, and instead reinforces behavior conducive to helping the clients overcome their depression, the therapist-client transactions will automatically generalize to the natural environment. For example, consider the following dialogue between client and therapist:

C: Our time will be up in five minutes. Then your next client will come in. I'm just part of your assembly line.

T: What do you mean? Are you thinking that you are just one of many clients and that, even though this hour is special to you, it isn't special to me?

C: Yeah. And it makes me angry. And you seem like a phony.

T: I can see why you might feel that way. What impresses me is that you were able to say it.

---

constant, and balancing. These three methods can be illustrated by a hypothetical experiment. Let us say that we are going to examine the effect of alcohol consumption on tension.

In the simplest of experiments, the independent variable is manipulated at two levels. These two levels usually represent the presence and absence of some treatment. The condition in which the treatment is present is commonly called the *experimental* condition; the condition in which the treatment is absent is called the *control* condition. In the experimental condition in our hypothetical research project, subjects are given 0.5 gram of alcohol per kilogram of body weight. The alcohol is administered as a mixture of vodka and tonic water. In the control condition, subjects are given the tonic water plain— no vodka. Thus, the alcohol is the independent variable; its presence or absence is manipulated by the researcher. The dependent variable is the subject's heart rate, which is the operational definition of tension in this study.

Other factors in the experiment that could influence the subjects' heart rate are controlled by *being held constant*. For instance, the instructions given for performing the tasks in the experiment, the tone of voice used by the experimenter in giving these instructions, the setting and the length of time in which the subjects are allowed to consume the drink, and other factors that can be held constant are identical in the two conditions. When all factors that could possibly be independent variables are held constant, no confounding is possible.

At least one set of factors cannot be held constant in this or any other experiment—the characteristics of the subjects tested. Researchers control factors that cannot be held constant by trying to *balance* the influence of these factors among the different experimental conditions. The most important balancing technique, **random assignment,** involves assigning subjects randomly to the different groups in the experiment. For example, if our hypothetical researchers were to assign all the male subjects to the

While the therapist might have tried to persuade the client that he was special or directed the discussion back to relevant issues in the environment, in FECT this would be a golden opportunity for the therapist to reinforce the client for his assertiveness. Because lack of assertion is a major part of this client's problem, his ability to be assertive with the therapist is significant. Equally significant is the FECT therapist's ability to recognize the clinically relevant behavior and reinforce it.

By training therapists to use FAP along with CBT, Kohlenberg hopes to enhance therapists' ability to use examples of faulty thinking in therapy sessions to modify depressive behavior. Therapists have been hired to be trained in both approaches, and experts in each are being used as supervisors. As depressives are randomly assigned to CBT (the control group) and FECT (the experimental group), the investigators will be able to assess the promise of FECT. Although only a handful of clients will be treated—not enough to apply the kind of statistical inference used in hypothesis testing—if FECT performs well relative to CBT, one can infer that FECT is promising and, therefore, worthy of formal hypothesis testing. Kohlenberg has also developed a system for coding therapist behaviors in the session, so that raters can be trained to code tapes of FECT and CBT and determine whether the therapists are restricting their FAP interventions to the FECT conditions. The coders are blind to which condition they are coding. This coding will determine the discriminability of the two treatments and lead to a system that can be used to code tapes in future studies comparing the two treatments.

Unlike formal experiments, in which the independent variable (in this case, treatment condition) must be kept constant throughout the duration of the study, it is expected that during treatment development, the FECT treatment will change as each case is intensely scrutinized. Regular observation of tapes by supervisors, meetings to discuss the cases, and information gleaned from informal observations will gradually shape a new, integrative manual for the FECT treatment. Thus, at the conclusion of the treatment development study, a new independent variable will emerge, and, if the experimental treatment is promising enough, it will be ready to be tested under formal experimental conditions.

Treatment development is an example of a type of pilot study. Pilot studies are usually preparatory investigations, preliminary inquiries, which are less time consuming and less expensive than full-blown experiments. They are designed to help prepare the investigators for formal hypothesis testing, by perfecting both independent and dependent variables so that, when the experiment occurs, the hypothesis will receive an optimal, internally valid test.

Pilot studies often comprise an important part of the treatment development process. But it is the interaction between scientists, therapists, and supervisors and the insights gleaned from this collaboration that are the most important components of the development of a new treatment.

vodka group and all the female subjects to the no-vodka group, gender differences would confound the experiment. If, however, the subjects were assigned randomly—by drawing lots, for example—then the researchers would maximize the likelihood that the two groups were equivalent on all measures other than the independent variable. (Note the difference between random assignment and random sampling, described earlier. In random sampling, subjects are chosen at random from a population, the goal being representativeness. In random assignment, already-chosen subjects are sorted at random into different experimental groups, the goal being balance among the groups.) It was the lack of random assignment that confounded the "executive monkey" experiment, discussed earlier.

In a properly conducted experiment, then, all variables other than the independent variable are either held constant or balanced. If it were not for the manipulation of the independent variable (the presence or absence of alcohol in the drink), the groups would be expected to perform similarly. Therefore, if the groups perform *differently,* the researchers can assume that the independent variable is responsible for the difference.

Minimizing the Effects of Expectations   A further problem in conducting experiments is that both the experimenter and the subjects may *expect* a certain outcome and act accordingly. For example, if subjects know that they are drinking alcohol, they are likely to expect certain effects: that they will feel relaxed, giddy, and so on. If subjects respond according to these expectations, called **demand characteristics,** it will be difficult to determine the effect of the alcohol. Similarly, the experimenters may have expectations and, consequently, may treat the subjects who have received alcohol differently than they treat those who are drinking plain tonic. For example, the experimenter may read the instructions more slowly to the "drinkers." The experimenter's observations of behavioral results may also be biased by the knowledge of the experimental conditions. For instance, the experimenter, in observing the "drinking" group, may be more likely to notice any unusual motor movements or slurred speech. The term used to describe these biases is experimenter effects.

Scientists have developed procedures to control for both demand characteristics and experimenter effects. One is the use of a *placebo control group*. A placebo (Latin for "I shall please") is a substance that looks like a drug or other active substance but is actually an inert, or inactive, substance. In our alcohol example, a placebo control group would receive a drink that would look, smell, and taste like the alcoholic drink but would contain no alcohol. Thus, if "alcoholic" effects could be noted in these subjects' behavior after they had had their drinks, the experimenters would know that demand characteristics played an important role in the subjects' behavior.

Placebo control groups are traditionally used for evaluating drug treatments, but they have also been used to assess various forms of psychotherapy. While other groups undergo specific therapies, the placebo control group receives a "theoretically inert" treatment (Hibbs, 1993; Taylor & McLean, 1993). That is, the placebo control group is taken through a procedure that, while sufficiently complicated to seem like psychotherapy, is unrelated to any recognized form of psychotherapy. If, as has happened, this group shows improvement comparable to that of subjects receiving recognized treatments, experimenters are at least alerted to the fact that therapeutic outcome is being affected by nonspecific (non-theory-related) factors, such as attention from the therapist.

Another way to minimize the influence of subjects' and experimenters' expectations is to use a **double-blind** procedure. In this technique, both the subject and the experimenter are kept unaware (blind) as to which treatment is being administered. In our alcohol study, we could achieve double-blind control by having two researchers: one to prepare the drinks and to code the glasses, and a second researcher to pass them out, recording which subject got which glass. As long as the first researcher did not know who got what drink and the second researcher did not understand the coding system, neither of them would know, when they got to the stage of observing the subjects' behavior, who was a "drinker" and who was not. The drinkers would be identified only later, when the code was compared with the record of who received what. At the same time, the drinkers would have no way of knowing whether they were receiving the alcohol or the placebo, hence the term "double-blind": both parties are in the dark.

Statistical Inference   Suppose that we have completed the alcohol study just described. Can we be reason-

In a double-blind study, the experimental substance and the placebo control are administered from coded containers. This procedure keeps both the experimenters and the subjects from knowing until afterward which subjects received which substance. The purpose is to prevent the expectations of the experimenter and of the subjects from affecting the study's results.

ably confident that the results are real, rather than simply the product of chance? To be confident that results are not due to chance, scientists often rely on **statistical inference**. They begin by assuming the **null hypothesis**, which, as the term implies, is the assumption that the independent variable has had no effect. Then they use probability theory to determine the likelihood of obtaining the results of their experiment if the null hypothesis were correct—that is, if the independent variable had had no effect. If the likelihood is small (conventionally, less than 5 times out of 100, or 0.05), they judge the result to be "statistically significant," reject the null hypothesis, and conclude that the independent variable did have an effect.

You can appreciate the process of statistical inference by considering the following situation. You and a friend have dinner together once a week, and you always toss a coin to see who will pay the bill. Curiously, your friend always has a coin ready, and so, she always does the tossing. Now, it would be convenient if you could examine the coin to see if it is unfairly weighted. But, since this might cause a problem in your relationship, the best you can do is test her coin indirectly by using the null hypothesis. That is, you assume that the coin is unbiased and then wait to see the results. If, over time, the coin tossing deviates from the expected 50-50 split of heads and tails more than chance would predict, you might conclude that there is something funny about your friend's coin. You don't know for sure that her coin is unfairly weighted, but you do know that the likelihood of your losing that often with a fair coin is less than 5 out of 100, or 0.05. Similarly, researchers would like to test any obtained result directly for significance, but usually the best they can do is compare their outcome to the outcome expected if chance alone were operating.

Statistical inference tells us only that a finding is believable. It does not tell us whether the finding is important. It is possible to obtain statistically significant differences between groups even when there is no substantial difference between those groups in the natural environment. This can be done, for example, simply by using very large numbers of subjects. If, in the alcohol study, we were to assign 5,000 subjects to the experimental group and 5,000 to the control group, almost any difference between the two groups would test out as statistically significant, though it might have no scientific meaning whatsoever (Jacobson, Follette, & Revenstorf, 1984).

Even if a statistically significant finding does represent a true difference between groups, that does not mean that the difference is great enough to have any practical consequence. When therapists read about research on new treatments, they want to know not just whether the findings are statistically significant, but whether they have **clinical significance**—that is, whether they can be of real help in treatment. Imagine, for example, a study of a new treatment for obesity, using subjects weighing about 300 pounds. If the experimental subjects (those trying the new treatment) lost an average of 10 pounds apiece and the control subjects lost no weight at all, that would be a statistically significant finding, but it would not be of much help to an obesity therapist's 300-pound patients.

This does not mean that tests of statistical significance are a waste of time. In some cases, they are a crucial protection against mistaking chance conjunctions for important relationships, but statistical significance is a minimum standard.

Research Designs

Research designs are the tools experimenters use to test hypotheses. Each design has its advantages and disadvantages. Asking a researcher whether one design is better than another is like asking a carpenter whether a screwdriver is better than a hammer. Which tool is best depends on the job to be done.

Correlational Research

In abnormal psychology, as in all science, the choice of research design involves ethical and practical considerations. For example, if we were interested in whether divorce increases a person's risk for depression, we could not randomly assign a group of people to get divorced and then wait to see if they developed depression.

A common solution to this problem is to examine groups that have been "treated naturally." That is, people who are divorced can be compared, as to their rate of depression, with those who have remained married. Such studies have been done, and they have shown that people who are separated or divorced are indeed much more likely than married people to become depressed (Bruce & Kim, 1992). Because this kind of research involves looking for correlations, or relationships, between subjects' characteristics and their performance, it is called **correlational research** (also *natural group research*).

One correlational design frequently used in research on abnormal behavior is the **case-control design**, in which people diagnosed as having a particular mental disorder—the *cases*—are compared with *controls,* or people who have not been diagnosed as having the disorder. For example, if schizophrenics and people chosen from the general

"Do people hate us because we dress this way or do we dress this way because people hate us?"

The Correlation Coefficient: A Measure of Predictive Strength

The correlation coefficient *(r)* is a measure of how well we can predict one variable if we know the value of another variable. For example, we might want to know how accurately we could predict students' success in college on the basis of their SAT scores.

The correlation coefficient has two characteristics, a direction and a magnitude. The *direction* can be either positive or negative. A positive correlation indicates that, as the value of one variable *(X)* increases, the value of the other variable *(Y)* also increases (see diagram A). The correlation between SAT scores and success in college should be a positive one. In a negative correlation, as the value of *X* increases, the value of *Y* decreases (see diagram B).

The higher a person's social class, the *less* likely that person is to be admitted to a mental hospital; social class and admission to mental hospitals are negatively correlated. Diagram C shows what happens when two variables are neither positively nor negatively correlated: as the value of *X* increases, the value of *Y* changes unpredictably. Because we have no ability to predict *Y* on the basis of *X*, the correlation coefficient in this situation is zero. For example, the relationship between eye color and mental illness represents a zero correlation; we could not predict the likelihood that a person would become mentally ill by knowing the person's eye color.

The *magnitude* of the correlation coefficient can range from 0 to 1.00. A value of +1.00 indicates a perfect positive correlation, and a value of −1.00 indicates a perfect negative correlation. Values between 0 and 1.00 indicate predictive relationships of intermediate strength. Remember, the sign of the correlation signifies only its direction. An *r* value of −0.46 indicates a stronger relationship than an *r* of +0.20.

One final word of caution: the correlation coefficient represents only the *linear* relationship between two variables. The linear correlation of *X* and *Y* in diagram D is zero, but the two variables are obviously related. A curvilinear relationship like that shown in diagram D exists between level of arousal and performance. Performance first increases with increasing arousal but then declines when arousal exceeds an optimal level.

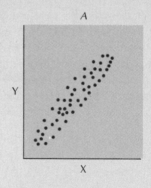

A

Y

X

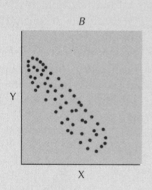

B

Y

X

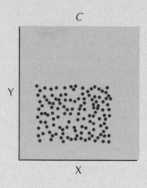

C

Y

X

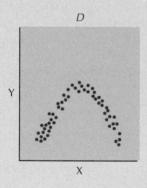

D

Y

X

population differ according to a specific measure of behavior, the difference may be an indicator of schizophrenia, as long as other characteristics are balanced across the two groups.

Correlational research designs are highly effective in meeting the first two objectives of the scientific method, description and prediction. Unfortunately, serious problems arise when the results of correlational studies are used as a basis of causal inference. People tend to assume that all three conditions for a causal inference (covariation of events, a time-order relationship, and elimination of plausible alternative causes) have been met when really only the first condition, variation, has been met. For instance, the evidence that divorced people are more likely than married people to become depressed shows that these two factors are correlated. Such a finding could be taken to mean that divorce causes depression. Before reaching that conclusion, however, we must be sure that the time-order condition has been met—namely, that divorce *preceded* the depression. Perhaps depressed people are more likely to get divorced because of the strain placed on the relationship by the depression. In other words, a demonstration of covariation offers no indication of the *direction* of a causal relationship. (For a discussion of the most common measure of covariation, the *correlation coefficient*, see the box above.)

Nor does covariation eliminate plausible alternative causes. The fact that two factors covary does not mean that one is the cause of the other. Perhaps they are both dependent on another factor altogether—the so-called **third-variable problem**. Perhaps the situation is not that divorce causes depression or vice versa but, rather, that both are caused by the stresses of poverty. The directionality and third-variable problems make it a treacherous enterprise to infer causation from correlations.

One partial solution to the third-variable problems is *matching,* or choosing subjects who are similar with regard to potentially relevant factors other than the factor of interest. The divorced and nondivorced subjects could be matched, for example, on income level. The idea, of course, is to end up with two groups that differ only in the matter of divorce. In a sense, matching is an application of the control technique of holding conditions constant. One problem with this approach is that matching may lead to such a restriction of the people included in the study that the groups may no longer be representative of the general population. If you were to compare the emotional disorders of college students with those of elderly people who had been matched with the students for general health and amount of education, you would probably be studying a very unrepresentative group of elderly people. A more serious problem with matching, however, is that the number of potentially relevant factors is usually so large that it is impossible to select two or more groups equal in all characteristics except the one of interest. In the divorce study, one might want to control many factors besides income—for example, gender, educational level, religion, ethnic origin, and number of children. Nonetheless, matching can be useful. If a relationship between divorce and depression persisted after divorced and married groups were matched on income level, then the researcher could reasonably conclude that income level alone was not responsible for the difference.

Alternatively, the researcher could revert to random selection. When there are many potentially confounding factors, the best choice is usually careful random selection or random selection within certain broad restrictions—in this case, for example, married people with family incomes of $50,000 to $100,000 *versus* divorced people whose predivorce family income was $50,000 to $100,000.

Longitudinal Studies One type of correlational research design is sufficiently distinct to warrant separate discussion. In these studies, called **longitudinal studies** (or *prospective studies*), the behaviors of the same subjects are studied on several different occasions over what is usually an extended period of time. Because the same people are tested several times, it is possible to specify more precisely the time-order relationship between factors that covary.

One of the most important forms of longitudinal research is the **high-risk design,** which involves the study of people who have a high probability of developing a disorder. For several decades, Sarnoff

Mednick and his research team (e.g., Cannon & Mednick, 1993) have been studying the development of people who are at high risk for schizophrenia because their mothers were schizophrenic and because this disorder seems to have a strong genetic component. The findings of Mednick's team will be discussed in detail in Chapter 13, but two points are worth noting here, as examples of what high-risk research can produce. First, the schizophrenic mothers whose children also became schizophrenic were more severely disturbed than were the schizophrenic mothers whose children did not become schizophrenic. Second, the mothers of the high-risk children who became schizophrenic were hospitalized—and, thus, separated from their families—while their children were young.

Mednick's longitudinal studies are an example of *genetic high-risk design:* the subjects are chosen because they are thought to be genetically predisposed to the disorder. Another type of high-risk design that has been used increasingly in research on abnormal behavior is the *behavioral high-risk design.* Here, subjects are chosen not because of genetic vulnerability but because they show a behavioral characteristic, of whatever origin, that is thought to make them vulnerable to a disorder. A good example of this design is the research of Loren and Jean Chapman and their associates (Allen, Chapman, Chapman, et al., 1987; Chapman & Chapman, 1987). The Chapmans selected a group of young people who, by virtue of their unusual thinking patterns as identified on a test, were considered prone to psychosis. After only a 2-year follow-up, the 60 people in their high-risk group had more psychotic and psychoticlike episodes than did those in the low-risk group (Chapman & Chapman, 1987). Three high-risk subjects had actually developed full-blown psychotic disorders, whereas none of the low-risk subjects had developed a psychotic disorder.

Longitudinal designs are not without problems when it comes to inferring causation. For example, in Mednick's study, to say that the child's schizophrenia was related to the severity of the mother's schizophrenia and to the timing of her hospitalization is not necessarily to say that separation from the mother or the degree of her psychopathology caused the disorder in the child. Perhaps the children who were later diagnosed as schizophrenic were already, in their early years, sufficiently impaired to cause increased emotional distress in their mothers, which in turn could have caused these mothers to be more severely disturbed and to be hospitalized sooner. Longitudinal studies, then, do not eliminate the question of causality, but they do enable researchers to gain a better understanding of the time course of the development they are investigating.

These children have spent their early years amid random violence in Belfast, Northern Ireland. Epidemiological studies would reveal the incidence of depression and anxiety disorders among children in this community. Such studies might also identify the kinds of buffers that protect children psychologically from extreme stress.

Epidemiological Studies

Epidemiology is the study of the frequency and distribution of disorders within specific populations. Key concepts in epidemiology are **incidence**, the number of new cases of the disorder in question within a given time period, such as a year; **prevalence**, the percentage of the population that has the disorder at a particular time; and **duration**, the average length of a given disorder. The simple formula is prevalence = incidence × duration. Thus, acute depression is a brief disorder with a high incidence, while schizophrenia is a lengthy disorder with a low incidence. Both have fairly high prevalence, but for different reasons. Epidemiological data, then, tell us how common a disorder is. They may also point researchers to significant relationships between the disorder and other variables, such as age, gender, and life circumstances. Such findings, in turn, may suggest causes. For example, the epidemiological finding that depressed people have higher rates of negative life events than do nondepressed people (e.g., Paykel, 1979b) has led to what is now the widely held hypothesis that life stresses may trigger depressive episodes in vulnerable people.

Epidemiological surveys, like other research designs, are prone to certain pitfalls. The most serious concern is that descriptions of a population based on a sample are dependent on the representativeness of the sample. Random sampling is the best technique currently available to ensure representativeness, but random sampling guarantees representativeness only when all the selected respondents take part in the survey. In one study, for example, a random sample of Canadian women was surveyed in order to obtain information on the prevalence of fears and phobias in women (Costello, 1982), but, as the research report points out, 16 percent of the women selected refused to participate. We have no way of knowing whether these women were more likely or less likely to have fears and phobias than were the women who agreed to participate. Perhaps the nonparticipants were generally more fearful and, therefore, unwilling to talk to a stranger. Or perhaps they were generally *less* fearful and, thus, able to be assertive in refusing to be questioned. Although the representativeness of a survey is compromised whenever the response rate falls below 100 percent, the fact is that the usual response rate is about 50 to 60 percent, and, however short of the ideal, this is generally considered acceptable in psychological research.

Experimental Designs

A "true" experimental design is one in which an independent variable is manipulated by the experimenter and a dependent variable is measured. Most research on the causes of abnormal behavior does not involve true experiments, for the reason stated earlier: ethical and practical considerations forbid our imposing the suspected cause (independent variable) on experimental subjects. However, there are types of true experiments that have advanced our understanding of abnormal psychology.

Clinical Trials   Clinical trials are studies of the effectiveness of treatments. In clinical trials, patients with a particular disorder are randomly assigned to one or more treatments, or to a treatment group *versus* an untreated control group. For example, researchers might assemble a group of people with dog phobias and randomly assign them to one of two treatment conditions, behavioral or psychodynamic therapy. The treatment would be the independent variable. The dependent variable might be a test, rating the severity of dog phobia. The test would be administered before and after treatment to determine which therapy is more effective.

Several forms of psychotherapy and drug treatment have been subjected to hundreds of clinical trials, and, when they pass the test, they are said to be "empirically supported" by controlled experimental research. Unfortunately, such research seldom pays enough attention to the matter of clinical significance. Though a treatment may, technically speaking, be "empirically supported," that does not mean it is really effective enough that therapists should drop the methods they are using and switch to this one. Still, clinical trials do constitute a form of true experiment, and one that may suggest not only useful treatments but also possible causes.

Analogue Experiments Another type of true experiment often used in psychopathology research is the analogue experiment. The researcher designs an experimental situation that is analogous to "real life" and that may serve as a model for how psychopathology develops and how it can be alleviated. The critical advantage of analogue experiments is that they permit the kinds of control necessary to identify causal relationships and, therefore, have high internal validity.

Hiroto and Seligman (1975), for instance, used an analogue experiment to test their hypothesis that the experience of failure can lead to depression. To one group of college students they gave a set of solvable problems; to another group they administered a set of unsolvable problems. Then they measured all the students' moods. They also asked them to perform a different, unrelated set of tasks. The students who had been given the unsolvable problems became sad and did not do as well on the later tasks as did the students who had worked with the solvable problems. Similar mood and performance deficits have been observed in people diagnosed as depressed. Therefore, the findings of this analogue experiment could be viewed as supporting the theory that depression is a form of "learned helplessness" (Nolen-Hoeksema, Girgus, & Seligman, 1992).

Another important advantage of analogue research is that, in the artificial, analogue setting, the experimenter can test variables that could not be manipulated with genuinely distressed people. To cause ordinary college students to become briefly depressed, as was done in the experiment just described, is ethically permissible, but one cannot risk making depressed people more depressed. On the other hand, the kinds of psychological problems that one can eth-

ically induce in an experiment may *not* be analogous to mental disorders (Suomi, 1982). In general, the more ethical an analogue experiment in abnormal psychology, the less analogous it is likely to be, but one cannot, for that reason, ignore ethics. To state the problem more concretely, failure to complete a set of unsolvable laboratory problems may not be comparable to real precursors of depression, such as the death of a close friend, but researchers cannot kill people's friends in order to produce a better analogue. This problem can be partially solved by developing animal models of psychopathology. For example, uncontrollable electric shock has been used with animal subjects as an analogue of the types of stressful experiences that are thought to cause ulcers and depression (Weiss, 1977, 1982). We saw this technique in the executive monkey experiment discussed earlier in this chapter.

Animal models offer several advantages (Suomi, 1982). Not only can researchers more closely mimic the severity of naturally occurring events; they can also gain almost complete control over the subject's developmental history (e.g., diet and living conditions) and even, through controlled breeding, its genetic endowment. Many important variables, therefore, can be held constant and, thus, can be prevented from confounding the experiment. Further, many behavioral and physiological procedures considered too intrusive to be used with human subjects (e.g., sampling brain neurotransmitters or cerebrospinal fluid) can be performed on animals. Also, because laboratory animals develop more rapidly and have shorter life spans than do human subjects, the long-term consequences of pathology and effectiveness of treatment can be assessed quickly. Animal models have been developed for drug addiction, anxiety disorders, and various other forms of psychopathology (King, Campbell, & Edwards, 1993). It should be added, however, that experimentation with animals has also become increasingly controversial on ethical grounds.

Though analogue experiments cannot be exactly like the real thing, they can come close to it, and it is on the degree of likeness that they are evaluated: how close to reality did they come? The answer to this question depends on how much we know about the real thing (Suomi, 1982). We still do not know the causes of many psychological disorders, let alone the cures. (That is what the researchers are trying to find out.) Consequently, many models can be validated only partially—in terms of the symptoms they reproduce, for instance. Even though, by manipulating certain variables, experimenters may reproduce the symptoms of a naturally occurring disorder, they still have not proved that the naturally occurring disorder issues from those same variables (Abramson &

The baby macaque on the left exhibits normal curiosity, while the one on the right, suffering from induced fetal alcohol syndrome, is listless and unresponsive. Such animal models of human pathology can make valuable contributions to our understanding of various disorders. Though animal research presents ethical problems, it will probably remain an important tool in determining the causes of psychopathology.

Seligman, 1977). When animal subjects are used, a nagging question is always present: just how similar is the behavior of any other animal species to that of the human species? In addition, it is unlikely that all forms of human psychopathology can be induced in animals.

The internal validity provided by analogue experiments must be weighed against the cost to external validity. As a general rule, experimental procedures that increase internal validity tend to decrease external validity (Kazdin & Rogers, 1978). Nevertheless, the search for causal relationships is best conducted under the tight controls of experiments with high internal validity.

The Single-Case Experiment

Experiments with multiple groups, particularly those in which subjects are randomly assigned to experimental conditions, are often considered the best means of establishing cause-and-effect relationships. But they have certain disadvantages for research in abnormal psychology (Hersen & Barlow, 1976). For example, ethical problems arise when researchers withhold treatment from subjects in order to provide a "control" group. Furthermore, it is sometimes difficult to assemble enough appropriate subjects for a group experiment. Finally, the average response of a group of subjects may not be representative of any one subject. These problems have led some researchers to turn to single-case experiments.

The **single-case experiment** resembles its cousin, the case study, in that it focuses on behavior change in one

person. However, it differs from the traditional case study in that it methodically varies the conditions surrounding the person's behavior and continuously monitors the behavior under those changing conditions. When properly carried out, the single-case experimental design has considerable internal validity.

The first stage of a single-case experiment is usually an observation, or *baseline*, stage. During this stage, a record is made of the subject's behavior before any intervention. A typical measure is frequency of behavior over a period of time, such as an hour, a day, or a week. For example, a record might be made of the number of tantrums thrown by a child or the number of panic attacks reported by a person with an anxiety disorder. (A potential drawback to this approach is that the mere fact of observation can change the behavior if the subject knows he or she is being observed, a problem known as Hawthorne effect.) Once behavior is shown to be relatively stable—that is, once there is little fluctuation between recording intervals—a treatment is introduced. The effect of the treatment is ordinarily evaluated by comparing baseline behavior with after-intervention behavior.

Single-case experiments can be set up in a number of ways, but the most common designs are described here.

ABAB Design   In the ABAB design, an initial baseline stage (A) is followed by a treatment stage (B), a return to baseline (A), and another treatment stage (B). Because treatment is removed during the second A stage, this design is also referred to as a *reversal design*. If behavior, after improving in the first treatment stage, reverts to baseline when the treatment is withdrawn and then improves again in the second treatment stage, it is fair to assume that the treatment was responsible for the behavior change. On the other hand, if only one baseline and one treatment stage were used (an AB design), any improvement in the B stage might be due to another factor.

Kelly and Drabman (1977) used an ABAB design when they tried to modify a socially undesirable behavior in a 3-year-old mentally retarded girl named Susan. For most of her life, Susan had had a habit of repeatedly sticking out her tongue. The experimenters were concerned that, left untreated, this behavior would make it difficult for Susan to be accepted by other people.

Baseline observations were made of the frequency of Susan's tongue thrusts during daily 10-minute sessions. Then came the treatment: a mildly aversive stimulus, lemon juice, was squirted on Susan's tongue whenever she stuck it out. Treatments lasted 10 minutes and continued for 9 sessions. Treatment was then withdrawn for 16 sessions. Finally, a second treatment stage was instituted, for another 16 sessions. A follow-up was conducted 6 months after the end of the ABAB treatment. Figure 3.2 shows the changes in Susan's behavior through alternating baseline and treatment conditions. As the graph shows, the lemon juice was successful in eliminating tongue thrusting, and the 6-month follow-up revealed no recurrence.

The withdrawing of treatment in the ABAB design may pose ethical problems. While Susan's return to sticking out her tongue in the second A stage was not cause for alarm, there are certain behaviors—such as head banging in severely disturbed children—for which it is not appropriate to halt an effective treatment. In such cases, other single-case experimental designs must be considered.

Multiple-Baseline Design   An experimental design that does not depend on interrupting treatment is the **multiple-baseline design**. In this procedure, the same treatment is aimed successively at several targets—usually several subjects, several behaviors in one subject, or several situational variants for one behavior. When the design is used across subject, a baseline is first established for each subject; then the intervention is introduced, first for one subjects, then for the next, and so on. If the intervention is responsible for changing behavior, then an effect should be observed in each subject immediately following treatment. Like the ABAB design, the multiple-baseline design rules out alternative explanations for behavior change by demonstrating that behavior responds *systematically* to the introduction of the treatment.

Dyer, Christian, and Luce (1982) used a multiple-baseline design to see whether children suffering from autism (Chapter 16) could be taught to "look before they leaped." Autistic children often seem to begin a task without paying any attention to its requirements. The researchers felt that this tendency could

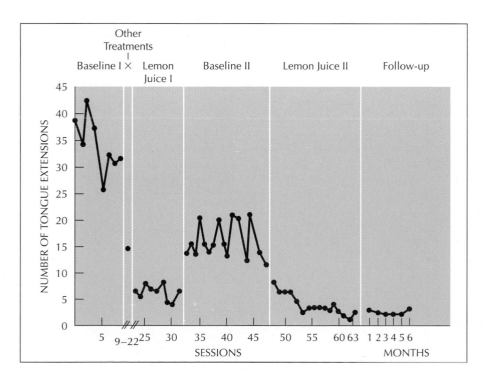

FIGURE 3.2   The ABAB procedure helped Susan, a mentally retarded 3-year-old, learn to stop sticking out her tongue. As the graph shows, squirting lemon juice on her tongue discouraged her habit (Lemon Juice I). When the lemon juice treatment was temporarily halted, her habit gained strength again (Baseline II), but then it declined once more when the lemon juice was reapplied (Lemon Juice II) (Kelly & Drabman, 1977).

be remedied by the use of a *response-delay* procedure, which requires the child to wait a predetermined amount of time before responding. The procedure was tried on three autistic children. In practical terms, it generally meant holding the child's hands for several seconds after he or she was presented with a discrimination-learning problem.

Multiple baselines for performance on the discrimination-learning tasks were established for the three children. The treatment was introduced first with one child, then with the second, and finally with the third. An examination of the behavioral records (Figure 3.3) shows that each child's discrimination learning immediately improved with the response-delay treatment.

Limitations of the Single-Case Design Like the traditional case study, the single-case experiment design

is weak in external validity. As each person is unique, it can be argued that there is no way of knowing whether the effect of a particular treatment on one person can predict its effect on other people. This problem may not be as serious as it appears, because the efficiency with which data can be collected from one subject often makes it easy to repeat the procedures with other subjects (Kazdin, 1978). Therefore, while generalizability is in no way guaranteed by the single-case design, it can easily be tested. Moreover, external validity can be enhanced by the use of a single *group* of subjects in a single-case experimental design, such as ABAB. Then it is possible to draw conclusions about the effect of the experimental variable not just on the individual subjects but on the population from which the sample was drawn.

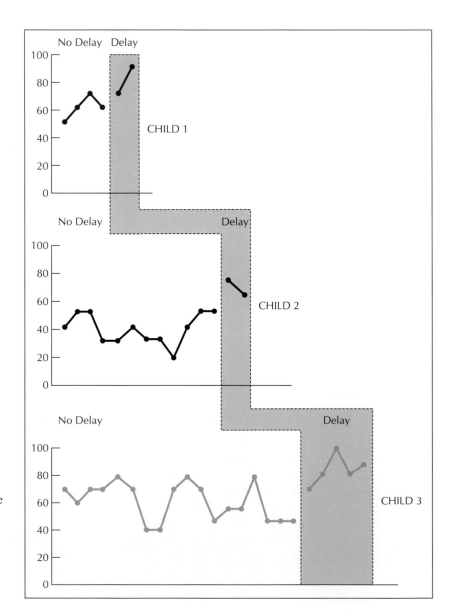

FIGURE 3.3 The multiple-baseline design was employed to see whether encouraging autistic children to pay attention to instructions before performing a discrimination-learning task would help them do better on the task (Dyer, Christian, & Luce, 1982). The multiple-baseline design has an important advantage over the ABAB design: it does not require the experimenter to interrupt a treatment that seems to be helpful.

KEY TERMS

ABAB design, 70	covariation of events, 59	high-risk design, 67	prevalence, 68
analogue experiment, 69	demand charactcristics, 63	hypothesis, 60	random assignment, 62
case-control design, 65	dependent variable, 61	incidence, 68	random sample, 60
case study, 61	double-blind, 64	independent variable, 61	replicate, 60
clinical significance, 65	elimination of plausible	internal validity, 59	representativeness, 59
clinical trials, 68	alternative causes, 59	longitudinal studies, 67	single-case experiment, 70
clinicians, 60	epidemiology, 68	multiple-baseline design, 71	statistical inference, 64
confounding, 59	experimenter effects, 64	null hypothesis, 64	third-variable problem, 66
control techniques, 61	external validity, 59	operational definitions, 61	time-order relationship, 59
correlational research, 65	generalizability, 59	placebo, 64	

SUMMARY

- The scientific method is characterized by the skeptical attitude of those who use it, by the objectives it is intended to meet (namely, reliable and valid description, prediction, control, and understanding of behavior), and by the specific procedures used to meet those objectives (hypothesis testing, definition formulation, and methods of control).

- Research that fails to eliminate alternative explanations of a phenomenon is said to be confounded. Only when no confounding is present is a study internally valid.

- The external validity of research depends on whether the findings can be generalized, or applied, to different populations, settings, and conditions. External validity increases as the representativeness of a sample increases. The best way to achieve a representative sample is to use a random sampling procedure. External validity also increases with frequent, successful replication of a study.

- Research often begins with the development of a testable, or falsifiable, hypothesis. To be testable, a hypothesis must be formulated in terms of concepts that have been given operational definitions so that they can be observed and measured.

- Generally, a hypothesis is tested in an experiment, in which three control techniques are used: manipulating the independent variable in order to measure its effects on the dependent variable; holding all other variables constant; and balancing uncontrollable factors—the personal characteristics of the subjects being tested—among all conditions.

- Often, the response of a placebo control group can either support or cast doubt on the supposed relationship between an independent and a dependent variable.

- Double-blind experiments, in which neither the subjects nor the experimenters know what treatment is being administered to whom, are used to minimize the effect of expectations on the study's results or on their interpretation.

- Many different research designs are used to investigate abnormal behavior. Prior to the testing of hypotheses, a phase of exploration, discovery, and observation is used to generate the hypotheses. One basis for hypothesis generation is the case study, the intensive description and analysis of a single person. Treatment development is also gaining recognition as a method of informal observation that is useful for generating hypotheses and the experimental methods for testing them.

- Correlational, or natural, group designs examine whether systematic differences exist between groups of people who have been treated "naturally." Major tasks in evaluating the results of correlational studies are to determine the direction of the causal relationship and to eliminate possible third variables that may cause differences between groups.

- Longitudinal studies examine the behavior of people over time. Although this design does not solve the problem of determining causality, it is more powerful than a correlational design, because assumptions of covariation and time-order relationships can be more easily tested.

- The high-risk design is a type of longitudinal research that follows people who are thought to be vulnerable to developing a disorder in the future.

- Epidemiological studies examine the incidence and prevalence of a behavioral disorder in a population. Such studies can help to determine whether the frequency of a particular disorder is related to other variables, which may be causes. A major concern in epidemiological surveys is the representativeness of the sample.

- In experimental designs, the experimenter manipulates an independent variable and measures a dependent variable.

- Analogue experiments, which place subjects in artificial situations that are analogous to real-life situations, permit the kind of experimental control that is useful in identifying causal relationships.

- Clinical trials are experimental designs used to evaluate treatments for behavior disorders. They involve randomly assigning patients to either experimental or control groups and examining whether or not the experimental treatment outperforms the comparison one.

- Single-case experimental designs monitor behavior change in an individual following an intervention that was introduced after a baseline (no-treatment) observation. Evidence for a causal relationship is obtained if the person's behavior changes systematically with the introduction of the treatment.

Part Two | THEORETICAL PERSPECTIVES

Chapter 4

In Chapter 1, we spoke briefly of the perspectives, or schools of theory and practice, in abnormal psychology. Those perspectives will be the subject of this and the next chapter. In the present chapter, we will focus on three perspectives that look for the causes of abnormal behavior primarily *inside* the individual. For the biological perspective, those causes are the functioning of the brain and other systems of the body; for the psychodynamic perspective, they are unconscious motives; for the cognitive perspective, they are more conscious thought processes. We will begin with the biological perspective, because it is the oldest.

The Biological Perspective

Long before recorded history, people associated abnormal behavior with things going on inside the head. But the brain does not permit easy access; therefore, theories about the organic bases of abnormal behavior remained for centuries in the realm of speculation. Today such theories are being built with concrete evidence. With the help of advanced technology, researchers can now flip a switch, see a moving picture of a living brain as it is functioning, and search such pictures for blood clots, tumors, and other possible causes of behavioral problems. The brain, then, is no longer the dark territory that it used to be. The same is true of other biological functions that affect our thoughts and emotions. Perhaps the greatest source of optimism and excitement in abnormal psychology in the past 30 years has been the tremendous advance in the study of the biological bases of behavior.

The biological perspective focuses on the interaction between behavior and organic functions. It is not a single, general theory but, rather, a collection of specific theories about specific pathologies. Most of these theories will be dealt with in the chapters that discuss the disorders in question. Our purpose here is to lay the groundwork by describing the kinds of biological mechanisms—the genes, the nervous system, the endocrine system—now being investigated by neuroscientists and by giving some picture of their research methods.

Fundamental to the **biological perspective** is the issue of the relationship between the physical and psychological aspects of our functioning—the so-called *mind-body problem.* Though most of us tend to regard our minds as things apart from our bodies, the two are really aspects of a single, complex entity. What the mind experiences affects the body. A stressful job can contribute to hypertension; a death in the family can alter the survivors' immune systems, making them illness-prone. Conversely, alterations in body chemistry can have massive effects on emotion and behavior. Physical and mental functioning cannot realistically be considered apart from each other.

It has long been recognized that certain abnormal behavior patterns are caused by organic factors. Two chapters of this book—Chapter 14, "Neuropsychological Disorders," and Chapter 16, "Mental Retardation and Autism"—are devoted largely to such patterns. But in recent years researchers have come increasingly to suspect—indeed, to show—that organic factors are involved in disorders *not* traditionally considered organic, such as anxiety and depression. The reverse is also true: researchers are discovering more and more ways in which what used to be regarded as purely organic illness is, in fact, related to psychological stress—a matter that is the subject of Chapter 8, "Psychological Stress and Physical Disorders." It is to the biological factors involved in this new research that we now turn.

Behavior Genetics

Every cell in the human body contains a mass of threadlike structures known as **chromosomes.** Coded on the chromosomes are all the instructions, inherited from the parents at the moment of conception, as to what proteins the body should produce. The proteins in turn determine what the body will become: brown-eyed or blue-eyed, tall or short, male or female. The individual units in which this information is carried are called **genes.** There are more than 2,000 genes on a single chromosome. In some cases, a given trait is controlled by a single gene. But the vast majority of human traits are *polygenic,* the products of the interaction of many genes.

It has long been known that genetic inheritance influences not only physical traits, such as eye color, but also behavior. What is not known is the *extent* to which genes control behavior. This is the famous nature-nurture question, and it is as unresolved in abnormal psychology as it is in any other branch of psychology. Researchers in **behavior genetics,** as this subfield is called, have methods of determining whether a behavioral abnormality is subject to genetic influence. But establishing the degree of genetic influence is a much thornier matter. As we just saw, most traits are controlled by the subtle interaction of many genes—and affected, furthermore, by other factors in the body chemistry, as well as by experience. Thus, the relationship of genes to traits is not a single link but a vast net of influences.

Because of these complexities, it is only in the past three decades that researchers have begun to make any genuine progress in relating genetics to behavior disturbances (Plomin, Owen, & McGuffin, 1994). To date, genetic defects have been shown to be directly responsible for a few forms of abnormality—for example, Down syndrome, a form of mental retardation. But such clear-cut cases of direct genetic causation are apparently rare. Instead, most genetically influenced disorders seem to fit what is called the **diathesis-stress model.** According to this model, certain genes or gene combinations produce a *diathesis,* or constitutional predisposition, to a disorder. If this diathesis is then combined with certain kinds of environmental stress, abnormal behavior will result. Studies within the past 30 years indicate that, just as a tendency to develop diabetes, heart disease, and certain types of cancer can be genetically transmitted, so can a predisposition to certain behavioral disturbances.

Clinical Genetic Studies   To understand the genetic evidence, one must understand the methods by which it is obtained. Every human being is born with a unique genotype—that is, a highly individual combination of genes representing the biological inheritance from the parents. This genotype interacts with the person's environment to determine the phenotype—that is, the person's equally unique combination of observable characteristics. The entire purpose of behavior genetics is to discover to what extent different behavioral disorders are due to genetic inheritance rather than environmental influence. This is done via three types of studies: family studies, twin studies, and adoption studies.

Family Studies   Family studies are based on our knowledge that different types of family relationships involve different degrees of genetic similarity. All children receive half their genes from one parent and half from the other. Thus, parents and children are 50 percent identical genetically. On average, any two siblings have approximately 50 percent of their genes in common. Aunts and uncles, one step further removed, are approximately 25 percent identical genetically to a given niece or nephew. And first cousins, yet another step removed, have approximately 12.5 percent of their genes in common.

With these percentages in mind, the genetic researcher puts together a sample of families containing one diagnosed case, referred to as the *index case,* or *proband case,* of the disorder in question. Then the researcher studies the other members of each family—grandparents, parents, children, grandchildren, siblings, aunts and uncles, cousins—to determine what percentage of persons in each of these relationship groups merits the same diagnosis as the index case. When all the families have been examined in this way, the percentages for each relationship group are averaged, so the researcher ends up with an average percentage of siblings sharing the index case's disorder, an average percentage of aunts and uncles bearing the index case's disorder, and so on. If it should turn out that these percentages roughly parallel the percentages of shared genes—if, for example, siblings prove approximately twice as likely as aunts and uncles to share the index case's disorder—then this would strongly suggest that predisposition to the disorder in question might be transmitted genetically. If you turn ahead to Figure 13.1 (page 388), you will see a graph summarizing family studies of schizophrenia. The figures clearly suggest that the more closely one is related to a person with schizophrenia, the more likely one is to develop schizophrenia.

Family studies are an important avenue of investigation into the genetic aspects of psychological disorder. Such research explores the extent to which the shared genes of parents, children, cousins, and other relatives affect the likelihood that any one member of a family will develop a disorder.

Such evidence, however, only suggests—it does not prove—genetic transmission. While a person has more genes in common with siblings than with aunts and uncles, he or she also has much more of the environment in common with siblings (same parents, same schools) than with aunts and uncles. Though recent research suggests that shared environment is not the primary cause of similarity between family members (Plomin, Owen, & McGuffin, 1994), it is still a potential confounding factor in family studies.

Twin Studies   The genes-versus-environment confusion is less troublesome in twin studies. Here the basic technique is to compare monozygotic and dizygotic twins. **Monozygotic (MZ) twins,** also called *identical twins,* develop from a single fertilized egg and, therefore, have exactly the same genotype. They are always of the same sex, have the same eye color, share the same blood type, and so on. In contrast, **dizygotic (DZ) twins,** also called *fraternal twins,* develop from two eggs fertilized by two different sperm. Therefore, DZ twins, like any pair of siblings, have only approximately 50 percent of their genes in common. As with ordinary siblings, one may be female and the other male, one blue-eyed and one brown-eyed, and so forth. Thus, while monozygotic twins are as likely as dizygotic twins to share the same environment, they have approximately twice as many genes in common.

From this configuration, one can guess the research design. The researcher assembles one group of index cases, each of whom is an MZ twin, and a second group of index cases, each of whom is a DZ twin. All the *co-twins* (the twins of the index cases) are then examined to determine how many of them are concordant—that is, share the same disorder—with their index twin. If the researcher should discover that the concordance rate for the MZ twins is considerably greater than that for the DZ twins, then this would be substantial evidence that predisposition to the disorder is genetically transmitted. And that, in fact, is what has been discovered in the case of both schizophrenia and bipolar (manic-depressive) disorder: a concordance rate three to five times higher for MZ twins than for DZ twins. Even more than the family studies, this is strong evidence for a hereditary factor in those disorders. At the same time, twin studies also provide good evidence for environmental causation. In the behavioral disorders for which genes have been shown to increase risk, they have not been found, on average, to account for more than half the difference between those with "genetic loading" and those without. Therefore, the environment is obviously an important influence as well (Plomin, Owen, & McGuffin, 1994).

Twin studies are beautifully simple in design but not in practice, the chief problem being that MZ twins are very rare. It is no easy task to assemble an adequate sample of MZ twins who have paranoid schizophrenia. Furthermore, the question of environmental influence cannot be eliminated altogether from twin studies, since MZ twins, so similar physically and always of the same sex, may be raised more alike than DZ twins.

Adoption Studies   Adoption studies attempt to make a decisive separation between genetic and environmental influence. As we have seen, as long as two relatives share the same environment—live under the same

Twin studies are revealing the concordance rate of various disorders in both MZ (identical) and DZ (fraternal) twins. Even when identical twins do not grow up in the same household, they are likely to have a great deal in common. These twins, separated at birth and reunited at age 31, had both become firefighters. Unfortunately, some twins also share a greater vulnerability to psychological disorders such as schizophrenia.

The Minnesota Study of Twins Reared Apart

One of the most extensive studies of twins reared apart began in 1979 at the University of Minnesota. Since that time, the Minnesota researchers have studied more than 100 sets of monozygotic and dizygotic twins from across the United States and around the world. The twins were all separated early in life, reared apart in their formative years, and reunited as adults. The researchers located the twin pairs through such means as adoption officials, friends and relatives of the twins, and the twins themselves, many of whom volunteered for the project, hoping to be reunited with a separated twin.

The idea behind the project is to collect information about the medical and social histories of each twin, assess each twin's current medical and psychological states, and then compare any differences or similarities within each twin pair. During a week at the research center, each participant undergoes intensive medical and psychological assessment, including a psychophysiological test battery, individual ability testing, measurement of special mental abilities, personality inventories, psychomotor assessment, a life stress interview, a life history interview, a twin relationship survey, a test of emotional responsiveness, and measurement of interests, values, and expressive style—answering more than 15,000 questions in the process (Segal, 1984). In addition, the researchers study the twins' rearing environments.

This study has so far yielded two unmistakable conclusions: genetic factors account for a large part of behavioral variability, and being reared in the same environment has only a negligible effect on the development of similar psychological traits (Bouchard, Lykken, McGue, et al., 1990). Of all the traits tested, IQ shows the highest correlation between monozygotic twins reared apart: a heritability factor of about 0.70. But other psychological traits, such as personality variables, social attitudes, and interests, have also shown strong correlations. The researchers have also begun to evaluate the degree of heritability for alcohol and drug abuse and antisocial behavior. Initial results have found a genetic component for drug abuse and for both child and adult antisocial behavior but not for alcohol abuse (Grove, Eckert, Heston, et al., 1990).

In sum, the study of twins at the Minnesota Center has found that correlations for monozygotic twins reared apart are about the same as those for monozygotic twins reared together. According to Bouchard and his associates, "Being reared by the same parents in the same physical environment does not, on average, make siblings more alike as adults than they would have been if reared separately in adoptive homes" (Bouchard, Lykken, McGue, et al., 1990, p. 227).

The twin studies, however, do not discount environment altogether. That is because people with the same genotype tend to seek out or be exposed to the same type of environment. What each of us finds a congenial environment is influenced by our genetic individuality. An energetic toddler will have different learning experiences from a passive toddler. An outgoing child will elicit different reactions from people than will a shy child. These varying experiences will certainly have an effect on psychological variability, but it is important to remember that many of these experiences are self-selected, a process directed by our genetic predispositions. Bouchard has shown that monozygotic twins reared apart tend to select very similar environments, and, to the extent that these experiences have an impact on their behavior, there is an interaction between heredity and environment. The old nature-versus-nurture argument should probably give way to a new understanding of nature *via* nurture.

Source: Based on Bouchard, Lykken, McGue, et al., 1990.

roof, pet the same dog, fight the same family fights—the fact that they share the same behavioral disorder cannot be attributed with certainty to genetic influence. But, if through adoption the environmental tie were broken, then any significant similarities in behavioral history should be entirely the result of the genetic tie. For example, if infants who were born of severely disturbed mothers and adopted into other families at birth developed that same disturbance at approximately the same rate as infants born of *and* raised by mothers suffering from that disorder, then the disorder must, to a large extent, be in the genes. Likewise, if a pair of MZ twins who were separated at birth and raised in different homes still showed a substantially higher concordance rate for a given disorder than did DZ twins raised together or separately, then this would constitute the firmest possible evidence for genetic transmission. (See the box above for a large-scale study of separated twins, though this research focused on personality in general.)

It is just such mother-child pairs and twin pairs that are the object of adoption studies. The adopted-twin studies are the less important of the two, because the samples are so small. (If it is difficult to assemble a group of MZ twins, all of whom have paranoid schizophrenia, imagine the difficulty of putting together a group of MZ twins, all of whom have paranoid schizophrenia *and* have been raised apart from their co-twins.) The mother-child adoption studies are somewhat easier to do, since a severely disturbed mother is likely to give up her child for adoption. Several such studies have been done, and, as we shall see, they now constitute our best evidence for the genetic transmission of a tendency toward bipolar disorder (Chapter 9) and schizophrenia (Chapter 13).

Molecular Genetic Studies Whereas clinical genetic studies aim to determine the extent of genetic inheritance in behavioral disorders, molecular genetic studies attempt to identify exactly which genes are involved. We know that genes located close to one another on a chromosome tend to be "linked," or inherited together. In *linkage analysis,* therefore, researchers use a *genetic marker,* a gene with a known location on the human chromosome set, as a clue to the location of a gene controlling a disorder. For example, if people who are color-blind—a trait whose controlling gene has been located—were unusually susceptible to bipolar disorder, we could assume that a gene related to bipolar disorder was located near the "color-blind gene," on the same chromosome. Linkage studies are now being actively pursued for schizophrenia, bipolar disorder, alcoholism, and panic disorder (Dunner, 1997; Plomin, Owen, & McGuffin, 1994).

The Central Nervous System

If behavioral abnormalities do result from some form of biological malfunction, then the likely place to look for such malfunction is the nervous system. The **nervous system** is a vast electrochemical conducting network that extends from the brain through the rest of the body. Its function is to transmit information, in the form of electrochemical impulses, among various cells throughout the body.

The nervous system has many divisions (see Figure 4.1), but its headquarters is the **central nervous system (CNS),** consisting of the brain and spinal cord. Of all the parts of the nervous system, the CNS is the one primarily responsible for the storage and transmission of information.

Logically, when there is a problem in the CNS, there is a problem in behavior. As we shall see in Chapter 14, any damage to the brain, whether from injury or disease, can cause a massive change in the personality. Recent research, however, has concentrated more on subtle chemical changes that may be implicated in psychopathology.

Neurons Like every other part of the body, the nervous system is made up of cells specifically adapted for its functions. Nerve cells, called **neurons,** have the following characteristic structural features (see Figure 4.2):

1. The *cell body,* which contains the nucleus. The chemical reactions that take place in the cell body provide the energy and the chemicals needed for the transmission of impulses.

2. The *dendrites,* short fibers branching out from the cell body. In most neurons, it is the dendrites that receive impulses from other neurons.

3. The *axon,* a long fiber stretching outward from the cell body. This is the passageway through which impulses are transmitted along the neuron on their way to other neurons or to the muscles and glands.

4. The *axon terminals,* the axon's branchlike endings, each with a buttonlike structure at its tip. It is through these buttons at the ends of the axon terminals that the impulse is transmitted to the next neuron.

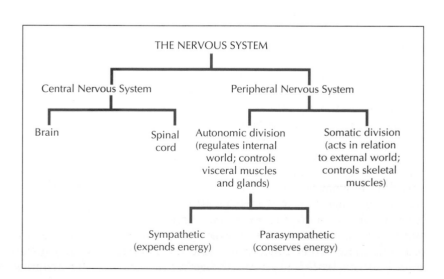

FIGURE 4.1 Diagram of the relationships among the parts of the nervous system.

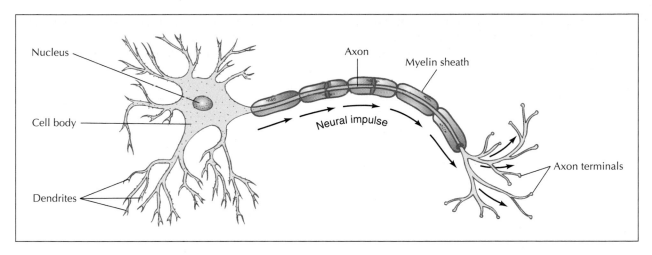

FIGURE 4.2 The structure of this motor neuron is typical of many other neurons. The dendrites, short fibers branching out from the cell body, receive impulses from other neurons and transmit them along the axon to the axon terminals. Impulses cross the gap at the end of each axon terminal, moving on to the next group of dendrites. In many neurons, a myelin sheath wrapped around the axon speeds the transmission of the impulses.

5. In some neurons, a *myelin sheath,* which is made up of fatty cells wrapped around the axon in segments. The myelin sheath speeds neural transmission by insulating the axon from other cells, just as traffic on an interstate is sped along by limiting the access of other roadways.

The typical pathway is as follows. Through its dendrites, a neuron receives an impulse from a neighboring neuron. (The number of neighboring neurons may range from one to several thousand.) The neuron then passes that impulse along its axon to the axon terminals. At the terminal, the impulse must leap a small gap, called the synapse, between the terminal button and the dendrite of the neuron that is to receive the impulse. This leap is accomplished by a chemical known as a neurotransmitter. If a sufficient amount of neurotransmitter crosses the synapse, the receiving neuron will "fire"—that is, send on the impulse.

Firing is an all-or-nothing response: if enough neurotransmitter is received, the neuron fires; if not, it doesn't. This is important, because changing the amount of neurotransmitter available in the synapse, even by a little bit, may determine whether the receiving neuron fires or not. In fact, most psychoactive drugs do exactly this: they affect the amount of neural activity by altering the amount of neurotransmitter in the synapse.

It is also important to note that not all impulses stimulate the nerve to fire. Some may inhibit transmission; that is, the impulse makes the receiving neuron *less* likely to fire. In a typical case, a receiving neuron is stimulated by both excitatory and in-

hibitory impulses. It will then tally the excitatory and inhibitory input and will or will not fire.

Thus, the information that our nervous system receives, and the way in which it will be acted on, is regulated by synaptic transmission. Synaptic transmission, in turn, is determined by the action of neurotransmitters. It is, thus, no surprise that the neurotransmitters have been a major focus of biological research in abnormal psychology.

Neurotransmitters In the cell body, amino acids from the protein we eat are converted into neurotransmitters. Then the neurotransmitters travel down

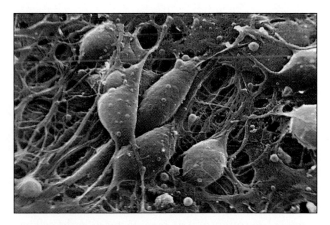

This is a false-color scanning electron micrograph (SEM) of neurons from the cerebral cortex. It clearly shows the large central cell body of each neuron, with a single axon extending from one end, and one or more smaller dendrites from the other.

the axon to the axon terminals. See Figure 4.3 for the rest of their life cycle. In the axon terminals, the neurotransmitters are stored in small sacs called *vesicles (Stage 1)*. When an impulse reaches the axon terminal, the neurotransmitter is released into the synapse, where it floods the gap and makes contact with special proteins called **postsynaptic receptors** on the surface of the receiving neuron. Molecules in the neurotransmitter fit into the postsynaptic receptors like a key into a lock, and this reaction causes a change in voltage in the receiving neuron, which will then either fire or not fire *(Stage 2)*. The neurotransmitter may then break down into its component amino acids, be reincorporated into the axon terminal through a process called *reuptake,* or remain circulating in the synapse *(Stage 3)*.

Receptors for neurotransmitters can change over time. If too much neurotransmitter is being released into the synapse, the postsynaptic receptors, to compensate, will decrease in number or become less sensitive to the neurotransmitter—a process called *down-regulation*. Or the opposite may occur: if the presynaptic neuron is not releasing enough neurotransmitter to carry the impulse, the postsynaptic receptors will undergo *up-regulation,* increasing in number or sensitivity. Biological researchers are now exploring the possibility that some behavioral disorders are due in part to faulty up- or down-regulation. Several drug treatments for those disorders are

thought to work by restoring smooth regulation (Hamblin, 1997).

Scientists have been aware of the existence of neurotransmitters only since the 1920s, and the study of their relation to psychological disorders is more recent still, beginning in the 1950s. This is now one of the most exciting areas of biological research in abnormal psychology. It is not yet known how many kinds of neurotransmitters exist in the human body—probably more than 50. The ones that seem to have important roles in psychopathology are the following (McGeer, Eccles, & McGeer, 1987; Stahl, 1996):

1. *Acetylcholine*. The first neurotransmitter discovered, acetylcholine is involved in transmitting nerve impulses to the muscles throughout the body. In the central nervous system, it may also be involved in attentional processes, in sleep disorders, and in Alzheimer's disease (Blokland, 1996).

2. *Dopamine*. This substance seems to be crucially involved in the regulation of motor behavior and in reward-related activities. Certain frequently abused drugs, such as stimulants, act on the dopamine system. Disturbed dopamine activity is thought to be related to schizophrenia.

3. *Enkephalins*. These substances seem able to act upon the opiate receptors in the brain (the parts

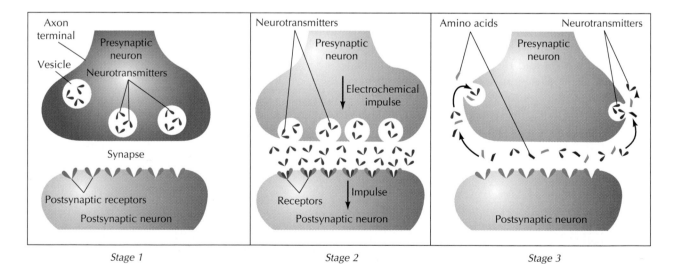

FIGURE 4.3

Stage 1: Neurotransmitters manufactured in the cell body are stored in vesicles in the axon terminal.

Stage 2: An electrochemical impulse passing through the presynaptic neuron causes the neurotransmitter to be released into the synapse, where it bonds with the receptors of the postsynaptic neuron, transmitting the impulse.

Stage 3: Some of the neurotransmitter breaks down into its original amino acids. Some is taken back up into the presynaptic neuron (reuptake) and re-stored in the vesicles. The remainder circulates in the extracellular environment.

that are affected by opium or related drugs). As such, they may be the body's "natural drugs."

4. *GABA (gamma-amino-butyric acid).* GABA is a neurotransmitter that works almost exclusively in the brain, inhibiting neurons from firing. Tranquilizing drugs that inhibit anxiety work by increasing the activity of GABA.

5. *Norepinephrine (NE).* In the autonomic nervous system, this substance is involved in producing "fight or flight" responses, such as increased heart rate and blood pressure. In the central nervous system, norepinephrine activates alertness to danger.

6. *Serotonin.* This neurotransmitter has an important role in constraint. Imbalances in serotonin and norepinephrine may be involved in severe depression, as well as in a number of other disorders, including anxiety disorders, obsessive-compulsive disorder, eating disorders, and alcoholism (Dubovsky & Thomas, 1995).

Drug Treatment Research on neurotransmitters is intimately linked with psychopharmacology, the study of the drug treatment of psychological disorders. Not all psychoactive, or behavior-affecting, drugs target the neurotransmitters, but many do, attempting to correct neurotransmitter imbalances at any one of several stages. If the goal is to increase the action of a neurotransmitter, drugs may be used to increase the level of the neurotransmitter in the synapse—for example, by slowing down its reuptake. If the goal is to suppress the action of a neurotransmitter, drugs may be used to attach to the postsynaptic receptors in place of the neurotransmitters, thus blocking them. Or drugs may be used to influence neurotransmitters via up- or down-regulation. But these are very delicate manipulations, still in the experimental stages. Indeed, in some cases researchers still do not know whether the neurotransmitter in question needs to be enhanced or suppressed.

Drugs are now the most common form of treatment for psychological disorders. In some cases, they are very effective, but they often have unwanted side effects. They also raise the question of whether the drug is merely treating the symptom, without addressing the cause. There are five main categories of drugs used in the treatment of abnormal behavior (see Table 4.1): antianxiety drugs, sedative-hypnotic drugs, antipsychotic drugs, antidepressant drugs, and antimanic/mood-stabilizer drugs. We will discuss these medications in the chapters on the relevant disorders.

The Anatomy of the Brain While behavior may be affected by chemical reactions at the finest level of brain activity, we also know that many behavioral abnormalities are related to the gross structure of the brain. Therefore, a knowledge of the anatomy of the brain is essential to an understanding of psychopathology.

The outermost part of the brain is an intricate, convoluted layer of "gray matter" called the *cerebral cortex* (see Figures 4.4 and 4.5). The external surface

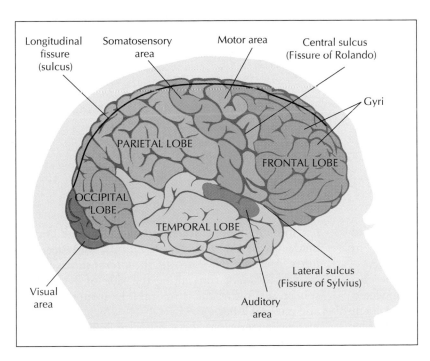

FIGURE 4.4 The four lobes of the cortex and the major fissures that separate them.

TABLE 4.1   Major Psychotherapeutic Drugs

Category	Chemical Structure or Psychopharmacologic Action	Generic Name	Trade Name
Antipsychotic drugs (also called major tranquilizers or neuroleptics)	Phenothiazines		
	Aliphatic	Chlorpromazine	Thorazine
	Piperidine	Thioridazine	Mellaril
	Piperazine	Trifluoperazine	Stelazine
		Fluphenazine	Prolixin
	Thioxanthenes		
	Aliphatic	Chlorprothixene	Taractan
	Piperazine	Thiothixene	Navane
	Butyrophenones	Haloperidol	Haldol
	Dibenzoxazepines	Loxapine	Loxitane
	Benzisoxazoles	Risperidone	Risperdal
	Dibenzodiazepines	Olanzapine	Zyprexa
		Clozapine	Clozaril
Antidepressant drugs	Tricyclic antidepressants (TCAs)		
	Tertiary amines	Amitriptyline	Elavil
		Imipramine	Tofranil
		Clomipramine	Anafranil
		Doxepin	Sinequan
	Secondary amines	Desipramine	Norpramin
		Nortriptyline	Pamelor
		Protriptyline	Vivactil
	Monoamine oxidase (MAO) inhibitors	Phenelzine	Nardil
		Tranylcypromine	Parnate
	Selective serotonin reuptake inhibitors (SSRIs)	Fluoxetine	Prozac
		Sertraline	Zoloft
		Paroxetine	Paxil
		Fluvoxamine	Luvox
	Others	Bupropion	Wellbutrin
		Venlafaxine	Effexor
		Nefazodone	Serzone
Antimanic/mood-stabilizer drugs		Lithium carbonate	Eskalith
		Carbamazepine	Tegretol
		Valproic acid	Depakene
Antianxiety drugs (also called minor tranquilizers)	Benzodiazepines	Chlordiazepoxide	Librium
		Diazepam	Valium
		Chlorazepate	Tranxene
		Oxazepam	Serax
		Lorazepam	Ativan
		Alprazolam	Xanax
		Clonazepam	Klonopin
	Azaspirodecanediones	Buspirone	BuSpar
Sedative-hypnotic drugs	Benzodiazepines	Triazolam	Halcion
		Temazepam	Restoril
		Flurazepam	Dalmane
	Imidazopyridines	Zolpidem	Ambien

of the cerebral cortex has many *sulci* (fissures) and *gyri* (ridges between sulci), which are "landmarks" in studying the brain. A major sulcus called the *longitudinal fissure* divides the brain along the midline into two hemispheres, the right and left brain, connected by the *corpus callosum,* a band of nerve fibers. Each hemisphere is further divided into four lobes. The *central sulcus* (or *fissure of Rolando*) divides the cor-

tex into the *frontal lobe* and the receptive cortex, made up of the *parietal, temporal,* and *occipital lobes.* Another major fissure, the *lateral sulcus* (or *fissure of Sylvius*), runs along the side of each hemisphere, separating the temporal lobe from the frontal and parietal lobes.

The functions of these different lobes have been the subject of much debate. The frontal lobes are a particular enigma, but it appears that they are related essentially to language ability, to the regulation of fine voluntary movements, and to higher cognitive functions such as judgment, planning, the ordering of stimuli, and the sorting out of information. In addition, the frontal lobes serve as a comparator organ—that is, they somehow allow us to look at our behavior and evaluate its appropriateness by seeing how it is perceived by others. This enables us to change our behavior when feedback suggests the need. The frontal lobes also serve to overcome psychological inertia (that is, they help tell us when to start and stop an action). Knowing the proper time to stop or change course is crucial to socially appropriate behavior. Finally, the frontal lobes, because they have two-way connections between the perception-processing centers and the emotion-processing centers, are key to the integration of emotion and cognition (LeDoux, 1993), which in turn is critical to mental health. Many mental disorders—depression, for example—involve a disruption of that relationship.

The temporal lobes control auditory perception and some part of visual perception. Furthermore, they clearly have some role in memory, for damage to the temporal lobes generally involves memory loss. The parietal lobes are the center of intersensory integration (e.g., the ability to visualize a cow upon hearing a "moo") and of motor and sensory-somatic functions. Damage to the parietal lobes frequently results in spatial disorientation and in loss of control over gross-motor behavior (e.g., walking). Finally, the occipital lobes appear to control visual discrimination and visual memory. Although the four lobes have been described separately, in fact they are intricately connected to one another, so the functions of each are affected by the functions of the others.

A cross section of the brain reveals other important structural features (see Figure 4.6). Particularly important in emotional functioning are the hypothalamus and the limbic structures. The *hypothalamus* controls hunger, thirst, and sexual desire; regulates body temperature; and is involved in states of emotional arousal. The *limbic structures,* interacting with the hypothalamus, control behaviors such as mating, fighting, and experiencing pleasure. The *amygdala,* one of the limbic structures, is involved in emotional responses, both positive (such as romantic attraction) and negative (such as "fight or flight" reactions) (LeDoux, 1993). The *hippocampus,* another limbic structure, operates on memory as well as emotion, which may help to explain why we remember emotionally charged experiences more clearly than neutral ones.

Buried in the middle of the brain is the *thalamus,* which relays input from the peripheral nervous sys-

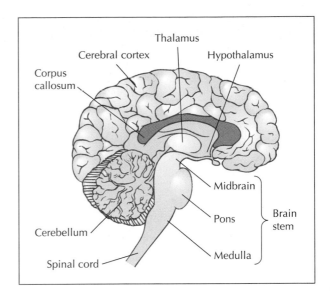

FIGURE 4.5   A cross section of the brain.

tem to other brain structures, including the frontal lobe and the limbic structures. Scientists have recently discovered direct connections between the thalamus and the amygdala, which may help to account for "automatic" emotional reactions such as phobias (Aggleton, 1992). Other brain structures include the *basal ganglia,* which are involved in carrying out planned, programmed behaviors; the *cerebellum,* which is involved in posture, physical balance, and fine-motor coordination; the *pons,* a relay station connecting the cerebellum with other areas of the brain and with the spinal cord; and the *medulla,* which regulates such vital functions as heartbeat, breathing, and blood pressure. The *brainstem* includes the pons, the medulla, and the *reticular activating system,* which extends through the center of the brainstem and regulates sleep and arousal. Within the brain are *ventricles,* cavities filled with cerebrospinal fluid.

Several of these brain structures are now the focus of intense study by researchers in abnormal psychology. Schizophrenia has been associated with abnormalities of size in various parts of the brain: enlarged ventricles and smaller frontal lobes, cerebrums, and craniums (skulls). Temporal-lobe malfunction may be responsible for the memory loss seen in Alzheimer's disease. The appetite-control function of the hypothalamus is being investigated in relation to obesity and bulimia. Basal ganglia abnormalities have been linked to conditions involving ritualistic behavior, such as obsessive-compulsive disorder. Damage to the limbic structures may lead to emotional problems and personality disturbance. These theories will be discussed in later chapters.

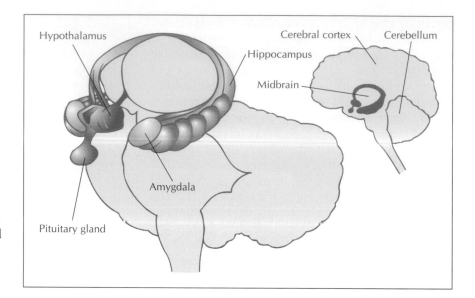

FIGURE 4.6   The limbic structures and hypothalamus. Coming from the Latin word for "border," *limbus,* the limbic structures, including the amygdala and the hippocampus, form a kind of dividing line between the cerebral cortex above and the midbrain and cerebellum below.

Measuring the Brain   For years, much of what was known about the relationship between structure and function in the brain was inferred from the behavior of brain-damaged patients. It was found, for example, that patients with damaged parietal lobes often could no longer walk; therefore, it was concluded that the parietal lobes had some control over gross-motor behavior. Or, on rare occasions, the functioning of the brain could be observed and tested in the course of brain surgery. Today, however, there are techniques that allow researchers to see inside the brain without surgically invading it.

A test that has been used for decades is electroencephalography (EEG), which we discussed in Chapter 2. EEG can be used to measure general brain activity, such as sleep patterns in people with insomnia, or to detect brain abnormalities such as epilepsy. It can also give a picture of the brain's responses to specific external events. In this case, the test is called *event-related potentials,* or *ERPs*. ERPs measure changes in brain activity as a consequence of specific sensory, cognitive, or motor stimuli. People with schizophrenia consistently show ERPs that are different from those of normal controls. The test can also help predict which hyperactive children will respond to stimulant medication (Hegerl & Herrmann, 1990; Javitt & Silipo, 1997).

In recent years, however, scientists have invented a number of extremely sophisticated techniques that produce an actual image of the brain, like a photograph. One such technique is **positron emission tomography (PET)**. In a PET scan, radioactive water molecules are injected into the bloodstream. Then a computerized scanner tracks the molecules on a screen as they are metabolized by the brain. Differences in metabolism in different parts of the brain show up as color contrasts on the screen, and these can point to brain damage—for example, from a stroke. They can also indicate whether patients with a known disorder are improving after drug treatment. A related technique, *single photon emission computer tomography (SPECT),* has also been used to measure blood flow and glucose metabolism in the brain.

While PET, like EEG, measures brain activity, two other techniques, **computerized tomography (CT)** and **magnetic resonance imaging (MRI)**, focus on brain structure. CT passes X rays through cross sections of the brain, measuring the density of tissue within each cross section. In patients with memory loss or language disorders, this can reveal tumors or lesions (tissue damage) that may be the root of the problem. In MRI, the most recently developed technology, the subject is enclosed in a magnetic field, which causes the hydrogen atoms in the brain to shift their positions. Then the magnetic field is turned off, and the atoms return to their original positions, leaving electromagnetic tracks, which, read by the computer, produce an image of the brain tissue. MRI, thus, works at a subatomic level (Scheele, Maravilla, & Dager, 1997). (It was originally called "nuclear magnetic resonance imaging," but the name was changed because the word *nuclear* frightened many patients [Raiche, 1994].) Because it works with such minute particles, MRI yields very precise images, like photographic negatives. A recently developed variation, *functional MRI (fMRI),* measures the magnetic action of blood oxygen and thus—like PET but, again, far more precisely—produces images of brain metabolism (David, Blamire, & Breiter, 1994).

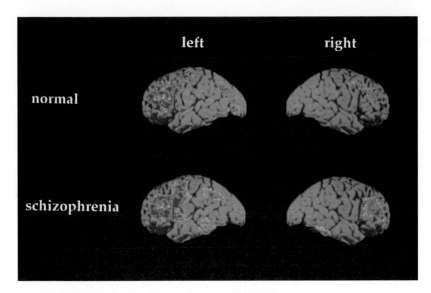

left   right

normal

schizophrenia

Positron emission tomography (PET) scans provide color images of the brain's activity. Shown here are images of the brain of a normal adult (top) and the brain of a schizophrenic patient (bottom) while each was speaking. Notice the greater activity in the left and right frontal lobes of the schizophrenic patient.

Each of these techniques has its strengths and weaknesses. EEG and ERPs, because they measure electrical activity, are far more precise at specifying the *timing* of brain activity. Indeed, they can record events in the brain within milliseconds of neuron firing. They are also inexpensive and completely noninvasive, with no radioactive tracers (PET), no X rays (CT), no powerful magnetic fields (MRI). CT, PET, and MRI are more expensive and more invasive, and they give less information about the timing of brain functions. Their great virtue is their ability to reveal brain structure and, in the case of PET and fMRI, the location of brain activity. The choice of technique usually depends on the purposes of the test—what the testers are trying to find—and, to a large extent, on the patient's financial resources.

Neuroscientists are now using these technologies to test hypotheses about various psychological disorders—schizophrenia, for example. As previously mentioned, schizophrenia has been linked to abnormalities in the size of various parts of the brain: enlarged ventricles, smaller frontal lobes, and so on. These findings, which will be discussed in Chapter 13, are largely the product of CT, PET, and MRI scans (Kotrla & Weinberger, 1995).

Psychosurgery The new neuroimaging technologies have also led to advances in psychosurgery, surgery aimed at reducing abnormal behavior. Early forms of psychosurgery, such as the prefrontal lobotomy (Chapter 1), were often harmful. In recent years, however, researchers have developed more refined psychosurgical techniques—techniques that destroy less brain tissue and, therefore, produce fewer and milder side effects. One procedure, called *cingulotomy*, involves inserting an electrode into the cingulate gyrus, a ridge of brain tissue lying above the corpus callosum. The electrode is then heated, creating a small lesion. The principle here is to disrupt pathways leading from the emotion centers of the thalamus and hypothalamus to the frontal lobe and, thus, to reduce the expression of emotion. Cingulotomy has proved effective for severe obsessive-compulsive patients who have not responded to other treatments (Baer, Rauch, Ballantine, et al., 1995). In another procedure, called *stereotactic subcaudate tractotomy*, a small, localized area of the brain is destroyed by radioactive particles inserted through small ceramic rods. The site varies with the nature of the disturbance. For depressed patients, it is the frontal lobe; for aggressive patients, it is the amygdala, a structure in the lower part of the brain.

Psychosurgery has been found to be effective with severe depression—and with intractable pain (Bridges, Bartlett, Hale, et al., 1994). Nevertheless, it is still extremely controversial, and, even in its newer, more conservative forms, it is used only when other treatments have failed. Its defenders claim that the benefits are substantial and the side effects relatively mild. Other observers doubt both claims and feel that the public should be very wary of such radical and irreversible treatments.

Lateralization: Effects on Language and Emotion One aspect of brain functioning that researchers are now studying is lateralization, the differences between the right and left hemispheres of the brain. Though the two hemispheres appear similar, they have pronounced differences in structure and function. To begin with, neuron connections between the brain and the peripheral nervous system are crossed, so each hemisphere controls the opposite side of the body.

This lateralization is most pronounced in right-handed males, but it is also seen in females and in left-handed males.

In the past, it was popular to assign neat "function" labels to the two sides of the brain. The left brain handled language; the right brain, visual-spatial skills. The left brain was "logical"; the right brain, "emotional." Today we know that these generalizations do not hold. Complex cognitive processes such as language and emotion require interplay among various parts of the brain, on both sides. Nevertheless, different *aspects* of these processes do seem to be localized on the left or right.

In the case of language, the left brain has long been recognized as the center of language production (Provins, 1997). Recently, however, areas in the right hemisphere have been found to affect "pragmatic" aspects of language, such as the understanding of context and the use of metaphors and humor (Hough, 1990; Kaplan, Brownell, Jacobs, et al., 1990).

As for emotion, many studies have shown that the perception of emotion is a right-hemisphere activity (Hellige, 1993). Indeed, it seems to be controlled by the area where the right temporal lobe meets the right parietal lobe. But this does not mean that emotion in general is headquartered in the right brain. Actually, it now appears that different emotions may be controlled by the right *and* left hemispheres. One EEG finding is that people with a history of depression tend to have reduced electrical activity in left-hemisphere emotion centers (Davidson, 1993). As we shall see in Chapter 9, researchers now believe that some people are biologically predisposed to depression. Possibly, the predisposition involves the disabling of protective mechanisms in the left brain.

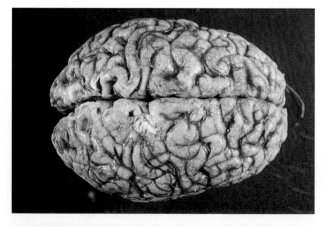

The two hemispheres of the brain, while symmetrical in appearance, do not divide so neatly when it comes to various brain functions. Strict lateralization is limited to just a few brain processes.

The Peripheral Nervous System: Somatic and Autonomic

While the central nervous system is the high command of the body's information network, the peripheral nervous system, a network of nerve fibers leading from the CNS to all parts of the body, is what carries out the commands. Look back at Figure 4.1. The peripheral nervous system has two branches. One is the somatic nervous system, which senses and acts on the external world. The somatic nervous system relays to the brain information picked up through the sense organs, and it transmits the brain's messages to the skeletal muscles, which move the body. The actions mediated by the somatic nervous system are actions that we think of as voluntary: picking up a telephone, crossing a street, tying one's shoes.

The second branch of the peripheral nervous system is the autonomic nervous system, and it is this branch that is of special interest to abnormal psychology.

The Autonomic Nervous System   While the somatic nervous system activates the skeletal muscles, the autonomic nervous system (ANS) controls the smooth muscles, the glands, and the internal organs. Thus, while the somatic division directs our more purposeful responses to environmental stimuli, such as crossing a street when the light turns green, the autonomic division mediates our more automatic responses, such as increased heart rate if we come close to being run over as we cross the street. Because the functions of the ANS tend to be automatic, it used to be known as the "involuntary" nervous system. And, though we now know that many autonomic functions can be brought under voluntary control, it is still true that this function—the regulation of heartbeat, respiration, blood pressure, pupil dilation, bladder contraction, perspiration, salivation, adrenaline secretion, and gastric-acid production, to name only a few—is generally carried out without our thinking about it.

The role of the ANS is to adjust the internal workings of the body to the demands of the environment. Like the central and the peripheral nervous systems, the ANS is subdivided into two branches—the sympathetic division and the parasympathetic division—which are structurally and functionally distinct (Figure 4.7).

The Sympathetic Division   The sympathetic division, consisting of the nerve fibers that emanate from the middle of the spinal cord, mobilizes the body to meet emergencies. To return to the example of crossing the street, if you were to see a car speeding toward you, you would automatically experience a sudden

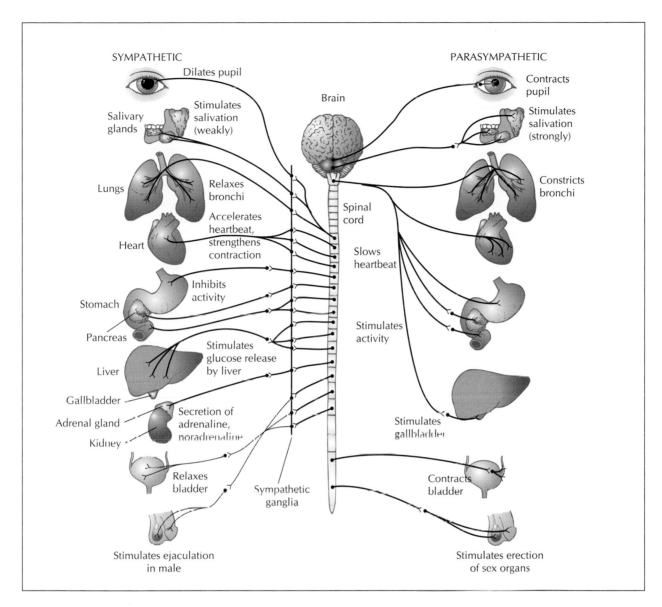

FIGURE 4.7 The sympathetic and parasympathetic branches of the autonomic nervous system (ANS) consist of nerve fibers emerging from the spinal cord.

increase in sympathetic activity, which in turn produces a number of physiological changes. The heart beats faster and pumps out more blood with each beat. The blood vessels near the skin and those that lead to the gastrointestinal tract constrict, increasing blood pressure and slowing digestion. At the same time, the blood vessels serving the large muscles—the muscles that will be needed for action—dilate, so they receive more blood. The pupils of the eyes also dilate, making vision more acute. Adrenaline is pumped into the blood, and this in turn releases blood sugar from the liver so that it can be used by the muscles. Breathing becomes faster and deeper so as to take in more oxygen. All these changes prepare the body for quick action. Of course, sympathetic

arousal is not always so intense, but, regardless of its intensity, the result is an adjustment of internal conditions so that the organism can make maximum use of whatever energy it has stored within it.

The Parasympathetic Division The **parasympathetic division**, which consists of nerve fibers emerging from the top and bottom of the spinal cord (Figure 4.7), is essentially opposite in function to the sympathetic division. While the latter generally gears up the body to use its energy, the parasympathetic division slows down metabolism and regulates the organs in such a way that they can do the work of rebuilding their energy supply. Thus, while sympathetic activity increases heart rate, parasympathetic activity decreases it; while sympathetic activity inhibits digestion, parasympathetic activity promotes it; and so on. The relationship between the two systems is complex, however, and sometimes they work together rather than in opposition (Bernston, Cacioppo, & Quigley, 1991). For example, the orienting response—when an infant instinctively turns toward its mother—involves a slowing of heart rate (parasympathetic activity) in combination with pupil dilation and increased sweating (sympathetic activity).

Because of its connection to arousal, the ANS is critically important in regard to stress-related disorders such as headaches, hypertension, and insomnia. As we shall see in Chapter 8, an important theory in the study of these disorders is that something has gone wrong in the regulation of the cycle connecting the brain to the ANS to the organ in question as they operate together in response to the environment.

The Endocrine System

Closely integrated with the central nervous system is the **endocrine system,** which is responsible for the production of **hormones,** chemical messengers that are released into the bloodstream by the endocrine glands and that affect sexual functioning, appetite, sleep, physical growth and development, the availability of energy, and emotional responses. For example, chronically low levels of thyroid activity result in anxietylike symptoms, such as tension and irritability, whereas low levels of pituitary activity result in depressionlike symptoms—fatigue, apathy, and so forth.

The headquarters of the endocrine system is the hypothalamus, which, as we saw, lies at the center of the brain. Just below the hypothalamus is the pituitary gland, called the "master gland" because it regulates hormone secretion by the other glands of the body.

Hormones may be involved in certain highly specific psychological disorders. One is major depression. Many studies suggest that, in depressed people, hypothalamus dysfunction leads to oversecretion of a chemical called corticotropin-releasing factor (CRF), which in turn leads to overactivation of the pituitary and adrenal glands (Pariante, Nemeroff, & Miller, 1997). At the same time, animal research indicates that harsh rearing conditions may result in chronically elevated CRF levels in adult life, thus creating a predisposition to depression (Coplan, Andrews, Rosenblum, et al., 1996). Hormone imbalances have also been implicated in bipolar disorder, eating disorders, and stress-related disorders.

Evaluating the Biological Perspective

The biological perspective is intuitively appealing. If the causes of abnormal behavior are understood as

even partly organic, this would help to relieve the stigma that still attaches to psychopathology. And, if psychopathology is biologically caused, then it might be biologically cured, through treatments quicker and less expensive than psychological therapy. But the greatest argument in favor of this perspective is simply its record of achievement. In the past few decades, biological researchers have made immense strides in understanding the relationship between physiological systems and psychological disorders. Such breakthroughs *have* led to the development of some effective drugs and to the invention of remarkable diagnostic tools such as CT, PET, and MRI. These, in turn, have provided the foundation for further discoveries.

But we must not embrace this approach uncritically. For example, it cannot be assumed that, if a psychological disorder is linked to biochemical abnormalities, such abnormalities are the cause of the disorder. They might be the result of the disorder. (Or both might be due to a third, unknown factor.) Similarly, we cannot infer the cause of a disorder from an effective treatment for it. Aspirin may relieve headaches, but that does not mean that headaches are caused by a lack of aspirin. Finally, not all biological treatments are successful. From medieval bleeding to modern psychosurgery, the history of abnormal psychology provides numerous examples of widely accepted biological treatments that later turned out to be ineffective or even dangerous. With these facts in mind, neuroscience researchers are careful to acknowledge the limitations and risks of any biological treatment.

Biological research in abnormal psychology also raises ethical questions. In the case of disorders that are linked to genes, such as schizophrenia, should we attempt to "repair" the defective genes if and when technology makes this possible? In the meantime, should we prohibit people with these disorders from having children? Can we even require that they be cautioned about the risk of passing on the disorder?

Another ethical problem has to do with symptom reduction and its consequences. Since the 1950s, for example, drugs have been available that control schizophrenia. While they do not cure the disorder, they eliminate its most dramatic symptoms, with the result that thousands of mental patients have been released from hospitals. But what have they been released to? Many of them end up on the street. Have drugs been used as a "quick fix," enabling us to put off the challenge of developing long-term community care for psychotic patients?

But it is not the fault of the biological perspective if its discoveries raise ethical problems. Einstein's theory of relativity also raised ethical problems, in the form of nuclear arms. It is up to societies to solve these problems. As for hasty conclusions about organic causation,

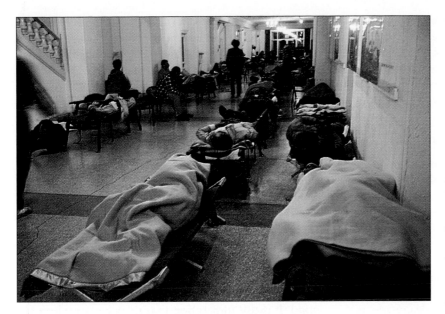

One of the unforeseen consequences of advances in neuroscience research has raised ethical questions: the release of disturbed people from hospitals with prescriptions for the drugs they need but without provisions for adequate follow-up care meant that many of these discharged patients would end up living on the streets and sleeping in public shelters.

it is rarely the researchers who make one-cause claims. As we saw, they tend to espouse the diathesis-stress model, acknowledging both organic and environmental causes. In recent years, the prestige of this model has been greatly boosted by the evidence for brain plasticity, the brain's capacity to shape itself in response to external events. Before, we knew that the environment worked together with brain chemistry to mold behavior. Now we know that the environment can actually alter brain chemistry—indeed, brain structure. Given this kind of interaction, it is no longer possible to consider biogenic and psychogenic causation as an either-or proposition. As a result, one may argue with this or that biological finding, but the biological perspective itself cannot be dismissed.

The Psychodynamic Perspective

The **psychodynamic perspective** is a school of thought united by a common concern with the dynamics, or interaction, of forces lying deep within the mind. Different psychodynamic theorists emphasize different aspects of mental dynamics, but almost all agree on three basic principles. First is that of psychic determinism: that much of our behavior is not freely chosen but, on the contrary, is determined by the nature and strength of intrapsychic forces. Second is the belief that such forces usually operate unconsciously—in other words, the true motives of our behavior are largely unknown to us. Third, most psychodynamic thinkers assume that the form these forces take is deeply affected by childhood experience, and particularly by relationships within the family.

The founding father of the psychodynamic perspective was Sigmund Freud, a neurologist who began his practice in Vienna in the 1880s. At that time, the most common complaint brought to the neurologist was hysteria, physical impairment—such as paralysis—for which no physical cause could be found. As we saw in Chapter 1, the idea that the origin of hysteria might be psychological rather than physiological had already been proposed. Convinced by this idea, young Freud set himself the task of discovering the specific psychological causes involved and of working out an effective cure. Within a few years, he had put forth the idea that hysteria constituted a defense against unbearable thoughts or memories. (The hand may be "paralyzed," for example, to overcome an urge to strike out.) From this seed grew his theory of psychoanalysis, by which, ultimately, he sought to explain not just hysteria but all human behavior, normal and abnormal.

The psychodynamic perspective is by no means bounded by Freud's theory. It is a large and living school of thought, by now more than a century old, built of proposals and counterproposals, propositions and refinements contributed by many theorists besides Freud. It is impossible, however, in the space of this chapter, to give appropriate coverage to the full range of psychodynamic theory.* Furthermore,

---

*Neither is it possible to do justice to Freud's views in one short chapter. The English edition of his collected writings, known as *The Standard Edition of the Complete Psychological Works of Sigmund Freud* (London: Hogarth Press, 1953–1974), fills 24 volumes. Furthermore, Freud constantly revised and refined his ideas throughout his long life. The reader should be aware that what is presented in this chapter is a condensation of a complex and extensive collection of theories.

Freud's theory, however much it has been revised, is still the foundation of psychodynamic thought. Therefore, we will give first and fullest consideration to Freud—that is, to the "classical" psychodynamic position. Then we will describe the ways in which later theorists have expanded this view.

The Basic Concepts of Freudian Theory

The Depth Hypothesis   The key concept of psychoanalysis, and Freud's most important contribution to psychology, is the depth hypothesis, the idea that almost all mental activity takes place unconsciously. According to Freud, the mind is divided into two levels. At the surface is the *perceptual conscious,* consisting of the narrow range of mental events of which the person is aware at any given instant. Beneath the perceptual conscious lies the unconscious, consisting of all the psychological materials (memories, desires, fears, etc.) that the mind is not attending to at that moment.

It was Freud's belief that the things we forget do not disappear from the mind. They simply go into the unconscious. Furthermore, much of this material is not passively forgotten. It is actively forgotten, forced out of consciousness—a process called *repression*—because it is disturbing to us. These censored materials may erupt into consciousness when psychological controls are relaxed—for example, when we are under hypnosis or when we are dreaming. But, during our normal waking hours, the contents of the unconscious are kept tightly sealed from our awareness. At the same time—and this is the crucial point—these unconscious materials always play some role in determining our behavior. When we choose one profession over another or marry one person rather than another, we do so not only for the reasons that we tell ourselves but also because of events from our past that are now hidden from us—a fascinating and disturbing notion.

The Necessity of Interpretation   If Freud was correct that the origins of our behavior are buried deep in the psyche, then psychology cannot confine itself simply to observing surface behavior. Rather, it must engage in interpretation, revealing the hidden, intrapsychic motives. Interpretation was Freud's primary tool. In all human behavior—actions, dreams, jokes, works of art—he saw two layers of meaning: the *manifest content,* or surface meaning, and the *latent content,* or true, unconscious meaning. The goal of his theoretical writings and of his therapy was to reveal, via interpretation, the latent content: the unconscious forces that cause people to do what they do.

In certain respects, this is an old and uncontroversial idea. For thousands of years, it has been understood that some decoding process, whether or not it

is called "interpretation," is indispensable to human communication. When someone you have asked for a date replies that he or she is busy for the next month, you naturally understand the message. This person does not want to go out with you. The ability to get along in human society depends on our ability to decode such statements. Interpretation, then, was not invented by Freud. What Freud invented was the idea that interpretation could be used to identify *unconscious* motives for our behavior.

The Structural Hypothesis: Id, Ego, and Superego
Some years after his formulation of the depth hypothesis, Freud constructed a second, complementary psychic schema, the so-called structural hypothesis. As we have seen, the defining characteristic of psychodynamic theory, as handed down from Freud, is its concern with the interaction of forces within the mind. It is this interaction that the structural hypothesis describes. Briefly, it states that the mind can be divided into three broad forces—the id, the ego, and the superego—and that these three forces are continually interacting with one another, often in conflict.

The Id   At birth, according to Freud's hypothesis, the energy of the mind is bound up entirely in primitive biological drives, to which Freud gave the collective term **id.** The id is the foundation of the psychic structure and the source from which the later developments of ego and superego must borrow their energy.

The drives that make up the id are of two basic types, sexual and aggressive—the former above all.* Freud saw the sexual drive as permeating the entire personality and subsuming, in addition to actual sexual behavior, a wide range of other life-sustaining pursuits, such as the need for food and warmth, the desire for the love of friends and family, and the impulse toward creativity. These and other positive desires, in Freud's view, were extensions and transformations of a basic sexual drive, which he named the **libido** and which he saw as the major source of psychic energy.

The id operates on what Freud called the *pleasure principle.* That is, it is utterly hedonistic, seeking only its own pleasure or release from tension and taking no account of logic or reason, reality or morality. Hungry infants, for example, do not ask themselves whether it is time for their feeding or whether their mothers may be busy doing something else; they want food, and so they cry for it. According to Freud, we are all, at some level, hungry infants.

---

*On the *number* of basic drives, Freud changed his theory many times. After 1920, he elevated aggression to the status of a basic drive, at least partly in response to the horrors of World War I.

In Freud's view, small children freely use aggression to get what they want because the id is not yet under the restraint of the ego and superego.

The Ego While the id can know what it wants, it has no way of determining which means of dealing with the world are practical and which are not. To fulfill these functions, the mind develops a new psychic component, the ego. The ego mediates between the id and the forces that restrict the id's satisfactions. Ego functions begin to develop shortly after birth and emerge slowly over a period of years.

Whereas the id operates on the pleasure principle, the ego operates on the *reality principle*—to find what is both safe and effective. When the id signals its desire, the ego locates in reality a potential gratifier for the desire, anticipates the consequences of using that gratifier, and then either reaches out for it or, if that gratifier is ineffective or potentially dangerous, delays the id's satisfaction until a more appropriate gratification can be found.

Imagine, for example, a 3-year-old girl playing in her room. The id signals that aggressive impulses seek release, and the girl reaches for her toy hammer. The ego then goes into action, scanning the environment. The girl's baby brother is playing nearby. Should she hit him over the head with her hammer? The ego, which knows from experience that this will result in the unpleasant consequence of punishment, says no and continues the scanning process. Also nearby is a big lump of clay. The ego determines that no harm will come from pounding the clay, and so the girl hits that instead. According to Freud, it is from the ego's weighing of these considerations that the mind develops and refines all its higher functions: language, perception, learning, discrimination, memory, judgment, and planning. All these are ego functions.

The Superego Imagine that three years later the same girl once again sits with hammer in hand, looking for something to pound. Again she considers her brother's head, and again she rejects that possibility. This time, however, she rejects it not only because it would result in punishment but because it would be "bad." What this means is that the child has developed a superego.

The **superego** is that part of the mind that represents the internalized moral standards of the society and, above all, of the parents. This superego, approximately equivalent to what we call "conscience," takes no more account of reality than the id does. Instead of considering what is realistic or possible, it embraces an abstract moral ideal and demands that the sexual and aggressive impulses of the id be stifled in order to conform to that ideal. It is then the job of the ego to find a way to satisfy the id without antagonizing the superego.

Thus, in the fully developed psychic structure, the ego has three fairly intransigent parties to deal with: the id, which seeks only the satisfaction of its irrational and amoral demands; the superego, which seeks only the satisfaction of its rigid ideals; and reality, which offers only a limited range of options.

When we consider the structural hypothesis, it is important to keep in mind that id, ego, and superego are not *things* in the mind or even parts of the mind, but simply names that Freud gave to broad categories of intrapsychic forces. It is difficult, in discussing these categories, not to speak of them as if they were actual entities—the id screaming for gratification, the superego demanding the opposite, and the ego running back and forth between them. But these are metaphors, nothing more.

The Dynamics of the Mind Through ego functions, as we have seen, the mind can usually mediate conflicts among id, superego, and reality. At times, however, either the id or the superego will threaten to overwhelm the ego's controls, resulting in unacceptable feelings or behavior. In response to this threat, the person experiences anxiety.

Anxiety, akin to what most of us call "fear," is a state of psychic distress that acts as a signal to the ego that danger is at hand. Anxiety can have its source in reality, as when you confront a burglar in your house. Or—and this was Freud's major concern—anxiety

Sigmund Freud's daughter Anna was a psychoanalyst in her own right; she was largely responsible for defining the defense mechanisms. Here, father and daughter are pictured together in 1928.

can originate in internal dynamics, in an id impulse that threatens to break through the ego's controls and cause the person to be punished, either by the superego (in the form of guilt) or by reality.

Anxiety can be managed in a number of ways. If a pregnant woman is afraid of childbirth, she can calm her fears by going to childbirth classes and learning how to cope with labor pains. However, the ego's solutions are not always so straightforward. Indeed, most anxiety is not even experienced consciously. It is kept closeted in the unconscious, and the danger is dealt with through the ego's employment of defense mechanisms.

Defense Mechanisms   The ego tends to distort or simply deny a reality (whether external or internal) that would arouse unbearable anxiety. This tactic is called a **defense mechanism,** and, as long as it works, the anxiety will not be experienced consciously. According to Freud, we all use defense mechanisms all the time. If we did not, we would be psychologically disabled, for the facts they conceal—of the primitive drives of the id, of the condemnations of the superego—would produce intolerable anxiety if they were constantly breaking through into the conscious mind. The defense mechanisms, then, serve an adaptive function. They allow us to avoid facing what we cannot face and, thus, to go on with the business of living.

If they become too rigid, however, they can defeat adjustment. When defense mechanisms force us never to leave the house or—to use a more ordinary example—to redirect onto our home life our problems at work, then we are sacrificing our adaptive capacities. Furthermore, if most of the ego's energy is tied up in

the job of maintaining defenses, then the ego will have little strength left for its other important functions, such as perception, reasoning, and problem solving. Defense mechanisms, then, are adaptive only up to a point. The basic defense mechanisms—described largely by Freud's daughter, Anna, also a prominent psychoanalyst—are as follows (Freud, 1946):

1. *Repression.*   In the process of **repression,** as we have already seen, unacceptable id impulses are pushed down into the unconscious and thereby robbed of their power to disturb us consciously. Thus, for example, a girl who is sexually attracted to her father will simply remove this intolerable thought from her consciousness. It may come up in her dreams, but in disguised form, and, once she wakes up, the dreams, too, are likely to be repressed.

One of the earliest of Freud's conceptualizations, repression is the most fundamental defense mechanism of psychodynamic theory. It is on the basis of this mechanism that Freud constructed his symbolic readings of human behavior, whereby a person's actions are viewed as masked representations of the contents of his or her unconscious. And Freud evolved his technique of psychoanalysis expressly in order to dredge up this repressed material—"to make the unconscious conscious," as he put it.

Repression is fundamental also in that it is the basis of all the other defense mechanisms. In every one of the defenses that we will describe, the "forbidden" impulse is first repressed; then, instead of acting on that impulse, the person engages in a substitute behavior that serves either as an outlet for the impulse, as an additional protection against it, or both.

2. *Projection.* In *projection*, unacceptable impulses are first repressed, then attributed to others. Thus, an internal threat is converted into an external threat. For example, a man whose self-esteem is threatened by his own preoccupation with money may accuse others of being money-hungry. This relieves his own moral anxiety and simultaneously enables him to throw the guilt onto others.

3. *Displacement.* Like projection, *displacement* involves a transfer of emotion. In this case, however, what is switched is not the source but the object of the emotion. Afraid to display or even to experience certain feelings against whoever has aroused them, the person represses the feelings. Then, when the opportunity arises, he or she transfers them to a safer object and releases them. A good example of displacement can be found in a story by James Joyce titled "Counterparts." In it a poor man spends the day suffering humiliations for which he cannot retaliate; then he goes home, discovers that his son has let the hearth fire go out, and on that pretext gives the boy a terrible beating.

4. *Rationalization.* Most defenses occur not in isolation but in combination (Erdelyi, 1985). In the example just cited, the pretext that the man used for beating his son illustrates another defense mechanism, *rationalization*. A person who engages in rationalization offers socially acceptable reasons for something that he or she has actually done (or is going to do) for unconscious and unacceptable motives. Rationalization is one of the most common defenses. According to Freud, we need to make ourselves "look good."

5. *Isolation.* We engage in *isolation* when we avoid unacceptable feelings by cutting them off from the events to which they are attached, repressing them, then reacting to the events in an emotionless manner. Isolation is a common refuge of patients in psychotherapy. Eager to tell the therapist what the problem is but unwilling to confront the feelings involved, patients will relate the facts in a calm, detached fashion ("Yes, my mother's death caused me considerable distress"), whereas it is actually the feelings, more than the facts, that need to be explored.

6. *Intellectualization.* Isolation is often accompanied by *intellectualization*: the person achieves further distance from the emotion in question by surrounding it with a smokescreen of abstract intellectual analysis ("Yes, my mother's death caused me considerable distress. Young children find it difficult to endure separation, let alone final separation, from their mothers," etc.).

7. *Denial.* *Denial* is the refusal to acknowledge an external source of anxiety. In some cases, the person will actually fail to perceive something that is obvious. For example, a woman who has been diagnosed as terminally ill may go on planning a lengthy trip to be taken when she is well again. Because it involves a drastic alteration of the facts, denial is considered a "primitive" defense. It is usually resorted to by children or by people facing a very serious threat (e.g., terminal illness or the death of a loved one).

8. *Reaction formation.* A person who engages in *reaction formation* represses the feelings that are arousing anxiety and then vehemently professes exactly the opposite. Thus, someone who claims to be disgusted by sexual promiscuity may be demonstrating a reaction formation against his or her own sexual impulses.

9. *Regression.* The mechanism of *regression* involves a return to a developmental stage that one has already passed through. Unable to deal with its anxiety, the ego simply abandons the scene of the conflict, reverting to an earlier, less threatening stage. In the extreme case, a regressed adult may be reduced to a babbling, helpless creature who has to be fed and toileted like a baby. On the other hand, well-adjusted adults often resort to minor regressive behaviors—whining, making childish demands, playing hooky from school or work—simply to take the edge off the pressures they are experiencing at the moment.

10. *Undoing.* In *undoing*, the person engages in a ritual behavior or thought in order to cancel out an unacceptable impulse. For example, some people with obsessive-compulsive disorder (Chapter 6) devise rituals, such as repeated hand washing, to dispel disturbing sexual thoughts.

11. *Sublimation.* *Sublimation*, the transformation and expression of sexual or aggressive energy into more socially acceptable forms, differs from all other defense mechanisms in that it can be truly constructive. The skill of a great surgeon, for example, may represent a sublimation of aggressive impulses. Likewise, Freud hypothesized that many of the beautiful nudes created by Renaissance painters and sculptors were the expression of sublimated sexual impulses.

The Stages of Psychosexual Development In Freud's view, the development of the personality is a process of **psychosexual development**, a series of stages in which the child's central motivation is to gratify sexual and aggressive drives in various erogenous (pleasure-producing) zones of the body: the mouth, the anus, and the genitals, in that order. The characteristics of the adult personality are a consequence of the ways in which conflicts over these id strivings are handled at each stage of development.

According to Freud, the oral stage is the first stage of psychosexual development. Infants put any and all objects they can into their mouths to gratify the urgings of the id.

The Oral Stage   The oral stage begins at birth. As the name indicates, the mouth is the primary focus of id strivings. Infants must suck in order to live. Soon, however, they are using their mouths to satisfy not only their hunger but also their libidinal and aggressive impulses. Breast, bottle, thumb, pacifier, toys—infants suck, bite, and chew whatever they can find in their search for oral stimulation. According to Freud and his followers, unsatisfied oral needs can lead to dependency in adulthood.

The Anal Stage   The anal stage usually begins in the second year of life. The libido shifts its focus to the anus and derives its primary gratification from the retaining and expelling of feces. The child's anal pleasures are barely established, however, before they are interfered with, through toilet training. Traditionally, Freudian theorists have regarded toilet training as a crucial event, since it is children's first confrontation with an external demand that they control their impulses. Suddenly their pleasures are brought under regulation. They are told when, where, how, and so forth. Toilet training, then, is the first difficult demand on the developing ego. If problems occur, the ego may experience considerable anxiety, and such anxiety can engender personality problems.

The Phallic Stage   In the phallic stage, which extends from about the third to the fifth or sixth year, the focus is shifted to the genitals, and sensual pleasure is derived from masturbation. Because of this newfound erotic self-sufficiency, the child in the phallic stage begins to develop a sense of autonomy, as opposed to the extreme dependence characteristic of earlier stages.

The phallic stage is held to be particularly crucial because it is the scene of the Oedipus complex,

named after Oedipus, the legendary king of Thebes, who unknowingly killed his father and married his mother. According to Freud (1905/1953), the child's extreme dependence on the mother during infancy culminates, during the phallic stage, in sexual desire for the mother. How this is resolved depends on whether the child is a boy or a girl. In boys, the incestuous desire leads to a recognition of the father's capacity for wrath, which in turn arouses **castration anxiety:** the boy fears that his father will punish him for his forbidden wishes by cutting off the guilty organ, his penis. This worry is supposedly confirmed by the boy's observations of female anatomy. Lacking penises, girls seem to him castrated, and he fears the same fate for himself. To allay his castration anxiety, he eventually represses the incestuous desire that aroused it. Instead of competing with the father, he identifies with him, internalizing the father's—and the society's—prohibitions against incest and aggression, thus building the foundations for the superego.

In girls, the situation is more complicated. In what has been called the Electra complex, a girl observes that she has been born without a penis. She experiences what Freud called *penis envy,* and this causes her to reorient her sexual interest toward her father. If she can seduce him, then at least vicariously she can obtain the desired organ. Of course, her desires are as futile as the boy's, and eventually she retreats back into her earlier, dependent identification with the mother.

Thus, eventually both boys and girls undergo identification with the parent of the same sex; in the process, they incorporate that parent's values, from which the superego develops. But, according to Freud, sexual differences in the Oedipal drama give rise to sexual differences in the superego. The boy's active struggle with ambivalence toward his father supposedly endows him with greater maturity, sounder judgment, and better self-control than girls are able to develop in their passive reversion to identification with the mother. (Freud's views on girls' development during this stage drew criticism that his theories are based only on male psychology. See the box on page 99, "Psychodynamic Theory and Female Development," for discussion and rebuttals of this aspect of Freud's theory.)

Latency and the Genital Stage   Usually between the ages of 6 and 12, the child goes through the **latency** period, during which sexual impulses seem dormant. Then, as the child enters puberty, sexual strivings are reawakened. Now, however, they are directed not at the child's own body, as in earlier stages, but toward others, in a new emotion combining altruistic feeling with the primitive sexual drive. This final phase of development, called the **genital stage,** ends with the

Psychodynamic Theory and Female Development

Freud, like all thinkers, reflected the values of his time. Nowhere is this more obvious than in his views on female development, which mirror—even defend—the sexual inequality of late nineteenth-century Europe.

Freud's theory of female psychology rests on the fact that a girl does not have a penis. According to Freud, the moment a child notices this basic anatomical difference, he or she begins to become, psychologically as well as biologically, a male or a female. A girl's realization that she has no penis produces ineradicable jealousy, or "penis envy." As Freud (1932/1974) wrote, "The discovery that she is castrated is a turning point in a girl's growth" (p. 105). What she turns toward from that moment on is a position of inferiority.

The process may be summarized as follows. Because she considers herself already "castrated," a girl never experiences and then overcomes castration anxiety. Her Oedipal experience lacks the cathartic resolution of a boy's Oedipal crisis. As a result, her superego (the fruit of a successfully resolved Oedipus complex) is stunted. Throughout her life, she remains narcissistic, vain, and, above all, envious, for she can never overcome her bitterness over her castration. Furthermore, lacking a strong, mature superego, she is culturally inferior, since the ability to contribute to the advance of civilization depends on the mechanism of sublimation, which in turn depends on the superego. Thus, while men work at lofty pursuits, women remain mired in feelings of inferiority and efforts to compensate for it. If a woman is lucky, she will be rewarded with the ultimate compensation, a baby; if the baby is a boy, "who brings the longed-for penis with him" (Freud, 1932/1974, pp. 150, 154), all the better. But any baby is only a substitute: because of women's perception of themselves as castrated, they remain, somehow, "other," a deviation from the norm of masculinity.

The opposition to this theory was first put forward in 1939 by post-Freudian theorist Karen Horney, who retorted that it is not little girls who perceive their condition as degraded. Rather, it is little boys—and the men they eventually become—who see their penisless counterparts as deficient. Horney also pointed out that, if girls are envious, what they probably envy is not a penis but, rather, the power that in most societies is reserved for men.

More recently, psychodynamic thinkers have proposed some sharply revised ideas of female development. What these thinkers have in common with Freud is the notion that the young child's attachment to its mother is of crucial importance to male or female development and that this attachment has a very different meaning for girls than for boys. Nancy Chodorow, in her book *The Reproduction of Mothering* (1978), stresses the differences between girls' and boys' early childhood environments. For both, the mother is the primary love object during early infancy. However, the girl's task is to internalize the feminine role, while the boy's task is to renounce an identification with femininity and differentiate from it in order to become masculine. Boys, therefore, place a premium on separation and individuation. Girls are less motivated to differentiate themselves and, consequently, have more difficulty with separation and individuation.

Another theorist in this mode is Carol Gilligan, author of *In a Different Voice* (1982), an influential book on girls' moral development. Like Chodorow, Gilligan sees boys' needs to separate from their mothers as responsible for a personality difference observable in adult men and women:

For boys and men, separation and individuation are critically tied to gender identity since separation from the mother is essential for the development of masculinity. For girls and women, issues of femininity or feminine identity do not depend on the achievement of separation from the mother or on the progress of individuation. Since masculinity is defined through separation while femininity is defined through attachment, male gender identity is threatened by intimacy while female gender identity is threatened by separation. Thus males tend to have difficulty with relationships, while females tend to have problems with individuation. (p. 8)

In this view, the key crisis of early childhood is not the phallic conflict, but Margaret Mahler's "separation-individuation" crisis (see page 103). Girls, according to this theory, do *not* grow up into morally inferior penis enviers. They may, however, grow into adulthood with a greater need for close human attachments than many men have.

---

attainment of mature sexuality, which to Freud meant not only heterosexual love but also maturity in a broad sense: "loving and working," as he characterized the hallmarks of healthy functioning.

Normal and Abnormal Behavior

Normal Personality Functioning In Freud's view, both the sane and the insane are motivated by the irrational id, with its reckless drives. Some people are simply more capable of controlling these drives. Their success in doing so depends largely on their psychosexual development, which, in the normal person, will have produced a healthy balance among the id, ego, and superego. This does not mean that the three forces coexist in perfect harmony. They are constantly conflicting, but the ego mediates. Thus, the key to adaptive behavior is ego strength. In times of stress, the ego may be weakened, in which case the defenses operate poorly, leaving us with a good deal of anxiety.

Or, under the influence of alcohol or other drugs, the superego's functioning may become weak and, thus, allow id impulses the upper hand. But eventually the balance of power among the three psychic components is restored, and the person is once again able to satisfy the demands of the id without flying in the face of reality or morality.

Abnormal Personality Functioning Like normal functioning, abnormal functioning is motivated primarily by irrational drives and determined by childhood experiences. Indeed, one of the central principles of psychoanalytic theory is that normal and abnormal behavior lie on a continuum. Abnormality is a difference in degree, not in kind. Dreams, fantasies, works of art, psychiatric symptoms, hallucinations—these are simply different stops on the same road.

What, then, is the difference between normal and abnormal? The difference is ego strength. As we just saw, the ego may be weakened by conflict, but normally it bounces back. In some cases, however, the conflict continues, creating more and more anxiety, which in turn creates more and more rigid defenses in the form of behaviors that seriously impede adaptive functioning. After a car accident, a woman begins to feel anxious about driving; soon she can't ride in a car even if someone else is driving; eventually she refuses to leave her house. Freud called such conditions neuroses.

In extreme cases, the ego's strength may be severely depleted (or severely underdeveloped from the start), drastically curtailing adaptive functioning. Defenses break down, flooding the psyche with id impulses and attendant anxiety. Emotions are cut loose from external events. Speech loses its coherence. Inner voices are mistaken for outer voices. This condition of ego collapse, known as **psychosis,** is the furthest reach of the structural imbalance.

The Descendants of Freud

As Freud's theory gained acceptance, young people traveled to Vienna from many countries to be analyzed by Freud and his followers. They then took his theory back with them, disseminating it through Europe and the United States. As it spread, Freudian theory changed. Many of Freud's pupils and their pupils constructed new theories, extending and modifying his principles.

In this elaboration of Freud's theory, three trends are especially noteworthy. The first is the pronounced emphasis on the ego. Freud, while by no means ignoring the ego, gave special attention to the id. In general, later contributors to psychodynamic thought shifted the spotlight to the ego. That is, they deemphasized sex, instincts, and determinism and

emphasized goals, creativity, and self-direction. Second, the post-Freudian thinkers tended to view the child's social relationships as the central determinant of normal and abnormal development. Again, this is hardly a subject ignored by Freud; the Oedipus/Electra complex is nothing if not a social drama. Still, Freud always viewed social interactions in relation to the strivings of the id. Later thinkers deemphasized the id and moved social interaction to center stage. Finally, later theorists tended to extend the period of critical developmental influences. Freud emphasized the phallic stage, and especially the Oedipus/Electra complex. Many subsequent thinkers have placed greater stress on infancy, while others see critical developmental junctures occurring well into adulthood.

Among the post-Freudian theorists, we will consider two of Freud's students who dissented from his ideas—Carl Jung and Alfred Adler; two theorists who focused on interpersonal issues—Harry Stack Sullivan and Karen Horney; and two psychoanalysts who were pioneers in "ego psychology"—Heinz Hartmann and Erik Erikson. Finally, we will discuss Margaret Mahler, Heinz Kohut, John Bowlby, and Mary Ainsworth, whose theories have had a great impact on the field as it exists today.

Carl Gustav Jung Freud's most cherished pupil, Swiss psychiatrist Carl Gustav Jung (1875–1961),

Carl Gustav Jung, a student of Freud, took a broader and more positive view of the unconscious than Freud did. Jung claimed that the unconscious is creative and includes not only the personal but also the collective unconscious, a set of universal human symbols.

broke with him early in his career, claiming that Freudian theory was unduly negative and reductive. The main focus of the disagreement was the nature of the libido. Whereas Freud saw the energy of the psyche as primarily sexual, Jung viewed the libido as a much broader force, comprising an autonomous "spiritual instinct" as well as a sexual instinct. There was a corresponding division in the two men's views of the unconscious. To Freud, the unconscious was a regressive force, pulling us back into infantile, id-directed behavior. To Jung, the unconscious was also a creative force. Jung (1935) argued, moreover, that the mind contains not just the personal unconscious (that is, biological drives and childhood memories) but also a *collective unconscious,* a repository of "archetypes," or symbols, expressive of universal human experiences. This set of symbols, shared by all humankind, is the source of mythology and art, whose unity across cultures is explained by their common origin.

Jung's therapeutic practices also differed from Freud's. In Freudian therapy, the primary goal is control: the rational ego taking control of the irrational id and directing it to constructive ends. In Jungian therapy, the goal is integration: the uniting of opposing tendencies (e.g., masculinity and femininity, extroversion and introversion) within the self so that the patient can become more "whole" and thereby more creative.

Alfred Adler   Another member of Freud's inner circle who eventually broke with him was Alfred Adler (1870–1937). Like Jung, Adler believed that Freud had placed undue emphasis on sexual instincts. In Adler's view, the primary motivator of behavior is not the sexual drive but a striving to attain personal goals and overcome handicaps. (It was Adler who coined the term *inferiority complex.*) Related to his interest in power is his concept of *masculine protest,* by which Adler (1917/1988) meant the unwarranted belief that men are inherently superior to women. According to Adler, masculine protest is the product not of penis envy or the Electra crisis but simply of an unequal society. Its consequences are smugness and callousness in men and pathological feelings of inferiority in women.

Adler's most important contribution, however, was his concern with the social context of personality. Psychological disturbance, he claimed, has its roots not so much in early childhood experiences as in people's present circumstances, particularly their relationships with others. Mature people are those who can resolve their power struggle and devote themselves selflessly to others. An active socialist, Adler was concerned not just with intimate social relationships but with society in general, which he hoped to serve through psychiatric means.

Alfred Adler, also a student of Freud, rejected Freud's heavy emphasis on the role of biological drives. Instead, Adler stressed the importance of viewing human beings in a social context.

Harry Stack Sullivan   The study of psychological disorder as a social phenomenon was carried forward by American psychiatrist Harry Stack Sullivan (1892–1949). Particularly crucial, in Sullivan's view, is the parent-child relationship. Children of rejecting parents develop severe anxiety about themselves—anxiety that makes it almost impossible for them, as they grow up, to weather the threats to the self that are part of almost any close relationship. For people with disturbed family relationships, other human beings pose too great a threat. The person wards them off either by engaging in rigid self-protecting behaviors (neurosis) or by withdrawing completely from the world of other people (psychosis). But, regardless of its severity, psychological disturbance is an anxiety-motivated flight from human relationships.

Aside from his elaboration of the social theory of psychopathology, Sullivan's other major contribution was in the treatment of severe mental disturbance, an area in which Freud and his early followers felt that psychoanalysis could be of little help. Sullivan was the first analyst to report significant success in the long-term psychoanalytic treatment of psychotics, and the warm, supportive approach that he developed for this purpose has served as a model for later therapies aimed at helping psychotics by placing them in a benign "milieu" (Chapter 13).

Karen Horney diverged from Freud in her theory of female psychology. Horney asserted that men and women differ psychologically not because of penis envy, but because of the limited opportunities society affords to women.

Karen Horney   Another post-Freudian thinker who focused on social relationships was Karen Horney (1885–1952). According to Horney (1937), psychological disturbance is the result of *basic anxiety,* a pervasive view of the world as impersonal and cold. This, in turn, is the product of a failed parent-child attachment. (Note how many post-Freudians conceptualize anxiety as stemming from a *lack* of parent-child intimacy, as opposed to the overintimacy postulated by the Oedipus/Electra complex.) Basic anxiety, as Horney saw it, leads to one of three "neurotic trends": *moving away* (shy, withdrawn behavior), *moving toward* (dependent, needy behavior), or *moving against* (hostile, aggressive behavior)—three patterns that cover most forms of psychopathology.

As the only woman among the early psychoanalytic thinkers, it was perhaps inevitable that Horney developed a theory of female psychology, one that departed from Freud's. (See the box on page 99.) Horney, like Freud, saw significant psychological differences between men and women, and competition between them, with men seeking to dominate women and women seeking to deceive and humiliate

men. But, while Freud attributed this to penis envy, Horney proposed the more direct interpretation that it is due to men's greater prestige and wider opportunities in society.

Heinz Hartmann   As we saw, a critical trend in post-Freudian theory has been an increasing emphasis on ego functions. A milestone in this line of thought was Heinz Hartmann's *Ego Psychology and the Problem of Adaptation* (1939). To Freud, the ego derived its energy from the id, and its role was to serve the id. Against this limited view of the ego's functioning, Hartmann (1894–1970) argued that the ego develops independently of the id and has its own autonomous functions—in other words, functions that serve *ego* strivings, such as the need to adapt to reality, rather than id strivings. In particular, the mind's cognitive (mental-processing) operations, such as memory, perception, and learning, are, in Hartmann's (1939) view, "conflict-free" expressions of the ego. The id and the superego may help induce a child to go to school, for example, but only a relatively pure ego motivation can explain how the child learns to solve an algebra problem. Hartmann also felt that Freud overemphasized the role of conflict in mental life. If, in many of its basic operations, the ego is working for itself rather than mediating battles between the id and its opponents, then the life of the mind also has a "conflict-free sphere."

Hartmann's ideas were instrumental in the founding of a whole new school of *ego psychology,* which has had a huge influence on psychoanalytic theory since World War II. Today many psychoanalytic writers focus on the ego and the interplay between its conflict-solving functions and its conflict-free functions, particularly cognitive processes. This shift has had the effect of bringing psychoanalysis closer to other branches of psychology, where cognitive processes have been commanding more attention in the past few decades.

Erik Erikson   An important extension of the new ego psychology and of the social analysis of personality was the developmental theory put forth by Erik Erikson (1902–1994). To Erikson, the major drama of development is the formation of the *ego identity,* an integrated, unique, and autonomous sense of self. The ego identity is the product of what Erikson called *psychosocial development.* Like Freud's theory of psychosexual development, of which it is a deliberate revision, Erikson's psychosocial development proceeds through a series of chronological stages. But these stages differ from Freud's. In the first place, there are more of them. To Freud, the personality is essentially formed by the age of 6 or 7; to Erikson, personality de-

Erik Erikson proposed a theory of psychosocial development that extended and expanded Freud's psychosexual stages. According to Erikson, personality development continues throughout a person's lifetime.

In Erikson's theory of psychosocial development, the primary task of the preschool child is to separate his or her identity from that of the mother. If successful, the child acquires the initiative to master a variety of skills.

velopment extends from birth to death. The second difference is the pronounced social emphasis of Erikson's theory, proclaimed in the term *psychosocial*. While Freud saw the individual psyche in near isolation (except for the influence of parents and siblings), Erikson saw personality development as deeply affected not only by the family but also by teachers, friends, spouses, and many other social agents.

Third and most important is the central role of the ego in Erikson's developmental progression. Freud's stages have to do with challenges to id strivings; Erikson's stages have more to do with challenges to the ego. At each stage, there is a crisis—a conflict between the individual and the expectations now imposed by society. The ego is then called upon to resolve the crisis by learning new adaptive tasks. In the second year, for example, the child is faced with toilet training, a challenge that may lead to a new sense of self-reliance or, if the training is poorly handled, to feelings of shame and self-doubt. Likewise, from the third to the fifth year, when the challenge confronting the child is that of separating from the mother, a successful resolution will lead to a new sense of initiative, whereas a troubled separation will foster guilt.

Through this process of conflict resolution, the ego identity—the image of oneself as a unique, competent, and self-determining individual—is gradually formed. Or, if the ego fails to master the crisis, this failure will hamper identity formation and may generate psychological disorders. Erikson believed, how-

ever, that a failure at one stage does not guarantee failure at future stages. In his scheme, the ego is a resilient force, and there is always a second chance. Erikson's theory, thus, is more hopeful than Freud's scheme, where a serious childhood trauma can handicap a person for life. In general, recent psychoanalytic thinking, because of its emphasis on the adaptive, problem-solving ego, is more optimistic than earlier psychoanalytic formulations.

Margaret Mahler Certainly the most influential concept in contemporary psychodynamic thought is that of **object relations**. In psychodynamic terminology, "objects" are the people to whom one is attached by strong emotional ties. For the child, obviously, the chief object is the primary caretaker, usually the mother. And, according to *object-relations theorists*, the most powerful determinant of psychological development is the child's interaction with the mother.

A very influential member of this school was Margaret Mahler (1897–1985). As she indicated when she titled her book *The Psychological Birth of the Human Infant* (Mahler, Pine, & Bergman, 1975), Mahler was concerned primarily with charting the process by which infants separate themselves psychologically from their mothers. Mahler saw newborns as having no sense of their own existence apart from their mothers. Then, at around 5 months, begins the long and sometimes wrenching process of *separation-individuation*. As conceptualized by

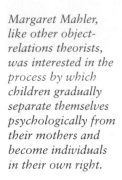

Margaret Mahler, like other object-relations theorists, was interested in the process by which children gradually separate themselves psychologically from their mothers and become individuals in their own right.

Mahler, separation-individuation involves several stages, each marked by greater independence and greater ambivalence, as the child vacillates between pleasure and terror over his or her new separateness from the mother. This ambivalence is finally resolved between the ages of 2 and 3, when children achieve *object constancy:* they internalize the image of the mother—fix her in their minds so that she is no longer losable—and are thereby freed to consolidate a separate identity.

This, however, is the ideal scenario. Separation-individuation can be disturbed by many factors—above all by the mother, if she either hurries or resists the toddler's move toward independence. In any case, Mahler felt that the success with which the separation-individuation process is navigated determines the child's psychological future, since the features of this first, crucial relationship will be repeated in later intimate relationships.

Heinz Kohut   Like Mahler, Heinz Kohut (1913–1981) was interested primarily in the psychological consequences of the parent-child relationship. In his practice as a therapist, Kohut encountered a great many patients who, though they shared similar problems—extreme demandingness and self-importance covering a very fragile self-esteem—seemed to fit no diagnostic category. He referred to this syndrome as *narcissistic personality disorder* (see Chapter 10). From his work with these patients, he built his so-called *self psychology.*

Kohut proposed that the development of the *self,* or core of the personality, depends on the child's receiving two essential psychological supports from the parents. One is the confirmation of the child's sense of vigor and "greatness." The other is a sense of calmness and infallibility: the feeling that there is nothing that the child can't handle. Parents communicate these things through the most ordinary daily behavior—by exclaiming over the artworks that their

children bring home from school and by assuring them, when they are nervous over a test, that they can surely pass it. "If the parents are at peace with their own needs to shine and succeed," Kohut wrote, "then the proud exhibitionism of the budding self of their child will be responded to acceptingly" (Kohut & Wolf, 1978, p. 417), and the child will develop a "healthy narcissism." But some parents cannot provide this support, and the result, for the child, is a damaged self. Thus, Kohut's theory, like Mahler's, differs from Freud's both in its interpersonal character and in its emphasis on cognitive and emotional rather than biological needs. Kohut and Mahler also place the critical events of early childhood well before the phallic stage, and this is the general trend in psychodynamic theory today.

John Bowlby and Mary Ainsworth   One of the most influential forces in psychodynamic thought today is *attachment theory,* developed by English psychiatrist John Bowlby (1907–1991) with collaboration from psychologist Mary Ainsworth (b. 1913). Attachment theory is another example of the post-Freudian emphasis on social relationships. Bowlby was trained as a psychoanalyst, but eventually he discarded instinct theory and began adopting concepts from animal studies and cognitive psychology. In his influential trilogy *Attachment* (1969), *Separation* (1973), and *Loss* (1980), he put forth his theory that the basic determinant of adult personality is *attachment,* the affectional bond between the child and its primary caretaker. To grow up mentally healthy, he wrote, "the infant and young child should experience a warm, intimate, and continuous relationship with his mother (or permanent mother substitute) in which both find satisfaction and enjoyment" (1951, p. 13). In Bowlby's view, attachment is an emotional need, as opposed to the physical needs that Freud stressed, and it need not always be pleasurable. (The child might be firmly disciplined.) Basically, what the parent provided was a "secure base" of care to which the child could return, plus encouragement to explore the world beyond that base.

Bowlby estimated that as many as one-third of all children did not have the kind of parenting that enabled them to form a secure attachment and that this predisposed them to problems in marriage and child rearing, for they would constantly perceive and interpret the behavior of those close to them according to the pattern of the old, faulty childhood attachment. He also believed that poor attachment led to adult disorders. For example, inadequate parental care could create the pattern of "anxious attachment" (insecurity, dependency), which in turn created a risk for phobias, hypochondriasis, and eating disorders. (People with "anxious attachment," Bowlby felt, were also apt to break down in the face of threats to later attachments.) Another pattern was "emotional detachment," the product not just of inadequate care but also of serious deprivation. Emotionally detached people, Bowlby felt, were at high risk for antisocial and hysterical personality disorders (Chapter 10).

Mary Ainsworth worked with Bowlby, beginning in the 1950s. Ainsworth (1967, 1982) conducted studies of infant-mother pairs in Uganda and the United States. Building on Bowlby's view, she theorized that a crucial component of attachment was the mother's sensitivity to the child's signals. Ainsworth also developed a reliable and valid method for testing attachment behavior: the so-called strange situation paradigm, in which children are observed as they are briefly separated from their mothers and exposed to strangers (Ainsworth & Wittig, 1969).

Prompted by attachment theory, researchers today are exploring the relationship between psychopathology and disturbed parent-child bonds. Many disorders, including anxiety, depression, personality disorders, and conduct and drug-use disorders, have been linked to failures in attachment (Allen, Hauser, & Borman-Spurrell, 1996; Main, 1996; Rosenstein & Horowitz, 1996).

The Psychodynamic Approach to Therapy

Though psychoanalysis as practiced by Freud is rarely used today, it is, nevertheless, the grandfather of all psychodynamic therapies. Therefore, we will give this technique first consideration and then discuss its modern variants.

Freudian Psychoanalysis   Freud's experience with his patients led him to conclude that the source of "neurosis" was anxiety experienced by the ego when unconscious material threatened to break through into the conscious mind. Thus, according to Freud, the proper treatment for neurosis was to coax the unconscious material out into consciousness so that the patient could at last confront it. Once acknowledged and "worked through," this material would lose its power to terrorize the ego. Self-defeating defenses could, accordingly, be abandoned, and the ego would then be free to devote itself to more constructive pursuits. As Freud succinctly put it, "Where id was, there shall ego be."

The client often lies on a couch, the better to relax, thus loosening the restraints on the unconscious, and the analyst typically sits outside of the client's field of vision. What the client then does is talk—usually for 50 minutes a day, 3 or 4 days a week, over a period of several years. The client may talk about his or her childhood, since it is there that the roots of the problem presumably lie, but present difficulties are also discussed. The analyst remains silent much of the time, so as not to derail the client's inner journey. When the analyst does speak, it is generally to *interpret* the client's remarks—that is, to point out their

This is Freud's office in Vienna, with the famous couch on which his patients reclined while he analyzed them. Freud's chair was at the head of the couch, out of the patient's view. The comforts of the couch (note the pillows and coverlets) and the removal of the analyst from the patient's line of sight were intended to free the patient from inhibition in discussing intimate matters.

This painting by Henri Rousseau is titled The Dream. *Psychoanalytic methods encourage the patient to report his or her dreams and then to free associate to the dream material. In light of the patient's associations, the analyst interprets the dream, revealing its latent content, which will presumably center on unconscious conflicts.*

possible connection with unconscious material. This dialogue between client and therapist turns on four basic techniques: free association, dream interpretation, analysis of resistance, and analysis of transference (Vaughan & Roose, 1995).

Free Association   Freud's primary route to the unconscious was free **association,** whereby the client simply verbalizes whatever thoughts come to mind, in whatever order they occur, taking care not to censor them either for logic or for propriety. The rationale is that the unconscious has its own logic and that, if clients report their thoughts exactly as they occur, the connective threads between verbalizations and unconscious impulses will be revealed. When such connections do become clear, the analyst points them out.

Dream Interpretation   A second important tunnel to the unconscious is dream **interpretation.** Freud believed that, in sleep, the ego's defenses were lowered, allowing unconscious material to surface. But defenses are never completely abandoned; therefore, even in dreams repressed impulses reveal themselves only in symbolic fashion. Beneath the dream's manifest content, or surface meaning, lies its latent content, or unconscious understory. For example, one client, a depressed woman whose mother was verbally and physically abusive, reported a dream in which she saw a horse in a fenced-in area. A monkey kept jumping onto the horse's back, and the horse couldn't shake it off. According to the analyst, the latent content was that the horse was the client and the monkey on her back was her mother's constant criticism. The fenced-in area stood for her restricted self-esteem as a result of her domination by her mother (Glucksman, 1995, p. 189).

This is a simplified example, for dream interpretation normally involves free association. After the dream is reported, the analyst asks the client to free associate to its contents, and the resulting associations are taken as clues to the meaning of the dream.

Analysis of Resistance   As clients are guided toward the unwelcome knowledge of their unconscious motivations, they may begin to show **resistance,** using various defenses to avoid confronting the painful material. They may change the subject, make jokes, or pick a fight with the analyst; they may even begin missing appointments. It is then the analyst's job to point out the resistance and, if possible, to interpret it—that is, to suggest what the patient is trying not to find out.

Analysis of Transference   As psychoanalysis progresses, with the client revealing his or her secret life to the analyst, the relationship between the two partners becomes understandably complex. In his own practice, Freud noted that, while he tried to remain neutral, many of his patients began responding to him with very passionate emotions—sometimes with a childlike love and dependency, at other times with hostility and rebellion. Freud interpreted this phenomenon as a **transference** onto him of his clients' childhood feelings toward important people in their lives—above all, their feelings toward their parents.

Transference is an essential component of psychoanalysis. In fact, traditional analysts maintain that, in order for the therapeutic process to be successful, clients must go through a stage, called *transference neurosis,* of reenacting with the analyst their childhood conflicts with their parents, for it is these repressed conflicts that are typically undermining their adult relationships. The belief is that, once these central emotions are brought out, clients have reached the core of the neurosis, which, with the analyst's help, they can then confront, evaluate realistically, and thereby overcome. This is a prime example of what psychoanalysts mean by the term "working through."

As we will see later in this chapter, it is possible to demonstrate the existence of transference in objective terms that can be evaluated in an experiment based on the perspective of cognitive psychology. See the box on page 114.

Modern Psychodynamic Therapy Most of today's psychodynamic therapists practice a considerably modified form of psychoanalysis, often based not only on Freud's theory but also on the theories of his followers. They depart from orthodox psychoanalytic techniques in several important respects. First, they generally take a more active part in the therapy session, dealing with the client face-to-face (the couch is seldom used) and speaking and advising much more extensively than Freud would have considered appropriate. Second, while the client's past is by no means ignored, modern psychodynamic therapists generally pay more attention to the client's present life, especially his or her personal relationships. Finally, most psychodynamic treatment today is briefer and less intensive than orthodox psychoanalysis. Therapist and client typically meet once or twice a week for anywhere from a few months to a few years. This broad category of therapy is probably the most common form of psychological treatment in the United States.

Evaluating the Psychodynamic Perspective

Psychodynamic Theory Versus the Medical Model Freud was trained in medicine, and the Freudian view of behavioral abnormalities as the symptoms of an underlying psychic disturbance is close to the medical model's approach to maladaptive behavior patterns as the symptoms of an underlying organic dysfunction. (Indeed, some recent psychodynamic writers have tried to integrate their approach with medical models [Gabbard, 1992; Glucksman, 1995].) However, Freud went to great pains to differentiate his theory from the medical view. He claimed that a medical education was of no use to the psychoanalyst—"The analyst's experience lies in another world from that of pathology, with other phenomena and other laws" (Freud, 1926/1953, p. 119)—and he urged the training of lay (nonphysician) analysts. Furthermore, he insisted that psychoanalysis could offer nothing comparable to a medical cure. Actually, despite its parallels with medicine, the psychodynamic perspective was the first of the purely psychological approaches to abnormal behavior—the first, that is, to regard abnormal behavior not as a moral, religious, or organic problem but as a problem in the history of the individual's emotional life.

Criticisms of Psychodynamic Theory

Lack of Experimental Support The most common criticism of the psychodynamic position is that most of its claims have never been tested in scientifically controlled experiments. Freud evolved his theories on the basis of clinical evidence—that is, observations of patients in therapy—and today psychodynamic writers still tend to rely on case studies to support their formulations. The problem with case studies is that they are open to bias. We can never know to what degree psychodynamic therapists' expectations color the patient's responses or their reporting of those responses.

The reason psychodynamic writers have depended on clinical evidence rather than controlled experiments is that most of the phenomena they deal with are too complex to be testable by current experimental techniques (Erdelyi & Goldberg, 1979). Furthermore, most of these phenomena are unconscious and, hence, inaccessible to direct testing. Nevertheless, some of Freud's most basic claims have been subjected to research and have been validated (Andersen, 1992; Fried, Crits-Christoph, & Luborsky, 1992; Holmes, 1978). Experiments have shown, for example, that dreams do allow people to vent emotional tension; that children do go through a period of erotic interest in the parent of the opposite sex, accompanied by hostile feelings toward the same-sex parent; that people do transfer feelings about those close to them in the past onto new people; and that bringing implicit perceptions and memories into conscious awareness does lead to more adaptive behavior. Likewise, recent research has shown that many of the basic methods of psychodynamic "insight" therapy do have the intended result of revealing core issues and fostering positive change (Anderson & Lambert, 1995; Bornstein, 1993; Grenyer & Luborsky, 1996).

In other cases, the evidence contradicts Freudian theory. For example, there is little or no support for Freud's claim that dreams represent wish fulfillment or that women regard their bodies as inferior to men's because they lack penises. (Most of Freud's conclusions regarding specifically female sexuality have been contradicted by research [Fisher & Greenberg, 1977].) However, the important point is that psychodynamic theory is not altogether closed to empirical testing and that, in some cases, it holds up well under such testing. Indeed, even without the intention of testing psychodynamic theory, experimental psychologists have turned up evidence in support of many of Freud's positions—for example, that most of our mental contents are unconscious (Miller, 1956); that under normal conditions some of our unconscious mental contents are accessible to us, while others are not (Bargh, 1989; Kihlstrom, 1987); and that most of the causes of our behavior are inaccessible to us (Nisbett & Ross, 1980; Nisbett & Wilson, 1977).

Dependence on Inference   A second, related criticism of the psychodynamic approach is that, because it assumes that most mental processes are unconscious, it must depend on inference, and inference can easily be mistaken. Indeed, the psychodynamic view of the relationship between behavior and mental processes is so complicated and indirect that behaviors could conceivably be taken to mean whatever the psychodynamic interpreter wants them to mean. If a 6-year-old boy expresses great love for his mother, this could be interpreted as a sign of Oedipal attachment. However, if the same 6-year-old boy expresses hatred for his mother, this could also be interpreted as an expression of Oedipal attachment, via reaction formation. It should be added, however, that responsible analysts rarely, if ever, draw conclusions on the basis of one piece of evidence alone.

Unrepresentative Sampling and Cultural Bias   Another point on which psychodynamic theory has been criticized is that it is based on the study of a very limited sample of humanity. In most of Freud's published cases, the patients were upper-middle-class Viennese women between the ages of 20 and 44 (Fisher & Greenberg, 1977). Though these people were adults, Freud drew from them his theories regarding the child's psyche. (He never studied children in any systematic way.) Though they had serious emotional problems, he drew from them his theories regarding normal development. Though they lived in a time and place in which overt expressions of sexuality, especially by women, were frowned upon, he concluded that their sexual preoccupations were typical of all human beings.

There is also the matter of Freud's cultural biases. He lived in a society in which social-class distinctions were rigidly observed, in which the family was dominated by the father, and in which women's opportunities were strictly limited. That these facts influenced his patients' thoughts is unquestionable. In addition, as Erich Fromm (1980) pointed out, they may have influenced Freud's interpretation of that evidence, leading him to see more repression, more sexual motivation, and more "penis envy" than are actually universal properties of the human psyche.

Reductiveness   It has been argued that psychodynamic theory has handed down to the twentieth century an exceedingly dismal vision of human life—a reductive vision—in which the human being is driven by animal instincts beyond his or her conscious control, in which people are virtually helpless to change themselves after the die is cast in early childhood, in which acts of heroism or generosity are actually disguised outgrowths of baser motives, and in which all that most people can know of their own minds is the surface, while the true causes of their behavior remain sealed up in the dark chambers of the unconscious.

Many of these positions, it should be recalled, have been substantially modified by later psychodynamic theorists. Furthermore, even if that were not the case, it is not the duty of science to produce a comforting picture of life, only a true one. As it happens, Freud found much to admire in the human psyche he envisioned. If the ego could fashion civilization out of the base materials the id provided, then the ego was a heroic force, indeed. Furthermore, if psychodynamic theory is deterministic, so (as we shall see) are most other schools of psychology. And the psychodynamic perspective does hold out the hope that, by acquainting ourselves with our inner lives, we can exercise greater control over our destinies. In short, it has pointed out the adaptive value of self-knowledge.

The Contributions of Psychodynamic Theory   Probably the greatest contribution of psychodynamic theory was that it helped to demythologize mental disorder. By arguing that the most "crazy" behaviors have their roots in the same mental processes as the most "sane" behaviors, Freud contributed greatly to the modern effort to treat the mentally disturbed as human beings rather than as freaks. Furthermore, by pointing out what he called the "psychopathology of everyday life"—the ways in which irrational and unconscious impulses emerge in dreams, in jokes, in slips of the tongue, in our ways of forgetting what we want to forget—Freud showed that the mentally disturbed have no monopoly on irrationality. This aspect of psychodynamic theory helped to establish the concept of mental health as a continuum ranging from adaptive to maladaptive rather than as a dichotomy of "sick" and "healthy."

Second, to the treatment of mental problems Freud contributed the technique of psychoanalysis, which then gave rise to the wide variety of psychodynamic therapies in use today. Even therapists who reject Freud's theory altogether reveal his influence in the consulting room. The now-traditional technique of a one-to-one patient-therapist relationship aimed at increasing the patient's self-knowledge—a technique that underlies almost every known form of psychotherapy—was essentially a Freudian invention.

While modern thinkers are still arguing with Freud, no one can deny his impact on the contemporary conceptualization, assessment, and treatment of abnormal behavior. It is Freudian theory that is responsible for the widespread assumption that abnormal behavior stems from events in the individual's past and that it occurs in response to unconscious and uncontrollable impulses. In terms of psychological assessment, the widely used projective tests, such as the Rorschach (Chapter 2), are based on the Freudian notion that behavior is symbolic and that what a person reads into a picture or an event is actually a reading of his or her own psyche.

The impact of psychodynamic theory has been felt far beyond the field of professional psychology. Freud directed the attention of the twentieth century to the gap between the outer life and the inner life—to dreams, fantasies, and memory, as well as to how these factors guide our behavior. In doing so, he changed not only psychology but art, literature, history, and education. Indeed, he altered popular thinking. Today, people who have never read a word by Freud show no hesitation in explaining their problems in terms of their childhood experience, in viewing their own children's development as crucial prefigurations of their adult lives, or in using such terms as *repressed, rationalization,* and *ego*—terms Freud coined to explain the human psyche. Freud radically altered the Western conception of the human mind. The same cannot be said of any other psychological theorist.

The Cognitive Perspective

Although the **cognitive perspective**, which views abnormal behavior as the product of mental processing, did not become important in abnormal psychology until the 1970s, cognitive functions such as memory, reasoning, and problem solving had been of interest to psychologists ever since psychology began (Craighead, Ilardi, Greenberg, et al., 1997). Cognition is important to abnormal psychology for two reasons. First, many psychological disorders involve serious cognitive disturbances. For example, severely depressed people usually cannot concentrate—a condition that makes them fail at tasks and, thus, feel more depressed. Schizophrenics also have severe cognitive problems; typically, they cannot think or use language clearly. Second, it is believed that certain cognitive patterns may not be symptoms but actual

causes of their associated disorders—a possibility that has given considerable impetus to cognitive research in the past few decades.

The Background of the Cognitive Perspective

The cognitive perspective grew out of the behavioral perspective, which we will discuss in the next chapter. For now, it is enough to know that the behaviorists, in a radical departure from psychodynamic thought, took the position that the most important causes of human behavior are not inside us, as Freud had claimed, but outside us, in the environment. In what is called *stimulus-response theory (S-R theory)*, they proposed that the environment provides stimuli and the organism responds. The responses that are *reinforced*—that bring us rewards or release us from discomfort—are those that we repeat. Behavior, then, is the product of learning.

However, whereas most behaviorists endorsed S-R theory, others questioned the wisdom of ignoring all mental processes: how is it, they asked, that the same stimulus can produce different responses in different human beings? For example, an avid golfer would find a tournament broadcast on TV exciting, but a nongolfer would find the same event utterly boring. Some other factor, in addition to the stimulus, must be influencing the response. Presumably, that other factor was cognition, or the mental processing of stimuli.

Given the variability of responses, some behaviorists questioned not only S-R theory but also the very principle of reinforcement. For example, Edward Tolman (1948) held that human beings learned not by reinforcement of trial-and-error responses but by perceiving the relationship among various elements of the task. Reinforcement, Tolman argued, affected learning by creating expectancies, inner "predictions" as to which responses would lead to rewards and punishments in which situations. As for the responses themselves, they were learned through mental processes independent of reinforcement. Tolman and Honzig (1930) demonstrated this principle by showing that, if rats were given a chance to explore a maze, without reinforcement, then later, when reinforcement was available, these rats would run the maze faster than other rats that had not had an opportunity to explore the apparatus. In other words, the rats had learned something without being rewarded for it.

Cognitive Behaviorism

Thus, behaviorism no sooner developed S-R theory than it produced a cognitive challenge to that theory. As we shall see, an alliance between these two, called *cognitive behaviorism,* has produced valuable results in the form of refined theories and treatments. The central claim of the cognitive behaviorists is that people's actions are often responses not so much to external stimuli as to their own individual mental processing of those stimuli. These theorists claim that, though cognitive events are not objectively observable, they are learned responses and, thus, are subject to the same laws as other behavior. Ultimately, theory and research on cognitive factors and their role in influencing behavior developed into a broader movement known as the cognitive perspective.

Besides its importance in providing new theories about behavior, the cognitive perspective has had a decided influence on the process of psychotherapy. In this chapter, we will see how two of the most influential cognitive theorists, Albert Ellis and Aaron T. Beck, developed their ideas about the role of cognition in abnormal behavior from working with clients in therapy. We will also briefly look at some of the principal techniques in cognitive therapy. More detail on cognitive therapies will be presented in chapters devoted to various disorders.

Albert Ellis: Irrational Beliefs   Albert Ellis (b. 1913) developed what has come to be known as *rational-emotive therapy,* which is based on the idea that psychological problems are caused not by events in the outside world but by people's reacting to such events on the basis of irrational beliefs. Ellis (1962) has proposed an ABC system to explain how this process works: A is the activating experience; B, the beliefs or thoughts that irrationally follow; and C, the consequences for the person, both emotional and behavioral. Ellis (1980) suggests that most problems stem from certain core irrational beliefs, such as

1. I must do well and win approval, or I rate as a rotten person.
2. Others must treat me considerately and kindly, or society and the universe should punish them.
3. I should be able to get all the things I want easily and quickly.

Most people, when they see these beliefs stated so bluntly, are able to recognize their irrationality, yet they react to many events as if such statements were entirely true and reasonable. For example, a person may become extremely upset and depressed about some minor failing (reflecting irrational thought number 1) or angry at some slight (reflecting irrational thought number 2). Ellis' therapy involves confronting and disrupting the irrational beliefs (B) so that the emotional and behavioral consequences (C) will change accordingly.

Aaron T. Beck: Cognitive Distortions   In a number of influential books and articles, Aaron T. Beck (b. 1921) has pointed out that psychological disorders are often associated with specific patterns of distorted thinking (1967, 1976; Beck, Emery, & Greenberg, 1985; Beck & Freeman, 1990). In depression, for example, the distorted thoughts center on a pessimistic view of the self, the world, and the future—the "negative triad," as Beck calls it. In anxiety, the distorted thoughts center on threats of danger. The cognitive distortions Beck has identified include magnification (seeing minor events as far more important than they are), overgeneralization (drawing a broad conclusion from little evidence), and selective abstraction (paying attention to only certain kinds of evidence while ignoring other, equally relevant information). These distortions operate automatically, without the person's being aware of them. Thus, a person who becomes extremely depressed at not receiving a birthday card from one family member, while receiving cards from many other relatives and friends, would probably be engaging in all three kinds of cognitive distortion. In Beck's therapy, clients are led to discover their distorted thoughts and to replace them with more reasonable and valid thoughts.

We will refer to Ellis and Beck in other chapters in this book. Now let us consider some of the cognitive processes that they and other thinkers within this perspective have identified as crucial to abnormal behavior.

Cognitive Appraisal

Cognitive theorists have argued that between stimulus and response comes the all-important process of cognitive appraisal. In this process, the person, before reacting, evaluates the stimulus in light of his or her own memories, beliefs, and expectations. It is this internal mental activity that accounts for the wide differences in individual responses to the same external stimulus. For example, two people giving a lecture may react quite differently to the stimulus of seeing several members of the audience get up and walk out in the middle of the talk. One may say to himself, "Oh, I must be boring them to tears. I knew I would make a bad lecturer." He responds to this cognitive appraisal by becoming anxious, perspiring, and perhaps stumbling over his words. Another lecturer, with a more positive view of herself and her speaking skills, interprets the departures as due to circumstances external to herself: "They must have a class to catch. Too bad they have to leave; they will miss a good talk" (Meichenbaum, 1975, p. 358). And she will proceed, unruffled, with her lecture.

Cognitive behaviorists believe that our cognitive appraisal of our competence affects our behavior in relevant situations. People who learn athletic skills in childhood are likely to feel confident about participating in sports—and perhaps other group activities—later in life.

In other words, what determines the response is not the stimulus itself but the person's interpretation of the stimulus. As Greek philosopher Epictetus put it, "Men are disturbed not by things but by the views they take of them"—a maxim that cognitive theorists are fond of quoting.

Attributions   One form of cognitive appraisal that has attracted a number of researchers is **attribution,** our beliefs about the causes of life events (Fiske & Taylor, 1991; Weiner, Frieze, Kokla, et al., 1971). Research in this area has focused on three dimensions of attribution: global/specific, stable/unstable, and internal/external. Consider, for example, a woman who was recently fired. The way she explains this event to herself will affect her emotional state. Internal attributions ("I can't handle pressure") are much more damaging to self-esteem than external attributions ("My boss was impossible to work for!"). Likewise, broad-based, or global, attributions ("I'm incompetent") are more destructive than specific attributions ("I don't belong in sales") and long-term, or stable, attributions ("I'll never get ahead") are more harmful than unstable attributions ("I picked the wrong job"). As we will see in Chapter 9, people who habitually attribute failures to global, stable, internal faults have an attributional style that makes them more vulnerable to feelings of hopelessness and helplessness, and ultimately more susceptible to depression (Abramson, Alloy, & Metalsky, 1995; Abramson, Metalsky, & Alloy, 1989).

Cognitive Variables Affecting Behavior   What types of processes are involved in cognitive appraisal? Walter Mischel (1973, 1979) has proposed five basic cate-gories of cognitive variables that help to determine individual responses to a given stimulus:

1. *Competencies.* Each of us has a unique set of skills, acquired through past learning, for dealing with various situations. If one person has learned to respond to pushiness by standing up for herself and another person has not, these two people will react differently when someone cuts in front of them in the checkout line at the supermarket.

2. *Encoding strategies.* Each of us has a special way of perceiving and categorizing experience. One woman, upon finding a copy of *Playboy* under her teenage son's mattress, may have a talk with the boy on the injustice of viewing women as sex objects. Another woman may regard the magazine as a normal sign of male puberty and just push it back under the mattress.

3. *Expectancies.* Through learning, each of us forms different expectations as to which circumstances are likely to lead to rewards and punishments. A student who has had very supportive teachers in math courses and one who has had very critical teachers will have different expectations about whether math courses are likely to be reinforcing.

4. *Values.* Each of us places different values on different stimuli. A person who values outdoor activities will find an invitation to go hiking more appealing than will someone who prefers watching TV.

5. *Plans and goals.* As a result of different learning histories, we also formulate different plans and goals, which then guide our behavior. If a store employee who hopes to become floor manager finds out that other employees are pilfering, he

might report this to his boss, whereas an employee who hates the store and intends to quit soon might keep quiet.

Albert Bandura (1977, 1982, 1986) also sees behavior as regulated primarily by cognition, but, whereas Mischel divides the cognitive territory into five categories of variables, Bandura has concentrated on one category, expectancies. Bandura distinguishes between two types of expectancies: (1) *outcome expectancies,* expectations that a given behavior will produce a certain result, and (2) *efficacy expectancies,* expectations that one will be able to execute that behavior successfully. Bandura claims that efficacy expectancies are the chief determinant of coping behavior and that they, in turn, are determined primarily by performance feedback from prior experience. Imagine, for example, that a woman who is afraid of flying must fly to a distant city for a job interview. Here the outcome expectancy is the woman's judgment as to how likely it is that the plane will get her to her destination. In this case, the outcome expectancy is quite high. But whether or not she will actually make the reservation depends more on her efficacy expectancy, her confidence as to whether she will actually be able to get on the plane and make the trip without incident. That confidence depends on how well she has managed similar stressful situations in the past.

Self-Reinforcement

Cognitive theorists agree with the behavioral position that behavior is molded by reinforcement and punishment, but they claim that the most potent rewards and punishments come not from the external environment but from the mind—in the form of self-approval and self-criticism. In some cases, this cognitive reinforcement can lead to external reinforcement ("I just made it through that frightening plane trip—I'll go buy myself an ice cream cone"), but more often it remains on the cognitive level, in the form of self-congratulation ("I did just fine") and increased self-esteem.

Information Processing

Information processing is a broad area of cognitive research concerned with how the human mind takes in, stores, interprets, and uses information from the environment. Cognitive researchers have learned, for example, to make a distinction between what they call automatic and controlled processing of information. *Automatic processing,* which seems to operate without conscious awareness or intention, yields quick, well-learned responses that remain stable over time. *Controlled processing,* on the other hand, re-

quires logic and consideration as the mind integrates new information and devises a response (Craighead, Ilardi, Greenberg, et al., 1997). When a child with a skinned knee goes crying to a parent, for example, the parent will engage in automatic processing—not a lot of thought but, rather, a quick succession of responses: consoling words, soap and water, bandage. But, when at age 14 the same child begins moping, coming in late from school, and spending time locked in his room, the parent, lacking any "formula" for this new problem, will have to engage in controlled processing. Many abnormal behavior patterns, such as phobias and other anxiety responses, can be viewed as the result of inappropriate automatic processing (McNally, 1995). Therapists have had some success in teaching people with these problems to convert to controlled processing (Kanfer & Hagerman, 1985).

As this talk of information processing suggests, many cognitive thinkers now take the computer as their model for the human mind. One great difference, however, between the computer and the human mind is that the former takes in information passively; whatever is put into it, it absorbs. The human mind, on the other hand, actively selects, and at times distorts, the information that it takes in. This fact makes cognitive research rather more slippery than computer studies.

Attention Human beings cannot possibly attend to, let alone process, all the information that bombards their senses at any given moment, so they take in only some information, the information that seems to them most important, and they filter out the rest. This mechanism, an indispensable adaptive function, is called **selective attention.**

Some forms of psychopathology may be due to a failure in selective attention. It has been proposed, for example, that many of the symptoms of schizophrenia, such as distorted perceptions and unwanted thoughts, stem from a breakdown in selective attention, with the result that the mind is flooded with information (Perry & Braff, 1994). Attention may be an important factor in other disorders as well. Depressives have been found to pay more attention to negative stimuli than do nondepressed people. (Kuiper, Olinger, & MacDonald, 1988). Likewise, people with anxiety disorders selectively attend to threatening information (Williams, Mathews, & McLeod, 1996). Furthermore, most psychiatric disorders involve increased self-focused attention (Ingram, 1990). That is, people with these disorders spend an inordinate amount of time brooding about themselves. In part, this is undoubtedly a result of their problems—they are experiencing anxiety attacks, sexual dysfunction, or whatever; therefore, they worry about themselves—but it may also be a cause, in that it seems to reduce their flexibility in considering how to solve their problems.

Organizing Structures   The mind doesn't just choose what information it will take in. It also arranges that information in lasting and meaningful patterns, which then affect how other information will be taken in.

Schemas   In the vocabulary of cognitive psychology, a schema is an organized structure of information about a particular domain of life—a structure that serves the person as a pattern for selecting and processing new information (Craighead, Ilardi, Greenberg, et al., 1997; Markus, 1977). Of particular interest to abnormal psychology are the *self-schemas,* the schemas that relate to our self-concept and identity. Most people have positive self-schemas—they see themselves as successful, talented, and well liked—and such a view is adaptive. It motivates people to pursue goals; it also protects them psychologically, causing them to focus on their successes and dismiss their failures as due to outside factors, such as bad luck. By the same token, negative self-schemas are maladaptive, eroding motivation and causing people to focus on their failures. According to Aaron Beck, depression is due primarily to self-schemas dominated by themes of worthlessness, guilt, and deprivation. Beck believes that anxiety, too, is caused by distorted self-schemas, in this case dominated by themes of threat and uncertainty.

The principle of schemas in cognitive psychology affords an opportunity to test a highly subjective concept of the psychodynamic perspective: transference. See the box "A Cognitive Approach to Transference" on page 114.

Beliefs   A related cognitive theory is Albert Ellis' view that anxiety and depression are due to irrational beliefs. If, for example, a woman believes that she must be approved of by everyone, she will spend inordinate amounts of time trying to please others, even to her own detriment. As a result, her behavior will appear odd and inappropriate. Furthermore, it will allow no expression of her true preferences and interests—a sacrifice that will eventually give rise to feelings of acute frustration.

The Cognitive Approach to Therapy

If cognitions are an important cause of abnormal behavior, it follows that such behavior can be treated by changing cognitions. To this end, cognitive theorists have developed a variety of techniques to increase coping skills, to develop problem solving, and to change the ways clients perceive and interpret their worlds. These techniques and the broader therapy in which they are applied are called **cognitive restructuring.**

Self-Instructional Training   A straightforward version of cognitive restructuring is *self-instructional training.* Developed by Donald Meichenbaum and his colleagues (Meichenbaum, 1977; Meichenbaum & Cameron, 1973), this technique concentrates on "self-talk," the things that people say to themselves before, during, and after their actions. The object is to change the pattern of self-talk in such a way that, instead of defeating the person, it helps him or her to cope with threatening situations.

In self-instructional training, therapists model "cognitive coping exercises." First, they voice defeating self-sentences, so as to alert clients to the kinds of thoughts that trigger and reinforce maladaptive behavior. Then they "answer back" with more constructive self-talk, thus showing clients how they can combat self-defeating thoughts. Once the therapist has modeled this sequence, the client imitates it. For example, a person with a fear of driving a car might say, "This is so dangerous. The minute I'm out of the driveway I could be killed. Wouldn't it be better just to stay home? But wait . . . millions of people drive cars every day without having accidents. And can't I be in control of my own safety by driving defensively? If I don't try, I'll end up stuck at home forever and never get to go where I want to go. I'll just do my best and I'll be fine!" Finally, clients are asked to practice pairing the behavior with self-talk and reinforcement through graduated performance assignments (driving farther from home each time or driving on busier roads, supporting each successful assignment with appropriate self-talk). Self-instructional training is a practical treatment aimed at straightforward problem solving and, as such, it is the most "behavioral" of the cognitive therapies. It does not require that the client understand or develop "insight" into his or her cognitive dysfunctions.

Ellis' and Beck's Cognitive Therapies   Other kinds of cognitive therapy call on the client to identify and analyze self-defeating cognitions, as well as to revise them. Perhaps the oldest such treatment is Albert Ellis' **rational-emotive therapy.** As we saw earlier, Ellis' basic contention is that emotional disturbances are the result not of objective events in people's lives but of the irrational beliefs that guide their interpretations of those events. To combat such beliefs, Ellis and his followers point out in blunt terms the irrationality of the client's thinking, model more realistic evaluations of the

A Cognitive Approach to Transference

According to psychodynamic theory, important people in our lives, such as our parents, are represented unconsciously in our memories and exert an influence on our thoughts and behavior. One such influence occurs in psychotherapy, where the conflicts and anxieties attached to these relationships can be unknowingly directed toward the therapist. Freud thought that his patients actually began to treat him as their father, a process that he called *transference*.

From the perspective of cognitive psychology, important people in our lives are represented in memory as schemas that contain not only memories of a person's appearance and identity but also potentially intense feelings toward the person. When we meet individuals who resemble people in our past, we assimilate the new people to the schemas we have formed from our past relationships. As a result, we expect people who resemble important others from our past to behave as those others did, and we experience feelings toward those individuals that are similar to the feelings associated with the people we already know. This expectation based on cognitive psychology is similar to the psychodynamic concept of transference; it was tested by Susan Andersen and her colleagues in several recent experiments.

In a pretest session held 2 weeks before the experiment (Andersen, Reznik, & Manzella, 1996), 80 undergraduate women were asked to describe 2 important people in their lives. One was to be someone whom "you like very much and feel very good about, someone in whose presence you feel happy and great about yourself, and someone you want to be close to." The other person was to be the exact opposite, someone they did not like and did not want to be close to. In each case, they were asked to disclose both favorable and unfavorable information about the person.

Unknown to these research participants, when they arrived for another presumably unrelated experiment that took place two weeks later, they were actually taking part in an extension of the pretest session. In the second session, they were told that they would meet a fellow student as part of a test of a new "buddy" system at their university. (No meeting actually took place.) Participants were then given a supposed description of the unknown other, so that the investigators could study the effects that this information might have on their meeting. For half of the participants, the description was actually taken from one of their two important relationships described two weeks earlier. The other half of the participants received one of the same descriptions that the first half received, but in this case the descriptions were not of someone they knew. In all cases, the descriptions included lists of both favorable and unfavorable characteristics of either someone who was strongly liked (positive person) or someone who was strongly disliked (negative person), as well as some more neutral characteristics that could apply to anyone.

Participants were asked to read the list of characteristics aloud one at a time. Unknown to the participants, their facial expressions were videotaped as they read each character-

---

client's situation (e.g., "So what if your mother didn't love you. That's *her* problem!"), instruct the client to monitor and correct his or her thoughts, rehearse the client in appraising situations realistically, and give homework assignments so that new ways of interpreting experience can be strengthened.

Similar in theory if not in tone is the version of cognitive therapy developed by Aaron Beck (1976). We have already discussed Beck's theory of depression: that it is caused by a "negative triad" of thoughts about the self, the world, and the future. To change such cognitions, Beck adopts a less didactic and more Socratic approach than Ellis, questioning patients in such a way that they themselves gradually discover the inappropriateness of their thoughts. We will discuss Beck's treatment for depression in detail in Chapter 9.

Constructivist Cognitive Therapy A slightly different version of cognitive therapy has been proposed by Michael J. Mahoney (1991). He calls this *constructivist cognitive therapy,* as opposed to the Beck and Ellis approaches, which he calls "rationalist."

To Mahoney, rationalist cognitive therapy depends too much on conscious, rational, verbal analysis and does not take sufficient account of emotion and other seemingly irrational components of behavior. According to Mahoney, people begin in childhood to *construct* their worlds out of their experience: their actions and the feedback they receive from those actions. If the cognitive patterns developed in this way are self-defeating, then constructivist cognitive therapy is a chance to construct new patterns. Self-exploration is an important part of the process. Among the techniques Mahoney recommends are writing (stories, poetry, journals, letters not to be mailed), observing oneself sitting in front of a mirror, and speaking in a "stream-of-consciousness" manner in the therapeutic setting. These techniques all aim at helping the client understand his or her characteristic way of viewing the world, in the hope of changing that view for the better.

Common Strategies in Cognitive Therapy The common element in all cognitive therapy is an attempt to istic. This procedure allowed the investigators to gauge the emotional reaction to the unknown person as the characteristics were revealed. Participants then completed a memory test for the descriptions by indicating their confidence that they had seen various characteristics. Some of these characteristics were descriptive of the participant's important other but had not been presented in the description the participant received earlier. This procedure enabled the investigators to see if the participants were using their schema-based knowledge of their important relationship to shape their expectations of the unknown person. Finally, participants rated how much they would expect to like the unknown person and disclose important personal information to the person and how much they would expect the person to like them.

As predicted, reactions to the unknown person were much stronger and more favorable when the descriptions resembled someone with whom the women had a positive relationship. For example, the women tended to smile more often in response to the unknown person's characteristics when the person resembled someone in their lives whom they liked than when the person resembled someone they disliked or someone they did not know. The women's expectations concerning the unknown person were also strongly influenced by the resemblance of the person to their important others. Women who received descriptions that resembled an important other expected to like the positive person much more than the negative person and wanted to get to know the person more. They also thought the positive person would like them more than the negative person. However, when exactly the same descriptions were evaluated by other participants for whom there was little resemblance to important others, reactions were much less extreme. For these students, the descriptions did not activate critical schemas of important people in their lives.

Another indication that participants transferred their feelings and expectations from their important others to the unknown person was observed in the memory results. Women who received descriptions that resembled their important others were more likely to misremember seeing descriptions that were not actually shown than were women who received descriptions that did not resemble an important other. This finding suggests that the women used their schemas to "fill in" their memories and their expectations of the unknown person.

In many respects, these results reproduce the phenomenon of transference in a simple laboratory analogue to what might occur in psychotherapy. From the psychodynamic perspective, the question of whether transference has taken place in a therapist-client relationship can be answered only qualitatively or subjectively. Cognitive psychology, on the other hand, proposes that the evaluation of transference can be addressed through answers to specific questions—a hypothesis that can be tested through experiment.

identify and alter the pattern of thought that is causing a client's maladaptive behavior. Cognitive therapists have devised a number of useful strategies aimed at identifying faulty cognitions and replacing them with more realistic ones. In hypothesis testing, clients are urged to test their assumptions in the real world. A depressed woman, for example, who insists that her friends no longer want anything to do with her might be urged to call a few friends on the phone and suggest a get-together. Did the friends refuse to talk to her? Did they all refuse her invitation?

In reattribution training, the client is helped to change distorted ideas of cause-and-effect and to attribute events to their causes in a realistic manner. In one reported case, for example, a lawyer facing a trial with the belief that a loss would be entirely his fault was asked by his therapist to estimate the relative importance of the factors that influence the outcome of a trial (jury composition, nature of the offense, appearance of the plaintiff and defendant, length of trial, competence of the judge and the opposing lawyer, and so on). He was, thus, able to realize that the verdict would be affected by many circumstances, several of them beyond his control (Bedrosian & Beck, 1980).

In the technique known as decatastrophizing, the client is asked to consider what would actually happen if his or her worst fear were realized. A client with a social phobia, for example, might say that he can't go to a party because he would feel foolish, no one would talk to him, and he would have a terrible time. "And what if that happened?" the therapist might ask. What is the *worst possible* result? That the client would leave the party early, without having spoken to anyone? And would that be a catastrophe, or would it simply be embarrassing? Questions like these help clients realize that their fears are exaggerated.

Evaluating the Cognitive Perspective

Criticisms of Cognitive Psychology Cognitive theory is open to the same criticism as any other theory depending on inference: that it is unscientific, because we can't actually observe the forces under discussion. And, as critics have pointed out, the history of cognitive theory—memory theory in particular—has been one in which hypothesized factors claimed to be central were eventually replaced by other hypothesized factors claimed to be central (Skinner, 1990; Watkins, 1990), inviting the question of how central they actually are, if they are so changeable. Whatever the hypothesized factors, noncognitive theorists are likely to deny not so much their existence as their centrality. According to behaviorists (e.g., Skinner, 1990), cognitions may be there, but they are only a product of reinforcement history; therefore, what we have to study is not the former but the latter. Likewise, psychodynamic theorists would certainly not deny the existence of cognitions or negative self-schemas, but they would say that these were the product of early family relationships and that it is those relationships, not their cognitive consequences, that constitute the root problem.

One major objection to the cognitive approach is that life is not always rational and that simply recognizing that one's view of life is based on "irrational" assumptions—as Ellis would have it—is not enough to produce therapeutic change. Sometimes dysfunctional thoughts persist, despite the client's best attempts to brand them as irrational and self-defeating. A second objection is that there are times when changing one's way of thinking about the world may not be appropriate or right. As Mahoney (1991) writes, "When the Roman slave Epictetus (A.D. 60–138) wrote his famous manual for how to be happy as a slave, he did not consider the possibility of social action against the practice of slavery" (p. 115). With certain realities of life—a poor work situation, an abusive marriage—changing one's view of the situation may not be the whole answer.

A final point about cognitive therapy, though not necessarily a shortcoming, is that we don't really know how it works (Whisman, 1993). With depressed patients, for example, does cognitive therapy actually reduce the frequency of their negative thoughts, or does it just teach them a new set of skills for dealing with such thoughts (Barber & DeRubeis, 1989)? It is possible that cognitive therapy's successes with depression actually have little to do with cognitive change. Perhaps the improvement in mood is due, instead, to the satisfaction of mastering therapeutic tasks or simply to the increase in pleasurable activities. Cognitive changes occur in cognitive therapy, but do they come before or after the changes in emotion and behavior? Preliminary studies indicate that they come before (Whisman, 1993), but these results are tentative. Cognitive therapy is the newest of the major treatment strategies, and more research is needed before we will understand its mechanisms.

The Contributions of Cognitive Theory   The cognitive approach has the virtue of focusing on specific, operationalized variables and of insisting on empirical evidence. At the same time, unlike other scientific approaches, such as behaviorism, it takes intangible processes—thoughts, emotions—into account. Using this approach, cognitive researchers have accumulated a large body of empirically based findings, with many useful models of the causes of abnormal behavior.

However, the strongest argument in favor of cognitive psychology is its therapy. Cognitive treatment is very practical. Its techniques can be described forthrightly and applied by any clinician—or even used by the person seeking help without the intervention of a therapist. (Anyone, for example, can use Meichenbaum's "self-talk" technique.) Moreover, cognitive therapy works, at least for some disorders.

Using the strategy of reattribution training, a cognitive therapist could help a lawyer who believed he was completely responsible for losing a trial to recognize that many factors, some beyond his control, affected the outcome.

Its most notable successes so far have been in the treatment of depression and panic disorder (Clark, Salkovskis, Hackmann, et al., 1994). Cognitive therapy has been found to be at least as effective as drugs in treating acute depression and seems to be more effective than drugs in reducing the likelihood of further depressive episodes (Hollon & Beck, 1994; Scott, 1996). Cognitive therapy has also proved helpful with substance dependence and some personality disorders (Beck & Freeman, 1990). Another advantage of cognitive therapy is that there are manuals describing how to administer and evaluate it. Beck and his colleagues, for example, have developed a detailed manual for the administration of cognitive therapy for depression (Beck, Rush, Shaw, et al., 1979). The manual has made it possible to train many therapists in this technique, as well as to conduct large-scale outcome studies.

KEY TERMS

anal stage, 98
anxiety, 95
attribution, 111
autonomic nervous system (ANS), 90
behavior genetics, 78
biological perspective, 78
castration anxiety, 98
central nervous system (CNS), 82
chromosomes, 78
cognition, 109
cognitive appraisal, 110
cognitive perspective, 109
cognitive restructuring, 113
computerized tomography (CT), 88
concordant, 80
decatastrophizing, 115

defense mechanism, 96
depth hypothesis, 94
diathesis-stress model, 79
dizygotic (DZ) twins, 80
dream interpretation, 106
ego, 95
endocrine system, 92
free association, 106
genes, 78
genital stage, 98
genotype, 79
hormones, 92
hypothesis testing, 115
id, 94
interpretation, 94
latency, 98
lateralization, 89
libido, 94
magnetic resonance imaging (MRI), 88

monozygotic (MZ) twins, 80
nervous system, 82
neurons, 82
neuroses, 100
neurotransmitter, 83
object relations, 103
Oedipus complex, 98
oral stage, 98
parasympathetic division, 91
peripheral nervous system, 90
phallic stage, 98
phenotype, 79
positron emission tomography (PET), 88
postsynaptic receptors, 84
psychoanalysis, 93
psychodynamic perspective, 93

psychopharmacology, 85
psychosexual development, 97
psychosis, 100
psychosurgery, 89
rational-emotive therapy, 113
reattribution training, 115
repression, 96
resistance, 106
schema, 113
selective attention, 112
somatic nervous system, 90
structural hypothesis, 94
superego, 95
sympathetic division, 90
synapse, 83
transference, 106
unconscious, 94

SUMMARY

- The biological perspective focuses on the interaction between people's physical and psychological functioning. The mind and body are two aspects of a single complex entity. Psychological stress and physical illness often influence each other.

- Behavior genetics is a subfield of psychology that attempts to determine the degree to which specific psychological disorders are genetically inherited. Only a few psychological disorders have a clear-cut genetic cause, but many disorders, including schizophrenia, apparently result from the interaction of environmental stressors and an inherited predisposition to the disorder. A person's observable characteristics, or phenotype, are the product of experience combined with his or her genotype, or genetic endowment. Through family, twin, and adoption studies, behavior geneticists try to assess heritability.

- The central nervous system (CNS), consisting of the brain and spinal cord, controls behavior by processing, transmitting, and storing information. Neurotransmitters mediate the transmission of impulses across the

synapse between two neurons, or nerve cells. Six neurotransmitters are implicated in psychopathology: acetylcholine, dopamine, enkephalins, GABA, norepinephrine, and serotonin. Drugs intended to alleviate a disorder by increasing the action of a given neurotransmitter may do so by slowing down its reuptake into the neurons' axon terminals, where it is made. A neurotransmitter's action may be suppressed by using a drug to attach to receptors on the neurons in the neurotransmitter's place.

- Drugs are now the most common of the biological treatments for abnormal behavior. The five main categories are antianxiety drugs, sedative-hypnotic drugs, antipsychotic drugs, antidepressant drugs, and antimanic/mood-stabilizer drugs.

- A major focus of biological research in abnormal psychology has been brain anatomy. The external surface of the cerebral cortex shows many fissures (sulci) and ridges (gyri). The longitudinal fissure divides the brain along the midline into two hemispheres, each containing four lobes with differentiated functions. Regulatory structures include the hypothalamus, limbic structures, thalamus, basal ganglia, cerebellum, and brainstem, a structure containing the pons, medulla, and reticular activating system. Psychological disorders have been traced to dysfunctions in many of these structures.

- Research on the relationship between brain anatomy and psychological functioning has been greatly aided by electroencephalography (EEG), positron emission tomography (PET), computerized tomography (CT), and magnetic resonance imaging (MRI).

- Psychosurgery is brain surgery performed for the purpose of reducing abnormal behavior when no organic brain disorders are present. Prefrontal lobotomy, in which brain tissue is destroyed in an effort to calm the behavior of extremely disturbed patients, was once common but is rarely performed today. Less destructive techniques are cingulotomy and stereotactic subcaudate tractotomy. Psychosurgery is controversial and is used only when other treatments have failed.

- Lateralization is the localization of functions in one hemisphere of the brain. Only a few, very limited functions are completely lateralized. Complex cognitive processes, such as language and emotion, involve interplay among parts of the brain in both hemispheres, although *aspects* of these processes are apparently lateralized. For example, in most people, the left hemisphere seems to control language production; the right hemisphere seems to be specialized for the subtle interpretation of language.

- The peripheral nervous system consists of the somatic nervous system and the autonomic nervous system (ANS). The somatic nervous system activates skeletal muscles and controls purposeful behavior. The autonomic nervous system activates smooth muscles, glands, and internal organs and controls such automatic responses as heart rate, respiration, and the release of adrenaline. The ANS adjusts the body to changing environmental demands through its sympathetic and parasympathetic branches. Sympathetic arousal prepares us for quick action in emergencies—for example, increasing heart rate, respiration, and blood sugar. The parasympathetic division slows metabolism and helps to restore the system to equilibrium. The ANS is associated with such stress-related disorders as hypertension and insomnia.

- The endocrine system influences emotional states, sexual functioning, energy availability, and physical growth and development by releasing hormones into the bloodstream from the hypothalamus, pituitary gland, and other endocrine glands. Glandular dysfunction may be involved in certain psychological disorders.

- The biological perspective presents problems of both causality and ethics. Finding that a genetic predisposition or chemical imbalance accompanies a given disorder does not mean that the organic factor is the only or even the principal cause of the disorder. Ethical concerns involve genetic engineering and the sometimes negative consequences of symptom reduction without adequate follow-up care. Neuroscientists have made great strides in developing diagnostic tools and discovering effective drug treatments for some disorders. Even for these disorders, however, researchers favor the diathesis-stress model, which studies the combined influences of environmental stress and biochemical factors.

- The psychodynamic perspective holds that much of our behavior is not the result of conscious choice but is driven by unconscious, internal forces, which often reflect our childhood experiences and family relationships.

- Sigmund Freud's theory of psychoanalysis laid the foundation for the psychodynamic perspective. The key concept in Freud's theory is the depth hypothesis, the idea that almost all mental activity takes place outside conscious awareness. The unconscious contains material that has been actively forgotten, or repressed.

- Freud held that psychology cannot limit itself to observations but must use interpretation to probe beneath manifest (surface) reasoning to identify latent (unconscious) motivations.

- Freud proposed the structural hypothesis, which divides the mind into three forces—id, ego, and superego. Present from birth, the id consists of primitive biological drives, the most powerful of which are sex and aggression. The id operates on the pleasure principle, ignoring reason, reality, and morality. The ego develops later and operates on the reality principle, seeking ways to gratify the id that are both safe and effective. The superego, which develops last, represents the moral standards of society and parents that the child internalizes. Rigid and uncompromising, the superego demands perfection. The ego's task is to satisfy the id without provoking the superego.

- The id, ego, and superego coexist in a state of dynamic tension, which may explode at any time. Anxiety results when the ego senses danger. Most anxiety is not experienced consciously but is held in check by defense mechanisms. Though often adaptive, overuse of defense mechanisms may interfere with thought processes and everyday functioning.

- Freud viewed personality as the product of childhood psychosexual development, from the oral and anal stages to the phallic, latency, and genital stages. At each stage, the child is forced to resolve conflicts between his or her biological urges and social restraints. Under- or overgratification at any stage may create anxiety and lead to maladaptive adult behavior.

- Freud believed that both normal and abnormal behavior result from interactions among the id, ego, and superego. A healthy adult has the ego strength to balance conflicting demands by the id and the superego. When the ego experiences too much conflict, however, it is weakened. This produces rigid behavior patterns, called neuroses. In extreme cases, the ego collapses and adaptive functioning ceases, a condition known as psychosis.

- Freud's theories were extended and modified by a number of other thinkers. Post-Freudian theorists tended to put less emphasis on the id and more on the ego; to focus less on sexual drives, or libido, and more on personal fulfillment and social relationships; and to pay less attention to childhood traumas and more to present circumstances and ongoing development.

■ Among the most influential post-Freudian theorists, many of whom were Freud's students, were Carl Jung, who believed that the unconscious is a creative as well as a regressive force and who thought of integration of personality components, not mere control by the ego, as the goal of personality development; Alfred Adler, who found the chief behavioral motivator to be the striving to attain personal goals and who believed that the source of psychological disturbance lies in people's relationships with others; Harry Stack Sullivan, who believed that psychological disturbance of any degree of severity is an escape from anxiety in forming human relationships that results from parental rejection; Karen Horney, who identified basic anxiety, resulting from poor parent-child intimacy, as a cause of several fundamental patterns of neurotic behavior; Heinz Hartmann, whose ego psychology recognized autonomous functions and strivings of the ego, especially in the mind's cognitive operations; and Erik Erikson, who saw the development of ego identity as a lifelong process. Influential thinkers in more contemporary psychodynamic theory have included Margaret Mahler, who attached profound importance to the process whereby infants separate from their mothers; Heinz Kohut, who developed the theory of self psychology, according to which parents' early support of the child is crucial to the child's developing a lasting calm and self-esteem; and John Bowlby and Mary Ainsworth, who collaborated in developing attachment theory, which stresses the attachment between the child and its mother (or primary caretaker) as the basis of secure adult attachments.

■ All psychodynamic therapy is based to some extent on Freudian psychoanalytic theory. In psychoanalysis, the client talks, and the analyst interprets possible connections with unconscious material. The process relies on free association, dream interpretation, and analysis of resistance and transference. Most psychodynamic therapists today practice a modified form of psychoanalysis that includes post-Freudian ideas. Most therapists now speak directly to the client much more than Freud would have considered appropriate. Still, the one-to-one therapist-client consultation Freud pioneered underlies almost every form of psychotherapy.

■ The psychodynamic perspective has been criticized for lack of experimental support, dependence on inference, unrepresentative sampling, cultural biases (especially relating to gender differences), and a negative portrait of human nature. But psychodynamic theory played a major role in demystifying abnormal behavior by exposing the irrationality of everyday life and showing that normal and abnormal behavior are not so much distinct categories as points on a continuum. Psychodynamic theory has also had an enormous impact on Western culture by calling attention to the inner world of dreams and fantasies.

■ The cognitive perspective in psychology begins with an interest in cognition, or the mental processing of stimuli. The early cognitive behaviorists argued that variations in responses to the same stimuli could be explained only in terms of cognitive events. They argued that psychological problems arise from irrational beliefs (Ellis) or distorted thinking (Beck).

■ The cognitive perspective holds that a person's response to a stimulus reflects the way he or she processes or appraises the stimulus, not the stimulus itself. Some attribution styles are more adaptive than others.

■ The cognitive perspective has been criticized for being unscientific to the extent that it is based on inference, and for mistaking secondary for primary causes. At the same time, the cognitive perspective is more scientific than some other perspectives in that it emphasizes operationalized variables and empirical measures of memory, association, and anticipation.

■ Cognitive therapy is based on the idea that, to change a pattern of maladaptive behavior, it is necessary to restructure the pattern of thoughts that maintains it. In self-instructional training, the client is taught to engage in more constructive self-talk. Rational-emotive therapy is aimed at identifying irrational assumptions that guide clients' interpretations of events and, thus, their behavior. Aaron Beck's cognitive therapy holds that emotional disorders are caused primarily by irrational, negative thoughts. Constructivist cognitive therapy uses self-exploration to gradually reveal new ways of thinking and feeling. Common strategies in cognitive therapy include hypothesis testing, reattribution training, and decatastrophizing.

■ Cognitive therapy is sometimes criticized for not recognizing that life can be irrational and that changing one's thinking is not always an appropriate response. On the other hand, it is very practical and often effective: its techniques can be described forthrightly and summarized in a manual.

Chapter 5

In the previous chapter, we considered three perspectives, the biological, psychodynamic, and cognitive, whose primary focus is on causes inside the individual, causes that cannot be observed. In this chapter, we will turn to three perspectives that focus on causes presumed to be external to the individual. For the behavioral perspective, the emphasis is on factors in the environment that influence behavior. For the family systems and sociocultural perspectives, the focus is also on environment but, more specifically, the family and social environments. These perspectives all share the assumption that, in order to understand behavior, one has to look outside the person for explanations.

All three are products of the twentieth century, and they arose in reaction to prior philosophies of behavior—behaviorism as a reaction to psychodynamic theory and to the introspective method, family systems and sociocultural theories as a reaction to psychiatry itself, with its tendency to view abnormal behavior as a problem in the person rather than in the social context.

The Behavioral Perspective

Perhaps the most fundamental assumption of psychodynamic theory is that what you see is not what you get. Behavior is only the surface of mental functioning; its substance lies beneath, in remote, unconscious processes. It is on this point that the **behavioral perspective**, which views behavior (except for genetically determined behavior) as the result of environmental experience, departs most radically from psychodynamic thought. Environmental experience, also called learning, is the sum total of all life experiences that the individual has been subjected to and which continue to impinge on his or her behavior—modifying it, refining, it, and changing it. For the behaviorists, the only causes of behavior other than genes are in the environment (Skinner, 1953). Faced with a student who is depressed after failing an exam, a psychodynamic theorist would take the exam as a jumping-off point for more fundamental explorations: how did failure during childhood affect his relationship with his parents? Faced with the same student, the behavioral theorist might be just as interested in childhood experiences, seen as learning history. But, in treating the depression, the behaviorist would be more concerned with *proximal* (nearby) causes, causes in the current environment. What were the consequences for the student of failing the exam? What circumstances in his current life situation may have caused the failure, and what current circumstances may now be operating to encourage the response of depression?

This difference in treatment focus is reflected in the methods of the two schools. Psychodynamic theorists, interested in the hypothetical inner reaches of the psyche, must often forgo scientific verifiability. The behaviorists' proximal focus, by contrast, is in part the result of their insistence on scientific method, more specifically on a method known as the experimental analysis of behavior.

The Background of Behaviorism

An important component of many psychological theories in the late nineteenth century was *introspection,* the study of the mind by analysis of one's own thought processes. It was in reaction to this trend that behaviorism arose, claiming that the causes of behavior were not in the depths of the mind but in the environment, first in the learning histories, then in the more proximal stimuli that elicited, shaped, reinforced, and punished certain responses. The explanation, in other words, lay in **learning**, the process whereby behavior changes in response to the environment.

Actually, psychological theorists, including psychodynamic thinkers, had long recognized the influence of learning on human character. But it was not until the early twentieth century that scientists began to uncover the actual mechanisms of learning, thereby laying the theoretical foundation for behaviorism. Especially crucial were the contributions of four scientists: Ivan Pavlov, John B. Watson, Edward Lee Thorndike, and, most important, B. F. Skinner.

Pavlov: The Conditioned Reflex   In conducting research with dogs, Ivan Pavlov (1849–1936), a Russian neurophysiologist, found that, if he consistently sounded a tone at the same time that he gave a dog food, the dog would eventually salivate to the sound of the tone alone. Thus, Pavlov discovered a basic mechanism of learning, the **conditioned reflex:** if a neutral stimulus (e.g., the tone) is paired with a nonneutral stimulus (e.g., the food), the organism will eventually respond to the neutral stimulus as it does to the nonneutral stimulus.

The implications of this discovery were revolutionary. Whereas it had always been assumed that human beings' reactions to their environment were the result of complicated subjective processes, Pavlov's finding raised the possibility that many of our responses, like those of the dogs, were the result of a simple learning process. In other words, our loves and hates, our tastes and distastes might be the consequences of nothing more mysterious than a conditioning process whereby various things in our environment became "linked" to other things to which we responded instinctively, such as food, warmth, and pain. Along with this different view of psychology came the possibility of testing such processes empirically, under controlled conditions.

Watson: The Founding of Behaviorism It is John B. Watson (1878–1958), an American psychologist, who is credited with founding the behavioral movement. This is not because Watson made major contributions to the theory of behaviorism but, rather, because he publicized a method for studying behavior and made it the battle cry for a new school of psychology aggressively opposed to subjective approaches.

In a now-famous article, "Psychology as the Behaviorist Views It," Watson (1913) made his position clear: "Psychology, as the behaviorist views it, is a purely objective, experimental branch of natural science which needs introspection as little as do the sciences of chemistry and physics" (p. 176). Watson argued that introspection was, if anything, the province of theology. The province of psychology was behavior—observable and measurable responses to specific stimuli. And the goal of psychology was the prediction and control of behavior.

Watson supported his rejection of the introspection method by demonstrating, in a classic experiment, that a supposedly subjective emotion such as fear could, like the salivation response of Pavlov's dogs, result from a simple, objective conditioning process. With the help of a colleague, Rosalie Rayner, Watson conditioned a fear of rats in an 11-month-old boy, Albert B. (Watson & Rayner, 1920). Before the experiment, Albert had no fear of the tame laboratory rats. On the first day of the experiment, the boy

was shown a white rat. Watson then struck an iron bar with a hammer, producing a very loud noise. The first time this happened, Albert was simply startled. As it happened again and again, he began to show signs of fright—crying, falling over, and crawling away from the rat. After 7 pairings of the rat and the noise, Albert showed these reactions in response to the rat alone, without the noise. Thus, a conditioned fear reaction had been established. Later tests showed that, without further conditioning, Albert produced these sorts of behaviors in response to a variety of stimuli similar to the rat: a rabbit, a dog, a sealskin coat, and a bearded Santa Claus mask. Commenting on these results, Watson argued that many of our "unreasonable" fears are established in the same way that Albert's was—through conditioning.

Thorndike: The Law of Effect Another psychologist of Watson's time was Edward Lee Thorndike (1874–1949), whose early experiments with animals had a decisive influence on learning theory. Unlike Pavlov and Watson, who had studied the relationships between behavior and the stimuli that preceded it, Thorndike was interested in the relationship between behavior and its *consequences*. If an organism is repeatedly presented with a pleasant or painful stimulus after making a given response, how will this affect the response?

In one experiment, Thorndike placed a hungry cat in a box equipped in such a way that, if the cat pulled a cord or pressed a lever, the door of the chamber flew open. When the cat escaped, it was given a piece of salmon to eat. In early trials, the cat often took a long time to get out of the box. Gradually, however, the escape time grew shorter and shorter until finally

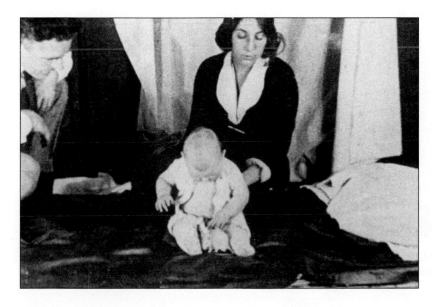

To support his claim that psychology is an objective science, John B. Watson and his colleague Rosalie Rayner conducted an experiment to condition "Little Albert" to fear rats. Watson's experiment is considered unethical by today's standards.

the cat was no sooner placed in the box than it exited and collected its reward. Thorndike concluded that the reason the cat learned the proper escape response was that this response had become associated with the food, which was the consequence of escaping. From this conclusion, Thorndike formulated what he called the **law of effect**, which states that responses that lead to "satisfying" consequences are strengthened and, therefore, are likely to be repeated, whereas responses that lead to "unsatisfying" consequences are weakened and, therefore, are unlikely to be repeated.

Though Thorndike used objective methods in his experiments, Watson did not consider him a behaviorist, for he used subjective terms such as *satisfying* and *unsatisfying* to describe his observations. For the early behaviorists, all references to inferred mental states were unscientific and, therefore, to be avoided, yet, despite its subjective wording, Thorndike's law of effect had laid down another fundamental principle of learning: the importance of reward in the learning process.

Skinner: Radical Behaviorism   Following the pioneering discoveries of Pavlov and Thorndike, many prominent psychologists—including Edwin Guthrie, Edward Chase Tolman, Clark Hull, and B. F. Skinner—contributed to the development of learning theory. Of these, the one who has had the most decisive influence on the behavioral perspective was B. F. Skinner (1904–1990).

Skinner created a version of behaviorism that was revolutionary in its implications and applicable to

B. F. Skinner, the founder of radical behaviorism, extended earlier behavioral theories and demonstrated their applicability to everyday life.

everyday life. First, he broadened behaviorism. Watson had declared that psychologists should study only what they could observe. Skinner referred to this as "methodological behaviorism" and set out to expand it. In his approach, which he called **radical behaviorism,** everything a person does, says, and feels constitutes behavior and, even if unobservable, can be subjected to experimental analysis. The skin, he said, was an arbitrary boundary. Whether behavior was public or private, it was still of interest to psychology.

Second, Skinner insisted on the practical applications of experimental analysis. He took Thorndike's law of effect and developed a method for predicting and influencing human behavior that focused on *environmental contingencies*. He demonstrated that our social environment is filled with reinforcing and punishing consequences, which mold our behavior as surely as the piece of salmon molded the behavior of Thorndike's cat (Skinner, 1965). Our friends and families influence us with their approval or disapproval. Our jobs influence us by offering or withholding money. Our schools influence us by passing us or failing us, thus affecting our access to jobs. Skinner stated outright what Pavlov had merely suggested: much of our behavior is based not on hypothetical processes occurring beneath the skin but on external contingencies. Furthermore, precisely because they *are* external, these contingencies can be altered to change our behavior. As we will see, this is a fundamental principle of behavioral treatment in abnormal psychology.

The Assumptions of Behavioral Psychology

Before we go on to discuss the mechanisms of learning, we will review the basic assumptions of behaviorism as it developed in the hands of the scientists whose work we just discussed.

The first assumption is that the task of psychology is, as Watson claimed, the study of behavior—the study of the responses that an organism makes to its learning history, to the aggregate of experiences that it has been subjected to throughout its life. Such experiences may be imposed from the outside, by the people, objects, and events in the organism's environment. They can also be internal, such as back pain, which may elicit the response of taking a pill. Likewise, responses may be external (e.g., pounding a table in anger) or internal (e.g., thinking "I'm not going to show her I'm angry").

A second basic assumption has to do with methodology. According to methodological behaviorism, both stimuli and responses are objective, empirical events that can be observed and measured and that *must* be observed and measured in order to qualify as scientific evidence. Hence, behavioral studies since Pavlov's time have always attempted to include careful measurement of responses. As we just saw, Skinner redefined behavioral study as including nonobservable events. But, regardless of whether a behavior was observable or not, its causes were to be found through an analysis of context, of events external to the organism.

A third assumption, formulated by Watson, is that the goal of psychology is the prediction and control of behavior. For behaviorists working in a laboratory, where they can set up and manipulate environmental circumstances, prediction and control are relatively easy to obtain. But, when the behaviorist moves out of the laboratory into the world at large, these goals become more elusive. The environmental stimuli of everyday life are infinitely more varied, complex, and uncontrollable than those of the laboratory, and individuals, even when studied under controlled conditions, have genetic constraints and learning histories that limit the influence of the scientist. The challenge of studying human beings, and especially of changing their behavior, tests the creativity of even the most well-trained behaviorists. As we will see, the behavior analyst often has to infer rather than directly observe causal relationships and must rely on empirical tests that are far less precise than Skinner's experimental analysis of behavior. Finally, there are ethical considerations. (Most behaviorists today would consider Watson's experiment with Albert B. to be out of ethical bounds.) Still, for behavioral psychologists, the objectives are to predict and influence behavior.

The final basic assumption of contemporary behaviorism is that the place to look for the real causes of behavior, at least those that are not genetically determined, is outside rather than inside the organism. Predictors of behavior that lie within the organism are not held to be causes; rather, they are the mechanisms by which the environment exerts its effects. This assumption is an article of faith. Thus, contemporary behaviorism is really less a theory than a method, one that makes possible the experimental analysis of behavior. That analysis is stated in terms of the mechanisms of learning, to which we will now turn.

The Basic Mechanisms of Learning

Respondent Conditioning According to behaviorists, all behavior that is not genetically determined is a function of either respondent or operant conditioning. *Unconditioned* responses are innate reflexes, such as blinking and salivation, that occur automatically when elicited by certain stimuli. It is possible, however, through the pairing of stimuli, to condition people to respond reflexively to an initially neutral stimulus, one that would not naturally have elicited the response. The learning of such a conditioned response is what is commonly referred to as **respondent conditioning** (or *classical conditioning*). An excellent example is one we discussed previously: Pavlov's dog experiment. Because a hungry dog salivates naturally —that is, without conditioning—when presented with food, the food is designated as an **unconditioned stimulus** (UCS) and the natural response of salivation as the **unconditioned response** (UCR). And, because the dog's salivation to the tone was the result of conditioning, the tone is called the **conditioned stimulus** (CS) and the salivation to the tone alone, without the food, the **conditioned response** (CR).

As we proceed up the evolutionary scale from animals to humans, classical conditioning plays less of a role. Even in humans, however, many behaviors can be attributed to classical conditioning. For example, adolescent and adult humans respond reflexively to erotic stimulation with sexual arousal. However, through the pairing of erotic and neutral stimuli, humans can learn to become sexually aroused by stimuli that would otherwise have posed no erotic potential. Verbal references to sex are one example. This makes the study of sexual behavior complicated, because everyone has a different learning history. One person's sexual fantasy may be another person's basis for disgust.

Operant Conditioning In respondent behavior, the organism responds passively to the environment; in operant behavior, as the name suggests, the organism *does* something, because in the past that action was associated either with desirable outcomes or with the avoidance of undesirable outcomes. Unlike respondent behavior, however, all operant behavior is the result of conditioning. In **operant conditioning** (also called *instrumental conditioning*), the likelihood of a response is increased or decreased by virtues of its consequences. Having taken a certain action, the individual learns to associate that action with certain consequences. This association between action and consequence is called a **contingency,** and it will direct the individual's behavior in the future: the person will repeat the behavior, or cease to engage in it, in order to obtain or avoid the consequence. This, of course, is Thorndike's law of effect, and a good example is Thorndike's cat. Human beings, like the cat, learn to do things as a function of their consequences.

Were it not for the salmon, Thorndike's cat would not have learned to press the lever. Were it not for the paycheck, some people would not go to work. Operant conditioning depends on **reinforcement,** the process by which events in the environment increase the probability of the behavior that preceded it. As Skinner pointed out, the world is full of reinforcers. The simplest type, the primary **reinforcer,** is one to which we respond instinctively, without learning, under the right conditions—for example, food (when we are hungry), water (when we are thirsty), warmth (when we are cold), and sex (when we are aroused). Most of the reinforcers to which we respond, however, are not simple primary reinforcers but, rather, conditioned **reinforcers** (also called *secondary reinforcers*), stimuli to which we have learned to respond through their association with primary reinforcers. Money is a good example of a conditioned reinforcer. We respond to it positively not because we have an instinctive liking for green pieces of paper printed with symbols but because those pieces of paper are associated with past reinforcers and signal the future delivery of further reinforcers.

Environmental contingencies operate on behavior in four basic ways. In positive reinforcement, a response followed by a consequence in the environment results in a strengthening of the response. Suppose a child dresses herself for school for the first time. Her parents praise her, and, following this praise, she dresses herself the next morning. Let us further suppose that later the praise stops, and the child stops dressing herself. It appears that the praise is functioning as a positive reinforcer. The evidence would be even stronger if a reinstitution of praise were to result in a resumption of self-dressing.

A second type of reinforcement process is **negative reinforcement.** In this case, the response is strengthened by *the avoidance or removal of an aversive stimulus.* (Negative reinforcement should not be confused with punishment, the suppression of a response through the presentation of an aversive stimulus. This mechanism will be discussed shortly.) To understand negative reinforcement, let us imagine that a student fails to study for an exam and, consequently, receives an *F.* If he then studies for the next exam, avoids an *F,* and then goes on studying for exams in the future, it appears that receiving an *F* constituted a negative reinforcer.

This process, also called *escape or avoidance learning,* can teach us some very useful behaviors, as in the example just cited. However, behaviorists feel that it may also be responsible for many patterns of abnormal behavior. For example, a little boy who is bitten by a dog may develop a dog phobia, a fear of all dogs. From that point on, he may simply run the other way whenever he sees a dog, and, every time he flees, the avoidance of being bitten will reinforce the running away. As a result, the dog phobia will be maintained indefinitely, because the boy never has a safe, happy experience with a dog to counteract the phobia.

Whereas reinforcement involves the strengthening of behavior, **punishment** describes the suppression of behavior. Typically, punishment is a process whereby behavior decreases in frequency following aversive consequences. For example, when we scold a child for hitting another child, we are hoping that scolding will function as a punisher. If the child subsequently hits less frequently, we have probably succeeded in finding an effective punisher.

Negative reinforcement and punishment are sometimes confused, for a number of reasons. First, similar consequences do not have similar effects on all people. For example, we think of scolding as a punishment, and, when we scold a child for aggressive behavior, we would expect the aggression to decrease. But, in some families, parental scolding actually results in *increased* aggression, a phenomenon called the *negative spiral* (Patterson, 1982). Thus, while the parent is trying to punish the child, the child is actually reinforced by the scolding. Another reason for confusion between the categories is that people find it hard to think of reinforcement as negative, so they just call "pleasant" situations reinforcement and "unpleasant" situations punishment. Keep in mind that behaviorists avoid defining reinforcers and punishers according to their apparent rewarding or punishing properties. Instead, reinforcers and punishers are determined empirically, by observing how they function in strengthening or weakening behavior. Reinforcement increases the likelihood of a response; punishment decreases the likelihood of a response.

The process of identifying reinforcing and punishing consequences is what behaviorists call *functional analysis.* Functional analysis is the primary method for determining which variables control behavior. If the behavior systematically varies according to your presenting and withholding certain consequences, you are demonstrating a functional relationship between the two. Such demonstrations are the hallmark of a behavior analysis.

Other Mechanisms Associated with Learning

In addition to defining respondent and operant conditioning, psychologists have identified a number of other mechanisms associated with learning. These mechanisms identify some of the processes involved in learning, help to explain its scope and complexity, and delineate the conditions under which it occurs.

Extinction One of the most important of these mechanisms is extinction, the elimination of a response by withdrawing whatever reinforcer was maintaining it. In respondent conditioning, as we saw, a CS comes to be paired with a UCS, creating a

CR. By the same token, the CR will extinguish if the CS is repeatedly presented *without* the UCS. Take, for example, the case of the dog-phobic child. Just as his fear was created by the pairing of the dog (CS) with the bite (UCS), so it will dissipate if he repeatedly encounters dogs that don't bite. (And that is how dog phobias are treated by behavioral therapists. The trick is to get the phobic person to play with friendly dogs so that extinction can take place.) As for operant behaviors, extinction simply requires the removal of the reinforcement that is maintaining the response. Such a process is probably involved in the normal child's gradual abandonment of infantile behaviors. Because parental attention often reinforces temper tantrums, the ending of attention during a tantrum often leads to extinction.

Generalization   Another important aspect of learning is generalization, whereby, once an organism has learned to respond in a certain way to a particular stimulus, it will respond in the same way to similar stimuli without further conditioning. In other words, the conditioned response automatically "spreads," or generalizes, to things that resemble the conditioned stimulus. Once again, we have already seen an example: Albert B's spontaneous fear of rabbits, dogs, seal-skin coats, and bearded Santa Claus masks once he was conditioned to fear the white rat.

Discrimination   The opposite side of the coin from generalization is discrimination—that is, learning to distinguish among similar stimuli and to respond only to the appropriate one. Pavlov, for instance, found at first that a number of different tones, close in frequency, elicited his dogs' salivation response; however, when only one of those tones was consistently accompanied by food, the dogs learned to salivate to that tone only. Likewise, people learn to discriminate between similar environmental events—between a friendly smile and a malicious grin—when one has reinforcing consequences and the other does not.

Discrimination learning helps to explain complex learning in humans. A *discriminative stimulus* is a cue telling the individual that a particular response is likely to be reinforced. For example, at a high school dance, if Jim asks Pam for her phone number, the social norms at this high school might suggest that Jim finds Pam attractive. To the extent that "being found attractive" is a reinforcer, and to the extent that Pam has similar feelings about Jim, the request for the phone number functions as a discriminative stimulus for the response of providing the phone number, a response likely to be reinforced by a subsequent phone call from Jim. However, the same request, made by Frank, does not function as a discriminative stimulus for the same response. Why? Because, for whatever reason, Pam does not give her phone number to Frank. She may not find him attractive, or she may have heard things about him that make her wary of him.

In functional analysis, discriminative stimuli form an important piece of the puzzle. They can be narrow and discrete, as in the request for the phone number, or they can be broad and all-encompassing. For example, the entire learning history of an individual can be considered a discriminative stimulus. At any rate, the addition of the discriminative stimulus to the description of contingency generates a **three-term contingency**: under certain conditions (e.g., certain learning histories, certain situations, all viewed as discriminative stimuli), certain responses are likely to be met with certain consequences (reinforcement, punishment, etc.) The addition of the discriminative stimulus complicates the relationship between behavior and its consequences, but all three terms are necessary for a complete behavior analysis.

Shaping   A process critical to operant conditioning is shaping, the reinforcement of *successive approximations* of a desired response until it finally achieves the desired form. Shaping is involved in the development of many of our skills. Imagine a child learning to dive. First, she sits on the edge of the pool, puts her head down, and just falls into the water. For this first step, she receives a pat on the back (positive reinforcement) from the swimming teacher, and she may be further reinforced by the experience of successfully executing the act. Then she may start from a standing position and even hazard a little push as she takes off. This effort will be reinforced by further approval from the teacher, by the pleasure of a smoother descent into the water, and by her own feelings of achievement. Soon she will be ready for the diving board and then for fancier dives, with external and internal rewards at every step of the way. Thus, throughout the process there is positive reinforcement of successive approximations of the diving response.

Learning to Follow Rules: Instructions as Discriminative Stimuli   Actually, it is unlikely that a swimming teacher would ask a child to learn by trial-and-error. Instead, the teacher would dive into the pool to show the child the proper technique and would then reward her with approval for imitating the performance. This type of learning—learning through imitation—is known as modeling (Bandura & Walters, 1963; Rosenthal & Bandura, 1978). Modeling is a common example of learning by exposure to **rules** or instructions. When behavior is governed by rules, following the rule is the behavior that is reinforced. Instructions are a type of rule. Modeling is a common form of instruction.

Modeling, like other rule-governed behavior, can occur without reinforcement. By watching his father use woodworking tools, this boy in the Philippines develops his own skills.

As in the diving lesson, so it is in human development in general, rules normally accompany shaping—that is, we are rewarded for successive approximations of a response that conforms to the rule. But the converse is not necessarily true. Many children get no pats on the back as they are learning how to dive; they simply watch someone else do it, and suddenly they, too, are doing it. Thus, learning can occur without verbal specification of rules. A striking characteristic of rule-governed behavior is that, unlike many other forms of learning, it can—and often does—occur without any obvious external reinforcement (Hayes, 1989). Rules and instructions add to the child's learning history and provide a wealth of discriminative stimuli. They send signals to the child that certain responses are likely to be reinforced.

A summary of the various learning mechanisms can be found in the box on page 129.

Abnormal Behavior as a Product of Learning

In the behavioral view, personality development is the result of the interaction between our genetic endowment and the types of experiences we are exposed to in living our lives. And, according to the behaviorists, this is as true of abnormal development as it is of normal development. We have already seen how a dog phobia could develop through respondent conditioning and be maintained through negative reinforcement. Similarly, depression may be due in part to extinction: if significant positive reinforcements are withdrawn—a job lost, a marriage ended—many of a person's behaviors simply extinguish, and he or she becomes inactive, withdrawn, dejected, and depressed.

Contemporary, or radical, behaviorism emphasizes the importance of the three-term contingency and de-emphasizes the simple connection between stimulus and response. The extinction theory of depression, for example, arose in the 1970s, with P. M. Lewinsohn as its leading proponent. Today Lewinsohn claims that extinction theory is no longer sufficient to account for depression. Instead, he and his colleagues have put forth a vicious-cycle theory involving many components, with stress leading to a disruption of ordinary behavior patterns, leading to reduced positive reinforcement (extinction theory), leading to increased self-awareness and self-criticism (cognitive processing), leading to feelings of hopelessness, leading to self-defeating behaviors that occasion further stress, thus taking the person through the cycle again (Lewinsohn, Hoberman, Teri, et al., 1985). Such explanations, favoring complexity over simplicity and attempting to incorporate all recent experimental findings, represent the coming of age of behavioral accounts of abnormal behavior. A radical behaviorist would emphasize each phase of the cycle as adding to the life experience and learning history of the depressive. Nevertheless, the causal emphasis would remain on external circumstances. The internal experiences in this cycle—for example, the feelings of hopelessness—would be considered part of the depressive response rather than a separate component in the causal chain.

With more complex, radical behavioral views, the emphasis has been increasingly on the entire life history of the individual, rather than simply on proximal causes. As a corollary, behaviorists avoid terms such as *normal* and *abnormal,* because these words imply an absolute distinction between something

	DEFINITION	EXAMPLE
RESPONDENT CONDITIONING	Pairing a neutral stimulus with a nonneutral stimulus until the organism learns to respond to the neutral stimulus as it would to the nonneutral stimulus	A child who has seen a taxicab strike a pedestrian learns to fear all taxis.
OPERANT CONDITIONING	Rewarding or punishing a certain response until the organism learns to repeat or avoid that response in anticipation of the positive or negative consequences	See specific examples below.
Positive Reinforcement	Increasing the frequency of a behavior by rewarding it with consequences the organism wishes to obtain	Students praised by parents for studying study more and do better in school. AA programs reward alcoholics with praise, hugs, and certificates when they meet sobriety goals.
Negative Reinforcement	Increasing the frequency of a behavior by removing a stimulus the organism wishes to avoid	A claustrophobic person goes on taking the stairs rather than the elevator, because he thereby avoids anxiety.
Punishment	Decreasing the frequency of a behavior by offering a consequence the organism wishes to avoid	A child molester, in treatment, views pictures of naked children, becomes aroused, then inhales ammonia and learns not to be aroused by this stimulus.
EXTINCTION	Decreasing the frequency of a behavior by unpairing UCS and CS or behavior and reinforcement	A teacher decides to ignore an autistic child's disruptions in class, and the disruptions decrease.
GENERALIZATION	Spontaneously transferring a conditioned response from the conditioned stimulus to similar stimuli	A woman, after having been raped, begins to fear all men.
DISCRIMINATION	Learning to confine a response only to particular stimuli	In therapy, a hopeless depressed person learns to distinguish situations that can be changed from situations that cannot.
SHAPING	Reinforcing successive approximations of a desired response until that response is gradually achieved	A mentally retarded person is taught to make his bed by being praised first for pulling up the sheets and smoothing them down, then for pulling up the covers and smoothing them down, then for tucking them in.
RULE-GOVERNED BEHAVIOR	Learning by following instructions	A person with a phobia for heights watches a model climb a fire escape and gradually learns to climb one herself.

healthy and something sick. In the behavioral view, there are no absolutes; behavior is defined within its context. The behaviorists also see all responses as united by the same principles of learning. At one end of the continuum we can, indeed, identify responses that make it difficult for people to conduct their lives successfully, but these responses do not differ qualitatively from more adaptive responses. Depressive behavior, as we just saw, may develop through the same mechanisms as any other category of behavior. Hence, behaviorists prefer to speak of "maladaptive" rather than "abnormal" behavior.

Likewise, behaviorists have traditionally been skeptical of the usefulness of labeling people according to diagnostic categories (e.g., phobia, schizophrenia, paranoia), because these categories, with their resemblance to medical diagnoses (e.g., pneumonia, cancer), seem to imply the medical model. That is, they suggest disease states—a suggestion that runs directly counter to the behaviorists' belief in the continuity of normal and abnormal. Furthermore, diagnostic categories group people based on similarities in form. For example, all those with similar depressive symptoms are called "depressed." However, to behaviorists, similar behaviors can serve a variety of functions, and one cannot assume that depressive behavior serves the same function for all people exhibiting it. Therefore, diagnostic labeling violates a basic tenet of behavior analysis: that the function of behavior, not the form, is the basis for prediction and influence. To the behaviorists, what is needed is not to put diagnostic labels on people but simply to specify as clearly as possible what the maladaptive behavior is, what contingencies may be setting the stage for and maintaining it, and how these contingencies may be rearranged in order to alter it (Hersen & Turner, 1984; Widiger & Costa, 1994).

In applying this sort of analysis to psychological abnormalities, the behaviorists do not claim that all such abnormalities are the result of learning alone, but only that learning may be an important contribution and that, *whatever the initial cause*, relearning may help to alter the behavior. For example, no one would claim that the basic cause of mental retardation is faulty learning, yet many mentally retarded people have been greatly helped by behavior therapies.

The Behavioral Approach to Therapy

One major influence of the behavioral perspective has been in the area of treatment. Behavior therapy attempts to alter abnormal behavior by making use of the same processes that presumably operate to produce normal behavior—reinforcement, punishment, extinction, discrimination, generalization, rules, and so forth.

Respondent Conditioning and Extinction Behavior therapy's respondent-conditioning techniques are aimed at changing how we feel—the degree to which we like, dislike, or fear certain aspects of the environment. All human beings, every day of their lives, are subject to respondent conditioning, sometimes with unfortunate results, so that they develop fears and desires that interfere with their functioning. When this happens, the maladaptive response can be therapeutically unlearned, either by removing the stimuli that reinforce it (extinction) or by pairing with incompatible positive or negative stimuli. Among the many techniques that employ these principles, we will describe two: systematic desensitization and exposure.

Systematic Desensitization First named and developed as a formal treatment procedure by Joseph Wolpe (1958), **systematic desensitization** is based on the premise that, if a response antagonistic to anxiety (such as relaxation) can be made to occur in the presence of anxiety-provoking stimuli, the bond between these stimuli and anxiety will be weakened and the anxiety will extinguish. Systematic desensitization involves three steps. In the first step, the client is given relaxation training. In the second step, therapist and client construct a **hierarchy of fears**—that is, a list of anxiety-producing situations in order of their increasing horror to the client. The following, for example, is the hierarchy of fears (in this case going from most to least frightening) established for a patient who was plagued by fears of dying (Wolpe & Wolpe, 1981, p. 54):

1. Seeing a dead man in a coffin
2. Being at a burial
3. Seeing a burial assemblage from a distance
4. Reading the obituary notice of a young person who died of a heart attack
5. Driving past a cemetery (the nearer, the worse)
6. Seeing a funeral (the nearer, the worse)
7. Passing a funeral home (the nearer, the worse)
8. Reading the obituary notice of an old person

THE FAR SIDE By GARY LARSON

"Now relax. . . . Just like last week, I'm going to hold the cape up for the count of 10. . . . When you start getting angry, I'll put it down."

9. Being inside a hospital
10. Seeing a hospital
11. Seeing an ambulance

Once the relaxation response and the hierarchy of fears have both been established, then the two can be combined in the third step, the actual desensitization. In some cases, the desensitization is conducted *in vivo*—that is, the client practices relaxing while actually confronting the feared stimuli in the flesh. Most desensitization, however, takes place in the consulting office and relies on imagery. Clients are asked to relax and then to imagine themselves experiencing, one by one, the anxiety-producing stimuli listed in their hierarchies, starting with the least frightening and moving upward. When the client arrives at an item that undoes the relaxation response, he or she is asked to stop imagining the scene, rest, reestablish the relaxation, and then try the scene again. (If this doesn't work, intermediate scenes may have to be inserted into the hierarchy.) Depending on the severity of the problem, treatment generally takes 10 to 30 sessions (Wolpe, 1976), with a few in vivo sessions at the end to make sure that the relaxation response carries over from the imagined situation to the real one. Systematic desensitization has proved effective with a wide variety of problems, notably phobias, recurrent nightmares, and complex interpersonal problems involving various fears—of social and sexual intimacy, aggressive behavior, social disapproval, rejection, and authority figures (e.g., Kazdin & Wilson, 1978).

Exposure   Despite its successes, systematic desensitization has now been largely replaced by exposure, which is simpler and apparently just as effective (Barlow, 1991). **Exposure** is similar to systematic desensitization, except that the relaxation training is eliminated. Patients are simply confronted with the experiences they fear, but in the absence of reinforcement, so that the maladaptive response (anxiety, avoidance) can extinguish. In the original, "cold-turkey" version of exposure, called *flooding*, the patient undergoes a prolonged confrontation with the feared stimulus—or, if that is not possible, with vivid representations of it—in a situation that does not permit avoidance (Levis, 1985). This technique was found to be particularly useful in the elimination of obsessive-compulsive rituals (Rachman & Hodgson, 1980). As we will see in Chapter 6, obsessive-compulsive rituals usually have to do with one of two themes: contamination and checking. When the fear is contamination, flooding involves having clients actually "contaminate" themselves by touching and handling dirt or whatever substance they are trying to avoid. This ordeal is combined with *response prevention*: the clients are forbidden to carry out their anxi-

ety-alleviating rituals (in this case, usually hand washing). The hoped-for result is that they will realize that the thing they fear actually poses no real threat. Flooding with response prevention apparently works well with anxiety-related disorders, but it is hard for patients to tolerate (Gelder, 1991). Today, instead of flooding, most behavior therapists use *graded exposure*. As in systematic desensitization, the client confronts the feared stimulus gradually, in steps. For example, people with dog phobias first watch videos of dogs, then enter a room where there is a caged dog, then stand in front of the cage, and so on, until, with the extinction of the fear, they are petting the dog.

Operant Conditioning   Operant conditioning, as we have seen, is learning via consequences. Under certain stimulus conditions, we produce a certain response, and the fact that this response is followed by positive or negative consequences provides an incentive for us to repeat or avoid that same response when next we are faced with the same stimulus conditions. Operant behavior, then, has three components: (1) the learning history, discriminative stimulus, or cue for a certain response, (2) the response, and (3) the consequences. Behavior therapists have found that, by altering any of these components, they can change maladaptive patterns of behavior.

The manipulation of the consequences of a response in order to change the frequency of that response is called **contingency management**. An interesting example involved 40 participants in a 6-month behavioral program for cocaine dependence (Higgins, Delaney, Budney, et al., 1991). All the participants had to have their urine tested for cocaine traces 3 times a week. After the test, half simply received their test results. The other half received rewards as well as results: every time their urine was "clean," they were given a voucher they could use to buy articles in local stores. For the first 3 months, the vouchers increased in value with each consecutive clean test. In the second 3 months, the vouchers were replaced by state lottery tickets. Both rewards worked very well. In the rewards group, 75 percent of the participants completed the whole 6-month program, as compared with 40 percent of the no-rewards group. Furthermore, the average length of continuous cocaine abstinence, as documented by the urine tests, was twice as long for the rewards group as for the no-rewards group. Clearly, behavior can be changed by managing its contingencies.

Multicomponent Treatment   Most forms of behavior therapy are administered as part of multicomponent treatment. A psychological disorder typically has many facets, and, as the person comes to live with the disorder, it develops more facets. Problem drinkers, for example, do not just have problems with drinking. Whether as a cause or a result of the drinking, they have problems with their marriages, their children, their jobs, their social skills, their expectations, and their self-esteem. The best treatments for substance dependence address all these difficulties, via different techniques. In the voucher program for cocaine abusers that we just described, the vouchers worked well, but their primary purpose was simply to keep the participants in the program, where, at the same time, they were receiving relationship counseling, instructions on avoiding cues for drug use, various kinds of skills training (drug refusal, problem solving, assertiveness), employment counseling, and help in developing new recreational activities. In such programs, the hope is that each kind of therapeutic change will bolster the others and, thus, in a holistic fashion, free the person from the disorder.

The New Radical Behavioral Therapies: Integrating Acceptance with Change   Over the past 15 years, radical and other behavior therapists have begun to emphasize "acceptance" as well as change, particularly in treating behavior disorders. In some cases, the approach is "integrative," combining behavioral principles with various philosophical perspectives. In other cases, the basis is simply radical behaviorism. But what unites these approaches is recognition of the limits of direct attempts to change. These therapists show their patients that in many cases the harder you try to alter a behavior, the more entrenched it becomes. The key to change, they suggest, may be letting go of the goal of change. But, all the while that they are initiating patients into this supposedly fatalist truth, they are also creating conditions that expose the patients to new, reinforcing contingencies, which may, in fact, generate change.

Perhaps the first acceptance-based version of behavior therapy was *dialectical behavior therapy (DBT),* developed by Marsha Linehan (1992) to treat borderline personality disorder (Chapter 10) and suicidal behavior. DBT integrates behavioral principles with Eastern religion and philosophy. It places a heavy emphasis on validation (i.e., acceptance) of the person and combines a variety of validation-fostering techniques with the traditional behavioral skills training.

The acceptance-based interventions have become popular alternatives to traditional behavior therapy in the past decade (Hayes, Jacobson, Follette, et al., 1994), and their influence is growing. It remains to be seen whether or not they will deliver on all they have promised.

Behavior Therapy: Pros and Cons   A commonly voiced criticism of behavior therapy is that it is superficial.

Because it does not dwell on the patient's past and does not have insight as a primary goal, it seems shallow to those who feel that therapy should lead to greater self-acceptance and self-understanding. This is a criticism that does not apply to the new acceptance-based treatments: some of these treatments place as much importance on the patient's past as do psychodynamic theories (Hayes, 1987; Hayes, Jacobson, Follette, et al., 1994; Jacobson & Christensen, 1996; Kohlenberg & Tsai, 1992). But, as noted, the results of the acceptance-based treatments are not yet in. In the meantime, the criticism does apply to traditional behavior therapy. Though early behavior therapists might have believed in the value of self-understanding, they felt it was too vague and grandiose an ideal to serve as a treatment goal. Behavior therapy aimed simply to provide people with the skills they need in order to deal more effectively with life. If this led to self-understanding, so much the better. But, if not, at least they could live a decent life.

A more serious version of the "superficiality" charge is the claim that behavior therapy can do patients harm by addressing only their symptoms and ignoring the "underlying cause." In such a case, the patient might be relieved of the symptom, only to be faced later with another and possibly worse symptom, because the underlying conflict has not been dealt with. This phenomenon, called "symptom substitution" by the critics of behavior therapy, has been largely disconfirmed. Usually, symptom relief leads to more general improvement rather than to symptom substitution (Bandura, Blanchard, & Ritter, 1969; Sloane, Staples, Cristol, et al., 1975).

Other critics of behavior therapy argue that it denies individual freedom—that behavior therapists move in and take control of the patient's behavior, manipulating it according to their own values. Actually, all psychotherapies involve some control by the therapist, whether that control is directed toward insight or reconditioning. Likewise, in all therapies, the therapist's values play an important part. Indeed, in this respect the only important difference between behavior therapy and the insight therapies is that, in the latter, the therapist's values are often implicit, whereas the clear spelling out of treatment goals in behavior therapy tends to make the therapist's values clear from the start.

How well does behavior therapy do in achieving its goal of behavior change? According to the evidence, it does quite well. Behavior therapy has a relatively good record in treating anxiety and phobias (Emmelkamp, 1994), insomnia (Lacks & Morin, 1992), obesity (Brownell & Wadden, 1992), alcohol and drug dependence (Nathan, Marlatt, & Loberg, 1978), depression (Jacobson, Dobson, Truax, et al., 1996), marital prob-

© Sidney Harris

lems (Jacobson & Addis, 1993), personality disorders (Linehan, 1992), conduct disorders (Patterson, 1982), autism (Lovaas, 1987), and other problems (Kazdin & Wilson, 1978). Aside from the fact that it often works, behavior therapy has other advantages as well. It tends to be faster and less expensive than other therapies. Its techniques can be taught to paraprofessionals and non-professionals, so therapy can be extended beyond the consulting room to hospital wards, classrooms, and homes. Finally, because behavior therapy is precise in its goals and techniques, it can be reported, discussed, and evaluated with precision.

Evaluating Behaviorism

For reasons previously outlined, behaviorists have forthrightly opposed competing theories of abnormal behavior: the medical model, the psychodynamic perspective, and even at times the cognitive perspective, which in some measure is an outgrowth of behaviorism. But these other theories are not just scientific constructs; they are outgrowths of some of our most deeply ingrained beliefs—for example, the belief that the psychologically disturbed are "different" from the rest of us (medical model) and that psychological disturbance has its roots deep in the psyche (phychodynamic theory). Hence, the disagreements between behaviorism and these other schools are not just quibbles over details. Radical behaviorism, in particular, constitutes a drastic revision of Western thought on the subject of human life. As such, it has been severely criticized.

Criticisms of Behaviorism

Oversimplification   A common objection to behavioral theory is that it constitutes a naive simplification of

human life. This criticism is based primarily on the work of early behaviorists such as Watson and Pavlov, in which human existence is reduced to small measurable units of behavior. Furthermore, critics claim that, by excluding the inner life from consideration, behaviorists have chosen to ignore all the deeper forces that distinguish human action from the behavior of experimental animals. Introspective theories sacrifice rigor for the sake of these intangibles; behaviorists, it is said, sacrifice the intangibles for the sake of rigor.

In the case of the early behaviorists, this charge has some justice, but not in the case of Skinner and his followers. The definition of behavior put forth by the radical behaviorists encompasses all of the so-called deeper workings of the mind tackled by the introspective theorists. Remember that, to the radical behaviorists, thinking and feeling are as important as overt action, and they are explainable in the same way. Contemporary behaviorists have not needed a new set of definitions and principles to explain complex human behavior, including subjective experience. They have simply made more complex use—for example, in the three-term contingency—of the principles discovered by the early behaviorists.

Determinism   The second major focus of criticism is the deterministic emphasis of behaviorism. According to behaviorists, all human behavior that is not genetically determined is the product of either respondent or operant conditioning. Thus, it is not free will but, rather, life experience that determines what we will do with our lives. Skinner (1965), for example, argued that the notion of human freedom was simply obsolete:

The free inner man who is held responsible for the behavior of the external biological organism is only a prescientific substitute for the kinds of causes which are discovered in the course of a scientific analysis. All these alternative causes lie *outside* the individual. . . . These are the things that make the individual behave as he does. For them he is not responsible, and for them it is useless to praise or blame him. (pp. 447–448)

Behaviorism does not lay the foundation for any kind of legal system, for any religious belief, or for any moral code. Law, religion, and morality have historically been based on the notion that we are capable of choosing between right and wrong, whereas, according to Skinner, whatever we do—whether we treat other people kindly or brutally, whether we behave ourselves or lie, cheat, and steal—we do these things because our evolutionary and learning histories have taught us to do them. Such ideas have been coldly received by theorists who emphasize free will and moral responsibility.

The Issue of "Control"   Finally, the word *control,* as used by the behaviorists, bothers many people, making them wonder if the behaviorists did not have some diabolical goal. Skinner, in particular, aroused fears with his descriptions of how all behavior is controlled by contingencies and his suggestion that we could lead happier lives if we would simply acknowledge these controlling variables and set about designing contingencies that would strengthen desirable behaviors. Though his proposal was that we could thereby increase ethical behavior, critics have worried that such "behavioral engineering," as they call it, could become the basis for a totalitarian regime, in which people would be coerced by reinforcement.

Actually, the term *control,* in the behavioral vocabulary, does not mean coercion. It means predictability and adherence to scientific laws, the same things that all scientists are interested in. If the behaviorists' concern with control is cause for alarm, then all psychologists should arouse the same misgivings, for all of them attempt to identify the factors that cause human beings to behave as they do. It is only because the behaviorists have focused on life circumstances—in other words, those that can be manipulated—that they have been the primary object of "mad scientist" suspicions.

It should be added that Skinner's belief in the power of the environment, exclusive of mental processes, has been a subject of endless controversy. Some believe that Skinner's beliefs have not been validated by research. The results of behavioral therapy, and particularly the high relapse rate among substance abusers (Nicolosi Molinari, Musicco, et al., 1991), have suggested to some that behavioral techniques are futile without the cooperation of the patient. Free or not, will is a critical factor in therapy, even behavioral therapy. However, to the radical behaviorists, these research findings do not invalidate the behavioral perspective. Rather, they simply suggest that, for many clinical problems, we have not yet found effective ways to influence long-standing maladaptive behavior.

The Contributions of Behaviorism   There is much that can justly be said in favor of behaviorism. In the first place, the objectivity of behavioral research is not a virtue to be slighted. A major problem with most of the other psychological perspectives is that their statements on human behavior are often vague, based more on inference than on fact, and open to the charge of bias. In contrast, the behaviorists' findings are expressed much more concisely and are based as closely as possible on actual, measurable evidence, with the result that they can easily be retested by other professionals. The value of such precision has not gone unnoticed. Most psychological research is now behavioral in method. That is, it is based on experimentation and on objective measurement. If inferred constructs are used, they are "operationalized,"—that is, defined in terms of concrete behaviors.

Second, while the behaviorists are accused of doing away with individualism, it can be argued that individualism is safer with the behaviorists than with psychologists of other schools of thought, for, unlike many other psychologists, the behaviorists recognize a broad range of responses as legitimate and are very sensitive to the adverse effects of labeling people as "abnormal."

Finally, as we saw, the treatment methods the behaviorists developed have produced some promising results, and with a wide range of disorders. In addition, substantial contributions have been made in education, business, and sports physiology through the application of behavioral principles. Such successes constitute a revolutionary achievement—one that has changed psychology forever, no matter how controversial its theories.

The success of behavior therapy has been minimized by its critics because the goals of early behavior therapy applications were relatively modest. Whereas a psychodynamic therapist might try to help patients find meaning in life or achieve self-knowledge, an early behavioral therapist would typically try to help them experience fewer panic attacks or fewer nights of insomnia—achievements that seemed small to early behaviorism's detractors. In answer, it might be said that such achievements were all that many patients wanted, and perhaps all they needed. But the limited-goals accusation has since been invalidated by the work of radical behaviorists. Their therapies take on the full range of clinical problems, including those ignored by the early behaviorists.

The Family Systems Perspective

Beginning in the 1950s, a creative group of maverick mental health professionals began to shake up the psychiatric establishment with a new and revolutionary way of looking at mental illness. The pioneers in this movement were Nathan Ackerman in New York; Jay Haley at the Mental Research Institute in Palo Alto, California, and his colleagues Donald Jackson and Virginia Satir; Murray Bowen in Washington, DC; and Lyman Wynne from the National Institute of Mental Health. Although their work began primarily in the area of schizophrenia, it quickly spread to the entire field of abnormal psychology. Today, the students and disciples of these pioneers number in the tens of thousands, and the **family systems perspective** has become a major force in the treatment of abnormal behavior.

Family Systems Theories

The founders began by formulating **family systems theories,** in which abnormal behavior is seen as the product of habitual relationship patterns, usually within the family. Like psychodynamic theories, family systems approaches recognized the importance of the family in determining the emotional well-being of each member. Like behaviorism, they looked to the context, the environment, for the causes of abnormal behavior. But family systems theory differed from other theories in that it viewed the behavior of a disturbed individual as a *reflection* of poor family functioning. Although one family member might be defined as the patient, in a sense that patient was merely a messenger, communicating to the world the problems existing in the family as a whole.

One of the earliest and most influential of the family systems approaches was *communication theory,* which posited that psychopathology results from faulty communications within the family, which can take a number of forms (Bateson, Jackson, Haley, et al., 1956; Watzlawick, Beavin, & Jackson, 1967). In *double-bind communication,* one family member presents another with a contradictory message; no matter how the other person responds, he or she is "wrong." For example, a mother may ask a child to kiss her but turn away when he tries to do so. Other patterns proposed by the communications theorists are *ambiguous messages,* in which one person makes a demand without indicating how it might be met; *hostile, runaway* exchanges, in which disagreement, instead of being negotiated, simply escalates from hostility to greater hostility, like a runaway train; and *silent schisms,* in which the family splits into factions, always engaged in an unacknowledged war.

Approaches based on communication theory focused on the role of family communication in driving other family members crazy. A variation on this theme was formulated somewhat later by Salvador Minuchin (1972, 1974). Minuchin's *structural theory* conceptualizes relationships in terms of *units,* individuals and alliances that serve some function within the group, and the *boundaries,* or psychological "fences," between them. According to Minuchin, problems within the family result from problems with its structural balance. Weak boundaries lead to "enmeshed" relationships: units that are supposed to have some distance from one another become too close, thereby disturbing their relationships with other units (see Figure 5.1). Overly rigid boundaries, on the other hand, create disengaged relationships between units, as, for example, in the "generation gap," where a wall is erected between the parents and the children.

A third major influence in family systems theory is the school of thought popularized by psychiatrist Murray Bowen (Papero, 1995). Bowen was influenced by psychoanalytic theory, but he translated psychoanalytic concepts into a family systems language. He proposed that the key to healthy functioning for a family member is the degree to which that person achieves *differentiation of self.* According to Bowen, differentiation requires the ability to *individuate* from other family members, to establish a separate identity, with the blessing of parents and children. Bowen and his followers believe that people search for partners in marriage who have achieved similar degrees of self-differentiation, and that children are generally limited in their ability to individuate by the degree of differentiation achieved by their parents.

Today, there is considerable overlap between the family systems approach and the behavioral perspective. Indeed, in the past two decades, behaviorism has spawned what might be called a family systems subschool, in which behavioral principles such as reinforcement and punishment are used to describe how marriage partners choose one another and how they construct their relationships with each other and their children (e.g., Jacobson & Christensen, 1996). Gottman (1994) has articulated a *balance theory* of marriage, whereby a certain ratio of positive to negative behaviors has to be maintained in marital exchanges in order for the couple to remain at low risk for divorce. Balance theory depends on the concept of *reciprocity,* or the tendency to respond to a partner's behavior in kind (Patterson, 1982). Many researchers have found that in happy couples each

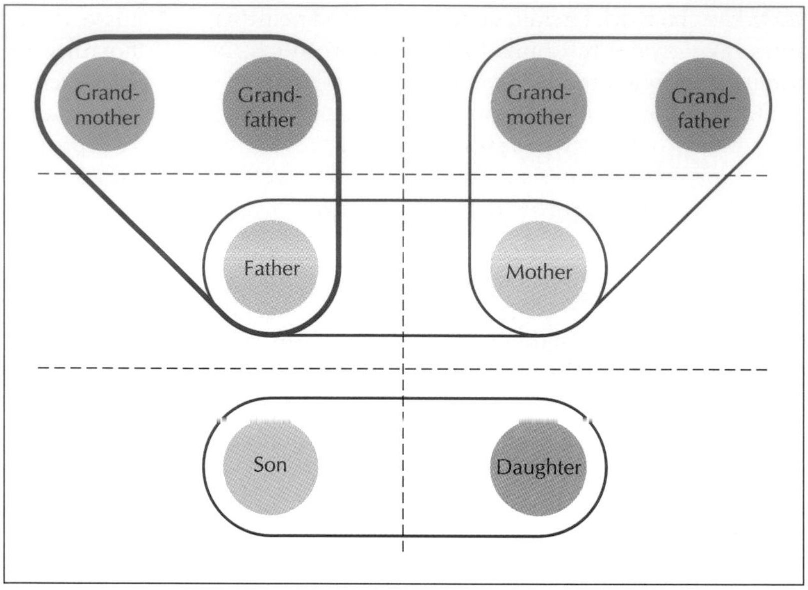

FIGURE 5.1   An "enmeshed" relationship. Minuchin's structural theory views the family in terms of units (solid lines) and boundaries (broken lines). In the family shown here, the boundary between the father and his parents has weakened, resulting in an enmeshed relationship that isolates him from the rest of the family.

partner is inclined to let negative behavior go by without the need to reciprocate in kind; in distressed couples, on the other hand, the partners are likely to respond to negative affect with negative affect of their own. Jacobson and colleagues have reported a similar phenomenon, known as *reactivity,* the tendency to respond to the immediate contingencies of the situation rather than the long-term contingencies (Jacobson, Follette, & McDonald, 1982). To explain this, Gottman (1979) uses a bank account metaphor. Imagine couples going through married life depositing positive behaviors into a bank account. The more positive deposits, the greater the reservoir of good faith; once the balance is high enough, negative behaviors do not result in a withdrawal of these deposits. But, if the deposits are low, almost any negative behavior will immediately result in a withdrawal—either reciprocal negative behavior or a decrease in positive behavior. Thus, happy couples don't exhibit as much reactivity as unhappy couples do. Another way of thinking about reactivity is that it is an operational definition of trust: the more partners trust one another, the less they need to get even. A provocation can occur without reciprocity, because the recipient has a history of mostly positive behavior, and the partners *trust* that, in the long run, positive behaviors will predominate.

Family Systems Theory and Abnormal Behavior

By the 1970s, these theories began to be applied to specific patterns of abnormal behavior. Coyne (1976b) and D. J. Kiesler (1983), for example, suggested that depression might be the product of a spi-

ral of complementary dominance and submission responses. Drawing on this work, Horowitz and Vitkus (1986) proposed the following five-step process:

1. The depressed person feels hopeless and inept.
2. The depressed person seeks reassurance from others, often through self-critical statements.
3. Others respond with complementary controlling statements (e.g., offering advice).
4. These controlling responses evoke further submissive behavior from the depressed person.
5. Others become frustrated with the depressed person's continued (or increased) negativity.

In other words, even though others may be sincerely trying to help the depressed person, they are unwittingly encouraging his or her symptoms via their complementary controlling behavior.

A number of other family variables have been linked to psychological disorders. Abnormal behavior patterns have been found to appear and disappear depending on the role the person occupies in the family (Jacobson & Christensen, 1996; Patterson, 1982; Sim & Romney, 1990; Vitkus & Horowitz, 1987). Patterson, in his *coercion theory,* has described how parents and children interact to produce adolescents with conduct disorders, through a complicated chain of events characterized by negative reinforcement. The family variable of *expressed emotion (EE),* or communications relaying criticism and overinvolvement, has proved helpful in explaining why patients hospitalized for schizophrenia and depression tend to relapse once they return home (Vaughn & Leff, 1976). The more EE from family members, the higher the risk of relapse. Finally, depression, anxiety disorders, and substance abuse have all been linked to marital problems (Jacobson, 1989).

These findings suggest that psychological problems are as much in the relationship as in the person, and that is the guiding principle of family therapy. Many family systems theorists go so far as to label the person seeking treatment as the "identified patient." In other words, he or she is merely the one who has been identified by the others as sick, whereas in truth it is the family that is "sick." At the very least, to borrow a term from Alcoholics Anonymous, the patient tends to have an "enabler," usually a parent or spouse, who, while seeming to be put upon, nevertheless helps to maintain the problem and has strong psychological reasons for doing so. Accordingly, family therapists prefer to treat the network, not the person, lest the network sabotage treatment, or, alternatively, lest someone in the network begin to suffer psychologically as the person in treatment improves. G. Greenberg (1977) cites the case of a woman who was in therapy for depression. As her symptoms lifted, her husband began phoning the therapist to complain of her worsening condition. As she continued to improve, the husband became increasingly distressed, eventually lost his job, and finally committed suicide. It would appear that, in this case, the husband's psychological well-being was dependent on his wife's continued depression.

Family and Couple Therapy

Family Therapy   Although **family therapy** originated in the 1950s, it has become popular only in the past 25 years or so. In 1962, there were only 3 professional journals devoted to family therapy; in 1990, 19 were published in the United States and 17 were published abroad (Sluzki, 1991). Family treatment is now a thriving field.

What most family therapies have in common, regardless of their theoretical orientation, is the assumption that, while one member of the family may have symptoms, the disturbance lies not merely in the symptomatic person but in the family unit as a whole. The family is seen as a system in which the whole is more than the sum of its parts.

There are a variety of approaches to family therapy. The oldest and historically the most influential is the **strategic approach** (Haley, 1976; Satir, 1967; Watzlawick, Beavin, & Jackson, 1967), which developed as an outgrowth of the double-bind theory of schizophrenia (see Chapter 13). Often, in order to shake up a faulty communication system, therapists use techniques known as *paradoxical intention* (Shoham-Salomon & Rosenthal, 1987). That is, the therapist instructs the family members to engage in whatever maladaptive pattern of behavior they are already engaging in. For example, if a father is constantly interrupting his daughter, the therapist tells the father that in the next session he is to interrupt the daughter every time she begins to speak. This approach has a way of upsetting the maladaptive pattern, and, thus forcing patients to find other, better ways of dealing with their problems.

A more widely used method today is **structural family therapy**, in which the therapist analyzes the family unit as a set of interlocking roles (Minuchin & Fishman, 1981). Like any group, family members

In family therapy, only one person may have symptoms, but the entire family is treated as a system in disarray.

create roles for one another: the disciplinarian, the scapegoat, the one who needs looking after, the one who is expected to take care of everyone else, and so on. These roles satisfy certain needs; furthermore, each member must go on enacting his or her role in order for the others to continue in their roles. Consequently, any effort on the part of an individual member to step out of an accustomed role will meet with resistance from the rest of the family. According to adherents of structural family therapy, such roles are the key to family disturbance. Indeed, some therapists contend that the reason one family member becomes "sick" is that the family role system requires a sick member (Minuchin, 1974). Structural family therapy, thus, concentrates on analyzing roles, along with the psychological purposes they serve, and on encouraging members to fashion more comfortable and flexible roles for themselves.

Other family therapies are offsprings of the major psychological perspectives. Since the mid-1980s, there has been a resurgence of psychodynamic family therapy, based on the idea that problems in current relationships are caused by unconscious impulses, defenses against them, and old expectations that need to be changed (Nichols & Schwartz, 1991). Transference relationships with the therapist are seen as revealing problems within the family or, alternatively, problems within the parents' families of origin. The techniques of psychodynamic family therapy are similar to those of individual therapy: listening and interpretation. Murray Bowen's version of family therapy (Papero, 1995) can be viewed as an extension of psychodynamic approaches, despite the different language system.

Behavioral family therapy has been primarily of two kinds. One involves training parents of conduct-disordered children to interact with their children in ways that decrease antisocial and increase prosocial acts (Miller & Prinz, 1990). In this type of therapy, parents are taught not to reinforce bad behavior by simply giving in when the child annoys them for long enough. They are also shown how to administer effective reinforcers and punishers. Such treatment are often quite successful (Kazdin, 1987). The other common form of behavioral family therapy is treatment to lower EE in the families of schizophrenic patients. This therapy, in which family members are taught how to solve problems in a calmer, less abrasive manner, significantly lowered the relapse rates of the schizophrenic patients involved (Falloon, Boyd, McGill, et al., 1982, 1985; Halford & Hayes, 1991).

Couple Therapy   Couple therapy is a growing field, not only for alleviating relationship problems and preventing divorce, but also as a primary or adjunct treatment for various forms of abnormal behavior. Troubled marriages almost invariably include communication problems. Indeed, in some cases, communication has broken down altogether. Thus, the establishment of an honest dialogue between the two partners is of top priority in most approaches to couple therapy. However, different approaches emphasize various facets of individual and relationship functioning. *Traditional behavioral couple therapy,* or *TBCT,* (Jacobson & Margolin, 1979) tries to emphasize homework assignments that increase positive behavior, in accord with Gottman's balance theory of marriage. The newer *integrative behavioral couple therapy,* or *IBCT,* (Jacobson & Christensen, 1996), in addition, tries to promote each partner's acceptance of the other. Insight-oriented couple therapy (Sharff, 1995; Wile, 1995) as-

Most approaches to couple therapy stress improving communication between partners.

sumes that if the partners can be brought to understand the "real" sources of their anger at each other, this will improve the marriage. Emotion-focused couple therapy (Johnson & Greenberg, 1995) sees marital conflict as a result of unexpressed and often unacknowledged emotion. As therapy allows for increased expression of primary emotions, the marriage is expected to become more intimate.

The most widely studied approach to couple therapy, and the only couple treatment "empirically validated" by the Division of Clinical Psychology in the American Psychological Association, is TBCT. As noted, its aim is to increase positive behavior between partners. Behavioral couple therapy began with the view that marital distress is the result of *coercion* (Patterson & Hops, 1972)—that is, the reciprocal use of aversive stimuli to influence the other person's behavior. In coercive marriages, spouses get each other to do things by means of complaints, accusations, and the like. In happy marriages, on the other hand, spouses get what they want from each other by selectively reinforcing desirable behavior with compliments, thanks, and more tangible rewards. Through the use of contingency management, communication skills training, and other techniques, TBCT teaches couples how to convert from coercion to *positive* reciprocity and how to improve their skills for solving problems and settling conflicts (Jacobson & Margolin, 1979; Jacobson & Prince, in press).

Some couple therapists have begun to adopt cognitive as well as behavioral techniques. The hope is that teaching partners communication skills may help them identify cognitive distortions in their dealings with each other. For example, a wife may find that comments she thought were neutral ("Did you pick up the things at the dry cleaner's?") are interpreted by the husband as highly critical ("Why are you always so lazy and forgetful?"). When couples are taught "expressive communication skills"—how to verbalize their feelings effectively—such misunderstandings can be brought into the open. In another borrowing from cognitive therapy, couple therapists have begun teaching partners problem-solving skills: how to identify a problem, think of possible solutions, discuss the pros and cons without emotional overreaction, and so on (Jacobson & Holzworth-Munroe, 1986). Cognitive restructuring has also been used in couple therapies, but it does not seem to increase the effectiveness of TBCT (Baucom & Epstein, 1990; Halford et al., 1993; Jacobson & Addis, 1993). In contrast, another attempt at expanding the horizon of TBCT seems to show promise in improving currently existing couple treatments. (See in the box on page 140.)

Another promising recent entry into the couple therapy arena is *emotionally focused marital therapy.*

As stated earlier, this kind of treatment aims at getting the partners to experience and express their emotions toward one another and, in particular, to tell one another what kind of relationship they truly want (Johnson & Greenberg, 1995).

Family and Couple Therapy: Pros and Cons   Couple and family therapies appear to be generally successful—more so, in some cases, than individual therapy. A thorough review of research in this area found that, out of 30 studies comparing family or couple therapy with individual or group treatment of the "identified patient," 22—or 73 percent—found couple or family therapy to be superior (Gurman & Kniskern, 1978). More recent reviews (Lebow & Gurman, 1995; Shadish, Montgomery, Wilson, et al., 1993) found that family therapy of various kinds was more effective than no treatment or other control conditions when measured by either family interactions of behavior ratings. But we need more outcome studies, especially studies comparing the effectiveness of different forms of couple and family therapy. The only approach whose results have been carefully examined is TBCT.

In view of the good showings by TBCT, the scope of this treatment is now being broadened. Prompted by evidence that depression is often related to marital warfare, some therapists have begun using TBCT when either the husband or the wife is depressed. Recent outcome studies indicate that, compared with individual therapy, this treatment can be as effective in reducing depression and more effective in reducing marital discord (Prince & Jacobson, 1995).

Evaluating the Family Systems Perspective

The family systems perspective appeals to psychodynamic theorists because, like psychodynamic theory, it emphasizes the importance of the family. However, it is also consistent with cognitive and behavioral perspectives because it focuses on environmental causation, it measures observable exchanges, and it can, therefore, be tested empirically. Therapists from most perspectives now agree that for many problems the best approach is to treat the couple or the family rather than just the "identified" patient.

Another contribution that family systems theory has made to psychotherapy in general is its analysis of the subtle and sometimes counterproductive workings of the patient-therapist relationship (Haley, 1963). Some practitioners of insight therapy, in the effort not to influence what the patient is saying, confine themselves to minimal feedback. In effect, they try to disappear. But, as interpersonal research has shown, therapists never disappear from their patients' awareness, and, when their responses are ambiguous—for

The Limitations of Change: An Acceptance-Based Approach to Couple Therapy

Most couple therapies are based on a belief that partners who have weathered many years of severe conflict and incompatibility can still make major changes in their relationship. This optimistic view has been especially prevalent among behavior therapists, who inherited Watson's faith in the power of the environment to modify behavior. To subscribe to the behavioral position, however, one need not be optimistic about the human potential for change. Radical behaviorism is silent regarding the malleability of the human organism. It simply states that, to the extent that people change, they do so because environmental contingencies have changed.

In recent years, Andrew Christensen and Neil S. Jacobson have developed a new and promising approach called integrative behavioral couple therapy, or IBCT (Jacobson & Christensen, 1996). This therapy, derived from a radical behavioral perspective, takes as its starting point the apparently pessimistic view that couples who have suffered years of destructive interactions will find it hard, if not impossible, to change their relationship. But Christensen and Jacobson substitute a new kind of optimism. They say that, if partners can learn to give up the struggle to change each other, paradoxically, many of the desired changes will emerge "spontaneously," as environmental contingencies alter and begin to support a more intimate relationship. Furthermore, through "acceptance work," areas of conflict can be turned into opportunities for intimacy. In the end, the couples are better off with those disagreements than they would be without them, or so the theory goes.

The therapeutic techniques used to foster acceptance fall into two basic categories: turning problems into strengths and tolerance. *Empathic joining* and *unified detachment* are both techniques for turning problems into strengths. In empathic joining, the effort is to change each partner's experience of the other's negative behavior from one of contempt or disgust to one of compassion and respect. For example, suppose John enters therapy convinced not only that Mary is uncommunicative, but also that she is uncommunicative because she is psychologically disturbed. Empathic joining techniques would give John opportunities to experience Mary's uncommunicativeness as just another endearing part of her and perfectly understandable, given Mary's experience with her own parents. Once John learns to love not just the parts of Mary he has always loved but even her communication difficulties, the environmental contingencies shape and reinforce her greater communicativeness.

Unified detachment serves the same purpose as empathic joining but comes at it from a different angle. In order to become more accepting of an area of conflict, partners are taught to regard the problem as an "it" rather than as something that one does to the other. In other words, they detach themselves from it and look at it together as a common enemy. In doing so, they become closer. For example, Frank had an extramarital affair. When his wife, Virginia, discovered this, she was both crushed and furious. Although Frank ended the affair and apologized, Virginia could not forgive him. Meanwhile, Frank, sensing her mistrust, found it difficult to be around her. The therapist gave Frank and Virginia the homework assignment of writing a joint letter to the third party, telling her together that the affair was over and explaining that they had decided to work together for a closer marriage. This joint effort both unified them and detached them from the shame and anger created by the betrayal.

In IBCT, turning problems into strengths is the ideal. The fall-back strategy is tolerance, whereby partners simply learn to put up with the things they came into therapy wanting to change. An example of a technique used to promote tolerance is *role-playing negative behavior.* In the therapy session, the partners practice conflictual interactions that are likely to come up in the future, thus preparing themselves for the inevitable slipups. These practice exercises are analogous to exposure techniques used in behavior therapy: they desensitize couples to the occurrence of negative behavior in the future, so that, when it does occur, it will seem simply a problem, not a catastrophe.

How effective is IBCT? In a preliminary study reported by Jacobson, Christensen, and their colleagues (1997), couples were randomly assigned either to IBCT or to TBCT. Whereas TBCT improved the marriages of 64 percent of the couples, as it typically does, IBCT was successful in 89 percent of the cases. These results must be viewed with caution, however. The sample size was small (20 couples), and it was impossible to determine the reliability of the differences between the 2 groups' results. Still, these are by far the most impressive outcomes ever reported in couple therapy research. Furthermore, at a 1-year follow-up, 30 percent of the TBCT couples had separated, whereas all the ICBT couples were still together.

This pilot study is a classic example of treatment development (Chapter 3). It showed that IBCT is promising and that therapists were able to keep IBCT and TBCT distinct. The experimenters also produced a manual for more definitive hypothesis testing (Jacobson & Christensen, 1996). As this book is being written, Jacobson and Christensen are providing a more definitive test of IBCT, with the largest sample of subjects ever used in a couple therapy clinical trial ($N = 180$), and two sites. If the preliminary findings are confirmed, this will validate the notion that acceptance is key in a happy long-term relationship. Hard as it is to teach two old dogs new tricks, it may be easier if you stop trying.

example, when they are silent—patients are likely to interpret this in a manner consistent with their symptoms (Wachtel, 1973). For example, a depressed patient thinks, "She disapproves of what I'm saying," and becomes more depressed. Such research has had its effect. As we saw in Chapter 4, psychodynamic therapy has gone through dramatic changes in the past few decades. It is now the norm for therapists to be more empathetic and responsive, less focused on that elusive goal, "objectivity," and less resistant to giving the patient explicit hope.

The family systems perspective has been criticized on three counts. First, most of its assertions have not been subjected to research. A second criticism is that family systems theory is limited in scope. Some current researchers in this area conceptualize the family or couple relationship as a factor that maintains, or even aggravates, psychological disorders, but not as the root cause, and it is partly for this reason—the modesty of its claims—that family systems theory has been so influential. However, it has yet to become a major, unified perspective. Rather, it has contributed to other, more dominant perspectives, particularly in the area of treatment, rather than taking a place alongside them. Third, although family therapy can be tested empirically, the vast majority of family therapists have little interest in proving scientifically that their techniques work. Many actually dismiss the need for research and training programs do not routinely train their students to be scientists. Therefore, the field remains dominated by charismatic lecturers. The facts supporting their claims are still few and far between.

The Sociocultural Perspective

Like the family systems and behavioral perspectives, the sociocultural perspective studies abnormal behavior in an environmental context. But, whereas family systems theorists confine their attention to the family environment, the sociocultural perspective views abnormal behavior as the product of broad social forces. The perspective embraces two interrelated theories—one straightforward, one more subtle.

Mental Illness and Social Ills

The more straightforward position is that psychological ills are the result of social ills, such as poverty. Epidemiological research has shown, for example, that rates of mental illness are much higher among the urban poor than in other segments of the population. Economic recessions also take their toll in mental illness. As unemployment rose in the late 1970s and early 1980s, admissions to mental hospitals, suicides, and deaths from stress-related ailments such as heart disease and cirrhosis of the liver rose significantly as well (Pines, 1982b).

Apart from poverty, many other injustices built into our society—the lack of any respected role for the aged, discrimination against minority groups and women, and homophobia (which in turn leads to condemnation of AIDS sufferers)—create stress that can lead to psychological disturbance. According to the sociocultural view, it should come as no surprise if a poor, ill-educated, and jobless teenager acts

Sociocultural theorists maintain that social conditions such as poverty and racial discrimination can lead to psychological disorders.

"wild" or if a lonely and idle 85-year-old woman is depressed. Rather than probe their psyches for an underlying psychological cause, we should address the obvious social causes. For example, poverty is a significant risk factor for psychopathology. In addition to experiencing more stress, the poor are less likely to have the personal resources and social support to cope with stress (Dohrenwend & Dohrenwend, 1981). Two epidemiological studies (Bruce, Takeuchi, & Leaf, 1991; Kessler, McGonagle, Zhao, et al., 1994) found that people in the lowest income groups had about *twice* the risk of developing an episode of a psychiatric disorder as people who were not poor.

Mental Illness and Labeling

As we saw in Chapter 1, the definition of *abnormal behavior* depends upon who is doing the defining. It is on this fact that the second sociocultural theory rests. Adherents to this theory claim that we may label people "mentally ill" not because of anything intrinsically pathological in their behavior but simply because they have violated social norms—a situation that the society cannot tolerate and that it handles by labeling and treating the people in question as if they were "sick." This theory has generated some interest in the process whereby people become labeled as mentally ill. How does the society choose which deviants it will designate as sick? And why do the people accept the label?

One theorist who has considered these questions at length is Thomas Scheff (1966, 1975). His analysis of the labeling process is as follows. Deviant behavior, whatever its cause, is extremely common. Most of it is transitory and is ignored by the society. However, certain forms of deviance, for one reason or another, come to the attention of the mental health establishment and are singled out as "mental disorders." Once singled out and labeled in this way, a person exhibiting such deviance is placed in the *social role* of a "mentally ill" person. And it is extremely likely that he or she will accept that role, for, as with any other social role (e.g., teacher, student, wife, husband), the society provides strong rewards for behavior consistent with the role and strong punishments for behavior inconsistent with the role. If, for example, a man who has once been labeled "mentally ill" tries to rejoin the world of the sane, he will find much to deter him—rejections from employment agencies, raised eyebrows from people who know about his "past," and so forth. Thus, according to Scheff, most people who are designated mentally ill ultimately embrace the role and settle back into what has been called the "career" of the mental patient (Goffman, 1959). In short, the label becomes a self-fulfilling prophecy.

Class, Race, and Diagnosis What kinds of behavior are most likely to identify a person as mentally ill? What do those socially learned stereotypes of mental illness consist of? A famous group of studies, the so-called New Haven studies (Hollingshead & Redlich, 1958; Myers & Bean, 1968), throws some light on this question, suggesting not only that psychological disturbance is a social phenomenon but that it is closely related to social class.

What the New Haven studies found was that, when people of lower socioeconomic levels suffered from behavior disturbances, they were more likely than middle-class people to be placed in state mental hospitals. The reasons were twofold. First, the lower-class people could not afford private outpatient care. Second, they tended to express their unhappiness in aggressive and rebellious behaviors. And these behaviors, while acceptable to other lower-class people as "normal" signs of frustration, appeared unacceptable—indeed, bizarre—to the mental health professionals who were diagnosing them, because those professionals came from higher socioeconomic brackets and, accordingly, had different ideas about what constituted normal responses to stress. Hence, people with lower socioeconomic backgrounds were more likely to be labeled as psychotic and to be hospitalized as a result. In contrast, people of higher socioeconomic levels tended not to be hospitalized, not only because they could pay for outpatient care but also because their "style" of deviance (e.g., withdrawal and self-deprecation) seemed to the doctors, coming from the same social class, less bizarre, Consequently, these people were diagnosed as having "neurotic" disorders—diagnoses that carry much less stigma—and, with the help of regular therapy, were able to return to their daily lives. Unlike the hospitalized and "psychotic" poor, they were given less of a "sick" role to fill and, thus, were more likely to improve.

In a review of research findings, Lopez (1989) showed that this principle applies to race as well as to class. In one study (Luepnitz, Randolph, & Gutsch, 1982), experienced therapists were given sets of hypothetical patient profiles and were asked to provided diagnoses. From therapist to therapist, the profiles were the same except for one factor: race. Patients identified as white in one set were said to be African American in another. The study found that, *with the same symptoms,* the African Americans were more likely to be diagnosed as alcoholic or schizophrenic, whereas the whites were more likely to be diagnosed as depressed. As in the New Haven studies, these different disorders carry different levels of stigma, have different prognoses, and lead to different treatments. Differences in race and class not only determine who is considered severely abnormal

African American Protest and the Mental Health Establishment

The treatment of African Americans forms a depressing chapter in the history of American mental health. On the one hand, the position of African Americans in our society exposes them to stresses—poverty, unemployment, poor housing, and family breakdown—that increase their risk for psychological disturbance. On the other hand, their protests against that situation have often been written off as signs of psychological disturbance (Landrine, 1988).

This story goes back many years. In the 1850s, physician Samuel Cartwright (1851/1981) described what he saw as two nerve disorders that afflicted slaves. In one, *drapetomania* (from the Greek *drapetes*, meaning "runaway"), the symptom was running away from one's owner.

The other, *dysathesia aethiopica*, was characterized by arguing with or attacking one's master, destroying plantation property, or refusing to work—in other words, failing to be a good slave.

Under slavery, it was repeatedly argued that freedom would endanger the mental health of African Americans (Deutsch, 1944). They were childlike creatures, it was said; therefore, they needed the care and supervision offered by the slave-holding system. After emancipation, unacceptable behavior by African Americans was often blamed on the withdrawal of such supports. At the same time, mentally disturbed African Americans were often barred from admission to mental hospitals (Dain, 1964). Usually, they were put in jail.

Such thinking has died hard. During the civil rights movement, it was theorized that, if African Americans were given the concessions they sought, this would deprive them of a "well-defined status" within the society and, thus, predispose them to mental illness (Wilson & Lantz, 1957). During the urban race riots of the 1960s, an article in the *Journal of the American Medical Association* discussed the possible role of brain pathology in causing the riots (Mark, Sweet, & Ervin, 1967). These are good examples of Thomas Szasz's point in *The Myth of Mental Illness:* psychiatry has often performed a policing role in the society, discrediting protest by calling it mental illness.

---

but also, by doing so, affect the person's chances for improvement (Braginsky, Braginsky, & Ring, 1969). The history of African Americans' treatment in American society illustrates some of the ways in which labeling is influenced by race and class (see the box "African American Protest and the Mental Health Establishment," above).

Those charged with developing diagnostic criteria have not ignored these problems. One proposal is to replace the current diagnostic system with a dimensional system (Chapter 2), classifying patients not according to disorders but simply on how they rate on variables such as depression or anxiety. Presumably, this would discourage stereotyping. Another possible solution, which has already been implemented in *DSM-IV,* is to inform diagnosticians about cultural variations in normal and abnormal behavior and to warn them against specific biases.

Prevention as a Social Issue

Because sociocultural theorists are concerned with the social and economic causes of psychological disorders, their approach to treatment revolves around community prevention programs. Three levels of prevention have been distinguished. The goal of *primary prevention* is to prevent the kinds of social ills that put people at risk for psychological disorders. *Secondary prevention* is aimed at modifying existing risk factors so that they do not lead to the development of

disorders. *Tertiary prevention* is actual treatment of disorders once they arise.

Chapter 1 raised some of the issues of prevention and social policy in its discussions of community mental health centers and deinstitutionalization. Chapter 19 will fully explore issues of prevention and social action.

Evaluating the Sociocultural Perspective

Almost no one in the mental health field would dispute the sociocultural theory that societal conditions contribute to psychological disturbance. Like all other perspectives, what distinguishes the sociocultural perspective from competing theories is a matter of emphasis. Whereas sociocultural theorists claim that socially engendered stress is the primary cause, other theorists say that it is secondary to other factors, such as learning history or ego strength. In turn, most sociocultural theorists readily concede the importance of learning history and ego strength but argue that these are influenced by social disadvantage.

The theory that psychological abnormality is a cultural artifact, maintained through labeling, is far more controversial. Differential labeling is not the only possible explanation for the disproportionate numbers of lower-class people who are diagnosed as psychotic. The phenomenon could be accounted for more simply via the socioeconomic-stress theory: because the poor have to cope with more serious stresses, they have more serious breakdowns. Another possible explanation is that severely disturbed people slip downward on the socioeconomic ladder—they tend to lose their jobs, for example—so that, whatever their original socioeconomic status, they are members of the lower class by the time they are diagnosed (Dunham, 1965; Kohn, 1973).

Integrating the Perspectives

Our review of the six theoretical perspectives has shown various ways of understanding the causes of psychological disorders. Traditionally, theorists have viewed these causes as occurring either inside the individual (biological, psychodynamic, or cognitive perspective) or outside the individual (behavioral, family systems, or sociocultural perspective). In recent years, many theorists have broadened their perceptions into a framework known as the **diathesis-stress model** (also called the *vulnerability-stress* or *biopsychosocial* model). This model recognizes that most disorders have a combination of internal and external causes.

According to the diathesis-stress model, various external factors, including stressful life events, early childhood traumas, brain injuries, and poor parenting, can accelerate the development of disorders in some people. However, when faced with the same external factors or stresses, some people are more vulnerable than others to developing a disorder. This vulnerability is determined by biological, personality, and cognitive predispositions known as "diatheses." Thus, the diathesis-stress model holds that environmental factors (stressors) trigger a predisposed person's vulnerability (diatheses) in such a way that the person develops a disorder (Abramson, Metalsky, & Alloy, 1989; Monroe & Simons, 1991; Walker & Diforio, 1997).

The diathesis-stress model informs the thinking of most researchers today, integrating the traditional perspectives into a broader, more contemporary approach. This approach is apparent in research on panic attacks, posttraumatic stress disorder, dissociative and somatoform disorders, depression, schizophrenia, eating disorders, and other disorders. We will discuss the interaction of internal and external causes as we examine these disorders later in this text.

KEY TERMS

behavior therapy, 130
behavioral perspective, 122
conditioned reflex, 122
conditioned reinforcers, 126
conditioned response, 125
conditioned stimulus, 125
contingency, 125
contingency management, 131
couple therapy, 138
diathesis-stress model, 144
discrimination, 127

exposure, 131
extinction, 126
family systems perspective, 135
family systems theories, 135
family therapy, 137
generalization, 127
hierarchy of fears, 130
law of effect, 124
learning, 122
negative reinforcement, 126
operant conditioning, 125

positive reinforcement, 126
primary reinforcer, 126
punishment, 126
radical behaviorism, 124
reinforcement, 125
respondent conditioning, 125
rules, 127
shaping, 127
sociocultural perspective, 141
strategic approach, 137

structural family therapy, 137
systematic desensitization, 130
three-term contingency, 127
unconditioned response, 125
unconditioned stimulus, 125

SUMMARY

■ The behavioral, family systems, and sociocultural perspectives differ from the three perspectives studied in the previous chapter in that they focus on causes external to the individual, emphasizing observable behavior and empirical research.

■ The behavioral perspective stresses immediate causes of behavior, rather than deep-seated, unconscious ones. Behaviorism was developed in the early twentieth century as a result of discoveries about the mechanisms of learning. Most important were Ivan Pavlov's demonstration that learning could be the result of the conditioned re-

flex, or simple association; John B. Watson's belief that psychology should be a natural, empirical science; Edward Lee Thorndike's law of effect (responses that lead to "satisfying" consequences are strengthened and likely to be repeated, while responses that lead to "unsatisfying" consequences have the opposite effect); and B. F. Skinner's radical behaviorism, according to which behavior includes all that a person does, says, and feels and which asserts that any kind of behavior can be predicted and influenced through knowledge of relevant environmental contingencies.

■ The basic assumptions of behaviorism are that psychology's task is to study behavior, or the responses an organism makes to stimuli on the basis of its learning history; that psychological research should be empirical, based on measurement; that the goal of psychology is the prediction and control of behavior; and that the real causes of any behavior that is not genetically determined lie outside the individual.

■ According to behaviorists, there are two basic ways of learning: respondent conditioning (an organism's learning to respond to a neutral stimulus as it would to a nonneutral one) and operant conditioning (an organism's learning to operate on the environment to obtain or avoid consequences). The frequency of behavior may be increased by positive or negative reinforcements or decreased through punishments.

■ Related learning mechanisms include extinction (through repeated unpairing of a conditioned stimulus and an unconditioned stimulus); generalization (responding to related stimuli in similar ways); discrimination (learning to differentiate among related stimuli); shaping (reinforcing successive approximations to a desired response); and rule-governed behavior (learning by following rules and instructions).

■ Behaviorists see all behavior as resulting in the same way from the interaction of our genetic endowment and our learning history. Thus, they prefer to speak of "maladaptive" rather than "abnormal" behavior and to avoid assigning people to specific diagnostic categories.

■ Radical behaviorism has increasingly focused on complex rather than simple causes of maladaptive behavior (such as the depressive response)—that is, on an individual's entire life experience and learning history rather than on specific proximal causes.

■ Behavior therapy uses the principles of learning to help patients change or unlearn maladaptive behavior, including self-defeating thoughts as well as inappropriate actions. Respondent-conditioning and extinction techniques (systematic desensitization, exposure) are used when the aim is to change emotional responses. Operant-conditioning techniques (such as contingency management) are used when the goal is to change overt behavior. Most forms of behavior therapy are administered as part of multicomponent treatment.

■ New radical behavioral therapies, combining principles of behaviorism with elements of various philosophies, often emphasize acceptance or validation of an individual's maladaptive behavior. In doing so, they may open up indirect avenues to change.

■ Behavior therapy is criticized for denying the client's freedom and uniqueness and for being superficial. However, it is effective in teaching people better skills to deal with life, it is often less expensive and faster than insight therapies, and it is precise in its goals and techniques.

■ Behaviorism challenges not only other theories of abnormal behavior but basic Western cultural notions. It has been criticized as oversimplified and deterministic and as a possible means of political coercion. At the same time, behavioral approaches to objectivity and experimentation have become the norm in psychological research, and behaviorism has largely destigmatized abnormal behavior. Behavior therapies have long been successful in achieving limited treatment goals, and radical behavioral therapists are now taking on the full range of clinical challenges.

■ Family systems theories, which are influenced in varying degrees by behaviorism and the psychodynamic perspective, maintain that the causes of abnormal behavior may be found in habitual relationship patterns, usually within the family. According to communication theory, psychopathology results from ambiguous, contradictory, or hostile family communication patterns. Minuchin's structural theory focuses on excessively weak or rigid boundaries between units within the family. Bowen proposed that an individual's healthy functioning depends on proper differentiation of self. Gottman's balance theory of marriage focuses on the balance between positive and negative behavior within a marriage and on partners' ability to withstand each other's negative behavior without a need to reciprocate in kind.

■ The guiding principle behind family therapy is that a family member's psychological problem resides as much in family relationships as in the person.

■ There are several types of family therapies. In the strategic approach, based on the communication-theory concept of the double bind, the therapist aims to force family members into awareness of the faults in their communication patterns. Structural family therapy concentrates on analyzing the role each member has within the family and on encouraging members to adopt more flexible roles. Psychodynamic family therapy employs the methods of listening and interpretation used in individual psychotherapy. In behavioral family therapy, parents can learn how to use reinforcers and punishers with conduct-disordered children, and families of schizophrenics a can learn calmer ways to solve problems.

■ The main goal in most couple therapies is the establishment of an honest dialogue between the two partners. The most studied therapy is traditional behavioral couple therapy (TBCT), which aims to increase positive behavior in accordance with Gottman's balance theory of marriage.

■ Couple and family therapies have been widely successful, often more so than individual treatment of a symptomatic family member or partner. TBCT, in particular, has been found as effective as individual therapy in treating a depressed partner.

■ Family systems theory has yet to become a major, unified psychological perspective, partly because its claims are too modest and partly because some of its findings have not held up under further study. Nevertheless, both family and couple therapies have won respect among therapists from all perspectives and have led to a reevaluation of the traditionally distant role of the therapist in psychotherapy.

■ The sociocultural perspective argues that the root of abnormal behavior lies not within the mind but in society.

One theory is that social ills, such as poverty and discrimination, push people into psychopathology. Another theory holds that labeling people as "mentally ill" tends to become a self-fulfilling prophecy. Additional research indicates that people's class and race influence the way in which their problems are diagnosed and the treatment they receive.

■ No one disputes that socioeconomic factors and cultural variables may contribute to psychological disturbance, but the extent to which these are causes or effects of abnormal behavior is a matter of debate. Particularly controversial is the theory that labeling alone may be responsible for the disproportionate occurrence of psychological abnormality among the poor.

■ Many theorists use a diathesis-stress model, which recognizes that most disorders have a combination of internal and external causes. According to this model, environmental factors trigger predisposed vulnerabilities in some individuals, so that these people develop a psychopathology, while those without such vulnerabilities do not. The diathesis-stress model provides a contemporary framework for synthesizing the theoretical perspectives.

Part Three | EMOTIONAL AND BEHAVIORAL DISORDERS

Chapter 6

A 27-year-old married electrician complains of dizziness, sweating palms, heart palpitations, and ringing of the ears of more than 18 months' duration. He has also experienced dry mouth and throat, periods of extreme muscle tension, and a constant "edgy" and watchful feeling that has often interfered with his ability to concentrate. These feelings have been present most of the time over the previous two years; they have not been limited to discrete periods. Although these symptoms sometimes make him feel "discouraged," he denies feeling depressed and continues to enjoy activities with his family.

Because of these symptoms, the patient had seen a family practitioner, a neurologist, a neurosurgeon, a chiropractor, and an ear nose-throat specialist. He had been placed on a hypoglycemic diet, had received physiotherapy for a pinched nerve, and had been told he might have "an inner ear problem."

He also has many worries. He constantly worries about the health of his parents. His father, in fact, had a myocardial infarction two years previously but is now feeling well. He also worries about whether he is "a good father," whether his wife will ever leave him (there is no indication that she is dissatisfied with the marriage), and whether he is liked by his co-workers. Although he recognizes that his worries are often unfounded, he can't stop worrying.

For the past two years, the patient has had few social contacts because of his nervous symptoms. Although he has sometimes had to leave work when the symptoms became intolerable, he continues to work for the same company he joined for his apprenticeship following high-school graduation. He tends to hide his symptoms from his wife and children, to whom he wants to appear "perfect," and reports few problems with them as a result of his nervousness (Spitzer, Gibbon, Skodol, et al., 1994, pp. 298–299).

At the heart of this young man's problem is anxiety, a state of fear that affects many areas of functioning. Anxiety involves three basic components:

1. *Subjective reports* of tension, apprehension, dread, and expectations of inability to cope

2. *Behavioral responses* such as avoidance of the feared situation, impaired speech and motor functioning, and impaired performance on complex cognitive tasks

3. *Physiological responses* including muscle tension, increased heart rate and blood pressure, rapid breathing, dry mouth, nausea, diarrhea, and dizziness

Anxiety is part and parcel of human existence. All people feel it in moderate degrees, and in moderate degrees it is an adaptive response. In the words of one researcher, "Without it, we would probably all be asleep at our desks" (Stephen M. Paul, quoted in Schmeck, 1982). We would also expose ourselves to danger. It is anxiety that impels us to slow down on a slippery road, to study for exams, and, thus, to lead longer and more productive lives. But, while most people feel anxiety some of the time, some people feel anxiety most of the time. For these people, it is not an adaptive response. It is a source of extreme distress, relievable only by strategies that limit freedom and flexibility.

In this chapter, we will focus on the anxiety disorders, characterized either by manifest anxiety or by behavior patterns aimed at warding off anxiety. Until 1980, the anxiety disorders were grouped with the somatoform and dissociative disorders (Chapter 7) under the single diagnostic heading of *neurosis*. This term was coined in the eighteenth century by a Scottish physician, William Cullen, to describe a general affliction of the nervous system that produced "nervous" behavior. Throughout the nineteenth century, people who were "sane" but nevertheless engaged in rigid and self-defeating behaviors were labeled neurotic and were thought to be the victims of some unidentified neurological dysfunction. Then, beginning around the start of the twentieth century, this biogenic view was gradually replaced by Freud's psychogenic view. To Freud, neurosis was due not to organic causes but, rather, to anxiety. As repressed memories and desires threatened to break through into the conscious mind, anxiety occurred as a "danger signal" to the ego. Neurotic behavior was either the expression of that anxiety or a defense against it.

The early editions of the *DSM* implicitly endorsed Freud's view by gathering all the so-called neurotic disorders into a single, anxiety-based category. Many people objected to this, however. The diagnostic manual, as they pointed out, was meant to be used by mental health professionals of all theoretical persuasions; therefore, to use a term that implied a psychodynamic interpretation was inappropriate. In response to these criticisms, *DSM-III* (1980) eliminated the "neurosis" heading and broke up the "neurotic disorders" into separate categories, based on the behavior patterns they involved—a practice that has survived into *DSM-IV*. Nevertheless, the term *neurosis* is still widely used in psychodynamic writings. And mental health professionals of many persuasions continue to use it as an indication of the *severity* of a psychological disorder, "neurotic" indicating the milder disturbances and "psychotic" the more debilitating ones.

In that sense of severity, the anxiety disorders are "neurotic" conditions. They do not destroy reality contact. People with anxiety disorders may misinterpret or overreact to certain stimuli related to their psychological problems, but in general they see the same world as the rest of us. And in most cases they still go about their daily rounds, carrying on fairly reasonable conversations, engaging in relationships with other people, and so on. They may cope poorly, but they cope.

Though the anxiety disorders may not be crippling, they still represent the single largest mental health problem in the United States (Kessler, McGonagle, Zhao, et al., 1994). They are more common than any other psychological disorder, and they can lead to more severe disorders, such as depression and alcoholism (Burke, Burke, & Rae, 1994). They may also lead to physical disorders, such as heart disease (Barlow, 1988; Wells, Golding, & Burnam, 1989) and, thus, to earlier death (Gräsbeck, Rorsman, Hagnell, et al., 1996).

In this chapter, we will describe the various syndromes that fall under the heading of "anxiety disorders." Then we will examine the theoretical perspectives on the anxiety disorders, together with the corresponding therapies.

Anxiety Disorder Syndromes

Anxiety can be experienced in a variety of ways. There are three basic patterns, however. In panic disorder and generalized anxiety disorder, the anxiety is unfocused; either it is with the person continually or it seems to descend "out of nowhere," unconnected to any special stimulus. By contrast, phobias, posttraumatic stress disorder, and acute stress disorder involve a fear aroused by an identifiable object or situation. Finally, in obsessive-compulsive disorder, anxiety occurs if the person does *not* engage in a thought or behavior that otherwise serves no purpose and may in fact be unpleasant and embarrassing.

Panic Disorder

We have already seen the general features of anxiety, in the example that began this chapter. In a **panic attack**, anxiety begins suddenly and unexpectedly and soon mounts to an almost unbearable level. The person sweats, feels dizzy, trembles, and gasps for breath. The pulse quickens and the heart pounds. Nausea, chest pains, choking, feelings of numbness, and hot flashes or chills are also common. To people in the grip of such an attack, the world may suddenly seem unreal *(derealization),* or they may seem unreal to themselves *(depersonalization).* Above all, they have a sense of inescapable doom—that they are going to lose control, go crazy, or even die. Indeed, patients are often first recognized as having panic dis-

order when they turn up in hospital emergency rooms claiming, despite evidence of good health, that they are dying of a heart attack (Katerndahl, 1996). Such catastrophic thoughts are central to panic disorder and help to distinguish it from other anxiety disorders (Noyes, Woodman, Garvey, et al., 1992). A panic attack usually lasts several minutes, though it may continue for hours. When it subsides, the person feels exhausted, as if he or she had survived a traumatic experience. Between attacks, the person may worry constantly about having another attack.

There are two kinds of panic attacks. In *uncued* (or *unexpected*) attacks, the attack seems to come "out of the blue," unconnected to any specific stimulus. In *cued* (or *situationally bound*) attacks, the attack occurs in response to a situational trigger, such as seeing a snake. This distinction is used in differential diagnosis, for, although panic attacks may occur in all the anxiety disorders, cued attacks are more characteristic of phobias, while uncued attacks are by definition present in panic disorder. According to *DSM-IV,* a person has **panic disorder** when he or she has had recurrent, uncued panic attacks, followed by psychological or behavioral problems—that is, persistent fear of future attacks, worry about the implications or consequences of the attacks, or significant changes in behavior (e.g., staying home from work) as a result of the attacks.

However, while uncued attacks are required for the diagnosis of panic disorder, panic disorder patients still report more cued than uncued attacks (Garssen, DeBeurs, Buikhuisen, et al., 1996), and many experts now believe that attacks said by patients to be uncued also have precipitating events —subtle changes, such as physical exertion, that cause some alteration in body chemistry (Craske, 1991). The onset of panic disorder is probably also more explainable than it seems to its sufferers. Most people diagnosed with panic disorder report one or more stressful events, generally involving injury, illness, or interpersonal conflict, in the year preceding the first attack (Shulman, Cox, Swinson, et al., 1994). Nevertheless, when victims report that their attacks are uncued, this in itself is important, for it helps to account for the victims' catastrophic feelings, their sense of going out of control. People with panic disorder cannot go anywhere—to work, to the movies, to the supermarket—without fearing that they may have an attack in front of everyone, and with help nowhere in sight.

Consequently, some may, in fact, cease to go anywhere—a complication of panic disorder called agoraphobia. Literally, **agoraphobia** means "fear of the marketplace." Actually, what the agoraphobic fears is being in any situation from which escape might be

Agoraphobia can become so severe that the person does not dare to venture outside the home for months—sometimes even years—at a time.

difficult, and in which help would be unavailable, in the event of panic symptoms. Agoraphobia is often preceded by a phase of panic attacks, the first of which is likely to have occurred outside the home. (Only 10.6 percent of first attacks occur at home [Shulman, Cox, Swinson, et al., 1994].) Eventually, the person becomes so afraid of having an attack, especially in a public place, that he or she begins to stay closer and closer to home. Some agoraphobics refuse to leave home unless someone goes with them; some are able to leave home to go to places in which they feel safe; others refuse to leave home at all.

Because so many panic disorder victims are also agoraphobic, *DSM-IV* lists agoraphobia as a complication of panic disorder. But the manual also classifies agoraphobia as a disorder in its own right, for many agoraphobics—indeed, two-thirds, according to one estimate—have no history of panic disorder (Eaton & Keyl, 1990). Conversely, many victims of panic disorder do not become agoraphobic. Finally, in a sample of panic disorder patients with agoraphobia, 90 percent were found to have reported agoraphobic avoidance *before* the first panic attack (Fava, Grandi, Rafanelli, et al., 1992). So while panic attacks often lead to agoraphobia, they are by no means a prerequisite.

What predicts whether a person with panic attacks will develop agoraphobic avoidance? One might guess that the determining factors would be the frequency and severity of the attacks, but this is appar-

ently not the case. Instead, avoidance seems to be linked to cognitive factors. Among panic disorder victims, those who believe that their attacks will be beyond their ability to cope and will lead to negative consequences are the ones most likely to become agoraphobic (Clum & Knowles, 1991).

An interesting fact about panic attacks is that they can be induced under laboratory conditions, with results closely resembling those of natural attacks. Furthermore, they can be induced in many different ways: by pharmacological agents such as sodium lactate, yohimbine, and caffeine; by breathing-related procedures such as exercise, hyperventilation, and carbon dioxide inhalation; and by behavioral procedures such as relaxation exercises or confrontation with a phobic stimulus. The panic-provoking agent that has been most extensively studied is sodium lactate, which produces panic attacks in 70 to 80 percent of panic disorder patients, compared with 0 to 10 percent of normal controls (Nutt & Lawson, 1992). It seems also to produce panic attacks in patients who have had panic attacks before, even though they have diagnoses other than panic disorder.

Groups at Risk Panic disorder is a common condition, affecting about 3.5 percent of Americans during their lifetime; agoraphobia is more common, with a prevalence of 5.3 percent (Eaton, Kessler, Wittchen, et al., 1994; Kessler, McGonagle, Zhao, et al., 1994). Also common is the occasional panic attack, experienced by over 7 percent of Americans in their lifetime (Eaton, Kessler, Wittchen, et al., 1994). Women are more likely than men to develop panic disorder, and they are far more likely than men to develop agoraphobia (Bekker, 1996; Yonkers & Gurguis, 1995). About three-quarters of agoraphobics are women. Panic disorder, with or without agoraphobia, tends to make its appearance in late adolescence or early adulthood—the median age of onset is 24 (Burke, Burke, Regier, et al., 1990)—though panic attacks occur in children as well and are common in adolescents (Ollendick, Mattis, & King, 1994). Only in the elderly is panic disorder uncommon, and onset in old age is very rare (Flint, Cook, & Rabins, 1996). In addition to age and gender, marital status is a factor in vulnerability. People who are separated or divorced are at greater risk for both panic disorder and agoraphobia (Wittchen & Essau, 1993).

The prevalence of panic disorder is similar across ethnic groups and cultures, but the symptoms vary. In Puerto Rico and other Caribbean cultures, "ataques de nervios" (panic attacks) frequently include shouting and weeping, whereas in equatorial Africa, people with panic attacks may report sensations of worms crawling in their heads (Kirmayer, Young, & Hayton, 1995).

Generalized Anxiety Disorder

As the name suggests, the main feature of generalized anxiety disorder is a chronic state of diffuse anxiety. *DSM-IV* defines the syndrome as excessive worry, over a period of at least six months, about several life circumstances. The most common areas of worry are family, money, work, and health (Rapee & Barlow, 1993). Many normal people worry about such things, but it is the excessiveness and uncontrollability of the worrying that makes it a disorder. We saw an example of generalized anxiety disorder in the case described at the beginning of this chapter. People with generalized anxiety disorder are continually waiting for something dreadful to happen, either to themselves or to those they care about, and this subjective condition spills over into their cognitive and physiological functioning. They feel restless and irritable; their hearts beat faster; they have difficulty concentrating; they tire easily (Thayer, Friedman, & Borkovec, 1996). Typically, they also suffer from chronic muscle tension and insomnia. And, in response to symptoms, many of them develop secondary anxiety—that is, anxiety about their anxiety—fearing that their condition will cause them to develop ulcers, lose their jobs, alienate their spouses, and so forth. Like panic disorder, generalized anxiety disorder usually comes in the wake of stressful life events (Newman & Bland, 1994).

Generalized anxiety disorder sounds as though it might be the "resting state" of panic disorder, and some researchers believe that this is the case—that these syndromes are two phases of a single disorder (Barlow, 1988). At the same time, there are strong grounds for separating them. In a comparison, Noyes and his colleagues found three major differences between the two syndromes. First, their symptom profiles differ. The symptoms of generalized anxiety disorder suggest hyperarousal of the central nervous system (insomnia, restlessness, inability to concentrate), whereas the symptoms of panic disorder seem connected to hyperarousal of the autonomic nervous system (pounding heart, rapid breathing, dizziness, nausea). Second, generalized anxiety disorder usually has a more gradual onset and a more chronic course than panic disorder. Finally, when these disorders run in families, they tend to run separately. First-degree relatives of people with generalized anxiety disorder are more likely to have generalized anxiety disorder than panic disorder; first-degree relatives of panic disorder patients are more likely to have panic disorder than generalized anxiety disorder (Noyes, Woodman, Garvey, et al., 1992).

Groups at Risk Though generalized anxiety disorder strikes all age groups, including the elderly (Schneider, 1996), most victims develop the condition fairly early in life; many report that they have always felt anxious. It is a common disorder, affecting as much as 5 percent of the U.S. population. It is twice as common in women as in men (Kessler, McGonagle, Zhao, et al., 1994; Rapee, 1991). People who are separated, divorced, or widowed are also at higher risk, as are the unemployed (Wittchen, Zhao, Kessler, et al., 1994). The rates are similar across a variety of cultures (Anderson, 1994).

Phobias

A **phobia** involves two factors: (1) an intense and persistent fear of an object or a situation that, as the person realizes, actually poses no real threat and (2) avoidance of the phobic stimulus. In some cases, the phobic stimulus is something that seems utterly harmless. Often, however, the stimulus is one that carries a slight suggestion of danger—for example, something that a child might be afraid of, such as dogs, insects, snakes, or high places. Nonphobic people may also avoid these things. Many of us, for example, distinctly prefer not to step out onto a fire escape and would never touch a snake, no matter how harmless. The difference between these reactions and a phobic reaction is, first, one of severity. While the normal person may feel apprehension at the sight of a snake, the snake-phobic person shows intense anxiety—escalated heart rate, sweating, and so forth—and may have a panic attack. Second, because of the severity of the anxiety response, phobic people, unlike others, must design their lives so that they avoid the thing they fear. Phobias are divided into two types, specific phobia, or fear of circumscribed objects or situations, and social phobia, or fear of social embarrassment.

Specific Phobia Among the more frequently seen types of **specific phobia** are **acrophobia**, fear of heights; **claustrophobia**, fear of enclosed places (e.g., elevators, subways); phobias of body injury; and animal phobias, particularly for dogs, snakes, mice, and insects. The most common are the animal phobias (Costello, 1982), but many people with these conditions do not seek help, for they can manage, without much difficulty, to avoid the animal in question. In general, the degree of impairment in phobia cases depends on the degree to which the phobic stimulus is a usual factor in the person's normal round of activities. Dog-phobic people are in a bad position, for dogs are a common sight. Fear of air travel might be more debilitating to a business executive than to a suburban homemaker. In other cases, the phobic stimulus is so rare a factor in the person's environment that it has little or no effect on daily activities. For example, a city dweller with a phobia for snakes need only avoid going to the zoo.

A commuter with claustrophobia would need to avoid this crowded subway car. Without an alternative method of transportation to work, he or she would need to seek treatment or risk jeopardizing his or her job.

Social Phobia   People suffering from **social phobia** avoid performing certain actions in front of other people, for fear of embarrassing or humiliating themselves. Common objects of social phobia are public speaking, eating in public, and using public bathrooms. Social phobia erodes self-confidence: to have to plan one's life in order to avoid encountering a stranger in the lavatory is a humiliating experience. But the basic problem with this phobia is that it restricts people's choices, forcing them into narrow channels of behavior. Thus, it may interfere seriously with work, as the following case shows:

> The patient was a 39-year-old, married, African American, female physician who described a long-standing history of becoming "really nervous" in large crowds, especially if the people were unfamiliar. Although unable to recollect the specific onset, she remembered being extremely shy in elementary and junior high school. At social functions, she typically would "hide out" in the bathroom. . . . She reported no close friends or confidants, was unwilling to get involved with people unless certain of being liked, and did not date until after college. She occasionally would consume alcohol prior to, and frequently during, social events to cope with her discomfort. When in stressful situations, she stuttered. For example, saying her name during introductions, whether to professionals or patients, was particularly difficult. Consequently, she avoided speaking on the telephone and introducing herself to others, often being perceived as brusque and somewhat rude. (Fink, Turner, & Beidel, 1996, p. 202)

These social fears had posed a constant stumbling block in her career:

> She . . . reported difficulty attending rounds as a medical student and giving oral presentations to professionals in her field. She described a constant desire to quit her residency training; and after 6 months into her training, she developed an intense fear of hospitals. She complained of nausea, headaches, and tachycardia [rapid heart rate] upon entering the lobby of a hospital. . . . She was frequently the only African American student in her classes and felt that White students excluded her from many activities. She also thought that the students and faculty viewed her as incompetent. . . . The fear was dramatically more intense when racial encounters involved White males. Because of her social-evaluative fears, she opted to forgo specialized residency training, leave the hospital environment, and work in a public health clinic. (Fink, Turner, & Beidel, 1996, p. 205)

In social phobia, the person's fears are more realistic than those of other phobia sufferers. Agoraphobics are not very likely to collapse or have a heart attack in a public place, but social phobics, precisely because they are fearful of social blunders, are likely to commit them. People with this disorder generally have low self-esteem. They often engage in cognitive distortions, holding themselves up to perfectionistic standards, thus magnifying their shortcomings (Juster, Heimberg, Frost, et al., 1996). Finally, as part of their anxiety response, they are prone to blush, sweat, and tremble (Uhde, Tancer, Black, et al., 1992). All these handicaps make them prone to social rejection, thus increasing their anxiety—a vicious cycle (Schneier, 1991; Taylor & Arnow, 1988).

Is social phobia just a specific phobia for social situations? Researchers think not. To begin with, social phobias are more pervasive than specific phobias. Rare is the social phobic who is afraid of only one situation. Usually, the anxiety spreads over many situations (Turner, Beidel, Dancu, et al., 1986). Indeed, what social phobics often fear is the disapproval of others in general, and this is not a phobic stimulus that can easily be avoided.

In consequence, social phobics are generally more impaired than are people with specific phobias. In one survey of social phobics (Turner, Beidel, Dancu, et al., 1986), 92 percent reported that anxiety had interfered with their careers, 64 percent said that it prevented them from attending social functions, and 50 percent admitted that they used alcohol or tranquilizers to calm themselves in social situations. The risk for alcohol and drug abuse in social phobia has been reported by other researchers as well (Fyer, 1990; Merikangus & Angst, 1995).

Distinguishing social phobia from other syndromes, such as agoraphobia, is sometimes difficult. Still, according to the research, there is a difference.

Agoraphobics are afraid of the actual symptoms of acute anxiety—afraid that they will scream, pass out, or have a heart attack. For social phobics, the fear is social. It is not the symptoms that scare them but the idea that someone will witness the symptoms and think poorly of them as a result. Furthermore, agoraphobics tend to seek out others for comfort; social phobics are comforted by avoiding others (Schneier, 1991; Turner & Beidel, 1989).

Like the patient described in the previous case, many social phobics recall having been shy as children (Stemberger, Turner, Beidel, et al., 1995). Shyness tends to run in families and probably has some genetic underpinning (Plomin & Daniels, 1986). There have not yet been any genetic studies on social phobia, but researchers have isolated a number of what seem to be high-risk parenting styles. Parents who are overprotective without being emotionally supportive; parents who are overconcerned with dress, grooming, and manners; and parents who discourage children from socializing, thus preventing them from learning social skills and mastering social fears—these three patterns are frequently reported by victims of social phobia (Bruch & Heimberg, 1994).

Groups at Risk Specific phobias often begin in childhood—the mean age at onset is between 11 and 17 (Boyd, Rae, Thompson, et al., 1990)—and they are common, affecting up to 11 percent of the general population. African Americans and Hispanics are at higher risk than other American ethnic groups, and women are twice as susceptible as men (Magee, Eaton, Wittchen, et al., 1996). Social phobia affects about 13 percent of Americans at some time in their lives, but here the distribution between sexes is more even. Social phobia usually begins in early adolescence, which seems logical, for that is believed to be the developmental stage at which children become acutely aware of how they are impressing others and, hence, become prone to embarrassment. The lesser a person's income or education, the greater the risk of both specific and social phobias (Magee, Eaton, Wittchen, et al., 1996), which, again, makes sense; the poor have reason to fear.

Obsessive-Compulsive Disorder

An **obsession** is a thought or an image that keeps intruding into a person's consciousness; the person finds the thought inappropriate and distressing and tries to suppress it, but still it returns. Similarly, a **compulsion** is an action that a person feels compelled to repeat again and again, in a stereotyped fashion, though he or she has no conscious desire to do so.

People suffering from either obsessions or compulsions—or, as is usually the case, from both—are said to have **obsessive-compulsive disorder.**

Mild obsessive-compulsive symptoms are common in the general population (Gibbs, 1996), as many people can attest. A song may keep playing in our heads; our minds may return again and again to the question of whether we fed the cat before going to work. But these thoughts pass, and we go on about our business. Pathological obsessions, on the other hand, do not pass; though the person tries to suppress them, they recur day after day. Furthermore, they often involve scandalous or violent themes—most obsessions revolve around contamination, violence, sex, or religious transgression, which makes them even more demoralizing to the people who have them.

Compulsions, though they may be as irrational and disruptive as obsessions, tend to have more neutral content. Indeed, they are often responses to obsessions—responses aimed at warding off the danger posed by the obsession—and, as such, they generally have overtones of duty and caution. The most common compulsions fall into two categories, cleaning rituals and checking rituals (Khanna & Mukherjee, 1992; Rachman & Hodgson, 1980). People who perform cleaning rituals are compelled again and again to stop whatever they are doing and go through some hygiene procedure—typically, hand washing. People with checking rituals are forced, with equal frequency, to interrupt their activities and go make sure they have done something that they were supposed to do. Some people, for example, no sooner get into bed than they have to get up and make certain they have

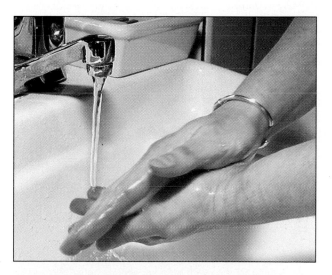

The cleaning rituals that often characterize obsessive-compulsive disorder go far beyond the requirements of ordinary hygiene. People who need to wash their hands dozens of times a day are severely restricted in their actions.

locked the front door or, worse yet, all the doors and windows in the house—a process that may be repeated seven or eight times until, exhausted and still uncertain, they at last fall asleep. Checking rituals are often responses to obsessions about harm to loved ones, while cleaning rituals often accompany obsessions about contamination. Whatever their routine, compulsives become extremely anxious if they are prevented, or try to prevent themselves, from engaging in it. They recognize that their compulsions are excessive, unreasonable, and perhaps even humiliating. Nevertheless, they give in to them to relieve their mounting anxiety. For example, in the movie *As Good as It Gets,* Jack Nicholson portrayed a person with both cleaning and checking rituals.

At its worst, obsessive-compulsive disorder can be completely disabling, as the person's life is given over to obeying the compulsion. Such was the situation in the following case. The patient was 19 years old, and the account was provided by his father:

> When George wakes in the morning . . . he feels that his hands are contaminated and so he cannot touch his clothing. He won't wash in the bathroom because he feels that the carpet is contaminated and he won't go downstairs until he is dressed. Consequently, I have to dress him, having first cleaned his shoes and got out a clean shirt, underclothes, socks and trousers. He holds his hands above his head while I pull on his underpants and trousers and we both make sure, by proceeding very cautiously, that he doesn't contaminate the outside of his clothing. . . . George then goes downstairs, washes his hands in the kitchen and thereafter spends about twenty minutes in the toilet. . . . I then have to stand in the doorway and supervise him, my main function being to give reassurance that he has not done anything silly to contaminate his clothing. Thankfully he is now managing on some occasions to cope in the toilet without my close supervision but I still have to be on call so that I can help him if he starts to panic for any reason. Incidentally, I have to put newspapers down on the floor of the toilet and change them daily to make sure that his trousers never come into contact with any contaminating substances. If he only wants to urinate then my task is made easier. I simply have to check his trousers and boots for splashes, sometimes getting down on my hands and knees with a [flashlight].
>
> Recently he has been checking that there are no pubic hairs on the floor and he asks me to get down on my hands and knees to check the floor meticulously. Basically he has to be completely sure that there is no contamination around because if he is not sure then he will start to worry and ruminate about it later on. He has to be completely sure and therefore needs a second opinion. As soon as he has zipped up his trousers I have to march in with a pad soaked in antiseptic and give the zip a quick once-over. When he washes his hands after toileting, he meticulously scrubs each finger and methodically works his way up as far as his

> elbow. I used to have to watch him at every step of the way but now he only calls me in occasionally. Sometimes he will have washed and dried his hands and then decides that he is not sure whether he washed properly. At this stage I usually have to supervise him so that when he is finished he is absolutely certain that the job has been done perfectly without missing a square inch of contamination. (Rachman & Hodgson, 1980, pp. 66–67)

This was just the patient's morning routine. The rest of the day followed a similar course.

In the past, it was assumed that obsessive-compulsive disorder was related to what is called obsessive-compulsive personality disorder, a personality type characterized by rigidity, overconscientiousness, and overconcern with detail. (The personality disorders will be the subject of Chapter 10.) This view was heavily influenced by the psychoanalytic theory that both syndromes were rooted in conflicts over toilet training and the associated issues of control and autonomy. But recent, well-controlled studies (Crino & Andrews, 1996) have shown that people with obsessive-compulsive disorder generally do not show obsessive-compulsive personality disorder as well. Instead, they are more likely to show traits associated with other personality disorders, such as withdrawal (avoidant personality disorder), dependency (dependent personality disorder), or self-dramatization (histrionic personality disorder) (Black, Noyes, Pfohl, et al., 1993; Crino & Andrews, 1996).

Obsessive-compulsive disorder should not be confused with the far more common problems of excessive drinking, eating, or gambling. We often hear people speak, for example, of "compulsive gamblers" or "compulsive eaters." These activities, however, are not compulsions. By definition, a compulsion is engaged in not as an end in itself but as a means of relieving the distress attendant upon *not* engaging in it. "Compulsive eaters" and "compulsive gamblers," while they may be pained by the consequences of these excesses, nevertheless pursue eating and gambling as ends in themselves.

However, obsessive-compulsive disorder does overlap with depression. Like depression, obsessive-compulsive symptoms respond to certain antidepressant drugs, clomipramine (Anafranil) and selective serotonin reuptake inhibitors (SSRIs). If obsessive-compulsive patients can be helped by antidepressant drugs, is their problem a mood disorder rather than an anxiety disorder? Perhaps so, for obsessive-compulsive patients sometimes show depressive reactions—guilt, dejection, feelings of helplessness—as strongly as they show anxiety (Gibbs, 1996). It is possible that obsessive-compulsives belong in an intermediate category, overlapping both the anxiety and mood disorders (Insel, Zahn, & Murphy, 1985; Sturgis, 1993).

Groups at Risk Obsessive-compulsive disorder was once thought to be very rare, but recent estimates suggest that it affects 2 to 3 percent of the population worldwide (Weissman, Bland, Canino, et al., 1994). People who are separated, divorced, or unemployed are at greater risk (Karno, Golding, Sorenson, et al., 1988). Men and women are equally at risk (Yonkers & Gurguis, 1995), though there is a curious sex differential in the nature of compulsions: young, single men are more likely to have checking rituals, whereas married women are more likely to have cleaning rituals (Khanna & Mukherjee, 1992; Sturgis, 1993). Obsessive-compulsive disorder usually appears in late adolescence or early adulthood—the median age of onset is 23 (Burke, Burke, Regier, et al., 1990)—but it may also begin in childhood (Swedo, Leonard, & Rapoport, 1992). In about 50 to 70 percent of patients, the onset of obsessions and compulsions begins after a stressful event, such as a pregnancy or the death of a relative (Kaplan & Sadock, 1991).

Posttraumatic Stress Disorder

Posttraumatic stress disorder is a severe psychological reaction, lasting at least one month and involving intense fear, helplessness, or horror, to intensely traumatic events—events involving actual or threatened death or serious injury to oneself or others. Such events include assault, rape, natural disasters such as earthquakes and floods, accidents such as airplane crashes and fires, and wartime traumas. Predictably, most of our knowledge of posttraumatic stress disorder comes from war survivors—people who survived Nazi concentration camps, the bombing of Hiroshima, or the daily agonies of combat during wars.

Posttraumatic stress disorder differs from other anxiety disorders in that the source of stress is an external event of an overwhelmingly painful nature, so the person's reaction, though it may resemble other anxiety disorders, seems to some degree understandable. Nevertheless, it is extremely debilitating. The person may go on for weeks, months, or years reexperiencing the traumatic event, either in painful recollection or in nightmares. In some cases, stimuli reminiscent of the event may cause the patient to return psychologically to the scene of the disaster and go through it all over again in his or her mind. Consequently, victims of posttraumatic stress disorder usually take pains to avoid being reminded of the trauma. At the same time, they seem to numb themselves to their present surroundings. They may find it difficult, for example, to respond to affection—a source of great pain to families of returning soldiers—or to interest themselves in things that they once cared for. Typically, they also show symptoms of heightened arousal, such as insomnia, irritability, and exaggerated startle responses. They may also show strong physiological reactions to any reminder of trauma. In one study of two groups of Vietnam veterans—the first diagnosed as having posttraumatic stress disorder, the second as suffering from other anxiety disorders—each of the subjects heard a taped account of his own war experiences. The change in heart rate in the posttraumatic stress disorder group was almost double that of the second group (Pitman, Orr, Forgue, et al., 1990).

Symptoms of posttraumatic stress disorder generally appear shortly after the trauma. In some cases, however, there is an "incubation period." For days or even months after the event, the person is symptom-free; then, inexplicably, the traumatic reaction begins to surface. In many cases, symptoms clear up by themselves within about 6 months; some however, linger for years. In a study of 1,098 Dutch veterans who had fought in the Resistance against the Nazis in World War II, it was found that, 50 years after the end of the war, 25 to 50 percent of these people were still suffering from posttraumatic stress disorder, and only 4 percent showed no symptoms at all (Op den Velde, Hovens, Aarts, et al., 1996). Similarly, in a survey of Vietnam war veterans, 15 percent of the men and 8.5 percent of the women were still suffering from posttraumatic stress disorder 15 or more years after the war (Schlenger, Kulka, Fairbank, et al., 1992; Weiss, Marmar, Schlenger, et al., 1992). On the other hand, severe posttraumatic stress symptoms may persist for only a few weeks, in which case they are classified as *acute stress disorder*. Acute stress disorder lasts from 2 days to 4 weeks. Beyond that point, it is reclassified as posttraumatic stress disorder.

Combat Since World War I, traumatic reactions to combat have been known by a succession of names: "shell shock," "combat fatigue," "combat exhaustion," and now "posttraumatic stress disorder." Actually, no one term is fitting, for stress reactions to combat differ markedly from one person to another (Rundell & Ursano, 1996). Some soldiers become depressed and curl up in their bunks, unable to move. Others experience anxiety, which escalates to panic attacks. Whatever the response, the precipitating stimulus is usually the same: a close escape from death, often with the added horror of seeing one's companions killed. Such traumas, however, are usually preceded by months or years of accumulated stress: fear, sleep deprivation, cold, heat, and numerous brushes with

More than other American conflicts, the Vietnam War is associated with lingering cases of posttraumatic stress disorder. Public acknowledgments of the courage of those who served, such as this memorial wall in New York City, were belated attempts to ease the veterans' return to civilian life.

death. Many soldiers seem to succumb not so much to a single trauma as to this constant piling up of stress. Indeed, many show no effects until they have returned to civilian life and are suddenly surprised by nightmares and nervous tremors. Their symptoms may be a problem not just for them but for their families as well. Research on Vietnam veterans has shown that those with posttraumatic stress disorder are more likely to show hostility and aggression toward their partners (Chemtob, Hamada, Roitblat, et al., 1994).

Many veterans of the Persian Gulf War have reported symptoms resembling those of posttraumatic stress disorder or acute stress disorder. Whether these symptoms are a result only of psychological trauma or also of exposure to dangerous chemical or biological agents has been a matter for debate. See the box "Persian Gulf War Syndrome" on page 159.

Civilian Catastrophe   Disaster is not confined to wartime. There are "civilian catastrophes" as well. Victims of a plane crash, an earthquake, a fire, or a flood, an assault, a rape, or a hijacking are also subject to posttraumatic stress disorder. Among the survivors of the Mount St. Helens eruption in 1980, most of those diagnosed with posttraumatic stress disorder still had this condition three years later (Shore, Tatum, & Vollmer, 1986).

An important component of the survivor's psychology is guilt (Joseph, Williams, & Yule, 1995). Many people, having barely escaped a disaster, begin to feel deep remorse that their lives were spared, as if, by taking up a place on the survivor list, they had caused others to die. This guilt was a theme reiterated

by the survivors of a devastating flood in 1972 at Buffalo Creek, West Virginia:

> One of our very close friends stayed drunk for almost five months because he could still hear his brother and sister screaming for their mother and his mother screaming "God help us" when the water hit them. Sometimes he talks with me about it and I get the impression that he feels bad because he lived through it all. He is only twenty years of age, but I guess sometimes he feels like a thousand years old. (quoted in Erikson, 1976, p. 171)

A similar sense of guilt has been observed in Hiroshima and concentration camp survivors and in combat troops.

The responses of the survivors of Hiroshima and the Nazi death camps are the extreme case, for these people suffered not only extreme physical peril but also the deaths of their families and friends, the loss of their homes, the obliteration of their whole world. Survivors of less complete disasters (e.g., near death in a fire or automobile accident), who can go home to their families and their accustomed surroundings, tend to recover more quickly and more completely, yet even these people, after getting over the acute phase of the traumatic reaction, may suffer irritability and have difficulty concentrating and resuming their former daily routines.

Groups at Risk   Posttraumatic stress disorder is fairly common. In a representative national sample of close to 6,000 people, between the ages of 15 and 54, almost 8 percent had had this disorder at some time in their lives, though, as is often the case with anxiety

Persian Gulf War Syndrome

Was the experience of soldiers in the Persian Gulf War of 1990–1991 different from that in other wars? The war was short, and relatively few Americans suffered casualties. Nevertheless, the Gulf War was quite stressful for most participants. In many cases, members of reserve units were pressed into service in a matter of days and transported to the Gulf for combat. More women than ever before served in combat functions, and more married men with children also served (Rundell & Ursano, 1996). And, for the first time in recent war, Americans fought in a theatre in which the enemy was suspected of having the capability of using massive doses of chemical and biological weapons.

It was not surprising that many veterans of the war experienced symptoms of stress and anxiety following their return. As this book goes to press, there is still disagreement about the source of these reactions. Many veterans have been labeled as experiencing a "Gulf War syndrome." As of 1997, more than 70,000 veterans (out of about 700,000) have signed up as possible sufferers of this syndrome. Many of the symptoms are characteristic of acute stress disorder and posttraumatic stress disorder: nightmares, trouble sleeping and maintaining normal routines, intrusive thoughts associated with traumatic combat events, and chronic fatigue. Many of these veterans also suffer from elevated levels of depression.

Recent research indicates that veterans of the Gulf War experience a range of symptoms, some of which may well have sources other than the stress of combat. For example, a study of 249 Gulf War veterans found that at least 25 percent had symptoms that could result from damage to the central nervous system (Haley, Thomas, & Hom, 1997), including problems in concentrating, muscle pain, and urinary incontinence. One hypothesis is that poisonous gases were released at various points during the war, some as a result of deliberate Iraqi chemical warfare and some as a result of bombings of enemy munitions depots. Although the gases that were released may not have produced immediate symptoms in soldiers, it is possible that these gases had a delayed effect, which is now appearing in Gulf War veterans. Other explanations involve overexposure to protective applications such as insect repellants.

Our experience in Vietnam, the last major war effort involving U.S. soldiers, suggests that chemical weapons can produce long-lasting effects. It was not for many years until research was able to determine the potential effects of Agent Orange on people. This chemical was sprayed by U.S. forces to defoliate enemy territory. Unfortunately, the chemical is toxic to people and animals and may have caused serious illness in many Vietnam veterans. It may take many years to determine if other toxic agents caused the many symptoms that Gulf War veterans continue to experience.

The Gulf War experience reinforces what we already knew from other wars: combat veterans suffer heightened levels of both acute and chronic stress disorders, these disorders are difficult to separate from the effects of potentially harmful biological agents, and we lack sufficient knowledge about these war-related traumas to be able to prevent them or reduce their impact on veterans.

---

disorders, people who were separated, divorced, or widowed were at higher risk, and women also were more susceptible. The survey also turned up some expectable differences in the nature of the precipitating trauma. For men, the traumas most often associated with posttraumatic stress disorder were combat exposure and seeing someone killed or badly injured. For women, the most frequently reported stressors were rape and sexual molestation (Kessler, Sonnega, Bromet, et al., 1995). Various researchers have reported rates of posttraumatic stress disorder as high as 80 percent in rape victims, 87 percent in survivors of childhood sexual abuse, and 54 to 88 percent in prisoners of war (Davis & Breslau, 1994; Sutker & Allain, 1996; Rodriguez, Ryan, Vande Kemp, et al., 1997). Nonwhites may also be at higher risk than whites (La-Greca, Silverman, Vernberg, et al., 1996).

As the survey rates show, however, not all people are disabled by traumatic experiences. Many soldiers, for example, go through grueling combat experiences and emerge with nothing more than a few bad dreams. What determines the severity of the response? As Table 6.1 indicates, the severity of the trauma is a significant factor. Among soldiers, for example, the greater the combat exposure and the threat of death, the greater the likelihood of posttraumatic stress disorder (Rundell & Ursano, 1996). The person's psychological strength before the trauma may be more important. In a study of volunteer firefighters who survived the huge wave of bushfires that hit southern Australia in 1983, Alexander McFarlane (1988, 1989) found that the intensity of exposure to the fire, the degree of perceived threat, and even the extent of personal losses did not predict posttraumatic stress disorder; what did predict it was pretrauma adjustment and family psychiatric history. Those who had been chronically distressed, especially in their personal relationships, and those with a greater family history of psychopathology were the most likely to develop posttraumatic stress disorder.

Victims of a natural catastrophe like the devastating earthquake of 1994 in Northridge, California, are at risk to develop posttraumatic stress disorder.

Related to this finding are the long-term studies by Zahava Solomon and her colleagues of Israeli soldiers who fought in the 1982 Lebanon war (Mikulincer & Solomon, 1988; Solomon, Mikulincer, & Benbenishty, 1989b; Solomon, Mikulincer, & Flum, 1988). These researchers found that coping styles and attributional styles (styles of assigning causes to events) had an important relationship to the soldiers' posttraumatic state. "Problem-focused coping," the effort to analyze problems or get help in dealing with them—as opposed to "emotion-focused coping" (wishful thinking, denial, emotional venting)—apparently served as good protection against posttraumatic stress disorder, as did a tendency to attribute events to controllable causes. As cognitive theorists would predict, those who felt (and acted) most helpless were the most vulnerable to long-term psychiatric effects. Other studies of disaster victims have found that people who assign external causes to events surrounding the disaster—in other words, those, who do not blame themselves—are better protected against posttraumatic symptoms (Joseph, Williams, & Yule, 1995).

Logically, another factor in risk for posttraumatic stress disorder is the environment to which the person returns after the trauma. In a study of 442 Miami schoolchildren who lived through Hurricane Andrew, LaGreca and her colleagues found that the children most likely to develop posttraumatic stress disorder were those who lacked adequate social support—for example, a parent in whom they could confide their fears—and those who, after the hurricane, were exposed to additional major stresses, such as the death or hospitalization of a family member (LaGreca, Silverman, Vernberg, et al., 1996).

Finally, the likelihood of posttraumatic stress disorder also depends on the nature of the trauma. Traumas caused by human actions, such as rape, tend to precipitate more severe reactions than do natural disasters such as floods, earthquakes, and hurricanes (O'Donohue & Elliot, 1992). Apparently, the nature of the symptoms also depends on the nature of the trauma. Studies of Vietnam veterans (Laufer, Brett, & Gallops, 1985) and of survivors of civil and terrorist violence in Northern Ireland (Loughrey, Bell, Kee, et al., 1988) indicate that *reexperiencing symptoms* (intrusive memories, nightmares, startle reactions) are most common in those who have witnessed or suffered acts of abusive violence, whereas *denial symptoms* (emotional numbing, difficulty in concen-

TABLE 6.1 Factors Affecting the Likelihood of Posttraumatic Stress Disorder

Features of the Trauma	Features of the Person	Features of the Posttrauma Environment
Intensity of exposure to trauma	Pretrauma psychological adjustment	Availability and quality of social support
Duration of exposure to trauma	Family history of psychopathology	Additional major stressors
Extent of threat posed by trauma	Cognitive and coping styles	
Nature of trauma: caused by humans or natural disaster	Feelings of guilt	

trating) are most common in those who have themselves participated in acts of abusive violence.

Problems in the Classification of Posttraumatic Stress Disorder

There are a number of questions about posttraumatic stress disorder as a diagnostic category (Davidson & Foa, 1991). To begin with, *DSM-IV* defines the disorder as a response to an event that involves "actual or threatened death or serious injury, or a threat to the physical integrity of oneself or others." But studies have found that more usual events, such as a miscarriage or the discovery of a spouse's affair, can also precipitate the symptoms of posttraumatic stress disorder (Helzer, Robins, & McEvoy, 1987). Currently, severe reactions to these more ordinary traumas are classified separately as *adjustment disorders*. But it is possible that they, too, should be called posttraumatic stress disorders.

A second problem with this diagnosis is that *most* victims of severe trauma show symptoms associated with posttraumatic stress disorder. Even if, in most people, the symptoms do not last for the month required to earn the diagnosis of posttraumatic stress disorder, we are still left with the question of whether a response that is almost universal should be designated as a psychological disorder (Solomon, Laor, & McFarlane, 1996).

A final problem with this diagnostic category is whether it should be grouped with the anxiety disorders. There are grounds for doing so. Not only is anxiety one of the foremost symptoms of posttraumatic stress disorder, but the disorder shares additional symptoms, such as fear-based avoidance, with the other anxiety syndromes (Davidson & Foa, 1991; Rothbaum, Foa, Murdock, et al., 1990). Furthermore, first-degree relatives of posttraumatic patients show a high rate of anxiety disorders (Davidson, Smith, & Kudler, 1989). But there is also an argument for placing posttraumatic stress disorder among the dissociative disorders (Chapter 7), for the defining characteristic of that group—the dissociation, or splitting off, of a part of experience or personality—is also seen in the "psychic numbing" and other denial symptoms of posttraumatic stress disorder patients. According to some researchers, however, posttraumatic stress disorder should not be classified with either the anxiety or the dissociative disorders. They argue that, because posttraumatic stress disorder is defined in large measure by its precipitating event, the trauma, it should be placed in a separate category of stress-related disorders (Davidson & Foa, 1991). But this may not be a good solution, either, for many forms of psychopathology—depression, dissociative disorders, and borderline personality disorder, to name a few—seem to be precipitated by trauma (McGorry, 1995).

Anxiety Disorders: Theory and Therapy

In Chapters 4 and 5, we presented a general overview of the various perspectives on psychological disturbance. In the present section, we will see how adherents of these perspectives interpret and treat the anxiety disorders.

The Psychodynamic Perspective: Neurosis

Psychodynamic writers call the anxiety disorders neuroses. (We will do the same in discussing this perspective.) Neurosis has been the major focus of psychodynamic theory, the subject of countless books and articles. Our discussion here is only an outline.

The Roots of Neurosis

As we saw in Chapter 4, Freud viewed anxiety as stemming not just from external danger but also from threatened breakdowns in the ego's struggle to satisfy the id without violating the demands of reality and the superego. This push and counterpush goes on all the time in normal lives and usually works well enough so that anxiety over the id impulse is never experienced consciously. In some cases, however, the anxiety is so intense that it *is* experienced consciously, with debilitating results. Or it is kept at bay only through the use of extremely rigid defense mechanisms. It is these situations that, according to psychodynamic theory, constitute neurotic behavior.

In cases where anxiety is experienced chronically and directly, without elaborate defense, what we see is generalized anxiety disorder. The cause is repressed, but the anxiety leaks through. In the panic attack, the cause—that is, the id impulse—moves closer to the boundaries of the conscious mind, resulting in an urgent buildup of anxiety. In phobia, the ego defends against the anxiety by displacing it, as in Freud's famous case of "Little Hans" (1909/1962). Hans was a 5-year-old Viennese boy who refused to go out into the street for fear that a horse from one of the city's many horse-drawn carriages would bite him. Freud's interpretation of the phobia was that Hans was caught up in a fierce Oedipal struggle. As usual in Oedipal conflicts, the boy's hostility toward his father was accompanied by intense anxiety that the father would retaliate by castrating him. Hans managed this by displacing his fear onto horses—a logical substitution, since his father would sometimes play "horsie" with him and had black glasses and a moustache reminiscent of the horses' black blinders and muzzles. Having made this substitution, Hans could relieve his anxiety by avoiding horses—a strategy, however, that left him phobic.

Psychodynamic thinkers may interpret obsessive-compulsive disorder in a number of ways, depending on the nature of the symptoms. In the case of a man obsessed with the fear that he will kill his wife in her sleep, psychodynamic theory would suggest that the unconscious aggressive impulse has, in fact, made its way into the conscious mind. On the other hand, cleanliness rituals and obsessions with germs would be interpreted as a reaction formation against wishes surviving from childhood and especially from the anal stage: the desire to soil, to play with feces, and to be generally messy and destructive.

To psychodynamic theorists, then, the anxiety disorders really differ only in the choice of defense, and some preliminary research supports this view. In a study of anxiety disorder patients (Pollock & Andrews, 1989), those with panic disorder were most likely to use displacement, reaction formation, and somatization (preoccupation with physical symptoms); those with social phobia tended to use displacement and devaluation (criticism of self and others); and those with obsessive-compulsive disorder relied on projection, acting out (childish, impulsive behavior), and undoing (making amends for a negative thought or action by some compensatory action). This theory that "defense style" determines the nature of the disorder is one of the strengths of the psychodynamic position. Other perspectives are not always clear on why anxiety takes one form over another.

A more recent psychodynamic explanation of the anxiety disorders comes from Bowlby's attachment theory. As we saw in Chapter 4, Bowlby claimed that disturbances in the parent-child bond could leave the child in a state of "anxious attachment" marked by dependency and insecurity. According to proponents of this theory, such children grow up vulnerable to anxiety disorders, especially panic disorder and agoraphobia. Retrospective studies of panic disorder patients do show that these people are disproportion-

ately likely to have childhood histories marked by separation anxiety, parental loss, or inadequate parenting in general (Shear, 1996; Silove, Manicavasagar, Curtis, et al., 1996).

Treating Neurosis The goal of psychodynamic therapy for the anxiety disorders, as for most disorders, is to expose and neutralize the material that the ego is defending against, so that the ego will be freed to spend its energy on more useful tasks. In Chapter 4, we outlined the basic techniques that orthodox psychoanalysis uses to achieve this goal. Patients are asked to lie on a couch and engage in free association, reporting whatever comes to their minds. They are also asked to describe their dreams. In both cases, the analyst delves beneath the manifest content of the patient's statements and interprets their latent content, or unconscious meaning. As this process goes forward, patients are expected to show **resistance,** or refusal to confront the unconscious conflict. They change the subject, begin missing appointments, and so forth. They also begin to develop **transference,** reenacting with the therapist the love and hostility they felt toward their parents. Both resistance and transference are also interpreted to the patient.

In the past few decades, however, psychodynamic therapists have moved toward briefer, face-to-face therapies, directed more at the present than at the past and aimed at specific symptoms. For example, Shear, Pilkonis, Clotre, et al. (1994) have experimented with an "emotion-focused" treatment for panic disorder. In this therapy, panic is seen as being related either to a feeling of being trapped (the result of being overprotected by others) or to a fear of being unable to get needed help (the result of being abandoned by others). Panic disorder patients, it is thought, tend to avoid pinpointing these feelings;

In traditional psychoanalysis, the client lies on a couch and the therapist sits out of his or her view (left). In the past few decades, however, psychodynamic therapists have shifted to face-to-face encounters with their clients (right).

the object of emotion-focused therapy is to get the patient to confront them and to understand how they may trigger panic attacks.

The Behavioral Perspective: Learning to Be Anxious

Behavioral researchers have challenged the psychodynamic argument that the anxiety disorders stem from unconscious conflict. In their view, these disorders arise from faulty learning.

How We Learn Anxiety   One important theory of anxiety disorders is that they are engendered through avoidance learning (Mowrer, 1948). This theory, already described briefly in Chapter 5, involves a two-stage process:

Stage 1. In the course of the person's experience, a neutral stimulus is paired with an aversive stimulus; thus, through respondent conditioning, the neutral stimulus becomes anxiety-arousing.

Stage 2. The person avoids the conditioned stimulus, and, because this avoidance results in relief from anxiety (i.e., negative reinforcement), the avoidance response, via operant conditioning, becomes habitual.

Imagine, for example, a man who periodically gets drunk and beats his young daughter. Soon the signs of the father's drinking (CS) will become paired in the child's mind with the pain of the beating (UCS), and she will experience anxiety (CR) at the first sign that her father has been drinking. Eventually, this anxiety may generalize to the father as a whole, drunk or sober, in which case he himself becomes the CS. Therefore, she avoids him, and, every time she does so, her anxiety is relieved, thus reinforcing the avoidance response. In time, the anxiety may generalize further—for example, to men in general. Again she responds with avoidance, and again avoidance produces negative reinforcement in the form of anxiety relief. Ultimately, this process may leave her, as an adult, with serious social problems.

In the view of many behaviorists, the disorders that we have discussed in this chapter are variations on avoidance-reinforced anxiety. Panic attacks, for example, are seen as extreme conditioned fear reactions to internal physiological sensations (Wolpe & Rowan, 1988); agoraphobia, which, as we have seen, often develops as a way of avoiding having a panic attack in public, is thus the product of Stage 2. In specific phobias, the avoidance strategy is less global—one need not become housebound in order to avoid elevators, for example—but the process is the same: the object becomes aversive through respondent conditioning

(e.g., a childhood experience of feeling smothered in a confined space), and then avoidance is learned through negative reinforcement. In obsessive-compulsive disorder, the anxious person has found that some action, such as hand washing, reduces his or her anxiety; the action, thus, becomes a form of avoidance, strengthened, once again, through negative reinforcement. In posttraumatic stress disorder, the psychological distress and heightened arousal that patients show in response to reminders of the trauma are the products of respondent conditioning, and their "psychic numbing" and amnesia for the event are the avoidance strategy.

This two-stage avoidance-learning theory has been buttressed by a number of studies. However, it has at least three problems. First, while some anxiety patients do report traumatic conditioning experiences (Merckelbach, de Jong, Muris, et al., 1996), others do not. Many phobics, for example, cannot remember any formative encounter with the object of their phobia. Second, traditional learning theory is hard put to explain why only very select, nonrandom types of stimuli typically become phobic objects. Guns, knives, and electrical outlets, for example, should be at least as likely as animals, heights, and enclosed spaces to be associated with traumatic conditioning experiences, yet the former are rare as phobic objects, while the latter are common. Why? Seligman (1971) proposed that, via natural selection, human beings may be "prepared" to fear certain stimuli that would have been threatening to our evolutionary ancestors—for example, as snakes would have been but as electrical outlets would not. This is an ingenious theory that has been supported by some experimental evidence, though it is contradicted by other evidence (Davey, 1995; Tomarken, Sutton, & Mineka, 1995).

A third and very serious problem with the avoidance-learning theory is that it focuses entirely on concrete stimuli and observable responses without concern for the *thoughts* that may be involved in anxiety. Many studies indicate that such an explanation is insufficient. A stimulus does not have to be experienced directly in order to arouse anxiety. People can acquire anxiety responses vicariously, by watching others react with pain to a given stimulus. For instance, children of spider-phobic parents are more likely than children of controls to show fear when viewing a film with spiders in it (Unnewehr, Schneider, Margraf, et al., 1996). Even monkeys can learn to be afraid just by watching other monkeys respond with fear to an unfamiliar object (Cook, Mineka, Wolkenstein, et al., 1985). In human beings, not even observation is required to feel fear. While walking through a high-crime neighborhood, you do not have to have seen someone mugged in that part of town. You need only have heard that that neighborhood is dangerous.

What do you feel when you look at this picture? One intriguing theory about the origins of anxiety is that natural selection may have predisposed humans to fear stimuli, such as heights, that our prehistoric ancestors would have had to avoid in order to survive.

What all this suggests is that cognitive processes play an important role in the acquisition of anxiety responses. Indeed, recent research indicates that, for most people suffering from agoraphobia, specific phobias, and social phobia, the fear was acquired through a combination of direct learning and cognitive processes, such as observation and exposure to negative information (Merckelbach, de Jong, Muris, et al., 1996). Cognitive processes may also determine the behavioral *response* to anxiety. Albert Bandura (1977, 1982) has shown that the best predictor of avoidance behavior is not the amount of anxiety experienced but, rather, *efficacy expectations*—people's expectations, based on past performance, as to how well they will be able to cope with the situation. Many actors and dancers, for example, suffer intense stage fright, some to the point of vomiting before performances, yet they still go onstage, presumably because they know from experience that they can perform well despite their anxiety.

A theory related to efficacy expectations is the *fear-of-fear* interpretation of panic disorder (Barlow, 1988). In this view, the physiological changes that accompany the panic attack—increased heart rate, sweating, and so forth—become conditioned stimuli for further panic attacks: when these changes start to occur, even for ordinary reasons, the person begins to feel afraid of a coming attack, and, in a classic spiral, the fear intensifies the physiological reactions and vice versa until the attack occurs. For example, many panic patients avoid exercise or sexual activity because the increased physiological arousal produces fear of an impending attack (Barlow, 1988). This fear of fear—also called "anxiety sensitivity"—is seen in many kinds of anxiety disorder but, above all, in panic disorder (Reiss, Peterson, Gursky, et al., 1986), and research indicates that it increases the risk for future panic attacks (Schmidt, Lerew, & Jackson, 1997).

Unlearning Anxiety   For the anxiety disorders, behaviorists have evolved a set of related techniques aimed at reducing anxiety through confrontation with the feared stimulus. In Chapter 5, we described **systematic desensitization** (Wolpe, 1973), in which the client draws up a "hierarchy of fears" and then imagines them, one by one, while in a state of deep muscle relaxation. Alternatively, the client might approach the feared stimulus *in vivo,* or in the flesh, also while in a state of relaxation.

Systematic desensitization worked well with specific phobias, but eventually behavioral therapists found that the relaxation-training component was often unnecessary. Clients could be helped simply through **exposure,** or confrontation (sudden or gradual) with the feared stimulus. For example, in one study of clients with blood or injection phobias, the clients were exposed to more and more threatening stimuli, such as pictures of hypodermic needles or blood stained pads, and then the actual objects. Meanwhile, they were instructed to keep their muscles tense so that their blood pressure would remain high enough to prevent them from fainting. Close to 90 percent of the clients were cured within five sessions (Ost, Sterner, & Fellenius, 1989). With obsessive-compulsive disorder, exposure is usually combined with "response prevention" (Riggs & Foa, 1993). A contaminant-fearing client not only is asked to handle the substances he or she fears but also is prevented from relieving the fear by performing a ritual. When this produces no disastrous results, presumably the anxiety would extinguish.

When exposure is imagined rather than *in vivo,* it often takes the form of **flooding,** in which the person is confronted with the feared stimulus for prolonged periods of time. In the case of the social-phobic physician described earlier in the chapter, the client and her therapist together wrote the following scene:

> It's daily rounds at the VA [Veterans Administration hospital]. Today's even more stressful than usual, because the chairman, a White, older male is participating on rounds. The other residents, interns, and medical students are showing off, quoting from the *New England Journal of Medicine* and talking all at once. The whole while, you are thinking to yourself, "I should be saying something." You really want to be at your best. The chairman looks around the group and says, "Before we start, why don't we go around the circle and say who we are." You immediately think, "What if the words don't come out?" ... You open your mouth to say your name, and the words just do not come out. You can't say your name! You feel hot and begin to sweat. Everyone is looking at you in horrified silence.... You hear the intern next to you say "This is Dr. XXXXX; she's having a bad day" ... You see the chairman lean to the person next to him and hear him say, "How can she function as a physician; she can't even say her own name. She's so incompetent that she can't even talk." Everyone continues to stare at you. You feel incredibly stupid. You feel inept. You are not cut out to be a physician, and everyone there knows it. (Fink, Turner, & Beidel, 1996, p. 204)

In weekly sessions, this narrative was read to the client, and she was asked to imagine it until her anxiety abated. As in many treatments using imagined stimuli, the client was also given *in vivo* assignments:

> She was specifically to initiate a set number of conversations and outings with her White neighbors and coworkers each week. While attending a professional conference, she was required to invite a White physician to lunch. She also had to invite her employer, a White, middle-aged, male physician to lunch. Finally, she engaged in therapist-directed, but not accompanied, exposure to hospitals. She was instructed to go to a highly avoided local hospital and remain there until she experienced a 50% reduction in her initial distress. (Fink, Turner, & Beidel, 1996, pp. 205–206)

Exposure techniques such as these have proved helpful with specific phobias, social phobia, panic disorder (with and without agoraphobia), obsessive-compulsive disorder, and posttraumatic stress disorder (Barlow & Lehman, 1996). Graded exposure is now the common denominator of behavioral treatments for the anxiety disorders. But is it sufficient? Probably only for specific phobias. With more complex anxiety disorders, exposure treatments generally work better than other treatments, but they are not wholly effective. Many cases of obsessive-compulsive disorder survive exposure therapy. Likewise, a review of reports on exposure therapy for agoraphobia

found that fewer than half the clients were functioning at normal levels by the end of treatment (Jacobson, Wilson, & Tupper, 1990).

There is now some hope that the effectiveness of exposure therapy may be increased by combining it with cognitive therapy (Heimberg, Salzman, Holt, et al., 1993). Social phobics have been treated in group therapy involving cognitive restructuring, together with exercises that push the client into social situations. Other researchers have developed a multicomponent "stress management" therapy for war veterans and rape victims suffering from posttraumatic stress disorder. This treatment involves not only exposure and cognitive therapy but also coaching in relaxation, anger management, and problem solving. We do not yet know how well these new, combined therapies work or, if they do work, which of the components, the behavioral or the cognitive, is the "active ingredient."

The Cognitive Perspective: Misperception of Threat

As we have seen, cognitive processes play a role in the development of anxiety disorders. To cognitive theorists, that role is central. According to their theory, the problem with anxiety disorder patients is that they misperceive or misinterpret stimuli, internal and external. What is not really threatening, these people *see* as threatening—hence their symptoms. (As the box "Anxiety and Selective Attention" on page 167 illustrates, these patients may actually have a way of *looking for* a threat in stimuli they are exposed to.) Although cognitive models have been proposed for each of the anxiety disorders, we will focus on panic disorder. This is because cognitive approaches to panic disorder have been especially successful and influential.

Anxiety as Misperception We noted earlier that many different kinds of stimuli—sodium lactate, hyperventilation, carbon dioxide inhalation, confrontation with phobic stimuli—have been found to provoke panic attacks. No single biological mechanism can account for the fact that all these different things produce panic. But there is a single cognitive mechanism that can explain it. If a person, upon experiencing unusual body sensations (which all these panic-inducing agents do produce), interprets such sensations catastrophically, as a signal that he or she is about to pass out or have a heart attack, then panic could result. (See Figure 6.1.)

Fundamentally, that is the cognitive interpretation of panic disorder. As we noted, most experts do not believe that panic attacks come "out of the blue."

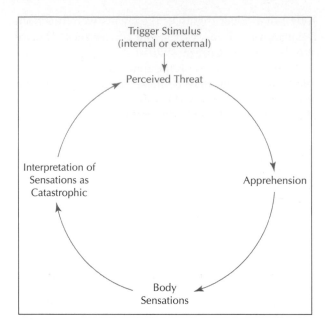

FIGURE 6.1   A cognitive model of a panic attack.

Often, upon investigation, an attack is found to have been preceded by an event that altered the person's physiological state in some way—for example, exercising, having sexual relations, drinking a beverage containing caffeine, or even getting up quickly from a seated position. Most of us, when we do these things, experience some internal adjustments—the heart skips a beat, breathing may become momentarily labored—but we ignore these sensations. Panic disorder patients do not ignore them; they interpret them as dangerous, which aggravates the sensations. As the sensations become more extreme, so does the interpretation, eventually mounting to the conviction of impending doom that characterizes a panic attack (Clark, 1993). Note that this formulation is related to, but slightly different from, the fear-of-fear theory. In fear of fear, the internal changes become a conditioned stimulus for the panic attack. In the cognitive model, the internal changes must be followed by an *interpretation* of those changes, a catastrophic interpretation, for the attack to ensue. Having developed the catastrophic interpretation, the person begins to pay even closer attention to internal sensations that might mean "danger"—which makes further attacks more likely. Meanwhile, the catastrophic interpretation persists because, by engaging in safety-seeking behaviors, the person never tests it. For example, a panic disorder patient may habitually hold on to a chair during a panic attack in order to prevent herself from collapsing. As a result, she never discovers that she wouldn't collapse if she were to let go of the chair (Salkovskis, Clark, & Gelder, 1996).

There is considerable experimental support for this model. Research has shown that panic disorder patients are more likely to misinterpret body sensations than are other anxiety disorder patients or normal controls (Clark, Salkovskis, Gelder, et al., 1988; Cox, 1996). In addition, activating negative interpretations of body sensations has been found to produce panic attacks in panic disorder patients. For example, in one study, panic disorder patients and controls were asked to read aloud a series of word pairs, some of which linked internal sensations with catastrophic experiences (e.g., *breathlessness/suffocate; palpitations/dying; collapse/insane*). Ten out of 12 of the panic disorder patients, but no recovered patients or normal controls, had a panic attack while reading these words (Clark, Salkovskis, Gelder et al., 1988).

Finally, some studies have shown that panic attacks can be prevented by decreasing patients' tendency to misinterpret internal sensations as catastrophic (Carter, Hollon, Carson, et al., 1995; Clark, Gelder, Salkovskis, et al., 1991). In one experiment, 20 panic disorder patients were asked to inhale carbon dioxide, which they knew might produce a panic attack, and they were all told that, when a light in front of them went on, they could use a dial attached to their chairs to adjust the carbon dioxide level. In fact, the dial did nothing; all the subjects received the same amount of carbon dioxide, but under differing cognitive conditions, because, as it turned out, the light went on for only half the subjects. Thus, the subjects in this experiment differed not in their actual control but in their sense of control. At the end of the experiment, the "controlling" subjects reported significantly fewer panic symptoms than those who had had no sense of control (Sanderson, Rapee, & Barlow, 1989).

This theory is not airtight, however. It does not explain, for example, why panic attacks that occur during sleep are often unconnected with dreams of any sort, let alone dreams of catastrophe (Ley, 1988a,b). Furthermore, certain studies have found that some panic disorder patients either do not report catastrophic cognitions until *after* the attack (Wolpe & Rowan, 1988) or do not report them at all (Rachman, Lopatka, & Levitt, 1988). And the theory does not explain how such catastrophic interpretations of body sensations develop in the first place.

The cognitive theorists' view of agoraphobia is simply an expansion of their view of panic disorder. For agoraphobia to develop out of panic disorder, what is needed is one further cognitive appraisal: that one cannot cope with the panic. In a study comparing panic disorder patients with and without agoraphobia, the agoraphobics, predictably, scored much lower on the perception of self-efficacy in coping with

Cognitive theorists believe that people with anxiety disorders have distorted perceptions of the world around them, and a number of studies suggest that this is the case. Not only do people with anxiety disorders pay more attention to threatening stimuli than to neutral or positive stimuli, but they choose their threatening stimuli according to the type of anxiety disorder they have.

The studies that produced these findings were ingeniously designed. Some rely on the Stroop task, which asks participants to name, as quickly and accurately as possible, the colors of the ink in which a series of words is presented (Stroop, 1935). Participants are not supposed to pay attention to the meaning of the words, only to their colors. In one study, however, people with generalized anxiety disorder took significantly longer to identify the colors of "threat" words than the colors of "nonthreat" words, such as *holiday* and *contented*. Participants whose concerns were predominantly physical hesitated over "physical threat" words, such as *disease* and *mutilated*. Those whose anxiety was primarily social paused for "social threat" words, such as *failure* and *inadequate* (Maidenberg, Chen, Craske,

et al., 1996; Mogg, Mathews, & Weinman, 1989). It has also been found that, after cognitive-behavioral therapy, generalized anxiety disorder patients show less attentional bias for threat words on the Stroop task (Mogg, Bradley, Millar, et al., 1995).

In another study, Vietnam combat veterans with posttraumatic stress disorder were slower than control participants to name the colors of words such as *bodybags*, *'Nam*, and *firefight* (McNally, Kaspi, Riemann, et al., 1990). They also took more time on Vietnam-related words than on other words that were emotionally charged, either positively (*love, pleasant, loyal*) or negatively (*germs, filthy, urine*—words selected because they relate to another anxiety disorder, obsessive-compulsive disorder).

Motor-vehicle accident victims with posttraumatic stress disorder were also slower than control participants to name the colors of accident-related words, such as *traffic* and *blood* but not of neutral or positive words (Harvey, Bryant & Rapee, 1996).

Similarly, in people with panic disorder, "fear" words (*panic, fear, anxiety*), "body sensation" words (*dizzy, heartbeat, faintness*), and "catastrophe" words (*death, heart attack, insane*) produced progressively greater inter-

ference with the speed of color naming than did neutral words (*polite, moderate, clever*). Control participants experienced a similar *pattern* of delay in naming the colors, especially of the "catastrophe" words, but the magnitude of interference for these and the other threat cues was much less for them (McNally, Riemann, & Kim, 1990).

Another paradigm used to measure this attentional bias involves homophones, words that sound alike but are spelled differently and mean different things. In one homophone study, anxious participants listened to a tape recording of words that might or might not be threatening, depending on which way they were spelled (*die/dye, slay/sleigh, foul/fowl*). After they heard each word, they were asked to spell it. The clinically anxious participants tended to choose the more threatening of the two possible spellings—to write *moan* instead of *mown* and *pain* instead of *pane*, for example (Mathews, Richards, & Eysenck, 1989). Presumably, these participants interpreted the world in the same way: a phone ringing in the night meant a death in the family; a boss's bad mood meant the person was going to be fired. Thus, through attentional bias, they created the dangers they feared.

panic (Telch, Brouillard, Telch, et al., 1989). Similarly, agoraphobic avoidance in the absence of panic attacks is seen as a consequence of the belief that one will not be able to cope if a symptom occurs away from home. It has also been found that prior history of mastery and control experiences is a predictor of agoraphobic avoidance. Not surprisingly, people who have faced difficulties and have overcome them are less likely to deal with panic attacks by avoidance, as happens in agoraphobia (Craske & Barlow, 1988).

Cognitive theorists see the remaining anxiety disorders as variations on this misinterpretation-of-threat theme. In specific phobia, it is the threat of the phobic object that is misinterpreted; in social phobia, it is the threat of disapproval from others; in posttraumatic stress disorder, it is the threat of things in the environment associated with the remembered trauma; in obsessive-compulsive disorder, it is the

threat of certain thoughts, which, in the person's eyes, will have catastrophic consequences if such consequences are not forestalled by the compulsive ritual.

Reducing Perceptions of Threat A revolution in the treatment of panic disorder was created when researchers and clinicians began focusing on the panic attacks themselves, rather than on the avoidance behavior that normally accompanies this disorder. Most of the recent cognitive treatments for panic disorder are based on the work of David Clark and his colleagues, who designed a therapy that has three main parts: identifying patients' negative interpretations of body sensations; suggesting alternative, noncatastrophic interpretations; and helping patients test the validity of these alternative explanations (Clark, Salkovskis, & Chalkley, 1985; Clark, Salkovskis, Hackman, et al., 1994). For example, patients may be taught an alternative interpretation for the body sensations they respond to with such fear, that the sensations are the result of something they can control: breathing. Patients are asked to hyperventilate. Then, when they begin to experience the same sensations that have triggered their panic attacks, this similarity is pointed out to them, and they are taught how to do slow, deep breathing that reduces the symptoms. For many patients, this is their first experience of controlling a panic attack—a lesson that is then buttressed by the therapist's teaching them new cognitions to use in combating the misperception of threat when an attack occurs outside the office. Together, patient and therapist also try to identify what the patient's attack "triggers" are. When the triggers are identified, the attacks seem more understandable, less terrifying. The patient may also be able to avoid some of them.

This therapy has proved highly successful. In five controlled studies, between 75 and 95 percent of the panic disorder patients became free of panic attacks after three months of cognitive therapy, and these improvements were maintained at one- and two-year follow-ups (Clark, 1991). Moreover, cognitive therapy compares favorably with behavioral and drug treatments for panic disorder, and, compared with these other forms of treatment, it appears to decrease the likelihood of relapse (Clark, 1991).

The only remaining question about this cognitive therapy is what makes it work. According to Clark and his colleagues, the basis of the improvement is a cognitive change. Meanwhile, David Barlow and his colleagues have developed a panic-control therapy that is similar to Clark's and apparently works just as well, but they attribute the success of their treatment to exposure—exposure to the feared stimuli as well as a kind of exposure that these researchers call "interoceptive conditioning," in which patients are exposed to their internal anxiety cues, such as hyperventilation and rapid heart rate (Barlow & Lehman, 1996). Whether the basic change mechanism is extinction through exposure (Barlow) or cognitive retraining (Clark), the fact remains that an effective treatment for panic disorder has been developed, and it is clearly the treatment of choice for this condition.

For generalized anxiety disorder, the best approach seems to be combined cognitive and behavioral therapy (Borkovec & Costello, 1993). Cognitive restructuring is used to help patients control their worrying. At the same time, behavioral strategies are used to teach them how to relax, to solve interpersonal problems, and to structure their lives more effectively. As we saw earlier, similar cognitive-behavioral treatments are now being tried with posttraumatic stress disorder.

The Biological Perspective: Biochemistry and Medication

Genetic Research Of all the anxiety disorders, the one that seems most likely to have a genetic basis is panic disorder (Crowe, 1991). The risk of panic disorder in the first-degree relatives of panic disorder patients is 8 to 21 percent, as opposed to 1 to 2 percent in the general population (Weissman, 1993). As we have seen, family studies offer the weakest form of genetic evidence, for they cannot separate environmental from genetic influence. But twin studies, which are more informative, have also implicated genes in panic disorder (Skre, Onstad, Torgersen, et al., 1993). In a Norwegian study, the concordance rate for panic disorder in MZ twins was 31 percent, as opposed to 0 percent for DZ twins (Torgersen, 1983).

For the other anxiety disorders, the genetic evidence is weaker but still significant. A well-controlled family study of adult obsessive-compulsive patients found that the rate of obsessive-compulsive disorder in their first-degree relatives was about 10 percent, as opposed to about 2 percent in the relatives of controls (Pauls, Alsobrook, Goodman, et al., 1995). Twin studies also indicate some genetic basis for obsessive-compulsive disorder: the concordance rate for compulsive behaviors has been found to be about twice as high in MZ twins as in DZ twins (Carey & Gottesman, 1981). As for specific phobias, a study of the first-degree relatives of phobics found them to be three to four times more likely to have phobias than first-degree relatives of normal controls (Fyer, Mannuzza, Chapman, et al., 1995). For social phobia, the evidence is sketchier, though here, too, there are indications that the disorder runs in families (Fyer, Mannuzza, Chapman, et al., 1995).

Posttraumatic stress disorder also seems to involve some genetic predisposition, if only toward psychological disturbance in general. Earlier in this chapter, we saw that a family history of psychopathology predicted which of the Australian firefighters succumbed to posttraumatic stress disorder after the 1983 bushfires (McFarlane, 1988, 1989). In a study of war veterans, it was found that, when combat exposure was high, a family history of psychopathology seemed to have no effect on whether a person would develop a posttraumatic syndrome; it was when combat exposure was low that the soldiers with a family history of psychopathology were at greater risk (Foy, Resnick, Sipprelle, et al., 1987). The anxiety disorder for which there is the weakest evidence of genetic influence is generalized anxiety disorder. Some twin studies have found a modest heritability (Kendler, Neale, Kessler, et al., 1992); others have found no heritability (Torgersen, 1983).

If anxiety disorders are inherited, *what* exactly is inherited? Probably a diathesis, or vulnerability, toward anxiety disorders in general rather than toward a specific syndrome is inherited. For instance, rats can be bred for "nervousness" (Barlow, 1988); apparently, so can human beings. As for what this nervousness consists of, that is an open question. Possibly it is an overly responsive autonomic nervous system (Eysenck, 1967) or an attentional bias for threat. (See the box on page 167.) Or it may be what is called "behavioral inhibition," a childhood tendency to withdraw from unfamiliar situations (Kagan, 1989; Rosenbaum, Biederman, Pollock, et al., 1994). Whatever it is, however, one should keep in mind that it is only a predisposition toward anxiety. Recall the Norwegian twin studies, in which there was a 31 percent concordance rate between MZ twins for panic disorder. This is an impressive figure, but it means that more than two-thirds of the MZ twins, people with exactly the same genetic endowment, were not concordant. Obviously, environment plays an important role.

The Role of Neurotransmitters For years, it was known that under many circumstances, anxiety can be relieved by drugs, such as Valium, that belong to a chemical group called the benzodiazepines. But how the benzodiazepines actually affect the brain's chemistry remained a mystery. Then, in 1977, it was discovered that the benzodiazepines attach to certain receptors on the neurons of the brain. This finding suggests that the brain may have a natural chemical, similar to the benzodiazepines, that regulates certain forms of anxiety. It follows, then, that abnormalities in the level of this chemical—too high or too low—may underlie some anxiety disorders.

Whatever the chemical process in question, it involves a neurotransmitter called GABA (gamma-aminobutyric acid), for it is GABA that is activated by the benzodiazepines (Costa & Guidotti, 1985). GABA is an inhibitory neurotransmitter; that is, once it is activated, it turns *off* the affected neurons. Presumably, this is the chemical basis of the benzodiazepines' ability to control some forms of anxiety: they signal GABA to shut off a certain measure of neural activity, including the activity of neurons that use norepinephrine and serotonin for neurotransmission.

It is doubtful, however, that a shortfall in the inhibitory action of GABA underlies all anxiety conditions, nor is stimulation of GABA the only way in which the benzodiazepines operate. Certain types of anxiety, those experienced as generalized tension, are more responsive to the benzodiazepines than are other anxiety conditions, such as panic disorder, which are more responsive to another class of drugs, the antidepressants. (Refer to Table 4.1 on page 86 for the classification of psychotherapeutic drugs.) This finding points to two conclusions. First, the chemical basis of panic disorder is probably different from that of generalized anxiety—a conclusion already suggested by the genetic evidence (Johnson & Lydiard, 1995). In other words, there is apparently more than one kind of anxiety, at least biochemically. Second, panic disorder may be more closely related to depression biochemically than to generalized anxiety. We know that the antidepressants in question enhance norepinephrine and serotonin transmission, which has been repeatedly implicated in depression. Presumably, norepinephrine and serotonin are also involved in panic disorder (Nutt & Lawson, 1992), a theory bolstered by the finding that panic disorder patients often show abnormalities in the functioning of those two neurotransmitters (Butler, O'Halloran, & Leonard, 1992). Another link between depression and panic disorder is that both are associated with abnormalities in the hypothalamic-pituitary-adrenal hormone system (Abelson, Curtis, & Cameron, 1996).

One hypothesis as to the biochemistry of panic disorder (Gorman, Liebowitz, Fyer, et al., 1989) is that panic attacks are triggered by increased neurological firing in a section of the brainstem known as the locus ceruleus, a major norepinephrine center. Several lines of evidence point to this specific location. First, as we saw earlier, panic attacks can be provoked in the laboratory by an infusion of the drug yohimbine, and we know that yohimbine raises the firing rate in the locus ceruleus. Second, studies have shown that monkeys have paniclike reactions in response to electrical stimulation of the locus ceruleus and that, if the locus ceruleus is removed, they become less vulnerable to anxiety-provoking stimuli (Redmond, 1977, 1979). Third, panic disorder patients show abnormal brainwave activity in the locus ceruleus in response to auditory stimuli (Levy, Kimhi, Barak, et al., 1996). Fourth, substances that reduce the locus ceruleus firing rate—and these include the drugs currently used for panic disorder—do prevent panic attacks. Nevertheless, these findings have been challenged. Researchers in the laboratory have now provoked panic attacks with a wide range of stimuli, not all of which are clearly connected even to the brainstem, let alone to the locus ceruleus. (For further discussion of the relation between anxiety and the locus ceruleus, see the box on page 170.)

A competing biochemical theory of panic disorder is the "suffocation false alarm hypothesis." There is a monitor in the central nervous system that signals impending suffocation in response to elevated levels of carbon dioxide and brain lactate. According to the suffocation false alarm hypothesis, some people's suffocation monitors are hypersensitive and produce

When is brain deterioration good news? According to some researchers, the decreased incidence of anxiety disorders in middle-aged people may be the result of deterioration in the locus ceruleus, a portion of the medulla oblongata, which in turn is part of the brainstem.

The medulla oblongata has long been known to control such functions as breathing and heart rate and to produce the neurotransmitters epinephrine (adrenaline) and norepinephrine. The locus ceruleus, in particular, appears to be responsible for norepinephrine production—70 percent of all cells with receptors for this neurotransmitter are located there. Although the locus ceruleus is a tiny mass at the base of the brain, it has extensive connections to many other parts of the nervous system.

Normally, the locus ceruleus acts as a sort of alarm system, producing increased amounts of norepinephrine in the face of stress and real or imagined danger. High activity levels in the locus ceruleus are characteristic of panic attacks, for example, and low activity levels may be associated with reckless behavior.

As the body ages, however, the locus ceruleus apparently undergoes changes that reduce the amount of anxiety the person experiences. Autopsies of people aged 40 to 60 indicate that the cells of the locus ceruleus begin to lose their bluish color after 40. The cells of the locus ceruleus also become clogged in middle age with neuromelanin, thought to be a waste product of norepinephrine. This excess of neuromelanin slows the cells' functioning and eventually kills them. As a result, norepinephrine production declines sharply in middle age. At the same time, there is an increase in the production of monoamine oxidase, an enzyme that breaks down norepinephrine, thereby reducing further the amount of norepinephrine available to the brain.

As norepinephrine declines, so does anxiety. Many middle-aged people report feeling less worried and more self-assured than when they were younger. Of particular interest to psychotherapists is the decline of drug addiction, bulimia, and anxiety disorders such as panic attacks in patients over age 40 (Flint, Cook, & Rabins, 1996). According to Dr. Stephen Roose, a psychiatrist at the New York State Psychiatric Institute, "As these cells [of the locus ceruleus] die, diseases that are pathologies of this brain system seem to burn out."

---

false alarms, which then produce panic attacks. For this hypothesis, too, there are several kinds of evidence. As we saw earlier, exposure to increased levels of either carbon dioxide or sodium lactate produces attacks in panic disorder patients. And, if carbon dioxide is implicated, this would help to explain the occurrence of panic attacks during relaxation and sleep, when carbon dioxide levels rise (Klein, 1996).

Obsessive-compulsive disorder has also been the object of intense biochemical study. There is a growing consensus that obsessive-compulsive disorder is connected to serotonin abnormalities, for drugs that selectively inhibit serotonin reuptake do relieve the symptoms of this disorder (Dolberg, Iancu, Sasson, et al., 1996; Pigott, 1996). At the same time, some dysfunction of the frontal lobe of the brain may also be involved, for PET scans of the brains of obsessive-compulsive patients in the process of glucose metabolism show abnormalities. Furthermore, when, in rare cases, obsessive-compulsive disorder has been treated by surgical disconnection of the frontal lobe, this has relieved the disorder (Mindus & Jenike, 1992).

Yet another line of research has to do with the basal ganglia, a region of the brain known to be involved with movement. Researchers have turned up a number of connections between obsessive-compulsive disorder and movement disorders thought to be caused by basal ganglia abnormalities. One such movement disorder is Tourette's syndrome, which produces tics—involuntary movements and verbalizations. Tourette's patients show a disproportionately high rate of obsessive-compulsive disorder, as do their relatives; conversely, obsessive-compulsive patients and their relatives are disproportionately likely to have tics (Pauls, Alsobrook, Goodman, et al., 1995). Meanwhile, PET scans of obsessive-compulsive patients have found abnormalities in the basal ganglia, and specifically in the caudate nucleus, which is thought to be the cognitive section of the basal ganglia (Baxter, Phelps, Mazziotta, et al., 1987). Perhaps obsessions are a sort of cognitive tic.

At this point, little is known about the biology of social phobia, but serotonin abnormalities may be involved (Tancer, 1993). Drugs that help relieve social phobia include those, such as Prozac and the benzodiazepines, that enhance serotonin neurotransmission through blocking serotonin reuptake (Prozac) or through blocking the inhibitory effect of GABA on serotonergic neurons (benzodiazepines) (Jefferson, 1996).

Even the anxiety disorder with the greatest "environmental" aspect is now being probed for biochemical underpinnings. Roger Pitman (1988, 1989) has put forth a hormonal theory of posttraumatic stress disorder. We know that hormones and neurotransmitters are involved in memory processes. According to Pitman, they may therefore be responsible for the intrusive memories that afflict posttraumatic patients. That is, the trauma may overstimulate stress-responsive hormones and neurotransmitters, with the result that the memory of the trauma becomes "overconsolidated" and cannot fade. This hypothesis locks in with the recent finding that victims of posttraumatic stress disorder tend to show hormone abnormalities indicative of an exaggerated response to stress (Yehuda, Levengood, Schmeidler, et al., 1996).

Whatever the specific biochemical processes involved in the anxiety disorders, these recent findings have given new impetus to research on neurotransmitters. And the newfound connection between neurotransmitters and anxiety states has generated renewed interest in the possible role of drugs in treating these disorders.

Drug Treatment

Minor Tranquilizers Among the **minor tranquilizers**, or drugs taken to reduce anxiety, the most popular are the **benzodiazepines**—particularly Valium (diazepam), Xanax (alprazolam), Ativan (lorazepam), and Tranxene (chlorazepate), and they are very popular, indeed. In 1989, American pharmacies filled over 52 million prescriptions for the antianxiety benzodiazepines (Shader, Greenblatt, & Balter, 1991)—that is one prescription for one out of every five men, women, and children in the United States. For a number of years, Valium was the most widely prescribed drug in the world. This wide use of antianxiety medications is often assumed to be a plague of modern life. As it happens, the percentage of people using drugs to control anxiety and insomnia has remained relatively stable over the past hundred years. The drugs themselves have changed—whereas people in the 1990s use benzodiazepines, people in the 1890s used bromides and opium-based compounds—but the use of drugs for these purposes was as widespread in the late nineteenth century as it is now (Woods, Katz, & Winger, 1987). In most cases, antianxiety drugs are prescribed by family doctors for people who are not in psychological treatment but are simply going through a hard time in their lives. Indeed, half the users of such drugs are people who are medically ill; the drug is prescribed to control the patient's emotional reactions to the illness (Maxmen & Ward, 1995). Antianxiety drugs are also widely used in conjunction with psychological treatment, particularly for the anxiety disorders.

Benzodiazepines are CNS depressants; they slow down the workings of the central nervous system, and, in doing so, they can create disturbing side effects. A common problem is daytime sedation in the form of fatigue, drowsiness, and impaired motor coordination (Maxmen & Ward, 1995). (Benzodiazepines are often implicated in falls in the elderly and in automobile and industrial accidents.) These drugs may also interfere with memory, particularly for events that occur after taking the drug. Finally, benzodiazepines may aggravate physical disorders involving breathing, such as congestive heart failure and sleep apnea, a disorder in which breathing repeatedly stops for 10 seconds or more during the night (Chapter 8). All these side effects are dose-dependent: the higher the dose, the greater the likelihood of problems (Maxmen & Ward, 1995). (Therefore, physicians try to prescribe the lowest effective dose.) The risk of side effects is also multiplied if benzodiazepines are taken in combination with other central nervous system depressants, especially alcohol. When combined with alcohol, benzodiazepines have a synergistic effect: each multiplies the other's power, placing the person at risk for an overdose.

Apart from side effects, a major drawback of benzodiazepines is the difficulty of **withdrawal**, or termination of the drug. When a benzodiazepine is taken in large doses, termination is often followed by *rebound*: the symptoms return with redoubled force. Thus, the person is likely to start taking the drug again in order to suppress the now-magnified symptoms (Maxmen & Ward, 1995). This has been a problem with Xanax. Xanax is very effective in the treatment of panic attacks (Shader & Greenblatt, 1993), but, when it is withdrawn, up to 90 percent of patients relapse, many of them experiencing worse panic attacks than they had before (Michelson & Marchione, 1991).

The difficulty of withdrawal is related to whether a drug is short-acting or long-acting—that is, how quickly it is absorbed into the bloodstream and how long it stays there. Long-acting benzodiazepines, such as Valium and Tranxene, tend to accumulate in the body over time, so that, the longer the person takes the drug, the higher the dose he or she is getting. By contrast, short-acting benzodiazepines, such as Xanax and Ativan, are usually eliminated from the system in less than eight hours. As a result, going "cold turkey" with a short-acting benzodiazepine is more likely to result in rebound and other withdrawal symptoms (Rickels, Schweizer, Case, et al., 1990). The long-acting benzodiazepines, however abruptly terminated, naturally eliminate themselves from the system bit by bit, with less disturbing effects.

However, even with long-acting benzodiazepines and a therapeutically tapered withdrawal, discontinuing these drugs is very hard for long-time users—people who have taken the drug daily for over a year. In a study of 63 benzodiazepine-dependent patients going through a gradual termination, only 63 percent of those on long-acting drugs—and worse, only 58 percent of those on short-acting drugs—were able to achieve a drug-free state (Schweizer, Rickels, Case, et al., 1990). For panic disorder patients, the figures are even less encouraging. In one study, only one-fourth of the panic disorder patients who had participated in a gradual benzodiazepine withdrawal program were drug-free at a 3-month follow-up, though, when the patients received cognitive-behavioral therapy in conjunction with the drug taper, their success rate tripled (Otto, Pollack, Sachs, et al., 1993). Here, then, is an example of a promising way to combine antianxiety medication with psychotherapy. Because Xanax works so quickly, it may be used for a brief period of time, with cognitive-behavioral therapy instituted as a longer-term solution while the drugs are withdrawn.

Because of the problems with benzodiazepines, physicians have tried treating anxiety disorders with other drugs. One alternative is BuSpar (buspirone), a recently introduced nonbenzodiazepine. BuSpar does not interact with alcohol and seems to be more selective in its effects on anxiety, though it is ineffective with panic disorder and only sometimes effective for generalized anxiety (Maxmen & Ward, 1995). But the major alternative to the benzodiazepines has been antidepressants.

Antidepressant Drugs   **Antidepressant drugs,** as the name indicates, are used to elevate mood in depressed patients. However, because antidepressants are often effective for panic disorder and obsessive-compulsive disorder (Rosenbaum & Gelenberg, 1991), we will begin our discussion of them in this chapter. The first important class of antidepressants to gain a wide following were the **MAO inhibitors,** including phenelzine (Nardil) and tranylcypromine (Parnate). The name of this class of drugs was based on the belief that they interfered with the action of the enzyme monoamine oxidase (MAO), which in turn degrades certain neurotransmitters, including norepinephrine and serotonin, in the nervous system. The MAO inhibitors are often quite effective in treating anxiety disorders. However, these drugs can also have adverse effects on the brain, the liver, and the cardiovascular system and, when combined with certain other drugs or foods—especially foods prepared by fermentation (e.g., beer, wine, some varieties of cheese)—can result in severe illness and even death. Because of these risks, the MAO inhibitors are recommended as the first medication to use with anxiety disorders only when they are clearly more successful than other medications. One such case is social phobia, for which Nardil seems to be the most effective drug.

For other anxiety disorders, the MAO inhibitors have proved less useful than another class of antidepressants, the **tricyclics,** so named for their three-ringed molecular structure. Commonly used tricyclics are Tofranil (imipramine), Elavil (amitriptyline), Sinequan (doxepin), and Anafranil (clomipramine). Tricyclics have proved quite effective with panic dis-

order and Anafranil has been used with some success in treating obsessive-compulsive disorder. However, the tricyclics can have unpleasant side effects: blurred vision, dry mouth, constipation, weight gain, drowsiness, and jitteriness. As many as 40 percent of anxiety-disorder patients cannot tolerate the tricyclics (Kunovac & Stahl, 1995).

The tricyclics are gradually being displaced by a newer class of antidepressants, the **selective serotonin reuptake inhibitors,** or **SSRIs.** Like the tricyclics, the SSRIs work by blocking neurotransmitter reuptake, but they zero in on only one neurotransmitter, serotonin (hence, their name). For reasons that are not well understood, this makes the SSRIs effective for many patients who have abandoned other antidepressants because of the side effects. There are several SSRIs on the market—Paxil (paroxetine) and Zoloft (sertraline) are two of the newer ones—but the best known, because it was the first, is Prozac (fluoxetine). Introduced in 1987, it soon became (and remains) America's most widely prescribed antidepressant.

Just as the SSRIs have replaced the tricyclics as the drug of choice for depression, they have now become the physician's favorite in the treatment of most anxiety disorders. Sixty percent of the physicians surveyed now start an anxiety-disorder patient with an SSRI rather than with Xanax, Nardil, or Tofranil (Lydiard, Brawman, & Ballenger, 1996). Because the SSRIs are still relatively new, there has been less research on them than on the other antidepressants,

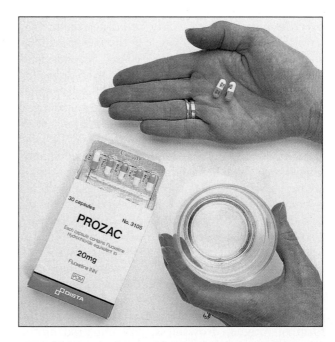

SSRIs like Prozac, long used to treat depression, are now frequently prescribed in the treatment of anxiety disorders as well.

but early reports indicate that they work very well with panic disorder and are helpful with social phobia, too (Lydiard, Brawman, & Ballenger, 1996). They have also shown some promise in the treatment of obsessive-compulsive disorder, though at this point the tricyclic Anafranil seems to be more effective (Greist, Jefferson, Koback, et al., 1995).

SSRIs, too, can have side effects. Prozac, for example, often causes headache, upset stomach, jitteriness, and sexual dysfunction. But these problems are generally easier for patients to tolerate than the side effects, such as weight gain and blurred vision, associated with the tricyclics. Jitteriness—which amounts to one of the symptoms of the anxiety the drug is meant to treat—is not common enough as a side effect to preclude using this antidepressant as an antianxiety drug; a way to avoid jitteriness is to start the patient at a low dose and then gradually increase the dose to the therapeutic level (the dose at which the drug relieves symptoms). Other side effects associated with the SSRIs are often mild or short-lived. None of the medications prescribed for anxiety is curative. At best, the drug suppresses symptoms. When the drug is removed, there is likely to be rapid relapse. Consequently, many experts have concluded that, unless patients want to remain on medication for the rest of their lives, they should consider psychotherapy, either alone or in combination with drugs, for psychotherapy *is* aimed at getting rid of the disorder permanently.

The most common criticism of antianxiety drugs, is not that they don't work well enough but that, by working as well as they do, they may invite people to avoid solving their problems. As Freud pointed out, anxiety is a *signal*. By taking antianxiety drugs, we suppress the signal, but we do not solve the problem. Indeed, the problem may become more serious as a result of our ignoring it. Taking antianxiety drugs, then, is like turning off a fire alarm because we can't stand the noise. Again, the solution seems to be psychotherapy, preferably in combination with drugs. The drugs, it is hoped, will relieve the symptoms to the point that patients can actually concentrate on the therapy. The therapy will then teach them new skills and help them to solve problems so that they can live their lives without anxiety.

For panic disorder, cognitive-behavioral therapy seems to have an 80 percent cure rate, a result at least as impressive as that of any medication, and the gains are maintained after the treatment is completed, which is not the case with any drug therapy. But preliminary results from a current large-scale study suggest that, when cognitive-behavioral therapy for panic disorder is combined with Tofranil, it is even more effective than cognitive-behavioral therapy alone and is better than Tofranil alone (Barlow & Lehman, 1996). If such results are confirmed, this will be a powerful argument for combining cognitive-behavioral therapy with drugs in treating panic disorder.

For the other anxiety disorders, the prospects for combined treatments are less clear. Obsessive-compulsive disorder, as we saw, is hard to treat, though both Anafranil and exposure techniques have had some success. This suggests that the best treatment would use both, but preliminary results from a study of such a treatment seem to favor behavioral therapy alone, without the drug (Foa & Liebowitz, 1995). For specific phobias and generalized anxiety disorder, cognitive-behavioral therapy remains the treatment of choice, while for social phobia, cognitive-behavioral therapy and Nardil seem to work equally well. The effectiveness of drug/psychotherapy treatments for these disorders, and for posttraumatic stress disorder, remains an unexplored question.

As a final caveat, there is some reason to be concerned about the concept of combining drugs and psychotherapy, however promising the preliminary results. As psychologists have discovered, learning is state-dependent (Ho, Richard, & Chute, 1978; Overton, 1984). What we learn in a given biological or psychological state does not fully generalize to other states. Thus, if, while taking antianxiety medication, we acquire new skills for dealing with stress, these skills will not necessarily survive the withdrawal of the medication.

KEY TERMS

acrophobia, 153
agoraphobia, 151
antidepressant drugs, 172
anxiety, 150
anxiety disorders, 150
benzodiazepines, 171
claustrophobia, 153
compulsion, 155
exposure, 164

flooding, 164
free association, 162
generalized anxiety disorder, 153
MAO inhibitors, 172
minor tranquilizers, 171
obsession, 155
obsessive-compulsive disorder, 155

panic attack, 151
panic disorder, 151
phobia, 153
posttraumatic stress disorder, 157
resistance, 162
selective serotonin reuptake inhibitors (SSRIs), 172
social phobia, 154

specific phobia, 153
systematic desensitization, 164
transference, 162
tricyclics, 172
withdrawal, 171

SUMMARY

- Anxiety disorders are characterized by either manifest anxiety or behavior patterns aimed at warding it off. The components of anxiety are a subjective sense of tension and fear, behavioral responses such as avoidance of a feared situation, and physiological responses such as increased heart rate and respiration.

- In panic disorder, a person experiences and/or intensely fears a series of panic attacks, sudden and unexpected onsets of severe anxiety. Physical sensations such as dizziness, trembling, and shortness of breath give rise to a feeling of impending catastrophe, such as total loss of control or death. Panic disorder can lead to agoraphobia, a fear of leaving the safety of home.

- The incidence of panic disorder is similar across ethnic groups and cultures. Panic disorder and, especially, agoraphobia are more common among women than among men. Most patients report one or more stressful life events in the year preceding their first attack.

- In generalized anxiety disorder, patients experience a chronic state of excessive and uncontrollable worry about important concerns in their lives. Although generalized anxiety disorder resembles a dormant state of panic disorder, the two disorders differ in their course and in their biological symptoms. Like panic disorder, generalized anxiety disorder tends to follow stressful life events. It is much more common among women than among men.

- A person with a phobia intensely fears some object or situation and persistently tries to avoid that stimulus. People with a specific phobia react to a particular object (such as a rat) or situation (such as an enclosed space). Social phobia, which is essentially a fear of the disapproval of others, is aroused by a social situation (such as public speaking) that the phobic perceives as carrying a risk of embarrassment or humiliation. African Americans and Hispanics are at greater risk for specific phobias than are other American ethnic groups, and women are more susceptible than men. The distribution of social phobia is closer to equal for the two sexes. The risk of both specific and social phobias is greater among people of lower income or education.

- People suffering from obsessive-compulsive disorder are bothered by recurring, often disturbing thoughts (obsessions) and/or stereotyped actions (compulsions) that they seem unable to control. Men and women are equally at risk for obsessive-compulsive disorder. The onset often follows a stressful event in one's life.

- Posttraumatic stress disorder is a severe reaction, involving intense fear, helplessness, or horror, to traumatic events that pose mortal danger to a person, such as natural disaster, assault, and combat. Victims typically reexperience the event for long periods of time, show diminished responsiveness to their surroundings, develop physical symptoms, and may suffer from depression, anxiety, irritability, and guilt. When the disorder is of short duration—a few days to a few weeks—it is classified as acute stress disorder.

- Psychodynamic theorists view the anxiety disorders as neuroses resulting from unconscious conflicts between id impulses and ego actions. The neurotic individual experiences conscious anxiety over these conflicts or keeps the anxiety at bay through rigid defense mechanisms. According to the theory, the style of a person's defenses is a key to revealing the nature and causes of the disorder. Treatment has traditionally focused on uncovering what the ego is trying to suppress and involves the techniques of free association, dream interpretation, and analysis of resistance and transference.

- Behaviorists attribute anxiety disorders to faulty learning, not unconscious conflicts. In the process of learning to avoid anxiety, people may also learn to associate a neutral stimulus with the anxiety-producing stimulus and then be conditioned to habitually avoid that stimulus. Behavioral therapy is directed at removing the symptoms of a disorder through such techniques as systematic desensitization and exposure.

- According to the cognitive perspective, people with anxiety disorders misperceive or misinterpret internal and external stimuli. Events and sensations that are not really threatening are interpreted as threatening, and anxiety results. Cognitive therapy aims at helping the patient to interpret body sensations in a noncatastrophic way.

- The biological perspective seeks genetic and biochemical links to anxiety. Some anxiety disorders, especially panic disorder, appear to have a genetic component. Recent evidence also suggests that brain chemistry and neurotransmitters influence some forms of anxiety.

- Antianxiety drugs, or minor tranquilizers, such as the benzodiazepines Valium, Xanax, Ativan, and Tranxene, are used to treat symptoms of many of the anxiety disorders. They are also used to relieve stress related to illness and medical treatment. Side effects of these drugs include daytime sedation, interference with memory, and aggravation of respiratory disorders. These drugs also act synergistically with alcohol and may produce a rebound effect upon withdrawal.

- Antidepressant drugs, those used to elevate mood in depressed patients, are often effective in treating panic disorder, obsessive-compulsive disorder, and social phobia. Among these are the MAO inhibitors (Nardil, Parnate) and the tricyclics (Tofranil, Elavil, Anafranil, Sinequan). These drugs are also associated with a number of side effects. The tricyclics are being replaced by SSRIs, especially Prozac, now the most widely prescribed antidepressant in the United States.

■ No antianxiety medication is curative. Drugs can only suppress the symptoms of an anxiety disorder, and only for as long as they are being taken. It is widely accepted that some form of psychotherapy is needed for getting rid of the anxiety permanently.

■ A combination of drugs and psychotherapy is often advantageous in treating anxiety disorders. The major drawback is that patients who are under medication when they learn skills for dealing with stress may not retain those skills after withdrawal of the medication.

Chapter 7

A well-dressed woman in her early thirties was brought to the hospital by the police after she was found wandering on an interstate highway. She had no identification with her. She spoke coherently but slowly and was apparently traumatized, but not psychotic. On the ward she seldom spoke, and she ate only when she was coaxed. When asked who she was, she would stare into space or shrug her shoulders with a gesture of despair. She was given the temporary name of Jane Doe, and, after four weeks of futile attempts to establish her identity, she was moved to a ward for chronic patients.

Jane was taken to the psychologist's office every day, but she barely responded to him, and she could not be hypnotized, because she would not close her eyes or concentrate on the procedure. Eventually the psychologist tried progressive relaxation, to which Jane responded well. After each relaxation session, the psychologist would pick up his office telephone and pretend to call a friend or relative. Then he would give Jane the phone and suggest that she make a call, but she always said that she didn't remember anyone's number. Finally, one day, after Jane had achieved a state of deep relaxation, the psychologist gave her the phone again and asked her just to punch in numbers at random. She did so, and after a while she was consistently punching the same area code and phone number, though she never waited for the ring. But the psychologist wrote down the number, and, taking the phone from Jane, he called it himself and gave the phone back to Jane, whereupon she got to speak to her mother in Detroit, 400 miles away. As it turned out, Jane was a highly skilled engineer who had wandered away from her home in Boston on the day when the movers came to move her household to another state, where she was supposed to be relocating. Jane's family arrived to pick her up the next day. (Adapted from Lyon, 1985.)

DB was a 33-year-old man who had a clerical job and lived with his parents. Seven years earlier, during military training, he had been hit in the right eye by a rifle butt. Thereafter he claimed that he was blind in that eye, though medical examinations indicated that the eye was functioning normally.

To find out whether DB was in fact receiving no information through his right eye, he was given a test during which his left eye was completely covered. The test involved a machine that emitted a buzz. The machine had three switches, only one of which could turn off the buzz, and with each trial the controlling switch changed at random. DB's hands were placed on the machine, and he was told that on each trial he was to try to turn off the buzz. What he was not told was that the machine also had a visual component: a screen showing three triangles, one of which was always pointed in a direction different from the other two. On each trial the controlling switch was the one under the twisted triangle. So the machine gave its user the right answer—if the user could see.

DB had 21 sessions with the machine. Four of those were control sessions: the screen was turned off, so that there were no visual cues. On these control sessions, DB pulled the right switch 39 percent of the time, roughly what one would expect by chance. But in the 17 experimental sessions, when the screen was on, he pulled the right switch 74 percent of the time—far greater than a chance percentage. Furthermore, when the visual cue was present, he took twice as long to pull the switch, indicating that he was processing information. DB's "blind" eye was clearly seeing, and he was reclassified as having a psychological, not a physical, disorder. (Adapted from Bryant & McConkey, 1989.)

According to current psychiatric terminology, these two cases represent different disorders. Jane Doe has dissociative amnesia, one of the dissociative disorders, which are disturbances of higher cognitive functions such as memory or identity. DB, on the other hand, has a conversion disorder, which is one of the somatoform disorders, characterized by physical complaints or disabilities for which there is no apparent organic cause.

Despite their different labels, conversion disorder and the dissociative disorders have much in common (Bowman & Markand, 1996; Kihlstrom, Tataryn, & Hoyt, 1993). First, both mimic actual neurological disorders—amnesia in the case of Jane Doe, blindness in the case of DB. Second, in both cases, the problem is not a neurological disability but a disruption of conscious awareness. Jane Doe knew her mother's telephone number, and DB could see with his right eye. In each case, the ability affected behavior, but neither Jane Doe nor DB was consciously aware of that ability.

Because of these similarities, conversion disorder and the dissociative disorders were grouped together for a long time in a broad category called "hysterical neurosis," **hysteria** being a psychogenic disorder that mimics a biogenic disorder. But, when the *DSM* abandoned the concepts of neurosis and hysteria in 1980, the dissociative disorders and conversion disorder became separated. The dissociative disorders now include only disturbances of higher cognitive functions. Conversion disorder, because it affects not cognitive functions but sensory functions (as in blindness) or motor functions (as in paralysis), has been moved into the category of "somatoform disorders," psychological disorders that take somatic, or physical, form. But, in view of their shared features and their historical connection, the present chapter will consider these two categories, and their theories and treatments, together.

Dissociative Disorders

As the name indicates, the **dissociative disorders** involve the dissociation, or splitting apart, of components of the personality that are normally integrated. As a result, some psychological function—identity, memory, perception of oneself or the environment—is screened out of consciousness. Many people, especially children and adolescents, have dissociative experiences—feelings of "strangeness," brief spells of memory loss or identity confusion—in the course of normal life (Rauschenberger & Lynn, 1995). In some measure, dissociation is an adaptive skill. For example, when we drive a car while having a conversation, what we attend to is the conversation, all the while screening out the psychological and motor functions involved in driving the car. However, if we have to attend to these functions—if, for example, the road suddenly becomes dangerous—we can do so. What was screened out can be called back. In the dissociative disorders, the screened-out function cannot be called back voluntarily. Furthermore, it is a critical function, such as our memory of past events or of who we are.

The dissociative disorders occur without any demonstrable damage to the brain. Instead, as we shall see, they have their origin in severe psychological stress and develop as a way of coping with that stress. In this regard, they are like posttraumatic stress disorder and acute stress disorder (Chapter 6), which often include dissociative symptoms and which may accompany dissociative disorders (Loewenstein, 1994). We will discuss four syndromes: dissociative amnesia, dissociative fugue, dissociative identity disorder, and depersonalization disorder.

Dissociative Amnesia

Amnesia, the partial or total forgetting of past experiences, may be caused by a blow to the head or by any one of a number of brain disorders. Some amnesias, however, occur without any apparent organic cause, as a response to psychological stress. In addition to medical tests for brain pathology, there are several ways of distinguishing between organic and dissociative amnesia (Sackeim & Devanand, 1991; Sivec & Lynn, 1995). First, dissociative amnesia is almost always *anterograde*, blotting out a period of time after the precipitating stress, whereas organic amnesia, particularly from a head injury, is usually *retrograde*, erasing a period of time prior to the precipitating event. Second, dissociative amnesia is often selective; the "blank" period tends to include events that most people would want to forget—either a trauma or perhaps an unacceptable action such as an extramarital affair. Third, people with dissociative amnesia are often much less disturbed over their condition than are those around them—an indifference that suggests relief from conflict. Fourth, most people with dissociative amnesia remain well oriented to time and place and have little problem learning new information, whereas organic amnesias typically involve some disorientation and difficulty with new learning. Finally, because the events forgotten in dissociative amnesia are simply screened out of consciousness rather than lost altogether (as is the case in organic amnesia), they can often be recovered under hypnosis or with the aid of sodium amytal, a barbiturate (Ruedrich, Chu, and Wadle, 1985).

Patterns of Memory Loss   There are five broad patterns of dissociative amnesia. First and most common is *localized amnesia*, in which all events occurring during a circumscribed period of time are blocked out. For example, a man who has survived a fire in

Dissociative amnesia is a popular plot device for Hollywood movies. In this scene from Alfred Hitchcock's Spellbound *(1945), psychiatrist Ingrid Bergman tries to help Gregory Peck recover his memory.*

which the rest of his family has died might have no memory of anything that happened from the time of the fire until three days later. Second is *selective amnesia,* in which the person makes "spot" erasures, forgetting only certain events that occurred during a circumscribed period of time. In the just described example, the man might recall the fire engines coming and the ambulance taking him to the hospital but forget seeing his children carried out of the house or identifying their bodies the next day. Third is *generalized amnesia,* in which, as in the case of Jane Doe, the person forgets his or her entire life. Though this is the kind of amnesia that tends to turn up in novels and movies, it is actually rare. A fourth pattern, also rare, is *continuous amnesia,* in which the person forgets all events that occur after a specific period up to the present, including events that occur *after* the onset of amnesia. For example, if the amnesia begins on Monday, the person does not know on Wednesday what he or she did on Tuesday, let alone prior events. Finally, in *systematized amnesia,* the person forgets only certain categories of information (e.g., all information about his or her family); other memories remain intact. While some patterns are more common than others, amnesia in general is rare. However, its incidence tends to spiral among victims of war and natural disasters. Indeed, many of the reported cases of amnesia have been soldiers in World War I and World War II (Loewenstein, 1991).

As noted, dissociative amnesias may involve no disorientation. The exceptions are generalized and continuous amnesia, in which all or much of the person's past is blocked out. Patients with these forms of amnesia do not know who or where they are, do not recognize family or friends, and cannot tell you their name, address, or anything else about themselves. In other words, their *episodic memory,* or memory of personal experience, is lost. Typically, however, their *semantic memory,* or general knowledge, is spared. For instance, a patient who cannot identify a picture of his wife is still able to identify a picture of John Kennedy (Kopelman, Christensen, Puffett, et al., 1994). *Procedural memory,* or memory for skills, is also usually intact. Amnesia victims can read and write, add and subtract.

In most cases, though, even episodic memory is only partially erased. **Explicit memories,** memories we are aware of, may be gone, but often the person shows evidence of having **implicit memories,** memories that he or she cannot call into conscious awareness but that still affect behavior. At the beginning of this chapter, we saw an example of this: Jane Doe's dialing the telephone number of the mother she didn't remember she had. Under the influence of implicit memory, many amnesia victims show strong reactions to things that recall the initiating trauma. In one reported case, the patient, a rape victim, had no conscious memory of the rape but clearly had unconscious knowledge of it. When shown a TAT card that depicted a person attacking another person from behind, he became extremely upset. Then he left the testing session to go to his room, where he attempted suicide (Kaszniak, Nussbaum, Berren, et al., 1988).

When dissociative amnesia occurs in novels and movies, it appears suddenly and dramatically, as the only symptom; it also disappears suddenly, with the person gratefully resuming his or her former life. This, apparently, is not the usual pattern. Many amnesias do remit suddenly, without treatment—others become chronic—but, even when they remit, they tend to recur. In a recent survey of 25 patients, almost half had had more than 1 episode of amnesia. Furthermore, their memory loss was accompanied by a wide range of other symptoms—above all, depression, headaches, and sexual dysfunction (typically, decreased sexual desire). Indeed, in most cases, the amnesia was discovered only on questioning; the presenting complaint was usually depression. As for what precipitated the first amnesic episode, this was retrospective evidence, which is always questionable—and more so, needless to say, in people with memory disorders—but 60 percent named childhood sexual abuse; 24 percent, marital trouble; 16 percent, a suicide attempt; 16 percent, disavowed sexual behavior such as adultery or promiscuity (Coons & Milstein, 1992).

Amnesia and Crime   Amnesia has created difficulties for the legal system (Saks, 1995). Crime victims who cannot consciously recall the crime are unable to offer what would be valuable testimony in court. A worse problem is that people *accused* of crimes often do not remember the event. One researcher (Schacter, 1986a, 1986b) found that between 23 and 65 percent of people charged with or convicted of homicide claim to have no memory of the crime. In such cases, alcohol or other drugs are often involved, so some of these amnesias may be drug-induced "blackouts." Others may be faked. But others are probably true dissociative amnesias, responses to the extreme emotional arousal surrounding the crime. Whatever the source, defendants claiming amnesia may be judged incapable of assisting in their own defense, in which case they may be judged incompetent to stand trial. If they are tried, they may qualify for the insanity defense, on the grounds that they committed the crime in an altered state of consciousness, in which they did not know what they were doing or that it was wrong (Saks, 1995). Such was the case in the 1993 trial of Lorena Bobbitt (Chapter 19), who claimed to have

In 1977, a man named William Stanley Milligan was arrested for the rape of three women in Columbus, Ohio. Two of the women positively identified him as the Ohio State University "campus rapist," and fingerprints found at the scene of one of the crimes matched his. It seemed to be an open-and-shut case. Not until Milligan twice tried to commit suicide in jail while awaiting trial did it occur to his lawyers that he might need psychiatric help.

The report of the examining psychologists and psychiatrists profoundly altered the nature of the case. At the time of the trial, they had identified at least 10 different personalities somehow coexisting within Milligan. These included the host, or core personality, Billy; Arthur, an emotionless Englishman, who dominated the other personalities; Ragen, a Yugoslavian known as the protector of women and children and the "keeper of hate"; Allen, an 18-year-old manipulator and con artist; Tommy, a 16-year-old antisocial personality, who was also a landscape painter and escape artist; Danny, 14, a timid painter of still lifes; 8-year-old David, who "absorbed" the pain and suffering of the others; Christene, a 3-year-old English girl; Christopher, her troubled 13-year-old brother; and Adalane, 19, an introverted lesbian.

Milligan was eventually found not guilty by reason of insanity—the first case of dissociative identity disorder to be acquitted of a major crime under that plea. Accordingly, he was sent to a mental hospital near Columbus, where he was placed under the care of David Caul, a psychiatrist who had experience in treating dissociative identity disorder.

Caul soon discovered more personalities, including 13 "undesirables." (Arthur called them this because they rebelled against his control.) One of the undesirables was the Teacher—the fusion of all 23 identities. Described as "Billy all in one piece," the Teacher had total recall of the events in Milligan's life. In his sessions with Caul, Milligan's personalities fused more and more into 1 competent person. Soon he was allowed unattended trips into town and weekend furloughs. These privileges, however, provoked anger from the people of Columbus, who still feared Milligan's potential for violent behavior.

Under the glare of unfavorable publicity and open public hostility, Milligan's personalities once again split apart. Aggressive personalities came to the fore, causing Milligan to be sent to a maximum-security institution. Eventually, after years of treatment, his personalities seemed to fuse, and he was released. He established a child-abuse prevention agency, worked as a farmer, and developed a career as an artist (Kihlstrom, Tataryn, & Hoyt, 1993).

Even though several experienced psychiatrists testified that Milligan had dissociative identity disorder, traceable to traumatic abuse suffered in childhood at the hands of his stepfather, many professionals and laypeople alike still suspect that Billy Milligan was faking. This disorder typically arouses such skepticism, sometimes justifiably.

In another case soon after Milligan's, Kenneth Bianchi, a man accused of a number of rape-murders in the Los Angeles area, claimed in an insanity defense that the crimes he was accused of were committed by one of his personalities, Steve Walker. The defense was undermined, however, by evidence that Bianchi was faking. (His alter egos were not consistent, for example.) He was convicted of multiple counts of murder.

In another twist, a Wisconsin man named Mark Peterson was accused of sexual assault by a dissociative identity disorder patient who said that only one of her personalities gave consent. (Another watched the event and another went to the police.) Peterson was eventually convicted under a law that makes it equivalent to rape to have sexual intercourse with a mental patient (Kihlstrom, Tataryn, & Hoyt, 1993).

These cases raise fascinating and difficult questions. Should a person be held responsible for crimes committed by a subordinate personality? Is a person the victim of a crime if one personality gives consent? The legal system has not yet come to a firm decision. But at present the courts generally consider people with dissociative identity disorder responsible for crimes committed by one personality if that personality knew right from wrong at the time of the crime (Appelbaum & Greer, 1994; Saks, 1995).

no memory of cutting off her husband's penis, and Bobbitt was acquitted on the grounds of temporary insanity. For other legal problems posed by the dissociative disorders, see the box above.

Dissociative Fugue

A condition related to amnesia is **dissociative fugue**, in which the person not only forgets all or most of his or her past but also takes a sudden, unexpected trip away from home. Fugue, then, is a sort of traveling amnesia, but it is more elaborate than amnesia. While people with amnesia, in their confusion, may wander about aimlessly, fugue patients are purposeful in their actions. Furthermore, while amnesia patients may also forget their identity, many fugue patients go one step further and manufacture a new one.

The length and elaborateness of fugues vary considerably. Some people may go no farther than the next town, spend the day in a movie house, check into a hotel under an assumed name, and recover by morning. Such modest adventures are the usual pattern. In rare cases, however, patients travel to foreign countries, assume a new identity, fabricate a detailed past, and pursue an altogether new life for months or even years. During the fugue, they appear fairly normal to observers. Finally, however, they "wake up," often after a jolting reminder of their former life or, as it appears in some cases, simply when they once again feel psychologically safe (Riether & Stoudemire, 1988). Fugue usually remits suddenly, and, when fugue victims wake up, they are completely amnesic for the events that occurred during the fugue. The last thing they may remember is leaving home one morning. This second-stage amnesia is what usually brings fugue victims to professional attention. They seek therapy only once the fugue ends, partly because they want to find out what they did during the fugue.

Like amnesia, fugue is generally rare but is more common in wartime and after natural disasters. Again, like amnesia, it tends to occur after a severe psychological trauma and—as the term (derived from the Latin word for "flight") suggests—seems to function as an escape from psychological stress. The following case shows both the precipitating trauma and the escape motivation. It also offers a good example of implicit memory:

> Bernice L., a middle-aged homemaker, had been raised in a stern, loveless, and extremely religious home. She grew up shy and anxious, but, when she went away to college, she began to bloom a little. This was largely the work of her roommate, a vivacious girl by the name of Rose P. who introduced Bernice to her friends, encouraged her to develop her talent for the piano, and in general drew her out. In their junior year, however, their friendship suffered a crisis. Rose became engaged to a young man with whom Bernice also promptly fell in love. When the man married Rose, Bernice lapsed into a severe depression. She returned home, but, at her parents' insistence, she eventually went back to school.
>
> Upon graduation, Bernice married a young clergyman to whom she felt little attraction but of whom her parents approved. They had 2 children and eventually settled in a small town not unlike her childhood home. Bernice had few satisfactions in life other than her children and her happy memories of her first 2 years in college. Then, when she was 37 years old, her younger child, a musically talented boy, died. The next day she disappeared, and for 4 years she could not be found.
>
> Later, with the help of a therapist, Bernice recalled some of the events of those 4 years. Totally amnesic for her past life, she had returned to her old college town. There, under the name of Rose P., she began giving piano lessons, and within 2 years she became assistant director of the local conservatory of music. She made a few friends, but she never spoke of her life, for it was still a complete blank to her. Then one day she was recognized by a woman who had known both her and Rose P. during college. Bernice's husband, now a minister in Chicago, was located, and reluctantly she returned to him.

> In therapy, Bernice's amnesia was finally dispelled. She resumed her old identity; readjusted to her husband, who proved patient and sympathetic; and settled down to life in Chicago. (Adapted from Masserman, 1961, pp. 35–37)

Dissociative Identity Disorder

Perhaps the most bizarre of the dissociative disorders is dissociative identity disorder (DID), formerly known as *multiple personality disorder*. In this pattern, the personality breaks up into 2 or more distinct identities or personality states, each well integrated and well developed, which then take turns controlling the person's behavior. (Sometimes called "split personality," dissociative identity disorder should not be confused with schizophrenia, which is an altogether different syndrome. See Chapter 13.) Amnesia is part of the pattern. At least 1 of the personalities is amnesic for the experiences of the other or others. The first case of DID to receive extensive professional attention—the case of "Miss Beauchamp," who may have had as many as 17 personalities—was reported by Morton Prince in 1905. Ever since, this disorder has held a certain fascination for the public, as shown by the immense popularity of Thigpen and Cleckley's *The Three Faces of Eve* (1957), both book and movie, and by the best-seller *Sybil* (Schreiber, 1974), about a girl with 16 personalities.

In DID, a distinction is usually made between the host, the personality corresponding to who the person was before the onset of the disorder, and the alters, the later-developing personalities. There are many different configurations of host and alters (Putnam, 1989). In the simplest pattern, called *alternat-*

The film The Three Faces of Eve *depicts a woman with dissociative identity disorder.*

ing personality, 2 identities take turns controlling behavior, each having amnesia for the thoughts and actions of the other. In a slightly more complex pattern, the alter knows about the host, but the host doesn't know about the alter. While the host is directing the person's behavior, the alter, fully aware of the thoughts and actions of the host, continues to operate covertly and to make its presence felt now and then. In such cases, the alter is said to be **coconscious** (Prince, 1905) with the host. When the coconscious alter finally surfaces, it can discuss in detail the interesting problems of the host. Meanwhile, the host only gradually becomes aware of the existence of the alter, usually by encountering the evidence of his or her activities. In one case (Osgood, Luria, Jeans, et al., 1976), the host, "Gina," first learned of the existence of her alter, "Mary Sunshine," when she began waking up in the morning to find cups with leftover hot chocolate in the kitchen sink. "Gina" did not drink hot chocolate. But even this is an atypically simple pattern. Most DID patients have far more than 1 alter—surveys have found an average of 13 per patient (Kluft, 1984; Putnam, Guroff, Silberman, et al., 1986)—and the host and alters often have complex patterns of coconsciousness. One personality may know about another, but not about a third; that third personality may be in league with a fourth and a fifth, but not with the sixth and seventh; and so on.

The pattern of an initially ignorant host and a coconscious alter was illustrated in *The Three Faces of Eve* (Thigpen & Cleckley, 1957):

Eve White was the host. She had no knowledge of the existence of her alter, Eve Black, although Eve Black had been alternating with Eve White for some years. Whenever Eve Black surfaced, all that Eve White could report was that she had "blackouts." Eve Black, on the other hand, was coconscious with Eve White, knew everything she did, and would talk about her with contempt. Eve White was bland, quiet, and serious—a rather dull personality. Eve Black, on the other hand, was carefree, mischievous, and uninhibited. She would "come out" at the most inappropriate times, leaving Eve White with hangovers, bills, and a reputation in local bars that she could not explain. During treatment, there emerged another alter, Jane, who was coconscious with both Eve White and Eve Black, though she had no memory of their activities prior to her appearance. More mature than the other two, Jane seemed to have emerged as the result of the therapeutic process.

Eve's problems with dissociative identity disorder did not come to an end in 1957 with the publication of *The Three Faces of Eve*. In 1975, a woman named Chris Sizemore, an apparently unremarkable middle-aged homemaker from Fairfax, Virginia, revealed that she was "Eve" and that Eve Black, Eve White, and Jane were only 3 of the many personalities with which she had struggled throughout her life. Indeed, Mrs. Sizemore had manifested 21 separate identities, each with its own speech patterns, habits, preferences, and moral code. The personalities invariably came in sets of 3, with considerable conflict among them. "If I had learned to sew as one personality and then tried to sew as another, I couldn't do it. Driving a car was the same. Some of my personalities couldn't drive."

In the early years, a particular personality would dominate for a period of several days. Later, Mrs. Sizemore's personality would change at least once a day. The transition from one personality to another was usually marked by a sudden and very painful headache. The headache would last for about 10 seconds, during which Mrs. Sizemore was conscious of nothing. When the pain disappeared, a new personality would be in control.

In 1977, Mrs. Sizemore reported that she was cured (Sizemore & Pittillo, 1977), a fact she ascribed to the eventual realization that all of her different personalities were truly parts of herself, not invaders from the outside. "You don't know how wonderful it is," she said, "to go to bed at night and know that it will be you that wakes up the next day." (Adapted from Nunes, 1975.)

Sizemore's recovery is atypical. In most cases, the disorder is chronic, though the frequency of personality switches decreases over time.

Types of Personalities As with Eve, many cases of DID involve personalities that are polar opposites: one conformist, duty-doing, "nice" personality and one rebellious, impulsive, "naughty" personality. In this respect, multiple personalities seem to be extreme cases of the normal conflict between self-indulgence and restraint—or, as the Freudians would put it, between id and superego. In surveys of dissociative identity patients by two teams of researchers, at least 50 percent of the patients reported drug abuse by an alternate personality; 20 percent claimed that an alternate personality had been involved in a sexual assault on another person, and 29 percent reported that one of their alternates was homicidal (Putnam, Guroff, Silberman, et al., 1986; Ross, Miller, Reagor, et al., 1990). Dissociative identity patients may do violence to themselves when one personality tries to kill another. Such "internal homicide" attempts were reported by more than half the people in the previously mentioned surveys.

But "good" versus "bad" is not the only pattern. In some cases, one personality encapsulates a traumatic memory, while the others are unaware of it. In other cases, the personalities may divide up the emotional life, one dealing with anger, another handling sadness, and so on. Often the personalities specialize in different areas of functioning, one for family relations, one for sex life, one for work, others for specific skills. And these patterns may overlap. For example, a personality that embodies the memory of an abusive father may also be the only one who can solve complex mathematical problems (Loewenstein & Ross, 1992). Most patients—85 percent in the Putnam survey—have at least one personality who is a child, and more than half of Putnam's subjects had at least one personality of the opposite sex. The younger the patient was when the first alter appeared, the more subordinates he or she is likely to have.

Childhood Abuse In the Putnam survey, only 3 out of 100 patients did not report some significant trauma in childhood. The most common was sexual abuse, reported by 83 percent of the patients, and, in 68 percent of the patients, this sexual abuse involved incest. Three-fourths of the patients also claimed to have suffered repeated physical abuse in childhood, and almost half reported having witnessed a violent death, usually of a parent or sibling, during their early years (Putnam, Guroff, Silberman, et al., 1986). The Putnam findings have been roughly duplicated by other studies (Loewenstein, 1994).

These nearly unanimous testimonies of abuse suggest that dissociative identity disorder may be a stratagem that terrified children use to distance themselves from the realities of their lives (Atchison & McFarlane, 1994). In support of this view, most patients report that the disorder began in childhood, at a time of severe trauma. (In the Putnam survey, 89 percent reported onset before the age of 12.) It should be kept in mind, however, that most of the evidence of childhood abuse is based on retrospective surveys of the patients or their therapists. Some experts (Frankel, 1990; Kihlstrom, Tataryn, & Hoyt, 1993; Piper, 1994a) are concerned that claims of abuse may be biased by current theories of DID. (Because some experts have hypothesized that the cause is childhood abuse, the therapist seeks, and the patient finds, memories of childhood abuse.) More important, there have been no prospective studies examining the outcomes of children who have been abused. Thus, we do not know whether abused children are more likely to develop DID than are nonabused children. Finally, we do not know whether the incidence or severity of childhood abuse is any greater for DID than for other psychological disorders, such as depression or borderline personality disorder (Chapter 10), for which childhood abuse has also been reported to be common. The recall of childhood abuse is itself a highly controversial issue. (See the box on pages 186–187.)

Even if a connection between childhood abuse and DID becomes established in the future, researchers will still be left with the task of identifying the mechanism by which one leads to the other. Many children are abused. Why do only some of them—the minority of them—develop multiple identities? Certain studies (Butler, Duran, Jasiukaitis, et al., 1996) have found that people with dissociative identity disorder are easier to hypnotize and in general more suggestible than either the general population or other psychiatric patients. Thus, it is possible that hypnotic susceptibility or something related to it, such as proneness to fantasy or the ability to focus attention narrowly, may make some people vulnerable to subdividing their identities under stress (Brenneis, 1996; Butler, Duran, Jasiukaitis, et al., 1996).

Problems in Diagnosis While dissociative identity disorder was once considered very rare, it is now reported much more frequently. In the words of one research team, writing in 1986, "More cases of MPD [multiple-personality disorder] [DID] have been reported within the last five years than in the preceding two centuries" (Putnam, Guroff, Silberman, et al., 1986, p. 285). And the vast majority of them have been reported in North America, where public interest in this disorder—aroused by books, movies, and magazine articles on cases such as Eve, Sybil, and Billy Milligan (see the box on page 181)—seems to run highest. Such circumstances, together with the fact that therapists have often used hypnosis in getting DID patients to switch from one personality to another, raise the possibility that the power of suggestion may be influencing some patients to convert severe but common disorders into more interesting "multiple personalities" (Piper, 1994a). Some experts (e.g., Merskey, 1995) believe that DID is more a fad than a legitimate syndrome.

Alternatively, the rise in the numbers of reported cases may reflect better recognition of the syndrome (Gleaves, 1996). DID patients suffer a wide variety of symptoms besides alternating personalities. Depression, suicidal behavior, insomnia, amnesia, sexual dysfunction, and panic attacks were all reported by more than half the people in the Putnam and Ross surveys. Many patients also "hear voices," the voices of their other personalities (Boon & Draijer, 1993). When such patients first come before a diagnostician, they report all these symptoms, and, if the diagnostician is unfamiliar with or skeptical about dissociative identity disorder, the patient may easily be diagnosed as suffering from some other disorder, such as schizophrenia or depression (Loewenstein, 1994). Indeed, in the Putnam and Ross surveys, an average of seven years passed between the time the subjects first contacted a mental health professional about symptoms related to dissociative identity disorder and the time when that diagnosis was applied.

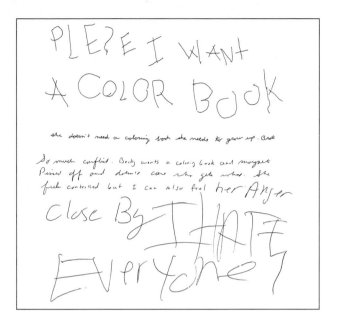

The same person—a dissociative identity disorder patient —produced these dramatically different handwriting samples under the influence of different personalities.

Other trends also have contributed to the rise in the number of DID diagnoses (Gleaves, 1996). One is the increased awareness and reporting of childhood sexual abuse, which, as we saw, is often thought to be a cause of DID. Another is the interest in the posttraumatic stress disorder—and, consequently, in trauma syndromes in general—that grew out of the Vietnam War. Finally, in the 1970s and 1980s, there was a growth in the field of cognitive psychology and, therefore, in such DID-related matters as memory and consciousness. All these factors helped to legitimize the disorder. In 1980, DID was first included as a distinct syndrome in the *DSM;* once it was listed, of course, it began to be more frequently diagnosed.

In recent years, even firm defenders of the DID diagnosis have become more concerned about false cases. For example, Ross (1997) now estimates that a quarter of the DID cases in the dissociative disorders unit that he directs are either faked or **iatrogenic** (induced by therapy). In a discussion of courtroom cases, Coons (1991) lists a number of criteria by which false cases might be distinguished from the true. Patients whose subpersonalities change over relatively short periods of time; patients who manifest subpersonalities only under hypnosis; patients whose personality switches are not accompanied by the usual signs (headache, altered appearance); patients who do not show the multiple symptomatology (depression, panic attacks, etc.) typical of dissociative identity disorder—in these cases, according to Coons, the diagnostician should strongly consider the

possibility of **malingering,** the conscious faking of symptoms in order to avoid responsibility. According to other DID experts (Kluft, 1991), however, it is very difficult to distinguish true cases from malingering. The cause of the DID diagnosis has not been helped by a number of highly publicized lawsuits recently brought against therapists by patients whom they treated for DID. In 1997, a patient, Patricia Burgus, received a settlement of $10.6 million from the Chicago hospital and doctors under whose care she came to believe that she had 300 personalities (Belluck, 1997).

In defense of the syndrome, a number of experts have reported that the physiology of DID patients—brain waves, PET scans, pain sensitivity, and skin conductance—may vary significantly depending on which personality is in charge (Atchison & McFarlane, 1994; Miller & Triggiano, 1992). For example, in a study of evoked brain potentials—that is, the brain waves elicited by various stimuli—Putnam (1984) compared 11 dissociative identity disorder patients with 10 controls who had been asked to simulate the disorder. In the true patients, the brain waves varied much more from personality to personality than they did in the controls. The different personalities of a single patient may also score very differently on standardized personality tests. These findings, however, do not rule out iatrogenesis. If a patient has been induced in therapy to develop several personalities, those personalities, encapsulating different emotions and cognitions, may well score differently on such tests (Merskey, 1995).

Depersonalization Disorder

Like fugue and dissociative identity disorder, **depersonalization disorder** involves a disruption of personal identity. Here, though, the disruption occurs without amnesia. The central feature of this syndrome is *depersonalization,* a sense of strangeness or unreality in oneself. People with depersonalization disorder feel as though they have become cut off from themselves and are viewing themselves from the outside, or that they are functioning like robots or living in a dream. The sense of strangeness usually extends to the body. Patients may feel as though their extremities have grown or shrunk, as though their bodies are operating mechanically, as though they are dead, or as though they are imprisoned inside the body of somebody else.

These feelings of strangeness in the self are often accompanied by **derealization,** a feeling of strangeness about the world: other people, like oneself, seem robotic, dead, or somehow unreal, like actors in a play. People experiencing depersonalization or derealization may also have episodes of *déjà vu* (French

In 1990, a jury in Redwood City, California, convicted a man, George Franklin, of murdering a child some 20 years earlier—a, verdict based on Franklin's daughter's claim that she had suddenly remembered witnessing the crime. This was only the most sensational of hundreds of recent cases of so-called *recovered memory*—memories of childhood abuse, particularly sexual abuse, that according to the rememberers were repressed and then eventually returned to consciousness. A number of people have sued their remembered abusers, and won. At the same time, "recovery specialists," therapists expert in excavating such memories, have published best-selling books, claiming that many people with psychological problems are suffering from buried memories of abuse.

Recovered memory has generated huge public interest, stimulated by magazine articles and television talk shows. This fascination, in turn, has prompted a wave of skepticism. According to some observers, many recovered memories of abuse are nothing more than the product of suggestion—and hypnosis—by irresponsible therapists. Such skepticism, however, is mild compared with the outrage of parents who say they have been wrongly accused. Some are fighting back in court, and not just against their children but also against the therapists in whose offices these alleged memories have surfaced. Patients, too, are suing their therapists. In the 1997 case described on page 185, former patient Patricia Burgus claimed that she was induced in therapy to produce false memories of being sexually abused, of abusing her own two sons, and of having belonged to a satanic cult whose activities included cannibalism. As noted, Burgus received a settlement of $10.6 million (Belluck, 1997). In 1995, the conviction of George Franklin was reversed, largely because of questions raised about the validity of his daughter's recovered memory.

How can false memories be distinguished from true ones? This question has prompted a flurry of research, which so far has established a few principles. First, it is apparently possible to forget and then remember a childhood trauma. In one study, researchers asked a random national sample of 724 adults whether they had experienced some form of trauma and, if so, whether they had ever forgotten this. Almost three-quarters said they had undergone a trauma. (The most common were assault, rape, or sexual molestation; natural disasters or car accidents; and the witnessing of assault or murder.) Almost a third of this group said that, at some point in their lives, they had forgotten all or part of the trauma (Elliott, 1997).

That study, however, relied on self-report. Another researcher, L. M. Williams (1994), began her study with records of documented abuse. Using a hospital's files on 206 girls, ages 10 months to 12 years, who had received medical treatment following verified sexual abuse in the early 1970s, Williams tracked down as many of those girls, now women, as she could and asked them if they would participate in a survey about women treated at that hospital. More than half consented, and, in the course of a 3 hour interview, they were asked about many things. But, when the question of childhood sexual abuse was put to them, 38 percent did not report the incident for which the hospital records showed they had been treated. Perhaps they were simply withholding this information, out of a sense of privacy. Probably not, says Williams, for two-thirds of these "nonreporters" told the interviewer about *other* episodes of childhood abuse. Of those who did report the documented abuse, 16 percent said there had been a time in the past when they did not remember it (Williams, 1995).

Thus, apparently people can forget true episodes of abuse. And, according to other recent research, they can also have false memories of abuse. The latter process seems to hinge on what is called *source amnesia*. In storing a memory, the brain distributes it among various areas—the sounds of the memory in one part, the sight of it in another part, and so on. Information

Eileen Franklin Lipsker testified about her recovered memory of having seen her father sexually abuse and murder her playmate 20 years before, when she was 8 years old. Her testimony resulted in her father's conviction, which was later reversed.

as to the *source* of a memory, when and where the thing happened—in life, in a movie, in a story told to the person—seems to be stored primarily in the frontal cortex, and this information is more fragile than other parts of memory. People often remember things but forget the source. For example, they may recognize a man's face but not recall where they know him from. Or they misidentify the source. (For example, they claim to remember an event from childhood when in fact they have only been told about it.)

According to some researchers, source amnesia is what is happening in many cases of recovered memory. The rememberers are not inventing the memory; they are simply misattributing it—to their own lives (Lindsay & Read, 1994). Where, then, does it come from?

One possibility is the media: the talk shows, magazine articles, and books mentioned earlier. An item of special interest to researchers is Ellen Bass and Laura Davis' *The Courage to Heal,* the so-called bible of recovery specialists. This 1988 book, which has no doubt given needed comfort to numerous survivors of childhood abuse, may also have confused many other people. One of its main premises is that a great number of people are victims of incest but don't realize they were abused. For readers who are in doubt, the book offers a list of things they might recall, ranging from the relatively harmless, such as being held in a way that made them uneasy, to the clearly criminal, such as rape. Then readers are told, "If you are unable to remember any specific instances like the ones mentioned above but still feel that something abusive happened to you, it probably did" (p. 21). Abuse can also be deduced from psychological symptoms, the authors claim, and they list the symptoms, including depression, self-destructive thoughts, low self-esteem, and sexual dysfunction—in other words, "symptoms" experienced by many people, including the children of irreproachable parents. *The Courage to Heal* has been repeatedly implicated in disputed memories of abuse.

Another possible source of suggestion is therapists. Psychologist Elizabeth Loftus reported a case in which a man, whose daughter claimed to have recovered memories of his molesting her, hired a private investigator to go to the daughter's therapist. The investigator pretended that she was seeking psychological help; her complaint was nightmares and insomnia. By the fourth session, the therapist had declared the investigator a probable incest survivor, a diagnosis she said was "confirmed on the basis of the 'classic symptoms' of body memory and sleep disorders. When the patient insisted that she had no memory of such events, the therapist assured her that this was often the case" (Loftus, 1993, p. 530). The therapist recommended that she read *The Courage to Heal.*

The fact that therapists specializing in recovered memory often unearth such memories through hypnosis and hypnotic age regression (telling the patient, under hypnosis, that he or she is now a child) only increases people's concerns about such therapy, for the research on memories obtained through hypnosis seriously questions their accuracy (Destun & Kuiper, 1996). Under hypnosis, for example, people have remembered being abducted by aliens (Gordon, 1991).

But can the memory of a traumatic event actually be planted in a person's brain? According to several recent studies, the answer is yes. In one experiment (Loftus, Feldman, & Dashiell, in press), the researchers were reluctant to instill a memory of sexual abuse, so they chose instead the widespread childhood fear of getting lost in a store. One 14-year-old subject, Chris, was told by his older brother, Jim, that their mother had lost Chris in a shopping mall when he was 5. Jim told Chris the story briefly, with few details. Then, for several days afterward, Chris was questioned about the episode, and he began to recover the memory. On the second day, he recalled how he felt when he was lost; on the fourth day, he reported what his mother had said to him when she found him. Within a few weeks, he remembered a great deal more:

I was with you guys for a second and then I think I went over to look at the toy store, the Kay-bee toy and uh, we got lost and I was looking around and I thought, "Uh-oh. I'm in trouble now." . . . I thought I was never going to see my family again. I was really scared you know. And then this old man, I think he was wearing a blue flannel, came up to me . . . he was kind of old. He was kind of bald on top . . . he had like a ring of gray hair . . . and he had glasses. (Loftus, 1993, p. 532)

When Chris was finally debriefed, he was incredulous. By that time, he remembered the "episode" very well.

But being lost is not the same as being molested. As noted, the researchers in this case did not feel it was safe to implant a memory of abuse, but such an experiment took place informally in the widely publicized case of Paul Ingram. Ingram, a county sheriff in Olympia, Washington, was arrested in 1988 after his 2 daughters, ages 18 and 22, claimed to have retrieved memories of being abused by him. Ingram was at first bewildered by the accusations, but gradually he claimed that he remembered episodes in which he had assaulted the girls. Soon the accusations escalated. One daughter, who had read books on satanic ritual abuse and had seen "satanic abuse" survivors on *Geraldo,* then remembered that Ingram had forced her to take part in satanic rituals—she estimated that she had attended 850 such events—in which babies were chopped up. Under prodding by police investigators, Ingram remembered the satanic rituals too.

Social psychologist Richard Ofshe, an authority on cults and mind control, was brought in by the prosecution to question Ingram. To determine how suggestible Ingram was, Ofshe told him a lie: that 1 of his daughters and 1 of his sons were now claiming that he had forced them to have sex with each other. As before, Ingram seemed puzzled at first, but, by his third meeting with Ofshe, he proudly produced a 3-page confession, describing how he had watched the 2 children have sex and including numerous details of their intercourse. Ofshe eventually concluded that all of Ingram's memories of the abuse he had inflicted were fantasies, the product of suggestion by the investigators questioning him. Ingram concluded the same thing—too late to retract his guilty plea. He was convicted of rape and sentenced to 20 years in prison (Wright, 1994).

No one involved in the recovered-memory controversy denies that children are sexually abused (including many whose memories of abuse require no recovery). Nor, in the face of the studies cited above, would most experts claim that all recovered memories of abuse are false. Clearly, some that are called true are false, with terrible consequences for the accused, and some that are called false are true, with the equally traumatic consequences for the accusers. What would be possible, however, is a commitment on the part of therapists to seek out confirming physical evidence. Such evidence can help separate false charges from the true (Bowers & Farvolden, 1996).

for "already seen"), the sense of having been in a place or situation before, when one knows that this is not the case. Or they may have the opposite experience, *jamais vu*, (French for "never seen"), the sense, when one is in a familiar place or situation, of never having encountered it before. In the view of cognitive psychology, depersonalization and derealization constitute a failure of recognition memory. The person is unable to match current experience with past experience, as might happen on entering a familiar room that has been redecorated (Reed, 1988). Depersonalization often involves reduced emotional responsiveness, a loss of interest in others and the world in general. Often it also involves reduced physiological responsiveness (Griffin, Resick, & Mechanic, 1997)—reduced heart rate and skin conductance. People afflicted with depersonalization do not lose touch with reality. They know that their perceptions of strangeness are wrong. Nevertheless, the perceptions are frightening. The person may feel that he or she is going insane.

Depersonalization can occur briefly in the course of normal life. When people wake up from sleep, when they have had a bad scare, or when they are very tired or practicing meditation, they may have a brief spell of depersonalization. Depersonalization also occurs as a component of other psychological disorders, particularly anxiety disorders, depression, and schizophrenia, and it is a common symptom of the other dissociative disorders (Simeon & Hollander, 1993). Finally, depersonalization often occurs after "near-death experiences," in which people are rescued at the last moment from drowning or other accidents. Some research indicates that the experience of depersonalization *during* a traumatic event is adaptive—that it decreases the risk of depression and anxiety after the event (Shilony & Grossman, 1993). Possibly, the sense that this is happening in a dream or to someone else protects the person from suffering the full impact of the trauma. At the same time, other evidence (Griffin, Resick, & Mechanic, 1997) suggests that people who develop pronounced feelings of depersonalization *after* a trauma are more likely to succumb to a full-blown posttraumatic stress disorder (Chapter 6).

A brief spell of depersonalization connected with a trauma does not, however, constitute depersonalization disorder. The diagnosis is made only when depersonalization (with or without a trauma) is severe and persistent enough to disrupt the person's life, as in the following case:

> Mr. B was a 37-year-old married professional man who had suffered from depersonalization disorder since age 10. He vividly recalled its acute onset on a day

> when he was playing football: he was tackled by another boy and suddenly felt that his body had disappeared. The depersonalization was initially episodic but became continuous by age 14. He described it as "not being in this world . . . I am disconnected from my body. It is as if my body is not there." The depersonalization was lessened when he was alone and almost disappeared in his wife's presence. All social settings made it much worse. He met criteria for schizoid personality disorder. As a child he had suffered marked emotional neglect. His parents fed and clothed him but never expressed emotion; he recalled hardly ever being touched or kissed. It is of interest that his sense of detachment only involved his body and not other aspects of the self. (Simeon, Gross, Guralnik, et al., 1997, pp. 1109–1110)

The onset of depersonalization disorder may be either sudden, as in this case, or gradual. The condition is usually chronic.

Groups at Risk for Dissociative Disorders

The prevalence of dissociative identity disorder, like most other aspects of that disorder, is a topic of controversy and awaits careful research. Some experts estimate prevalence to be as high as 3 percent of the general population (Ross, Joshi, & Currie, 1991); others place it far lower. DID is anywhere from 3 to 9 times more common in women than in men (Loewenstein, 1994), and, according to the research, most of these women are already deeply troubled. The Putnam group's survey found that at the time of diagnosis, almost 90 percent of its sample was suffering from depression, and more than half had histories of substance abuse and suicide attempts (Putnam, Guroff, Silberman, et al., 1986). Although, as noted, its victims say that DID begins in childhood—and some child cases have been identified (Peterson & Putnam, 1994)—DID tends not to be diagnosed until the patient is in his or her twenties or thirties. The symptoms generally look the same across cultures (Atchison & McFarlane, 1994; Sar, Yargic, & Tutkun, 1996), but not across age groups. Children, it seems, are less likely to have clear-cut alters, but very likely to show amnesia and trancelike states. Without the alters, they may fail to be diagnosed with DID and yet still be at high risk. A new diagnostic category—"dissociative disorder of childhood," stressing amnesia and trance, together with abrupt shifts in behavior—has been proposed to cover this condition (Peterson & Putnam, 1994).

As for depersonalization disorder, specialists agree that it is rare. Like DID and other dissociative disorders, it seems to be more common in women than in men (Simeon, Gross, Guralnik, et al., 1997). The condition is seen worldwide, but in some cultures it is not regarded as a disorder but as a legitimate trance or spirit possession (Castillo, 1997).

Dissociative Disorders: Theory and Therapy

Most theories of the dissociative disorders begin with the assumption that dissociation is a way in which people escape from situations that are beyond their coping powers. As for how the process occurs, and how the resulting disorders should be treated, these questions receive different answers.

The Psychodynamic Perspective: Defense Against Anxiety

It was in the late nineteenth century that the dissociative disorders were first extensively studied. A pioneer in this research was French psychologist Pierre Janet (1929), who originated the idea of mental dissociation. Under certain circumstances, Janet claimed, one or more divisions of mental functioning could become split off from the others and operate outside conscious awareness. Janet called this phenomenon *désagrégation,* which was translated into English as "dissociation" (hence, the name of this category). Janet and others considered the dissociative disorders a subdivision of hysteria. But it was left to Janet's contemporary, Sigmund Freud, to enunciate a *cause* of dissociation in the theory of hysteria that was to become the basis for his entire theory of the mind.

Dissociation as Defense Freud, as we have seen, believed that many basic human wishes were in direct conflict with either reality or the superego and that the result of this conflict was painful anxiety. To protect the mind against the anxiety, the ego repressed the wish and mounted defenses against it. The dissociative disorders—indeed, all the neuroses—were simply extreme and maladaptive defenses. Dissociative amnesia, for example, is regarded by Freudian theorists as a simple case of repression. Fugue and dissociative identity disorder are more complicated, in that the person also acts out the repressed wish directly or symbolically—the fugue patient goes off and has adventures, the person with dissociative identity disorder becomes a different, "forbidden" self—while the ego maintains amnesia for the episode, thus protecting the mind against the strictures of the superego.

This theory has on its side the observation that dissociative disorders do appear to operate in such a way as to grant wishes that the person could not otherwise satisfy (as illustrated in the case histories of Bernice and Eve). There is also some research support for the anxiety-relief hypothesis. One recent study found that dissociative patients experience less intrapsychic conflict than alcoholic patients (Alpher, 1996). But, with its strict division between conscious and unconscious, the Freudian model does not seem to offer an adequate explanation of dissociative identity disorder, in which the "forbidden" self does not, in fact, remain unconscious but, instead, seizes the consciousness. Several writers (Brenner, 1996; Kluft, 1992; MacGregor, 1996) have put forth more complex theories of DID in line with current psychodynamic thinking. Kluft's hypothesis is that this condition develops when a child with a special capacity to dissociate—that is, to focus intensely on one thing to the exclusion of others—is exposed to overwhelming stress. Imagine, for example, a young girl who has an imaginary companion (as many DID patients report having had [Sanders, 1992]). If she were sexually abused and no adult were available to minister to her distress, she might expand the imaginary companion to contain the abuse experience, thus walling it off from herself. (This would help to account for the frequent reports of child subordinates in multiple personality.) She might also develop a third, punitive personality, based on the abuser, as a refraction of her guilt feelings, as well as a "protector" personality, in answer to her need for protection. Over time, this constellation could be expanded to contain and enclose other upsetting experiences. The subpersonalities might remain dormant for years, but, under the stress of later traumas, they could emerge as overt, alternating personalities—in other words, dissociative identity disorder.

Treating Dissociation Psychodynamic therapy is the most common treatment for the dissociative disorders. When trauma is involved, or thought to be involved, the treatment generally proceeds in three stages. Stage 1 involves settling the patient down: establishing an atmosphere of trust and helping the patient to gain some mastery over the dissociative symptoms. Then, in Stage 2, the traumatic memory is recovered and grieved over. Stage 3 is devoted to the reintegration of the traumatic memory, so that the patient no longer has to use dissociation to wall it off (Herman, 1992; Kluft, 1996).

Exposing the repressed memory may be no easy task, however. After all, the whole thrust of the dissociative disorders is to protect that material from exposure. In amnesia, fugue, and DID, the traditional method of bringing forth the lost material has been hypnosis. (Barbiturates may achieve the same effect.) Under hypnosis, fugue and amnesia patients often

Although hypnosis is an effective method for bringing forth dissociated material, it has drawbacks. In some cases it creates or aggravates dissociative symptoms. In others, the memory-retrieval brought on by hypnosis may retraumatize the client.

reveal the events covered by the amnesia, and people with DID bring forth subordinate personalities. Indeed, some cases of dissociative identity disorder are *discovered* through hypnosis. A disadvantage of hypnosis is that in some cases it seems to bring on or exacerbate dissociative symptoms (Destun & Kuiper, 1996). But, because it also uncovers dissociated material, many treatments for dissociative identity disorder still rely on this method (Putnam & Loewenstein, 1993). Another concern is that the memory-retrieval may be retraumatizing—particularly when it takes the form of *abreaction,* or the intense reexperiencing of the event—and unnecessarily prolonged, plunging the patient again and again into a state of emotional crisis. Some therapists now avoid abreactions (Ross, 1997). Kluft (1996) has proposed a technique called "fractionated abreaction," in which the memory is retrieved only gradually, in small parts, while the therapist encourages mastery and discourages surrender to emotion.

Therapeutic outcome studies (Coons, 1986; Kluft, 1988) indicate that this may be a long process. As we pointed out earlier, fugue tends to remit without treatment, and dissociative amnesia may also. Hence, the usual goal of therapy in these disorders is to recover and integrate the lost material so that the patient doesn't suffer a relapse. But DID is far more stubborn. The more alters, the more difficult it is to integrate them into a single personality (Kluft, 1986), and, when integration is achieved, it can crumble in the face of stress or if, as sometimes happens, another, previously undetected personality surfaces. A recent 2-year follow-up of patients treated for DID found that they showed marked improvement in a wide variety of symptoms, including dissociative

symptoms (Ellason & Ross, 1997). Those who had achieved integration were significantly more improved, but they appear to be a minority. By 1 count, only 38 of the 153 patients who began treatment for DID achieved a stable integration of their personalities (Piper, 1994b).

The Behavioral and Sociocultural Perspectives: Dissociation as a Social Role

Learning to Dissociate The dissociative disorders constitute a problem for learning theory, for it is almost impossible to discuss these disorders without invoking concepts such as awareness and identity—indeed, they are fundamentally disorders of awareness and identity—and such concepts are not part of the behaviorist's vocabulary (Sackeim & Devanand, 1991). What the behaviorists have done is to conceptualize the dissociative disorders as a form of learned coping response, with the production of symptoms in order to obtain rewards or relief from stress.

According to the behaviorists, the dissociative disorders, like many other psychological disorders, are the result of a person's adopting a social role that is reinforced by its consequences (Seltzer, 1994). In amnesia, fugue, and dissociative identity disorder, the rewarding consequence is protection from stressful events. Fugue, for example, gets its victims away from situations painful to them, and amnesia for the fugue protects them from painful consequences of their actions during the fugue. Note the similarity between this interpretation and the psychodynamic view: in both cases, the focus is on motivation, and the motivation is escape. The difference is that in the psychodynamic view the process is unconscious, whereas in the behavioral view dissociative behavior is maintained by reinforcement, like any other behavior.

Like the behaviorists, sociocultural theorists see dissociative symptoms as the product of social reinforcement. In a theory put forth by Spanos (1994), for example, dissociative identity disorder is a strategy that people use to evoke sympathy and escape responsibility for certain of their actions. Those actions, they say, were performed by some other, nonresponsible part of themselves. According to Spanos, this process is aided by hypnosis: patients learn the "hypnotic role" and in that role produce the kind of behavior that the clinician hypnotizing them seems to want. Once they produce it, the clinician validates it with an "expert"diagnosis, and that diagnosis results in a number of possible rewards: relief from distress, an ability to control others, permission for misbehavior, and even, in some cases, avoidance of criminal proceedings. The clinician is rewarded, too, by attention: he or she has uncovered another case of this celebrated disorder. Thus, having created the disorder, both therapist and patient come to believe in its existence, for they have good reason to do so.

To test this hypothesis, Spanos and his colleagues designed an experiment based on the case of Kenneth Bianchi, the so-called Hillside strangler, who raped and murdered several women in the Los Angeles area during the early 1980s. (See the box on p.181.) Upon arrest, Bianchi claimed he was innocent, and he was sent for a psychiatric evaluation, during which he supposedly showed evidence of dissociative identity disorder. What happened was as follows. First, Bianchi was hypnotized. Then the clinician described the situation to him as one in which another, hidden "part" of him might emerge. Bianchi was given an easy way to signal the arrival of that part. The clinician said to him:

> I've talked a bit to Ken but I think that perhaps there might be another part of Ken that I haven't talked to. And I would like to communicate with that other part. And I would like that other part to come to talk to me . . . And when you're here, lift the left hand off the chair to signal to me that you are here. Would you please come, Part, so I can talk to you . . . Part, would you come and lift Ken's hand to indicate to me that you are here . . . Would you talk to me, Part, by saying "I'm here"?
>
> (Schwarz, 1981, pp. 142–143)

Bianchi answered yes and then had the following exchange with the clinician (B=Bianchi; C=clinician):

> C: Part, are you the same as Ken or are you different in any way?
>
> B: I'm not him.
>
> C: You're not him. Who are you? Do you have a name?
>
> B: I'm not Ken.
>
> C: You're not him? Okay. Who are you? Tell me about yourself. Do you have a name I can call you by?
>
> B: Steve. You can call me Steve.
>
> (Schwarz, 1981, pp. 139–140)

"Steve" went on to say that, with the help of a cousin, he had murdered a number of women and that Ken knew nothing either about him (Steve) or about the murders. When he was released from his hypnotic state, Bianchi was "amnesic" for all that Steve had said. He then pleaded not guilty by reason of insanity, the insanity being dissociative identity disorder. (The defense failed.)

What Spanos and his colleagues did was to subject a number of college students to variations on the procedure Bianchi went through. The students were instructed to play the role of accused murderers, and they were divided among three experimental condi-

Kenneth Bianchi, the "Hillside Strangler," made an unsuccessful attempt to prove that he was not guilty by reason of insanity, in the form of dissociative identity disorder.

tions. In the "Bianchi condition," the subjects were hypnotized and then put through an interview taken almost verbatim from the Bianchi interview. In a second, "hidden-part condition," the subjects were also hypnotized, after which they were told that under hypnosis people often reveal a hidden part of themselves. However, in contrast to the Bianchi condition, that hidden part was not directly addressed, nor was it asked whether it was different from the subject. In the third, control condition, the subjects were not hypnotized, and they were given only vague information about hidden parts of the self.

After these experimental conditions were set up, all the subjects were questioned about whether they had a second personality. They were also asked about the murders. In the Bianchi condition, 81 percent of the subjects came up with second personalities that had different names from themselves, and in the majority of cases this second personality admitted guilt for the murders. In the hidden-part condition, only 31 percent revealed second personalities with new names, though, here again, the majority of second personalities confessed to the murders. In the control condition, only 13 percent confessed to the murders, and no one produced a new personality with a different name.

Thus, it appears that, when the situation demands, people who are given appropriate cues can manufacture a subordinate personality and will shift blame onto it. Furthermore, in keeping with Spanos' theory, the students who produced a second personality in some measure came to believe in it or at least knew how to design it skillfully. In a second session, when these "multiple-personality" subjects were given the same personality test twice, one time for each personality, their new alter personalities tested very differently from their host personalities (Spanos, Weekes, & Bertrand, 1985). Recall that this finding of differences between alters on personality tests has been put forth as support for the genuineness of DID. But apparently such differences can also be manufactured.

According to Spanos and others (Brenneis, 1996), what these findings suggest is that most cases of dissociative identity disorder are strategic enactments. Many of these patients are highly imaginative people, with rich fantasy lives. And, as we saw, they are very susceptible to suggestion and hypnosis. If such people were placed in difficult circumstances from which "multiple personality" would help them escape and if, under hypnosis or even without hypnosis, an admired authority figure (the therapist) were to give them the suggestion that they might have a subordinate personality and were to tell them how such a personality could be expressed, they could, in fact, develop one and come to believe in it.

Nonreinforcement   According to behavioral and sociocultural theory, the way to treat dissociative symptoms is to stop reinforcing them. In a case of dissociative identity disorder, for example, therapists, friends, and family members would express no interest in the alters. At the same time, they would expect the patient to take responsibility for actions supposedly produced by the alters. Using such an approach with a woman who reported alters, Kohlenberg (1973) found that the alters' behaviors became less frequent when they were not reinforced. The therapist may also help patients deal with emotions that they are presumably pushing off onto alters. In one case, a passive patient, L, had a very aggressive alter, "Toni." Once L was given assertiveness training and taught how to express anger, Toni disappeared (Price & Hess, 1979). Actually, a number of psychodynamic therapists have recommended ignoring alters, on the grounds that work with alters takes time away from the patient's serious, present problems (McHugh, 1992).

The Cognitive Perspective: Memory Dysfunction

Cognitive theorists view the dissociative syndromes as fundamentally disorders of memory. In each case,

what has been dissociated is all or part of the patient's "autobiography." As we have seen, the patient's skills (procedural memory) and general knowledge (semantic memory) are usually intact. What is impaired is the patient's episodic memory, or record of personal experience. As we have also seen, it is only partially impaired. Patients may still show evidence that they have implicit memory of their past. What they don't have is explicit memory for the dissociated material, the ability to retrieve it into consciousness.

Retrieval Failure   What causes this selective impairment of explicit episodic memory? Two cognitive theories have been proposed. One has to do with what is called *state-dependent memory*. A number of studies have shown that people have an easier time recalling an event if they are in the same mood state as the one they were in when the event occurred (Blaney, 1986; Bower, 1994). Hence, memories established in an extreme emotional state—for example, the kind of severe traumatic reaction that is thought to set off dissociative amnesia and fugue—may be "lost" simply because they are linked to a mood that is not likely to recur. A dramatic case of state-dependent memory is that of Sirhan Sirhan, the man convicted of killing Robert F. Kennedy. In the waking state, Sirhan claimed amnesia for the crime, but under hypnosis his mood became more and more agitated, as it had been during the crime, and in this state he not only recalled the murder but reenacted parts of it (Bower, 1981).

Such a mechanism may also help to explain dissociative identity disorder. Typically, the different personalities are characterized by different mood states. Therefore, state dependency may lead one personality to have amnesia for the experiences of another. By the same token, situations that produce strong emotion may cause a shift from one personality to a different personality, one with moods and memories consistent with that emotion. For example, if a quiet-tempered patient is made angry, this may cause a sudden shift to a hostile subordinate personality, for that is the personality that can process and express the anger (Bower, 1994).

A second cognitive theory of dissociation has to do with *control elements,* facts about oneself under which other information is categorized and which, therefore, can activate or inhibit the retrieval of that other information. According to Schacter and his colleagues, a person's name may be the ultimate control element of episodic memory. If the name is forgotten, the life is forgotten. Schacter and his team, for example, described a case in which a patient hospitalized for amnesia had almost no episodic memory. He

Sirhan Sirhan gave dramatic evidence of state-dependent memory. In his normal waking state, he said he did not remember having killed Senator Robert F. Kennedy, but in an agitated state under hypnosis he remembered and even reenacted the murder.

knew, however, that he had a nickname, "Lumberjack," and that he had worked for a messenger service. As it turned out, it was his co-workers at the messenger service who had given him that nickname. Thus, remembering the name he had at work, he could remember his work, but, not remembering his real name, he could not remember the rest of his life (Schacter, Wang, Tulving, et al., 1982). This theory is supported by the finding that in some cases, but not all, amnesia remits once the person is confronted with his or her name (Kaszniak, Nussbaum, Berren, et al., 1988).

Improving Memory Retrieval   To date, there has been little work on cognitive therapy for dissociative disorders. Nevertheless, many therapists use cognitive mechanisms in treating dissociative patients. For example, in the case of Jane Doe at the beginning of this chapter, the therapist was appealing to her implicit memory when he asked her to punch in telephone numbers at random. Other patients have been asked to state the first name that comes to mind or to say which of a list of cities "rings a bell," the hope

being that the name or city will be the patient's own, arising from implicit memory. There is also the possibility that retrieved facts will act as control elements, releasing the information stored under them. State dependency has also been appealed to. As in the case of Sirhan Sirhan, many therapists have tried to reinstate strong emotions in their patients, first under hypnosis and then in the waking state, in order to spring the lock on state-dependent memories.

The Biological Perspective: Brain Dysfunction

The dissociative disorders, as we have pointed out, involve psychiatric symptoms that look like the product of neurological disease but are thought instead to be the result of psychological processes. Are they? According to neuroscience researchers, some so-called dissociative disorders may be neurological disorders after all. According to one theory (Sivec & Lynn, 1995), the dissociative syndromes may be a by-product of undiagnosed epilepsy (Chapter 14). Epileptic-type seizures have been associated with dissociative identity disorder ever since the disorder was first described (Charcot & Marie, 1892). Conversely, some victims of epilepsy have reported dissociative experiences such as blackouts, fugues, depersonalization, déjà vu, and feelings of demonic possession following seizures. This theory may apply to certain dissociative conditions, but it is unlikely to explain DID, in which the symptoms are far more elaborate than the dissociative experiences reported by epileptics. Furthermore, as we saw, DID is far more common in women, whereas epilepsy is more frequently diagnosed in men.

   A second hypothesis has to do with the hippocampus (Chapter 4), a part of the limbic system. Recent evidence suggests that memories are divided among different parts of the brain, according to the sensory modality through which they were acquired. (For example, visual information is stored in the occipital cortex, tactile information in the sensory cortex, and so on.) When a memory needs to be retrieved, it is apparently the hippocampus that brings the memory elements back together and integrates them. But stress can derail this process. In autopsies of monkeys and in MRI scans of human beings, it has been shown that stress can lead to structural changes in the hippocampus, including the atrophy of cells. Stress can also trigger the release of neurotransmitters that are highly concentrated in the hippocampus—a process that is thought to interfere with the encoding and retrieval of memories. Thus, if dissociative disorders originate in stress and if the stress is chronic—as would be the case, for example, with long-term child abuse—this might alter the functioning of the hippocampus to the point where it could no longer unite memory elements. The result would be amnesia or, in DID, the isolation of different memories in different states of consciousness (Bremner, Krystal, Charney, et al., 1996; Bremner, Krystal, Southwick, et al., 1995). In support of this hypothesis, it has been found that electrical stimulation of the hippocampus and nearby regions of the brain produces symptoms that resemble dissociation.

Finally, it has been suggested that, at least in depersonalization disorder, there may be some abnormality in serotonin functioning. Patients with depersonalization disorder tend to have migraine headaches (Chapter 8), and serotonin has been implicated in migraines. Second, episodes of depersonalization can be brought on by marijuana, and marijuana intoxication is also thought to involve an alteration in serotonin levels. It has also been shown that drugs that lower serotonin levels can induce depersonalization, while selective serotonin reuptake inhibitors (SSRIs), which increase serotonin levels, have been found to relieve depersonalization disorder in some patients (Simeon, Stein, & Hollander, 1995).

It should be kept in mind that none of these hypotheses rule out psychological causation. What neuroscience researchers are speculating about is the neurological processes underlying dissociative states. Such processes, in their view, could be activated by psychological stress as well as by neurological disease or injury (Sackeim & Devanand, 1991).

Drug Treatment   Little in the way of biological treatment has been developed for the dissociative disorders. The barbiturate sodium amytal can be used as an alternative to hypnosis to aid in the recovery of memories, although the reliability of such memories is no better than with hypnosis. As noted, SSRIs such as Prozac (Chapter 6) have helped in some cases of depersonalization disorder, although their usefulness for this condition has never been evaluated in controlled studies (Simeon, Stein, & Hollander, 1995). As researchers gain more knowledge about stress-induced changes in memory function, it is hoped that they will be able to develop medications for the dissociative disorders.

Somatoform Disorders

The primary feature of the somatoform disorders is that, as the name suggests, psychological conflicts take on a somatic, or physical, form. Some patients complain of physical discomfort—stomach pains, breathing problems, and so forth. Others show an actual loss or impairment of normal physiological function: suddenly they can no longer see, swallow, or move their right leg. In either case, there is no organic evidence to explain the symptom, while there *is* evidence (or at least a strong suspicion) that the symptom is linked to psychological factors. We will discuss five syndromes: body dysmorphic disorder, hypochondriasis, somatization disorder, pain disorder, and conversion disorder.

Body Dysmorphic Disorder

Many of us are preoccupied with our appearance. We worry that we are too fat or too thin, that we have too little hair or hair in the wrong places, that our nose is too big, that our ears are too prominent, and so on. Such concerns are normal, particularly during adolescence. Some people, however, are so distressed over how they look that they can no longer function normally. Such people are said to have body dysmorphic disorder, defined as preoccupation with an imagined or a grossly exaggerated defect in appearance.

Most people with this condition complain of facial flaws, such as the quality of the skin or the shape of the nose. Another common complaint is thinning hair. But any part of the body, or several parts at once, may be the focus of the concern. People with body dysmorphic disorder are not delusional (though they may eventually become so). If confronted, they usually concede that they are exaggerating. Nevertheless, they suffer great unhappiness. They may spend several hours a day looking in mirrors and trying to correct the defect—recombing the hair, picking the skin. In one reported case, a woman spent hours each day cutting her hair to try to make it symmetrical (Hollander Liebowitz, Winchel, et al., 1989). People with this disorder may try to

A person with body dysmorphic disorder may spend hours in front of a mirror every day, trying to fix an imagined or highly exaggerated flaw in appearance.

camouflage the imagined defect—for example, by growing a beard to cover "scars." Some resort to plastic surgery, which, however, rarely satisfies them. Many of them repeatedly seek reassurance. (Again, this does not reassure.) To avoid being seen, they may drop out of school, quit their jobs, avoid dating, and become housebound. In severe cases, the person may contemplate or even attempt suicide (Phillips, McElroy, Hudson, et al., 1995), as in the following case:

> Karen is a 17-year-old Caucasian woman who was hospitalized after attempting suicide. She attributed her suicide attempt to concerns about her appearance. Since age 13 she had been excessively preoccupied with her "large" nose, "small" breasts, and "ugly" hair. In reality, Karen was an attractive woman.... She described her concerns as "very, very distressing—an obsession. They're so horrible I get suicidal; it's why I overdosed. I couldn't stand the pain any more." She thought about her appearance "every second of every day," and she checked mirrors, store windows, and other reflecting surfaces for several hours a day. She also frequently compared her appearance with that of others and asked her mother "a million times a day" whether she looked okay. She avoided being photographed and destroyed any photographs that were taken of her. When she was complimented on her attractive hair, Karen felt angry because she assumed the comments "were a way they can avoid commenting on my ugly face and body." As a result of her appearance concerns, Karen avoided social interactions and dating, failed some courses, and eventually dropped out of school. A rhinoplasty [nose surgery] did not diminish her concerns; she worried less about her nose but more about her breasts. (Phillips, Atala, & Albertini, 1995, pp. 1216–1217)

The onset of body dysmorphic disorder is usually gradual and may begin with someone making a negative comment on the person's appearance. A history of having been teased as a child, of having once had a disfiguring condition (e.g., severe acne), or of being unloved by parents may place people at risk for the disorder. The media, with their emphasis on physical beauty, probably also contribute to the development of this condition (Phillips, 1996a). Unless it is treated, body dysmorphic disorder tends to be chronic.

Not surprisingly, the disorder is associated with social phobia; it is also associated with depression— four out of five patients have experienced major depression—and it can sometimes be treated with antidepressant drugs. Another related syndrome is obsessive-compulsive disorder, which turns up in the histories of almost a third of body dysmorphic patients. It is possible that body dysmorphic disorder is a form of obsessive-compulsive disorder. Both conditions involve obsessional thinking as well as compulsive behaviors (e.g., mirror checking); both tend to appear in adolescence and to be chronic; both may respond to the same drugs, such as Prozac; in some cases, both occur in the same families. But there are also important differences between the two syndromes. The most obvious is the content of the preoccupations: body dysmorphic patients are focused on their appearance, while obsessive-compulsives are usually concerned with danger or contamination. Also, body dysmorphic patients generally show lower self-esteem, greater shame, and more concern over rejection by others than do obsessive-compulsives (Phillips, McElroy, Hudson, et al., 1995; Simeon, Hollander, Stein, et al., 1995).

Hypochondriasis

The primary feature of **hypochondriasis** is a gnawing fear of disease—a fear maintained by constant misinterpretation of physical signs and sensations as abnormal. Hypochondriacs have no real physical disability; what they have is a conviction that a disability is about to appear. Hence, they spend each day watching for the first signs, and they soon find them. One day the heart will skip a beat, or the body will register a new pain. This is then interpreted as the onset of the disease. Often, when they appear at the doctor's office, hypochondriacs have already diagnosed their condition, for they are usually avid readers of articles on health in popular magazines. And, when the medical examination reveals that they are perfectly healthy, they are typically incredulous. Soon they are back in the doctor's office with reports of further symptoms, or they may simply change doctors. Some go through several doctors a year. Others resort to "miracle" cures or try to cure themselves, either with strenuous health regimens or with pills, of which they typically have large collections.

It should be emphasized that hypochondriacs do not fake their "symptoms." They truly feel the pains they report; they are convinced that their records of their heart irregularities are accurate (although research has found that hypochondriacs are no more accurate than controls in detecting their own heartbeats [Barsky, Brener, Coeytaux, et al., 1995]). They are sincerely afraid that they are about to succumb to some grave disease, and in consequence they suffer terribly, not just from anxiety but also from depression (Noyes, Kathol, Fisher, et al., 1994). Insofar as they cannot be reassured by the medical evidence, their fears are irrational. However, these fears do not have the bizarre quality of the disease delusions experienced by psychotics who report that their feet are about to fall off or that their brains are shriveling. Hypochondriacs tend to confine their anxieties to more ordinary syndromes, such as heart disease or

Molière's comedy The Imaginary Invalid *was written in the seventeenth century, a time when hypochondriasis was widely regarded as a common, inevitable disease of civilization.*

cancer. Hypochondriac fears are also different from obsessive-compulsive fears of contamination and disease. Obsessive-compulsives know that their fears are groundless, and they try to resist them. Hypochondriacs find their fears quite reasonable and don't see why others question them (Barsky, 1992a).

Several developmental factors may predispose a person to hypochondriasis. Hypochondriacs are more likely than others to have suffered, or to have had a family member who suffered, a true organic disease, thus making their fears, however unfounded, at least understandable (Barsky, Wool, Barnett, et al., 1994; Robbins & Kirmayer, 1996). And, if the sick person in their past was a parent, their symptoms often resemble the parent's (Kellner, 1985). There is also some evidence that people who had overprotective mothers are more likely to be hypochondriacs (Baker & Merskey, 1982; Parker & Lipscombe, 1980). Finally, many hypochondriacs have histories of childhood physical or sexual abuse (Barsky, Wool, Barnett, et al., 1994; Salmon & Calderbank, 1996).

Somatization Disorder

A third somatoform pattern is **somatization disorder,** characterized by numerous and recurrent physical complaints that begin by age 30, that persist for several years, and that cause the person to seek medical treatment but cannot be explained medically. Somatization disorder resembles hypochondriasis in that it involves symptoms with no demonstrable physical cause, yet the disorders differ in the focus of the patient's distress. What motivates the hypochondriac is the fear of disease, usually a specific disease; the "symptoms" are troubling not so much in themselves but because they indicate the presence of that disease. In contrast, what bothers the victim of somatization disorder is actually the "symptoms" themselves. There is also a difference in the patients' approaches to the symptoms. Whereas hypochondriacs may try to be scientific, measuring their blood pressure several times a day and carefully reporting the results, victims of somatization disorder usually describe their symptoms in a vague, dramatic, and exaggerated fashion. Finally, the two disorders differ in the number of complaints. Hypochondriacs often fear a particular disease; therefore, their complaints tend to be limited. In somatization disorder, on the other hand, the complaints are many and varied (Schmidt, 1994). Indeed, *DSM-IV* requires that the patient present at least four pain symptoms, two gastrointestinal symptoms, one sexual symptom, and one symptom that mimics neurological disorder, such as blindness, dizziness, or seizures, before this diagnosis can be made. Like hypochondriacs, somatization patients tend to engage in "doctor shopping," going from physician to physician in search of the one who will finally diagnose their ailments (Ford, 1995).

Though the complaints for which they are diagnosed are not organically based, somatization patients may develop actual organic disorders as a result of unnecessary hospitalization, surgery, and medication. In one case (Pitman & Moffett, 1981), a patient had averaged one hospitalization per year for the preceding 39 years.

Like hypochondriasis, somatization disorder is often accompanied by depression and anxiety (Gureje, Simon, Ustun, et al., 1997). In other respects, somatization patients resemble dissociative patients. They, too, are highly hypnotizable (Bliss, 1984), and, like dissociative identity patients, they tend to report histories of sexual abuse (Pribor, Yutzy, Dean, et al., 1993).

Pain Disorder

Many people experience pain on a daily basis. For example, 10 to 15 percent of adults in the United States have some form of work disability as a result of back pain alone (American Psychiatric Association, 1994). In some cases, however, even when an organic disorder is present, the pain seems to be more severe or persistent than can be explained by medical causes, and psychological factors are assumed to play a role as well. Such cases are diagnosed as **pain disorder.** In support of the psychogenic explanation, pain disorder patients tend to have psychiatric symptoms. In a sample of 283 chronic pain patients, more than half met the criteria for a personality disorder (Chapter 10), and between a half and two-thirds suffered from anxiety, depression, or both (Fishbain, Goldberg, Meager, et al., 1986).

Of course, the psychological problems of these patients may be the result of rather than—or certainly in addition to the cause of their pain, but there are indications that the pain has a psychological basis. For one thing, the patients' descriptions of their pain tend to differ from those of patients whose pain is thought to be primarily organic. They have a harder time localizing the pain; they tend to describe it in emotional terms (e.g., "frightening") rather than sensory terms (e.g., "burning"); and they are less likely to specify changes in the pain—for example, that it is worse at night or when they are walking. Finally, they tend to see the pain as their disorder, rather than as a symptom of a disorder (Adler, Zamboni, Hofer, et al., 1997). Like hypochondriacs, many pain disorder patients have what seems to be a predisposing family history, such as parents who suffered from chronic pain or who were overconcerned with their children's health (Scharff, 1997).

Conversion Disorder

In hypochondriasis and somatization disorder, there is no physical disability, only fear of or complaints about illness or disability. In **conversion disorder,** there *is* an actual disability: the loss or impairment of a motor or sensory function, although, again, there is no organic pathology that would explain the disability. Conversion symptoms vary considerably, but among the most common are blindness, deafness, paralysis, and anesthesia (loss of sensation)—often partial but sometimes total (Turner, Jacob, & Morrison, 1985). Also common are conversion symptoms that mimic physical illnesses, such as epilepsy or cancer (Bowman & Markand, 1996), though the choice of symptoms varies with the culture. For example, some men in non-Western cultures show *couvade,* a condition in which they experience pains similar to their wives' labor pains during childbirth (Iezzi & Adams, 1993). Like the "symptoms" involved in hypochondriasis and somatization disorder, conversion symptoms are not supported by the medical evidence, but neither are they faked. They are involuntary responses, independent of the person's conscious control. At the same time, they contradict the medical facts. Upon examination, for example, the eyes are found to be perfectly free from defect or damage, yet the person is unable to see.

Conversion disorder, formerly known as "hysteria," has played a central role in the history of psychology. As we saw in Chapter 1, it was named and described by Hippocrates, who believed that it was confined to women, particularly childless women. In Hippocrates' view, hysteria was caused by the wanderings of a uterus that was not being put to its proper use. Idle and frustrated, the uterus traveled around inside the body, creating havoc in various organ systems. The Greek word for uterus is *hystera,* hence the term *hysteria.*

In the nineteenth century, hysteria served as the focal point for debate between psychogenic and biogenic theory. It was the cure of this disorder through hypnosis that laid the foundation for Freud's theory of the unconscious. Interestingly, Freud's explanation of hysteria stressed the same factor as Hippocrates': sexual conflict. Today, many psychologists reject the sexual interpretation, but it is generally agreed that conversion disorders are the result of *some* psychological conflict. According to this view, the conversion symptom serves two important psychological purposes. First, it blocks the person's awareness of internal conflict; this is called the **primary gain.** In addition, it confers the **secondary gain** of excusing the person from responsibilities and attracting sympathy and attention.

One reason psychologists tend to accept the conflict-resolution hypothesis is that many conversion patients (about one-third) seem completely unperturbed by their symptoms—a response known as **la belle indifférence,** or "beautiful indifference." Whereas most people would react with horror to the discovery that they were suddenly half-blind or could no longer walk, "indifferent" conversion patients are undismayed. Typically, they are eager to discuss their symptoms and describe them in the most vivid terms, but they do not seem eager to part with them. This paradoxical reaction, like the equanimity of people suffering from dissociative amnesia, has been interpreted by psychodynamic theorists as a sign of relief once the newfound disability supplies a defense against unconscious conflicts and thereby reduces anxiety.

Conversion disorders represent something of a philosophical paradox. On the one hand, the patient's body appears to be in good health. Biologically, conversion patients *can* do whatever it is they say they can't do. And often they can be made to do it, either by trickery or under hypnosis or drugs such as sodium amytal. Further evidence for their lack of organic pathology is that the symptoms are often selective. Conversion "epileptics," for example, seldom injure themselves or lose bladder control during attacks, as true epileptics do. Likewise, in conversion blindness, patients rarely bump into things. Furthermore, victims of conversion blindness, when given visual discrimination tests, often perform either much better or much worse than if they had answered merely at random—a result indicating that they *are* receiving visual input (Kihlstrom, Barnhardt, & Tataryn, 1991). In short, all evidence points to the conclusion that the patient's body is capable of functioning properly. On the other hand, conversion patients, by definition, are *not* consciously refusing to use parts of their bodies. The response is involuntary.

This situation is something like the memory problem in dissociative disorders. Just as dissociative patients lose explicit memory but retain implicit memory, so conversion patients lose explicit perception but still show implicit perception. As in the case of DB at the opening of the chapter, these patients show clear evidence that their supposedly disabled organs are, in fact, operating normally, but they are not aware of those operations. The organ's functioning has been dissociated, as it were, from the patient's conscious awareness (Kihlstrom, Barnhardt, & Tataryn, 1991).

The following case illustrates la belle indifférence, together with other features of conversion disorder:

Mr. Sione is a 50-year-old minister from Western Samoa. He is quite famous there as a biblical scholar and leader in the religious community. Over a period of several months he began experiencing weakness in his legs to the point where he was unable to walk. He was excused from some of his duties at the high school where he teaches. He continued to give lectures but did not have to mete out corporal punishment to students, which is a common form of punishment in Samoa. He previously had been given the task of paddling students because the principal knew that he would be fair and not as harsh as some other teachers. . . .

In Hawaii, he underwent some neurologic tests without any pathological findings. His neurologist told him he could walk and attempted to lead him about the room. At this point, Mr. Sione collapsed on the floor, unable to support his own weight. A psychiatrist was called to consult. Further history revealed two prior episodes of leg weakness. Once as a teenager he had fallen out of a tree and spent several weeks in bed. He recalled this time fondly, saying that he had never received so much attention from his family, since he was from a large family and often felt ignored. . . .

While in Hawaii for the medical evaluation, he seemed to be having a great time. His wife, with whom he had a good relationship, had come with him. When not undergoing tests, she would help him get around the hospital. The psychiatrist noted that he avidly watched violent television shows. As they discussed this topic over a couple of sessions, it became clear that he was fascinated by violence but at the same time he found it quite repugnant. He began to talk about the conflict he experienced in Samoa over being the teacher who was supposed to physically punish students. He felt this was against his religious training, even though it was culturally accepted. He also worried that he might secretly enjoy the punishment that he inflicted and felt aghast at this possibility. As his stay in Hawaii neared an end, the psychiatrist said he was allowed to return to work, in a wheelchair if necessary, but under no circumstances would he be permitted to mete out corporal punishment to students. He accepted this prohibition. He was able to walk onto the departing airplane that week and was able to return to teaching. (Chaplin, 1997, pp. 60–70)

In this instance, the conflict-resolution function is obvious. In the words of the writer who presented the case, Steven L. Chaplin, "the conversion symptom afforded [Mr. Sione] the opportunity to solve a difficult psychological dilemma. When the consulting psychiatrist was able to offer an alternative solution, the need for the disabling symptoms was resolved" (1997, p. 80).

Conversion, Malingering, or Organic Disorder? With conversion disorder, differential diagnosis is both important and tricky. First, malingering must be ruled out, which is often hard to do. However, malingerers are usually cautious and defensive when questioned about their symptoms, because they are afraid of being caught in a lie. Conversion patients, on the other hand, are typically candid and, as we noted, sometimes talk eagerly and at length about their disabilities. Furthermore, precisely *because* they are unaware that their organs are functioning normally, conversion patients sometimes innocently reveal this. Most malingerers, for example, would not be foolish enough to claim blindness and then catch a ball thrown in their direction, but a conversion patient might do this (Kihlstrom, Barnhardt, & Tataryn, 1991).

Second and more difficult is the task of ruling out an actual organic disorder. In some cases, the symptoms constitute "neurological nonsense," as Charcot put it—that is, they directly contradict what we know about the nervous system. For example, in *glove anesthesia,* patients report that the entire hand is numb, from the tips of the fingers to a clear cutoff point at the wrist (see Figure 7.1)—in other words, the area covered by a short glove—whereas, if they were suffering from a true neurological impairment, the area of numbness would run in a narrow stripe from the lower arm through one or two of the fingers.

These, however, are the easier cases. In others, the symptoms are uncannily similar to those of true organic disorders. Nevertheless, there may still be certain signs that suggest conversion disorder. (Note the similarity between these criteria and those for distinguishing dissociative from organic amnesia.) These include the following:

1. *Rapid appearance of symptoms, especially after psychological trauma.* Organic disorders tend to surface more gradually.
2. *La belle indifférence.* Organic patients are more likely to be upset over their symptoms.
3. *Selective symptoms.* If "paralyzed" legs move during sleep, the paralysis is presumably not organic.

These criteria, in addition to specialized medical tests, are usually the basis for the diagnosis of conversion disorder. However, they are not foolproof—a fact that research has made embarrassingly clear. In a study involving 30 patients, 80 percent were eventually found to have a diagnosable medical disorder as the underlying cause of symptoms originally diagnosed as conversion (Gould, Miller, Goldberg, et al., 1986). Clearly, a substantial proportion of "conversion disorders" are, in fact, neurological disorders in their early stages, when they are hardest to detect (Marsden, 1986).

Conversion disorder is usually described as rare. It is possible, however, that what is rare is merely the *diagnosis* of conversion disorder. Conversion patients, after all, believe they have a medical problem. Therefore, they go to physicians, not to psychotherapists. As we have noted, differential diagnosis is tricky. Furthermore, many physicians may associate conversion disorder with the more bizarre symptoms of late-nineteenth-century hysteria—glove anesthesia, inability to swallow, paralysis—thus allowing the more ordinary conversion symptoms that tend to turn up

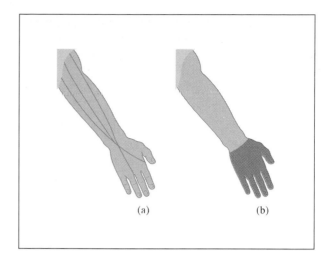

FIGURE 7.1   A patient with glove anesthesia—that is, numbness in the whole hand, ending at the wrist—will be suspected of having conversion disorder. The skin areas served by nerves in the arm are shown in A. Glove anesthesia, shown in B, cannot result from damage to these nerves.

today, such as back trouble or blurred vision, to slip by unnoticed. In short, it seems likely that, while many "conversion disorders" are actually organic, many conditions diagnosed as organic are actually conversion disorders (Jones, 1980).

Groups at Risk for Somatoform Disorders

Body dysmorphic disorder is a relatively new *DSM* category, and there are no reliable figures on its prevalence. Such figures may be slow in coming; according to some researchers, victims are ashamed of the disorder and tend not to seek treatment. Most patients are unmarried, and the average age of onset is 16 (Phillips, 1996a), with some childhood cases occurring as well. The disorder seems to be equally common in males and females, and this is also true of hypochondriasis.

By contrast, somatization disorder is seen far more often in women than in men (Martin, 1995). This condition is reasonably common, occurring in an estimated 2.8 percent of people contacting health centers worldwide (Gureje, Simon, Ustun, et al., 1997), but researchers have found that, apart from aches and pains, which are universal, the symptoms reported vary from culture to culture. In a recent study, sexual and menstrual symptoms figured in somatization disorder only in the West; complaints of body odor only in Japan; body heat and coldness only in Nigeria; and kidney weakness only in China (Janca, Isaac, Bennett, et al., 1995). Full-scale somatization disorder occurs more frequently among less-educated people (Ford, 1995) and in cultures in which the verbal expression of emotional distress is frowned upon (Raguram, Weiss, Channabasavanna, et al., 1996), suggesting that sociocultural factors play a role in the disorder.

Because its diagnosis is so problematic, conversion disorder's prevalence is open to question, but one estimate is that 5 to 14 percent of all consultations in a general medical setting are for conversion symptoms (Iezzi & Adams, 1993). The disorder is twice as common in women as in men. As with somatization disorder, there is also a socioeconomic risk factor. The poorer, the less educated, and the less psychologically sophisticated a community, the greater the prevalence of conversion disorder. Rural rather than urban populations also tend to produce conversion cases (Chaplin, 1997; Ford, 1995). Not surprisingly, patients in such communities tend to report more bizarre symptoms, whereas more sophisticated patients generally report symptoms that resemble true organic diseases. With conversion disorder, as with other somatoform disorders—and the dissociative disorders—a history of childhood trauma seems to increase vulnerability (Bowman & Markand, 1996).

Somatoform Disorders: Theory and Therapy

The Psychodynamic Perspective: Defense Against Anxiety

Somatizing as Conflict Resolution   As we saw in Chapter 1, Freud and Josef Breuer found that, if hysterical patients could be induced under hypnosis to talk uninhibitedly about their childhoods and their present problems, their symptoms subsided somewhat. Out of this treatment, Freud independently evolved his theory of the "conservation of energy," which stated that strong emotions that were not expressed would lead to somatic symptoms. The distressing memories that Freud's patients revealed to him were often of childhood seduction. In the beginning, Freud assumed that these seductions had actually occurred. Later, he came to believe that they were usually fantasies generated during the Oedipal period. Real or imagined, however, the episodes seemed to be reawakened in the mind by the sexual feelings accompanying puberty. The result was anxiety, leading in turn to repression of the memory, leading in turn to physical symptoms, which both expressed the wish and prevented its fulfillment. But sexual feelings were not the only cause; hostility, too, could lead to hysteria. A hysterical paralysis, for instance, could be

a defense against the expression of violent feelings. (Recall the case of Mr. Sione.) In Freud's opinion, the effectiveness of this mechanism in blocking both the impulse and the person's awareness of the impulse accounted for la belle indifférence. The symptoms relieved the anxiety; therefore, the person was not in a hurry to get rid of them.

In the psychoanalytic view, hypochondriasis, somatization disorder, and body dysmorphic disorder are also defenses against the anxiety produced by unacceptable wishes. Hypochondriacs, Freud reasoned, were people who, deterred by the superego from directing sexual energy onto external objects, redirected it onto themselves. Eventually, this self-directed sexual energy overflowed, transforming itself into physical symptoms. Other psychoanalytic thinkers have blamed hostility rather than sexual desire. In one theory (Brown & Vaillant, 1981), hypochondriacs are angry over having been unloved or hurt. Rather than express their grievances, they displace them onto the body, imagining *it* to be hurt. Similar conflict-resolution theories have been offered for somatization disorder and body dysmorphic disorder (Kellner, 1990; Phillips, 1996a). In all of the somatoform disorders, psychodynamic theorists also see a strong element of regression. Beset by anxiety, the person regresses to the state of a sick child, in which he or she hopes to receive attention, "babying," and relief from responsibilities—in other words, secondary gains. The primary gain is the relief of anxiety.

This conflict-resolution model of somatoform disorders is an old and famous theory, intuitively appealing. But, as usual with psychodynamic theories, it is hard to test. Furthermore, there is some evidence against it. For example, as noted earlier, only about one-third of conversion patients seem to show la belle indifférence. That leaves two-thirds who are often very alarmed over their sudden disabilities. Studies show that hypochondriasis and somatization disorder also tend to involve high levels of expressed anxiety (Gureje, Simon, Ustun, et al., 1997; Noyes, Kathol, Fisher, et al., 1994). If the function of the somatoform disorders is to relieve psychological suffering, they do not seem to be doing a good job—a fact which casts some doubt on the psychodynamic interpretation.

Uncovering Conflict   Psychodynamic treatment for the somatoform disorders involves roughly the same "talking cure" that led to Freud's theory of these syndromes. As usual in psychodynamic therapy, the patient is induced to release the repression, thus bringing into consciousness the forbidden thoughts and memories. Presumably, the somatic symptoms will then subside, and the ego's energy, formerly tied up in maintaining the symptoms, will be free to pursue more constructive ends. With the dissociative disorders, as we saw, hypnosis is often used to bring forth the repressed material. With the somatoform disorders, the therapist is more likely to ask the patient to produce this material in his or her normal conscious state, either through free association or simply through candid discussion.

There is no evidence, however, that this psychodynamic approach is any more effective than other therapies for somatoform disorders. In general, the somatoform disorders are not particularly responsive to treatment, nor do they generally improve without treatment. One study found that, on a 4-year follow-up, 63 percent of the conversion patients and 92 percent of the somatization patients still merited those diagnoses (Kent, Tomasson, & Coryell, 1995). It may be that the best treatment for somatization patients is simply low-level medical care: brief physical examinations, supportive talks. This does not cure the disorder, but it helps to prevent patients from seeking more invasive cures, thus harming themselves with unnecessary surgery or drugs (Smith, Monson, & Ray, 1986a). Supportive group therapy may also be of use. A recent study found that somatization patients who attended eight group therapy sessions reported better physical and mental health on a 1-year follow-up than did patients who received standard medical care (Kashner, Rost, Cohen, et al., 1995).

The Behavioral and Sociocultural Perspectives: The Sick Role

Illness is not just a biological dysfunction. It also has social components (Mechanic, 1962). People who are ill are justified in adopting the "sick role." They can stay home from work or school; they are relieved of their normal duties; others are expected to be sympathetic and attentive to them. According to behavioral and sociocultural theorists, somatoform disorders are inappropriate adoptions of the sick role (Pilowsky, 1994).

Learning to Adopt the Sick Role The sick role also involves sacrifices: loss of power, loss of pleasurable activities. Why would people want to give up these things for long? The behaviorists say that their learning histories have probably made the rewards of the sick role more reinforcing than the rewards of illness-free life. According to Ullmann and Krasner (1975), two conditions increase the chances that a healthy person will adopt the sick role. First, the person must have had some experience with the role, either

Did Elizabeth Barrett Browning (1806–1861) suffer from a somatoform disorder? Behavioral and sociocultural theorists might say that she adopted the "sick role." Following a minor accident at the age of 15, she spent 25 years as an invalid, cared for at home by her family. She experienced a rapid and nearly total recovery when she married fellow-poet Robert Browning.

directly, by being ill, or indirectly, by having the sick role modeled. Many people with somatoform disorders meet this condition. Hypochondriasis, somatization, and conversion patients are all likely to have had early personal or family histories of physical illness or somatic symptoms (Barsky, Wool, Barnett, et al., 1994; Robbins & Kirmayer, 1996). The second condition, according to Ullmann and Krasner, is that the adoption of the sick role must be reinforced. This, too, has been found to be the case with somatoform patients. Many have childhood histories of receiving attention and sympathy during illness—recall the case of Mr. Sione on page 198—and research suggests that this operant-conditioning process predisposes them to adopt the sick role as a coping style in adult life (Schwartz, Gramling, & Mancini, 1994). Respondent conditioning may also play a part. The autonomic nervous system, which controls breathing, heart rate, and numerous other bodily functions (Chapter 4), is subject to conditioning, so, if anxiety is paired, for example, with minor heartbeat irregularities, as it may be in an illness-preoccupied household, then anxiety can come to *trigger* that symptom, which in turn will cause further anxiety, then further symptoms—in other words, the beginning of hypochondriasis (Kellner, 1985).

Sociocultural theorists also regard somatoform disorders as a case of role adoption, but they focus less on the family than on larger cultural forces. In the sociocultural view, the likelihood of people's using the sick role as a coping style depends on their culture's attitudes toward unexplained somatic symptoms. If this theory is correct, then rates of somatoform disorder should vary from culture to culture. They do, and in ways consistent with cultural values. Somatization and conversion disorder are more prevalent in non-Western cultures and in less-industrialized cultures—India, China, Nigeria, Libya, Mexico—cultures in which the expression of emotional distress in psychological terms is less accepted, more stigmatized (Raguram, Weiss, Channabasavanna, et al., 1996). In the United States, as we saw, conversion and somatization disorder are more common in rural communities and in lower socioeconomic groups, in which, again, psychological expressions of emotional problems may be frowned on. Thus, people in these communities and groups may be encouraged to somaticize unhappiness rather than psychologize it (Goldberg & Bridges, 1988).

Treatment by Nonreinforcement   As with dissociative disorders, the behavioral treatment of somatoform disorders is usually two-pronged. First, the therapist withdraws reinforcement for illness behavior. Second, the therapist tries to build up the patient's coping skills, a lack of which is presumably part of the reason for resorting to the sick role. One short-term treatment for 17 people with hypochondriasis and illness phobia (disabling fear of illness) emphasized the withdrawal of reinforcement, particularly the negative reinforcement (via anxiety relief) that the patients obtained through reassurance seeking. When they sought reassurance from the therapist, they were given none, and their families were instructed to give them none. In a 5-year follow-up, about half the patients located were symptom-free (Warwick & Marks, 1988).

As for building coping skills, behavioral treatments often include social-skills training, in which patients are taught how to deal effectively with other people, and assertiveness training, which teaches patients how to show strength—how to make requests, how to refuse requests, how to show anger when necessary. For many people, the sick role may be a way of making demands on others, and of evading their demands, without taking responsibility for such actions. ("Because I am sick, you have to do things for me and I don't have to do things for you.") Behaviorists try to teach people how to manage social give-and-take without such blackmail.

In treating conversion disorders, the therapist often tries to provide a face-saving mechanism so that patients can give up the "illness" without having to face the accusation that they were never ill to begin with. This mechanism may be a placebo drug or physical therapy. In any case, the placebo is there to provide a socially acceptable reason for the cure; the cure, meanwhile, is effected through a change in reinforcement. This was the case with Mr. Sione, who was "prohibited" by his doctor from inflicting corporal punishment on his students, the very thing that probably brought on his symptoms.

For chronic pain disorder, behavioral therapists have used such techniques as relaxation and contingency management to decrease pain medication, to reduce verbal reports of pain, to discourage "sick" behaviors, and to increase activity levels. Recent evidence suggests that such treatment is quite effective, especially when combined with cognitive restructuring (Wilson & Gil, 1996).

The Cognitive Perspective: Misinterpreting Bodily Sensations

Overattention to the Body   Recall the cognitive interpretation of panic disorder (Chapter 6): it is essentially a problem of misinterpretation. The cognitive view of hypochondriasis and somatization disorder is roughly the same. According to several theorists, people with these disorders have a "cognitive style" predisposing them to exaggerate normal bodily sensations and catastrophize over minor symptoms. Given these tendencies, they misinterpret minor physiological changes as major health problems (Barsky, 1992b; Salkovskis & Clark, 1993). When, for example, these patients are under stress and experience indigestion, they say, "I may have undetected stomach cancer" rather than "I am nervous." In support of this idea, it has been shown that hypochondriacs focus more attention on bodily sensations, catastrophize more readily about symptoms, hold more false beliefs about disease, and fear aging and death more than do nonhypochondriac psychiatric patients or normal controls (Barsky & Wyshak, 1989; Barsky, Wyshak, & Klerman, 1990). Likewise, body dysmorphic patients selectively attend to minor physical flaws and catastrophize about how these will cause them to be rejected (Phillips, 1996a; Veale, Gournay, Dryden, et al., 1996). Such cognitive biases lead them to mirror-checking, reassurance-seeking, and avoidance of social situations with rejection potential, all of which increase their misery.

It has also been found that "somatizers," or people with a high rate of medically unexplainable somatic complaints, have correspondingly high rates of negative affect: pessimism, self-blame, general unhappiness (Pennebaker & Watson, 1991). If this negative affect were combined with difficulty in expressing emotion, a trait that apparently runs high in somatization disorder patients (Cohen, Auld, Brooker, et al., 1994), then the person would be all the more likely to redirect distress onto the body—an explanation consistent with Freud's.

Treatment: Challenging Faulty Beliefs   Recent reports show that hypochondriacs can be helped by a combination of cognitive therapy (revising thinking habits) and behavioral therapy (change in reinforcement). Salkovskis and Warwick (1986), for example, have described their treatment of a man who, because he had developed a harmless rash, was convinced that he had leukemia. He inspected the rash constantly, spent hours reading medical textbooks, and discussed his problem incessantly with his family. He eventually became suicidal and was hospitalized. The therapists got the patient to agree that his condition had one of two explanations: (1) he was suffering from a deadly illness, not yet diagnosed, or (2) he had a problem with anxiety. In view of the strong evidence for the second hypothesis, the therapists persuaded the patient to test it by altering the conditions that might be maintaining his anxiety. This meant that he would stop reading medical books, stop checking the rash, and stop seeking reassurance. The hospital staff, the family doctor, and the family were also instructed to stop giving reassurance. His hypochondriacal anxieties swiftly declined. Other cognitive therapists have reported success with hypochondriacs by teaching them to distract themselves from bodily sensations and to reattribute such sensations to benign causes rather than fatal diseases (Barsky, 1996).

Cognitive-behavioral therapies have also proved effective for pain disorder (Wilson & Gil, 1996) and body dysmorphic disorder. In the latter case, for example, patients are confronted with their presumed physical flaws and are prevented from seeking reassurance—the behavioral technique of exposure. Meanwhile, they undergo cognitive restructuring, in which they are taught how to challenge faulty assumptions (e.g., "I must look perfect in order to be loved") and how to redirect their attention away from their appearance (Rosen, Reiter, & Orosan, 1995; Veale, Gournay, Dryden, et al., 1996).

The Biological Perspective: Brain Dysfunction

Genetic Studies   We have already discussed the fact that people with somatoform disorders tend to have family histories of somatic complaints. Is it possible that this is the product not of learning but of genes?

A hypochrondriac might spend hours every day reading about suspected illnesses in medical textbooks. Cognitive therapies can relieve the anxieties of people with hypochondriasis by helping them to reattribute their bodily sensations to harmless causes rather than deadly diseases.

Guze and his colleagues have conducted several family studies of somatization disorder, with intriguing results. First, it appears that, among the first-degree relatives of patients with somatization disorder, the women show an increased frequency of somatization disorder, while the men show an increased frequency not of somatization disorder but of antisocial personality disorder, a personality pattern characterized by chronic indifference to the rights of others (Chapter 17). Furthermore, somatization disorder and antisocial personality are seen together in the same person much more frequently than we would expect by chance. These findings have led to the hypothesis that somatization disorder and antisocial personality disorder may be the product of similar genetic endowment and that what determines whether a person with this endowment will be a somatizer or an antisocial personality is his or her sex (Guze, Cloninger, Martin, et al., 1986; Lilienfeld, 1992).

Of course, the basis of these family patterns need not be genetic. It could be environmental. To document the genetic factor more clearly, twin and adoption studies are needed. One twin study (Torgersen, 1986), conducted in Norway, found that the MZ twins had a higher concordance rate for somatoform disorders than the DZ twins. The sample was small, however, and there was reason to believe that the MZ twins shared not only more similar genotypes but also more similar environments than did the DZ twins. In an adoption study conducted in Sweden, the researchers tracked down the medical and criminal histories of the biological and adoptive parents of 859 women with somatization disorder. The results seemed to show not 1 but 2 patterns, depending on whether the woman was a "high-frequency somatizer" (frequent somatic complaints, but few kinds of complaints) or a "diversi-form somatizer" (less frequent complaints, but of a more diverse nature). The biological fathers of the high-frequency somatizers showed disproportionately high rates of alcoholism; the biological fathers of the diversiform somatizers showed disproportionately high rates of violent crime (Bohman, Cloninger, von Knorring, et al., 1984; Cloninger, Sigvardsson, von Knorring et al., 1984). These findings, though preliminary, support the suggestion that there is a genetic factor in somatization disorder and that the factor is somehow linked to antisocial behavior (Lilienfeld, 1992).

Brain Dysfunction and Somatoform Disorders The essential mystery of conversion disorder—that, while the body is functioning normally, the conscious mind does not know this—has been the subject of some neuroscientific research. Tests of brain waves in people with conversion anesthesias, blindness, and deafness clearly indicate that these patients' brains are receiving normal sensory input from their "disabled" organs. If you prick the finger of a person with glove anesthesia, this message does arrive in the cerebral cortex, as it is supposed to. Likewise, electrical stimulation of the movement centers of the brain does produce normal movement in patients with conversion paralysis. In other words, there seems to be no blockage of the neural pathways between the brain and the peripheral organs. Why, then, can't conversion patients consciously feel sensations or initiate movement?

Presumably the problem lies in the *processing* of sensory signals in the cerebral cortex, for it is that processing that would bring the signal into conscious awareness. Conversion patients seem to have suppressed some stage of cerebral processing (Marsden, 1986). In support of this hypothesis, several studies of conversion patients with loss of sensory function have revealed high levels of inhibitory (transmission-suppressing) action in the cerebral cortex in response to sensory stimuli (Hernandez-Peon, Chavez-Ibarra, & Aguilar-Figueroa, 1963; Levy & Mushin, 1973). Such a slowdown in processing might be caused by a shock to the brain. Some evidence indicates that

hypoxia (oxygen deprivation) and hypoglycemia (low blood sugar) can bring on conversion symptoms (Eames, 1992).

Another interesting finding has to do with lateralization, the difference between the right and left hemispheres of the brain (Chapter 4). In a study of 430 patients with conversion disorder, somatization disorder, and other psychological disorders involving somatic complaints, it was found that 70 percent had their symptoms on the left side of the body (Bishop, Mobley, & Farr, 1978). Because the left side of the body is controlled by the right side of the brain, this suggests that somatoform disorders may stem from dysfunction in the right cerebral hemisphere, a possibility that has since been supported by other neurological studies (Flor-Henry, Fromm-Auch, Tapper, et al., 1981; James, Singer, Zurynski, et al., 1987).

In body dysmorphic disorder, it is possible that there is some abnormality in serotonin functioning. The evidence for this is still sketchy. Basically, it consists of the finding that drugs that decrease serotonin transmission exacerbate body dysmorphic symptoms, while drugs that increase such transmission relieve symptoms (Phillips, 1996b). But more may be discovered as research on serotonin continues. At the same time, it must be reemphasized that the discovery of a neurological basis for a psychological disorder does not rule out a psychological basis. If the neurons of body dysmorphic patients are not processing serotonin properly, or if the brains of conversion patients are inhibiting sensory input, this may be for psychological reasons.

Drug Treatment Like the biological findings, biological treatments for somatoform disorders are scarce and preliminary. Antidepressant drugs seem to help some patients. In one study, 70 percent of the body dysmorphic patients improved markedly when given SSRIs such as Prozac or Zoloft, but these findings need to be followed by controlled studies comparing SSRI treatment with placebo treatment (Phillips, 1996). For pain disorder, tricyclic antidepressants (Chapter 6) have been found to decrease subjective ratings of pain, but their long-term effectiveness has not yet been established (Wilson & Gil, 1996).

KEY TERMS

alters, 182
amnesia, 179
body dysmorphic disorder, 194
coconscious, 183
conversion disorder, 197
depersonalization disorder, 185

derealization, 185
dissociative amnesia, 181
dissociative disorders, 178
dissociative fugue, 181
dissociative identity disorder (DID), 182
explicit memories, 180
host, 182

hypochondriasis, 195
hysteria, 178
iatrogenic, 185
implicit memories, 180
la belle indifférence, 197
malingering, 185
pain disorder, 197
primary gain, 197

secondary gain, 197
somatization disorder, 196
somatoform disorders, 194

SUMMARY

- Dissociative disorders occur when stress causes components of the personality, which are normally integrated, to split apart, or dissociate. As a result, a critical psychological function is screened out of consciousness. These disorders disturb only the higher cognitive functions, not sensory or motor functions.

- In dissociative amnesia, psychological stress screens out the memory function. The loss of memory typically applies to a period of time *after* the precipitating stressful event, is selective, does not reduce the amnesiac's ability to learn new things, is not disorienting or disturbing to the amnesiac, and is recoverable.

- A related condition is dissociative fugue, in which a person not only forgets all or some of the past but also takes a sudden, unexpected trip and often assumes a new identity.

- In dissociative identity disorder (DID), formerly known as multiple personality disorder, a person develops two or more distinct identities or personality states that take turns controlling the person's behavior. At least one of the personalities is amnesic of the other(s). In some cases, the various personalities display significant physiological differences.

- Depersonalization disorder involves a persistent sense of strangeness or unreality about one's identity. The person may feel like a robot or an actor in a dream. Such feelings are often accompanied by derealization, a sense of strangeness about the world and other people. Those suffering with this disorder recognize the strangeness of their feelings and may fear they are going insane.

- Gender is a risk factor in DID and depersonalization disorder, which are more common in women than men. Some cultures view depersonalization disorder as a legitimate, trancelike state and not as a disorder.

- In the psychodynamic view, dissociative disorders are extreme and maladaptive defenses against the anxiety produced by repressed wishes. Psychodynamic therapy—the most common treatment for these disorders—aims at identifying the repressed material and reintegrating it into the personality.

- Both behaviorists and socioculturalists hold that a person adopts the symptoms of a dissociative disorder in order to get the reward of protection or relief from stress. These theorists believe that reinforcement maintains the dissociative behavior. Accordingly, the way to treat dissociative symptoms is to stop reinforcing them.

- Cognitive theorists view these disorders as impairments of episodic memory, or one's record of personal experience. Cognitive therapy uses various cognitive techniques to trigger and release memories.

- Some neuroscience researchers hypothesize that the dissociative disorders are a by-product of undiagnosed epilepsy. Others suggest involvement of the hippocampus or changes in levels of serotonin. Biological therapies are undeveloped.

- The primary feature of the somatoform disorders is that psychological conflicts take on a somatic, or physical, form.

- A person with body dysmorphic disorder is so preoccupied with an imagined or a grossly exaggerated defect in appearance that he or she cannot function normally. This syndrome is associated with obsessive-compulsive disorder and depression.

- In hypochondriasis, a person maintains a chronic fear of disease by misinterpreting physical signs and sensations as abnormal. Hypochondriacs do not fake their symptoms; they are genuinely convinced they are ill.

- In somatization disorder, a person has physical complaints that begin by age 30, persist for several years, and cannot be medically explained. The complaints are many, varied, and dramatic and are not focused on a particular disease, as in hypochondriasis.

- For people with pain disorder, the pain seems more severe or persistent than can be explained by medical causes. Patients have difficulty localizing the pain, describe it in emotional rather than sensory terms, and often do not specify changes in the pain.

- In conversion disorder, an actual disability, such as blindness or paralysis, exists with no medical basis. The condition is produced involuntarily, but it is generally agreed that conversion disorders provide relief for an internal conflict.

- The risk factors for somatoform disorders include gender, education level, and socioeconomic status. Body dysmorphic disorder and hypochondriasis are equally common in men and women, but somatization and conversion disorders are more prevalent in women. The symptoms of somatization disorder vary across cultures.

- From the psychodynamic perspective, the somatoform disorders are defenses against the anxiety caused by unacceptable wishes. All contain a strong element of regression, or return to a childlike state, that will elicit care from others. Therapy aims at uncovering what is repressed and resolving the conflicts the repression is creating.

- Behavioral and sociocultural theorists believe the somatoform disorders represent inappropriate adoptions of the "sick role" in order to reap its rewards (attention, relief from responsibility, etc.). Treatment calls for not reinforcing illness behavior and for developing the patient's coping skills.

- Cognitive theorists attribute the somatoform disorders to a cognitive style that exaggerates normal bodily sensations and makes catastrophic interpretations of minor symptoms. Cognitive therapy calls on patients to challenge their faulty beliefs and cease seeking reassurance from others, who would give negative reinforcement to their claims.

- Neuroscience researchers have found evidence for a genetic role in somatization disorder and some evidence of brain dysfunction in conversion disorder. However, biological treatments are scarce.

EXIT

CHAPTER 8

In a recent experiment, Sheldon Cohen and his colleagues asked 420 volunteers to fill out questionnaires about the amount of stress they had been coping with during the preceding year. Then 394 of the subjects were given nose drops containing cold viruses, and the remaining 26 were given placebo drops. They were quarantined and watched, to see who caught colds. Some of the experimental subjects came down with colds, while others did not. That was to be expected—people's immune responses differ. What was not expected, however, was how clearly these people's immune responses reflected the psychological pressures they had been under. The more stress a subject had reported on the pretest questionnaire, the more likely he or she was to catch the cold (Cohen, Tyrrell, & Smith, 1991).

This was a watershed study. For years psychology had acknowledged the existence of psychophysiological disorders (also called *psychosomatic disorders*)—that is, illnesses influenced by emotional factors. But it was generally believed that there were only a few such illnesses. These conditions, including asthma, ulcer, hypertension, and migraine headaches, were listed in the *DSM* as "psychophysiological disorders," the assumption being that all other illnesses were purely organic. Increasingly, this assumption came under attack, as evidence accumulated that widely diverse medical conditions were affected, if not caused, by psychological factors. Accordingly, in the 1980s, *DSM-III* dropped the list of psychophysiological disorders in favor of a comprehensive category—"psychological factors affecting physical condition"—that could be applied to any illness. Still, the importance of such factors was bitterly contested. In June 1985, the highly respected *New England Journal of Medicine* published an editorial dismissing most reports of psychological influence on physical health as "anecdotal." "It is time to acknowledge that our belief in disease as a direct reflection of mental state is largely folklore," the editorial concluded (quoted in Kiecolt-Glaser & Glaser, 1991). Particularly in the case of cancer and infectious diseases such as colds, theories of psychological influence were viewed with great skepticism. Then, four years after the *New England Journal of Medicine* editorial, a competing journal published the results of a carefully controlled study showing that breast cancer patients who were given supportive group therapy in addition to their medical care survived almost twice as long, after the beginning of treatment, as those not receiving group therapy (Spiegel, Bloom, Kraemer, et al., 1989). Two years after that, the Cohen group's findings about stress and the common cold were published—in the *New England Journal of Medicine*. Today there are very few experts who still doubt that

the workings of the mind influence the health of the body. In the words of *DSM-IV*, "Psychological . . . factors play a potential role in the presentation or treatment of almost every general medical condition," including eating disorders, high-risk behaviors, and compliance with medical recommendations (American Psychiatric Association, 1994, p. 676*).

The conceptualization of the role of psychological factors in physical illness has not only broadened in recent years; it has become far more complex. Researchers now recognize that, even if an illness is caused by a purely physical factor, that illness in turn *causes* emotional stress. Surveys have found that about 20 percent of people in the hospital, for whatever illness, have a diagnosable depressive syndrome (Rodin & Voshort, 1986). There is no question that these emotional factors in turn affect the course of the illness—how serious it will become and whether and how quickly the patient will recover. In sum, many professionals are coming to believe that physical illness can no longer be studied apart from psychological factors.

This more *holistic*, or unified, concept of body and mind has led to the development of a new research discipline, **health psychology** (also called *behavioral medicine*). Three major historical trends have met in health psychology. The first is the previously mentioned trend toward holistic thinking: the recognition that our way of living and state of mind affect our physical well-being. In a survey of articles published between 1977 and 1993, researchers estimated that three behavioral factors—tobacco use, alcohol use, and diet and exercise—accounted for 38 percent of all deaths in 1990 (McGinnis & Foege, 1993). The second is the recognition that psychological and lifestyle factors can be used to prevent, as well as treat, illness. The third is the discovery that certain treatments pioneered by behavioral psychology, such as biofeedback and relaxation training, can relieve stress-related physical ailments.

In this chapter, we will first review the history of the concept of mind *versus* body. Then we will discuss psychological stress: how it is defined and how it influences illness, particularly via the immune system. Finally, we will examine the interaction of mind and body in certain illnesses, and we will describe the current psychological perspectives on the nature of that interaction.

Mind and Body

What is the relationship between the mind and the body? This question—the **mind-body problem**—has

---

*Reprinted with permission from the *Diagnostic and Statistical Manual of Mental Disorders*, Fourth Edition. Copyright © 1994 American Psychiatric Association.

been under debate for centuries. Logically, it would seem that mind and body are essentially the same thing. *Mind,* after all, is simply an abstract term for the workings of the brain. And the brain not only is part of the body but also is directly connected by nerves to all other parts of the body. Therefore, whatever is going on "mentally" inside a person is also going on physically, and vice versa. Most of the time, however, we are unaware of the activity going on in our brains. We are conscious only of the *effects* of that activity—effects that we think of as "mental," not physical. This is undoubtedly one reason we tend to regard the mind as something apart from the body (Schwartz, 1978).

Whatever the reason, the prevailing opinion for centuries has been that mind and body are separate entities—interrelated, perhaps, but still independent. This *dualism* of mind and body is often said to have originated with Greek philosopher Plato, in the fifth century B.C., but it undoubtedly reaches much further back, to prehistoric peoples' efforts to explain death. In death, they observed, the body remained, yet it was no longer alive. Something, then, must have departed from it. That something—the mind, soul, or spirit—was clearly separate from the body.

Incorporated into the Jewish and Christian religions, mind-body dualism was handed down from ancient times to the Middle Ages and the Renaissance. In the early seventeenth century, French philosopher René Descartes described mind and body as altogether independent entities—the mind spiritual, the body physical. Descartes' influential theories, together with the discoveries of Galileo and Sir Isaac Newton, laid the foundation of modern scientific rationalism. In this view, nature was a vast, self-powered machine. To explain its operations, one need not—indeed, should not—resort to philosophical or religious concepts. Nature could be explained only by reference to its internal parts—that is, only through empirical evidence, things that could be observed and measured.

Of course, there were many illnesses whose empirical causes were not known. Might they involve factors that could not be observed? The question was sometimes asked. But, in the late nineteenth century, with the discovery by Louis Pasteur and others that germs caused disease, such doubts were largely dispelled. The causes of illness were indeed observable; all we needed were better microscopes. Some exceptions were still recognized. Over the years, physicians repeatedly noted a connection between certain disorders, such as high blood pressure and psychological tension, so the list of "psychophysiological disorders" was drawn up. They were the exceptions, though. Organic causation was the rule.

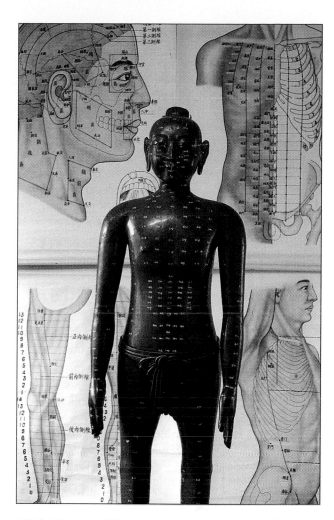

While Western philosophy and medicine separated the mind from the body, Eastern cultures, such as the Chinese, have always joined them. This Sung Dynasty (tenth through thirteenth centuries) bronze statue was used to teach acupuncture, a pain-relieving technique based on the connections between the brain and the rest of the nervous system.

Only in the past half-century has this assumption been called into serious question. In the 1960s, it was discovered that physiological functions such as blood pressure and heart rate, which were once considered completely involuntary (i.e., the province of the body, not of the mind), could be influenced voluntarily. And, if the mind could affect the beating of the heart and the dilation of blood vessels, why could it not also affect such processes as the growth of cancer cells? The remainder of this story was told at the beginning of the chapter. As recent research has demonstrated, psychological factors *can* affect the growth of cancer cells, as well as many other disease processes, down to the common cold. The list of "psychophysiological disorders" is now gone from *DSM-IV;* the course of all illnesses is thought to be potentially influenced by psychological factors. Kept apart for centuries, mind and body are increasingly considered one.

In this chapter, we will take the position that mind and body are, in fact, one. What people experience as a mental event, such as sadness, is also a physical event, whether they realize it or not. Likewise, physical events, such as the firing of neurons in the brain, trigger mental events. It is not so much that the one causes the other as that they cannot, in truth, be separated. As one researcher explained, the words *psychological* and *physical* refer not to different phenomena but to different ways of talking about the same phenomenon (Graham, 1967, p. 52).

Psychological Stress

Defining Stress

The term **stress** is frequently used in many different ways. Some writers, such as W. B. Cannon (1936), define it as a *stimulus:* stress consists of environmental demands that lead to physical responses. This definition has been adopted by many later researchers and has generated a number of studies on how various life events, such as divorce or losing a job, affect people. An interesting question in this line of research has to do with positive life events. According to some researchers, not just divorce but also marriage, not just losing a job but also taking one, can be stressful enough to tax one's health (Holmes & Rahe, 1967). Other researchers have pointed to the usefulness of minor positive events such as gossiping with friends or getting a good night's sleep as buffers against stress (Lazarus, Kanner & Folkman, 1980).

A second definition holds that stress is a *response.* On the basis of extensive research, Hans Selye (1956, 1974) described a "general adaptation syndrome," which divides the body's reaction into three successive stages: (1) alarm and mobilization—a state of rapid, general arousal in which the body's defenses are mobilized; (2) resistance—the state of optimal biological adaptation to environmental demands; and (3) exhaustion and disintegration—a stage reached when the body loses its ability to cope with prolonged demands.

Finally, some cognitive theorists define stress not as stimulus or response but as the *interaction between the stimulus and the person's appraisal of it,* a process that determines the person's response (Lazarus & Folkman, 1984). This theory will be discussed later, under the cognitive perspective.

What Determines Responses to Stress?

Regardless of whether stress is a response, a stimulus, or an appraisal of a stimulus, the fact remains that different people experience it differently. Why do some people cope well with stress and others fall ill? And why do some people fall ill with migraines, others with high blood pressure or backaches?

Stimulus Specificity   One of the earliest indications that people's responses to stress are keyed to the type of stress involved came from a rather bizarre experiment (Wolf & Wolff, 1947). In 1947, a patient named Tom who had experienced severe gastrointestinal damage underwent surgery, and with his permission the surgeon installed a plastic window over his stomach so that its internal workings could be observed. In subsequent sessions with Tom, the investigators found that his flow of gastric juices decreased when he was exposed to anxiety-producing stimuli and increased when he was exposed to anger-producing stimuli. This experiment showed that gastric activity (and, by extension, ulcer) was related to emotional states, as researchers had long suspected. It also established the principle of **stimulus specificity**—that different kinds of stress produce different kinds of physiological response. This principle has since been confirmed by other investigators. Different emotions—fear, anger, disgust, sadness, happiness—have been shown to have significantly different effects, not only on gastric activity but also on heart rate, blood pressure, muscle tension, respiration rate, and other physiological functions (Levenson, 1992; Schwartz, Weinberger, & Singer, 1981). Researchers have pinpointed subtler distinctions as well. Apparently, the physiological reaction differs, depending on whether we are anticipating a stressful event or actually undergoing it, as students may verify in the case of final exams. It also differs according to whether the stress is short term or long term (Weiner, 1994). Finally, the reactions in question are extraordinarily complex. It is not just a matter of changes in heart rate or breathing. Different stressors produce whole, distinctive *patterns* of physiological response, involving not just autonomic activity but also different facial expressions, brain-wave changes, and hormone secretions (Weiner, 1994).

Individual Response Specificity   Physiological responses to stress not only depend on the kind of stress, they also depend on the person responding. Whether as a result of genes or learning (probably both), people appear to have characteristic patterns of physiological response, which carry over from one type of stress to another—a phenomenon called **individual response specificity.** The first hint of this fact came in an experiment in which a group of people with a history of cardiovascular complaints (e.g., high blood pressure) and a group of people with a history of muscular complaints (e.g., backache) were both exposed to the same painful stimulus. Though the stressor was the same, the cardiovascular group responded with greater changes in heart rate than did the muscular group, while the muscular group showed greater changes in muscle tension than did the cardiovascular group (Malmo & Shagass, 1949). What this suggested—and it has since been confirmed—is that, in responding to stress, people tend to favor one physiological system.

It also appears that some people respond more intensely to stress in general. In an intriguing experiment, it was found that whether or not a 10-month-old baby would cry when its mother left the room could be predicted from the baby's EEG brain-wave pattern as tested earlier, when the mother was in the room. Infants whose EEGs showed *hemispheric asymmetry,* or more activity on one side of the brain—in this case, more activity in the right frontal area than in the left—were the most likely to cry when their mothers exited (Davidson & Fox, 1989). This same pattern of asymmetry has also been observed in shy 3-year-olds and in depressed adults (Davidson, 1992). Possibly, it reflects an innate hypersensitivity to stress.

Stimulus Versus Individual   There is an apparent contradiction between individual response specificity and stimulus specificity. If people have characteristic patterns of response that carry over from stressor to stressor, how can patterns of response vary with changes in the stressor? This seems improbable only if we think of physiological response to stress as a simple process. But, as we saw, it is an extremely complex process, and many variables influence the final response. The two variables we are considering—the person and the stressor—operate simultaneously (Engel, 1960; Engel & Bickford, 1961). As described, the flow of gastric juices tends to increase with anger and decrease with anxiety; here we see stimulus specificity. The *degree* of increase and decrease, however, is subject to individual response specificity. That is, "gastric reactors" may show extreme increases and decreases; "cardiac reactors," on the other hand, may show only mild gastric changes, concentrating instead on heart-rate changes. And if, as the hemispheric asymmetry research suggests, some people are generally heavy reactors to stress, then this factor, too, would influence the response.

How Stress Influences Illness

Over the years, research has established a connection between stress and illness. The study discussed at the opening of this chapter—the Cohen group's investigation of colds—is a good example, and it has been

built upon by later researchers. For example, the Cohen group found that levels of stress predicted not only who developed cold symptoms but also who became infected (as revealed by levels of antibodies in the blood), whether or not they developed symptoms (Cohen, Tyrrell, & Smith, 1991). Later, another research group (Stone, Bovberg, Neale, et al., 1992) found much the same thing. They exposed 17 subjects to a cold virus, and all 17 became infected, but only 12 went on to show cold symptoms. As in the Cohen study, the subjects had filled out stress questionnaires, and what the questionnaires revealed was that those who came down with the colds were those who had experienced the most "major life events," both positive and negative, in the preceding year. Thus, if, as we have so often been told, colds strike when we are "run-down," there is more to this than staying up late. Even positive changes in our lives can run us down.

A more dramatic example has to do with sudden cardiac death (SCD), a form of heart attack that kills 450,000 people per year in the United States. Most people who die of SCD are found to have an underlying heart disease, but only about one-third show evidence of the coronary occlusion (blockage in the arteries of the heart) that causes most heart attacks. Rather, SCD is primarily an electrical accident that occurs when the heart's large, steady contractions give way to rapid, irregular contractions known as fibrillations. Vulnerability to SCD seems to be associated with long-term psychological stress (Kamarck & Jennings, 1991). Furthermore, in about 20 percent of cases, SCD is connected to an experience of great emotion, such as sudden surprise, anger, grief, or even happiness (Lane & Jennings, 1995). Other kinds of heart disease are also associated with stress. Heart patients often show constriction of the coronary arteries and reduced blood flow during acute stress; these effects can also be produced by laboratory stressors such as having to solve difficult arithmetic problems or give a speech about one's personal life (Lane & Jennings, 1995). Conversely, some people who are especially reactive to stress seem to be at high risk for heart disease—a subject that we will come to later in this chapter.

Stress and illness are clearly related, but what is it that mediates the relationship? How are thought and emotion translated into physical breakdown?

Changes in Physiological Functioning

Stress and the Autonomic Nervous System   What are the physiological changes associated with stress? To attempt an answer, we must look again at the autonomic nervous system (ANS). As we saw in Chapter 4, the ANS controls the smooth muscles, the glands, and the internal organs, regulating a wide variety of functions—among them heartbeat, respiration, blood pressure, bladder contraction, perspiration, salivation, adrenaline secretion, and gastric acid production—to allow the body to cope with the ebb and flow of environmental demands. In general, the sympathetic division mobilizes the body to meet such demands by speeding up heart rate, constricting the blood vessels near the skin (thereby raising blood pressure), increasing adrenaline flow, and so forth. And, in general, the parasympathetic division reverses these processes, returning the body to a resting state so that it can rebuild the energy supply depleted by sympathetic activity (see Figure 4.7, page 91).

Several decades ago, W. B. Cannon (1936) proposed that stress resulted in a massive activation of the entire sympathetic division: increased heart rate and blood pressure, fast breathing, heavy adrenaline flow, dilated pupils, inhibited salivation and digestion. Regardless of the nature of the stress or of the person, the physiological response, according to Cannon, was the same generalized sympathetic arousal. That hypothesis has been confirmed in broad outline.

The ANS also contributes to the *fight-or-flight response,* a primitive response to threats and challenges seen in all animals. Actually a combination of several physical and emotional responses, such as a rapid increase in heartbeat, the fight-or-flight response is designed to prepare the organism to fight for or flee for its life. Generally, the sympathetic system is aroused and the parasympathetic system suppressed during this response.

Changes in the Immune System

In the studies of colds, as we saw, not all the people who were exposed to the virus became infected, and not all the people who became infected developed symptoms—in both cases, only those who had been under greater stress. Clearly, the factor mediating this connection was the **immune system,** the body's system of defense against infectious disease and cancer. The job of the immune system is to distinguish between "self" and "nonself" within the body and then to eliminate "nonself." The primary agents of the immune system are small white blood cells, called *lymphocytes,* that patrol the body, identifying foreign substances and either attacking them or producing specially adapted proteins, called *antibodies,* that undertake the attack. In either case, the first stage of attack involves the immune particle's attaching itself to the foreign particle, which it can do only if its chemical structure fits that of the invader. As a result, in order to stay healthy, the body has to circulate a vast number of different lymphocytes, each adapted for a different virus, bacterium, or other invader.

Scientists have only just begun their inventory of the immune system, but this research has accelerated rapidly in the past decade. One reason is the AIDS epidemic. The AIDS virus kills its victims by destroying immune cells, thus leaving the body undefended against illness. Obviously, if we knew more about the immune system, we might find a cure for AIDS. Another stimulus to research on immune functions has been the effort to save lives through organ transplants. A major frustration in organ transplant surgery is that the immune system often perceives the new organ as "nonself" and rejects it. Again, if we had more detailed knowledge of the immune system, we would be in a better position to control this response. Finally, a critical factor in the stepping up of research on immune functions has been the research on stress and illness. The study of the immune system as a link between stress and illness has evolved into a subspecialty of health medicine, **psychoneuroimmunology,** or **PNI.**

In most PNI research, immune responses are studied by means of blood samples. Blood is taken from the subjects; then white blood cells are isolated and exposed to *mitogens,* compounds that mimic the action of foreign substances in the body. Healthy white blood cells, upon encountering mitogens, will begin multiplying and secreting attack compounds. Less healthy white blood cells will do this less efficiently. Thus, by recording the number and behavior of white blood cells in people who are under stress and then comparing those results with white-blood-cell action in the same people when they are under less stress or in control subjects, researchers can draw conclusions about the relationship between stress and immune function.

In this research, then, immune function is the dependent variable, stress the independent variable. PNI research has focused on three broad categories of stressors: naturalistic major events, naturalistic minor events, and laboratory stressors.

Naturalistic Major Events Needless to say, the major real-life events that are most likely to produce stress—divorce, a death in the family—cannot be arranged for experimental purposes, nor, in most cases, can they be studied prospectively; they are too infrequent and unpredictable. But, by assembling and studying subjects after the event, researchers have been able to establish that major life stresses do, indeed, penetrate to the immune system.

One of the earliest studies to demonstrate this principle involved 26 people whose spouses had recently died. The subjects' blood was tested 2 weeks after the death of the spouse and then again 6 weeks after the death. On the second trial, the responsiveness

Caring for a spouse with Alzheimer's disease can be extremely stressful. Witnessing a loved one turning into a virtual stranger over time, a process called "living bereavement," has been shown to weaken the immune system in the same way that ordinary bereavement does.

of these people's white blood cells to mitogens was significantly lower than that of the controls (Bartrop, Luckhurst, Lazarus, et al., 1977). Most of us have heard of people dying of a "broken heart" after the death of a loved one, and this phenomenon has been documented by research (Lynch, 1977). Possibly one of the avenues by which the heart is broken is the immune system.

For many of the subjects in the study just cited, the spouse's death was sudden. What is the immune response to the long-term stress of watching a family member die slowly? A major health problem in the United States today is Alzheimer's disease, an organic brain disorder that strikes the elderly and causes *dementia,* a progressive breakdown of mental functioning involving memory loss, agitation, and irrational behavior (Chapter 14). There is no cure for Alzheimer's; in most cases, neither is there a speedy end. Patients may survive for 20 years. Many are placed in nursing homes, but some are cared for by their families, a situation that is often extremely stressful for the caregivers. Day by day, they watch

the personality of a spouse, father, or mother disintegrate. This process has been described by caregivers as a "living bereavement," and, like ordinary bereavement, it taxes the immune system, as one study showed. Janice Kiccolt-Glaser and her colleagues studied a group of 69 men and women who had been taking care of a spouse with Alzheimer's dementia for an average of 5 years. During the year-long interval between the beginning of the study and the follow-up, the caregivers, compared with controls, showed decreases in 3 different measures of cellular immunity. They were also ill for more days with respiratory infections (Kiecolt-Glaser, Dura, Speicher, et al., 1991). This study provided the first good evidence that chronic stress led to chronically depleted immune function.

Naturalistic Minor Events   Interesting as these studies are, they have limited bearing on the question of how the immune system responds to ordinary, daily stress: traffic jams, family arguments, bounced checks. Until recently, these "naturalistic minor events" were rarely studied by PNI researchers. (Indeed, human beings were rarely studied by PNI researchers. Most experiments involved rodents.) Then, in 1982, Kiecolt-Glaser and her co-workers began looking at the immune responses of Ohio State University medical students during final examinations. The students' blood was tested periodically throughout the academic year, including the tense three-day final-exam period. On every measure of response studied— the numbers of different kinds of immune cells, the cells' activity, their secretions—immune functioning decreased during the exam period. On one measure, the production of chemicals that activate the so-called natural-killer (NK) cells, which fight tumors and viruses, immune activity dropped by as much as 90 percent during the exam period. In a later study, the medical students' blood showed increased levels of the stress-response hormones adrenaline and noradrenaline during both waking and sleeping hours over the course of the exam period. It is possible that these hormone changes were responsible in part for the immune-function changes (Glaser, Pearson, Bonneau, et al., 1993; Kiecolt-Glaser & Glaser, 1991). For more on the link between minor stress and illness, see the box on page 214.

Laboratory Stressors   When researchers study real-life stressors, there are many factors they can't control. Perhaps some third variable was affecting the immune functions of the Alzheimer's patients' caregivers. Out of respect for such possibilities, experimenters studying real-life stress have to be cautious in drawing cause-and-effect conclusions. By using laboratory

Minor Stresses and Illness

In exploring the links between psychological stress and physical illness, researchers have tended to concentrate on the impact that major stressors have on the human body. Divorce, a death in the family, the loss of a job, a move to a distant city—these and other major life events cause tremendous stress and put a person at increased risk of becoming ill (Holmes & Rahe, 1967; Selye, 1976). Happy occasions—getting married, receiving a promotion, going on vacation may also cause stress, but they are much less likely to result in illness.

More recently, researchers have begun to look into the role that less dramatic events play in the stress-disease connection. Surprisingly, the daily hassles of life—getting caught in traffic jams, waiting in lines, losing the car keys—may be more stressful than major unpleasant events (Lazarus, 1980). In fact, continual mild stress has been found to be a better predictor of declines in physical health—and of depression and anxiety—than major life events (DeLongis, Coyne, Dakof, et al., 1982).

Other studies have shown that stress affects the body's defenses against herpes viruses. Unlike most other common viruses, which the immune system actually eliminates from the body, herpes viruses, once they enter the system, remain there for life. Most of the time, they are inactive, but they may flare up now and then, producing cold sores, genital herpes, mononucleosis, or other illnesses, depending on which herpes virus is involved. In medical students who have been infected with herpes viruses, immune activity against the virus has been shown to drop during final exams and then to rise again during summer vacation (Glaser, Pearson, Bonneau, et al., 1993).

Stress apparently affects not only one's defenses against already present herpes viruses but also one's risk of being infected in the first place. In one experiment, a group of West Point cadets was tracked for four years after they entered the academy. None of these students had been infected with the Epstein-Barr virus, which causes mononucleosis, before going to West Point. But in the course of the four years a number of them became infected. Those who did—and those who spent longest in the infirmary—tended to be the ones who, on an earlier test, had shown three risk factors for stress: high motivation for a military career, poor grades, and fathers who were "overachievers" (Kiecolt-Glaser & Glaser, 1991).

stressors, on the other hand, researchers can control conditions in such a way as to eliminate confounding variables. They can also observe the response to stress *as it occurs* and, thus, study its internal dynamics.

In an interesting study, 30 subjects were given 2 hard tasks to perform. One was an arithmetic problem. Starting with a 4-digit number (e.g., 4,269), the subjects had to subtract 13 repeatedly in their heads and announce the results (4,256, 4,243, 4,230, . . ."). All the while, an experimenter urged them to work faster. The second task was the so-called Stroop color-word test, in which the subjects were shown, on a video monitor, the names of colors appearing in a different color. (For example, the word *blue* might appear printed in red.) Subjects are asked to ignore the word on the screen and just report the color that the word was printed in—a difficult task made even harder by the fact that each presentation was accompanied by a taped voice naming various colors randomly connected to the one on the screen. The subjects in the PNI experiment worked at these tasks for 20 minutes, after which blood samples were taken. The samples showed significantly reduced immune functioning, compared with that of the controls, who did not perform the tasks. An hour later, blood was taken again, and again it showed depleted immune activity. Thus, immune responses to stress are not necessarily brief, transient effects (Stone, Valdimarsdottir, Katkin, et al., 1993).

For all its advantages, laboratory research has the disadvantage that its conditions are not those of ordinary life. The Stroop color-word test is not among the trials that most people endure in their daily existences. However, one experiment, again by the Kiecolt-Glaser team, went fairly far in duplicating an important source of real-life stress: marital conflict. Ninety recently married couples were admitted to a hospital research unit for 24 hours. By means of an interview and questionnaire, 2 or 3 topics of conflict were identified for each couple. Then the couples were asked to discuss these problems and try to resolve them during a 30-minute session. The session was videotaped, and blood samples were taken several times in the course of it. (The couples had been outfitted with catheters.) The videotapes were later rated on various measures—negative behavior, positive behavior, problem-solving behavior, avoidant behavior—by independent raters, and these results were compared with the results of immune-function tests on the blood samples. What the researchers found, in general, was that the more negative behavior, such as arguing or accusing, a subject showed, the more likely he or she was to show reduced immune functioning. Interestingly, immune changes were not found to be related to positive, problem-solving, or avoidant behaviors, only to negative behaviors. Another curious finding was that women were more likely than men to show negative immune changes.

As in the stress-task experiment, the immune effects were not transient. They were still present 24 hours after the taped session (Kiecolt-Glaser, Malarkey, Chee, et al., 1993).

Feedback Loops Stress produces direct physiological effects, and those effects have other effects. The body's functions—digestion, respiration, circulation—are not single-component operations. They are systems of many parts, each of which sends the others **feedback,** or information about regulating the system. Especially important in theories of stress and illness is **negative feedback,** in which the turning *on* of one component in a system leads to the turning *off* of another component. According to Gary Schwartz's (1977) *disregulation model,* stress-related illness occurs when there is a disruption in the negative-feedback cycle. Consider the case of blood pressure. In response to threats in the environment, the brain causes the arteries to constrict. In doing so, it depends on the *baroreceptors,* pressure-sensitive cells surrounding the arteries, to signal when blood pressure is running too high. But various circumstances, such as chronic stress or genetic predisposition, may blunt the responsiveness of the baroreceptors, so they fail to provide this crucial negative feedback. When that happens, a regulated system becomes a disregulated system, and the result is illness—in this case, chronically high blood pressure.

Another influential theory, developed by Herbert Weiner (1994), concerns the **oscillations,** or rhythmic back-and-forth cycles, of the various systems in the body. Such oscillating cycles control almost all bodily functions. Breathing, blood pressure, heartbeat, temperature, digestion, menstruation, sleep, the production of hormones, neurotransmitters, immune cells—all go up and down on a number of time scales, whether second by second, day by day, or month by month. These cycles, too, are controlled by negative feedback. Indeed, that is what keeps them oscillating: turning on in one cycle leads to turning off in another, and vice versa. (For example, the turning off of sleep results in the turning on of stomach contractions, so we want breakfast.) According to Weiner, stress may throw a system out of rhythm; in which case, the other systems are also affected. After the disruption, the system may find a new rhythm, or it may become chronically irregular. In either case, the result may be a disease process. For example, people who work late shifts suffer chronic disruptions of their sleep cycle. On workdays they wake up in the afternoon; on days off, if they want to see their families and friends, they wake up in the morning. This irregularity apparently takes its toll, and not just on sleep. Long-term night-shift workers have more gastrointestinal problems

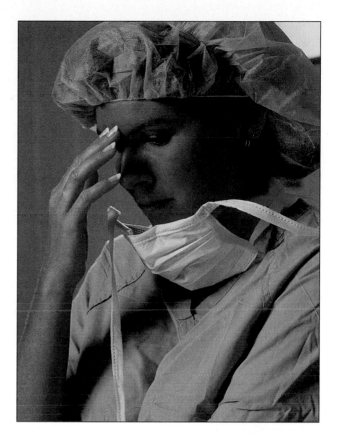

Medical interns once epitomized the kind of chronic irregularities in work schedule—many hours on duty alternating with a few hours off—that can result in stress-related illness. Now that such fatigue has been shown to interfere with patient care, many teaching hospitals are scheduling shorter and more regular shifts for their interns.

and more illness than people who work day shifts (Rutenfranz, Haider, & Koller, 1985).

Schwartz's model, then, focuses more on the failure of a single component, which then disregulates the system as a whole. Weiner's model concentrates from the beginning on the system—on the whole body as a finely tuned network of oscillating systems, all vulnerable to stress.

Changes in High-Risk Behavior

Schwartz's and Weiner's theories are models—comprehensive, abstract descriptions. On a more concrete level, stress may contribute to illness by causing people to behave in a way that puts them at risk for illness. For example, people with adult-onset diabetes can usually maintain their health by taking medication and following a special diet. As studies (Brantley & Garrett, 1993) have shown, however, diabetics who are under stress are likely to stray from their diets and forget their pills, with the result that they may fall ill.

Stress can also interfere with preventive measures against disease. In a study of women who engaged in self-initiated exercise, the subjects exercised fewer days, skipped planned exercise sessions, reported lower levels of confidence in meeting their exercise goals, and were less satisfied with their exercise sessions during periods of high stress (Stetson, Rahn, Dubbert, et al., 1997). Ironically, 70 percent of the women reported that they used exercise to manage stress. But, in order to see the chain leading from stress to high-risk behavior to illness, it is hardly necessary to look to this kind of study. As anyone knows, stress may lead to smoking, drug use, sleep loss, overeating, and undereating, and any of these will increase the risk of illness.

Stress may also encourage its victims to report illness. People whose lives are going smoothly tend to overlook health problems; people who are under pressure are more likely to call the doctor. This is one reason for the association between stress and illness—which is not to say that such reports of illness are exaggerated. On the contrary, this connection illustrates one of the few beneficial effects of stress: it causes people who are at risk to seek help earlier, with the possibility that they may receive needed treatment or learn to change their behavior, for example, by eating more healthfully or starting an exercise regimen.

Psychological Factors and Physical Disorders

As we saw, psychological factors can affect any physical disorder. We will discuss only a few conditions in which the influence of mental processes has been of special concern to researchers, beginning with coronary heart disease and high blood pressure, which have been linked strongly to psychological factors. The evidence on the relationship between stress and cancer, AIDS, and other conditions covered in this section is progressively less conclusive.

Coronary Heart Disease

The heart, a muscle that pumps blood throughout the body, is fed by the major arteries, which supply it with oxygen and nutrients. Those arteries can become occluded, or blocked, by *atherosclerosis,* or the formation of fatty deposits on the inside walls of the arteries. The deposits build up over the years, causing the formation of scar tissue and calcium deposits that restrict the passage of blood, sometimes leading to a heart attack. More often, a blood clot (thrombus) suddenly blocks a coronary artery at a narrow point, cutting off the blood supply to part

of the heart (ischemia) and causing a *myocardial infarction,* or heart attack. In some people, the heart's electrical impulses become disorganized, and blood circulation ceases, causing sudden cardiac death.

Coronary heart disease, brought about by atherosclerosis and manifested as either heart attack or sudden cardiac death, is usually manifested when the heart's oxygen demands exceed the available supply. Transient reductions in the oxygen supply due to exercise or stress can cause *angina pectoris,* or chest pain; more enduring reductions can cause a myocardial infarction. But, in individuals who have not yet been diagnosed with coronary artery disease, routine testing can often identify the disease before a major event. Electrocardiograms administered while a subject exercises can reveal "silent" ischemia, most often due to undiagnosed atherosclerosis.

Coronary heart disease is the number one cause of death in the United States and other industrialized countries of the West. Although the underlying pathogenic process, coronary atherosclerosis, begins early in life, the expression of the disease—heart attack or sudden cardiac death—often occurs in mid- to late adulthood. The development, expression, and course of the disease represents a complex interplay of biological, psychological, and social factors. Traditional risk factors for coronary heart disease include a family history of the disease, increasing age, gender (males are more at risk than females), high blood levels of cholesterol, high blood pressure, cigarette smoking, obesity, physical inactivity, and diabetes mellitus. Research indicates that stress and some personality traits are also risk factors for coronary heart disease. Day-to-day lifestyle, including diet, exercise, and stress level, has an important impact on the progression of the disease (Smith & Leon, 1992), as the following case history suggests:

Mr. Smith, a fifty-year-old auto worker was 20 percent overweight, smoked, ate the typical American diet (high in animal fat and low in fruits, vegetables, and fiber), and lived a sedentary lifestyle. The primary wage earner of his family, he had two children in college. Recently his company had decided to downsize, threatening Mr. Smith's job. For the next month, he had experienced episodic tightness in his chest, primarily when he exerted himself and after meals. He attributed the tightness to indigestion.

One Friday in January, Mr. Smith received a pink slip. The next week there was a big snowfall. After a large breakfast, during which he argued with his wife about how he was spending his time, Mr. Smith decided to shovel the driveway. Experiencing tightness in his chest, he attributed it to indigestion and continued to work. But within a few minutes, the feeling had become more oppressive, expanding into a pain that radiated down his left arm. Overwhelmed, Mr. Smith fell to his knees, clutching his chest, and passed out. His wife, who had been watching from the window, called 911 immediately. At the emergency room, physicians diagnosed a myocardial infarction ("heart attack") and admitted him for diagnostic tests. After returning home, Mr. Smith began a cardiac rehabilitation program that included exercise, diet modification, and advice on smoking cessation and stress management.

Over the next six months, Mr. Smith stopped smoking, lost more than ten pounds, and found a new job. Though he no longer experiences chest pain, he worries about having another heart attack. He practices the relaxation techniques he learned through a stress management class regularly. He also is learning cognitive strategies for managing his anger and fear. While maintaining his new eating habits and exercise regimen is a struggle, Mr. Smith is getting a great deal of support from his wife and children, who have modified their own diets to match his "heart healthy" diet. (J. Haythornthwaite, Johns Hopkins University, personal files)

Men whose jobs are repetitive and unchallenging have been shown to be at an increased risk of developing coronary heart disease. This risk can be decreased by introducing variety into the work and by offering men a greater role in making decisions about their work.

Since the 1960s, the death rate from heart attacks has declined steadily, as has the apparent number of initial acute myocardial infarctions (heart attacks). Improved emergency services may have contributed to the reduced death rate. More important, some major risk factors have declined, including dietary intake of animal fat and cholesterol and cigarette smoking. The detection and management of high blood pressure have also improved, and physical activity levels may have increased.

Research on nonhuman primates has demonstrated the link between social environment/status and atherosclerosis (Manuck, Marsland, Kaplan, et al., 1995). In socially dominant males, a moderately high-risk diet combined with an unstable social environment produced twice the amount of coronary atherosclerosis than normal. That is, the stress of retaining a dominant social status in a constantly changing social environment contributed to the disease. Later work demonstrated that activation of the sympathetic nervous system (SNS) contributed to atherosclerosis. Dominant males, placed in an unstable social environment and given a medication that blocked specific SNS activity, did not develop increased atherosclerosis, suggesting that the medication protected the heart by reducing the physiological response to stress. In a similar unstable social environment, unmedicated dominant males exhibited large increases in heart rate during social encounters. In these studies, researchers found sex differences in the impact of social status on the development of atherosclerosis. Subordinate female animals showed greater atherosclerosis, regardless of the stability of their social environment. Overall, these studies demonstrate the

potential effects of social stress in facilitating the development of coronary artery disease.

In humans, researchers have used a variety of epidemiological methods to examine the relationship between social and occupational stress and the development and progression of coronary heart disease (Krantz, Contrada, Hill, et al., 1988). In a large, prospective study done over a 6-year period, Karasek and colleagues (1981) found that the Swedish men who described their work as psychologically demanding and scored low on a scale measuring latitude in decision making were at increased risk of developing symptoms of coronary heart disease and eventually dying from it. Men whose jobs were characterized by low intellectual demands were also at increased risk. These findings were independent of age, educational level, smoking, and obesity (Karasek, Baker, Marxer, et al., 1981). More recent studies suggest that a demanding work environment is not as important as low control in predicting increased risk of coronary heart disease (Bosma, Marmot, Hemingway, et al., 1997). These findings suggest that giving employees more variety in their work, and more input into decisions about their work, may decrease their risk of coronary heart disease.

Large cardiovascular and neuroendocrine responses have been observed in response to both laboratory stressors (for example, the mental arithmetic and Stroop color-word tests described on page 214) and naturalistic stressors (for example, public speaking and driving in traffic). These acute cardiac responses, which are referred to as cardiovascular reactivity, have long been thought to contribute to the development and expression of coronary heart disease (Krantz & Manuck, 1984). The most compelling support comes from the primate experiments on social environment and social dominance just described. However, some recent studies have provided more direct support in humans. For example, Barnett and colleagues (1997) studied men and women referred to an atherosclerosis prevention clinic over a 2-year period. Among 136 untreated individuals, the magnitude of the blood pressure response to a Stroop color-word test significantly predicted the progression of carotid atherosclerosis (Barnett, Spense, Mamick, et al., 1997).

In the book *Type A Behavior and Your Heart* (1974), Friedman and Rosenman advanced the thesis that coronary heart disease, along with other cardiovascular disorders, tends to strike a specific kind of personality, which the authors called **Type A.** Type A people are aggressive achievers. They talk, walk, and eat rapidly and are highly impatient. They fidget in frustration if kept waiting at an elevator or a traffic light. They finish other people's sentences for them. They pride themselves on getting things done in less time than other people, and they measure their own performance by rigorous standards. In short, they keep themselves under heavy pressure—pressure that eventually takes a toll on their cardiovascular systems.

In an impressive longitudinal study, 2,249 male executives between the ages of 39 and 59 were evaluated and followed for 9 years (Rosenman, Brand, Jenkins, et al., 1975). Approximately half were identified as Type A and the other half as Type B (the more relaxed, patient executive). Of the 257 men who had heart attacks during the 9 years, 178 were Type A, while only 79 were Type B—a striking 2-to-1 differential. Soon, however, conflicting findings began to appear. In a study of heart-attack survivors, the Type As actually lived longer than the Type Bs (Ragland & Brand, 1988). Other studies have also indicated that workaholic Type As are not in as much danger as was

once thought. There seems to be no correlation between heart disease and the impatient struggle to accomplish ever more work. There is, however, a correlation between heart disease (with depression) and high levels of anger, hostility, and aggression—qualities often seen in Type A people (Booth-Kewley & Friedman, 1987). More recent research has focused on the possibility that hostility is the pathogenic component of the Type A pattern. Research has confirmed the link between heart disease and hostile or negative beliefs and attitudes toward others, including cynicism, distrust, and denigration (Matthews, 1988; Miller, Smith, Turner, et al., 1996).

Numerous studies have demonstrated correlations between hostility and the severity of coronary heart disease; some have demonstrated a relationship between hostility, the development of coronary heart disease, and premature mortality (Miller, Smith, Turner, et al., 1996). Hostility is thought to contribute to the development of heart disease through frequent, intense episodes of physiological arousal. A number of laboratory studies support this notion: individuals who score high on measures of hostility show larger-than-normal cardiovascular and neuroendocrine responses to a wide variety of stressful situations, particularly those that involve interpersonal challenges (Smith, 1992).

Cardiovascular reactivity has also been implicated in the expression of coronary heart disease. For example, in one study, individuals suffering from stress-induced myocardial ischemia were found to be more than twice as likely as others to experience a cardiac event, including death, bypass surgery, and angioplasty, over the next 2 years (Jiang, Babyak, Krantz, et al., 1996). In another study, subjects wore an ambulatory ECG monitor and kept diaries for 48 hours, noting feelings of happiness, sadness, tension, and frustration. After adjustment for physical activity and time of day—factors known to affect myocardial functioning—investigators showed that emotional distress in the form of tension, frustration, or sadness increased the risk of transient myocardial ischemia by a factor of 2 (Guilette, Blumenthal, Babyak, et al., 1997).

Anger has been shown to be particularly stressful for patients with cardiovascular disease. In one study, patients were asked to recall an event that had recently evoked their anger. Recalling the event reduced the functioning of their hearts more than did exercising, giving a brief speech, or performing mental arithmetic (Ironson, Taylor, Boltwood, et al., 1992). In a more recent study of survivors of myocardial infarction, investigators found that episodes of intense anger can actually trigger a heart attack (Mittleman, Maclure, Sherwood, et al., 1995).

Hypertension

Of all the physical disorders commonly associated with psychological stress, chronically high blood pressure, known as **hypertension,** is the most common and the most dangerous. An estimated 15 percent of the population of the United States suffers from this cardiovascular disorder, which in turn predisposes them to other deadly cardiovascular disorders, heart attack and "stroke" (MacMahon, Peto, Cutter, et al., 1990). Untreated hypertensives have an average life expectancy of between 50 and 60 years, compared with 71 years for the population at large.

We saw earlier how hypertension illustrates the principle of disregulation (Schwartz, 1977): breakdown in one component leads to breakdown in the system as a whole. The function of the cardiovascular system, consisting of the heart and the peripheral blood vessels, is to pump blood through the body, carrying nutrients where they are needed and carrying wastes where they can be disposed of. Every heartbeat represents a contraction of the heart; with each contraction, blood is pushed out of the heart and through the blood vessels. At the same time, the blood vessels are contracting and dilating in response to internal and external stimuli. The blood pressure—that is, the pressure that blood exerts on the walls of the blood vessels—is a function of several variables, but one of the most important, at least in hypertension, seems to be the degree of constriction in the blood vessels (Forsyth, 1974). When a normal person's blood pressure rises too high, the baroreceptors convey this information to the brain; in response to this negative feedback, the brain then relaxes the constricted vessel walls. In hypertensives, however, the regulatory mechanism fails to work, with the result that the blood vessels remain chronically constricted and, hence, the blood pressure chronically high.

Why does this happen? In a small percentage of cases, 10 to 15 percent, hypertension is linked to an identifiable organic cause, usually kidney dysfunction (Shapiro & Goldstein, 1982). In the remaining cases, known as **essential hypertension,** there is no known organic cause. Many different factors have been suggested.

One factor in the development of essential hypertension is environment. It may be that some essential hypertensives live in environments that are particularly rich in the kinds of stressors that increase blood pressure. Long-term exposure to stressful occupations has been linked to hypertension, while long-term exposure to low-stress environments has been associated with an absence of the age-associated increase in blood pressure typically observed in Western societies. For instance, air traffic controllers working in high-volume control centers were found to have significantly higher rates of hypertension than members of a control group who performed other jobs in the same work environment (Cobb & Rose, 1973). And, over the course of 20 years, Italian nuns living in a cloistered community did not show the expected age-related increase in blood pressure that was found in a control group of women (Timio, Verdecchia, Venanzi, et al., 1988).

In light of these findings, it is interesting to note that essential hypertension is twice as common among African Americans as it is among Caucasians. While this disparity may be a function of genes, diet, or other factors, one might also hypothesize that African Americans as a group are exposed to greater stress than Caucasians (Anderson, 1989). A study of African Americans in Detroit found that those living in high-stress areas—neighborhoods with lower income, higher unemployment, higher divorce rate, higher crime rate—had higher blood pressure than those living in low-stress areas (Harburg, 1978).

Essential hypertension may also be due in part to individual response specificity. In other words, genes or experience may have programmed the brain to respond to different kinds of stress with increases in blood pressure. Recent research has focused on subjects assumed to be at risk for hypertension, including people with at least one hypertensive parent and people who had mildly elevated blood pressure in childhood or early adulthood. When confronted with demanding behavioral and cognitive tasks, such people do experience greater cardiovascular reactions than people without a family history of hypertension (Fredrikson & Matthews, 1990). Research suggests that elevated blood pressure and hypertension may be related to the way in which individuals express affect, particularly its inhibition, as well as to defensiveness and high levels of negative affect, such as anger. Defensiveness appears to be the strongest predictor of blood pressure (Jorgensen, Johnson, Kolodziej, et al., 1996).

Because high blood pressure produces no immediate discomfort, many hypertensives are unaware of their condition, with the result that it may go untreated for years. Furthermore, those who are aware that they have hypertension are often unaware that circumstances in their family lives or work environments may be aggravating it. Like the aforementioned baroreceptors, they have adapted to the stress and no longer see it as stressful. Often, it takes a crisis—a situation in which blood pressure and environmental pressures simultaneously increase dramatically—before such patients will take seriously the connection between their blood pressure and their way of life and consider changing the latter. In many

Even for young people, the stress of living in a dangerous, drug-ridden neighborhood such as New York City's south Bronx raises the risk for developing essential hypertension.

cases, family and work circumstances are not all that need changing. A number of physical factors—above all, smoking, obesity, and high salt intake—have been shown to aggravate hypertension. Obese people are three times more likely to be hypertensive than people who are not overweight (Van Italli, 1985). As for smoking, it apparently combines synergistically with hypertension to create a high risk of coronary heart disease (Kannel & Higgins, 1990).

Cancer

Cancer is one of the greatest challenges that the human body has ever posed to medical science. This disease accounts for almost one-quarter of all deaths in the United States, and it is gaining ground. Death rates from other major killers such as heart disease and strokes have been decreasing, but death rates due to cancer have actually risen 20 percent in the past three decades (American Cancer Society, 1994).

For a long time, it was believed that, whatever physical disorders might be associated with psychological stress, cancer was not one of them. Now, as recent studies have established, cancer *is* one of them. At the beginning of this chapter, we mentioned one such study, involving breast cancer patients who, in addition to their medical treatment, attended weekly group therapy for a year (Spiegel, Bloom, Kraemer, et al., 1989). The therapy sessions addressed various matters. The women were taught by the group leaders how to control pain through self-hypnosis; they were also advised on how to communicate with their families and how to be assertive with their doctors.

But the main function of the group was to give the women a chance to express their feelings and support one another. They discussed their family problems, their physical distress as a result of chemotherapy and radiation, and their fear of dying. Eventually, they developed strong bonds. They visited one another in the hospital, wrote poems together, and even, at one point, moved their meeting to the home of a dying member. As we saw, these women were found, on follow-up, to have survived twice as long as controls after the beginning of treatment. What kept them alive? The experimenters speculate that the advice and sympathy the subjects received may have influenced them to follow health regimens better— eat, exercise, take medication—and, thus, live longer. But in the experimenters' opinion a major factor was simply social support. It is a well-established fact that married cancer patients survive longer than unmarried cancer patients (Goodwin, Hunt, Key, et al., 1987), but even families, out of worry and grief, may be of limited psychological use to a dying member. The women in this study had each other, and apparently that helped them to fight breast cancer.

Other researchers have found the same thing with people suffering from malignant melanoma, a form of skin cancer that can be cured in its early stages but tends to recur. In a study of 68 patients, 34 controls were given medical treatment only; the remaining 34 subjects were given medical treatment and group therapy—in this case, only 6 sessions—focused on education, stress management, coping skills, and psychological support. Recontacted 5 to 6 years later, the groups showed widely different health records. Twice

The "Aliveness Project" in Minneapolis helps AIDS patients reduce stress, in an effort to relieve some of their symptoms.

as many of the controls had had a recurrence of malignant melanoma, and 3 times as many of the controls had died (Fawzy, Fawzy, Hyun, et al., 1993).

Thus, group therapy seems to help some cancer patients. Possibly one of its crucial benefits is that it encourages active coping as opposed to helplessness. Animal studies have shown a close correlation between helplessness and the growth of cancer cells. In one study, Sklar and Anisman (1979) implanted tumor cells in rats and then divided the rats into three groups. One group received electric shocks that they could escape by pressing a bar. The second group received inescapable shocks, and the third group, no shocks. The experimenters found that the tumors grew more quickly in the rats given inescapable shocks than in either of the other groups. In a later study, with much the same design, the cancer cells were implanted in smaller doses, so that the animals' immune systems could conceivably combat them. The results were quite striking: the rats given the inescapable shocks were only half as likely to reject the cancer and were twice as likely to die of it as the escapable-shock and no-shock groups (Visintainer, Volpicelli, & Seligman, 1982). Generalizing from rats to human beings is always problematic, but it is likely that helplessness will be a major concern of future PNI research on cancer.

Whatever the relationship between cancer and life stress, cancer itself—finding out one has it, dealing with the family, going through treatments—is a major life stress, one that can affect behavior in a way that influences the person's chance of survival. Eating habits, alcohol consumption, the taking of medica-tion—all of these behaviors are vulnerable to stress. Psychological treatment for cancer patients is still in its early stages. (As noted, it was only recently recognized that psychological treatment helps cancer patients.) But in the future such treatment should probably place more emphasis on these practical issues (Anderson, Kiecolt-Glaser, & Glaser, 1994).

AIDS

Acquired immune deficiency syndrome, or **AIDS,** was first identified in 1981. It is caused by the **human immunodeficiency virus (HIV),** which is communicated via the blood, semen, vaginal secretions, or breast milk of an infected person, either during unprotected sex, through a shared hypodermic needle, from a contaminated blood transfusion, or (in the case of a newborn whose mother is infected) in the womb. Once the virus becomes active, it attacks the immune system, leaving the person open to various infections, including Kaposi's sarcoma, a form of cancer rare in people unexposed to HIV. But HIV can remain dormant for a long time before becoming active. Some people are said to have been HIV-positive for 20 years before developing symptoms. To date, more than 612,000 Americans have been diagnosed with AIDS—the epidemic is far worse in other countries —and 379,258 Americans have died of AIDS (Centers for Disease Control, 1997). More will die in the years to come. Between 1 and 2 million Americans are estimated to be HIV-positive, but this figure may be unrealistically low, for many people have not yet been tested. Indeed, the largest risk group, heterosexual men and women having unprotected sex with multiple partners, has a testing rate of only 35 percent (Berrios, Hearst, Coates, et al., 1993).

In view of the evidence that psychological stress affects the immune system, we might assume that stress would speed the course of AIDS, a disease centered in the immune system. The findings are contradictory, however. Some studies have found no relationship between stress and the progress of HIV infection (Kessler, Foster, Joseph, et al., 1991; Rabkin, Williams, Remien, et al., 1991). Others have found more vigorous immune responses in HIV-positive men with more active coping styles (Goodkin, Blaney, Feasler, et al., 1992). As for the medical benefits of psychological treatment, most efforts have been focused on one potential benefit, the avoidance of high-risk behavior. There have been a number of cognitive-behavioral skills-training programs designed to discourage unsafe sex. Typically, these programs include several components: instructions about safe and unsafe sex; assertiveness training (to enable people to say no to unsafe sex); problem-solving training (to teach people to anticipate and avoid risk factors such as alcohol or drug use); and reinforcement of behavior change. Such programs, so far aimed primarily at homosexual men (Kelly & Murphy, 1992) and sexually active teenagers (Rotheram-Borus, Koopman, & Haignere, 1991), have reported good results.

Headache

Stress has long been implicated in chronic headaches, including the very severe form known as **migraine headache.** Migraines differ from ordinary headaches —often called **muscle-contraction headaches,** or *tension headaches*—in that they are usually localized on one side of the head and are far more intense. A migraine attack further differs from a tension headache in that it is sometimes preceded by an *aura,* or spell of perceptual distortion, often involving strange visual sensations such as flashing lights or blind spots. Finally, in migraine, unlike tension headaches, head pain is typically accompanied by other symptoms: physical (nausea, vomiting), cognitive (confusion), and affective (depression, irritability). Intolerance to light and sound are also common. Migraine attacks range from bearable discomfort to complete immobilization. They may last from several hours to several days and may occur as frequently as every day or as infrequently as once every few months.

In recent years, theories of migraine have shown a dramatic shift from psychological to organic causation. For the past half-century, migraine was thought to be the product of a stress-induced cardiovascular process involving the constriction and dilation of the blood vessels in the head (Wolff, 1948). As for the psychological causes behind this cardiovascular quirk, there were various theories, ranging from descriptions of a "migraine personality" to speculations about female emotional instability. (Migraine is twice as common in women as in men.)

Recently, however, these theories have been essentially scrapped, together with the idea that migraine is a cardiovascular disorder. According to newer findings (Raskin, Hosobuchi, & Lamb, 1987), migraine is a neurological disorder involving a dysfunction in the operation of the neurotransmitter serotonin. A number of signs pointed researchers in this direction. For one thing, the most effective drugs for migraine are all connected to serotonin, whereas they are not directly connected to blood-vessel function. Furthermore, serotonin and its chemical counterpart, norepinephrine, are both linked to depression and sleep disturbances, which in turn are linked to migraine and are commonly seen in families with a susceptibility to migraine. The connection between migraine and serotonin was also signaled by a curious accidental experiment. Fifteen people with no history of migraine, but with intractable back pain, were given electrode implants in their brains as a treatment for their back problems. All of them developed severe migraine. According to Raskin and colleagues (1987), the site of the electrode implantation was near the region of the brain where serotonin is most active.

No one knows as yet the precise nature of the presumed serotonin dysfunction. Perhaps, in migraine sufferers, the body simply produces too little serotonin. Or perhaps the available serotonin is destroyed too quickly by enzymes as it crosses the synapses between the nerve cells. Another possibility is that the receptors responsible for taking up serotonin are not accepting enough of it. In any case, the serotonin hypothesis has unleashed a great flurry of research, and more refined hypotheses are expected shortly.

If effective drugs are developed, they will be welcome, for migraine is a common disorder, afflicting approximately 18 million people in the United States alone. The fact that two-thirds of these people are women—and that their attacks tend to appear in adolescence and disappear after menopause—suggests that hormonal changes associated with the menstrual cycle are also involved in migraine. And underlying all these organic factors is presumably some measure of genetic causation, for as many as 90 percent of migraine sufferers have a family history of the disorder.

None of this means that stress is not involved in migraine. Many different stimuli—bright lights, red wine, changes in atmospheric pressure—can precipitate a migraine, but one of the most common triggers is minor stress (Brantley & Jones, 1993). In one study, it was found that the best predictor of migraines was stress one to three days prior to the headache. For muscle-contraction headaches, the best predictor was stress on the same day (Mosley, Penizen, Johnson, et al., 1991). What the serotonin research suggests is simply that migraine is one of many physical disorders involving both organic and environmental causes.

Obesity

Eating behavior, like most other bodily functions, is regulated by feedback loops. In highly simplified terms, the sequence is as follows. When the body is in need of nourishment, it sends hunger signals to the brain. Then, as we eat, other internal signals alert the brain that the body is satiated, at which point we put down our forks. This is the normal regulatory cycle. It, too, can succumb to disregulation, however. The feedback may fail to reach the brain, or the brain may receive the feedback but still respond inappropriately. In either case, the cycle is thrown off, and the person either fails to eat when the stomach signals hunger or goes on eating when the stomach signals satiety.

The first of these two patterns of disregulation—chronic failure to eat, to the point of extreme malnutrition—is known as *anorexia nervosa*. Because it normally begins in adolescence, we will discuss it under childhood and adolescent disorders (Chapter 15). We will turn our attention now to the second and far more familiar pattern, obesity.

Obesity is a socially defined condition. Strictly speaking, the term refers to an excessive amount of fat on the body, but every culture has its own idea of what is excessive. What would have been regarded as a healthy adult in the nineteenth century would now be called a fat person; conversely, to nineteenth-century eyes, the thinness of today's fashion models would seem grotesque. Our society, actually, is caught in a curious paradox. Perhaps in no other culture has thinness been so highly prized, and obesity so prevalent. Researchers estimate that 24 percent of American men and 27 percent of American women are more than 20 percent overweight (Brownell & Wadden, 1992). The prevalence of obesity increases with age and is highest among lower socioeconomic groups (Brownell, 1982).

Obesity is not good for the body. It increases the likelihood of digestive disease, cardiovascular disease, adult-onset diabetes, and cancer (Brantley & Garrett, 1993; Bray, 1984). But does this make an "abnormal" condition? It certainly does not by the statistical-rarity criterion, as we have just seen. However, it might be defined as such according to the

The line that separates obesity from normal weight varies across cultures and centuries. More than a few of today's Americans wish they could have lived in seventeenth-century Europe, when Rubens' voluptuous nudes represented the ideal of female beauty. (Men have had their turn in other ages—in the early decades of this century, for example, when a protruding abdomen was a sign of a man's success and prosperity.)

norm-violation criterion, the norm being thinness. Above all, the "abnormality" of obesity would be related to the personal-discomfort criterion. In many sectors of our society, obesity is viewed as "a state verging on crime" (Rodin, 1977a). As a result, the obese not only suffer the consequences of their socially defined unattractiveness—ranging from a mild sense of inferiority to extreme social and sexual maladjustment—but they must suffer shame as well. This is personal discomfort, indeed, and it pushes many people into therapy.

What causes obesity? In part, the reasons are directly physiological. Excess weight is not necessarily due to excessive eating. Many obese people eat moderately and still remain fat, while many thin people can "eat anything" and still stay thin—an injustice of which overweight people often complain. Factors that influence body weight include genetic differences, such as the resting metabolic rate and number of fat cells, and behavioral differences, such as caloric intake, eating habits, and activity level (Brownell &

Wadden, 1992). And, while activity level can be altered by exercise programs, metabolic rate is in large measure genetically determined. Furthermore, once a person becomes overweight, the added pounds *further* lower the metabolic rate. (That is, once the weight is gained, fewer calories are needed to keep it on than were needed to put it on.) To make matters worse, dieting also tends to lower the metabolic rate, with the result, ruefully noted by many dieters, that one can count calories religiously and still not lose weight (Rodin, 1981). In sum, certain bodies are apparently born to carry more fat than others.

However, obesity is due not to physiology alone but to an interaction of physiological and psychological factors. A number of studies indicate that obese people are far more responsive than others to any food-relevant stimulus: the taste of food (Nisbett, 1968), the sight and smell of food (Rodin, 1981; Schachter, 1971), the clock indicating that it is mealtime (Schachter & Gross, 1968), and, presumably, television commercials and magazine advertisements. Other experiments suggest that overweight people may also have a problem with the transmission of feedback from the stomach to the brain. When normal people are asked how hungry they are, their answers correlate strongly with the frequency of their stomach contractions. When overweight people are put to the same test, the correlation is much weaker (Stunkard & Koch, 1964).

It is hard to say, however, whether the disregulation observed in these experiments was actually due to obesity. Most overweight people are dieters, and whatever disregulation they show may be the result not of excess weight but of dieting. Several experiments have found that obese people who are not dieters do not show overresponsiveness to food cues (Herman & Mack, 1975; Ruderman & Wilson, 1979). On the other hand, overresponsiveness and many of the other peculiarities said to characterize the eating behavior of the obese *are* found in people who are of normal weight but are chronic dieters (Klajner, Herman, Polivy, et al., 1981). There is now solid evidence that chronic dieting may lead to disregulation. People who, whether or not they are overweight, have been kept from their normal eating pattern are more likely to engage in binge eating (Wardle, 1980), are more likely to eat in response to stress (Cools, Schotte, & McNally, 1992; Heatherton, Herman, & Polivy, 1991), and are more likely to go on eating once they have violated the dietary restraint (Ruderman, 1986)—facts that will sound familiar to anyone who has been on a diet. This disregulation may eventually lead to the chronic pattern of binge eating known as bulimia (Polivy & Herman, 1985). Bulimia will be discussed, with anorexia, in Chapter 15.

Such findings, together with the physiological evidence previously described, have caused many weight-reduction programs to shift their emphasis from dieting to exercise. Exercise presumably does not interfere with the regulatory cycle that controls eating. On the other hand, it does burn up calories, suppress the appetite, and increase the metabolic rate, so, even when one is not exercising, calories are being burned faster. But exercise alone may not be enough. Recent research indicates that the most effective weight-reduction programs are those that focus on several components—typically, dietary changes, problem solving, and peer support as well as exercise—and that extend over a long period, such as a year. As for the maintenance of weight loss, those who go on exercising are the most likely to keep the pounds off (Craighead & Agras, 1991).

In addition to advocating weight reduction for the obese, many experts feel that what our society needs is a broader definition of physical attractiveness, so that beauty is not confined to the thinnest end of the spectrum of human body types. Many moderately heavy people have nothing wrong with them, either physically or psychologically. On the other hand, it is possible that dieting has acquired an undeservedly bad name in recent years. "The 1990s are taking shape as an antidieting decade," weight expert Kelly Brownell has written (1993, p. 339). Popular magazines regularly publish articles critical of weight consciousness, and antidieting books are appearing. A statistic often cited in such writings is that 95 percent of all diets fail. That figure, however, is over 30 years old (Stunkard & McLaren-Hume, cited in Brownell, 1993) and was derived from people in university-based treatment programs—people who were heavier, showed more psychological disorders, and were more likely to be binge eaters than overweight people in general (Brownell, 1993). In fact, it is not at all clear how successful most diets are; research is badly needed on this question. In the meantime, it appears that the perils of dieting have been exaggerated. According to one review (French & Jeffrey, 1994), dieting is not usually associated with nutritional deficiencies, adverse physiological reactions, severe psychological reactions, or the development of eating disorders. Such problems can arise, but ordinarily they don't.

Sleep Disorders

Common sleep disorders include insomnia, circadian rhythm disorders, nightmares, night terrors, and sleepwalking. The last three tend to afflict children; therefore, they will be discussed under childhood disorders in Chapter 15.

Insomnia   Insomnia, the chronic inability to sleep, is rarely discussed in textbooks on abnormal psychology except as a symptom of other disorders, such as depression, yet, for an extremely large number of people, sleeplessness is the sole complaint, and one that causes severe physical and psychological distress. Sleeping problems affect an estimated 14 to 25 percent of the population. Women are at higher risk than men, and older people are at considerably higher risk than younger people.

There are three broad patterns of insomnia. Some people take an extremely long time to fall asleep; others fall asleep easily but awaken repeatedly during the night; others fall asleep easily but wake up much too early in the morning (e.g., 3 or 4 A.M.) and are unable to fall asleep again. At some point in our lives, each of us has probably experienced one of these difficulties. The term *insomnia* is applied only if the problem persists and the person's daily functioning is clearly disturbed—by fatigue, irritability, inability to concentrate, and so forth—as a result.

Sleep disturbance is almost always a source of concern for the person experiencing it, and this concern leads to what is called *anticipatory anxiety*. The minute the person gets into bed, or even while undressing, he or she begins to worry: Will I be able to sleep? Will it be like last night? And, since worry of any kind impedes sleep, the person probably *will* have another night like last night. Hence, insomnia is a classic example of the vicious cycle.

Insomnia can stem from many factors, including drugs, alcohol, caffeine, nicotine, stress and anxiety, physical illness, psychological disturbance, inactivity, poor sleep environment, and poor sleep habits (Bootzin & Perlis, 1992). It may also be a subjective matter in part. Many insomniacs underestimate the amount of sleep they get, at least as measured by instruments such as EEGs. When the gap between reported and measured sleep is extreme, this condition is called *sleep-state misperception*. Some cases of sleep-state misperception seem to be due to an inability to distinguish between sleep states and going-to-sleep states. People who go on thinking, during sleep, about problems that were on their minds during the day are likely to believe that they weren't sleeping but were still in that twilight stage between waking and sleep (Engle-Friedman, Baker, & Bootzin, 1985). Actually, what insomnia experts call sleep, based on EEG brain-wave patterns, is simply an operational definition. People who are "asleep" by EEG criteria often, if you wake them up, say that they are awake. Still, this happens far more often with insomniacs than with good sleepers

This multiple-exposure image conveys some of the frustration and exhaustion of insomnia. Treatment of this condition with hypnotic drugs is tricky, because withdrawal from "sleeping pills" can involve the return of insomnia, along with the onset of other symptoms.

(Borkovec, Lane & VanOot, 1981). And, by measures other than the EEG, some of these insomniacs *are* awake. In one experiment, a group of insomniacs "slept" (by EEG criteria) while, every four or five minutes, a voice on a tape, speaking at normal volume, said a letter of the alphabet. If awakened and asked to repeat the last letter spoken, some of the subjects were able to give the right answer (Engle-Friedman, Baker, & Bootzin, 1985). Such evidence suggests that, at least for some insomniacs, the critical problem may be hypervigilance. That is, they are less able than the rest of us to turn off the sounds of the night while asleep.

Until recently, the most widely used **hypnotics,** or sleeping pills—Dalmane (flurazepam), Halcion (triazolam), and Restoril (temazepam)—were benzodiazepines, which cause numerous problems: daytime sedation, memory loss, a synergistic effect with alcohol, and a high rebound rate upon withdrawal (Maxmen & Ward, 1995). Like the benzodiazepines prescribed for anxiety, they differ in their effects, depending on whether they are short- or long-acting. Dalmane, because it is long-acting, produces more daytime grogginess but less rebound. Halcion, because it is short-acting, has the opposite profile: it causes less grogginess but it can involve severe rebound—not just insomnia but acute daytime anxiety, sometimes escalating to panic attacks. Restoril is intermediate between short- and long-acting, but it does not reach its peak effectiveness until more than an hour after it is taken. Therefore, Restoril is generally prescribed when the sleep problem consists of waking during the night, Halcion when the problem is *falling* asleep. Dalmane is often avoided because of the daytime grogginess, but it is resorted to if the patient doesn't respond to the other drugs.

All the benzodiazepine hypnotics have the additional disadvantage of altering the "architecture" of sleep—our passage through the various stages of sleep in the course of the night. In particular, they all suppress REM sleep, with the result, in some cases, that the patient experiences REM *rebound*—restless sleep, nightmares—when he or she tries to go to bed without taking the drug. And, in most cases, withdrawal from the drug means a return to insomnia (Maxmen & Ward, 1995).

Because of these drawbacks, and because benzodiazepines are often diverted onto the illegal drug market, efforts have been made to stem their use. Some drugs have been removed from the market. (Halcion's side effects and rebound potential have caused it to be banned in Britain.) In other cases, laws have been changed to make these drugs harder to prescribe. In New York State, for example, benzodiazepines can be obtained only through "triplicate prescription." For every prescription, there must be three copies: the physician keeps one, the pharmacy retains the second, and a third is sent to the state regulatory agency. This cumbersome procedure, with its implication of supervision, was intended to discourage physicians from prescribing benzodiazepines, and it has done so. But, while the number of benzodiazepine prescriptions has diminished, the number of prescriptions for barbiturates, which are generally more dangerous, has increased (Shader, Greenblatt, & Balter, 1991). Apparently, when people cannot sleep, drugs are what they turn to, though behavioral therapy has proven to be more effective than medication for severe insomnia.

An encouraging recent development has been the introduction of Ambien (zolpidem), a hypnotic that is not a benzodiazepine. Ambien is short-acting and is absorbed very quickly. Therefore, it is useful primarily for sleep-onset disorders. Most crucial, however, is the fact that it has far fewer side effects than the benzodiazepines. It does not have a synergistic effect with alcohol; it does not alter the architecture of sleep; it does not produce rebound or severe withdrawal. As a result, it is now very popular. In 1994, less than a year after its approval by the FDA, Ambien became the most frequently prescribed hypnotic in the United States.

Most sleep-inducing drugs are ineffective when used over a long period, and many of them have undesirable side effects. Hence, there is a great need for treatments that can compete with drugs. Insight therapy may be helpful for those whose insomnia is part of a larger psychological problem, but, for those whose major or only problem is insomnia, the best route now available is probably behavioral therapy, which typically combines learning to relax with strengthening the habit of falling asleep at bedtime (Bootzin & Perlis, 1992).

Circadian Rhythm Disorders   **Circadian rhythm disorders** occur when people try to sleep at times that are inconsistent with circadian rhythms, the cycles dictated by their "biological clocks." Sometimes the disorder is due to work shifts. We noted earlier that many late-shift workers try, on their days off, to wake up at the same time as their friends and families, thus derailing their sleep cycles. Other workers' cycles are disturbed by rotating shifts. In both cases, the result is often reduced sleep, drowsiness on the job, and health problems. But circadian rhythm disorders are not limited to shift workers. Many people, for no external reason, fall asleep earlier or later than seems to them normal or desirable. They get a good night's sleep, but not when they want to. Age is often a factor in this pattern. Many young people lie awake at

2 A.M., while old people fall asleep after dinner and then wake up at 3 A.M. Such problems, which can be very distressing, are sometimes treated by *chronotherapy*, which involves moving bedtime later and later in regular increments. For example, a "night person" who regularly goes to sleep at 3 A.M. is told to put off going to sleep until 6 A.M., then the next day until 9 A.M., and so on, until, by moving bedtime around the clock, he or she reaches the desired bedtime. Once the target bedtime is reached, however, it must be adhered to strictly, for there is a tendency to drift back to the former pattern (Czeisler, Richardson, Coleman, et al., 1981). Another therapy that appears promising for circadian rhythm disorders is light treatment. To move bedtime earlier, the person is exposed to bright light in the morning; to move bedtime later, lights are used in the evening. This treatment is still new, but it has been shown to help shift workers, jet-lag sufferers, "night people," and elderly people suffering from early-morning waking (Bootzin, Manber, Perlis, et al., 1993; Czeisler, Kronauer, Allen, et al., 1989).

Groups at Risk

Gender

Although, in the United States, coronary heart disease is the leading cause of death for both men and women, the risk is higher for men. In animal studies, the male primates that were fed an atherogenic diet (a diet high in saturated fat and cholesterol) developed coronary heart disease in greater numbers than did the females on the same diet (Kaplan, Adams, Clarkson, et al., 1984). Two primary hypotheses have been proposed to explain gender differences in the risk of coronary heart disease (Matthews, 1989). One is that reproductive hormones, particularly estrogen, exert a protective effect on lipids and blood pressure in females. There is moderate support for this hypothesis. Women whose ovaries have been surgically removed generally show higher rates of coronary heart disease, compared with those of control groups. Postmenopausal women also show higher rates of coronary heart disease than premenopausal women. And, finally, women who take hormone replacement therapy show reduced rates of coronary heart disease, compared with women who do not.

The second hypothesis is that men more frequently engage in potentially health-damaging behaviors, including smoking and drinking alcohol. But epidemiological studies suggest that the differential rates of coronary heart disease among men and women are not attributable to the effects of these behavioral risk factors. Matthews (1989) has proposed a more complicated, interactive model in which men and women differ in their experience of stressors (in their number, frequency, and type), as well as in their cardiovascular, neuroendocrine, and metabolic responses to stressors. Over time, the complex interplay of these differences produces different rates of coronary heart disease in the two genders. There is some support for this model. In laboratory studies of married couples solving problems, the women's cardiovascular responses were found to be associated with their husbands' expressions of hostility rather than with their own hostility, while the men's cardiovascular responsivity was more associated with their own hostility (Smith & Brown, 1991). In a similar study, the wives showed greater reductions in immune function in response to a marital discussion than did their husbands (Kiecolt-Glaser, Malarkey, Chee, et al., 1993).

Race

As a group, African Americans experience higher infant mortality rates, a shorter life expectancy, and higher rates of death from homicide, cancer, stroke, diabetes, and liver disease than do Caucasian Americans. They also have higher rates of hypertension than whites and, consequently, higher rates of morbidity and mortality from coronary heart disease, stroke, and renal disease. Finally, African Americans have higher rates of obesity than whites (Kumanyika, 1987), as well as higher blood pressure—a difference that applies to both men and women.

The data on racial differences in cardiovascular reactivity (thought to be a potential risk factor for coronary heart disease) are mixed. Some studies show hyperreactivity among African Americans, while others do not. African Americans are generally more sensitive to sodium, which suggests that the typical Western diet, high in sodium, is particularly deleterious to them. Blood pressure changes in response to stressful stimuli may have a different underlying pathophysiology in different racial groups (Anderson, 1989).

Finally, race influences socioeconomic status in the United States: African Americans have significantly lower socioeconomic status than whites on all measures (Anderson & Armstead, 1995). As is noted in the following section, socioeconomic status is an important predictor of health. At almost all levels, African Americans show higher mortality and morbidity rates than whites, a disparity that is particularly striking at the low end of the socioeconomic scale (Anderson & Armstead, 1995).

Socioeconomic Status

Socioeconomic status—education, income, and employment level—has long been identified as a factor in determining health. Individuals of low socioeconomic status show poorer health and greater risk of early death than those of high socioeconomic status (see Figure 8.1). While health behaviors—smoking, diet, exercise, and obesity—differ according to socioeconomic status, they do not fully account for the disparity between groups, nor do documented differences in access to and quality of medical care (Adler, Boyce, Chesney, et al., 1993). Some data suggest that the association between socioeconomic status and health may be a function of the greater emotional impact of stressful life events on individuals of lower socioeconomic status, compared with those of higher status (Anderson & Armstead, 1995).

The relationship between socioeconomic status and coronary heart disease is independent of other traditional risk factors and appears to affect the development and progression of coronary heart disease. Though coronary heart disease rates have been declining in recent years, epidemiological studies suggest that the declines may be specific to high socioeconomic groups. Low socioeconomic status is associated with other risk factors for coronary heart disease, including smoking, obesity, elevated cholesterol levels, and hypertension. But those factors do not fully account for the consistently negative relationship observed between socioeconomic status and coronary heart disease (Kaplan & Kell, 1993). Recent data suggest that differences in the psychological aspects of the work environment, particularly low control over decision making and low skill requirements, may account for the inverse relationship between socioeconomic status and coronary heart disease (Marmot, Bosma, Hemingway, et al., 1997).

Finally, a few studies of survival and recovery from acute cardiac events suggest an association between socioeconomic status and survival. For example, in one study, social class was inversely associated with functional improvement in the year following an acute myocardial infarction (Ickovics, Viscoli, & Horwitz, 1997). The effects of social class were found to be independent of the subjects' medical history, age, race, mental state, and life stress, as well as the severity of their heart attacks. Similar findings have been observed in patients who underwent cardiac diagnostic tests: over a 5-year period, lower socioeconomic status was associated with increased risk for death from coronary heart disease (Williams, Barefoot, Califf, et al., 1992).

Stress and Illness: Theory and Therapy

The Behavioral Perspective

Respondent Versus Operant   For years it was generally accepted that autonomic responses were involuntary. Therefore, if conditioning were involved in the disregulation of these responses, it would have to be respondent conditioning, for operant conditioning requires that the organism be capable of voluntarily modifying responses in order to obtain rewards or avoid punishments. We now know that respondent conditioning can have a powerful effect on physio-

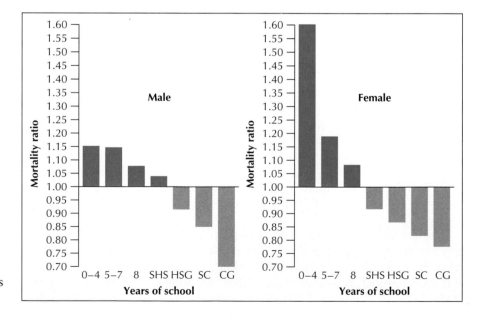

FIGURE 8.1   Mortality ratio (observed to expected deaths) by education. SHS indicates some high school; HSG, high school graduate; SC, some college; and CG, college graduate. (Journal of the American Medical Informatics Association (JAMIA) June 1993)

logical responses. A problem with cancer patients, for example, is that in response to chemotherapy they develop conditioned nausea and immune dysfunction. In a study of 20 women receiving chemotherapy for ovarian cancer, the women were tested first at home and then at the hospital. Even though the hospital tests were done before the chemotherapy, the women still showed an increase in nausea and a decrease in immune activity—clearly a conditioned response and one that does not aid in recovery (Bovjberg, Redd, Maier, et al., 1990).

Until about 30 years ago, such respondent behaviors were all that behaviorists could point to as an explanation for stress-related illness, and they were not a very comprehensive explanation. Then, in the 1960s, a series of breakthrough experiments with rats showed that not only heart rate but also blood pressure and urine formation could be modified through operant conditioning (Miller, 1969). One rat was even taught to dilate the blood vessels in one ear and, at the same time, constrict the blood vessels in the other ear in response to a cue (Di Cara & Miller, 1968). Clearly, some autonomic responses could not only be controlled but controlled with great precision.

This discovery had two important consequences. First, it helped to explain how learning could operate in the development of physical disorders: if the disorder had any rewarding consequences, then these consequences might be maintaining the disorder through operant conditioning. Second, whether or not voluntary control was involved in the development of the disorder, it could be enlisted to relieve the disorder.

Biofeedback, Relaxation, and Exercise Since these early experiments, it has been found that the physiological responses underlying many physical disorders can be partially controlled if patients are first trained to recognize these responses in their bodies—to know what it "feels like" when their heart rate or blood pressure, for example, goes up and down. Given this information, the patient can then *make* it go up and down. This training is known as **biofeedback training.** Migraine patients, for example, are hooked up to a machine that gives them feedback on temperature and blood flow in their hands. (Whatever the implications of the serotonin hypothesis, many migraine patients obtain relief when blood flows away from the head toward the periphery [Blanchard & Andrasik, 1985].) The patients, in other words, are given immediate feedback on their bodily functioning, and then, through a process we do not yet understand, they begin to exert control over this functioning—a control that it is hoped will extend beyond the biofeedback laboratory, into their daily lives. Indeed, biofeedback has proved quite

helpful with headaches (NIH Technology Assessment Panel, 1996).

Another technique that behaviorists have used extensively in stress-relief programs is **relaxation training.** There are several procedures for inducing deep muscle relaxation, but perhaps the most popular is *progressive relaxation,* developed by E. Jacobson (1938). In this technique, the client, going from muscle group to muscle group within the body, is instructed to contract the muscles, to hold them that way for about 10 seconds, and then to release them, thus achieving a state of relaxation. The object is to teach the person, first, how to distinguish between tension and relaxation and, second, how to achieve the latter. With practice in this technique, many people, as soon as they feel themselves going tense, can relax their bodies—a great aid in combating stress. Relaxation training has been used for years, successfully, in treating a wide variety of conditions—depression, anxiety disorders, insomnia—that involve stress. Researchers have found that it can also stimulate immune functioning, as has been shown in studies of older people (Kiecolt-Glaser, Glaser, Williger, et al., 1985) and of HIV patients (Rutenfanz, Haider, & Koller, 1985).

Finally, exercise can relieve stress, as was shown in an interesting experiment with men who had signed up for HIV testing. Half these men were assigned to a 5-week aerobic exercise program, the other half to no intervention. Then they waited for their HIV-status results. Their immune functions were tested a week before they received their results and again a week after. Not surprisingly, many of the men who were found to be HIV-positive showed decreased immune activity, together with anxiety and depression, but, as it turned out, these were the men in the no-intervention group. The results for the HIV-positive men in

Research has shown that exercise can reduce stress and bolster the immune system.

the exercise group were roughly the same as for the men who were HIV-negative: no emotional or immunological change (LaPerriere, Antoni, Schneiderman, et al., 1990).

The Cognitive Perspective

Predictability and Control   With stress, as with anxiety, the cognitive theorists have pointed out that there is more to the process than simply stimulus and response. Two cognitive variables that seem to be particularly important in stress reactions are the person's ability to predict the stressful stimulus and his or her sense of control over the stimulus. As research has shown, predictable stimuli are less stressful than unpredictable stimuli. This principle was borne out during the London blitz of World War II. Londoners, who were bombed regularly and frequently, experienced very few serious stress reactions, whereas people in the countryside, who were bombed far less frequently but unpredictably, often responded with severe anxiety (Vernon, 1941).

Even more important than predictability, however, seems to be the sense of control. Remember the rats who were implanted with cancer cells. Remarkably, the rats who were able to control the shock were as likely to reject the cancer as those who received no shock (Visintainer, Volpicelli, & Seligman, 1982). This study's applicability to humans as well has been shown experimentally. The point is not just that by coping we can actually solve the problems that create stress; coping also affects our physiological responses to stress. Researchers have found that decreased catecholamine levels, which are associated with depression, were also associated with subjective judgments of inability to cope and that, as people's sense of their coping ability increased, so did their catecholamine level (Bandura, Taylor, & Williams, 1985). According to PNI researchers, coping also affects the immune system. Poor coping suppresses immune responses; good coping enhances them (Kiecolt-Glaser, Fisher, Ogrocki, et al., 1987). Thus, effective coping not only keeps people healthy; it probably also helps them get better once they fall ill (Rodin & Salovey, 1989).

In all cases, however, according to cognitive researchers, coping is connected to cognitive processes and is determined by cognitive styles. This interaction is the focus of the model of stress developed by Richard Lazarus and his research group (Folkman, Lazarus, Dunkel-Schetter, et al., 1986; Lazarus & Folkman, 1984). The model describes stress not as something in the person or something in the environment but as a dynamic, mutually reciprocal, bidirectional relationship between the two, involving six basic factors. One is the *environmental event* itself.

Another is the *primary appraisal* of that event, in which the person decides whether he or she has anything at stake in the event. The event may be irrelevant (the person has no stake in the event), benign-positive (a good stake), or stressful (a potentially bad stake). A third factor in Lazarus' model is *secondary appraisal;* having decided that there is something at stake, the person determines whether he or she can influence the situation. The fourth factor is *coping,* which may be either problem-focused (taking action to change the situation) or emotion-focused (e.g., seeking social support). Coping and appraisal are linked in a constant back-and-forth dynamic: the person appraises, copes, appraises the feedback, copes again, and so on. The fifth factor involves the *outcomes of coping.* These may be physiological (ANS arousal, immune system activation), behavioral (changes in high-risk behaviors), and cognitive (changed goals or beliefs). Finally, the sixth factor consists of *health outcomes,* such as illness or if one copes effectively prevention, illness reporting, and/or recovery. Conceptually, the value of this model is its interactive nature, but it also has a practical benefit: because it is broken down into multiple factors, with multiple reappraisals, it offers second and third chances for improved coping.

Stress Management Intervention   Cognitive principles have been put into practice in so-called stress management programs (Meichenbaum & Jaremko, 1983). The goal of such programs is to pinpoint the cognitive and environmental sources of the patient's stress and then to build up the skills that he or she needs in order to cope with those stressors. If the person complains of being pushed around by others, for example, assertiveness training can help the person avoid being pushed around. Likewise, people who feel overwhelmed by demands on their time may be given help with time management. Most patients are also instructed in muscle relaxation, either through the contracting-and-relaxing technique or through meditation. The newer psychological treatments for people with serious illnesses often involve such training. Stress management was part of the Fawzy team's group therapy for malignant melanoma patients, for example (Fawzy, Fawzy, Hyun, et al., 1993).

Similar programs have been used with Type As, teaching them how to cope with stress more effectively. In one such program, for example, a group of Type As who had survived one heart attack were trained in relaxation, self-control, and goal setting. Over a 3-year period, only 7 percent of these subjects suffered a second heart attack, compared with 13 percent of a control group that received only the customary medical treatment (Friedman, Thoresen, Gill, et al., 1986).

The addition of stress management and psychosocial intervention to routine cardiac rehabilitation programs has been shown to reduce patients' psychological distress (depression and anxiety) and to lower their heart rate, blood pressure, and cholesterol levels (Linden, Stossel, & Maurice, 1996). Over a 2-year period, cardiac patients who received psychosocial intervention along with routine cardiac rehabilitation showed a lower death rate and a 46 percent reduction in nonfatal cardiac events. This analysis of many studies suggests that such interventions are quite powerful, despite wide variability in length and type of treatment and in the person delivering it.

Cognitive-behavioral stress management intervention has also been provided to gay men awaiting the results of their HIV tests (Antoni, Baggett, Ironson, et al., 1991). The program included relaxation training, cognitive restructuring, assertiveness training, and health education; a group of control subjects received no intervention. Psychological distress and immune functioning were assessed after 5 weeks of treatment, before notification of the test results, and again 2 weeks after notification. In the control group, the HIV-positive subjects showed twice the level of depression as the HIV-positive subjects in the stress management program. Although the HIV-positive subjects in the control group showed no change in their immune function following notification, the HIV-positives in the intervention program actually improved their immune function. The individuals who practiced relaxation more frequently showed the greatest improvement in their immune function.

The Psychodynamic Perspective

Psychological Inhibition Psychodynamic theorists, as we have seen, regard most behavior as symptomatic of buried emotional content. Thus, it comes as no surprise that the psychodynamic school was the first to recognize that psychological difficulties might contribute significantly to physical illness. Traditionally, psychodynamic theorists have referred to stress-related physical disorders as *organ neuroses*. As the term suggests, psychodynamic theory regards these disorders as caused by the same mechanisms—repression, anxiety, defense—that cause the anxiety, somatoform, and dissociative disorders. Accordingly, they would be treated by the same therapy: excavation of the repressed material, catharsis, the working out of better defenses. Where a serious physical illness is involved, however, a psychodynamic therapist would also insist on the patient's receiving medical treatment at the same time.

Psychodynamic theorists regard family interactions as central to stress-related physical disorders, as they are to all other psychological disorders. And they may be correct, for these disorders tend to run in families. Migraine and hypertension are more common in families of people with these disorders than in the population at large, though this might be a function of shared genes rather than, or as well as, shared emotional distress.

Inhibition of the expression of emotion has long been thought to contribute to the development of many "psychosomatic" diseases, including cancer and hypertension. Recent work has extended this concept to psychological inhibition, or the inhibition of emotional, social, and behavioral impulses. In a study of gay men, Steve Cole and colleagues (1996) found that, over a 5-year period, the men who did not reveal their homosexuality were at increased risk of developing infectious diseases and cancer. The rate of disease incidence increased in proportion to the degree to which the individuals concealed their homosexuality (Cole, Kemeny, Taylor, et al., 1996). These effects were found to be independent of other factors, including demographic variables, depression, other negative affect, and the tendency to inhibit emotions. In another study, the same group of investigators found that, in HIV-positive gay men who concealed their homosexuality, the infection progressed faster than in those who did not conceal their sexual orientation.

The Value of Catharsis A psychodynamic principle that has been confirmed by PNI research is the value of emotional catharsis to physical health. In one experiment, 50 undergraduates at Southern Methodist University were asked to keep journals for 20 minutes a day for 4 days. Half the students agreed to write about personal or traumatic events, and some of the entries they produced were quite painful: accounts of homesickness, family quarrels, family violence. The other half of the students were asked to write on trivial topics, which were assigned each day. (On one day, they were asked to describe the shoes they were wearing, on another to tell about a party they had recently attended.) At the beginning of the experiment, there were no differences in immune function between the groups, but there were by the end. The immune cells of the traumatic-journal students were more active than those of the trivial-journal students, and these differences had an impact on health. Six weeks after the journal keeping, the experimenters checked the students' health center records for the period before and after the journal assignment. Compared with the trivial-journal students, the traumatic-journal students showed a significant drop in clinic visits after the experiment (Pennebaker, Kiecolt-Glaser, & Glaser, 1988).

These results have been supported by experiments with other groups of students (Esterling, Antoni, Kuman, et al., 1990) and with working adults, who showed a reduction in sick days after keeping "traumatic" journals (Pennebaker, 1990). For many people, expressing emotion is a healthy activity. According to James Pennebaker (1993), the originator of this research, what is most crucial is the expression of *negative* emotion. This was confirmed by the Fawzy group's malignant melanoma study. In that experiment, the group-therapy patients who showed the best outcomes in terms of recurrence and survival were those who had expressed the most emotional distress before beginning the therapy (Fawzy, Fawzy, Hyun, et al., 1993).

The Family Systems Perspective

Several theorists claim that a major source of physical illness is the stress imposed by modern industrial societies. One such stress is the disruption of marriage and the family. The number of single-person households in the United States has multiplied many times in the past century. And, according to an impressive array of findings, people living alone, if they have no regular social support, are depriving themselves of potent protection against illness. As we saw earlier, married cancer patients survive longer than the unmarried, and there is good evidence that social support also helps people combat many other illnesses, as well as injuries (Cohen, Doyle, Skoner, et al., 1997; House, Landis, & Umberson, 1988; Uchino, Caccioppo, & Kiecolt-Glaser, 1996). There is also strong evidence that people without social support are more prone to disease. Among the leading causes of premature death in our society are heart disease, cancer, stroke, cirrhosis of the liver, hypertension, and pneumonia. For each of these disorders, without exception, premature death rates are significantly higher in the unmarried than in the married. In the case of coronary heart disease, our society's major killer, the death rate, depending on age group, is 2 to 5 times higher among the unmarried (Lynch, 1977). While the lack of an intimate relationship may predispose people to disease, the *loss* of such a relationship may be an even greater health hazard. In a study of 400 cancer patients, 72 percent had suffered the loss of an important personal relationship within 8 years prior to the diagnosis of cancer, compared with 10 percent of a control group for a comparable period (LeShan, 1966a).

Recent analyses of data collected in a 70-year longitudinal study concluded in 1991 have confirmed that individuals who remain married live longer than those who experience divorce or separation—but not longer than those who never marry (Tucker, Friedman, Wingard, et al., 1996). The impact of a marital breakup was evident, despite the number of years the subjects had been married. The researchers concluded that marital breakup was a stressful event that had long-term health risks, risks not entirely reduced by remarriage. But the apparent protective effects of marriage may be due partially to selection factors, which account for the stability of a marriage. The subjects who exhibited low conscientiousness in childhood or who had witnessed their parents' divorce were less likely to remain married, and more likely to die sooner, than the others.

The Sociocultural Perspective

In addition to the breakup of the family, other broad changes in our society appear to be affecting the susceptibility of certain groups to particular illnesses. For example, ulcers were once 4 times as prevalent among men as among women. This ratio has now been reduced to about 2 to 1, presumably because more women are now doing the same work as men and, therefore, are exposed to the same stressors. As this change in the workplace continues, it is possible that the sex differential for ulcers will disappear altogether. Likewise, if the fact that African Americans are twice as likely as whites to develop hypertension is due to the stresses of being a disadvantaged minority rather than to genes (or to a salt-heavy diet, another possibility), this ratio, too, may be equalized as opportunities are equalized.

The Biological Perspective

Genetic Predisposition   As we have seen, stress-related physical disorders tend to run in families—a fact that suggests genetic risk. This is true of migraine and hypertension. As we saw earlier, people with at least one hypertensive parent show greater cardiovascular reactions to stress than do people without a family history of hypertension. This evidence is supported by twin studies, which have found exaggerated reactivity to be more commonly shared between MZ twins than between DZ twins or siblings (Rose & Chesney, 1986). Because we know from longitudinal studies that people with heightened cardiovascular reactivity are at risk for hypertension (Menkes, Matthews, Krantz, et al., 1989), early identification and treatment of stress-reactive people should help to prevent this disorder. The cardiovascular reactivity hypothesis may also help in early intervention. Type As tend to breed Type As (Plomin & Rende, 1991), so it is possible to identify and help them before they develop the heart problems to which some of them are clearly predisposed.

PNI and Interactive Theories Apart from genetic risk, the major concern of recent biological research has been a matter that we have already discussed at length in this chapter: the immune system. The PNI findings, combined with interactive models such as those of Schwartz, Weiner, and Lazarus, have basically overturned our conceptualization of stress and illness. In other chapters of this book, there may be close ties between the various perspectives, but in this chapter the division into perspectives indicates nothing more than slight differences of focus. No one in the field claims that there is one cause, or even one kind of cause. The subject itself—stress and illness—is interactive, and the most promising theories are all cat's cradles of intersecting causes. Consider Fig-

ures 8.2 and 8.3, which were adapted from the work of Sheldon Cohen (of the cold research) and Gail Williamson. Figure 8.2 shows the relationship between stress and the onset of infectious disease. Figure 8.3 shows the relationship between stress and the reactivation of latent pathogens (disease-causing agents), such as HIV or a herpes virus. For purposes of clarity, feedback loops are not indicated, but, even in this simplified form, what the figures show are highly intricate systems, including physical, behavioral, and emotional causes. Researchers on stress and illness face a complicated problem but, by accepting this fact, they have begun producing very exciting findings.

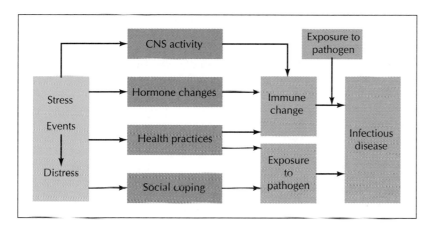

FIGURE 8.2 Model for the relationship between stress and the onset of infectious disease. (Adapted from Cohen & Williamson, 1991, p. 8)

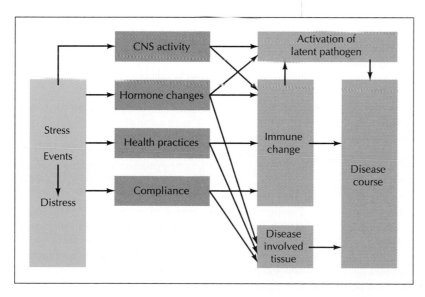

FIGURE 8.3 Model linking stress to the reactivation of latent pathogens and to the severity of the ongoing disease. (Adapted from Cohen & Williamson, 1991, p. 8)

KEY TERMS

acquired immune deficiency
    syndrome (AIDS), 221
biofeedback training, 229
circadian rhythm disorders,
    226
coronary heart disease, 216
essential hypertension, 219
feedback, 215

health psychology, 208
human immunodeficiency
    virus (HIV), 221
hypertension, 219
hypnotics, 226
immune system, 212
individual response
    specificity, 210

insomnia, 225
migraine headache, 222
mind-body problem, 208
muscle-contraction
    headaches, 222
negative feedback, 215
obesity, 223
oscillations, 215

psychoneuroimmunology
    (PNI), 212
psychophysiological
    disorders, 208
relaxation training, 229
stimulus specificity, 210
stress, 210
Type A, 218

SUMMARY

- The mind-body problem—the relationship between mental and physical processes—has been debated for centuries. Until recently, science endorsed dualism, drawing a sharp line between physical and psychological disorders. Stress-related illnesses were regarded as exceptions to the rule. However, new research has demonstrated that state of mind influences diseases ranging from the common cold to cancer. Health psychology, or behavioral medicine, takes the holistic view that mind and body are one and that the course of *any* illness can be influenced by psychological factors.

- Stress can be defined in terms of the stimulus, the person's response, or the person's appraisal of the stimulus. Physiological reaction to stress depends on the specific type of stress, the person's characteristic mode of responding to stress, and his or her general level of reactivity.

- Researchers who study the physiological changes associated with emotion focus on the autonomic nervous system (ANS), which mobilizes the body to meet environmental challenges and then (usually) reverses these processes to permit the body to build energy resources. Some of the most interesting research comes from the subfield of psychoneuroimmunology (PNI). The immune system defends the body against "invaders" by circulating a large and varied number of small white blood cells, called lymphocytes, that identify foreign bodies and either attack them directly or produce antibodies to do so. When the immune system is not functioning properly, health is compromised. PNI research has shown that immune functioning may decline after major events, whether sudden shock (the death of a spouse) or chronic stress (caring for a spouse with Alzheimer's); minor events (such as final exams); and laboratory stressors (frustrating tests, induced marital conflict).

- Researchers who study coronary heart disease, hypertension, cancer, AIDS, headaches, obesity, and sleep disorders have paid special attention to psychological factors. Coronary heart disease, the number one cause of death in the United States, is influenced by a complex interplay of biological, psychological, and social factors, including family history of the disease, lifestyle, and stress level. Hypertension, or chronic high blood pressure, has been linked to anger and hostility, occupa-

tional stress, and family history. Cancer may not be caused by stress, but several studies have found that cancer patients who participate in group therapy, as well as receive medical treatment, live longer than controls, perhaps because they are better able to overcome feelings of hopelessness. With AIDS, however, therapy may be more successful in preventing risky behavior than in slowing progress of the disease. Migraine headache, once thought to arise from psychological causes, is now thought to be largely biogenic. Obesity is influenced by both genetic factors, such as metabolic rate, and behavioral factors, such as eating habits and activity level. There is no single explanation of sleep disorders (insomnia and circadian rhythm problems), but behavioral therapies often are the most effective treatment.

- Gender, race, and socioeconomic status put certain groups at risk for disease. Men are at higher risk for coronary heart disease than are women. African Americans are at higher risk than whites for a wide range of diseases, from hypertension and heart disease to diabetes. And people of low socioeconomic status are particularly prone to coronary heart disease.

- The behaviorist perspective emphasizes the role of respondent and operant conditioning in the disregulation of ANS responses. Behavioral therapists treat many disorders with biofeedback, relaxation training, and exercise, which can stimulate the immune system.

- The cognitive perspective emphasizes the person's ability to predict stressful events and his or her sense of control. Lazarus' dynamic model identifies six factors in coping with stress, from the event to the health outcome. Stress management programs help people to pinpoint the stage at which they experience stress and to develop appropriate coping skills.

- Psychodynamic theorists emphasize the role of unconscious conflicts; the goal of psychodynamic therapy is catharsis. Research shows that catharsis, in "traumatic" journals or group therapy, can boost immune function and aid recovery, even from cancer.

- Family systems theorists emphasize the role of the family in supporting health. Couples who remain married for life, for instance, live longer than those who separate or divorce.

- The sociocultural perspective focuses on the role of social change—especially family breakdown and women's entry into the workforce—in stress-related physical disorders.

- The biological perspective emphasizes the role of heredity and, increasingly, the immune system in stress and illness. It highlights complex patterns of interaction among psychological and biological factors.

Chapter 9

Paula Stansky was a 57-year-old woman, widow and mother of four children, who was hospitalized . . . because, according to her children, she was refusing to eat and take care of herself.

The patient . . . was described as a usually cheerful, friendly woman who took meticulous care of her home. . . . About two months prior to her hospitalization, however, her younger children reported a change in their mother's usual disposition, for no apparent reason. She appeared more easily fatigued, not as cheerful, and lackadaisical about her housework. Over the course of the next few weeks, she stopped going to church and canceled her usual weekly bingo outing with neighborhood women. As the house became increasingly neglected and their mother began to spend more time sleeping or rocking in her favorite chair, apparently preoccupied, the younger children called their married brother and sister for advice. . . .

When her son, in response to the telephone call, arrived at her house, Ms. Stansky denied that anything was wrong. She claimed to be only tired, "possibly the flu." For the ensuing week, her children tried to "cheer her up," but with no success. After several days had gone by without her taking a bath, changing her clothes, or eating any food, her children put her in the car and drove her to the hospital. . . .

On admission, Ms. Stansky was mostly mute, answering virtually no questions except correctly identifying the hospital and the day of the week. She cried periodically throughout the interview, but only shook her head back and forth when asked if she could tell the interviewer what she was feeling or thinking about. She was agitated, frequently wringing her hands, rolling her head toward the ceiling, and rocking in her chair. . . . Her children indicated that during the past week she had been waking up at 3:00 A.M., unable to fall back to sleep. She also seemed to them to have lost considerable weight. (Spitzer, Skodol, Gibbon, et al., 1983, p. 118)

Many of us go through occasional periods of dejection, where life seems grey and nothing seems worth doing. Some of us have also known the opposite state, a mood of excitement and recklessness in which we become feverishly active and think we can accomplish anything. In other words, **depression** and **mania**, in mild and temporary forms, are part of ordinary existence. In some cases, however, such mood swings become so prolonged and extreme that the person's life is seriously disrupted. These conditions are known as the **mood disorders,** or *affective disorders, affect* meaning "emotion."

The mood disorders have been recognized and written about since the beginning of the history of medicine. Both depression and mania were described in detail by Hippocrates in the fourth century B.C. As early as the first century A.D., Greek physician Aretaeus observed that manic and depressive behaviors sometimes occurred in the same person and seemed to stem from a single disorder. In the early nineteenth century, Philippe Pinel (1801/1967), the reformer of Paris' mental hospitals (Chapter 1), wrote a compelling account of depression, using Roman Emperor Tiberius and French King Louis XI as illustrations. Depression has also been vividly described by some of its more famous victims. In one of his recurring episodes of depression, Abraham Lincoln wrote, "If what I feel were equally distributed to the whole human family, there would not be one cheerful face on earth."

Though they have been scrutinized for centuries, however, the mood disorders still remain something of a mystery. What is known about them will be outlined in the first section of this chapter. In the second section, we will turn our attention to suicide, which is often the result of depression. Finally, we will describe the theory and treatment of mood disorders according to various perspectives.

Depressive and Manic Episodes

One of the most striking features of the mood disorders is their episodic quality. Within a few weeks, or sometimes within a few days, a person who has been functioning normally is plunged into despair or is scaling the heights of mania. Once the episode has run its course, the person may return to normal or near-normal functioning, though he or she is likely to have further episodes of mood disturbance. The nature of the episode (whether depressive or manic), its severity, and its duration determine the diagnosis and often the treatment—matters we will discuss. For now, let us examine the typical features of severe depressive and manic episodes.

Major Depressive Episode

In some cases, a psychological trauma plunges a person into a **major depressive episode** overnight, but usually the onset of depression is gradual, occurring over a period of several weeks or several months. The episode itself typically lasts several months and then ends, as it began, gradually (Coryell, Akiskal, Leon, et al., 1994).

The person entering a depressive episode undergoes profound changes in most areas of his or her life—not just mood but also motivation, thinking, and physical and motor functioning. The following are the characteristic features of the major depressive episode, as described by *DSM-IV:*

1. *Depressed mood.* Almost all severely depressed adults report some degree of unhappiness, ranging from a mild melancholy to total hopelessness. Mildly or moderately depressed

people may have crying spells; severely depressed patients often say they feel like crying but cannot. Deeply depressed people see no way that they or anyone else can help them—a type of thinking that has been called the **helplessness-hopelessness syndrome.**

2. *Loss of pleasure or interest in usual activities.* Aside from depressed mood, the most common characteristic of a major depressive episode is loss of pleasure and, therefore, lack of interest, in one's accustomed activities. This loss of pleasure, known as **anhedonia,** is generally far-reaching. Whatever the person once liked to do—in the case history at the beginning of the chapter, for example, keep house, play bingo, go to church— no longer seems worth doing. Severely depressed patients may experience a complete "paralysis of the will"—an inability even to get out of bed in the morning.

3. *Disturbance of appetite.* Most depressives have poor appetite and lose weight. A minority, however, react by eating more and putting on weight. Whatever the weight change, whether loss or gain, that same change tends to recur with each depressive episode (Kendler, Eaves, Walters, et al., 1996).

Abraham Lincoln, whom many historians consider the greatest U.S. president, was subject to recurring bouts of severe depression.

4. *Sleep disturbance.* Insomnia is an extremely common feature of depression. Waking up too early and then being unable to get back to sleep is the most characteristic pattern, but depressed people may also have trouble falling asleep initially, or they may awaken repeatedly through- out the night. As with eating, however, sleep may increase rather than decrease, with the patient sleeping 15 hours a day or more. Depressives who sleep to excess are usually the same ones who eat to excess (Kendler, Eaves, Walters, et al., 1996).

5. *Psychomotor retardation or agitation.* Depression can usually be "read" immediately in the person's motor behavior and physical bearing. In the most common pattern, **retarded depression,** the patient seems overcome by fatigue. Posture is stooped, movement is slow and deliberate, gestures are kept to a minimum, and speech is low and halting, with long pauses before answering. In severe cases, depressives may fall into a mute stupor. More rarely, the symptoms take the opposite form, **agitated depression,** marked by incessant activity and restlessness—hand-wringing, pacing, and moaning.

6. *Loss of energy.* The depressive's reduced motivation is usually accompanied by a sharply reduced energy level. Without having done anything, he or she may feel exhausted all the time.

7. *Feelings of worthlessness and guilt.* Typically, depressives see themselves as deficient in whatever attributes they value most: intelligence, beauty, popularity, health. Their frequent complaints about loss—whether of love, material goods, money, or prestige—may also reflect their sense of personal inadequacy. Such feelings of worthlessness are often accompanied by a profound sense of guilt. Depressives seem to search the environment for evidence of problems they have created. If a child has trouble with schoolwork or the car has a flat tire, it is their fault.

8. *Difficulties in thinking.* In depression, mental processes, like physical processes, are usually slowed down. Depressives tend to be indecisive, and they often report difficulties in thinking, concentrating, and remembering. The harder a mental task, the more difficulty they have (Hartlage, Alloy, Vázquez, et al., 1993).

9. *Recurrent thoughts of death or suicide.* Not surprisingly, many depressives have recurrent thoughts of death and suicide. Often, they say that they (and everyone else) would be better off if they were dead.

Manic Episode

The typical **manic episode** begins rather suddenly, over the course of a few days, and is usually shorter than a depressive episode. A manic episode may last from several days to several months and then usually ends as abruptly as it began. *DSM-IV* describes the prominent features as follows:

1. *Elevated, expansive, or irritable mood.* The mood change is the essential, "diagnostic" feature of a manic episode. Typically, manics feel wonderful, see the world as an excellent place, and have limitless enthusiasm for whatever they are doing or plan to do. This expansiveness is usually mixed with irritability. Manics often see other people as slow, doltish spoilsports and can become quite hostile, especially if someone tries to interfere with their behavior. In some cases, irritability is the manic's dominant mood, with euphoria either intermittent or simply absent.

2. *Inflated self-esteem.* Manics tend to see themselves as extremely attractive, important, and powerful people, capable of great achievements in fields for which they may, in fact, have no aptitude whatsoever. They may begin composing symphonies, designing nuclear weapons, or calling the White House with advice on how to run the country.

3. *Sleeplessness.* The manic episode is almost always marked by a decreased need for sleep. Manics may sleep only two or three hours a night and yet have twice as much energy as those around them.

4. *Talkativeness.* Manics tend to talk loudly, rapidly, and constantly. Their speech is often full of puns, irrelevant details, and jokes that they alone find funny.

5. *Flight of ideas.* Manics often have racing thoughts. This is one reason they speak so rapidly—to keep up with the flow of their ideas. Manic speech also tends to shift abruptly from one topic to the next.

6. *Distractibility.* Manics are easily distracted. While doing or discussing one thing, they notice something else in the environment and abruptly turn their attention to that, instead.

7. *Hyperactivity.* The expansive mood is usually accompanied by restlessness and increased goal-directed activity—physical, social, occupational, and often sexual.

8. *Reckless behavior.* The euphoria and grandiose self-image of manics often lead them into impulsive actions: buying sprees, reckless driving, careless business investments, sexual indiscretions, and so forth. They are typically indifferent to the needs of others and think nothing of yelling in restaurants, calling friends in the middle of the night, or spending the family savings on a new Porsche.

The following is a clear-cut case of a manic episode:

> Terrence O'Reilly, a single 39-year-old transit authority clerk, was brought to the hospital in May, 1973, by the police after his increasingly hyperactive and bizarre behavior and nonstop talking alarmed his family. He loudly proclaimed that he was not in need of treatment, and threatened legal action against the hospital and police.
>
> The family reported that a month prior to admission Mr. O'Reilly took a leave of absence from his civil service job, purchased a large number of cuckoo clocks and then an expensive car which he planned to use as a mobile showroom for his wares, anticipating that he would make a great deal of money.
>
> He proceeded to "tear around town" buying and selling the clocks and other merchandise, and when he was not out, he was continuously on the phone making "deals." He rarely slept and, uncharacteristically, spent every evening in neighborhood bars drinking heavily and, according to him, "wheeling and dealing." Two weeks before admission his mother died suddenly of a heart attack. He cried for two days, but then his mood began to soar again. At the time of admission he was $3000 in debt and had driven his family to exhaustion.... He said, however, that he felt "on top of the world." (Spitzer, Skodol, Gibbon, et al., 1983, p. 115)

For a condition to be diagnosed as a manic episode, it must have lasted at least a week (or less, if hospitalization is required) and must have seriously interfered with the person's functioning. A briefer and less severe manic condition is called a *hypomanic episode*. On occasion, patients meet the diagnostic criteria for both manic episode and major depressive episode simultaneously. (For example, they show manic grandiosity and hyperactivity, yet weep and threaten suicide.) This combined pattern is called a *mixed episode*.

Mood Disorder Syndromes

Major Depressive Disorder

People who undergo one or more major depressive episodes, with no intervening periods of mania, are said to have **major depressive disorder.** This disorder is one of U.S. society's greatest mental health problems. Its prevalence in the United States during any given month is close to 4 percent of men and 6 percent for women.

The lifetime risk—that is, the percentage of Americans who will experience major depression at some point in their lives—is about 17 percent (Blazer, Kessler, McGonagle, et al., 1994). Depression is second only to schizophrenia in frequency of admissions to American mental hospitals (Olfson & Mechanic, 1996). As for the nonhospitalized, private physicians report that as many as 12 to 48 percent of their patients suffer from depression (Barrett, Barrett, Oxman, et al., 1988), and those patients are more debilitated—lose more workdays, spend more time in bed—than patients with many chronic medical conditions, such as diabetes or arthritis (Hays, Wells, Sherbourne, et al., 1995). As grave as the situation is, it is getting worse. Each successive generation born since World War II has shown higher rates of depression (Burke, Burke, Roe, et al., 1991; Klerman, 1988). Major depression is now the fourth leading cause of disability and premature death worldwide (Murray & Lopez, 1996). According to some experts, we are in an "age of depression."

Course In about 80 percent of all cases of major depression, the first episode is not the last (Judd, 1997). The more previous episodes a person has had, the younger the person was when the first episode struck, the more painful events he or she has endured recently, the less supportive the family has been, and the more negative cognitions he or she has, the greater the likelihood of recurrence (Belsher & Costello, 1988; Lewinsohn, Roberts, Seeley, et al., 1994). Over a lifetime, the median number of episodes per patient is four, with a median duration of four and a half months per episode (Judd, 1997; Solomon, Keller, Leon, et al., 1997).

The course of recurrent depression varies considerably. For some people, the episodes come in clusters. For others, they are separated by years of normal functioning. As for the quality of the normal functioning, that also varies. Some people also return to their **premorbid adjustment**—that is, their level of functioning prior to the onset of the disorder. As for the others, one study of people who had been symptom-free for 2 years found that they still showed serious impairment in job status, income, marital adjustment, social relationships, and recreational activities (Coryell, Scheftner, Keller, et al., 1993). Depression also affects the immune system, leaving its victims more susceptible to illness (Schleifer, Keller, Bartlett, et al., 1996). All of these effects make it difficult for people coming out of a depressive episode to resume their former lives. Indeed, some research indicates that the symptoms and behaviors characteristic of a depressive episode actually generate stressful life events, which in turn can maintain the depression and produce a cycle of chronic stress and impairment

(Daley, Hammen, Burge, et al., 1997; Monroe & Simons, 1991). Thus, people snap back, but many of them do not snap back entirely, just as scar tissue is not the same as the original tissue. Not surprisingly, the longer a depressive episode lasts, the less likely it is that the person will fully recover (Keller, Lavori, Mueller, et al., 1992).

Groups at Risk for Depression   Certain groups within the population are more susceptible than others to major depression. The rate for Caucasians is higher than for African Americans, for separated and divorced people than for married people (Blazer, Kessler, McGonagle, et al., 1994), and for women than for men. Indeed, the risk for women is one and a half to three times higher than for men (Eaton, Anthony, Gallo, et al., 1997)—a fact that investigators have tried to explain with theories ranging from hormonal differences to the changing social role of women. One promising theory has to do with differences in the way men and women respond to depressed moods. According to Susan Nolen-Hoeksema (1987, 1991), women, when they are "down," tend to ruminate on this, focusing on the depression, wondering why it is happening and what it will lead to. Men take the opposite tack: they try to distract themselves. Because the evidence indicates that rumination exacerbates and prolongs depression, whereas distraction relieves it, women are likely to have longer and more serious depressions (Just & Alloy, 1997). For a more comprehensive theory of the female disadvantage with regard to depression, see the box on page 242.

As for age, it was once thought that the middle-aged and the elderly were the high-risk groups. But recent

Women are about twice as likely as men to experience depression. A possible explanation for this difference in prevalence is that women tend to analyze their depression, whereas men are more likely to try to distract themselves from it.

Why Do Gender Differences in Depression Emerge in Adolescence?

Women are about twice as likely as men to develop a serious depression, but, curiously, the same is not true of boys and girls. Prior to age 14 or 15, the two genders are at equal risk. (If anything, boys show a slightly higher risk.) What happens to girls in adolescence to make them so much more prone to depression?

To answer that question, Susan Nolen-Hoeksema and Joan Girgus (1994) have tentatively proposed an interactive model. According to this model, girls already carry a heavier load of risk factors for depression from childhood, but it is not until those factors are activated by the special challenges of adolescence that they crystallize into a greater vulnerability to depression. In defense of this theory, the researchers list a number of characteristics associated with depression: a negative attributional style, a tendency to ruminate on depression, helplessness, avoidance of aggression, and avoidance of dominance in groups. Though all these characteristics correlate with depression in both males and females, girls show them to a greater extent than boys long before adolescence.

Then, in adolescence, new risk factors arise, and it is the combination of these with the prior risks that tips the balance. One new risk, for example, is shame about one's body. Research has shown that boys value the physical changes associated with puberty more than girls do (Brooks-Gunn, 1988). Boys like their newly muscled shoulders; girls, on the other hand, tend to be distressed by the gain in body fat, and they often find menstruation embarrassing. Such "body dissatisfaction" is associated with depression (Allgood-Merten, Lewinsohn, & Hops, 1990). So is sexual abuse and rape, another puberty-connected risk factor that is far more serious for girls than for boys. It is estimated that girls aged 14 to 15 have a higher risk of being raped than any other age or sex group (Hayman, Stewart, Lewis, et al., 1968).

Finally, it is in adolescence that girls begin to confront most directly the restricted role carved out for them by their society. Many adopt the role quickly. Youngsters of both genders show less interest in school as they pass from sixth to seventh grade, but girls show a sharper drop in academic ambition (Hirsch & Rapkin, 1987). By the time they enter college, women are sorting themselves into less lucrative, less competitive fields. In 1986 to 1987, American women received only 15 percent of the bachelor's degrees awarded in engineering, whereas they took 76 and 84 percent of the bachelor's degrees in education and nursing, respectively (National Center for Education Statistics, 1989). In many cases, women actively choose these fields—that is the work they truly want. In other cases, however, it is probable that the choice is made because these are "women's fields," with less competition from men.

Apparently, girls who accept the narrowed role prescribed for women are at higher risk for depression (Girgus, Nolen-Hoeksema, Paul, et al., 1991). According to studies done in the 1970s, girls who defied such role expectations were *also* more prone to depression (Gove & Herb, 1974)—no doubt a reflection of the widespread disapproval of assertive women. That standard is surely changing, but not overnight. In one study, female leaders, especially those who behaved in stereotypically masculine, aggressive ways, were still rated more negatively and viewed as less normal than equally assertive male leaders (Eagly, Makhijani, & Klonsky, 1992).

If they encountered the challenges of adolescence with no disadvantage, girls might weather them well enough. But, because they are already handicapped by a higher load of risk factors, they are less likely to cope well. And so, according to Nolen-Hoeksema and Girgus (1994), they may develop the patterns that will make them, from then on, twice as vulnerable to depression as men.

research indicates that growing old does not increase one's susceptibility to depression (Roberts, Kaplan, Shema, et al., 1997). If anything, it is the young who are at risk. The peak age at onset for major depression is now 15 to 19 years for women and 25 to 29 years for men (Burke, Burke, Regier, et al., 1990), though the disorder may strike at any age, even in infancy.

The symptom picture differs somewhat, depending on age group (Harrington, 1993). In depressed infants, the most striking and alarming sign is failure to eat. In older children, depression may manifest itself primarily as apathy and inactivity. Alternatively, it may take the form of separation anxiety, in which the child clings frantically to parents, refuses to leave them long enough to go to school, and is haunted by fears of death (or of the parents' deaths). In adolescents, the most prominent symptoms are sulkiness, negativism, withdrawal, complaints of not being understood, and perhaps antisocial behavior and drug abuse (Cantwell, 1982; Goodyer, 1992)—in other words, an exaggeration of normal adolescent problems. (See Chapter 15 for further discussion of depression in childhood.) In the elderly, lack of pleasure and motivation, expressions of hopelessness, and psychomotor retardation or agitation are common signs, as are delusions and hallucinations (Brodaty, Peters, Boyce, et al., 1991).

Bipolar Disorder

Whereas major depression is confined to depressive episodes, **bipolar disorder,** as the name suggests, involves both manic and depressive phases. In the usual case, bipolar disorder first appears in late adolescence in the form of a manic episode. The subsequent episodes may occur in any of a variety of patterns. The initial manic episode may be followed by a normal period, then by a depressed episode, then a normal period, and so forth. Or one episode may be followed immediately by its opposite, with normal intervals occurring only between such manic-depressive pairs. In a less common pattern, called the *rapid-cycling type,* the person (usually a woman) switches back and forth between depressive and manic or mixed episodes over a long period, with little or no "normal" functioning between. This pattern, which tends to have a poor prognosis (Bauer, Calabrese, Dunner, et al., 1994), turns up in about one-fourth of bipolar patients in response to antidepressant medication (Altshuler, Post, Leverich, et al., 1995).

The addition of manic episodes is not the only thing that differentiates bipolar disorder from major depression. The two syndromes differ in many important respects (Bebbington & Ramana, 1995; Goodwin & Jamison, 1990). First, bipolar disorder is much less common than major depression, affecting an estimated 0.8 to 1.6 percent of the adult population (Kessler, McGonagle, Zhao, et al., 1994). Second, the two disorders show different demographic profiles. Unlike major depression, bipolar disorder occurs in the two sexes with approximately equal frequency, and bipolar disorder is more prevalent among higher socioeconomic groups. Third, while people who are married or have intimate relationships are less prone to major depression, they have no advantage with respect to bipolar disorder. Fourth, people with major depression tend to have histories of low self-esteem, dependency, and obsessional thinking, whereas people with bipolar disorder are more likely to have a history of hyperactivity (Winokur, Coryell, Endicott, et al., 1993). Fifth, the depressive episodes in bipolar disorder are more likely to involve a pervasive slowing down—psychomotor retardation, excess sleep—than are those in major depression. Sixth, the two disorders differ in their course. Episodes in bipolar disorder are generally briefer and more frequent than are those in major depression. Seventh, the two conditions differ in prognosis. In general, bipolar disorder creates greater impairment and has a worse long-term outcome (Gitlin, Swendsen, Heller, et al., 1995; Goldberg, Harrow, & Grossman, 1995). Finally, bipolar disorder is more likely to run in families. On the basis of these clues, many researchers think that the two disorders, similar as they may appear, spring from different causes.

We may, however, be looking at more than two disorders. Some patients have a manic or mixed

In the film Mr. Jones, *Richard Gere portrays a man suffering from bipolar disorder.*

episode—or a series of such episodes—with no subsequent depressive episode. Such cases, though they involve only one "pole," are nevertheless classified as bipolar disorder, because, apart from the absence of depressive episodes, they resemble the classic bipolar disorder. (Some researchers suspect that they are simply cases of insufficient follow-up.) Alternatively, some patients have both depressive and manic phases but in the latter are hypomanic rather than fully manic. In recognition of these two patterns—and the need to assemble research groups to test whether they are different disorders—*DSM-IV* has divided bipolar disorder into two types. In *bipolar I disorder,* the person has had at least one manic (or mixed) episode and usually, but not necessarily, at least one major depressive episode as well. In *bipolar II disorder,* the person has had at least one major depressive episode and at least one hypomanic episode but has never met the diagnostic criteria for manic or mixed episode.

The following is a case of bipolar I disorder, involving both full-blown manic and depressive episodes:

At 17 [Mrs. M. had] suffered from a depression that rendered her unable to work for several months. . . . At 33, shortly before the birth of her first child, the patient was greatly depressed. For a period of four days she appeared in coma. About a month after the birth of the baby she "became excited" and . . . signed a year's lease on an apartment, bought furniture, and became heavily involved in debt. Shortly thereafter, Mrs. M. became depressed and returned to the hospital in which she had previously been a patient. After several months she recovered and . . . remained well for approximately two years.

She then became overactive and exuberant in spirits and visited her friends, to whom she outlined her

Streams of Fire: Bipolar Disorder and Creativity

The "mad genius" is an ancient idea, but recently it has been restated by Kay Jamison, a professor of psychiatry at Johns Hopkins School of Medicine. In her 1992 book, *Touched with Fire: Manic-Depressive Illness and the Artistic Temperament*, Jamison argues that artists show an unusually high rate of mood disorder and that this is part of what makes them creative. To assemble her evidence, Jamison studied the lives of a large group of British and Irish poets born between 1705 and 1805. Her conclusion was that they were 30 times more likely to have suffered manic-depressive illness, 20 times more likely to have been committed to an asylum, and 5 times more likely to have killed themselves than were members of the general population. Jamison studied not just poets but artists in many media: Baudelaire, Blake, Byron, Coleridge, Dickinson, Shelley, Tennyson, Whitman, Balzac, Conrad, Dickens, Zola, Handel, Berlioz, Schumann, Tchaikovsky, Michelangelo, van Gogh, Gauguin—all these, Jamison believes, probably suffered from serious mood disorders.

Neither is the evidence confined to past centuries. Jamison provides a list of major American poets of the twentieth century: Hart Crane, Theodore Roethke, Delmore Schwartz, John Berryman, Randall Jarrell, Robert Lowell, Anne Sexton, and Sylvia Plath. Of these, five won the Pulitzer prize, and five committed suicide. All eight were treated for depression, and all but one were treated for mania. Many of Jamison's creative manic-depressives also had family histories of mood disorder. Lord Byron, who once described his brain as "a whirling gulf of fantasy and flame," had a great-uncle known as "Mad Lord Byron" and a father known as "Mad Jack Byron." His mother had violent mood swings; his maternal grandfather, a depressive, committed suicide.

Together with these sad histories, Jamison describes the creative benefits of mania. For one thing, it instills confidence. It also allows its victims to work uninterruptedly for long hours. (Earlier studies of outstanding artists and scientists have shown that, whatever their mental status, they have one trait in common: the ability to work hard for many hours at a stretch [Roe, 1952].) But, above all, the euphoria, the hyperintense perceptions, the feeling of bursting inspiration that accompanies mania provide rich material for art. Novelist Virginia Woolf wrote, "As an experience madness is terrific...and in its lava I still find most of the things I write about." Composer Hugo Wolf described his blood as "changed into streams of fire."

"These are people who have had emotional experiences that most of us have not had," says Jamison, and in their work they give us the benefit of what they discover through those experiences: "We ask artists to go over the edge emotionally on our behalf" (quoted in Keiger, 1993, p. 40).

Some observers find Jamison's conclusions more romantic than scientific, particularly insofar as they involve "diagnosing the dead" on the basis of the anecdotal (and often apocryphal) evidence of biographies. There were no *DSM* criteria in the nineteenth century, let alone before; consequently, it is hard to know whether the eccentricities of people such as "Mad Jack Byron" constitute the same condition that we call bipolar disorder. Also, famous artists' lives have been very heavily scrutinized, and this may lead to distortion.

---

plans for reestablishing different forms of lucrative business. She purchased many clothes, bought furniture, pawned her rings, and wrote checks without funds. She was returned to a hospital. Gradually her manic symptoms subsided, and after four months she was discharged. For a period thereafter she was mildly depressed. In a little less than a year Mrs. M. again became overactive.... Contrary to her usual habits, she swore frequently and loudly, created a disturbance in a club to which she did not belong, and instituted divorce proceedings. On the day prior to her second admission to the hospital she purchased 57 hats.

During the past 18 years this patient has been admitted and dismissed from the hospital on many occasions. At times, with the onset of a depressed period, she has returned to the hospital seeking admission. At such times she complained that her "brain just won't work." She would say, "I have no energy, am unable to do my housework. I have let my family down; I am living from day to day. There is no one to blame but myself." During one of her manic periods, she sent the following telegram to a physician of whom she had become much enamored: "To: You; Street and No.: Everywhere; Place: the remains at peace! We did our best, but God's will be done! I am so very sorry for all of us. To brave it through thus far. Yes, Darling—from Hello Handsome. Handsome is as Handsome does, thinks, lives and breathes. It takes clear air. Brother of Mine, in a girl's hour of need. All my love to the Best Inspiration one ever had." (Kolb, 1982, pp. 376–377)

Dysthymic Disorder and Cyclothymic Disorder

There are many people who are chronically depressed or who chronically pass through depressed and expansive periods but whose condition is not severe enough to merit the diagnosis of major depressive disorder or bipolar disorder. Such patterns, if they last for two years or more, are classified as dysthymic disorder and cyclothymic disorder, respectively.

Dysthymic disorder involves a mild, persistent depression. Dysthymics are typically morose, pes-

Schoolteachers and bus drivers may also feel, now and then, that their brains are licked with fire, but, because they are not artists, they are less likely to interest the public in this fact. Partly because the "mad genius" stereotype—and because mad geniuses make lively reading—artists' biographers tend to stress the extravagant and the pathological.

However, Jamison's findings have been supported in some measure by studies of living people. Andreasen (1987) surveyed 30 writers taking part in the University of Iowa's Writer's Workshop and found that fully 80 percent had met the *DSM* criteria for a major affective disorder. In a later study, Richards and her colleagues found that the bipolar and cyclothymic patients and their normal first-degree relatives scored significantly higher on creativity than did either the normal controls or the people with psychiatric diagnoses other than mood disorder. An interesting aspect of this study was that the research team used a much broader and more "normal" definition of creativity than other researchers have used. The subjects who were involved in social and political causes, who showed a special flair for business, who worked at hobbies—they, too, got points for creativity. The researchers concluded that the most creative people were not those with or without bipolar disorder but those in between, the cyclothymics and the even milder, "subclinical" moody types, together with the normal first-degree relatives of people with pronounced mood disorders (Richards, Kinney, Lunde, et al., 1988).

(Left) Novelist Virginia Woolf (1882–1941) struggled with what was probably bipolar disorder throughout her adult life. She finally drowned herself. (Right) Peter Ilyich Tchaikovsky (1840–1893), one of the most popular and influential Russian composers of the nineteenth century, suffered severe depressions.

simistic, introverted, overconscientious, and incapable of fun (Akiskal & Cassano, 1997). In addition, they often show the low energy level, low self-esteem, suicidal ideation, and disturbances of eating, sleeping, and thinking that are associated with major depression, though their symptoms are not as severe or as numerous (Klein, Kocsis, McCullough, et al., 1996). The syndrome is about half as common as major depressive disorder.

Cyclothymic disorder, like dysthymic disorder, is chronic. For years, the person never goes longer than a few months without a phase of hypomanic or depressive behavior. Because the pattern is mild and persistent, as in dysthymia, it becomes a way of life. In their hypomanic periods, which they come to depend on, cyclothymics work long hours without fatigue—indeed, with their mental powers newly sharpened—before lapsing back into a normal or depressed state. It has been suggested that cyclothymia and bipolar disorder are especially common in creative people and help them get their work done. (See the box on pages 244–245.)

Both dysthymia and cyclothymia have a slow, insidious onset in adolescence and may persist for a lifetime. In this sense, they are like the personality disorders, the subject of our next chapter. Far closer, however, is the link with the major mood disorders. Like people with major depressive disorder or bipolar disorder, dysthymics and cyclothymics have relatives with higher-than-normal rates of mood disorders. Also, dysthymia and cyclothymia show the same gender distribution as their graver counterparts. Dysthymic disorder, like major depression, is one and a half to three times more common in women, whereas in cyclothymic disorder, as in bipolar disorder, the genders are at equal risk (Kessler, McGonagle, Zhao, et al., 1994). Finally, patients with dysthymia and cyclothymia tend to show the same neurophysiological abnormalities and the same reactions to antidepressant drugs, as people with major depressive disorder and bipolar disorder (Akiskal, Judd, Lemmi, et al., 1997). About 10 percent of dysthymics go on to develop major depressive disorder, and 15 to 50 percent of cyclothymics eventually show bipolar disorder.

Dimensions of Mood Disorder

In addition to the important distinction between bipolar disorder and depressive disorder, there are certain *dimensions,* or points of differentiation, that researchers and clinicians have found useful in classifying mood disorders. We shall discuss three dimensions: psychotic-neurotic, endogenous-reactive, and early-late onset.

Psychotic Versus Neurotic   As we saw in Chapter 6, psychological disorders may be described, in terms of severity, as either psychotic or neurotic—a distinction that hinges on the matter of reality contact. Neurotics do not lose their ability to interact with their environment in a reasonably efficient manner. Psychotics do, partly because their thinking processes are often disturbed by *hallucinations,* or false sensory perceptions, and *delusions,* or false beliefs. This same neurotic-psychotic distinction is often applied to depression. In psychotic depression, hallucinations, delusions, and extreme withdrawal effectively cut the tie between the person and the environment. Manic episodes can also have psychotic features. Mrs. M.'s letter to her doctor (page 244) qualifies as evidence of psychotic-level thought disturbance. However, many cases of major depression and bipolar disorder—and, by definition, all cases of dysthymia and cyclothymia—remain at the neurotic level.

Are neurotic- and psychotic-level mood disorders two different entities altogether? The traditional position is that they are. For example, Kraepelin (Chapter 1), in his original classification system, listed all incapacitating mood disorders under the heading "manic-depressive psychosis," which he considered an organic illness distinct from neurotic-level mood disturbances. Many theorists still hold to this position, and there is some evidence to support it. Psychotic depressives tend to differ from nonpsychotic depressives not just in reality contact but also in psychomotor symptoms, cognitive deficits, biological signs, family history, and response to various treatments (Coryell, 1996; Jeste, Heaton, Paulsen, et al., 1996).

Other theorists argue that the distinction between neurotic and psychotic depression is quantitative rather than qualitative. This theory, known as the continuity hypothesis, rests on the idea that depression appears, above all, to be an exaggerated form of everyday sadness (Flett, Vredenberg, & Krames, 1997). According to the proponents of the continuity hypoth-

esis, psychotic depression, neurotic depression, dysthymia, and normal "blues" are simply different points on a single continuum. The findings that people with low-level mood disorders—not just dysthymics and cyclothymics but also people with "subsyndromal" symptoms (symptoms not severe enough to merit diagnosis)—are at risk for more severe depression and have relatives with higher rates of mood disorder lends some support to the continuity hypothesis (Angst & Merikangus, 1997).

Endogenous Versus Reactive   Many proponents of the continuity hypothesis believe that all mood disorders are largely psychogenic. Those who hold to the Kraepelin tradition, on the other hand, generally believe that only the neurotic forms are psychogenic. They regard the psychotic forms as biogenic.

Basic to the latter point of view is a second dimension of mood disorder: the endogenous-versus-reactive dimension. Originally, the terms *endogenous* and *reactive* were intended to indicate whether or not a depression was preceded by a precipitating event, such as a death in the family or the loss of a job. Those linked to such an event were called reactive; those not linked were called endogenous (literally, "born from within"). According to adherents of Kraepelin's position, neurotic depressions were generally reactive and therefore psychogenic, while psychotic depressions were generally endogenous and therefore biogenic.

As it turns out, however, the distinction is not so easily made. The research indicates that *most* depressive episodes, including those in bipolar patients, are preceded by stressful life events (Cui & Vaillant, 1996; Johnson & Miller, 1997), but it is often unclear whether such events were, in fact, a major cause. In many cases, there is a precipitating event for a first episode but not for later episodes (Brown, Harris, & Hepworth, 1994; Frank, Anderson, Reynolds, et al., 1994). As a result of these confusions, the terms *endogenous* and *reactive,* despite their dictionary meanings, are now generally used not to indicate the absence or presence of precipitating events but to describe different patterns of symptoms. Patients who show pronounced anhedonia together with the more *vegetative,* or physical, symptoms (e.g., early-morning waking, weight loss, psychomotor changes) and who describe their depression as different in quality from what they would feel after the death of a loved one are classified as endogenous, or, in *DSM-IV's* terminology, as having "melancholic features." Those whose disturbance is primarily emotional or cognitive are called reactive, or without melancholic features.

The endogenous-reactive distinction made on the basis of symptoms does seem to describe a genuine difference. Endogenous patients differ from reactive

Having the comfort and support of a family member can help a person to avoid the onset or relapse of depression that is associated with uncontrollable losses such as death.

patients in their sleep patterns. They are also more likely than reactive patients to show the biological abnormalities that we will describe later in this chapter and to respond to biological treatments, such as electroconvulsive ("shock") therapy (Rush & Weissenburger, 1994). Accordingly, some researchers still suspect that endogenous cases are more biogenic, but this has not been established, and there is some evidence to the contrary. For example, if endogenous depression were more biochemically based, then we would expect endogenous patients to have greater family histories of depression than do reactives, but numerous studies have shown that they do not (Rush & Weissenburger, 1994). Researchers are still investigating this question intensively, and it is partly to help them assemble research groups that the *DSM* requires diagnosticians to specify whether or not a depression has melancholic features.

When depression is preceded by a clearly precipitating event, that event is usually an uncontrollable loss—being laid off from work, losing one's home—and particularly, an interpersonal loss (Cronkite & Moos, 1995). "Exit events"—death, separation, divorce, a child's leaving home—rank high among stressors associated with the onset of depression (Paykel & Cooper, 1992). By the same token, if a person has a close relationship, and, therefore, someone to confide in, he or she is less likely to succumb to depression in the face of stressful life events (Cronkite & Moos, 1995). The same principles hold for people recovering from depression. Stress, particularly stress connected with exit events and other losses, is associated with relapses, while social support, particularly in the form of a confidant, is associated with continued recovery, even in the face of stress (Lewinsohn, Hoberman, & Rosenbaum, 1988; Paykel & Cooper, 1992).

Early Versus Late Onset   In the past few years, evidence has been steadily accumulating that age at onset is an important dimension of mood disorder. The earlier the onset of the disorder, the more likely it is that the person's relatives have, or have had, mood disorders. Some of the findings are quite remarkable. In a study of children of people with major depression, when the parent's age at onset was under 20, the lifetime risk of major depression in the child was almost twice as great as the risk when the parent's age at onset was over 30 (Weissman, Warner, Wickramaratne, et al., 1988). Early-onset patients are also more likely to have children and other relatives who are alcoholic (Kupfer, Frank, Carpenter, et al., 1989).

Early onset affects not just the relatives but also the person with the early onset. In a study of dysthymics, 94 percent of the early-onset group graduated to major depression, compared with 55 percent of the late-onset group—again, about a 2-to-1 ratio (Klein, Taylor, Dickstein, et al., 1988). Likewise, in a study of major depressives, the early-onset patients were more likely to show personality disorders (Chapter 10) as well (Fava, Alpert, Borus, et al., 1996).

In general, then, the earlier the onset, the harder the road, both for the person and for the rest of the family. These findings may suggest that early-onset patients have a higher "genetic loading" for mood disorder. Alternatively, the higher rates of depression in the relatives of early-onset patients could be due to environmental effects. Relatives of early-onset cases have lived with a depressed person for a longer period of time. In particular, children of an early-onset depressed parent have had greater opportunity to learn depressive behaviors from the parent.

Comorbidity: Mixed Anxiety-Depression

One important trend in the study of depression is the increasing evidence of the comorbidity, or co-occurrence, of depressive and anxiety disorders (Pini, Cassano, Simonini, et al., 1997). The symptomatologies of the two disorders show considerable overlap. Both include weeping, irritability, worry, fatigue, insomnia, low self-esteem, dependency, poor concentration, and feelings of helplessness (Alloy, Kelly, Mineka, et al., 1990). Indeed, people diagnosed with either anxiety or depression are likely to meet the diagnostic criteria for the other as well, either simultaneously *(intraepisode comorbidity)* or at different times in their lives *(lifetime comorbidity)*. People in these two diagnostic groups also tend to respond to the same antidepressant drugs (Fyer, Liebowitz, & Klein, 1990), share similar endocrine abnormalities (Heninger, 1990), and have family histories of both anxiety and depressive disorders (Merikangus, 1990; Weissman, 1990). These findings have reignited an old debate over whether depression and anxiety are, in fact, two distinct entities or whether they are somewhat different manifestations of the same underlying disorder.

The comorbidity findings have also led to a proposal that a new category, "mixed anxiety-depression," be included in the *DSM*. This would make the *DSM* consistent with the World Health Organization's *ICD-10,* which has such a category. More important, it would provide a diagnostic label for people who have mixed symptoms of anxiety and depression but who do not meet the *DSM-IV* criteria for either disorder alone. There are many such people, and they may be at risk for more severe mood and anxiety disorders, especially if they are not given appropriate treatment (Stein, Kirk, Prabhu, et al., 1995; Zinbarg, Barlow, Liebowitz, et al., 1994). Having no diagnostic label for them makes appropriate treatment less likely. And, of course, if these people do represent an important category of psychopathology, then having no diagnostic label gives us a false picture of the field.

Suicide

People take their lives for many reasons, but a very common reason is depression. The lifetime risk of suicide among people with mood disorders is estimated at 19 percent (Goodwin & Jamison, 1990). Among people who commit suicide, an estimated 55 percent were depressed before the fatal attempt (Isacsson & Rich, 1997).

The Prevalence of Suicide

Accurate statistics on the prevalence of suicide are difficult to obtain, because many people who commit suicide prefer to make their deaths look accidental. It has been estimated that at least 15 percent of all fatal automobile accidents are actually suicides, for example (Finch, Smith, & Pokorny, 1970). In 1990, the last year for which census statistics are available, there were just over 30,000 suicides reported in the United States (National Center for Health Statistics, 1993). In the general population, it has been estimated that eight people attempt suicide for every one who commits suicide (Leenaars & Wenckstern, 1991), which would mean that each year perhaps a quarter of a million people in the United States attempt suicide. Many statisticians and public health experts would consider these figures far too low. As Figure 9.1 shows, other countries have far higher rates—Hungary's is almost four times that of the United States—and recent studies suggest that the worldwide rate is increasing (Harrison, 1997). But even at 30,000 per year, suicide is the eighth most common cause of death in this country.

Groups at Risk for Suicide

Certain demographic variables are strongly correlated with suicide. Twice as many single people as married people kill themselves—widowed and divorced people, in particular, are at higher risk—and childless women are more likely to commit suicide than are those with children (Hoyer & Lund, 1993). In general, the likelihood of a person's committing suicide increases as a function of age, especially for men. Three times as many women as men attempt suicide, but three times as many men as women succeed in killing themselves. The fact that men choose more lethal methods, such as shooting themselves, is one of the reasons more men die (Garland & Zigler, 1993). (Only in China do women commit suicide more frequently than men—a fact that may be related to the low status of women in Chinese society [Harrison, 1997].) Apart from depressed people, drug-abusers are at higher risk (Shaffer, Gould, Fisher, et al., 1996), as are people with a history of childhood physical or sexual abuse (Wagner, 1997; Yang & Clum, 1996).

According to a demographic summary put together by Shneidman and Farberow in 1970, the *modal suicide attempter* (i.e., the person who most commonly attempts suicide and survives) is a native-born Cau-

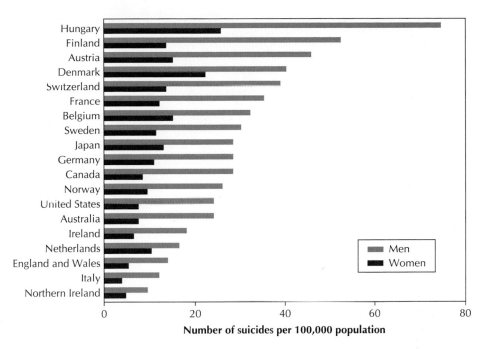

FIGURE 9.1
Age-adjusted suicide rates per 100,000 population for people aged 15 to 74, as of 1987 or most recent date available. (Mościcki, 1995, p. 140, based on World Health Organization statistics)

casian woman, a homemaker in her twenties or thirties, who attempts to kill herself by swallowing barbiturates and gives as her reason either marital difficulties or depression. In contrast, the *modal suicide committer* (i.e., the person who succeeds in taking his or her own life) is a native-born Caucasian man in his forties or older who, for reasons of ill health, depression, or marital difficulties, commits suicide by shooting or hanging himself or by poisoning himself with carbon monoxide (see Figures 9.2 and 9.3).

These generalizations still hold (Maris, 1992), but there have been some recent shifts in suicide-related variables, particularly regarding age. Suicide rates among men aged 15 to 34 have increased in the past few decades (Silverman, 1997). Older men are still more likely than younger men to kill themselves, but the gap is narrowing. The racial picture is also changing. Though Caucasian men are still at higher risk than African American men, suicide among African American men is on the rise (Mościcki, 1995; Silverman, 1997).

Teenage Suicide Of special concern among groups at risk are teenagers, whose suicide rate has risen 200 percent since 1960. In 1987, suicide became the second leading cause of death (after accidents) among 15- to 19-year-olds (Gould, Shaffer, Fisher, et al., 1992). As many as 7 to 16 percent of high school students have made at least one suicide attempt (King, 1997). For many of their elders, this is hard to understand. How can people who "have their whole lives ahead of them" want to take those lives?

In some measure, the answer probably lies in the special circumstances of adolescence, the fact that, while teenagers may be exposed to situations as stressful as those facing adults, they lack the resources—emotional self-control, problem-solving capacity, mobility, money—that adults can marshal in order to find

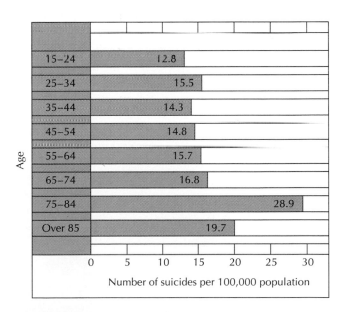

FIGURE 9.2 U.S. suicide rates by age. The largest number of suicides occurs in people between 75 and 84 years of age; in this group, there are 28.9 deaths per 100,000 of population. (U.S. Bureau of the Census, 1990)

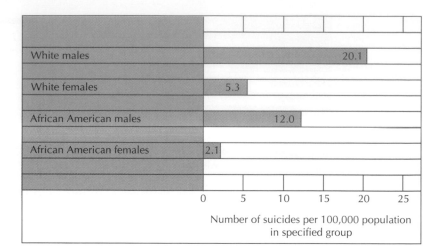

FIGURE 9.3   U.S. suicide rates by race and gender. Suicide occurs most frequently among white males, least frequently among African American females. (U.S. Bureau of the Census, 1990)

relief (Reynolds & Mazza, 1994). At the same time, teenagers today seem to have more cause for distress. Depression and substance abuse, two powerful risk factors for suicide, are both on the rise among adolescents (Lewisohn, Rohde, Seeley, et al., 1991).

Apparently, another major risk factor for adolescent suicide is trouble within the family (Wagner, 1997). One "psychological autopsy" compared 120 teenage suicide victims with 147 controls matched for age, gender, and ethnic group. Compared with the controls, the suicide victims scored higher on several risk factors: depression, substance abuse, school problems, and social isolation. But another important difference between the two groups was the level of disturbance within the families. The suicide victims' families had suffered more suicides; they also showed poorer parent-child communications (Gould,

Fisher, Parides, et al., 1996; Shaffer, Gould, Fisher, et al., 1996). Another study found that, compared with the families of controls, the families of adolescent suicide attempters showed more conflict, more childhood sexual abuse, and poorer parental care (Beautrais, Joyce, & Mulder, 1996).

Thus, the problems of suicidal teenagers are often rooted in their families' problems. But, for the teenagers, the difficulties are multiplied: they are still dependent on their families for love and support that may not be forthcoming, and many are too young to seek out professional help for themselves. Only one-fifth of the teenagers who attempt suicide receive even medical attention, let alone psychotherapy, following their attempt (King, 1997). These young people may, indeed, feel that there is no solution to their problems.

Teenage suicide has reached epidemic proportions in the United States. The episode shown here ended well, with the guard talking the young woman back into the building.

Myths About Suicide

Common as it is, suicide is still surrounded by an aura of mystery and by a number of popular misconceptions. One of the most unfortunate myths about suicide is that people who threaten to kill themselves will not carry out the threat—that only the "silent type" will pull it off. This is not true. In a study of 71 completed suicides, more than half the victims had clearly communicated their suicidal intent within 3 months before the fatal act (Isometsä, Henriksson, Aro, et al., 1994). When people threaten suicide, they should be taken seriously.

Another myth is that people who attempt suicide and fail are not serious about ending their lives—they are just looking for sympathy. On the contrary, about 40 percent of all suicides have made a previous attempt or threat (Maris, 1992), and, the more prior attempts, the greater the likelihood of a completed suicide (Goldstein, Black, Nasrallah, et al., 1991).

People's emotional reactions to suicide—fear, horror, curiosity, incomprehension—have given it the status of "unmentionable" in the minds of many, a taboo that is strengthened by the Judeo-Christian prohibition against taking one's own life. Hence, a third myth about suicide is that one should never speak of it to people who are depressed. According to this notion, questioning depressives about suicidal thoughts will either put the idea into their heads or, if it is already there, give it greater force. In opposition to this belief, most clinicians agree that encouraging patients to talk about suicidal wishes helps them to overcome such wishes.

Suicide Prediction

When someone commits suicide, family and friends are often astonished—which shows how often they are oblivious to the signs. As we just saw, most suicidal people clearly communicate their intent. For example, they may say, "I don't want to go on living" or "I know I'm a burden to everyone." But even those who don't announce their plans usually give signals (Shneidman, 1992). Some withdraw into an almost contemplative state. Others act as if they were going on a long trip. Others give away their most valued possessions. Sometimes the expression of suicidal intent is less direct, however clear in retrospect. For example, a depressed patient leaving the hospital on a weekend pass may say, "I want to thank you for trying so hard to help me." Failure to pick up such signs may be due in part to the fact that depressives who commit suicide tend to do so as they are coming out of their depression. It is not clear whether they seem less depressed because they have made the deci-

sion to commit suicide or whether, being less depressed, they at last have the energy to act upon their suicidal wishes.

Predictably, suicide is often directly related to stress. There is some evidence that the nature of the stress may vary over the life cycle. One study found that interpersonal conflicts, rejections, and separations most often precede suicide in younger people, whereas economic problems are more critical in middle age, illness in old age (Rich, Warsradt, Nemiroff, et al., 1991). Like the onset of depression, suicide attempts are frequently preceded by "exit" events.

Cognitive variables may be among the most useful predictors of who will attempt suicide. Not surprisingly, the cognitive variable most frequently associated with serious suicidal intent is hopelessness (Glanz, Haas, & Sweeney, 1995). In a 10-year follow-up study of hospitalized patients who expressed suicidal thoughts, hopelessness turned out to be the best single predictor of who would eventually kill themselves (Beck, Steer, Kovacs, et al., 1985), and this has proved true with outpatients as well (Beck, Brown, Berchick, et al., 1990). From accounts of people who survived suicide attempts, together with research on those who died, suicide expert Edwin Shneidman (1992) put together a "suicidal scenario," a summary of elements that are usually present in the decision to take one's own life:

1. A sense of unbearable psychological *pain,* which is directly related to thwarted psychological *needs*

2. Traumatizing *self-denigration*—a self-image that will not include tolerating intense psychological pain

3. A marked *constriction* of the mind and an unrealistic narrowing of life's actions

4. A sense of *isolation*—a feeling of desertion and the loss of support of significant others

5. An overwhelmingly desperate feeling of *hopelessness*—a sense that nothing effective can be done

6. A conscious decision that *egression*—leaving, exiting, or stopping life—is the *only* (or at least the best possible) solution to the problem of unbearable pain (pp. 51–52)

As this summary shows, many people who commit suicide imagine that it is the only way out of an unbearably painful situation—a conviction that is often clear in the notes they leave. In a study comparing real suicide notes with simulated notes written by a well-matched control group, Shneidman and Farberow (1970) found that the writers of the genuine notes expressed significantly more suffering than the control group. Suicidal anguish is evidently hard to feign. Interestingly, though, the genuine suicide notes also contained a greater number of neutral statements—lists of things to be done after the suicide has taken place, and so forth. Both the ring of authentic hopelessness and the neutral content are illustrated in the following two genuine suicide notes:

> Barbara,
> I'm sorry. I love you bunches. Would you please do a couple of things for me. Don't tell the kids what I did. When Theresa gets a little older, if she wants to cut her hair please let her. Don't make her wear it long just because you like it that way. Ask your Mom what kind and how much clothes the kids need and then buy double what she says. I love you and the kids very much please try and remember that. I'm just not any good for you. I never learned how to tell you no. You will be much better off without me. Just try and find someone who will love Theresa and Donny.
>
> Love Bunches—Charlie
> P.S. Donny is down at Linda's
> Put Donny in a nursery school

> Dear Steve:
> I have been steadily getting worse in spite of everything and did not want to be a burden the rest of my life.
>
> All my love,
> Dad
> My brown suit is the only one that fits me.

Not all suicides feel unqualified despair, however. According to Farberow and Litman (1970), only about 3 to 5 percent of people who attempt suicide are truly determined to die. Another 30 percent fall into what the researchers call the "to be or not to be" group—those who are ambivalent about dying. Finally, about two-thirds of suicide attempters do not really wish to die but, instead, are trying, through the gesture of a suicide attempt, to communicate the intensity of their suffering to family and friends. Regarding the last two groups, it bears repeating that their mixed feelings do not mean that they are not in danger. As we saw, many of those who are not determined this time will be more determined next time (King, 1997).

Suicide Prevention

As we just pointed out, most people who attempt suicide do not absolutely wish to die. It was on the basis of this finding, together with the fact that suicide attempters are often reacting to crises in their lives, that the first telephone "hot lines" for potential suicides were established in the late 1950s. Hot-line staffers, often volunteers, try to "tune in" to the caller's distress while presenting arguments against suicide and telling the caller where he or she can go for professional help. Another preventive effort, this one aimed specifically at the newly high-risk adolescent population, involves school-based programs. Here, teachers, parents, and the teenagers themselves are given workshops in which they are informed of the "warning signs" of suicide and are told how and to where to refer someone who seems to be in danger.

Unfortunately, neither of these efforts has been especially successful. Communities with suicide hot lines appear to have lower suicide rates only for one group—young white women, the most frequent hot-line users—and, even for them, the decrease is slight (Rihmer, 1996). As for the school-based programs, they seem to be minimally effective in changing attitudes and coping behavior, particularly in boys (Shaffer, Garland, & Vieland, 1991), who are less likely than girls to turn to the kind of social and professional support that such workshops recommend (Overholser, Evans, & Spirito, 1990). It is probable, furthermore, that school-based programs are not reaching their target population. The adolescents most at risk for suicide—delinquents, substance abusers, runaways, incarcerated teenagers—are the ones least likely to be in school, let alone paying close attention to a suicide-prevention workshop.

Mood Disorders: Theory and Therapy

Because depression is far more common than mania, most theories of mood disorder have concentrated on depression and suicide, and the therapies focus on depression.

The Psychodynamic Perspective

Reactivated Loss   The first serious challenge to Kraepelin's biogenic theory of mood disorder came from Freud and other early psychoanalytic theorists, who argued that depression was not a symptom of organic dysfunction but a massive defense mounted by the ego against intrapsychic conflict. In his now-classic paper "Mourning and Melancholia" (1917/1957) Freud described depression as a response to loss (real or symbolic), but one in which the person's sorrow and rage in the face of that loss remain unconscious, thus weakening the ego. This formulation was actually an elaboration of a theory put forth by one of Freud's students, Karl Abraham (1911/1948, 1916/1948). Abraham had suggested that depression arises when one loses a love object toward whom one had ambivalent, positive and negative, feelings. In the face of the love object's desertion, the negative feelings turn to intense anger. At the same time, the positive feelings give rise to guilt, a feeling that one failed to behave properly toward the now-lost love object.

Severe stress and feelings of hopelessness drive some people to attempt suicide. This desperate man seized a gun and threatened suicide from the back seat of a police car. He later surrendered.

Because of this guilt—and because of early memories in which the primary love object was symbolically "eaten up," or incorporated, by the infant—the grieving person turns his or her anger inward rather than outward, thus producing the self-hatred and despair that we call depression. In the case of suicide, the person is actually trying to kill the incorporated love object. "Anger in" has escalated to "murder in."

While "anger in" still figures importantly in traditional psychoanalytic discussions of depression and suicide, modern theorists have expanded and revised this early position. There are now many psychodynamic theories of depression, yet they share a certain number of core assumptions (Bemporad, 1988; Blatt & Homann, 1992). First, it is generally believed that depression is rooted in a very early defect, often the loss or threatened loss of a parent (Bowlby, 1973). Second, the primal wound is reactivated by a recent blow, such as a divorce or job loss. Whatever the precipitating event, the person is plunged back into the infantile trauma. Third, a major consequence of this regression is a sense of helplessness and hopelessness —a reflection of what was the infant's actual powerlessness in the face of harm. Feeling incapable of controlling his or her world, the depressive simply withdraws from it. Fourth, many theorists, while perhaps no longer regarding anger as the hub of depression,

feel that ambivalence toward introjected objects (i.e., love objects who have been "taken in" to the self) is fundamental to the depressive's emotional quandary. Fifth, it is widely agreed that loss of self-esteem is a primary feature of depression. Otto Fenichel (1945) described depressives as "love addicts," trying continually to compensate for their own depleted self-worth by seeking comfort and reassurance from others. This leads to the sixth common psychodynamic assumption about depression: that it has a functional role. It is not just something that people feel but something that they *use*, particularly in the form of dependency, in their relationships with others.

Like most psychodynamic theories, these assumptions are not fully open to empirical validation, but two claims have been tested. First, a high level of dependency on others does appear to characterize some depressed persons, and these highly dependent people are more likely to become depressed when they experience social rejections (Coyne & Whiffen, 1995). Second, research has examined the role of parental loss, though the results are mixed. There is evidence for the link. Women who have lost their mothers in childhood through either death or separation are apparently more likely to succumb to depression (Harris, Brown, & Bifulco, 1990), and depressed patients who have suffered a serious childhood loss, particularly separation from a parent, are more likely to attempt suicide (Bron, Strack, & Rudolph, 1991). But many researchers now believe that the crucial risk factor, at least for depression, is not so much parental loss as poor parenting (Kendler, Neale, Kessler, et al., 1992a; Lizardi, Klein, Ouimette, et al., 1995). Recent research has focused especially on a parenting pattern called *affectionless control*—that is, too much protectiveness combined with too little real care. This pattern may leave children feeling chronically helpless and overdependent. As adults, when they encounter stress, they are more vulnerable to depression because they feel helpless (Rapee, 1997).

Repairing the Loss In Chapter 6, we described the basic psychodynamic treatment for the "neuroses." Such treatment is used for neurotic-level depression as well. Through free association, dream analysis, and analysis of resistance and transference, the therapist tries to uncover the childhood roots of the current depression and to explore the patient's ambivalent feelings toward the lost object, both primal and current.

As we have noted, however, today's psychodynamic therapists tend to be more directive than their predecessors, as well as more concerned with the patient's present circumstances than with the past. Hence, many therapists focus less on childhood trauma than on the current cause of the depression and on how the patient uses the depression in his or her dealings with others. This pragmatism is even more pronounced in short-term therapy. Klerman and his co-workers have devised a treatment, based on the work of Harry Stack Sullivan (Chapter 4), called *interpersonal psychotherapy*, or *IPT*. In this 12- to 16-session therapy, therapist and patient first identify the core problem. The 4 most common core problems are assumed to be grief, interpersonal disputes (e.g., a failing marriage), role transition (e.g., retirement), and lack of social skills. Once the problem is identified, however, therapist and patient do not spend time on interpretation or analysis. Instead, they attack the problem directly through discussion of possible solutions and strategies for carrying out those solutions (Klerman, Weissman, Rounsaville, et al., 1984). Recent studies indicate that IPT does prevent relapses in formerly depressed patients who have discontinued drug treatment (Frank, Kupfer, Perel, et al., 1990). It also appears to be moderately effective in helping people who are depressed (Elkin, Shea, Watkins, et al., 1989). Although IPT has not been subjected to as many studies as either cognitive or behavioral therapy for depression, it seems to work just as well, at least in the short run (Shea, Elkin, Imber, et al., 1992). For severely depressed patients, it may be even more effective than either cognitive or behavioral treatments (Elkin, Shea, Watkins, et al., 1989).

Psychodynamic treatment of the suicidal patient tends to follow the same lines as treatment for depression, but with special emphasis on emotional support. With potential suicides, therapists are careful to avoid doing or saying anything that could be viewed as rejection. In their analysis of the patient's behavior, they are likely to interpret suicidal threats as an appeal for love, whether from the therapist or from others.

The Behavioral Perspective

Like the psychodynamic perspective, the behavioral perspective on depression and suicide is a collection of theories. We will discuss the two major approaches, one focusing on external reinforcers and the other on interpersonal processes.

Extinction Many behaviorists regard depression as the result of extinction (Ferster, 1973; Lewinsohn, 1974). That is, once behaviors are no longer rewarded, people cease to perform them. They become inactive and withdrawn—in short, depressed.

What causes the reduction in reinforcement? Lewinsohn (1974) has pointed out that the amount of positive reinforcement a person receives depends on three broad factors: (1) the number and range of stimuli that are reinforcing to that person; (2) the availability of such reinforcers in the environment; and (3) the person's skill in obtaining reinforcement. Sudden changes in a person's environment may affect any one of these factors. A new and reluctant retiree, for example, may find that the world outside the office holds few things that are truly reinforcing. Or a man whose wife has recently died may find that, whereas he had the social skills to make a success of marriage, he is at a loss in the dating situation. In their new circumstances, these people simply do not know how to obtain reinforcement; therefore, they withdraw into themselves.

A number of studies by Lewinsohn and his colleagues have produced results consistent with the extinction hypothesis. For example, one objection to this hypothesis has been the widely held assumption that depressives are immune to reinforcement; it is not that they lack sources of pleasure but, rather, that they have lost the ability to experience pleasure. It has been found, however, that even severely depressed people show an elevation of mood if they learn to decrease the frequency of unpleasant events and increase the frequency of pleasant activities (Lewinsohn, Sullivan, & Grosscup, 1980). Depressives also lack skill in obtaining reinforcement, as

Lewinsohn suggested. Depressed people are much less adept than nondepressed people at interacting with others (Segrin & Abramson, 1994). They are also less skillful at coping with the impediments to reinforcement. Not surprisingly, this is all the more true of suicide attempters. When a group of teenagers, hospitalized after a suicide attempt, was compared with a group of distressed but nonsuicidal teenagers, the suicidal subjects were far more likely to use social isolation as their way of coping with problems (Spirito, Overholser, & Stark, 1989). Suicidal adolescents are also likely to avoid problems, to see them inaccurately, and to respond to them in a more emotional fashion (Sadowski & Kelley, 1993). Of course, poor coping and avoidance of problems mean that these people are less likely to get help.

Aversive Social Behavior Some research has found that depressives are more likely than nondepressives to elicit negative reactions from people with whom they interact (Coyne, 1990; Segrin & Abramson, 1994), and this finding has formed the basis of interpersonal theories of depression. According to one theory, depressives have an aversive behavioral style in which, by constantly seeking reassurance, they try to force "caring" behavior from people who, they feel, no longer care enough. Instead of love, however, what depressives are likely to get from their put-upon families and friends is shallow reassurance of the "now, now" variety or, worse, rejection, which simply aggravates their depression (Coyne, 1976b; Joiner & Metalsky, 1995). Depression, then, is a cry for help, but one that rarely works. An alternative interpersonal theory is that depressives actually seek out rejection, for this is more familiar and predictable to them than positive feedback (Giesler, Josephs, & Swann, 1996). In response, they are rejected, and this deepens their depression (Joiner, 1995).

In support of these interpersonal hypotheses, some studies have found that rejecting responses from friends and family do tend to maintain or exacerbate depression (Joiner, 1995; Swann, Wenzlaff, Krull, et al., 1992). For example, Hooley and Teasdale (1989) found that the depressed patients whose spouses were critical toward them were more likely to suffer a relapse of depression in the next nine months than were those with more accepting spouses. However, it is not clear that depressives' interpersonal style predates the onset of their depression. Some evidence suggests that this style is only present during the depressed episode and goes away when the depressed person recovers (Rohde, Lewinsohn, & Seeley, 1990). Whether or not it predates the depression, though, depressives' poor interpersonal skills probably help to maintain their depression.

Increasing Reinforcement and Social Skills In keeping with the extinction theory of depression, behaviorists in the 1970s developed treatments aimed at increasing the patient's rate of reinforcement. Fensterheim and Baer (1975), for example, described what was essentially a project for the relearning of pleasure. First, patients were urged to imagine a gratifying action—eating an ice cream cone, reading a detective story, anything that seemed remotely appealing to them. Then they made an "appointment" with themselves to perform this action. When the time of the appointment arrived, they had to perform the action, whether or not they felt like it. Patients repeated this process a number of times, all the while keeping a record of their responses to their "pleasure excursions." The goal was not only to increase the patients' contact with reinforcers but also to retrain them in the experience of pleasure.

Another important thrust in the behavioral treatment of depression has been **social-skills training.** As we have seen, depressives are not popular with others—a problem that social-skills training aims to remedy directly by teaching basic techniques for engaging in satisfying social interactions. Patients are shown how to initiate a conversation, how to keep eye contact, how to make small talk, how to end a conversation—in other words, the nuts and bolts of socializing. Such behaviors are often modeled for patients, after which they are practiced through role playing. The therapist, for example, might pretend to be a guest at a party with whom the patient must open a conversation.

Most behavioral treatments for depression are multifaceted, using the techniques previously described, together with others. For example, Lewinsohn and his colleagues have put together a treatment that includes self-monitoring of mood and activities, instruction in positive coping self-statements, and training in a variety of areas—coping skills, social skills, parenting skills, time management—with the aim of decreasing unpleasant experiences and increasing pleasant experiences (Lewinsohn & Gotlib, 1995). Similar multifaceted programs have been used with suicidal patients. For example, Liberman and Eckman (1981) have reported a successful evaluation of a behavioral program for repeated suicide attempters that includes social-skills training, anxiety management, and contingency contracting with family members regarding family disputes.

In evaluating the effectiveness of any treatment (behavioral or otherwise) for depression, one must keep in mind that 85 percent of depressed people recover from an episode within a year, even with no treatment. Furthermore, drug studies indicate that 20 to 40 percent of outpatient depressives recover in

2 to 4 months, even if all they receive is a placebo. Thus, it is relatively easy to design a therapy that ends with a substantial rate of recovery. There is going to be substantial recovery, anyway.

Many of the behavioral therapies of the 1970s and 1980s showed promise, but none of them was tested rigorously—that is, through randomized trials comparing the behavioral therapy with drug therapy and with placebo "treatment." Because, as we will see, there are effective antidepressant drugs that are much less expensive than psychotherapy, the latter has to outperform these drugs (and placebos) in order to justify its use. None of the behavioral therapies described passed such a test. Alternatively, because none of the drugs actually *cures* depression—that is, prevents relapses as well as lifts current mood—psychotherapy could prove its usefulness by showing that it does prevent recurrence, but at this point none of the behavioral therapies has met this standard.

In fact, with the rise of cognitive therapy in the 1980s, most behavioral therapies that did not include a cognitive component were laid aside. Cognitive therapy swept the field, and most behaviorists joined the trend, creating combined cognitive-behavioral treatments that included pleasure enhancement and social-skills training, as well as cognitive retraining.

The Cognitive Perspective

As we saw earlier, depression involves a number of changes: emotional, motivational, cognitive, and physical. Cognitive theorists hold that the critical variable is the cognitive change. In all cognitive formulations, it is the way people *think* about themselves, the world, and the future that gives rise to the other factors involved in depression.

Helplessness and Hopelessness   In a cognitive-learning model of depression, Martin Seligman (1975) has suggested that depression may be understood as analogous to the phenomenon of **learned helplessness.** This phenomenon was first demonstrated with laboratory dogs. After exposing a number of dogs to inescapable electric shocks, Seligman and his colleagues found that, when the same dogs were later subjected to escapable shocks, they either did not initiate escape responses or were slow and inept at escaping. The investigators concluded that, during the first phase of the experiment, when the shocks were inescapable, the dogs had learned that the shock was *uncontrollable*—a lesson they continued to act upon even in the second phase of the experiment, when it was possible to escape the shocks (Maier, Seligman, & Solomon, 1969).

After further research on learned helplessness in animals and humans, Seligman noted that this phenomenon closely resembled depression. He therefore proposed that depression, like learned helplessness, was a reaction to inescapable or seemingly inescapable stressors, which undermined adaptive responses by teaching the person that he or she lacked control over reinforcement. This formulation is consistent with the finding that, when there is a clear, precipitating event for a depression, it is often an uncontrollable loss. Learned helplessness also fits with certain neuroscience findings. For example, depressed patients who see themselves as helpless tend to show higher levels of MHPG, a product of norepinephrine metabolism (Samson, Mirin, Hauser, et al., 1992). As we will see, norepinephrine abnormalities are often found in depressed people. In addition, PET scans of people doing unsolvable problems—which tend to produce learned helplessness—show that learned helplessness is associated with increased brain activity in the limbic system. The limbic system is also implicated in the processing of negative emotions such as depression (Schneider, Gur, Alavi, et al., 1996).

Note the difference between the learned helplessness theory and extinction theory. In extinction theory, the crucial factor is an objective environmental condition, a lack of positive reinforcement; in learned helplessness theory, the crucial factor is a subjective cognitive process, the *expectation* of lack of control over reinforcement. One should also note the connection between learned helplessness theory and the psychodynamic theory of early loss. The evidence for the psychodynamic theory—for example, that women who lost their mothers in childhood tend to show greater helplessness—is also evidence for the learned helplessness theory.

When it was originally formulated, the learned helplessness model had certain weaknesses. As Seligman and his colleagues pointed out, the model explained the passivity characteristic of depression but did not explain the equally characteristic sadness, guilt, and suicidal thoughts. Neither did it account for the fact that different cases of depression vary considerably in intensity and duration. To fill these gaps, Abramson and her colleagues adapted the model from a helplessness to a hopelessness theory. According to their view, depression depends not just on the belief that there is a lack of control over reinforcement (a *helplessness expectancy*) but also on the belief that negative events will persist or recur (a *negative outcome expectancy*). When a person holds these two expectations—that bad things will happen and that there is nothing one can do about it—he or she becomes hopeless, and it is this hopelessness that

According to the theory of learned helplessness, people who experience an uncontrollable loss like the death of a parent would be more likely to become depressed.

is the immediate cause of the depression (Abramson, Metalsky, & Alloy, 1989).

But what is the source of the expectations of helplessness and negative outcomes? According to the researchers, these expectations stem from the *attributions* and *inferences* people make regarding stressful life events—that is, the perceived causes and consequences of such events. People who see negative life events as due to causes that are (1) permanent rather than temporary, (2) generalized over many areas of their life rather than specific to one area of their functioning, and (3) internal, or part of their personalities, rather than external, or part of the environment, are at greatest risk for developing hopelessness and, in turn, severe and persistent depression. Likewise, people who infer that stressful events will have negative consequences for themselves are more likely to become hopeless and depressed. In fact, Abramson and her co-workers have proposed that "hopelessness depression" constitutes a distinct subtype of depression, with its own set of causes (negative inferential styles combined with stress), symptoms (passivity, sadness, suicidal tendencies, low self-esteem), and appropriate treatments. Thus, what was once a cognitive-learning formulation has been refined in this theory to an explicitly cognitive formulation. This theory also applies to suicide. Hopelessness is the best single predictor of suicide—even better than depression (Glanz, Haas, & Sweeney, 1995).

In the past decade, the revised hopelessness theory has begun to be tested, with mixed results. On the positive side, it has been found that depressives are more likely than controls to explain negative events by means of the kind of attributions listed in the previous paragraph (Joiner & Wagner, 1995; Sweeney, Anderson, & Bailey, 1986). Moreover, attributional style can help predict who, in a given sample, has

been depressed in the past (Alloy, Lipman, & Abramson, 1992), who will become depressed in the future when exposed to stress (Abramson, Alloy, & Metalsky, 1995; Alloy, Abramson, Murray, et al., 1997; Robinson, Garber, & Hillsman, 1995), and who, having recovered from depression, will relapse (Ilardi, Craighead, & Evans, 1997). It also predicts who, in a group of depressed people, will recover when exposed to positive events (Needles & Abramson, 1990). Other studies have shown that the reason a combination of stress and negative attributional style predicts depression is that this combination predicts hopelessness. It is hopelessness which, in turn, predicts depression (Alloy & Clements, in press; Metalsky, Joiner, Hardin, et al., 1993). Finally, people who show this combination also exhibit many of the symptoms said to be part of the hopelessness-depression subtype (Alloy, Just, & Panzarella, 1997). At the same time, there is conflicting evidence. For example, some researchers have found that the stress-plus-negative-attributions combination did not necessarily lead to depression (Cole & Turner, 1993; Hammen, Adrian, & Hiroto, 1988). To summarize, most of the evidence argues that attributional style and hopelessness play a role in depression. What is not clear is whether they actually help *cause* the depression.

Negative Self-Schema A second major cognitive theory of depression, Aaron Beck's negative self-schema model, evolved from his findings that the hallucinations, delusions, and dreams of depressed patients often contain themes of self-punishment, loss, and deprivation. According to Beck, this negative bias—the tendency to see oneself as a "loser"—is the fundamental cause of depression. If a person, because of childhood experiences, develops a cognitive "schema" in which the self, the world, and the future are viewed in a negative light, that person is then predisposed to depression. Stress can easily activate the negative schema, and the consequent negative perceptions merely strengthen the schema (Beck, 1987; Haaga, Dyck, & Ernst, 1991).

Recent research supports Beck's claim that depressives have unusually negative self-schemas (Teasdale, Taylor, Cooper, et al., 1995) and that these schemas can be activated by negative cues. In one interesting study, depressed and normal subjects performed an emotional Stroop task (Chapter 4): they were shown positive and negative self-descriptive adjectives and were asked to name the color of ink the adjectives were printed in. When, prior to the Stroop task, the subjects were exposed to another series of negative self-statements (e.g., "I often feel judged"), the depressed subjects were significantly slower at naming the ink colors for the negative adjectives on the Stroop task (Segal, Gemar, Truchon, et al., 1995). Presumably, their negative self-schemas were primed in the first stage and then, on the Stroop task, went into action.

Other studies indicate that depressives—and people at high risk for depression—selectively attend to and remember more negative than positive information about themselves (Alloy, Abramson, Murray, et al., 1997; Gotlib, Gilboa, & Sommerfield, in press). Still other research suggests that depressives may have two distinct negative self-schemas, one centered on dependency, the other on self-criticism (Nietzel & Harris, 1990). For those with dependency self-schemas, stressful social events—in other words, situations in which their dependency would be most keenly felt—lead to depression. For those with self-criticism schemas, failure should trigger depression. Researchers testing this hypothesis have found that it works better for dependency self-schemas and social events than for self-criticism schemas and failure (Coyne & Whiffen, 1995).

An interesting finding is that, while depressives may be more pessimistic than the rest of us, their pessimism is sometimes more realistic than our optimism. Lewinsohn and his colleagues put a group of depressives and two control groups through a series of social interactions and then asked the subjects (1) how positively or negatively they reacted to the others and (2) how positively or negatively they thought the others reacted to them. As it turned out, the depressives' evaluations of the impression they had made were more accurate than those of the other two groups, both of whom thought they had made more positive impressions than they actually had (Lewinsohn, Mischel, Chaplin, et al., 1980). To quote the report of another Lewinsohn research team, "To feel good about ourselves we may have to judge ourselves more kindly than we are judged" (Lewinsohn, Sullivan, & Grosscup, 1980, p. 212).

We may also have to judge ourselves more capable than we are. Alloy and Abramson (1979) found that depressives, in doing an experimental task, were far more accurate in judging how much control they had than were nondepressed subjects, who tended to overestimate their control when they were doing well and to underestimate it when they were doing poorly. Thus, in certain respects it may be that normal people, not depressives, are cognitively biased—and that such bias is essential for psychological health (Alloy & Abramson, 1988; Haaga & Beck, 1995). Research supports this view. Alloy and Clements (1992), for example, tested a group for bias in judging personal control. They found that the subjects who had been inaccurately optimistic about their personal control when they were first tested were less likely than more realistic subjects to become depressed a month later in the face of stress.

While these studies strongly suggest that cognitive variables play a role in depression, it is by no means clear that the role is causal (Haaga, Dyck, & Ernst, 1991). However, as we have seen before, a factor need not be causal in order to be useful in treatment.

Cognitive Retraining   Aaron Beck and his co-workers have developed a multifaceted therapy that includes behavioral assignments, modification of dysfunctional thinking, and attempts to change schemas. It is the alteration of schemas that is considered most important. According to Beck's theory, this is what will inoculate the patient against future depressions. First, however, the therapist attacks the present depression, through "behavioral activation"—that is, getting the patients to get out and engage in pleasurable activities—and by teaching them ways of testing dysfunctional thinking. On a form (Figure 9.4), patients are asked to record their negative thoughts, together with the events that preceded them. Then they are to counter such thoughts with rational responses and record the outcome (Young, Beck, & Weinberger, 1993).

A refinement of cognitive retraining is *reattribution training,* which aims to correct negative attributional styles (Beck, Rush, Shaw, et al., 1979). In this approach, patients are taught to explain their difficulties to themselves in more constructive ways ("It wasn't my fault—it was the circumstances," "It's not my whole personality that's wrong—it's just my way of reacting to strangers") and to seek out information consistent with these more hopeful attributions (Alloy, Clements, & Kolden, 1985). A similar approach has been used with suicidal patients. Beck and his colleagues see this as a way of correcting negative

DATE	SITUATION Describe: 1. Actual event leading to unpleasant emotion, or 2. Stream of thoughts, daydream, or recollection, leading to unpleasant emotion.	EMOTION(S) 1. Specify sad/ anxious/ angry, etc. 2. Rate degree of emotion, 1–100.	AUTOMATIC THOUGHT(S) 1. Write automatic thought(s) that preceded emotion(s). 2. Rate belief in automatic thought(s), 0–100%.	RATIONAL RESPONSE 1. Write rational response to automatic thought(s). 2. Rate belief in rational response, 0–100%.	OUTCOME 1. Rerate belief in automatic thought, 0–100%. 2. Specify and rate subsequent emotions, 1–100.

Explanation: When you experience an unpleasant emotion, note the situation that seemed to stimulate the emotion. (If the emotion occurred while you were thinking, daydreaming, etc., please note this.) Then note the automatic thought associated with the emotion. Record the degree to which you believe this thought: 0% = not at all; 100% = completely. In rating degree of emotion: 1 = a trace; 100 = the most intense possible.

FIGURE 9.4 Form for "daily record of dysfunctional thoughts," as used in the cognitive treatment developed by Beck and his co-workers. (Young, Beck, & Weinberger, 1993, p. 250)

bias. As the research cited previously suggests, it may also be a way of instilling positive bias. In any case, it seems to combat hopelessness.

In some encouraging evaluations, cognitive therapies have been shown to be at least as effective as drug therapy, and perhaps superior to drugs at 1-year follow-up (Dobson, 1989; Hollon, Shelton, & Davis, 1993). A combination of cognitive-behavioral therapy and drugs may have a slight advantage when compared with either treatment by itself (Hollon, DeRubeis, Evans, et al., 1992). Some experts interpret the evidence as indicating that cognitive-behavioral therapy, unlike drug therapy, has a relapse-prevention effect (Evans, Hollon, DeRubeis, et al., 1992), but there is considerable debate about this (Jacobson & Hollon, 1996; Klein, 1996). There is also some question as to whether cognitive-behavioral therapy works as well as drugs for severely depressed patients (Sotsky, Glass, Shea, et al., 1991; Thase, Simons, Calahane, et al., 1991).

Furthermore, there is controversy about the mechanisms by which cognitive-behavioral therapy produces change. As noted, Beck's treatment is multifaceted, including behavioral activation together with cognitive tasks. A recent study by Jacobson and his colleagues found that the behavioral activation component of cognitive-behavioral therapy worked as well as the entire treatment package, both at alleviating depression and at preventing relapse (Gortner, Gollan, Jacobson, et al., in press; Jacobson et al., 1996). Thus, it could be that cognitive-behavioral therapy is just as effective without its cognitive components.

The Sociocultural Perspective

Society and Depression One of the first scholars to study suicide scientifically was French sociologist Émile Durkheim, writing in the late nineteenth century (1897/1951). Durkheim saw suicide as an act that occurred *within a society* and, in some measure, under the control of that society. Today, it is widely recognized that socioeconomic factors affect suicide rates. In 1932, at the height of the Depression, the suicide rate in the United States almost doubled in one year. During the recession of the 1970s, it rose again (Wekstein, 1979).

An even more dramatic indicator of social determinants of hopelessness is the rise in rates of depression in the past century. The first clear evidence of this phenomenon came from a study conducted in the mid-eighties (Robins, Helzer, Weissman, et al., 1984). The researchers surveyed 9,500 people randomly selected from urban and rural areas to see how many had had an episode of serious depression in their lives. In the 20- to 25-year-old group, 5 to 6 percent had at least 1 episode; in the 25- to 44-year-old group, the rate was higher: 8 to 9 percent. That made sense—the longer you have lived, the greater your chance of having experienced depression. But what were the researchers to make of the fact that the 70-year-olds in the survey showed a rate of only 1 percent? The people who had lived the *longest* had the least experience of depression. These results were essentially duplicated by a study of close relatives of depressed patients (Klerman, Lavori, Rice, et al., 1985). Even among people at risk for depression, the young adults were 6 times as likely as the over-65 group to have had a depressive episode, and these findings, too, have been confirmed (Blazer, Kessler, McGonagle, et al., 1994; Lewinsohn, Rohde, Seeley, et al., 1993). The conclusion is that the prevalence of depression in the United States has increased steadily, and the age of onset has dropped precipitously, in the past hundred years.

Why? Presumably, social change has something to do with it. We know, for example, that rates of depression tend to be lower in highly traditional social groups. Depression does not seem to exist, for instance, in a New Guinea tribe called the Kaluli (Scheiffelin, 1984). And, among the Amish living in Pennsylvania, the incidence of major depression is one-fifth to one-tenth the rate of depression among people living in Baltimore, only 100 miles away (Egeland & Hostetter, 1983). The common denominator of the Kaluli and the Amish is that each is a traditional, tight-knit, nonindustrialized community with stable families, a stable social structure, and long-held customs and beliefs. In our society, on the other hand, what we see predominantly is change, as people move away from their families, away from their birthplaces, and up and down the socioeconomic ladder. As Martin Seligman (1988) notes, "The modern individual is not the peasant of yore with a fixed future yawning ahead. He (and now she, effectively doubling the market) is a battleground of decisions and preferences" (p. 91). What this means is that young people today cannot rely on the support systems that were in place in their grandparents' day: the family, the church, the traditions and customs that once dictated choices. People must rely on themselves, and, if the answer is not there, apparently, a sense of helplessness sets in, greatly increasing the risk of depression. (For sociocultural factors that may contribute to women's increased vulnerability to depression, see the box on page 242.)

Changing the Society   As we saw earlier, there have been some attempts—hot lines, school programs—at preventing suicide on the social level, but they have not been especially effective. A recent review of such programs suggests that efforts might be better spent attacking the social problems most closely associated with suicide: delinquency, truancy, substance abuse, teen pregnancy, and family distress (Garland & Zigler, 1993). Several researchers have also called for stricter gun-control laws (Lester & Murrell, 1980) and for educating journalists about the possible imitative effects of suicide coverage. There is some evidence, though mixed, that highly publicized suicides may negatively inspire others, particularly young people who share characteristics such as age, gender, and race, with the celebrity suicide (Velting & Gould, 1997). In 1977, for example, there was a significant increase in suicide by gunshot in Los Angeles County during the week following comedian Freddie Prinze's suicide by gunshot (Berman, 1988).

The Biological Perspective

Genetic Research   Family studies have shown that first-degree relatives of people with major mood disorders are much more likely than other people to develop these disorders. For major depression, their risk is $1\frac{1}{2}$ to 3 times higher, and for bipolar disorder it is fully 10 times higher, than that of the general population (Strober, Morrell, Burroughs, et al., 1988). As we have seen, the family risk for both conditions is even greater when the index case had an early onset. Although unipolar patients are found among the relatives of bipolar patients, the reverse seldom occurs (Winokur, Coryell, Keller, et al., 1995)—further support for the theory that the two syndromes spring from different causes. Finally, suicide also runs in families, even when the association with depression is controlled (Brent, Bridge, Johnson, et al., 1996).

As we know, it is difficult in family studies to separate environmental from genetic influence. However, twin studies also support the role of genetic inheritance in the mood disorders and suicide. In a review of genetic research on mood disorders in twins, M. G. Allen (1976) found that the concordance rate for bipolar disorder was 72 percent among monozygotic twins, as compared with 14 percent among dizygotic twins. The concordance rate for unipolar disorder was 40 percent among monozygotic twins, as compared with 11 percent among dizygotic twins. The difference between the bipolar and unipolar concordance rates among monozygotic twins (72 percent versus 40 percent) suggests that genetic factors are more important in bipolar disorder than in depression. But more recent twin studies indicate that genes play a crucial role in major depression as well. According to this research, 40 to 45 percent of the difference in depression rates between MZ and DZ twins is attributable solely to genes. The rest of the difference, the results indicated, is due to individual-specific environment—in other words, life events specific to each member of the twin pair—and not at all to shared environmental factors such as social class, parental childrearing practices, or early parental loss (Kendler, Neale, Kessler, et al., 1992a, 1993; McGuffin, Katz, Watkins, et al., 1996). Even more current research suggests that the way genes increase risk for major depression is by increasing the person's sensitivity to stressful life events (Kendler, Kessler, Walters, et al., 1995).

But the most impressive evidence for the heritability of mood disorders comes from adoption studies. In a study of the biological and adoptive parents of bipolar adoptees as compared with the biological and adoptive parents of normal adoptees, Mendlewicz and Rainer (1977) found a 31 percent prevalence of mood disorders in the biological parents of the bipolar adoptees, as opposed to 2 percent in the biological parents of the normal adoptees—a striking difference. A more recent study (Wender, Kety, Rosenthal, et al., 1986), this time of the biological and adoptive parents, siblings, and half-siblings of adoptees with a broad range of mood disorders, found that the prevalence of unipolar depression was 8 times greater—and the suicide rate 15 times greater—in the biological relatives of the mood disorder cases than in the biological relatives of the normal adoptees. These two studies constitute firm support for a genetic component in both bipolar and unipolar mood disorder.

An important new direction in the genetic study of mood disorders is linkage analysis (Chapter 4). In an intriguing linkage-analysis study, blood samples were taken from every person in an 81-member Amish clan. Then, for each subject, the researchers isolated the DNA molecule and searched the molecule for evidence of a characteristic that tended to be inherited with bipolar disorder. They found what appeared to be the characteristic on chromosome 11. Furthermore, when they compared the chromosomes of the 19 family members diagnosed as suffering from psychiatric disorders (primarily bipolar disorder) with those of the 62 members considered psychiatrically well, they consistently found a difference at chromosome 11 (Egeland, Gerhard, Pauls, et al., 1987).

Unfortunately, other studies have had mixed results. Some have failed to show linkage between bipolar disorder and markers on chromosome 11 (Gill, McKeon, & Humphries, 1988; Hodgkinson, Sherrington, Gurling, et al., 1987). Some show linkage to genes on other chromosomes (Berrettini, Ferraro, Goldin, et al., 1997). Rather than viewing these results as a negation of the Amish study, however, many scientists see them as an indication that bipolar disorder is not a single disease but a group of related diseases, with a variety of genetic (and environmental) causes that await identification. In the 1990s, the National Institutes of Health has been sponsoring a project to map the entire human chromosome set, the Human Genome Project, most of which remains unexplored. As this project proceeds,

Research among the Amish has turned up a linkage between a chromosomal characteristic and bipolar disorder. Such studies can shed light on the heritability of mood disorders.

we may see the emergence of genes that are consistently linked to bipolar disorder.

Neurophysiological Research   Given that organic factors are implicated in the mood disorders, the next question is, *what* organic factors? According to neurophysiological researchers, the problem may have to do with biological rhythms. As we have seen, sleep disturbance is one of the most common symptoms of depression. Depressives also consistently show abnormalities in their progress through the various stages of sleep (Benca, Obermeyer, Thisted, et al., 1992), possibly as a result of overarousal (Ho, Gillin, Buchsbaum, et al., 1996). One such abnormality is shortened rapid eye movement (REM) latency—that is, in depressives the time between the onset of sleep and the onset of REM sleep, the stage of sleep in which dreams occur, is unusually short. And this characteristic may indicate a biological vulnerability to depression, for depressives who have shortened REM latency (1) are more likely to have the endogenous symptom pattern and to respond to antidepressant drugs, but not to psychotherapy, (2) tend to go on showing shortened REM latency, even after the depressive episode has passed, (3) are likely to have first-degree relatives who also have shortened REM latency, and (4) are more likely to relapse (Buysse & Kupfer, 1993; Giles, Biggs, Rush, et al., 1988).

These sleep disturbances, together with the hormonal abnormalities associated with depression, suggest that in depressives the "biological clock" has somehow gone out of order—a hypothesis that Ehlers and her colleagues have combined with the findings on loss and depression to produce an integrated biopsychosocial theory. According to this theory, our lives are filled with social "zeitgebers" (literally, "time givers"): personal relationships, jobs, and other responsibilities and routines that help to activate and regulate our biological rhythms. Having someone with whom you sleep, for example, helps to enforce your sleep rhythms. When he or she goes to bed, so do you. Consequently, when an important social zeitgeber is removed from a person's life—when a spouse dies, for example—the removal may not only produce an important loss but also may disrupt the body's circadian rhythms, or biological cycles, leading to a range of consequences (sleep disturbance, eating disturbance, mood disturbance, hormonal imbalance) that we call depression (Ehlers, Frank, & Kupfer, 1988). In keeping with this disrupted-rhythm theory, some evidence suggests that depriving a depressed patient of sleep, particularly of REM sleep, may have a therapeutic effect (Liebenluft & Wehr, 1992; Wehr, 1990).

One form of depression that may be closely related to the body's biological rhythms is **seasonal affective disorder,** or **SAD.** Beginning with Hippocrates, physicians over the centuries have noted that many depressions come on in winter. In the late nineteenth century, surgeon and Arctic explorer Frederick Cook made the connection between this phenomenon and light exposure. In the Eskimos, and also in the members of his expeditionary team, Cook observed a depressed mood, together with fatigue and decreased sexual desire, during the long, dark Arctic winter. Recently, this seasonal depression, which includes not only increased sleeping but also increased eating and a craving for carbohydrates, has been added to the *DSM*. Many people experience it in a mild degree. In order for the diagnosis of SAD to be made, however, the patient must meet the criteria for major depressive episode; remission as well as onset must be keyed to the seasons, and the pattern must have lasted for at least 2 years. There is a summer version of SAD, but the winter version is much more common, and, as Cook suspected, the latter seems to be tied to the much shorter photoperiod, or period of daylight, during the winter (Young, Meaden, Fogg, et al., 1997). Women are at far higher risk—60 to 90 percent of patients are female—and so are the young. The average age of onset is 23 (Oren & Rosenthal, 1992). Recent studies suggest that the disorder has a genetic component (Jang, Lam, Livesley, et al., 1997).

The most promising current theory of SAD is that it is caused by a lag in circadian rhythms; thus, during the day, the person experiences the kind of physical slowdown he or she should be undergoing at night (Teicher, Glod, Magnus, et al., 1997). About three-quarters of SAD patients improve when given the same kind of light therapy that is used for circadian rhythm sleep disorders (Chapter 8): exposure to bright artificial light for several hours a day (Oren & Rosenthal, 1992). In some cases, light therapy, if it is applied at the first sign of symptoms, can actually prevent a full-blown episode (Meesters, Jansen, Beersma, et al., 1993). If this circadian-rhythm theory is correct, then light therapy should work best if it is applied in the morning, because extra morning light advances circadian rhythms, whereas extra evening light does not. Unfortunately, the evidence for this prediction is mixed, and it seems that a combination of morning and evening light therapy is most effective (Lee, Blashko, Janzen, et al., 1997).

Neuroimaging Research   Recent CT and MRI studies suggest that mood disorders involve abnormalities in brain structure. People with mood disorders tend to show enlargement of the ventricles and the sulci (the spaces between brain tissues). They also show re-

Sometimes the treatment for a troubling disorder is as blessedly simple as a few extra hours of sunshine each day. Many people with the aptly named SAD, or seasonal affective disorder, benefit from sitting in front of an ultraviolet light box for a prescribed amount of time during the short days of winter.

duced volume in the frontal lobe, the cerebellum, and the basal ganglia, all of which are brain regions thought to be involved in mood regulation (Elkis, Friedman, Wise, et al., 1995; Soares & Mann, 1997).

Biochemical Research   At present, perhaps the most vital area of research on mood disorders is biochemistry. There are two major biochemical theories.

Hormone Imbalance   One biochemical theory is that depression is due to a malfunction of the hypothalamus, a portion of the brain known to regulate mood. Because the hypothalamus affects not only mood but also many other functions that are typically disrupted in the course of a depression, such as appetite and sexual interest, some researchers (e.g., Holsboer, 1992) suggest that the hypothalamus may be the key to depressive disorders. If so, the abnormality may have to do with the control of hormone production. The hypothalamus regulates the pituitary gland, and both the hypothalamus and the pituitary control the production of hormones by the gonads and the adrenal and thyroid glands. There is substantial evidence that in depressives there is some irregularity in this process. In the first place, depressives often show abnormal hormone levels. Second, people with abnormal hormone activity often show depression as a side effect. Third, CT scans show that many depressives have enlarged pituitary and adrenal glands (Nemeroff, Krishnan, Reed, et al., 1992). Fourth, postmortem studies of the brains of depressed patients show abnormalities in the neurons of the

hypothalamus (Purba, Hoogendijk, Hofman, et al., 1996). But perhaps the best evidence is that depression can sometimes be effectively treated by altering hormone levels. In certain cases, for example, induced changes in thyroid output have aided in recovery from depression; in others, administering estrogen, a sex hormone, has proved an effective treatment (Bauer & Whybrow, 1990).

Hormone imbalances appear to be particularly characteristic of endogenous and psychotic depressions. Indeed, such imbalances can be used to help differentiate between endogenous and reactive cases, and between psychotic and nonpsychotic cases, via a technique called the **dexamethasone suppression test** (**DST**). Dexamethasone is a drug that in normal people suppresses the secretion of the hormone cortisol for at least 24 hours. However, endogenously and psychotically depressed patients, who seem to secrete abnormally high levels of cortisol, manage to resist the drug's effect as long as they are in the depressive episode (Nelson & Davis, 1997). This is the basis for the DST. Depressed patients are given dexamethasone, and then their blood is tested at regular intervals for cortisol. The nonsuppressors—those whose cortisol levels return to high levels within 24 hours despite the drug— are classed as endogenous or psychotic. Since the DST was developed, researchers have discovered other interesting things about nonsuppressors. They tend not to respond to psychotherapy (or placebos); they tend to show nonsuppression in later depressive episodes as well; if they continue to show nonsuppression after treatment, this predicts relapse. All these facts support the notion that DST nonsuppression is a marker of a more endogenous depression (Thase, Dubé, Bowler, et al., 1996). Nonsuppression also seems to be tied to social facts. Among baboons, DST nonsuppressors are likely to be isolated, socially subordinate individuals. It is possible that the high stress associated with low social rank causes the nonsuppression (Sapolsky, Alberts, & Altmann, 1997). On the other hand, nonsuppression may be linked to behaviors that create a social disadvantage.

An important finding in the research on hormone imbalances is that such imbalances occur both in major depression and in depressive episodes of bipolar disorder. Genetic research, as we noted, suggests that major depression and bipolar disorder are two distinct syndromes, with different causes. For this reason, it seems unlikely that the hormonal abnormalities common to both syndromes constitute a *primary* cause. (A good possibility is that they are caused by the neurotransmitter imbalances that we will discuss next [Delgado, Price, Heninger, et al., 1992; Holsboer, 1992].) Neither does the stubborn cortisol production of the DST nonsuppressors seem to be a primary cause of depression, for DST nonsuppression is also seen in many other disorders, including schizophrenia, obsessive-compulsive disorder, eating disorders, and alcoholism (Thase, Frank, & Kupfer, 1985). At the same time, the fact that hormones can sometimes relieve depression suggests that in certain, perhaps atypical, cases, hormone imbalance may play a causal role.

Neurotransmitter Imbalance   The second important theory of biochemical research has to do with the neurotransmitters norepinephrine and serotonin. According to the **catecholamine hypothesis,*** increased levels of norepinephrine produce mania, while decreased levels produce depression (Schildkraut, 1965). The only way to test this hypothesis directly would be to analyze brain-tissue samples of manics and depressives to determine whether their norepinephrine levels are, in fact, abnormally high and low, respectively. Because this cannot be done without damage to the brain, we have to rely on indirect evidence. That evidence consists of findings that drugs and other treatments that relieve depression or produce mania increase the level of norepinephrine in the brain, while drugs that produce depression or alleviate mania reduce the level of norepinephrine in the brain (Miller, Delgado, Salomon, et al., 1996; Schildkraut, 1972).

This research is spurred by the hope that the action of the drugs will tell us something about the process by

which mood disorders develop in the first place. As we saw in Chapter 4, when an impulse travels down a neuron and reaches its end, this neuron, the *presynaptic* neuron, releases the neurotransmitter into the synapse that lies between it and the next, or *postsynaptic,* neuron. The neurotransmitter bonds with the receptors of the postsynaptic neuron, thereby transmitting the impulse. Some of the neurotransmitter is taken back up into the presynaptic neuron—a process called reuptake. (Review Figure 4.3, page 84.)

The tricyclics, a class of drugs widely used for depression, generally work by blocking the reuptake of norepinephrine (and serotonin) by the presynaptic neuron. Superficially, this suggests that depression may be due to too-rapid reuptake or to inadequate secretion. However, the picture is probably more complicated than that. First of all, recent research indicates that, if depressives have a problem with norepinephrine function, it has to do not with the presynaptic receptors, which appear to operate normally, but with the postsynaptic receptors, which appear to be undersensitive to norepinephrine (Halper, Brown, Sweeney, et al., 1988; Heninger, Charney, & Price, 1988). Second, some newer, and effective, tricyclics do not work by blocking reuptake; they increase norepinephrine levels by more subtle means. The fact that tricyclics generally take 2 weeks to start relieving symptoms suggests that their success has to do not with immediate effects, such as blocking reuptake, but with long-term effects—specifically, the enhancement of proteins that affect the atrophy or growth of the neurons (Duman, Heninger, & Nestler, 1997).

As the research suggests, neither does the system have to do with norepinephrine alone. Serotonin is probably involved as well. It has been shown, for example, that L-tryptophan, an amino acid that increases serotonin levels, is an effective treatment for *both* mania and depression. Furthermore, when recovered depressives—and recovered SAD patients—are put through a procedure that depletes their tryptophan levels, their depressive symptoms return (Bremner, Innis, Salomon, et al., 1997; Lam, Zis, Grewal, et al., 1996). Another connected finding is that children who have major depression, together with children whose parents have the disorder, show abnormalities in their response to drugs that enhance serotonin (Birmaher, Kaufman, Brent, et al., 1997). Finally, PET scans show that the brains of depressed patients have a reduced responsiveness to serotonin (Mann, Malone, Diehl, et al., 1996). Thus, serotonin is probably involved, together with norepinephrine, in the mood disorders.

Serotonin has been implicated in suicide as well. As we saw in the discussion of adoption studies, the

*This theory is so-called because norepinephrine belongs to a group of structurally similar molecules called the *catecholamines.*

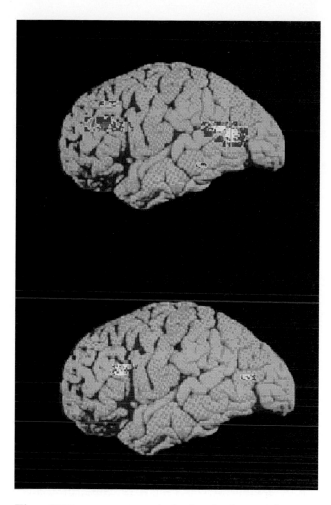

These PET scans compare the brain of a depressed person (top) with the brain of a person whose depression has been treated (bottom). Regions shown in red and yellow depict areas of low brain activity in the depressed individual. The healthy brain treated for depression shows that metabolic activity and blood flow has resumed in the affected areas.

biological relatives of adoptees with mood disorders appear to be 15 times more likely to commit suicide than the biological relatives of control adoptees. This argues very strongly for an inheritable risk for suicide, even apart from depression. It has been proposed that a decreased flow of serotonin from the brainstem to the frontal cortex may be associated with suicide, independent of depression—indeed, with impulsive, aggressive behavior as well. In support of this hypothesis, tests of the cerebrospinal fluid of suicide attempters, particularly those who have chosen violent methods, have found evidence of abnormally low serotonin activity (Mann, McBride, Brown, et al., 1992). In addition, postmortem analyses of suicides have found subnormal amounts of serotonin and impaired serotonin receptors in the brainstem and frontal cortex (Arango & Underwood,

1997). Should this hypothesis gain further support, it is possible that in the future we will have special drug therapies for people who attempt suicide.

A newer biochemical theory of depression is that depressive episodes, especially those triggered by stress, are caused by the atrophy, or death, of certain neurons in the hippocampus (Chapter 4), a region of the brain involved in emotion, learning, and memory as well as in the regulation of sleep, appetite, and cortisol function. According to this hypothesis, antidepressant drugs reverse this atrophy by increasing the expression of a gene, the so-called *brain-derived neurotrophic factor,* that promotes neuron growth (Duman, Heninger, & Nestler, 1997).

A Summary of Biochemical Findings It seems indisputable that norepinephrine, serotonin, and hormone abnormalities are all involved in the mood disorders, and the most compelling current theories differ only in the emphasis they give to each of these three factors. What is most likely is that mood disorders are due to a complex interaction of genetic, neurophysiological, biochemical, developmental, cognitive, and situational variables (Kendler, Kessler, Neale, et al., 1993; Whybrow, Akiskal, & McKinney, 1984).

Whatever the biological perspective ultimately contributes to uncovering the cause of mood disorders, it has already contributed heavily to their treatment—a matter to which we now turn.

Antidepressant Medication The most common therapy for depressed patients, whether or not they are receiving other kinds of therapy, is drugs. The three major classes of *antidepressant medication*—the **MAO inhibitors,** the **tricyclics,** and the **selective serotonin reuptake inhibitors (SSRIs)**—have already been described in Chapter 6, in relation to the anxiety disorders, and the most commonly used drugs within those classes were listed in Table 4.1 on page 86. All three classes seem to work by increasing levels of the neurotransmitters that we have just discussed, the MAO inhibitors by interfering with an enzyme (MAO) that degrades norepinephrine and serotonin, the tricyclics by blocking the reuptake of norepinephrine and serotonin, the SSRIs by blocking the reuptake of serotonin alone.

The prescription of these drugs is a matter of balancing symptom relief against side effects. As we saw in Chapter 6, the MAO inhibitors have the most troubling side effects, but, for certain types of depression—especially "atypical depression," characterized by excessive sleeping and/or eating—they tend to work better than other antidepressants. The tricyclics can also have unpleasant side effects. Another disadvantage with the tricyclics is that they do not begin to take effect for about 2 weeks—which, for a severely depressed person, is a long time to wait. Finally, it is relatively easy to overdose on tricyclics, and this makes them dangerous to prescribe for suicidal patients. Still, the tricyclics have proved successful with 50 to 70 percent of depressed outpatients. Although it is estimated that 30 percent of these patients would have improved in that time period, anyway, the response rate was still better than with placebos (Thase & Kupfer, 1996).

In the past decade, however, most of the excitement in drug treatment for depression has been over the SSRIs, which have gradually displaced most other antidepressants. The SSRI that has received the most attention is Prozac (fluoxetine). Introduced in 1987, by 1993 it had been prescribed for more than 10 million people in the United States (Barondes, 1994). Together with other SSRIs, Prozac can also have side effects, primarily headache, upset stomach, and sexual dysfunction. Furthermore, in a small number of cases, it seems to produce anxiety and insomnia. Finally, determining the correct dose is a delicate procedure. Prozac's *half-life,* the amount of time it stays in the system, is very long: 7 days (Agency for Health Care Policy and Research, 1993). Therefore, patients who take the drug daily are gradually increasing its level in the bloodstream, a process that can lead to overdose. Unfortunately, the symptoms of Prozac overdose resemble the symptoms of depression, so there is a danger, when the signs of overdose appear, that the patient will increase the dose, thinking that what is needed is simply more of the drug (Cain, 1992).

Because of these complications, Prozac has probably peaked in popularity. Physicians are now switching to SSRIs with short half-lives, particularly Paxil (paroxetine) and Zoloft (sertraline). It seems that Paxil and Zoloft not only reduce the risk of overdose but are less likely to produce anxiety and insomnia. All of the SSRIs approved for use in the United States are as effective as the tricyclics in combating depression.

What is remarkable about the SSRIs, however, is the claim that they sometimes do far more than eliminate depression. In certain reported cases, the drug is said to transform the personality. Patients who have always suffered from fear of rejection, low self-esteem, and social awkwardness are suddenly confident, decisive, and full of energy and hope. This ability to make people "better than well" was the subject of Peter Kramer's 1993 book *Listening to Prozac,* which in turn boosted that drug's popularity. In Kramer's view, Prozac's apparent power to alter longstanding personality characteristics raised the possibility that what we think of as personality—our core characteristics as human beings—might be more biologically based than had been imagined. This now

seems a naive notion. Prozac's ability to relieve depression—or even to alter personality, if it does so—might be due to the chemical effects of the drug, but it might also be due to the expectations raised by the prescribing physician, or even by the publicity attendant on the drug. (See the box on page 267.)

Two newer antidepressants are Effexor (venlafaxine) and Serzone (nefazodone). Effexor is like a tricyclic, but without the unpleasant side effects. (Its side effects are closer to those of the SSRIs.) Although it has been under investigation for only a short time, it may turn out to be the drug of choice for severe depressions; it has already been shown to outperform SSRIs in two studies with hospitalized patients (Thase & Kupfer, 1996). Serzone has a unique biochemical structure, but it effectively increases available norepinephrine and serotonin, just like the tricyclics. It, too, has the same side-effect profile as the SSRIs, with one important exception: no sexual dysfunction. Preliminary research suggests that Serzone may be just as effective as the other antidepressants (Thase & Kupfer, 1996).

A substantial minority of patients do not respond to the first antidepressant given to them. Ordinarily, they are then switched to another. It appears that, on average, 40 percent of patients not responding to a tricyclic respond to an SSRI, and vice versa. In cases in which both tricyclics and SSRIs have failed, an MAO inhibitor or Wellbutrin (bupropion), another new antidepressant, may work. For many years, the use of Wellbutrin was delayed because, in a small number of cases, it caused seizures. However, careful regulation of dosage can minimize this risk, and Wellbutrin has few other side effects and seems to work quite well (Thase & Kupfer, 1996).

All these antidepressants are effective not only with major depressive episodes but also with chronic major depression (episodes lasting more than two years), dysthymia, and "double depression," in which major depression is superimposed on dysthymia (Kocsis, Friedman, Markowitz, et al., 1996; Thase, Fava, Halbreich, et al., 1996). They are also helpful for people with chronic low-grade depression. Such people, however, are the ones least likely to be given antidepressants, because psychiatrists and family doctors tend to assume that these long-lasting depressions are best treated by psychotherapy. (Alternatively, such patients, if they show any anxiety—which they usually do—are given antianxiety drugs, for physicians seem to pay more attention to anxiety symptoms than to depression.) Nevertheless, many victims of chronic depression can get immediate relief from antidepressants. Ideally, most of them should probably have psychotherapy as well, in the hope of preventing relapse and to deal with the problems created in their lives by the depression.

Drug Therapy Versus Psychotherapy

The recent successes of psychopharmacology have created a sometimes bitter controversy within the field of psychological treatment. Certain advocates of drug therapy speak as if drugs were on their way to making behavioral and insight therapies obsolete. In the words of psychiatrist Paul Wender, one day "every disease is going to be [seen as] a chemical or an electrical disease" (quoted in Gelman, 1990, p. 42). Indeed, some experts believe that personality itself may come to be seen as a biological phenomenon. As Peter Kramer (1993) puts it, "When one pill at breakfast makes you a new person,... it is difficult to resist the suggestion, the visceral certainty, that who people are is largely biologically determined" (p. 18).

To many psychotherapists—people who have spent their careers treating psychological disturbance as part of the deepest problems of living—such statements seem naive and presumptuous. An editorial in the *Journal of the American Psychoanalytic Association* called attention to the dangers of "the recent and forceful biologization of everything from cigar smoking to love (a deficiency of phenylalanine treatable by chocolate in the absence of the loved person)" (Shapiro, 1989a). Some experts also fear that psychotherapists may be becoming like internists, "managing" depression, for example, the way internists manage hypertension, by prescribing drugs and monitoring their effects, while the root cause of the depression goes unexplored. As noted earlier, to suppress symptoms is not necessarily the wisest course. By definition, symptoms are symptoms *of* something.

On the side of the drug-therapy advocates, it must be said that the root cause of some depressions may, in fact, be biochemical—that biochemical imbalance is what the symptoms are signaling and what the drugs are correcting. Furthermore, as we have seen, in some cases they correct it very efficiently. Drug treatment for certain disorders is now so widely regarded as effective that *not* to prescribe drugs for these disorders can be viewed as malpractice. (In a celebrated case, a doctor suffering from bipolar disorder sued a Maryland hospital for treating his illness with psychotherapy rather than drugs. The case was settled out of court.)

Does drug therapy, in fact, work better than psychotherapy? Most of the research on this question has to do with depression. One large-scale review of outcome studies concluded that both biological and psychological therapies are effective treatments for depression, though the most effective treatment is a combination of the two (Free & Oei, 1989; Thase, Greenhouse, Frank, et al., 1997). The Agency for Health Care Policy and Research (1993) conducted a review of the literature on the treatment of depression and came to four conclusions. First, about half of depressed outpatients show marked improvement from medication. Second, the most appropriate patients for medication are those who have the most severe symptoms, plus recurrent episodes and family histories of depression. Third, psychotherapy—particularly cognitive, behavioral, and interpersonal—is effective for mild to moderate depression. Fourth, combined treatment should be considered for more severe depressions and for those that have not improved with psychotherapy or drug therapy alone.

While these recommendations have been criticized for overstating the effectiveness of medication, in a sense they are nothing new, for they repeat a long-held principle: that the treatment of choice depends on severity. Ever since the introduction of the phenothiazines in the 1950s, it has been widely believed that, in general, the most severely disturbed patients needed drugs, while the less severely disturbed needed psychotherapy. It should be added, however, that this principle is now being challenged. Some researchers (e.g., Hollon, DeRubeis, Evans, et al., 1992) have found that the most severe depressions are as likely to yield to cognitive therapy as to drug therapy. As for the idea that the least severe depressions are those that require psychotherapy, much of the controversy surrounding Prozac has to do with Prozac's challenge to that point. Sensitivity to criticism, low self-esteem, fear of rejection: these mild, nagging problems, which have for so long been thought the province of psychotherapy, not drugs, are exactly what Prozac seems to relieve—a fact that is causing "a rethinking of fundamental assumptions in psychiatry" (Barondes, 1994, p. 1102).

One preliminary finding is that drug therapy, when it is discontinued, is more likely than psychotherapy to be followed by relapse. In a study of medication *versus* cognitive therapy for depression, it was found that the two worked equally well during the acute phase of the depression but that, once the treatment ended, the patients in the medication group were more likely to have subsequent depressions (Hollon, Shelton, & Loosen, 1991). This result, however, was not replicated by a later, large-scale study, which found roughly equal relapse rates for all treatment conditions (Shea, Elkin, Imber, et al., 1992).

It may be that the wave of the future is combined treatment. Even if there is a clear biochemical abnormality, and one that can be corrected biochemically, the patient is still left with the damage that has been done to his or her life by the disorder. People who have been depressed on and off for years often have wrecked marriages, strained family relations, and few friends. While the drug may help to relieve the symptoms of the disorder, psychotherapy may be needed to repair the results of the disorder.

Furthermore, a psychological disorder is never *just* biochemical. Recall the levels of causality discussed in Chapter 3. All behavior is multidetermined. Drug therapy and psychotherapy are two different ways of approaching mental events. With gradual adjustments, the two therapies may be able to work together. While the defenders of psychotherapy often feel called upon to protect psychology against the incursions of biology, Freud, who was certainly a defender of psychotherapy, repeatedly predicted that this treatment would ultimately be served by biological research. "Let the biologists go as far as they can," he said, "and let us go as far as we can—one day the two will meet" (quoted in Gelman, 1990, p. 42).

Antimanic Medication While there are many competing drugs in the antidepressant market, the field of *antimanic medication* is dominated by one medication, **lithium**. Lithium is administered as lithium carbonate, a natural mineral salt that has no known physiological function (Schou, 1997). For some reason, however, this simple salt is capable of ending swiftly and effectively about 70 percent of all manic episodes. In approximately 40 percent of cases, lithium also terminates depressive episodes in bipolar patients. When bipolar depressive episodes are unresponsive to lithium, physicians usually prescribe either Wellbutrin or an SSRI, because they do not make patients sleepy, and unimpaired alertness seems to speed recovery in bipolar patients.

Currently, the great virtue of lithium is preventive: when taken regularly, in a maintenance dose, it is generally effective in eliminating or at least in diminishing mood swings in bipolar disorder (Schou, 1997). It is not easy, however, to determine what the maintenance dose is, because for most patients the effective dose is close to the toxic dose, which can cause convulsions, delirium, and in rare cases death. An overdose is generally preceded by clear warning signs, such as nausea, alerting the patient to discontinue the drug. Still, because of its potential dangers, patients who take lithium must have regular blood tests to monitor the level of the drug in their systems. Another problem with lithium is that, when people have taken it for more than 2 years, stopping it often results in a new manic episode within 2 to 3 months (Suppes, Baldessarini, Faedda, et al., 1991). Because of these risks, researchers have been trying to develop

other drugs for mania. An anticonvulsant, Tegretol (carbamazepine), has been found to be effective for about a third of manic patients (Small, Klapper, Milstein, et al., 1991).

Thus far, we have discussed only acute treatment response, the ability of these medications to relieve a current episode of mania or depression. Most psychiatrists now feel that, after an acute phase, there should be a "continuation" phase, in which the patients are maintained for 6 months to a year on the medication that helps them. Continuation therapy results in a 30 to 40 percent lower risk of relapse during the period in which the drug is continued. Usually, if a patient has responded positively to antidepressants and has remained free of depression through the continuation phase, he or she is assumed to have recovered from the episode that led to the treatment (Thase & Kupfer, 1996).

Electroconvulsive Therapy For reasons that are not completely understood, electric shock, when applied to the brain under controlled circumstances, seems to help relieve severe depression. This type of treatment, known as **electroconvulsive therapy** (**ECT**), involves administering to the patient a shock of approximately 70 to 130 volts, thus inducing a convulsion similar to an epileptic seizure. Typically, therapy involves about 9 or 10 such treatments, spaced over a period of several weeks, though the total may be much lower or higher.

This technique was first discovered in the 1930s (Bini, 1938). Since that time, it has become clear that, like antidepressants, the shock affects the levels of

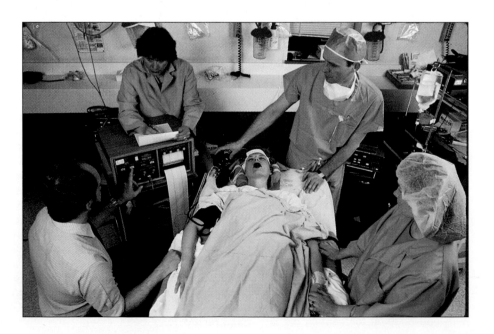

Electroconvulsive therapy is a controversial treatment with potentially serious side effects, but it has been shown to help many severely depressed people.

norepinephrine and serotonin in the brain, but theories as to its exact mode of operation are as various and incomplete as those regarding the antidepressants (Mann & Kapur, 1994). At present, all we know is that electric shock apparently *does* work, and quite well, for many seriously depressed patients (Abrams, 1992; American Psychiatric Association, 1990).

Like other biological treatments, ECT has its complications. The most common side effect is memory dysfunction, both anterograde (the capacity to learn new material) and retrograde (the capacity to recall material learned before the treatment). Research indicates that, in the great majority of cases, anterograde memory gradually improves after treatment (Hay & Hay, 1990). As for retrograde memory, there is generally a marked loss one week after treatment, with nearly complete recovery within seven months after treatment. In many cases, however, some subtle memory losses, particularly for events occurring within the year preceding hospitalization, persist beyond seven months (Squire, Slater, & Miller, 1981). And, in very rare cases (e.g., Roueché, 1974), such persisting losses are not subtle but comprehensive and debilitating. The probability of memory dysfunction is less if ECT is confined to only one hemisphere of the brain (Hay & Hay, 1990), the one having less to do with language functions—as we saw in Chapter 4, this is usually the right hemisphere—and this approach has proved as effective as bilateral shock (Horne, Pettinati, Sugerman, et al., 1985).

Another problem with ECT is that, although the treatment is painless (the patient is anesthetized before the shock is administered), many patients are very frightened of it. And, in some cases, ward personnel have made use of this fear, again for "patient management," telling patients that, if they don't cooperate, they will have to be recommended for an ECT series.

These problems have made ECT a controversial issue over the years. Defenders of ECT point out that many studies have found it highly effective—more effective, in fact, than antidepressants (Mann & Kapur, 1994; National Institute of Mental Health, 1985). Furthermore, unlike antidepressants, it works relatively quickly—an important advantage with suicidally depressed patients. On the other hand, ECT has vociferous critics, who consider it yet another form of psychiatric assault on mental patients. In support of this view, the voters of Berkeley, California, in 1982 passed a referendum making the administration of ECT a misdemeanor punishable by a fine of up to $500 and 6 months in jail. While the courts later reversed the ban, the fact that the voters passed it indicates the strength of opposition to this treatment.

Though the controversy over ECT is not settled, it has had its impact on practice. State legislatures have established legal safeguards against the abuse of ECT, and in general the technique is being used less frequently than it was in the 1960s and 1970s. At the same time, a 1990 report of the American Psychiatric Association concluded that ECT *was* an effective treatment for serious depressions and should be used, particularly in cases in which other treatments, such as psychotherapy and antidepressant medication, have failed.

KEY TERMS

agitated depression, 239
anhedonia, 239
bipolar disorder, 242
catecholamine hypothesis, 264
comorbidity, 248
continuity hypothesis, 246
cyclothymic disorder, 245
depression, 238

dexamethasone suppression test (DST), 263
dysthymic disorder, 244
electroconvulsive therapy (ECT), 268
endogenous, 246
helplessness-hopelessness syndrome, 239
learned helplessness, 256

lithium, 268
major depressive disorder, 240
major depressive episode, 238
mania, 238
manic episode, 240
MAO inhibitors, 265
mood disorders, 238

premorbid adjustment, 241
reactive, 246
retarded depression, 239
seasonal affective disorder (SAD), 262
selective serotonin reuptake inhibitors (SSRIs), 265
social-skills training, 255
tricyclics, 265

SUMMARY

■ People who suffer from the major mood disorders—disorders of affect, or emotions—experience exaggerations of the same kinds of highs and lows all human beings experience. Mood disorders are episodic: the depressive or manic episode often begins suddenly, runs its course, and may or may not recur. Thinking, feeling, motivation, and physiological functioning are all affected.

■ A major depressive episode is characterized by depressed mood (the helplessness-hopelessness syndrome), loss of pleasure in usual activities, disturbance of appetite and sleep, psychomotor retardation or agitation, loss of energy, feelings of worthlessness and guilt, difficulty remembering or thinking clearly, and recurrent thoughts of death or suicide.

■ A major manic episode is characterized by an elated, expansive, or irritable mood combined with inflated self-esteem, sleeplessness, talkativeness, flight of ideas, distractibility, hyperactivity, and reckless behavior.

■ Major depressive disorder is one of the most common mental health problems in the United States. It affects women more often than men, Caucasians more than African Americans, and separated and divorced people more than married people. People with bipolar disorder experience mixed or alternating manic and depressive episodes. Many others suffer from dysthymic disorder (milder but chronic depression) or cyclothymic disorder (recurrent depressive and hypomanic episodes). Demographic, family, and individual case patterns suggest that different mood disorders may have different etiologies.

■ Mood disorders differ along several dimensions, including psychotic versus neurotic; endogenous (from within) versus reactive (a response to loss); and early versus late onset. Evidence of comorbidity, especially mixed anxiety-depression, is increasing.

■ People suffering from depression are at high risk for suicide. Single people are more likely than married people to kill themselves. Although more women than men attempt suicide in most countries, more men succeed in killing themselves. Teenagers are at risk for suicide due to a complex set of factors, including family problems. People who threaten to commit suicide often attempt to do so; people who attempt suicide, but fail, often try again. Encouraging people to talk about suicidal thoughts often helps them overcome these wishes. Among factors that predict suicide, hopelessness—the belief that there is no other escape from psychological pain—stands out. Suicide hot lines and school-based prevention programs often do not appeal to the people who need them most.

■ Most theories and treatments for mood disorders focus on depression (not mania) and suicide. Psychodynamic theorists, beginning with Freud, trace depression to an early trauma that is reactivated by a recent loss, bringing back infantile feelings of powerlessness. Some see depressives as "love addicts" who attempt to compensate for their low self-esteem by seeking reassurance from others. But dependency on a loved one can turn to anger and guilt. According to this view, suicidal people are attempting to destroy another person whom they have incorporated into their own psyches. Empirical studies lend some support to the association of depression with dependency and with early loss of a parent or poor par-

enting. Psychodynamic treatment of depression aims not only to unearth the early trauma but also to examine how the patient uses depression in dealing with others. A short-term therapy that uses this approach is interpersonal therapy.

■ There are two prominent behaviorist perspectives on depression and suicide. According to one view, the extinction hypothesis, depression results from a loss of reinforcement, often exacerbated by a lack of skill in seeking interpersonal rewards. According to a second view, depressives elicit negative responses by demanding too much reinforcement in inappropriate ways. However, which comes first, depression or aversive behavior, is debatable. Behavioral therapies focus on increasing self-reinforcement and on teaching social and other skills.

■ The cognitive perspective also has two main theories of depression and suicide. One focuses on learned helplessness (the belief that one cannot control or avoid aversive events) combined with hopelessness (the feeling that negative events will continue and even increase). Hopelessness, in particular, is a predictor of suicide. A second cognitive theory traces depression and suicide to negative schemas, or images, of the self, the world, and the future. But, again, whether these feelings are a cause or consequence of depression is debatable. Cognitive therapists seek to correct negative thoughts and attributions by such methods as cognitive training and reattribution training.

■ The sociocultural perspective attempts to explain historical changes and cross-cultural differences in the rates of depression and suicide. One view is that rapid social change, one of the defining characteristics of modern life, deprives people of necessary social supports.

■ The biological perspective holds that, whatever the contribution of early or current emotional and/or social stress, mood disorders are at least partly organic. Some neuroscientists study families, twins, and adopted children and their biological and adoptive parents to discover the degree to which mood disorders are inherited. There is strong evidence that vulnerability to mood disorders and suicide runs in families. Some neuroscientists look at seasonal fluctuations in mood. Some examine CT, MRI, and PET scans for abnormalities in structures or regions thought to be involved in mood regulation. And some focus on biochemistry, especially hormonal imbalances and the neurotransmitters norepinephrine and serotonin. Today the most common treatment of major depression is the use of antidepressant medication (MAO inhibitors, tricyclics, and selective serotonin reuptake inhibitors [SSRIs]. Many depressed patients receive antidepressants in addition to another kind of therapy.

Chapter 10

Eccentric Personality Disorders
  Paranoid Personality Disorder
  Schizotypal Personality Disorder
  Schizoid Personality Disorder
Dramatic/Emotional Personality Disorders
  Borderline Personality Disorder
  Histrionic Personality Disorder
  Narcissistic Personality Disorder
Anxious/Fearful Personality Disorders
  Avoidant Personality Disorder
  Dependent Personality Disorder
  Obsessive-Compulsive Personality Disorder
Groups at Risk
  Comorbidity
  The Dispute over Gender Bias
  Cultural Bias
Personality Disorders: Theory and Therapy
  The Psychodynamic Perspective
  The Behavioral Perspective
  The Cognitive Perspective
  The Sociocultural Perspective
  The Biological Perspective

Ms. C, a 36-year-old woman, was referred to the day hospital Borderline Personality Disorders Treatment Program after her fourth hospitalization for depression and suicidality. Ms. C had not known her father. She was raised by her mother, who had a polysubstance dependence. Her relationship with her mother was described as negligent and distant. She had two brothers. The oldest brother abused her sexually for 3 years after she was 13 years old. The abuse ended when he was drafted into the army. She denied any feelings of anger or bitterness toward him and in fact described substantial feelings of fondness and affection. He died while serving in Vietnam.

She obtained good to excellent grades in school but had a history of indiscriminate sexual behavior, substance abuse, and bulimia nervosa (her common method for purging was to attempt to swallow a belt, thereby inducing vomiting). Her first treatment was at the age of 19 years. She became significantly depressed when she discovered that her fiancé was sexually involved with her best friend. Her hospitalization was precipitated by the ingestion of a lethal amount of drugs. After this hospitalization, she began to mutilate herself by scratching or cutting her arms with broken plates, dinner knives, or metal. The self-mutilation was usually precipitated by episodes of severe loneliness and feelings of emptiness.

She had an active social life and a large network of friends. However, her relationships were unstable. She could be quite supportive, engaging, and personable but would overreact to common conflicts, disagreements, and difficulties. She would feel intensely hurt, depressed, angry, or enraged and hope that her friends would relieve her pain through some gesture. However, they typically felt frustrated, annoyed, or overwhelmed by the intensity of her affect and her reactions.

Her sexual relationships were even more problematical. She quickly developed intense feelings of attraction, involvement, and dependency. However, she soon experienced her lovers as disappointing and neglectful, which at times had more than a kernel of truth. Many were neglectful, unempathic, or abusive, but all of them found the intensity of the inevitable conflicts and her anger to be intolerable. (Widiger & Sanderson, 1997, p. 1304)

Many of the psychological disorders that we have discussed so far arise like physical disorders in the sense that their sufferers, having once been "well," find themselves "ill," and in a specific way. They can no longer look at a dog without fear; they can no longer find reason to be happy. By contrast, the personality disorders are conditions that have generally been with the person for many years and have to do not so much with a specific problem, such as dog phobia or depression, as with the entire personality. To quote the *DSM-IV* definition, a personality disorder is "an enduring pattern of inner experience and behavior that deviates markedly from the expectations of the individual's culture, is pervasive and inflexible, has an onset in adoles-

cence or early adulthood, is stable over time, and leads to distress or impairment" (American Psychiatric Association, 1994, p. 629).* This disorder, then, has to do with stable traits. To quote *DSM-IV* again, "*Personality traits* are enduring patterns of perceiving, relating to, and thinking about the environment and oneself that are exhibited in a wide range of social and personal contexts. Only when personality traits are inflexible and maladaptive and cause significant functional impairment or subjective distress do they constitute Personality Disorders" (American Psychiatric Association, 1994, p. 630). Because personality disorders are so generalized and of such long standing, people with these disorders may not see their condition as a problem that can be treated; it is just who they *are*. Typically, they are very unhappy, though in some cases they may give less pain to themselves than to those who have to deal with them—their families, co-workers, and so forth.

There is considerable debate over the value of the personality disorders as diagnostic categories. In the first place, most of these categories are not particularly reliable. Though diagnosticians generally agree that a given case is one of personality disorder—as opposed, say, to depression or schizophrenia—they frequently disagree on *which* personality disorder they are confronting. What one calls "schizoid personality disorder" another may call "advoidant personality disorder" or something else. Furthermore, in the past, the diagnostic criteria for the personality disorders had narrow boundaries. While not specific enough to ensure high reliability, the criteria were too specific to cover many of the people thought to have personality disorders, so these people were shunted into residual categories such as "mixed" or "atypical" personality disorder. In the 1987 revision of the *DSM*, the diagnostic categories were broadened, with the result that their coverage increased—together with their overlap (Morey, 1988). In turn, the next revision, the *DSM-IV*, has made the diagnostic criteria more specific (Gunderson, 1992). It is hoped that this will control the overlap.

Such diagnostic problems have led some experts to propose that people with personality disorders be classed not by diagnostic categories but by dimensional ratings (Chapter 2). In other words, people would be rated on such things as dominance *versus* submission or novelty seeking *versus* novelty avoiding. Ms. C., for example, would be identified not as having borderline personality disorder but simply as having a high score on aspects of antagonism and

*Reprinted with permission from the *Diagnostic and Statistical Manual of Mental Disorders,* Fourth Edition. Copyright © 1994 American Psychiatric Association.

neuroticism, plus other ratings that might be relevant to her problem. (Costa & Widiger, 1994). While such a system would no doubt increase reliability, it would also create difficulties in communication among psychological professionals and probably in treatment decisions as well.

Another problem has to do with the assumption, clearly stated in the *DSM-IV* definition, that human beings have stable personality traits. This assumption has been vigorously attacked by behaviorists, who argue that human behavior is influenced as much by the situation the person is in at the moment as by his or her presumed traits (Mischel & Peake, 1982). Other experts (Epstein, 1983; Kenrick & Funder, 1988), while acknowledging situational influence, have shown that people do tend to act in certain ways with a relatively high frequency over time. (A student who cheats on one test is more likely than others to cheat on the next test, though the situation will also influence that decision.) Indeed, some people act in certain ways with an extraordinarily high frequency—in other words, they are rigid—and these are precisely the people who are said to have personality disorders. Nevertheless, the problem of situation specificity, like that of diagnostic overlap, was addressed in *DSM-IV*, and one diagnostic category, "passive-aggressive disorder," was removed because of evidence that this pattern was often a situational

reaction rather than a stable personality disposition (Gunderson, 1992).

DSM-IV lists 10 personality disorders, 9 of which will be described here. (The remaining syndrome, antisocial personality disorder, will be covered in Chapter 17.) The diagnostic manual organizes the personality disorders into 3 "clusters": odd/eccentric personality disorders, dramatic/emotional personality disorders, and anxious/fearful personality disorders (see Figure 10.1).

Odd/Eccentric Personality Disorders

People with *odd/eccentric personality disorders* have some traits in common with victims of schizophrenia and delusional disorder (Chapter 13), though they do not show the decisive break in reality contact that characterizes those very grave conditions.

Paranoid Personality Disorder

The defining characteristic of **paranoid personality disorder** is suspiciousness. We all feel suspicious in certain situations and with certain people, often for good reasons. However, paranoid personalities feel suspicious in almost all situations and with almost all people, usually for poor reasons. And, when they are confronted with

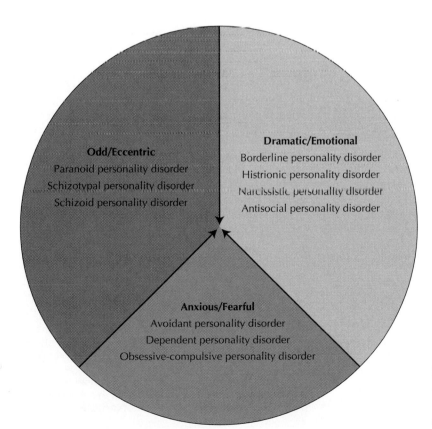

FIGURE 10.1
Clusters of personality disorders. (Antisocial personality disorder will be discussed in Chapter 17.)

Someone who is continually suspicious that people engaged in casual conversation are plotting against him or her, like the woman pictured here, exhibits a key characteristic of paranoid personality disorder.

evidence that their mistrust is unfounded, they typically begin to mistrust the person who brought them the evidence: "So he's against me too!"

Such an attitude, of course, involves an impairment in cognitive functioning. Paranoid personalities are constantly scanning the environment for evidence to support their suspicions—and constantly finding such evidence. If two people are talking together near the coffee machine, or if the mail is late, or if the neighbors are blaring music at midnight, this is taken as evidence of personal hostility.

This suspiciousness has equally drastic effects on emotional adjustment, for it stands in the way of love and friendship. Paranoid personalities typically have few friends. They may have an "ally," usually someone in a subordinate position, but eventually they begin distrusting that person, too, and look for another ally—a process that repeats itself. Some paranoid personalities become very isolated; others join fringe political groups. Their work record is often spotty. They tend to be hypercritical, stubborn, and controlling, and they often become embroiled in hostile disputes, which may escalate to lawsuits. With all these interpersonal problems, however, paranoid personalities rarely turn up in psychotherapists' offices, for they see their difficulties as coming from without rather than within. For this reason, it is difficult to estimate the prevalence of this disorder.

Despite similarities in name and in the defining trait of suspiciousness, paranoid personality disorder should not be confused with paranoid schizophrenia or delusional disorder, which are psychoses—that is, severely disabling disorders, involving loss of reality contact. Paranoid personality disorder is not as disabling. It should be added, however, that researchers have found paranoid personality disorder to be significantly more common among the biological relatives of schizophrenics than in the population at large (Nigg & Goldsmith, 1994). Therefore, different as the two disorders are, there may be some genetic relationship between them.

Schizotypal Personality Disorder

The person with **schizotypal personality disorder** seems odd in his or her speech, behavior, thinking, and/or perception, but not odd enough for a diagnosis of schizophrenia. For example, speech may ramble, but never to the point of actual incoherence, as is often the case with schizophrenics. Or the person may report recurrent illusions, such as feeling as if his of her dead mother were in the room—a situation different from that of the schizophrenic, who is more likely to report that the dead mother *is* in the room. Schizotypal personalities may also show magical thinking, claiming that they can predict the future, read the thoughts of others, and so on. Like paranoid personalities, they may become involved with fringe groups—astrology enthusiasts, self-proclaimed alien-abduction survivors—and isolated from anyone who does not share this interest. Often, such people also have childhood histories of having been teased and excluded because of their peculiar behaviors, as was the case of the following woman:

Ms. G is a 60-year-old woman who has never been married and lives by herself with 13 cats. Ms. G's appearance is strange, and her behavior is obviously eccentric. Although she has an endearing quality and is likable, anyone who sees her immediately senses that she is "different." Ms. G dresses in a crazy quilt of colors in an eclectic style that favors the 1920s. She has never been able to work, but she lived on an inheritance from her parents until she was in her 40s and since then has been supported by disability payments and welfare. Ms. G was raised in a devout Roman Catholic home and believes that she is destined to receive a visitation from the Virgin Mary, as the children at Lourdes did. She is constantly on the lookout for messages or clues that she believes will reveal to her when and where the visitation will occur. For example, she carefully reviews the most ordinary statements made by individuals (e.g., the checker at the grocery store or the clerk at the post office) to see whether their words have hidden and deeper meanings. Ms. G experiences almost constant feelings of depersonalization and derealization: She says she feels as if she is not connected to herself and as if she is a character in a movie. She is fascinated by the subject of out-of-body experiences and describes frequent episodes of astral travel. Her apartment is filled with signs and refuse she has collected over the years. Despite her odd beliefs, Ms. G is not delusional and is able to acknowledge that she may be mistaken in her beliefs. She often feels that other people are talking about her when she leaves the apartment but acknowledges that this may be because of the unusual way she dresses. For this reason and because she is extremely stilted and shy in social situations, Ms. G generally goes out only at night to avoid talking to others or meeting them in the elevator. She sneaks in and out of her apartment surreptitiously and does her shopping at the 24-hour store at 3 A.M. when hardly anyone is there.

Ms. G had a maternal uncle who was schizophrenic. She has been very shy and retiring since she was a child and says that she was always "odd" and never fit in with her brothers or sisters or fellow students. Although her siblings have suggested at various times over the years that Ms. G seek some sort of psychiatric treatment, she has refused. Ms. G is brought in for evaluation at this time because she was picked up by the police after she took a figure of the Virgin Mary from a religious supply store without paying for it, claiming that she was meant to have it. When the policeman insisted that Ms. G must return the statue, she became argumentative, irritable, and threatened to strike him. At this point she was handcuffed and brought to the emergency room.

Ms. G has four brothers and two sisters. To varying degrees, they have tried to remain in contact with her over the years. She has rejected most of their overtures, however, and is irritated at each one of them for different reasons. She says she feels more comfortable alone. Although in earlier years she used to be invited to family gatherings for holidays, her brothers and sisters have long since abandoned their attempts to get her to participate in these social occasions. For the past 15 years she has lived in almost complete isolation, except for an occasional phone call from one of her brothers or sisters. Her siblings have arranged for her to receive disability and welfare payments, however, and also provide her with hand-me-down clothes. (Frances & Ross, 1996, pp. 288–289)

Schizotypal personality disorder was added to the *DSM* in 1980 as part of an effort to improve the reliability of the diagnosis of schizophrenia and to study its relation (if any) to other conditions. In schizophrenia, diagnostic lines are often hard to draw. In the "classic" case, the person appears decidedly odd in many respects: speech, thought, perception, emotion, social behavior, motor behavior, and so on. However, many cases are not classic ones. For example, the person seems either only marginally odd in a number of respects or very odd in only one respect, social withdrawal. These two patterns, classified in the past as subtypes of schizophrenia, are now labeled as personality disorders: schizotypal personality disorder and schizoid personality disorder, respectively.

Schizoid Personality Disorder

The defining characteristic of **schizoid personality disorder** is a severely restricted range of emotions that is most notably associated with social detachment. Schizoid personalities appear to have little or no interest in relationships: they are often distant from their families, they rarely marry, and they have no close friends. In the contacts they do have with others, they seem not to experience the emotions that are part of ordinary social life: warmth, pleasure, disappointment, hurt. They also seem to take little pleasure in solitary activities. In the most severe cases, the ability to experience positive emotional experiences such as joy, happiness, gaiety, and pleasure is completely lacking. (Such an absence of pleasurable emotions is known as *anhedonia*.) If questioned, schizoids may claim that they have friends, but these usually turn out to be superficial acquaintances. They may try to make a friend, but the effort will founder on their inability to show the expected warmth and emotional investment.

Because of their self-absorption, schizoid personalities may appear absentminded—"out of it," so to speak. However, they do not show the unusual thoughts, behaviors, or speech patterns seen in the schizotypal personality. And, unlike schizotypal personalities, they may be quite successful in their work if it requires little social contact.

A further distinction between the schizoid and schizotypal personality disorders is susceptibility to schizophrenia. There is evidence that schizotypal personality disorder is more common in the families of diagnosed schizophrenics than in the population at large (Nigg & Goldsmith, 1994). Furthermore, schizotypal personalities tend to respond to the same medications as schizophrenics (Schulz, Schulz, & Wilson, 1988), a finding which suggests a biological relationship between the two disorders. Thus, schizotypal personalities may be at risk, genetically or otherwise, for schizophrenia, but this is apparently not as likely with schizoid personalities (Nigg & Goldsmith, 1994).

Dramatic/Emotional Personality Disorders

People with *daramatic/emotional personality disorders* tend to show behavior that is attention-seeking, demanding, and erratic.

Borderline Personality Disorder

Borderline personality disorder was illustrated in the case history that opened this chapter. First proposed by psychodynamic theorists (e.g., O. F. Kernberg, 1975)—and still questioned by some other theorists (e.g., Siever & Davis, 1991)—this category has received a great deal of attention in recent years (Clarkin, Marziali, & Monroe-Blum, 1991; Gunderson & Phillips, 1991). Morey (1991) describes the disorder as a syndrome involving four core elements:

1. *Difficulties in establishing a secure self identity.* Borderline personalities have an unstable sense of self and are therefore heavily dependent on their relationships with others in order to achieve a sense of identity, of self-hood. Hence, they have a hard time being alone and tend to be devastated when a close relationship comes to an end. The character played by Glenn Close in the movie *Fatal Attraction* resembles borderline personality and, in particular, exemplifies this catastrophic response to the end of a relationship.

2. *Distrust.* As dependent as they are on other people, borderline personalities are also suspicious of those people and expect to be abandoned or victimized by them. Given their difficult behavior, they may well be (Kroll, 1988). This combination of dependence and mistrust creates a profound ambivalence in the borderline personality's feelings for others. A friend who is idolized one moment may be attacked the next.

3. *Impulsive and self-destructive behavior.* Borderline personalities are typically impulsive and unpredictable in their actions. When they cut loose, they often engage in self-destructive behavior such as drug abuse, reckless driving, fighting, and promiscuity. They are also given to making manipulative suicide threats.

4. *Difficulty in controlling anger and other emotions.* This is a very prominent feature of borderline personalities. They exist in a state of perpetual emotional crisis, the primary emotions being grief and anger.

The intense emotionalism of borderline patients has led some researchers to suggest that borderline personality, like mood disorders, may be due to abnormalities in the limbic system, the part of the brain that regulates emotions (Kling, Kellner, Post, et al., 1987). Many theorists have raised the question of whether borderline personality is not a form of depression. A number of borderline patients meet the diagnostic criteria for depression, and there is some evidence, though not conclusive, that mood disorders may be more prevalent in the families of borderline personalities (Gunderson & Elliott, 1985). There is also some overlap between borderline personality disorder and dissociative identify disorder, formerly

Glenn Close's character in the movie Fatal Attraction *provides an example of borderline personality disorder.*

called multiple personality disorder (Putnam, 1989), and both sets of patients tend to report childhood histories of physical and sexual abuse (Herman, Perry, & van der Kolk, 1989). It has been suggested that many people said to have dissociative identity disorder are actually misdiagnosed borderline patients.

Among patient populations, borderline is one of the most frequently diagnosed personality disorders, and it is said to be especially hard to treat, for the borderline patient's intense ambivalence is, of course, redirected onto the therapist.

Histrionic Personality Disorder

The essential feature of **histrionic personality disorder** is self-dramatization—the exaggerated display of emotion. Such emotional displays are often clearly manipulative, aimed at attracting attention and sympathy. Histrionic personalities "faint" at the sight of blood, dominate an entire dinner party with the tale of their recent faith healing, are so "overcome" with emotion during a sad movie that they have to be taken home immediately (thus spoiling their companions' evening), threaten suicide if a lover's interest cools, and so forth. To themselves, they seem sensitive; to others, after the first impression has worn off, they usually seem shallow and insincere.

Their interpersonal relationships, then, are usually fragile. Initially, upon meeting a new person, they seem warm and affectionate. Once the friendship is established, however, they become oppressively demanding, needing their friends to come right over if they are having an emotional crisis, wondering why no one called them after a traumatic visit to the dentist, and generally taking without giving. They are typically flirtatious and sexually provocative, but their characteristic self-absorption prevents them from establishing any lasting sexual bond.

Histrionic personality disorder seems, at times, like a portrait of women as drawn by a misogynist: vain, shallow, self-dramatizing, immature, overdependent, and selfish. Most reports indicate that at least two-thirds of people diagnosed with the disorder are women (Corbitt & Widiger, 1995). (See the box on pages 284–285 for a discussion of the possibility of sexual bias in *DSM* criteria for personality disorders.)

Narcissistic Personality Disorder

The personality syndrome most commonly diagnosed in a number of psychoanalytic centers in recent years has been the so-called narcissistic personality (Millon & Davis, 1996). Largely because of the interest of the psychoanalytic community (Lion, 1981), this category was added to the *DSM* in 1980. The essential feature of **narcissistic personality disorder** is a grandiose sense of self-importance, often combined with periodic feelings of inferiority (Kernberg, 1975; Kohut, 1966). Narcissistic personalities brag of their talents and achievements, predict for themselves great successes—a Pulitzer prize, a meteoric rise through the company ranks—and expect from others the sort of attention and adulation due to one so gifted. However, this apparent self-love is often accompanied by a very fragile self-esteem, causing the person to "check" constantly on how he or she is regarded by others and to react to criticism with rage or despair. (Alternatively, in keeping with their sense of self-importance, narcissistic personalities may respond to personal defeats with nonchalance.)

Narcissistic personalities are poorly equipped for friendship or love. They characteristically demand a great deal from others—affection, sympathy, favors—yet they give little in return and tend to show a striking lack of empathy. If a friend calls to say that he has had an automobile accident and cannot go to

The term narcissistic personality disorder comes from the ancient Greek legend of Narcissus, a handsome boy who fell in love with his own reflection in a pool of water. In the painting shown here, Francois LeMoyne depicts Narcissus admiring himself.

the party that night, the narcissistic personality is likely to be more concerned over the missed party than over the friend's well-being. Narcissistic personalities are also given to exploitation, choosing friends on the basis of what they can get from them. Their feelings about such friends tend to alternate between opposite poles of idealization and contempt, often depending on how flattering the friend has been lately. Not surprisingly, in view of these facts, narcissistic personalities tend to have long histories of erratic interpersonal relationships, and it is usually failures in this area that bring them into therapy.

Narcissistic personality disorder resembles histrionic personality disorder. Some theorists have even suggested that they are simply the masculine (narcissistic) and feminine (histrionic) versions of a common underlying trait. (As histrionic personality disorder is diagnosed more frequently in women, narcissistic personality disorder is found more frequently in men.) The two types are distinguishable, however, in the nature of their attention-seeking. What the narcissistic personality wants is admiration; what the histrionic personality wants above all is concern. Consequently, while histrionic personalities sometimes make dramatic shows of helplessness—tears, desperate phone calls, suicide threats—the narcissistic personality would be too proud to display such vulnerability (Widiger & Sanderson, 1997).

In the past decade or two, a number of articles and books have been written about narcissistic personality disorder from two opposite perspectives: the psychoanalytic and social learning points of view. Psychoanalytic theory suggests that such personalities are compensating for inadequate affection and approval from their parents in early childhood (Kernberg, 1975; Kohut, 1972). The social learning perspective (Millon & Davis, 1996) sees this disorder as created by parents who have inflated views of their children's talents and, therefore, have unrealistic expectations.

Anxious/Fearful Personality Disorders

The *anxious/fearful personality disorders,* as their name indicates, all involve nervousness and worry. They differ in the object of the worry and in the behaviors used to cope with it.

Avoidant Personality Disorder

Like schizoid personality disorder, **avoidant personality disorder** is marked by social withdrawal. However, the avoidant personality withdraws not out of inability to experience interpersonal warmth or closeness but out of fear of rejection. This category, derived from a theoretical model of personality developed by Millon (1981), has as its essential feature a hypersensitivity to any possibility of rejection, humiliation, or shame. For most of us, making new friends is somewhat difficult; for avoidant personalities, it is supremely difficult, because, though they want to be loved and accepted, they expect not to be. Therefore, they tend to avoid relationships unless they are reassured again and again of the other's uncritical affection. Even then, they remain watchful for any hint of disapproval. Not surprisingly, avoidant personalities generally have low self-esteem. They typically feel depressed and angry at themselves for their social failure. On the other hand, like schizoid personalities, they may be successful professionally if the profession does not require social skills. Indeed, their work may serve as a refuge from loneliness.

Avoidant personality disorder is difficult to differentiate from social phobia, and many patients receive both diagnoses. The distinction between the two is normally made on the grounds of how pervasive and

Fear of rejection leads people with avoidant personality disorder to withdraw from social relationships and situations.

chronic the person's condition is. While people with social phobia may recall having been shy as children, avoidant personalities typically report extreme timidity and withdrawal as far back as they can remember. While social phobics' fears are often restricted to specific situations (e.g., public speaking), so that they have some relief, avoidant personality disorder is more engulfing, affecting almost every day of the person's life (Widiger, Mangine, Corbitt, et al., 1995), as can be seen in the following case of a 43-year-old man:

> Timid and easily daunted, [Mr. X] avoids new experiences in order to avoid feeling inadequate, embarrassed, or even slightly uncomfortable. He would like to date. Through his work with the Library Association he has contact with many single women (perhaps with similar problems) who would probably be most delighted by an invitation; but he lacks the courage to ask someone out. He would be terrified if the woman said yes, and humiliated if she said no. . . .

> Mr. X's professional life is also in a rut. He would advance to a more stimulating and responsible position at a university library if he were more productive, but for 10 years he has worked and reworked his master's thesis for eventual publication in book form. Each time he has written a "final draft" the fears about exposing his work prevent his moving the project forward, and he decides to make one more revision. Even if the thesis were published, he realizes that he might be once again passed over for a promotion because his supervisors have openly stated that he lacks the air of authority to supervise others. Mr. X does not deny their assessment. . . .
>
> [According to Mr. X's family, he was] a timid, easily startled baby from birth and, unlike his siblings, was upset by any minor changes in the nursery or dietary routine. He had difficulty adjusting to babysitters, playgroups, and kindergarten. Whereas many of the first graders were more excited than frightened about entering school, Mr. X cried piteously each morning his mother left him with the teacher. . . .
>
> Later in grade school, Mr. X was regarded as an outsider and was teased by the other boys for being a "scaredycat." To relieve the loneliness, Mr. X would usually be able to find a close friend—sometimes a boy, sometimes a girl—who was also outside the "in groups" and who also felt frightened. Along with this capacity to always find at least one close friend, Mr. X's other saving grace has been his ability to perform research by doggedly pursuing every small reference until a given subject has been thoroughly mastered. Because of this ability, he was an exceptionally fine graduate student and was encouraged to go on for a doctorate degree. He declined on the grounds that doctoral candidates were too competitive (i.e., intimidating) and that he would be comfortable living at a level that was more relaxed. He now realizes that in seeking comfort he has found boredom and loneliness. (Perry, Frances, & Clarkin, 1990, pp. 324–326)

Dependent Personality Disorder

The defining characteristic of **dependent personality disorder**, as the name indicates, is dependence on others (Bornstein, 1993). Fearful or incapable of making their own decisions, dependent personalities turn over to one or two others—for example, a spouse or parent—the responsibility for deciding what work they will do, where they will go on vacation, how they will handle the children, what people they will associate with, even what they will wear. Underlying this self-effacement is a fear of abandonment. For most of us, waiting for a friend who is late is an inconvenience or annoyance. For the dependent personality, it is an emotional catastrophe: the long-dreaded sign that the friend no longer cares. Because of the fear of abandonment, the dependent personality, often a woman, tolerates her husband's infidelities, drunkenness, even physical abusiveness for fear that, should she protest,

he will leave her. This passivity breeds a vicious cycle. The more the dependent personality lets others control and abuse her, the more helpless she feels, and these feelings in turn further discourage her from taking any self-respecting action.

While dependent personalities share with borderlines an intense fear of abandonment, the two disorders are otherwise distinct, and borderline personality disorder is far more disabling. Dependent personalities do not generally engage in the reckless or self-mutilating behavior characteristic of borderline personalities. Furthermore, dependent personalities may find peace in a stable relationship if the other person can tolerate their submissiveness. (Some spouses apparently find it attractive.) By contrast, the borderline personality's distress is not relieved by a relationship. Indeed, it may become worse when the person is involved with someone and discovers that the feelings of emptiness remain (Gunderson, 1984, 1996).

The following history illustrates the basic features of dependent personality:

> Matthew is a 31-year-old single man who lives with his mother and works as an accountant. He seeks treatment because he is very unhappy after having just broken up with his girl friend. His mother had disapproved of his marriage plans, ostensibly because the woman was of a different religion. Matthew felt trapped and forced to choose between his mother and his girl friend, and since "blood is thicker than water," he had decided not to go against his mother's wishes. Nonetheless, he is angry at himself and at her and believes that she will never let him marry. . . .
>
> Matthew works at a job several grades below what his education and talent would permit. On several occasions he has turned down promotions. . . . He has two very close friends, whom he has had since early childhood. He has lunch with one of them every single workday and feels lost if his friend is sick and misses a day.
>
> Matthew is the youngest of four children and the only boy. He was "babied and spoiled" by his mother and elder sisters. He had considerable separation anxiety as a child—difficulty falling asleep unless his mother stayed in the room, mild school refusal, and unbearable homesickness when he occasionally tried "sleepovers.". . . He has lived at home his whole life except for one year of college, from which he returned because of homesickness. (Spitzer, Gibbon, Skodol, et al., 1994, pp. 179–180)

Obsessive-Compulsive Personality Disorder

The defining characteristic of **obsessive-compulsive personality disorder** is excessive preoccupation with orderliness, perfectionism, and control. Obsessive-compulsive personalities are so taken up with the mechanics of efficiency—organizing, following rules, making lists and schedules—that they cease to be efficient, for they never get anything important done. In addition, they are generally stiff and formal in their dealings with others and find it hard to take genuine pleasure in anything. For example, they may spend weeks or months planning a family vacation, deciding what the family will see and where they will eat and sleep each day and night, and then derive no enjoyment from the vacation itself. Typically, they spoil it for the others as well by refusing to deviate from the itinerary, worrying that the restaurant will give away their table, and so forth.

This personality disorder should not be confused with obsessive-compulsive disorder, which, as we say in Chapter 6, is one of the anxiety syndromes. Though a superficial similarity—the shared emphasis on rituals and propriety—has led to their having similar names, the two conditions are quite different. In the personality disorder, compulsiveness is not confined to a single sequence of bizarre behaviors, such as constant hand washing but is milder and more pervasive, affecting many aspects of life. Furthermore, while obsessive-compulsive disorder is not common, obsessive-compulsive personality disorder is fairly common (more so in men than in women). People suffering from obsessive-compulsive disorder generally do not also show obsessive-compulsive personality disorder.

People with obsessive-compulsive personality disorder tend to be "workaholics," but they may have trouble at work for their perfectionism prevents them from making decisions and meeting deadlines. On the other hand, there are some jobs in which perfectionism is an asset. Many obsessive-compulsive personalities are quite successful in their careers and have sacrificed their personal lives to that end. Typically, they seek treatment only after their condition has left them with a series of divorces, a depression due to loneliness, or a physical disorder resulting from years of stress.

People with obsessive-compulsive personality disorder spend their days vigorously resisting any sudden change in plans. By contrast, sufferers of *impulse-control disorders* regularly disrupt their own lives when they experience urges to perform destructive behaviors and act on them. These disorders do not belong to the personality disorders or any other group of major syndromes (see the box on p. 283).

Groups at Risk

Comorbidity

Table 10.1 gives the estimated prevalence rates for the personality disorders within the community at large and within clinical settings—that is, among people being treated for psychological disorders. As the table shows, personality disorders are rare in the general population but at times very common—in the case of histrionic personality disorder, 10 times more common—in clinical populations.

Thus, one group at risk for personality disorders is people in psychological treatment, not necessarily for a personality disorder. Most people with personality disorders do not seek help for that condition. It has been with them since childhood; it feels normal, if not comfortable. In any case, it seems unsolvable. What brings them into treatment is usually a more specific problem, perhaps a sexual disorder or marital conflict, and it is only in treatment that the personality disorder is identified. Borderline personalities tend to turn up in substance-abuse, eating-disorder, and

TABLE 10.1 Estimated Prevalence Rates and Gender Differences for Personality Disorders			
PERSONALITY DISORDER	**PREVALENCE**		**GENDER COMPARISON**
	Community	**Clinical**	
Paranoid	.5–2.5%	2–20%	M>F
Schizotypal	3%	2–5%	M>F
Schizoid	.5–1%	2–5%	M>F
Borderline	2%	8–15%	F>M
Histrionic	1–3%	10–15%	F>M
Narcissistic	1%	2–16%	M>F
Avoidant	1%	5–25%	M=F
Dependent	2–4%	5–30%	F>M
Obsessive-compulsive	1%	3–10%	M>F

Adapted from American Psychiatric Association (1994) and Widiger & Sanderson (1997).

Personality disorders are pervasive, penetrating all areas of the sufferers' lives. But other disorders involve patterns of impulsive behavior in just one aspect of life and do not seem to be part of other major syndromes. *DSM-IV* calls these patterns the **impulse-control disorders**, their essential feature being the failure to resist impulses to act in a way harmful to oneself or others. The disorders included in this category, together with the behavior involved, are *intermittent explosive disorder* (destructiveness), *kleptomania* (theft of objects not needed for personal use or monetary value), *pyromania* (setting fires for pleasure or tension relief), *trichotillomania* (compulsively pulling out one's own hair), and *pathological gambling* (also called compulsive gambling). For the first three, prevalence, where it is known, is low. (Kleptomania, for example, seems to occur in only about 5 percent of identified shoplifters.) Pathological gambling and trichotillomania are more common and deserve discussion.

Estimates of the number of compulsive gamblers in the United States range from 1.1 million (Blume, 1987) to 9 million people (Gamblers Anonymous). Pathological gamblers are more likely to be men than women, and they seem to share certain personality characteristics: above-average intelligence and education; competitiveness; and a need for challenge, stimulation, and risk taking (Peck, 1986). As with other disorders, pathological gambling seems to develop in stages, with predictable crises. In the earliest phase, the persona tends to win and continues to win as beginner's luck is replaced by increasingly skillful betting and playing. The gambler becomes more and more confident and excited. Eventually, the "big win" occurs, in an amount that may exceed a year's salary. In the typi-cal case, this sets off the compulsion (Custer & Custer, 1978).

The winning phase gives way to the second phase, losing. The gamblers begin betting compulsively and "chasing," or betting more and more to get back the money they lost. Betting poorly and heavily, they fall deeply into debt. Having run through their income and savings, they begin borrowing, buoyed by the irrational belief that they will soon win and repay the debt. Most report that the initial experience of borrowing is not depressing—on the contrary, it feels like the big win.

As debts mount, so do personal consequences. Like alcohol-dependent people who hide bottles around the house, pathological gamblers often try to conceal their losses from their families. At the same time, they may manipulate family and friends to pay off pressing debts. Divorce, imprisonment, and job loss become increasing threats. Some confess their problem to family members and are "bailed out." Like the first stage of borrowing, however, the bailout generally does not rein in the gambler. Rather, It is exhilarating, like the big win.

The gambler then enters the final phase: desperation. Gambling continues with "all-consuming intensity and apparent disregard for family, friends, and employment" (Moran, 1970). Gamblers commonly suffer from depression, irritability, hypersensitivity, and restlessness during this stage. Many compulsive gamblers recover in self-help groups such as Gamblers Anonymous, but mental health professionals have taken little interest in the problem. With treatment facilities almost nonexistent and compulsive gambling so widespread, people who suffer from this ruinous disorder do not get the help they need, despite the fact that it can be treated (Blume, 1987).

Unlike pathological gambling, trichotillomania shares many characteris-tics with obsessive-compulsive disorder (discussed in Chapter 6), and can even be treated with similar drugs. Most trichotillomanics pull out the hairs on their heads—in severe cases, this can produce large bald spots—but they may also pull at their eyebrows, eyelashes, pubic hair, and facial hair. Like people with compulsions, trichotillomanics recognize their behavior is senseless, try to resist it, eventually succumb, and, once they succumb, obtain tension relief until the urge strikes again. There is also some evidence for a biological connection between the two syndromes. For example, first-degree relatives of trichotillomanics are at increased risk for obsessive-compulsive disorder. Furthermore, trichotillomania, like obsessive-compulsive disorder, responds to certain antidepressant drugs—those that block serotonin reuptake—and not to other antidepressants.

On the other hand, there are significant differences between the two disorders. Trichotillomania is more common in women than in men, a pattern not seen in obsessive-compulsive disorder. In a survey of more than 2,500 college freshmen, 1.5 percent of the males and 3.4 percent of the females reported symptoms of trichotillomania (Christenson, Pyle, & Mitchell, 1991). Also, trichotillomanics, unlike people with obsessive-compulsive disorder, do not seem to experience clear obsessions before engaging in their compulsive behavior (Jaspers, 1996; Mansueto, Stemberger, Thomas, et al., 1997). Instead of dispelling frightening thoughts, they gain pleasure, gratification, or relief when they give in to their impulses. However, the relief is temporary. Like compulsive gamblers, trichotillomanics must live with the results of their behavior long after the impulse has passed and the harm has been done.

mood-disorder clinics; avoidant personalities in anxiety-disorder clinics; dependent personalities in mood-disorder clinics and marriage counseling. While the condition for which the treatment was sought—the anxiety disorder or mood disorder—is listed as the Axis I diagnosis (see Chapter 2) and the personality disorder as the Axis II diagnosis, in fact, it is the personality disorder that has predisposed the

Politics and Personality Disorders

Certain personality disorders—histrionic, dependent, and borderline—are diagnosed more frequently in women, while others are diagnosed more frequently in men. Such gender imbalances are seen in many psychological disorders: schizophrenia (more common in men), major depressive disorder (more common in women), dissociative identity disorder (far more common in women), alcohol abuse (far more common in men). In the case of the personality disorders, however, some observers feel that the imbalance lies less in psychological than in political facts.

Marcie Kaplan (1983), for example, has pointed out that the *DSM* criteria for histrionic personality disorder—emotionalism, attention-seeking, seductiveness, suggestibility—resemble an age-old stereotype of women. *The Penguin Dictionary of Proverbs*, (1983), in its section on women, lists 104 old sayings on the subject of the female character, including its emotionalism ("Early rain and a woman's tears are soon over"); shallowness ("Women have long hair, and short brains"); deceitfulness ("Women naturally deceive, weep and spin"); and capriciousness ("Because is a woman's reason"). The dictionary offers no section on the qualities of the male character.

In other words, the society defines women as histrionic and then, when they act histrionic, diagnoses them as disturbed. In Kaplan's view, the same

situation pertains to dependent personality disorder: the society places women in a position of dependency and then labels them disturbed when they show dependency.

When *DSM-III* was being revised in the 1980s and 1990s, such political questions were hotly debated, and not just apropos of the histrionic and dependent personality disorders. It was proposed, for example, that the manual add a new category: self-defeating personality disorder, characterized by chronic pessimism and self-destructive behavior. Actually, this was just a variant of the "masochistic personality disorder" that had been mentioned in passing, and without a formal listing, in *DSM-III*. When it was suggested that masochistic personality disorder be formally listed in *DSM-IV*, many people objected: first, because such a category might give renewed credence to the old psychoanalytic idea that many people, particularly women, wish to be abused and, second, because the diagnosis could be used to blame victims of abuse—again, particularly women—for their victimization (Walker, 1984).

Partly in answer to these concerns, the name of the proposed syndrome was changed from "masochistic" to "self-defeating" personality disorder, but that did not settle the dispute. There were protest demonstrations, threats of legal action (Coalition Against Misdiagnosis, 1986; Rose-

water, 1986), and angry articles in the press. Finally, self-defeating personality disorder was dropped from consideration for *DSM-IV*.

At the same time that this controversy was going on, there was a parallel dispute over another proposed syndrome, "sadistic personality disorder." Basically, this proposal was a response to the debate over self-defeating personality disorder. If some people were abused because they had personality traits that invited abuse, then presumably some people *inflicted* abuse because they had personality traits tending in that direction—hence, sadistic personality disorder. However, this category, too, was opposed on the grounds of potential misuse against women. If "self-defeating personality disorder" could be invoked to excuse abusers on the grounds that they were simply responding to the masochistic needs of their victims, "sadistic personality disorder" could be used to excuse abusers on the grounds that they couldn't help it—they had a personality disorder that made them assault people. Eventually, this category, too, was dropped.

Did the framers of *DSM-IV* simply cave in to political pressure? According to some research, a significant proportion of abused women do show a long-standing pattern, if not of placing themselves in harm's way, then at least of failing to get out of the way. In a study of 119 women in a battered

---

person to the Axis I condition. In the usual case, it also makes that condition much more severe.

The Dispute over Gender Bias

Another risk factor in the diagnosis of personality disorders is gender. Look again at Table 10.1. For five of the personality disorders listed, men are at higher risk; for three, women are at higher risk. Some of the differentials are extreme. Women account for three-quarters of diagnosed borderlines (Widiger & Trull, 1993) and for two-thirds of diagnosed histrionic personalities (Corbitt & Widiger, 1995). They are also at greater risk for dependent personality disorder. None

of these female risk factors is greater than the male risk factor for antisocial personality disorder (Chapter 17), in which men outnumber women three to one; however, because of the nature of the power imbalance in our society, the female-heavy categories are the ones that have drawn the most attention. In no other area of abnormal psychology has the question of diagnostic bias against women been debated as bitterly as in the personality disorders. (See the box above).

It is possible that diagnosticians do view men and women differently. If so, this may be an extension of the fact that men and women behave differently. Personality disorders are maladaptive exaggerations women's shelter, Snyder and Fruchtman (1981) identified 4 patterns of abuse, at least 1 of which seemed to suggest a personality disorder. All the women in this group had suffered substantial neglect and abuse as children. As adults, almost half of them had been abused by people other than their current abuser, and 27 percent of them had been abused by their husbands *before* marrying them. Finally, 60 percent of this group rejected the shelter's offers of intervention and returned home to their assailants. As was detailed in an article on controversies over the *DSM-IV* personality disorders (Widiger, 1995), many investigators have concluded that a history of victimization in childhood can produce chronic, pervasive attitudes of self-blame, together with an expectation of abuse and behaviors that make abuse more likely—in other words, an overall cognitive-emotional-behavioral pattern that we would call a personality disorder. Likewise, there is evidence that some abusers (again, people likely to have been abused in childhood) show a long-standing, pervasive pattern of sadistic thought and behavior (Gay, 1989; Spitzer, Fiester, Gay, et al., 1991). Such evidence might have been enough to obtain listings for these categories if sensitive political issues had not been involved (Walker, 1989).

But domestic violence is now an exceedingly sensitive political issue, and the publicity surrounding the 1995 trial of football star O. J. Simpson, accused of killing his former wife, made it even more pressing. When a behavior is designated as the product of psychological disturbance, people tend to regard it as a problem merely in the person rather than in the society—a point that sociocultural theorists have repeatedly stressed. Furthermore, the person showing the behavior tends to be *excused* from both moral and criminal responsibility (See Chapter 18, "Legal Issues in Abnormal Psychology.") For both these reasons, many observers feel that to describe proneness toward violence (seen more frequently in men) and proneness toward submitting to violence (seen more frequently in women) as psychological syndromes simply perpetuates those problems.

Whatever the "right" answer, this dispute illustrates a point we have made before: diagnosis, like any other social institution, is influenced by politics—by shifting power relations among social groups. It is no accident that it was in the 1980s, in the wake of the gay rights movement, that homosexuality was deleted from the *DSM*'s list of sexual deviations. Neither is it surprising that feminist issues are now at the forefront of diagnostic controversy. In such debates, however, it is not always easy to determine where a group's best interests lie. If a diagnostic category describes a behavior specific to your subgroup, is this good or bad for you? On the one hand, it may stigmatize your group. (This was the argument with regard to homosexuality.) On the other hand, it may encourage the study and treatment of a condition that is, in fact, a cause of suffering to many in your group. This was the argument for listing self-defeating personality disorder. If such a disorder exists most commonly in women, then preventing its recognition and treatment is a serious disservice to women (Widiger, 1995).

Finally, however, the question that must be asked about any diagnostic category is not whether it is good for one group or another but whether it is good for science—whether is describes a condition that actually exists. The fact that a diagnostic category has a high potential for misuse does not mean that it is scientifically invalid (Fiester, 1991). This is not to say that the self-defeating and sadistic personality disorders were known to be valid. The research on both was preliminary. Neither should it be thought that politically disadvantaged groups are the only ones with political agendas. If some women have nonscientific reasons for rejecting "self-defeating personality disorder," some men may have nonscientific reasons for endorsing it.

of personality traits that, when not exaggerated, are normal and useful: modesty in dependent personality, self-assertion in narcissistic personality, and so on. We know that, whether because of nature or nurture, men and women, as groups, differ in such traits (Feingold, 1994). Despite manifold exceptions, women in general are more tender, more emotional, and more empathic than men. Men, in general, are more assertive, more confident, and more tough-minded than women. Therefore, it is no surprise that personality disorders involving emotionalism (histrionic, borderline) are more frequently diagnosed in women and that those involving self-importance (narcissistic) or callousness (antisocial) are more common in men. As anthropologists have pointed out, every culture has its own "idiom of distress"—a range of symptoms from which members of that culture choose when they are in psychological trouble. Viewed metaphorically as two cultures, the two genders are employing their unique idioms of distress.

However, the fact remains that those idioms are related to social injustices. It is partly because women are more emotional that they have historically been given less power and freedom than men. Thus, one can argue that, by focusing on gender-specific traits in defining personality disorders, the psychiatric establishment is perpetuating injustice and opposing the current movement toward liberation of both genders from confining roles.

The makers of the diagnostic manual have not been indifferent to this argument. For example, in *DSM-III-R,* the 1987 edition of the manual, one of the diagnostic criteria for histrionic personality disorder was "overly concerned with physical attractiveness" (American Psychiatric Association, 1987, p. 347). This was a valid indicator for the presence of the disorder. Nevertheless, it involved a subjective judgment. (Who is to say that a person is *overly* concerned with physical attractiveness?) It also seemed to stigmatize women's greater concern with their appearance. (Is there something wrong with wearing makeup?) In any case, the criterion involved a female-related characteristic and, therefore, raised the possibility that women might be overdiagnosed with histrionic personality disorder.

In attempting to solve this problem, some commentators pointed out that men, too, try to get attention by means of physical appearance, but they do it differently. Thus, in *DSM-IV,* the criterion was changed to "consistently uses physical appearance to draw attention to self" (American Psychiatric Association, 1994, p. 658). And, to encourage nonbiased application of the criterion, the manual gave not just a female example but also a male one: "A man with this disorder may dress and behave in a manner often identified as 'macho' and may seek to be the center of attention by bragging about athletic skills" (American Psychiatric Association, 1994, p. 656).

It is unlikely, however, that such a revision will equalize the distribution of the histrionic personality disorder diagnosis. And there remains the problem of whether it is possible to create "gender-blind" criteria for disorders related to gender stereotypes. As noted, those stereotypes have had their effect. In general, men and women do specialize in those traits. It is questionable whether the diagnostic manual should be based on a hypothetical future in which that is not the case, rather then reflecting present-day reality. In the meantime, however, *DSM-IV* strongly cautions against the overapplication of the personality disorder diagnoses to one gender.

Cultural Bias

Some of the same questions apply to the diagnosis of personality disorder in various ethnic subgroups. What seems normal behavior to a young Hispanic male may seem "macho" to a non-Hispanic diagnostician. What a Japanese American woman sees as normal wifely submissiveness may look like dependent personality disorder to a non-Japanese. Part of the definition of personality disorder in *DSM-IV* is

that the behavior in question "deviates markedly from the expectations of the individual's culture" (American Psychiatric Association, 1994, p. 663), but how well do diagnosticians know the patient's culture, and how thoroughly can they suppress the values of their own culture? On the other hand, as was pointed out in Chapter 2, there is also the danger that diagnosticians bending over backwards to respect the patient's supposed cultural values will fail to treat a serious disorder. Such problems are far from solved, but the fact that *DSM-IV* now warns diagnosticians about them is already a mark of progress.

Personality Disorders: Theory and Therapy

The Psychodynamic Perspective

Character Disorders Psychodynamic theorists interpret personality disorders, which they call "character disorders," as stemming from disturbances in the parent-child relationship. The more severe syndromes, such as borderline personality, are thought to originate in the early, pre-Oedipal relationship between infant and mother (or other caretaker), and particularly in what Mahler called the *separation-individuation* process (Chapter 4), in which children learn to separate from their mothers and regard themselves, and others, as individual persons. A troubled separation-individuation could lead to a poorly defined sense of self, a central problem in borderline personality, or narcissistic personality.

Whatever the root of the problem, the final result, as in all psychological disorders according to the psychodynamic view, is a weakened ego and, therefore, poor adaptive functioning. Psychodynamic theorists see people with character disorders as falling somewhere between neurotics and psychotics in terms of ego strength. (In other words, they function better than psychotics and worse than neurotics.) In all the character disorders, normal "coping" behavior, the province of the ego, has broken down, to some extent, and has been replaced by erratic, distorted, or deviant behavior. The borderline personality falls apart in times of stress; the dependent personality is constantly ceding decisions to others. These breakdowns in coping behavior affect the broad range of ego functions—perception, memory, language, learning. Obsessive-compulsive personalities shift all mental energy into planning; paranoid personalities shift all energy into perception, scanning the environment for signs of who is against them.

Narcissistic personality disorder has been the subject of intense study and controversy in psychodynamic circles. Otto Kernberg (1975), along with *DSM-IV,* sees the basic pattern as a combination of grandiosity and feelings of inferiority that is primary; the grandiosity is merely a defense against childhood feelings of rage and inferiority. Heinz Kohut (1966, 1972, 1977), on the other hand, sees the grandiosity as primary—the expression of a "narcissistic libido" that, for various reasons, has evaded the neutralizing efforts of the ego. When the narcissistic personality shows rage and wounded self-esteem, these are reactions to blows to the grandiose self-image.

A prominent theme of current object-relations theory is that the self-image is the product of the child's "introjection," or incorporation, of the parents' attitudes, particularly their attitudes toward the child. Parents who give their children unconditional love instill in them strong self-esteem. Parents who have ambivalent feelings toward their children and treat them inconsistently create in them ambivalent, conflicted self-images. This mechanism has been invoked as an explanation for narcissistic personality disorder (Gabbard, 1994; Kohut, 1977). Children who are generally ignored by their parents but who are flooded with praise and attention when they do something the parents are proud of are likely to grow up hungry for attention and convinced that they can win it only through success. But the need is never satisfied, for it never heals the original wound of the parents' indifference, hence the relentless attention-seeking of the narcissistic personality.

Psychotherapy for Personality Disorders   Because people with personality disorders are often not distressed by their behavior, they tend not to seek treatment. When they do end up in a therapist's office, it is often not on their own initiative but, rather, because they have been induced into marriage counseling or family therapy because of a spouse's complaints or a child's emotional problems. In such situations, they are generally resistant to treatment. And, even when they do experience sufficient unhappiness to enter treatment on their own, they tend to see the problem as external to them rather than internal—an attitude that bodes ill for insight-oriented therapy.

Psychodynamic therapists often take a more directive, more parental approach with personality-disorder patients than with other patients. Waldinger and Gunderson (1987) list a number of basic tenets common to the psychodynamic treatment of borderline personality: the therapist is more active, more likely to block acting-out behavior, more focused on the present than on the past, and more concerned with connecting feelings and actions than is the case in the usual insight therapy.

However, psychodynamic therapists still look to insight as the mechanism of change. As the personality-disorder patient begins deploying his or her characteristic patterns of behavior in the therapy hour, the therapist gently and empathically points out the distortions in the pattern and asks the patient what, in his or her childhood experience, might have created such a need for admiration (narcissistic personality disorder), fear of rejection (avoidant), devotion to perfectionism (obsessive-compulsive), or need for nurturance (dependent). As with much psychodynamic therapy, this may be a slow process.

The Behavioral Perspective

Many behaviorists, as we saw, object to the very concept of personality disorder, because it implies fixed personality traits. However, as pointed out in a review of behavioral work in this area (Turkat & Levin, 1984), the personality disorders can be usefully addressed by behaviorists if the diagnostic terms are understood as "descriptors of classes of behavior that have been learned and can be changed" (p. 497). This position is actually not so different from the behaviorists' approach to other, less trait-bound disorders. As for how these "classes of behavior" are learned, the behaviorists point, as usual, to eliciting stimuli and reinforcing consequences.

Skills Acquisition, Modeling, and Reinforcement   In a study of borderline personality, Marsha Linehan (1987) claims that many borderline patients come from families that show "invalidating syndrome," "the tendency to invalidate affective experiences and to oversimplify the ease of solving life's problems" (p. 264). These are families that expect children to be cheerful and to understand that, if they fail, it is their fault. Such parents do not coddle. As a result, the child is never able to obtain sympathy for minor upsets. The only thing that get such parents' attention is a major emotional display, so that is what the child learns to produce. Furthermore, because these parents do not address minor sorrows, their children never learn the emotional skills that other children do when they take their problems to their parents: how to calm themselves down, how to comfort themselves. Such children, Linehan argues, may logically grow to show the kind of constant and uncontrollable emotional turbulence we call borderline personality.

In addition to skills acquisition—or failure of skills acquisition—reinforcement and modeling may also play a role in the development of personality disorders. For example, dependent personality disorder might result from a childhood in which assertiveness was repeatedly punished, histrionic personality

The behavioral perspective on personality disorders emphasizes positive parent-child interaction, such as reinforcement as shown here. If a parent does not address minor joys and sorrows, the child may establish inappropriate patterns of behavior.

disorder from parental indulgence of temper tantrums, and obsessive-compulsive personality disorder from consistent rewards for neatness, rule following, and other "goody-goody" behaviors (Millon & Davis, 1996). In other cases, parental modeling of the behaviors in question might be as important as rewards and punishments.

New Learning   In handling personality disorders, behaviorists have operated on the assumption that, because most of these disorders can be seen as inappropriate social behavior, what the patients' need is social-skills training. Avoidant and dependent personalities can apparently benefit greatly from social-skills and assertiveness training (Stone, 1993). Histrionic patients, too, have been given social-skills training, with special attention to interacting with the opposite sex, because most of them complain of

troubled romances (Kass, Silver, & Abrams, 1972). Behavioral techniques have also been used to teach empathic behavior to histrionic patients (Woolson & Swanson, 1972).

With borderline patients, Linehan (1993) has used a more comprehensive treatment, which she calls **dialectical behavior therapy.** Already described briefly in Chapter 5, dialectical behavior therapy combines social skills training with coaching in how to regulate emotions and tolerate distress. For example, patients are taught the Zen technique of *mindfulness,* as a form of relaxation. In mindfulness, one begins by trying to listen only to one's breathing. If negative thoughts intrude (as usually happens with borderline personalities), patients are told not to criticize themselves for this but simply to accept the negative thoughts and return to their breathing. This technique is useful not only in teaching patients how to relax when in the grip of negative feelings—a major achievement for borderline patients—but also in instilling in them an acceptance of life's disappointments, hence the "dialectical" nature of this therapy: one takes a step back, into acceptance of pain, in order to take a step forward, out of pain. Linehan reports that so far this therapy has been successful in reducing suicidal threats and self-destructive behavior in the women patients whom she and her colleagues have treated (Linehan, Heard, & Armstrong, 1993).

The Cognitive Perspective

Faulty Schemas   Cognitive theory holds that our thoughts, emotions, and behavior are organized by underlying schemas, structures of information that we have in our minds about various domains of life (Chapter 4). In keeping with this assumption, cognitive theorists interpret the personality disorders as the product of distortions or exaggerations in the schemas. Because faulty schemas are "structuralized," or woven into a person's normal cognitive processes (Beck, Freeman, Pretzer, et al., 1990), the person does not recognize them as faulty. On the contrary, the distortions generate perceptions, and even situations, that confirm the schemas. They may also help someone to survive in a job or marriage, which in turn would increase his or her investment in the schemas.

Consider, for example, obsessive-compulsive personality. For people who fit this label, a central belief of the self-schema may be "I am basically overwhelmed, so I need strict systems and rules in order to function." This belief, in turn, generates the view that others, who do not show the same system-bound behavior, are incompetent or irresponsible, and their incompetence makes the obsessive-compulsive personality even more insistent on rules.

"See—It's not impossible for an obsessive-compulsive to get a responsible job."   © Sidney Harris

Other common beliefs of the obsessive-compulsive personality are "I have to drive myself and others relentlessly" and "Everything must be done perfectly." When, life being what it is, things are not done perfectly, the obsessive-compulsive personality's response is guilt over his or her own failures and anger over others' derelictions. This produces a constant state of tension, stifling pleasure, affection, and spontaneity. Thus, the final result is emotional distress and ineffective behavior, both traceable to the faulty beliefs.

According to cognitive theorists, such beliefs are acquired through learning—often through modeling—and may be a response to developmental conditions. (Perfectionistic parents, for example, could breed a child's obsessive-compulsive personality.) What distinguishes the beliefs peculiar to personality disorder, however, is not just their dysfunctional character—for many of us hold unhelpful beliefs— but their rigid character. In the cognitive view, schemas normally exist on a continuum from compelling to noncompelling. Many of us, for example, have schemas about nutrition that are on the relaxed end of the scale, whereas our schemas about child-rearing are likely to be much more compelling—that is, based on firmly held beliefs. In personality-disorder patients, most schemas are pushed to the compelling end of the range. The beliefs are rigid and admit no exceptions.

Altering Schemas   Because the schema is seen as the root of the problem, the goal of cognitive therapy is to induce the patient to alter the schema. In the case of

personality disorders, in which habits are old and deeply ingrained, cognitive therapists generally do not try to tear down the schema altogether. Rather, they opt for the more realistic goal of getting the patient to modify, reinterpret, or camouflage the schema (Beck, Freeman, Pretzer, et al, 1990; Freeman, 1989; Freeman & Leaf, 1989).

With obsessive-compulsive personality, for example, modifying the schema might mean inducing the patient to confine his or her perfectionism to the job and not let it spill over into the home, where the patient might be destroying family harmony over such matters as the proper way to make a bed or mow a lawn. Reinterpreting a schema means putting it to more functional use. Thus, the therapist might guide an obsessive-compulsive personality into a line of work in which perfectionism would be more appropriate and less of a nuisance to others. Finally, "schematic camouflage" involves teaching patients socially acceptable behaviors that they can use simply to ease their way in situations in which their habitual rigidity is likely to cause them difficulties. For instance, if they must always have their steak done exactly medium rare when they go to a restaurant, the therapist can teach them, through social-skills training, how to be very specific in ordering and how to complain effectively if the order comes back wrong.

The Sociocultural Perspective

While other theorists look to the individual psyche for the explanation of the personality disorders, sociocultural theorists feel that these conditions are the products of large-scale social processes—processes that ensure the advantage of certain social groups and the disadvantage of others. Accordingly, they argue that psychologists should devote their efforts to changing the society rather than trying to change its victims (Holland, 1978).

An illustration is the feminist critique of dependent personality disorder (Brown, 1992). According to this view, to diagnose a psychological disorder in women who are clinging and submissive is to blame the victim. It is the society that has created this condition in women, by denying them the power a person needs in order not to be submissive. Giving therapy to women for this condition is like treating a contaminated food system by giving antibiotics to the people who get sick from it. Until the contamination in the system is addressed, it will go on poisoning people.

Such reasoning was also the grounds for the opposition to the proposed new category of self-defeating personality disorder (review the box on pages 284–285): to call self-defeating behavior in women an individual problem, or a "disorder," is to deflect attention from the social injustice that is the true source of the problem.

The Biological Perspective

Genes and Personality   As we have seen, the swing of the pendulum in the early twentieth century toward seeing human behavior as the product of environmental influence has in some measure been reversed in the late twentieth century. With the rise of neuroscience research, we are returning, with empirical findings, to the pre-twentieth-century belief that much of human behavior is biologically based. Some of these findings have been quite dramatic. For example, in a study comparing MMPI scores of MZ and DZ twins—some raised together, some raised apart—it was found that the contribution of environment was small or negligible on all but 2 of the 14 personality scales (Tellegen, Lykken, Bouchard, et al., 1988). The experimenters concluded that only 50 percent of measured personality difference among their subjects was due to environmental difference. The rest they attributed to genetic difference.

If genetic factors are so powerful in forming the normal personality, presumably they are also involved in personality disorder (Nigg & Goldsmith, 1994). An important line of research on this question has to do with the relationship of personality disorders to Axis I disorders that have a genetic component. Some researchers (Siever & Davis, 1991) have proposed that the personality disorders are just "characterological" versions of Axis I disorders—that

avoidant personality, for example, is a form of social phobia, schizotypal personality is a variant of schizophrenia, borderline personality is a version of mood disorder, and so on. This argument is supported by the family studies cited earlier. As we saw, schizotypal personality disorder and schizophrenia tend to run together in families, as do borderline personality disorder and depression.

Drug Treatment   Another finding suggestive of a connection between the personality disorders and Axis I conditions is that personality disorders can sometimes be alleviated by the drugs used for their Axis I counterparts. Schizotypal patients have been helped by low doses of phenothiazines, the class of drugs most often used for schizophrenia (Silver, 1992). Borderline and avoidant personalities often respond to antidepressants (Coccaro, 1993). Some personality disorders have no drug treatment as yet, but that may change.

Drugs and Diagnosis   These treatment links, together with the family studies, have raised questions about the diagnostic system. Should personality disorder patients be reclassified as having the corresponding Axis I disorder? As we pointed out, the distinction between personality disorders and Axis I conditions such as the anxiety and mood disorders is usually made on the grounds that a personality disorder is more chronic and pervasive. The person has had the disorder for most of his or her life, and it affects

Studies have shown that personality traits, as well as personality disorders, are largely genetically determined.

nearly every aspect of his or her functioning. But, if a chronic and pervasive avoidant personality disorder clears up in response to the drugs used in treating social phobia, why shouldn't we regard it as a chronic and pervasive social phobia? In the words of the man who chaired the *DSM-IV* work group on anxiety disorders, "One may have to rethink what the personality disorder concept means in an instance where six weeks of phenelzine [Nardil] therapy begins to reverse long-standing interpersonal hypersensitivity" (Liebowitz, 1992, p. 251).

But the fact that two disorders respond to the same drug does not indicate that they are the same disorder. Aspirin relieves both colds and menstrual cramps, but that doesn't mean that a cold is a form of menstrual cramps. It means that aspirin treats a symptom common to both, pain. As for avoidant personality disorder's responsiveness to Nardil, Nardil is an antidepressant. If we were going to revise the classification system according to the results of drug treatment, we would have to reclassify avoidant personality disorder—and social phobia—as a form of depression.

KEY TERMS

avoidant personality disorder, 280
borderline personality disorder, 277
dependent personality disorder, 281

dialectical behavior therapy, 288
histrionic personality disorder, 278
impulse-control disorder, 283

narcissistic personality disorder, 279
obsessive-compulsive personality disorder, 281
paranoid personality disorder, 275

personality disorder, 274
schizoid personality disorder, 277
schizotypal personality disorder, 276

SUMMARY

- A personality disorder is a long-standing, pervasive, rigid pattern of thought, feeling, and behavior that impedes functioning and causes unhappiness for the person and, usually, the people around him or her. Because personality disorders are difficult to diagnose reliably and because their definition depends on the concept (opposed by some theorists) of stable traits, there is debate over the value of this diagnostic category. Nevertheless, it is useful as a description of people with a generally maladaptive "style."

- *DSM-IV* lists 10 personality disorders, which it informally groups into "clusters": odd/eccentric (paranoid, schizotypal, and schizoid personality disorders); dramatic/emotional (borderline, histrionic, narcissistic, and antisocial personality disorders); and anxious/fearful (avoidant, dependent, and obsessive-compulsive personality disorders). Antisocial personality disorder is of broad social and clinical interest and is a subject of much study apart from other personality disorders.

- The odd/eccentric personality disorders in some ways resemble schizophrenia and delusional disorder but are not accompanied by the severe disability and loss of reality contact associated with those conditions. Paranoid personality disorder is marked by suspicion of people in almost all situations. In schizotypal personality disorder, the person's speech, behavior, thinking, and/or perceptions are disturbed. In schizoid personality disorder, eccentricity is confined to social withdrawal: schizoid individuals seem unable to form attachments or to experience the kinds of emotions that would enable them to sustain or take pleasure from relationships, and they often seem unable to experience positive emotions, such as joy or happiness, in any situation.

- The dramatic/emotional personality disorders are characterized by attention-seeking, demanding, and erratic behavior; people with these disorders tend to experience failures in interpersonal relationships because of their difficult behavior. Elements of borderline personality disorder include problems in forming a secure self-identity, distrust, impulsive or self-destructive behavior, and difficulty in controlling anger and other emotions. Symptoms of borderline personality disorder to some degree overlap those of depression and those of dissociative identity disorder. The dominant feature of histrionic personality disorder is self-dramatization, often clearly intended to attract attention and sympathy. Narcissistic personality disorder is characterized by exaggerated self-importance, often combined with fragile self-esteem.

- The anxious/fearful personality disorders involve worry in various forms and behaviors for coping with it. The essential feature of avoidant personality disorder is hypersensitivity to the possibility of rejection, humiliation, or shame; the result is a recoil from others and, typically, loneliness and regret. Dependent personality disorder is characterized by excessive dependence on others, to the point of submissiveness; it is built on a fear of abandonment. Obsessive-compulsive personality disorder is defined by excessive preoccupation with orderliness, perfectionism, and control, at the cost of real effectiveness and of spontaneity in interpersonal relationships. Though similar in name and in some appearances to the anxiety syndrome know as obsessive-compulsive disorder, obsessive-compulsive personality disorder differs from that disorder because, like many personality disorders, it is more pervasive, affecting many aspects of life.

- A group that is perhaps most at risk for personality disorders is people in psychological treatment. Personality disorders are not usually the disturbances for which people seek or are admitted for treatment, but their very high incidence in clinical populations suggests that they are what predispose patients to their Axis I conditions—such as anxiety disorders, mood disorders, and substance abuse.

- Gender is a risk factor in most of the personality disorders. Men are at greater risk than women for many of the personality disorders and are at far greater risk for antisocial personality disorder. Women are at far greater risk for borderline and histrionic personality disorders and at greater risk for dependent personality disorder. The disorders that more often affect women receive undue attention, and arguments over the existence of gender bias are more intense in the area of the personality disorders than in any other area of psychological diagnosis. One side of the argument is that men and women in a given culture do behave differently, and their maladaptive behaviors are likely to be exaggerations of the genders' respective behaviors under ordinary circumstances. On the other hand, the criteria for personality disorders are not free of subjective elements, and, given the power imbalance between the genders in society, women may more often be misdiagnosed with personality disorders.

- Diagnosis of personality disorders across ethnic and cultural boundaries is also a sensitive matter. Behavioral traits that are taken for granted in one ethnic group may seem maladaptive to diagnosticians from another group or from the majority culture; professionals who are overly concerned with respecting a patient's cultural values may fail to treat a serious disorder.

- Psychodynamic theorists trace personality disorders, which they call character disorders, to disturbances in the early parent-child relationship, leading to a weak ego; in terms of ego strength, they consider people with character disorders to fall between neurotics and psychotics. In all the character disorders, normal coping behavior, governed by the ego, breaks down and is replaced by erratic, distorted, or deviant behavior.

- Insight-oriented therapy, a slow process under the best of circumstances, may seem to hold little promise for treatment of personality disorders. People with the disorders do not often seek treatment of their own initiative; rather, they may be induced into counseling because of marital or family problems and tend to see the problem as something external to themselves. Nevertheless, psychodynamic therapists will regard the insight approach as the road to change. Therapists often take a directive approach, pointing out the patient's maladaptive behavior patterns as they arise in the therapy session and gently prodding the patient to look for their origins in his or her childhood experience.

- Behavioral theorist generally reject the concept of personality disorders because it implies the existence of stable personality traits—an assumption they do not endorse. They regard the disorders as types of behavior that have been learned and, thus, can be changed; they focus on the maladaptive modeling and reinforcement and the lack of skills acquisition that led to the behaviors. Social-skills training is a major part of behavior therapy for the personality disorders. Marsha Linehan's dialectical behavior therapy combines social-skills training with coaching in regulating emotions and tolerating distress; it has been successful in treating self-destructive behavior in women with borderline personality disorder.

- The cognitive perspective holds that personality disorders are products of distortions or exaggerations in the schemas that structure the information in our minds. The faulty beliefs are rigid and admit no exceptions. Cognitive therapy is directed at modifying faulty schemas (learning how to keep them from interfering with one's life); reinterpreting the schemas (learning how to put them to constructive use); or camouflaging them (learning socially acceptable behaviors to perform in difficult situations as a substitute for annoying behaviors).

- Sociocultural theorists emphasize the role of large-scale social processes as background for the personality disorders—processes that create advantage and disadvantage for different groups. For example, the feminist position that diagnosis of dependent personality disorder in women is an instance of blaming the victim, in a society that denies women the power to avoid submissiveness, is consistent with sociocultural theory. Sociocultural theorists argue that psychologists should strive to change society instead of trying to change its victims.

- The biological perspective focuses on genetic and physiological factors that may contribute to personality disorders. The biological position is supported by research that links specific personality disorders with some of the more typical Axis I disorders that are known to have a genetic component. For example, schizotypal personality disorder and schizophrenia tend to run together in families, as do borderline personality disorder and depression. Some successes in drug treatment, too, have tended to support these findings: both schizotypal patients and schizophrenics have been helped by phenothiazines, and borderline personalities are sometimes helped by antidepressants. However, response to the same medication is far from proof that two disorders are variants of the same condition.

Chapter 11

A forty-five year-old white male, who works as a construction foreman during his sober periods, completed eight years of education. . . . He started drinking at the age of eighteen. . . .

He described himself as a "spree" drinker, but his heavy-drinking episodes now last three to four weeks and occur about six times a year. During these drinking periods, according to his statement, he consumes at least a quart of whiskey, a gallon of wine, and one to three six-packs of beer per day. He has had loss of memory and times of extreme shakes and hallucinations on a "few" occasions. He has had so many arrests for public drunkenness that he cannot even estimate their number. He has also had one arrest for drunk driving. He reports that both of his brothers are also alcoholics. His father drank heavily for years but was dry for the year before his death.

On his first known admission five years ago, the patient denied that he had been drinking heavily and said he had only a few beers a day. He was brought to the hospital by his wife because he was talking to the television, hearing strange music, and seeing bugs and snakes. He was detoxified. On his next admission, two years ago, he said that he had not been working more than a day or two at a time and that his wife supported him by working as a manager at a local department store. . . . [After a few days in the hospital] he requested a long pass to "look for work," and when he was told that he wasn't ready to leave the hospital, he returned to his room, dressed and left.

A year later his wife brought him to the hospital because she had returned from work to find him unconscious on the floor. His heart was pounding furiously, and he was blood-red in color and gasping for breath. After sobering up in the hospital . . . he swore that he was "willing to do anything to get better."

Everyone was convinced, and eight days later he was given a one-day pass to visit his wife before entering the alcohol treatment program. He returned sober from the pass, but he must have brought a bottle with him, since the next morning he was intoxicated and unable to begin the treatment program. He left the hospital two days later against the advice of the staff. (Jellinek, 1946)

To many people, the very word *drug* has connotations of danger, yet most Americans use some form of **pyschoactive drug**—that is, a drug that alters one's psychological state—either occasionally or regularly. Most confine themselves to legal drugs such as alcohol, nicotine, and caffeine, which, precisely because they *are* legal, tend not to be looked upon as drugs. However, as can be seen in the preceding case history, legal drugs can damage people as severely as illegal drugs.

Psychoactive substances do not invariably cause harm. When they are prescribed by physicians, they can be very helpful. In many societies, and in subcultures of our own society, they are an integral part of social and religious ritual. Neither is occasional recreational use, in small doses, necessarily the road to

destruction. Certain drugs are an important source of harmless pleasure, as anyone knows who has ever enjoyed a beer at a ball game. It is when drug use becomes habitual and when it begins to erode the person's normal functioning—work, studies, relationships with others—that it is redefined as "abuse." As functioning continues to decline, and as use of and recovery from the drug come to occupy a major portion of the person's life, "abuse" is redefined as "dependence."

In the past few decades, drugs have become a major focus of social concern, as evidenced by the recent proliferation of alcohol- and drug-treatment centers and of educational programs aimed at the prevention of abuse. Particularly in the 1980s, with the appearance of "crack," a cheaper, more powerful, and highly addictive form of cocaine, social anxiety escalated feverishly. A nationwide anticrack campaign claimed billboards and television commercials. Efforts were made to mandate urine testing for holders of high-responsibility jobs in order to detect drug users. The sense of emergency has not died down. A recent *Newsweek* poll indicated that, after crime and the economy, drug abuse was the American people's leading social concern (Fineman, Turque, Rosentiel, et al., 1996). However, in the early 1980s, cocaine use among high school students, the targets of the anticrack campaign, actually increased very little, if at all. Alcohol was then and is now America's number-one drug problem. And social alarm, though it may ultimately contribute to prevention, may have so far done more harm than good, creating a "war on drugs" whose major effect has merely been to put poor, young drug users in jail. Meanwhile, those who control the illegal drug trade tend to go free, and effective treatments for drug abusers have only begun to be developed.

In this chapter, we will first describe the common features of drug dependence. Then we will discuss alcohol and nicotine, the most easily available and most widely abused drugs in our society. Finally, we will examine other varieties of drugs: depressants, stimulants, hallucinogens, and marijuana. Theories as to the cause and treatment of abuse will also be covered.

Though our chapter will go drug-by-drug, it is important to keep in mind that in many cases drugs are not used individually. Some drug users like to combine effects, a common combination being marijuana and alcohol. Other drug users switch repeatedly from one drug to another. As a result, the current trend in drug-treatment centers is to deal with patients as people who seek *a* drug experience—any alteration in their state of consciousness—rather than to worry over whether they are abusing alcohol, heroin, or another drug.

The Nature of Substance Dependence and Abuse

The discussion of drug abuse is hampered by the fact that neither the society nor the mental health profession has yet agreed on a clear and consistent terminology. For years it was customary to distinguish physiological and psychological need. Drug use that had altered the body's chemistry to the point where its "normal" state was the drugged state, so that the body required the drug in order to feel normal, was called **addiction.** By contrast, the psychological dimension of drug abuse—the abuser's growing tendency to center his or her life on the drug—was called *psychological dependence.* These definitions, however, were not accepted by all professionals. (Indeed, recent editions of the *DSM* reserve the term *dependence* specifically for conditions that involve addiction.) Furthermore, as methods for detecting "withdrawal symptoms" became more precise, researchers discovered that all psychoactive drugs had both physiological and psychological effects. The two could not be separated.

In response to these confusions, *DSM-IV* has placed both the physical and psychological manifestations of pathological drug use under two diagnostic categories: "substance dependence" and "substance abuse." Both problems are defined in terms of behavioral criteria. In other words, the problem lies not in the drug but in the way a person uses the drug. By itself, the fact that a person takes a drug—whether legal or not—does not necessarily indicate dependence or abuse. The drug may or may not be physiologically addictive. Substance use becomes abuse or dependence when the pattern of use begins causing problems in the person's life.

A person qualifies for the diagnosis of **substance dependence** when he or she meets any three of the following seven criteria:

1. *Preoccupation with the drug.* A great deal of time is spent in activities necessary to obtain the substance (e.g., theft), in taking the substance (e.g., chain smoking), or in recovering from its effects.
2. *Unintentional overuse.* Problem users begin to find repeatedly that they have taken more of the drug than they intended.
3. *Tolerance.* As noted, habitual drug use alters the body chemistry. The body adjusts to the drug, so that the usual dose no longer produces the desired effect—a phenomenon called **tolerance.** (Some alcoholics, for example, can drink a quart of whiskey a day without seeming intoxicated.) As tolerance develops, the person requires larger

and larger amounts of the drug in order to achieve the desired biochemical change.
4. *Withdrawal.* With prolonged use, the body eventually *requires* the drug in order to maintain stability. If the drug level is decreased, the person undergoes **withdrawal,** psychological and physical disruptions ranging from mild anxiety and tremors to acute psychosis and, in extreme cases, death. Consequently, the person often takes the drug in order to avoid or relieve withdrawal symptoms.
5. *Persistent desire or efforts to control drug use.* Many drug-dependent people repeatedly quit and repeatedly relapse. Drug dependence is a chronic disorder.
6. *The abandonment of important social, occupational, or recreational activities for the sake of drug use.* Many of life's major functions—work, friendship, marriage, childrearing—conflict with heavy drug use and may be given up as a result.
7. *Continued drug use despite serious drug-related problems.* Many people go on smoking despite emphysema or taking narcotics despite a long record of drug-related arrests. This is no longer recreational use.

The difference between substance dependence and **substance abuse** is one of degree. Substance abuse is essentially a pattern of maladaptive drug use that has not progressed to full-blown dependence. According to *DSM-IV,* a person qualifies for this diagnosis if he or she shows any one of the following:

1. Recurrent, drug-related failure to fulfill major role obligations (e.g., absenteeism from school or work, neglect of children)

In tolerance—one of the major criteria for substance dependence—a person requires more of the drug to achieve the same biochemical change.

2. Recurrent drug use in physically dangerous situations (e.g., drunk driving)

3. Drug-related legal problems (e.g., arrests for disorderly conduct)

4. Continued drug use despite social or interpersonal problems (e.g., marital quarrels) caused by the effects of the drug

Alcohol Dependence

For thousands of years, alcohol has been the traditional "high" of Western culture. And, unlike most of the other drugs we will discuss in this chapter, it can be purchased legally in all but a few parts of the United States. For both of these reasons, alcohol is the most widely used of all the psychoactive drugs. In 1995, 52 percent of Americans aged 12 or older used alcohol. About 16 percent engaged in "binge drinking," meaning that they took 5 or more drinks on the same occasion within a month. And about 6 percent were "heavy drinkers," defined as having had 5 or more drinks on the same occasion on at least 5 different days in the past month (Substance Abuse and Health Services Administration, 1996).

The Social Cost of Alcohol Problems

It is impossible to determine exactly how much damage is done to society at large as a result of alcohol dependence and abuse. Easier to measure is the amount of money it costs. It is estimated that alcohol-related automobile accidents cost the American economy more than $13.8 billion in 1994.

Even more—$70 billion—is lost to the economy due to decreased work productivity. Workers with drinking problems are slower and less efficient, lose time on the job, make hasty decisions, and lower the morale of their coworkers. They are also more likely to become prematurely disabled and to die young.

As for their medical costs, more than $20 billion is spent annually on medical treatment and support services for alcoholics. Alcohol-dependent employees cost their companies the equivalent of 25 percent of their salaries (Alcoholism Council of Greater New York, 1987). Approximately 40 percent of all occupied beds in American hospitals are filled by people with ailments linked to alcohol consumption. And the ill effects of alcohol are not limited to the drinker if the drinker is pregnant. Babies born to mothers who drink during pregnancy run a substantial risk of having *fetal alcohol syndrome,* a pattern of damage involving bodily malformations, mental retardation, and delayed development (see Chapter 16).

Finally, $12 billion is lost annually in alcohol-related motor vehicle accidents (National Safety Council, 1992). The effects of alcohol on the nervous system—and, consequently, on the drinker's behavior—are directly proportionate to the amount of alcohol in the bloodstream. This latter factor is called the **blood alcohol level,** which is expressed in terms of the amount of alcohol in relation to a specific volume of blood. Table 11.1 indicates the approximate relationship between alcohol intake and blood alcohol level. Note that there is a gender difference. Women have less body fluid (but more fat) per pound of body weight. Therefore, if a 150-pound woman and a 150-pound man have 5 drinks apiece, she will have a

Some of the social costs of alcohol abuse are beyond measurement. Five passengers died and more than 100 were injured when the driver of this New York City subway train drove it off the tracks in 1991. It was later determined that he had been intoxicated.

TABLE 11.1 Relationships Among Gender, Weight, Oral Alcohol Consumption, and Blood Alcohol Level

ABSOLUTE ALCOHOL (OUNCES)	BEVERAGE INTAKE*	BLOOD ALCOHOL LEVELS (MG/100ML)					
		Female (100 lb)	Male (100 lb)	Female (150 lb)	Male (150 lb)	Female (200 lb)	Male (200 lb)
1/2	1 oz spirits[†] 1 glass wine 1 can beer	0.045	0.037	0.03	0.025	0.022	0.019
1	2 oz spirits 2 glasses wine 2 cans beer	0.09	0.075	0.06	0.05	0.045	0.037
2	4 oz spirits 4 glasses wine 4 cans beer	0.18	0.15	0.12	0.10	0.09	0.07
3	6 oz spirits 6 glasses wine 6 cans beer	0.27	0.22	0.18	0.15	0.13	0.11
4	8 oz spirits 8 glasses wine 8 cans beer	0.36	0.30	0.24	0.20	0.18	0.15
5	10 oz spirits 10 glasses wine 10 cans beer	0.45	0.37	0.30	0.25	0.22	0.18

Source: Ray (1983).

*In one hour.

[†]100 proof spirits.

higher blood alcohol level than he and, consequently, will be more intoxicated.

In all states, a person with a blood alcohol level of 0.10 percent is considered by law to be intoxicated. As Table 11.2 indicates, a driver with a blood alcohol level of 0.10 percent is less cautious, less alert, and slower to react than a nondrinking driver. As the blood alcohol level rises, so does the level of impairment. A nighttime driver who has had several drinks is also laboring under a severe visual handicap; it has been shown that visual recovery from glare slows down as blood alcohol level increases (Sekuler & MacArthur, 1977).

The relationship between blood alcohol level and motor vehicle accidents is all too clear:

On the night of January 29, 1996, Templeton, a fourth-year medical student, was returning home to New York from interviews for residencies in Pennsylvania. Driving on a four-lane highway, within the speed limit and with his seat belt on, he was struck head-on by a car going in the opposite direction. Both drivers died on impact. The man driving the other car had been arrested twice for driving under the influence (DUI). The first time, he was allowed to keep his car and his license, even though he never paid the fine. The second time, he was jailed for resisting arrest, escaped, stole his impounded car, and fled the state in order to avoid his day in court. On the night he killed Dr. Templeton, and himself, he was driving south in a northbound lane. He was drunk. (Adapted from Templeton, 1997)

This case is not atypical. Research has shown that the vast majority of men killed in car accidents were drunk at the time. Of these, 73 percent were chronically heavy drinkers, and most had a history of DUI convictions and license suspensions (Kennedy, Isaac, & Graham, 1996). Other studies have clearly documented that a bad driving record is related to alcohol abuse, which in turn increases the risk of injury (Voas, Holder, & Gurenewald, 1997). One emergency room survey of people surviving car accidents found that 68 percent were drunk at the time of the accident (Voas, Holder, & Gurenewald, 1997). Those with previous arrests, hospital admissions, criminal records, and histories of drug abuse

TABLE 11.2	Blood Alcohol Level: Physiological and Psychological Effects

Blood Alcohol Level (%)	Effect
0.05	Lowered alertness; usually good feeling; release of inhibitions; impaired judgment
0.10	Less caution; impaired motor function
0.15	Large, consistent increases in reaction time
0.20	Marked depression in sensory and motor capability, decidedly intoxicated
0.25	Severe motor disturbance, staggering; sensory perceptions greatly impaired
0.30	Stuporous, but conscious—no comprehension of world around them
0.35	Equivalent to surgical anesthesia
0.40	Probable lethal dose

Source: Adapted from Ray (1983).

were much more likely to be drunk at the time of the accident.

Even if alcohol abusers don't drive, they can still cause serious damage. As we have mentioned, alcohol increases the likelihood of injuries on the job. (This is especially true on farms.) Alcohol also contributes to the incidence of physical assault and sexual offenses. Alcohol use is involved in at least 30 percent of all the corroborated assaults in which tissue damage occurs and in 30 percent of the deaths (O'Farrell & Murphy, 1995). In the area of sexual offenses—pedophilia and forcible rape—alcohol use accounts for 90 percent of the drug-related sexual offenses. Impaired judgment also increases the likelihood of unprotected sex, with the possible consequences of pregnancy and sexually transmitted diseases, including AIDS.

The Personal Cost of Alcohol Dependence

The Immediate Effects of Alcohol Pharmacologically, alcohol is considered a depressant. It slows down and interferes with the transmission of electrical impulses in the higher brain centers, areas that control, organize, and inhibit some of our complex mental processes. And it is this release from control that helps people to relax, to stop worrying about what other people think of them, and to have a good time.

The initial effect of alcohol may be to stimulate rather than to depress. With a drink or two, people often become more talkative, more active. By the time the blood alcohol level reaches 0.03 to 0.06

percent, two types of effects occur. First, mood and social behavior change. Some people become depressed and remorseful; others become amorous or belligerent. The second effect is that judgment is impaired. Amorous types begin making wanton remarks to strangers, belligerent types start fights, and so forth. As the blood alcohol level continues to rise, the depressant effect of alcohol becomes more obvious. People slow down, stumble, and slur their words. Their judgment is further impaired, and they tend to engage in even more reckless behavior. "Depressive" drunks, for example, may begin loudly confessing their sins and failures.

For a long time, it was believed that the "bad" behaviors associated with drinking, particularly sexual indiscretion and belligerence, resulted directly from the physiological effect of alcohol on the brain. Presumably, alcohol impeded the brain's inhibition functions, and the "real person" came out. To quote the old Latin saying, *"In vino veritas"*—"In wine, truth." But experiments in which the behavior of people who have drunk alcohol is compared with the behavior of people who merely think they have drunk alcohol suggest that the disinhibiting effect has as much to do with the predictions made by the drinkers (and others) about how the alcohol is going to affect them. These predictions are often expressed as expectancies, which in turn reflect learned beliefs about what alcohol does to people. Increased sexual arousal, in particular, seems to be less a product of alcohol's chemical effects than of the drinker's expectancy that alcohol enhances sexual performance (Hull & Bond, 1986). Likewise, those who voice beliefs that alcohol unleashes aggressive behavior are apparently the ones most inclined to engage in and excuse such behavior (Critchlow, 1986), though the alcohol has its effect too (Bushman & Cooper, 1990). The broader context must also be taken into account—not just the drink but the fact that the drinker is at a party or in a bar. Barrooms, as we know, are where brawls may occur. Therefore, for those inclined in that direction, the expectancies associated with both the drink and the barroom may help produce brawling.

The Long-Term Effects of Alcohol Abuse Because it can relieve tension, alcohol is often resorted to as a means of coping with, or at least enduring, life's problems. The ironic result is that alcohol abusers end up with more problems than they had before and fewer resources for dealing with them. Hence, they drink more. Hence, they have more problems—a classic vicious cycle. In the process, their mental acuteness is lost; memory, judgment, and the power to concentrate are all diminished. As their capabilities

Pictured here (from left to right) are a healthy liver, a liver that is fatty from alcohol disease, and a liver that is cirrhotic with alcohol disease.

are eroded, so is their self-esteem. They neglect and alienate their friends. Often unable to work, alcohol abusers typically feel guilty toward their families, but at the same time they may take out their problems on the family. Child abuse, for example, is often connected with alcohol abuse. Alcohol also impairs sexual functioning and is one of the leading causes of impotence. Whether as cause or result of their drinking, alcohol abusers also have very high rates of other psychiatric disorders, especially antisocial personality disorder, depression, and anxiety disorders (Ross, Glaser, & Germanson, 1988; Roy, DeJong, Lamparski, et al., 1991).

As serious as the psychological consequences are the physiological effects. Habitual overuse of alcohol can cause stomach ulcers, hypertension, heart failure, cancer, and brain damage. Another common consequence is cirrhosis of the liver, which is now the ninth leading cause of death in the United States (Debakey, Stinson, Grant, et al., 1996). In addition, alcohol dependence often entails malnutrition. Alcohol is high in calories, which provide energy, but it is devoid of any known nutrient. Because alcohol-dependent people typically eat little and unselectively, their protein and vitamin intake tends to be dangerously insufficient. In extreme cases, they may develop Korsakoff's psychosis (Chapter 14), a severe memory disorder thought to be caused by vitamin B deficiency.

An infrequent but terrifying complication of chronic alcohol dependence is *delirium tremens*—literally, meaning "trembling delirium" and better known as the DTs. This severe reaction is actually a withdrawal symptom, occurring when the blood alcohol level drops suddenly. Deprived of their needed dosage, patients with the DTs tremble furiously, perspire heavily, become disoriented, and suffer night-

marish delusions. This condition usually lasts for three to six days, after which the patient may vow never to take another drink—a vow that in many cases is broken shortly after discharge from the treatment center.

In short, alcohol abuse is very damaging to health. Death rates are much higher for alcohol abusers than for nonabusers—two to four times higher in the case of men, three to seven times higher in the case of women (Edwards, 1989).

The Development of Alcohol Dependence

There is considerable variability in how people become alcohol-dependent, but some common patterns have been noted. While certain people develop abusive drinking patterns quite rapidly, most go through a long period of social drinking, during which they gradually increase the quantity and frequency of their drinking and come to rely on the mood-altering effects of alcohol. As consumption increases, many people begin to experience "blackouts," periods in which, under the influence of alcohol, they remain conscious and carry on in a fairly normal fashion but of which they have no memory the following day. In social situations, the alcoholic-to-be may also begin "sneaking drinks" (e.g., stopping at the bar on the way to the men's room) in order to keep ahead of the others without letting them know. Another serious danger sign is morning drinking, to get oneself "going."

Whatever the pattern, most people headed for alcohol dependence eventually find that they have trouble stopping themselves once they start drinking and that, as a result, they are drunk at least 2 or 3 times a week. Some abusers, however, remain "spree" drinkers, staying sober for long periods but then, often in response to stress, going on "benders," alcoholic binges lasting several days. Jellinek (1946), who described many of these patterns, claimed that the total itinerary, from the beginning of heavy drinking to complete defeat by alcohol, took 12 to 18 years, but for many people the route is shorter. The course of alcohol dependence has interesting parallels with the course of another devastating behavioral disorder, compulsive gambling (review the box on impulse-control disorders on page 283).

Groups at Risk for Alcohol Abuse and Dependence

Different social groups have different patterns of alcohol consumption. Interestingly, people with higher incomes are more likely to use alcohol. (*Gallup Poll Monthly,* 1992). So are people with more education. If you have a college degree, chances are (68 percent) that you drink; if you have less than a high school education, chances are that you don't (42 percent). On the other hand, less-educated Americans are almost twice as likely to drink to excess (Substance Abuse and Mental Health Services Administration, 1996), so the distinction between use and abuse is an important one.

Other important risk factors have to do with gender, racial and ethnic origin, religion, and age.

Gender   In every way, men are more involved with alcohol than women are. About 60 percent of American men, as opposed to 45 percent of women, use alcohol, and about 32 percent of men, as opposed to 11 percent of women, use it to excess (Substance Abuse and Mental Health Services Administration, 1995). There are also marked differences between the genders in patterns of use and abuse. First, women usually begin drinking later in their lives, experience their first intoxication later, develop dependence later, and go to facilities with shorter histories of drinking problems than do men. Women are more likely than men to cite a stressful event as precipitating the problem, and they are more likely than men to have a problem-drinking spouse or lover. Alcohol-dependent women are much more likely than their male counterparts to drink alone, but, when women do drink with someone else, it is likely to be a person close to them. Conversely, men are more likely than women to drink in public places and with strangers. Women also drink large amounts less often, do less bender and morning drinking, and have shorter drinking bouts. Finally, women more frequently combine alcohol with other substances—tranquilizers, barbiturates, amphetamines, hypnotics, and antidepressants, or nonprescription drugs (Gomberg, 1997).

It is not clear whether these divergent drinking patterns have to do more with the social role differences or with biological differences between men and women. In favor of the first hypothesis, it should be added that, although the rate of alcohol abuse among women still lags far behind the rate for men, it has risen steadily in recent years—a fact that some experts attribute to the increase in the number of women entering the workforce and taking on high-pressure jobs formerly reserved for men. Other writers, however, argue that what has risen is not the number of women with drinking problems but the number of women seeking help for alcohol abuse, rather than drinking in secret (Weisner & Schmidt, 1992).

Race, Ethnicity, and Religion   White Americans have a higher rate of alcohol use (56 percent) than either Hispanics (45 percent) or African Americans (41 percent) (Substance Abuse and Mental Health Services Administration, 1996). As for patterns of abuse, however, the picture becomes more complicated. The U.S. Department of Health and Human Services (1991) has reported that white teenagers and young adults are more likely to have alcohol-related problems than are African Americans their age. But, between ages 30 and 39, rates of alcohol abuse for African American men rise rapidly, surpassing rates for white men. Interestingly, as African American males' incomes rise, their rates of alcohol abuse fall; the reverse is true for white men. As for women, African American women are far more likely to abstain from alcohol than are white women. The fact that income and gender override race suggests that the differences between whites and African Americans are the result of different social conditions, not inherited genetic differences.

Within racial patterns, there are ethnic patterns. Men of Irish extraction are more at risk than men of Italian extraction. Hispanic men (especially Mexican American and Puerto Rican men in their thirties or older) have higher rates of alcohol abuse and dependency than either African American or white males. Most Hispanic women either abstain or drink infrequently. Native American men have the highest rate of alcohol abuse of all American racial and ethnic groups (U.S. Department of Health and Human Services, 1991). In fact, the American Indian Policy Review Commission declared alcohol abuse "the most severe and widespread health problem among Indians today" (Dorris, 1989). Alcohol is implicated in 40 percent of all Native American deaths, including accidents, liver disease, homicide, and suicide. Almost all crimes for which Native Americans are jailed or imprisoned are alcohol-related (Yetman, 1994).

Charlie Parker (phenobarbital/heroin/ alcohol), died age 34

Billie Holiday (narcotics), died age 44

Hank Williams (alcohol), died age 29

Elvis Presley (barbiturates/alcohol), died age 43

Jimi Hendrix (multiple drug overdose), died age 27

Shannon Hoon (cocaine), died age 28

Substance dependence is a problem for people in most professions, but in popular music it can be said to be a tradition, or a plague. Various explanations have been put forward: Musicians keep late hours; they work in nightclubs, where alcohol and nicotine are all around them (and other drugs are often available as well); many of them grew up poor, and the poor are at greater risk for substance dependence. The habit is more likely to destroy talent than to nourish it. The musicians pictured here all had their careers shortened by substance dependence. Their average age at death was 34.

Why should this be so? Alcoholic beverages were first introduced to Native Americans by European traders. Because they had not encountered alcohol before, Native Americans had no cultural norms defining its proper use. The traders were given to binge drinking and drunken brawls, and their behavior provided the model. Later, it seems, heavy drinking became a form of social protest for Native Americans, as well as an escape from a world in which their cultures, lands, and livelihoods were being destroyed (Dorris, 1989; Yetman, 1994). On most Native American reservations today, substandard living conditions, high rates of unemployment, and extreme poverty are still the norm, and rates of alcohol abuse remain high.

Another cultural correlate of alcohol abuse is religious affiliation. One religious group that seems particularly resistant to alcohol problems is, predictably, conservative Protestants, who have a notably high percentage of alcohol abstainers and a notably low percentage of heavy drinkers. There are also few alcohol abusers among Orthodox

Religious affiliation is one cultural correlation of alcohol use, with the percentage of abstainers versus abusers varying from one religious group to another. Across all religious groups, however, it seems that regular attendance at religious services correlates highly with alcohol abstinence.

Jews, who drink wine but in controlled and primarily religious settings (Goodwin & Gabrielli, 1997; Snyder, 1958). Catholic, Reform Jewish, and liberal Protestant groups all contain a fairly high proportion of alcohol users, with the Catholics leading the other groups in the percentage of heavy drinkers. In all religious groups, it appears that attendance at religious services correlates highly with abstinence.

Age   Rates of general alcohol use in the United States have remained stable in recent years, but not, it seems, within age groups. Adults appear to be drinking less; young people, more. (Table 11.3 summarizes some of these differences.) America's children start drinking at a younger age, drink more often, and get drunk more often than most adults realize. By sixth grade, significant numbers of young people have at least tried alcohol, and the proportion of young drinkers increases with each grade. In one survey, 70 percent of high school seniors said they had tried alcohol, and 50 percent had used alcohol during the previous 30 days. Of those who had drunk recently, more than 60 percent had become intoxicated (Hansen, 1993).

The proportion of young people who drink regularly and heavily climbs during college. A 1994 survey found that almost half of all college students go in for binge drinking. (See the box on page 305.) Why, when adults are drinking less, are students drinking more? One answer is advertising—billboards and commercials proclaiming that "it's Miller time" or that "the night belongs to Michelob." These images and slogans are so much a part of our environment that we hardly think about them—which makes their impact more insidious. Most of the ads, especially those for beer, associate alcohol use with success and happiness. They do not show young drinkers throwing up at the dormitory or crashing their cars into telephone poles. They show them going on dates, wearing smart clothes, and looking vivacious, sexy, and athletic.

TABLE 11.3	Prevalence of Frequent Heavy Drinking in Different Age Groups			
AGE (YEARS)	**GENDER**	**RACIAL/ETHNIC GROUP (%)**		
		WHITE	**AFRICAN AMERICAN**	**HISPANIC**
18–29	Male	31	16	17
	Female	7	6	2
30–39	Male	21	17	26
	Female	8	5	2
40–49	Male	19	14	11
	Female	7	6	2
50–59	Male	17	20	12
	Female	1	2	8
60+	Male	4	5	3
	Female	1	1	0
Average	Male	19	15	17
	Female	5	4	3

Source: Adapted from *U.S. Department of Health and Human Services: National Household Survey, 1984, Health Status and Minorities and Low Income Groups,* 3rd Edition. Washington, DC, U.S. Government Printing Office, 1991. Reprinted by permission of American Psychiatric Press, Inc.

National Public Radio reporter David Baron, researching a story about drinking among college students, went to a student party in Boston. Introduced to a freshman named Brian, he asked him how much he had had to drink. "Five or six pints of Guinness and then two or three beers, so far," Brian answered. "Are you expecting to have more?" Baron asked. "Yes, uh-huh," Brian replied.

In a nationwide survey of almost 18,000 college students, Henry Wechsler (1994) of Harvard School of Public Health found that half the males and 40 percent of the females engaged in "binge drinking," defined as having 5 drinks in a row for men, 4 for women. The vast majority of these students saw nothing wrong with their behavior. Indeed, less than 1 percent felt they had an alcohol problem, yet the binge drinkers were far more likely than their sober classmates to have been injured, to have gotten in trouble with the police, and to have missed classes because of alcohol. They were also 7 times more likely to have had unprotected sex, 10 times more likely to have driven after drinking, and 11 times more likely to have fallen behind in their schoolwork than nonbingers. Clearly, they had a problem, whether they thought so or not.

Beer busts on campus, and their destructive effects, are nothing new. The major revelation of the Wechsler survey was the degree to which campus alcohol abuse imposes hardships on *nonabusers*, the students who are trying to study while the party is going on. The survey found that at heavy-drinking schools nondrinkers and moderate drinkers were two to three times more likely to report physical assault, sexual harassment, destruction of their property, and interruption of their sleep and studies by drinkers. On some campuses, students reported that Thursday through Sunday the dormitory halls were loud with drunks, the bathrooms unusable. Female students claimed that they woke up Sunday after Sunday to find a strange man in their roommate's bed. (Often, the man was strange to the roommate too.) To deal with such problems, certain colleges have now set up "substance-free" dorms. Others have stepped up controls on campus parties, banning kegs and sending out roving patrols of campus police to check on underage drinkers.

Why do some students engage in binge drinking? Studies have shown that binge drinking is associated with difficulties in making the transition from being a family member to being an independent adult. Other researchers have found that young people who had conduct problems in high school are more likely to be binge drinkers in college, especially if they are male and join fraternities. Another critical factor, it seems, is the person's attitude toward drinking (Baef, Kiulalany & Marlatt, 1995). A fairly recent study (Hansen, 1993) evaluated 12 risk factors for alcohol use among young people: low self-esteem, poor coping skills, and the like. As it turned out, the factor that had the highest correlation with alcohol use was normative beliefs, specifically the belief "that alcohol use and abuse is prevalent and acceptable among young people" (Hansen, 1993, p. 57). In the past, programs to discourage high school students from abusing alcohol have tried *affective approaches:* stress management, confidence building, and other strategies for fostering emotional strength. Today, such programs are shifting to *social-influence approaches,* which place greater emphasis on changing attitudes and building resistance to peer pressure (Hansen, 1993).

That peer attitudes influence drinking is clear from the wide variations the Wechsler survey found in different student bodies' drinking patterns. It was the small residential colleges and large universities of the northeastern and north central states that had the highest rates of binge drinking. The large regional or research universities in the South and West had lower rates. Women's colleges and African American colleges also had fewer binge drinkers. These variations seem to indicate that the school subculture can encourage or discourage alcohol abuse, which in turn suggests that nonabusers might start trying to make their voices heard. Many people, and probably most young people, do not wish to be killjoys. But, just as nonsmokers have begun objecting to secondary smoke, victims of the secondary effects of alcohol abuse should probably begin speaking out.

However, advertising is not the only factor. Parents often loudly condemn the use of illegal drugs but send a mixed message about alcohol abuse. "Don't drink and drive" can easily be interpreted to mean "It's okay to get drunk, but don't drive." The message from peers is typically less mixed—indeed, decidedly pro-abuse—and, according to research (Hansen, 1993), such attitudes are the primary risk factor for alcohol use.

Treatment of Alcohol Dependence

The treatment of alcohol dependence begins with **detoxification**—that is, getting the alcohol out of the person's system and seeing him or her through the withdrawal symptoms. Detoxification can be done at home, under outpatient care, though it is often undertaken in the hospital. The patient is usually given a tranquilizer, such as Serax (oxazepam), for about a week to prevent the seizures that can sometimes follow a "cold-turkey" termination of chronically high alcohol consumption. At the same time, large amounts of vitamins and liquids are administered daily to counter nutritional deficiency and dehydration.

Through this process, the toxic effects of alcohol are eliminated from the system and the body is returned to a near-normal state. That, however, is only a prelude to the behavioral changes that are the major goal of alcohol rehabilitation—the effort to turn a person with a disrupted social, family and professional life into an integrated, self-sustaining, coping member of society. This is no easy task. Because rehabilitation touches so many aspects of the alcohol-dependent person's life, the better-designed alcohol rehabilitation treatments are multimodal, combining many strategies.

Multimodal Treatments In the best multimodal programs, patients are provided with occupational therapy, to help them learn or relearn job skills; relaxation training, to teach them how to reduce tension without alcohol; group and individual therapy, to help them learn something about themselves and to show them how to relate to others without drinking; family and marital therapy, to resolve the problems at home that may have contributed to and/or resulted from their drinking; and job counseling, to get them back to work. These various forms of treatment are given concurrently, and most, if not all, patients participate in them daily. That, however, is the ideal scenario. In practice, most alcohol treatments, inpatient or outpatient, consist of group therapy twice a week plus educational films and Alcoholics Anonymous meetings.

Sometimes hospitals' treatment programs supply an additional deterrent to drinking, in the form of a drug called Antabuse. Antabuse (disulfiram) is a chemical that interferes with the normal metabolic processing of alcohol for about two days after the medication is taken. When the Antabuse taker drinks alcohol, a toxic by-produce of alcohol metabolism, acetaldehyde, accumulates in the bloodstream, causing flushing, increased heart rate, and intense nausea. Antabuse treatment is based on the assumption that it will help alcoholics to avoid impulsive drinking (Baekeland, Lundwall, Kissen, et al., 1971), because, if they want to take a drink without becoming violently ill, they must stop taking the Antabuse at least two days in advance. The drug thereby provides artificial support for the patient's "will power." However, the support is artificial. Once out of the hospital, many alcoholics simply stop taking the drug. Also, it is not clear that Antabuse is particularly effective for those who go on taking it. A national study comparing recovering drinkers who were prescribed Antabuse with controls who received a placebo found no difference in relapse rates between the two groups (Fuller, 1990).

Support Groups: Alcoholics Anonymous One part of most successful rehabilitation programs is support groups. Expatients may meet one or more times a week for three to six months, or they may go on meeting indefinitely. This continued contact reminds people recovering from alcohol dependency that they need not battle their problem alone—that help is available. Furthermore, the follow-up meetings give them the opportunity to continue working on their problems and to learn additional interpersonal coping skills.

The most widely known of these regular meeting programs is Alcoholics Anonymous, better known as AA. The AA program started in the mid-1930s and has since spread around the world. AA operates on two basic tenets: (1) once an alcoholic, always an alcoholic and (2) an alcoholic can never go back to "normal" drinking. AA sees alcoholism as a lifelong problem; to combat it, the alcoholic must abstain from drink. For help in this difficult task, AA offers not just its regular meetings, at which members come together, usually several times a week, to air their problems, but also its famous "sponsor" system. New members are assigned a sponsor from among the regular members. If the new member has an overpowering urge to drink, he or she can call the sponsor, who will then give support over the phone or even stay with the new member until the crisis passes. Sponsors also help new members to begin the so-called Twelve Steps to recovery, which, while spiritual in focus, involve some very practical measures, such as self-examination, admission of fault, and the making of amends.

AA appears to have an extremely high dropout rate. Less than 10 percent of people who go to an

Support groups such as Alcoholics Anonymous can be helpful to recovering substance abusers by reminding them that they are not alone.

AA meeting continue in treatment, become abstinent, and stay abstinent for a year (Tonigan, Toscova, & Miller, 1996). However, for those who stay with AA, the program does seem to work. In one study that followed 100 patients 1 month and then 6 months after treatment, those who continued to go to meetings drank significantly less (Tonigan, Toscova, & Miller, 1996). Not surprisingly, those who were most confident, most highly motivated, and most active in their coping methods were more likely both to continue with AA and to benefit from the program (Morgenstern, Labouvie, McCrady, et al., 1997). Still, given the high dropout rates and the poor quality of much of the research on AA, it would be premature to say that the program is effective (Tonigan, Toscova, & Miller, 1996).

Outpatient and Brief Treatments The past two decades have seen a tremendous growth in residential care for people who are alcohol-dependent. There are units in the Veterans Administration hospitals and in the psychiatric and general hospitals. In addition, the United States now has more than 400 private residential treatment facilities (Moore, 1985), some of them, such as the Betty Ford Center, highly visible. It is questionable, however, whether alcohol-dependents need to be hospitalized round the clock. Outpatient and day-hospital programs have also been expanding in recent years, and several studies have found no difference in relapse rates between outpatient and inpatient programs—a fact which seems to hold regardless of whether the choice between inpatient and outpatient was made by the patient or by random assignment (McKay, Alterman, McLellan, et al., 1995). Partly because of such findings, and also because inpatient care costs 5 to 10 times more than outpatient care (Alterman, O'Brien, McLellan, et al., 1994), most insurance programs are now reluctant to pay for full hospitalization except when the patient has clear medical or psychiatric problems beyond alcohol dependence.

At the same time, the trend throughout the psychotherapy field toward brief treatments has also hit alcohol rehabilitation. One of the resulting treatments—which, according to its developers, can work in as few as four sessions—is **motivational interviewing** (Miller & Rollnick, 1991). As its name suggests, motivational interviewing is a question-and-answer method aimed at increasing the patient's motivation to change. Ambivalence is the norm among substance-dependent people: they want to live drug-free, and they don't. Motivational interviewing tries to shift them toward wanting to, so that they become ready to give up the drug. The style of interviewing follows five principles: (1) show compassion for the patients; (2) help them see the ways in which their lives are not going well; (3) avoid arguing with them; (4) for the time being, let them hold on to whatever mechanisms they are using to avoid changing, whether rationalizations ("I can't stop drinking until I meet a woman") or distortions of reality ("I don't really have a drinking problem); (5) help them develop confidence that they can change. Most of these principles are achieved through the therapist's asking questions. Here is a sample dialogue:

Therapist: How many beers would you like to be drinking per day?
Client: One at most.
Therapist: How many beers do you think you're now drinking per day?
Client: Two.
Therapist: For the next week, keep track. It may be useful to us later.

A week later, the therapist asks about the assignment:

Therapist: What did you find out?
Client: I'm drinking more than I want to be.
Therapist: How much?

FRAMES is the acronym used by motivational interviewers to describe the treatment process: Feedback, Responsibility, Advise, Menu (of alternative strategies for changing drinking), Empathy, and Self-efficacy. The therapist provides feedback in a nonconfrontational, reflective manner and lets the client guide the direction and speed of change.

Relapse Prevention A very important recent trend in alcohol rehabilitation is **relapse prevention.** Most alcoholics who stop drinking, even for years, do eventually slip and take a drink again at some point. The goal of relapse prevention is to lessen the likelihood of such "slips" and, when they happen, to prevent them from turning into full-scale relapses.

The "relapse prevention" movement was given its greatest boost from the cognitive behavioral model generated by Marlatt and his colleagues (Marlatt & Gordon, 1985). This was the first and most influential cognitive-behavioral approach to substance abuse (it will be discussed more fully later in the chapter). It can lead a clinician in a variety of directions; thus, the relapse prevention (RP) model has spawned numerous treatment programs for a variety of addictions. The RP model can be used in conjunction with other models of treatment. It is not just a set of techniques but also a theory of relapse. The model states that the risk for relapse begins with a high-risk situation: any threatening circumstance that makes the former addict afraid of losing control, therefore being at risk for drinking—for example, a recovered alcoholic who unexpectedly ran into his exwife at a party where alcohol was served. Anything that produces unpleasant feelings, social pressure, or conflict with another person can trigger the risk for relapse. The high-risk situation generates a variety of internal reactions, according to the model. Patients with good coping skills end up feeling confident that they can refrain from relapsing, despite the high-risk situation. This confidence helps protect them from relapsing. In contrast, those without good coping skills are less confident in their abilities to resist the temptation. Instead, they look to the drug to lead them out of the troubled waters of risk. Once they slip and have a drink, they experience an "abstinence violation effect" (AVE). Having acted in a way that directly contradicts their commitment to abstinence, they feel guilty, out of control, and thus continue to drink. RP techniques suggested by Marlatt and Gordon include identifying in advance and later avoiding high-risk situations; analyzing the chain of thoughts leading to alcohol use in high-risk situations; making constructive lifestyle changes, such as choosing friends who do not drink; and learning that "one drink does not make a drunk." In other words, just because you have slipped does not mean you are doomed to relapse.

How effective are treatment programs based on the RP model? Although results have not been consistent, relapse prevention treatments do appear to make relapses rarer and milder (Carroll, 1996). In the few studies that have compared relapse prevention treatments with AA, the absolute success rates seem to be about the same (Ouimette, Finney, & Moos, 1997).

Matching   Recall the finding, described earlier, that certain kinds of patients—those with more confidence, higher motivation, and more active ways of coping—tend to do best in AA. Most experts agree that alcoholics are a heterogeneous group. Hence, it would seem, treatment would be more likely to work if, by **matching,** patients could be directed to the program that best fit their characteristics. For example, some experts have argued that treatment should be tailored to the patient's "readiness to change" (Annis, Schober, & Kelly, 1996). When motivation is low, a treatment aimed at that problem, such as motivational interviewing, might be the answer, whereas patients already committed to changing should be channeled into more demanding programs. Other characteristics that have been proposed as a basis for matching are demographic variables (e.g., age, gender, racial/ethnic group), intelligence, severity of abuse, presence or absence of other psychological disorders, and strength of social network (whether the patient has supportive family or friends).

Among experts in substance dependence, the belief in matching is strong, but not until recently was that belief tested, in Project MATCH, the most ambitious and expensive treatment outcome study ever conducted in the field of alcohol rehabilitation. In this experiment, large groups of alcoholics in different cities were randomly assigned to three different treatments: motivational interviewing, a program modeled on AA, and a cognitive-behavioral treatment based on relapse prevention. Then they were followed for a year to see how well the treatment worked. Meanwhile, on the basis of 10 characteristics often targeted in matching, a number of predictions were made: for example, that the least motivated patients would do best in motivation interviewing; that patients with the least psychopathology were expected to benefit more from AA; and that motivational interviewing (MI) was expected to be inferior for patients with severe alcohol problems. In all, there were 16 predictions, and almost none of them were borne out. All the treatments were somewhat effective and about equally effective, but not according to any principles of matching (Project MATCH Research Group, 1997).

Do the results of Project MATCH prove that the matching hypothesis is utterly unfounded? Not necessarily, but they do raise doubts about this widely cherished belief. The study also shows once again that alcohol dependence is very hard to treat. Follow-up studies indicate that, of those who enter treatment, inpatient or outpatient, only about 30 percent stop drinking permanently. The others resume some level of drinking and require ongoing care. We are not even close to identifying truly effective therapies for alcohol-dependent people, let alone discovering which therapy works best for whom.

Nicotine Dependence

One out of every four American adults is a smoker (Schmitz, Schneider, & Jarvik, 1997). Fewer people smoke than drink, but a much higher proportion of smokers become dependent. As a result, nicotine dependence is the most common form of drug dependence in the United States. However, discussions of psychoactive drugs often give little if any attention to nicotine, for, of all the psychoactive drugs, it is the least destructive *psychologically.* Indeed, it appears to do no psychological damage whatsoever. The disorder "nicotine dependence," as defined by *DSM-IV,* refers primarily to those who want to stop smoking but cannot.

Tobacco contains nicotine, which has apparently paradoxical effects on the central nervous system. On the one hand, it stimulates the system by elevating the blood pressure and increasing the heart rate. At the same time, it has a calming effect. This effect is not just psychological—the product of the pleasure of indulging a habit. Animal studies have shown that injections of nicotine reduce aggression. In any case, nicotine does not seem to impair mental functioning. What it impairs is the smoker's health.

The Antismoking Movement

For generations, the use of nicotine products was considered a "vice," and children were warned that smoking would "stunt their growth." Not until 1964, in the famous "Surgeon General's Report" (U.S. Public Health Service, 1964), did the public receive compelling evidence that smoking is a major health hazard. Since 1964, further studies have confirmed this report. Current research shows that, each year, more than 400,000 Americans die prematurely from tobacco-induced diseases, including lung cancer (136,000 deaths), coronary heart disease (115,000 deaths), and chronic obstructive lung disease, such as emphysema (60,000). Smoking has killed more Americans than all wars and all automobile accidents in the country's history (Schmitz, Schneider, & Jarvik, 1997).

Tobacco users are not the only ones who are harmed by smoking. In 1992, the Environmental Protection Agency reported that each year *secondhand smoke* causes 3,000 deaths from lung cancer, contributes to respiratory infections in babies (7,500 to 15,000 of whom require hospitalization), and triggers new cases of asthma in 8,000 to 26,000 young children (Cowley, 1992a). Furthermore, congressional hearings held in the spring of 1994 revealed that tobacco companies not only suppressed research that showed smoking to be a health hazard but also halted research designed to isolate the addictive ingredients in cigarettes. Critics claim that the companies have deliberately raised the level of nicotine in their products to make them even more addicting. Tobacco company executives counter that the reason is to enhance taste (Hilts, 1994).

These findings have resulted in legislation banning cigarette advertisements from radio and television and requiring that each pack of cigarettes sold in this country carry an advertisement of its own potentially lethal effects. In recent years, there has been a marked increase in antismoking legislation. Smoking is banned in most movie theaters, stores, and office buildings, as well as on public transportation systems and in many restaurants. Current legislative proposals include limiting the amounts of nicotine and tar in cigarettes and enforcing stricter control over distribution (especially to young people).

The tobacco companies have vigorously opposed antismoking legislation, which they compare to Prohibition—the ban on alcohol that led to the growth of a black market. At the congressional hearings in 1994, the top executives of America's seven largest tobacco companies all testified that they did not believe cigarettes were addictive. But all said they would rather their own children did not smoke—prompting columnist Anna Quindlen (1994) to quip, "They were simply in the business of selling the stuff to other people's sons and daughters" (p. 23).

Nevertheless, the antismoking message has gotten through. The proportion of adult Americans who smoke dropped from 45 percent in 1954 to 25 percent in 1997. People who still use tobacco smoke fewer cigarettes than before (Schmitz, Schneider, & Jarvik, 1997). (See Figure 11.1.) And, while many people are quitting, fewer are starting: the percentage of high school seniors who smoke daily dropped from 27 percent in 1975 to 19 percent in 1993 (Johnston, O'Malley, & Bachman, 1994). Some, however, have taken up smokeless tobacco (chewing tobacco and snuff) instead. According to one survey, 9 percent of male high school seniors used smokeless tobacco during a sample 30-day period in 1993 (Johnston, O'Malley, & Bachman, 1994). Many adolescents apparently believe that smokeless tobacco is safe, which is not the case. While it is not associated with lung cancer, it is associated with throat and mouth cancer.

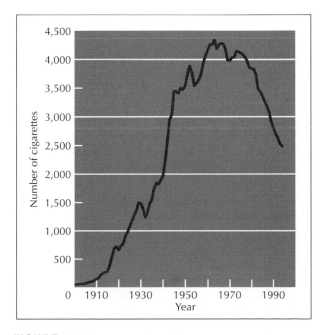

FIGURE 11.1 Cigarette consumption, per capita, in the United States, 1900–1994.

Legal Remedies

In the past few years, both the public and the government have begun pressuring the tobacco industry at unprecedented rates. The federal government has brought lawsuits; in many states, the tobacco companies have been hit by class action suits as well. Antismoking advocates and public policy makers have formed advisory committees to guide such litigation. Antismoking groups have also been lobbying for increases in federal excise taxes on cigarettes and for curbs on overseas marketing to countries, especially in the Third World, where the dangers of smoking are still not widely understood.

The most far-reaching and controversial outcome of this campaign was an agreement reached between the federal government and the tobacco companies in early 1997. An industry that until recently has not even conceded that smoking was bad for one's health agreed to pay $368 billion for public health benefits—the largest legal settlement ever paid by a private industry. The federal government was also given some power to regulate the tobacco industry in the future. In return, the government agreed to disallow further lawsuits against the tobacco companies.

Many public health advocates feel that the tobacco industry got off too lightly. As they point out, $368 billion may sound like a lot of money, but it is not nearly enough to reimburse Medicare, Medicaid, the Veterans Administration, and other health programs for the money they have spent, and are spending, on smoking-related illnesses. Indeed, when spread over 25 years—the amount of time the tobacco companies have to make these payments—the sum represents less than 15 cents per dollar for the $100 billion per year of medical costs due to smoking. In return for this partial compensation, the tobacco industry now has protection, guaranteed at least until the year 2000, from legal attempts to stop them from marketing a deadly substance. (Actually, it is only class action suits that will be disallowed, but that effectively eliminates lawsuits. Most individuals cannot afford, alone, to sue tobacco conglomerates.) Finally, the tobacco companies did not even have to admit that for years they had lied to the American public, by suppressing evidence that nicotine was addictive.

Nevertheless, $368 billion is a large amount; it will do some good. (Part of it will be used to provide health coverage for uninsured children.) And, with this dramatic settlement, the fact that nicotine is a dangerous drug, one that requires government regulation, was put squarely before the public.

However, fighting smoking still remains an urgent public health problem. Of special importance is the need to prevent teenagers from taking up tobacco.

(Tax increases raising the price of a pack of cigarettes by one to two dollars would help greatly.) Such efforts are bound to be opposed. Many states depend on tobacco for their economic stability; in those states, a political candidate who is not willing to fight tobacco regulation cannot get elected. The tobacco industry is also powerful enough to influence government officials from nontobacco states. Thus, this will be a long struggle.

Nicotine Dependence: Theory and Therapy

Learning or Addiction?   Why tobacco should have such a firm hold over so many people is not at all clear. Behavioral theorists see it as a learned habit maintained by a number of reinforcers—the stimulant effects of nicotine, the pleasure associated with inhaling and exhaling smoke, the experience of tension reduction in social situations, the enhanced image of oneself as "sophisticated," or perhaps all of these, the primary reinforcer varying from smoker to smoker (O'Leary & Wilson, 1975). However, these reinforcers seem rather weak to maintain such a dangerous habit.

Is smoking, then, a physiological addiction? For years, some experts doubted this. For one thing, there was no evidence of tolerance; many people go on smoking a pack a day for decades. And the withdrawal symptoms experienced by those who stop smoking—irritability, anxiety, restlessness, difficulty in concentrating, decreased heart rate, craving for nicotine, overeating (White, 1991)—seem mild compared with those of addictions such as alcohol.

In the early 1980s, however, Stanley Schachter presented impressive evidence in support of the addiction hypothesis. In a number of studies, Schachter and his colleagues found that smoking does not calm smokers or elevate their mood, nor does it improve their performance over that of nonsmokers. On the other hand, *not* smoking, or an insufficient nicotine level in the bloodstream, causes smokers to perform considerably worse than nonsmokers. Schachter concluded that smokers get nothing out of smoking other than avoidance of the disruptive effect of withdrawal and that it is for this reason—avoidance of withdrawal—that they smoke (Schachter, 1982).

In support of this conclusion, Schachter and his coworkers have good evidence that smokers regulate their nicotine levels in order to ensure that withdrawal symptoms do not occur. In one experiment, smokers increased their cigarette consumption when low-nicotine cigarettes were substituted for their regular, high-nicotine brands. In another experiment, a group of smokers was given vitamin C, which lowers the nicotine level in the bloodstream. (Vitamin C acidifies the urine and so increases the rate at which nicotine is excreted.) Once again, the subjects compensated by smoking more. Schachter suggests that this mechanism may explain why people smoke more when they are under stress. Stress, like vitamin C, acidifies the urine. Thus, smokers under stress would have to increase their nicotine intake in order to maintain their usual nicotine level and thereby fend off withdrawal.

Treatment   Treatment programs for smokers tend to report high relapse rates, and relapse is apparently even more common for those who try to quit on their own: according to one survey, only 10 to 20 percent are still abstinent a year later (Lichtenstein & Glasgow, 1992). Mark Twain summed it up neatly. He could stop smoking easily, he said; he had done so hundreds of times. Recent years have seen the development of a number of new treatments, from cognitive-behavioral therapy to antidepressants to various mechanisms— chewing gum, skin patches, nasal sprays, and inhalers—for introducing nicotine into the bloodstream without tobacco use. So far, none of these methods has proved especially successful. Much hope was invested in the nicotine-replacing methods, and they do seem slightly more effective than older treatments. One study, for example, found a 26 percent success rate with nicotine chewing gum at six-month follow-up, as opposed to 19 percent without the gum (Fortmann & Killen, 1995). But with this, as with other treatments, the vast majority of quitters relapse.

Why are some people able to break the habit and others not? Research suggests that a number of factors—motivational, cognitive, social—predict who, having quit smoking, will remain abstinent. Not surprisingly, the higher the person's motivation, the less likely a relapse (Marlatt, Curry, & Gordon, 1988), and it makes a difference whether the motivation is intrinsic (the person truly wants to stop smoking) or extrinsic (the person would happily go on smoking but wants to get the family off his or her back). Intrinsic motivation works better than extrinsic motivation (Curry, Wagner, & Grothaus, 1990). Two cognitive factors that predict continued abstinence are self-efficacy (Garcia, Schmitz, & Doerfler, 1990)— whether the person believes that he or she can actually succeed—and the use of coping mechanisms. Those who struggle actively with the desire to smoke—by talking to themselves, by calling up thoughts of emphysema and lung cancer, by substituting exercise or gum chewing—are most likely to conquer it (Bliss, Garvey, Heinold, et al., 1989). Another psychological factor that may affect nicotine dependence is depression. One study found that more than 50 percent of smokers who made repeated unsuccessful attempts to quit met the diagnostic criteria

Nicotine-replacement mechanisms such as the patch have not proved particularly successful in helping smokers to quit.

for major depressive disorder (Glassman, 1992). This is one reason antidepressants are now being tried as a smoking-cessation aid.

In an effort to study the relapse process more closely, Shiffman and his colleagues developed little computers that could be connected to the palm of the hand so that people who had quit smoking could record their temptations and the results on the spot (Shiffman, Paty, Gnys, et al., 1996). Using this methodology, the researchers discovered a number of predictors of the ability to resist temptation. We have already discussed one: cognitive coping strategies. People who struggle with themselves mentally are more likely to win. Another factor that influences the likelihood of relapse is mood. Bad moods weaken resistance. But the most powerful predictor of relapse is the environment—whether the person is in a place where cigarettes are available, where smoking is allowed, and where there are other people smoking. Thus, those who manage to quit don't seem to be different types from those who fail. They are simply the ones who are exposed to more high-risk situations.

Other studies, too, have pointed to the power of the environment. Cigarettes are one of the most heavily advertised consumer products on the market. In 1996, tobacco companies paid New York advertising agencies $500 million to promote smoking in the United States alone. Often their ads are targeted at the groups that are the most likely to smoke and the least likely to quit—women, African Americans, Hispanics, young people, and the international market (Barry, 1991). Although it is difficult to prove cause and effect, the data suggest that advertising pays off. For example, smoking rates have declined more sharply for men than for women—not because fewer women quit smoking but because more teenage girls and young women have taken up the habit (Firoe, Novotny, Pierce, et al., 1989). The fact that women are less likely than men to participate in sports, more likely than men to want to lose weight, and more inclined to view cigarettes as relaxing all contribute to this trend (Waldron, Lye, & Brandon, 1991). Tobacco companies capitalize on "femininity" by featuring sexy young women in their ads and naming their cigarettes "thins," "lights," and "slims." But advertising also can be used to "sell" quitting. Smoking rates dropped twice as fast in California as in the nation as a whole after that state launched a media antismoking campaign (Cowley, 1992b).

The smoker's immediate environment also has an impact. People whose spouses and friends smoke are more likely to relapse than people who travel in smoke-free circles (Morgan, Ashenberg, & Fisher, 1988). Would-be quitters benefit more from spouses who support them with positive behaviors such as compliments and praise than with negative behaviors such as nagging (Cohen & Lichtenstein, 1990).

Other Psychoactive Drugs

For the person in search of a potent psychoactive drug other than alcohol, a wide variety of drugs—depressants, stimulants, hallucinogens—can be equally destructive if they are used habitually. Most of these drugs are nothing new. Opium has been easing people's pain for almost 9,000 years. And until recently many of these drugs were sold legally, over the counter, in the United States. In the nineteenth century, countless self-respecting women thought nothing of taking laudanum, a form of opium, to help them sleep. During the Civil War, morphine was commonly administered as a cure for dysentery and other

ailments, with the result that many soldiers returned from the war as morphine addicts. At the beginning of this century, the major ingredient in the best-selling cough syrups was a recently discovered miracle drug called heroin.

Eventually, however, controls began to be imposed. In 1914, Congress passed the Harrison Act, making the nonmedical use of the opiates illegal. Marijuana was made illegal in some states in 1937, and other states followed. Most of the drugs that we will discuss in the remainder of this chapter cannot be legally purchased for recreational purposes. They must be obtained either from a doctor or from illegal sources. Many people do obtain them, however. Figure 11.2 illustrates trends in drug use among college students. Prevalence rates for most drugs declined during the 1980s but began to increase again starting around 1990. In contrast, the use of legal drugs (alcohol and cigarettes) has remained fairly constant throughout this period.

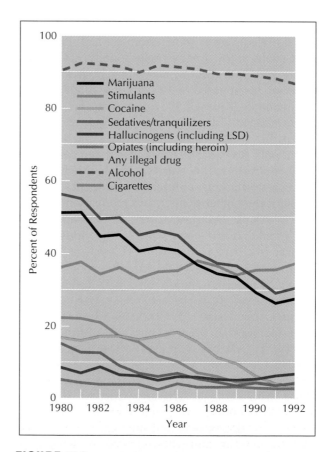

FIGURE 11.2 Trends in drug use among college students. Drug use declined during the 1980s but began to rise again around 1990. In contrast, alcohol and cigarette use remained fairly constant throughout this period.

Depressants

As we have seen in the case of alcohol, a **depressant** is a drug that acts on the central nervous system to reduce pain, tension, and anxiety; to relax and disinhibit; and to slow intellectual and motor reactivity. Along with alcohol, the major depressants are opiates, sedatives, and tranquilizers. All have a number of important effects in common: tolerance develops; withdrawal symptoms occur; and high dosages depress the functioning of vital systems, such as respiration, and thus may result in death.

Opiates The **opiates** are drugs that induce relaxation and reverie and provide relief from anxiety and pain. Included in this group are opium, the derivatives of opium, and chemically synthesized drugs that imitate certain effects of opium.

The grandfather of the opiates is **opium,** a chemically active substance derived from the opium poppy. Early in the nineteenth century, scientists succeeded in isolating one of the most powerful ingredients in opium. This new opiate, which they called **morphine** (after the Greek god of dreams, Morpheus), was soon widely used as an *analgesic,* or pain reliever. As the years passed, however, it became clear that morphine was dangerously addictive. Thus, scientists went back to work, trying to find a pain reliever that would not cause addiction. In 1875, this research culminated in the discovery, by Heinrich Dreser (who also discovered aspirin), that a minor chemical change could transform morphine into a new miracle drug, **heroin,** much stronger than morphine and presumably nonaddictive—an assumption that turned out to be cruelly mistaken.

The final entry in our list of opiates is **methadone,** a synthetic chemical developed by the Germans during World War II, when they were cut off from their opium supply. Methadone differs from other opiates in 3 important ways. First, it is effective when taken orally, so injection is not necessary. Second, it is longer-acting. Heroin, for example, takes effect immediately and is active for only 2 to 6 hours. Methadone, by contrast, takes effect slowly—likewise, its effects taper off slowly—and it is active for 24 to 36 hours. Third, because of its slow onset and offset, methadone satisfies the craving for opiates without producing an equivalent euphoria, or "high." For this reason, it is now used as a replacement drug in the treatment of heroin addicts.

Our discussion will focus on heroin, which is the most widely abused opiate in the United States. Through the early 1970s, heroin use increased each year. In 1972–1973, there were 500,000 to 600,000 opiate abusers in the United States, most of them on heroin. Since then, the percentage of heroin users in the country seems to have remained constant.

Heroin is normally taken by injection, either directly beneath the skin ("skin-popping") or into a vein ("mainlining"). The immediate positive effects of mainlining heroin are twofold. First is the "rush," lasting 5 to 15 minutes. As one addict described it, "Imagine that every cell in your body has a tongue and they are all licking honey" (Ray, 1983). The second effect is a simple state of satisfaction, euphoria, and well-being, in which all positive drives seem to be gratified and all negative feelings—guilt, tension, anxiety—disappear completely. As noted, this artificial paradise lasts only 2 to 6 hours, after which the heroin addict needs another injection.

Such are the positive effects. The negative effects are even more impressive. In the first place, not all people have the "honey-licking" experience. All users respond initially with nausea, and for some, this response outweighs the euphoric effects. Second, if heroin use becomes regular, both addiction and tolerance develop. As with alcohol and nicotine, people dependent on heroin must continue dosing themselves in order to avoid withdrawal symptoms, and as in alcoholism, this eventually requires larger and more frequent doses.

Third, should withdrawal take place, it can be a terrible experience. Withdrawal symptoms begin about four to six hours after the injection and vary in intensity according to the dosage regularly used. The first sign of withdrawal is anxiety. Then comes a period of physical wretchedness, something like a bad case of flu, which lasts one to five days. The symptoms generally include watering eyes, a runny nose, yawning, hot and cold flashes, tingling sensations, increased respiration and heart rate, profuse sweating, diarrhea and vomiting, headache, stomach cramps, aches and pains in other parts of the body, and possibly delirium and hallucinations as well—all this combined with an intense craving for the drug. In hospital settings, however, withdrawal symptoms are far less dramatic, for they are relieved by other drugs.

Most people believe that repeated exposure to opiates automatically leads to long-term addiction. An alternative view is that drug use represents a means of adapting to major stresses in one's life; if these stresses are temporary, the addiction is also likely to be (Alexander & Hadaway, 1982). For instance, many soldiers became dependent on heroin while serving in Vietnam, but few of them continued the habit once they returned home (Bourne, 1974). Similarly, most people who are given opiates in the hospital do not become addicted after they have left the hospital (Melzack, 1988).

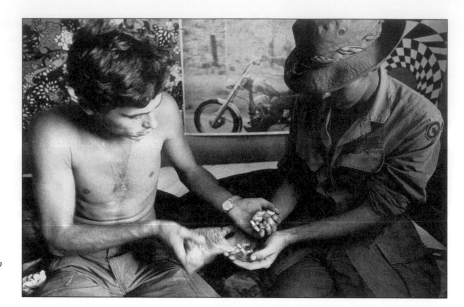

Heroin is highly addictive, but addiction to it may depend on the person's situation. Most soldiers who abused the drug in Vietnam gave it up once that extremely stressful experience was behind them.

Barbiturates   The **barbiturates,** including Nembutal (pentobarbital) and Seconal (secobarbital), are a group of powerful *sedative,* or calming, drugs whose major effects are to alleviate tension and bring about relaxation and sleep. These drugs are legally prescribed by some physicians as sleeping pills. They are sold illegally on the street as "downers" to provide an alcohol-like experience without the alcohol taste, breath, or expense.

Barbiturates have long been the drug of choice for suicide attempts. An overdose first induces sleep and then stops respiration. Furthermore, the overdose need not be made up solely of barbiturates. Both barbiturates and alcohol are depressants, so their combined impact is multiplied in what is called a **synergistic effect.** If a barbiturate is taken with alcohol, the effect is four times as great as that of either of the drugs taken alone (Combs, Hales, & Williams, 1980). The person who combines the two drugs runs the risk, intentionally or unintentionally, of becoming a suicide-overdose statistic. This was the cause of the well-publicized deaths of Judy Garland and Marilyn Monroe. Today, partly because of their danger, barbiturates are less widely prescribed, but, as noted, they are still sold illegally and continue to be implicated in many suicides.

The use of barbiturates by the young is generally recreational and sporadic. Among older people, barbiturate use typically begins as a way of relieving insomnia. As we shall see, however, barbiturates, along with other depressants, tend over time to aggravate rather than relieve sleeping problems. Thus, the person takes more and more of the drug and eventually becomes addicted.

In their effects, which generally last from three to six hours, barbiturates are similar to alcohol. Like alcohol, they disinhibit, induce relaxation and mild euphoria, and impair judgment, speech, and motor coordination. Like alcohol-dependent people, barbiturate addicts exhibit an unsteady gait, slurred speech, diminished intellectual functioning, and confusion. Again like alcohol, the barbiturates, though they are technically depressants, often have a stimulating effect, especially if they are taken with the expectation of having fun rather than of getting sleep (Wesson & Smith, 1971). Indeed, one of the major concerns of those who study barbiturates is the relationship between aggression and Seconal, a favored barbiturate of the young. For most people, however, the stimulating effect is only an early phase of barbiturate intoxication and wears off within a half hour. A final area of similarity between barbiturates and alcohol is withdrawal. Withdrawal from barbiturate addiction is similar to withdrawal from alcohol dependence and is equally unpleasant. Without medical supervision, either can result in death.

Tranquilizers and Nonbarbiturate Sedatives   Within the past decade, the dangers associated with barbiturates have led to their widespread replacement, as a prescription sleeping medication, by such nonbarbiturate sedatives as Dalmane and Halcion. At the same time, **tranquilizers** such as Tranxene (chlorazepate) and Valium (diazepam), which have long been used in the treatment of anxiety disorders and stress-related physical disorders, are also prescribed for insomnia.

All these drugs have essentially the same problems as the barbiturates. They are habit-forming and they have serious side effects, including drowsiness, breathing difficulties, and impaired motor and intellectual functioning. The elderly are particularly vulnerable to the dangers of tranquilizers and nonbarbiturate sedatives, for they are more likely to have disorders the drugs can aggravate—respiratory disorders and kidney and liver ailments (Institute of Medicine, 1991). Taken in high doses over a long period, these drugs can also create symptoms very close to those of major depression. Finally, like barbiturates, tranquilizers and nonbarbiturate sedatives have a synergistic effect in combination with other depressants, though the risk of accidental suicide is not as great.

As with barbiturates, dependence on nonbarbiturate sedatives often begins with a sleeping problem. The person takes the drug and initially obtains some relief. After about 2 weeks of continuous use, however, tolerance develops, and the usual dose no longer produces a good night's sleep. However, at this point many people go on taking the drug. First, by this time their difficulties in sleeping may not only have returned; they may be worse than before. Prolonged drug use often creates what is called *drug-induced insomnia,* a pattern of fitful and disrupted slumber, without any deep sleep. Faced with this new problem, many users reason that, if they needed pills before in order to sleep, now they really need them. Second, these drugs suppress *rapid eye movement (REM) sleep,* the stage of sleep in which dreams occur. If, after a week or more of drug-induced sleep, users try to sleep without the medication, they are likely to experience a *REM rebound*—a night of restless dreaming, nightmares, and extremely fitful sleep—after which they may go back to the drug simply to avoid a repetition of such a miserable night. (Dalmane is the only one of these drugs that suppresses REM sleep but does not produce a REM rebound, because it stays in the bloodstream for more than 24 hours. As a result of its prolonged effect, however, it produces daytime hangover and sedation effects.)

Thus, although the drug soon loses its effectiveness against the original sleeping problem, the usual solution is not to abandon the drug but to take more of it. Once the person increases the dose to about two to three times the normal sleep-inducing dose, addiction begins to develop. From that point on, the drug becomes a way of life.

Tranquilizers, of course, are taken not just for insomnia but for generalized anxiety (Chapter 6)—anxiety that is often the result of high-pressure jobs and an overstressful environment. Possibly for this reason, minor tranquilizers are among the most commonly prescribed drugs in this country, with more than 70 percent of the prescriptions written not by psychiatrists but by general-practice physicians—in other words, family doctors (Clinthorne, Cisin, Balter, et al., 1986). While the majority of people who take tranquilizers develop no problems, many suffer side effects and some do become dependent.

Stimulants

The **stimulants** are a class of drugs whose major effect, as the name indicates, is to provide energy, alertness, and feelings of confidence. We have already discussed one widely used stimulant, nicotine. Another is the caffeine that we take in with our coffee, tea, and cola drinks. Far more powerful are the amphetamines, which can be obtained only by prescription or "on the street," and cocaine, which must be bought illegally.

Amphetamines The **amphetamines** are a group of synthetic stimulants—the most common are Benzedrine (amphetamine), Dexedrine (dextroamphetamine), and Methedrine (methamphetamine)—which reduce feelings of boredom or weariness. Suddenly users find themselves alert, confident, full of energy, and generally ready to take on the world. The amphetamines depress appetite—hence their use by people with weight problems. When taken in small doses for brief periods, they improve motor coordination—hence their use by professional athletes. And they inhibit sleepiness—hence their use by college students preparing for exams. Contrary to campus wisdom, however, they do not improve complex intellectual functioning (Tinklenberg, 1971a). The amphetamine user may experience a number of physical effects, including elevated blood pressure, racing heartbeat, fever, headache, tremor, and nausea. Psychologically, the user may feel restless, irritable, hostile, confused, anxious, or, briefly euphoric (Kaplan & Sadock, 1991).

As long as they are taken irregularly and in low doses, amphetamines do not appear to pose any behavioral or psychological problems. As with most other psychoactive drugs, the problems arise from high doses and habitual use. Once use becomes habitual, tolerance develops, and higher doses become necessary. At the far end of the amphetamine-abuse spectrum are the "speed freaks," people who inject liquid amphetamine into their veins for periods of three to four days, during which they neither eat nor sleep but remain intensely active and euphoric to the point of mania. This heightened activity level can easily lead to paranoid and violent behavior.

Of special importance to the student of abnormal psychology is the resemblance between the effects of amphetamine abuse and the symptoms of paranoid schizophrenia (Chapter 13). Under the influence of heavy doses of amphetamines, people may express the same delusions of persecution seen in the paranoid schizophrenic (Bell, 1973; Snyder, 1979). This amphetamine psychosis, the closest artificially induced counterpart to a "natural" psychosis, appears to be unrelated to any personality predispositions and is thus assumed to be the direct result of the drug. Accordingly, research is now in progress with both animals and human beings to determine whether paranoid schizophrenia may be caused by the same chemical changes that amphetamines induce in the brain.

Cocaine Unlike the synthetic amphetamines, **cocaine** is a natural stimulant; it is the active ingredient in the coca plant. An "in" drug in the 1920s, cocaine again became very fashionable in the 1970s. Its popularity peaked in the mid-1980s at 5.8 million users and then declined to 1.3 million users in the United States by 1995 (preliminary estimates, National Institute on Drug Abuse, 1997). In its classic form, cocaine is sold as a powder, which may be injected but is usually "snorted"—that is, inhaled into the nostrils, where it is absorbed into the bloodstream through the mucous membranes. The rush produced by a snort of cocaine takes effect in about 8 minutes and lasts about 20 minutes. A more elaborate procedure is "freebasing," in which the powder is heated with ether or some other agent—a process that "frees" its base, or active ingredients—and is then smoked. This method carries the psychoactive ingredients to the brain more quickly and thereby delivers a more rapid high than snorting or even injection.

Until recently, cocaine was quite expensive; consequently, its regular users tended to be middle- and upper-class white-collar workers and executives. (It was also favored by entertainment celebrities, whose glamour attached itself to the drug.) But, with the development of the variant form called **crack cocaine**, this drug is now within the buying power of people on weekly allowances. (A vial of 0.1 gram of crack may sell for as little as 50 cents.) Crack is a form of freebased cocaine that is sold in small chunks, or "rocks," which are smoked in a pipe. Because it is freebased, crack is exceptionally powerful, producing in seconds an intense rush (stronger than that of regular cocaine), which wears off within 20 minutes.

Cocaine intoxication is characterized by excitement, intense euphoria, impaired judgment, irritability, agitation, and impulsive sexual behavior. Physically, the user's blood pressure and heart rate increase. If a high dose is taken, seizures and cardiac arrest may result. Some people develop transient periods of paranoia from cocaine use, and those who do may be at higher risk of developing psychosis in the future (Satel & Edell, 1991).

As with amphetamines, tolerance develops with regular use of cocaine, and prolonged heavy use is followed by severe withdrawal symptoms. In a study of 14 "binge" users, Gawin and Kleber (1986) charted the withdrawal symptoms in 3 distinct phases (Figure 11.3). The first phase, known to cocaine users as the "crash," begins horribly. Within a half hour of the final cocaine dose, the person experiences a mounting depression and agitation combined with an intense craving for the drug. These

Readily available and cheap, crack has brought cocaine— once considered a drug for an overpaid young elite— within reach of just about everyone. As a result, thousands of lives have been devastated since the crack epidemic began in the 1980s.

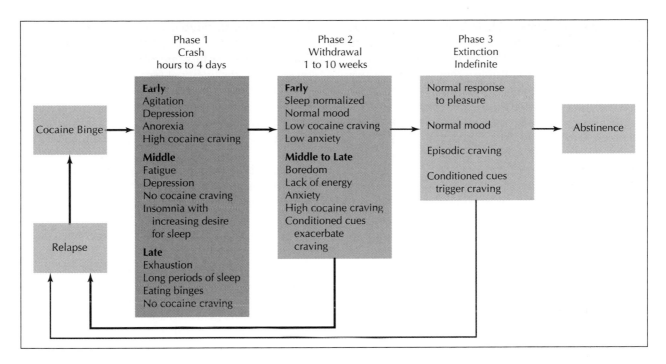

FIGURE 11.3 The three phases of cocaine withdrawal. As the symptom lists show, the craving for cocaine disappears in phase 1, only to reappear in phase 2 and then dissipate very gradually. The arrows at the bottom indicate the likelihood of relapse: strong in phase 2, moderate in phase 3. (Gawin & Kleber, 1986)

feelings then change to fatigue and an overwhelming sleepiness, which last several days. In the second, or "withdrawal" phase, the person returns to deceptively normal functioning, which then gives way to a fluctuating state of boredom and listlessness, mixed with anxiety. At this point, strong cocaine cravings return, and the person may begin another binge. If not, the withdrawal phase passes in 1 to 10 weeks. It is followed by phase 3, "extinction," in which the person regains normal functioning, though with occasional cocaine cravings, usually in response to some conditioned stimulus, such as seeing old cocaine-using friends. Such episodic cravings may recur indefinitely.

Hallucinogens

The **hallucinogens** are a class of drugs that act on the central nervous system in such a way as to cause distortions in sensory perception—hence their name, which means "hallucination producers." Unlike the stimulants or depressants, they achieve their effect without substantial changes in level of arousal. Tolerance develops rapidly to most hallucinogens, but there is no evidence that they are physiologically addictive. There are many hallucinogens, including mescaline, psilocybin, PCP, and, best known of all,

LSD. Despite this variety, rarely can any hallucinogen other than LSD or PCP be bought on the street.

LSD Albert Hoffman, a Swiss chemist, first synthesized **LSD (lysergic acid diethylamide)** in 1938. Five years later, after working one morning with his new chemical, he had an interesting experience:

> Last Friday . . . I was forced to stop my work in the laboratory . . . and to go home, as I was seized by a peculiar restlessness associated with the sensation of mild dizziness. On arriving home, I lay down and sank into a kind of drunkenness which was not unpleasant and which was characterized by extreme activity of imagination. As I lay in a dazed condition with my eyes closed (I experienced daylight as disagreeably bright) there surged upon me an uninterrupted stream of fantastic images of extraordinary plasticity and vividness and accompanied by an intense, kaleidoscope-like play of colours. This condition gradually passed off after about two hours. (Hoffman, 1971, p. 23)

Hoffman guessed that this experience might have been due to his having ingested some of the new chemical on which he was working, so he purposely swallowed a small amount of LSD and found that he had guessed correctly.

LSD and the other hallucinogens seem to work by interfering with the processing of information in the nervous system. That is their attraction and their danger. They can produce a kaleidoscope of colors and images. They can give the user a new way of seeing things. For example, they can produce changes in body image and alterations in time and space perception (Kaplan & Sadock, 1991). And they may open up new states of awareness, allowing the user to find out things about the self that were never imagined before. These are potentially attractive benefits. The problem arises with people who are unable to process or accept the new kinds of perceptions induced by hallucinogens. The person whose grasp on reality is not firm, who derives great support from the stability of the surrounding world, or who has emotional problems may suffer negative effects, possibly for years, from any of the hallucinogens.

The hallucinogens are most harmful when they produce a "bad trip," in which the user becomes terrified and disorganized in response to distorted perceptions. Such an experience is not quickly forgotten. For some people, the drug-induced disruption of their relationship with reality is so severe that they require long-term therapeutic assistance (Frosch, Robbins, & Stern, 1965). Also, a small percentage of regular LSD users suffer "flashbacks"—spontaneous recurrences, when not under the drug, of hallucinations and perceptual distortions that occurred under the drug—a phenomenon that may disrupt their functioning. Flashbacks and other disruptions of visual processing can recur for as long as eight years after LSD use (Abraham, 1983; Abraham & Wolf, 1988). They are more likely to occur when the former LSD user is under stress, fatigued, or ill (Kaplan & Sadock, 1991).

PCP   PCP (phencyclidine), or "angel dust," is a hallucinogen that surfaced in the 1970s and was widely used because it was cheap, easily available, and often mixed with (or misrepresented as) other substances. The drug soon acquired a bad reputation. For one thing, overdoses were common and extremely toxic. In one large mental health facility in Washington, DC, PCP poisoning accounted for one-third of inpatient admissions between 1974 and 1977, outstripping even alcoholism (Luisada, 1977). A more serious risk was PCP's "behavioral toxicity," the tendency of users to harm themselves—through burns, falls, drowning, automobile accidents—and to endanger others as a result of the paranoia and perceptual distortions produced by the drug. These problems discouraged many users, and PCP consumption has been declining steadily since the late 1970s.

Marijuana and Hashish

Marijuana and **hashish** are often classified as hallucinogens, yet they deserve separate treatment. In the first place, their effects are considerably milder than those of the hallucinogens previously described. For this reason, they are often referred to as "minor hallucinogens," while LSD, PCP, mescaline, and the others are called "major hallucinogens." Second, although the major hallucinogens may be widely used, the use of marijuana and hashish is far more common. More than 1 of every 2 Americans between the ages of 18 and 25 has tried marijuana (National Institute on Drug Abuse, 1989), and many, having tried it, have become frequent users. Marijuana use among the young increased dramatically in the 1970s, peaked in 1979 and 1980, and has been declining slowly since then, though it is still America's most popular illegal drug.

Marijuana and hashish are both derived from cannabis, a hemp plant that grows, cultivated and wild, in many countries, including the United States. Marijuana consists of the dried and crushed leaves of cannabis. Though it is usually rolled into a cigarette, or "joint," and smoked, it can also be eaten. Hashish, derived from the resin rather than the leaves of cannabis, is five or six times stronger than marijuana. Like marijuana, it can be eaten, but it is usually smoked in a specially designed pipe.

In both forms, the active ingredient is the same: THC (delta 9, tetrahydrocannabinol), which most researchers agree is not physiologically addictive. THC has 2 consistent physiological effects. The first is an accelerated heart rate. As the dose increases, so does the heart rate, which may go up to 140 to 150 beats per minute. The second change is a reddening of the whites of the eyes. Both effects disappear as the drug wears off.

The behavioral effects of marijuana have been studied in a variety of situations. The impact of a mild marijuana high on simple behaviors is either nil or minimal. The person can easily turn on the television, dial a phone number, make a pot of coffee, and so forth. However, as the complexity of the task increases, as speed of response becomes more important, and as a more accurate sense of time and distance is required, the impairment of ability from a single-joint marijuana high becomes more apparent. It has been clearly established that driving under the influence of marijuana is dangerous (Hollister, 1988).

Having discussed the physiological and behavioral effects, we now come to the major reason for using marijuana and hashish—the psychological effects. These have been summarized by Tinklenberg (1975):

Initial effects of cannabis at low doses usually include euphoria, heightening of subjective sensory experiences, alterations in time sense, and the induction of a relaxed, laissez-faire passivity. With moderate doses, these effects are intensified with impaired immediate memory function, disturbed thought patterns, lapses of attention, and a subjective feeling of unfamiliarity. (p. 4)

It should be noted that the latter group of reactions is generally not at all disturbing. The individual simply feels "spaced out"—a not unpleasant experience for most people under relaxed conditions. Many marijuana users report being totally absorbed in their drug experience while it is happening. During these episodes of total involvement, the person's perceptual, imaginative, and cognitive resources are completely engaged (Fabian & Fishkin, 1981).

There is also a negative side to marijuana: it can heighten unpleasant experiences. The drug may intensify an already frightened or depressed mood until the person experiences acute anxiety. This is most likely to happen to an inexperienced user who takes a large dose and is unprepared for its effect (Grinspoon, 1977). At high levels of THC intake, the effects and the dangers are similar to those of LSD. Some people experience sensory distortions, depersonalization, and changes in body image—all of which can result in a panic reaction and a fear of "going crazy." At this point, intervention by a professional or a trained lay therapist becomes necessary, and short-term psychotherapy may eventually be required. These severe reactions to the use of THC are the exception, however, not the rule, and they generally occur only at the higher dose levels.

Is Marijuana Dangerous? Much less clear than the short-term effects of high doses of THC use are the long-term effects of low doses. Can regular use of marijuana or hashish cause psychological or physiological damage? This question has polarized scientists (Grinspoon & Bakalar, 1997). For scientists, there are four areas of specific concern.

The first has to do with the effect of prolonged heavy marijuana use on blood levels of the male sex hormone, testosterone. There seems to be general agreement that regular marijuana use (about nine joints a week) for six or more months results in a reduction of the testosterone level in the blood (Grinspoon & Bakalar, 1997). The degree of testosterone reduction is directly related to the amount of marijuana smoked. But even the 40 percent reduction in testosterone reported in the original study of this problem (Kolodny, Masters, Kolodner, et al., 1974) does not seem to be enough to impair significantly the sexual activity of males *with established patterns of sexual activity.* Nevertheless, variations in sex-hormone level have a greater impact on the sexual activity of men who have not yet stabilized their patterns of sexual behavior. Therefore, it is possible, though it has not been proved, that heavy, chronic marijuana use by young, sexually inactive men could result in impaired sexual functioning.

The second question is whether marijuana use suppresses immune reactions, the body's mechanisms for fighting off the invasion of foreign substances such as germs. The evidence is fairly solid that chronic marijuana smoking does impair the functioning of one part of the immune system (Gold, 1997). However, this impairment has yet to show any recognizable clinical effect. Therefore, as with the testosterone problem, the significance of the immune response effect is unclear.

A third concern is the effect of marijuana smoke on the lungs. A report commissioned by the Institute of Medicine (1982) indicates that chronic marijuana use may injure the lungs. Because marijuana smoke contains about 50 percent more carcinogenic hydrocarbon than does tobacco smoke and because laboratory exposure of human lung cells to marijuana smoke produces changes that are characteristic of early cancer, health authorities are concerned that heavy, prolonged marijuana use could lead to lung cancer.

A fourth problem centers on the psychological effect of chronic marijuana use. Some professionals feel strongly that prolonged use of marijuana eventually results in impaired judgment, apathy, and—as with the more potent drugs—a focusing of one's existence on the drug experience. Related to this thinking is the argument that those who begin by smoking marijuana will go on to more dangerous drugs, such as heroin. However, a comparison of the figures on frequency of marijuana use and narcotics use shows that very few marijuana smokers make the transition to narcotics. As for general deficits that may result from prolonged use, the first study of long-term use among Americans found no cognitive effects after more than 7 years of extremely heavy use (Schaeffer, Andrysiak, & Ungerleider, 1981). Intellectual functioning among these 10 adults was above average and virtually identical with that shown in tests they had taken 15 to 20 years previously. There *is* evidence that *amotivaational syndrome*—apathy, loss of ambition, difficulty in concentrating—does exist among marijuana smokers, but there is some indication that it may be primarily an accentuation of preexisting behavior patterns (Maugh, 1982).

In sum, the issues are clear, but the answers are not. Testosterone levels go down, but sexual activity may not. One immune response is suppressed, but there is no observable effect. The personality may be affected, but the evidence is incomplete. The only thing that we know for sure about long-term marijuana smoking is that it increases the likelihood of respiratory ailments.

Marijuana as a Medical Treatment   There is compelling evidence that marijuana is useful in treating certain medical disorders (Voth & Schwartz, 1997). Particularly in cancer patients undergoing chemotherapy, it seems to decrease nausea and increase appetite, thus speeding recovery as well as relieving suffering. It has also been reported to help glaucoma and AIDS patients. As a result, ballot initiatives in some states have made marijuana available by medical prescription for certain disorders. But, because of the continuing debate over the risks of marijuana use, these state initiatives have been condemned by Attorney General Janet Reno, Secretary of Health and Human Services Donna Shalala, and President Clinton (Kassirer, 1997). The public seems to be in favor of allowing physicians to weigh the potential risks and benefits and to advise their patients accordingly. In 1986, a special committee appointed by the Drug Enforcement Administration (DEA) arrived at the same conclusion, but its recommendation was overruled by the DEA. Similar debates are going on in Europe (Dean, 1995). It is ironic that, while morphine, an addictive drug with a potential for lethal overdose, can be prescribed for medical patients, such patients are not allowed to use marijuana, whose only established risk is the possibility of respiratory illness after years of regular use.

Groups at Risk for Abuse of Illegal Drugs

As we will discuss in the section on the sociocultural perspective, abuse and dependence on illegal substances are highly related to race, class, education level, gender, and socioeconomic status. African American and Hispanic men who are poor, relatively uneducated, and either under- or unemployed are at particularly high risk.

In addition to these sociocultural factors, medically ill patients, patients with coexisting mental disorders, and those afflicted with chronic pain are also at greater risk for drug abuse than others (Beeder & Millman, 1997; Novick, Haverkos, & Teller, 1997; Portenoy & Payne, 1997). Patients with both physical and mental illnesses often medicate themselves with illegal substances in order to heal their physical or psychic pain, whereas chronic pain patients often get hooked on the high more than the pain relief provided by controlled prescription painkillers.

The use of anabolic steroids continues to plague the sports world as athletes from the elite to the amateur take the drug to bulk up or boost their performance (see box on page 321).

Substance Dependence: Theory and Therapy

In our discussions of alcohol and nicotine, we have already described a number of theories and treatments that pinpoint those drugs. But research findings strongly suggest that certain principles apply to substance dependence in general, regardless of the substance (McLellan, Alterman, Metzger, et al., 1994). Therefore, this section will focus on the overall problem of drug dependence.

The Psychodynamic Perspective

Current psychodynamic thinking about substance dependence stresses the *homeostatic* function of drugs—that is, their ability to restore equilibrium in the face of painful emotions (Brehm & Khantzian, 1997).

Drugs and Conflict   For adolescents suffering anxiety over having to take on new, adult roles, drugs can ease adaptation in the short run, especially if an adolescent lacks good role models and adequate coping skills. The choice of drug depends in part on the defense the adolescent it trying to bolster. For those with low self-esteem, amphetamines can provide feelings of power. For those frightened by social interactions, heroin can ease social withdrawal.

Related to this interpretation is the idea of substance abuse as "self-medication"—for example, in the case of Vietnam veterans who abuse heroin or barbiturates. According to current psychodynamic thinking, the establishment of self-care—the ability to control and calm one's emotions—is a crucial task of early childhood, and it is dependent on adequate nurturing. If parents are cold and underprotective, the child will have no caring skills to internalize and, thus, will grow up susceptible to the artificial calming effects of drugs.

Acquiring Self-Care   Psychodynamic therapy for substance-dependent people aims at remedying self-care skills. For example, in a brief "supportive-expressvie" therapy developed by Luborsky (1984), cocaine abusers are given psychodynamic interpretations, to bring up the painful emotions that the drugs are suppressing; then they are given supportive suggestions, to show them how to deal with those

Anabolic Steroids: Not for Athletes Only

Anabolic steroids have stalked the fringe of sports for 40 years, mostly in the shadows, illuminated for seconds by the sudden spotlight of breaking news:

- Chinese female swimmers test positive in 1994.
- NFL guard attempts suicide after flunking drug test in 1991.
- Canadian sprinter Ben Johnson is stripped of Olympic medal and world record in 1988.

Time moves on, and as once-celebrated names disappear from the media, steroids move back into the shadows, where as many as a million Americans take them every day, swallowing them and injecting them into their muscles. The majority of users are not elite athletes; they have moved on to more sophisticated drugs, harder to detect. The new converts to anabolic steroids are construction workers, cops, and lawyers, adding muscle to look good; and teenagers, bulking up to earn a spot on the team.

Vanity and glory were not the drugs' intent. Anabolic-androgenic steroids are a synthetic version of testosterone, the male hormone that occurs naturally in the body. Developed in the 1930s in Germany, they were used to help patients with wasting disorders to rebuild their bodies. Today their legitimate use is limited: they are prescribed primarily as androgens in treating men whose testes, through accident or disease, have lost the ability to produce testosterone.

Steroids' shadow life began early. Use by athletes was first confirmed when the success of Soviet weight lifters at the 1954 Vienna championships was traced to steroids. Within 10 years, they were widely used in all strength areas of sports. Popularity spread quickly to professional and college football players; to runners and jumpers in track and field; to skiers, swimmers, and cyclists; and to anybody else looking for artificial help. Bodybuilders embraced them most; use throughout competitions became common. Their most celebrated star, Arnold Schwarzenegger, admitted to using them in 1972.

Sports' governing agencies first moved against steroids, mostly on the basis that they afforded an unfair advantage; they were banned in collegiate and Olympic competition in the mid-1970s. By 1991, Congress had declared steroids a controlled substance, making illicit use and trafficking federal offenses.

The drugs' value was widely accepted within sports. They added lean muscle mass to athletes in training and helped them work harder and require less recovery time. But their worth outside sports has been debated; many medical and government officials insisted that their impact was psychological. The debate hurt the establishment's credibility. Doctors and drug officials insisted that gains from steroids were limited, while Ben Johnson pumped up on steroids and ran the 100 at the Olympics in a time still unmatched a decade later.

That credibility suffered even further with official claims of the drugs' risks. In women, certain effects of taking high levels of male hormone were predictable: acne, deepening voice, and proliferation of facial and body hair. Men may experience the paradoxical side effects of enlarged breasts and high-pitched voice. But doctors warned of heart attacks, strokes, and severe liver and kidney damage. While in varying degrees many of these were linked to steroid abuse, they were rare enough that few users knew anyone suffering serious side effects.

The problem has been that little solid research exists on the hazards of long-time, high-dose steroid use, and none is anticipated soon: no medical ethics board would risk a controlled study administering 100 times the therapeutic dose of steroids, the amount taken by many athletes.

While the best available knowledge contends that steroids are not killers, no one suggests they are safe. "You've got to look at the history of hormones and the ever-present possibility of delayed, adverse effects," says Gary Wadler, a trustee of the American College of Sports Medicine and clinical associate professor at Cornell University Medical College. "I have great concerns for what we're

going to see 10 to 15 years down the road." Wadler draws comparisons with DES, a synthetic female hormone, that had been used to stabilize pregnancies in women who had had repeated miscarriages; a generation later, their daughters showed increased rates of vaginal cancer. High-dose use of the corticosteroid cortisone put patients at risk for hip fractures 15 years later.

Other potential adverse medical effects of steroid abuse are reduction of HDL cholesterol (the beneficial kind) and increased total cholesterol, testicular shrinkage, decreased spermatogenesis, reduced testosterone production, benign and malignant liver tumors, liver chemistry abnormalities, alterations in tendons, and dependency syndrome, as well as the risk (from sharing needles) of AIDS and hepatitis. Among teenage users, premature closure of the growth plates in the long bones has been proved.

This last effect is particularly disturbing in light of the expansion of steroid use from elite athletes to teenagers. Boys using steroids to swell their muscles may also be stunting their growth. According to Charles Yesalls, professor of health policy and administration and sports science at Penn State University, "Between 250,000 and 500,000 adolescents in the country have used or are currently using steroids," and 38.3 percent of them began by age 15.

Add to all the other risks a wide range of possible behavioral changes, including increased irritability, aggressiveness, euphoria, sleeplessness, and recklessness. "Maybe one person of 20 will be very susceptible to these side effects," says Harrison Pope (Pope & Katz, 1990), who has studied the effects of anabolic steroids. "In rare cases, people on steroids have become homicidal, committed murder." The phenomenon occurs just often enough that it has its own name—"roid rage." Its existence, according to Pope and his research partner, David L. Katz, means that these drugs pose "a greater-than-expected public health problem, both for users and for society at large."

emotions. The goals are to build up patients' intrapsychic strength and to improve their relationships with the other people in their lives. Currently, this approach is being evaluated in comparison with several other treatment strategies (Crits-Christoph, Siqueland, Blaine, et al., 1997)—a rare attempt to validate psychodynamic therapy for substance dependence. But psychodynamic treatment is not widely used in drug rehabilitation, partly because there have been so few efforts to demonstrate its effectiveness.

The Behavioral Perspective

Psychological and Biochemical Rewards   Traditionally, behaviorists have viewed alcohol dependence as a powerful habit maintained by many antecedent cues and consequent reinforcers. Several suggestions have been offered as to what the primary reinforcer might be: social approval, ability to engage in relaxed social behavior, avoidance of physiological withdrawal symptoms, or reduction of psychological tension. For years, tension reduction was considered a prime suspect. According to this view, all of us have our share of troubles—anxiety, self-doubt, depression, guilt, annoyance. In the process of trying to reduce our psychological discomfort, some of us take a drink, and if this works, then alcohol use becomes associated with the alleviation of psychological pain and is likely to be repeated. Eventually, of course, excessive drinking may itself create further psychological distress, especially guilt, which in turn will be alleviated by more drinking. Thus, the vicious cycle begins. This theory has also been applied to drug dependence in general.

The tension-reduction hypothesis has received some support from animal research. In a classic study (Conger, 1951), laboratory rats were given an electric shock whenever they came near their food dishes. As a result, the rats showed hesitation, vacillation, and other signs of inner conflict when they approached their food, yet when they were injected with alcohol, they went up to their food dishes with no signs of conflict. Other animal studies, however, have not consistently supported the tension-reduction hypothesis.

Today, behavioral theories of alcohol dependence are generally based not so much on negative reinforcement, the reduction of unpleasant states, as on positive reinforcement, the creation of pleasant states. As we will see, neuroscience researchers have discovered that one of alcohol's effects on the central nervous system is to release the neurotransmitters dopamine and norepinephrine, together with endorphins, the body's "natural opiates." In a combination of learning theory and biochemical theory typical of contemporary psychology, many behaviorists now believe that these chemical rewards are the prime reinforcers of excessive drinking, though tension reduction and other kinds of maladaptive coping are thought to be involved as well.

Learning Not to Abuse Drugs   The early behavioral programs for substance dependence relied primarily on aversion conditioning: for example, alcohol was paired with an unpleasant stimulus, usually electric shock or induced nausea. Such programs had some initial success but also a heavy relapse rate (Lemere & Voegtlin, 1950). Drop-outs were common as well.

The problems with these treatments, presumably, was that, while they suppressed the behavior, they did nothing to alter the conditions that elicited and maintained it. Whatever the rewards of excessive drinking, compensation for poor coping skills is probably involved as well. Under the influence of drugs, coping skills deteriorate further, while stresses (e.g., unemployment, marital conflict) increase. The object of current behavioral programs is to remedy this broad adjustment problem, usually through a combination of cognitive and behavioral techniques. The alcoholism is still addressed directly. Patients are taught to identify cues and situations that lead to drug taking, and through role playing and practicing, they are taught alternative responses. But they are also taught new ways of dealing with life: how to solve problems and, by training in relaxation and social skills, how to cope with stress. Such programs have helped many people to stop abusing drugs, but they are not superior to other treatments (including other cognitive-behavioral treatments) that we will discuss shortly (Sobell, Toneatto, & Sobell, 1990).

In Chapter 5, we mentioned the innovative work of Higgins and his colleagues in applying reinforcement theory to the treatment of cocaine abusers (Higgins, Delaney, Budney, et al., 1991). In the contingency management program these researchers set up, patients were given regular urine tests to determine whether they were cocaine-free. After each test that they passed, they received points worth 15 cents each. The points were then converted into vouchers that the patients could use to buy what they wanted in various neighborhood stores participating in the program. Each time they passed a test, the number of points increased. (Conversely, patients who failed the urine test not only got no points but, on their next test, dropped down to the original rate of points-per-test-passed and had to work their way back up again.) Meanwhile, for three months the patients also had weekly therapy in which they were given counseling on employment and family relations, advice in finding recreational activities that were not drug-

Nearly three-quarters of male wife-beaters meet the criteria for alcohol dependence, and many are drunk when the abuse occurs. Behavioral couple therapy has been shown to reduce domestic violence substantially.

related, and help in identifying and avoiding high-risk situations. Finally, if friends or family were available, they were informed of the test results and instructed to reward test-passing with reinforcements that were planned beforehand.

This carefully designed program had mixed results. On the one hand, only a minority of the participants remained drug-free throughout the three months. On the other hand, the group did better than a comparison group in an AA-like program. Further research has consistently shown that the vouchers played a significant role in keeping patients in the program. Thus, material rewards, plus what the researchers called "community reinforcement"—the participation of the friends, families, and stores—did seem to work for some people, though it is not known how long such gains last. Perhaps this approach gives cocaine abusers a good start, after which they need other kinds of support to prevent relapse.

The Family Systems Perspective

Whether as cause or result, substance dependence is very often associated with problems in the family. Therefore, some experts have suggested that couple or family therapy might be a good way to treat both problems. If domestic relations are repaired, maybe the ex-abuser will be less likely to relapse.

Behavioral Couple Therapy   Behavioral couple therapy, either alone or in combination with individual counseling, has been used for many years as a treatment for alcohol dependence. There is some evidence that this ap-

proach reduces drinking, and there is very good evidence that it reduces problems in the relationship.

One such problem may be domestic violence. Almost three-quarters of wife-beaters meet the criteria for alcohol dependence, and many are drunk when they attack (Brookoff, O'Brien, Cook, et al., 1997). It appears that behavioral couple therapy can substantially reduce such violence. In a study of male alcoholics, the men's rates of domestic violence were significantly higher than in the general population during the year before treatment. After behavioral couple therapy, the violence decreased markedly, and this reduction was directly related to reductions in drinking. In general, the patients who stopped beating were the ones who stopped drinking (O'Farrell & Murphy, 1995).

Recently, behavioral couple therapy has been tried with other kinds of drug abusers. In one study, illegal-drug abusers who were receiving individual therapy were randomly assigned to either receive or not receive behavioral couple therapy as well. Then all these men were evaluated after the therapy and reevaluated at regular intervals for a year. Compared with the couples where only the drug-abusing husband received therapy, those for which the couple therapy was added showed greater improvements in marital happiness and fewer days of separation. In addition, the men in the couple-therapy group used fewer drugs, reported longer periods of abstinence, were less often arrested, and spent less time in the hospital. Unfortunately, as is so often the case in drug treatment, the gains began to diminish during the follow-up period (Fals-Stewart, Birchler, & O'Farrell, 1996).

Family Therapy   Interestingly, 60 to 80 percent of drug-dependent people, and especially those who are under 35, either live with their parents or contact a parent at least once a day. Almost all drug-dependent people are in touch with a parent at least once a week. This is true not only in the United States but also in Puerto Rico, England, Italy, and Thailand. What it suggests is that family therapy makes sense for drug abusers. On one hand, the family may be willing to help in the abuser's treatment. On the other hand, it may be the family that needs treating. It often turns out that the parents are also drug-dependent (Stanton & Shadish, 1997).

Family therapy seems especially promising in the case of teenagers. A good example is the home-based, "multi-system" treatment that Henggeler and his associates have developed for substance-abusing delinquents and other difficult adolescents. In this treatment, the therapists basically collaborate with the family, but it is not just the family that is drawn in. All the institutions surrounding the adolescent—school, work, peers, community—are viewed as interconnected systems influencing the family and, therefore, the adolescent's problem. Thus, all are used, as in the following instance:

> Frank, 15 years old, was an alcoholic and a delinquent. He often stayed out all night with his friends, drinking and committing robberies. This was not an abnormal pattern in his neighborhood. The community had a thriving criminal subculture, and that is what was available by way of recreation for local teenagers. Frank's mother was single, socially isolated, devoid of parenting skills, and depressed. She felt powerless to control the boy. Still, she placed great value on education (she had finished high school), and she was pained over Frank's indifference to school. The therapists assumed that, if the boy was to stop misbehaving, the mother had to take a stronger hand. After treating her depression with medication and cognitive therapy, they gave her lessons in effective parenting. Her church, her extended family, and her neighbors were all engaged to provide her with social support. Gradually, the mother began setting curfews for Frank and rewarding him for good behavior. She got him involved in various community activities, and the boy set vocational goals for himself. Thus, a new context, prosocial rather than antisocial, was created for him. Both his delinquency and his alcohol abuse stopped. (Adapted from Henggeler, Pickrel, Brondino, et al., 1996.)

The Cognitive Perspective

Thinking About Drugs   As we saw earlier, people's expectations about the effects of alcohol play a role in whether they will use and abuse alcohol (Goldman, Brown, & Christiansen, 1987). Through modeling—the example of parents, peers, and people on television and in movies—children develop *alcohol expectancies,* beliefs about the effects of alcohol consumption. These expectancies congeal into a schema that, later, when the opportunity to drink arises, will determine how the person will use alcohol and how he or she will act under its influence. According to research, the major positive expectancies that people hold about alcohol are that it transforms experiences in a positive way, that it enhances social and physical pleasure, that it enhances sexual performance, that it increases power and aggressiveness, that it facilitates social assertiveness, and that it reduces tension (Brown, Goldman, Inn, et al., 1980). People also hold certain negative expectancies about alcohol—specifically, that it impairs performance and encourages irresponsibility (Rohsenow, 1983)—but, for many people who have problems with alcohol, the positive expectancies outweigh the negative, so they drink, often to excess.

In support of this view, it has been shown that young adolescents' expectations about alcohol do significantly predict whether they will begin drinking, even when other known predictors—age, religious observance, parental drinking patterns—are controlled (Goldman, Brown, & Christiansen, 1987). Such expectations also predict whether they will go on to problem drinking (Christiansen, Smith, Roehling, et al., 1989; Stacy, Newcomb, & Bentler, 1991). It has been shown, in addition, that heavier drinkers have stronger positive expectancies about alcohol than do light drinkers (Brown, Goldman, & Christiansen, 1985). But, while expectancy theory is persuasive on the subject of why people *begin* to drink, it is not as good at explaining why some of them go on to become alcohol-dependent. In the words of one researcher, "Expected consequences may play a greater part in influencing a teenager's first drink than in influencing an alcoholic's millionth drink" (Leigh, 1989, p. 370). By the millionth drink it is the rare person who would still be nursing hopes of good times and enhanced sexual power.

Expectancies seem to be a more complicated issue than was once thought. It matters whether suppressing the urge to drink inhibits expectancies or enhances them (Palfai, Monti, Colby, et al., 1997)—for example, making the next drink seem even *more* likely to produce fun. Another factor is memory: how well the person makes the connection between drinking cues and outcome expectancies (Stacy, 1977). Finally, temperament has an effect on how one responds to expectancies. If the expectancy is of having a new thrill, the response will depend on whether the person is a novelty seeker or a harm avoider (Galen, Henderson, & Whitman, 1997).

Cognitive-Behavior Therapy Cognitive therapy was added to behavior therapy for substance abuse in the 1980s because improvements from behavior therapy alone were usually temporary. It wasn't so hard to get people to give up drugs for a few weeks or a few months; the problem was to make the change last. Estimated relapse rates ranged from 50 to 90 percent (Brownell, 1986). As we saw in our discussion of alcohol rehabilitation, Marlatt and his colleagues (Marlatt & Gordon, 1985), in their relapse prevention model, placed great emphasis on the *abstinence violation effect,* whereby former drinkers who suffer a lapse say to themselves, "Well, I had a drink—I might as well get drunk." According to Marlatt and his group, such people have been indoctrinated by the "disease" or "loss of control" concept of drinking: once you have a drink, you have to get drunk. Needless to say, such a view provides a handy excuse for a relapse. Most cognitive theory and therapy for substance dependence in the past decade has been aimed at countering the abstinence violation effect. "Slips" are now seen as *part* of the recovery. (Some therapists even guide their patients through "planned slips.") The goal is to control the cognitive responses to the slip so that it does not initiate a relapse.

Researchers are now beginning to identify specific factors that lead to relapse. These fall into three categories: individual (intrapersonal), environmental (situational), and physiological. In the first category, negative emotional states such as stress, anger, depression, and anxiety are among the strongest determinants of relapse, accounting for an estimated 30 percent of relapses across the substance-dependence disorders (Cummings, Gordon, & Marlatt, 1980). Interestingly, the relationship between stress and relapse seems to be reciprocal (Brown, Patterson, Grant, et al., 1995). Areas of stress created by the drug problem are most likely to sabotage abstinence. (For example, if drugs have put your job at risk, problems on the job are most likely to send you back to drugs.) Finally, it should come as no surprise that "psychosocial vulnerability" —poor coping skills, lack of social support, perceived inability to resist temptation—place people at higher risk for relapse (Brown, Patterson, Grant, et al., 1995).

On the basis of findings such as these, McAuliffe (1990) developed a program to help substance-dependent people head off negative emotional states by refining their coping skills. In McAuliffe's study, 168 recovering heroin addicts were randomly assigned either to the usual aftercare treatment or to a specially designed relapse-prevention program involving 2 weekly meetings—1 led by a professional counselor, 1 by a recovering addict—for 6 months. In the meetings, the experimental subjects were taught strategies for dealing with former drug-using com-

Research has shown that areas of stress created by drug abuse are most likely to undermine abstinence. For instance, if drug abuse jeopardizes a person's job, stress at work is most likely to lead to a relapse.

panions, with drug offers, and with job and family problems. They were also taught how to make new friends and develop drug-free recreational activities, as well as how to respond to slips. At a 1-year follow-up, the subjects in the relapse-prevention program were significantly more likely to be completely abstinent or suffering only rare slips than were those who had only the traditional aftercare.

In addition to negative emotional states, motivation and commitment are key factors in the prediction of relapse (Hall, Havassy, & Wasserman, 1990). Bolstering motivation and assessing motivation— does the person really want to quit, or has the boss delivered an ultimatum?—should become part of relapse-prevention programs in the future (Hall, Havassy, & Wasserman, 1991).

Apart from individual factors, environmental contingencies figure heavily in relapse risk. Possibly the key environmental factor is social support, its presence or absence. Relapses are often precipitated by interpersonal conflict—for example, family quarrels. Conversely, the recovering substance abuser can be greatly helped by encouragement from family, friends, and coworkers. Another source of social support is self-help groups such as Alcoholics Anonymous and Narcotics Anonymous, which offer the kind of understanding that only fellow sufferers can extend. At the same time, these groups teach their members how to cope with environmental contingencies. For example, two notorious predictors of lapses and relapses are exposure to the drug and social pressure from users (Shiffman, 1982). Alcoholics Anonymous and other self-help groups offer members advice on how to avoid or control such cues. This kind of contingency management can greatly increase a person's chances of remaining drug-free.

As for physiological factors, withdrawal cravings can lead swiftly to a slip, especially if they are combined with risk-laden individual and environmental factors. People who are angry or depressed, or who are spending the evening with old drinking buddies, will have a far harder time withstanding physiological pressures to return to the drug. In addition, it may be true that a lapse places the would-be abstainer on a slippery slope. Research with animals suggests that the ingestion of small amounts of drugs creates a "priming effect," activating conditioned physiological responses that lead to further drug consumption (Carroll & Comer, 1995). Another area of interest for physiological researchers has been the substitution of new, benign addictions, such as physical exercise.

When a truly effective treatment is found, it will probably combine all these factors: intrapersonal, situational, and physiological. In the meantime, cognitive-behavioral treatment based on relapse prevention does continue to show promise, though it may not be any more successful than the competing psychosocial treatments: motivational interviewing, AA-type programs, and contingency management (Carroll, 1996).

The Biological Perspective

Genetic Studies   Most of the genetic research on substance dependence has focused on alcohol, and most of the findings suggest that some people inherit a predisposition to problems with this drug. One type of evidence comes from cross-cultural studies. It has been reported, for example, that the Japanese, Koreans, and Taiwanese respond with obvious facial flushing and clear signs of intoxication after drinking amounts of alcohol that have no detectable effect on Caucasians (Harada, Agarwal, Goedde, et al., 1982; Wolff, 1972). Such ethnic differences have led some investigators to conclude that sensitivity to alcohol is related to genetic factors, possibly affecting the autonomic nervous system.

Goodwin and his coworkers have conducted an even more revealing study with a group of male adoptees (Goodwin, Schulsinger, Hermansen, et al., 1973). Each of the men in the index group had been separated in infancy from his biological parents, one of whom had been hospitalized at least once for alcohol dependence. Many more of the index children grew up to have drinking problems and to seek psychiatric treatment than did a matched control group of adoptees whose biological parents were not alcohol-dependent. However, the rate of drinking problems among the men in the index group was less than would be expected if their drinking pattern were due solely to genetic factors. Furthermore, in a compan-

ion study, the adopted-away daughters of alcohol-dependent parents showed no difference in their rate of drinking problems either from that of controls or from that of their nonadopted sisters (Goodwin, Schulsinger, Moller, et al., 1977). Still, the finding for the adopted sons clearly suggests some measure of genetic influence.

Additional support for the existence of a genetic factor comes from findings that the sons and brothers of severely alcohol-dependent men run a 25 to 50 percent risk of becoming alcohol-dependent themselves and that there is a 55 percent concordance rate for dependence in MZ twins, compared with 28 percent for same-sex DZ twins (Hrubec & Omenn, 1981; Kaprio, Koskenvuo, Langinvainio, et al., 1987; Schuckit & Rayses, 1979). Again, genes are obviously not the only factor. As is clear from the fact that 45 percent of the MZ twins were discordant, environment plays its part. However, as suggested by the adoption studies of Goodwin and his colleagues, the genetic component appears to be stronger for men than for women. Twin studies have also suggested that the heritability of alcohol dependence is greater for men than for women. One research team, for example, selected a sample of twins in which a member of each pair was known to be alcohol-dependent or alcohol-abusing. Then the researchers determined whether the other member of each twin pair had problems with alcohol. In all, they compared 85 male MZ twin pairs with 96 male DZ twin pairs—and 44 female MZ twin pairs with 43 female DZ twin pairs—on rates of alcohol dependence and abuse (McGue, Pickens, & Svikis, 1992). They found higher concordance rates for alcohol dependence and abuse for male MZ (76.5 percent) than male DZ (53.6 percent) twins, but no difference in concordance rates for female MZ (38.6 percent) versus DZ (41.9 percent) twins.

Additional adoption studies by Cloninger and his colleagues have complicated the picture further (Bohman, Sigvardsson, & Cloninger, 1981; Cloninger, Bohman, & Sigvardsson, 1981). According to these researchers, a susceptibility to alcoholism is inherited, but in two different ways. What this research group calls Type 1 susceptibility affects both men and women and follows the diathesis-stress model. That is, in order for the genetic susceptibility to lead to actual alcohol dependence, there must be environmental stress—above all, the stresses associated with low socioeconomic status. Type 2 susceptibility is far more heritable—it seems to be independent of environmental influences—and is passed from father to son. In Type 2, it is very rare for either the mothers of alcohol-dependent sons or the daughters of alcohol-dependent fathers to be dependent themselves, whereas the heritability from father to son is about 90 percent. The two types also differ in their age at onset—Type 2 generally beginning in adolescence, Type 1 in adulthood—and they differ dramatically in severity. Type 1 is rarely associated with criminal behavior; these drinkers tend to be dependent, quiet-living people. By contrast, Type 2 alcohol-dependent men are impulsive and aggressive, prone to brawling, reckless driving, and other criminal behavior. They also seem to be significantly more prone to depression and suicide (Buydens-Branchey, Branchey, & Noumair, 1989). Thus, it seems likely that there is more than one genetic factor involved in drinking problems and that at least one is sex-linked.

A final indicator of heritability is the fact that experimenters have been able to breed rats with a taste for alcohol. The best known are the so-called P rats—alcohol-preferring rats—developed by Ting Kai Li and his associates (Li, Lumeng, McBride, et al., 1987; Murphy, Gatto, Waller, et al., 1986). While most rats find alcohol distasteful, the P rats not only prefer alcohol solutions to water but will drink to intoxication, and they develop tolerance. They will also do tasks in order to gain access to alcohol. The fact that these behaviors were developed through selective breeding strongly suggests that genes are at work in human drinking problems as well.

Biochemical Studies

Endorphins In the early 1970s, scientists discovered that nerve cells in the brain have *opiate receptors*, sites to which opiates such as heroin and morphine attach themselves. The fit between the opiates and the receptors is so perfect that researchers suspected the brain must produce a natural substance that the receptors were intended to fit. This suspicion led in 1975 to the discovery of *enkephalins*, brain chemicals that are similar to morphine and that do, indeed, fit the opiate receptors (Goldstein, 1976). Several of these substances have been given the name **endorphins**, meaning "morphine within."

Endorphins may account for a number of mind-body phenomena that have puzzled scientists for many years. For one thing, they may underlie our natural control of pain and our natural experience of pleasure. It has long been known that stimulation of certain parts of the brain can produce pleasure and help control intractable pain. The stimulation seems to cause the brain to produce more endorphins. (If acupuncture controls pain—a point that is still being debated—it may do so via the same mechanism.) Endorphins may also be the mechanism by which placebo drugs can relieve pain. Possibly the person's learning history—the linking of pain-relieving drugs with endorphin produc-

The "runner's high" is produced by the release of endorphins—natural brain chemicals that cause feelings of pleasure—in response to exertion. Morphine and other opiates produce the same biochemical reaction.

tion—creates a conditioned response whereby simply being told that a drug will relieve pain releases the endorphins that will do the job.

More to the point of this chapter, endorphins may also explain physiological dependence on drugs. It is possible that, when external opiates are taken, the brain ceases to produce internal opiates, or endorphins. The person thus becomes entirely dependent on external opiates for the relief of pain and the achievement of pleasure. Withdrawal symptoms, accordingly, occur during the time between the cessation of external opiate consumption and the resumption of internal opiate production.

Recently, scientists have discovered that the opiate receptor sites can be occupied by substances that prevent both opiates and endorphins from attaching themselves to the receptors. One such opiate antagonist is naltrexone, which has been used under the brand name Revia in the treatment of opiate addiction. When a person on Revia takes an opiate, the opiate has no effect—it neither produces a rush nor reduces withdrawal symptoms. The hope is that the repeated experience of taking an opiate without any effect will eventually break the addiction.

Dopamine   A second important theory has to do with the neurotransmitter dopamine. According to this theory, most of the abused drugs, including alcohol, amphetamines, cocaine, and opiates, stimulate the dopamine-producing neurons in the median forebrain bundle, a complex neural pathway that connects the midbrain to the forebrain (Wise, 1988). This increased dopamine production is what creates the drug's positive effects (euphoria, stimulation) and thus, by reinforcement, the risk of addiction. Animal research has provided some support for this theory. Rats that have been trained to administer opiates, alcohol, and amphetamines to themselves stop using these drugs if they are given a chemical that blocks the synthesis of dopamine. Presumably, once dopamine production is turned off, the drugs are no longer reinforcing. Such dopamine-suppressing chemicals can also block the stimulant effects of alcohol and amphetamines in human beings (Engel & Liljequist, 1983; Wise, 1988). If the implications of this research prove to be correct—that is, if a variety of addictive drugs all turn out to deliver their rewarding effects via dopamine—this means that one drug may satisfy the urge for a different drug. In turn, that might mean that people who have conquered an addiction to one drug, such as heroin, would be at risk for relapse from even occasional use of any other dopamine-mediated drug, such as alcohol, cocaine, or even caffeine.

Drug Treatment for Drug Dependence   Several medications are now being prescribed to reduce cravings and other withdrawal symptoms in people coming off drug dependence. One of the most widely studied is Revia, which is being used not just for opiate dependence but also for alcoholism. In one experiment in which a group of alcoholics who had been through detoxification were randomly assigned either to Revia or to a placebo, the Revia group reported fewer cravings and lower relapse rates (O'Brien, Volpicelli, & Volpicelli, 1996). Unfortunately, some people seem not to respond to Revia, and many people fail to take the pills (Volpicelli, Rhines, Rhines, et al., 1997). Two other drugs, buspirone and acamprosate are also being tried in alcohol rehabilitation, and they, too, show some promise. But none of these drugs is a panacea, and all have to be combined with one of the psychosocial treatments, such as cognitive-behavior therapy or AA.

A more familiar drug is methadone, which is at the center of many drug rehabilitation programs. As we saw earlier, methadone is a synthetic opiate, and like other opiates, it is highly addictive. It does not produce the extreme euphoria of heroin, but it does satisfy the craving for heroin and prevent withdrawal symptoms. In short, what methadone maintenance programs do, at best, is switch people from dependence on heroin, in the form of three to four injections daily (with the attendant risk of AIDS), to dependence on methadone, in the form of one oral dose per day. This relieves them of their "doped" behavioral symptoms and of the need to steal in order to finance their habit.

Methadone maintenance programs have had substantial success, particularly in terms of controlling the public health and public safety problems associated with drug abuse—notably AIDS and crime. At the same time, methadone does not prevent its takers from becoming dependent on alcohol, barbiturates, or other drugs. Furthermore, methadone maintenance programs do not have a good track record in keeping patients off heroin once the methadone is discontinued (Woody, McLellan, Luborsky, et al., 1995).

The Sociocultural Perspective

All the treatments for substance abuse that we have examined so far target the individual abuser and his or her immediate environment, and none of them is notably effective. Perhaps no form of psychotherapy is strong enough to combat a problem that has so much to do with political systems and cultural practices.

Drugs and Poverty   As we discussed in the section on groups at risk for abuse of illegal drugs, drug dependence in the United States has been gradually shaped by a legacy of racism and poverty. Together, these two forces have created a breeding ground for illegal drugs, the ghetto. Even though illegal drug use has declined overall since the 1970s, and though people of all races and classes abuse drugs, African American and Hispanic communities have been disproportionately victimized by drug abuse. In turn, drug abuse has ravaged those communities.

The forces that stabilize drug use have accelerated in the 1990s. At all levels of government, there have been cuts in programs aimed at the well-being of the inner cities. Meanwhile, American corporations—and, consequently, jobs—have continued leaving the cities for greener pastures in the suburbs or in Third World countries. The result has been a dramatic decline in the standard of living among the poor in American cities. In the 1980s, crack cocaine came along, to stymie both drug rehabilitation and the criminal justice system. None of the attempted solutions to the crack problem, or to the heroin epidemic

Needle-exchange programs, which allow heroin users to trade in their used needles for clean ones to help reduce the spread of HIV, are an example of harm reduction. Rather than ending drug use, harm reduction policies attempt to control the damage that drug use does to society at large.

surrounding it, seems in any way sufficient. There is not enough money and not enough hope, either among drug users or in the society at large.

When drugs are available and opportunities for drug-free personal fulfillment are not, drugs will be used. What is there to lose? In an environment where the legal paths to financial success are virtually nonexistent, how surprising is it that drug dealing is a high-status profession in the inner city? Compared with the ending of racism and poverty, any treatment discussed in this chapter has to be viewed as little more than a side issue. Given the mood of the American public, what can mental health professionals do to curb drug dependence?

To make matters more complicated, a new drug-related problem arose in the 1980s: the spread of AIDS. Injecting drugs intravenously is a primary way of contracting the AIDS virus, and female IV users may not only contract the virus but pass it on to their children during pregnancy. Finally, as we have stated, there is an inevitable correlation between drugs and crime. Heroin and cocaine addicts must come up with a substantial amount of money every day to support their habits. They are generally unemployable; therefore, unless they are independently wealthy, they must steal. Addicts are responsible for millions of dollars worth of property crimes annually. As many as 20 percent of inmates in federal prisons committed their offenses in order to obtain drugs. More than 5 percent of the murders committed in this country are directly related to the sale of narcotics.

Harm Reduction   Assuming that the United States and other Western countries continue to be more concerned with balanced budgets than with poverty and racism, what is left as a solution at the policy level? One answer is *harm reduction,* a set of inter-

ventions that concentrates not on ending drug dependence but on controlling the harm that drug dependence does to the society at large. First introduced in the Netherlands in the 1980s, harm-reduction policies attempt to integrate drug abusers into the larger society and to distinguish between use and abuse. Harm reduction began when it was first discovered that HIV was often transmitted through the sharing of needles for drug injection. We might prefer that HIV-infected people not use drugs, but, if they do, we would prefer that they not spread this deadly disease in the process, hence the beginning of needle-exchange programs, whereby heroin addicts trade in their contaminated needles for clean ones. Harm-reduction advocates also want to reduce the criminal activity that results from drug abuse. One proposal is to legalize drugs and dispense them to addicts under medical supervision and at nominal cost. Such a system was tried in Great Britain during the 1970s and 1980s. Opponents of this approach claim that it simply encourages addiction, and the apparent increase in the number of British addicts during the 1980s seemed to support this argument. It was because of this increase that the British system was abandoned. However, defenders of legalization claim that it is the only reasonable way to prevent addicts from doing as much harm to society as they do to themselves.

Despite some successes reported in Holland, Australia, and Switzerland, harm-reduction policies have been slow to catch on in the United States. As regards drugs, American politicians seem wedded to a philosophy of zero tolerance. Needle-exchange programs offer a good example. Contaminated needles spread about one-third of all new AIDS cases nationwide. Drug use accounts for two-thirds of new cases of HIV among women, and more than half of those among children, who, as noted, contract it from their mothers in the womb. More than 60 cities now have needle-exchange programs, and there is evidence that these programs reduce the spread of HIV without increasing drug use. The American Medical Association and other groups have called for the legalization of needle exchange. Nevertheless, needle-exchange programs are illegal in most states, and in 1988, Congress made it a crime for federal funds to be used for such programs.

While harm reduction has gained little support, some efforts are being put into the *prevention* of drug abuse. Drug education is now common in the schools and the workplace. Television commercials show movie stars and sports heroes warning teenagers against drugs, and advertisements in buses and subways tell people who already have drug problems where they can go for help, what number they can call, before they become defeated. Such efforts probably do some good, but the most obvious way to prevent drug abuse is to end poverty.

KEY TERMS

addiction, 297	endorphins, 327	methadone, 313	relapse prevention, 307
amphetamines, 315	hallucinogens, 317	morphine, 313	stimulants, 315
barbiturates, 314	hashish, 318	motivational interviewing, 307	substance abuse, 297
blood alcohol level, 298	heroin, 313		substance dependence, 297
cocaine, 316	LSD (lysergic acid diethylamide), 317	opiates, 313	synergistic effect, 314
crack cocaine, 316		opium, 313	tolerance, 297
depressant, 313	marijuana, 318	PCP (phencyclidine), 318	tranquilizers, 314
detoxification, 305	matching, 308	psychoactive drug, 296	withdrawal, 297

SUMMARY

- Psychoactive drugs are substances people use to alter their psychological state. *DSM-IV* defines two categories of pathological drug use—substance dependence and substance abuse—on the basis of problems a drug is causing in a person's life. Either diagnosis depends on behavioral criteria rather than on whether the drug is dangerous or illegal.

- A diagnosis of substance dependence requires that a person meet three of the following criteria: preoccupation with the drug; unintentional overuse; tolerance (progressively larger doses are needed to achieve the same effect); withdrawal symptoms when the drug is not used; persistent efforts to control use, followed by relapse; abandonment of important social, occupational, or recreational activities that interfere with drug use; and continued use despite serious drug-related problems.

- A diagnosis of substance abuse requires that a person meet one of four criteria: recurrent, drug-related failure to meet social role obligations; recurrent use in dangerous situations (e.g., drunk driving); drug-related legal problems; continued use despite social or interpersonal problems.

- Alcohol, legal and sanctioned by custom, is one of the most widely abused drugs. The social and personal costs of its abuse are enormous. A depressant, alcohol interferes with the higher brain centers, which control behavior. After one or two drinks, a person may become talkative and active; as blood alcohol level rises after more drinks, there are changes in mood and behavior, and very high levels lead to stupor, unconsciousness, and, ultimately, death. Whether a person becomes amorous, aggressive, or sad when drinking heavily depends largely on the individual's expectancy of the effect of drink. Long-term overuse can cause heart disease, cirrhosis of the liver, and brain damage; withdrawal may cause DTs (delirium tremens), a severe reaction characterized by trembling, delusions, and disorientation. Other results of long-term abuse include loss of self-esteem, inability to work, family violence, and depression and other psychiatric disorders.

- Most alcohol-dependent persons develop their abuse patterns over a long period, during which they gradually rely more and more on the mood-altering effects of alcohol and continually increase their drinking.

- Alcohol use and abuse patterns and the relationship between them vary in American society according to social class, gender, race and ethnicity, religion, and age. Rates of drinking to excess are increased among less-educated Americans. Use and abuse are higher among men than among women. Relative rates of drinking between whites and African Americans also vary by age and gender. African American women are less likely to drink than white women, and white teenagers are more likely to abuse alcohol than are African American teenagers; however, alcohol-abuse rates are higher for African American men in their thirties than for white men the same age. Native American men are particularly at risk. Rates of drinking have been decreasing among older people but rising among young people.

- Treatment of alcohol dependence begins with detoxification: getting the person free of alcohol and through the withdrawal symptoms. Further rehabilitation requires significant behavior changes. An ideal treatment would be multimodal, combining occupational therapy, relaxation training, individual and group psychotherapy, job training, and support groups such as Alcoholics Anonymous (AA). In practice, most clients mainly attend group therapy and AA meetings.

- Motivational interviewing, a form of short-term psychotherapy, is a question-and-answer method aimed at getting substance-dependent persons to overcome ambivalence toward living drug-free. Relapse prevention based on a cognitive-behavioral approach has gained importance: patients learn to recognize and avoid situations that could put them at risk of relapse, to cope with the unavoidable high-risk situations, and to prevent slips from becoming relapses.

- Cure rates for all forms of alcohol treatment are low. Highly motivated patients with good coping methods benefit from AA, but only small numbers of those who begin going to AA stay abstinent for a year. Relapse prevention treatment also has a low success rate. Matching clients to therapies—motivational interviewing, AA, relapse prevention-based cognitive-behavioral treatment—according to their readiness to change has also been disappointing.

- Although fewer people now smoke than drink, a higher number of smokers become dependent. Nicotine is a drug that both stimulates and calms users. Smoking leads to premature deaths from heart disease, lung cancer, and other respiratory disorders—not only in smokers but in the people (especially children) around them. Health warnings, social pressure, and legislation banning smoking in public places have led a significant number of smokers to quit, but advertising targeted at vulnerable groups encourage others to start.

- The cause of nicotine dependence is unclear. Behavior theorists proposed that smoking is a learned habit reinforced by pleasurable sensations and associations. Stanley Schachter and colleagues found evidence that the only benefit smokers receive from nicotine is avoiding the mainly psychological withdrawal symptoms that result from quitting smoking.

- Relapse rates are high among those quitting smoking. Factors affecting relapse rate include the motivational, the cognitive (whether one believes one can quit), and the social (whether cigarettes are available and whether spouses and friends are smokers). Depression was also found to be common among smokers who had repeatedly attempted to quit and failed. Methods of helping people quit now include cognitive-behavior therapy, antidepressants, and nicotine replacement mechanisms such as patches; nicotine replacement has a slight but measurable advantage.

- Other psychoactive drugs fall into three main categories: depressants, stimulants, and hallucinogens. Most of these drugs can be obtained only by prescription or illegally. The depressants include opiates (e.g., morphine and heroin), which induce relaxation, euphoria, and usually addiction; barbiturates (e.g., Nembutal and Seconal), which induce sleep but, combined with alcohol, may cause death; and tranquilizers (e.g., Valium), which reduce anxiety but may lead to dependence. While most of these drugs have medical uses, all can be abused. Overuse of depressants leads to tolerance; withdrawal is extremely uncomfortable and often dangerous.

- The stimulants increase energy, alertness, and feelings of confidence. This category includes amphetamines (e.g., Benzedrine and Dexedrine), which in high doses may lead to induced psychosis; cocaine (and crack cocaine), which produces a rapid but short-lived "high"; and caffeine. Regular or heavy use of amphetamines or cocaine leads to tolerance, addiction, and withdrawal symptoms upon quitting.

- The hallucinogens cause distortions in sensory perception. While LSD may induce "bad trips" and "flashbacks," it does not appear to be addictive. PCP is a behavioral toxin that often induces risky and/or violent behavior. While usually classified as hallucinogens, marijuana and hashish are milder, producing euphoria, heightened sensory experiences, and a relaxed, timeless state. They can also heighten negative feelings and experiences and can impair activities (such as driving) that require quick and accurate judgments. Research on the effects of marijuana on testosterone and sexual activity, the immune system, and personality has not produced consistent findings, but smoking marijuana does increase the incidence of respiratory ailments. Marijuana is not known to be addictive; severe responses are rare except at high dose levels.

- Marijuana may be effective in relieving the suffering of persons undergoing chemotherapy and may have some use in treating AIDS and glaucoma patients. However, its use as a prescription drug remains illegal in most states.

- Rates of dependence on and abuse of illegal drugs vary with race, class, gender, and educational and socioeconomic status; underemployed or relatively uneducated African American and Hispanic men are a particularly high-risk group. Also at greater than average risk for drug abuse are those who take medication: people with medical illnesses and mental disorders or with chronic pain.

- Current psychodynamic thinking about substance abuse in general focuses on drug use as a way to establish self-care, or the ability to control and calm one's emotions—normally, a capability acquired in early childhood. Psychodynamic therapy for drug rehabilitation, thus, aims at building up patients' intrapsychic strength; its effectiveness has not been widely demonstrated.

- Traditional behavior theories emphasized tension reduction (negative reinforcement) as a cause of alcohol abuse; a vicious cycle ensues when an individual learns that taking a drink relieves psychological discomfort and then more drinking leads to more discomfort. More recent theories emphasize pleasure seeking (positive reinforcement), the reinforcer being natural substances in the central nervous system released as a result of alcohol consumption. The theories have been applied to substance abuse in general. Behavior therapies for substance abuse teach patients to recognize cues that lead to drug-taking and to develop alternative means of solving problems and coping with stress.

■ Therapies associated with the family systems perspective—behavioral couple therapy and family therapy—are especially applicable to substance dependence because of the damage drug use does to families. Behavioral couple therapy has shown results in both reduced drug use and improved marital happiness, but relapse remains a problem. Family therapy has been found promising for teenaged drug users.

■ Cognitive theorists focus on alcohol expectancies—the ideas people develop early in life, by watching the example of others, about their future alcohol-use patterns and their likely response to alcohol. People with excessive positive expectancies may be at greater risk for excessive drinking. Cognitive therapy has recently focused on countering the abstinence violation effect: the sense of failure after a lapse in abstinence, which creates vulnerability to relapse. It is expected that a truly effective relapse-prevention method will address intrapersonal factors (handling stress and anxiety), situational factors (presence or absence of social support), and physiological factors (resisting cravings).

■ Neuroscience studies suggest that genetic factors might predispose individuals to alcohol dependence. There may be a particular type of inherited susceptibility that affects males only.

■ Brain chemistry plays a special role in drug dependence. One theory holds that use of opiates decreases the production of endorphins, the brain's natural opiates and, thus, creates a craving for external opiates; another holds that opiates and other addictive drugs increase the brain's production of dopamine, causing a surge of pleasure that the user seeks again.

■ Medication can reduce withdrawal symptoms from some drugs, as well as relapse rates. Revia, combined with psychosocial treatments, has been effective in treating people coming off dependence on alcohol and opiates, and BuSpar shows promise in alcohol rehabilitation. Methadone, a synthetic opiate that blocks cravings for heroin but doesn't produce the doped behavioral symptoms, has been very successful in keeping users off heroin for the duration of its use.

■ The sociocultural perspective stresses the political and social causes of drug abuse (such as racism, poverty, and lack of opportunity) and suggests that solutions must go beyond treating individual users. Although public budget reductions and migration of jobs from cities have undercut efforts to relieve the causes of drug abuse, harm-reduction policies could still control the damage that drug dependence does to society. An example is needle-exchange programs for heroin users to lessen the spread of HIV; the programs are illegal in most states.

Chapter 12

Mr. and Ms. Albert are an attractive, gregarious couple, married for 15 years, who present in the midst of a crisis over their sexual problems. Mr. Albert, a successful restaurateur, is 38. Ms. Albert . . . is 35. She reports that throughout their marriage she has been extremely frustrated because sex has "always been hopeless for us." . . .

The difficulty is the husband's rapid ejaculation. Whenever any lovemaking is attempted, Mr. Albert becomes anxious, moves quickly toward intercourse, and reaches orgasm either immediately upon entering his wife's vagina or within one or two strokes. He then feels humiliated, recognizes his wife's dissatisfaction, and they both lapse into silent suffering. . . .

Mr. Albert has always been a perfectionist, priding himself on his ability to succeed at anything he sets his mind to. . . . His inability to control his ejaculation is a source of intense shame, and he finds himself unable to talk to his wife about his sexual "failures." Ms. Albert is highly sexual, easily aroused by foreplay, but has always felt that intercourse is the only "acceptable" way to reach orgasm. Intercourse with her husband has always been unsatisfying, and she holds him completely responsible for her sexual frustration. . . .

In other areas of their marriage, including rearing of their two children, managing the family restaurant, and socializing with friends, the Alberts are highly compatible. Despite these strong points, however, they are near separation because of . . . their mutual sexual disappointment. (Spitzer, Gibbon, Skodol, et al., 1994, pp. 266–267)

While human sexual tastes are extremely broad, life in society places limits on them. To begin with, people must cope with the needs of their sexual partners. Rapid ejaculation may be satisfactory for some men but not for the women they are having sex with, as the case illustrates. Some sexual patterns, such as child molesting, are designated as crimes. A number of other sexual behaviors (e.g., cross-dressing), while they involve no harm to others, nevertheless transgress social norms and are therefore considered psychological disorders—in the eyes of many people, shameful disorders. There are very few categories of abnormal behavior to which society attaches as much stigma as sexual disorders.

The disorders that we will cover in this chapter are grouped according to the aspect of sexuality that they interfere with:

1. *Sexual dysfunction:* disruption of the sexual response cycle or pain during intercourse

2. *Paraphilias:* sexual desires or behaviors involving unusual sources of gratification

3. *Gender identity disorders:* dissatisfaction with one's own biological sex and a desire to change to the opposite sex

Before discussing sexual behaviors, however, we must first look at our sexual norms and the extent to which they actually reflect our sexual makeup and behavior.

Defining Sexual Disorders

Compared with other cultures, Western culture has been sexually repressive. For example, while the ancient Greeks not only tolerated but actually glorified homosexuality, the Judeo-Christian tradition that supplanted Greco-Roman civilization has, for the most part, condemned same-sex relationships. Today, church doctrine on sexual morality has relaxed somewhat. Nevertheless, most present-day denominations still place restrictions on sexual activities that circumvent or replace *coitus,* or penile-vaginal intercourse, within the context of marriage.

Western sexual mores are derived not only from religious dogma but also from the writings of experts on mental health and *sexology,* the scientific study of sexuality. Some writings were notably open-minded. Magnus Hirschfeld, a German sexologist of the late

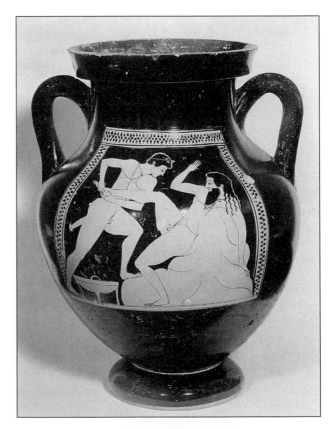

The definition of sexual "normality" has always varied between cultures and across time. In ancient Greece, for example, male homosexuality was considered a normal adjunct to heterosexual marriage.

nineteenth and early twentieth centuries, argued that homosexuality was a normal form of sexual orientation and that the rights of homosexuals should be protected. Hirschfeld also proposed a theory of "intermediaries," people who did not fit the normal (and, in those days, strict) dichotomy of male and female but, instead, combined "masculine" and "feminine" traits (Bullough & Bullough, 1993). Other experts were far more restrictive, however. One of the most influential early psychiatric works on sex, Richard von Krafft-Ebing's *Psychopathia Sexualis* (1886/1965a) condemned masturbation as a psychologically dangerous practice. In his opinion, masturbation halted the development of normal erotic instincts and, thus, led to homosexuality. Krafft-Ebing regarded homosexuality as a form of psychopathology. In his view, and in Freud's, the only genuinely healthy, mature, and normal sexual outlet was coitus. Succeeding generations of psychologists and psychiatrists concurred. In *DSM-II,* published in 1968, people whose sexual interests were "directed primarily toward objects other than people of the opposite sex [or] toward sexual acts not usually associated with coitus" were classified as suffering from sexual disorders.

This rather narrow definition of sexual normality has served for many centuries to help guarantee the continuation of the human species and the survival of the family structure. However, there is little to indicate that human beings are programmed biologically to confine their sexual gratification to coitus. On the contrary, while the sex drive itself is inborn, the direction that it will take is partly a result of socialization. While Western culture considers the female breast an erotic object, many societies consider it sexually neutral. While homosexuality is generally frowned on in our society, in other societies it is not only accepted but actually institutionalized as the proper sexual outlet for adolescent boys (Herdt & Stoller, 1990).

As for freedom of sexual expression, an instructive contrast is provided by two small villages, one in Polynesia and one on an island off the coast of Ireland. In the Irish village of Inis Beag, a researcher (Messenger, 1971) who interviewed the inhabitants over 19 months found that they had no apparent knowledge of tongue kissing, oral-genital contact, premarital coitus, or extramarital coitus. The idea of a man putting his mouth on the woman's breast, or the woman stimulating the man's penis with her hand, was also unheard of. Intercourse was considered a health risk and was achieved quickly, without removing underwear. Female orgasm was apparently unknown. By contrast, in the same year another researcher (Marshall, 1971) reported that, on the

Polynesian island of Mangaia, copulation was "a principal concern of the Mangaian of either sex" (p. 116). Mangaians began full-scale sexual activity at about 13 years, after receiving detailed and enthusiastic instruction from their elders. Sexual technique and sexual anatomy were objects of connoisseurship: "The average Mangaian youth has fully as detailed a knowledge . . . of the gross anatomy of the penis and vagina as does a European physician" (Marshall, 1971, p. 110). For males, the average rate of orgasm at age 18 was 3 per night, 7 nights a week; at age 28, 2 per night, 5 to 6 nights a week. Women had a higher rate, since the male's goal in intercourse was to bring the woman to orgasm several times before he himself reached climax. All Mangaian women were orgasmic. When told that many European and American women do not experience orgasm, Mangaians typically asked whether this did not impair their health. In short, the definition of what is sexually normal and abnormal in Mangaia was almost the opposite of that in Inis Beag. These two cultures are extremes—perhaps the most sexually permissive and the most sexually repressive societies known to Western research. But they illustrate a crucial point: human sexual behavior, viewed across cultures, is extremely variable.

Within a culture, attitudes toward sexuality may change over time. Our own society is far more open about sex today than it was just a few decades ago, for example. Even in less tolerant times, however, sexual behavior does not necessarily conform to declared standards of sexual morality or normality. The famous Kinsey reports (Kinsey, Pomeroy, & Martin, 1948; Kinsey, Pomeroy, Martin, et al., 1953) revealed that many Americans had engaged in culturally prohibited sexual activities. More than 90 percent of the males Kinsey interviewed had masturbated; over 80 percent of the men and 50 percent of the women in his samples had participated in premarital sex; and oral sex was not a rare occurrence. In the 1940s and 1950s, when the Kinsey reports were published, these findings were shocking to many people. Today, they would be considered unremarkable.

In part because of research, in part because of the general social climate, the 1960s and 1970s brought widespread questioning of traditional sexual morality in the United States. Prohibitions on such activities as premarital sex, masturbation, and oral-genital sex were relaxed. Homosexuality, too, was reconsidered, not only by the public but also by the mental health establishment. In its early editions, the *DSM* listed homosexuality as a sexual disorder, along with pedophilia, fetishism, sadism, and so forth. Then in 1973 the board of trustees of the American Psychiatric

Gay rights groups have worked to maintain homosexuality as a "normal form of sexual life." Research finds no justification for considering homosexuality as a pathological pattern.

Association voted to drop homosexuality per se from the list. The trustees' report described homosexuality as "a normal form of sexual life" (American Psychiatric Association, 1974). Still, the *DSM* retained a category called "ego-dystonic homosexuality disorder" for individuals who *themselves* rejected their homosexuality and wanted to become exclusively heterosexual. Many psychologists, together with gay rights groups, objected to this category as well. In their view, homosexuals who rejected their sexual orientation did so because they had internalized negative stereotypes —stereotypes reinforced by psychiatric labeling, even in the milder form of "ego-dystonic homosexuality disorder." At the same time, more and more research was accumulating to show that there was no justification for regarding homosexuality as a pathological pattern. As these studies showed, homosexuals are no more prone to psychopathology than are matched groups of heterosexuals (Hooker, 1957; Paul, Gonsiorek, & Hotvedt, 1982; Saghir & Robins, 1969; Saghir, Robins, & Walbran, 1969). Moreover, there is no "typical" homosexual personality; homosexuals, both male and female, differ as much from one another in personality as do heterosexuals (Hooker, 1957; Wilson, 1984). In response to such findings— together with the fact that "ego-dystonic" homosexuality was rarely diagnosed, anyway—the APA in 1986 voted to drop homosexuality from the *DSM* altogether. Today, in *DSM-IV*'s listing of sexual disorders, there remains a residual category, "sexual disorder not otherwise specified," to cover problems not included in other categories, and one of the examples given is "persistent and marked distress about sexual orientation," but otherwise the manual makes no reference to homosexuality.

Nevertheless, the catalog of psychiatrically recognized sexual disorders remains a long one. The remainder of this chapter is devoted to these conditions.

Sexual Dysfunctions

In the past three decades, our society has seen two major upheavals in sexual attitudes. First came the "sexual revolution" of the 1960s and 1970s, with a new openness about sex and a new interest in sexual satisfaction—giving it and getting it. Sex manuals became best-sellers. Movies and television began showing explicit sex scenes. Popular magazines, even "family" publications such as *Reader's Digest,* began running articles on how to improve your love life.

In the 1980s, the fervor died down somewhat. In part, this was probably just the passing of a trend. (It is also possible that the trend was more in the media than in the population—see the box on page 339.) But a crucial factor was the rapidly spreading AIDS epidemic. "Casual sex" lost its allure. Many people sought, instead, to settle down with one partner. Others opted for abstinence (Ingrassia, 1994). But, for those having sex, the emphasis was on safe sex, with sports and entertainment stars, not to speak of school health services, broadcasting the message.

The campaign for safe sex has not quelled the interest in good sex, however. Though more people are now confining their sex lives to a single relationship, the lesson of the 1960s has not been forgotten: today's young and middle-aged adults, particularly the women, have far higher expectations for sexual satisfaction than their parents did. This change has had many beneficial effects. It has eased the flow of

Sex in America: Myths and Reality

From what Americans see in the movies, on television, and, above all, in advertising, a person might easily conclude that everyone else in the country has a vigorous, varied, even exotic sex life and that he or she is the only one home alone on Saturday night. But the findings of more than a sample of the recent so-called Sex in America Survey (Laumann, Gagnon, Michael, et al., 1994), studying a sample of more than 3,500 Americans aged 18 to 59, should offer comfort. The central finding of this study was that Americans are far more conservative sexually than has been thought.

Of those surveyed, only 56 percent of the men and 29 percent of the women had had more than 4 sexual partners since age 18. (One-fifth of the men and almost one-third of the women reported having had only 1 sexual partner since age 18.) Over a lifetime, the typical American male seems to have had 6 partners; the typical female, 2. And however many partners they have had, most of them are faithful to the one they marry. Nearly 75 percent of the married men and 85 percent of the married women said they had never had sex outside their marriage.

Not only do most Americans have limited sexual histories; they also have less sex than might have been guessed. In terms of frequency, the population breaks down, roughly, into thirds. About one-third reported having sex twice a week or more often; another third, a few times a month; another third, a few times a year or not at all. And the people doing it most often (and most frequently reaching orgasm when they do it) were the married. Almost 40 percent of the married people, compared with 25 percent of the unmarried, said they had sex at least twice a week. Swinging singles were the exception, not the rule.

According to the survey, homosexuality, too, is less prevalent than is often claimed. Only 7.1 percent of the men and 3.8 percent of the women reported that they had ever had sex with someone of their own gender. (Only 2.7 percent of the men and 1.3

percent of the women said they had done so within the past year.) Masturbation was also less common than one might imagine. Only 63 percent of men and 42 percent of women said they had masturbated within the past year, and, curiously, the people who masturbated the most were not those who were deprived of other outlets. On the contrary, they were the ones who were also having the most partnered sex.

Another finding was that American tastes in sex acts are far from kinky. In a list of 14 acts, the one most often rated as very appealing by the women (78 percent) and the men (83 percent) was coitus. Next in line, in a near-tie for both the men and women, were watching one's partner undress and receiving oral stimulation. Finally, the age at which Americans lose their virginity has dropped in the past few decades, but not by much: 6 months. For Americans born in the decade 1933–1942, the average age of deflowering was about 18. For those born 20 to 30 years later, it was about 17½.

While the survey exploded many popular notions, it confirmed others:

- Men are more likely than women to have sex on the mind. Among the respondents, 54 percent of the men but only 19 percent of the woman said they thought about sex every day.

- There is such a thing as a pickup establishment. People who meet in bars are far more likely to end up in bed together before the month is out than people who meet at school, at work, or even at a private party.

- There was a free-love boom in the 1960s. The percentage of people who reported having had more than 20 sexual partners was significantly higher for the generation that came of age in the 1960s.

- The AIDS crisis has caused people to be more careful. Of those who reported having had five or more sexual partners

within the past year, three-quarters said they had changed their sexual behavior by having fewer partners, getting an HIV test, or using condoms more scrupulously.

- With aging, women have a harder time finding a sexual partner than men. By age 50, 22 percent of the women, as compared with 8 percent of the men, had no sexual partner. The good news is that women—and men—who have no sexual partners think less about sex and often report that they are happy and fulfilled without it.)

The survey also revealed interesting differences between ethnic and religious groups. For example, age at first intercourse varies along ethnic lines. Half of African American males have lost their virginity by age 15, half of Hispanic males by about 16½, half of African American females by about 17, and half of white and Hispanic females by about 18.

The methodology of the Sex in America survey has been highly praised. Unlike the Kinsey studies, which, conducted in less candid times, often had to rely on special groups, such as college fraternities, in order to find people willing to talk about their sex lives, this was a truly random sample, highly representative of the general population. And almost 80 percent of those contacted—in other words, not just the sexually talkative (therefore, presumably, the sexually active)—agreed to participate. Nevertheless, any self-report survey is limited by what people choose to report, and obviously a survey of sexual behavior has greater problems in this regard. According to one of the researchers, Stuart Michaels, the subject on which distortion was most likely was homosexual behavior: "There is probably a lot more homosexual activity going on than we could get people to talk about" (quoted in Elmer-DeWitt, 1994).

information about sex, has increased sexual communication between partners, and has dispelled anxiety over harmless sexual practices. At the same time, however, it has ushered in new forms of anxiety. Many sexually normal people now worry about the adequacy of their sexual "performance." The concern with gratification has also resulted in psychology's devoting considerable attention to sexual dysfunctions, disorders that prevent the person from having satisfactory sex.

Forms of Sexual Dysfunction

Sexual dysfunctions are disorders involving either a disruption of the sexual response cycle or pain during intercourse. The contemporary study of sexual dysfunction began, appropriately, in the 1960s, with the work of William Masters and Virginia Johnson at the Reproductive Biology Foundation in St. Louis. When Masters and Johnson began their research, studies of sexuality were rare, and clinicians who dealt with sexual problems were rarer still. However, since the publication of Masters and Johnson's *Human Sexual Response* (1966) and *Human Sexual Inadequacy* (1970), the number of researchers, therapists, and journals specializing in sexuality has grown enormously. One result has been a more sophisticated understanding of sexual dysfunctions. In the past, any lack of sexual interest or arousal in males was called "impotence." Similarly, the pejorative label "frigidity" was applied to almost every female sexual complaint. Today psychologists recognize a variety of specific difficulties. In *DSM-IV*, most of the sexual dysfunctions are grouped according to the phase in the sexual response cycle in which they occur.

Sexual Desire Disorders   The first phase of the sexual response cycle is the *desire* phase, or interest in having sex. Masters and Johnson paid little attention to sexual desire, because it could not be measured physiologically, but more recent researchers have focused on this elusive problem (Rosen & Leiblum, 1990). The two disorders of the desire phase are basically two degrees of negativity toward sex.

Hypoactive Sexual Desire Disorder   People with **hypoactive sexual desire disorder** are generally uninterested not only in sexual activity but even in sexual fantasy. What constitutes low desire, however, has to be decided within the context of age, gender, and cultural norms. The most common biological factors in hypoactive desire are pain, illness, and reduced testosterone, the hormone that controls sexual interest in both sexes. As for psychological factors, these may include depression, stress, ambivalence about sex, and conflict in the relationship. Not surprisingly, low desire is often accompanied by disorders of other response phases, especially arousal disorder in women and erectile disorder in men. In the Sex in America survey (see the box on page 339), one-third of the women and one-sixth of the men reported a persistent lack of interest in sex in the past year. This is now the most common complaint of couples seeking treatment for sexual dysfunction, and, about half the time, the low-desire member is a man. For most therapists, hypoactive desire is the most difficult sexual dysfunction to treat, especially in men.

Sexual Aversion Disorder   The person with **sexual aversion disorder** is not just uninterested in sex but also disgusted or frightened by it and, therefore, actively avoids it. This problem is far more common in women than in men and is often the result of sexual trauma, such as rape or childhood sexual abuse, though it may also follow a period of dyspareunia, or pain during sex. About one-fourth of people with sexual aversion disorder also have panic disorder (Chapter 6).

Sexual Arousal Disorders   During *arousal,* the second phase of the response cycle, feelings of sexual pleasure are accompanied by muscular tension and vascular engorgement, or increased blood flow. In men, this creates an erection. In women, the genitals swell and the walls of the vagina secrete lubricant. Disruptions of this phase take two forms, one male and one female.

Female Sexual Arousal Disorder   The presence of **female sexual arousal disorder** is best indicated by insufficient vaginal lubrication. In the Sex in America study, about one-fifth of the women surveyed reported a problem with lubrication during the preceding year (Laumann, Gagnon, Michael, et al., 1994). While there are few known biological causes of arousal disorder in women, there are manifold psychological causes, including emotional distress, a history of sexual trauma, and lack of trust in one's partner.

Male Erectile Disorder   Until recently, **male erectile disorder,** formerly known as *impotence,* was the one form of sexual dysfunction most often brought to the therapist's office; therefore, it was the one that received the most attention. Over the years, there have been heated debates as to whether its causes are physical or psychological. In fact, most erection problems seem to have multiple causes (Buvat, Buvat-Herbaut, Lemaire, et al., 1990). Age may be a contributing factor. In the general population, about 10 percent of men report serious problems with erections, but in the over-50 population the prevalence rises to 20 percent (Laumann, Gagnon, Michael, et al., 1994). Common medical causes of erectile disorder are diabetes, multiple sclerosis, and kidney disease, but any physical illness can impair erections. So can various medications, together with most forms of substance abuse. (Alcoholism is often accompanied by erectile disorder.) The range of psychological causes is equally broad: performance anxiety, stress, depression, underlying paraphilia, avoidance of intimacy, sexual inexperience, and unresolved anger toward one's sexual partner. Of these, the most common cause is performance anxiety, though that problem is normally enmeshed in others, as in the following case:

> Abe and Layla were an Egyptian couple in their mid-thirties who had been married for 10 years. They presented with an erection problem that had developed when they had moved to the United States several years before. In the initial evaluation, Layla reported that she had never enjoyed sex but that she had never told Abe about this because she felt that she should not expect to enjoy sex. She had been raised in a strict Muslim household and had never been taught about sex or discussed it with anyone. Once she arrived in the United States, however, she began to learn more about sex, mainly from women's magazines and from talking with her new American friends. She understood that sex could be very different from what she had experienced and that it could be exciting for her as well. Abe, too, began to see that sex could be different than the quick, passionless encounters they had had, but this realization made him feel inadequate sexually. He imagined that American men were much better lovers than he. He was also worried about his wife's growing frustration with their sexual relationship. His self-doubt quickly developed into performance anxiety, and he began to lose his erection during sex. (Adapted from Carroll, Northwestern University Medical School, clinical files.)

Orgasmic Disorders Once a critical threshold of sexual stimulation has been achieved, the person enters the third phase of the sexual response cycle, *orgasm.* In both men and women, orgasm is manifested by a muscular contraction of the genitals and the internal sex organs at 0.8-second intervals. In men, this is accompanied by an ejaculation of semen from the penis. Either sex may fail to reach orgasm, though men are more likely to complain of reaching it too soon.

Female Orgasmic Disorder When a woman has trouble reaching orgasm, she is said to have **female orgasmic disorder.** This problem has received a great deal of attention over the years, though some of the concern may have been due to an insistence on "vaginal orgasm." (See the box on page 342.) Whatever the definition, a persistent problem in achieving orgasm was reported by almost one-fourth of the women in the Sex in America survey (Laumann, Gagnon, Michael, et al., 1994). Common causes include other sexual problems (especially sexual arousal disorder), inadequate sexual stimulation, and anxiety about sex. However, an increasingly frequent cause is the use of antidepressant drugs, particularly SSRIs such as Prozac, Zoloft, and Paxil.

Male Orgasmic Disorder Male inability to reach orgasm, or **male orgasmic disorder,** is less common, reported by only 8 percent of men (Laumann, Gagnon, Michael, et al., 1994); therefore, it has been less studied. This condition, too, may be caused by antidepressant drugs, though it appears that some men just have a constitutionally high threshold for orgasm. Another common cause is an inability to "let go" with a sexual partner. Many men who cannot achieve orgasm with a partner can do so by masturbating.

Premature Ejaculation Far more common—indeed, the most common male sexual complaint, reported by almost one-third of men (Laumann, Gagnon, Michael, et al., 1994)—is the opposite problem, **premature ejaculation,** in which the man reaches orgasm before, on, or shortly after penetration. Traditionally, premature ejaculation has been regarded as due to psychological factors, but recent research suggests that there may be biological causes as well (Metz, Pryor, Nesvacil, et al., 1997).

Sexual Pain Disorders Two forms of sexual dysfunction, dyspareunia and vaginismus, do not fit into the response-cycle typology.

Dyspareunia Pain during sexual activity, or **dyspareunia,** was reported by 14 percent of the women—but only 3 percent of the men—in the Sex in America survey (Laumann, Gagnon, Michael, et al., 1994). Such pain is usually due to gynecological or urological problems, but it may also be a conditioned response to sexual trauma.

Vaginismus An exclusively female problem is **vaginismus,** in which the muscles surrounding the outer part of the vagina contract involuntarily when attempts are made to insert the penis. This makes intercourse either impossible or painfully difficult. Like dyspareunia, vaginismus often turns out to be a consequence of sexual trauma, as in the following case:

What Is Normal Sexual Response in a Woman?

One of the most common complaints women bring to sex therapists is a socially defined dysfunction: they reach orgasm not through intercourse but only through manual or oral stimulation of the clitoris or only when intercourse is combined with manual stimulation. The designation of this pattern as somehow less than normal is due in part to our society's moral strictures against masturbation; intercourse may be normal, but "touching" yourself (or being touched) is not. It is also reflected in an old Freudian distinction between "clitoral" and "vaginal" orgasms. According to Freud, only the woman who has "vaginal" orgasms is sexually normal and psychologically mature.

Many sex researchers feel that this definition of sexual normality is absurd. (It is also male-centered: because men reach orgasm through intercourse, women should.) All orgasms, no matter how they are achieved, constitute the same physical process, and there is no evidence that women who require direct stimulation to achieve orgasm are any less healthy or mature than those who do not. Women who reach orgasm during intercourse receive indirect stimulation of the clitoris: their partner's pubis (the bony structure behind the penis) rubs against their genitals, and penile thrusting pulls the clitoral hood back and forth. Many, possibly most, women require the more intense, *direct* stimulation of the clitoris, but the physiological mechanism of the orgasm is identical in both instances.

To say that direct clitoral stimulation is less healthy or less normal than indirect stimulation is, in the words of psychologist Joseph LoPiccolo (1977), "to draw almost mystical distinctions between the male pubis and the male hand" (p. 1239). Thus, according to LoPiccolo,

A woman who can have coital orgasm if she receives concurrent manual stimulation of her clitoris does not have secondary orgasmic dysfunction; she is normal. Similarly, a woman who regularly has orgasm during manual or oral stimulation . . . and who enjoys intercourse even though orgasm does not occur during coitus, is a candidate for reassurance about her normality rather than for sex therapy. (p. 1239)

As Helen Singer Kaplan (1974) pointed out, female sexual response, like most human traits, is extremely variable. Women reach orgasm from erotic fantasy alone, from brief foreplay, from coitus, from manual or oral stimulation of the clitoris without coitus, from coitus combined with manual stimulation, or from intense stimulation such as that provided by a vibrator. About 10 percent of women never experience orgasm, and, although they may justifiably seek professional help if they are distressed by this, any pattern of response can serve as the foundation for a happy sexual relationship. Of course, women who are dissatisfied with their response pattern should seek sex therapy, for the pattern may well be changeable. But those who are satisfied sexually yet worry that they do not fit some definition of "normal" should save their money. There is no single normal pattern.

Joan, 34 years old, presented with a complaint of being unable to undergo a pelvic examination because of anxiety. It soon came out that she had an additional problem. She was in a serious relationship with a man to whom she felt close, but, whenever they attempted intercourse, they were prevented by vaginismus. She felt little sexual pleasure and avoided sexual contact as much as possible.

Joan reported that when she was 10 years old her stepfather had rubbed her breasts and genitals and had inserted his finger into her vagina on a number of occasions. In high school she had avoided relationships with boys. In college, feeling peer pressure to be sexually active, she had had several bad sexual experiences, including an occasion of date rape during a party. After college, she had had a series of short-term relationships, which she had invariably ended when the man approached sex.

In therapy, she had a difficult time discussing her sexual history. She felt that it was wrong to talk about sex. She also said that she felt "dirty," and she imagined that she had a sexually transmitted disease, though there was no evidence of this. Treatment first focused on getting her to feel safe enough to discuss her past abuse. She reported that she had always felt that she was to blame for this, because she hadn't

struggled. Therapy revealed that she had long mistrusted men and expected that they would eventually hurt her. (Adapted from Carroll, Northwestern University Medical School, clinical files.)

Diagnosing Sexual Dysfunction

In categorizing sexual problems, the *DSM-IV* distinguishes between **lifelong dysfunction** (one that has existed, without relief, since the person's earliest sexual experiences) and **acquired dysfunction** (a dysfunction that develops after at least one period of normal functioning). In the case of Abe and Layla, for example, Abe had an acquired erectile disorder. It also distinguishes between **generalized dysfunction,** a dysfunction that is present in all sexual situations at the time of diagnosis, and **situational dysfunction,** which, as the term indicates, is one that occurs only in certain situations or with certain partners. For example, a woman with a generalized orgasmic disorder never experiences orgasm, while a woman with a situational orgasmic disorder may reach orgasm when masturbating alone but not while having sex with a partner. (But review the box above for problems in defining situational orgasmic disorder in women.)

It is very important to note that, according to *DSM-IV*, no sexual dysfunction can be diagnosed without evidence that the person's condition "causes marked distress or interpersonal difficulty." In other words, if a person has no interest in sex or no arousal or no orgasm—or even vaginismus—and this does not cause unhappiness or disrupt a relationship, then the person does not have a sexual dysfunction. Furthermore, the term *sexual dysfunction* applies only to problems that persist over time. Occasional episodes of "sexual failure" are normal. When a person is tired, sick, upset, intoxicated, or simply distracted, sexual responsiveness may be dulled. Neither should the label of sexual dysfunction be applied to the common occurrence of premature ejaculation, fleeting erections, or missing orgasms in young people who have not yet established a regular pattern of sexual activity and are so concerned with "doing it right" that they cannot fully enjoy sex. The myths that sex comes naturally and that a couple should be able to achieve mutual ecstasy under any and all conditions are frequent causes of sexual problems. Therapy often reveals that one episode of failure leads to another simply because the first episode created so much anxiety that sexual responsiveness is impaired on the next occasion. The second failure aggravates the anxiety, further undermining sexual performance, and so on, until a regular pattern of sexual failure is established. Furthermore, such anxiety is communicable: sexual anxiety is often found in both members of a couple. Vaginismus and lifelong erectile disorder, or premature ejaculation and female orgasmic disorder, are often seen together in couples.

Groups at Risk for Sexual Dysfunction

As Tables 12.1 and 12.2 show, the more education and money a person has, the less likely he or she is to suffer from a sexual dysfunction, as from other major problems. However, there are exceptions within this rule. For example, the rich are somewhat more likely than the middle class to report sexual problems, but the poor are far more likely than either group. Tables 12.1 and 12.2 also reveal striking racial and ethnic differences. In general, African American people—and, according to other studies, African American men in particular—are at higher risk for sexual dysfunction than the population as a whole, though the situation varies within the dysfunction. Asian Americans, for example, are almost twice as likely as African Americans to have problems reaching orgasm.

Prevalence also varies with gender. As can be seen in Figure 12.1, women greatly outnumber men in disorders involving pain during sex, inability to achieve

TABLE 12.1	Frequency of Sexual Dysfunction in Men by Education, Race/Ethnicity, and Income						
STATUS	**SEXUAL DYSFUNCTION**						
	Pain During Sex	**Sex Not Pleasurable**	**Unable to Orgasm**	**Lack of Interest in Sex**	**Anxiety About Performance**	**Climax Too Early**	**Unable to Keep an Erection**
Education							
Less than high school	4.6	14.7	12.7	22.3	23.2	36.0	15.4
High school graduate	4.1	5.7	8.2	13.2	17.3	32.5	9.5
Some college	2.1	8.9	7.9	15.7	17.8	24.4	10.2
Finished college	2.2	6.6	6.5	15.7	10.9	25.8	9.1
Advanced degree	1.7	5.2	6.8	13.3	14.5	24.1	9.3
Overall	3.0	8.0	8.3	15.7	16.9	28.5	10.4
Race/ethnicity							
White	3.0	7.0	7.4	14.7	16.8	27.7	9.9
African American	3.3	15.2	9.9	20.0	23.7	33.8	14.5
Hispanic	2.0	8.2	10.9	16.7	7.1	25.0	8.9
Asian/Pacific Islander	0.0	6.3	18.8	14.7	15.6	31.3	9.4
Overall	3.0	8.1	8.2	15.7	17.0	28.5	10.4
Income							
Poor	5.5	15.3	15.9	25.4	20.5	29.7	14.0
Middle	2.8	6.0	7.2	13.0	15.3	28.0	9.1
Rich	1.9	9.1	6.1	15.0	14.2	30.3	11.3
Overall	2.9	7.5	7.9	14.6	15.6	28.6	10.0

Source: Adapted from Laumann, Gagnon, Michael, et al., 1994, p. 370.

TABLE 12.2 Frequency of Sexual Dysfunction in Women by Education, Race/Ethnicity, and Income

STATUS	SEXUAL DYSFUNCTION						
	Pain During Sex	Sex Not Pleasurable	Unable to Orgasm	Lack of Interest in Sex	Anxiety About Performance	Climax Too Early	Trouble Lubricating
Education							
Less than high school	16.1	25.8	30.0	43.2	16.2	17.4	14.0
High school graduate	16.8	22.2	28.0	35.4	11.8	11.7	19.5
Some college	14.5	20.5	22.4	32.0	10.4	9.3	19.2
Finished college	9.6	18.4	19.1	27.9	8.3	6.2	19.3
Advanced degree	9.3	16.5	13.3	23.4	13.3	4.1	23.7
Overall	14.3	21.2	24.0	33.4	11.5	10.3	18.8
Race/ethnicity							
White	14.7	19.7	23.2	30.9	10.5	7.5	20.7
African American	12.5	30.0	29.2	44.5	14.5	20.4	13.0
Hispanic	13.6	19.8	20.3	34.6	11.7	18.4	12.0
Overall	14.4	21.2	24.1	33.4	11.5	10.3	18.8
Income							
Poor	16.2	23.3	27.4	39.7	20.0	18.2	13.9
Middle	14.5	21.5	23.6	32.0	10.2	10.6	19.0
Rich	11.4	17.3	20.8	27.5	11.7	4.4	23.7
Overall	14.3	21.1	23.8	32.5	12.0	10.8	18.9

Source: Adapted from Laumann, Gagnon, Michael, et al., 1994, p. 371.

orgasm, and lack of interest, pleasure, or arousal. On the other hand, men are more likely to feel anxiety about sex—probably because the "performance" pressures on them are greater—and they are almost three times more likely to complain of climaxing too early. As noted, premature ejaculation is the most common male sexual complaint. (As we will see, it is also one of the most treatable sexual complaints.)

Sexual Dysfunction: Theory and Therapy

The Psychodynamic Perspective

As we saw in Chapter 4, Freud claimed that mature genital sexuality was the product of successful resolution of the Oedipus complex. Accordingly, classical psychodynamic theory tends to attribute sexual dysfunction to unresolved Oedipal conflicts. This line of thinking can be seen in the interpretation of impotence offered by Otto Fenichel (1945):

> Impotence is based on a persistence of an unconscious sensual attachment to the mother. Superficially no sexual attachment is completely attractive because the partner is never the mother; in a deeper layer, every sexual attachment has to be inhibited, because every partner represents the mother. (p. 170)

Similarly, psychoanalytic formulations of female orgasmic disorder tend to stress the role of continued penis envy.

More current psychodynamic approaches to sexual disorders have focused instead on disturbances in object-relations as underlying most sexual dysfunctions (Scharff & Scharff, 1991).

Psychodynamic therapy for sexual dysfunction follows the same principles as psychodynamic treatment in general: uncovering the conflict and "working through" it, primarily via analysis of defenses. While there is no evidence from controlled studies that such an approach actually relieves sexual dysfunction, for many years it was the only form of treatment that was generally available. Certain authorities who took other approaches (Ellis, 1962; Wolpe, 1958) argued that sexual dysfunction, instead of being analyzed as a symptom of underlying conflict, should be attacked directly, by altering either the behavior in question or the attitudes surrounding it. But this was a minority view. Then in 1970 came the publication of Masters and Johnson's *Human Sexual Inadequacy,* outlining a systematic, short-term approach to direct symptomatic treatment. This approach, described in the next section, revolutionized sex therapy.

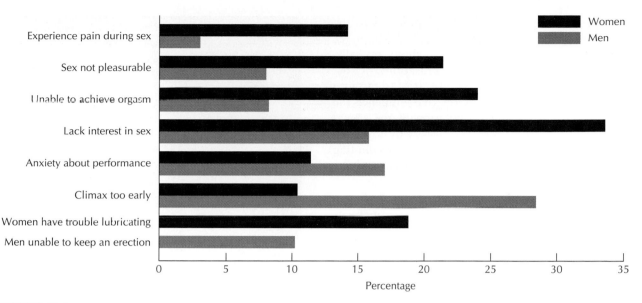

FIGURE 12.1 Sexual dysfunction by gender. (Adapted from Laumann, Gagnon, Michael, et al., 1994, p. 369)

The Behavioral and Cognitive Perspectives

Learned Anxiety and the Spectator Role Behavioral theories of sexual dysfunction have focused consistently on the role of early respondent conditioning, in which sexual feelings are paired with shame, disgust, fear of discovery, and especially anxiety over possible failure, all of which then proceed to block sexual responsiveness (Kaplan, 1974; Wolpe, 1969). This is also the position of Masters and Johnson, though they do not associate themselves with behaviorism or with any other theoretical school. According to Masters and Johnson (1970), any one of a number of painful experiences can cause a person to worry that he or she will be unable to perform adequately—will not achieve erection, will reach orgasm too quickly or not quickly enough, or whatever. As a result of this anxiety, the worried partner assumes what Masters and Johnson call the **spectator role.** That is, instead of simply relaxing and experiencing pleasure, the person is constantly watching and judging his or her performance. And, with cruel irony, the performance is almost inevitably a failure, because the person's tense and critical attitude blunts his or her responsiveness to sexual stimuli.

As for the factors that first trigger performance anxiety and lead to the adoption of the spectator role, Masters and Johnson (1970) point to several possibilities: religious and sociocultural taboos on sexual feelings, particularly for women; disturbance in the marriage; parental dominance of one partner; over-

use of alcohol; and, finally, early psychosexual trauma, which can range from molestation and rape to ordinary humiliation, such as the following:

> During the patient's first sexual episode the prostitute took the unsuspecting virginal male to a vacant field and suggested they have intercourse while she leaned against a stone fence. Since he had no concept of female anatomy, of where to insert the penis, he failed miserably in this sexually demanding opportunity. His graphic memory of the incident is of running away from a laughing woman.
>
> The second prostitute provided a condom and demanded its use. He had no concept of how to use the condom. While the prostitute was demonstrating the technique, he ejaculated. He dressed and again fled the scene in confusion. (p. 177)

If sexual dysfunction stems from faulty learning, so that sexual arousal comes to be associated with anxiety, then presumably it may be curable through new learning that gradually breaks down and eliminates this association. This idea is the basis of Masters and Johnson's treatment strategy and of most current behavioral sex therapies.

Assessment Crucial to direct treatment is proper assessment, for that is how the therapist finds out what factors are lurking behind the sexual problem. In assessment, every effort is made to include both members of the sexual relationship, in order to take into account all the biological, psychological, interpersonal, and cultural factors impinging on the case. After a description of the problem has been developed, the therapist typically explores with the couple their "sexual script" (Gagnon, Rosen, & Leiblum, 1982): who does what to whom, sexually, and what thoughts, emotions, and sensations each associates with sex. The therapist also tries to tap into social norms and cultural mores that influence the couple's behavior. A full formulation of the sexual problem also includes a detailed history of how each member developed his or her sexuality, including learned attitudes, patterns of sexual arousal, and any episodes of sexual trauma.

Direct Symptomatic Treatment In the treatment itself, the couple is retrained to experience sexual excitement without performance pressure.* Training usually takes the form of *sensate focus exercises.* During the period devoted to these exercises, the partners observe a ban on sexual intercourse. Instead, they simply devote a certain amount of time to gentle stroking and caressing in the nude, according to instructions given by the therapist. Very gradually, the allowed sexual play is increased, but always without performance demands.

The purpose of sensate focus exercises is not only to allow the partners to rediscover their natural sexual responses without anxiety but also to improve their communication. In the course of the exercises, each provides the other with feedback—what feels good, what doesn't feel good. The sharing of such information, aside from its crucial value in allowing the partners to satisfy each other, also deepens their trust in each other, which may have been sorely damaged by years of unhappy sex. After a period of sensate focus exercises, the couple is given more specific exercises, aimed directly at the disorder in question.

For premature ejaculation, many therapists prescribe the so-called start-stop technique (Semans, 1956). In this procedure, the woman stimulates the man's penis until he feels ready to ejaculate, at which point he signals her to stop. Once the need to ejaculate subsides, she stimulates him again, until he once again signals her to stop. Once the need to ejaculate subsides, she stimulates him again, until he once again signals her to stop. Repeated many times, this technique gradually increases the amount of stimulation required to trigger the ejaculation response, so that eventually the man can maintain an erection for a longer time. The "squeeze" technique, in which the

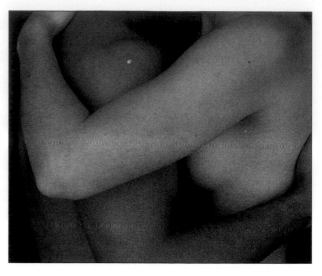

Sensate focus exercises are designed to help partners rediscover their natural sexual responses and provide feedback to each other.

woman squeezes the shaft of the man's penis when he feels close to ejaculation, has a similar effect.

With erectile disorder, the therapist, to eliminate anxiety, may actually tell the patient to try *not* to have an erection while he and his partner are going through their sensate focus exercises. This technique of forbidding the behavior that the patient is trying to accomplish is called *paradoxical instruction.*

Instructed not to have an erection, the patient may find himself sufficiently free of anxiety that he begins to respond to the sexual stimuli and, thus, has the "prohibited" erection. Once this happens, the therapist "permits" the couple, in very gradual stages, to proceed further and further toward intercourse, always with the warning that the techniques "work best" if the man can prevent himself from having an erection. In the end, intravaginal ejaculation is "allowed" only after it has already occurred because the man could not stop himself (LoPiccolo & Lobitz, 1973).

The most effective treatment for lifelong orgasmic dysfunction in women (Andersen, 1983; LoPiccolo & Stock, 1986) begins with education on female sexual anatomy and self-exploration exercises designed to increase body awareness. Then the woman is taught techniques of self-stimulation, perhaps with the aid of an electric vibrator and/or erotic pictures and books. This approach is based on the belief that masturbation enables a woman to identify the signs of sexual excitation, to discover which techniques excite her, and to anticipate pleasure in sex. When she has achieved orgasm alone, the therapist recommends sensate exercises with her partner, gradually incorporating the "orgasm triggers" she used alone. She may be encouraged to use a vibrator while her partner is present and to

---

*When the person seeking therapy does not have a partner, or when the partner is unwilling, Masters and Johnson, together with other therapists, have sometimes provided surrogate partners. However, this practice is controversial. Indeed, it has been called prostitution. Furthermore, in the case of unwilling partners, the relationship is unlikely to benefit from what the willing partner learned with a surrogate. It is rarely used these days.

engage in the fantasies that arouse her when she is masturbating. Teaching her partner what stimulates her is an essential element of this program. Treatment of women with situational orgasmic disorder is similar. For women with sexual aversion disorder, these procedures are often combined with systematic desensitization. As with male sexual problems, the goal is to remove the pressure to perform and to encourage, instead, the simple experience of pleasure.

Cognitive Psychology and Direct Treatment Masters and Johnson popularized the concept of direct treatment of sexual dysfunction: attacking the symptom itself, without extensive exploration of its psychic roots. At the same time, their concern is not just with the couple's sexual behavior but also with the partners' thoughts about sex—and about each other. Throughout this therapy, the emphasis is on the *couple*. During the assessment phase, the therapist explores the beliefs and experiences that may have led to the present dysfunction. Shame-ridden memories are discussed with comforting matter-of-factness; repressive attitudes are challenged outright; the person is encouraged to appreciate his or her sexuality. Resentments and fears that may have blocked communication are aired. As with the sensate focus exercises, the aim here is not just to increase the flow of information but also to restore a sense of trusting collaboration between the partners.

Following Masters and Johnson's lead, cognitive psychologists have further explored the mental processes underlying sexual response—for example, the development of attitudes that can block arousal. Wincze (1989) cites the case, not an unusual one, of a man who learned when he was young the difference between "good girls" and "bad girls." He knew that his wife was a "good girl," a respectable woman, but her desire for sex confused and inhibited him because it was "bad-girl" behavior. This man also believed that in order to approach his wife sexually he needed to be fully aroused; it did not occur to him that arousal might develop in the *course* of sexual intimacy. Between these two beliefs, this man and his wife, both in their thirties, had had intercourse only once in the seven months before they sought treatment (at the wife's urging).

Cognitive therapists have also developed treatments that aim directly at attitudes and beliefs hostile to sex. For women, common interferences include negative attitudes toward the body ("Does he think I'm fat?") and worries about the propriety of sexual expression ("If I act too eager, he won't respect me"). But thoughts need not be antisexual in order to interfere with sex. Worries about work or children can also block sexual responsiveness. Often, cognitive

therapists urge patients to allow sexual stimuli into their lives—for example, by reading erotic literature or giving some time each day to sexual thoughts. Such techniques are not confined to strictly cognitive therapy. Almost all sex therapists try to attack negative cognitions. Conversely, cognitive therapy is often combined with other approaches, particularly behavioral "direct treatment."

Multifaceted Treatment

Some sex researchers are dissatisfied with the theory that sexual dysfunction is caused by faulty learning. As they point out, millions of sexually untroubled people have been exposed to learning of this sort. Many people, perhaps most, were taught that sex was dirty. For many people, the first attempt at intercourse was painful and embarrassing. (Indeed, for many people, the attempt failed.) And many people have unhappy marriages—yet their sexual functioning remains stubbornly normal. Obviously, the cause of sexual dysfunction involves more than bad experiences and repressive attitudes. Consequently, some sex therapists, while using the kind of direct treatment outlined in this section, combine it with an exploration of intrapsychic or relationship factors that may be causing sexual dysfunction, or at least helping to maintain it.

Kaplan: Remote Causes The sex therapists who came after Masters and Johnson tended to probe psychological factors more systematically and more deeply. Helen Singer Kaplan (1974), for example, argued that sexual dysfunction was probably due to a combination of immediate and remote causes. *Immediate causes* are factors such as performance anxiety, overconcern about pleasing one's partner, poor technique, lack of communication between partners, and marital conflict—the sort of causes on which Masters and Johnson concentrated. Such factors, Kaplan claimed, are potent stressors, but in most cases they are not enough to undermine sexual functioning unless they are combined with (or based on) *remote causes* of sexual dysfunction: intrapsychic conflicts that predispose the person to anxiety over sexual expression. These conflicts are essentially the same as those the psychodynamic theorists blame for sexual dysfunction: infantile needs, deep-seated guilt, and—above all—unresolved Oedipal struggles.

On the basis of this theory, Kaplan (1974, 1979) devised a combined "direct" and psychodynamic treatment that she called "psychosexual therapy." She agreed with other direct therapists that behavior should be the primary focus of treatment and that unconscious conflicts, even when they are obvious to

Helen Singer Kaplan, a noted sex therapist, devised a multifaceted treatment for sexual dysfunction that she called psychosexual therapy.

the therapist, should be bypassed as long as the patient is responding to the direct treatment. But, in some instances, she argued, the remote causes prevent the patient from responding to therapy. In such cases, Kaplan felt, brief "insight" therapy is called for. Furthermore, in many instances the direct therapy itself brings to the surface psychological problems that the patient has been blocking through avoidance of normal sexual functioning. Indeed, it is extremely common for patients to progress well in direct therapy until they are just on the edge of reaching their goal, at which point they seem to experience a flood of anxiety and begin to resist treatment. Kaplan interpreted this response as a last-ditch attempt to maintain psychological defenses against whatever conflict has been blocking sexual responsiveness. And she claimed that at this point psychodynamic exploration of the patient's conflict was necessary before direct therapy could be resumed.

Family Systems Theory: The Function of the Dysfunction

A central principle of Masters and Johnson's treatment was that the patient was the *couple:* to solve the sexual problem, the therapist had to address the psychological conflicts between the partners. Other therapists confront the psychological components of sexual dysfunction via family systems theory, the analysis of relationships as systems of interlocking needs (Chapter 5). According to this approach, sexual dysfunction, distressing though it may be to the

couple, usually has an important function in the couple's total relationship—that is, it serves psychological purposes for both partners (Heiman, LoPiccolo, & LoPiccolo, 1981). Consider, for example, low sexual desire on the part of the man, a problem that is turning up more and more frequently in sex therapy (Kaplan, 1974; Schover & LoPiccolo, 1982; Spector & Carey, 1990). Low sexual desire often has a number of causes. If the relationship in question involves conflicts over power and control, with the woman tending to dominate, then the man's lack of interest in sex may be his way of preserving some area of control for himself. At the same time, the woman, though she may complain of the man's sexual indifference, may also be deriving benefits from it. By seeing him as weak, for example, she maintains power in the relationship.

According to systems therapists, such secret payoffs underlie many cases of sexual dysfunction and must be dealt with if the problem is to be relieved. The therapist generally addresses the "function of dysfunction" from the beginning of treatment, asking patients to describe the benefits they derive from the problem, warning them that they may feel considerable fear when the problem begins to lessen; analyzing this fear, once it appears, as the product of a shaken system; and helping them to devise a better system. Such analysis, like Kaplan's, is combined with direct treatment.

Results of Cognitive-Behavioral Direct Treatment

Though success rates for cognitive-behavioral direct treatment have rarely matched the outcomes claimed by Masters and Johnson (1970) in their early work, they are still good (Hawton, 1992; Heiman, 1997). For female arousal and orgasmic disorder, self-stimulation exercises have been very successful, especially in the case of lifelong rather than acquired dysfunctions. For vaginismus, a gradual program of relaxation and dilation of the vagina, either by fingers or by dilators, is effective in 75 to 100 percent of cases. For male erectile disorder, the basic cognitive-behavioral techniques—sensate focus exercises, relaxation, and systematic desensitization—work with about two-thirds of patients (Hawton, 1992; Wylie, 1997). For premature ejaculation, the stop-start technique is helpful in about three-quarters of cases. There have been no controlled outcome studies of treatment of low desire in either men or women. Low desire in men seems especially difficult to alter; some men may simply have a constitutionally low level of sexual interest. However, treatment of this dysfunction is still in its early stages, and it is unlikely that any one therapy will be best for the majority of patients, male or female, because the range of factors underlying the problem is so broad.

Outcome studies have addressed the treatment setup as well. While Masters and Johnson (1970) popularized the idea of an intensive, live-in, two-week program, with the couple receiving counseling from two co-therapists, one male and one female, later research has not supported these requirements. It appears that once-a-week sessions, in the couple's home city, are sufficient; that one therapist works as well as two; and that no matching of patient and therapist by gender is necessary. (On the other hand, Masters and Johnson's insistence on having both members of the couple in therapy has been strongly supported.) Research has also shown that group therapy is useful with certain dysfunctions, notably female orgasmic disorder and male erectile disorder. Instructional books are helpful, too. Finally, in keeping with systems theory, it does seem that combining relationship therapy with direct treatment is very beneficial (Hawton, 1992; Heiman & Meston 1997).

The Biological Perspective

In 1970, Masters and Johnson asserted that 95 percent of erectile failures were psychological, not physiological or organic, in origin. Today researchers are not so sure (Krauss, 1983; LoPiccolo, 1992). In some cases, organic causes are known. Erectile disorder may be the result of diabetes, heart disease, kidney disease, or alcoholism. A variety of medical treatments—renal dialysis, tranquilizers, antidepressants, medications for hypertension—can also interfere with erection. Long-term use of oral contraceptives can reduce the female sex drive. Female dyspareunia may be caused by vaginal infections, ovarian cysts, or lacerations or scar tissue resulting from childbirth (Sarrel, 1977). Other organic factors—hormonal deficiencies, neurological impairment, neurotransmitter imbalances—are suspected contributors to sexual dysfunction.

In the 1970s and early 1980s, many sex researchers concentrated on developing diagnostic tools for differentiating between psychological and organic sexual dysfunction. They invented devices for measuring vasocongestion in the genital region; they devised tests of the sensory threshold in the genital area. Research on *nocturnal penile tumescence* (NPT) attracted a good deal of attention. Men have erections during rapid-eye-movement (REM) sleep, the stage of sleep associated with dreams. NPT research is based on the assumption that, if a man has erections while he is asleep but not during sexual encounters, his problem is primarily psychological in origin.

Today, however, researchers are questioning the very concept of differentiating the organic from the psychological cases (LoPiccolo, 1992). Rather,

Recent advances have been made in biological therapy, especially for erectile disorder. One technique is the vacuum pump, which is used for enhancing erections.

they believe that many, if not most, cases of sexual dysfunction involve *both* psychological and physiological factors. A mild organic impairment—perhaps one that cannot be detected by current techniques, or one not yet known to be associated with sexual functioning—may make a person vulnerable to sexual dysfunction. But whether that person actually experiences sexual difficulties may depend on psychological factors, learning, and/or sexual technique. This would help to explain, for example, why some people who have been taught that sex is sinful or who had humiliating early experiences with sex function normally, while others do not. Research and clinical experience have shown that some cases of sexual dysfunction are purely psychological, some primarily organic, and many others the result of interacting organic and psychological factors.

Over the past decade, considerable progress has been made in developing biological treatments, particularly for erectile disorder. One technique is the vacuum pump for enhancing erections. This works by placing the penis in a cylinder and pumping out the air to create a vacuum, thus drawing more blood into the penis. A band is then placed at the base of the penis to hold the blood in. This technique has proved helpful in many cases (Turner, Althof, Levine, et al., 1991). Another treatment involves the man's injecting a vascular dilation agent (either papaverine or phentolamine) into his penis when he wants an erection. The penis becomes erect within 30 minutes of the injection and remains erect for 1 to 4 hours. Many men have reported satisfaction with this method (Turner, Althof, Levine, et al., 1989), but there is some question about its long-term use, because a substantial number of patients develop nodules on their penises as a side effect. Researchers are now experimenting with a variation on this technique: inserting the vasodilator, in pellet form, into the urethra, where it is absorbed into the tissue of the penis. A third treatment involves taking (by mouth) a drug called yohimbine, which has long had a reputation as an aphrodisiac. Yohimbine stimulates the secretion of norepinephrine and thereby increases the firing rate of nerve cells in the brain. Therefore, it is possible that the drug corrects neurotransmission problems that are causing the erectile disorder. Yohimbine treatment shows a small but consistent tendency to enhance erections in men who have erectile disorder, but not in men who are functioning normally (Caey & Johnson, 1996).

For men who do not benefit from medications or sex therapy, penile prosthesis is available. In one type, a semirigid rod is surgically inserted into the penis. This makes the penis permanently stiff enough for intercourse. At the same time, the rod is bendable enough for the penis to look normal under clothing. In another type of prosthesis, a water-filled bag is surgically inserted into the abdomen and connected by tubes to inflatable cylinders that are inserted into the penis. When the man wants an erection, he pumps the bag, causing the water to flow into the penile cylinders and thus engorge the penis. Follow-ups on penile prosthesis recipients (Steege, Stout, & Culley, 1986; Tiefer, Pedersen, & Melman, 1988) indicate that most of them, if they had to do it over again, would choose the prosthesis, primarily for the repair of their self-esteem, but that their sexual satisfaction was still not equal to what they enjoyed before they developed erection problems.

The newest medical treatment for erectile disorder is via oral medications such as sildenifil and apomorphine, which seem to help in some cases regardless of whether the erection problem is due to organic or psychological factors. These drugs act peripherally, that is, in the tissue of the penis itself, to trigger relaxation of the smooth muscle of the penis, which results in vascular enlargement and produces an erection. But further research is needed before these drugs can be considered more than experimental.

Another recent advance in medical treatment is the use of SSRI antidepressants for premature ejaculation. As noted, many people taking SSRIs for depression develop delayed orgasm as a side effect. By the same token, these drugs help control premature orgasm (Assalian & Margolese, 1996).

A major trend in today's sex therapy is the integration of biological and psychological treatment. For example, even in cases of erectile disorder in which there is clearly an organic cause, treatment with injections works better if the psychological aspects of the problem are also addressed, and if the couple are helped to incorporate the injection process into their "sexual script." For almost everyone, sex is a tender matter, and even the most purely organic problem has psychological consequences—embarrassment, nervousness—that cannot be addressed by purely organic treatments.

Paraphilias

The sexual revolution has expanded our definition of normal sexual behavior. Premarital sex, oral sex, homosexuality—behaviors that were spoken of in whispers, if at all, a generation ago—are now discussed casually by many people. This does not mean, however, that all barriers have fallen. According to *DSM-IV*—and, it is safe to assume, according to most members of our society—normal sexuality still consists of a nondestructive interplay between consenting adults.

A number of recognized sexual patterns deviate from this standard. These patterns are called **paraphilias** (from the Greek *para*, meaning "beside" or "amiss," and *philia*, meaning "love"). We shall discuss the following:

1. **Fetishism:** reliance on inanimate objects or on a body part (to the exclusion of the person as a whole) for sexual gratification

2. **Transvestism:** sexual gratification through dressing in the clothes of the opposite sex

3. **Exhibitionism:** sexual gratification through display of one's genitals to an involuntary observer

4. **Voyeurism:** sexual gratification through clandestine observation of other people's sexual activities or sexual anatomy

5. **Sadism:** sexual gratification through infliction of pain and/or humiliation on others

6. **Masochism:** sexual gratification through pain and/or humiliation inflicted on oneself

7. **Frotteurism:** sexual gratification through touching and rubbing against a nonconsenting person

8. **Pedophilia:** child molesting—that is, sexual gratification, on the part of the adult, through sexual contact with prepubescent children

Some paraphiliacs—most important, child molesters—are defined by the law as *sexual offenders*. That is, their acts are grounds for criminal prosecution. There has been much debate over whether another

Most paraphilic behaviors occur in mild form in daily life. For example, this billboard caters to mild voyeurism.

category of sexual offenders, rapists, should be included in the *DSM* among paraphilics. In the end, this was not done, lest rapists be excused from criminal responsibility on the grounds of having a mental disorder. Clearly, however, a person whose preferred stimulus for arousal is sexual coercion would meet the criteria for paraphilia. (Rape will be discussed in Chapter 17.)

At the same time, a distinction must be made between paraphilias that involve harm to others and those that are essentially victimless, such as fetishism and transvestism. Other paraphilias fall between the two poles: they may or may not cause harm, depending on the circumstances.

It is important to note that most of these behaviors occur in mild, playful, or sublimated forms in what we call everyday life. Sexually explicit movies, videos, and television programs—magazine and billboard advertisements, too—cater to what might be called normal voyeurism. It is only when the unusual object choice becomes the central focus and *sine qua non* of the person's arousal and gratification that the pattern is generally deemed abnormal by the society and by diagnosticians. Similarly, many people have fantasies involving sexual aggression, but it is only when these impulses are acted upon that they are labeled pathological.

Fetishism

Fetishism is a good example of a "spectrum disorder," one that exists on a continuum ranging from normal to abnormal, with many variations in be-

tween. It is not unusual, of course, for people to concentrate sexual interest on a particular attribute of the opposite sex. Certain women consider the male buttocks to be particularly important, while many men are fascinated by large breasts. Other men prefer as sexual partners women who are stylishly dressed, and the sight of a pair of underpants held together with a safety pin can leave them discouraged sexually. In general, however, such people, despite their preferences, do not disregard the rest of the person and can respond to conventional sexual stimuli.

Further along the continuum, we can place the following case, reported by von Krafft-Ebing (1886/1965a):

A lady told Dr. Gemy that in the bridal night and in the night following her husband contented himself with kissing her, and running his fingers through the wealth of her tresses. He then fell asleep. In the third night Mr. X produced an immense wig, with enormously long hair, and begged his wife to put it on. As soon as she had done so, he richly compensated her for his neglected marital duties. In the morning he showed again extreme tenderness, whilst he caressed the wig. When Mrs. X removed the wig she lost at once all charm for her husband. Mrs. X recognized this as a hobby, and readily yielded to the wishes of her husband, whom she loved dearly, and whose libido depended on the wearing of the wig. It was remarkable, however, that a wig had the desired effect only for a fortnight or three weeks at a time. It had to be made of thick, long hair, no matter of what colour. The result of this marriage was, after five years, two children, and a collection of seventy-two wigs. (pp. 157–158)

Mr. X's "hobby" still falls in the middle of the continuum, for, once the wig was present, he was interested in intercourse with his wife. In most cases of fetishism that come to the attention of diagnosticians, sexual absorption in a single body part—a pattern known as *partialism*—or, more commonly, fascination with an inanimate object has totally crowded out any interest in normal sexual interplay with another human being. Much of the person's life is occupied with collecting new examples of his favored object.

Most fetishes are closely associated with the human body. Common choices are fur, women's stockings, women's shoes, women's gloves, and especially women's underpants. More exotic fetishes have also been reported. Bergler (1947) cited the case of a man whose major source of sexual gratification was the sight of well-formed automobile exhaust pipes. The fetishist's sexual activity, typically, consists of fondling, kissing, and smelling the fetish and masturbating in the process.

Transvestism

Transvestism is similar to fetishism—indeed, *DSM-IV* calls it "transvestic fetishism"—in that it involves a fascination with inanimate objects. But transvestites go one step further and actually put on their fetish, which is the clothing of the opposite sex. Once cross-dressed, transvestites typically masturbate privately or have heterosexual intercourse, though they may also enjoy appearing publicly in their costumes.

Transvestites usually do not come into conflict with the law, and in recent years social attitudes toward transvestism have eased somewhat. Indeed, nightclubs featuring transvestite performers have become increasingly popular. Partly as a result of this social tolerance, there has been little psychological investigation of transvestism. However, some insight into the psychology of the transvestite has been provided by Bentler and his colleagues, who, with the help of a national transvestite organization, administered standardized personality tests to a large sample of male transvestites (Bentler & Prince, 1970; Bentler, Shearman, & Prince, 1970). These tests revealed what a number of clinicians had already suspected: as a group, transvestites appear to be no more prone to psychological disturbance than the population at large. Not surprisingly, however, they tend to have marital problems. Most women, upon discovering their husbands' transvestism, are very distressed; many such marriages end in divorce. But some women tolerate their husbands' transvestism and incorporate it into the sexual relationship, as in the following case:

Curtis is a 29-year-old married contractor who has a secret. When he goes to work each morning he wears a pair of women's panties. He began cross-dressing as a young boy when he would sneak into his older sister's room and put on her panties or bra. Eventually, he stole some women's underwear from the girls locker room at school. He wore the panties while he masturbated. When Curtis left home and went to college he began wearing women's panties under his clothes every day and continued to use them to masturbate.

He dated infrequently in college until he met Sally. She was kind and he enjoyed being with her. Curtis had his first sexual experience with a woman when he and Sally had sex one night during his junior year. As their relationship progressed, Curtis felt he could no longer hide his secret from her. One night he told Sally that he wore women's panties under his clothes. She seemed confused about why he needed to wear the panties, but was not very upset about the fact that he wore them. Tentatively, Curtis asked her if she would be willing to let him wear the panties while they were having sex. Sally nodded, and said, "I guess so, if that makes you happy." A year later they were married. During the first few years of their marriage Curtis continued to wear panties during sex. His wife periodically went shopping and brought home new panties for him as the old ones wore out. (Fauman, 1994, p. 295)

Transvestism is thought to be relatively rare, but the reported rarity may be due to lack of public exposure or public alarm. Many transvestites lead quiet, conventional lives, cross-dressing only in their bedrooms and never appearing on talk shows or in therapists' offices. Thus, the pattern may be more common than is assumed.

Transvestism is often confused with other forms of cross-dressing. There are two primary reasons a man will dress in women's clothing: first, for sexual pleasure and, second, for the purpose of assuming a female role. It is men in the first category who are transvestites. (However, many transvestites, as they grow older, come to associate cross-dressing more with a sense of calm and well-being than with sexual arousal.) Men in the second category, who are dressing as women not for sexual arousal but to take on the role of a woman, are not transvestites. This group includes "drag queens," who are almost always homosexual men who simply enjoy playing with the female role, and female impersonators, who assume female roles as part of a performance.

Transvestites are also sometimes confused with transsexuals, or people with gender identity disorder. As we will see, such confusion is justified by the facts. There appears to be a continuum between pure transvestism (sexual arousal associated with the fetish of cross-dressing) and transsexualism (the desire to change one's gender). While most transvestites are

Cross-dressing is seen in transvestites, in transsexuals, and also in homosexual "drag queens."

content, outside the sexual setting, with being men, others experience a persistent desire to become female, and some go on to seek sex reassignment surgery.

Another related phenomenon is **autogynephilia,** from the Greek *auto-* (self), *gyne-* (woman), and *philia* (love). In this pattern, the man depends for sexual arousal on the fantasy of being a woman (Blanchard, 1989). When asked which of three images—a nude male, a nude female, or himself as a woman—is most exciting sexually, the autogynephilic chooses the third. Some of these men label themselves as homosexual and say that they enjoy fantasies of making love to a man, but, when the fantasy is explored, it usually becomes clear that the other man in the fantasy is mainly a prop. The primary sexual stimulus is the image of the self as a woman. Autogynephilia probably underlies many cases of transvestism. That is, the man probably cross-dresses in order to support the fantasy of being a woman.

Exhibitionism

Exhibitionism and voyeurism are the two sex offenses most often reported to the police. They are usually treated harshly by the courts, on the assumption that, if treated leniently, the offender will graduate to more serious sex crimes. Studies of sex offenders indicate that more than 10 percent of child molesters and 8 percent of rapists began as exhibitionists (Abel, Rouleau, & Cunningham-Rathner, 1984). But most exhibitionists are not dangerous; they do not attempt to have sexual contact with their victims.

The typical exhibitionist is a young man, sexually inhibited and unhappily married (Blair & Lanyon, 1981; Mohr, Turner, & Jerry, 1964). Experiencing an irresistible impulse to exhibit himself, he usually goes to a public place, such as a park, a movie theater, or a department store, or simply walks down a city street and upon sighting the appropriate victim—typically, a young woman, though sometimes a young girl—shows her his penis. The penis is usually, but not always, erect. The exhibitionist's gratification is derived from the woman's response, which is generally shock, fear, and revulsion, although exhibitionists also enjoy victims who show excitement. Observing the reaction, the exhibitionist experiences intense arousal, at which point he may ejaculate spontaneously or masturbate to ejaculation. Usually, however, he goes home and then masturbates while fantasizing about the event. (In some instances, the episode is not followed by ejaculation; the exhibitionist merely obtains psychic relief.) Although an encounter with an exhibitionist may involve no physical harm, it can be very upsetting for an adult and traumatic for a child.

In some cases, exhibitionism occurs as a symptom of a more pervasive disturbance, such as schizophrenia, epilepsy, senile brain deterioration, or mental retardation. But most exhibitionists turn out to be simply shy, submissive, immature men who have uncommonly puritanical attitudes about sex (Witzig, 1968), particularly about masturbation. Furthermore, they often experience feelings of social and sexual inferiority and serious doubts about their masculinity (Blair & Lanyon, 1981). Thus, it has been suggested, they display their genitals for shock value in a desperate effort to convince themselves of their masculine prowess (Blane & Roth, 1967; Christoffel, 1956), all the while arranging the circumstances so that the victim is unlikely to respond positively and, thus, make sexual demands on them. In the rare instance in which the victim shows indifference or scorn rather than the expected shock and dismay, the exhibitionist is generally cheated of sexual gratification. Indeed, it has been suggested that the best "cure" for exhibitionism would be to educate the public not to respond to it.

Voyeurism

An element of voyeurism, as of exhibitionism, is usually involved in normal sexual activity. In recent years, sexually oriented magazines and videos have provided more or less "acceptable" outlets for those who derive pleasure from looking. The traditional definition of voyeurism distinguished true voyeurs—or "peeping Toms," as they are sometimes called—as people for whom the pleasure of looking interferes with normal sexual interplay with another person. Actually, voyeurism often occurs alongside normal sexual interplay. Thus, a realistic definition of voyeurism must take into account social sanctions against violating the privacy of others. In practice, then, a voyeur obtains gratification from watching strangers, in violation of their sexual privacy. This usually means watching women who are undressing or couples engaged in sex play. The risk involved in watching strangers may be a desirable adjunct to the voyeur's pleasure. The danger of being discovered, perched on the fire escape or balcony adds to the sexual thrill of the peeping, which usually leads to masturbation.

Like exhibitionism, voyeurism seems to provide a substitute gratification and a reassurance of power for otherwise sexually anxious and inhibited males. Voyeurs, like exhibitionists, are often withdrawn both socially and sexually, with little in their developmental histories to support the learning of more appropriate interpersonal skills. Again, like exhibitionists, most voyeurs are harmless, but not all: 10 to 20 percent of them go on to rape the women they peep at.

Sadism and Masochism

There appears to be an element of aggression in even the most "natural" sexual activity. Human beings, like most other mammals, sometimes bite and scratch during intercourse, and aggressive sexual fantasies—of raping or of being raped—are common (Masters & Johnson, 1966). Conversely, a sexual element often underlies aggression. Both men and women have reported becoming sexually excited at boxing matches and football games or while watching fires or executions—a fact that has led some theorists to propose that our society's preoccupation with violence may be sexually motivated.

In sadism and masochism, however, the element of physical and/or psychological cruelty—inflicting and being subjected to it, respectively—assumes a central role in sexual functioning. Both disorders are named for literary figures who publicized the sexual pleasures of cruelty. The term *sadism* is taken from the name of the Marquis de Sade (1740–1814), whose novels include numerous scenes featuring the torture of women for erotic purposes. Masochism is named for an Austrian novelist, Leopold von Sacher-Masoch (1836–1895), whose male characters tended to swoon with ecstasy when physically abused by women.

Jeffrey Dahmer (center) was one of the most notorious multiple murderers in U.S. history. His killings were sex-related, centering on sadistic abuse of and necrophilic sex with young men whom he abducted and drugged.

Individual patterns of sadism turn up primarily in men. The degree of cruelty may range from sticking a woman with a pin to gruesome acts of mutilation, numerous examples of which can be found in von Krafft-Ebing's *Psychopathia Sexualis* (1886/1965a). Between these two extremes are sadists who bind, whip, bite, and cut their victims. For some, the mere sight of blood or the victim's cries of pain are sufficient to trigger ejaculation; for others, the act of cruelty merely intensifies arousal, which eventually leads to rape. Similarly, the masochist may need to suffer only a mild pain, such as spanking or verbal abuse, or may choose to be chained and whipped. And, like the sadist, he or she may reach orgasm through the experience of pain alone, or the abuse stage may serve simply as "foreplay," leading eventually to intercourse. Masochists without sadistic partners usually have to resort to prostitutes, some of whom specialize in abusing clients. Sadists without partners may prey on prostitutes or other unwary women.

In many cases, however, sadists and masochists do have complementary partners, with whom they share a **sadomasochistic** relationship. In some of these pairings, one partner is always the sadist, the other always the masochist. Alternatively, both partners may enjoy both sadism and masochism, in which case they switch between the two. According to a survey of male readers of a sadomasochistically oriented magazine (Moser & Levitt, 1987), most sadists and masochists are heterosexual, well educated, reasonably affluent, given to switching between sadism and masochism, and undisturbed by their specialized tastes. Other sadists and masochists are homosexuals; in fact, there is a substantial so-called S-and-M segment within the homosexual subculture. To serve sadomasochists, many underground newspapers carry advertisements by sadists and masochists seeking partners and stating their special requirements. Likewise, in many large American cities there are "sex shops" that specialize in selling sadomasochistic equipment.

In sadism and masochism, the line between normal and abnormal may be hard to draw. Just as with the sexual dysfunctions, *DSM-IV* requires evidence of distress of interpersonal difficulty, so with all the paraphilias one of the diagnostic criteria is that the person's sexual pattern has caused "clinically significant distress or impairment in social, occupational, or other important areas of functioning." By this standard, mutually consenting S-and-M partners who are satisfied with their sexual pattern and who show no disturbance in other aspects of their lives are not candidates for diagnosis, though most people would probably consider their behavior to be abnormal.

Frotteurism

New in *DSM-IV* is a separate listing for frotteurism (from the French word *frotter,* "to rub"), in which the person obtains gratification by touching or rubbing against a nonconsenting person. Frotteurs usually operate in crowded places, such as buses or subways, where they are more likely to escape notice and arrest. Typically, the frotteur touches the person's breasts or genitals or rubs his own genitals against a person's thighs or buttocks. Part of the excitement for the frotteurist, as with most sexual offenders, is the sense of power over the unsuspecting victim that the act produces.

Pedophilia

Children, by definition, lack the knowledge and experience to consent to sexual relations. Thus, pedophilia (from the Greek, meaning "love of children") involves a violation of the rights of the child, who may suffer serious psychological harm as a result. The pedophile may (in order of increasing rarity) covertly or overtly masturbate while caressing the child, stroke the child's genitals, masturbate between the child's thighs, have the child stimulate him or her manually or orally, or attempt intercourse. The pedophile may entice a group of children to participate in sexual activities and pose for pornographic pictures, using peer pressure to maintain secrecy (Burgess, Groth, & McCausland, 1981). Some pedophiles look for jobs or volunteer positions that involve extensive contact with children (Abel, Lawry, Karlstrom, et al., 1994).

An estimated 10 to 15 percent of children and adolescents have been sexually victimized by an adult at least once (Lanyon, 1986). Prepubescent children are more likely than older adolescents to be victimized, and girls twice as likely as boys. Although cases of female sexual abuse of children do turn up, they are rare: most pedophiles are male (Finkelhor, 1984). The stereotype of the child molester includes a number of myths, however. First, the typical pedophile is not a "dirty old man" who lives on the margins of society. In most cases, he is an otherwise law-abiding citizen who may escape detection precisely because he does not appear disreputable. Although ranging in age from the teens to the seventies, most pedophiles are in their twenties, thirties, or forties. Many are also married or divorced, with children of their own. Second, most child molestation is not committed by strangers lurking about the schoolyard. The offender is usually acquainted with the victim and his or her family; indeed, many are related to the victim (Conte & Berliner, 1981). Third, child molestation usually does not entail physical violence. Rather, the offender uses his authority as an adult to persuade the child to acquiesce (Finkelhor, 1979). Fourth, child molestation usually is not an isolated event but consists of repeated incidents with the same child. The molestation may begin when the child is quite young and recur over 5 or 10 years before it is discovered or broken off (Finkelhor, 1979). A final interesting point about pedophilia is that it is usually accompanied by other paraphilias. In a survey of over 500 paraphiliacs, most of them pedophiles, half the respondents reported engaging in 4 or more paraphilias (Abel, Becker, Cunningham-Rathner, et al., 1988).

Several researchers feel that a distinction should be made between situational and preference molesters (Howells, 1981; Karpman, 1954). *Situational molesters* are people with more or less normal, heterosexual histories who most of the time prefer adult sexual partners. Their child molesting is impulsive—it is usually a response to stress—and they may view it with disgust. Incest offenders are usually of this type, rather than true pedophiles. By contrast, *preference molesters,* people who actually prefer children as sexual partners, are generally not married, prefer male children, and do not view their behavior as abnormal. For these people, child molesting is a regular sexual outlet. Their contacts with children are planned, not impulsive or precipitated by stress. Whether or not they are preference molesters, pedophiles who specialize in male children have a much higher rate of recidivism, or repeat offenses (American Psychiatric Association, 1994). In the survey mentioned earlier (Abel, Becker, Cunningham-Rathner, et al., 1988), the pedophiles who preferred boys averaged about 150 victims; those who preferred girls averaged about 20 victims.

The causes of pedophilia seem to vary (Finkelhor & Araji, 1986). Sometimes it is associated with arrested psychological development: experiencing himself as a child, with childish emotional needs, the pedophile is most comfortable relating to children. Other pedophiles may be so isolated socially or so timid that they are unable to establish adult heterosexual relationships and turn to children as substitutes. In still other cases, an early experience of arousal with other children may become fixed in the person's mind. Finally, because about half of pedophiles were themselves molested as children (Dhawan & Marshall, 1996), some may be trying to restore feelings of control by reenacting their histories, with the roles reversed.

Children usually do not report their victimization immediately; they are afraid their parents will blame them. Molestation is generally discovered when an adult becomes suspicious, when the child tells an adult other than his or her parent, or when a physician sees signs of sexual abuse (Finkelhor, 1979). But children "tell" adults about their problem in indirect ways (Browne & Finkelhor, 1986). Most studies of child victims report varying degrees and combinations of sleep and eating disorders, fears and phobias, difficulties at school, and inappropriate sexual behavior. The effects do not go away when the abuse stops. Adults who were sexually exploited as children frequently exhibit depression, dissociative disorders, self-destructive behavior, feelings of being isolated and stigmatized, and distrust of others. Tragically, women who were sexually abused as children are more likely than other women to be physically abused by their husbands or other partners as adults (Finkelhor, 1984; Herman, 1981).

Some types of child abuse seem to do more psychological harm than others. A review of empirical research found that the negative psychological impact of abuse was worse if it occurred at an early age, if it continued over a long period of time, if there was a close relationship to the perpetrator, and if the abuse was severe or violent (Kendall-Tuckett, Williams, & Finkelhor, 1993). On the basis of clinical experience, Groth (1978) argued that, if the abuse continues over a period of time, if it involves violence or penetration, or if the molester is closely related to the child, the risk of severe trauma is that much greater. According to MacFarlane (1978), any collusion or suggestion of collusion on the part of the child increases the risk. If the child cooperates to some degree, if he or she is older and aware of the taboo violation, or if the child's disclosure is met by parental anger or accusation, the psychological damage will be worse.

Incest, or sexual relations between family members, has been prohibited, in varying degrees, by virtually all human societies throughout their known histories. Explanations of this universal taboo range from the argument that it encourages families to establish wider social contacts to the contention, supported by scientific studies, that inbreeding fosters genetic defects in offspring.

Despite the taboo, incest does occur. Alfred Kinsey (Kinsey, Pomeroy, & Martin, 1948; Kinsey, Pomeroy, Martin, et al., 1953) reported that only 3 percent of his sample had had incestuous relations. More recent studies indicate that the rate of incest in the general population is much higher: 7 to 17 percent (Finkelhor, 1994; Greenwald & Leitenberg, 1989; Hunt, 1974).

One study (Russell, 1986) concluded that father-daughter incest is "the supreme betrayal": more than twice as many victims of fathers reported being extremely upset and suffering severe long-term effects

Therapeutic artwork attempts to help children express difficult feelings. Children who were molested drew these pictures.

as victims of all other incest perpetrators combined. Other researchers (Kendall-Tuckett, Williams, & Finkelhor, 1993) have also found that abuse by a father or stepfather is more damaging than any other form of abuse. What kind of man would assault his daughter? One who is promiscuous and unselective in his sexual partners? Research suggests not. Cavallin (1966) reports that the typical incestuous father confines his extramarital sexual contacts to his daughter, or perhaps to several daughters, beginning with the eldest. Far from being indiscriminately amoral, such fathers tend to be highly moralistic and devoutly attached to fundamentalist religious doctrines (Gebhard, Gagnon, Pomeroy, et al., 1965). Father-daughter incest tends to occur in connection with a troubled marriage. The man may abuse his wife (as well as his children) and then turn to the daughter sexually when the wife rejects his advances. The wife may pretend not to notice because she is afraid of her husband's violence. She is often isolated from other family members, due to chronic illness or infirmity. In many cases, the victim assumes the caretaking role in the family, even acting as a surrogate wife. Some mothers blame their daughters for threatening to break up the family (Herman, 1981).

Not surprisingly, the impact on the daughter can be profound. The long-term effects reported by incest victims are similar to those of nonincestuous child molestation: lowered self-esteem, self-blame, and self-hatred; a tendency to be vengeful or passive; emotional coldness and lack of responsiveness; negative feelings about physical closeness; and the belief that other people would think ill of them if the incest were known. Incest victims are also at higher risk for a range of psychological disorders, especially depression, anxiety, suicidality, and substance abuse (Kendall-Tuckett, Williams, & Finkelhor, 1993; Russell, 1996).

Groups at Risk for Paraphilias

According to *DSM-IV*, most of the paraphilias are all but exclusively male aberrations. The only exception is masochism, but even there the male-female ratio is 20 to 1. Some writers believe this is because female sexuality is repressed in the process of socialization, with the result that most women never develop truly normal or truly abnormal forms of sexual expression. It should be added, however, that data on the prevalence of the paraphilias generally come from arrest records, and women are much less likely than men to be arrested, or even reported, for unconventional sexual behavior. (Should a woman choose to undress regularly in front of a window, neighbors may disapprove, but they are unlikely to call the police.) Still, these facts do not account for the vastly greater numbers of male paraphiliacs. There seems to be a true difference between the sexes in this respect. Sociobiologists (e.g., Wilson, 1987) have proposed that natural selection breeds into males an instinctive desire to inseminate as many partners as possible and that this instinct makes men more responsive to a greater variety of sexual stimuli. Other researchers have suggested that the difference between the sexes in risk for paraphilias may be due to male-female differences in brain structure (Flor-Henry, 1987). If so, this might help to explain the early onset of most paraphilias. Half of paraphilic adults report that their pattern developed before age 18 (Abel, Osborn, Anthony, et al., 1992).

Paraphilias: Theory and Therapy

The Psychodynamic Perspective

Oedipal Fixation According to Freudian theory, paraphilias represent a continuation into adulthood of the diffuse sexual preoccupations of the child. In Freud's words, young children are "polymorphously perverse"—that is, their sexual pleasure has many sources: sucking, rubbing, defecating, displaying themselves, peeping at others. Furthermore, according to Freud, children are capable of any number of defensive maneuvers in attempting to deal with the castration anxiety and penis envy endemic to the Oedipal period. Thus, psychodynamic theorists generally consider paraphilias to be the result of fixation at a pregenital stage. In general, with paraphilias as with sexual dysfunctions, it is the Oedipal stage, with its attendant castration anxiety, that is considered the major source of trouble.

In keeping with this theory, transvestism has been interpreted as a denial of the mother's presumed castration. Dressed in the clothes of a woman but still equipped with a penis underneath, the transvestite can unconsciously convince himself that his mother did not suffer castration after all and that, therefore, he need not fear the same fate for himself (Nielson, 1960). Similarly, Fenichel (1945) viewed sadism as an attempt, through cruelty and aggression, to take the part of the castrator rather than that of the castrated and thus to relieve anxiety. Indeed, castration anxiety is often seen as paramount in any paraphilia case that involves the avoidance of coitus.

Other psychodynamic interpretations of paraphilias have stressed the person's inability to disentangle and control his or her basic id impulses. Thus, sadism has been explained as a continuation of the child's confusion of sexual and aggressive impulses. Similarly, masochism may be seen as a redirection onto the self of aggressive impulses originally aimed at a powerful, threatening figure.

Group and Individual Therapy In individual psychotherapy or psychoanalysis, the treatment of paraphilia follows the usual procedure of uncovering the conflict and "working through" it. A variation on this technique—group therapy—has been used as a substitute for imprisonment in the cases of some rapists, pedophiles, and other criminal offenders. The group technique has the advantage of placing the troubled person in a situation where he can take comfort from the knowledge that he is not "the only one"—a reassurance that can hasten his confrontation of his problem. In addition, group therapy saves costs.

Although successful treatment of paraphilias through group therapy, individual psychotherapy, and psychoanalysis has been reported (e.g., Cohen & Seghorn, 1969), such cases are the exceptions. Psychodynamic therapy for sex offenders has been found to be largely ineffective (Knopp, 1976). Such patients may have committed hundreds of offenses before they

enter treatment, and, when they do begin therapy, it is nearly always because they have been required to by the courts. Their motivation to stay out of jail, hence their motivation to lie to the therapist—to claim that they are responding to treatment, thinking normal sexual thoughts, engaging in normal sexual acts—is often high. But their motivation to change may be very low. Having convinced a therapist (and perhaps themselves) that they are "cured," they often slip back into their old patterns.

The Behavioral Perspective

Conditioning The simplest behavioral interpretation of sexual deviations is that the deviation results from a respondent-conditioning process in which early sexual experiences, particularly masturbation, are paired with an unconventional stimulus, which then becomes the discriminative stimulus for arousal. For example, if a child experiences sexual arousal in connection with the help of a furry toy or a pair of women's underpants, this may lead to fetishism.

In the case of sadism and masochism, behavioral theorists have noted that sex, aggression, and the experience of pain all involve strong emotional and physiological arousal. Hence, it has been proposed that the sadist and the masochist are simply persons who never learned to discriminate among the various types of arousal. Another learning theory of masochism is that the child may have been cuddled and loved by his parents only after being punished, with the result that physical affection and punishment became paired. More recent behavioral theories of the paraphilias tend to stress cognitive factors as well as, or in preference to, direct conditioning. Albert Bandura (1986), for example, has argued that parents may knowingly or unknowingly model unconventional sexual behavior.

Unlearning Deviant Patterns New programs for the treatment of sex offenders take the complex nature of sexual behavior into account. A multifaceted approach combines elements of traditional psychotherapy with specific techniques for dealing with sexual issues. The goal is to change the patient's sexual arousal patterns, beliefs, and behavior (Abel, Osborn, Anthony, et al., 1992; Hudson, Marshall, Ward, et al., 1995).

Treatment begins with steps to bring deviant sexual behavior under temporary control. A man who drinks to reduce his inhibitions may be required to join Alcoholics Anonymous; a child molester is required to abandon any job or recreational activities that bring him into contact with children; an incestuous father may be required to move out of his home temporarily.

Behavioral techniques are then used to eliminate deviant arousal. One such technique is called *stimulus satiation*. Suppose the patient is an exhibitionist who preys on young girls. He is asked to collect pictures of girls that arouse in him an urge to expose himself and to arrange them in order from the least to the most exciting. He is also told to collect "normal" sexual materials, such as erotic pictures from *Playboy*. Then he is instructed to take these materials home and masturbate while looking at the normal stimuli and to record his fantasies verbally with a tape recorder. Two minutes after he has ejaculated (or after 10 minutes if he does not), he must switch to the deviant stimuli, begin masturbating again, no matter how uninterested he is, and continue for 55 minutes. However, if he should become aroused again during this time, he switches his attention back to the normal pictures of adult women and ejaculates again while focused on normal sex. Therefore, he focuses on deviant stimuli only while he is not aroused and is not feeling any physical pleasure. The patient is required to repeat this procedure 3 times a week for at least a month, moving from the stimuli that excite him least to those that stimulate him the most. His tapes are analyzed carefully. If his fantasies with normal stimuli are confined to such exhibitionist acts as looking at an adult woman and being looked at by her, he is encouraged to imagine physical contact with her. After 10 to 15 sessions, most sex offenders find the deviant stimuli boring or even aversive (LoPiccolo, 1985).

Stimulus satiation may be combined with other procedures. In *covert sensitization*, the patient is taught to indulge in a deviant fantasy until he is aroused and then to imagine the worst possible consequences—his wife finds him engaged in sex play with a child, he is arrested in front of his neighbors, the arrest makes headlines, his son attempts suicide, and so on (Barlow, 1993). In *shame aversion therapy*, the patient is required to rehearse his paraphilic behavior—to exhibit himself or, if he is a transvestite, to dress in women's clothing—in the therapist's office, while the therapist and the patient's wife observe and comment. (This technique is so distressing that it is used only when other techniques seem to fail.)

However, deviant sexual behavior, once suppressed, is not automatically replaced by normal behavior. The final task of behavior therapy is to build an appropriate sexual orientation. Sex offenders often lack basic social and sexual skills. Treatment of unmarried offenders includes training in making conversation, maintaining eye contact, using empathy skills, listening, asking for a date, and making socially acceptable sexual advances. Married sex offenders often report that their sexual relationships with their wives are good or adequate, but further

probing usually reveals that sex is infrequent and stereotyped, lacking in playful, erotic activities. The partners are taught to do sensate exercises, to communicate their desires, and to explore new sexual experiences. Weekly therapy for at least a year is recommended for most sex offenders. Follow-up sessions every two weeks or once a month should continue for another year or year and a half. Thereafter, the patient should be reassessed every six months for three to five years.

Even this refined, intensive, long-term therapy does not guarantee a cure, however. Recently, behavioral therapy for sex offenders has placed less emphasis on a comprehensive (and often elusive) cure than on simple relapse prevention—that is, teaching people how to prevent themselves from committing the offense again. Relapse prevention involves training patients to avoid situations that place them at risk, showing them how to interrupt thought chains that lead to the offense and persuading them that having the impulse to commit the offense does not mean they must commit it—they can exert voluntary control through behavioral strategies. Reports on such programs indicate that they are successful in preventing relapses both in pedophiles and in rapists (Furby, Weinrott, & Blackshaw, 1989; Marshall & Pithers, 1994; Pithers & Cumming, 1989).

The Cognitive Perspective

Learning Deviant Attitudes As noted in the section of sexual dysfunction, the cognitive perspective holds that, while we are born with a sex drive, the way that drive is expressed depends on the attitudes we develop in childhood. A great deal of childhood sexual experimentation crosses "normal" boundaries. Children peep and display themselves, for example. If such behavior is reinforced—if, for example, a young boy's exhibiting himself to a girl is met with a reaction of pleasure or curiosity—this will foster attitudes ("Girls like this," "I can get attention this way") that lead to its adult repetition.

One attitude common to sex offenders is a tendency to "objectify" their victims, regarding them simply as potential sources of gratification rather than as human beings with feelings of their own (Abel, Gore, Holland, et al., 1989). Such beliefs are widespread in our society. According to cognitive theory, if they are combined with other predisposing factors—uncorrected childhood norm violation, lack of parental modeling of normative sexual values, poor self-esteem, poor social skills, and poor understanding of sexuality—they may well lead to sexual deviation (Malamuth, Heavey, & Linz, 1993; Ward, Hudson, Johnston, et al., 1997).

Combating Deviant Beliefs   The cognitive treatment for paraphilias is essentially the same as that for sexual dysfunction: the procedure is to identify the deviation-supporting beliefs, challenge them, and replace them with more adaptive beliefs (Murphy, 1990). As usual, this cognitive restructuring is typically combined with behavior therapy, just as behavior therapy and most psychological therapies now incorporate cognitive techniques.

A mental process to which cognitive therapists have recently given great attention is objectification of the victim, for, as long as sex offenders think in that way, they are likely to repeat the offense. (And at least in the case of pedophiles, the more they repeat the offense, the greater the degree of objectification [Abel, Gore, Holland, et al., 1989]—a vicious cycle.) Many programs for sex offenders now include "victim awareness" or "victim empathy" training, in which offenders are confronted with the emotional damage done to sex-offense victims. In one program, sex offenders are asked to imagine what one of their victims was thinking during the assault (Wincze, 1989). They may also be assigned to read books, listen to audiotapes, and view videotapes in which victims of child molesting describe their experience of the episode and its psychological consequences. The attackers often respond to these descriptions with great surprise, saying such things as, "I didn't think it would hurt her [a six-year-old]; she had already been abused by someone else" (Hildebran & Pithers, 1989). Another technique is role reversal: the therapist takes the role of the offender, while the offender takes the role of an authority figure and argues against the sexually aggressive belief system (Abel, Osborn, Anthony, et al., 1992).

The Biological Perspective

Because sexual arousal is controlled in part by the central nervous system, it is possible that paraphilias are related to neurological disorders. A number of researchers have investigated this question, but without conclusive results (Blumer & Walker, 1975; Rada, 1978). Whatever its role in causation, however, there is no question (other than the ethical one) that biology can be used in the treatment of sexual deviation. In various European countries, both castration and brain surgery have been used with dangerous sex offenders (usually rapists and pedophiles), this "treatment" usually being offered as an alternative to imprisonment. (Abel, Osborn, Anthony, et al., 1992) Another route is the use of antiandrogen drugs, which decrease the level of testosterone, a hormone essential to sexual functioning. Antiandrogen treatment is now widely used with chronic offenders in Europe and the United States, and it does seem to decrease arousal and thereby reduce recidivism (Bradford, 1990; Bradford & Pawlak, 1993). In a study of 3 chronic pedophiles, 1 of whom had averaged 1 offense weekly for 40 years, all were able to control their behavior after antiandrogen treatment combined with psychotherapy (Wincze, Bansal, & Malamud, 1986). Antidepressants have also proved effective in treating paraphilias, particularly in cases involving shame and depression (Kafka & Pretky, 1992).

To assess arousal in such studies, and to detect deviant (usually pedophile) attraction in men who have been arrested on sex-offense charges but deny any deviant pattern, a technique called *penile plethysmography* is often used. In penile plethysmography, an apparatus attached to the penis measures erection while the subject is exposed to the presumed erotic stimulus via slides, films, or audiotapes ("You are baby-sitting your neighbors' little girl for the evening" [Freund & Blanchard, 1989]). This technique seems to have some validity, though it is not foolproof (McConaghy, 1989). Many men are able to suppress deviant arousal in the laboratory, while others are sufficiently traumatized by being arrested on a sex charge that they temporarily lose their arousal capacity. Furthermore, the invasive nature and high cost of laboratory techniques makes them impractical for other purposes, such as screening job applicants. Researchers have developed a noninvasive test, involving self-report and a few simple physiological measures, to screen people applying for positions that involve close contact with children (Abel, Lawry, Karlstrom, et al., 1994).

Gender Identity Disorders

The gender **identity disorders** (GID) are a group of patterns characterized by a central dilemma, that of having a gender identity, or sense of gender, opposite to one's biological gender. GID is defined by two features, **gender dysphoria** (unhappiness with one's own gender) and a desire to change to the other gender. GID is apparently quite rare. Some European studies indicate that it occurs in only 1 out of 30,000 men and 1 out of 100,000 women (American Psychiatric Association, 1994).

The phenomenon of gender-crossing has been known since ancient times (Bullough & Bullough, 1993). A famous story in Greek and Roman mythology is that of the wise man, Tiresias, who was changed by a god from a man to a woman as a punishment for killing two snakes that were copulating. (As a result of his double experience, he was called in to settle a dispute among the gods as to which gender had more pleasure in love-making. When he said women had more pleasure, Hera, the queen of the gods, became angry and blinded him.) History offers many examples of people who at times took the role of the opposite sex, including at least one Roman emperor, the first governor general of New York, and the first surgeon general of the United States. The historical record also shows that, as a rule, men presented themselves as women mainly for sexual purposes, while women have crossed gender primarily to gain the power and freedom of men. Some cultures (not including our own) have made broad allowances for this. In many native North American societies, for example, there was an institutionalized role, the berdache, for men who dressed and acted as women.

Harry Benjamin (1964), an endocrinologist, coined the term transexual to refer to people seeking to change their gender by means of hormones or surgery. In the 1960s, a large number of people began to request gender-reassignment surgery, and many physicians were willing to perform this. Today, the enthusiasm over gender-reassignment has waned, but around the world there are still programs that offer psychological and medical help to transsexuals. While in past decades many clinicians treating GID regarded it as akin to borderline personality disorder or even psychosis, recent research indicates that most GID patients do not manifest any other psychological disorder. When given personality tests—the MMPI, for example—they do not show significantly more abnormal profiles than the general population (Cole, O'Boyle, Emory, et al., 1997).

Patterns of Gender Identity Disorder

Among adults with GID, there are three basic patterns, each with its characteristic history:

1. *Homosexual male-to-female transsexuals* are usually girlish from childhood. As they grow, they are attracted to men as sex partners. They do not find cross-dressing sexually exciting. They have tried to live as homosexuals but are not satisfied, because they want men to be attracted to them as *women*.

2. *Homosexual female-to-male transsexuals* show essentially the same pattern, with the genders reversed: boyish behavior in childhood, attraction to women (though they may date boys in adolescence), no sexual excitement from cross-dressing, adult effort to live as a lesbian, and dissatisfaction due to wanting to be loved as a man.

3. *Heterosexual male-to-female transsexuals* have a different history. Typically, they do not show feminine behavior as children. (Indeed, they are often hyper-masculine.) They are sexually attracted to women, but, from adolescence on, they are more aroused by transvestism and by imagining themselves as women (autogynephilia). They have tried to live as heterosexuals and are often married, but they are dissatisfied.

GID is categorized as either "of childhood and adolescence" or "of adulthood." The childhood version is far more common. At some point in childhood, about 1 percent of boys and 3 percent of girls express a desire to be of the opposite gender (Zucker & Bradley, 1996).

Richard Raskin, a physician and professional tennis player, had gender reassignment surgery and became Renee Richards.

Interestingly, very few of these children grow up to be transsexual adults. In a major study by Green and his colleagues, 66 boys who were taken to a mental health clinic because they said they wanted to be girls were followed up through late adolescence of adulthood. Three-quarters of them developed into homosexuals or bisexuals. Only 1 became an adult transsexual (Green, 1987). Clearly, most children with gender dysphoria resolve their gender dilemma before adulthood.

The Psychodynamic Perspective

After their change in gender identity, some seek sexual relations with men, while others prefer women and live as lesbians. Psychodynamic theorists have usually attributed GID to a disturbance in the parent-infant bond. In the case of males, this is said to be an overlong, symbiotic relationship with the mother, thus creating a female identity in the infant. Female GID, on the other hand, is thought to be due to the mother's physical or emotional absence, with the result that the girl identifies with her father instead. There has been some controversy over whether the disorder is due to an intrapsychic conflict and whether, therefore, it can be treated by the usual psychoanalytic route of conflict-resolution. Stoller (1975) has argued that the "blissful symbiosis" with the opposite-sex parent is part of the core identity—in other words, not based on conflict and not open to change. Meyer (1979), on the other hand, sees GID as the result of a serious developmental failure—indeed, a condition akin to psychosis—and believes that psychoanalysis is the appropriate treatment.

The Behavioral Perspective

Behavioral theorists interpret GID as the result of a long, subtle process in which the child's gender-role behavior is shaped toward the opposite gender by an important caretaker. The treatment that follows from such a theory is to stop reinforcement for cross-gender behavior and increase reinforcement for gender-appropriate behavior. Four decades ago, John Money and his colleagues proposed a different but related theory, based on the "imprinting" of birds by their caretakers. In this model, GID is the result of an imprinted "gender fixation" on the opposite-sex parent, occurring during a critical developmental period and then stamped in through reinforcement (Money, Hampson, & Hampson, 1957).

The Biological Perspective

Biological researchers have also turned their attention to GID (Hoenig, 1985). One hypothesis attrib-

utes the disorder to hormone imbalance. Research has shown that both male and female rats can be reprogrammed to show the sexual behavior of the opposite gender if they are given the hormones that control sexual arousal in the opposite gender (Beach, 1957). This research is hard to apply to human beings, however, because one cannot know the gender identity of a rat. Furthermore, tests on GID patients have not turned up evidence of hormone abnormalities. Other biological researchers have suggested that GID may be related to a difference in the brain. Several studies have found that transsexuals are likely to show EEG abnormalities, especially in temporal-lobe functioning. Temporal lesions have been associated with paraphilias, and it is possible that they are involved in GID as well.

Gender Reassignment

Because the problem in GID is a discrepancy between gender identity and physical gender, one solution is to change the identity to fit the body. A number of psychodynamic and behavioral therapists have tried this, in keeping with the theories previously outlined, but there is no empirical evidence for the effectiveness of such treatment.

The alternative is to change the body to fit the gender identity, a process called **gender reassignment** that has developed over the past 30 years. The Harry Benjamin International Gender Dysphoria Association (HBIGDA, 1990), a group devoted to studying and treating GID, recently published a set of standards of care that probably represents the ideal scenario. After a detailed evaluation by a mental health professional trained and experienced in the treatment of GID, patients are given at least 3 months of psychotherapy to help them understand what their options are and decide what they actually want. If they still choose gender reassignment, they are given hormone treatment to initiate physical changes. Next comes the most critical phase, the so-called real-life test. In this phase, patients must live completely in the desired gender, dressing, working, and presenting themselves in that role for a minimum of a year, the goal being to make the person understand, before any irreversible changes are made, what it means to occupy that role. Psychotherapy and hormone treatment are continued during this period. For male-to-female patients, the hormones (estrogen) typically result in decreased beard growth, changes in fat distribution, breast development, and voice changes. For female-to-male transsexuals, the hormone (testosterone) produces facial-hair growth, a deepening of the voice, muscle development, breast reduction, and enlargement of the clitoris.

After a year in the real-life test, the person may proceed to surgery. In male-to-female surgery, the testicles are removed, together with the body of the penis, and the skin of the genitals is inverted to create a neo-vagina. The surgeon can also fashion an approximation of external sex organs: labia and a clitoris. In addition, the patient may be given breast implants, and the trachea may be shaved to raise the pitch of the voice. For female-to-male transsexuals, the genital surgery, involving the creation of a neo-phallus, is much more difficult, but in many cases it has been possible to build a penis almost indistinguishable from one produced by nature. Female-to-male patients may also have hysterectomies and breast-reduction surgery.

The outcome of such surgery has been the subject of more than 70 empirical studies (Carroll, 1997). The single most consistent finding is that gender reassignment produces an improvement or a satisfactory outcome in between two-thirds and nine-tenths of patients (Abramowitz, 1986; Green & Fleming, 1991). The areas in which patients report the most improvement are self-satisfaction, interpersonal relationships, and psychological health. They report less improvement in their work life, and the impact on their sexual functioning is still unclear. Nevertheless, these are encouraging results.

There have also been some casualties, people who regretted the surgery or afterwards had serious psychological breakdowns. (There have been suicides, too.) The rate of poor outcomes seems to be about 8 percent (Abramowitz, 1986). It is rarely clear, however, whether a poor outcome is due to the gender reassignment or to preexisting problems in the person's life. If poor outcome is defined simply as regretting the surgery, this seems to occur in less than 1 percent of female-to-male and less than 2 percent of male-to-female transsexuals.

Outcome is influenced by a number of factors, notably the nature of the therapy. Research has found that, the longer the patient is kept in the real-life test phase and the more realistic his or her expectations, the better the result (Botzer & Vehrs, 1997). In addition, some categories of patients are likely to have more positive results. Female-to-male reassignment seems to yield more satisfaction than male-to-female, and, in the male-to-female group, those who began as homosexuals have better results than those who were heterosexual. Not surprisingly, the person's prior psychological health is also a predictor of success. Patients with a history of serious psychological disturbance are not likely to be fully cured by gender reassignment (Abramowitz, 1986; Bodlund & Kullgren, 1995; Botzer & Vehrs, 1997; Green & Fleming, 1991). Satisfaction is also more likely for those who have family and social support, as in the following case:

Joe was a 45-year-old steelworker when he presented with a request for gender-reassignment surgery. He was married and had a 10-year-old daughter. He lived in a blue-collar community, in which he was well known and where he served as president of the local bowling league. He reported that at the age of 7 he had begun to cross-dress in his older sister's clothes several times per week. This was not sexually exciting to him at the time—he simply enjoyed it—but, when he reached puberty, he began to masturbate while cross-dressed, usually fantasizing about himself as a woman. He was attracted to girls of his own age and began to date. After high school, he tried to rid himself of his urge to cross-dress and went into the army in order to make himself "more of a man." He stopped cross-dressing for several years, but the autogynephilic fantasies remained. After discharge from the service, he had several relationships with women and eventually met his future wife, Barbara.

After several months of dating, Joe told Barbara of his cross-dressing urges. She was concerned but supportive. They had a satisfying sexual relationship in the beginning. After they married, he continued to cross-dress in secret. On several occasions, he threw out his women's wardrobe and stopped cross-dressing. Over time, however, his unhappiness with being male increased. He became overweight and made no attempt to stay healthy. The sexual excitement of cross-dressing decreased, but he felt a strong urge to go out in public as female. He became very depressed.

Joe stated that he wanted gender-reassignment surgery as soon as possible. After a careful evaluation, he was given psychotherapy focusing on his gender dysphoria and possible resolutions to it. In therapy, he considered the options of trying to rid himself of his cross-dressing, living as a male and cross-dressing occasionally, or making the transition to female. Part of his therapy included his wife, who said she would support whatever decision he made. Eventually, he decided on gender reassignment. At this point, he started taking female hormones and prepared to make the transition to living as female. He began to "come out" to his family and friends. The most difficult times for him were when his friends shunned him for his decision to change. His daughter was included in family sessions in order to help her understand the changes her father was going through. She began to call his hormones his "happy pills," because they made him happier.

On New Year's Day, Joe "came out" to the bowling league as Josephine. The following month, she was re-elected as president of the league, though she had to move from the men's league to the co-ed league. After 2 years of therapy and one year of taking hormones and living as a woman, she was re-evaluated for appropriateness for surgery. By this time, she had developed breasts and had gone through extensive electrolysis. She had lost 70 pounds and had given up smoking in order to look and feel better. She had legally changed her name and gender on all her identification. She and her wife had divorced but lived in

2 halves of the same duplex. She continued to act as a parent to her daughter, who now called her "Aunt Joey." Her genital surgery went well and there were no major complications. One year after surgery, on a follow-up evaluation, Josephine admitted that there had been some difficult times, especially with other people's negative reactions. Also, she had not yet been able to form a satisfying relationship with a man. She stated, however, that she was much happier living as a woman than she had been as a man and was very glad to have been able to accomplish her "dream." (Adapted from Carroll, Northwestern University Medical School, clinical files.)

Just as our understanding of homosexuality has changed in the past few decades, so has our view of GID. What was once seen by clinicians as a serious mental disorder is now regarded as a variant of gender experience. Today, for most professionals working with GID, the task is simply to help patients decide on their own resolution to their gender dilemma.

KEY TERMS

acquired dysfunction, 342
autogynephilia, 353
dyspareunia, 341
exhibitionism, 350
female orgasmic disorder, 341
female sexual arousal disorder, 340
fetishism, 350
frotteurism, 350

gender dysphoria, 360
gender identity disorders (GID), 360
gender reassignment, 362
generalized dysfunction, 342
hypoactive sexual desire disorder, 340
incest, 356
lifelong dysfunction, 342

male erectile disorder, 340
male orgasmic disorder, 341
masochism, 350
paraphilias, 350
pedophilia, 350
premature ejaculation, 341
sadism, 350
sadomasochistic, 355
sexual aversion disorder, 340

sexual dysfunctions, 340
situational dysfunction, 342
spectator role, 345
transsexual, 361
transvestism, 350
vaginismus, 341
voyeurism, 350

SUMMARY

- Sexual disorders are among the most stigmatized behaviors in society. Western culture generally regards heterosexual relations as the only acceptable form of sexual activity and tends to view all other forms as abnormal. However, views of sexual activity vary greatly among different cultures and can change within a society over time.

- Sexual dysfunctions are disorders which, over a long period of time, disrupt the sexual response cycle or cause pain during intercourse. They are grouped according to the phase of the sexual response cycle in which they occur: hypoactive sexual desire disorder and sexual aversion disorder (desire phase); female sexual arousal disorder and male erectile disorder (arousal phase); and orgasmic disorder and premature ejaculation (orgasm phase). Other disorders, which don't disrupt a specific part of the cycle, include dyspareunia and vaginismus (sexual pain disorders). Studies have shown that several types of sexual dysfunction are common.

- The risk factors for sexual dysfunction include gender, race, education, and socioeconomic status. However, differences in reporting sexual problems have complicated these findings. Generally, women are more likely than men to suffer from disorders of sexual pain and arousal. Premature ejaculation is the most common male sexual complaint.

- The psychodynamic perspective links sexual dysfunction to an unresolved Oedipal conflict among males and to penis envy among females. Though psychodynamic approaches were not proven effective, for many years they were the only treatment widely available.

- Masters and Johnson believe that sexual dysfunction results from performance anxiety, which causes the worried partner to become more of a spectator than a participant. Their work in the 1970s revolutionized the sex therapies, especially behavioral ones.

- Research has shown that behavior and cognitive therapies are quite effective. The behavioral theory maintains that, if sexual dysfunction results from learned anxiety, then the problem can be cured through new learning. Direct symptomatic treatments, especially sensate focus exercises, are used to treat sexual dysfunctions through the behavioral method. Cognitive psychologists focus on attitudes and thoughts about sex that can block arousal.

- Some therapists use a multifaceted approach, combining direct treatment with an exploration of attitudes or problems in the relationship. Family systems therapy focuses on relationship therapy as part of the treatment of sexual dysfunction.

- Researchers believe that sexual dysfunction may result from a combination of organic and psychological factors. New biological therapies have been developed, especially for male erectile disorders, over the past decade. A significant trend in sex therapy is the integration of biological and psychological factors.

■ In the paraphilias, the person is aroused by something other than what is usually considered a normal sexual object or activity. Males are much more likely than females to develop a paraphilia.

■ In fetishism, inanimate objects or a body part is used for sexual gratification, generally replacing all interest in normal sexual activity.

■ Transvestites seek sexual gratification by wearing clothing of the opposite sex, often at home. Most are heterosexual, but transvestism often leads to marital problems if discovered by the spouse.

■ Exhibitionists display their genitals to an involuntary observer. Exhibitionists receive gratification from the observer's response—often shock or fear.

■ Voyeurism is the observation of other people's sexual activity or anatomy, unbeknownst to the subject. Voyeurs receive sexual gratification from the thrill of watching or the danger of being discovered.

■ Sadism and masochism—inflicting pain on others and subjecting oneself to pain, respectively—are sometimes difficult to classify as paraphilias, because in a consenting sadomasochistic couple there is generally no social or occupational distress or impairment.

■ In frotteurism, a person obtains sexual gratification by touching or rubbing against a nonconsenting person. Frotteurs tend to be adolescents or young adults.

■ Pedophiles are adults who seek sexual gratification through sexual contact with children. Though pedophiles rarely cause physical harm to children, they can create severe emotional distress in their victims. Pedophilia has several causes, including arrested psychological development, social isolation, and childhood sexual abuse. Unfortunately, children rarely tell their parents that they have been abused.

■ Incest, sexual relations between family members, is a crime, not a psychological disorder, but it can have severe mental effects on the victim. Incest is most common between father and daughter, and the effects on the victim include low self-esteem, depression, anxiety, substance abuse, and difficulties in sexual adjustment as adults.

■ The psychodynamic perspective maintains that paraphilias result from Oedipal fixation and the associated castration anxiety. Psychodynamic therapy has not been shown to be effective.

■ Behavioral therapists believe that paraphilias are caused by respondent conditioning and the modeling of unconventional sexual behavior. Therapy involves removing the abnormal stimulus from the patient and then using a technique such as stimulus satiation, covert sensitization, or shame aversion therapy. Behavioral therapy for paraphilias has demonstrated moderate success.

■ The cognitive perspective links paraphilias to attitudes developed in childhood. Offenders often "objectify" their victims. Therapy concentrates on identifying the deviation-supporting beliefs and replacing them. Therapists also try to increase the attacker's empathy for the victim.

■ Neurological research on the causes of paraphilias has been inconclusive. However, biological treatments, including antiandrogen drugs, seem to be effective.

■ Gender identity disorders are a group of patterns defined by unhappiness with one's own gender and a desire to change to the other gender. A person with gender identity disorder believes that he or she was born into the wrong biological gender.

■ Psychodynamic theorists attribute gender identity disorder to a disturbance in the parent-infant bond and view psychoanalysis as the treatment. Behavioral theorists see it as the result of an influential caretaker shaping a child's gender-role behavior and work on stopping the reinforcements. Biological researchers have looked for EEG abnormalities. Therapies based on changing the person's identity to fit the body have generally been ineffective.

■ People with gender identity disorders who seek to change their gender are known as transsexuals. Some transsexuals elect to undergo gender-reassignment surgery, which involves a long period of therapy, hormonal treatment, a period of living as the desired gender, and then genital surgery. Gender reassignment improves self-satisfaction, relationships, and psychological health in over two-thirds of transsexuals. The nature of the therapy, the person's mental health history, and the amount of social support influence the level of success.

Part Four | PSYCHOTIC AND NEUROPSYCHOLOGICAL DISORDERS

Chapter 13

In his *Lectures on Clinical Psychiatry* (1904/1968), Emil Kraepelin (Chapter 1) describes the case of a woman he called the "widow":

> The widow, aged thirty-five, . . . gives full information about her life in answer to our questions, knows where she is, can tell the date and the year, and gives proof of satisfactory school knowledge. . . . For many years she has heard voices, which insult her and cast suspicion on her chastity. They mention a number of names she knows, and tell her she will be stripped and abused. The voices are very distinct, and, in her opinion, they must be carried by a telescope or a machine from her home. Her thoughts are dictated to her; she is obliged to think them, and hears them repeated after her. She is interrupted in her work, and has all kinds of uncomfortable sensations in her body, to which something is "done." In particular, her "mother parts" are turned inside out, and people send a pain through her back, lay ice-water on her heart, squeeze her neck, injure her spine, and violate her. . . .
>
> The patient makes these extraordinary complaints without showing much emotion. She cries a little, but then describes her morbid experiences again with secret satisfaction and even with an erotic bias. She demands her discharge, but is easily consoled, and does not trouble at all about her position and her future. Her use of numerous strained and hardly intelligible phrases is very striking. She is ill-treated "flail-wise," "utterance-wise," "terror-wise"; she is "a picture of misery in angel's form," and "a defrauded mamma and housewife of sense of order." They have "altered her form of emotion." She is "persecuted by a secret insect from the District Office. . . ." Her former history shows that she has been ill for nearly ten years. (p. 157)

The "widow" offers a good illustration of psychosis. As we have noted previously, the **psychoses** are a class of psychological disorders in which reality contact—the capacity to perceive, process, and respond to environmental stimuli in an adaptive manner—is radically impaired, with the result that the person cannot meet the ordinary demands of life. The psychoses, then, are the most severe of all the psychological disorders. Most of the conditions that we have discussed in earlier chapters allow for some measure of adaptive functioning. An acute psychotic episode does not. For this reason—and because the behavior of people with psychoses is disturbing to others—they are often hospitalized.

There are three main groups of psychoses:

1. *The mood disorders,* characterized, as their name indicates, primarily by disturbances of *mood* (but remember that not all mood disorders are psychotic)
2. *Schizophrenia,* considered to be primarily a disturbance of *thought*

3. *Delusional disorder,* in which the essential, and possibly the only, abnormality is a limited system of *delusions*

Mood disorders have already been described in Chapter 9. The present chapter will focus on the two other main types of psychosis, schizophrenia and delusional disorder, with special emphasis on the former, as it is far more common. First we will describe these disorders. Then we will discuss theories and treatment.

Schizophrenia

Schizophrenia is the label given to a group of psychoses in which deterioration of functioning is marked by severe distortion of thought, perception, and mood; by bizarre behavior; and by social withdrawal.

The Prevalence of Schizophrenia

Between 1 and 2 percent of people in the United States have had or will have a schizophrenic episode (Kendler, Gallagher, Abelson, et al., 1996). In other countries, the rates are similar (American Psychiatric Association, 1994). At present, there are about a million actively schizophrenic people in the country. Such people occupy about half the beds in U.S. mental hospitals (Kaplan & Sadock, 1991). Many other schizophrenics have been released from the hospital—either to smaller facilities or simply into the community. (It has been estimated that as many as one-third of homeless people are schizophrenic [American Psychiatric Association, 1997].) But about half of those discharged for the first time return to the mental hospital within two years (Kaplan & Sadock, 1991). The estimated cost of schizophrenia to our society is about $19 billion in health care alone (American Psychiatric Association, 1997). Clearly, this disorder constitutes an enormous public health problem.

The History of the Diagnostic Category

Although schizophrenia has probably been with us for thousands of years, it was not described as a distinct disorder until 1896, when Emil Kraepelin proposed that there were three major types of psychosis: manic-depressive psychosis, paranoia, and *dementia praecox,* a syndrome marked by delusions, hallucinations, attention problems, and bizarre motor behavior. Kraepelin believed that dementia praecox normally began in adolescence and led to irreversible mental breakdown—hence his term for the disorder, which is Latin for "premature mental deterioration."

Emil Kraepelin (1856–1926), a German psychiatrist, was the first to describe schizophrenia as a distinct disorder, calling it "dementia praecox." The term schizophrenia *was coined by Eugen Bleuler in 1911.*

While Kraepelin's description of the disorder has lasted, the name he gave it was soon replaced. In 1911, Swiss psychiatrist Eugen Bleuler, a highly influential teacher and writer, pointed out that dementia praecox was actually a poor description. In the first place, the disorder was not necessarily premature; many patients did not develop symptoms until well into their adult years. Second, most patients did not proceed to complete mental deterioration. Some remained the same year after year; others improved; others improved and relapsed. Bleuler (1911/1950), therefore, proposed a new term, *schizophrenia,* meaning "split mind" (from the Greek *schiz-,* or "divide," and *phren,* or "mind"). Actually, Bleuler's term also poses problems, because many people mistake it to mean multiple personality, or dissociative identity disorder (Chapter 7), which is an entirely different condition. What Bleuler was referring to was not a splitting of the personality into two or more personalities but, rather, a split among different psychic *functions* within a single personality. In the mind of the schizophrenic, emotion, perception, and cognition cease to operate as an integral whole. Emotions may split off from perception, perception from reality. As Bleuler put it, "The personality loses

its unity" (p. 9). A former schizophrenic quoted by Mendel (1976) described the experience more concretely: "The integrating mental picture in my personality was taken away and smashed to bits, leaving me like agitated hamburger distributed infinitely throughout the universe" (p. 8).

The Symptoms of Schizophrenia

DSM-IV lists five characteristic symptoms of schizophrenia: delusions, hallucinations, disorganized-speech, disorganized or catatonic behavior, and "negative symptoms," meaning a reduction or loss of normal functions such as language and goal-directed behavior. If a person has shown two or more of those signs for at least a month and has been noticeably disturbed for at least six months, the diagnosis is schizophrenia.

In cases in which the episode has lasted for less than a month, the diagnosis is *brief psychotic disorder.* When it has lasted more than a month but less than six months, the diagnosis is *schizophreniform disorder.* Only when the episode exceeds the six-month cutoff line is the diagnosis of schizophrenia made.

For the sake of discussion, we will break down the symptoms of schizophrenia into separate categories. Keep in mind, however, that in reality they are not separate, for they influence one another. If a person's thought processes are derailed, this affects mood; if mood is disturbed, this affects behavior. And, while all schizophrenics display some of these symptoms some of the time, no schizophrenic displays all of them all of the time. Indeed, some diagnosed schizophrenics often behave quite normally.

Disorders of Thought and Language

I'm a doctor, you know. . . . I don't have a diploma, but I'm a doctor. I'm glad to be a mental patient, because it taught me how to be humble. I use Cover Girl creamy natural makeup. Oral Roberts has been here to visit me. . . . This place is where *Mad* magazine is published. The Nixons make Noxon metal polish. When I was a little girl, I used to sit and tell stories to myself. When I was older, I turned off the sound on the TV set and made up dialogue to go with the shows I watched. . . . I'm a week pregnant. I have schizophrenia—cancer of the nerves. My body is overcrowded with nerves. This is going to win me the Nobel Prize for medicine. I don't consider myself schizophrenic anymore. There's no such thing as schizophrenia, there's only mental telepathy. . . . I'm in the Pentecostal Church, but I'm thinking of changing my religion. I have a dog at home. I love instant oatmeal. When you have Jesus, you don't need a diet. Mick Jagger wants to marry me. I want to get out the revolving door. With

Jesus Christ, anything is possible. I used to hit my mother. It was the hyperactivity from all the cookies I ate. (Quoted in S. Sheehan, 1982, pp. 72–73.)

This is a transcript of a schizophrenic woman's attempt at conversation in a hospital ward. The disordered language of schizophrenics, with its odd associations and rapid changes of subject, is presumably a clue to their disordered thought processes. Some experts on schizophrenia have tried to distinguish between disturbances of thought and disturbances of language, but such distinctions are possible only at a theoretical level. Language is the expression of thought. Conversely, our primary clue to thought is language. Therefore, we will consider the two functions together. First, we will discuss disturbances in the *content* of schizophrenic thought, known as delusions, and then we will discuss abnormalities in the *form* schizophrenic thought takes.

Delusions   Delusions, or firmly held beliefs that have no basis in reality, may accompany a variety of psychological conditions—mania, depression, organic syndromes, drug overdose—but they are extremely common in schizophrenia (Butler & Braff, 1991), affecting three-quarters or more of hospitalized schizophrenic patients (Harrow, Carone, & Westermeyer, 1985).

Most schizophrenics do not seem to realize that other people find their delusional beliefs implausible (Harrow, Rattenbury, & Stoll, 1988). Neither will they abandon their delusions in the face of contradictory evidence—a point that was vividly demonstrated some years ago by psychologist Milton Rokeach. In 1959, Rokeach had three men, each of whom claimed to be Jesus Christ, transferred to the same ward of a hospital in Ypsilanti, Michigan. For two years, the "three Christs" lived together, sleeping in adjacent beds, sharing the same table in the dining hall, and working together in the hospital laundry room while Rokeach observed them. His purpose was "to explore the processes by which their delusional systems of belief and their behavior might change if they were confronted with the ultimate contradiction conceivable for human beings: more than one person claiming the same identity" (Rokeach, 1964, p. 3). In other words, would any of them figure out that all three of them couldn't be Jesus? The following is an excerpt from one of their first encounters:

"Well, I know your psychology," Clyde said, "and you are a knick-knacker, and in your Catholic church in North Bradley and in your education, and I know all of it—the whole thing. I know exactly what this fellow does. In my credit like I do from up above, that's the way it works."

"As I was stating before I was interrupted," Leon went on, "it so happens that I was the first human spirit to be created with a glorified body before time existed."

"Ah, well, he is just simply a creature, that's all," Joseph put in. "Man created by me when I created the world—nothing else."

—*Did you create Clyde, too?* Rokeach asked.

"Uh-huh. Him and a good many others."

At this, Clyde laughed. (Rokeach, 1964, pp. 10–11)

After two years of daily contact, each of the three men still firmly believed that he alone was Jesus Christ. Most delusions fall into certain patterns:

1. *Delusions of persecution:* the belief that one is being plotted against, spied upon, threatened, or otherwise mistreated, particularly by a conspiracy

2. *Delusions of control* (also called *delusions of influence*): the belief that other people, forces, or perhaps extraterrestrial beings are controlling one's thoughts, feelings, and actions, often by means of electronic devices that send signals directly to the brain

3. *Delusions of reference:* the belief that one is being referred to by things or events that, in fact, have nothing to do with one. For example, schizophrenics may think that their lives are being depicted on television or in news stories.

4. *Delusions of grandeur:* the belief that one is an extremely famous and powerful person. Such delusions may crystallize into a stable delusional identity, with the person claiming, for example, that he or she is Joan of Arc, or, as with Rokeach's patients, Jesus Christ.

5. *Delusions of sin and guilt:* the belief that one has committed "the unpardonable sin" or has inflicted great harm on others. Schizophrenics may claim, for example, that they have killed their children.

6. *Hypochondriacal delusions:* the unfounded belief that one is suffering from a hideous physical disease. The hypochondriacal delusions of schizophrenics differ from the fears seen in hypochondriasis (Chapter 7) in that they refer not to recognized diseases but to bizarre afflictions. While hypochondriacs may complain of brain tumors, for instance, schizophrenics claim that their brains are full of mold or are being carried away in pieces.

7. *Nihilistic delusions:* the belief that one or others or the whole world has ceased to exist. The patient may claim, for example, that he or she is a spirit returned from the dead.

Vaslav Nijinsky (1889–1950), the great Polish-Russian ballet dancer, is shown here on the left, a few years before he was diagnosed as schizophrenic. The drawing of staring eyes was done by Nijinsky while he was in an asylum. Nijinsky remained a chronic schizophrenic for the last 30 years of his life.

Finally, many schizophrenics complain that their thoughts are being tampered with in some way. Such delusions, related to delusions of control, include

1. *Thought broadcasting:* the belief that one's thoughts are being broadcast to the outside world, so that everyone can hear them
2. *Thought insertion:* the belief that other people are inserting thoughts, especially obscene thoughts, into one's head
3. *Thought withdrawal:* the belief that other people are removing thoughts from one's head

These particular delusions seem to be highly specific to schizophrenia—in any case, they are not seen in people with psychotic mood disorders (Junginger, Barker, & Coe, 1992)—and they may represent an effort by schizophrenics to explain to themselves the mental chaos that this disorder entails. Many schizo-

phrenics, for example, experience what is called *blocking:* in the middle of talking about something, they suddenly fall silent, with no memory of what they were talking about. Such an experience is as disturbing to a schizophrenic as it would be to anyone else, and one way to explain it is to say that someone is stealing the thoughts out of one's head. Some researchers believe that many schizophrenic delusions represent "normal" explanations for abnormal experiences (Maher & Spitzer, 1993).

Loosening of Associations   As we saw earlier, it was for the quality of psychological "splitting"—a disconnection between different ideas or different mental functions—that Bleuler named the disorder schizophrenia. One of the clearest demonstrations of this splitting is the rambling, disjointed quality of the language produced by schizophrenic patients, particularly the younger ones (Harvey, Lombardi, Liebman, et al., 1997). Normal speech tends to follow a single train of thought, with logical connections between ideas. By contrast, schizophrenic speech often shows a **loosening of associations.** Ideas jump from one track to another, with the result that the person wanders further and further away from the topic. When the problem is severe, speech may become completely incoherent.

We do not know exactly what mental processes cause this confusion in speech, but it is likely that the problem lies in the mind's way of dealing with associations. In communicating with one another, people make many mental associations, both to the statements of those they are speaking to and to their own statements. Before speaking, however, they "edit" these associations, selecting the ones that are most relevant to the topic and discarding the others. In the schizophrenic mind, this process seems to break down, so that the speaker follows his or her own private train of associations, without editing for relevance (Docherty, Hawkins, Hoffman, et al., 1996).

This does not mean that schizophrenics cannot give a straight answer to a direct question. They can make very common primary associations to a given stimulus about as easily as normal people. It is the more subtle secondary associations that many schizophrenics cannot make without becoming confused and incoherent. This phenomenon was illustrated in an experiment conducted by Cohen and his colleagues. A group of normal subjects and a group of schizophrenics were shown two colored disks and were asked to describe one of the colors in such a way that a listener who was also looking at those two colors could pick out the one being described. When the colors were quite dissimilar, the schizophrenics did about as well as the normal subjects. For example, when one color was red and the other a purple-blue, they described the second one as purple or blue. In the next stage of the experiment, however, the two colors were quite similar, requiring that the speaker make subtle associations in order to describe the difference between the two. Faced with this task, the normal speakers managed to refine their associations in such a way as to indicate which color they meant. The schizophrenics, on the other hand, began reeling off associations that, while quite vivid, failed to convey the appropriate information:

Normal
Speaker 2:   My God, this is hard. They are both about the same, except that this one might be a little redder.

Normal
Speaker 3:   They both are either the color of canned salmon or clay. This one here is the pinker one.

Schizophrenic
Speaker 2:   This is a stupid color of a shit ass bowl of salmon. Mix it with mayonnaise. Then it gets tasty. Leave it alone and puke all over the fuckin' place. Puke fish.

Schizophrenic
Speaker 3:   Makeup. Pancake makeup. You put it on your face and they think guys run after you. Wait a second! I don't put it on my face and guys don't run after me. Girls put it on them.

(Cohen, Nachmani, & Rosenberg, 1974, p. 11)

What is it that pushes schizophrenics off the track? Some experts believe that, once schizophrenics make a given association, they cannot let go of it, as normal people can, and search for a more appropriate association. They get "stuck" on the first association, and the remainder of the response is "chained" off that first association, without any concern for relevance to the topic at hand. In other words, schizophrenics are at the mercy of their associative processes. In the examples just given, for instance, both of the schizophrenic speakers made a first association—one to salmon, one to pancake makeup—but then, instead of refining it in order to explain the difference between the two colors, they went off on trains of private associations to that first thought. (The same sort of loose associations show up in milder form in the biological relatives of schizophrenics [Kinney, Holzman, Jacobsen, et al., 1997].) This characteristic seems to be related to another peculiarity of schizophrenic thinking, a difficulty in grasping context. Recent EEG studies have found that, when schizophrenics have sentences read to them, they often show abnormal, event-related potentials when they get to the last word of the sentence. What this suggests is that they do not understand the context well enough to process the last word (Nestor, Kimble, O'Donnell, et al., 1997). As with the color-association test, it seems that schizophrenics have trouble "seeing the forest for the trees."

Poverty of Content   The result of loosened associations is that schizophrenic language may convey very little. Though the person may use many words, all grammatically correct, he or she communicates poorly. This **poverty of content** can be seen in the following excerpt from a letter by a schizophrenic patient:

> Dear Mother,
>   I am writing on paper. The pen which I am using is from a factory called "Perry & Co." This factory is in England. I assume this. Behind the name of Perry Co. the city of London is inscribed; but not the city. The city of London is in England. I know this from my school days. Then, I always liked geography. My last teacher in that subject was Professor August A. He was a man with black eyes. I also like black eyes. There are also blue and gray eyes and other sorts, too. I have heard it said that snakes have green eyes. All people have eyes. There are some, too, who are blind. These blind people are led about by a boy. It must be terrible not to be able to see. There are people who can't see and, in addition can't hear. I know some who hear too much. One can hear too much. (Quoted in Bleuler, 1911/1950, p. 17.)

Bleuler, who first published this letter, points out that the only common denominator of the ideas expressed in it is that they are all present in the patient's awareness: London—geography lesson—geography teacher—his black eyes—gray eyes—green snake eyes—human eyes—blind people—deaf people—and so on. The letter says much, and all very properly, but it conveys little, for it lacks any unifying principle beyond the irresistible linkage of associations.

Neologisms As we pointed out earlier, the confused speech of schizophrenics is generally interpreted as the product of confused thinking. However, some researchers have suggested that certain peculiarities of schizophrenic language may result not from radical thought disturbances but simply from an inability to retrieve commonly agreed-upon verbal symbols. That is, what schizophrenics have to say may be reasonable enough; they just can't find the right words with which to say it (Alpert, Clark, & Pouget, 1994; Barch & Berenbaum, 1996).

This hypothesis might account for the rare appearance in schizophrenic speech of words and phrases not found in even the most comprehensive dictionary. These usages, called **neologisms** (literally "new words"), are sometimes formed by combining parts of two or more regular words. Or the neologism may involve the use of common words in a new way (Willerman & Cohen, 1990). In either case, what is interesting about neologisms is that, while they are sometimes unintelligible, at other times they manage to communicate ideas quite vividly, as can be seen in the following transcript (possible intended meanings are indicated in brackets):

> TH.: Sally, you're not eating supper tonight. What's the problem?
> PT.: No, I had belly bad luck and brutal and outrageous. [I have stomach problems, and I don't feel good.] I gave all the work money. [I paid tokens for my meal.] Here, I work. Well, the difference is I work five days and when the word was [when I am told to work] but I had escapingly [I got out of some work]. I done it for Jones. He planned it and had me work and helped me work and all and had all the money. He's a tie-father [a relative]. Besides generation ties and generation hangages [relationships between family generations—the way generations hang together] . . . he gave love a lot. I fit in them generations since old-fashion time [since long ago]. I was raised in packs [with other people] . . . certain times I was, since I was in littlehood [since I was a little girl] . . . she said she concerned a Sally-twin [my twin sister]. She blamed a few people with minor words [she scolded people], but she done goodship [good things]. I've had to suffer so much. I done it United States long.

> TH.: Sally, is there anything else you want to tell me before you go?
> PT.: Well, I expect there's a lot of things, but I would know what they were, especially the unkind crimery [the bad things]. (Hagen, Florida State University, clinical files)

Clanging Another oddity sometimes found in the speech of schizophrenics (and of manics as well) is **clanging**, the pairing of words that have no relation to one another beyond the fact that they rhyme or sound alike. Clanging may be related to the associational problem just discussed. In this case, however, the basis for the associations is sound rather than sense. Hence, clanging speech is often closer to nonsense verse than to rational communication.

The following is a transcript of a conversation between a therapist and a schizophrenic patient who was particularly adept at clanging. (About half of all his daily speech was rhymed.) As the transcript shows, clanging often involves neologisms:

> TH.: How are things going today, Ernest?
> PT.: Okay for a flump.
> TH.: What is a flump?
> PT.: A flump is a gump.
> TH.: That doesn't make any sense.
> PT.: Well, when you go to the next planet from the planet beyond the planet that landed on the danded and planded on the standed.
> TH.: Wait a minute. I didn't follow any of that.
> PT.: Well, when we was first bit on the slit on the rit and the man on the ran or the pan on the ban and the sand on the man and the pan on the ban on the can on the man on the fan on the pan. [All spoken very rhythmically, beginning slowly and building up to such a rapid pace that the words could no longer be understood.]
> TH.: What's all that hitting your head for . . . and waving your arms?
> PT.: That's to keep the boogers from eatin' the woogers. (Hagen, Florida State University, clinical files)

Word Salad In some cases, schizophrenic language seems to show a complete breakdown of the associational process, so it becomes impossible for the listener to trace any links between successive words and phrases. This extreme situation is illustrated in the following statement, made by the same patient whose clanging was previously quoted:

> It's all over for a squab true tray and there ain't no music, there ain't no nothing besides my mother and my father who stand alone upon the Island of Capri where

there is no ice, there is no nothing but changers, changers, changers. That comes like in first and last names, so that thing does. Well, it's my suitcase, sir. I've got to travel all the time to keep my energy alive. (Hagen, Florida State University, clinical files)

Appropriately, this type of speech, in which words and phrases are combined in what appears to be a completely disorganized fashion, is referred to as **word salad.** Unlike neologisms, word salad suggests no effort to communicate. Neither does it appear to reflect a train of tangential association. Neither are the words even connected on the basis of sound, as in clanging. Word salad, then, is the ultimate in schizophrenic splitting. Nothing is related to anything else.

Disorders of Perception

My eyes became markedly oversensitive to light. Ordinary colors appeared to be much too bright, and sunlight appeared dazzling in intensity. When this happened, ordinary reading became impossible, and print seemed excessively black.

Objects appeared to be far away and flat. If I spoke to anyone, the person in question looked to me like a cutout picture without any relief. (Benioff, 1995, p. 88)

Many schizophrenic patients, like the one quoted here, report changes in perception, including visual illusions, disturbingly acute hearing, inability to focus attention, difficulty in identifying people, and difficulty in understanding what other people are saying. Schizophrenics have also reported changes in smell, complaining that their own body odor is more pronounced and more unpleasant, that other people smell stronger, and that objects have peculiar smells (Kaplan & Sadock, 1991). Among the many perceptual oddities involved in schizophrenia, two are of special concern: the breakdown of selective attention and the experience of hallucinations.

Breakdown of Selective Attention Normal people exercise selective attention without thinking about it. That is, they decide what they want to focus on in the environment and then concentrate on that, with the result that sensory data from the thing they are interested in register forcibly in the mind, while extraneous data (the sound of the air conditioner in the classroom, the earrings on the student in the front row) are confined to the edge of consciousness. Schizophrenics, however, seem unable to engage in this normal selection process—a fact that was noted by Kraepelin and Bleuler. Today, a century later, many researchers feel that the breakdown of selective attention underlies

most of the other symptoms of schizophrenia. McGhie and Chapman (1961), two major proponents of this theory, ask us to imagine what would happen if the mind ceased to exercise selective attention:

Consciousness would be flooded with an undifferentiated mass of incoming sensory data, transmitted from the environment via the sense organs. To this involuntary tide of impressions there would be added the diverse internal images, and their associations, which would no longer be coordinated with incoming information. Perception would revert to the passive and involuntary assimilative process of early childhood, and, if the incoming flood were to carry on unchecked, it would gradually sweep away the stable constructs of a former reality. (p. 105)

In consequence, the person would see an altered world, make odd associations, produce bizarre speech, experience inappropriate emotions—and, it is easy to imagine, work out strange beliefs and strange behavior patterns as a defense against the sensory overload. The result would be what we call schizophrenia. One patient of McGhie and Chapman (1961) testified to his attention problems in simple and poignant terms:

My thoughts get all jumbled up. I start thinking or talking about something but I never get there. Instead I wander off in the wrong direction and get caught up with all sorts of different things that may be connected with the things I want to say but in a way I can't explain. People listening to me get more lost than I do. (p. 108)

Hallucinations Added to the perceptual problems of schizophrenics is the fact that many of them perceive things that are not there. Such perceptions, occurring in the absence of any appropriate external stimulus, are called **hallucinations.** Auditory hallucinations are apparently the most common, occurring in 70 percent of schizophrenic patients (Cleghorn, Franco, Szechtman, et al., 1992), and certain types of auditory hallucinations are especially characteristic of schizophrenia, notably the experience of hearing two or more voices conversing with one another or of hearing voices that keep a running commentary on the patient's thoughts or behavior. After auditory hallucinations, visual hallucinations are the most frequent, followed by hallucinations of the other senses (Ludwig, 1986). While some schizophrenics recognize that their hallucinations are not real—that the voices are only in their heads—others are not sure (Frith, 1992), and a fair percentage, presumably the more severely psychotic, are convinced that their hallucinations are perceptions of real events. (Schizophrenics also disagree on whether hallucinations are harmful or beneficial—see the box on page 377.)

Hallucinations: Terror or Comfort?

Most experts on schizophrenia now believe that hallucinations are at least partly the result of neurological dysfunction. Nevertheless, as we have seen repeatedly, patients don't just have symptoms. They also have reactions to symptoms, and if those reactions are positive—if the symptom serves a purpose in the person's life—they may feed the disorder.

This might be the case with some hallucinating psychotics. Miller and her colleagues interviewed 50 hallucinating patients about their attitudes toward their hallucinations. Surprisingly, more than half the subjects reported that hallucinating had some advantages. Many claimed that their hallucinations were soothing. In the words of 1 patient, "If I can keep it low, it's relaxing, like having a radio on" (Miller, O'Connor, & DiPasquale, 1993, p. 586). Others said that the hallucinations provided companionship ("I was lonely; I wanted some friends" [p. 586]), that they served protective functions ("I hallucinated shooting my dad instead of actually shooting him.... I'm not in prison" [p. 586]), that they bolstered self-esteem, that they made it easier to get attention and disability payments,

and that they even helped with work ("When I do greeting cards, sometimes the voices make out the verses" [p. 586]). Ten out of the 50 patients said they would like to go on hallucinating as long as they could control the hallucinations.

At the same time, all but one of the patients also reported that their hallucinations had negative effects, preventing them from earning a living ("I've never been able to have a job because of this" [p. 587]), interfering with their activities ("The voices...try to help, but they may say do it in a different way than the boss" [p. 587]), upsetting them emotionally, damaging their social relationships and their self-esteem ("Every time I see the visions, they look so handsome; I feel worse about myself, since I'm uglier" [p. 587]); and interfering with their sex lives ("It got in the way of sex; I feel like I'm on TV" [p. 587]). Two-thirds of the patients said that they would prefer not to hallucinate, even if they could make the hallucinations come and go at will.

Thus, a clear majority of the patients wanted to be rid of their hallucinations, but a sizable minority did not, and the latter proved more resis-

tant to treatment. These interviews were conducted when the subjects entered the hospital for treatment. When they were released—after a mean stay of about two months—the researchers interviewed them again, to see if they were still hallucinating. Those who were had certain things in common. First, they were more likely to have olfactory hallucinations, or hallucinations of odors. (This is consistent with the finding that olfactory hallucinations may be associated with "pleasure centers" in the limbic structures of the brain [McLean, 1986].) Second, they were more likely to report that they could predict the onset of their hallucinations via an inner warning signal—a feature that probably makes hallucinations less threatening. Finally, those who were still hallucinating upon release tended to be the ones who, upon admission, had reported the most positive effects for their hallucinations. As the researchers point out, this last correlation does not prove a causal connection—that valuing one's hallucinations perpetuates them—but it certainly raises the question.

Schizophrenics, then, have not only a perceptual problem but also a reality-monitoring problem, and this in turn may be related to their difficulties in exercising selective attention. Their inability to screen out irrelevant stimuli may make it hard for them to tell the difference between self-generated and externally generated sounds and, thus, to distinguish between real voices and imaginary ones (Brebion, Smith, Gorman, et al., 1996). On the other hand, some voices "in the head" may be more than imaginary: they may be the patient's own voice, speaking subvocally—that is, with activation of the larynx but with no audible sound. PET scans of schizophrenics taken while the subjects were having auditory hallucinations have shown a pattern of activity in the language regions of the brain that is similar to the activity seen in the brains of normal subjects speaking in and listening to their own voices (Woodruff, Wright, Bullmore, et al., 1997).

Disorders of Mood While schizophrenia is considered to be primarily a disturbance of thought, it often

involves disturbances of mood as well. However, schizophrenic mood abnormalities have little in common with the psychotic mood disorders. As we saw in Chapter 9, the mood disorders involve either deep depression or manic elation, or an alternation between the two. Some other patients have either a manic or a major depressive episode while also showing the symptoms of schizophrenia. This intermediate syndrome is called *schizoaffective disorder* and has an intermediate prognosis. That is, schizoaffective patients fare somewhat better than schizophrenics, on the average, and somewhat worse than mood disorder patients (Davidson & McGlashan, 1997). However, in schizophrenia, there are generally two patterns of mood disorders.

One is a reduced emotional responsiveness, known either as **blunted affect** (when the patient shows little emotion) or **flat affect** (when the patient shows no emotion). In either case, this reduction of emotion is often accompanied by *anhedonia*, a reduced experience of pleasure. The second major pattern of schizophrenic mood disturbance is inappropriate affect, the expression of emotions unsuitable to the situation. For example, the patient may giggle while relating a painful memory or show anger when given a present. Usually, however, the inappropriateness is subtler. A number of studies have shown that schizophrenics tend to use the same gestures, show the same facial expression, and gaze at the listener in the same way regardless of whether the emotion they are describing is happy, sad, or angry. Furthermore, in all these situations, their gestures, facial expression, and gaze tend to be similar to those that nonschizophrenic people use when describing something happy (Knight & Roff, 1985). Thus, here again, the problem for schizophrenics seems to be one of differentiation. This is true even for those with blunted affect. Recent research suggests that such patients have difficulty only in expressing different emotions, not in feeling them (Berenbaum & Oltmanns, 1992; Kring & Neale, 1996).

Disorders of Motor Behavior   The following portrait of a schizophrenic ward shows a mix of behaviors that might be observed daily in hundreds of schizophrenic wards throughout the country:

> In the day room Lou stands hour after hour, never saying a word, just rubbing the palm of his hand around and around the top of his head. Jerry spends his day rubbing his hand against his stomach and running around a post at the same time. Helen paces back and forth, her head down, mumbling about enemies who are coming to get her, while Vic grimaces and giggles over in the corner. Virginia stands in the center of the day room, vigorously slapping her hand against her dress, making a rhythmical smacking sound, which, because of its tireless repetition, goes unnoticed. Nick tears up magazines, puts bits of paper in his mouth, and then spits them out, while Bill sits immobile for hours, staring at the floor. Betty masturbates quietly on the couch, while Paul follows one of the young nurse's aides on her room check, hoping to get a chance to see up her dress as she leans over to smooth a bed. Geraldine is reading her Bible; Lillian is watching television; and Frank is hard at work, scrubbing the floor. (Adapted from Hagen, Florida State University, clinical files)

In some cases, such as the last three in this example, schizophrenic motor behavior appears perfectly normal. In other cases, such as those of Betty and Paul, it is merely inappropriate to the setting. However, certain repetitive motor behaviors, such as the head rubbing, dress smacking, and paper tearing in the quoted case, are clearly abnormal. The act of engaging in purposeless behaviors repetitively over long periods of time is called **stereotypy**.

Schizophrenics sometimes show frenetically high levels of motor activity, running about, thrashing their arms, upsetting furniture, and generally expending a good deal of energy. Much more common, however, is the opposite: inactivity. In the extreme case, schizophrenics may lapse into a *catatonic stupor*, remaining mute and immobile for days on end

Social Withdrawal   As we shall see, an early sign of schizophrenia is emotional detachment—a lack of attention to or interest in the goings-on of the external world. Preoccupied with their own thoughts, schizophrenics gradually withdraw from involvement with the environment. Above all, they withdraw from involvement with other people. Note that, in spite of the wide range of behaviors taking place on the ward described in the case study, there is one behavior that is strikingly absent: social interaction. Rarely do schizophrenic patients engage in small talk. Often they act as if others do not exist.

This may be due in part to their social handicaps. They are less adept than nonschizophrenics at picking up interpersonal cues—that is, at understanding what the other person is feeling or trying to do (Penn, Corrigan, Bentall, et al., 1997). Many of them also have problems with gaze discrimination: they think other people are looking directly at them when this is not the case (Rosse, Kendrick, Wyatt, et al., 1994). Given these problems, it is no surprise that they recoil from social interaction.

The social withdrawal of schizophrenics is related to their attention problems as well (Green, 1996). The mental havoc that presumably results from the attention deficit would make communication very difficult, and, as we have seen, schizophrenics communicate poorly. Knowing that they are unlikely to make themselves understood—and knowing, furthermore, that people may treat them very curtly—schizophrenics may choose to focus on anything rather than other people.

The Course of Schizophrenia

Schizophrenia, like some other disorders, seems to follow a regular course, or progression of stages, through time. The course of the disorder has traditionally been divided into three phases: the prodromal phase, the active phase, and the residual phase.

The Prodromal Phase   In some cases, the onset of schizophrenia is very sudden. In a matter of days, a reasonably well-adjusted person is transformed into a hallucinating psychotic. In other cases, functioning deteriorates gradually for years before any clearly

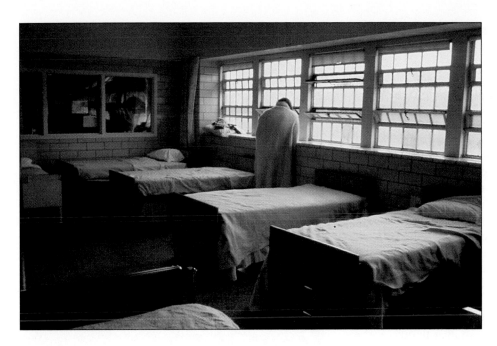

Social withdrawal is one of the leading symptoms of schizophrenia.

psychotic symptoms appear. This slow downhill slide is known as the **prodromal phase**.

During the prodromal phase, incipient schizophrenics generally become withdrawn and socially isolated. Often, they cease to care about their appearance or hygiene, forgetting to bathe, sleeping in their clothes, and so on. Performance in school or at work begins to deteriorate; the person shows up late, if at all, and seems careless and inattentive. At the same time, emotions begin to seem shallow and inappropriate. Eventually, family and friends note a change in the person. Sometimes, however, the disorder proceeds so gradually that it is not remarked upon until the person begins acting very bizarrely—dressing in odd ways, collecting trash, talking to invisible companions. By this time, the active phase has begun.

The Active Phase In the **active phase**, the patient begins showing prominent psychotic symptoms—hallucinations, delusions, disorganized speech, severe withdrawal, and so forth. The symptoms outlined earlier in this chapter describe the active phase of schizophrenia. As we noted, however, no one patient is likely to show all those symptoms.

The Residual Phase Just as onset may occur almost overnight, so may recovery. Ordinarily, however, what recovery there is is gradual. In most patients, the active phase is followed by a **residual phase**, in which behavior is similar to that of the prodromal phase. Blunted or flat affect is especially common in this period. Speech may still ramble, hygiene may still be poor, and, while outright hallucinations and delusions may have dissipated, the person may continue to have unusual perceptual experiences and odd ideas, claiming, for example, to be able to tell the future or to have other special powers. In consequence, holding down a job is still difficult for most schizophrenics in the residual phase.

In some cases, the residual phase ends with a return to perfectly normal functioning, or "complete remission," as it is known in the psychiatric vocabulary. This is not the usual outcome, however. Many patients remain impaired to some degree, and many go on to have further psychotic (i.e., active-phase) episodes, with increasingly impaired functioning between episodes. An extensive, long-term follow-up study of more than 1,000 schizophrenics by Manfred Bleuler (1978), the son of Eugen Bleuler, found that approximately 10 percent of the schizophrenics remained schizophrenic for the rest of their lives, 25 percent returned to and maintained normal functioning, and 50 to 65 percent alternated between the residual phase and a recurrence of an active phase. Other long-term studies have produced similar findings (Davidson & McGlashan, 1997). As one might expect, relapses tend to be triggered by stressful life events (Norman & Malla, 1993a, 1993b).

Another sad truth revealed by longitudinal studies is that schizophrenics tend to die about 10 years younger than other people (Jeste, Gladsjo, Lindamer, et al., 1996) and that their suicide rate is very high. Between 20 and 42 percent of schizophrenic patients attempt suicide, and 10 to 15 percent succeed. Suicide is more likely for those who are more suspicious and delusional and, not surprisingly, for those who are more aware that they are ill (Amador, Friedman, Kasapis, et al., 1996; Fenton, McGlashan, Victor, et al., 1997).

The Subtypes of Schizophrenia

Ever since the days of Kraepelin and Eugen Bleuler, schizophrenia has been divided into subtypes, based on behavior. Patients were described not merely as schizophrenic but as catatonic schizophrenics, paranoid schizophrenics, and so forth. These subtypes are often problematic for the diagnostician. If, upon intake, a schizophrenic patient claims that he is a famous person pursued by enemies, he will probably be classified as paranoid schizophrenic. But if two weeks later he no longer speaks of enemies but will not move from his chair, should he be reclassified as a catatonic schizophrenic?

Despite the difficulties, subtype diagnoses may ultimately be of value. As we saw in Chapter 3, the process of sorting patients into restrictive diagnostic groups is essential to research. Though at present we do not know whether different patterns of schizophrenic behavior issue from different causes and call for different treatments, we can never find out unless we study groups of patients with similar behavior patterns. And this means sorting them into subtypes.

DSM-IV lists five subtypes. One of these, the "undifferentiated" type, is a miscellaneous category, used for patients who do not fit into any of the other categories or who fit into more than one. Such patients are common. Another category, the "residual" type, is for patients who have passed beyond the active phase. This leaves three categories that actually describe active-phase symptomatology: disorganized, catatonic, and paranoid schizophrenia.

Disorganized Schizophrenia   Of all the varieties of the psychologically disturbed, the disorganized schizophrenic is the one who best fits the popular stereotype of a "crazy" person. Three symptoms are especially characteristic of **disorganized schizophrenia.** First is a pronounced incoherence of speech; it is the disorganized schizophrenic who is most likely to produce neologisms, clang associations, and word salad. Second is mood disturbance. Some disorganized schizophrenics have flat affect; others act silly—giggle, make faces, and so on. The third key symptom is disorganized behavior, or lack of goal orientation—for example, a refusal to bathe or dress. Though these three signs may define the subtype, most disorganized schizophrenics run the gamut of schizophrenic symptomatology. Their motor behavior is strikingly odd. They may also experience hallucinations and delusions, though these are often confused and fragmen-

(Top) This painting was done by a young schizophrenic man in the early stages of the disorder. The sad, partially faceless woman alone in the desert suggests loss of identity and loss of meaning. (Bottom) Another schizophrenic patient made this painting of the earth being split apart by lightning—perhaps the person's effort to picture his own, internal disintegration.

tary, unlike the more coherent imaginings of the paranoid schizophrenic. Furthermore, most disorganized schizophrenics are severely withdrawn, utterly caught up in their own private worlds, and at times almost impervious to whatever is happening around them.

The onset of disorganized schizophrenia is usually gradual and tends to occur at a relatively early age (Fenton & McGlashan, 1991). The distinguishing mark of the onset—withdrawal into a realm of bizarre and childlike fantasies—is illustrated in the following case of a professional golfer:

John joined the Army [when he was in his teens]. In boot camp he would sit for hours in a garage where jeeps and other motor vehicles were kept and talk to the cars. He would "dance" and act out animated soliloquies. He was sent to the base psychiatrist who tested his urine for illicit substances. His drug tests were all negative and John was given a discharge "for the convenience of the government." . . .

John returned to the town where his parents had now retired. He got a job at the local golf course. Within months of his employment there, he came to believe that an older woman who ran a concessions stand was "spying" on him and was telling co-workers that John was having sex with an underage high school girl working at the pro shop for the summer. . . . He was noted by co-workers and golfers alike to be "strange," to smile and grimace inappropriately, and occasionally to make no sense when he spoke. A greens keeper made the comment that he always avoided John because "he just goes on and on, and I don't know what he is talking about; he tells jokes that aren't funny, but he nearly breaks a rib laughing. I just have to get away from the guy."

John came to the attention of the authorities when he threatened to hit the older woman with a golf club. [He was hospitalized and later released.] . . .

Three years later, the pope came to San Francisco and John decided that he wanted an audience with him. Church officials told John that this was not possible. . . . [He then decided that] the pope was the Antichrist. John believed that he should warn the faithful that the pope was an impostor, and he concocted a scheme of lying down in front of the pontiff's motorcade and stopping traffic.

The police arrested John before he could get within three-hundred yards of the pope's motorcade. They transferred him to a psychiatric facility. . . .

During this second hospitalization, John had a marked thought disorder with some loose associations, some neologisms, and tangential phraseology: "The Pope is the Vicar of Christ, and since Vicary Street is near the highway, I felt that roads had something to do with it . . . you know, the macadam as in Adam and the Sistine Chapel and that picture of the trans-fingeration," he said. (Booth, 1995, pp. 166–169)

Catatonic Schizophrenia Once a common disorder but now quite rare (Morrison, 1991), **catatonic schizophrenia** has as its distinguishing feature a marked disturbance in motor behavior. Sometimes this disturbance takes the form of **catatonic stupor,** or complete immobility, usually accompanied by *mutism,* the cessation of speech; the patient may remain in this condition for weeks. Some catatonics assume extremely bizarre postures during their stupors. They may also show *waxy flexibility,* a condition in which their limbs, like those of a rubber doll, can be "arranged" by another person and remain in whatever position they are placed. However, catatonia is not limited to decreases in motor activity. Many catatonics alternate between periods of immobility and periods of frenzied motor activity, which may include violent behavior. In either form, catatonic schizophrenia

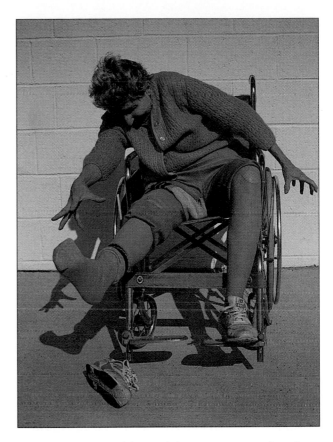

The woman pictured here exhibits catatonic rigidity, the stiff and bizarre postures assumed by patients with catatonic schizophrenia.

often involves medical emergencies. When excited, patients may injure themselves or others; when stuporous, they must be prevented from starving.

Though catatonic immobility suggests passivity, it may in fact be quite "active." To hold for hours the bizarre postures that catatonics often assume requires an extraordinary expenditure of energy. Furthermore, while some patients assume waxy flexibility, others strenuously resist any effort on the part of others to move their limbs—a feature known as *catatonic rigidity.* Similarly, though catatonia seems to suggest extreme withdrawal, it is clear that many patients are well aware of what is going on around them. Some show **echolalia,** parroting what is said by others; some show *echopraxia,* imitating the movements of others. Finally, in many patients one sees what is called *catatonic negativism.* That is, they not only refuse to do what is requested of them but consistently do just the opposite, indicating that they understand very well the nature of the requests.

The following case of a 22-year-old mathematics student illustrates the odd motor behavior of catatonic patients, together with their potential for violence:

Anna was brought to the psychiatric hospital by the police for an emergency admission after she had attacked a child. She had walked up to a 9-year-old girl at a bus stop and tried to strangle her. Some passersby fortunately intervened, restraining Anna, and called the police. At first she fought violently and tried to get at the child, but then suddenly she became motionless and rigid as a statue, with one arm stretched out toward the child and a wild stare on her face. When the police arrived, it was difficult to get her into the car, because she would not move and resisted attempts to move her. She almost had to be carried to the police car and forced into it. . . .

When she was brought to the ward, she remained standing just inside the entrance and resisted invitations to go further. She refused to have anything to eat and would not go to the examination room. She remained standing rigid, with her right arm stretched out in front of her, staring at her hand. She did not answer questions or respond in any way to the ward assistants. After several hours she finally had to be taken to her room and put in bed with the use of mild force. She lay in bed in the position where she had been placed, staring at the ceiling. . . . The next morning Anna was found standing rigid again, this time behind the door. She had urinated on the floor in the corner of the room. . . .

Anna's sister turned up and informed the physician that the family had been concerned about Anna for some time. For the last 2–3 months she had seemed reclusive and odd, with recurrent episodes of muteness and staring that lasted for several minutes. Several times she made peculiar statements that "children are trying to destroy mathematics" or "rational figures have a hard time." She stopped going to the university and stayed in her room, leaving it only for a walk in the evening. (Üstün, Bertelsen, Dilling, et al., 1996)

Paranoid Schizophrenia   The defining characteristics of paranoid schizophrenia are delusions and/or hallucinations of a relatively consistent nature, often related to the themes of persecution and grandeur. The delusions can range from a jumble of vague suspicions to an exquisitely worked-out system of imagined conspiracies. In either case, they are often accompanied by hallucinations—especially auditory hallucinations—supporting the delusional belief. When, in the classic case, the theme is persecution, it is often combined with the theme of grandeur.

Paranoid schizophrenia is far more common than either the disorganized or the catatonic type. A 1974 survey of more than 8,000 hospitalized schizophrenics found that close to half were diagnosed as paranoid (Guggenheim & Babigian, 1974). Paranoid schizophrenics are also, in the main, more "normal" than other schizophrenics. They perform well on cognitive tests (Strauss, 1993). They have better records of premorbid adjustment, are more likely to be married, have a later onset, and show better long-term

outcomes than do other kinds of schizophrenics (Fenton & McGlashan, 1991; Kendler, McGuire, Gruenberg, et al., 1994; Nicholson & Neufeld, 1993).

Though the active phase of paranoid schizophrenia usually does not appear until after age 25, it is typically preceded by years of fear and suspicion, leading to tense and fragile interpersonal relationships. The onset and development of paranoid schizophrenia are illustrated in the following case of a man hospitalized at the age of 36. He had begun expressing paranoid ideas about 10 years earlier:

Most of the content related to his girlfriend, beginning with plausible claims that she was being unfaithful to him. The paranoid ideation soon evolved to include totally unfounded accusations of her having a sexual relationship with one of his brothers. Within a few weeks, the allegations had progressed to include more bizarre claims, such as the belief that his girlfriend was having sex with dogs and farm animals and that she had been setting fires all over town. . . .

Over the next few years, . . . he would seclude himself in his room for days at a time, with multiple locks on his bedroom door, and his parents reported that he would frequently talk aloud in his room. He slept with a gun under his bed and a knife by his side. Such periods would often last several weeks at a time. These would be intermixed with periods of relative calm. . . .

[When he was finally hospitalized, he explained what he was afraid of.] He was convinced that his enemies had been coming into his house at night and raping him while he slept. He said that this had been occurring off and on over the previous several months and probably longer and that this was the reason for the elaborate locks on his bedroom door and the weapons under his bed. While in the hospital, he slept more during the day than at night, which he admitted was because of his ongoing concerns about being sexually assaulted while sleeping at night. Although he continued to deny frank hallucinations, he ultimately described having "dog ears" and explained that this enabled him to hear conversations that were going on far in the distance. He also admitted to concerns that his audio equipment had been tampered with in such a way that "the wrong lyrics come out of the music." Finally, he had entertained the idea that some sort of an electrical device had been placed in his body that allowed his enemies to hear everything he said, but he was not convinced this was true. (Flaum & Schultz, 1996, pp. 812–813)

The Dimensions of Schizophrenia

The subtypes we have just discussed are a classic way of looking at schizophrenia, but research has yet to prove that they are valid groupings—that is, that the schizophrenias they delineate are, in fact, different disorders, springing from different causes, requiring different treatments, and so forth. Accordingly, researchers have looked for other ways in which to organize information about schizophrenia. Today, discussions of this disorder are generally framed not according to subtypes but in terms of "dimensions." Like spatial dimensions (width, length), *dimensions* of schizophrenia are measures of continuous variation and are thus less exclusive than subtypes. With dimensions, patients are never "in" or "out"; they fall somewhere on the dimension. In practice, however, dimensions, too, tend to sort patients into groups. It is possible that their advantage over subtypes is simply that the groups they yield have so far proved more meaningful. The three that have received the most attention are the process-reactive dimension, the positive-negative symptoms dimension, and the paranoid-nonparanoid dimension.

Process-Reactive, or Good-Poor Premorbid As we noted, there is considerable variation in the onset of schizophrenia. Some patients go through an extended prodromal phase. Others go from normal functioning to full-blown psychosis almost overnight. This dimension of variation has traditionally been known as the process-reactive dimension. The cases in which onset is gradual are called *process schizophrenia.* Those in which onset is sudden and apparently precipitated by a traumatic event are called *reactive schizophrenia.*

This dimension has a long history, beginning with Kraepelin and Eugen Bleuler. These two theorists believed that the onset of the psychoses was a clue to their cause. The biogenic psychoses, because they were the result of an abnormal physiological *process,* would presumably have a gradual onset. By contrast, the psychogenic psychoses, because they were *reactions* to traumatic experiences, would appear suddenly, hence the terms *process* and *reactive.* Today, many researchers view the process-reactive dimension more as a continuum than as a dichotomy. Indeed, some now prefer to speak not of a process-reactive dimension but of a **good-poor premorbid dimension**—that is, in terms of how well the patient was functioning before the onset of the active phase. Actually, the good-poor premorbid dimension is basically the same as the process-reactive dimension, minus the causal implications. To describe onset is to describe premorbid adjustment, and vice versa.

Although there is some disagreement over the usefulness of the process-reactive dimension, there is general agreement as to what the terms describe. The process (or poor-premorbid) case typically involves a long history of inadequate social, sexual, and occupational adjustment. Process schizophrenics typically did not belong to a group of friends in school, did not date regularly during adolescence, did not continue their education after high school, never held a job for longer than two years, and never married (Haas & Sweeney, 1992; Kaplan & Sadock, 1991). Furthermore, there appears to have been no precipitating event—no sudden stressor such as a divorce or a job change—immediately preceding the active phase. Rather, the history usually reveals a gradual eclipse of thoughts, interests, emotions, and activities, until the person becomes so withdrawn that he or she is hospitalized.

In contrast, histories of reactive (or good-premorbid) schizophrenics are apparently normal. The patient fit in at home and at school, had friends, dated, and got along well in general. The onset of the schizophrenic symptoms usually occurs after a clearly precipitating event and is sudden and spectacular, often involving hallucinations and delusions. Such patients also tend to show extreme panic and confusion, for they are as horrified as everyone else over what has happened to them.

Premorbid adjustment has been useful in predicting which patients will recover and which will not (American Psychiatric Association, 1997). Poor-premorbid schizophrenics are more likely to have long hospitalizations and, when discharged, to require rehospitalization—than are good-premorbid patients.

Positive-Negative Symptoms Of all the dimensions of schizophrenia, the one that has attracted the most research attention in recent years—and, therefore, the one that will be most important in our discussion of the possible causes of schizophrenia—is the **positive-negative symptoms dimension. Positive symptoms,** characterized by the presence of something that is normally absent, include hallucinations, delusions, bizarre or disorganized behavior, and positive thought disorder such as incoherence. **Negative symptoms,** characterized by the absence of something that is normally present, include poverty of speech, flat affect, withdrawal, apathy, and attentional impairment (Andreasen, Arndt, Alliger, et al., 1995). The positive-negative symptoms dimension seems to parallel the good-poor premorbid dimension. Patients with negative symptoms are more likely to have had poor premorbid adjustment. And, like poor-premorbid patients, they tend to have an earlier onset (Castle & Murray, 1993) and a worse prognosis (Fenton & McGlashan, 1994). Indeed, they are the ones most likely to have an "unremitting course"—that is, never to recover. Positive and negative symptoms also seem to be associated with different kinds of cognitive problems. Patients with negative symptoms do worse on tests involving the processing of visual stimuli. Patients with positive symptoms do worse on tests that require the

TABLE 13.1	Summary of Differences Between Positive-Symptom (Type I) and Negative-Symptom (Type II) Schizophrenia	
	Positive (Type I) Schizophrenia	**Negative (Type II) Schizophrenia**
Symptoms	Delusions Hallucinations Incoherence Bizarre behavior	Poverty of speech Flat affect Social withdrawal Apathy
Premorbid adjustment	Good	Poor
Onset	Tends to be later	Tends to be earlier
Prognosis	Relatively good	Poor
Structural brain abnormalities	Absent	May be present
Drug response	Good	Poor
Gender distribution	More likely to be women	More likely to be men

processing of auditory stimuli, especially language (Buchanan, Strauss, Breier, et al., 1997).

These findings have led to increased speculation that there may be two biologically distinct types of schizophrenia, of which the one with negative symptoms is more like Kraepelin's original dementia praecox. Some researchers (Crow, 1989; Lenzenweger, Dworkin, & Wethington, 1989) have distinguished two such types. (See Table 13.1.) **Type I schizophrenia** is characterized by positive symptoms and tends to respond to medication. **Type II schizophrenia** is characterized by negative symptoms (and associated with structural abnormalities in the brain) and according to some research does not respond as well to typical antipsychotic medication (Earnst & Kring, 1997). As we will see, the two types also seem to fit differently into the "dopamine hypothesis," the leading biochemical theory of schizophrenia.

However, these two categories are not as tidy as they sound. Often, a typical "Type I" characteristic will turn up in an otherwise "Type II" patient. Some schizophrenics show positive and negative symptoms at the same time. Others initially show negative symptoms and then develop positive symptoms, or the reverse. In the latter case, the negative symptoms may be secondary. That is, they may develop as a *response* to the primary symptoms: under the pressure of frightening hallucinations (positive symptom), the patient withdraws socially, speaks little, and assumes a flat affect (negative symptoms). But it is very hard to determine whether negative symptoms are primary or secondary. To add to the complexity, some researchers now feel that there may be another important dimension, a "disorganized-nondisorganized" dimension, on which patients do not necessarily line up neatly into Type I and Type II (Arndt, Andreasen, Flaum, et al., 1995; Toomey, Kremen, Simpson, et al., 1997).

Paranoid-Nonparanoid   On the **paranoid-nonparanoid dimension**, the criterion of classification is the presence (paranoid) or absence (nonparanoid) of delusions of persecution and/or grandeur. Some studies have found the paranoid-nonparanoid dimension to be related to the process-reactive dimension (Fenton & McGlashan, 1991). As we saw, paranoid schizophrenics tend to have better premorbid adjustment, later onset, and better outcomes. They also resemble reactive schizophrenics in being more intact intellectually. Thus, the paranoid-nonparanoid dimensions, like the process-reactive, the good-poor premorbid, and the positive-negative symptoms, has had prognostic value and may aid in the development of theories as to the causes of schizophrenia.

Groups at Risk for Schizophrenia

Although schizophrenia occurs in all cultures, symptoms differ depending on the culture. While paranoid schizophrenics in industrial societies may fear the police, their African counterparts are more likely to think they are pursued by a sorcerer (Takeshita, 1997). Also, prognosis differs among cultures, with schizophrenic patients faring better in less-industrialized societies (Jablensky, Sartorius, Ernberg, et al., 1992). The emphasis on competition and self-reliance in industrial societies makes them a hard place for a recovering schizophrenic. Developing countries, with their stable social structures and their emphasis on family and interdependence, seem to offer a better halfway house (Takeshita, 1997).

Within industrialized societies, there are certain known risk factors. Schizophrenia is more likely to be found in people of lower IQ and in people who are unemployed and unmarried; it is also more likely to be diagnosed in city-dwellers (American Psychiatric

Association, 1997; Kendler, Gallagher, Abelson, et al., 1996). In the United States, African Americans have a higher rate of schizophrenia than whites, though it is not known whether this is due to actual differences or to diagnostic bias (Strakowski, Flaum, Amador, et al., 1996).

Age, too, is involved in risk. Schizophrenia normally strikes in adolescence or early adulthood, and the timing of onset is related to outcome. Early-onset cases, particularly those beginning in adolescence, have a worse prognosis (Eaton, Mortensen, Herman, et al., 1992). For men, the median age of onset is mid-twenties; for women, late twenties (Haas & Sweeney, 1992). Some researchers believe that the female sex hormone, estrogen, delays onset in women (Kulkarni, 1997).

Gender affects more than onset; it also determines vulnerability. Men are one and a half times more likely than women to develop schizophrenia (Iacono & Beiser, 1992a, 1992b). The genders also express the disorder differently (Symanski, 1996). Male schizophrenics are more likely to be withdrawn and to exhibit negative symptoms; women are more likely to have affective and positive symptoms (Castle & Murray, 1993; Gur, Petty, Turetsky, et al., 1996). In addition, men tend to have poorer premorbid adjustment, poorer response to medication, and worse prognosis (Meltzer, Rabinowitz, Lee, et al., 1997). Finally, schizophrenic men are less likely than women to have a family history of schizophrenia (Goldstein, Faraone, Chen, et al., 1990) but are more likely to have had birth complications and to show brain abnormalities (Nopoulos, Flaum, & Andreason, 1997), and the brain abnormalities they show are different from those typically seen in schizophrenic women (Reite, Sheeder, Teale, et al., 1997). These findings suggest that men and women may be differentially at risk for different types of schizophrenia, with men more susceptible to process, poor-premorbid, Type II schizophrenia and women more susceptible to reactive, good premorbid, Type I schizophrenia.

Delusional Disorder

The Symptoms of Delusional Disorder

Sarah P., 15 years old, was taken to a therapist because she kept running away from home, but apart from her disappearances she seemed a well-adjusted teenager. The therapist, trying to forge a bond with Sarah's father, asked him about his work. He replied that he had recently left a job of 18 years because of conflict with the union leadership:

The conflict had been so severe, he reported, that union officials were still persecuting him. In fact,

he whispered, they had implanted a minute radio receiver in his head through which they transmitted all manner of disgusting messages to him. Specifically, these messages told him to sexually molest various women, including his daughter.

Mr. P. became increasingly agitated as he spoke. The union had surrounded him with agents that tempted him. For example, a secretary at work persistently leaned over the filing cabinet in a way that suggested he was supposed to rape her. He, however, was onto their game and had resisted all of their efforts to get him to engage in these despicable behaviors. They had targeted him years ago, but he had been strong enough to ignore their behavior and to continue to work until he was able to get a new job at the same rate of pay. After all, he had a family to support.

The therapist later discussed the father's delusions with the mother. She said that she knew all about them:

She had long since stopped trying to talk him out of them, since her experience had been that he had only gotten more agitated when they discussed it. It was better, she had discovered, to gently change the subject after sympathizing with how difficult the situation must be for him. She reported that he had never behaved inappropriately, had never missed work, had never even spoken about his odd ideas to anyone other than to herself as far as she knew.

The therapist, with the wife's help, tried to persuade the father to take some antipsychotic medication. He refused. However, since Sarah's running away was no doubt connected to her father's state of mind, an arrangement was made for her to move in with her mother's sister. (Adapted from Bernheim, 1997, pp. 132–134.)

Mr. P.'s major symptom, a system of delusions, is something that we have already discussed under the heading of paranoid schizophrenia. In paranoid schizophrenia, however, the delusional system is simply one item in a cluster of abnormalities, all of which may function independently of one another. In delusional disorder, on the other hand, the delusional system is the fundamental abnormality. Indeed, in some cases, the delusional system is the *only* abnormality; in all other respects, the person seems quite normal. Other patients may show some disturbances of mood, but only as a consequence of the delusional system. (For example, they may explode in anger at complete strangers, but only because they suspect those strangers of spying on them, flirting with their spouses, or whatever.) In other words, it is assumed that, if there were no delusions, there would be no abnormality. Furthermore, whatever other symptoms the person shows, they do not include the characteristic symptoms of schizophrenia, such as

Jane H., a schizophrenic patient with auditory hallucinations, painted this picture while in an art therapy program. Particularly striking are the rather sinister eyes of the central figure, together with the many hands surrounding him.

loosening of associations, incoherence, or thought broadcasting. Finally, in this disorder the delusions are generally less bizarre than those of the paranoid schizophrenic. As with Mr. P., the person may claim to be pursued by enemies, but not by enemies from outer space.

As for the content of the delusions, *DSM-IV* lists five categories. The classic type, just seen in the case of Mr. P., is the *persecutory type*, involving the belief that one is being threatened or maltreated by others. In the *grandiose type*, as the name indicates, the person believes that he or she is endowed with extraordinary power or knowledge. In the *jealous type*, the delusion is that one's sexual partner is being unfaithful. In the *erotomanic type*, the person believes that someone of high status—the president of the company or of the United States—is in love with him or her. Finally, the *somatic type* involves the false

conviction that one is suffering from a physical abnormality or disorder.

Groups at Risk for Delusional Disorder

Delusional disorder differs from schizophrenia in striking more women than men and in having a later onset, between ages 25 and 45 (Manschreck, 1992). It is also far less common. For schizophrenia, as we saw, the lifetime risk is 1 to 2 percent; for delusional disorder, it is 0.3 percent (Evans, Paulsen, Harris, et al., 1996). It is possible, of course, that many more cases exist. We have all probably encountered a few candidates for this diagnostic label: ignored geniuses, self-styled prophets, radio talk show callers who have a detailed scheme for solving the world's problems. Because such people tend to have relatively good contact with reality, apart from their isolated delusional systems, many of them remain within the community and never see a therapist. Those who present themselves for treatment often do so not of their own volition but at the insistence of others.

Problems in the Study of Schizophrenia

So far, we have described schizophrenia and related psychoses, but we have not touched upon the cause or treatment of schizophrenia. Those topics will occupy the remainder of this chapter. First, however, it must be pointed out that schizophrenia involves special problems for researchers. In no other area of research is there greater danger of having one's research confounded by a third variable. Most of the schizophrenics available for research purposes are (1) hospitalized and (2) taking antipsychotic drugs. Consequently, any interesting differences that turn up between these subjects and nonhospitalized, nonmedicated controls may well be a function not of schizophrenia but of the medication or of the overcrowding, poor diet, difficult sleeping conditions, lack of exercise, and lack of privacy that are routine conditions of hospitalization (Blanchard & Neale, 1992).

A graver problem is that researchers do not agree on what actually constitutes schizophrenia—what the primary pathology is. Consider the analogy of a leg fracture. The fracture produces pain, a bent leg, and a limp. But, of these three symptoms, only the first two are primary—direct results of the broken bone. The limp is a secondary symptom, a strategy that the person adopts in order to cope with the primary symptom of pain. Likewise, in schizophrenia, there is little doubt that, among the recognized symptoms of the disorder, some are primary and others merely reactions to the primary symptoms. But which is which? Is social withdrawal the primary pathology, as some theorists believe, or do schizophrenics withdraw simply because their thought disorders make it difficult for them to communicate with others? Are delusions a primary symptom, or are they, as suggested earlier, merely the schizophrenic's way of explaining the chaos of his or her thoughts? Answering these questions is crucial to research on schizophrenia. Until we know what the basic disorder is, we stand little chance of discovering its cause.

Another vexing problem for schizophrenia researchers is finding what are called **differential deficits**, deficits specific to the disorder in question (as opposed to other disorders) and presumably central to it. Because schizophrenia has many debilitating symptoms, schizophrenics have problems with many different kinds of tasks, but such problems do not necessarily tell us about schizophrenia in particular (Chapman & Chapman, 1973, 1978). For example, if a researcher were to give a group of schizophrenics a driving test, they would probably not do as well as controls, but that does not mean that bad driving is causally related to schizophrenia. In order to show a differential deficit in schizophrenia, research must be able to show that, on two carefully constructed tasks, differing only in subtle ways, schizophrenics perform poorly on one and not on the other. Such findings are often very hard to produce, but the question of which deficits represent the core of schizophrenia cannot really be addressed without them.

Schizophrenia: Theory and Therapy

No one in the field of schizophrenia research believes that the disorder stems from a single cause. Clearly, it has multiple sources, and one of them is already known. It is well established that genetic factors are partially, but not wholly, responsible for the development of schizophrenia. Consequently, most researchers have adopted a *diathesis-stress model* (Chapter 5), which states that schizophrenia is due to the combination of a genetically inherited *diathesis,* or predisposition, and environmental *stress*. The various perspectives use this model in accordance with their specialties, some focusing on the diathesis, others on the stress, but always keeping other factors in mind as well.

The Biological Perspective

One of the most exciting areas of abnormal psychology today is biological research in schizophrenia. For years, neuroscientists concentrated primarily on the schizophrenic diathesis: first establishing its existence and then trying to discover what it actually consists

of in biological terms. Today they are also investigating biological stressors that might activate that diathesis. A vast amount of work remains to be done, but the evidence accumulated so far has revolutionized our understanding of this disorder.

Genetic Studies   The idea that schizophrenia might be passed from parent to child goes back at least as far as the eighteenth century. By the late nineteenth century, when biogenic theories were popular, the genetic hypothesis was endorsed by Kraepelin, Eugen Bleuler, and many other experts on schizophrenia. But it was not until about 30 years ago that researchers were able to design studies sophisticated enough to test the hypothesis scientifically. The evidence produced by these studies is extremely persuasive. In the words of David Rosenthal (1970), one of the foremost authorities on the genetics of abnormal behavior, "The issue must now be considered closed. Genetic factors do contribute appreciably and beyond any reasonable doubt to the development of schizophrenic illness" (pp. 131–132). The studies leading up to this conclusion are family, twin, and adoptive studies.

Family Studies   The earliest studies of the genetics of schizophrenia were family studies. Their findings, together with those of more recent research, clearly indicate that, the more closely one is related to a schizophrenic, the more likely one is to develop schizophrenia. Figure 13.1 shows the data published by Gottesman in 1991. As may be seen from this graph, children of 1 schizophrenic parent have a 13 percent chance, and children of 2 schizophrenic parents ("offspring of dual matings") have a 46 percent chance of becoming schizophrenic, as compared with a prevalence of 1 to 2 percent in the general population—a striking differential. According to a recent review of family studies, a person with a schizophrenic first-degree relative is almost 10 times likelier to develop schizophrenia than a person with no schizophrenia in the immediate family (Kendler & Diehl, 1993).

However, as we have seen in previous chapters, any psychological similarity among family members may be due to shared environment rather than shared genes. For more precision in controlling the environmental factor, we must turn to twin and adoption studies.

Twin Studies   In twin studies conducted since 1960, the average concordance rate for schizophrenia in MZ twins is approximately 46 percent, three times greater than the 14 percent average concordance rate for DZ twins (Gottesman, 1996). As more recent studies have improved in research methodology, the concordance rates for both MZ and DZ twins have dropped, but

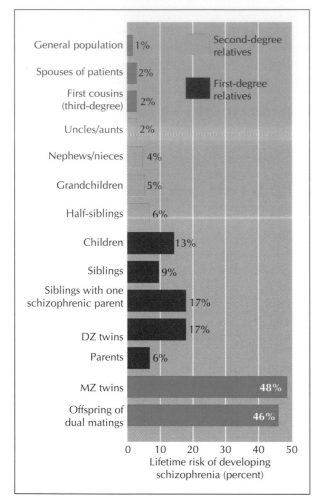

FIGURE 13.1   Lifetime risk of developing schizophrenia for the relatives of people with schizophrenia. The kinds of relatives are listed at the left. The children of a schizophrenic person have a 13 percent risk; the siblings of a schizophrenic, a 9 percent risk; and so on. These figures are averages of statistics compiled by family and twin studies in Europe between 1920 and 1987. (Gottesman, 1991)

proportionately. The MZ-DZ concordance ratios still lie between 3 to 1 and 5 to 1. Moreover, the MZ-DZ concordance difference tends to be greater when the index twin has more severe symptoms (Gottesman, 1991). It also varies with the nature of the index twin's symptoms. When the index twin has prominent negative symptoms, the MZ-DZ concordance difference is greater than when the index twin has prominent positive symptoms (Dworkin & Lenzenweger, 1984). This finding supports the validity of the Type I–Type II distinction and the belief that Type II has a stronger genetic component.

Such data must be considered strong evidence for the genetic hypothesis. However, as we saw, twin studies, too, are subject to objections. To begin with, the researcher is dealing with a small sample. (There are not that many schizophrenic MZ twins in the world.) Second, as we saw, some researchers feel that MZ twins share not only a more similar genotype but also a more similar environment than DZ twins, in that the MZ twins are always the same sex, tend to be dressed alike, and so forth. Hence, it is possible that here, too, the differential may be due to environment as well as genes.

Indeed, even if MZ twins are separated at birth and reared apart, they still share the same *intrauterine* environment. Given the recent evidence that some kind of prenatal damage—injury, exposure to a virus—may contribute to schizophrenia, the high concordance rates for MZ twins may be due to a shared intrauterine environment as well as to shared genes. One study found that the concordance rates for the MZ twins who shared the same placenta was almost double the concordance rate for the MZ twins who had separate placentas (Davis & Phelps, 1995). That is a striking finding, and good evidence that an intrauterine factor is involved in schizophrenia.

In an effort to distinguish between genes and environment, several researchers have studied the offspring of MZ twins who are discordant for schizophrenia (Gottesman & Bertelsen, 1989; Kringlen & Cramer, 1989). The logic of these studies has to do with the fact that, because MZ twins are genetically identical, they must transmit to their children the same genetic risk for schizophrenia, regardless of whether they themselves are schizophrenic. Thus, all the cousins have the same genetic risk. They do not all grow up under the same conditions, however. The children of the schizophrenic twin have the experience of being raised by a schizophrenic parent; the children of the other twin do not. Therefore, if both twins' children develop schizophrenia at approximately the same rate, this is very strong evidence for genetic transmission.

That is what these studies have found. In one study (Gottesman & Bertelsen, 1989), the risk for schizophrenia and schizophrenic-like disorders in the children of the schizophrenic twin was 16.8 percent; in the children of the nonschizophrenic twin, it was 17.4 percent. As might be expected, the differential was far greater in the children of the discordant DZ twins, who had only half their genes in common. Using the same research design, the researchers found that the children of the schizophrenic DZ twins were at a 17.4 percent risk; the children of their nonschizophrenic co-twins were at a 2.1 percent risk.

Again, this is good evidence for genetic transmission, and, again, there is a problem with it: the samples were very small. As noted, schizophrenic MZ

These quadruplets, the Genain sisters, were studied intensively for genetic causes of schizophrenia. All four had the disorder, with a wide range of severity.

twins are rare. But these twin studies are backed up by another kind of research with far larger samples: adoption studies.

Adoption Studies   As we have seen, the subjects of adoption studies are children who were adopted away from their biological families in infancy and, thus, have the genetic endowment of one family and the environmental history of another. If such a study could show that children who were born to schizophrenic mothers but were adopted in infancy by psychologically normal families still developed schizophrenia at approximately the same rate as the children who were born of one schizophrenic parent and were not adopted away, then again this would be very strong evidence for the genetic hypothesis.

Such studies have been done, and such were the findings. In a pioneering study, Heston (1966) located 47 adoptees who had been born to hospitalized schizophrenic mothers. He also gathered a matched control group of 50 adoptees whose mothers were not schizophrenic. From a large variety of sources—mostly firsthand interviews—information was gathered on all these subjects. A file was then compiled on each subject, all identifying information was removed, and diagnoses were made by several independent psychiatrists. The results were that schizophrenia was found only in the children of schizophrenic mothers. The rate for schizophrenia among this group was 16.6 percent, very close to the 13 percent figure for children who were born of a schizophrenic parent and not adopted away.

Another study that has produced immensely influential findings was begun in 1963 in Denmark by David Rosenthal and his colleagues (Rosenthal, Wender, Kety, et al., 1968). Through various central registries that have been maintained by the Danish government for about 50 years, the investigators identified 5,500 adoptees and 10,000 of their 11,000 biological parents. Then they identified all of the biological parents, called the *index parents*, who had at some time been admitted to a psychiatric hospital with a diagnosis of either schizophrenia or affective psychosis. The 76 adopted-away children of these parents *(index children)* were then matched with a control group of adopted children whose biological parents had no history of psychiatric hospitalization. Eventually, 19 percent of the index children versus 10 percent of the control children were diagnosed as having definite or possible schizophrenia (Gottesman & Shields, 1982). Perhaps of greater interest is the finding that 28 percent of the index children, compared with 10 percent of the control children, showed schizophrenic characteristics (Lowing, Mirsky, & Pereira, 1983).

Using the same Danish records, the same investigators (Kety, 1988; Kety, Rosenthal, Wender, et al., 1968, 1975) did another study with a different design. In the same group of 5,500 adoptees from Copenhagen, 33 were identified as having psychiatric histories that warranted a diagnosis of schizophrenia. A matched control group of nonschizophrenic adoptees was selected from the same records. Then 463 biological and adoptive parents, siblings, and half-siblings were identified for both the index and control groups, and these relatives were interviewed to determine whether they had ever suffered from schizophrenia. As it turned out, the rate of schizophrenia in the biological relatives of the index cases was about double (21.4 percent) that in the biological relatives of the control cases (10.9 percent), whereas the rates of schizophrenia in the adoptive relatives of the index and control cases were about the same (5.4 versus 7.7 percent). Thus, adopted children who later become schizophrenic are much more likely to have biological, rather than adoptive, relatives with schizophrenia. This finding, since confirmed (Kety, Wender, Jacobsen, et al., 1994), is persuasive evidence that there is a genetic component to schizophrenia.

Mode of Transmission   If there is a genetic component, where does the genetic abnormality lie? One viewpoint is that one or a few major genes are responsible for transmitting the risk, and some initial studies did succeed in linking schizophrenia to specific genes. But later studies have failed to support such connections (Kendler & Diehl, 1993). Consequently, many researchers now suspect that schizophrenia is caused not by one gene but by a variety of genetic subtypes and that what they produce is not one disorder but a range of similar disorders that, for want of evidence, are grouped into a single category (Kendler & Walsh, 1995). Researchers are now trying to identify "genetic markers," or simpler related traits, for these subtypes. (See the box on page 391.)

Another view is that schizophrenia is the product not just of many genes but of their combination with environmental factors. Genetic and environmental disadvantages combine until a certain threshold is reached. Beyond that threshold, the person develops schizophrenia (Gottesman, 1996). There is evidence for this view. For example, an adoption study that is still in progress (Tienari, Wynne, Moring, et al., 1994; Wahlberg, Wynne, Oja, et al., 1997) has found that its adoptees' risk for schizophrenia correlates not only with the psychiatric history of their biological parents but also with the psychological functioning of their *adoptive* families. Not surprisingly, the latter correlation is strongest when the adoptee is the child of a schizophrenic mother and therefore genetically at risk. Thus, this study, while supporting the role of genes, connects it back to the diathesis-stress model.

Genetic High-Risk Studies   A vast number of studies have been conducted with children who have been born to schizophrenic parents and who have shown at least some symptoms of schizophrenia. These studies have revealed a wealth of information, but they are almost always contaminated by methodological problems. If, for example, you wanted to identify significant events in the background of a child who is now showing schizophrenic symptoms, your theoretical notions might well bias your attention toward certain details of the child's history. Furthermore, if you interview people who have known the child—parents, grandparents, and so forth—their recollection will be influenced by what they know of the child's present condition. Retrospective information is always questionable.

The solution would be to conduct a *prospective* study—a longitudinal study (Chapter 3)—testing and interviewing a large, random sample of children at regular intervals over a period of time. Then, when some of these children developed schizophrenia, you would already have on file a reliable record of their physiological, psychological, and social histories and could begin searching for correlations. There is one problem with such a project, however. As we have seen, only 1 to 2 percent of the general population develops schizophrenia. Hence, in order to end up with a reliable sample of schizophrenics, you would have to include thousands of children in your study, making it prohibitively expensive and time-consuming.

In the early 1960s, Mednick and Schulsinger made a breakthrough in schizophrenia research by devising a longitudinal project that would resolve most of the problems just outlined (Mednick, 1970). Recognizing the impossibility of studying a random sample of normal children, the investigators turned to the **genetic high-risk design** (Chapter 3). That is, they chose as their sample 200 children who, by virtue of being born of schizophrenic mothers, were already genetically vulnerable to schizophrenia. As we have seen, such children stand about a 13 percent chance of developing the disorder. Thus, the investigators could predict that the number of eventual schizophrenics in their high-risk group would be large enough to permit meaningful comparisons with low-risk control children—children not born of schizophrenic mothers.

Mednick (1971) lists the following advantages of this research design over that of previous studies:

1. The children have not yet experienced the confounding effects of the schizophrenic life, such as hospitalization and drugs.

2. No one—teacher, relative, child, or researcher—knows who will become schizophrenic, which eliminates much bias from testing and diagnosis.

3. The information is current; the researchers do not have to depend on anyone's recollection.

4. There are two built-in groups of controls for the children who become ill: the high-risk subjects who stay well and the low-risk subjects. (p. 80)

By 1989, the children in the project had reached a mean age of 42 and were therefore past the major risk period for the onset of schizophrenia. (Remember that onset tends to occur in adolescence or early adulthood.) In the high-risk group, 16 percent had developed schizophrenia—approximately the expected figure—and another 26.5 percent had

Eye Tracking as a Marker for Schizophrenia

For researchers trying to locate the genetic bases of schizophrenia, a major problem is that the symptoms of this disorder are all complex behaviors, controlled by many genes, not to mention environmental influence. Social withdrawal, attention problems, odd perceptions—these experiences are quite removed from the protein-coding functions of any single gene. To study the genetics of schizophrenia via family tendencies toward such symptoms is, in the words of one researcher, "like studying the genetics of color blindness through familial tendencies to run traffic lights" (Cromwell, 1993).

A more profitable approach is to try to find in the schizophrenic population an unusual trait that may have a simpler and more direct link with genes. Such a trait, called a *genetic marker*, may be much less disabling than the main symptoms of schizophrenia—indeed, it may be utterly benign—but it could lead researchers to the genes that produce the disabling symptoms.

One of the hypothesized genetic markers for schizophrenia is an abnormality in what is called *smooth-pursuit eye tracking*. Most people can follow a moving object with their eyes in a smooth, continuous line while keeping their heads still. (Try this. Move your finger like a pendulum and track it with your eyes while keeping your head in a fixed position.) Many schizophrenics, however, cannot do this. Their eyes travel not in a smooth line but in a saccadic, or jerking, pattern (Levy, Holtzman, Matthysse, et al., 1993)—a characteristic that is probably related to a specific neurological abnormality.

Schizophrenics with deviant eye tracking have other things in common as well. Compared with schizophrenics who show normal eye tracking, they are more likely to have negative symptoms—flat affect, poverty of speech, anhedonia. They do not perform as well on tasks controlled by the frontal lobes of the brain (Clementz, McDowell, & Zisook, 1994; Ross, Thaker, Buchanan, et al., 1996). They are more likely to have relatives with poor eye tracking, and those relatives tend to show schizophrenic-like traits, such as odd social behav-ior (Keefe, Silverman, Mohs, et al., 1997). Finally, schizophrenics with poor eye tracking are less likely to recover (Katsanis, Iacono, & Beiser, 1996).

Interestingly, people with schizotypal personality disorder (Chapter 10) are also unusually prone to deviant eye tracking, as are their relatives (Siever, Friedman, Moskowitz, et al., 1994). This is an important finding. As we will see, children who have a genetic risk for schizophrenia but do not develop the disorder often show schizotypal personality disorder.

What all this evidence suggests is that there is a specific subgroup of schizophrenics with a similar genetic abnormality, or pattern of abnormalities. It seems likely that the defect involves one major gene, a recessive gene, together with a number of less potent genes that can aggravate or mitigate the effect of the major gene (Iacono & Grove, 1993). Researchers are trying to locate a genetic marker for schizophrenics with normal eye tracking.

---

developed a *schizophrenic-spectrum* disorder—that is, a disorder related to schizophrenia. (In most cases, it was schizotypal personality disorder—see Chapter 10.) In the low-risk group, by contrast, only 2 percent had developed schizophrenia, and only 6 percent had developed a schizophrenic-spectrum disorder (Parnas, Cannon, Jacobsen, et al., 1993). The researchers (e.g., Olin & Mednick, 1996) list the factors that separate the high-risk children who developed schizophrenia from the high-risk and low-risk children who remained normal:

1. *Home life.* Their home lives were less stable, they had less satisfactory relationships with their parents, and their mothers were more likely to be irresponsible and antisocial.

2. *Early separation and institutionalization.* They were more likely to be separated from their mothers in the first year of life, and they spent more time in institutions.

3. *School problems and criminal behavior.* They had behavior problems. The males were more domineering, aggressive, and unmanageable in school, and they were more likely (as were their mothers) to have arrest records. The females were more likely to be lonely, passive, nervous, and sensitive to criticism.

4. *Attention problems.* They showed less ANS habituation to the environment—that is, they had more difficulty "tuning out" incidental stimuli.

5. *Birth complications.* They were more likely to have experienced complications before or during birth, and those who had such complications were more likely to show brain atrophy.

This project has inspired many similar projects, and there is now intense activity in genetic high-risk research. Between the Mednick group and other research teams, the findings in this list have been confirmed and extended (Erlenmeyer-Kimling, Adamo, Rock, et al., 1997; Mirsky, Kugelmass, Ingraham, et al., 1995). A number of researchers have found a history of attention problems—for example, an inability to screen out repetitive stimuli, such as the ticking of a clock—in high-risk children who eventually become schizophrenic (Hollister, Mednick, Brennan, et al., 1994). Neurological tests and studies of home movies suggest that these children may also show poor motor coordination and negative facial expressions (Walker, Grimes, Davis, et al., 1993). There is further evidence that these children's mothers are more disturbed—they developed schizophrenia at an earlier age, were more likely to have been hospitalized during the child's early years, were more prone to childbirth-related psychosis, and had more unstable relationships with men (Olin & Mednick, 1996). Finally, both the Mednick group and other groups have accumulated further evidence that prenatal or birth trauma, and particularly prenatal viral infection, is an important dividing line between high-risk children who develop schizophrenia and high-risk children who don't (Cannon, Mednick, Parnas, et al., 1993).

What do all these findings amount to? First, they support the role of genetic inheritance. Second, the high rate of attention problems constitutes further support for the idea that attention deficits are a primary symptom of schizophrenia. Finally, and perhaps most important, the results of the high-risk studies offer suggestions as to the kinds of stress that may be especially likely to convert a schizophrenic diathesis into schizophrenia. Disrupted home lives, disabled mothers, institutionalization—these misfortunes may be the product of the genetic defect, but they also produce massive stress. As for prenatal and birth trauma, this is now a major concern to researchers trying to pinpoint the environmental pressures that may tip the balance in high-risk children.

Behavioral High-Risk Studies   A second type of high-risk study uses the **behavioral high-risk design** (Chapter 3), which selects high-risk people not on the basis of genetics but on the basis of behavioral traits that are thought to be associated with the disorder in question. Using this design with schizophrenia has the advantage of yielding a more representative sample of future schizophrenics. (Only about 5 to 10 percent of schizophrenics have a schizophrenic parent. The genetic high-risk studies, thus, represent only a small portion of the schizophrenic population.) Loren and Jean Chapman and their colleagues have used the behavioral high-risk design to screen a large number of college students for those prone to perceptual abnormalities and magical thinking (Allen, Chapman, Chapman, et al., 1987; Chapman & Chapman, 1985). Their screening mechanism is a test called the Perceptual Aberration–Magical Ideation Scale, or Per-Mag Scale, in which the subjects respond true or false to such statements as "Sometimes I've had the feeling that I am united with an object near me" and

"The hand motions that strangers make seem to influence me at times." Perceptual abnormalities and magical thinking seem to have a genetic basis (Grove, Lebow, Clementz, et al., 1991) and often turn up in the early histories of people diagnosed with schizophrenia. The Chapmans' goal is to discover whether this link holds up prospectively as well as retrospectively, and their method is to track the psychiatric progress of people who score high on the Per-Mag Scale.

They have already produced interesting findings. In a 10-year follow-up, 10 of their 182 high-risk subjects had developed a full-blown psychosis, as compared with only 2 of their 153 low-risk subjects (Chapman, Chapman, Kwapil, et al., 1994). But, for firmer results, we must await later follow-ups. The Chapmans' subjects are now only about 35 years old and are, therefore, still at risk for a first-time psychotic episode.

One potential problem with the Per-Mag Scale is that the people it selects are at risk not just for schizophrenia but for other psychoses as well. Still, researchers have been able to relate the cognitive idiosyncrasies measured by the scale to a wide range of schizophrenic characteristics. Compared with low Per-Mag scorers, high Per-Mag scorers show more hallucinations, delusions, and social withdrawal, more thought disorder and communication deviance, and more attention problems (Coleman, Levy, Lenzenweger, et al., 1996; Lenzenweger, Cornblatt, & Putnick, 1991). They also have more first-degree relatives who have been treated for schizophrenia (Lenzenweger & Loranger, 1989a).

Brain Imaging Studies   As we saw in Chapter 4, the study of the brain has been revolutionized in recent years by the development of new brain imaging technologies: PET, which measures brain functioning, and CT and MRI, which measure brain structure. Through these methods, researchers have been able to identify certain characteristic abnormalities in the brains of schizophrenics. To begin with, CT and MRI scans have shown that in chronic schizophrenics brain size is smaller than normal (Ward, Friedman, Wise, et al., 1996). In addition, they have demonstrated that chronic schizophrenics' brain ventricles —the cavities containing the cerebrospinal fluid— tend to be enlarged (Raz, 1993) and that this particular sign is related to cognitive impairment (Golden, Moses, & Zelazowski, 1980), poor response to drug treatment (Luchins, Lewine, & Meltzer, 1983), poor premorbid adjustment (Weinberger, Cannon-Spoor, Potkin, et al., 1980), and more negative than positive symptoms (Gur, Mozley, Shtasel, et al., 1994). It is also more likely to be found in male schizophrenics

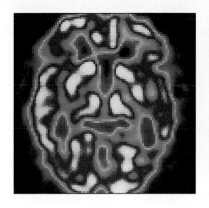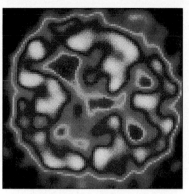

The PET scan at left shows brain activity in a normal person; the image at right shows the temporal lobe of a hallucinating schizophrenic. Normal brain metabolic activity produces a roughly symmetrical pattern in the yellow areas of the left and right cerebral hemispheres. In contrast, the visual areas (in yellow) of the schizophrenic are more active, possibly as a result of the hallucinations.

than in females (Flaum, Arndt, & Andreasen, 1990). These findings have been supported by postmortem analyses of schizophrenic brains (Heckers, 1997). As noted, it is chronic patients who tend to show enlarged ventricles. Therefore, it is possible that this abnormality is not so much a cause of schizophrenia as a result of the disorder—or a result of the cumulative effects of antipsychotic drugs. On the other hand, recent studies have reported similar abnormalities in first-episode schizophrenics (Lim, Tew, Kushner, et al., 1996).

If ventricles are enlarged, this suggests that the brain structures lying near those ventricles may also be affected. Brain imaging studies, together with postmortem studies, have found abnormalities in three specific systems: the frontal cortex, the temporal lobe–limbic structures, and the basal ganglia (Bogerts & Falkai, 1995; Heckers, 1997). Several PET scan studies have found that, when schizophrenics are given brain metabolism tests while they are performing cognitive tasks requiring the selective-attention and other problem-solving abilities of the frontal lobe, many of them show abnormally low frontal-lobe activity (Carter, Mintun, Nichols, et al., 1997). Furthermore, their frontal cortexes seem to have fewer synapses, making neural transmission more difficult (Glantz & Lewis, 1997). These patients tend to be those with negative symptoms. By contrast, patients with positive symptoms often show abnormalities in the temporal lobes or limbic structures (Marsh, Harris, Lim, et al., 1997). Thus, positive symptoms and negative symptoms seem to stem from different parts of the brain—further evidence for the Type I–Type II theory. But, as usual, the picture is not simple. Both positive-symptom and negative-symptom patients show abnormalities in the basal ganglia (Siegel, Buchsbaum, Bunney, et al., 1993). Furthermore, some patients show abnormalities in the *connections* among all three of the brain systems in question. This may explain why so many patients have both positive and negative symptoms (Buchsbaum, Someya, Teng, et al., 1996).

Prenatal Brain Injury The histories of schizophrenics show an abnormally high rate of birth complications (Geddes & Lawrie, 1995), and as we saw, high-risk children who develop schizophrenia are likelier than those who don't to have suffered a prenatal or birth complication. Could this be a stressor that, at least for some people, helps to convert the genetic diathesis into schizophrenia? Several lines of evidence point to such a conclusion.

One involves MRI and postmortem studies. The structure of the normal human brain is asymmetrical—a feature that develops in the second trimester (fourth through sixth months) of pregnancy. During that period, the frontal and temporal lobes become larger on the right than on the left, and other regions grow larger on the left than on the right. But in MRI and postmortem studies, many schizophrenic patients do not show this normal asymmetry, particularly in the language and association areas of the brain (Barta, Pearlson, Brill, et al., 1997). This suggests that their brains may have suffered trauma during the second trimester.

There are other hints of early prenatal brain damage. Damage to fetal brain tissue leads to a tissue-repair response called gliosis, but this response occurs only in the third trimester, not before. Thus, when the brain shows structural abnormalities *without* evidence of gliosis, such changes must have occurred before the third trimester. And that is what postmortem examinations of schizophrenic patients have shown: structural changes without gliosis (Bogerts, 1993). Other postmortem studies point specifically to the second trimester. During that period, neurons in the developing brain migrate from the walls of the ventricles to a temporary structure called the subplate in order, eventually, to form the association areas of the cerebral cortex. Those areas are responsible for the ability to make appropriate associations between things, a function that is radically disrupted in schizophrenia. And postmortem examination of schizophrenic brains has shown

Is Schizophrenia an Infectious Disease? The Viral Hypothesis

Is schizophrenia caused, in part, by infection? Certainly not in the way that the common cold is, or the virus would have been discovered long ago. Yet certain research findings raise the possibility that to some degree, in some people, schizophrenia is due to viral infection.

First put forth by Torrey and Peterson in 1976, the *viral hypothesis* states that, if infection is involved in schizophrenia, it cannot be the sole cause. It must interact with other causes, probably genetic abnormalities. Furthermore, such a virus could not be fast-acting, like the viruses that cause measles and chicken pox. It would have to be one of the "slow" viruses, which can remain latent within the body for years before any symptoms appear (Kirch, 1993). Slow viruses are known to be involved in other mental disorders, such as Jakob-Creutzfeldt disease, which involves progressive mental deterioration.

What is the evidence for the viral hypothesis? One well-established finding (Tam & Sewell, 1995; Torrey, Bowler, Rawlings, et al., 1993) is that people with schizophrenia are significantly more likely than other people—including people with "neurotic"-level disorders—to have been born in the winter. (See Figure 13.2.) Many viral infections show a peak incidence in the spring and winter months, so it is possible that the

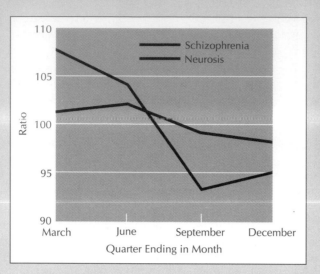

higher rate of schizophrenia in people who were winter babies is due to the fact that they were more likely to have been exposed to a virus in the late prenatal period (winter) or shortly after birth (spring).

Further support for the viral hypothesis comes from research on the relationship between schizophrenia and epidemics. One large-scale study followed up people who were exposed prenatally to the influenza epidemic that swept Helsinki, Finland, in 1957. As it turned out, those who were exposed in the second trimester were significantly more likely to have developed schizophrenia than either those who were not exposed or those who were exposed in the first or third trimester (Mednick, Machon, Huttunen, et al., 1988). In another study, mothers of schizophrenic patients were asked about infections during their schizophrenic child's gestation. The women reported more infections (especially influenza) during the sec-

FIGURE 13.2 Schizophrenia and winter births: ratio of observed to expected numbers of births by quarter of the year for patients with a diagnosis of schizophrenia and neurosis and born between the years 1921 and 1960. A ratio of 100 means that the expected number of births occurred during that quarter. (Adapted from Hare, Belusu & Adelstein, 1979)

ond trimester than during the first and third combined (Wright, Takei, Rifkin, et al., 1995). Also, CT scans of the brains of schizophrenic patients have found an association between enlarged ventricles and exposure to influenza during the second trimester (Takei, Lewis, Jones, et al., 1996). Note how these findings link up with the suggestions of second-trimester brain damage that have been produced by other studies. Further research on the relationship between schizophrenia and epidemics has shown conflicting results, however. Many studies have found a correlation (Venables, 1996), but some have not (Susser, Lin, Brown, et al. 1994).

All the evidence for the viral hypothesis is circumstantial. If a virus is involved in schizophrenia, it has yet to be identified. Nevertheless, it is possible that for some people this is the stressor, or one of the stressors, that interacts with genetic vulnerability to produce schizophrenic symptoms.

---

evidence of some disruption in the neural migration that forms the association areas—a problem that could have occurred only in the second trimester (Akbarian, Kim, Potkin, et al., 1996).

Finally, twin studies have also found signs of problems during the second trimester. MZ twins have nearly identical fingerprints, with only minor variations. In MZ twins who are discordant for schizophrenia, however, fingerprint differences are greater than in

normal MZ twins (Davis & Bracha, 1996). These twins, then, are abnormally different from each other in two ways: fingerprints and mental functioning. Fingerprints are established during the second trimester, so, if both abnormalities were caused by the same prenatal disturbance, which is logical, that disturbance must have happened during the second trimester. (One theory about the nature of the prenatal disturbance is examined in the box above.)

Biochemical Research: The Dopamine Hypothesis A biochemical abnormality has long been suspected of causing schizophrenia. The biochemical theory that has attracted the most attention in the past three decades is the dopamine hypothesis, which posits that schizophrenia is associated with excess activity in the parts of the brain that use dopamine as a neurotransmitter. The major line of evidence for the dopamine hypothesis comes from research on the antipsychotic drugs, particularly the phenothiazines, which we will discuss later in this chapter. These drugs have been dramatically effective in controlling schizophrenic symptoms. An interesting finding is that the antipsychotic drugs are most effective on symptoms such as thought disorder and withdrawal, are moderately effective on hallucinations, and are ineffective on neurotic symptoms such as anxiety (Tamminga, 1997). In other words, these drugs seem to act on fundamental schizophrenic symptoms; therefore, many researchers feel that their chemical activity should provide a clue to the chemical activities underlying schizophrenia. The drugs work by blocking the brain's receptor sites for dopamine. That is, they reduce the activity of the parts of the brain that use dopamine to transmit neural impulses (Holcomb, Cascella, Thaker, et al., 1996), hence the dopamine hypothesis: schizophrenia is connected to excess dopamine activity.

Another piece of evidence involves the stimulants amphetamine and methylphenidate, both of which are known to increase dopamine activity in the brain. As we saw in Chapter 11, amphetamines can produce psychotic states similar to schizophrenia, and so can methylphenidate. Furthermore, when these drugs are given to schizophrenic patients, the patients' symptomatology becomes more dramatic (Faustman, 1995). Here, then, we see another connection between schizophrenia and increased levels of dopamine activity. A final link has been provided by postmortem examinations. A number of postmortem studies have found increased brain dopamine and an increased number of dopamine receptors in the limbic structures of deceased schizophrenic patients (Goldsmith, Shapiro, & Joyce, 1997). Many of these patients, however, had been taking antipsychotic medication, and that may have caused the increase. PET scans of the brains of living schizophrenics who have not been taking antipsychotic drugs have produced inconsistent results. Some have shown an increased number of dopamine receptors in the limbic structures (Wong, Gjedde, Wagner, et al., 1986); some have not (Hietala, Syvälahti, Vuorio, et al., 1994).

This focus on dopamine has suggested a conceptual link between schizophrenia and Parkinson's disease (Chapter 14), a neuropsychological disorder that pro-

duces uncontrollable bodily tremors. Parkinson's disease is known to be caused, in part, by a deficiency of dopamine in certain parts of the brain, and drugs that increase dopamine levels are quite effective in reducing tremors in Parkinson's patients. However, these drugs can also produce schizophrenia-like symptoms (Tamminga, 1997). Conversely, antipsychotic drugs often produce a Parkinson's-like movement disorder called **tardive dyskinesia** as a side effect.

Thus, many lines of evidence converge to support the dopamine hypothesis. It is mostly indirect evidence, however. Other than the postmortem data and the PET scan findings, both of which have been challenged, there is no direct evidence that schizophrenics do, in fact, experience dopamine abnormalities (Lieberman & Koreen, 1993). And, if they do, there are probably different patterns of abnormality (Davis, Kahn, Ko, et al., 1991). It is only Type I schizophrenics, those with positive symptoms, who seem to have excess dopamine activity in the limbic system (Goldsmith, Shapiro, & Joyce, 1997). According to some studies, Type II schizophrenia is related to dopamine *underactivity* in the frontal lobe (Meador-Woodruff, Haroutunian, Powchik, et al., 1997). Moreover, the dopamine underactivity in the frontal lobe may lead to the dopamine overactivity in the limbic structures (Breier, Davis, Buchanan, et al., 1993).

At the same time, there is some evidence *against* the dopamine hypothesis (Davis, Kahn, Ko, et al., 1991). For example, when schizophrenics are first given antipsychotic drugs, their response (if they respond) is gradual, building over a period of about six weeks, yet it takes only a few hours for the drugs to block dopamine receptors in the brain. If schizophrenia were merely the result of activity in these neural tracts, the patients' improvement would also come within a few hours (Pickar, 1988). Furthermore, clozapine, a medication that works on many patients who do not respond to other antipsychotic drugs, has only a weak effect on dopamine receptors. Its primary action is to block serotonin receptors (Nordström, Farde, Nyberg, et al., 1995). Many experts now believe that it is not dopamine alone but an interaction between dopamine and serotonin activity that underlies schizophrenic symptoms (Kapur & Remington, 1996). Meanwhile, new studies suggest that yet another neurotransmitter system, the glutamate system, is also involved (Bartha, Williamson, Drost, et al., 1997). It seems likely that the biological explanation of schizophrenia, if it is ever arrived at, will be a highly complex one, involving a combination of biochemical imbalances—and different combinations both for different types of schizophrenia and for different phases of any single case of schizophrenia.

Chemotherapy As their name indicates, the **antipsychotic drugs** (also called *neuroleptics*) are used to relieve symptoms of psychosis: confusion, withdrawal, hallucinations, delusions, and so on. The most widely used group of antipsychotic drugs has been the **phenothiazines,** including Stelazine, Prolixin, Mellaril, and above all Thorazine (chlorpromazine). In general, antipsychotic drugs are quite effective at reducing schizophrenic symptoms (Shader, 1994). As a result, they have radically altered the conditions under which schizophrenics live. Patients who would have been in straitjackets 30 years ago are now free to roam hospital grounds. And many patients are sufficiently calm and functional to be released altogether, though they must go on taking the medication.

At the same time, these drugs have had an enormous impact on schizophrenia research. It was the effort to find out how the phenothiazines worked that led biochemical researchers to the dopamine hypothesis. Today, research on new, non-phenothiazine antipsychotics is leading to refinements of that hypothesis. These newer drugs often work better than phenothiazines for Type II, negative-symptom patients, the group most likely to show the brain abnormalities previously discussed. In other words, the dopamine-blocking phenothiazines are good at correcting positive symptoms, such as hallucinations and delusions, but are less good at relieving negative symptoms. This has led to a new hypothesis (Lingjaerde, 1994)—actually, it is a revival of an old hypothesis, put forth by Eugen Bleuler—that positive symptoms are secondary and the negative symptoms primary: that schizophrenic reality-distortions (e.g., hallucinations) are a consequence of information-processing problems, presumably originating in abnormal brain development.

While antipsychotic drugs have revolutionized the theory and treatment of schizophrenia, they are not without problems. First, a substantial proportion of the schizophrenic population, 20 to 40 percent, get little or no relief from them (Tamminga, 1997). Second, long-term use of phenothiazines can have serious side effects. In producing calm, these drugs can also produce apathy, reducing the patient to a "zombie"-like state. They can also cause constipation, blurred vision, dry mouth, muscle rigidity, and tremors. But the gravest side effect is tardive dyskinesia, a muscle disorder causing uncontrollable grimacing and lip-smacking. The prevalence of tardive dyskinesia in schizophrenics maintained on antipsychotic drugs is estimated at 20 to 30 percent (Gelenberg, 1991). Unlike other side effects, tardive dyskinesia cannot be relieved by other drugs, and it does not disappear when the antipsychotic medication is discontinued. Such problems often discourage patients from taking their antipsychotic medication, in which case they may soon be back in the hospital (Frances, Docherty, & Kahn, 1996).

These complications have sent researchers back to the laboratory to develop other antipsychotic medications. One recently marketed drug is Clozaril (clozapine), which seems to help patients unresponsive to phenothiazines, while posing a far lower risk of tardive dyskinesia. Unfortunately, Clozaril poses a slight risk of something else—agranulocytosis, a potentially fatal blood disease—which means that patients taking the drug have to have their blood monitored weekly (Baldessarini & Frankenburg, 1991). Another new drug, Risperdal (risperidone), is biochemically similar to Clozaril; therefore, like Clozaril, it carries only a slight risk for tardive dyskinesia, but it poses no risk of blood disease. Compared with the phenothiazines, both Clozaril and Risperdal are apparently as effective in reducing positive symptoms, but their great virtue is that they seem to be more effective in alleviating negative symptoms, such as apathy, anhedonia, and blunted affect. Many people believe that these newer drugs and their offshoots will eventually replace the phenothiazines as first-line medications for schizophrenia (Green, Marshall, Wirshing, et al., 1997).

Still, there is a limit to what any medication can accomplish when there are defects in brain development. Patients who are released from the hospital under the calming influence of antipsychotic drugs usually make only a marginal adjustment to life on the outside. Once outside, they often stop taking the drugs, in which case they may have to be readmitted. Thus, although antipsychotic drugs have definitely reduced the number of chronically hospitalized patients, it has been argued that they have merely replaced long-term hospitalization with "revolving door" admission. This, however, is not the fault of the medication—no one ever claimed that the antipsychotic drugs *cured* schizophrenia—but, rather, society's failure to provide community services for released patients.

The Cognitive Perspective

While neuroscience researchers concern themselves with both the diathesis and the stressor components of the diathesis-stress model, most cognitive theorists focus exclusively on the diathesis. As we know, a prominent symptom of schizophrenia is attention dysfunction. Remember the words of the patient quoted earlier: "My thoughts get all jumbled up. I start thinking or talking about something but I never get there." Since the time of Kraepelin and Eugen Bleuler, many researchers have suspected that this attention problem is the primary pathology in schizophrenia, with the other symptoms developing as results of the attention problem. And that, in brief, is the position of today's cognitive researchers. Cognitive theorists do not claim that attention deficits are the root cause of schizophrenia. In their view, the cause is biological. What they do claim, however, is that the psychological function most impaired by the biological abnormality is attention and that the attention problem, in turn, creates a predisposition to schizophrenia by making it hard for the person to cope with environmental stress (Nuechterlein & Dawson, 1984a, 1984b). Imagine, for example, a family with a highly charged, negative emotional atmosphere or a family in which the parents tend to give confusing messages. (As we will see, these are two circumstances that, according to family systems theorists, may contribute to schizophrenia.) A child with normal cognitive skills would probably be able to navigate the emotional perils of such a family, but a child who has difficulty focusing attention (and, hence, difficulty in solving problems) might well respond by becoming overaroused and disorganized—a condition that over time could develop into psychosis (Nuechterlein, Dawson, Gitlin, et al., 1992; Perry & Braff, 1994).

The goal of cognitive research in schizophrenia has been to determine the exact nature of the attention problems of schizophrenics and to relate these problems to other features of the disorder. Researchers have identified two distinct patterns, overattention and underattention.

Overattention We have already described the breakdown in selective attention that is seen in many schizophrenics. These patients "overattend" to the stimuli in their environment; they cannot focus on one thing and screen out the others. This phenomenon appears to be related to Type I, positive-symptom schizophrenia (e.g., Cornblatt, Lenzenweger, Dworkin, et al., 1985), and, according to current cognitive theory, the positive symptoms of Type I patients—hallucinations, delusions, incoherent speech—are the product of their overattention (Braff & Geyer, 1990; Perry & Braff, 1994). The reason these patients are confused and disorganized is that their information-processing functions are overburdened, and their nervous system overaroused, by stimuli that they cannot screen out (Dawson, Nuechterlein, & Schell, 1992). The reason their speech is full of irrelevant associations is that, unlike normal people, they cannot filter out such associations (Docherty, Hawkins, Hoffman, et al., 1996). Auditory hallucinations, according to this theory, are explainable as traces of real sounds that the patient hears but cannot eliminate from con-

To test the poor-selective-attention hypothesis, researchers had a series of stories, several of them including distractions, read to schizophrenic, manic, and normal subjects fitted with headphones. As the hypothesis would predict, the subjects with schizophrenia did worse than the manic and normal subjects in recounting the stories only when the distraction was introduced.

sciousness, and delusions arise as the patient's effort to account for these and other bizarre perceptions (Maher & Spitzer, 1993).

Many studies have documented the poor selective attention and consequent distractibility of schizophrenics (Braff, 1993). In one experiment (Wielgus & Harvey, 1988), schizophrenic, manic, and normal subjects were fitted with headphones, and eight successive stories were read to them in one ear by a male voice. During four of the stories, however, a distraction was introduced: at the same time that the subjects heard the story from the male voice in one ear, they were told a different story by a female voice in the other ear. The subjects' task was to repeat back word-for-word the story that was being told to them by the male voice. As the poor-selective-attention hypothesis predicts, the schizophrenics did worse than the other subjects only when the distraction was introduced. The problem uncovered by this experiment is a good example of a differential deficit.

The inability of schizophrenics to filter out irrelevant stimuli has been documented in neurophysiological tests as well. In one experiment, schizophrenics were given the task of pressing a button when they heard a tone of a given frequency. Again, however, a distraction was introduced: on some trials, a tone of a different frequency was also sounded. As predicted, this distraction impaired the schizophrenics' performance more than the performance of the controls. Furthermore, the schizophrenics responded to the distracting tones with abnormally large brain waves of the kind that signal that the brain has focused its attention on an environmental stimulus. In other words, the schizophrenics, whatever their effort to focus on the target stimulus, were significantly distracted by the interfering stimulus (Grillon, Courchesne, Ameli, et al., 1990). Finally, it has also been shown that, when an experiment is set up in such a way that picking up interfering stimuli *improves* performance, schizophrenics outperform nonschizophrenics (Salo, Robertson, Nordahl, et al., 1997; Spitzer, Weisker, Winter, et al., 1994). Here again is a differential deficit, and a remarkable one. When schizophrenics do better on a task than normal people, we are presumably tapping into something fundamental to schizophrenia (Braff, 1993).

As noted, this particular attention problem, the inability to screen out distractions, has been found to correlate with Type I, positive-symptom schizophrenia but not with Type II, negative-symptom schizophrenia (Cornblatt, Lenzenweger, Dworkin, et al., 1985; Wielgus & Harvey, 1988). The connection with Type I schizophrenia has also been demonstrated on a biochemical level. Type I, as we just saw, seems to be related to overactivity of dopamine transmission in subcortical areas of the brain. Following this lead, Swerdlow and his colleagues injected rats with dopamine in subcortical areas of the brain, thus creating the kind of dopamine overactivity that is presumed to underlie Type I schizophrenia. The rats responded by showing the kind of selective-attention problems seen in Type I schizophrenia. Furthermore, the attention problems of both Type I schizophrenics and dopamine-injected rats can be decreased by antipsychotic drugs that decrease dopamine activity (Swerdlow, Braff, Taaid, et al., 1994).

Underattention   Whereas Type I schizophrenics seem to be overattentive, Type II schizophrenics appear to be underattentive to external stimuli. This fact has been repeatedly demonstrated in studies of the *orienting response,* a pattern of physiological changes (involving galvanic skin response, blood pressure, pupil dilation, heart rate, and brain waves) that is thought to indicate that the brain has allocated its central attentional resources to the perception and processing of a stimulus. In a review of such experiments, Bernstein (1987) found that 40 to 50 percent of the schizophrenics, when presented with a stimulus of moderate intensity, failed to show a normal orienting response and more recent studies have confirmed this finding (Hazlett, Dawson, Filion, et al., 1997). Schizophrenics also tend to show abnormally low-magnitude brain waves in response to unexpected sounds—another indication of underattention (Catts, Shelley, Ward, et al., 1995).

Another kind of study that has been used to measure underattention employs what is called the *backward-masking paradigm.* The subject is shown a visual stimulus, the so-called target stimulus, quickly or indistinctly. Then, after an interval, this is followed by a "masking stimulus," such as a picture of a grid. When the masking stimulus comes right after the target stimulus, it "masks" the target stimulus: the subject does not register recognition of the target stimulus. But, as the time interval between the presentation of the target stimulus and the masking stimulus is increased, the subject becomes more and more likely to remember the target stimulus. For many schizophrenics, however, the interval between the two has to be stretched far longer than for normal subjects before the target stimulus registers on the consciousness (Saccuzzo, Cadenhead, & Braff, 1996). In other words, these schizophrenics seem to have deficient perception of and responsiveness to environmental stimuli. Recent research indicates that schizophrenics also have other "working memory" deficits, making it hard for them to hold information in their minds long enough to process it (Granholm, Morris, Sarkin, et al., 1997). According to cognitive theorists, such underattention is what leads to negative symptoms such as flat affect and social withdrawal (Braff, 1993). This conclusion is quite logical. If a person's perception of the environment is dulled, he or she may become apathetic and withdrawn.

In keeping with this hypothesis, both deficient orienting responses and poor performance on backward-masking tasks have been found to correlate with negative symptoms such as blunted affect, withdrawal, and motor retardation, as well as with other factors in the Type II profile, such as poor premorbid adjustment and poor prognosis (Braff, 1993; Slaghuis & Bakker, 1995). They do not correlate with positive symptoms, however. Indeed, the orienting responses of positive-symptom schizophrenics are more likely to be abnormally high than abnormally low. Of course, these findings give further support to the Type I versus Type II hypothesis. There do, in fact, seem to be at least two distinct schizophrenic patterns, one marked by overattention and one by underattention.

Vulnerability   If cognitive theorists are correct in claiming that biologically based attention problems create a vulnerability to schizophrenia, then these abnormalities should be present not just in active-phase schizophrenics but also in remitted (recovered) schizophrenics, in their biological relatives, and in people designated as being at risk for schizophrenia (Cornblatt & Keilp, 1994). They are. As we saw in our discussion of Mednick's high-risk children, one of the five characteristics separating those who developed schizophrenia from those who didn't was a history of selective-attention problems. Likewise, remitted schizophrenics, relatives of schizophrenics, children of schizophrenic parents, and people thought to be at risk for schizophrenia by virtue of showing schizophrenic-like personality features all show significantly high rates of selective-attention dysfunction (Braff, 1993; Finkelstein, Cannon, Gur, et al., 1997). Many remitted schizophrenics and high-risk people also show lowered orienting responses (Hazlett, Dawson, Filion, et al., 1997). For more solid confirmation of the attention-dysfunction hypothesis, we must await the outcomes of further longitudinal studies of high-risk children. But it seems clear already that, if "preschizophrenic" people are to be treated, attention deficits are a logical target.

Cognitive Therapy   Cognitive therapy for schizophrenic patients is only in its earliest stages. There are two basic approaches, one addressing the processes of schizophrenic thought, the other addressing its content.

The "process" approach, called *cognitive rehabilitation,* uses techniques borrowed from rehabilitation therapy for brain-injured people, such as stroke patients. The idea is to give patients tasks calling upon defective cognitive skills—memory, attention, social perception—and to build up those skills by means of instructions, training, prompting, and even monetary rewards. In one program, for example, patients were given tests that involved sorting objects into categories, to improve attention and conceptual understanding. To build social perception, they were shown slides of people engaged in various activities and were asked to make judgments about what the people were doing and what the emotional tone of the slides were: friendly, unfriendly, and so on. Studies have shown that this approach, combined with other techniques, does improve cognitive functioning and reduce symptoms (Brunner, Rider, Hodel, et al., 1995).

The other cognitive approach is aimed directly at schizophrenic hallucinations and delusions. Using basically the same techniques as cognitive therapy for nonpsychotic patients, the therapist leads the patient into a questioning of the thought. (Are those voices really coming from the outside? Is there actually a conspiracy against the patient?) For example, one patient who was hearing voices saying that she was going to be killed was asked to wear heavy, industrial earmuffs; if she could still hear the voices, then she had to consider the possibility that the voices were coming from her own mind (Chadwick, Lowe, Horne, et al., 1994). Then the therapist suggests alternative explanations. Typically, such therapy also includes teaching the patient coping devices for dealing with the unwelcome thoughts—for example,

listening to music to drown out "voices" (Tarrier, Harwood, Yusopoff, et al., 1990).

These therapies have come up against a number of problems. Whatever gains are made may not generalize to other areas of cognition, let alone to mood or behavior. Furthermore, on follow-up, the gains may be lost (Penn & Mueser, 1996). Still, both the "process" and "content" approaches remain promising and need to be carefully evaluated.

The Family Systems Perspective

The environmental stresses contributing to the development of schizophrenia may be biological—for example, prenatal brain injury—but it is likely that social factors are involved as well. Such environmental stressors have been the focus of the theories of schizophrenia coming from the other psychological perspectives.

The major concern has been trouble in the family. If, in Mednick's high-risk studies, one factor separating the high-risk children who developed schizophrenia from those who didn't was attention problems, another was an unstable family life. In that group, family disruption was probably due in part to genetic factors. The mothers of the high-risk children all had a history of schizophrenia, which does not bode well for parent-child interactions. But, according to family theorists, psychological tensions in the home may also be a stress factor in schizophrenia, and not just for the children of schizophrenic mothers.

Expressed Emotion   A hostile atmosphere seems to permeate the homes of many children who develop schizophrenia. Earlier researchers often focused on the personality traits of the family members, notably the mother. Today, researchers are more interested in what the people in the family say to one another—something that is more easily measured. In a number of studies (e.g., Miklowitz, Goldstein, Neuchterlein, et al., 1995), families of hospitalized schizophrenics have been rated on expressed emotion (EE) toward the patient. In these studies, the EE rating was based on two factors—the level of criticism and the level of emotional overinvolvement—in the remarks made by a key relative (e.g., the father, the mother, the spouse) in an interview regarding the patient shortly after his or her admission. For example, the sister of a 36-year-old schizophrenic patient remarked:

> To me [schizophrenia] is a totally selfish illness. . . . Rachel could, if she really wanted to, pull herself out of it. But it's as though she wants to . . . go into hospital. . . . I feel that she should care enough about other people to keep herself well . . . because it worries my father, it worries my family, it worries my

The film Shine *is based on the life of pianist David Helfgott, who suffers from schizophrenia.*

brother, and it worries me. To me that is enough to try to keep yourself well. (Brewin, MacCarthy, Duda, et al., 1991, p. 552)

Nine to 12 months after a group of high-EE patients were discharged, they were followed up to see who had relapsed. Interestingly, of all the factors on which the patients varied, the family EE was the best single predictor of relapse: patients who lived with high-EE relatives were 3 to 4 times more likely to have been rehospitalized than patients who lived with low-EE relatives (Linszen, Dingemans, Nugter, et al., 1997; Miklowitz, Goldstein, Doane, et al., 1989). Thus, EE seems to influence relapse risk. In turn, EE is influenced by family members' attributions regarding the patient's condition. Logically, high-EE relatives tend to be those, like the woman quoted earlier, who hold the patient responsible for his or her condition (Weisman, López, Karno, et al., 1993).

Some studies (e.g., Parker, Johnston, & Hayward, 1988) have failed to confirm the link between schizophrenia and high family EE. Still, many EE studies do suggest that a negative and emotionally charged family atmosphere may be related to both the onset and the course of schizophrenia. Other researchers feel that EE should be considered not as a contributor to the development of schizophrenia but specifically as a contributor to relapse—as a measure of the environmental stress that the remitted schizophrenic is exposed to when he or she returns home. In support of this idea, it has been shown that schizophrenics show higher autonomic arousal in the presence of high-EE relatives than in the presence of low-EE relatives (Tarrier, Barrowclough, Porceddu, et al., 1988).

Communication Deviance   Some experts feel that the heart of the interpersonal disturbance lies in the matter of communications between parent and child. In a classic theory put forth in the 1950s, Bateson and his co-workers proposed that schizophrenia might be the product of *double-bind communication*, a kind of no-win interchange, illustrated in the following account:

> A young man who had fairly well recovered from an acute schizophrenic episode was visited in the hospital by his mother. He was glad to see her and impulsively put his arm around her shoulders, whereupon she stiffened. He withdrew his arm and she asked, "Don't you love me any more?" He then blushed, and she said, "Dear, you must not be so easily embarrassed and afraid of your feelings." The patient was able to stay with her only a few minutes more and following her departure he assaulted an aide. (Bateson, Jackson, Haley, et al., 1956, p. 251)

The double-bind situation, then, is one in which the mother gives the child mutually contradictory messages (e.g., both rejection and affection in the case just cited), meanwhile implicitly forbidding the child to point out the contradiction. Whichever message the child acts upon, he or she is the loser. Bateson and his colleagues proposed that the type of mother most likely to engage in double-bind communication was one who found closeness with her child intolerable but who also found it intolerable to admit this to herself. Thus, she would push the child away, but, when the child withdrew, she would accuse the child of not loving her.

This theory, while less discussed today, helped to generate a line of more empirical research, and the research has indeed shown that families of schizophrenics tend to have unusual communication patterns (Wynne, Singer, Bartko, et al., 1975). Their verbal exchanges are variously described as blurred, muddled, vague, fragmented, and incomplete (Velligan, Mahurin, Eckert, et al., 1997). Here, for example, is a recorded exchange between a schizophrenic woman and her parents:

Daughter: (complainingly) Nobody will listen to me. Everybody is trying to still me.

Mother: Nobody wants to kill you.

Father: If you're going to associate with intellectual people, you're going to have to remember that still is a noun and not a verb.

(Wynne & Singer, 1963, p. 195)

Many current studies describe this phenomenon in terms of **communication deviance (CD)**, measured according to the number of deviant or idiosyncratic responses on a test such as the TAT or Rorschach. In one study, CD in parents proved a good predictor of whether their adolescent children would be diagnosed as schizophrenic 15 years later (Goldstein, 1987). The finding (Miklowitz, Strachan, Goldstein, et al., 1986) that communication deviance seems to correlate with expressed emotion—relatives that are high-EE are also high-CD—has given added impetus to this line of research.

These findings can be interpreted in a number of different ways, however. Given that schizophrenia in the child correlates with deviant communications in the family, there may still be no causal relationship between the two factors, for both may be the result of a third variable, such as a shared genetic defect (Miklowitz, Velligan, Goldstein, et al., 1991) or shared attention problems (Velligan, Mahurin, Eckert, et al., 1997). Furthermore, even if there is a causal relationship between the two, we are faced with the chicken-and-egg problem: while disturbed family communications—and a negative emotional climate—may have fostered the child's disorder, it is equally possible that the child's disorder has fostered the high levels of CD and EE. That the families of schizophrenic patients tend to express painful emotions is no surprise. Indeed, in the case of EE, most researchers today view the correlation with schizophrenia simply as a broad, interactive process, with the patient's symptoms causing the family to feel and vent negative emotions, which in turn exacerbate the patient's symptoms, thus creating a vicious cycle (Rosenfarb, Goldstein, Mintz, et al., 1995).

There is one further problem in evaluating the EE and CD findings. If the family setting is of major importance in the development of schizophrenia, why does one child in the family grow up schizophrenic while another turns our normally? It may be that the one who grows up schizophrenic is more vulnerable biologically to the emotional stress of a hostile family environment. But we do not know whether this is the case.

Despite these difficulties, most experts have not discarded the idea that the family may figure in the development of schizophrenia—only the claim that the family *alone* can engender the disorder. Again, the emphasis today is on diathesis and stress, and family hostility is still high on the list of stressors that could help to determine whether a schizophrenic diathesis is translated into schizophrenia.

Treatment for Families The findings regarding EE and CD have prompted the development of treatments for the families of schizophrenic patients. In 1 study, researchers spent several weeks with the families of 18 schizophrenic patients, studying the family members' difficulties in dealing with the patient and with each other. Then the families were taught a step-by-step method of working out problems, from planning a dinner menu to coping with major crises. The families were also briefed on schizophrenia, so that they would be less alarmed and distressed by the patient's symptoms. At a 9-month follow-up, only 1 patient from the 18 experimental-group families had relapsed, compared with 8 patients from 18 families in which the patient had received only individual treatment. These results held through a 2-year follow-up as well, so the gains seem to last (Falloon, Boyd, McGill, et al., 1985). In another study, high-EE families were counseled in how to make their interactions with the patient calmer and less negative. A year later, only 20 percent of the patients from these families had relapsed, compared with 41 percent of the patients from high-EE families that had received no treatment (Hogarty, Anderson, Reiss, et al., 1986).

Another line of research has addressed the question of whether therapy for the family can reduce the patient's need for medication. In one study, the subjects, all of whom had just been released from the hospital after an acute psychotic episode, were divided into three medication conditions: continued high dose, continued low dose, or dose varying according to symptoms. Then, in each group, the families were given either "applied family management"—the intensive problem-solving approach previously described—or a "family placebo," in which the therapist held monthly meetings with the family but made no attempt to teach them relapse-prevention skills. The result was that the low-dose and adjusted-dose patients showed higher relapse rates regardless of which type of therapy their families received (Schooler, Keith, Severe, et al., 1997).

According to the diathesis-stress model, a healthy family environment may prevent the onset of schizophrenia in a person with a genetic predisposition to the disorder.

Many studies have shown that family therapy does lower the risk of relapse, but at this point it seems that no one form is more effective than others. On the other hand, early reports show that intensive problem-solving therapy applied to groups of families meeting together, as opposed to single families, may be superior to the other approaches (McFarlane, Lukens, Link, et al., 1995).

The Behavioral Perspective

Learned Nonresponsiveness   The behaviorists have offered environmental theories of schizophrenia. According to Ullmann and Krasner (1975), for example, schizophrenics are people who, because of a disturbed family life or other environmental misfortunes, have not learned to respond to the social stimuli to which most of us respond. As a result, they cease to attend to these stimuli and begin taking their behavioral cues from other, idiosyncratically chosen stimuli. In consequence, they tend to become objects of disciplinary action and social rejection, leading to feelings of alienation and to the belief that others are out to "get" them. Hence, their behavior becomes even more bizarre. And if, as may happen, they are rewarded for bizarre responses—through attention, sympathy, or release from responsibilities—such responses are likely to become habitual.

There is some support for this hypothesis. It has been shown, for example, that, like the learned behaviors of normal people, the "crazy" behaviors of schizophrenics are sometimes produced in situations where they will lead to rewards. But this does not prove that those behaviors originated through reinforcement. Today, in view of the neuroscience findings, most behaviorists use learning theory not to explain the development of schizophrenia—they, too, tend to believe that it develops in part from biological causes—but to reduce schizophrenic symptoms.

Relearning Normal Behavior   Whatever the cause of schizophrenic behavior, it may be that mental health settings encourage such behavior by reinforcing "craziness" and not reinforcing adaptive responses. If so, then reversing that reinforcement pattern should lead to improvement. Historically, this has been one goal of behavioral treatment of schizophrenia.

Direct Reinforcement   Early behavioral treatments were straightforward applications of the principles of operant conditioning. That is, they attempted to change behavior by changing the consequences of behavior. Let us look at a specific case:

> Mr. C.'s most obnoxious behaviors were: urinating and defecating on the floor, shouting, swearing, name-calling, begging cigarettes, demanding other things, striking at other patients. It . . . seemed evident that Mr. C.'s inappropriate conduct usually was followed by some kind of staff attention. Two procedures for eliminating Mr. C.'s disruptive behavior were [implemented]. 1. Social attention should no longer be given following inappropriate behavior. 2. Social attention and cigarettes . . . would be the consequence of socially acceptable behavior. (Sushinsky, 1970, p. 24)

Modest though it was, this treatment program proved effective. In two weeks, Mr. C.'s "obnoxious" behaviors disappeared. Furthermore, he began striking up conversations and participating in rehabilitation therapy.

Procedures that involve the giving or withholding of the tangible reinforcers are surrounded by a number of ethical and legal questions (Chapter 18). There is no question, however, that such procedures can change behavior. Researchers have succeeded in instituting or increasing speech in mute and near-mute patients through the use of such simple reinforcers as fruit, chocolate, and magazines (Thomson, Fraser, & McDougall, 1974).

The Token Economy Some hospitals have extended operant-conditioning procedures to entire wards, using a system called the token economy. In a **token economy** patients are given tokens, points, or some other kind of generalized conditioned reinforcer in exchange for performing certain target behaviors, such as personal grooming, cleaning their rooms, or doing academic or vocational-training tasks. The patients can then exchange the tokens for any number of backup reinforcers, such as snacks, coffee, new clothes, or special privileges. The procedure is very much like that which operates outside the hospital: we earn money by performing specified tasks and then exchange this money for the privileges and goods that we want. Token economies have proved very useful in helping patients—even the most dysfunctional "chronic" patients—improve their behavior to the point where they can be released from the hospital (Paul & Lentz, 1977).

Social-Skills Training Many operant-conditioning programs have been aimed largely at improving patients' behavior *within* the hospital. Today, with the greater emphasis on release, attention has shifted to helping patients learn skills that will enable them to live on the outside—making friends, holding down a job, and the like. Foremost among such treatments is social-skills training.

As we have seen, most schizophrenics are socially inept. They withdraw and speak little, or else they speak a lot, but about bizarre things. **Social-skills training** aims to alleviate this problem by teaching patients conversation skills, eye contact, appropriate physical gestures, smiling, improved speech intonation—in general, characteristics that make a person attractive to others (Bellack & Mueser, 1993; Smith, Bellack, & Liberman, 1996). Such training is usually done in groups and is highly structured. A crucial component is role-playing, in which patients, under the therapist's supervision, practice their new skills. Typically, the patients are also given homework assignments and complete them with an assigned "buddy."

How effective is social-skills training? One study (Wallace & Liberman, 1985) compared social-skills training with an alternative treatment, holistic health therapy. The patients in the social-skills program worked with a problem-solving model on how to receive, process, and give interpersonal communications. The holistic-therapy patients spent as many hours in treatment as the social-skills patients, but their time was devoted to jogging, meditation, yoga, group discussions of stress control, and the development of positive expectations. Both groups showed

In exchange for keeping their rooms neat, grooming themselves, or performing other specified behaviors, these schizophrenic patients are receiving tokens as reinforcers. In turn, they can trade the tokens for specific privileges.

significant improvement in schizophrenic symptoms, and the improvements were approximately equal. Not surprisingly, the social-skills group showed better social skills, but it is still not known whether the social skills acquired in this or similar programs actually generalize to the patients' daily lives (Penn & Mueser, 1996). If they do not, this may be the fault of their daily lives. Implicit in social-skills training is the belief that the natural environment will reinforce the patients' improved skills, but most schizophrenics do not live in a natural environment. If they are not hospitalized, they tend to live in hostels with many other chronic psychiatric patients—an environment unlikely to reward normal sociability. Nevertheless, research now in progress suggests that some patients who receive social-skills training do retain the skills and make a better adjustment in the community than those who have not had social-skills training (Marder, Wirshing, Mintz, et al., 1996).

The Sociocultural Perspective

None of the treatments described thus far actually cures schizophrenia. Medication, family therapy, social-skills training—at best, they prevent relapse and help the patient to make some adjustment within the community. But in most cases schizophrenia is a recurring disorder. Released patients require many kinds of assistance, ideally from many kinds of professionals. Short of a cure for schizophrenia, what is most needed in this field is long-term, multifaceted support programs within the community.

One such program was part of a study that took place in Madison, Wisconsin (Test & Stein, 1978). Patients seeking psychiatric hospitalization were randomly assigned either to brief hospitalization (the median stay was 17 days), with typical aftercare, or to a community treatment service not involving hospitalization. In the latter service, the staff helped the patients find an acceptable community residence if staying at home was not feasible, and they showed them how to find jobs or places in sheltered workshops if they were unemployed. They also created an individually tailored treatment program for each patient, based on an assessment of what coping skills that particular patient was lacking. Treatment took place *in vivo*—that is, in the patients' homes, places of work, and neighborhood haunts. For 14 months, the staff maintained daily contact with the patients, calling them, dropping by, offering suggestions, and in general actively helping them make their way in the community. At the end of the 14-month experimental period and again upon follow-up 1½ years later, the community treatment patients showed better adjustment (e.g., fewer days unemployed) than

the hospitalized patients. Upon 2-year follow-up, however, the advantage of the community treatment program began to narrow. This finding suggests that community treatment, if it is to be successful, must maintain active involvement with patients long after their crises have passed.

This program gave rise to an approach called *assertive community treatment,* or *ACT,* that is now being tried in a number of cities in the United States and Great Britain. In ACT, the released patient is contacted frequently and can draw on the services of a wide range of professionals—not just mental health workers—all based in the community, where they are readily available. A recent analysis of the existing research concluded that ACT programs reduce symptoms, improve social functioning, and facilitate independent living (Scott & Dixon, 1995). They may also reduce the overall cost of caring for schizophrenics— that was part of their goal—but this is not yet clear.

Another recently developed community-based treatment is *personal therapy,* a one-on-one case-management treatment designed to fit the special emotional circumstances of the schizophrenic. Personal therapy focuses on control of emotions, the goal being to avoid the kind of emotional escalation that leads to relapse. But the teaching of emotional control is carefully spaced over three stages in order not to burden patients with tasks for which they are not ready. During one stage, for example, patients are taught "internal coping," a strategy for identifying internal signs of upcoming stress. Only later are they taught how to meet the stress. A crucial aspect of personal therapy is that it is long term, lasting from around the time of discharge for about three years.

The preliminary outcomes of personal therapy are promising. While relapse rates depend on whether patients are living with a family or on their own, the treatment does seem to result in less interpersonal anxiety and improved social relationships. These effects increase through the three-year treatment period, whereas the effects of most other treatments peak at one year and then decline as the patient starts to relapse (Hogarty, Greenwald, Ulrich, et al., 1997; Hogarty, Kornblith, Greenwald, et al., 1997). If these results hold up, we may have to acknowledge that a brief treatment model, or any model that provides limited services in deference to managed care, simply doesn't fit the needs of a severe, recurring disorder such as schizophrenia.

Unitary Theories: Diathesis and Stress

For a time, the breakthroughs in genetic research on schizophrenia seemed to cast doubt on environmental theories altogether. But, while the genetic findings seem unchallengeable, they are obviously not the whole story. As Seymour Kety (1970), one of the foremost genetic researchers, has pointed out, schizophrenia cannot be entirely controlled by genes, for, if it were, the concordance rate for MZ twins would be 100 percent. Not only is it not 100 percent but, as we saw, it is only 46 percent. Likewise, while having a schizophrenic first-degree relative increases one's risk of developing the disorder, it is by no means a necessary condition: 81 percent of people with schizophrenia have no schizophrenic parent or sibling (Gottesman, 1991).

Such are the findings that have led today's researchers to look for *both* genetic and environmental causes—in other words, to adopt the diathesis-stress model. But many questions remain. If there is a genetically inherited diathesis, what, exactly, is the genetic defect? And what is its primary expression? That is, what are the psychological functions that it directly impairs? Finally, what are the stresses most likely to convert such a diathesis into schizophrenia? In an extensive review of the research, Mirsky and Duncan (1986) list the prime suspects: (1) feelings of clumsiness and a sense of being "different" as a result of attention deficits; (2) increased dependence on parents as a result of being impaired; (3) poor academic performance and poor coping skills, again as a result of the basic organic impairment; (4) stressful family interactions, including high expressed emotion; (5) communication deviance in the family, leading to difficulty in communicating with people outside the family and, hence, to increased isolation; and (6) frequent hospitalization of a parent or other family members. In view of later re-

search, prenatal brain injury should probably be added to this list.

A number of studies (e.g. Norman & Malla, 1993a, 1993b) have shown that schizophrenic relapses tend to be preceded by an increase in stressful life events. These events look more like triggering events than like fundamental causes, but what is interesting is that the researchers now not only acknowledge diathesis-stress interaction but they also try to examine it. We have looked at other such studies in this chapter—notably, Mednick's high-risk studies. Another example is the Davis and Bracha group's study of fingerprints in MZ twins discordant for schizophrenia; here the hypothesized cause is both environmental (prenatal brain injury) and genetic. The diathesis-stress model has also led researchers to ask what happens to people who inherit a genetic vulnerability to schizophrenia but do not develop schizophrenia. Some studies indicate that in such cases the genetic diathesis is often expressed as schizotypal personality disorder. As we noted, this syndrome was commonly seen in those of Mednick's high-risk children who did not develop schizophrenia.

The recent breakthroughs in the study of schizophrenia have been very exciting, yet each new discovery has made the disorder seem more complicated. If the causes had proved to be wholly genetic or wholly environmental, research would have been far easier. But, framed as a diathesis-stress interaction—and one that probably involves many different kinds of genetic diathesis, together with many kinds of stress—the disorder poses a highly intricate problem, one that will occupy researchers for many years to come.

KEY TERMS

active phase, 379
antipsychotic drugs, 396
behavioral high-risk design, 392
blunted affect, 377
catatonic schizophrenia, 381
catatonic stupor, 381
clanging, 375
communication deviance (CD), 401
delusional disorder, 385
delusions, 372
differential deficits, 387

disorganized schizophrenia, 380
dopamine hypothesis, 395
echolalia, 381
expressed emotion (EE), 399
flat affect, 377
genetic high-risk design, 390
good-poor premorbid dimension, 383
hallucinations, 376
inappropriate affect, 378

loosening of associations, 373
negative symptoms, 383
neologisms, 375
paranoid-nonparanoid dimension, 384
paranoid schizophrenia, 382
phenothiazines, 396
positive-negative symptoms dimension, 383
positive symptoms, 383
poverty of content, 374

process-reactive dimension, 383
prodromal phase, 379
psychoses, 370
residual phase, 379
schizophrenia, 370
social-skills training, 403
stereotypy, 378
tardive dyskinesia, 395
token economy, 403
Type I schizophrenia, 384
Type II schizophrenia, 384
word salad, 376

SUMMARY

- Schizophrenia is the label given to a group of relatively common psychoses characterized by severe distortion of thought, bizarre behavior, and social withdrawal.

- *DSM-IV* identifies five characteristic symptoms of schizophrenia: delusions, hallucinations, disorganized speech, disorganized or catatonic behavior, and negative symptoms (a reduction in or loss of normal language and other functions). To be diagnosed with schizophrenia, a person must have shown two or more of these disturbances for at least a month and must have been functioning abnormally for at least six months.

■ Disorders of thought and language include delusions and loosening of associations between concepts. Loosening of associations results in language marked by poverty of content, neologisms, clanging, and word salad.

■ Disorders of perception produce a breakdown of selective attention, which some experts believe constitutes the basic pathology in schizophrenia. Hallucinations are often another perceptual problem for schizophrenics.

■ Disorders of mood in schizophrenia may take two forms. One is blunted or flat affect (reduced or absent emotional responsiveness). The other form is inappropriate affect (emotional expression unsuited to the situation).

■ Schizophrenics may display a wide variety of disorders of motor behavior. The behaviors range from merely inappropriate to bizarre.

■ Social withdrawal is an early sign of schizophrenia. This condition is exacerbated by difficulty in maintaining appropriate interpersonal behavior.

■ Schizophrenia follows a fairly regular course, involving three stages: (1) the prodromal phase, marked by a gradual social withdrawal and deterioration of functioning; (2) the active phase, marked by overt signs of psychosis; and (3) the residual phase, in which gross psychotic symptoms recede, but functioning remains impaired. Some patients experience a complete remission, but most remain impaired to a greater or lesser degree.

■ Schizophrenics may be classified into subtypes according to symptomatology. The three main subtypes are (1) disorganized schizophrenia, characterized by incoherent speech, mood disturbance (either flat affect or extreme silliness), and disorganized behavior; (2) catatonic schizophrenia, characterized by extremes of motor behavior (i.e., immobility or hyperactivity); and (3) paranoid schizophrenia, characterized by delusions and/or hallucinations of persecution and grandeur.

■ Today, classification of schizophrenics by symptomatology is considered less valid than classification along certain dimensions—an approach that allows for continuous variation in, rather than the mere presence or absence of, symptoms.

■ One dimension is the process-reactive dimension, in which cases with a gradual onset (process, or poor-premorbid) are distinguished from those with a rapid onset precipitated by a traumatic event (reactive, or good-premorbid).

■ The positive-negative symptoms dimension distinguishes those with new and abnormal behaviors (positive symptoms), such as hallucinations, delusions, and bizarre behaviors, from those with abnormal "nonbehaviors" (negative symptoms), such as withdrawal, flat affect, and poverty of speech. This dimension is now the focus of considerable research, because its two patterns may represent two biologically distinct disorders: Type I schizophrenia (positive symptoms) and Type II schizophrenia (negative symptoms).

■ A third dimension is the paranoid-nonparanoid dimension. This dimension indicates the presence or absence of paranoid delusions.

■ The symptoms of and prognosis for schizophrenia differ across cultures. Recovery is easier in developing countries, which maintain a stronger emphasis on social interdependence and family support. In industrialized societies, schizophrenia is more likely to strike males, people of lower IQ, and unemployed or unmarried people. It first appears in adolescence or early adulthood.

■ Delusional disorder, another category of psychosis, resembles paranoid schizophrenia in that the most prominent symptom is a system of delusions. In delusional disorder, however, the delusions are the fundamental abnormality, from which any other abnormalities emanate, and in many cases they are the patient's only symptom. Furthermore, if the patient does have other symptoms, they do not include the characteristic symptoms of schizophrenia (e.g., loosening of associations and incoherence). The delusions are more plausible and less bizarre than those found in paranoid schizophrenia.

■ Delusional disorder also differs from schizophrenia in prevalence and onset. It is far less common, it strikes more women than men, and it has a later onset.

■ Scientists have encountered several obstacles in trying to understand the causes of schizophrenia. Researchers don't agree on the primary pathology. The difficulty of discriminating between primary symptoms and secondary symptoms adds to the problem of diagnosis. The hospitalization and medication most schizophrenics receive could actually produce some of the unique features of schizophrenia. The difficulty in discovering differential deficits for schizophrenics further complicates research.

■ The biological perspective has convincingly indicated that genetic factors contribute to the development of schizophrenia. Genetic studies on schizophrenia in families, twins, and adopted children have produced very strong evidence for a genetic component of schizophrenia. Scientists have used deviant eye tracking, a trait unique to some schizophrenics, as a marker when trying to find a genetic cause of schizophrenia.

■ Brain scans of schizophrenic sufferers have shown several abnormalities. These irregularities may be a result of the medication schizophrenics receive, but it is believed that they are a cause of the disease, as the findings also appear in first-episode schizophrenics.

■ Another possible cause of the disorder is prenatal brain injury, specifically in the second trimester, when the brain undergoes important developmental stages. Studies showing that babies exposed to illnesses in their second trimester are more likely to develop schizophrenia than are babies exposed in their first or third trimester or those not exposed to an illness prenatally have added support to this theory.

- The dopamine hypothesis, a theory based on biochemical research, states that schizophrenia is related to excess dopamine activity in the brain. The theory has been disputed by some researchers, and it is probable that a biological cause for the disorder will involve not one but many biochemical imbalances. Antipsychotic drugs are quite effective at reducing the symptoms of schizophrenia.

- Cognitive theorists believe that the primary problem in schizophrenia is a biologically based attention deficit, with other symptoms developing as a result of this problem. It is believed that Type I schizophrenia is related to overattention, the inability to screen out irrelevant stimuli. Type II schizophrenics, however, appear to be underattentive to external stimuli, as seen in their abnormal orienting responses. In support of these theories, researchers have found attention deficits in active and remitted schizophrenics, in their relatives, and in high-risk preschizophrenics. Cognitive therapy is designed to rehabilitate deficient cognitive skills and to reduce hallucinations and delusions.

- Family systems theorists propose that psychological tensions in the home may be a stress factor in causing schizophrenia. Studies on expressed emotion (based on levels of criticism and emotional overinvolvement) of close relatives of schizophrenics have shown that a negative and highly emotional family atmosphere may lead to the onset of, or a recurrence of, schizophrenia. Communication deviance in parents has proved a good predictor of schizophrenia in adolescents. Family therapists empha-

size the need to work with the families of patients to prevent recurrences of the disorder.

- The behavioral perspective sees schizophrenics as people who do not respond to normal social stimuli due to environmental factors. Behaviorists feel that schizophrenics may continue their abnormal behaviors if they are rewarded for them; therefore, treatment aims at changing the behaviors by reversing the reinforcement. Patients are rewarded only for normal behaviors. Behavioral treatments include direct reinforcement, token economies, and social-skills training.

- Sociocultural theorists promote long-term, multifaceted support for released patients, to complement the relapse prevention function addressed by the other therapies. Assertive community treatment programs enable patients to draw on the services of a wide range of professionals in the community. Personal therapy provides one-to-one case-management treatment.

- Although there are many different perspectives on the causes and treatment of schizophrenia, most researchers now recognize that environmental and genetic factors interact in the causation of schizophrenia. Hence, many adopt the diathesis-stress model, which states that a predisposition to schizophrenia is inherited but that the disorder must be triggered by environmental stresses, such as poor coping skills and high expressed emotion and communication deviance within the family.

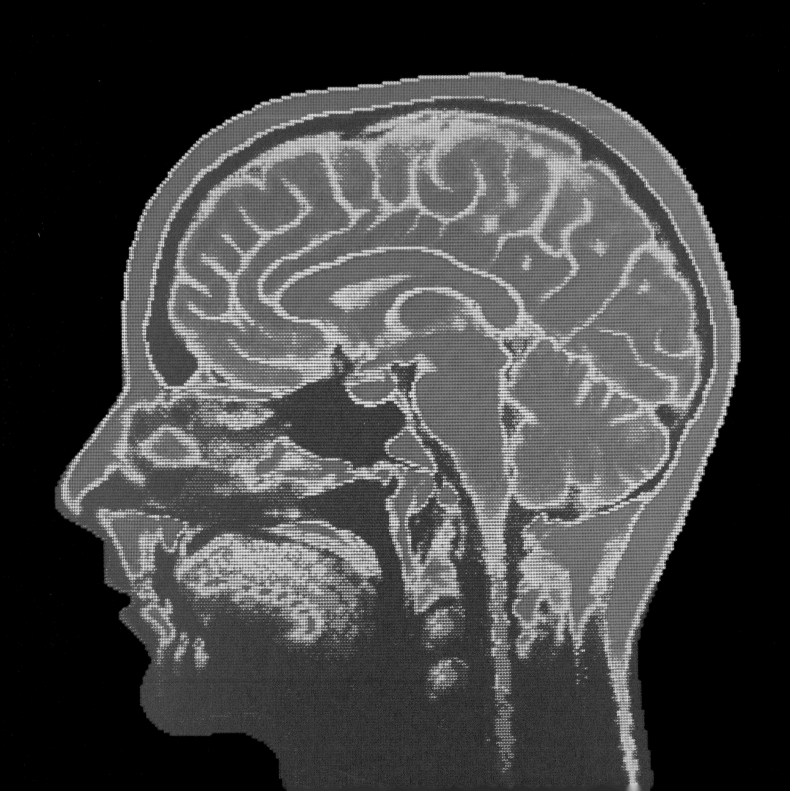

Chapter 14

Problems in Diagnosis
    Identifying an Acquired Brain Injury
    Specifying the Type of Injury
    Specifying the Site of the Damage
Types of Acquired Brain Injuries
    Cerebral Infection
    Brain Trauma
    Cerebrovascular Accidents: Strokes
    Brain Tumors
    Degenerative Disorders
    Nutritional Deficiency
    Endocrine Disorders
    Toxic Disorders
The Epilepsies
    Causes of Epilepsy
    Types of Seizures
    Psychological Factors in Epilepsy
    Groups at Risk
    Treatment of Epilepsy

Mrs. L., a 76-year-old widow and former secretary, lived alone in a small midwestern town. Though her two daughters and one son lived in other parts of the country, they spoke with her on the telephone and visited her regularly. Over the last two years they had noticed increasing anxiety and depression in their mother, as well as some change in her thinking and memory. Mrs. L.'s face had become rather unexpressive, and she shuffled when she walked. At first her children interpreted these changes as the result of old age. However, as their mother became more and more sad, they became concerned.

Finally they took her to a psychiatrist, who noted her recent weight loss and difficulty sleeping. He placed Mrs. L. on the antidepressant medication Prozac, which brought a mild improvement in her mood. Because of her shuffling gait, the psychiatrist referred her to a neurologist, who observed a "masked" facial expression and decreased arm swing. Concluding that they were symptoms of Parkinson's disease, he ordered an MRI scan of Mrs. L.'s head, which revealed a small tumor in the meninges overlying her brain. The neurologist judged the tumor to be largely incidental, however.

Approximately two months later, Mrs. L. developed a stomach virus, with vomiting and diarrhea. Shortly after that she began telling her children that she had been seeing them in her home, lying dead on the living room floor. At first she tried to talk to the images, but receiving no response, she gradually gave up. She later reported feeling mildly agitated that the images were not responding to her, though she did seem to understand that they could not be real. The family contacted the psychiatrist, who interpreted the images as mood-congruent hallucinations associated with depression. He increased Mrs. L.'s antidepressant medication and added an antipsychotic drug, Olanzepine.

Over the next three weeks Mrs. L.'s ability to care for herself deteriorated rapidly, and she became uncommunicative. One of her daughters returned home to help her dress, eat, and bathe. Again the family contacted the psychiatrist, who recommended that Mrs. L. be hospitalized. Because Mrs. L. had not responded to medication, soon after hospitalization she was considered for electroshock therapy (ECT). But first she was referred for neuropsychological testing, which revealed serious impairments of her visual perception. Mrs. L. could not copy even simple geometric figures, and her ability to learn and retain new information was impaired, as was her ability to focus and sustain her attention.

A neurologist was asked to reevaluate the possibility that the small tumor in Mrs. L.'s meninges could be contributing to her visual hallucinations, which had not ceased. While he felt that the tumor was only incidental, he noted that her hallucinations, disturbance of visual perception, decline in memory, poor attention and concentration, and Parkinson's-like symptoms could indicate a variant of Alzheimer's disease, possibly Lewy body disease. Because such patients are particularly sensitive to antipsychotic medications, the neurologist and neuropsychologist encouraged the psychiatrist to discontinue the Olanzepine. Mrs. L. was placed on a medication called Aricept, which is used

to treat Alzheimer's disease. Within days Mrs. L.'s hallucinations ceased. She was discharged to a nursing home, where her initiative and ability to care for herself began to improve. Three weeks later she left the nursing home to return to her family's care. (Smith, The Mayo Clinic, personal files)

Most of the disorders that we have discussed in this book so far are thought to be either partly or largely psychological, the result of the person's relations to his or her experience and environment. By contrast, the **acquired brain injuries,** as their name tells us, are by definition biological. They are directly traceable to the destruction of brain tissue or to biochemical imbalances in the brain, and they have a major effect on cognitive processes such as memory. This is not to say that these disorders are "purely" biological. The form such syndromes take depends in part on psychosocial factors—above all, what sort of personality the person has and what his or her living situation is. Likewise, the treatment of acquired brain injuries (also known as neuropsychological disorders) is psychological as well as medical. Rehabilitation programs typically involve not just physicians but psychologists, social workers, occupational therapists, physical therapists, and speech therapists.

Acquired brain injuries constitute a major health problem. At present they account for one-fourth of all first admissions to mental hospitals in the United States. In this chapter, we will first examine the difficulties of diagnosing acquired brain injuries. Then we will discuss the symptoms and the known causes of the major syndromes.

Problems in Diagnosis

There are four major problems in the diagnosis of an acquired brain injury: (1) deciding whether the syndrome is in fact an acquired brain injury or simply a psychological disorder; (2) if it is an injury, determining the cause of the pathology; (3) if the damage is localized (i.e., restricted to a specific area of the brain), determining the location; and (4) deciding how psychosocial factors influence the disorder's symptoms, and whether medical treatment or psychological therapy can modify them. None of these decisions is a simple matter.

Identifying an Acquired Brain Injury

The symptoms of acquired brain injury closely resemble those of psychological disorders. Disorientation, impaired intellectual functioning, and inappropriate affect are well-recognized symptoms of both schizophrenia and brain injury, for example. Diagnosis in such cases may not be easy, at least initially. Furthermore, the symptoms of a brain injury may be complicated by emotional disturbances developing *in response* to the impairment. Look again at the opening case. When the onset of a brain injury is gradual, secondary emotional problems may be present long before the person gets to the hospital. When people find themselves taking the wrong bus, calling the wrong phone numbers, or making embarrassing mistakes on the job, they tend to become anxious and depressed, so, by the time they see a diagnostician, they may have *both* a brain injury and a psychological disorder.

Before the development of modern diagnostic techniques such as magnetic resonance imaging, or MRI (Chapter 4), it was exceedingly difficult to differentiate between brain injury and psychological disorders. Often it was not until the autopsy that a patient whose symptoms had been curiously resistant to several years of psychotherapy was found to have a brain tumor (Patton & Sheppard, 1956; Waggoner & Bagchi, 1954). Such was the case with composer George Gershwin. Young and seemingly healthy, Gershwin one day lost consciousness momentarily while conducting a concert of his works. In the months that followed, he began to act peculiarly. He was irritable and restless, and he had terrible headaches. At the urging of his family, he entered a hospital for a complete physical examination and was declared "a perfect specimen of health" (Ewen, 1956, p. 298). He then began daily treatment with a psychotherapist, who decided that what Gershwin needed was rest and seclusion. The rest seemed to help, for about a month. Then Gershwin collapsed and went into a coma. He was rushed to a hospital, where exploratory surgery located an inoperable brain tumor. Gershwin died that same day, at the age of 38.

The reverse mistake—diagnosing a psychological problem as a brain injury—also occurs, especially with elderly patients. Physicians may diagnose dementia (an acquired brain injury) when in fact the person is suffering from depression brought on by the loss of a spouse, health problems, money problems, or any of the many difficulties faced by older people (Gurland, Dean, Craw, et al., 1980).

The differential diagnosis of brain injury and psychological disturbances is crucial. Many brain injuries can be treated, but only if they are recognized for what they are. Misdiagnosis can be fatal. Sound practice calls for a diagnostician to rule out brain injury before concluding that a disorder is psychological in origin. Diagnosticians can draw on a number of resources: direct observation of the patient, a detailed history of the onset and progress of the symptoms,

Before MRI and other sophisticated diagnostic techniques became available, brain disorders were even harder to diagnose than they are now. George Gershwin (1898–1937), composer of such classics as An American in Paris *and* Porgy and Bess, *was thought to be mentally ill when he began behaving strangely. Exploratory surgery revealed a fatal brain tumor.*

interviews with the patient's family and physician. In addition, diagnosticians usually put the patient through a series of tests: neurological tests to assess reflexes, which may be faulty if there is damage to the nervous system; EEGs, brain CT scans, and chemical analyses of cerebrospinal fluids; and, finally, neuropsychological tests, such as the Halstead-Reitan Battery and others that are specifically designed to detect impairment. Newer technologies such as MRI and PET (positron emission tomography) scans offer even better detection of brain pathology and are fast becoming the primary means of diagnosis (Bigler, Yeo, & Turkheimer, 1989; Jernigan, 1990; Pykett, 1982; Theodore, 1988a, 1988b). Most of these tests are discussed in Chapters 2 and 4.

Specifying the Type of Injury

If a man appears in an emergency room with a revolver in his hand and a bullet hole in his head, the physician on duty will have little difficulty determining the source, to say nothing of the presence, of brain damage. In most cases, however, it is even more difficult to specify the source of the impairment—tumor, poisoning, infection, "stroke," whatever—than to distinguish between psychological disorders and acquired brain injuries, yet the accurate identification of a brain injury is essential, as it is on this decision that treatment is based. A physician does not wish to treat for a brain tumor, only to discover that the patient actually has lead poisoning.

Several possible sources of confusion can make diagnosis difficult. In the first place, the symptoms of the various brain injuries overlap considerably. If it is determined that a patient's amnesia is due to injury, this condition could still be caused by a number of pathologies, each requiring different treatment. Second, just as different injuries may produce the same symptoms, so the same injury may produce widely different symptoms, depending on its *location* in the brain. A brain tumor may cause a speech disorder in one patient, double vision in another, emotional lability in a third. Furthermore, the source of the brain injury is only one of the many factors determining the patient's behavioral responses to the disease. The patient's age, general physical condition, prior intellectual achievements, premorbid personality, emotional stability, and social situation—as well as the nature, location, and extent of the brain damage—affect the symptoms. A patient who is rigid and pessimistic, uninsured, or alone in the world may respond to unwelcome symptoms with panic or total dejection. On the other hand, a patient who has money, family, and a resilient disposition may show a surprisingly moderate response, even to a severe impairment. From this bewildering array of variables, the diagnostician must ferret out the single primary variable: the source of the brain injury.

There is one final problem in determining the source of acquired brain injuries. As with so many of the psychological disorders, there are many brain injuries about which very little is known. Unfortunately, the better-understood syndromes are often the rarest, while many of the most common injuries remain baffling.

Delirium Delirium differs from other acquired brain injuries in that it remits quickly, leaving most patients unharmed. It is very dramatic, however. **Delirium** is a transient, global disorder of cognition and attention. Delirious patients are profoundly confused. Their thinking is disorganized, even dreamlike. In about half of all cases, hallucinations and delusions (usually of persecution) are present, and, when they are, patients may harm themselves or others as they attempt to escape or fight the imagined enemy. Some patients are hyperalert, others lethargic and drowsy, and these disturbances extend to the sleep cycle. Patients are often drowsy during the day and awake and agitated at night. Emotional lability is common, running the gamut from apathy to the extremes of fear and rage. The onset of delirium is sudden, and its severity fluctuates during the course of the day. (Most patients are worse at night.) In the typical case, the delirium passes within a month, recovery is complete, and the patient is partially or totally amnesiac for the whole episode.

Delirium is caused by a widespread disruption of cerebral metabolism and neurotransmission. It is a common condition in older people, and, when it strikes the elderly, the cause is often intoxication from medication, even ordinary medication in prescribed doses. (Older people may respond to drugs very differently than the young.) Another common cause is surgery. Surgery produces delirium in 10 to 15 percent of older patients (Seymour, 1986), and certain kinds of surgery pose a far greater risk. (Heart surgery provokes delirium in 24 to 32 percent of older patients.) Other causes are withdrawal from alcohol or other drugs, head injury, sleep loss, malnutrition, and psychological stress, such as the death of a spouse or relocation to a nursing home.

A final common cause is physical illness, such as heart attack or pneumonia, of which delirium is often the main presenting symptom in the elderly. To quote one expert, "Acute confusion [delirium] is a far more common herald of the onset of physical illness in an older person than are, for example, fever, pain, or tachycardia" (Hodkinson, 1976). For this reason, it is very important that the delirium not be misdiagnosed. It is often mistaken for dementia, particularly in patients who already have dementia. (As with other acquired brain injuries, these two can coexist in the same patient.) But, if delirium is not recognized as such, the possibility of underlying physical illness is ignored, perhaps with fatal results. The treatment of delirium is the removal of its cause—withdrawal of the intoxicating medication, treatment of the underlying physical illness, or whatever. Patients who are agitated may also be given sedatives (Lipowsky, 1989).

Specific Cognitive Impairments Acquired brain injury can produce specific impairments in a variety of cognitive areas. The most common signs of acquired brain injury are the following:

1. *Impairment of attention and arousal.* The person may be unaware of his or her own body and surroundings, unable to tell who he or she is, what the date is, and so forth. These impairments are often quite similar to delirium.

2. *Impairment of language function.* The person may have difficulty speaking coherently, understanding the speech of others, reading, and the like.

3. *Impairment of learning and memory.* The person may experience difficulty learning and retaining new information. He or she may also forget events of the distant past or, more typically, of the very recent past—an impairment called **amnesia.** To fill in the gaps in memory, the person may invent stories.

4. *Impairment of visual-perceptual function.* The person may be unable to recognize everyday objects for what they are—name them, use them correctly, or draw them.

5. *Impairment of motor skills.* The person may suddenly become paralyzed, unable to move an arm or a leg or to produce speech. Or he or she may lose the ability to coordinate movements or manipulate objects correctly, a disorder called **apraxia.** Patients with apraxia may try to write with a pair of scissors or light a match by striking the wrong end (Hécaen & Albert, 1978).

6. *Impairment of executive function, or the ability to plan, initiate, sequence, monitor, and stop complex behaviors.* The person may make inappropriate decisions—to drive unsafely, to give money away to strangers, or to walk out of the house in pajamas. He or she may move quickly and inappropriately from apathy to hostility or from laughing to weeping.

7. *Impairment of higher-order intellectual function.* The person may have difficulty performing mental tasks that draw on general knowledge, such as numerical calculation.

Impairments of language function, termed **aphasia,** are common. The diagnosis of aphasia depends on fluency of speech, comprehension, and the ability to repeat phrases and sentences (Cummings, 1985). Patients with *fluent aphasia* produce streams of incoherent speech. Syllables are reversed, word order is jumbled, and so on. Patients with *nonfluent aphasia* have difficulty initiating speech and respond to questions with one-word answers, short phrases, and long pauses. Aphasia patients also differ in their ability to understand speech (ranging from good to poor) and their ability to repeat speech correctly (also ranging from good to poor).

When the patient is aphasic, the diagnostician can usually say with some precision where it is that the brain is injured. In most people, language is controlled largely by the left hemisphere (Chapter 4). Aphasia is caused by damage to this hemisphere. Fluent aphasia is produced by injury closer to the rear of this hemisphere, nonfluent aphasia by injury closer to the front of the hemisphere. When damage is limited to the left frontal lobe, comprehension is usually pre-

served. When damage extends to the regions behind the frontal lobe, comprehension is impaired.

Impairments of the ability to recognize familiar objects are called **agnosia.** In his book *The Man Who Mistook His Wife for a Hat and Other Clinical Tales* (1985), Oliver Sacks described the case of Dr. P., a professor of music, who had developed visual agnosia. Dr. P. often failed to recognize his students' faces, yet, when they spoke, he knew immediately who they were. At the same time, he saw faces that didn't exist: he patted the tops of fire hydrants as if they were the heads of children. An ophthalmologist examined Dr. P. and, finding nothing wrong with his eyes, recommended that he see Sacks, a neurologist. Sacks found Dr. P. "a man of great cultivation and charm, who talked well and fluently, with imagination and humor" (p. 8). Gradually, however, it became clear that there was something seriously wrong with him. He was able to see but not to make sense of his perceptions. He could identify a cube, a dodecahedron, and other complex geometric forms, but, when Sacks handed him a rose, he was baffled:

"About six inches in length," he commented. "A convoluted red form with a linear green attachment."

"Yes," I [Sacks] said encouragingly, "but what do you think it *is*, Dr. P.?"

"Not easy to say." He seemed perplexed. . . .

"Smell it," I suggested, and he again looked somewhat puzzled, as if I'd asked him to smell a higher symmetry. (p. 12)

When Sacks handed him a glove, he was again bewildered:

"A continuous surface," he announced at last, "infolded on itself. It appears to have"—he hesitated—"five outpouchings, if this is the word." (p. 13)

On one occasion, as he was preparing to leave Sacks' office, Dr. P. reached for his wife's head and tried to lift it off, mistaking his wife for a hat. Interestingly, although Dr. P.'s visual sense was totally impaired, his musical sense remained intact. He was able to function in everyday life by composing eating songs, dressing songs, and bathing songs, which guided his actions. Dr. P.'s symptoms were due to brain injury in the visual-processing region of the brain.

Dr. P. was an unusual patient in that his symptoms were so isolated and specific. Most patients show a combination of disabilities. Thus, it is the rare case in which the diagnostician can accurately specify one spot, and one spot alone, in which the damage has occurred. Nevertheless, an educated guess must be made as to the site or sites.

Dementia *DSM-IV* describes **dementia** as the impairment of at least two cognitive functions, resulting in a decline from a higher level of performance that compromises a person's occupational or social functioning. Some dementias are caused by infectious diseases, such as syphilis or AIDS: see page 416. Others are degenerative—that is, caused by progressive physical deterioration. Degenerative dementia is described in more detail on page 423.

In diagnosing an acquired brain injury such as dementia, the clinician classifies it according to its cause—trauma, infection, poisoning, or whatever. The one exception to this classification system is epilepsy, which, because its cause is in some cases unknown, is classified by its symptomatology. This chapter will follow the same organizational plan.

Specifying the Site of the Damage

We mentioned earlier the matter of determining the location of the brain damage. This is the third important problem in diagnosis. In the case of some brain injuries, such as the degenerative disorders, the problem may not apply, for the damage is usually diffused throughout the brain. But, with many other injuries, such as "strokes" and brain tumors, damage may be restricted to one specific area, leaving the rest of the brain relatively unaffected. When this is the case, it is essential to determine the site of the injury, for treatment depends on this information. Obviously, a surgeon who is about to operate on a brain tumor needs to know where the tumor is. Such knowledge also guides rehabilitation. Therapists who know where the damage is can retrain patients to use the damaged parts or can teach them to compensate by developing undamaged parts.

Physiological measures such as the EEG can sometimes give vague hints as to the location of the brain injury. The patient's symptoms and history provide further hints. As we saw in Chapter 4, certain areas of the brain are known to control certain behaviors. Likewise, certain types of injury are dissociated with certain areas of the brain. Using this knowledge, a neurologist may be able to determine the location of the damage on the basis of how the patient is acting and how he or she performs on neuropsychological tests.

Today, CT, PET, and MRI are the primary methods of pinpointing the site of brain damage (Bigler, Yeo, & Turkheimer, 1989; Jernigan, 1990; Pykett, 1982; Theodore, 1988a, 1988b). See Chapter 4 for a description of the detailed information these tests can provide and Chapter 2 for an explanation of their use in diagnosis.

Types of Acquired Brain Injuries

Cerebral Infection

Behavior disorders can result from infections that damage and destroy the neural tissue of the brain. Cerebral infections can be caused by bacteria, viruses, protozoa, or fungi. There are three major categories of brain infection: cerebral abscess, encephalitis, and meningitis.

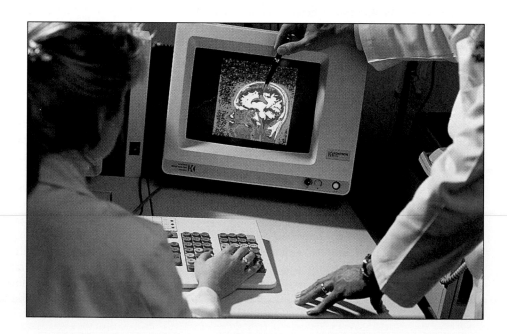

Computerized scans can help pinpoint the site of brain damage.

Cerebral Abscess   A cerebral abscess, like an abscess in any other part of the body, is an infection that becomes encapsulated by connective tissue. Because it cannot drain and heal like an infection on the outside of the body, it simply continues to grow inside the body. Brain abscesses usually occur when an infection in another part of the body travels to the brain or when a foreign object such as a piece of shrapnel enters the brain, introducing germs. With improved measures for preventing infection after injury, cerebral abscesses have become rare.

Encephalitis   Encephalitis is a generic term meaning an inflammation of the brain. Infections which lead to encephalitis can be caused by viral or nonviral agents. One form, *epidemic encephalitis*, also known as "sleeping sickness," was widespread following World War I. Its most striking symptoms are profound lethargy and prolonged periods of sleep, often for days or even weeks at a time. In their periods of wakefulness, however, patients might become extremely hyperactive, irritable, and then breathless and unable to sleep. Other symptoms include convulsive seizures and delirium—a state of excitement and disorientation marked by incoherent speech, restless activity, and often hallucinations. Epidemic encephalitis often leads to death. In those who survive—and especially in children, who are more susceptible—the disease often leaves an altered personality, in many cases a sociopathic personality.

The virus responsible for epidemic encephalitis, while still active in certain areas of Asia and Africa, is now virtually unknown in Europe and North America. However, there remain scores of viruses that can cause other types of encephalitis. Typically transmitted by such animals as mosquitoes, ticks, and horses, these viruses produce many of the same symptoms as epidemic encephalitis—lethargy, irritability, seizures—and often lead to death or, in those who survive, brain damage.

Mad Cow Disease   Mad cow disease is one of several fatal infectious diseases, called *spongiform encephalopathies*, that attack the brain in both animals and humans. Over the past decade, the disease has hit herds of cattle in Great Britain and may have spread to some consumers who ate the contaminated beef. In human beings, this type of encephalopathy is called Creutzfeldt-Jakob disease. While recent cases of Creutzfeldt-Jacob in Great Britain may be linked to mad cow disease, in most cases the source of the infection cannot be identified (Brown, 1997).

In the past, Creutzfeldt-Jakob disease afflicted mostly the middle-aged, but recently it has been seen

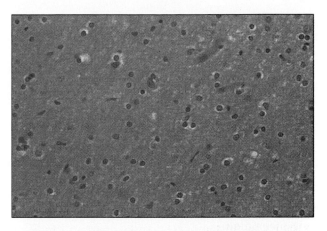

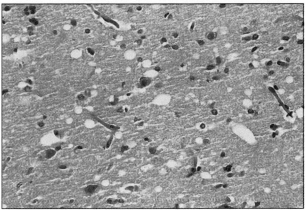

(Top) A normal human brain. (Bottom) The brain of a patient with Creutzfeld-Jakob disease. Note the spongelike, or "spongiform," characteristic of the brain tissue.

in much younger people, with an average age of 27. The first signs of infection are memory loss or confusion, sometimes accompanied by behavioral change or difficulty walking. As the disease progresses, visual perception and motor skills deteriorate rapidly, and the patient falls into dementia. Death occurs about 4 months after the onset of the illness.

Autopsies of these patients have revealed widespread degeneration of brain tissue. Plaques composed of prions, or protein deposits, have encrusted or replaced what were once normal neurons. Though further research remains to be done, scientists strongly suspect that the prion is the cause of the infection.

The form of Creutzfeldt-Jakob disease that is linked to mad cow disease has an incubation period of 10 to 15 years. The disease is comparatively rare, given the widespread consumption of beef in Great Britain. Why it has affected relatively few British citizens is still a mystery to researchers, as is the relatively young age of most of its victims (Brown, 1997).

Meningitis   Another type of cerebral infection is **meningitis,** an acute inflammation of the *meninges,* the membranous covering of the brain and spinal cord. As in cerebral abscess, these foreign bodies may be introduced into the brain either through an infection elsewhere in the body or by an outside agent entering the skull. Among the psychological symptoms usually observed in meningitis are drowsiness, confusion, irritability, inability to concentrate, memory defects, and sensory impairments. In milder cases, the primary infection may be effectively eliminated, but residual effects such as motor and sensory impairments and, in infants, mental retardation are not uncommon.

Neurosyphilis   Neurosyphilis, the deterioration of brain tissue as a result of syphilis, was once far more common than any of the forms of encephalitis. As we saw in Chapter 1, it was not until the late nineteenth century that the degenerative disorder called **general paresis** was finally linked to syphilis. Throughout the previous centuries, syphilis had raged unchecked through Europe, taking a huge toll in infant mortality, blindness, madness, and death. Among its more famous victims were Henry VIII and most of his many wives, and probably Christopher Columbus. Indeed, it is thought that the disease was introduced into Europe by Columbus' crew, who were apparently infected by the natives of the West Indies (Kemble, 1936).

With the development of such early detection procedures as the Wasserman test and with the advent of penicillin, the incidence of syphilis decreased dramatically in the late 1940s and the 1950s. Today, general paresis accounts for less than 1 percent of all first admissions to mental hospitals in the United States.

AIDS Dementia   Every year, *AIDS dementia* develops in about 15 percent of all those diagnosed with AIDS, or acquired immunodeficiency syndrome (Grant & Martin, 1994). Often, it appears in the late stages of the disease, but it may also occur as an early symptom, as in the following case (McArthur, Hoover, Bacellar, et al., 1993):

> Ted is a 32-year-old man who is a talented artist. He has been Human Immunodeficiency Virus (HIV)–positive for 8 years. Two of his close friends have died during the last year from active AIDS. Ted has had AIDS-related complex (ARC) with weight loss, fever, night sweats, fatigue, depression, and generalized lymphadenopathy for 2 years without other serious medical problems. Six months ago he developed [pneumonia], which was treated successfully.

> Three months ago his lover, Randy, noted that Ted was becoming forgetful and had difficulty concentrating on his artwork. Gradually, his memory impairment worsened and he began to have problems painting. He described the problem to Randy, "I can't seem to make the brush go where I want it to go. My hands don't work right." Ted complained of a constant headache and depression. He became increasingly confused and finally, in frustration, stopped trying to paint. The diagnosis is Dementia Due to HIV Disease. (Fauman, 1994, p. 63)

The early symptoms of AIDS dementia sometimes go unnoticed or are mistaken for other problems, physiological or psychological. In many cases, cognitive changes are the first sign of AIDS. At first patients may seem forgetful, apathetic, withdrawn, and either depressed or anxious or both. Later, they become confused, disoriented, and uncoordinated. At this point, the disorder is likely to be recognized as an acquired injury. In the final stages, the patient may go blind, have seizures, become mute, and lapse into a coma (Holland & Tross, 1985).

The HIV virus tends to invade the central nervous system early in the illness. In one study of patients in the early stages of AIDS, the virus was found in the cerebrospinal fluid of about half the subjects (McArthur, Cohen, Seines, et al., 1989; Sonnerborg, Ehrnst, Bergdahl, et al., 1988). But, while the HIV virus will attack the brain itself, AIDS dementia is often caused by other infectious agents, because the body's weakened immune system allows a multitude of pathogens to gain a foothold. The damage done to the brain seems to be diffuse rather than confined to a single area; as yet, there is no known way to reverse it. Over months or years, the dementia usually grows progressively worse.

Groups at Risk   Often, the source of cerebral infection is unknown. Encephalitis can be caused by many common illnesses, including measles, mumps, and influenza. People who are infected with the Epstein-Barr or herpes simplex virus can also develop encephalitis. In the case of herpes encephalitis, risk factors that place persons at risk for herpes infection also place them at greater risk for encephalitis. Similarly, groups at risk for HIV infection are at greater risk than the general population for developing dementia.

Another common source of infection is organisms that are transmitted through insect and rodent bites. For example, California and western equine encephalitis are mosquito-borne, while Rocky Mountain spotted fever is carried by a tick. Though all three of these diseases are prevalent throughout the United States, other types of encephalitis are found only in specific regions. For example, "valley fever," which is transmitted by rodents, occurs mainly in the Southwest; St. Louis encephalitis is generally found in the southern states. And Lyme disease, which can involve either encephalitis or meningitis, is prevalent mainly in New England. Thus, people who live in those regions—especially those who spend considerable time outdoors—are at greater risk than are those who live in other regions.

Treatment of Cerebral Infections　　The treatment of brain injuries that are caused by infection depends on the type of infection. Most bacterial infections are treatable with antibiotics. Cerebral fungal infections are also treatable, if they are identified correctly. Viral infections are more challenging to treat. Steroids can sometimes help the body to fight off a viral infection, and strong drugs such as Acyclovir may help to control infections such as herpes encephalitis. But some infections, such as Creutzfeldt-Jakob disease, the variant of mad cow disease, are largely untreatable (Ashe, Rosen, McArthur, et al., 1993).

Some researchers believe that, in the early stages, the course of an HIV infection of the central nervous system may be reversible (Grant & Martin, 1994). For this reason, they emphasize the importance of both proper diagnosis and timely drug therapy. Certainly, any secondary infections that may contribute to AIDS dementia can and should be eliminated. Antidepressants and tranquilizers may relieve some of the symptoms of the disorder. But, above all, people with AIDS dementia need a safe and structured environment and the help of friends, family members, and health-care workers such as home health aides. Memory aids (a list of numbers by the phone, a note by the door reminding the patient to turn the oven off) may help patients to cope with forgetfulness. Helpers may be needed to take over tasks such as driving, shopping, and preparing meals. In the final stages of the disorder, most patients must be moved to a hospice or nursing home.

Brain Trauma

More common than brain infection is **brain trauma,** or injury to brain tissue as a result of jarring, bruising, or cutting. With a prevalence of 200 per 100,000 population (Sorenson & Kraus, 1991), traumatic head injury is the leading cause of disability and death in children and young adults (National Institute of Neurological Disorders and Stroke, 1989).

A brain injury can have huge consequences. Every year, about 2,000 survivors lapse into a persistent vegetative state, and another 5,000 develop epilepsy (National Institute of Neurological Disorders and Stroke,

1989). These are the more serious cases; 80 percent of head injuries are classified as mild. But even in that group, more than three-quarters of victims show long-term disabilities. Almost all of them report verbal problems, and more than half have impaired memory (Sorenson & Kraus, 1991). Other persistent symptoms are fatigue, sleep disturbances, poor attention and concentration, slowed reactions, emotional ups and downs, and social and moral failures such as selfishness and callousness (Gronwall, Wrightson, & Waddell, 1990). In general, brain-injury survivors constitute a very troubled population, and a hidden one. They do not look disabled, and partly for that reason they often receive little understanding, let alone adequate treatment. But many of them are unable to live normal lives. One-third of brain-injured adults are unemployed 6 months after the injury (McMahan & Flowers, 1986), and they may remain so. They also have trouble sustaining marriages and friendships.

Brain trauma is subdivided into three categories: concussion, contusion, and laceration.

Concussion　　In the case of a **concussion,** the blow to the head jars the brain, momentarily disrupting its functioning (see Figure 14.1). The usual result is a temporary loss of consciousness, often lasting for only a few seconds or minutes, after which the person is typically unable to remember the events immediately preceding the injury. A familiar instance of concussion is a knockout in a boxing match. Concussions occur frequently, too, during football games, a problem discussed in the box on page 418.

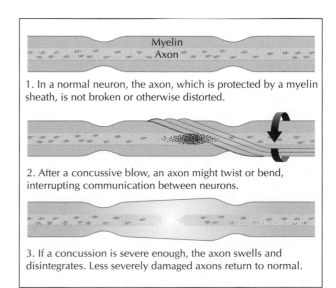

1. In a normal neuron, the axon, which is protected by a myelin sheath, is not broken or otherwise distorted.

2. After a concussive blow, an axon might twist or bend, interrupting communication between neurons.

3. If a concussion is severe enough, the axon swells and disintegrates. Less severely damaged axons return to normal.

FIGURE 14.1　　Anatomy of a concussion.

Concussions in Football: What City Am I In?

In September 1997, 3 days after sustaining his third concussion in 10 months, 49ers quarterback Steve Young decided to play it safe and sit out a game against the St. Louis Rams. A year earlier, Young had suffered a concussion so serious that it left him confused about what city he was playing in (Maiocco, 1997; Puzzanghera, 1996). Among pro football players, such incidents are not unique. In 1994, Merril Hoge, a running back for the Chicago Bears, was hit in the head during a preseason game in Kansas City. When the team trainer asked him if he knew where he was, he replied, "In Tampa Bay." "How do you know that?" the trainer asked. "I can hear the ocean," Hoge replied (quoted in King, 1994, p. 92).

Head injuries are common on the football field. Between 1989 and 1993, according to data from 28 teams in the National Football League (NFL), 341 different players suffered 445 concussions (Farber, 1994). Head injuries dog unprofessional football players as well: each season a quarter of a million high school football players suffer concussions (Farber, 1994). The problem, says Dr. Julian Bailes, a neurosurgeon for the Pittsburgh Steelers, is "almost epidemic"; each year about 10 high school players die from head injuries (quoted in Puzzanghera, 1996).

Most concussions do not end lives or even careers. Still, according to many experts, repeated concussions pose a risk of lasting neurological damage. Cowboys quarterback Troy Aikman cannot remember his team's victory in the NFC championship game in 1994 (Puzzanghera, 1996).

New York Jets wide receiver Al Toon suffered as many as 13 concussions over the course of his 8-year career and was finally forced to retire in 1992. Interviewed 2 years later, he reported that he was still chronically tired and irritable, and he could not watch his children on a carousel without becoming dizzy (Farber, 1994).

Once a player has sustained one concussion, he is four times as likely to suffer a second—a statistic that squares with the players' perceptions. "With every succeeding concussion, it seemed to be easier and easier to get a subsequent one," former Stanford University quarterback Don Bunce, now a sports physician, has said of his own experience on the field (quoted in Puzzanghera, 1996). Sometimes a hit to another part of the body is enough to damage the brain.

As concern over football head injuries has increased, so has awareness that the injuries are not always accidents—that defensive players sometimes engage in "head-hunting." That is, they aim for the head. Such bloodthirstiness is rewarded by coaches. "At every level, the harder you hit, the more you get patted on the back," according to Los Angeles Ram Fred Stokes (quoted in King, 1994, p. 29). Rough play is also rewarded by teammates: few on-the-field celebrations are more exuberant than those reserved for a hard hit on an opponent, regardless of whether the hit stopped him. This machismo culture tends to silence the head-hunters' victims. In the past, many players have refused to be taken out of a game after a concussion (Farber, 1994). "If we get knocked in the head it's embarrassing to come to the side-

line and say 'Hey, my head's feeling funny,'" Young once explained (quoted in Farber, 1994, p. 45).

Presumably, it is the job of the team medical staff to keep injured players off the field, but minor concussions can easily escape notice. "The symptoms are subjective," explains Bailes. "If you have a swollen ankle or a swollen knee, it's a physical part of the body, but if the brain is not processing information correctly maybe only you know that if you're the athlete" (quoted in Puzzanghera, 1996). Bunce concurs. "Right after you get hit there's sort of a stunned experience, then you often come back to the huddle and you have difficulty remembering plays," he recalls. "As time goes on, the more serious side effects of the concussion occur. That's when the brain further swells, you start getting a headache, which can be very intense. You often get blurred vision. You start getting nauseated" (quoted in Puzzanghera, 1996).

To deal with the increasing number of head injuries, the National Football League formed a special subcommittee in 1995. The next year the National Athletic Trainers Association and the NFL Players Association joined to sponsor a conference on the problem. And Bunce says a new helmet is being designed that will spread the impact of a head blow to the shoulders (Puzzanghera, 1996). Finally, *Sports Illustrated* football writer Peter King (1994) has proposed harsh penalties for head-hunting. But, even if such reforms are adopted, the NFL will still have to struggle to deliver in a reasonably safe fashion a product that is intrinsically violent.

In general, the longer the person remains unconscious after the blow, the more severe the posttraumatic symptoms and the less likely it is that the victim will recover completely. In addition to experiencing headaches and dizziness, the person may display apathy, depression, irritability, and various cognitive problems (poor memory, poor concentration). In less severe cases, these symptoms disappear within the span of a few days to a few months, but in some cases, aftereffects may still be experienced months or even years later.

Contusion In a contusion, the trauma is severe enough that the brain is not just jarred; it is actually bruised. The person typically lapses into a coma for several hours or even days and afterward may suffer convulsions and/or temporary speech loss. Further-more, on awakening from the coma, contusion victims may fall into a state of disorientation called **traumatic delirium,** in which they may imagine, for example, that the hospital staff are enemies or kid-nappers. These symptoms generally disappear within a week or so, but a very severe contusion or repeated contusions can result in permanent emotional insta-bility and intellectual impairment. Again, the length of the period of unconsciousness is useful in predict-ing the severity and duration of the posttraumatic symptoms.

The effects of repeated head injuries, such as those suffered by boxers, can result in cumulative damage. The effects can be manifested years later, in *dementia pugilistica* (better known as the punch-drunk syn-drome), which involves memory lapses, loss of coor-dination, dizziness, tremors, and other physical and psychological impairments. One study of a small sample of former prizefighters found that 87 percent exhibited abnormalities on at least two of four mea-sures (Casson, Seigel, Sham, et al., 1984). Re-searchers have also found structural changes in the brains of former boxers, including abnormalities sim-ilar to those found in Alzheimer's disease (Lampert & Hardman, 1984). Indeed, head injury may be a risk factor for Alzheimer's disease, although research is not conclusive on this point (Graves, Larson, White, et al., 1994).

Laceration In a **laceration,** a foreign object, such as a bullet or a piece of metal, enters the skull and directly ruptures and destroys brain tissue. Lacera-tion is potentially the most serious form of brain trauma, though its effects depend on the site of the damage. Lacerations in certain areas of the brain result in death or extreme disability, while damage to other areas may have relatively minor conse-quences. Periodically, the newspapers report a case in which a person who has been shot in the head simply waits for the external wounds to heal and then resumes normal functioning, going about his or her daily business with a bullet or two lodged in the brain. Such cases are rare, however. Normally, a cerebral laceration results in physical impairment or personality change, whether major or minor.

The following classic case, reported in 1868, illus-trates the subtle, variable, and unpredictable effects of cerebral laceration (see also Figure 14.2):

Phineas P. Gage, age twenty-five and strong and healthy, was the popular foreman of a railroad excava-tion crew. While he was working at a site, an explosion drove a tamping iron into the left side of his face and

up through his skull. Thrown onto his back by the force of the blast and by the entry of the rod, Gage con-vulsed, but he quickly regained speech and was placed in a cart, in which he rode in a sitting position for three-quarters of a mile to his hotel. He got out of the cart by himself and walked up a long flight of stairs to his room. Although bleeding profusely, he remained conscious during the doctor's ministrations. Soon af-terward he appeared completely recovered physically, but his personality had undergone a radical change. The equilibrium between his intellectual faculties and his instincts seemed to have been destroyed. He was now inconsiderate, impatient, and obstinate, and yet at the same time capricious and vacillating. He also began indulging in the grossest profanity. The change in temperament was so extreme that his employers had to replace him. To his friends he was simply "no longer Gage." (Adapted from Harlow, 1868, pp. 330–332, 339–340)

Groups at Risk Two-thirds of victims of brain trauma are male; the highest-risk age group is 15- to 24-year-olds (Kraus, Black, Hessol, et al., 1984). Chil-dren and the elderly are also at risk, usually through falls (Lezak, 1995). Indeed, falls are the second most common cause of head injury.

The most common cause of brain trauma, account-ing for over half of all serious head injuries, is automo-bile and motorcycle accidents. Many of these injuries could be prevented. It is estimated that the incidence of brain trauma could be reduced by one-fourth if all cars were equipped with air bags (Jagger, Vernberg, & Jones, 1987). It could also be reduced if people would not drive after drinking. More than half of all head-in-jury survivors have a documentable blood alcohol level at the time of the accident (Sparedo & Gill, 1989).

Treatment of Brain Trauma For many patients, head injuries can be devastating: they face the arduous task of relearning how to walk, talk, or dress. For others, the deficits are more subtle. Often, the frontal lobes are involved; these patients may lose control over their emotions or their ability to be-have in a socially appropriate manner. Depending on the severity of the injury, then, rehabilitation of head injury can range from intensive inpatient treatment, including coma management and resi-dential rehabilitation, to periodic outpatient treat-ment (Malec & Basford 1996).

Cerebrovascular Accidents: Strokes

A third category of brain disorder includes the disor-ders due to a **cerebrovascular accident (CVA)**—better known as a **stroke**—in which blockage or breaking of the blood vessels in the brain results in injury to brain tissue. CVAs are common—indeed, they are the third leading cause of death in the United States. In many cases, the occurrence of the CVA is marked by *stroke syndrome,* the acute onset of specific disabilities involving the central nervous system. The person wakes up from a nap or sits down to dinner, and suddenly he or she can no longer speak, understand speech, move the right side of the body, or perform another CNS-controlled function. In some cases, the stroke victim dies immediately or within days. In other cases, the victim not only lives but does not show stroke syndrome. Many people apparently have what are called "silent strokes," small CVAs that occur in less critical regions of the brain and that have a less noticeable effect on behavior, though the person may find that certain functions, such as memory, are gradually eroded. CVAs are found in 25 percent of routine autopsies, and many of these are silent strokes. There are two broad categories of CVAs: infarction and hemorrhage.

Infarction   In infarction, the supply of blood to the brain is somehow cut off, resulting in the death of brain tissue fed by that source. The two most common causes of infarction are thrombosis and embolism. In an **embolism,** a ball of something such as fat, air, or clotted blood breaks off from the side of a blood vessel or in some other way enters the bloodstream and floats upward until it reaches a blood vessel too narrow to let it pass. At that point, it blocks the vessel, cutting off the blood flow. In a **thrombosis,** fatty material coating the inside of a blood vessel gradually builds up until it blocks the flow of blood in that vessel. Predictably, these two different causes produce different kinds of onset. When a CVA results from an embolism, onset is usually sudden, with dramatic symptoms: the person may collapse, suffer seizures, become paralyzed. In thrombosis, the onset may be more gradual.

Hemorrhage   Aside from infection, the other major category of CVA is cerebral **hemorrhage,** in which a blood vessel in the brain ruptures, causing blood to

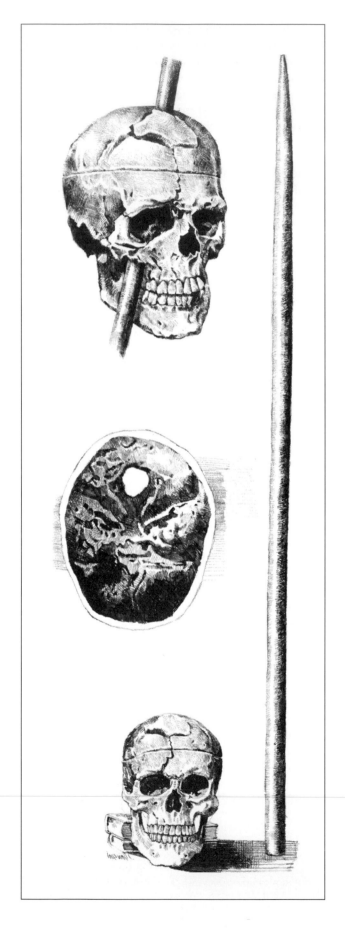

FIGURE 14.2   The cerebral laceration suffered by Phineas Gage is illustrated in these drawings, which are adapted from original sketches done by Dr. Harlow, the physician who attended Gage. The drawings show the relative sizes of the skull and the tamping iron that passed through it. The top drawing shows the position in which the iron lodged; it also shows the large section of the skull that was torn away and later replaced. The middle sketch, an upward view of the inside of the skull, shows the hole made by the iron, partially filled in by new bone deposit.

spill out into the brain tissue. When the hemorrhage occurs inside the brain, it is usually traceable to hypertension. A sudden increase in blood pressure—such as is associated with cocaine abuse—can also contribute to a hemorrhage.

When a hemorrhage occurs in the space around the brain, it is usually due to an aneurysm, or bulge in the wall of the blood vessel. Many such hemorrhages can be traced back to congenital aneurysms. That is, the patient was born with a weakened artery wall, which ballooned and eventually ruptured with age. Aneurysms may be as small as a pea or as large as a plum. They are common—they turn up in 2 percent of autopsied adults (Merritt, 1967)—and, if they do not lead to hemorrhage, they may produce no symptoms whatsoever.

The Effects of a Stroke The aftereffects of a stroke depend on the nature of the stroke—infarction or hemorrhage, embolism or thrombosis, hemorrhage within or around the brain—together with the extent of the damage and, above all, the location of the damage. The most common effects are aphasia, agnosia, apraxia, and paralysis, usually of one limb or one half of the body (because a stroke occurs in one brain hemisphere). Of all forms of stroke, the most common is infarction due to thrombosis, usually in the left-middle cerebral artery. Because the left hemisphere of the brain regulates language, aphasia is a very common effect of stroke. And, because most people are right-handed, and the left side of the brain controls the right side of the body, many stroke patients suffer motor impairments in their dominant hand or leg.

These disabilities (whether they result from CVAs or from any other organic brain disorder) are usually accompanied by some degree of emotional disturbance, partly the result of injury and partly a psychological response to the new impairment. Depression is the most common reaction, seen in 40 percent of patients (Robinson, 1997). Another common reaction is emotional lability: the patient may pass from laughing to weeping in an instant. The response depends greatly on the premorbid personality. People with compulsive tendencies are generally intolerant of any reduction in their abilities and, therefore, may become very depressed after a stroke. Likewise, suspicious natures are exacerbated by the sudden helplessness that accompanies a stroke. Such people may develop paranoid symptoms, accusing others of making fun of them, of stealing their belongings, and so forth. The symptomatology, then, is the result not just of a specific disorder in a specific part of the brain but also of this disorder's *working on* a specific personality.

Half of first-stroke patients die within five years, usually from another stroke (Terént, 1993). This is a

A therapist works with a patient to improve motor functions impaired by a stroke.

harsh statistic, but in fact it represents a medical victory. Stroke survival rates have almost doubled since the 1940s (Whisnant, 1993), and they are still improving. In patients who survive, some of the behavioral symptoms may disappear spontaneously, while others can be remedied through rehabilitation. And, as the disability is remedied, so in most cases is the attendant emotional disturbance. Some CVA patients recover completely, but most continue to labor under some form of impairment for the rest of their lives. In general, the younger the patient and the smaller the area of brain damage, the better the chance of recovery.

Groups at Risk The clearest risk factor for CVAs is age. Between the ages of 60 and 80, the risk increases almost eightfold. In people over 75, the rate of first stroke is almost 20 times that of the general population: 2,000 as opposed to 114 per 1,000 population (Terént, 1993). That is because the incidence of physical conditions that weaken the blood vessels—above all, hypertension, heart disease, and atherosclerosis, or thickening of the walls of the blood vessels—increases with age.

Another risk factor is gender. Men are more vulnerable than women by a ratio of 1.3 to 1 (Kurtzke, 1980). The women's advantage is due in part to the fact that estrogen seems to protect against atherosclerosis, but even after menopause, when estrogen levels fall, women are still somewhat less susceptible to strokes, and hormone-replacement therapy may restore their former advantage. Other higher-risk groups are diabetics, people with a family history of strokes, and African Americans, who bear twice the stroke risk of most other ethnic groups (Singleton & Johnson, 1993).

Those are the uncontrollable risk factors. In addition, there are several other conditions that make people vulnerable to this disorder. High cholesterol and obesity increase stroke risk; smoking almost doubles it; hypertension increases it from two to five times (Boysen, 1993). All these factors can be controlled.

Treatment of Stroke   Fearing heart attack, most people tend to seek medical attention quickly when they experience chest pain. However, people often ignore the first signs of stroke. A tingling or weakness on one side of the body, a drooping face, difficulty understanding or expressing oneself—all may be signs of a stroke. The importance of seeking treatment at the first appearance of such symptoms cannot be overemphasized. Recently, medications have been developed which can limit the effects of a stroke, if they are administered in a timely manner (Albers, 1997).

Brain Tumors

Brain tumors are classified as either metastatic or primary. **Metastatic brain tumors** originate in a different part of the body and then metastasize, or spread, to the brain. Usually, they develop from cancer of the lung, breast, stomach, or kidney and travel to the brain through the blood vessels. By contrast, **primary brain tumors,** as their name suggests, are tumors that originate in the brain. Some primary tumors are *intracerebral*—that is, they grow inside the brain. Others are *extracerebral,* growing outside the brain but inside the skull, often in the meninges. Intracranial tumors are more frequently seen in adults; extracranial tumors, in children. Brain tumors in general are common. Every year about 20,000 new primary brain tumors are diagnosed, and another 20,000 people are diagnosed as having metastatic brain tumors (Segal, 1991).

Although the actual cause of tumors has not yet been determined, their clinical course is clear. For some reason, a few cells begin to grow at an abnormally rapid rate, destroying the surrounding healthy brain tissue and resulting in a wide variety of psychological symptoms. In most cases, the first signs are subtle and insidious—headaches, seizures, visual problems, neglect of personal hygiene, indifference to previously valued activities, and failures of judgment and foresight. With the progressive destruction of brain tissue, the patient eventually develops at least one of the more obvious symptoms: abnormal reflexes; blunting of affect; disorientation in regard to time, place, and/or person; poor memory and concentration; double vision; and jerky motor coordination. The kind and severity of symptoms are directly related to the location of the tumor in the brain: the functions controlled by that section are probably impaired earlier and more severely than other functions. However, as the tumor grows, pressing against other sections, their functioning too are affected.

Any tumor that continues to grow, untreated, in the brain will eventually cause extreme physical distress (splitting headaches, vomiting, seizures), along with personality changes that may reach psychotic proportions. Just before death, the patient may become overtly psychotic and, finally, lapse into a coma.

Groups at Risk   Not much is known about risk factors for brain tumors. About all that can be said is that some types of cancer, such as lung cancer, metastasize to the brain; a significant risk factor for lung cancer, of course, is smoking.

Treatment of Brain Tumors   Several types of tumors can be removed surgically, and in many cases they are. However, because the surgery itself can cause additional brain damage, the physician may choose to avoid it. Surgeons are especially reluctant to operate on the language areas and on the major motor areas. In such cases, radiation treatment may be used, though this, too, can destroy brain tissue. In other cases, surgery, chemotherapy, and radiation are used in combination, both to remove the growth and to prevent future growths.

Degenerative Disorders

Degenerative disorders are syndromes characterized by a general deterioration of intellectual, emotional, and motor functioning as a result of progressive pathological change in the brain. As usual with organic brain disorders, symptoms vary, depending on the site of the damage (Cummings & Benson, 1992). Disorders caused by deterioration of the cerebral cortex produce memory disturbances, impaired comprehension, naming difficulties, and environmental disorientation. Until the late stages of the disease, gait, posture, muscle tone, and reflexes are usually unimpaired. Alzheimer's disease is such a disorder. In disorders caused by deterioration of the subcortical regions of the brain (below the cerebral cortex), the usual symptoms are concentrating and difficulty in solving problems, mood swings, and motor disturbances. Huntington's chorea and Parkinson's disease are disorders of this type. Still other disorders are caused by vascular disease that affects both the cortical and subcortical regions of the brain. These disorders are characterized by abrupt onset, stepwise deterioration—that is, deterioration in a series of downward plateaus—and focal symptoms, such as aphasia. Vascular dementia is an example of this last category.

Aging and Dementia   Psychologists used to think that **dementia,** or severe mental deterioration, was a final stage of aging that would occur in everyone who lived long enough. Today, we know that dementia is the result of degenerative brain disorders that affect only a small minority of the aged. Approximately 4 to 7 percent of people over 65 have definite signs of dementia. Prevalence rises with age, however: among people over 85, about 30 percent show dementia (Johansson & Zarit, 1991; Kokmen, Beard, Offord, et al., 1989). Fortunately, even at such advanced ages, most people have little or no evidence of degenerative brain disorder—no pronounced loss of memory, impaired reasoning, or impaired judgment.

Almost all old people experience some psychological changes simply as a function of aging. Although the precise biological processes are still not clear, it seems that all behavior mediated by the central nervous system slows down as the body ages (Birren, 1974; Salthouse, 1985). Old people in general experience a slowing of motor reactions, a lessened capacity to process complex information, and decreased efficiency in memory and in the learning of new material. These changes are part of the *normal* process of aging; they are no more pathological than wrinkles or gray hair. By contrast, the degenerative diseases known collectively as dementias, are pathological; they are the direct result of a severe organic deterioration of the brain. Dementias account for more hospital admissions and for more inpatient hospital days than any other psychiatric disorder among elderly people (Cummings & Benson, 1992). The most common dementias are Alzheimer's disease and Lewy body disease.

The diagnosis of these syndromes is a complicated matter. A host of treatable problems, including other illnesses, reactions to medication, and depression, can mimic the symptoms of dementia. Furthermore, Alzheimer's disease is sometimes difficult to distinguish from other dementias. The courses of these disorders do differ: for instance, vascular dementia involves a stepwise deterioration, whereas in Alzheimer's the deterioration is smooth and gradual. But, usually, when the patient comes for diagnosis, most of the course is in the future, and there is considerable overlap between symptoms. As yet, there is no sure medical test for Alzheimer's disease; the disorder cannot be diagnosed conclusively until postmortem examination. To make matters worse, many dementia patients have *both* Alzheimer's and Lewy body disease (see explanation of Lewy body disease beginning on page 424) or vascular dementia. A final source of confusion is one mentioned earlier: the symptoms in any case of acquired brain injuries have everything to do with the patient's premorbid personality and psychosocial history, the availability of outside supports, and any number of other intangible factors. This is particularly true of the elderly. Two patients with the same disorder may behave quite differently.

Alzheimer's Disease   The most common form of dementia, and one of the most tragic, is **Alzheimer's disease.** Autopsies of patients with this disorder reveal both *neurofibrillary tangles* (twisted and distorted nerve fibers) and *senile plaques* (microscopic lesions in the neurons). Alzheimer's can occur as early as age 40, but its prevalence increases with age. It is estimated that, in the United States, 4 to 5 percent of people over age 65, and 20 percent over 85, suffer from Alzheimer's (Johansson & Zarit, 1995).

The primary symptoms of Alzheimer's disease are cognitive deficits—particularly, loss of memory for recent events. An Alzheimer's patient may be able to tell you the names of all the people in the office where she worked 50 years ago, and all their children's names, but not what she ate for breakfast that morning. As the disease worsens, there is loss of memory for distant events as well. The characteristic early signs of the disease are irritability and failure of concentration and memory, with mild difficulty in recalling names and words. Patients may also have problems with perception and spatial orientation.

The cognitive deficits of Alzheimer's patients create major difficulties for them and their families (Zarit, Orr, & Zarit, 1985). Usually, complex behaviors such as playing poker or balancing the checkbook are disrupted first, but eventually simple, daily behaviors such as bathing and dressing also degenerate. Patients may also do things that are disturbing or simply stressful to their caregivers. They may ask the same question over and over; they may confuse night and day. Some forget that they have turned on the bath water or have lit the stove; some wander off and get lost; some become violent. As they weaken physically, they are likely to become bedridden. At this point, they may have little awareness of their

Former President Ronald Reagan suffers from Alzheimer's disease, the most common form of dementia.

surroundings. The rate of progression of the disease is highly variable. In some people, severe impairment and death occur between 3 and 5 years after onset, while other patients live 15 years or more after onset.

One of the "hottest" areas of recent neuroscience research has been the genetics of Alzheimer's disease. Family patterns strongly suggest that the disorder is controlled in part by genes, but in a complex way, involving not just 1 genetic abnormality but several (Hardy, 1993). The normal human cell contains 23 pairs of chromosomes, each of which has been numbered and partially "mapped" as to which genes it contains. The first breakthroughs in genetic research on Alzheimer's had to do with chromosome 21. It is a well-documented fact that almost all people with Down syndrome (Chapter 16), a disorder caused by the addition of a copy of chromosome 21, develop Alzheimer's disease if they live past age 40 (Zigman, Schupf, Zigman, et al., 1992). Thus, Alzheimer's researchers were alerted to the possible involvement of chromosome 21, and their interest was further piqued by the discovery that the production of amyloid, the substance at the core of the senile plaques found in the brains of Alzheimer's patients, is controlled by genes on chromosome 21 (Goldgaber, Lerman, et al., 1987). Finally, in 1987, researchers at

Massachusetts General Hospital announced that they had found abnormalities on chromosome 21 in 4 families with a long history—145 cases—of Alzheimer's disease (St. George-Hyslop, et al., 1987).

However, efforts to replicate those findings were only partly successful. Today, while it is accepted that chromosome 21 may be involved in some cases of Alzheimer's, interest has shifted to 2 other chromosomes: chromosome 14, which is associated with early-onset (before age 60) cases, and chromosome 19, which is implicated in many late-onset cases. But this is not the end of the story. The Germans of the Volga region and their American descendants, who have a strong inherited pattern of Alzheimer's, do not seem to show abnormalities at any of the identified sites on chromosomes 21, 14, or 19, so other chromosomes are probably involved as well.

To account for this heterogeneity, researchers have proposed the so-called amyloid-cascade hypothesis (Hardy, 1993). According to this hypothesis, the key element in the onset of Alzheimer's disease is the buildup of toxic levels of one kind of amyloid, beta amyloid, in the brain, but this buildup can be caused by the breakdown of any one of several regulatory mechanisms, each controlled by a different gene. Researchers have discovered, for example, that beta-amyloid accumulations (and a high risk for Alzheimer's) are linked to variations in a protein, ApoE (apolipoprotein E), that is controlled by genes on chromosome 19 (Corder, Saunders, Strittmatter, et al., 1993). That protein, however, is only one element in the long chain of reactions that, according to the cascade theory, constitutes the brain's processing of beta amyloid. Thus, ApoE is one link that can break; in which case, the fault lies on chromosome 19. But other links, controlled by other genes, may also break.

Thus, Alzheimer's is one of those disorders, like schizophrenia, for which researchers have identified multiple contributing factors but no single cause. And, as with schizophrenia, many researchers feel that in any given case the causes probably are multiple. Gatz and her colleagues, for example, have proposed a "threshold model" for Alzheimer's, whereby genetic risk together with any combination of other risk factors—head injury, exposure to toxic substances, alcohol abuse, poor nutrition, even lack of mental stimulation—gradually brings the person closer to a threshold beyond which symptoms begin to appear (Gatz, Lowe, Berg, et al., 1994).

Lewy Body Disease   Today, Alzheimer's disease is a relatively well-known cause of dementia in the elderly. But, recently, researchers have identified another, less well-known disorder, **Lewy body disease,**

which may now be the second most common degenerative brain disease. Lewy body disease affects an estimated 15 to 25 percent of elderly patients who suffer from dementia (McKeith, Galasko, Kosaka, et al., 1996). The disorder gets its name from the presence of microscopic rounded structures called *Lewy bodies* in neurons throughout the brain. Composed mostly of altered neurofilaments, Lewy bodies also contain a protein called Ubiquitin, whose function is to break down abnormal cellular proteins (Kalra, Bergeron, & Lang, 1996).

Because the presence of Lewy bodies is usually confirmed only by autopsy, clinicians must rely on an analysis of the patient's symptoms to diagnose the disease. The task is complicated by the fact that, in some cases, the symptoms of Lewy body disease are similar to those of Alzheimer's. Indeed, the same plaques and tangled neurons associated with Alzheimer's are found in the brains of about 50 percent of those with Lewy body disease. Furthermore, in many cases, Lewy body disease is followed by Parkinson's disease. Lewy body disease may be linked genetically to both Alzheimer's and Parkinson's (Kalra, Bergeron, & Lang, 1996). Given the overlapping symptoms, the classification of the disorder is still a matter of controversy; some researchers consider Lewy body disease to be a variant of Alzheimer's or Parkinson's, while others do not (Cercy & Bylsma, 1997).

In a recent study, researchers compared the symptoms of 112 subjects diagnosed at autopsy with Alzheimer's, Lewy body, or Parkinson's disease. They found that depression and hallucinations were more common among the subjects with Lewy body disease than among those with Alzheimer's: 50 percent of the Lewy body subjects had been depressed, compared with only about 14 percent of the Alzheimer's subjects: about 61 percent of the Lewy body subjects had suffered hallucinations, compared with only about 35 percent of those with Alzheimer's. The subjects with Parkinson's disease showed the same rates of depression and hallucination as those with Lewy body disease. Delusions were much more common among the subjects with Lewy body disease than among those with Parkinson's, but not those with Alzheimer's (Klatka, Louis, & Schiffer, 1996).

Perhaps the most distinguishing symptom of Lewy body disease is the day-to-day fluctuations in the patient's mental state. Hallucinations, confusion, agitation, and delusions come and go, often in a matter of minutes. Unexplained falls and transient clouding or loss of consciousness are also distinctive. (These symptoms do not fit well with *DSM-IV* criteria, which require the exclusion of delirium before a diagnosis of dementia is made.) Like Alzheimer's,

Lewy body disease occurs most often in the elderly. All cases eventually progress to dementia, and most involve memory impairment followed by symptoms of Parkinson's disease, particularly rigidity (Kalra, Bergeron, & Lang, 1996).

Vascular Dementia   As we saw earlier, an infarction is a kind of stroke in which blood flow in the brain becomes blocked, resulting in damage to the area of the brain fed by the blood vessels in question. (The damaged area is called an *infarct.*) **Vascular dementia** is the cumulative effect of a number of small strokes of this kind, eventually impairing many of the brain's faculties. The physical signs of vascular dementia are blackouts, heart problems, kidney failure, hypertension, and retinal sclerosis (a scarring of the retina of the eye). Common psychological symptoms are language and memory defects, emotional lability, and depression. Psychosis may also develop, typically with delusions of persecution. As noted, some of these symptoms overlap those of Alzheimer's, making diagnosis difficult.

Alzheimer's disease, Lewy body disease, and vascular dementia all affect mainly the elderly. The degenerative disorders to which we now turn—Huntington's chorea and Parkinson's disease—afflict the middle-aged or, in the case of Huntington's, young adults.

Huntington's Chorea   **Huntington's chorea** is one of the very few neurological disorders definitely known to be transmitted genetically. It is passed on by a dominant gene from either parent to both male and female children. Forty to 70 cases of Huntington's chorea occur in every 1 million people (Cummings & Benson, 1992).

The primary site of the damage that causes Huntington's chorea is the basal ganglia, clusters of nerve-cell bodies located deep within the cerebral hemispheres and responsible primarily for posture, muscle tonus, and motor coordination. However, the first signs of the disease are not so much motor impairments as vague behavioral and emotional changes. In the typical case, the person becomes slovenly and rude, and his or her moods become unpredictable and inconsistent, running the gamut from obstinacy, passivity, and depression to inexplicable euphoria. Intellectual functions, particularly memory and judgment, are also disrupted. As the disease progresses, delusions, hallucinations, and suicidal tendencies commonly appear (Boll, Heaton, & Reitan, 1974).

In addition to developing these psychological problems, the patient eventually begins to show the characteristic motor symptoms—an involuntary, spasmodic jerking of the limbs—to which the term *chorea* (from the Greek *choreia,* meaning "dance") refers. This sign appears to indicate irreversible brain damage (James, Mefford, & Kimbell, 1969). From then on, patients show increasingly bizarre behavior. They may spit, bark out words (often obscenities) explosively, walk with a jerky or shuffling gait, and smack their tongues and lips involuntarily. Eventually, they lose control of bodily functions altogether. Death is the inevitable result, occurring, on average, 14 years after onset.

Parkinson's Disease   First described in 1871 by James Parkinson (who suffered from it), **Parkinson's disease** also involves damage to the basal ganglia, particularly the region known as the substantia nigra. The cause of this condition is unknown, although it has been attributed to a variety of factors, including heredity, encephalitis, viruses, toxins, deficient brain metabolism, and head trauma. The illness occurs most frequently in people between the ages of 50 and 70.

The primary symptom of Parkinson's is tremor, occurring at a rate of about four to eight movements per second. The tremors are usually present during rest periods but tend to diminish or cease when the patient is sleeping. Interestingly, patients can often stop the tremors if someone orders them to do so, and for a short time they may even be able to perform motor activities requiring very fine muscular coordination. Such remissions are always temporary, however, and the patient once again lapses into the typical rhythmic jerking of arms, hands, jaws, and/or head.

Another highly characteristic sign of Parkinson's is an expressionless, masklike countenance, probably due to difficulties initiating movement and slowed motor responses. Parkinson's patients also tend to walk, when they *can* walk, with a distinctive slow, stiff gait, usually accompanied by a slight crouch.

Approximately 40 to 60 percent of Parkinson's disease patients also experience psychological disturbances. These include problems with memory, learning, judgment, and concentration, as well as apathy and social withdrawal. As many as half of Parkinson's patients also develop dementia. In more severe cases, there may be highly systematized delusions and severe depression, including suicidal tendencies. However, it is difficult to determine whether these symptoms are due directly to the brain pathology or simply to patients' distress over their physical helplessness.

Groups at Risk   We have seen that the incidence of dementia increases with age. Because women live longer than men, many more women than men will experience dementia. However, at any given age, the percentage of men and women who will develop dementia is the same (Kokmen, Beard, O'Brien, et al., 1993).

Former boxing champion Mohammed Ali, shown here lighting the torch at the 1996 Summer Olympic Games in Atlanta, is afflicted with Parkinson's disease.

Both age and gender are related to the type of dementia an individual is likely to develop. Patients with pure Lewy body disease (uncomplicated by symptoms of Alzheimer's) tend to be identified at a younger age than those with Alzheimer's, many of them before they develop dementia. Patients with mixed symptoms of Lewy body and Alzheimer's tend to be older, and most are demented when they are first seen (Cercy & Bylsma, 1997). Though women as a group live longer than men, men are twice as likely as women to develop Lewy body disease (Kalra, Bergeron, & Lang, 1996). In the retrospective study described, most of the subjects diagnosed with Lewy body disease at autopsy were male, while most of those diagnosed with Alzheimer's were female (Klatka, Louis, & Schiffer, 1996).

Research also suggests that educational level may affect either the incidence or rate of diagnosis of Alzheimer's disease. Several studies have suggested a connection between the disease and limited education, perhaps because education can affect performance on the diagnostic tests administered to patients to detect cognitive impairment. In a follow-up study of nearly 600 subjects of 60 years of age or older, researchers found that the risk of dementia was higher among subjects of low educational level and/or low lifetime occupational achievement. The risk was highest among subjects with both a low educational level and low lifetime achievement (Stern, Gurland, Tatemichi, et al., 1994). Researchers were unsure whether these factors merely increased the likelihood of diagnosis or they somehow contributed to the onset of the disease.

Vascular dementia occurs in about 3 percent of people over 65 (Cummings, 1987). An estimated 53 percent of stroke patients also go on to develop vascular dementia. The major risk factor for the disorder is high blood pressure. Eighty percent of vascular dementia patients have a history of hypertension; for this reason, African Americans are probably at greater risk for vascular dementia than are other ethnic groups. Other risk factors are diabetes, obesity, and smoking.

Huntington's chorea is a genetic disorder, and the defective gene has been identified. There is now a test that can identify carriers, and it may eventually be possible, through genetic engineering, to treat them before symptoms develop.

Treatment of Degenerative Disorders   It is known that in Alzheimer's disease the production of the neurotransmitter acetylcholine is disrupted. Therefore, presumably, the symptoms might be relieved if levels of acetylcholine could be raised. Following this reasoning, researchers developed a drug, tacrine—its brand name is Cognex—that blocks acetylcholine reuptake. The first drug specifically approved for treating Alzheimer's patients, Cognex went on the market in the early 1990s amid a great blast of publicity. The results were disappointing, however. Only 20 to 30 percent of patients on Cognex showed any benefits. Furthermore, the benefits were modest and, in some cases, transient (Farlow, Gracon, Hershey, et al., 1992), while the side effects, including liver problems, were serious.

A newer drug, Aricept (also called Donepezil) seems more promising. In a recent study, subjects treated with the drug showed improved scores on the cognitive subscale of the Alzheimer's Disease Assessment Scale. Those who received the drug also showed less decline over the 14 weeks of the study than did members of the control group, who received a placebo. Moreover, Aricept did not have an adverse effect on subjects' liver function (Rogers, Friedhoff, Apter, et al., 1996). For this reason, Aricept has now largely replaced Cognex in the treatment of Alzheimer's disease.

Another treatment that shows promise is a daily dose of 2,000 IU of vitamin E. In a 2-year study of more than 300 subjects, vitamin E slowed the progression of Alzheimer's disease among subjects with moderately severe impairment. Patients who took the vitamin lived longer, were institutionalized later, and retained the ability to perform basic activities longer than those who took a placebo (Sano, Ernesto, Thomas, et al., 1997). Other drug regimens—estrogen replacement therapy in older women, anti-inflammatory drugs and other drugs that inhibit the immune system—are apparently related to a decreased risk for Alzheimer's, but those findings are still speculative.

At present, then, there is no cure and little treatment for Alzheimer's disease. Behavior therapy techniques may suppress some symptoms. Tranquilizers may also be useful, though in some patients they make the symptoms worse. The most common treatment is custodial care, often in a nursing home. Still, many patients are able to remain at home with their families, especially if the families can rely on professional support services. The development of such services (see the box on page 428) is one of the most hopeful avenues in the treatment of degenerative brain diseases.

We have seen that high blood pressure, diabetes, obesity, and smoking are risk factors for vascular dementia. Better control of these problems may help in the prevention of vascular dementia, but, as with Alzheimer's, there is no cure. Once the damage has occurred, decline is irreversible.

Parkinson's is unusual among degenerative disorders in that it can be treated with some success. The substantia nigra is involved in dopamine synthesis, so, when this area degenerates in the course of Parkinson's, the patient's dopamine levels drop. Drugs that increase the amount of dopamine can in most cases control the tremor and other motor symptoms for several years, though they cannot cure the disease. Unfortunately, the beneficial effects of these medications decline with long-term use.

Nutritional Deficiency

Malnutrition—or, specifically, insufficient intake of one or more essential vitamins—can result in neurological damage and, consequently, in psychological disturbances. Two common syndromes in less industrialized nations are beriberi, due to thiamine deficiency, and pellagra, due to niacin deficiency, but improvements in diet have largely eliminated these conditions from the American population. More commonly seen in this country is Korsakoff's psychosis.

Korsakoff's psychosis is considered irreversible. Alcoholics are the most common victims because of

Caregivers: The Hidden Victims of Dementia

Caring for a patient with dementia can be brutally taxing. What follows is the record of a typical day in the life of a young woman living with her husband, her seven-year-old son, and her grandmother, a dementia patient:

The caregiver's day began at 5 A.M. when she got up and did light housekeeping chores. At 6, she prepared breakfast for her husband, and they had breakfast together. At 6:30, she woke her son up and began helping him get ready for school. From that time until 8, she either did chores or was with her son. At 8, she began the bathwater for her grandmother. Her grandmother got up at 8:15 and she assisted her with her bath and then with dressing. At 8:45, she fixed breakfast for her grandmother and gave her medications. After breakfast, her grandmother sat in a rocker and watched television until about 10:15. During this time, she talked to an ornamental Santa Claus (it was a few days before Christmas), calling it by her great-grandson's name. The caregiver did not intervene and was not disturbed by this behavior. She was cleaning in the kitchen during this time. From 10:15 to 12, the caregiver did housekeeping chores and the patient followed her around. She asked repeatedly to go out and see Fred (her deceased husband). The caregiver made excuses why they could not go out, which satisfied the patient. She also gave the patient a snack during this period. At noon, the patient laid down on the couch and rested. The caregiver then did some laundry. Her grandmother called to her a few times during this period, and she would then go to her to tuck her in again.

The afternoon and evening followed the same pattern, except that the woman was now looking after her son as well as her grandmother and handling friction between the two. At one point,

the patient became agitated because of the noise her great-grandson was making while playing, and she hit him on the head with a newspaper. The caregiver intervened, but the patient denied doing anything.

Finally, by 10:30 P.M., the woman got both the son and the grandmother into bed:

From 11:10 to 11:20, the caregiver had a cup of tea and watched television. At 11:20, her husband came home, and she fixed him supper. They talked until 12:10 A.M. and then went to bed. At 2:00 A.M., her grandmother called for assistance to go to the bathroom, and then had difficulty going back to sleep. To calm her, the caregiver talked with her about Christmases they had spent together in the past when the caregiver was a child. At 2:30, they both went back to bed, and the caregiver slept until 5 A.M. (Zarit, 1992, pp. 3–15)

As noted, many dementia patients, such as those with Alzheimer's, may live for 15 years or more after the onset of symptoms. Almost everyone agrees that the best situation for such patients is to remain with their families when possible, but this places a huge burden on the family. Even if patients are not agitated, as they often are, they still require constant supervision, and many of them sleep so little that they need close to 24-hour care.

In consequence, the family members suffer considerable stress (Gatz, Bengston, & Blum, 1990), and not just in the caregiving situation. They may have to give up their leisure activities and social lives; indeed, they may have to quit their jobs. (The woman in the above case did.) Or, if they go on working, they must struggle to divide their time between the requirements of the job and those of the patient, while their spare minutes are often spent arguing over the phone with other relatives over what should be done with the patient. Such a situation can lead to what researchers have called an "erosion of the self-concept" (Pearlin, Mullan, Semple, et al., 1990). The caregiver feels that he or she no longer has a self; it has been parceled out for use by others. Predictably, Alzheimer's caregivers are at higher-than-average risk for psychological disorders (Zarit, 1994). They also show lowered immune responses and are, therefore, more susceptible to physical disorders (Kiecolt-Glaser, Dura, Speicher, et al., 1991).

How can the caregivers be cared for? As soon as possible after the diagnosis of a degenerative brain disorder, the family members should meet with the professional who can advise them. This may be a psychologist, a social worker, or a representative of the Alzheimer's Association or another, similar organization. Such a professional can tell them what to expect as the disease progresses, teach them simple behavior-management techniques for coping with agitation, and direct them to services that can give them relief, such as adult day care and overnight respite care. (In the latter, the patient stays for short periods in a hospital or nursing home. This can free the family to take a vacation.) Legal and financial counseling is usually critical, so that families can plan how to manage the expense of caring for a dementia patient. And, if there is conflict among the family members, as there typically is in this stressful situation, they can be referred for family counseling, which is often very effective for relatives of dementia patients (Mittelman, Ferris, Steinberg, et al., 1993; Whitlatch, Zarit, & von Eye, 1991).

Finally, caregivers can join a support group. Support groups have been found to be very helpful to people with a wide range of problems— cancer patients, drug abusers, families of drug abusers, and so on. They can also be useful to families of dementia patients, providing them with tips, fellowship, and the kind of understanding that can come only from people in the same situation.

Comprehensive counseling and support benefit patients as well as their caregivers. In a recent study of more than 200 Alzheimer's patients and their caregivers, researchers found that, in families that received such services, caregivers were able to care for patients at home (rather than placing them in a nursing home) almost a year longer than were caregivers in a control group. Caregivers who belonged to the group that received counseling and support were only about two-thirds as likely as those in the control group to place their spouses in a nursing home (Mittelman, Ferris, Shulman, et al., 1996).

their notoriously bad diets. It is generally agreed that the primary pathology in this disorder is due to a deficiency of vitamin B_1, or thiamine (Brion, 1969; Redlich & Freedman, 1966).

There are two classic behavioral signs of Korsakoff's psychosis, anterograde amnesia and confabulation. *Anterograde amnesia* is the inability to incorporate new memories, and *confabulation* is the tendency to fill in memory gaps with invented stories. In response to questioning, for example, patients may placidly offer a nonsensical account of why they are in the hospital, if indeed they admit that the place is a hospital. Such patients usually seem calm and affable, while their total unawareness of the fantastic quality of their stories reveals a psychotic impairment of judgment. This impairment gradually spreads to other aspects of psychological functioning. In addition to having these memory deficits, many alcoholics experience a more generalized intellectual decline. Like the degenerative diseases previously discussed, chronic alcoholism can lead to deficits in most cognitive abilities (Cummings & Benson, 1992).

Endocrine Disorders

The **endocrine glands** are responsible for the production of hormones. When released into the bloodstream, the hormones affect various bodily mechanisms, such as sexual functions, physical growth and development, and the availability of energy. Disturbances in the endocrine system, and particularly in the thyroid and adrenal glands, can give rise to a variety of psychological disorders.

Thyroid Syndromes Overactivity of the thyroid gland—a condition called *hyperthyroidism,* or *Graves' disease*—involves an excessive secretion of the hormone thyroxin, which gives rise to a variety of physical and psychological difficulties. Psychological symptoms accompanying the disorder may include severe apprehension and agitation, hallucinations, excessive motor activity, sweating, and other symptoms suggestive of anxiety. Former president George Bush and his wife, Barbara, both suffer from Graves' disease.

Opposite to hyperthyroidism in both cause and effect is *hypothyroidism,* sometimes referred to as *myxedema,* in which underactivity of the thyroid gland results in deficient production of thyroxin. Hypothyroidism may be due to iodine deficiency, a problem that has become much less common in the United States since the advent of iodized table salt. People suffering from hypothyroidism are frequently sluggish, have difficulties with memory and concentration, and appear to be lethargic and depressed.

Again, however, symptomatology depends greatly on premorbid personality. The same is true of hyperthyroidism.

Adrenal Syndromes Chronic underactivity of the cortex, or outer layer, of the adrenal glands gives rise to *Addison's disease,* which involves both physical and psychological changes. Again, the psychological symptoms vary considerably according to the person's premorbid adjustment. Some patients just seem moderately depressed; others experience debilitating extremes of depression, anxiety, and irritability. Appropriate medication can relieve the symptoms of even a severe case of Addison's disease, restoring the person to normal functioning.

When the adrenal cortex is excessively active, several disorders may arise, one of which is *Cushing's syndrome.* This relatively rare disorder usually affects young women. Like the other endocrine disorders, Cushing's syndrome involves both physical symptoms—in this case, obesity and muscle weakness—and psychological difficulties, especially extreme emotional lability, with fluctuations in mood ranging from total indifference to violent hostility.

Toxic Disorders

Various plants, gases, drugs, and metals, when ingested or absorbed through the skin, can have a toxic, or poisonous, effect on the brain. Depending on the person, the toxic substance, and the amount ingested, the results of such brain poisoning range from temporary physical and emotional distress to psychosis and death. One sign that is almost always present in the toxic disorders is delirium.

Lead An especially tragic form of toxic brain disorder is lead poisoning. The excessive ingestion of lead causes a condition called lead **encephalopathy,** in which fluid accumulates in the brain, causing extreme pressure. Early symptoms include abdominal pains, constipation, facial pallor, and sometimes convulsions and bizarre behaviors such as hair pulling. In severe cases, the symptoms may be similar to those of psychosis, including hallucinations. The most common victims of lead poisoning are children, who may become mentally retarded as a result. As we will see in Chapter 16, children with mental retardation are more often exposed to lead than other children are (Grant & Davis, 1989).

Consumer advocacy groups have identified a number of sources of lead contamination, including old, lead-lined water pipes, lead-based paint on children's toys and furniture, old plaster walls, candles with lead-core wicks, certain electric tea kettles that

Children who eat lead-based paint chips may fall victim to lead poisoning and become mentally retarded as a result.

release lead from soft solder joints when heated, pottery glazes from which foods that contain acetic acid (e.g., grape juice) can leach lead, exhaust from automobiles that burn leaded gasoline, and industrial pollution. As can be seen from this list, the issue of metal poisoning often involves a conflict between the needs of industry and the needs of the person.

Other Heavy-Metal Toxins   The "industry versus the individual" conflict also crops up in two of the more common varieties of heavy-metal poisoning, mercury and manganese poisoning. Victims of these toxic disorders are usually those whose jobs bring them into close daily contact with mercury and manganese. However, other victims are simply unwitting citizens whose food or air has been contaminated by industrial wastes containing metallic toxins. One notorious source of such poisoning is fish taken from waters polluted by mercury wastes from nearby factories. In Japan, thousands of people have been permanently paralyzed and brain-damaged as a result

of eating mercury-contaminated fish (Kurland, Faro, & Siedler, 1960).

Early signs of brain damage due to mercury poisoning are memory loss, irritability, and difficulty in concentration. As the disease progresses, the individual typically develops tunnel vision (i.e., loss of peripheral vision), faulty motor coordination, and difficulty in speaking and hearing. In extreme cases, these symptoms lead to paralysis, coma, and death. Manganese poisoning is manifested in motor and speech impairments, restlessness, and emotional instability. Some experts believe that the personality changes that accompany both types of poisoning are often simply pathological exaggerations of the individual's premorbid personality traits.

Psychoactive Drugs   As we saw in Chapter 11, abuse of psychoactive drugs such as alcohol, opiates, and amphetamines can cause severe psychological disturbances. Other drugs have also been implicated in brain damage. In recent years, for example, the inhalation of aerosol gases and the fumes of certain glues has become a popular source of a "high" among adolescents. Unfortunately, the toxins in these gases and fumes tend to accumulate in the users' vital organs and can cause permanent damage, not only to the liver and kidneys but also to the brain, resulting in psychological deterioration and, in extreme cases, death.

Carbon Monoxide   Carbon monoxide, an odorless, tasteless, and invisible gas usually inhaled with automobile exhaust fumes, combines with the hemoglobin in the blood in such a way as to prevent the blood from absorbing oxygen. The usual result of this process is a swift and rather painless death, which makes carbon monoxide inhalation a favored means of suicide. Patients who survive, however, suffer a number of psychological consequences, typically including apathy, confusion, and memory defects. While these symptoms may clear up within two years, some patients suffer permanent mental damage (Kolb, 1982).

The Epilepsies

Approximately 0.6 percent of Americans suffer from the disease called epilepsy (Hauser & Hesdorfer, 1990). **Epilepsy** is a broad term covering a range of disorders. In all of them, however, the primary symptom is spontaneous seizures caused by a disruption of the electrical and physiological activity of the brain cells. This abnormal activity, which can usually be documented by an EEG recording, in turn disrupts the functions controlled by the affected part of the brain.

Causes of Epilepsy

Any condition that interferes with the brain's functioning, altering brain-wave patterns, can provoke epilepsy. This may happen at any time in life, beginning with prenatal life. People with severe seizures often have a history of trauma or anoxia (oxygen deprivation) at birth. But the most common cause is head injury (Meinardi & Pachlatko, 1991). This linkage is probably due in part to the fact that most cases of epilepsy have their onset during childhood or adolescence—a period in which, as noted earlier, there is a high risk for head injury. When epilepsy begins in middle age, a more likely cause is brain tumor; when it strikes in older age, it is often due to one of the cerebral vascular diseases that older people are prone to, such as stroke or cerebral arteriosclerosis (Annegers, 1993).

Cases such as these, in which the origin of the seizures can be identified, are known as **symptomatic epilepsy.** More common in the general population (Meinardi & Pachlatko, 1991), however, is **idiopathic epilepsy,** epilepsy in which the origin of the seizures is unknown. In many idiopathic cases, there is a family history of seizures, so genetic factors are probably involved (Anderson & Hauser, 1991).

Types of Seizures

There are two basic categories of seizures. The first is partial seizures, which originate in one part of the brain rather than in the brain as a whole. In a **simple partial seizure,** cognitive functioning remains intact. The person may experience sensory changes, such as stomach trouble or a strange smell, and/or motor symptoms on one side of the body. (For example, the fingers on one hand may start twitching.) Some people also report minor psychological changes, such as hearing a tune repeat itself again and again in their heads. But even in the midst of the seizure the person can still speak, understand speech, and think straight.

By contrast, a **complex partial seizure,** the most common form of seizure (Annegers, 1993), interrupts cognitive functioning. Such attacks are often preceded by an *aura,* or warning, which the person may be able to describe only in vague terms (e.g., "a funny feeling"). Then, as the seizure begins, the person can no longer engage in purposeful activity and does not respond normally. What he or she does instead is highly variable. Some patients seem to fall into a stupor; others engage in *automatisms,* repetitive, purposeless movements such as fumbling with their clothes; others have been known to break into a run. But, whatever the activity, the person is not thinking

normally; neither can he or she speak coherently. Complex partial seizures usually last more than 10 seconds, often for several minutes. They are sometimes called "temporal-lobe seizures" because they tend to arise in the temporal lobe, but they can originate in other parts of the brain as well.

While partial seizures begin and often remain in only one part of the brain, **generalized seizures,** the second major category of epileptic seizures, either involve the entire brain at the outset (primary generalized seizures) or soon spread from one part of the whole brain (secondary generalized seizures). Among the primary type are **absence seizures,** previously called *petit mal* ("little illness"). These attacks are usually seen in children rather than in adults. Absence seizures come without warning and typically last only a few seconds. During that period, children with these seizures seem to absent themselves from their surroundings. Their faces may take on a "spaced-out" look; they stop moving and speaking; if spoken to, they cannot respond. Then, as abruptly as it started, the seizure ends, whereupon some children are confused, while others, unaware of what has happened, simply resume whatever they were doing before.

Tonic-clonic seizures, found in both children and adults, are another type of generalized seizure. Sometimes heralded by an aura, these attacks typically begin with a tonic, or rigid, extension of the arms and legs. This is followed by a clonic, or jerking, movement throughout the body. The jerking gradually diminishes until the attack ends, at which point the person usually feels confused and sleepy. People can bang their heads or otherwise harm themselves during a tonic-clonic seizure, so hard objects should be moved out of the way, if possible. The only other way bystanders can help people having such seizures is to move them onto their sides, so that, if they vomit, the vomit will not back up into the air passages. (Contrary to popular wisdom, one should not put anything into their mouths to prevent them from swallowing their tongues; people cannot swallow their tongues.) Once known as *grand mal* ("great illness") seizures, tonic-clonic seizures are the most dramatic form of epileptic attack, and they are what most people think of when they think of epilepsy, though they are not the most common type.

Seizures starting in one part of the brain may spread to other parts. A simple partial seizure may develop into a complex partial seizure; a complex partial seizure, into a generalized tonic-clonic attack. In the latter case, the attack may look very much like a primary tonic-clonic seizure, but it is important for diagnosticians to distinguish between them, because each requires a different kind of drug.

Fyodor Dostoyevsky, a Russian novelist, suffered from tonic-clonic seizures, as does the hero of his novel The Idiot, *Prince Myshkin.*

Psychological Factors in Epilepsy

It is not just during seizures that the epilepsy disrupts the brain's functioning. Even between seizures, irregular brain waves often persist, interfering with concentration and learning. The most common complaint of people with epilepsy is that they have poor memories. This is due to the fact that most epilepsies involve the temporal lobes, and related structures, and these are the areas of the brain most related to memory. Despite these difficulties, however, many patients perform quite well in life, and some show great achievements. Julius Caesar, Fyodor Dostoyevsky, and Vincent van Gogh all reportedly suffered from epilepsy.

It was once thought that there was such a thing as an "epileptic personality." But, in view of the fact that people with epilepsy have widely different kinds of seizures, beginning at different ages and occurring with different frequencies, there is little reason to believe that they would have similar personality traits. In any case, there are no data to support such a claim. However, people with epilepsy do share problems that other people do not face. Consider the following firsthand account of a tonic-clonic attack by writer Margiad Evans:

> The food was on the table, the oil-stove lit. I picked up the coffee percolator to fill it. Just as I reached the sink and was standing in the doorway, I found I could not move, could not remember what I wanted to do. It seemed a long time that I stood there (actually perhaps a few seconds) saying to myself, "This is nothing. It will be all right in a moment and I shall remember *all the rest.*" Then I felt my head beginning to jerk backwards and my face to grimace. Then the percolator fell from my hand into the sink. But still some dogged part of me kept saying, "All this is really controllable." I was still conscious and felt violent gestures and spasms were shooting all over me, even till I felt my knees give and I fell down on the concrete floor. As I went, it shot through me, the astonishment: "As bad as this then?"
>
> The next thing I remember was the B ___s' kitchen and Betty B ___ . . . giving me tea and talking to me in the tone mothers use to little children coming out of nightmares. (Quoted in Kaplan, 1964, pp. 346–347.)

Such an experience, even if the person has had it many times, is nonetheless unsettling and damaging to self-esteem. Therefore, it is no surprise that people with epilepsy are more prone to anxiety and depression than is the general population (Dodrill, 1992).

Groups at Risk

As has been noted, groups that are at risk for other acquired brain injuries, particularly head injury, tumor, and stroke, are at higher risk for epilepsy than is the general population. These types of risk have to do with age—a relatively young age for head injury, a relatively advanced age for stroke—as well as gender (men are at higher risk for stroke than are women) and the presence of certain medical conditions, such as hypertension.

There is some evidence that gender may also affect the outcome of surgical treatment of epilepsy. In a study of 118 epileptic patients, researchers found that the women experienced a significant improvement in verbal memory after a lobectomy, while the men experienced a significant decline (Trenerry, Jack, Cascino, et al., 1995). In a similar study, researchers found that the women, but not the men, experienced a decline in visual memory following a lobectomy (Trenerry, Jack, Cascino, et al., 1996). These differences in the outcome of surgery appeared to be related to differences in the volume of the hippocampus in the men and women, as determined by MRI.

Treatment of Epilepsy

Most people with diagnosed seizure disorders take antiepileptic drugs, most commonly Depakote, Dilatin, Tegretol, or phenobarbital. If used as prescribed, these drugs suppress seizures in about 80 percent of patients (Richens & Perucca, 1993). Many patients also report side effects—notably, slowed movements and a general feeling of being "drugged down." Antiepileptic medication is designed to alter the functioning of the nervous system so as to prevent seizures; if it also affects other behaviors, such as fully normal motor responses, that is not surprising. But side effects can often be reduced if the medication is taken correctly (Dodrill, 1993).

When drugs are not successful in controlling the seizures, surgery may be recommended. The most common type of surgery involves the removal of the focal epileptic area, the area where the attacks are known to originate. But this type of surgery can be done only when the area is focal: known and limited. (Thus, the seizures must be partial rather than generalized.) Furthermore, the focal area must be one that can be removed without major damage to the person's mental faculties. Epilepsy surgery is becoming more common, but it is still performed on no more than perhaps one out of a hundred patients. Of these, 40 to 80 percent are seizure-free after surgery (Engel, Van Ness, Rasmussen, et al., 1993), and many report dramatic improvements in their lives as a result.

KEY TERMS

SUMMARY

- Unlike most disorders discussed in this book, which have largely psychological causes, acquired brain injuries are directly caused by destruction of brain tissue or by biochemical imbalances in the brain. There are four main problems in diagnosing acquired brain injuries: (1) is the disorder, in fact, an acquired brain injury? (2) if so, what caused the injury? (3) what part of the brain is damaged? And (4) how are psychosocial factors influencing the symptoms, and can they be modified?

- There are seven major symptoms of acquired brain injury: impairments of attention and arousal, language function, learning and memory, visual-perceptual function, motor skills, executive function, and higher-order intellectual function. The similarity of many of these symptoms to those of certain psychological disorders makes a correct diagnosis very difficult.

- There are three general types of acquired brain injury: delirium, specific cognitive impairments, and dementia. Delirium is a transient, global disorder of cognition and attention that is often caused by physical illness. Besides confusion and disorganization, it may include hallucinations and delusions. Most patients recover from delirium within a month. The second general type of injury, specific cognitive impairment, is focal—that is, restricted to a certain aspect of behavior. For instance, amnesia is an impairment of memory, usually of the very

recent past. Other specific cognitive impairments include aphasia (impairment of the language function), apraxia (impairment of the ability to coordinate movements or manipulate objects), and agnosia (impairment of the ability to recognize familiar objects). The third general type of brain injury, dementia, involves the lasting impairment of at least two cognitive functions, which causes a compromising decline in a person's occupational or social functioning. Some dementias are caused by infections, others by progressive physical deterioration.

- Acquired brain injuries are usually classified by their cause. Cerebral infection, brain trauma, stroke, tumors, degenerative disorders, nutritional deficiency, endocrine disorders, and toxic disorders are the major causes of brain injury.

- There are three main forms of cerebral infection: abscess, encephalitis, and meningitis. In a cerebral abscess, an infection becomes encapsulated within the brain. Encephalitis is an inflammation of the brain. Meningitis is an inflammation of the meninges, the covering of the brain and spinal cord. Recently, AIDS dementia, a cerebral infection that can be caused by either the HIV virus or a secondary infection, has reached epidemic proportions, while neurosyphilis, which can now be prevented by antibiotics, has become rare. Mad cow disease is a cerebral infection whose cause has not yet been determined.

- Brain trauma, physical injury to brain tissue, is the leading cause of disability and death in young adults; children and the elderly are also at risk, mainly due to falls. There are several forms of brain trauma: concussion, contusion, and laceration. In a concussion, a blow to the head jars the brain, often causing a brief loss of consciousness. A contusion is a bruise on the brain tissue, generally resulting in a coma of several hours or days. In a laceration, a foreign object enters and destroys brain tissue. Consequences vary, depending on the location of the damage.

- Cerebrovascular accidents (CVAs), or strokes, result from a blockage or the breaking of a blood vessel in the brain. The two main types of strokes are infarction and hemorrhage. In an infarction, the brain's blood supply is cut off due to a thrombosis or an embolism. A hemorrhage occurs when a blood vessel in the brain ruptures. The effects of a stroke depend on the location and extent of the damage to the brain. Risk of a stroke increases with age, because of the increased prevalence of conditions which weaken blood vessels.

- There are two types of brain tumors: metastatic tumors, which originate elsewhere in the body and spread to the brain, and primary tumors, which originate in the brain. Some primary tumors are intracerebral—that is, they grow inside the brain—while others are extracerebral, or located outside the brain, often in the meninges. Little is known about the risk factors for brain tumor, other than that smoking is a risk factor for metastatic brain tumors.

- Degenerative disorders are characterized by a general deterioration of intellectual, emotional, and motor functioning. Symptoms vary, depending on the site of the damage. The degenerative disorders include Alzheimer's disease, Lewy body disease, and vascular dementia, all of which affect mainly the elderly, as well as Huntington's chorea and Parkinson's disease, which more often strike in middle age. While all elderly people experience normal psychological changes as a function of aging, only a small percentage of the aged suffer from dementia.

- Alzheimer's disease is characterized by a loss of memory for recent events, and eventually for long-past events. It can be definitively diagnosed at autopsy by the presence of senile plaques and neurofibrillary tangles in the brain. Lewy body disease, which in the early stages often involves delirium, is quite similar to Alzheimer's in the later stages. It can be diagnosed at autopsy by the presence of rounded structures, called Lewy bodies, in the brain. Alzheimer's disease, which affects more women than men, and Lewy body disease, which affects more men than women, may be genetically related. Vascular dementia, whose symptoms closely resemble those of Alzheimer's and Lewy body disease, is the cumulative effect of a number of small strokes. It is particularly common in people with high blood pressure.

- Huntington's chorea is a genetically transmitted degenerative disease involving damage to the brain's basal ganglia. The disease begins with mood changes and progresses to paralysis and death. Parkinson's disease, also resulting from damage to the basal ganglia, is characterized by tremors and slowed motor responses. Treatment with drugs can control symptoms but cannot cure the disease.

- Malnutrition, specifically vitamin deficiency, can lead to neurological damage. Patients with Korsakoff's psychosis, a disease commonly associated with alcoholism, suffer from memory deficits.

- Disturbances in the endocrine system can produce many psychological problems. Thyroid syndromes, resulting from a malfunctioning thyroid gland, include hyperthyroidism and hypothyroidism. Abnormalities in the adrenal glands may give rise to Addison's disease and Cushing's syndrome.

- Toxic substances absorbed into the body may cause brain damage, with results ranging from temporary emotional distress to death. Toxic disorders almost always produce delirium. Lead and other heavy metals, some psychoactive drugs, and carbon monoxide all are toxic agents which may cause brain damage.

- The epilepsies are characterized by sudden seizures caused by a disruption of activity in brain cells. While in some cases the cause of epilepsy can be determined (usually a head injury or brain tumor), generally the origin of the seizures is unknown. There are two broad types of seizures: partial seizures, which start in only a portion of the brain, and generalized seizures, which involve the entire brain. The most common form, a complex partial seizure, interrupts cognitive functioning for up to several minutes. Between seizures, epileptics often complain of poor memories. Though the disease can interfere with concentration and learning, many epileptics are treated with drugs which suppress seizures. If the drug treatment is unsuccessful, surgery can sometimes be performed to control the seizures.

Part Five | DEVELOPMENTAL DISORDERS

Chapter 15

D.J., a five-year-old boy, was referred for treatment by his kindergarten teacher because, among other problems, he soiled his pants almost every day at school. Aside from the burden this placed on the teacher, it caused the child to be teased and excluded by the other children.

D.J.'s home situation was tense and chaotic. He was one of five children, ranging in age from nine years to six months. Both parents were employed full-time, the father working during the day and caring for the children at night, the mother taking the opposite shift. They were hard-pressed financially and could not afford child care. During the interview with the parents, the mother appeared depressed. She complained of constant fatigue, and she said she had been plagued by crying spells since the birth of the last child. The father was merely angry over the school's "meddling." In his view, D.J.'s problem was minor and reflected his boredom with the school program.

The developmental history revealed that D.J. had never fully achieved bowel control. His early toilet training was disrupted by various upheavals at home. (The family moved several times; the father was laid off and then held several temporary jobs; two more babies were born.) Since that time the parents had tried various approaches to D.J.'s soiling—yelling, spanking, sitting the child on the toilet after meals, sometimes for as long as two hours—but to no avail. The parents claimed that, in addition to soiling, D.J. was disobedient and aggressive at home. A medical examination revealed no organic problems. (Adapted from Bierman, Pennsylvania State University, personal files)

The disorders of childhood and adolescence include a wide range of problems. Some, such as soiling, as described in the case study, involve a failure to pass a developmental milestone "on time." Others, such as stuttering, involve a disruption of a developmentally acquired skill. Still others are simply psychological disorders that normally have their onset prior to adulthood (e.g., anorexia nervosa) or that afflict children as well as adults (e.g., depression).

Why must the disorders of childhood and adolescence be studied apart from adult disorders? To begin with, many of them have no counterpart in adult psychopathology. (Even when they do parallel adult disorders, and bear the same name, as in the case of depression, they manifest themselves differently in children.) But it is not just that children have different disorders; the entire phenomenon of psychological disturbance is different in children from what it is in adults. In the assessment of adult disorders, for example, age is often a relatively unimportant matter, whereas it is crucial in the assessment of troubled children and adolescents. A 2-year-old who assaults the new baby in the house is acting normally; a 10-year-old who does the same thing is not.

A second difference has to do with the question of what is normal. The period from infancy through adolescence involves so many rapid changes that the most stable of children may develop temporary psychological problems. It is often difficult for parents to decide when such problems require treatment. The lines between normal and abnormal are further blurred by the conflicting perceptions of parents, teachers, and doctors and by shifting cultural norms. Many parents and doctors today are fairly relaxed about masturbation, for example, but a few generations ago a child who masturbated was considered at risk for serious problems.

Third, the disorders of childhood and adolescence differ in course and outcome from adult psychological disorders. The less severe childhood disorders are often transitory. Children are more likely than adults, for example, to recover from phobias. This is partly because children change so rapidly and partly because they are so dependent on and responsive to their social environment.

Finally, unlike many troubled adults, most children do not think of themselves as having treatable psychological disorders. Even though they may be very upset by their problems, they do not ordinarily seek therapy. If they get it, they do so through the intervention of adults. Therefore, it is important for adults to be able to recognize the disturbances that children are prone to.

We will begin with general issues in childhood and adolescent psychopathology. Then we will turn to the individual disorders. Finally, we will examine the various theories and treatments of these disorders.

Issues in Child Psychopathology

Prevalence

It is estimated that one out of every five children and adolescents has a moderate or severe psychological disorder (Brandenburg, Friedman, & Silver, 1990; McDermott & Weiss, 1995). When do the troubles begin? Are problems likely to surface at some ages rather than others? Surveys of mental health clinics show that admission rates begin to increase gradually at age six or seven—a fact that is probably related to school entry. Problems that can be ignored or endured at home may not be tolerated in the classroom, and teachers, in general, are more prone than parents to conclude that a child needs treatment. Furthermore, starting school may itself be stressful enough to create or aggravate psychological problems. Until adolescence, psychological disturbance in general is more common in boys than in girls (Zahn-

Waxler, 1993)—a difference that is not yet clearly understood. In adolescence, however, the girls dominate certain categories, as we will see.

Classification and Diagnosis

In *DSM-IV,* disorders of childhood and adolescence, like adult disorders, are classified by syndromes, with the hope that this will help to relate individual cases to other, similar cases. An alternative classification method involves grouping together the preadult problems that tend to occur together in the same children or the same age groups. This is called the *empirical method,* because it was developed by asking parents, teachers, and clinicians to fill out checklists describing the types of problems experienced by children at different ages.

Empirical studies indicate that there are four major categories of childhood and adolescent disorders:

1. *Disruptive behavior disorders,* involving impulsive, aggressive, and other kinds of "acting-out" behaviors
2. *Disorders of emotional distress,* in which the main problem is mental suffering, usually in the form of anxiety or depression
3. *Habit disorders,* disruptions of daily physical habits such as eating, sleeping, and elimination
4. *Learning and communication disorders,* involving difficulties with such skills as reading, writing, and speaking

The empirical method is not inconsistent with *DSM-IV.* Indeed, most of the *DSM-IV* diagnostic categories can be grouped under these four headings. Clinicians who treat children are wary of diagnostic labels, however. First, as we noted, children change rapidly. Second, they may not fit neatly into any one category. As was shown in the opening case of D.J., a child may have both a habit disorder (soiling) and a disruptive behavior disorder. Likewise, many children who are overanxious also have sleeping problems, many children who are depressed are also disruptive, and so on.

Long-Term Consequences

People who treat disturbed youngsters hope that by doing so they are not only relieving a childhood disorder but also heading off an adult disorder. But do childhood disorders actually predict adult disorders? If so, by treating the one, can we prevent the other?

The answer to the first question depends on what kind of predictability we are looking for. The clearest and rarest, instance of predictability is *stability,* in

The diagnosis of a childhood psychological disorder depends not only on the kind of behavior involved but on the age of the child. An occasional outburst of aggression is normal in young children, but by adolescence such behavior may well be a sign of psychological disturbance.

which a childhood disorder simply persists into adulthood in the same or a similar form. One childhood problem that tends to remain stable is antisocial behavior. Antisocial behavior in adolescence is often followed by antisocial personality disorder in adulthood (Lahey, Loeber, Hart, et al., 1995; Robins & Price, 1991).

Another type of predictability is *continuity of developmental adaptation.* In this case, the childhood problem handicaps later development not by persisting in the same form but by setting the child on a skewed developmental path, which then leads to other, later disorders that may bear little resemblance to the original one. For example, infants who develop avoidant or resistant relationships with their parents are prone to become highly oppositional at age two and highly disruptive at age three or four. In turn, disruptive behavior during the transition into the school years (ages five to seven) places a child at risk for more extreme behavioral problems and for learning disorders. In such a case, we cannot say that the learning disorder represents a continuation of the infant avoidance, but it does seem that the early problem may have established a maladaptive pattern of development, with the form of maladaptiveness changing over time.

A third kind of predictability has to do with an early disorder's creating *reactivity to particular stressors*. For example, a young child who becomes depressed upon losing a parent is not necessarily on the road to adult depression. Still, this early loss may make the person more reactive to later, similar losses (e.g., divorce) and, thus, render him or her more vulnerable to adult depression. In general, childhood disorders of emotional distress, such as depression or anxiety, are not stable—they tend to clear up—but they have some predictive value on the continuity-of-development and reactivity-to-stress scales, particularly if they involve poor peer relations (La Greca & Fetter, 1995; Parker & Asher, 1987). Thus, if we consider the three kinds of predictability together, the answer to our earlier question is yes, some childhood disorders do predict adult disorders, though often indirectly.

As for the second question—whether treatment can prevent childhood disorders from leading to adult disorders—the answer is that no one knows for sure. Clearly, treatment helps in the short term. Outcome studies have found psychotherapy to be about as successful with children as with adults (Casey & Berman, 1985; Weisz, Weiss, Alicke, et al., 1987), though it is more helpful for girls than for boys and less helpful with problems of social adjustment than with problems of other kinds. Children who receive psychotherapy do better than children who receive none, and all types of therapy—play and nonplay, individual and group, children only and children plus parents—seem equally effective. Thus, some children and adolescents respond well to treatment, which suggests that treating them will help to prevent adult disorders.

Disruptive Behavior Disorders

The **disruptive behavior disorders** are characterized by poorly controlled, impulsive, acting-out behavior in situations where self-control is expected. The ability to control one's behavior depends on a number of skills developed over time. No one expects hungry infants to show restraint—to wait patiently and refrain from crying. During the toddler and preschool years, however, expectations are raised. Children of this age are asked to learn to inhibit behavior on command ("Don't touch that electric outlet!") and to moderate their behavior in consideration of other people's feelings ("Don't take her toy—play with this one"). Such learning is slow and involves many lapses in the form of disobedience, aggression, and temper

tantrums. Nevertheless, it proceeds. By the time they enter school, most children have developed the self-control skills necessary for compliant and organized behavior in the classroom and for responsive, nonaggressive interactions with peers. Those who have not developed these skills, who continue to be disruptive, impulsive, and aggressive, are at high risk for school adjustment difficulties, learning problems, and peer rejection. Among the disruptive behavior disorders listed by *DSM-IV*, the two most important are attention deficit hyperactivity disorder and conduct disorder.

Attention Deficit Hyperactivity Disorder

Dennis, an eight-year-old boy, was referred for treatment by his school psychologist. According to his teachers, he was uncooperative and disruptive in the classroom. He grabbed his classmates' pens and rifled through their desks. He talked incessantly, except when he was asked a question; then he would not answer. He fidgeted and squirmed constantly. He often got into fights with his classmates and had few friends. He seemed comfortable only with younger children.

These reports from school were seconded by Dennis' parents, who said that he was chronically disobedient and always in motion. He climbed on the furniture and, if reprimanded, did not seem to remember the prohibition a minute later. He was also very distractible, they said. He could never concentrate long enough to finish a chore or complete a homework assignment. (Eisen, Fairleigh Dickinson University, 1997, personal files)

In almost every elementary school, there are a few children who cannot sit still, cannot finish a task, cannot wait their turn, cannot focus their attention for longer than a minute or two. A few decades ago, researchers began to suspect that this pattern, characterized primarily by excess motor activity and short attention span, might be due to brain damage. It was known, for example, that certain kinds of brain infection produced restless motor activity. Furthermore, many children who manifested this pattern also showed "soft," or ambiguous, neurological signs that could suggest brain damage, and a small percentage of them showed definite signs of neurological impairment. On this evidence, the pattern was labeled "minimal brain dysfunction" (MBD). Still, no one could say exactly what the dysfunction was. Furthermore, there was (and still is) a strong trend away from labeling disorders according to cause when that cause has not been definitely established. In time, therefore, the syndrome was given a new name, *hyperactivity*, which had to do with its symptoms rather than its presumed cause. Eventually, however, those who studied the disorder came to feel that the

A child with ADHD (attention deficit hyperactivity disorder) lives in a state of incessant, purposeless activity and finds it almost impossible to concentrate.

short attention span was as fundamental a symptom as the hyperactivity. Accordingly, the syndrome is now called **attention deficit hyperactivity disorder, or ADHD.**

Between 3 and 5 percent of elementary school children are said to have ADHD (Barkley, 1990), with boys outnumbering girls by about 9 to 1. Thus, it is a common diagnosis. It is also a controversial one. Some experts believe that it is too readily applied to children whom parents and teachers find difficult to control (McArdle, O'Brien, & Kolvin, 1995).

We have already described the typical behavior of the ADHD child. The disorder's most salient features are incessant restlessness and an extremely poor attention span, leading in turn to impulsive and disorganized behavior. These handicaps affect almost every area of the child's functioning. Even the most trivial human accomplishments—setting a table, playing a card game—depend on the ability to set goals, plan ahead, organize one's behavior, and postpone gratification. It is this ability that is most strikingly absent in the ADHD child. Thus, the characteristic motor behavior of these children is often distinguished less by its excessiveness than by its haphazard quality. Most children are more physically active than adults—according to ratings by their parents and teachers, one-quarter to one-half of children and adolescents are restless and fidgety—but their getting up and down and running back and forth are usually directed toward a goal (McArdle, O'Brien, & Kolvin, 1995). By contrast, the incessant activity of ADHD children seems purposeless and disorganized. Furthermore, a normal child can, if motivated, sit still and concentrate; an ADHD child finds this almost impossible to do.

This inability to focus and sustain attention has a ruinous effect on academic progress. Children with ADHD have great difficulty following instructions and finishing tasks. Often, they cannot even remember what they set out to do. Consequently, no matter how intelligent they are, they tend to have severe learning problems. They are also extremely disruptive in the classroom, making incessant demands for attention. (Typically, it is not until such children enter school that their problem is recognized. What parents can put up with, a teacher with 25 pupils and a lesson plan to complete usually cannot.) By adolescence, 25 to 35 percent of ADHD children have received some form of special education.

ADHD children also show poor social adjustment. They disrupt games, get into fights, refuse to play fair, and throw temper tantrums. Such behavior does not make them popular. Of course, it also strains the parent-child relationship. ADHD takes its toll on self-care, trustworthiness, and independence (Stein, Szumowski, Blondis, et al., 1995)—all the areas that the child is supposed to be mastering in order to become a social being.

Not all ADHD children have all these symptoms. In some, the problem is much more one of inattention than hyperactivity; in others, the opposite. Accordingly, *DSM-IV* divides the syndrome into three subtypes: the *predominantly inattentive type*, the *predominantly hyperactive/impulsive type*, and the *combined type*. Most ADHD children are the combined type—that is, they have the full range of symptoms. Some studies (Barkley, DuPaul, & McMurray, 1990; Biederman, Newcorn, & Sprich, 1991) have shown that children of the combined type are more likely than those of the other two types to have problems with other children, to engage in antisocial behavior, and to be placed in special education classes. ADHD children also differ in the constancy of their symptoms. In some, the problem behaviors occur only at home or only at school, while the child shows adequate adjustment in the other setting. These situational ADHD children generally have less serious difficulties and a better prognosis than do pervasive ADHD children, who show their symptoms in all settings.

As for general prognosis, a recent review of 20 outcome studies (Klein & Mannuzza, 1991) indicates that most ADHD children still show the disorder in adolescence; indeed, 18 to 30 percent still show it as adults (Mannuzza & Klein, 1992). In adolescence, ADHD may branch out into the pattern of antisocial behavior known as conduct disorder (see the next section). According to teacher rating scales, 85 percent of children with conduct disorder also meet the criteria for ADHD (Pelham, Gnagy, Greenslade, et al., 1992). As for later adjustment, a study of young men who had had ADHD in childhood showed that, compared with controls, they had significantly higher rates of conduct or antisocial personality disorders (27 versus 8 percent), drug-use disorders (16 versus 3 percent), and full ADHD syndrome (31 versus 3 percent). Cognitive problems such as poor concentration tend to persist into adolescence, with predictable academic results: poor grades, expulsion, early withdrawal from school (Weiss & Hechtman, 1993). It is not yet clear whether cognitive disabilities continue into adulthood, but the adult lives of former ADHD children are marked by their poor academic records (Barkley, 1990).

Conduct Disorder

> Derek, 15 years old, was referred to treatment by his school counselor and by a juvenile detention officer. He had a history of shoplifting and vandalism (throwing rocks at windows, breaking into cars). He hung out with his friends day and night. He frequently smoked marijuana. He was sexually promiscuous. At school, where he showed up infrequently, he was withdrawn and contributed little. He rarely did any homework and was failing all his courses.
>
> Derek's parents were divorced, and his mother, who had remarried and was living out-of-state, had little contact with him. He lived with his father, who reported that Derek could not be trusted: he lied constantly and, when confronted, felt no remorse.
>
> Before going into treatment, Derek had been placed on six-month probation by the juvenile court. He was also on the verge of being expelled from school. (Adapted from Kearney, in press)

Some children seem indifferent to the rights of others. Rather than yield to anyone else, they argue, threaten, cheat, and steal. They may also go in for reckless behavior—setting fires, jumping off roofs—and for gratuitously cruel behavior. As they grow older, they graduate to the violation of major social norms. They are no longer just throwing blocks; they are committing assault and rape. At this point, usually in adolescence or preadolescence, they are given the diagnosis of **conduct disorder.**

The *DSM-IV* criteria for this diagnosis are grouped under 4 categories: aggression against people or animals (bullying, fighting, mugging, committing rape), destruction of property (vandalism, fire setting), deceitfulness or theft (lying, shoplifting, breaking and entering), and other serious violations of rules (being absent from school, running away from home). If a person is under 18, has committed any 3 of these infractions (in any category) in the past year, and shows poor adjustment at home or at school, he or she qualifies for the diagnosis of conduct disorder.

Like ADHD, conduct disorder is one of the most common syndromes of childhood and adolescence, with an estimated prevalence of 4 to 16 percent in the under 18 population (Cohen, Cohen, Kasen, et al., 1993). And, as with ADHD, boys greatly outnumber girls by a ratio of anywhere from 4 to 1 to 12 to 1 (Zoccolillo, 1993). In addition to gender, age of onset seems to be important in conduct disorder. Indeed, *DSM-IV* requires that diagnosticians specify whether a given case falls into the *childhood-onset type* (at least 1 symptom prior to age 10) or the *adolescent-onset type* (no symptoms before age 10). People of the childhood-onset type are usually male; they are more likely to be physically aggressive; they tend to have few, if any, friends. They are also more likely to graduate from conduct disorder to adult antisocial personality disorder (Chapter 17). Teenagers with adolescent-onset conduct disorders are less aggressive, generally have friends—indeed, they may be valued gang members—and are less likely to become antisocial personalities as adults. (See the box on page 443.) The prognostic value of age of onset has been confirmed by research (Fergusson, Horwood, & Lynskey, 1995; Tolan & Thomas, 1995). One study, for example, tested a group of adults who had had pronounced conduct disorders as children to see if they met the criteria for antisocial personality disorder. The subjects who did meet the criteria constituted 48 percent of those whose symptoms began after age 12, 53 percent of those whose symptoms appeared between 6 and 12, and 71 percent of those whose symptoms surfaced before age 6 (Robins, 1991). But the children with conduct disorders who do not

Antisocial Adolescents: Are There Two Types?

Most criminal offenders are teenagers. A graph that plots crime rate against age would produce a curve that rises sharply from age 11, peaks at 17, and declines fairly steeply in the twenties. This pattern does not represent just a few adolescents who commit many offenses. Rather, it represents a tenfold increase in the number of young criminals. Arrest statistics do not even begin to tell the story of how prevalent delinquency is in adolescence. Using self reports of deviant behavior, researchers have found that antisocial behavior appears to be a normal part of teenage life (Elliott, Ageton, Huizinga, et al, 1983). A study of more than 1,000 boys in New Zealand showed that, between the ages of 11 and 15, about one-third of the sample committed delinquent acts (Moffitt, 1991).

The good news is that the steep decline in offenders in early adulthood means that, for most delinquents, antisocial behavior is temporary and age-specific. T. E. Moffitt (1993) suggests that the pool of adolescent delinquents in society actually conceals two very distinct types of individuals: a very large group whose antisocial behavior is limited to adolescence and a much smaller group that persists in antisocial behavior over the life course, from childhood through adulthood. According to Moffitt (1991), these two types may be indistinguishable during adolescence: her New Zealand study found that the two types did not differ in the variety of laws they broke, the frequency of delinquency, or the number of times they appeared in juvenile court. But a look at the *preadolescent* history of the offenders does offer a way to distinguish between the persistent and temporary types.

From early childhood, persistent types are marked by continuity in antisocial behavior, which may have its origins in disruptions in neuropsychological functions. The antisocial child's aggressive behavior tends to create situations that only reinforce the antisocial tendencies, especially in unsupportive environments. Options for learning prosocial behavior narrow until the persistent antisocial behavior becomes fixed. The behavior may take different forms at different ages: the child who bites and hits at age 4 may be shoplifting at age 10, stealing cars at 16, robbing people at 22, and abusing a child at 30. This behavior takes place in all kinds of situations—at home, at school, at work, in shops (Patterson, 1993). The more stable and continuous the antisocial behavior, the more extreme the forms it takes.

Those whose delinquency is limited to adolescence differ from the persistent types in many important ways. Most significantly, their behavior is marked by *discontinuity*—their delinquent behavior tends to begin abruptly and end just as quickly. Moreover, unlike their persistent peers, they are discriminating: the temporary delinquents behave antisocially only in situations in which doing so seems rewarding to them; if prosocial behavior is more rewarding, they will engage in that. In other words, their antisocial behavior is adaptable and flexible rather than rigid and stable, as in the case of the persistent types.

The motivations of the two types also differ. For persistent offenders, biological deficits combined with disadvantageous environmental factors produce antisocial behavior that is pathological and abnormal. By contrast, for the temporary types, delinquent behavior is normative. It is a matter of conformity to the group. Moffitt (1993) believes that most delinquents start behaving antisocially in adolescence when they feel the gap between their physical maturity and the social maturity they will not attain until adulthood. Delinquent acts appear to be a way to gain adult power and status. The crimes of the temporary delinquents tend to be those that symbolize adult privilege or release from parental control, such as vandalism, substance abuse, and theft, whereas persistent offenders are more likely to commit victim-oriented offenses, such as violence and fraud. As teenagers grow out of their maturity gap, most of them come to see that the negative consequences of their acts outweigh the rewards, and this realization gradually extinguishes the delinquent behavior.

Moffitt's theory of the two types of adolescent delinquents, if true, indicates that it is futile to study the peak period of delinquent activity in order to learn more about the antisocial individual who will go on to lead a life of crime. Rather, we should single out cases that begin in childhood, even infancy, and follow these antisocial individuals in longitudinal studies. Her theory also suggests that we should learn more about what effects biological age, attitudes about maturity, and access to antisocial peer models have on nondelinquent teenagers.

develop antisocial personality disorder are still more likely to become "ordinary" criminals. Some studies (e.g., McCord, 1979; Zoccolillo & Rogers, 1991) have found that 50 to 70 percent of juvenile offenders are arrested again as adults.

Whatever their future prospects, children with conduct disorders are cause for grave social concern. Whether in gangs or on their own, these children commit serious crimes. Over 50 percent of those arrested in the United States in 1995 for violent crimes were under 18 (U.S. Bureau of the Census, 1997). Even more alarming is the fact that the rate of violent crime by juveniles increased by almost 50 percent between 1980 and 1995 (U.S. Bureau of the Census, 1997)—a rise that was probably due, however, not just to antisocial tendencies but to the increased availability of firearms.

Together, the disruptive behavior disorders, ADHD and conduct disorder, are the most predictive of childhood disorders, the ones most likely to be followed by adult maladjustment. This may be due to something inherent in these disorders, or it may be due to a third variable: the fact that many of these children—those with conduct disorders and those with aggressive forms of ADHD—tend to come from disorganized and unhappy families. However, the poor prognosis for the disruptive behavior disorders is also certainly due in part to the process described earlier: continuity of developmental adaptation. The behaviors involved in ADHD and conduct disorders cause immense disruptions in the lives of the children who have these disorders, damaging their academic performance, their social lives, and their relationships with their families—in other words, all the critical areas of a child's existence. It is not easy to recover from such setbacks.

Groups at Risk for Disruptive Behavior Disorders

Far and away the strongest risk factor for the disruptive behavior disorders is gender (Robins, 1991). As we saw, boys outnumber girls 9 to 1 in ADHD; in conduct disorder, the differential is similar. The genders also express conduct disorders differently. In boys, the most common symptoms are fighting, stealing, committing vandalism, and having school problems. In girls, the predominant behaviors are lying, being truant, running away from home, shoplifting, using drugs, and engaging in prostitution. But the most striking difference is that boys are more prone to physical aggression.

Like so many other gender issues, these findings have been the subject of recent debate. Why are girls less prone than boys to antisocial behavior? One possibility is that the difference is, to some extent, an artifact of reporting. Boys are more likely to be suspected of antisocial acts and, therefore, more likely to get caught (Zahn-Waxler, 1993). Also, the crimes in which girls specialize, such as shoplifting, are taken less seriously than those in which boys specialize—notably, assault. Another argument is that boys, more than girls, are socialized to be antisocial. In some measure, conduct disorder is just a pathological exaggeration of the behaviors—boldness, fearlessness, the ability to take action—for which boys, and not girls, have been traditionally rewarded in our society. Also, because boys are more likely than girls to be physically punished (Lytton & Romney, 1991), they may simply be doing what was done to them. Finally, it has been suggested that natural selection programmed males and females differently—because they are responsible for bearing and rearing children, females are subject to selective pressure for gentleness and empathy, while males are selected for lesser sensitivity, the better to protect the family. Thus, women became "worriers"; men, "warriors" (Dawkins, 1976; Zahn-Waxler, 1993).

Whatever the truth of these hypotheses, there is no question that socioeconomic factors also play a part in conduct disorders. Parental unemployment, family disruption, inadequate schools, and subcultural approval of criminal acts—in other words, all the correlates of poverty—are also correlates of conduct disorder (Richters & Martinez, 1993).

Disorders of Emotional Distress

In contrast to the acting-out involved in the disruptive behavior disorders, the disorders of emotional distress are "internalizing" disorders. The conflict is turned inward; the major victim is the child. Disorders of emotional distress are difficult to diagnose in the younger age groups, because children lack the verbal and conceptual skills to tell us what they are feeling. Their emotions have to be guessed at on the basis of their behavior. If a child refuses to go to school, for example, we may infer "school phobia"—and we may be wrong. School-avoidant children may not fear school; they may just find staying at home more rewarding (Kearney & Silverman, 1996). Nevertheless, in the absence of advanced verbal skills, children's behavior is still the best clue to their emotions.

The accurate assessment of anxiety and depression becomes far easier by adolescence, when children are capable of talking about their feelings. Indeed, the high prevalence of disorders of emotional distress in adolescents, relative to younger children, may be due simply to the fact that adolescents are capable of verbalizing these problems. In any case, there is no doubt that both young children and adolescents experience severe emotional distress, in the forms of anxiety and depression.

Anxiety Disorders

The *DSM* used to have a separate list of "anxiety disorders of childhood and adolescence." Now all but one of those categories have been merged with adult anxiety syndromes, on the grounds that they are simply the childhood versions of those disorders—disorders which, indeed, generally begin prior to adulthood.

Separation Anxiety Disorder

> Matt, an eight-year-old boy, was brought into treatment by his mother because of his fears of being separated from her. Matt refused to be left at home alone. He was afraid that he would be kidnapped or that his parents would be killed in a car accident. He also refused to be left alone in his room at night and was demanding that his parents let him sleep in their bed.
>
> Matt usually went to school, but on protest, and he often turned up at the nurse's office complaining of headaches and stomach aches. During the school day he would use the nurse's phone to call his mother several times a day at her office. Matt had friends and enjoyed playing with them, but only if his mother was in close proximity.
>
> When she brought Matt in, the mother reported that she was very frustrated by her inability to quiet the boy's fears. She also said that she was utterly exhausted by him. (Eisen, Fairleigh Dickinson University, 1997 personal files)

Separation anxiety—intense fear and distress upon being separated from parents (or other caregivers)—is seen in almost all children toward the end of the first year of life. It peaks at about 12 months and then gradually disappears. In some children, however, it does not disappear but persists well into the school years. Or, in the more typical pattern, it disappears on schedule and then reappears, at full intensity, later in childhood, usually after the child has undergone some kind of stress, such as the death of a pet or a move to a new school or new neighborhood. This condition, essentially a phobia of being parted from parents, is known as **separation anxiety disorder**. It is the one childhood anxiety syndrome that is still listed separately in *DSM-IV*, under "disorders of childhood and adolescence."

In extreme cases, children with this disorder cannot be separated from their parents by so much as a wall and will shadow them from room to room. In most cases, however, all that the child asks is to be allowed to stay at home, with the parent in the house. But, even with their parents present, children with this disorder may be haunted by fears of horrible things—kidnapping or murder—that may befall them or their parents if they are separated. They generally have sleeping problems as well, since sleep means separation; consequently, they may reappear night after night to crawl into bed with the parents. If banished from the parents' bedroom, they are likely to camp outside the door.

Children with this disorder are typically clinging and demanding, putting considerable strain on their parents. Parent-child conflicts, then, are common with separation anxiety disorder and they exacerbate it, because the parents' annoyance makes the child all the more fearful of abandonment. In addition to experiencing family conflicts, these children also suffer in other areas. They may refuse to attend school; consequently, their academic progress comes to a halt. Furthermore, because they cannot go to school or to other children's houses, they make no friends or they lose the friends they had.

The estimated prevalence of separation anxiety disorder is between 4 and 13 percent of children and adolescents (Bell-Dolan & Brazeal, 1993). By definition, it appears before age 18, generally before puberty, and lasts for several years, with fluctuating intensity. Indeed, it may last beyond age 18. Adults with separation anxiety disorder either refuse to move out of their childhood home or, if they succeed in establishing a new family, are as anxious about separating from their spouses and children as they formerly were about being parted from their parents.

Social Phobia Social phobia, or fear of social or performance situations in which embarrassment may occur, was discussed in Chapter 6. As we saw, it tends to have its onset in adolescence, but it may also begin in childhood, at which time it typically takes the form of a paralyzing fear of strangers—peers as well as adults. This disorder affects about 1.5 percent of children and adolescents (Benjamin, Costello, & Warren, 1990).

Like separation anxiety, fear of strangers is normal in very young children, beginning around eight months. But most children grow out of it by age two and a half. Older children may still be standoffish with people they don't know—averting their gaze, pretending not to hear questions, and so forth—but eventually they warm up to the new person and resume their normal behavior. Children with social phobia, on the other hand, do not warm up. When addressed by a stranger, they may be struck mute. When a new person enters the room, they typically take refuge at the side of a familiar adult. When pushed into a situation with many new people, they simply withdraw into a corner, blushing and tongue-tied, until rescued, or, depending on their age, they may burst into tears or even throw a tantrum (Vasey, 1995). As in adults, however, social phobia in children is not necessarily generalized to all social situations. It may be restricted to one or two circumstances, or greatly heightened by them. In social-phobic children, the most common fear is public speaking—reading aloud or giving an oral report, for example.

Social-phobic children, unlike those with separation anxiety disorder, are often well adjusted at home and have normal relationships with their parents. But

Children with social phobia fear strangers and new situations, leading them to cling to a parent or familiar adult.

at school they are painfully withdrawn. This usually interferes with their academic progress, and it prevents them from making friends. Social phobia is possibly more painful for children than for adults, because children do not have the option of avoiding feared situations altogether. (They are required to go to school.) Furthermore, they may not understand the source of their anxiety, and usually they do not know, as adult social phobics do, that it is excessive.

Generalized Anxiety Disorder   What was once called "overanxious disorder," a childhood syndrome, is now considered the childhood version of generalized anxiety disorder. In the typical case of generalized anxiety disorder, it begins well before adulthood. (According to *DSM-IV*, most people with generalized anxiety disorder claim that they have been overanxious all their lives.) In children and adolescents, the disorder often takes the form of anticipatory anxiety about performance situations. Will they pass the test? Will they be picked for the baseball team? If so, will they get hurt playing ball?

As these worries suggest, such children tend to have severe doubts about their own capabilities—doubts that lead them to constantly seek approval.

This complex of worry and self-doubt may be the result of family dynamics. There is some evidence that children with generalized anxiety disorder tend to come from families in which parental love is made conditional on consistently "good" behavior.

Whatever its cause, the pervasive anxiety of these children tends to breed failure. Because anticipatory anxiety robs behavior of its spontaneity, it often creates the very problems that were anticipated. Terrified lest they fail a test or be excluded from a classmate's birthday party, overanxious children run a higher risk of failing and being excluded. Such failures tend to lead to further anxiety and further failure—the familiar vicious cycle (Eisen & Engler, 1995; Rapee & Barlow, 1991).

Childhood Depression

For years the fact that children suffered depression was overlooked—or, when it was pointed out, it was denied (Carlson & Garber, 1986). Still today, parents and teachers often fail to notice depression in children, even children who report severe depressive feelings, including suicidal thoughts (Tarullo, Richardson, Radke-Yarrow, et al., 1995). Physicians, too, commonly fail to spot suicidal intent in young people (Slap, Vorters, Khalid, et al., 1992). Now, however, psychologists recognize the existence of childhood depression, though there is disagreement as to its manifestations. According to some research, the symptoms are similar to those of adult depression: a sad or hopeless mood, a negative view of life, concentration problems, and so on (Mitchell, McCauley, Burke, et al., 1988; Prieto, Cole, & Tageson, 1992). But, as developmental psychologists have pointed out, children express these symptoms differently than adults do—by clinging to their parents, refusing to go to school, or expressing exaggerated fears (of their parents' deaths, for example). Older children may sulk, withdraw from family activities, and retreat to their rooms. They may have trouble in school, become slovenly, or engage in delinquent acts. In both children and adolescents, depression may appear as merely one symptom of another emotional disorder or of conduct disorder (Compas, Ey, & Grant, 1993).

Still, clear-cut depressions are not rare in the underage population. Community surveys of children and adolescents have found the prevalence of clinical depression to be between 2 and 5 percent (Cohen, Cohen, Kasen, et al., 1993; Kashani, Carlson, Beck, et al., 1990; Lewinsohn, Hops, Roberts, et al., 1993). Adolescents may be somewhat more vulnerable than younger children. In school-age children in general, 1 percent are depressed enough to express clearly suicidal thoughts (Larsson & Melin, 1992), but adolescents are more likely to contemplate, attempt, and complete a suicide. As we saw in Chapter 9, adolescent suicides have increased alarmingly in recent years. Follow-up studies of people diagnosed as depressed in childhood indicate that they are also at risk for mood disorders as adults. Therefore, they could probably benefit from early detection and treatment (Harrington, Fudge, Rutter, et al., 1990).

Groups at Risk for Disorders of Emotional Distress

Girls are more likely to experience separation anxiety disorder, social phobia, and generalized anxiety disorder (Eisen, Kearney, & Schaefer, 1995). Young boys are more vulnerable to depression. In the early years, the differences between the genders in risk for anxiety and mood disorders are not striking. By adolescence, however, the picture changes. Teenage girls are twice as likely as teenage boys to experience disorders of emotional distress (Cohen, Cohen, Kasen, et al., 1993). Perhaps by this time the genders have been socialized into their "worrier" and "warrior" roles and express their problems accordingly.

Eating Disorders

Since Freud's time, psychologists have interpreted eating as a crucial part of development, because children's feelings about eating are bound up with their feelings about those who feed and sustain them—their parents and others. For the same reason, experts tend to view eating disorders as a reflection of emotional conflicts. We will discuss three conditions: anorexia nervosa, bulimia nervosa, and childhood obesity.

Anorexia Nervosa

Defined as a severe restriction of food intake caused by a fear of gaining weight, **anorexia nervosa** is overwhelmingly a disease of adolescent girls and young women. From 85 to 95 percent of anorexics are female, and in most cases the onset is between ages 12 and 18, though it may also occur in prepuberty or as late as age 30. Anorexia is a rare disorder, with annual incidence probably less than 1 in 100,000 population, but it is apparently becoming more common (American Psychiatric Association, 1994; Lucas, Beard, O'Fallon, et al., 1991). Unlike most psychological disorders, it is physically dangerous. About one-third of anorexics remain chronically ill, and an estimated 5 percent die (Steinhausen, 1994).

Predictably, the most dramatic physical sign of anorexia is emaciation. Bliss and Branch (1960) cite the case of a woman whose weight dropped from 180

Gymnast Christy Henrich, pictured here with her boyfriend, developed anorexia after being told she was too heavy to make the United States Olympic squad. She died in 1994, at age 22, from multiple organ failure caused by her eating disorder.

to 60 pounds. Not all cases are that severe, however, and not all involve a *loss* of weight. The cutoff line in the *DSM-IV* criteria is a body weight less than 85 percent of what is normal for the patient's age and height, whether that condition is the result of the patient's losing weight or simply not gaining weight as she grew. Aside from low weight, the other criteria are an intense fear of becoming fat, an unrealistic body image, and, in girls, *amenorrhea*, or suspension of menstrual periods. All these symptoms must be present for the person to be diagnosed as anorexic.

In behavioral terms, anorexics usually follow one of two patterns. In the *restricting type*, they simply refuse to eat (and perhaps overexercise as well). In the *binge-eating/purging type*, they eat, sometimes voraciously, but compensate by making themselves vomit or by using laxatives or other purgatives. Some patients report that they are so repelled by food that they never experience normal sensations of hunger, but they are the exceptions. Most anorexics clearly have normal appetites, at least in the early stages of the disorder (Marrazzi & Luby, 1986). Indeed, they may become preoccupied with food, collecting cookbooks, preparing elaborate meals for others, and so forth.

Apart from low weight, fear of obesity is perhaps the most typical feature of anorexia. According to one expert, a better name for the disorder would be "weight phobia" (Crisp, 1984). Despite overwhelming evidence to the contrary—clawlike hands, skull-like faces, protruding ribs—anorexics insist that they are too fat and need to lose weight. This distorted body image, together with an iron determination to correct the supposed fatness, is critical to the development of the disorder. Some anorexic women have a history of obesity (Schlundt & Johnson, 1990), and anorexia often follows a period of dieting, as in the following case:

At 15, Alma had been healthy and well-developed, had menstruated at age 12, was five feet six inches tall, and weighed one hundred twenty pounds. At that time her mother urged her to change to a school with higher academic standing, a change she resisted; her father suggested that she should watch her weight, an idea that she took up with great eagerness, and she began a rigid diet. She lost rapidly and her menses ceased. That she could be thin gave her a sense of pride, power, and accomplishment. She also began a frantic exercise program, would swim by the mile, play tennis for hours, or do calisthenics to the point of exhaustion. Whatever low point her weight reached, Alma feared that she might become "too fat" if she regained as little as an ounce....

When she came for consultation [at age twenty] she looked like a walking skeleton, scantily dressed in shorts and a halter, with her legs sticking out like broomsticks, every rib showing, and her shoulder blades standing up like little wings.... Alma insisted that she looked fine and that there was nothing wrong with being so skinny. (Bruch, 1978, pp. 1–2)

Because anorexia so often occurs in adolescence, the point in development when secondary sexual characteristics emerge and when many people embark on sexual relationships, some experts interpret anorexia as a way of avoiding an adult sexual role and especially the possibility of pregnancy (Bruch, 1985). The fact that amenorrhea sometimes *precedes* the weight loss (Halmi, 1974), and therefore may be psychogenic rather than the result of malnutrition, supports this hypothesis. But, even if anorexia does not aim to suppress sexuality, that is certainly one of its effects. Menstruation stops, the sex drive disappears, and breasts and hips shrink. Many anorexic women barely look female.

Another suspected cause of anorexia is family warfare, with self-starvation serving as a daughter's weapon against her parents. Few actions can bring parents to surrender as quickly as a child's refusal to eat. Clinicians often find disturbed relationships between parents and anorexic children, a connection that supports the family hypothesis. In one reported case, the patient confessed that she felt "full of my mother—I feel she is in me" (Bruch, 1978, p. 12). In starving herself, then, she was possibly laying siege to the "inner mother." But, as with other disorders, disturbed family relationships may be the effect rather than the cause (Bemis, 1978). Families are not usually harmonious when one member is starving herself to death. Whatever the cause of anorexia, family therapy, as we will see later in the chapter, is one of the most promising forms of treatment.

Bulimia Nervosa

People who engage in the uncontrolled binge eating plus compensation that was described under anorexia but who do not meet the other criteria for anorexia, such as low body weight or amenorrhea, are said to have **bulimia nervosa.** Bulimics regularly go on binges, during which they consume extraordinary amounts of food, often sweet, high-calorie food—a whole cake, a quart of ice cream—until they are uncomfortably, even painfully, full. Then, in 9 out of 10 cases, they make themselves vomit by sticking their fingers or another instrument down the throat to stimulate the gag reflex. Some bulimics, instead of vomiting, use laxatives, diuretics (drugs that induce urination), or enemas. Still others do not purge themselves but try to compensate by fasting or exercising.

Like anorexics, bulimics base their self-esteem in large measure on their body shape. (This is one of the diagnostic criteria.) Consequently, their binges are surrounded by shame. Most of them binge alone, in secret, and try to hide its traces from their families or roommates. Binges are often triggered by stress or unhappiness and are followed by greater unhappiness. Bulimia can also have physical consequences—not only unstable weight but amenorrhea and rotted teeth. (Repeated vomiting overexposes the teeth to stomach acid.)

Bulimia resembles anorexia not just in symptomatology but in other ways as well: it usually has its onset in late adolescence or early adulthood; it tends to appear after or during a period of dieting; and it is overwhelmingly a female disorder. In clinic and population samples, at least 90 percent of bulimics are female. But bulimia is far more common than anorexia, affecting 1 to 3 percent of adolescent girls and young women (Weltzin, Starzynski, Santelli, et al.,

1993). The disorder tends to persist for several years, appearing and disappearing, but its long-term outcome is not yet known (Lewinsohn, Hops, Roberts, et al., 1993). For years a part of campus pathology, bulimia has only recently begun to be seriously studied.

Childhood Obesity

Obesity in children has not generated the alarm that anorexia and bulimia have in recent years, yet it is a far more common problem. The estimated prevalence of obesity in children and adolescents is 20 percent (Campaigne, Morrison, Schumann, et al., 1994). In children, as in adults, excess weight can contribute to physical disorders, but a special concern with children is the psychological consequences. Adults have ways of coping with the shame that our society attaches to being overweight. For a child, on the other hand, teasing by peers and humiliating visits to the "husky" department of clothing stores may be crushing to self-esteem. This problem is especially acute for girls. In boys, low self-esteem is more likely to be associated with being too thin than with being overweight (Pierce & Wardle, 1993).

As we pointed out in Chapter 8, obesity is probably due to a combination of physiological factors—metabolic rate and exercise patterns—and psychological variables such as responsiveness to food cues. This is as true for children as for adults. But a factor that experts on childhood obesity take very seriously is the family routine: the balance of physical exercise *versus* television-watching in their leisure time, the balance of broiled fish *versus* macaroni and cheese at the dinner table. Parents are usually brought into the child's treatment right away, and their cooperation has great influence on the child's success in returning to and maintaining a normal weight (Foreyt & Goodrick, 1993; Israel, Silverman, & Solotar, 1986).

Groups at Risk for Eating Disorders

As we have pointed out, anorexia and bulimia are, for the most part, female disorders; they are as much the specialty of girls as conduct disorders are the specialty of boys. Why should females be so anxious about weight? Many experts blame the culture and, above all, the fashion and advertising industries. Over the past few decades, cultural ideals of female attractiveness, as reflected in magazine advertisements, have increasingly favored thinness, and it is in that same period that anorexia and, above all, bulimia have emerged as major public health problems (Killen, Taylor, Hayward, et al., 1996; Williamson, Kahn, Remington, et al., 1990). The recent increase in the incidence of these disorders may be due in part to

Obesity in children can have negative physical and psychological consequences. Studies have shown that parental involvement and modification of family routines can positively affect the success of a child's treatment.

greater public awareness and, hence, increased reporting, but it is surely due also to the fact that most of the fashion models on whom American girls base their notions of beauty resemble starvation victims.

The risk for eating disorders now seems to be spreading to preteenage groups. In one study, almost a third of the nine-year-old girls reported a fear of being fat, and almost half said they were dieting or trying to control their food intake (Mellin, Irwin, & Scully, 1992). The fact that such attitudes and behaviors correlate with psychological problems—lower self-esteem, greater depression—has only increased alarm over the eating disorders (Killen, Hayward, Wilson, et al., 1994).

As a result, experts are now trying to identify girls who are at risk. This includes those with "partial syndromes"—that is, those who meet some of the criteria for anorexia or bulimia but not enough to receive the diagnosis. Between 35 and 50 percent of girls referred for treatment of eating disorders have only partial syndromes (Shisslak, Crago, & Estes,

1995). Others who may be vulnerable are those who report being worried about their weight, skipping meals, experiencing a loss of control while eating, feeling guilty after eating, and believing that others see them as overweight (Williams, Schaefer, Shisslak, et al., 1986). The hope is that, by pinpointing such factors, programs—for example, nutritional education in schools—can be instituted to prevent full-syndrome eating disorders from developing.

Elimination Disorders

Like eating, toilet training can be an arena of intense conflict for a child. Toilet training is one of the first points in development at which children have to comply with demands that run counter to their natural impulses. Sometimes these demands are extreme, for our society insists that children achieve control over elimination at an early age. When children fail to pass this developmental milestone, they are diagnosed as having either enuresis (lack of bladder control) or encopresis (lack of bowel control).

Enuresis

Enuresis usually is defined as a lack of bladder control past the age when such control is usual. In this country, most children achieve daytime control between the ages of two and three and nighttime control a year later, but many are much slower. Most children who fall behind in bladder control have trouble with nighttime control—bed-wetting. Daytime wetting is much less common and may be the sign of a more serious psychological problem.

As for the age that separates normal "accidents" from enuresis, this varies with the clinician making the decision. *DSM-IV* specifies only a minimum age: no child under the age of 5 may be given this diagnosis. In addition, the child must be wetting his or her pants or bed at least twice a week or, if the frequency is less, must be suffering serious distress or impaired functioning (e.g., humiliations at school) as a result of the wetting. According to *DSM-IV*, the prevalence of enuresis at age 5 is 7 percent for boys and 3 percent for girls; at age 10, it is 3 percent for boys and 2 percent for girls.

Enuresis may be primary or secondary. Children with *primary enuresis* have never achieved bladder control; whenever they have to urinate, day or night, they wet their pants. Primary enuresis may last until middle childhood, and in rare cases it persists well beyond that point. (At age 18, the prevalence of enuresis is still 1 percent for males.) Some authorities have suggested that the condition may stem from organic,

possibly genetic, abnormalities (Bakwin & Bakwin, 1972). By contrast, children with *secondary enuresis* achieve bladder control and then lose it, almost always as a result of stress. The birth of a baby brother or sister, with the insecurity this often provokes, is probably the most common cause. Whether treated or not, secondary enuresis is usually temporary.

Most enuretic children are not emotionally disturbed (Christophersen & Edwards, 1992). When an emotional problem is present, it is usually a consequence, not a cause, of the wetting. When the enuresis occurs in isolation—that is, not as part of a larger problem—it usually responds well to treatment. Treatment may be warranted, for enuresis can cause problems. Children who wet their pants are likely to be ridiculed by their schoolmates. They may also have problems with their parents, who typically begin to resent being awakened in the night to change wet sheets. Rejecting or ridiculing the child only adds to the child's problems. Reassurance is a better tactic. Another is to keep a clean set of sheets and nightclothes next to the child's bed. Even a six-year-old can be taught, when the bed is wet, to change pajamas, sheets, and rubber pad. This preserves the parents' peace and the child's self-respect.

Bed-wetting almost always clears up, but it may clear up slowly. Many normal children are still wetting their beds at age 12, and, as noted, the causes may be organic. About three-quarters of enuretic children have a first-degree relative who was also enuretic, and the concordance rate is higher in MZ twins than in DZ twins (*DSM-IV*).

Encopresis

When the elimination problem is lack of bowel control rather than of bladder control, the condition is called **encopresis**. Encopresis and enuresis may occur together—about one-quarter of encopretic children are also enuretic—and in some ways the two syndromes are alike. Encopresis, too, is classified as either primary (control is never achieved) or secondary (control is mastered and then lost). In the primary form, it may have an organic basis. It is more common in boys than in girls. Finally, even more than enuresis, encopresis can earn a child mockery from peers and wrath from parents, compounding whatever problems he or she has.

However, encopresis is far rarer. Its prevalence— 1 percent of five-year-olds (Doleys, 1989)—is one-fifth that of enuresis. And it is a more serious problem. It rarely appears in isolation; usually, it occurs as part of a larger disorder, such as a disruptive behavior disorder, or in the context of severe family problems. (We saw such family problems, together with the social disgrace attendant on encopresis, in the case of D.J. at the opening of the chapter.) A substantial percentage of encopretic children are abused children, though, again, this may be a result rather than, or as well as, a cause of the encopresis.

Childhood Sleep Disorders

Of the sleep disorders listed in *DSM-IV,* the ones that are most common in children are insomnia, nightmares, night terrors, and sleepwalking.

Insomnia

Probably the most common response to stress in early childhood is insomnia, usually in the form of difficulties falling asleep or staying asleep. We have already discussed insomnia in Chapter 8, and much of what was said there applies to children as well as adults. Childhood insomnia is special, however, in that, as with other childhood disorders, it is not the person with the problem but his or her parents who decide if treatment is needed. Some parents dismiss a child's insomnia as attention-getting behavior. (As a result, many cases of true childhood insomnia probably go unreported.) The sleeping problem may, in fact, have physiological causes—for example, sleep apnea, a breathing disorder (Chapter 2), or a digestive problem such as colic. On the other hand, it is most often related to worries (Horne, 1992), particularly worries attendant on beginning school. Insomnia is endemic in children who are starting school, and it generally clears up by itself. About one-third of four-

and five-year-olds—but only 15 percent of six-year-olds and 8 percent of ten-year-olds—wake up repeatedly during the night (Klackenberg, 1982).

Nightmares and Night Terrors

Another common complaint is **nightmares,** which seem to occur more frequently in childhood than in the later years. Between 10 and 50 percent of children aged three to five have nightmares often enough to concern their parents (American Sleep Disorders Association, 1990). Less prevalent, but more disturbing, are sleep **terrors,** also called *night terrors,* which occur in 1 to 6 percent of children and are very rare in adults (Thorpy & Glovinsky, 1987). Children having nightmares show no particular physiological arousal, and they may or may not be awakened by the dream. In any case, when they do wake up, they are usually able to describe the dream in detail—how big the monster was, what its cave looked like—and they soon calm down. By contrast, children in the throes of a sleep terror show intense physiological arousal (sweating, hyperventilation, racing heart) and wake up in a panic, screaming. They are very hard to comfort, and usually they cannot say what the problem is or describe any sort of dream. The next morning, they have no memory of the episode. Sleep terrors, then, are far more harrowing than nightmares. They are also timed differently, because they arise out of a different stage of sleep (slow-wave sleep) than do nightmares (REM sleep). Sleep terrors occur during the first few hours of sleep; nightmares, closer to morning (Bootzin, Manber, Perlis, et al., 1993; Mindell & Cashman, 1995).

Night terrors are a rare and puzzling sleep disorder. The child awakens in a state of panic, but has no memory of the incident the next day.

Sleepwalking

Sleepwalking, or somnambulism, is another sleep disturbance that is much more common in the young. Less than 1 percent of adults sleepwalk, but between 15 and 30 percent of healthy children have at least 1 episode of sleepwalking, and 2 to 3 percent have frequent episodes (Thorpy & Glovinsky, 1987), with prevalence peaking at about age 12. Children who sleepwalk typically fall asleep, and, then, without waking up, they get out of bed an hour or 2 later and perform a complex action such as making a sandwich or even dressing and leaving the house. (They rarely go far, however.) Their eyes are open, and they do not bump into things. The episode may last anywhere from 15 seconds to 30 minutes, after which the sleepwalker usually returns to bed (Aldrich, 1989). Contrary to popular belief, sleepwalkers are not acting out their dreams. Like night terrors, sleepwalking occurs during non-REM sleep, which is not a period of dreaming.

Most experts do not regard sleepwalking in children as a serious problem. Generally, they advise parents to make sure the front door is locked and, if they find their children sleepwalking, not to wake them up—this often frightens them—but just to guide them back to bed (Barlin & Quaynum, 1986; Bootzin, Manber, Perlis, et al., 1993).

Learning and Communication Disorders

Learning Disorders

When a person's skill in reading, writing, or mathematics is substantially below what would be expected for his or her age, education, and intelligence and when this interferes with the person's adjustment, the problem is said to be one of the three **learning disorders**. Children with *reading disorder* (also known as *dyslexia*) read slowly and with poor comprehension, and, when reading aloud, they drop, substitute, or distort words. Children with *disorder of written expression* typically have a number of writing problems: poor paragraph organization; faulty spelling, grammar, and punctuation; illegible handwriting. In *mathematics disorder*, the child may fail to understand concepts, to recognize symbols, or to remember operations (e.g., to "carry" a number). In any case, the problem comes out wrong.

Anywhere from 5 to 15 percent of school-age children, the majority of them boys, are said to have learning disorders (Silver, 1991), but prevalence figures are probably not very accurate, because clinicians disagree on the definition of this syndrome. Mentally retarded children and children with im-

paired vision or hearing are excluded from the category, but that still leaves an extremely heterogeneous group. As many as one-quarter of children with conduct disorders, ADHD, and depression also have diagnosable learning disorders (Durrant, 1994). Various medical conditions, such as lead poisoning and fetal alcohol syndrome, involve learning disorders. And, while *DSM-IV* specifies that children whose school problems stem from lack of opportunity, poor teaching, and "cultural factors" should not receive this diagnosis, many of them do. At present, the diagnostic group probably runs the gamut from brain-damaged children to children with no quiet place to do their homework.

Though children with impaired vision and hearing are supposed to be excluded from the category, it is clear that many cases of learning disorder do involve distortions of visual and auditory perception. Indeed, disturbed visual perception is the most common problem of children in this category. Many have trouble focusing on lines of type on a page. Some cannot copy words from the chalkboard correctly. Some cannot tell *mop* from *map*, N from M, or a circle from a triangle.

As for problems of auditory perception, children with learning disorders often have to struggle to distinguish the sounds of different words or to make simple associations between the words they hear (Hulme & Roodenrys, 1995). Some may not be able to identify the sound of, for example, a car horn honking or a dog barking. When perceptual problems accompany a learning disorder, they usually occur in more than one system—visual, auditory, and haptic (touch and movement). It is the prevalence of such perceptual difficulties that has led many experts to believe that learning disorders are neurologically based.

Some children with learning disorders also show disturbances in memory and other cognitive functions. Many cannot recall from one day to the next what they have learned in school—a problem that is painfully frustrating to them and to their teachers. They may also have difficulties with sequential thinking and with organizing their thoughts. The cognitive aspects of learning disorders have been the subject of much research in recent years.

The memory lapses associated with learning disorders may be related to attention deficits. As noted, some children with learning disorders also have ADHD, but even those who don't, often have short attention spans. While children with learning disorders do worse than normal children at recalling important information, they do better at recalling irrelevant information (Felton & Wood, 1989). This suggests that their problem may lie not with remembering things but with paying attention to things that they will be expected to remember. Like other children, children with learning disorders get better at focusing attention as they grow older, but they lag two to four years behind. Some experts believe that learning disorders are fundamentally a problem of delayed development, and findings such as these support that theory. The signs of a learning disorder vary with each child and with the child's age (see the box on page 454).

Because children with learning disorders do poorly in school, they are often seen as failures by their teachers, parents, and peers. In consequence, they usually show low self-esteem and low motivation by age nine (Bjorkland & Green, 1992; Heavy, Adelman, & Smith, 1989), a problem which then worsens with time and with further failures. (According to *DSM-IV*, their school dropout rate is 40 percent. They also tend to have employment problems as adults.) Children with learning disorders, especially girls, are usually less popular with their peers than are other children, a disadvantage that is probably due to a number of factors. On the one hand, frustration and anxiety may cause these children to act in ways that alienate people. On the other hand, their social success may be undermined by the same cognitive problems that impede their academic success. A child who can't remember the rules of a game tends to be left out of games.

Groups at Risk for Learning Disorders

Boys are more likely than girls to develop learning disorders, though reading disorder occurs at equal rates in both sexes (*DSM-IV*). Poverty, low socioeconomic status, and membership in a minority group also put children at a higher risk for learning disorders (Barona & Faykus, 1992; Council for Exceptional Children, 1994; McDermott, 1994).

Historically, learning disorders have been a "middle-class" disorder. In the 1970s and 1980s, white, middle-class children were disproportionately placed in classes for children with learning disorders, while African American children were disproportionately placed in classes for the educable mentally retarded (Kessler, 1988). In 1971, the student body in classes for children with learning disabilities was 96.8 percent white and 3.2 percent African American, while classes for the educable mentally retarded where 34.2 percent white, 65.2 percent African American (Barona & Faykus, 1992).

More recently, schools have recognized that many standardized tests discriminate against certain groups and that being labeled "mentally retarded" can be a stigma. As educators have tried to move more children into school placements that optimize learning,

the class and race differences between children with learning disorders and mentally retarded children have diminished. However, they have not disappeared; as of 1990, minorities made up 32 percent of the school-age population, 47 percent of the students in classes for the educable mentally retarded, and 30 percent of students enrolled in programs for children with learning disabilities (Council for Exceptional Children, 1994).

The definitions, causes, and symptoms of learning disorders often merge confusingly. Children with the same symptoms may have different underlying disorders, and the same disorder may produce different symptoms in different children. Some people have attributed learning disorders to birth injuries; others, to genetic defects, dietary deficiencies, environmental problems, or poor teaching (Myers & Hammill, 1990; Taylor, 1989). It has also been suggested that learning disorders are only an extreme variation of normal development. In any case, the cause is not yet known; neither is it likely to be just one cause. Approaches to treatment are extremely varied, from diets and drugs (for children who also have ADHD) to special instructional techniques. The outlook for children with learning disorders is as variable as the conditions that gather under the umbrella term.

Communication Disorders

Delayed Speech and Other Gaps In Communication

Most children say their first words within a few months after their first birthday, and by 18 to 24 months they put together 2- and 3-word sentences. A few months' delay in this schedule rarely signals a problem, but a prolonged delay is reason for worry. It may be an early sign of an organic disorder, such as deafness, autism, or mental retardation (Chapter 16), or it may stem from environmental causes.

In other cases, speech develops on time, but there are gaps in the child's communication skills. Some children have problems with *articulation:* they do not enunciate clearly, or they go on talking baby talk long after it is normally abandoned. Others have difficulties with *expressive language*—that is, with putting their thoughts into words—either because their vocabularies are limited or because they have a hard time formulating complete sentences. Both these patterns can cause a child to be treated "like a baby." The child may also become very frustrated when he or she is not understood. But both patterns tend to clear up by themselves during the grade school years.

More serious and typically longer-lasting are delays in *receptive language*—that is, in understanding the language of others. This type of disability can be disastrous for a child in school. Surrounded by

Starting school can be difficult for young children. It's even harder for the up to 20 percent of school-aged children who may have a neurological deficit (mild to severe) that makes it difficult to read and write (Fletcher, Shaywit, Shankweiler, et al., 1994). Fortunately, in the United States parents have a right to have public schools evaluate their children for learning disabilities after age three. There are no absolute signs of learning disability; they vary with age and the individual. However, if a child seems to lag in comparison with the child's peers, an evaluation should be considered.

In preschool, learning-disabled children may have problems with language or concentration. These children may start talking later than their peers and have slow-growing vocab-ularies. They may also have trouble learning lists of words like number words, the alphabet, or the days of the week. Sounds of words can be confusing, and many of these children have trouble pronouncing and rhyming words. In addition, these children are often restless and distractible, and they have problems following directions. They may avoid tasks that require sitting still or concentrating such as solving puzzles, drawing, or cutting (Lyon, 1996).

When learning-disabled children reach kindergarten, their symptoms begin to show up in their schoolwork. Students up to the fourth grade make consistent language errors in their spelling and reading classes, such as reversing letters (p/q) or inverting them (u/n), and they may have trouble learning which letters represent which sounds. Some children cannot hold a pencil well, which only makes their writing worse. Attention problems may express themselves as impulsiveness, or an inability to follow directions or learn about time. The children may have poor recall and trouble learning any new skill (Lyon, 1996).

Of course, not all children who have a hard time in school have a learning disability. Poor hearing, eyesight, and muscular diseases can all interfere with learning as well. Children who may be learning disabled also need to be screened for psychological problems, including anxiety, depression, and attention deficit hyperactivity disorder. Distractible, impulsive children may simply be having problems at home—problems that can affect schoolwork but that need to be solved outside the classroom (Bryan & Bryan, 1990).

---

fast-paced verbal messages that others are obviously understanding while he or she is not, the child may become overwhelmed with frustration. Special education techniques are usually necessary for children with receptive language deficits.

Stuttering   The interruption of fluent speech through blocked, prolonged, or repeated words, syllables, or sounds is called **stuttering**. Hesitant speech is common in young children. Therefore, as with so many other childhood disorders, it is often difficult to decide when stuttering is a serious problem. Persistent stuttering occurs in about 1 percent of the population and in about 4 times as many boys as girls. It is most likely to appear between the ages of 2 and 7 (with peak onset at around age 5) and seldom appears after age 11.

Many children outgrow stuttering as their motor skills and confidence increase. Even those who do not outgrow it completely eventually tend to stutter less or only in stressful situations. About 40 percent of stutterers are estimated to overcome the problem before they start school, and 80 percent overcome it by late adolescence. Even those who do not fully outgrow it stutter less, or only in stressful situations, as they grow older (Couture & Guitar, 1993).

Organic theories of stuttering are popular in some quarters. One hypothesis is that stuttering stems from a problem with the physical articulation of sounds in the mouth and larynx (Agnello, 1975; Kerr & Cooper, 1976). But many psychologists today think that stuttering is psychogenic. Stuttering may be created unwittingly by parents who become so alarmed at their children's mild speech hesitations that they make the children anxious about speaking (Levine & Ramirez, 1989). The children's anxiety further disturbs their speech, which in turn makes them more anxious, and so on, until a chronic problem has been created. Other theorists have proposed different scenarios, but almost all agree that anxiety is important in creating, maintaining, and aggravating stuttering.

Disorders of Childhood and Adolescence: Theory and Therapy

Many people feel that treating childhood disorders is a matter of special urgency, not only to relieve the suffering of the children in question, but also in the hope of nipping these disorders in the bud, so that they don't persist into adulthood.

The Psychodynamic Perspective

Conflict and Regression   As a rule, psychodynamic theorists interpret childhood developmental disorders as stemming from a conflict between, on the one hand, the child's sexual and aggressive impulses and, on the other hand, the prohibitions imposed by the parents and by the developing superego. For example, nightmares may result when forbidden wishes, repressed during the waking hours, surface in the child's dreams. This process can then give rise to insomnia, with the child refusing to go to sleep for fear that the unacceptable desire will once again be reenacted in dreams.

In much the same way, encopresis can be interpreted as a disguised expression of hostility. A child who is caught in a power struggle with the parents over toilet training or anything else needs some release for aggressive feelings. To express them directly would arouse too much anxiety, so, instead, he or she inflicts on the parents the annoyance of cleaning up dirty pants.

Enuresis, on the other hand, is usually interpreted as a sign of regression. As we saw earlier, secondary enuresis is often precipitated by the birth of a sibling. In such cases, according to psychodynamic theory, the wetting constitutes an envy-motivated regression to the new baby's level—a way of letting parents know that older children need as much attention as new babies. Even if the stressor is something altogether different, such as the death of a grandparent or the beginning of school, it is still interpretable as regression: a retreat to an earlier and less threatening stage of development.

Anorexia, too, is often viewed as regression by psychodynamic writers. As we saw earlier, anorexia has been interpreted as a strategy for avoiding adult sexuality. According to psychodynamic theorists, the young woman, unable to meet the demands of sexual maturity, regresses to an earlier stage. Here, however, she is caught in a dilemma, for, among very young children, according to Freudian theory, eating is associated with sexual pleasure; indeed, it may also be associated with pregnancy. (For lack of better information, many small children believe that women become pregnant via the mouth.) Hence, the young woman, to avoid the disturbing sexual thoughts associated with food, refuses to eat (Freud, 1958; Szyrynski, 1973).

This classic psychodynamic interpretation has been challenged by ego psychologists who feel that anorexia has less to do with repressed instincts than with the adolescent's drive for autonomy. Bruch (1978), for example, sees anorexia as a "desperate struggle for a self-respecting identity" (p. 1) on the part of girls who for years have been dominated by their mothers. In childhood, these girls submit, becoming perfect, well-behaved daughters, but in adolescence they strike back by refusing to eat. This refusal constitutes both a rejection of the mother and a last-ditch attempt at self-determination. In effect, the girl is saying, "I will control my own life, even if it means starving to death." In support of this view, anorexic girls have repeatedly been described as shy, conscientious, and obedient prior to the onset of the disorder (Bruch, 1985; Goodsitt, 1985).

Play Therapy   For children, as for adults, psychodynamic theorists feel that the best treatment is one that allows patients to bring to the surface and "work through" their unconscious conflicts. However, procedures for achieving this are tailored to the child's developmental level and, therefore, differ somewhat from adult psychotherapy.

A very popular technique is play therapy. Here, instead of asking young patients what the problem is,

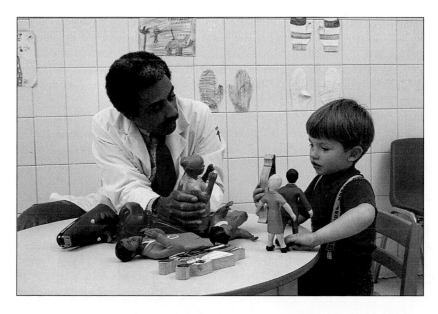

Very young children lack the ability to articulate what is troubling them. Through play therapy, they can express themselves nonverbally.

the therapist provides them with drawing materials and toys, on the assumption that whatever is troubling them will be expressed in their drawings and games. Typically, the therapist's office looks something like a small-scale nursery schoolroom, with blocks, crayons, and clay. Other essentials are toys for expressing aggression and dolls and puppets for play-acting family conflicts. Play therapy can be adapted to the theories of the therapist. As used by Anna Freud (1965), who was the best-known exponent of child psychoanalysis, it was closely modeled on adult psychoanalysis. The child was seen four or five times a week, and interpretations were an important part of the therapeutic exchange. For example, if a child were to comment, "You must see a lot of kids in this office," the therapist might respond, "Would you like to have me all to yourself?" Interpretations are geared to the child's level, however. Furthermore, the child is given more affection and support than an adult would receive in psychoanalysis. Less orthodox psychodynamic therapists generally see the child once or twice a week and place less emphasis on insight than on the venting of forbidden feelings.

Therapists treating children usually have a good deal of contact with parents. In some cases, the parents may be drawn in as "cotherapists," adopting at home techniques taught to them by the therapist. In other cases, all members of the family may be involved in therapy. Whatever the techniques used, the therapist's conversations with the parents may help to resolve family conflicts that have been maintaining the child's problem.

While such methods are generally characteristic of psychodynamic treatment of children, the specific approach varies with the tastes of the therapist, the age of the child, and the nature of the problem. With an anorexic whose life is in danger, a highly directive approach may be used; with an enuretic child, a looser, less directive approach. In treating a preschooler, the therapist may have regular contact with the parents; in treating an adolescent at war with her parents, the therapist may limit conversations with the parents, so as not to forfeit the child's trust. In all cases, the technique depends on the child's needs.

The Behavioral Perspective

Inappropriate Learning From the behavioral point of view, childhood disorders usually stem from either inadequate learning or inappropriate learning. For example, inadequate learning—that is, a failure to learn relevant cues for performing desired behaviors—may play a role in primary enuresis: the child may never have learned to identify the physio-

logical cues associated with a full bladder. In support of this idea, some researchers have found that enuresis can be successfully treated by teaching the child to recognize those cues (Houts, Berman, & Abramson, 1994). As for the development of problems through inappropriate learning—that is, the reinforcement of undesirable behavior—the behaviorist's prime example is the conduct disorders. Children with conduct disorders often come from poor, violence-ridden neighborhoods, where being "tough" with others may be the quickest route to social prestige, especially within a gang. In addition, there is little doubt that modeling plays a role in the conduct disorders. Aside from the influence of gangs, parents may themselves be models of antisocial behavior, especially through indifferent or abusive treatment of the child.

In Chapters 5 and 6, we discussed the importance of avoidance learning—the reinforcement of avoidance behavior by the removal of an aversive stimulus such as anxiety—in the development of phobias. Behaviorists believe that this same mechanism— together with direct reinforcements associated with staying home (parental attention, home cooking, television)—may also explain separation anxiety disorder and social phobia.

Relearning To replace the child's maladaptive responses with adaptive behaviors, behavior therapists use the entire behavioral repertoire: reinforcement, extinction, punishment (usually in the form of the withdrawal of rewards), modeling, respondent conditioning, and so on. To begin with the simplest technique, respondent conditioning, a classic example is the treatment of nocturnal enuresis by means of the so-called Mowrer pad. This device, invented by psychologist O. H. Mowrer, is a liquid-sensitive pad connected by a battery to an alarm. Any moisture on the pad sounds the alarm, awakening the child (Mowrer & Mowrer, 1938). Although theoretically the child should learn to awaken in anticipation of the alarm, many children learn instead to sleep throughout the night, neither awakening nor wetting.

In treating anxiety disorders in children, as in adults, behaviorists have used systematic desensitization (Kendall, Flannery-Schroeder, Panichelli-Mindel, et al., 1997) and exposure techniques. An early example of exposure therapy was Mary Cover Jones' famous treatment of the boy Peter's fear of furry animals by bringing a rabbit closer and closer to him while he was eating candy (Chapter 5).

Modeling has also proved very valuable in the treatment of phobias. The child watches the therapist or another person play with a dog, handle a snake, or deal in a relaxed manner with whatever it is that the child fears. Then, in successive steps, the child tries it, and the phobia gradually extinguishes (Barrios & O'Dell, 1997).

Operant-conditioning programs have been successful in the treatment of ADHD. One classroom program, for example, combined extinction of problem behaviors, such as the distracting of one's schoolmates, with reinforcement of more positive behaviors, such as remaining seated long enough to finish a task (Patterson, 1965). Such operant techniques have proven as effective as drugs in controlling the disruptiveness of ADHD children (Barkley, 1990). Operant conditioning has also been used in the treatment of anorexia nervosa: when anorexic patients are hospitalized and their privileges are made contingent upon eating, they almost invariably gain weight. But, once they are released from hospital treatment programs, they tend to relapse unless programs involving the family are also developed (Levendusky & Dooley, 1985). Parents, teachers, and other adults are a critical part of most behavioral programs.

One application of operant conditioning that has proved useful for certain behavior disorders is the token economy, a technique that we have discussed in relation to schizophrenia (Chapter 13). With children, it is used just as with adults. Desirable behavior is rewarded with stars, points, or a token that the child can save and later exchange for candy, a turn with a special toy, or another coveted reward. Token systems have proven successful in institutions for delinquent children and in schoolrooms (Kazdin, 1993).

The Cognitive Perspective

Negative Cognitions in Children Cognitive theorists argue that in children, as in adults, problem behaviors can stem from negative beliefs, faulty attributions, poor problem solving, and other cognitive factors. Depression offers a good example. Depression in a child is usually precipitated by disruption in family life—for example, parental separation. But, according to cognitive theory, the real trigger is not the event but the cognitive factors that come into play around it. When parents separate, the children need to be reassured that this is for the best. Often, however, they get the opposite message, as one parent succumbs to depression and, by modeling depressive cognitive strategies—helplessness, hopelessness, self-blame—inadvertently teaches the children to adopt the same way of thinking. Many children of recently separated parents believe that they are responsible for the breakup. And, in general, depressed children tend to have at least one depressed parent.

Changing Children's Cognitions Cognitive therapy is now being used for a wide range of childhood disorders. In the early 1970s, Meichenbaum and Goodman (1971) pioneered cognitive therapy for ADHD children, the goal being to teach them to modify their impulsiveness through self-control skills and reflective problem solving. This was done by means of self-instructional training, whereby the person is taught to modify his or her "self-statements" before, during, and after a given action. The therapist models appropriate self-statements in the face of a task: defining the problem ("What do I have to do?"), focusing attention ("Keep working at it"), guiding performance ("Now I have to add the numbers in the right column and carry the first digit"), evaluating performance ("Did I do it right?"), correcting errors ("That's wrong—let's go back"), and rewarding oneself for good performance ("I did a good job"). Then the child attempts the task, using the same or similar self-statements as a guide.

Self-instructional training has now been used by many therapists working with ADHD children. A review of 23 studies (Abikoff, 1985) indicates that the method works well for specific tasks and for a while, though the child's newly learned skills do not generalize as widely as was hoped and can vanish if not carefully reinforced. The technique is still being experimented with, however, and has served as a model for similar therapies aimed at improving the reading, writing, penmanship, and arithmetic skills of children with learning disorders (Lloyd, Hallahan, Kauffman, et al., 1991).

An important focus of cognitive therapy for depressed children is attribution retraining: teaching children to make attributions that are less internal ("It wasn't my fault"), less stable ("It won't always be this way"), and less global ("Not everything is bad"). Cognitive therapists also teach depressed children—and often their parents—how to increase their activity levels, how to solve problems effectively, and how to improve their "affective communication"—in other words, how to share their feelings. Social-skills training may also be used with a depressed child.

The usefulness of cognitive therapy depends greatly on the child's age. For most children under seven or eight, cognitive retraining cannot be used, because the child cannot understand the technique. For older groups, too, the procedures have to be adapted in such a way as to interest the child. Cognitive therapists have used cartoons with empty thought and speech bubbles to induce children to identify fearful thoughts and to combat them through self-talk (Kendall, 1990). Another technique is the so-called STOP acronym: *S* stands for "scared"; *T* stands for "thoughts," which the patients identify; *O* is for "other thoughts," coping thoughts, which they substitute; *P* is for "praise," which they then give themselves for mastering their fears (Silverman, 1989). Using these methods, Eisen and Silverman (in press) have successfully treated generalized anxiety disorder in young children.

As with adult disorders, cognitive techniques are often combined with behavioral strategies. Cognitive-behavioral treatment has had considerable success with bulimia (Wilson & Fairburn, 1993). One program reduced binge-eating averages by 70 percent (Oesterhed, McKenna, & Gould, 1987).

The Family Systems Perspective

The family systems perspective, as we saw in Chapter 5, sees the family as a miniature social system in which each member plays a critical role. According to this view, a childhood disorder is a signal of a disturbance in this system. The child may have the symptoms, but it is the family that is "sick" (Haley, 1963; Satir, 1967).

Consider the case of one highly intelligent boy of 14, who was referred for treatment because he was doing poorly in school. When the family was seen together, it soon became clear that there were problems between the mother and father. The mother repeatedly belittled the father, comparing him unfavorably with the son. The father, in turn, was gruff with his wife, and, despite his apparent concern about his son's academic difficulties, he made it clear that he doubted the virility of any boy who spent too much time with books. The boy, then, was caught in a struggle between his parents. He wanted to do well in order to please his mother, yet, by succeeding academically, he would become a sissy in his father's eyes. Worse yet, he would give his mother a reason to prefer him to his father, thus further straining the father-son relationship, hence the boy's academic problems.

According to family therapists, such family psychopathology underlies many childhood disorders and must be dealt with if the child's problems are to be relieved. This is not to suggest that other therapists ignore family dynamics. (We have just seen how cognitive therapists implicate parent-child relations in childhood depression.) The difference is one of emphasis. Rather than concentrating on the present family interaction, a psychodynamic therapist handling the case just described might search for deeper, earlier conflicts. (This case would lend itself to analysis of the Oedipal contest.) The behavioral therapist might emphasize the reinforcement patterns of the one-to-one relationship between father and child and between mother and child rather than exploring the

Cognitive therapists sometimes use cartoons with empty thought and speech bubbles, like the one pictured here, to help children express and combat fearful thoughts.

complex triangular interaction among the three family members.

Anorexia is one disorder that has been treated successfully through family therapy. Minuchin and his colleagues, who have been working with anorexics for years, claim that these girls' families tend to share the same characteristics: overprotectiveness, rigidity, and a superficial "closeness," covering a good deal of unexposed anger and resentment. The girl's anorexia, then, serves an important function for the family. It gives them a "safe" target for the expression of frustration and thus makes it possible for them to avoid open conflict over their true grievances. Because it performs this essential service, the anorexia is subtly and unwittingly encouraged by the family (Minuchin, Rosman, & Baker, 1978).

In order to relieve the anorexia, the family problems must first be relieved. To this end, the researchers propose "family therapy lunch sessions." Minuchin (1974) describes one such session with a hospitalized anorexic teenager and her parents. First, the therapist allows both parents to try to get their daughter to eat. Inevitably, they fail, and the therapist points out to them why, in terms of intrafamily struggles, the child is responding in this way. Then the therapist, who interprets the girl's refusal to eat as a fight for independence within the family, tells the patient she has triumphed over the parents and can savor that triumph, but to stay alive she must eat. After a time, this strategy begins to work; the patient begins eating surreptitiously. Once the patient is released from the hospital, the parents are instructed to use behavior-modification techniques at home. The girl must eat enough to gain a certain amount of weight each week. If she falls short of the goal, she must remain in bed.

Approximately 85 percent of those on whom this method has been tried show a lasting recovery (Minuchin, Rosman, & Baker, 1978)—a far better outcome than other therapies have achieved. Family therapy is now widely used for childhood disorders and has had some remarkable successes.

The Sociocultural Perspective

Can cultural patterns determine the shape that a childhood disorder will take? Weisz and his colleagues, pursuing this question, compared the records from mental health clinics in Thailand and the United States. These are two very different cultures. Americans place a high value on independence and open expression, whereas Thais, in keeping with Buddhist principles, value spontaneity less than the ability to maintain harmonious relations with others. And the American and Thai children in the Weisz team's sample conformed to these principles. The American children were more likely to have disorders of "undercontrolled behavior"—disruptiveness, fighting, temper tantrums—while the Thai children tended to have "overcontrolled-behavior" disorders such as anxiety, sleeping problems, and somatic complaints, particularly headaches (Weisz, Suwanlert, Chaiyasit, et al., 1987b).

This sample, however, was limited to children who had used mental health clinics. To find out if the same principles applied to the general population, Weisz and his colleagues later interviewed parents of school-age children in the two countries (Weisz, Suwanlert, Chaiyasit, et al., 1987a, 1993). They found a slightly different pattern. Again, problems of overcontrol—"sulks a lot," "has dizzy spells"—were more common in the Thai children than in the American children, but there was no difference in the incidence of undercontrol problems. Interestingly, though, the Thai children's undercontrol was more controlled than the American children's. They tended to show more subtle and indirect forms of acting-out—attention problems, cruelty to animals—whereas the American children used more direct forms, such as cruelty to other children. Thus, the principle still applied: even when they are violating norms, children heed norms.

What this suggests with regard to childhood disorders is the same point that sociocultural theorists have repeatedly made regarding adult disorders: to find the cause (and the cure), we should look to the culture as well as to the individual. Particularly in the case of the conduct disorders, sociocultural theorists are impatient with purely psychological explanations. As we saw, risk for conduct disorders correlates strongly with poverty-related factors: parental unemployment, family disruption, bad schools, and gang subcultures. In addressing the disorder, therefore, the society should attend to those matters. Another factor that may contribute to conduct disorder is the degree of violence in today's movies and on television. Children imitate aggressive acts that they see on television (Liebert, Neale, & Davison, 1973), and horror movies have been implicated in a number of serious crimes committed by children. For nearly 3 million children, exposure to violence happens in their own homes. Child abuse has been linked to a host of serious emotional problems in children (Chapter 17).

Two other syndromes to which cultural norms probably contribute are anorexia and bulimia—a matter we have discussed. Very few experts would argue that anorexia and bulimia are wholly due to cultural influence, but it is worth noting that anorexia is far rarer among the Chinese (Lee & Chiu, 1989) and among African Americans (Dolan, 1991)—two groups that, in general, do not subscribe to the hyperthin female ideal—than it is among American whites.

The Biological Perspective

There have been a number of heated disputes between biogenic and psychogenic theorists in the area of childhood disorders. Biological causes have been proposed for encopresis and enuresis. (As noted, three-fourths of enuretic children have a first-degree relative who was also enuretic.) Likewise, it has been proposed that anorexia may be due to a disturbance in the biological hunger response. With anorexia, however, recent research points to both biological and psychological causes. The cerebrospinal fluid of severely underweight anorexics has been found to contain abnormally high levels of neuropeptide Y, a neurochemical that is known to signal the hunger response. Furthermore, when these anorexics regain their normal weight, their neuropeptide Y levels also return to normal. Thus, it seems that anorexics *are* physiologically hungry—indeed, very hungry. However, psychological factors (such as fear of gaining weight) appear to override this physical need (Kaye, Berrettini, Gwirtsman, et al., 1990; Leibowitz, 1991).

Of all the disorders that we have discussed in this chapter, the one that seems most likely to have a biological basis is ADHD. As we noted earlier, the term *minimal brain dysfunction* is no longer widely used to describe this syndrome, and some researchers believe that ADHD is psychogenic. Nevertheless, the neuroscience perspective has contributed an effective drug treatment for the disorder. Most children with ADHD have a "paradoxical response" to stimulant drugs—above all, to amphetamines. While amphetamines "speed up" normal people, so they behave like hyperactive children, the same drugs slow down hyperactive children, so that they behave more like normal people. Furthermore, stimulants work with both the inattentive types, increasing their powers of concentration, and the hyperactive types, reducing their fidgetiness and impulsiveness. Studies have found that as many as three-fourths of ADHD children who are put on stimulants show dramatic improvements in attention span, social behavior, and self-control (DuPaul & Barkley, 1990; Gilberg, Melander, Liis von Knorring, et al., 1997).

Many children with ADHD are now on daily doses of amphetamines, usually either Dexedrine or Ritalin. Indeed, 3 to 5 percent of the school population takes Ritalin (Crossette, 1996). Some experts have strongly objected to this. For one thing, the drugs may have adverse side effects, including weight loss, insomnia, and high blood pressure. Second, they do not actually cure the disorder. General behavior may improve, but academic performance usually does not (Barkley, 1989), and the prognosis for the child remains the same. No drug can compensate for the accumulated deficits in the child's problem-solving skills. Such skills must be taught after attention has been improved by medication, thus requiring a combination of approaches (Arnold, Abikoff, Cantwell, et al., 1997; DuPaul & Barkley, 1993). Third, if parents, schools, and physicians become accustomed to using drugs for "problem children," the possibilities for abuse are frightening. It is all too easy to imagine medication being administered to *all* problem children, including those whose disruptive behavior is a response to family conflicts or simply to a boring school program.

These objections are important, and it is generally agreed that drugs must be prescribed with great caution. And, as mentioned earlier, some behavioral programs have been as effective as drug therapy (Barkley, 1990). Nevertheless, because amphetamines do, in general, have beneficial effects on the adjustment of ADHD children, they are still widely used, often in conjunction with behavior therapy.

KEY TERMS

anorexia nervosa, 447
attention deficit hyperactivity disorder (ADHD), 441
bulimia nervosa, 448
childhood depression, 446
conduct disorder, 442

disruptive behavior disorders, 440
encopresis, 450
enuresis, 450
generalized anxiety disorder, 446
learning disorders, 452

nightmares, 451
play therapy, 455
self-instructional training, 457
separation anxiety disorder, 445
sleep terrors, 451

sleepwalking, 452
social phobia, 445
stuttering, 454

SUMMARY

- The disorders of childhood and adolescence include a wide range of problems. Many of them have no parallel to adult disorders, and those that do (such as depression) may manifest themselves differently in children. Disorders of childhood are fairly common, become more prevalent with age, and are more common in boys up to adolescence.

- Empirical studies identify several general classes of childhood disorders: disruptive behavior disorders, involving impulsive, aggressive, acting-out behaviors; disorders of emotional distress, such as anxiety and depression; the disruption of habits such as eating, elimination, and sleeping; and learning and communication disorders.

- Childhood disorders may affect adult adjustment. A disorder may simply persist into adulthood in a similar form, as in the case of antisocial behavior, or a child's disorder may set him or her on a path that becomes a maladaptive pattern. Finally, childhood disturbances may create a reactivity to stressors, leaving the child at risk for problems later in life. Treatment (and prevention) of childhood disorders may help to prevent adult disorders.

- Two common disruptive behavior disorders are attention deficit hyperactivity disorder (ADHD) and conduct disorder. Children with ADHD lack the ability to focus their attention for more than a brief period and exhibit a variety of impulsive and disruptive behaviors. Some

ADHD children show more inattentiveness, and some, more hyperactivity, but most of them combine the two.

- A preadolescent or adolescent child who persistently violates social norms—stealing, lying, running away from home, destroying property, and so on—is said to have a conduct disorder. The younger the age of onset, the more serious the problem, both in childhood and adulthood.

- Boys are at a far higher risk than girls for developing disruptive behavior disorders. The genders also express conduct disorders differently. Boys are more physically aggressive and are prone to fighting, stealing, and vandalism, while girls choose less violent behaviors such as lying, being truant, running away from home, and shoplifting. These differences maybe an artifact of reporting, a side effect of socialization, or the result of natural selection. For both genders, socioeconomic factors, such as parental unemployment, that correlate with poverty are also associated with a higher risk of conduct disorder.

- Disorders of emotional distress are "internalizing" disorders: the child turns the conflict inward and becomes depressed or anxious. Children may suffer from many of the same anxiety disorders as adults, such as social phobias and generalized anxiety disorder; in addition, young children may experience separation anxiety disorder when having to part from their parents, however briefly. Depression in childhood may manifest itself like adult depression, or it may show up as problems at school, delinquency, or exaggerated fears. By adolescence, girls are twice as likely as boys to experience disorders of emotional distress.

- Eating disorders tend to be prompted by a distorted body image. They include anorexia nervosa, involving severely restricted food intake and substantial weight loss; bulimia nervosa, a pattern of binge-eating followed by induced vomiting or elimination; and obesity. Far more girls than boys are diagnosed with eating disorders.

- Elimination disorders include enuresis (lack of bladder control) and, more rarely, encopresis (lack of bowel control). Among the childhood sleep disorders are insomnia, nightmares, sleep terrors, and sleepwalking.

- Learning disorders involve inadequate development of learning skills, such as reading, writing, or mathematics. Children with these problems may have abnormal visual or auditory perception or memory problems. Boys with learning disorders outnumber girls. Historically, learning disorders have been over-diagnosed in white, middle-class children and under-diagnosed in minorities.

- Communication disorders include delayed speech and stuttering. Sometimes speech develops on time but with gaps in skills such as articulation, expressive language, and the ability to understand others.

- According to the psychodynamic perspective, disorders originate in a conflict between a child's impulses, on the one hand, and parents' prohibitions and the developing superego on the other. Treatment aims at allowing the child to bring unconscious conflicts to the surface and deal with them.

- Behaviorists focus on actual problem behaviors and the environmental variables that have conditioned them. They believe that children's behavioral problems usually stem from either inadequate or inappropriate learning. The behavioral treatment for both conduct and anxiety disorders makes use of the entire behavioral repertoire: reinforcement, extinction, withdrawal of rewards, modeling, respondent conditioning, and systematic desensitization.

- Cognitive theorists believe that some children's disorders may be caused by negative beliefs, faulty attributions, poor problem solving, and other cognitive factors. Cognitive therapy often focuses on teaching the child to make more positive and functional attributions. Self-instructional training may also be provided. Cognitive therapy is generally practiced with older children and adults, as most children under seven cannot understand the techniques used.

- The family systems perspective views the family as a miniature social system, in which each person plays a critical role. One branch of this perspective, family theory holds that a child may manifest a disorder, but it is the family that is "sick." Treatment involves an exploration of the interaction among all family members.

- From the sociocultural perspective, cultural patterns help to determine the shape a disorder will take. Treatment and prevention entail tackling social problems, such as inadequate schools, poverty, family disruption, unemployment, and exposure to violence or to unrealistic ideals of beauty.

- The biological perspective ascribes some developmental disorders to biological factors. Because ADHD has responded to medical treatment, it is assumed to be the developmental disorder most likely to have biological causes. Even so, there are strong arguments against using drugs to treat children's psychological disturbances.

Chapter 16

Mental Retardation

Levels of Mental Retardation

Genetic Factors

Environmental Factors

Mental Retardation in Adults

Groups at Risk for Mental Retardation

Autism

Symptoms of Autism

Theories of Autism

Groups at Risk for Autism

Society and People with Developmental Disabilities

Public Policy

Community Integration

Quality of Life

Support for the Family

Employment

Prevention and Therapy

Primary Prevention

Secondary Prevention

Behavior Therapy

Cognitive Therapy

Pharmacological Therapy

Psychotherapy

Controversial Treatments

Joan, a 35-year-old woman with mild mental retardation, lived at home with her aging parents and her brother. In school she had been a "slow learner," and she finally dropped out of high school in her sophomore year. At the time of her evaluation, she had been employed as a factory worker for 10 years, but she could never console herself for not having graduated from high school. Two years earlier she had started taking classes for a high school equivalency exam. When she arrived at the clinic, she had just taken the exam and failed it, scoring only 156 when the minimum passing score was 225.

Joan saw herself as "different" and stupid. All her shortcomings she saw clearly; all her good qualities she brushed aside. She was quite angry at her family. She felt they ignored her presence in family conversations and that they limited her independence. For example, they wouldn't let her go visit her cousin alone because they were afraid she would get lost. Above all, she blamed them for not allowing her to finish high school and for discouraging her high school equivalency studies. What she wanted most of all was to "finish high school like other people."

Aside from her anger at her family, Joan's most prominent emotion was depression. She had no friends and, other than needlepoint, no hobbies. She felt tired most of the day but had trouble sleeping at night. She also had a poor appetite and suffered crying bouts. She said she felt sad and lonely most of the time. (Adapted from Reiss, 1985, pp. 173–174)

Mental retardation, the name given to a condition of impaired intelligence and adaptive functioning, is not a single disorder with a single cause. It may be due to genetic abnormalities, to damage to the brain before or at birth, or—some experts believe—to deprivation in childhood. Its manifestations are as varied as its causes. In this country, people with mental retardation range from those who grow up, marry, and live on their own, going to work during the week and to the movies on Saturday night, to those who cannot learn, speak, or care for themselves in any way.

Although there are no absolute statistics on the prevalence of mental retardation, mental retardation affects approximately 2 percent of the U.S. population (Hodapp & Dykens, 1996). However imprecise this estimate, it signifies an enormous problem for society.

In this chapter, we will first discuss the definition and causes of mental retardation. Then we will describe a syndrome, autism, that usually involves retardation. Finally, we will look at the social issues surrounding retardation and autism, together with methods of prevention and therapy.

Mental Retardation

As defined by *DSM-IV*, mental retardation involves three criteria:

1. Significantly subaverage general intellectual functioning, determined using one or more of the standardized intelligence tests (criterion A)
2. Significant limitations in adaptive functioning in at least 2 of 11 adaptive skills areas (criterion B)
3. Onset before 18 years of age (criterion C)*

In criterion B, the term *adaptive functioning* refers to the person's ability to cope with life's demands and live independently, according to the standards of his or her age group, community, social class, and culture. To meet this criterion, the person must show limitations in at least two of the following adaptive skill areas: communication, self-care, home living, social/interpersonal skills, use of community resources, self-direction, functional academic skills, work, leisure, health, and safety (American Psychiatric Association, 1994). Several things should be noted about this definition. First, it requires that any person diagnosed with mental retardation show serious deficits in *both* intellectual and adaptive functioning. A child who scores low on an IQ test but who functions well in his or her community is not a candidate for this diagnosis. Second, mental retardation by definition manifests itself in childhood, and it is by judging the child in comparison with his or her age-mates that the diagnosis is made. Finally, the definition says nothing about cause. In the majority of cases, mental retardation is due to a deficit or dysfunction of the nervous system, but in many cases the exact cause cannot be shown, and diagnosis does not depend on its being shown.

Levels of Mental Retardation

Intelligence test scores have an approximately normal distribution, generally with 100 as the mean and 15 as the standard deviation (a measure of the dispersion of scores above and below the mean). In diagnosing mental retardation, the cutoff point between normal and "significantly subaverage intellectual functioning" is about 2 standard deviations below the mean—that is, an IQ of about 70. People whose scores fall below that line may be diagnosed with mental retardation if their adaptive skills are also impaired. In addition, it has been traditional in the past few decades to specify the person's "level" of retardation: mild, moderate, severe, or profound. The following descriptions of these four levels are based on Harris (1995).

1. *Mild Retardation*   About 85 percent of all cases of retardation are classified as mild retardation—a condition that, because it is mild, is often not recognized until the person enters school. In terms of crite-

*Reprinted with permission from the *Diagnostic and Statistical Manual of Mental Disorders*, Fourth Edition. Copyright © 1994 American Psychiatric Association.

Roughly 85 percent of people with mental retardation have a mild form of the disorder. These men with mild retardation in Amman, Jordan are learning woodworking skills that will help them live productively and independently.

rion A, this level of retardation is equated with an IQ of 50–55 to 70. As young children, people with mild mental retardation develop more slowly and need help longer with self-care tasks such as eating, dressing, and toilet training. By adolescence, though, they can function independently in most areas of life. They speak fluently and can usually read easy material and do simple arithmetic. As adults, they may need someone who can act as an advisor, particularly with regard to money management. Most can hold a job and have friends; some can also marry and have children.

2. *Moderate Retardation* Moderate retardation is usually evident by age two or three; it is equated with an IQ of 35–40 to 50–55. By about age six, such children can feed themselves with cup and spoon, cooperate with dressing, begin toilet training, and use some words and recognize shapes. By adolescence, they have good self-care skills and can carry on simple conversations, read a few words, and do simple tasks. In the past, people with moderate retardation were often institutionalized, but today many live in the community, in special residences or with their families.

3. *Severe Retardation* Severe retardation is equated with an IQ of 20–25 to 35–40. People with severe mental retardation can learn some self-care skills and, with proper training, can perform jobs in a sheltered workshop or daytime activity center. Training is especially valuable at this level, because it can make the difference between institutionalization and a more productive and happy life in a family or residence group. People with severe mental retardation do, however, require considerable supervision. They can understand language, but many have trouble speaking, and their reading and number skills are not sufficient for normal living.

4. *Profound Retardation* Profound retardation is equated with an IQ below 20 or 25. People with profound mental retardation can carry out some self-care activities and can sometimes perform tasks in a daytime activity center, but they require extensive supervision and help. Language is a severe problem; they may understand a simple communication, but they have little or no ability to speak. Many people with profound mental retardation remain institutionalized, usually because of severe behavior problems or multiple physical handicaps. Because of increased susceptibility to disease, people in this category often die in childhood or adolescence.

It should be added that these descriptions of the four levels of retardation are only broad generalizations. Even as generalizations, their value has been questioned. *DSM-IV* lists them, but the American Association on Mental Retardation (AAMR) manual argues against these groups because they are based partly on IQ, which is only one measure of functioning. Furthermore, they assume more consistency between IQ scores and adaptive behavior than many people show. Two people with IQs of 60 may differ as much in their coping ability as two people with IQs of 100. In sum, these descriptions give too much weight to IQ.

The AAMR recommends that diagnosticians not apply the IQ criterion until deficits in adaptive behavior have been established. Instead, the association recommends a classification based on levels of required support or assistance. According to these guidelines, mild retardation would be indicated by the need for "intermittent" assistance and/or success-ful functioning in work and marital relationships. Moderate retardation would be associated with "limited" assistance and/or success in elementary school. Severe mental retardation would be indicated by the need for extensive assistance and/or the acquisition of only basic communication, work, and self-help skills. Finally, profound retardation would be associated with the need for "pervasive" assistance and/or the achievement of only basic self-care skills under close supervision (Schalock, Stark, Snell, et al., 1994).

Genetic Factors

In some cases, particularly the severest cases, mental retardation can be attributed to a specific biological factor. But the mechanism by which that factor produces retardation is seldom understood. Furthermore, two people may have the same medical diagnosis yet be at very different levels of retardation. Finally, there is the problem of differential diagnosis. It is not always clear weather a diagnosis of retardation, autism, emotional disturbance, or learning disability is appropriate in any given case. All four conditions may result in generally impaired or deficient behavior and development, and the conditions are not mutually exclusive. Mental retardation and emotional disturbance, for example, may be present in the same person.

More than 300 organic or genetic anomalies are associated with retardation. We will discuss only a few of the more common and better-known syndromes.

Chromosomal Abnormalities   Since the early twentieth century, it has been known that certain forms of mental retardation are "X-linked"—that is, they are genetically inherited via the X chromosome, which also determines sex. But it was not until 1969 that H. A. Lubs, a researcher at the University of Miami School of Medicine, described the cause. In certain individuals, Lubs noted, the X chromosome shows a weak spot, where it appears to be bent or broken (Figure 16.1). This condition, which is called **fragile X syndrome**, occurs in about 1 out of every 1,000 to 2,500 births (Hagerman, 1992). People with fragile X syndrome have certain pronounced physical characteristics—large, prominent ears; an elongated face; and, in males, enlarged testicles. Many are hyperactive and may also show characteristics of autism: hand biting, limited speech, and poor eye contact. (Accordingly, some are diagnosed with autism.) In men, because they have only one X chromosome, this syndrome is more likely to have severe consequences; almost all males with fragile X experience some impairment in cognitive function, with the majority

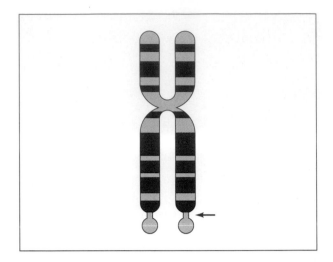

FIGURE 16.1   Schematic drawing of the fragile X chromosome. The arrow points to the fragile site. (Hagerman & McBogg, 1983)

falling into the moderate-retardation category. In women, because there are two X chromosomes, with the possibility that a normal one may mask the effects of the abnormal one, the risk of mental retardation is less (Sherman, 1996).

About as common as fragile X syndrome is **Down syndrome**, which occurs in approximately 1.5 out of every 1,000 births (Simonoff, Bolton, & Rutter, 1996). This condition is named after Langdon Down, the British physician who first described it in 1866. Typical traits of Down syndrome are slanting eyes; a flat nose; a small, round head; an extra fold of skin on the upper eyelids; a small mouth with drooping corners; a thickened, protruding tongue; short, stubby fingers; poor muscle tone; and, in almost all cases, mental retardation. Most people with Down syndrome have IQs of 50 or less. They are also susceptible to serious cardiac and respiratory diseases, with the result that their life expectancy is shorter than average. With advances in medicine, however, a child with Down syndrome who survives the first few months has a good chance of living into adulthood (Carr, 1994).

While Down syndrome was described in the mid-nineteenth century, its genetic basis was not discovered until the mid-twentieth century. In 1959, French geneticist Jerome Lejeune and his colleagues reported that people with Down syndrome almost always have an extra chromosome in pair 21, or **trisomy 21** (see the photo on page 467). This extra chromosome is thought to be caused by an error in cell division in the mother's ovum.

Together, fragile X and Down syndrome account for one-fourth of all cases of mental retardation,

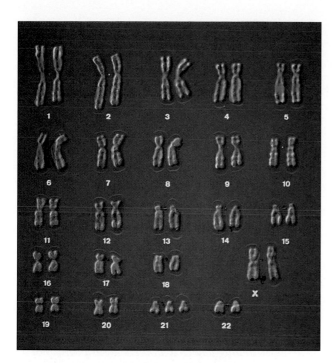

This false-color karyotype shows the pairs of chromosomes in a female with Down syndrome. Note the presence of an extra chromosome in pair 21, or trisomy 21.

though their incidence—and that of the many other chromosomal abnormalities that can cause retardation—may eventually be reduced through genetic counseling. Because fragile X is inherited, those at risk are people with a family history of X-linked retardation. As for Down syndrome, the risk is directly related to the mother's age: for women aged 20 to 24, the chances are about 1 in every 1,400 births; for women aged 30, 1 in every 900 births; for women aged 40, 1 in every 100; and, for women over the age of 45, about 1 in 25 (Thompson, McInnes, & Willard, 1991). In genetic counseling, high-risk prospective parents are advised as to the chances of an abnormal birth. If the woman is already pregnant, chromosomal abnormalities in the developing fetus can often be identified through a clinical procedure called amniocentesis, which involves extracting and analyzing a portion of the amniotic fluid in which the fetus is growing. Amniocentesis is now routinely recommended for pregnant women over 35, to screen for Down syndrome. When the tests reveal abnormalities, many couples are faced with difficult decisions about maintaining the pregnancy.

Metabolic Disturbances Another form of genetic defect results in metabolic disturbances. One of the best known is phenylketonuria (PKU), which occurs in about 1 in every 10,000 to 15,000 live births

(Nyhan & Haas, 1993). The cause of PKU appears to be a defective recessive gene, which leaves the child deficient in phenylalanine 4-hydroxylase, a liver enzyme that is needed to metabolize the amino acid phenylalanine. In consequence, phenylalanine and its derivatives accumulate in the body and eventually damage the developing central nervous system. The result is usually severe retardation, hyperactivity, and erratic and unpredictable behavior. Fortunately, this disorder can be detected soon after birth. Most states require that newborns be tested for PKU. A special, low-phenylalanine diet from infancy to at least age six can often prevent or at least minimize neurological damage (MacMillan, 1982).

Another metabolic disorder is Tay-Sachs disease. This disorder, transmitted by a recessive gene, is a defect of lipid metabolism, due to the absence of the enzyme hexosominidase A in the brain tissues. It is usually detected between four and eight months and is confined largely to children of Eastern European Jewish ancestry. It is characterized by progressive deterioration to the point of complete immobility, with isolated episodes of convulsions. Tay-Sachs disease is untreatable. Even under intensive hospital care, only 17 percent of afflicted infants survive beyond four years, and death is virtually certain before the age of six (Sloan, 1991).

Environmental Factors

Genes are one factor that can cause retardation. The other crucial influence on the developing brain is the environment, both prenatal—the environment of the uterus—and postnatal—the physical and social world surrounding the child in his or her early years.

Prenatal Environment

Congenital Disorders Mental retardation can be caused by **congenital disorders,** disorders acquired during prenatal development but not transmitted genetically. Until recently, three common congenital causes of mental retardation were rubella (German measles), syphilis, and a hormonal imbalance called thyroxine deficiency. Children affected by congenital rubella may be born with various impairments, including brain lesions, which usually result in mental retardation. Congenital syphilis, under certain circumstances, causes hydrocephalus, or excessive cerebrospinal fluid, which results in retardation. Thyroxine deficiency causes cretinism, a condition marked by serious mental retardation and physical disabilities. If a pregnant woman's diet lacks iodine, or if the thyroid of the fetus is damaged during birth, thyroxine deficiency will result. Thanks to widespread immunization for rubella, premarital and prenatal blood tests for syphilis (which responds to penicillin), and the availability of iodized table salt, these congenital diseases are now rare.

More common today are congenital disorders that result from the transmission of the HIV virus from an infected mother to her unborn child. Encephalopathy (the degeneration of brain tissue), meningitis, and lymphoma are among the congenital disorders that can result from in utero HIV infections (Belfer & Munir, 1997). These disorders lead to developmental declines, including cognitive delays and delays in the development of language and motor skills, as well as to declines in adaptive functioning (Pearson, Doyle, Pickering, et al., 1996). Ultimately, they produce mental retardation. The National Institutes of Health estimate that in utero transmission of the HIV virus can be reduced from about 25 percent to as low as 8 percent of at-risk children if HIV-positive mothers are given a drug called zidovudine during pregnancy and delivery, and their newborn infants are treated with the drug for the first six weeks of life (Belfer & Munir, 1997).

Drugs In the early 1960s, a new drug, thalidomide, was introduced in Europe and Canada to relieve morning sickness in pregnant women. Thalidomide did help with morning sickness; unfortunately, it had other effects as well. Many of the women who took the drug gave birth to babies with mental retardation and severely malformed limbs. Thalidomide was swiftly removed from the market, but it had far-reaching effects, and not just for the families of these unfortunate children. The thalidomide scandal helped to raise worldwide consciousness as to the potentially damaging effect that any drug taken during pregnancy can have on the developing fetus.

As many studies have shown, that includes alcohol. When a pregnant woman takes a drink, the alcohol enters the fetus's bloodstream almost immediately, slowing down the workings of the central nervous system (Landesman-Dwyer, 1981). Repeated exposure to this experience can damage the fetus. Even women who are only "social drinkers" are more likely than nondrinkers to have babies of lowered birth weight, whose growth, IQ, motor skills, attention, and social performance may later suffer (Niccols, 1994). As for women with alcoholism, their babies are at high risk for a complex of physical and behavioral defects known as **fetal alcohol syndrome, or FAS.** FAS involves distinctive facial characteristics (short eye slits, drooping eyelids, short nose, narrow upper lip), retarded physical growth, and, frequently, mental retardation. In fact, the majority of people of any age with fetal alcohol syndrome have IQs between 40 and 80 (Niccols, 1994). Approximately

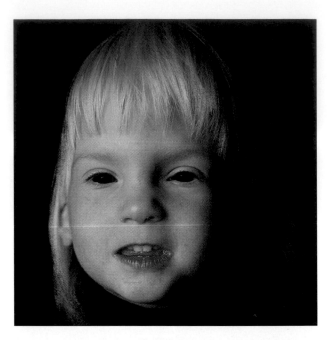

Babies born to drug-addicted mothers show a variety of ill effects, which often include low birth weight, irritability, and mental retardation. The child shown here displays the facial features typical of fetal alcohol syndrome, including a flattened bridge, missing indentation below the nose, and a barely formed upper lip.

1 to 3 out of every 1,000 babies born in the United States shows FAS (Niccols, 1994). If children with less severe impairments are included, the incidence may rise to 1 in every 300 (Harris, 1995).

Illegal drugs have equally profound effects on the fetal brain, as has been seen in the increasing number of "crack babies"—babies prenatally addicted to cocaine—that have been born since crack cocaine entered the illegal drug market in the mid-1980s. These babies are likely to show retarded growth at birth (Hadeed & Siegel, 1989). Their brain development may also be affected. They tend to be either overexcited or depressed; they develop language more slowly (van Baar, 1990); and they are less responsive to toys (Rodning, Beckwith, & Howard, 1989). The extent of retardation among crack-using mothers is not yet fully understood; more research is needed. There is no shortage of potential subjects, however. It has been estimated that, in the United States, among women aged 18 to 25, roughly 1 out of 5 uses illicit drugs; every year, half a million or more unborn children may be exposed to cocaine, marijuana, or some other substance (Harris, 1995).

Whatever damage these babies suffer is probably the result not just of prenatal environment but of a subtle interaction of prenatal and postnatal disadvantages. Cocaine-exposed babies tend to be born into families that are poor and unstable and that lack adequate health services (Mayes, Granger, Bornstein, et al., 1992; Zuckerman & Frank, 1992). Their mothers are more likely to be clinically depressed (Hawley & Disney, 1992), not to mention cocaine-addicted and, therefore, unlikely to offer the kind of stimulating interaction required for adequate brain development. In addition, such babies, because of the effects of the cocaine, are harder to care for—they are often overexcited or depressed—and this probably does not endear them to their mothers. In one study, substance-abusing women were observed with their babies at three months and then nine months after birth. In general, these women were less responsive to their babies' needs than were women who did not take drugs (Rodning, Beckwith, & Howard, 1992).

Malnutrition Another prenatal factor that can contribute to retardation is maternal malnutrition. A number of studies conducted in poorer countries have shown that prenatal malnutrition due to vitamin and mineral deficiencies later affects both a child's physical and behavioral development (Barrett & Frank, 1987). This is bad news; among poor families in the United States, 20 to 24 percent of African American and Hispanic babies may be affected by iron-deficiency anemia (Pollitt, 1994). Such dietary deficiencies can stunt physical growth (Tanner, 1990), cause delays in motor and intellectual development, and contribute to behavioral problems such as anxiety (Valenzuela, 1990), irritability, inattentiveness, listlessness, and lethargy.

Several recent studies have shown that, to overcome prenatal nutritional deficits, a combination of dietary supplements and social or intellectual stimulation is required. In one study, the progress of severely malnourished children who participated in a 3-year home-visiting program was compared with that of children of similar nutritional status who were not visited. At 14 years of age, the children who had participated in the program scored significantly higher on the WISC verbal scale than those who had not (Grantham-McGregor, Powell, Walker, et al., 1994). In another study, fetally malnourished infants who were placed in an intellectually supportive environment for the first 3 years of life did significantly better on measures of intellectual, behavioral, and social development than another group raised in a nonsupportive environment (Zeskind & Ramey, 1981). And, in a study of Colombian infants at risk for malnutrition, a combination of food supplements and home visitation proved effective in reducing the number of children whose growth was severely

retarded, compared with that of a control group (Super, Herrera, & Mora, 1990).

Malnutrition probably does not operate alone, however, for it is often seen in conjunction with other retardation-associated factors. Drug-addicted mothers, for example, also tend to suffer from malnutrition, thus placing their babies at a double risk.

Postnatal Environment

Toxins Various substances, if they enter the child's bloodstream during infancy or childhood, can cause neurological damage resulting in retardation. A sad example is the DPT vaccine, which is routinely given to children to protect them from diphtheria, pertussis, and tetanus. In a very small number of children, the pertussis component in the vaccine causes adverse reactions, including brain damage. DPT vaccination is thought to account for about 50 new cases of severe retardation per year.

A far higher risk of retardation is posed by lead poisoning (Chapter 14). Lead-based paint, though its use is now prohibited, is still to be found on the walls of older housing, particularly in low-income housing projects. If paint chips, or particles of household dust or soil that contain lead, are eaten by a child on a regular basis, lead deposits accumulate in the tissues and interfere with brain-cell metabolism, resulting in permanent damage. Retardation due to lead poisoning is usually severe (Grant & Davis, 1989). Lead can affect children prenatally as well, if the mother is exposed to it. One study found that children with elevated lead levels in their umbilical-cord blood showed slower mental development through age two (Ballinger et al., 1987). Another study found that of 64 retarded children, 11 were born into homes with high concentrations of lead in the tap water, compared to none in a matched group of normal children (Beattie, Moore, Goldberg, et al., 1975).

Physical Trauma Another potential cause of mental retardation is trauma to the brain as a result of accidents or child abuse. Children who are repeatedly beaten may suffer irreversible brain damage. The brain can also be harmed during birth. If labor is rapid and the baby's head compresses and reexpands so quickly that it hemorrhages, or if labor is slow and delivery by forceps injures the brain, retardation can occur. Another birth hazard is hypoxia, or insufficient oxygenation of the baby's blood. If anesthesia is improperly administered, if the mother is hypertensive, if labor is prolonged, or if the umbilical cord ruptures, hypoxia can result; even if it occurs only for a short period, it can cause mental retardation.

The Effects of Deprivation   Lead-based paint, as we just saw, is more common in poor neighborhoods. So are malnutrition and drug abuse. Furthermore, children who are at risk for retardation are less likely to receive appropriate treatment if they are poor. These facts alone might account for the disproportionately high incidence of mental retardation among children from disadvantaged backgrounds. At the same time, it has been proposed that, in the absence of an identifiable physical cause, some cases of mild retardation may be due to the psychological handicaps of growing up in a deprived setting. According to this view, children who lack a stable home, proper parental care, intellectual stimulation, and adequate language models and who are exposed to low expectations for life advancement and feelings of hopelessness suffer a kind of mental impoverishment that is not organic but that is measurable with intelligence tests (Garber & McInerney, 1982). Such impoverishment is sometimes called *pseudo-retardation,* on the grounds that the primary disturbance is emotional, not intellectual. Although every aspect of poverty, including substandard housing, inferior education, and discrimination, can contribute to emotional disturbance, and thus, to impaired learning, it is the decreased level of stimulation—of varied sensory experiences; of verbal communication; of one-on-one, parent-child interaction—that is thought to be most closely associated with poor intellectual development.

This hypothesis stresses psychological, as opposed to organic, factors. However, a report issued by the Carnegie Corporation (1994) suggests that what begin as psychological factors *become* physical factors. As we saw in Chapter 8, the long-held distinction between mind and body has become increasingly blurred as advances in neuroscience have permitted researchers to observe the physical processes involved in "mental" events and vice versa. The research summarized by the Carnegie report constitutes a further stage in the collapse of the mind-body distinction. It also supports the concept of **brain plasticity,** that experiences can alter the structure and function of the brain. The research indicates that what infants learn, and don't learn, from their environments has a substantial effect on the physical development of their brains.

At birth, the formation of the neurons, or brain cells, is virtually complete. What is not finished is the *organization* of the neurons, the wiring up of one neuron to the next, via the synapses (Chapter 4), to create the brain's intricate structure. (A neuron may have up to 15,000 synapses.) Broadly speaking, the newborn brain consists of an immense tangle of neurons. Then, in the period after birth, this mass is "sculpted." Some neurons die; others remain. Those

Studies have shown that an infant's sensory environment is critical to his or her brain development. A positive, stimulating sensory environment builds a more complex and efficient brain.

that remain develop synaptic connections to some cells and not to others. Through this process, the brain develops the circuitry that will allow it to process environmental stimuli for the rest of its life.

What is most critical about this process is that it seems to occur very early. In the first few months after birth, the number of synapses between neurons increases, twentyfold, from 50 trillion to 1,000 trillion (Kolb, 1989). By the time children are walking, they may have developed most of the neural connections they will ever have. PET studies have shown that the biochemical patterns of a one-year-old's brain are qualitatively similar to those of a young adult's brain (Chugani, 1993). The second crucial point is that the formation of the neural synapses is heavily influenced by the environment, and this includes not only long-recognized biological factors such as nutrition but also psychological factors—above all, sensory experience. "The brain uses information about the outside world to design its architecture" (Carnegie Corporation, 1994, p. 8). A rich, stimulating, and benign sensory environment builds a more complex and efficient brain (Chugani, Phelps, & Mazziotta, 1987). A barren environment produces a less efficient brain. Furthermore, environmental stress seems to activate hormones that impede brain functioning (McEwen, 1992).

The consequences of these findings for disadvantaged children are grimly stated by the Carnegie report: "Studies of children raised in poor environments—both in this country and elsewhere—show that they have cognitive deficits of substantial magnitude by eighteen months of age" (Carnegie Corporation, 1994, p. 8). Those studies, so far, have consisted of observational and cognitive tests, but their findings seem to be on the verge of confirmation by brain scan technology. If they are confirmed, this will be bad news indeed, for such cognitive deficits, the report adds, may not be fully reversible. On the contrary, they may be cumulative. One study, for example, tracked the progress of 2 groups of inner-city children, one that had been exposed since early infancy to good nutrition, toys, and playmates versus a second group that had been raised in a less stimulating environment. By age 12 these factors had had a measurable impact on brain functioning, and by age 15 the difference between the groups was even greater (Campbell & Ramey, 1994).

Most of these findings are quite recent and difficult to apply definitively to mental retardation. "Cognitive deficits" are not necessarily retardation. Nevertheless, the research does suggest that children raised in poverty are at high risk.

Teenage Mothers   In recent years, a factor that has placed the children of the poor at greater risk for developmental delays is the increase in teenage pregnancy. Among the industrialized nations, the United States has one of the highest rates of adolescent pregnancy (Newberger, Melnicore, & Newberger, 1986)—twice as high as England's, seven times higher than that of the Netherlands. Every year, in this country, more than a million adolescent girls become pregnant, and half of these pregnancies go to term.

Children themselves, these girls are rarely equipped to raise children. To begin with, most are unmarried (Williams & Pratt, 1990) and, therefore, bear the burdens of parenthood alone—or oblige their own parents (or, frequently, their mothers) to share the burden. Furthermore, they are usually poor and, as a result of their premature motherhood, become poorer. Almost half of all teenage mothers—in the case of unmarried teenage mothers, three-quarters—go on welfare within four years of the birth of the child (Carnegie Corporation, 1994). In addition, teenage mothers, because they are caught

up in the developmental struggles of adolescence, are unlikely to have the psychological stability, ego control, and attentiveness that underlie parental competence—a fact that has been borne out by observations of these girls in interaction with their children. According to a number of studies, adolescent mothers, compared with adult mothers, are less sensitive to their children's cues, less likely to interact with their children verbally, less likely to praise them, and more likely to criticize and punish them (Borkowski, Whitman, Passino, et al., 1992).

At the same time that they receive lesser care, the children of adolescent mothers suffer greater exposure to factors associated with developmental disabilities. Maternal use of drugs and alcohol, poor prenatal care, poor nutrition, low birth weight, maternal ignorance regarding child development, low maternal IQ—all these factors, known to predispose children to developmental delays, are more common with teenage motherhood. To take only the last factor, the average IQ of teen mothers who choose to raise their children has been estimated at 85 (Borkowski, Whitman, Passino, et al., 1992).

It should come as no surprise, then, that mild mental retardation turns up more frequently—according to one estimate, three times more frequently—in the children of adolescent mothers (Borkowski, Whitman, Passino, et al., 1992; Broman, Nichols, Shaughnessy, et al., 1987). To what extent is this attributable to the mother's age alone, as opposed to the problems so often seen in the lives of teen mothers, such as poverty, single parenthood, and interrupted education? In a study that controlled for those factors, the IQ differences between the children of teen mothers and those of adult mothers narrowed, with mean scores of 91 to 94 for the children of young teenagers, 95 to 98 for those of older teens, and 98 to 101 for those of adults (Belmont, Cohen, Dryfoos, et al., 1981). Nevertheless, those other disadvantages do tend to exist in the lives of teenage mothers, widening the gap between their children and those of adult mothers.

Institutionalization   If, as has been proposed, mild retardation may be due in part to a nonstimulating environment, and particularly to a lack of stimulating interaction with parents, then an obvious test case would be institutionalized children. The pioneering work in this area was done by René Spitz (1945). Spitz found that children cared for in an institutional setting by professional nurses showed an average loss in developmental quotient from 124 to 72 within a year. In research done even earlier, Skeels and Dye (1938–1939) found that the IQs of 13 children with mental retardation increased an average of 27.5 points over 2 years after they were moved from an overcrowded orphanage to living conditions in which they became the center of attention. They also found that 12 average to dull-normal children who remained at the orphanage decreased in IQ by an average of 26.2 points during the same 2 years.

There has been considerable debate over the meaning and methodology of both these studies. Nevertheless, more recent research has confirmed the negative impact of institutions. In comparisons of children reared at home with those reared in institutions, those who lived at home, with or without mental retardation, seemed to show improved mental development, especially in language, which seems to be a prime casualty of institutionalization. And children who had spent their early years in an institution were found to be more restless and disobedient than children in a control group (Hodges & Tizard, 1989). On the other hand, much depends on the kind and quality of institutional care. Kibbutz children in Israel and children in well-staffed, high-quality residences seem to suffer little or no deprivation (Kohen-Raz, 1968; Moyles & Wolins, 1971).

Mental Retardation in Adults

Many people with mental retardation grow up to lead relatively happy and useful adult lives, but many others do not, for retardation involves an increased susceptibility both to further brain disorders and to emotional disturbance.

Down Syndrome and Alzheimer's Disease   In years past, people with Down syndrome rarely lived beyond middle age, with the result that their aging process was little studied. Today, however, more and more people with this disorder are surviving into middle and even old age. One of the consequences of this development has been the discovery of a link between Down syndrome and Alzheimer's disease. In people with Down syndrome, furthermore, Alzheimer's strikes unusually early. To quote a recent review of research on this subject, "Virtually all adults with Down syndrome over 40 years of age have Alzheimer's disease" (Zigman, Schupf, Zigman, et al., 1993, p. 63). This is clearly the result of their abnormal genetic endowment, though the biochemistry of the connection is not yet fully understood.

In some respects, Alzheimer's in a person with Down syndrome is no different from Alzheimer's in other people, though, because of Down-related behavioral deficits, it may be harder to diagnose. In general, the onset of Alzheimer's in people with Down syndrome is marked by behavioral regression. That is, the skills they have learned, often with great difficulty—gross motor skills, toileting, dressing and grooming, eating, speaking—begin to crumble, often necessitating their removal from home or from relatively open residential programs into more restricted living arrangements. Some proceed to dementia. In any case, this is a cruel burden overlaid on an already difficult life (Prasher & Chung, 1996).

Mental Retardation and Other Mental Disorders   People with mental retardation are also at risk for a variety of other mental disorders, including attention deficit hyperactivity disorder, disruptive behavior disorders, feeding and eating disorders, schizophrenia and other psychotic disorders, bipolar disorder, and anxiety disorders (Szymanski & Kaplan 1997). They are also at greater risk for drug abuse today than in the past, due to increased contact with the general population (Christian & Poling, 1997). In addition, adults with mental retardation are vulnerable to depression (Szymanski & Kaplan, 1997), a typical case being the one described at the opening of this chapter. When the person's IQ is over 50, the symptoms of emotional disturbance are much like those of people with normal intelligence. Depressed people with mild retardation report sadness, self-blame, and sleeping and eating problems, just like those without retardation. When IQ is lower, emotional disturbance is harder to detect, but there are special scales for diagnosing psychopathology in people with mental retardation (e.g., Reiss, 1992; Reiss & Valenti-Hein, 1990).

Why are people with mental retardation more subject to depression than people without mental retardation? A likely reason is simply their social position (Reiss & Benson, 1985): the fact that many people avoid them, that they must watch others succeed where they themselves fail, that they cannot have the same privileges as others. The day when a teenager with mental retardation sees his younger brother come home with a driver's license—something that he himself will never have—can be a bitter one, and the cumulative impact of these small, day-to-day sorrows can have serious emotional consequences.

Though treatment is available and effective, most people with mental retardation do not get to make use of treatment. In many cases, the emotional difficulties of people with mental retardation are not even diagnosed—a problem that is due in part to "diagnostic overshadowing": because the intellectual deficit is so obvious, the emotional dysfunction is ignored (Reiss, Levitan, & Szysko, 1982). Another problem is that people with mental retardation who have emotional disturbances fall through a crack in the service-delivery system—between agencies that serve people with mental retardation and those that serve the mentally ill. Recognizing this situation, researchers and clinicians are now trying to recast their thinking about mental retardation in terms of the "whole person." In recent years, several model mental health programs have been set up for persons with mental retardation, but many more are needed.

Groups at Risk for Mental Retardation

There are several risk factors for mental retardation. One of the most significant is gender: males tend to outnumber females by approximately 1.6 to 1, due largely to the prevalence of fragile X syndrome, which affects boys more dramatically than girls. However, other gender-linked disorders also have a disproportionate effect on males. Another risk factor is age. The prevalence of mental retardation appears to peak at age five to six years, due primarily to increased cognitive testing and a need for intellectual capability in school. Mental retardation is not usually first diagnosed later in life, because a person's adaptive behavior generally increases over time.

A third important risk factor is socioeconomic status. In general, mild mental retardation is somewhat more prevalent in families with low incomes than in families with high incomes. This risk factor is related to parental intelligence and the amount of intellectual stimulation the child receives. However, socioeconomic status does not seem to be related to the more severe forms of mental retardation. A related risk factor may be minority group status. For example, compared with other ethnic groups, African Americans have a higher incidence of mild mental retardation. Factors such as testing bias and environmental and cultural background may help to explain this phenomenon.

Finally, prenatal and perinatal variables are major risk factors for mental retardation. As we saw, maternal age is closely related to the prevalence of Down syndrome. In addition, exposure to disease, drugs, toxins, incompatible blood types, maternal emotions, anoxia, and malnutrition can affect the development of a child's central nervous system before or during birth. Many different genetic and metabolic disorders can also contribute to mental retardation (Hodapp & Dykens, 1996; Szymanski & Kaplan, 1997).

Autism

Of all the conditions that involve mental retardation, one that deserves special attention, by virtue both of its fame and its severity, is autism. It has long been recognized that some children are profoundly disturbed, sometimes from earliest infancy. For years

Dustin Hoffman's protrayal of Raymond Babbitt, a man with autism and savant syndrome, in the movie Rain Man *earned him an Academy Award.*

such children were often thought to have schizophrenia, because their symptoms in some ways resembled those of adults with schizophrenia. Then, in 1943, American psychiatrist Leo Kanner argued that within this group one could recognize a distinct syndrome, different from schizophrenia. Because its main symptom seemed to be the inability to relate to anyone outside of oneself, Kanner called the syndrome **early infantile autism**, from the Greek *autos,* "self." According to Kanner, autism was inborn and showed itself by age two and a half years.

Today, as a result of Kanner's discovery, the diagnostic ground has shifted. The diagnosis of schizophrenia in childhood is now rare; most psychotic disorders in children are considered instances of autism. Prevalence figures vary, largely because there is a great deal of variation in symptoms and therefore considerable disagreement as to what should be called autism as opposed to "autistic-like" conditions. Strictly defined, autism occurs in about 2 out of every 10,000 births. Using less stringent criteria, the disorder is thought to occur in 4 or 5 out of every 10,000 births (Bryson, 1997; Harris, 1995).

Despite the broad range of behaviors covered by the term *autism*, there are four symptoms that are almost invariably present: social isolation, mental retardation, language deficits, and stereotyped behavior.

Symptoms of Autism

Social Isolation

> A beautiful, enigmatic child tiptoes into your waiting room, his gaze averted from you. Instead of a toy, he clutches a strange, dirty, dangling string which he twirls from time to time. When you start to examine him, he shrinks from your touch, particularly disturbed by your hands touching his head. He stares out the window instead of noticing you or your office. He seems alone, totally self-preoccupied. (Coleman, 1989, p. 1)

One striking abnormality common to all people diagnosed with autism is impaired social behavior (Rapin, 1991; Waterhouse, 1994; Waterhouse, Wing, & Fein, 1989)—a problem implied, as we saw, in the very name of the syndrome. Many children with autism withdraw from all social contact into a state of what has been called "extreme autistic aloneness." As infants, they do not demand attention from others—a rare trait in a baby—and are difficult to hold and cuddle because they stiffen or go limp when they are picked up. The recoil from personal contact is even sharper in older children, who may behave as though other people simply do not exist. As with other characteristics of autism, however, the degree of social isolation varies. Many toddlers with autism show an attachment to their mothers; they cling to the mother and, when strangers are present, hover near her (Sigmund & Mundy, 1989). Furthermore, even when social isolation is extreme, this does not mean that the child shows no emotion. Children with autism may exhibit rage, panic, or inconsolable crying, but often in response to things that an observer cannot identify.

Partly on the basis of their social variability, Lorna Wing (Wing & Attwood, 1987; Wing & Gould, 1979) has proposed that children with autism can be subclassified into three types. In the *aloof* type, the child rarely makes a spontaneous social approach, except to get something he or she wants, and rejects approaches from others. In the *passive* type, the child does not initiate contact, but he or she responds if someone else makes the contact and structures the interaction. In the *active-but-odd* type, the child approaches others but in a peculiar, naive, or one-sided way. According to Wing and her colleagues, other characteristics of children with autism vary consistently with these "social types": aloof types move, play, and communicate in certain ways, passive types in other ways, and so on—a claim that has been at least partially validated (Castelloe & Dawson, 1993). It is possible that what we call autism is not one disorder but several. Subclassification schemes such as Wing's are an effort to make some sense out of the diversity of symptoms and, if different disorders are involved, to assemble the research groups necessary to find that out.

Mental Retardation   Most children with autism have mental retardation. About 76 to 89 percent have an IQ of less than 70 (Bryson, Clark, & Smith, 1988; Gillberg, 1991; Steffenburg & Gillberg, 1986). But children with autism differ from other children with mental retardation in the nature of their cognitive deficits. Children with autism do quite a bit better, for example, on tests of sensorimotor ability, such as finding hidden figures, than on tests of social understanding and language; children with mental retardation tend to perform more evenly on all such tests (Shah & Frith, 1983). When children with autism receive therapy to improve their social relationships, their mental retardation does *not* improve as well (Rutter, 1983). Therefore, in children with autism, mental retardation is a primary cognitive problem, not merely a result of their social withdrawal.

In rare cases, people with autism and mental retardation show signs of above-average intelligence in one limited area, such as art or music. Such people are called savants. The box on page 475 describes the case of Nadia, a savant child who displayed remarkable artistic ability.

Language Deficits   More than half of all children with autism do not speak at all. Others babble, whine, scream, or show echolalia—that is, they simply echo what other people say. Some children with autism aimlessly repeat snatches of songs, television commercials, or other bits of overheard language. Those who do speak can communicate only in a limited way (Bailey, Phillips, & Rutter, 1996). Some use pronouns strangely, referring to themselves in the second person ("you") or third person ("he," "she"). Still others speak extremely literally. In essence, children with autism cannot communicate *reciprocally*, cannot engage in the usual give-and-take of conversation.

The severity of language problems in children with autism is an excellent indicator of prognosis. Children most likely to benefit from treatment have developed some meaningful speech by the age of five years (Gillberg & Steffenburg, 1987; Kobayashi, Murata, & Yoshinaga, 1992; Venter, Lord, &

Savant Syndrome

In rare cases, a person with greatly diminished mental skills shows extraordinary proficiency in one isolated skill a phenomenon known as **savant syndrome**. Until recently, savant syndrome was thought to be associated with retardation, but it is likely that savants actually have autism, not mental retardation. The abilities of savants are often so wildly exaggerated by the press that the phenomenon is often regarded with some skepticism. However, scientists, too, have observed and described savants (e.g., Viscott, 1970).

How do these remarkable skills develop? Perhaps by way of compensation. Just as the blind may develop particularly keen hearing, so a child with autism may compensate by becoming "overproficient" in one salvaged skill. Alternatively, the source of savants' abilities may be purely biological. That is, one area of the brain may be rendered abnormally efficient by the same structural change that rendered the rest of the brain abnormally inefficient. Another possibility is that, when such abilities appear in association with autism, they are produced by the intense concentration typical of children with autism. Whatever its source, the savant phenomenon makes an enigmatic disorder, autism, seem even more enigmatic.

In almost all reported cases, the skill in question is based on memory or calculation. There have been several reports of children who, if given a date, could say immediately what day of the week it fell on. Others can recite columns of numbers from the telephone book after one reading. Raymond (played by Dustin Hoffman), the hero of the movie *Rain Man,* was a "calculator savant." There have also been several reports of musical savants—not surprising, because music, like numbers, involves intricate systems. Some years ago, an English psychiatrist, Lorna Selfe (1978), reported a truly unusual case—a drawing savant.

Nadia, the second of three children born to a Ukrainian couple living in England, was clearly abnormal from an early age. She did not speak, and she did not seem even to notice other people, with the exception of her mother and a few others. Most of her days were spent tearing paper into thin strips or performing some other ritualistic activity. Her diagnosis was autism.

When Nadia was three, her mother had to be hospitalized for several months. When the mother returned, the child was overjoyed. Inexplicably, she began to draw. What she drew was equally inexplicable—figures of

A rooster drawn by Nadia when she was about three and a half.

astonishing beauty and sophistication. For the next three years, Nadia produced drawing after drawing. She refused to use color; only a ballpoint pen would do. She drew on any kind of paper she could find, including boxes. She sketched with the utmost concentration, then sat back, surveyed the result, and wiggled her hands and knees with pleasure.

At the same time, Nadia was being taken on the round of clinics and special schools. She was enrolled in several programs but made no progress. Then, around age 6½, she began speaking and stopped drawing. At the time when this case was written up, Nadia was 10 years old. She had acquired a small vocabulary, was responsive to a limited circle of people, and could even handle simple mathematics. When asked to draw a picture, she could produce one, but it had none of the genius of her earlier work. As mysteriously as it had appeared, her remarkable artistic talent had vanished.

Recent research on savant drawing ability has shown that children like Nadia can construct patterns from segmented components at the same level as children of high intelligence (Pring, Hermelin, & Heavey, 1995). Researchers have also found that savant abilities sometimes decline as the symptoms of autism improve (Bailey, Phillips, & Rutter, 1996). Perhaps these findings help to explain the changes in Nadia's savant abilities over time.

Schopler, 1992). A child's intellectual development is another excellent indicator of his or her prognosis. Children with autism who do not have mental retardation (about one-fourth of those with autism) also tend to be those who have begun to speak meaningfully by age five years and who adjust better as adults.

Stereotyped Behavior Many children with autism tend to repeat a limited number of movements endlessly, ritualistically, and without any clear goal. These self-stimulating movements—twirling, tiptoeing, flapping the hands, rocking, tensing parts of the body—may involve the fine or gross muscles of the hands, face, trunk, arms, and legs. Left to themselves, many children with autism, especially those who are institutionalized, spend a great deal of time in these bizarre forms of self-stimulation.

Some of these repetitive movements cause physical harm. Head banging and hand biting are not uncommon. Children with autism have also been known to pull out their hair, bite off the ends of their fingers, and chew their shoulders down to the bone, often crying out in pain as they do so. Why do children with autism engage in such self-stimulatory and self-injurious behaviors? According to Durand (1990), children with developmental disabilities, especially those with mental retardation and without language, often engage in maladaptive behavior to communicate desires to others or to obtain certain kinds of reinforcement. Specifically, these children often seek sensory reinforcement, escape from aversive situations (such as a boring educational routine), attention from others, and/or positive tangible reinforcement, such as food or a toy.

Motor mannerisms are not the only area in which children with autism show an intense and narrow focus. They may have a favorite activity—tearing paper, spinning the wheels on a toy car—in which they lose themselves for hours every day. With toys and other objects, they tend to interest themselves in the part rather than the whole—not the car, for example, but just the wheels. They are also likely to resist any change in their surroundings and routines. Toys must always be put in the same place on the same shelves. Breakfast must be an unvarying ritual of egg first, vitamin pill second, and then toast. If the child senses that any step has been skipped, he or she may respond with a tantrum. Clinicians have noted that many normal children, when they are about two and a half years old, insist on sameness in routines. They have suggested, therefore, that the development of children with autism may stall at this point.

All these problems—the ritual behaviors, the self-absorption and bizarreness, the intellectual and social deficits—appear in the following case:

I first observed Jennie when she was seven years old, in a small classroom at a school for children with severe disabilities. An uncommunicative and unresponsive child, Jennie rarely made eye contact with anyone. If left alone she would put her hands over her throat, stick out her tongue, and make strange noises. Unless her attention was diverted, she would continue this way for hours, standing or rocking back and forth in her chair. If someone got too close to Jennie, she might grab the person's jewelry or eyeglasses and fling them across the room. Jennie did not like new experiences. One day she slapped a new intern who had approached her shortly after entering the room.

Though Jennie did not speak, she did understand and comply with simple requests to get her lunch or use the bathroom. She had a picture book with photographs of items she might want or need—a lunch box, a cookie, a glass of water, a favorite toy, or the toilet—and used it to communicate when she was asked to. But Jennie seemed unable or unwilling to discriminate between colors, to understand the concept of yes versus no, or to follow commands that included more than one step (for example, "Clap your hands and touch your nose"). Her former teachers reported that, though she could learn the difference between red and blue in the classroom, she could not transfer her learning to a different setting.

Despite her poor cognitive skills, Jennie's life skills were relatively good. She could put on her winter jacket with help and could use the toilet without difficulty, as long as she was reminded to put her clothes on again afterward. Still, Jennie needed constant supervision, mostly for her own safety. She tended to be oblivious of danger and could not be trusted to leave alone a hot stove.

Jennie's parents told me that she "had always been like this." They had noticed that Jennie was different when as an infant she resisted being held, and later when she failed to talk by the age of three years. At first they had thought she was deaf, but medical tests indicated that her hearing was normal. They had enrolled Jennie in her current school at age four years and reported that her behavior had improved greatly since then. Limited psychological testing and extensive observations over the past three years had largely confirmed Jennie's impaired cognitive and social skills. Jennie was diagnosed with both autism and mental retardation. (Adapted from Kearney, 1998)

Some children with autism improve enough by the time they are grown to hold down jobs and even live alone, though they are still aloof and still have language problems and poor social judgment. As for the remainder—that is, the vast majority of children with autism—most do improve with treatment but rarely enough to allow them to live outside a special residence when they reach adulthood, let alone on their own (Gillberg, 1991; Kobayashi, Murata, & Yoshinaga, 1992; Venter, Lord, & Schopler, 1992).

Theories of Autism

Explanations of autism have changed radically in the past few decades. Popular in the 1950s and 1960s was the psychodynamic view that autism was caused by cold, rejecting parents (e.g., Bettelheim, 1967)—a theory that, after adding grief and guilt to the lives of parents already coping with a difficult situation, has now been repudiated by research. Researchers are now focusing on brain dysfunction, investigating what factors may be involved, and on the cognitive perspective, examining the consequences of the presumed physical flaw.

The Biological Perspective

Genetic Research   As we noted in Chapter 13, a great deal of sophisticated and productive research has been carried out on the genetics of schizophrenia. In recent years, similar studies of autism have been done, despite the difficulty of finding large samples of twins. Researchers who scoured Great Britain, for example, found 11 pairs of monozygotic (MZ) twins and 10 pairs of dizygotic (DZ) twins in which at least 1 twin had autism (Folstein & Rutter, 1977). Of the MZ group, 4 of 11 were concordant. Of the DZ group, none was concordant. Even when a subject with an MZ twin who had autism was *not* diagnosed with autism, he or she was likely to be markedly impaired in language or cognition.

Three additional twin studies have essentially replicated these findings. A study based on a nationwide survey of clinics, schools, and parent organizations in Great Britain found a concordance rate of 50 percent for MZ twins and 0 percent for DZ twins. The concordance rates for cognitive/social disorder in this sample were 86 percent and 9 percent, respectively (Rutter, Macdonald, Le Couteur, et al., 1990). A follow-up study based on an earlier twin sample plus a new sample showed a concordance rate of 60 percent for MZ twins and 0 percent for DZ twins (Bailey, Le Couteur, Gottesman, et al., 1995). And a study done in the Nordic countries found a concordance rate of 91 percent for MZ twins and 0 percent for DZ twins. Concordance rates for cognitive disorder in this sample were 91 percent and 30 percent, respectively (Steffenburg, Gillberg, Hellgren, et al., 1989).

Even in non-twin siblings of children with autism, the rate of autism is about 3 to 7 percent (Bailey, Phillips, & Rutter, 1996). Findings differ with respect to the incidence of milder impairments among siblings of children with autism, however. In one study, 12 percent of the siblings of children with autism showed impairments in social interaction, compared with 0 percent of the siblings of children with Down syndrome (Bolton & Rutter, 1990). But, in another study, no difference was found between the rate of social or cognitive problems in siblings of children with autism and the rate in siblings of children with Down syndrome or low birth weight (Szatamari, Jones, Tuff, et al., 1993).

Whatever the genetic components that are involved, they are likely to differ with differing kinds of autism. One family study found that the patients with autism who were most likely to have siblings with autism or mental retardation were the ones who had the most severe retardation (Baird & August, 1985). Another study indicates that patients with autism who show the best functioning tend to come from families with a history of mood disorder (DeLong, 1992). In fact, several studies have found that major affective disorder is three times as common among parents of children with autism as among parents of children with tuberose sclerosis or epilepsy. Though the hardship of caring for a child with autism might be suspected as a contributing factor in major affec-

tive disorder, in nearly two-thirds of such parents, onset of the disorder precedes the birth of a child with autism (Bailey, Phillips, & Rutter, 1996).

Chromosome Studies   As was pointed out earlier, fragile X syndrome is associated not just with mental retardation but with autism. Two recent studies have found that the prevalence rate among patients with autism is 2.5 to 7 percent (Bailey, Phillips, & Rutter, 1996; Hagerman, 1992). Other abnormalities, such as tuberose sclerosis and anomalies on chromosome 15, are also associated with autism, though none so strongly as fragile X (Bailey, Phillips, & Rutter, 1996).

Biochemical Studies   In autism, as in schizophrenia (Chapter 13), a major focus of research today is the role of neurotransmitters. But a recent study found that children with autism do not necessarily have abnormally high levels of serotonin and dopamine, as was once thought (Tsai & Ghaziuddin, 1997). Whatever their role in the development of autism, these two neurotransmitters may play a role in its treatment. When children with autism receive stimulants such as the amphetamines, which increase dopamine, their symptoms of hyperactivity, ritualistic behavior, and self-stimulation get worse (Young, Kavanagh, Anderson, et al., 1982). Dopamine-inhibiting drugs such as the phenothiazines mitigate many of the symptoms of autism, including self-mutilation and repetitive motions, although they are less effective with autism than with schizophrenia (Campbell, Overall, Small, et al., 1989; Tsai, 1992).

Congenital Disorders and Birth Complications   While genetic factors are implicated in many cases of autism, this does not rule out nongenetic factors. Several birth complications appear to be related to autism, including pregnancy at an advanced age, bleeding after the first trimester, the use of medication during pregnancy, and the presence of meconium in the amniotic fluid (Tsai, 1987). According to Tsai and Ghaziuddin (1997), rubella, depressed immune function, autoimmune mechanisms, and problematic immune regulation may also be related to autism, though not necessarily in a cause-and-effect manner. But, in most cases of autism, congenital disorders and birth complications probably are not the primary causes of the disorder. Furthermore, congenital disorders may be related to genetic factors.

Neurological Research   Most researchers believe that, whatever its ultimate cause, autism results from a range of deficits in the brain. In the first place, most of the characteristic signs of autism—impaired language development, mental retardation, bizarre motor behavior, underreactivity and overreactivity to sensory input, responsiveness to touch and movement as opposed to auditory and visual stimuli—are related to the functioning of the central nervous system. Second, as many as 25 percent of persons with autism, particularly adolescents, develop seizure disorders, which are known to originate in the central nervous system (Klin & Volkmar, 1997; Volkmar & Nelson, 1990). Third, neurological examinations of children with autism sometimes reveal abnormalities such as poor muscle tone, poor coordination, drooling, and hyperactivity.

A fourth line of evidence has to do with neurophysiology. Two general types of research have been conducted: *EEG* and *ERP* studies. Electroencephalograms of people with autism are difficult to obtain, for the test requires more cooperation than many such people can give. Nevertheless, Minshew (1991) has reported that about 50 percent of persons with autism display abnormal EEGs. And a recent study showed that children with autism show reduced EEG activity in the frontal and temporal regions of the brain, compared with that of normal children (Dawson, Klinger, Panagiotides, et al., 1995). ERP studies are concerned with event-related potentials: how the brain waves of people show patterns of reaction to various sensory stimuli. ERP studies of people with autism have shown abnormalities of attention to both novel stimuli and language stimuli (Courchesne, Townsend, Akshoomoff, et al., 1994; Dunn, 1994). Taken together, EEG and ERP studies strongly suggest a neurological impairment in people with autism.

Fifth, autopsies of the brains of people with autism have revealed certain abnormalities in the cerebellum and in the limbic system, which is known to be involved in cognition, memory, emotion, and behavior. Specifically, the neurons in the limbic system appear to be smaller and more tightly packed. In some areas, their dendrites—the branching arms through which they receive signals from adjacent neurons—are shorter and less complex (Figure 16.2). Both these conditions are typical of earlier stages of prenatal brain maturation (Bauman & Kemper, 1994). In other cases, an abnormally low density of Purkinje cells, which are responsible for inhibiting the action of other brain cells, has been found. Such an abnormality may explain the stereotyped and overactive behavior sometimes seen in persons with autism. Finally, some researchers have found *megalencephaly* (an overly large brain size) in people with autism (Bailey, Phillips, & Rutter, 1996).

Another hopeful line of investigation has to do with brain-imaging techniques, such as MRI and PET scans. Although the results of many such studies conflict, researchers have identified some possible causal

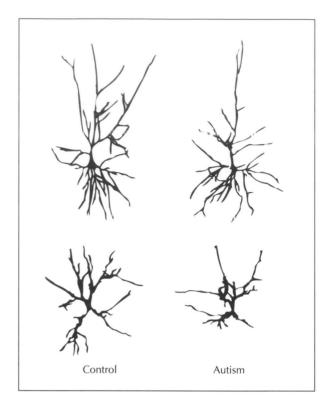

FIGURE 16.2   Photographic reproductions of neurons in a normal (control) brain and in the brain of a person with autism. In the upper pair, note the difference in the number of dendrites. In the lower pair, note the difference in dendrite length. (Adapted from Bauman & Kemper, 1992)

influences in autism, including enlarged ventricles in the brain (Bailey, Phillips, & Rutter, 1996; Minshew & Dombrowski, 1994). Scientists are now using brain-imaging techniques to develop interesting new hypotheses about causes of autism.

The Cognitive Perspective   No one denies that children with autism have problems affecting their capacity to imitate and comprehend, to be flexible and inventive, to form and apply rules, and to use information—in other words, to cope with the world. Cognitive theories hold that the cognitive problems of children with autism are primary and cause their social problems (Rutter & Bailey, 1993).

Recent investigations have focused on four broad areas of cognitive function: executive function, categorization and memory, social understanding, and theory of the mind. With respect to executive function, many researchers have noted that people with autism have great trouble solving problems, planning initiatives, controlling their impulses, maintaining attention, monitoring their performance, and inhibiting inappropriate behavior (Ozonoff, 1995).

Studies of categorization and memory have shown that people with autism also have difficulty forming new concepts and understanding new information based on those concepts. In particular, they have difficulty forming prototypes with which to categorize objects, so they tend to overrely on rules. Like people with amnesia, people with autism tend to show deficits in short- and long-term memory, which may be linked to dysfunctions in the amygdala and hippocampus (Bachevalier, 1994; DeLong, 1992; Klinger & Dawson, 1996).

The social understanding of children with autism is hampered by the fact that they do not attend to other people's emotional or attentional cues. In essence, their ability to comprehend gestures such as pointing or looking is severely impaired. They also have trouble understanding others' emotions and facial expressions (Hobson, 1993; Sigman, 1995).

A final cognitive hypothesis is that the fundamental problem of children with autism is that they have no theory of the mind—that is, they cannot appreciate the existence of purely mental states, such as beliefs or desires, and therefore cannot predict or understand behavior based on such states. In one study, for example, normal children and children with autism or mental retardation were given the following task concerning two dolls, Sally and Anne (Baron-Cohen, Leslie, & Frith, 1985). Sally, they were shown, put her marble in her basket and left. While Sally was gone, Anne took the marble out of the basket and hid it. When Sally returned, the children were asked where Sally would look for the marble. Over 80 percent of the children both with and without retardation answered, "In the basket," but only 20 percent of the children with autism gave the obviously correct answer. It was not that they could not remember, but they could not take another person's point of view. The lack of this critical skill undoubtedly contributes to the social isolation of children with autism.

Children with autism vary in their success with theory-of-the-mind tasks. Normal children develop a theory of the mind at around 18 months; about 20 percent of cases of autism have their onset at that time. Fein and Waterhouse (1990) have suggested that the theory-of-the-mind explanation may apply to that subgroup—their development becomes abnormal at that point—but that it is less likely to apply to children with autism who show abnormal social development in their first year of life. Another study has suggested that, in people with autism, the ability to solve theory-of-the-mind problems may be related to verbal ability (Yirmiya, Solomonica-Levi, Schulman, et al., 1996). Finally, some data suggest that the ability to solve this type of problem can be

taught to persons with autism who are of normal intelligence (Ozonoff & Miller, 1995).

Groups at Risk for Autism

Socioeconomic status and ethnocultural background are *not* major risk factors for autism. Gender *is* a significant risk factor, however, for males with autism generally outnumber females by a 3 or 4 to 1 margin. This finding may be related to the risk factors for mental retardation. Specifically, females with autism generally have more severe forms of mental retardation, and more severe symptoms of autism, than males with autism. Conversely, though, females with autism but not mental retardation have fewer problems than males with autism but not mental retardation.

Another risk factor for autism is the presence of the disorder in siblings. The prevalence of autism in siblings of children with autism is 3 percent, a rate that is substantially higher than that of the general population. This finding, in addition to the much higher rates of concordant autism in monozygotic but not dizygotic twins, raises the specter of genetic influences as a substantial risk factor for autism (Hodapp & Dykens, 1996; Klinger & Dawson, 1996; Szymanski & Kaplan, 1997).

Society and People with Developmental Disabilities

Our society is designed for people with at least average coping skills, people who can park a car, pay a bill, fill out an income tax form. Most people with mental retardation cannot handle such tasks. Indeed, most cannot care for themselves on their own. Some remain at home with their families, which is usually to their advantage, but many families cannot cope with a disabled member, and those that are willing are generally hard-pressed. People with mental retardation need special schooling, special jobs (if they can hold jobs), special psychological supports. If the family cannot provide such things, should it be the responsibility of the society to do so? Our discussion of these social issues will cover developmental disabilities as a whole, which include mental retardation and autism.

Public Policy

In the past 30 years, there have been tremendous charges in the field of mental retardation. To begin with, parent groups—above all the Association for Retarded Citizens (ARC), founded in 1950—have vigorously lobbied federal and state governments and have obtained not only large increases in funding but also legislation guaranteeing the right of people with mental retardation to a free education geared to their abilities. Second, these same parent organizations, along with other advocacy groups, have increasingly taken their grievances to the federal and state courts, whose decisions have substantially altered the treatment of people with retardation in this country. Finally, the number of professionals in the field of mental retardation has expanded greatly, a reflection of the discovery that people with mental retardation respond well to behavior therapy. This finding has generated a new mood of hope, attracting to the field a large number of young clinical psychologists. At the same time, several university-affiliated centers for training and research have been established to train these professionals and to teach them to work in interdisciplinary teams.

This new activism has brought about sweeping changes in public policy toward people with mental retardation. Whereas society once all but ignored them, today certain principles have been established, which, though by no means fully implemented, are guiding public institutions toward the granting of full citizens' rights to people with mental retardation. There are five basic principles:

1. *Free and appropriate education.* Public schools must create educational programs for people with retardation, so that they can learn with the maximum independence consistent with their abilities.

2. *Individualization.* Services should not be based on textbook descriptions of people with

retardation; they should be tailored to the person—what he or she needs and can do.

3. *Timely progress reviews.* People with mental retardation, once placed in a program, should not be left there indefinitely but should have their progress reviewed regularly, with at least one comprehensive annual evaluation.

4. *Community integration.* Services for people with mental retardation should be provided in the least restrictive environment consistent with the person's disabilities.

5. *Human rights.* The law should protect people with mental retardation from abuse in residential programs and facilitate lawsuits to obtain needed services. In keeping with this principle, the federal government has established a protection and advocacy commission in each state to provide legal help for people with retardation.

For many years, children with mental retardation were essentially excluded from the public school system. Then, in the early 1970s, decisions in a number of class-action suits required that local school systems provide special education for children with retardation. Finally, in 1975, this requirement became effective nationwide when Congress passed Public Law 94-142, guaranteeing to every citizen under the age of 21 a free public education appropriate to his or her needs. P.L. 94-142 has been responsible for a great increase in special education programs since the late 1970s. These programs are carefully tailored to the person, in keeping with the requirement that public education be "appropriate" to each child's needs. Typically, the school system has what is

Ideally, the "mainstreaming" of children with mental retardation into regular public-school classrooms has educational and social benefits for the normal children as well as for those with retardation.

called an individualized education program (IEP). The school holds a multidisciplinary conference to identify the handicaps of children requesting special education and to review the progress of those already receiving such services. The committee then formulates, in writing, an IEP for each child, and the appropriate services are provided.

The law has stimulated some highly innovative programs. One concept, for example, is the "cascade system." Nine educational programs, beginning with a regular classroom in a regular school and ending with a hospital setting, are designed to accommodate individual needs and to provide for progression from one level to another. Upward mobility is the goal, and it is to be achieved by constant periodic evaluation, so that assignment to a particular cascade level does not become a life sentence. Many children with mental retardation as noted, have been mainstreamed into regular classes. (They are usually given modified tasks.) Other children may spend part of the school day in the regular class and part in a special class. Children who need more help and guidance may attend a special day school or live in a residential school. Such programs, however, are by no means the norm. Though P.L. 94-142 mandates special education for all children with disabilities, Congress has not provided full funding for the implementation of the law, and many communities have been unable or unwilling to find the necessary funds.

In the case of children with autism, designing an appropriate education program may be a harder task, because of these children's special disabilities. Their need for an unvarying routine is not easy to meet in a classroom, even a special classroom, and their ritualistic movements may leave little room in their attentional field for what the teacher is trying to say. Furthermore, as noted earlier, they tend not to respond to social reinforcement (e.g., the teacher's approval), which is the usual form of classroom reinforcement (Harris & Handleman, 1997; Schreibman, 1994).

Community Integration

Some of the most important changes in recent years have been those under the heading "community integration." As recently as 1970, virtually all services for people with retardation were segregated from services for people without mental retardation. Children with mild and moderate retardation attended special education classes separate from the classes for other children. People with severe and profound retardation were sent off to large institutions, which, because they were outside the community, provided their own educational, medical, and psychological services. The effect of this segregation was to deprive

people with mental retardation of any real participation in the life of the society. The principle of community integration holds that people with retardation should be educated in the public schools and, when they get sick, they should go to the same hospitals as everyone else. They should be able to go to the same movie theaters, the same bowling alleys, the same restaurants as everybody else.

In some measure, this is now being achieved. Not only are children with mental retardation being educated in their local schools, but many in the mild-retardation category have been mainstreamed into regular education classes. As for residential facilities, community planning has shifted from a model of institutional care to one of residence within the community (Polloway, Smith, Patton, et al., 1996).

A wide range of assisted-living arrangements is now available, from *supported living arrangements*, in which supervision is generally provided only in the evening, to *community living facilities*—small- to medium-sized residential centers with round-the-clock supervision—and *intermediate-care facilities*, or medium-sized residences for groups of about six people. Each type of community-living facility can care for people who function on several different levels. For example, someone with severe mental retardation but no major medical or behavioral problems might be successful in an intermediate-care facility, while someone with only moderate mental retardation but severe physical problems and self-injurious behavior might not be able to live there. Large state institutions still care for those who cannot function satisfactorily in community settings. But, as increasing numbers of community living centers are being established, more and more people are being moved out of the state institutions. This is an extremely heartening development. Large institutions, as we saw in previous chapters, can have damaging effects on the people they are supposed to care for, not only because so many of them offer dreary and even cruel living conditions but because they do not allow patients to use the skills they have. Consequently, those skills tend to disappear. The great virtue of community-living centers is that they challenge residents to use and develop their coping abilities.

Quality of Life

Over the past 10 years, one of the most intensely researched and discussed topics in the field of developmental disabilities has been the quality of life of people with disabilities. What is quality of life? Felce and Perry (1995) have suggested that it is a multidimensional concept that includes physical, material, social, and emotional well-being, as well as personal development and activity. Though these 5 dimensions are general enough to apply to almost anyone, individual differences should inform any assessment of quality of life.

Research shows that the size of a person's residential setting is not as important as the quality of life of the people who live within that setting. Because one key measure of quality of life is choice, some of the new research has focused on the choices people with developmental disabilities are allowed to make within their living arrangements. In one study, the degree of choice residents enjoyed was found to be correlated with adaptive, and to some extent maladaptive, behavior (Kearney, Durand, & Mindell, 1995b). Providing residents with some choice in their activities can affect the degree to which they participate in activities, the way they behave during the activities, and their perceptions of them (Harchik, Sherman, Sheldon, et al., 1993).

Given the difficulty of communicating with many people who have developmental disabilities, how can the degree of choice that is offered to them be measured? There are several methods, including interviews, questionnaires, pictures, and direct observation (Kearney & McKnight, 1997). For use in group homes for people with severe disabilities, Kearney, Durand, and Mindell (1995a) have developed the Resident Choice Assessment Scale. Ways have also been developed to implement or enhance the opportunity to make choices in programs and residences for those with developmental disabilities. Residents can be taught choice-making skills, and staff members can learn to facilitate their choice making (Kearney & McKnight, 1997).

Support for the Family

When a child is diagnosed with mental retardation or autism, the parents usually suffer terrible grief. In the past, the diagnosis was usually accompanied by a recommendation that a child be institutionalized. Today, even in the case of children with profound retardation, the recommendation is likely to be the opposite: that the parents try to care for the child at home. If they do so, however, they need supportive training and counseling (Dunst, Johanson, Trivette, et al., 1991).

Children with mental retardation, of course, have many of the same needs as normal children. They need to be fed, to be loved and held, to be given structure and discipline. Like normal children, they need to interact with other children and with adults to develop social skills, and they must be encouraged to be as independent as possible. But children with retardation also have special needs. They may be

physically handicapped. They are often teased or shunned by other children. They learn more slowly. In recent years, efforts have been made to teach parents simple behavioral techniques for dealing with these problems (Harris, Alessandri, & Gill, 1991; Schreibman & Koegel, 1996). Through reinforcement, parents can help children with retardation to develop speech. Through shaping, they can help them master complex behaviors such as self-feeding and using the toilet. Such home training not only increases the child's skills; it also tightens the parent-child bond by making the parents feel that they can actually do something concrete to help the child.

The adolescent with mental retardation presents additional concerns to the family and community. Parents must walk a narrow line between the child's need for independence and his or her lack of maturity. They must help the child to deal with physical changes, with sexual feelings, with threats to self-esteem (an especially difficult task if the child is aware of being "different"), and with a peer group that is outgrowing him or her. The extent to which these problems become an issue depends, of course, on the level of retardation. They are of greatest concern for parents of teenagers with mild and moderate retardation.

As the adolescent nears adulthood, the family and community must consider carefully the extent to which he or she will be able to live independently. Although parents may be confident of their ability to provide for a young child with mental retardation, they become uneasy when they think about the stresses and demands placed on the adult with mental retardation. One of the most complex issues is that of sex and marriage.

Historically, attitudes toward the sexual development of people with mental retardation have favored complete desexualization, physically and emotionally (Perske, 1973). Relationships between men and women with mental retardation were discouraged, and involuntary sterilization was common. Today, a more humane approach is taken. The trend is toward the belief that people with mental retardation, like normal people, have a right to sexual development and that they can be taught sexual behavior appropriate to their level of functioning. Programs exist to teach social and relationship skills to young adults with mental retardation and to educate them about AIDS and HIV risk reduction (Scotti, Nangle, Masia, et al., 1997; Whitehouse & McCabe, 1997). With some assistance from families or social agencies, many people with mild retardation can marry and maintain regular social functioning. When sterilization is considered, usually only as a last resort, a great deal of thought is given to the ethical issues involved in the decision (Elkins & Andersen, 1992).

Employment

Federal and state laws provide that people with mental retardation must have opportunities for useful employment, whether or not in the types of jobs other people hold. In practice, this means that, whatever their residential placement, people with mental retardation must be offered planned daytime programs or supported employment (Wehman & Kregel, 1995). In the case of people with severe or profound retardation, such daytime activities may be very simple, but many people with mild and some with moderate retardation do hold paying jobs, some in ordinary work environments, others in special work centers, called **sheltered workshops**, tailored to their needs.

It has long been assumed that people with retardation belong to America's socioeconomic surplus population—that most of them either can't or don't want to work or, if they do work, that they are the first to lose their jobs when the payroll is being cut. But this is no longer the case. Many, if not most, people with mental retardation do want to work (Test, Hinson, Solow, et al., 1993). Furthermore, when properly placed, they make good employees and consequently are not necessarily the first to be fired when jobs become scarce (Nietupski, Hamre Nietupski, VanderHart, et al., 1996). Interestingly, research also indicates that, when they are fired, it is often not because of a failure to do the job but because of a lack of social skills. The obvious conclusion is that vocational training for people with mental retardation must cover social skills as well as vocational skills—and training programs now tend to include them.

Prevention and Therapy

One of the most significant developments in the field of mental retardation is the idea that treatment can make a decisive difference in the lives of people with mental retardation. Whereas early detection of chromosomal and congenital abnormalities is available to help couples at risk and expectant parents, who may then seek counseling about the pregnancy, the new hope in the therapeutic community is to improve the quality of life of children and adults with mental retardation (Campbell, Schopler, Cueva, et al., 1996; Kearney & McKnight, 1998).

Primary Prevention

A major breakthrough in the prevention of mental retardation has been the advent of genetic analysis and counseling. Couples at risk for abnormal births can be identified, informed of the risk, and advised how to proceed. The gene for Tay-Sachs disease, for example, occurs in about 1 of every 30 people of Eastern European Jewish descent. If one carrier marries another, their chances of having a child with the disease are 1 in 4. A simple blood test can identify carriers, who can then get advice from a genetic counselor. Genetic analysis can also identify abnormalities in the developing fetus. If fragile X, Down syndrome, or another abnormality is detected, the parents may choose to terminate the pregnancy.

Secondary Prevention

When a child is at risk for a condition that could lead to mental retardation, secondary prevention, or early intervention, can do much to minimize its effects. We have already described several medical procedures that fall under this heading, including low-phenylalanine diets for PKU children and thyroid treatments for infants with missing or damaged thyroid glands. There are also psychological therapies. In infant stimulation therapy, for example, babies with mental retardation—for example, children with Down syndrome—are played with intensively several hours a day to stimulate their language acquisition, problem-solving skills, and achievement motivation. Parents do most of the teaching, aided and guided by a special education teacher and other child development specialists who observe the child periodically at home or at school and suggest and demonstrate activities to be added to the child's regimen. The key to these children's development is the amount of stimulation, exercise, and encouragement they receive as they strive to master the skills that come more easily to youngsters without mental retardation. Infant stimulation activities may be as simple as mothers talking to and making eye contact with their babies. Mothers can encourage use of the long muscles, helping the babies to sit up and lift their heads. (Children with Down syndrome are often strikingly "loose jointed" and have poor muscle tone.) Activities and equipment become more sophisticated as the child progresses. Many "graduates" of early intervention programs are able to feed and dress themselves, talk fluently, and participate in most children's activities. Some have learned to read and have acquired other academic skills (Hanson, 1987; Pines, 1982a).

Infant stimulation programs have been expanded to include children whose only apparent risk factor is poverty. If it is true, as the research assembled by the Carnegie report suggests, that the conditions associated with poverty can lead to mild retardation, could helping poor families early lessen the risk? This has been the goal of family-support programs instituted in various American cities in the 1980s and 1990s. In one such program, called Avance, that serves 2,000 Mexican American families yearly in and around San Antonio, Texas, parents are given special help with their infants for 2 years. Evaluations of Avance have shown that mothers who have been in the program are more affectionate and positive with their children, encourage the children's speech more, and provide a more stimulating environment than mothers who have received no special services (Johnson, Walker, & Rodriguez, 1993). The Carnegie report also calls for a broad range of other reforms—promotion of family planning; inclusion of child development courses in high school curricula; and improvement of prenatal-care services, parental-leave benefits, and child-care facilities—to help break the link between poverty and developmental delay. (We will discuss prevention issues more fully in Chapter 19.)

Behavior Therapy

Of all the services for people with mental retardation, almost none has generated more enthusiasm than the application of learning principles to training and behavior management. Behavioral techniques are being used extensively and with good success in the home, in schools and workshops, in institutional settings, and with both children and adults. They can be taught to parents, teachers, therapists, and hospital staffs, and they can be used for a variety of purposes.

The three basic techniques of behavior therapy are shaping (reinforcing successive approximations of desirable behavior), chaining (teaching the person to finish the task and then gradually expanding the number of steps required to finish), and using stimulus control (teaching that a behavior should occur in some situations but not in others). These methods have proved successful in the training of people with mental retardation in many areas, including self-help and adaptive skills, language and communication skills, and leisure and community skills, as well as in the replacement of maladaptive behaviors.

Self-Help and Adaptive Skills   Training in self-help and adaptive skills is designed to teach daily living skills such as feeding, dressing, and toileting. This type of training involves (1) the breaking down of the task into small steps, (2) backward or forward chaining, and (3) substantial feedback and reinforcement. In addition, in daytime programs, behavior therapists have been able to teach adults with mental retardation the skills necessary for holding a job. Token economies have been especially successful in vocational training programs, improving job performance rates (Rusch & Mithaug, 1980) and on-the-job social behavior (Eilbracht & Thompson, 1977)

and inculcating work habits, such as arriving on time, punching in and out, and taking breaks and lunch periods at the right times.

For people with severe mental retardation, especially those confined to institutions, behavior therapy is considered one of the most appropriate and effective techniques for teaching self-help skills (Grabowski & Thompson, 1977; Matson & Andrasik, 1982; Watson & Uzzell, 1981). The results, for both patients and staff, can be startling. Incontinence, for example, is a persistent problem in institutions for people with severe mental retardation. Cleaning up not only consumes most of the staff's time but makes assignment to these wards undesirable, so patients receive little friendly attention from the staff. Furthermore, patients who are incontinent generally cannot leave the ward. Toilet training not only improves patients' hygiene and promotes positive interactions with the staff but also opens new worlds; toilet-trained people can go out of the ward to other parts of the building or onto the grounds for outdoor recreation (McCartney & Holden, 1981).

Language and Communication Skills   In early childhood, one of the most important applications of behavior therapy has been in language acquisition (Grabowski & Thompson, 1977). Research into patterns of language acquisition by both normal children and children with mental retardation has yielded information that has allowed for the construction of step-by-step behavioral sequences to teach both speech and comprehension. Shaping and verbal imitation are typically used to train people who are mute. Sign language and picture books, through which people with receptive language can communicate by pointing, are also useful. Finally, caregivers can be taught to recognize the communicative body movements of those they care for. Such training in communication is designed to enhance language skills, to improve the prognosis for those with developmental disabilities, and to reduce behavior problems.

Leisure and Community Skills   Training in leisure and community skills is designed to improve the quality of life of people with mental retardation and to help them adapt to new surroundings. This type of training typically involves modeling, prompting, giving feedback, and using reinforcement. Examples include guided social contact in recreational settings, game-playing, use of the telephone, money management, skills in choosing clothes, and cooking skills. Vocational, social-skills, and assertiveness training procedures are sometimes used as well (Kohler & Strain, 1997).

Participating in social and recreational activities such as the Special Olympics can be an important part of therapy for individuals with mental retardation.

Procedures for developing appropriate responses, whether in leisure pursuits, communication, or self-help, depend first and foremost on conquering children's insensitivity to social reinforcement. To learn from others, children must regard others as important. In some cases, however, maladaptive behaviors must be extinguished using other means before positive behaviors can be taught.

Replacement of Maladaptive Behaviors   Treatments for maladaptive behaviors such as aggression and self-injury include time-outs, differential reinforcement of other behavior, and differential reinforcement of incompatible behavior. Children may also be taught sign language to reduce the need to communicate using maladaptive behaviors. For instance, they can learn to sign for a drink rather than to push someone to get his or her attention. Punishment-oriented treatments such as response cost, aversives, and overcorrection may also be used (Didden, Duker, & Korzilius, 1997; Harris, 1996; Lovaas & Buch, 1997).

The effectiveness of such techniques seems to depend on what behavior is being eliminated, as well as its function. Self-mutilating responses such as head banging may eventually extinguish if social attention is withdrawn when they occur. But some behaviors seem to be maintained by internal rather than external rewards, in which case withdrawing social attention will have little if any effect. For example, ritualistic motor behaviors motivated by sensory reinforcement are highly resistant to extinction. In some cases as well, the therapist may resort to punishment, usually in the form of spankings or, in cases of extremely self-

destructive behavior, electric shock. Ivar Lovaas (1970) conducted research on the use of electric shock in treating maladaptive behaviors, and as he points out, it is extremely effective in eliminating self-mutilating behavior. He argues that disturbed children are more likely to respond to therapy when they are treated like people—that is, rewarded, punished, and generally held responsible for their behavior—rather than like patients. Lovaas has also pointed out that, if self-destructive behavior is *not* eliminated by some kind of treatment, the child may spend long periods of time tied down in restraints, which is a punishment in itself and which makes it impossible for the child to participate in any other kind of therapy.

For such therapeutic changes to be maintained, the environment must support them. Follow-up reports indicate that responses learned in the treatment laboratory often do not generalize to the school or the home (Koegel & Rincover, 1977; Nordquist & Wahler, 1973). And some children, especially those who are returned to institutions after their treatment, relapse completely. There is no question that institutions foster such relapses, because in many institutional settings patients are expected to act inappropriately and no rewards are given for acting otherwise.

Most behavior therapists have no illusion that they are transforming children with developmental disabilities into normal children (Margolies, 1977). Rather, their aim is to provide these children with enough adaptive responses so that they can graduate from custodial care to a more useful and fulfilling existence, albeit in a "special" class. Critics of behavioral therapy for children with such disabilities have claimed that its products are no better than performing robots (Bettelheim, 1967), and in some instances this seems to be the case. For example, one child, when asked, "What did you have for breakfast?" would tell you that she had had "eggs, toast, jelly, juice, and milk" even on days when she had had no breakfast at all. In short, she had no understanding of the concept; she was simply responding with a programmed answer. In many other instances, however, behavioral treatment has resulted in the development of responses that are spontaneous as well as appropriate. Substantial gains have been made in eliminating self-mutilating and bizarre motor behavior and in developing language, self-help, and social skills.

Cognitive Therapy

Cognitive therapy for people with developmental disabilities focuses on five primary areas: self-instructional training, correspondence training, self-management and self-monitoring, self-control, and problem solving. These therapies usually supplement behavior therapy.

Self-instructional training involves the development of self-regulatory speech that is useful in academic, leisure, and vocational skills. To get through routine tasks and difficulties, students are trained to control their actions by controlling what they say to themselves before, during, and after the action. One group of researchers (Rusch et al., 1985), for example, reported on the use of self-instructional training with two women with mental retardation who had jobs as kitchen helpers in a university dormitory. Both these women enjoyed their jobs, but both had received feedback that they were doing certain things wrong. Specifically, they were forgetting to wipe the counters and to check and restock supplies. Thus, they were taught to make a series of statements to themselves on the job: first a question ("What does the supervisor want me to do?"), then an answer to that question ("I am supposed to wipe the counters, check the supplies, and restock the supplies"), then a performance-guiding statement ("Okay, I need to wipe the counter," etc.), then a self-reinforcement ("I did that right"). The statements, together with the accompanying actions, were first modeled for the women by a therapist. Then the women copied the therapist's performance, first saying the statements out loud, then whispering them, then instructing themselves covertly, without speaking. Both women improved and kept their jobs.

Variations on self-instructional training have been used to teach children with mental retardation to do arithmetic problems (Johnston, Whitman, & Johnson, 1980), to help mothers with mental retardation to handle their babies (Tymchuk, Andron, &

Rahbar, 1988), to teach dating skills to adults with mental retardation (Muesser, Valenti-Hein, & Yarnold, 1987), and to teach a janitor with mental retardation to control his anger on the job (Benson, 1986). Not surprisingly, in all these reports, the subjects were in the mild-retardation category. The technique seems simple, but it is often just such simple skills—knowing what to do when a baby has a fever, knowing not to yell at one's boss—that people with mental retardation need to remain in normalizing situations (a mother-child relationship, a job) rather than be relegated to the fringes of society.

Correspondence training involves the use of rewards for action-oriented verbal statements. For instance, students are rewarded for completing tasks they have promised to do or for telling the truth about a task just completed. The idea is to encourage students to associate their verbal statements with their past and future actions. Correspondence training may be used to promote both academic and social behaviors.

Training in self-management and self-monitoring involves teaching students to regulate their own behavior, to decide whether their performance has been adequate or inadequate, and to reward themselves accordingly. This type of training can be used to bolster leisure activities, control stereotypic behavior, and improve on-task behavior.

Training in self-control involves delayed gratification of impulses—for example, giving large rewards for waiting and small rewards for immediate gratification. To cope with the waiting, students learn to make appropriate self-statements.

Finally, training in problem solving is a generic process that involves learning to define a problem, develop possible solutions, choose the best of these solutions, implement it, and decide whether the solution was effective. The procedure may be enhanced with visual prompts and imagery (Whitman, 1994; Whitman, Scherzinger, & Sommer, 1991).

Pharmacological Therapy

Pharmacotherapy is commonly used for people with developmental disabilities. Major drug therapies for treating people with mental retardation include psychotropic drugs, which are useful in managing disruptive or aggressive behavior, and anticonvulsive medications, which are used to control seizures. Aman and Singh (1991) estimate that 50 to 67 percent of people with mental retardation are receiving medication for these types of problems; 30 to 50 percent take psychotropic drugs; and 25 to 35 percent take anticonvulsants.

Other drugs have been tried to treat autism. In view of the fact that some people with autism show

Facilitated communication, in which people with autism are helped to express themselves with the use of keyboards, has generated both hope and controversy. Is the speech pathologist helping the children communicate their own ideas or unconsciously conveying ideas through them?

abnormally high levels of serotonin, it was hoped that they might be helped by serotonin-reducing drugs. One such drug, fenfluramine, was given to two boys with autism, a three-year-old and a five-year-old, for three months. Both improved noticeably in their speech, social behavior, and IQ scores (the three-year-old's IQ nearly doubled). When the treatment was stopped, the gains held for at least six weeks but, after three months, began to diminish (Geller, Ritvo, Freeman, et al., 1982). Fenfluramine appears now to be useful primarily in controlling overactive or stereotypic behaviors; it is not helpful in treating the core social and language deficits inherent in autism (Campbell, 1988; Campbell, Adams, Small, et al., 1988).

Psychotherapy

For years it was believed that people with mental retardation could not benefit from psychotherapy (Fine, 1965), because they lacked the intellectual sophistication to discuss their problems in psychodynamic terms. But, with the development of less insight-oriented therapies, there are now many forms of psychological treatment that can help people with mental retardation: supportive psychotherapy (Fine, 1965), group psychotherapy (Szymanski & Rosefsky, 1980), family therapy, and a modified form of Carl Rogers' client-centered therapy (Prouty, 1976). Group therapy is often used in inpatient settings, to help clients gain insight into their problems and to enhance their social supports. Family therapy may also be useful with parents who are

raising children with mental retardation; procedures such as contingency management and token economies can be taught. In addition, family therapy can focus on educating family members about a person's condition, changing family dynamics that curtail development, and building social support networks for family members. For someone with mental retardation who is considering raising a family, marital counseling and parent training may be helpful (Barrett, Walters, Mercurio, et al., 1992; Kearney & McKnight, 1998).

Controversial Treatments

Apart from those just discussed, other therapies are being tried, with mixed results and sometimes in the face of vigorous opposition. A new treatment called *facilitated communication* was tried in the early 1990s. Supposedly, facilitated communication enables people with motor and speech problems to communicate by typing letters on a keyboard or pointing to letters on a letter board as a "facilitator" helps to guide their hands (Biklen, 1990). These claims, which raised the possibility that beneath their communication problems autistic people were secretly leading rich mental lives, created much hope and publicity. However, a number of experimental studies (e.g., Moore, Donovan, Hudson, et al., 1993) have failed to support the claims. One report concluded that subjects' seemingly sophisticated responses were reactions to the demand characteristics of the facilitators—the facilitators were "putting words into their client's hands" (Eberlin, McConnachie, Ibel, et al., 1993).

In another controversial treatment, *auditory training,* patients are hooked up to a training machine for an hour a day over a 10-day period. The machine, which plays specially selected music, is supposed to retrain patients' attention, altering the structure of the left brain, which controls language and speech, in the process. The effectiveness of this method has never been validated by controlled studies, however. Until such studies are conducted, the benefits of auditory training will remain entirely conjectural (Amos, 1993; Campbell, Schopler, Cueva, et al., 1996).

Still another treatment, *megavitamin therapy,* involves the ingestion of high doses of vitamin B_6 and magnesium. But megadoses of vitamin B_6 can damage the nerves in the hands and feet (Bendich & Cohen, 1990), while doses low enough to ensure against side effects seem not to influence subjects' behavior (Tolbert, Haigler, Waits, et al., 1993). This therapy remains controversial.

KEY TERMS

SUMMARY

- Mental retardation, which affects about 2 percent of the U.S. population, is defined as involving significantly subaverage general intellectual functioning, determined using standardized intelligence tests; significant limitations in adaptive functioning in at least 2 of 11 adaptive skill areas; and onset before age 18 years. Four levels of retardation are generally recognized: mild, moderate, severe, and profound.

- About 85 percent of people diagnosed with mental retardation fall into the category of mild retardation. As adults they can often lead relatively independent lives. People with moderate mental retardation can learn to care for themselves but do not become independent. People with severe or profound retardation require considerable supervision.

- Many physical or genetic anomalies are associated with retardation, including chromosomal abnormalities, such as fragile X syndrome and Down syndrome, and metabolic disturbances, such as phenylketonuria.

- Environmental factors also contribute to mental retardation. In the prenatal environment, congenital disorders (such as rubella), drugs (such as cocaine and alcohol), and maternal malnutrition can cause retardation. In the postnatal environment, important causal factors include reactions to toxins, physical trauma, and the psychological handicaps of growing up in a deprived setting. The last may cause, or at least foster, cultural-familial retardation, a condition for which children of teenage mothers are especially at risk. Research suggests that what begin as psychological factors may become physical factors through effects on the developing brain. Institutionalization can also have profound effects on intellectual functioning.

- As adults, people with mental retardation are susceptible to other organic brain disorders (such as Alzheimer's disease) and emotional disturbance. Many forms of psychological treatment can help those with retardation, if they can find access to the treatment.

- Groups most at risk for mental retardation are males, young people, and people of low socioeconomic status. Males with mental retardation outnumber females with mental retardation by about 1.6 to 1, due largely to the greater prevalence of gender-linked disorders such as fragile X syndrome in males. The diagnosis of mental retardation peaks at age 5 to 6 years, around the time children enter the primary grades and encounter increased cognitive demands. Mild retardation is more prevalent in families with low incomes than in those with high incomes. Statistically, African Americans are at greater risk for mild mental retardation than are other ethnic groups, though testing bias and environmental and cultural factors may explain their higher incidence rate.

- Autism, normally recognizable in early childhood, is a profound disturbance with four basic symptoms: social isolation, mental retardation, language deficits, and stereotyped, ritualistic behavior. Many children with autism insist on preserving the sameness of their environment. Only a small percentage make a good adjustment as adults.

- Autism may have a genetic component; it has been associated with fragile X syndrome. It almost certainly has a biochemical component, for many children with autism show abnormally high levels of serotonin and dopamine. Congenital disorders and complications in pregnancy and birth are closely associated with autism. Neurological studies suggest that the basic deficit in autism lies in the limbic system or in the frontal and temporal regions of the brain. An abnormally low density of Purkinje cells, enlarged ventricles, and megalencephaly, or an enlarged brain, are also suspected as causes of autism.

- Cognitive researchers argue that cognitive abnormalities are the primary problem in autism. Recent investigations have focused on four broad areas of cognitive function: executive function, categorization and memory, social understanding, and theory of the mind. Some researchers suspect that children with autism have no theory of the mind, or appreciation of the existence of purely mental states, such as beliefs or desires; therefore, they cannot predict or understand others' behavior.

- Gender is a significant risk factor for autism: males with autism outnumber females with autism by 3 or 4 to 1. The high prevalence of the disorder among males may be related to the risk factors for mental retardation. Another risk factor for autism is the presence of the disorder in siblings. Socioeconomic status and ethnocultural background are *not* risk factors for autism.

- Opportunities for people with mental retardation have expanded greatly in recent years. Five principles have been established: (1) people with mental retardation are entitled to free and appropriate education; (2) services for them should be individualized; (3) their progress should be evaluated regularly; (4) their lives should be integrated into the community, not segregated from it; and (5) the law should protect them from abuse and deprivation. The education of children with mental retardation has been upgraded, but children with autism are difficult to educate because of their ritualistic behaviors and lack of response to social reinforcement.

- Parents today are normally urged to try to care for a child with mental retardation at home, though they need support in order to handle the problems involved. In the child's early years, parents can use behavioral techniques to teach self-care, self-discipline, and academic skills. In adulthood, some people with mental retardation may be able to live on their own or in assisted living arrangements, and some may marry. Many can also work, either in ordinary jobs or in sheltered workshops. Their quality of life, especially the degree of choice they enjoy, is an important influence on their adjustment.

- Efforts are being made to prevent mental retardation through genetic counseling and improved prenatal care and to minimize the effect of retardation when it occurs (e.g., through infant stimulation programs). Mental retardation can also be treated through behavior therapy, cognitive therapy, pharmacological therapy, and psychotherapy. Behavior therapy includes training in self-help and adaptive skills, language and communication skills, and leisure and community skills; it is also used to replace maladaptive behaviors. One form of cognitive therapy, self-instructional training, is especially helpful; it involves teaching people with mental retardation to deal with routine tasks and difficulties by talking themselves through the process step-by-step. Self-rewards, self-management, self-monitoring, and problem-solving techniques can also be taught through cognitive therapy. Pharmacological therapy involves the use of psychotropic drugs to manage disruptive or aggressive behavior and anticonvulsants to control seizures. Psychotherapy for people with mental retardation includes supportive therapy, group therapy, family therapy, and a modified form of client-centered therapy.

Part Six | SOCIETAL AND LEGAL ISSUES

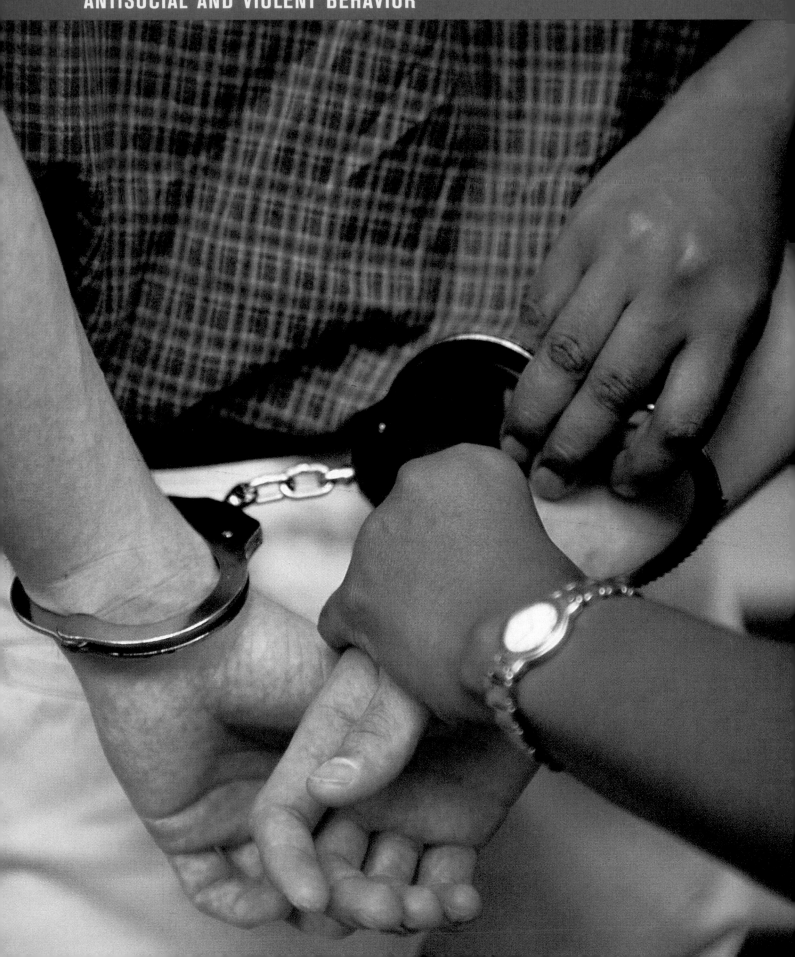

Chapter 17

George was born and raised in a rural Midwestern community. His father was a drifter and a con man who spent most of his time away from home. When he was home, he was violent toward all other family members: his wife; George; and George's older sister, Rita. George's mother made her living as a prostitute and supported her family by meeting her customers at the family home. George was abused both physically and sexually by a number of her patrons, and many of them abused his mother as well. In fact, George's most cherished childhood memory was of a violent event that occurred when he was 12. One night, he heard noises coming from his mother's bedroom and realized his mother was being beaten by one of her customers. George got his father's shotgun, ran up to his mother's bedroom and pointed the gun at the customer's head, saying, "Lay a hand on her again and I'll blow your head off."

George felt powerful that day. He began to see life as a game, and all human beings as things to be used. While in high school, George ran away from home to live with his father, and he was left alone most of the time. He happily spent his teenage years developing his skills as a con man, satisfying his sexual appetites, and consuming illegal drugs. As time went on, George talked himself out of numerous arrests. Even when 19-year-old George killed his fiancée, and was convicted of involuntary manslaughter, he got probation. At that point, he decided to join the navy.

It was in the navy that he first met Vicky. He was in a bar, drinking with his buddies, when a beautiful blonde woman walked in. George watched the others stare; then he bet each of them $100 that he could get Vicky to marry him within six months. They all accepted his wager, and he picked up Vicky that night. George immediately sensed Vicky's vulnerabilities and made up stories that made it seem as if he shared her dreams. She fell in love with him instantly. Soon afterward, he managed to impregnate her by poking a hole in a condom.

Vicky had already been married once, and had no intention of marrying again, before she became pregnant. But she wanted a family, and she loved George. They married, and he won his bet.

George began to beat Vicky after the baby was born. Before he began to give her bruises and black eyes, he called her names, such as "slut" and "bitch," and he told this thin, beautiful woman that she was fat and ugly. Over the next four years, the abuse gradually escalated, until George was assaulting Vicky four times a year, degrading her and threatening to kill her on a daily basis. Vicky was quite certain that, if she tried to leave, George would kill her and himself. Also, her job did not pay a living wage, so she was financially dependent on George.

Vicky did escape from George, and today she is alive and well. But not all are so lucky. Most battered women eventually get out of abusive relationships, but fear, economic insecurity, and social isolation often make escape time-consuming, difficult, and potentially life-threatening (Jacobson & Gottman,

1998). George was a batterer, and his abuse of Vicky was domestic violence. George also met *DSM-IV* criteria for "antisocial personality disorder," a syndrome marked by a tendency to harm other people. This may seem like a strange way to define a mental illness. Clearly, George did not feel he was suffering from a disorder. He was able to talk his way out of arrests, pick up women on a whim, and generally get what he wanted, yet George attacked the people closest to him again and again.

Violent offenders who assault, rape, or commit domestic violence may think their actions are justified, or the result of free choice. However, research has shown strong sociocultural correlates for these violent behaviors. Psychologists today are challenged by questions as to how to treat the "disease" of violence, which may be a natural outgrowth of our society's attitudes toward women, masculinity, and sex. Biological, cognitive, and behavioral factors also seem to influence violent behavior.

Not all violence is associated with *DSM-IV* disorders. People—generally men—who commit rape or domestic violence can behave normally in other aspects of their lives; otherwise, it would be very easy for their victims to avoid them. Instead, both rape and domestic violence are extremely widespread, and millions of women in the United States are assaulted each year.

This chapter is about antisocial and violent behavior, examining antisocial personality disorder, rape, and domestic violence. We will emphasize both antisocial violence toward strangers and violence in intimate relationships. There has always been a great deal of debate as to whether violence per se constitutes evidence of mental illness. But there is no question that violent crime is a major social problem in the United States.

Antisocial Personality Disorder

People suffering from the personality disorders that we have studied so far may inconvenience their families and friends considerably, but usually they harm themselves more than they harm others. The defining trait of **antisocial personality disorder (APD)**, by contrast, is a predatory attitude toward other people—a chronic indifference to and violation of the rights of one's fellow human beings.

Antisocial personality disorder is by no means an unusual phenomenon. It affects about 1 percent of females and 4 to 6 percent of males among the general population, according to *DSM-IV* and epidemiological research (Cloninger, Bayone, & Przybeck, 1997; Kessler, McGonagle, Zhao, et al., 1994; Robins,Tipp,

& Przybeck, 1991). Furthermore, because antisocial behavior often involves criminal behavior, this disorder raises the whole issue of the relationship between abnormal psychology and crime. For these reasons—and because it is the most reliably diagnosed of the personality syndromes—we will discuss this disorder in this chapter.

Characteristics of the Antisocial Personality

DSM-IV's list of criteria for the diagnosis of antisocial personality disorder can be summarized as five basic points:

1. *A history of illegal or socially disapproved activity beginning before age 15 and continuing into adulthood.* Usually by the time of puberty—or, in the case of boys, earlier—the person has begun his or her career of antisocial behavior, in the form of truancy, delinquency, theft, vandalism, lying, drug abuse, running away from home, and/or chronic misbehavior in school. As adults, people with antisocial personalities may graduate to prostitution, pimping, drug dealing, and other crimes.

2. *Failure to show constancy and responsibility in work, sexual relationships, parenthood, or financial obligations.* People with antisocial personalities lack steadiness and a sense of obligation. They tend to walk out on jobs, spouses, children, and creditors.

3. *Irritability and aggressiveness.* People with antisocial personalities are easily riled, and they express their anger not just in street brawls but also often in abuse of mates and children.

4. *Reckless and impulsive behavior.* Unlike "normal" criminals, people with antisocial personalities rarely engage in planning. Instead, they tend to operate in an aimless, thrill-seeking fashion, traveling from town to town with no goal in mind, falling into bed with anyone available, and stealing a pack of cigarettes or a car, depending on what seems easiest and most gratifying at the moment.

5. *Disregard for the truth.* People with antisocial personalities lie frequently and easily. Cleckley (1976) offered the following example:

> In a letter to his wife, at last seeking divorce and in another city, one patient set down dignified, fair appraisals of the situation and referred to sensible plans he had outlined for her security. He then added that specified insurance policies and annuities providing for the three children (including their tuition at college) had been mailed under separate cover and would, if she

had not already received them, soon be in her hands. He had not taken even the first step to obtain insurance or to make any other provision, and, once he had made these statements in his letter, he apparently gave the matter no further thought. (p. 342)*

As is usually the case with the *DSM* criteria, only some, not all, of these characteristics need be present in order for the case to be diagnosed as antisocial personality disorder. However, a history of antisocial behavior during both adolescence and adulthood must be present. Also, in keeping with the policies of the diagnostic manual, this list confines itself to verifiable behaviors.

Antisocial Behavior and Psychopathy

The question of the relationship between psychological disturbance and **antisocial behavior,** behavior that violates the rights of others, forms an interesting chapter in the history of psychology. Until about 200 years ago, criminals were generally treated as criminals, with little thought as to their psychological well-being. In the eighteenth and nineteenth centuries, clinicians such as Philippe Pinel and Benjamin Rush began to speculate that certain cases of immoral and criminal behavior might be subtle forms of mental illness. In 1835, an English psychiatrist, J. C. Prichard, identified a condition that he called "moral insanity," which he described as "a form of mental derangement in which the intellectual functions appear to have sustained little or no injury, while the . . . moral or active principles of the mind are strangely perverted or depraved" (Preu, 1944, p. 923). In the late nineteenth century, such people came to be called "psychopaths," and, in keeping with the biogenic thinking of the period, it was assumed that their problem was a hereditary defect. Then, with the rise of sociology in the twentieth century, researchers began, instead, to stress the influence of social conditions. Accordingly, "psychopaths" were relabeled "sociopaths" (Birnbaum, 1914), the implication being that the problem lay not in the person but in the person's relationship to society.

Thus, while its causes were still being disputed, antisocial behavior was absorbed into abnormal psychology. There were no longer any criminals, just disturbed people. Yet many criminals seem to commit their crimes for simple and relatively understandable reasons—to supplement their incomes, to punish someone who has done them wrong, and so forth. Should these people also to be regarded as psychologically disturbed? In

---

*Reprinted with permission from the *Diagnostic and Statistical Manual of Mental Disorders*, Fourth Edition. Copyright © 1994 American Psychiatric Association.

FIGURE 17.1   A hostile, sociopathic patient made this doodle of a bloody knife being plunged into a female breast. On a subsequent occasion, only the face within the circle was shown to the patient, and he identified it as his mother's.

Courtesy of C. Scott Moss.

early editions of the *DSM*, there was some hedging on this point. *DSM* swung from one direction to the other but has now settled in the middle. Some people who engage in antisocial behavior are psychologically "normal," and others are not. However, has the *DSM-IV* actually succeeded in clearly distinguishing between normal criminals and people with APD? In the research conducted to determine the criteria for APD in *DSM-IV*, 70 percent of those in prison met *DSM-IIIR* criteria for APD (Widiger, Cadoret, Hare, et al., 1996). Like *DSM-IIIR*, *DSM-IV* bases the diagnosis of APD largely on behavior that is common among criminals and fails to include the interpersonal and emotional characteristics traditionally associated with psychopathy. When such *psychopathic* characteristics as a lack of empathy, an inflated sense of one's self-importance, and a glib, superficial interpersonal style were included in diagnostic considerations, only 28 percent of the prison inmates qualified as psychopaths (Widiger, Cadoret, Hare, et al., 1996). This suggests that the diagnosis of APD has moved *closer* to reliably identifying criminals, but further from the classic notion of psychopathy (Hare, 1996; Zagon, 1995).

Despite *DSM-IV*'s omissions, many experts have held on to the term *psychopathy* for a *subgroup* of

people diagnosed with APD to emphasize the more subjective portraits that they consider part and parcel of some of the antisocial personalities. For example, Cleckley, who treated psychopaths for many years, devoted an entire book, *The Mask of Sanity* (1976), to a description of this disorder and does not distinguish between APD and psychopathy. (His conceptualization, updated and expanded by Hare and his colleagues, formed the basis, in part, for *DSM-IV*'s debate about whether to include psychopathy as a subgroup of those with APD [Hare, 1993; Hart & Hare, 1997; Widiger, Cadoret, Hare, et al., 1996]). According to Cleckley, psychopaths differ from normal people, including "normal" criminals, not only in their actions but also in their emotions, motivations, and thought processes. First, their misdeeds are not just impulsive but almost unmotivated—or, rather, not motivated by any understandable purpose. Their behavior, therefore, often has a perverse or an irrational quality. Cleckley (1976) cites the case of a teenager whose exploits included "defecation into the stringed intricacies of the school piano, the removal from his uncle's automobile of a carburetor for which he got 75 cents, and the selling of his father's overcoat to a passing buyer of scrap materials" (p. 65). This lack of purposefulness, Cleckley claims, is what makes most psychopaths unsuccessful criminals. However, as Lykken (1995) notes, there are some psychopaths who are "successful" and do not end up getting caught and going to prison. He suggests that successful psychopaths have higher IQs, come from relatively privileged backgrounds, and exhibit the superficial charm and ability to "con" that is often associated with psychopathy.

Second, according to Cleckley, psychopaths have only the shallowest emotions. Through lack of love, lack of loyalty, and, above all, lack of empathy—an inability to imagine what might be the feelings of the child they have left alone all day in an empty house or the friend whose credit cards they have stolen—they are able to ignore what most people would regard as obligations. Neither do they feel anxiety or remorse over such actions, for they are as deficient in guilt as they are in other basic emotions. Zax and Stricker (1963) report the case of a boy who killed a neighborhood child by shooting her in the head:

> He spoke of the incident . . . in a nonchalant, unfeeling way, and was very suave and unnaturally composed in explaining why he was on the ward. He said, "I was showing her the gun. I didn't know it was loaded. She turned her head and it got her in the temple. I told the police that I was very sorry. You're to find out if there is anything mentally wrong with me. I thought I'd have to go to reform school." (p. 240)

A third aspect of Cleckley's portrait is poor judgment and failure to learn from experience. Psychopaths, he argues, do not make the connection between their actions and the consequences of those actions. Or, as later theorists (Newman, 1997) have refined the concept, antisocial personalities (and psychopaths) are bad at **passive avoidance learning**, learning to stop making a response that results in punishment. Once punished for an action, normal people learn either not to repeat the action or to repeat it in such a way that they will not be caught. In contrast, people with antisocial personalities may repeat an offense again and again, and in the same manner, even though they have been punished for doing so.

Finally, according to Cleckley, *most psychopaths are able to maintain a pleasant and convincing exterior.* Because of their lack of anxiety and guilt, they can lie, cheat, and steal with remarkable poise, as in the following case:

A 28-year-old man began serving a two-year sentence for armed robbery. Although psychological tests revealed some psychotic thinking, his behavior was calm and controlled. He was thought to be faking the psychotic symptoms. However, he began to cause trouble and become very aggressive shortly thereafter. He flooded the entire unit of the prison, spat on staff members, and threw fecal matter and urine at other inmates.

He was then transferred to a maximum security prison and put in solitary confinement. But even though he had neither clothes nor bed to sleep on, he continued to cause trouble. For example, he managed to strip his cell of its surface and make himself a knife out of these materials, just a day after a session with the ward psychiatrist, when he had seemed remorseful, controlled, and contrite. He blamed the guards for his violent behavior, rather than himself. In the past, he had a documented record of repeatedly trying to act "crazy" and get transferred to a psychiatric unit, from where he would ultimately escape. He managed to convince all mental health professionals that he had psychiatric problems, although no one could describe exactly what they were. Yet these "problems" kept him from being severely punished for his aggression.

Finally, the weary staff transferred the man to a forensic psychiatric unit. The workers making the transfer wore riot gear as they held him, tranquilized him with a benzodiazepine, put him in a straight jacket, and took him away.

From that time on, the 28-year-old thief was cooperative. He took his anti-psychotic medication, and showed dramatic improvement in his social functioning. He was later transferred to a more comfortable facility specializing in the long-term care of criminals who were chronic mental patients. Previously, a very similar sequence of actions had gotten him paroled. Would it happen again? (Coacheer & Fleming, 1996)

A psychoanalyst might interpret this case as evidence that many psychopaths have underlying psychoses

and, if properly treated, can be managed if not rehabilitated. On the other hand, this inmate made a much better life for himself by behaving as if he were crazy and was reinforced for doing so, again and again. At one time or another, many psychopaths display psychotic behavior.

The debate about whether someone is clinically antisocial, simply a criminal, or a psychopath is by no means settled. There is considerable overlap and not always perfect agreement about whether an individual best fits one category rather than another. Hart and Hare (1989) reported findings that are representative of those in the literature. They found that 50 percent of the men sentenced to a psychiatric unit within a prison met *DSM-III* criteria for APD, while only 13 percent met the criteria for psychopathy, based on Hare's widely used Psychopathy Checklist (Hare, 1993). In addition to the largely behavioral criteria used to identify APD, Hare and his colleagues require that psychopaths have additional qualities such as a lack of empathy, a glib and superficial demeanor, and a distorted sense of their own self-importance that makes them seem arrogant.

The decision to confine the diagnosis in *DSM-IV* to APD, and not include the extra criteria necessary for a diagnosis of psychopathy, was based in large part on research conducted by Widiger and others (Widiger, Cadoret, Hare, et al., 1996). However, the results of that research were far from conclusive, and the ultimate decision to ignore the term *psychopathy* in *DSM-IV* seems to have been motivated primarily by the desire to maximize the likelihood of a reliable diagnosis by clinicians (Widiger, Cadoret, Hare et al., 1996). There is good reason to believe that a subgroup of antisocial people are psychopaths, and it could still prove to be important to separate them from those with APD but no psychopathy (Hare, 1996; Zagon, 1995).

In this chapter, we will attempt to maintain the distinction, assuming that there is overlap between APD and psychopathy but treating the literature on psychopathy separately. This division facilitates both areas of research and may have treatment implications. For example, Cornell and colleagues (Cornell, Warren, Hawk, et al., 1996) found that, in a sample of prison inmates (most of whom probably had APD), those who committed **instrumental aggression** were much more psychopathic than those whose aggression was **reactive agression**. This distinction is common in the aggression literature, and it refers to whether or not the aggression is goal-oriented (instrumental) or hostile and a response to a perceived provocation (reactive). Psychopaths appear to be particularly prone to instrumental aggression. When they attack, they are calm, controlled, and goal-oriented. This profile is

Serial Killers

People with antisocial personality disorder generally commit violence as a way of getting something they want—sex, drugs, money, and so on. One group of psychopaths commits violence for the sake of violence—simply for the joy of killing. Serial killers, from Jack the Ripper to Ted Bundy, have both fascinated and terrified us for at least a century, yet, although experts from the FBI claim to be able to profile serial killers, and more and more seem to be emerging each year, they are still far too few in number for systematic research (DeHart & Mahoney, 1994). People who kill strangers because they are, for example, young women in their twenties with long, blonde hair are commonly thought by society to be psychotic. However, from what is known, although most serial killers are psychopathic, they are not typically psychotic.

Serial killing is probably more common than most people think (Holmes & DeBurger, 1985). Today, approximately 20 percent of all homicides in America are committed without apparent motive, whereas in 1966 the percentage was only 6 percent. From 1960 to 1983, the solution rate for homicides dropped from over 90 percent to 76 percent. Law enforcement officials believe that many of the unsolved and apparently motiveless crimes were committed by serial murderers. Serial killers are not motivated by any material or rational gain but, rather, kill for reasons that are related to idiosyncratic goals. The victims are usually strangers, and they have symbolic importance to the perpetrator, who kills without the slightest remorse.

The first serial killer in recorded history was Gilles De Rais, a fifteenth-century nobleman, who killed more than 800 children. He was also a sexual sadist who gained a great deal of pleasure from mutilating children, then having sex with them after they were dead. In fact, most serial killers today are sexual sadists (Drukteinis, 1992; Warren, Hazelwood, & Dietz, 1996). They are aroused by controlling and degrading others, and the arousal is unmistakably sexual—including a variety of painful sex acts, sexual bondage, and intentional torture.

Serial killers may confine their killing to a particular region, or they may move from one place to another. John Wayne Gacy of Chicago was a respected businessman who may have killed as many as 33 boys and buried them in various parts of his house. Before getting caught, many geographically stable serial killers maintain reputations as well-respected pillars of the community. It takes a long time to catch these killers, because none of the usual motives exist. By contrast, Ted Bundy began in Washington, moved to Utah, then went to Colorado, and was ultimately executed in Florida. He even escaped from prison while in Colorado, and he spent time in Chicago, East Lansing, and Louisville before ending up in Tallahassee. Many believe that Bundy killed more than 300 young women.

Holmes and DeBurger have suggested that there are five types of serial killers. First is the visionary type. These killers have psychotic symptoms, including hallucinations and delusions. Harvey Carignan killed dozens of women, and he appeared to believe that he was following God's orders. He perceived women as evil, and he believed he was told to eliminate evil in the world. Second, there is the mission-oriented type, which tries to eliminate a certain type of person. Often, the killer views such a person

typical of serial killers, who elaborately plan their murders. (See the box above.) Criminals in general, though, including nonpsychopathic APDs, are more prone to acts of rage and more likely to be motivated by revenge. Psychopaths are also much more likely to lie and be deceptive in their dealings with people than are other antisocial criminals (Seto, Khattar, Lalumiere, et al., 1997).

Finally, we should not overlook the overlap between APD and substance abuse (Strain, 1995). At least 50 percent of people meeting the criteria for substance abuse also have antisocial personalities. The question of which is primary—the antisocial behavior or the drug use—may have important implications for etiology, as well as for treatment. To what extent do people with antisocial personalities drink and use drugs to acquire the reinforcers associated with them? To what extent do drug abusers "look" antisocial simply because of their substance abuse? These are important but as yet unanswered questions.

Antisocial Behavior in Juveniles

Antisocial behavior is not confined to adults. In fact, most antisocial adults were delinquents during their adolescent and preadolescent years (Farrington, 1995; Monahan, 1996; Raine, Venables, & Williams, 1995; Strain, 1995). Moreover, homicide rates among boys, both adolescent and preadolescent, are much higher in the United States than anywhere else in the world (Potter & Mercy, 1997). But the problem of antisocial behavior is hardly confined to the United States. For example, in a widely publicized 1993 case in Liverpool, England, two 10-year-old boys abducted a 2-year-old boy named James Bulger from a shopping mall, walked him 2½ miles to a railroad track, stoned him to death, and then laid his body on the track, where it was cut in half by the next train. The boys then went home, stopping in at their favorite video store on the way. Such incidents are receiving more and more attention in the media, and with good reason. Despite reports of declining crime rates and stable rates of fatal as unworthy to live with other humans. Serial killers who murder prostitutes are often in this category. Third, there is the hedonistic type. Hedonistic serial killers get great pleasure and excitement from murder and often leave bizarre physical evidence behind. For example, in 1984, a poor alcoholic was found dead; a crutch had been inserted 17 inches into his rectum. For many, the enjoyment has a sexual component. Sexual mutilation is common, as are necrophilia and the removal of body parts. Hedonistic types sometimes target men as well as women. These killers are typically quite intelligent and hard to catch. Fourth, there is the power/control-oriented type. The pleasure of killing comes from the power and control. Ted Bundy was a classic example of this type. The pleasure is not based primarily on sex but on domination. While both hedonistic and power/control serial killers are typically psychopaths, the goal of the latter is not pleasure but an inflated sense of self-importance.

What general statements can be made about serial killers? Most are white males 25 to 34 years of age. They tend to be charming, charismatic, intelligent, and psychopathic. They tend to choose one type of victim, one that is vulnerable and easy to control. For example, all of Bundy's victims were young women with dark, long hair, parted in the middle. There is a typical "con" that is used to gain access to the victim. The killings tend to be elaborately planned, and the weapons chosen bring them into physical contact with their victims: knives, fists, and so on. Interestingly, their plans become less sophisticated and less elaborate over time, as the acts seem more and more driven by desperation, less calculated. Like many of the perpetrators of violence, many serial killers were abused as children and, as adults, are dependent on drugs or alcohol. In fact, sadistic fantasies are often enhanced by such intoxication.

Catching serial killers poses major problems for law enforcement. It is possible that, in the past decade, the number of serial killers has tripled, as the overall murder rate has doubled. At least 5,000 people per year are killed by serial killers. There are probably between 30 and 100 serial killers currently at large in the United States.

Because so many serial killers were born out of wedlock and suffered difficult childhoods, it is interesting to speculate on motives. One of the more interesting, if unproven, theories is Hale's (1994) view that the victims of serial killers bring back memories of people who humiliated the killers early in life. The humiliation turns into rage, but the relief is only temporary because the memories continue. Thus, so must the killings.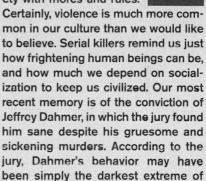

Perhaps serial killers represent the extreme end of a continuum, people who are untamed even by a society with mores and rules. Certainly, violence is much more common in our culture than we would like to believe. Serial killers remind us just how frightening human beings can be, and how much we depend on socialization to keep us civilized. Our most recent memory is of the conviction of Jeffrey Dahmer, in which the jury found him sane despite his gruesome and sickening murders. According to the jury, Dahmer's behavior may have been simply the darkest extreme of human possibility. (See Chapter 18 for a fuller discussion of the insanity defense.)

as well as nonfatal assaults in the United States, violence has been increasing among children and adolescents. Older adolescents and young adults are more likely to be arrested for violent crimes than is any other age group. About 50 percent of violent crimes are committed by males between the ages of 15 and 24 (Potter & Mercy, 1997).

Juvenile delinquency comes under the heading of "conduct disorders" in *DSM-IV* and is grouped not with the personality disorders but with the disorders of childhood and adolescence. Therefore, we discussed it in Chapter 15.

Still, juvenile delinquency raises some very urgent psychological issues which are pertinent to any discussion of antisocial and violent behavior. Most important are questions of cause and prevention. What is it that "hardens" children to the point at which they can engage in antisocial acts? Conduct disorders have a well-established connection with antisocial personality and with adult antisocial behav-

ior in general. In one important study, Farrington (1995) followed 411 children in South London from ages 8 to 32. He found that antisocial behavior in childhood was a good predictor of adult antisocial personality. These findings were consistent with earlier longitudinal studies conducted in the United States (Loeber & Dishion, 1983; Robins, 1966). Farrington also identified several factors in young children (ages 8–10) that led to delinquency, including poor impulse control, low intelligence, other criminals in the family, poverty, and bad parenting. Other studies have indicated that much training in delinquent behavior goes on in friendships between adolescent males (Dishion, Spracklen, Andrews, et al., 1996) and that physical fighting during preadolescence is a strong predictor of adolescent conduct disorder (Loeber, Green, Keenan, et al., 1995).

It was such research that led to the inclusion of childhood antisocial behavior among the criteria for adult antisocial personality. According to the current definition, as we saw, antisocial personality disorder begins before age 15. Therefore, all people with antisocial personalities, by definition, were once teenagers with conduct disorders. It is important to remember, however, that the reverse is not true: most teenagers with conduct disorders do *not* grow up to have antisocial personalities or even to engage in "normal" antisocial behavior (Rutter, 1997). With continuing research, we may discover what distinguishes juveniles with "normal" antisocial behavior from those who will have continuing conduct disorders.

Because most adults with APD were conduct-disordered as adolescents, the adolescents with conduct disorder who straighten out and overcome their own criminal history are of great interest. Research on such populations has just begun. Raine, Venables, and Williams (1995) have identified biological factors in 15-year-old boys with conduct disorders that "protect" them from developing into adult criminals: high levels of physiological arousal and a strong orienting response. These physiological signs usually indicate chronic levels of nervousness, tension, and guardedness. It may be that adolescent delinquents who have not developed the ability to commit crimes calmly and without fear are eventually cured of their criminal tendencies. In the Raine study, the boys were followed for 14 years. By age 29, most adult criminals have emerged. Thus, a valuable marker for biological protection from criminality in a high-risk population may have been identified for the first time.

Antisocial Personality Disorder: Theory and Therapy

Sociocultural, cognitive, behavioral, and biological perspectives have influenced the understanding and treatment of APD. Generally, these perspectives are not incompatible: sociocultural factors are aspects of society that create "risk" in the culture for antisocial and violent behavior. But those factors don't make all of us equally likely to be violent. Individual differences in upbringing, peer relations, and socialization affect the probability that a person will be violent. When individuals are violent, the violence is associated with observable changes in the brain and elsewhere in the body. Depending on one's perspective, many factors could be seen as playing a causal role. In short, nature and nurture do not operate independently of one another. Genetic effects often operate by increasing the risk that people will be exposed to environments that increase antisocial behavior. At the very least, genetic differences affect how susceptible people are to maladaptive environmental influences

(Rutter, 1997). The environment is all-important, because it forms the bridge between genetic influences and learning history. Thus, we will start by looking at how society can prompt antisocial behavior.

The Sociocultural Perspective

The injustices built into our society contribute dramatically to the development of criminal behavior. These conditions also foster antisocial personality disorder. From a public health perspective (Potter & Mercy, 1997), in subcultures affected by poverty, racism, and other forms of oppression, antisocial behavior is encouraged in various ways. There is tremendous status associated with material success, but white males have greater opportunities to gain access to that success. Given the importance in our culture of money and prestige, it is hardly surprising that, as legitimate access to society's rewards are blocked, people who do not have access to them resort to antisocial behavior to achieve their goals. In the inner cities, millions of young men and women have abandoned all hope of attaining the American dream, or even finding a job that pays a living wage. Instead, the path to status is to obtain material goods and power through antisocial behavior.

The beginning of these influences can be seen as early as preschool (Shaw & Winslow, 1997). Children model their parents' behavior, and they become "hardened" after a childhood characterized by child abuse and neglect (Widom, 1997). When, as adolescents, the key to high status is to join violent, drug-dealing gangs, those gangs become a training ground for acquiring APD (Cairns, Cadwallader, Estell, et al., 1997). Peer influences are important not only when it comes to delinquency but also in associated behaviors such as drug abuse (Thornberry & Krohn, 1997).

In high-risk environments, a variety of biological, psychological, and social factors converge to increase the probability of APD: poverty, unemployment, racism, and oppression, as well as the biological factors discussed in a later section. For example, Raine and colleagues (Raine, Brennan, Mednick, et al., 1996) looked at 397 male subjects during the first year of life and followed them until they were 20–22 years of age. Some of these subjects had problematic prenatal care or other problems related to their mothers' pregnancies; others were poor; and a third group was both poor and showed signs of early defects related to their mothers' pregnancies and their births. APD was much more common in the poor men who also had mothers who had had problematic pregnancies. In fact, over 70 percent of the crimes committed by the men in this sample were done by men in this last group.

The Behavioral Perspective

Behaviorists point to many of the environmental influences we've just discussed as sources of APD, including peer influences, child abuse, poverty, and parenting (Eron, 1997). The difference between the sociocultural and behavioral perspectives is one of emphasis. Sociocultural models stress the societal conditions that create environments conducive to the development of APD, while behaviorists focus on the individual's specific environments: in particular, on one's family. For example, children who are beaten by their parents, and grow up seeing their parents beat each other, are likely to learn that beating is a viable method of getting what you want (Widom, 1997). Many people with antisocial personalities have fathers who themselves have antisocial personalities. However, children are also influenced by the media (Huesmann, Moise, & Podolski, 1997). Many studies indicate that, when children watch aggressive acts on film or television, they may initiate the violence they have seen if an appropriate situation arises shortly thereafter. The horror movie *Child's Play 3* was implicated in the murder of James Bulger. In the climax of that movie, Chucky, the homicidal doll, has his face stained with blue paint. Apparently, both of James Bulger's 10-year-old murderers saw *Child's Play 3* on video shortly before they abducted him. As they walked him to the railroad tracks, the attackers stopped to buy a can of blue paint, which they then threw at him while throwing the bricks that killed him.

Parental reinforcement—or the lack thereof—may also play a role in the development of antisocial personality. Studies of children who seldom engage in antisocial behavior have shown that the parents of these children consistently reinforce **prosocial behavior**—that is, behavior that encourages social interaction. Helpfulness, cooperation, and affection are rewarded, and antisocial behavior is punished or ignored (Patterson, 1982). In the case of parents whose children have conduct disorders, a different pattern emerges. First, when such parents respond to their children, the response tends to be a punishing one. Second, the positive reinforcement that the parents provide is generally not related to prosocial behavior. In contrast, antisocial behavior is systematically reinforced by patterns of parental reciprocity of children's negative behavior, until a point at which the parents give up, thus ultimately reinforcing the entire coercive cycle: coercion followed by withdrawal of coercion.

Such parents, according to behaviorists, not only model aggression but also teach children that there is no connection between their positive behavior and the treatment they receive. Consequently, the children become desensitized to social stimuli, such as rules and laws, that indicate to people what the consequences of their behavior are. They do as they please, assuming that the outcome of their positive behavior will be determined not by their actions but by an arbitrary force such as luck. Negative behavior, on the other hand, is unwittingly reinforced through coercive family cycles.

Antisocial behavior may also be learned through direct positive reinforcement. It may win approval from peers and attention from parents and school

At the turn of this century, when government offered fewer social welfare programs than is the case now, poor children sometimes committed crimes, such as theft and truancy, out of need. Today such behavior is likely to be labeled antisocial.

authorities, while prosocial behavior goes unnoticed by elders and is ridiculed by peers.

The Cognitive Perspective

Cognitive theorists have contributed to our understanding of antisocial behavior primarily by focusing on social information processing (Dodge & Schwartz, 1997). It is apparent that antisocial children and adolescents are not good at reading social cues, deciding on appropriate responses, and problem solving effectively in social situations. Some of this work suggests that child abuse produces antisocial behavior by causing impairments in these social information-processing mechanisms. To understand their environment, people pay attention to the cues in their environment, then interpret those cues. If cues are construed in a hostile way despite benign intent, aggression becomes more likely. After interpretation, children review their goals and decide if they have been able to obtain them; an angry child might be inclined to choose aggressive goals. Then children search their memories for ideas as to how to respond; aggression is more likely if the child has a wide range of aggressive responses in his or her past repertoire. Upon finding possible responses, the child must decide which response to make; the decision to be aggressive is typical for an antisocial boy. Finally, the child acts; if the child's verbal and motor skills are deficient, the action is more likely to be antisocial.

Dodge and Schwartz (1997) describe an example of a boy whose schoolmate has just spilled paint on him. The boy looks at the other child to see whether it was done on purpose, relying on nonverbal cues. The boy might falsely conclude that other child spilled the paint intentionally. The boy's goal might become to get even, and the boy's decision might be to spill paint on the schoolmate. Deficiencies in any or all of these processes have been shown to be associated with antisocial behavior.

According to cognitive theorists, faulty thinking is acquired through learning and may be a response to developmental conditions. What distinguishes the beliefs peculiar to APD, however, is not just their dysfunctional character—for many of us hold unhelpful beliefs—but their unchanging character. The beliefs are rigid and admit no exceptions.

The Biological Perspective

Genetic Factors   Twin and adoption studies have produced evidence that heredity plays a role in criminal behavior, especially among middle-class criminals (Carey & Goldman, 1997). In fact, the literature consistently shows that identical twins are more likely than their fraternal counterparts to be concordant in criminal behavior and that adopted twins separated at birth are more likely to be concordant with one another than with their adopted siblings. However, the studies are also consistent in showing that the environment affects behavior as well.

What about the comorbidity between APD and other *DSM-IV* disorders? Genetic research suggests that the overlap among APD, alcoholism, and other drug addictions are part of the same heritability factor. Moreover, what seems to be inherited is a general vulnerability toward antisocial behavior, not a specific vulnerability toward violence. The family environment also emerges as important, as the other perspectives suggest. Unfortunately, generalization to the urban poor from current literature would be premature. Most of the well-designed studies have been done in the Scandinavian countries, which have social welfare systems in place and a predominance of middle-class people. In the United States, the environment may play a much greater role in APD among the poor and working classes, with genetics playing a much smaller role. In fact, popular theories, such as **evolutionary psychology,** suggest as much (Daly & Wilson, 1997).

This term refers to a theory that criminal behavior has become part of our genetic makeup, and can explain much of the violent crime that occurs in contemporary culture. According to this theory, all of us have the genotype, or potential, to become criminals. It is the environment that pulls the criminal behavior out of us, given this genetically based potential. Since poverty, racial discrimination, and hopelessness characterizing American inner cities are all stimuli for the enactment of this genetic potential, evolutionary psychology attempts to explain why violent crime is more common in the inner cities.

Physiological Abnormalities   There is reason to believe that people with antisocial personalities have a defect in brain functioning (Raine & Buchsbaum, 1996). Between 31 and 58 percent of all people with antisocial personalities show some EEG abnormality (Deckel, Hesselbrock, & Bauer, 1996), including increased activation in the left hemisphere of the frontal lobe. This increased activation, combined with scores on motor tests, suggest that impaired functioning in the prefrontal lobe may be the biological manifestation of the link between APD and substance abuse. Both antisocial behavior and substance abuse may be particularly reinforcing to those who show increased prefrontal activation. APD may be partly the product of "cortical immaturity"—that is, delayed development of the cerebral cortex, the topmost layer of the brain and the seat of most of its "higher" functions. If this is the case, then we might expect a person with APD to become better behaved with age; as the person grew older, the brain would finally mature and, consequently, antisocial behavior would diminish. This does, in fact, seem to be true in many cases (Lahey & Loeber, 1997). Many men with APD show marked behavioral improvements as they grow older.

However, if this cortical immaturity exists, what is the mental function that it impairs? According to one school of thought, it is the capacity for fear. Most of the abnormal slow-wave activity in people with antisocial personalities comes from the temporal lobe and the limbic system, two parts of the brain that control memory and emotion. This finding suggests that the essential defect in antisocial personality disorder may be an inability to respond normally to fear-inducing stimuli, leading in turn to an inability to inhibit responses that will result in punishment. This suggestion may help to explain the resistance of people with antisocial personalities to passive avoidance learning—the fact that they can be punished again and again for the same offenses yet never learn how to avoid the punishment.

An alternative explanation of the same phenomenon is "underarousal." This theory suggests that people with APD are not fearless but are simply underaroused stimulus-seekers (Raine, 1997). Theorists see antisocial behavior as a form of stimulus seeking. At present, it is not clear which of the two theories better explains the lack of arousal that accompanies APD.

Some recent research has given rise to a different, complementary theory: that people with antisocial personalities have information-processing problems that make it hard for them to switch their attention from cues for reward to cues for punishment (Barratt, Stanford, Kent, et al., 1997). For example, recent work by Barratt and colleagues looked at prison inmates who met the criteria for APD. The prisoners were further subdivided into impulsive aggressives and nonimpulsive aggressives. Those who showed impulsiveness along with aggression also were deficient in verbal ability and information processing, while the nonimpulsive prisoners did not exhibit these deficits. Impulsivity also seems to be related to low levels of serotonin, one of the brain's most important neurotransmitters (Virkkunen, Goldman, Nielsen, et al., 1995).

Taken together, these findings suggest that we may now understand at least part of the physiological substrate that constitutes APD. Perhaps the most exciting area of physiological research in APD involves using internal responses to predict subsequent antisocial behavior. For example, it has been established

that men with APD are underaroused. But how far back in childhood does underarousal appear? Does underarousal at an early age predict subsequent antisocial behavior? The answer appears to be yes. Raine, Venables, and Mednick (1997) examined 3-year-old children to see whether their heart rates would predict subsequent antisocial behavior. Indeed, the aggressive 11-year-olds had lower resting heart rates at age 3 than did the nonaggressive 11-year-olds. There is a growing body of evidence that resting heart rate is partly inherited and reflects both fearlessness and underarousal. It is an important early biological marker for aggression.

However, where do these biological markers come from? Are they really inherited, learned at an early age, or associated with prenatal and birth complications? Again, Raine and his colleagues appear to have a tentative answer (Raine, Brennan, & Mednick, in press). They had discovered that birth complications, combined with bad parenting, made it more likely that 18-year-olds will be violent. These 18-year-olds were followed until they were 34 years of age. The 34-year-olds continued to show evidence for the biosocial interaction (both bad parenting and birth complications contributed), but only for violent crime. The investigators were also able to determine that this interaction was not caused or mediated by other psychiatric disorders, and that it was found only for the violent adults who had a history of violence going back to adolescence.

Therapy

Although APD is not well understood, recent years have seen progress based on all four of the theoretical perspectives. Unfortunately, treating APD is even harder than understanding it. No therapy has demonstrated efficacy with APD. There are some isolated examples of successes with Beck's cognitive behavior therapy reported in the literature (Davidson & Tyrer, 1996; Southern-Gerow & Kendall, 1997), but there is not much reason to be hopeful. Criminals and noncriminals with APD seldom seek therapy, tend not to be motivated to change, and seem to be limited in their capacity to change. One potentially promising development is in the use of pharmacotherapy for violence (Karper & Krystal, 1997). Penick and colleagues (Penick, Powell, Campbell, et al., 1996) reported that some men with APD who were also alcoholics responded well to antidepressant medication, at least through a six-month follow-up. The researchers found that it was the men who also had a mood disorder, either depression or anxiety, who responded to the antidepressants. Thus, medications may have promise with a subgroup of men with APD: those with mood disorders who also abuse alcohol. It is also of interest that mood disorders are common in this population, despite the stereotype that APD types have a limited range of emotional responses.

What is true for APD is even more true for psychopathy. Psychopaths are even more likely than other criminals to reoffend after they get out of prison (Rice, 1997). Treatment programs designed to make psychopaths less dangerous may actually backfire and make them more dangerous. Although some psychologists argue that anger-management training combined with pharmacotherapy may be a viable treatment for psychopaths (Kristiansson, 1995), there is no empirical foundation for such claims.

Most experts in the field seem to agree that the only real way to stop APD is by preventing it from starting (Guerra, Attar, & Weissberg, 1997; Hawkins, Arthur, & Olson, 1997; Mulvey & Wooland, 1997; Offord, 1997; Reid & Eddy, 1997). In fact, even prevention may be difficult, if three-year-old boys are destined to be antisocial, as was the case in the study by Raine and colleagues. However, what is relevant to middle-class samples may not be as germane to American inner-city youth. It could very well be that, in the absence of an aggression-producing environment, biological variables are the primary predictors of APD. However, when the environment is stressful enough, it can provoke aggression in all of us (Wilson & Daly, 1997). Stressful environments will be best served by prevention programs. For example, if there were better health care for poor women, there would be fewer birth complications, and probably less depression among new mothers. This in and of itself would reduce the onset of antisocial behavior in children. In our discussion of prevention (Chapter 19), we will revisit questions related to violence.

Rape

Rape, or sexual intercourse with a nonconsenting partner, is a common crime. About 100,000 rapes are reported to the police each year (Greenfeld, 1997), but national surveys suggest that the actual incidence of rape is between 6 and 15 times higher than that (Koss, 1996), for most rapes go unreported. In a survey of more than 6,000 college students (Koss, Gidycz, & Wisniewski, 1987), 27.5 percent of the women reported experiencing and 7.7 percent of the men reported perpetrating an act that met the legal definition of rape (which includes attempted rape), though almost none of these crimes were reported. Another survey, this one of female rape victims, found that only 21 percent of the stranger rapes and only 2 percent of the acquaintance rapes had been re-

ported (Koss, Dinero, Seibel, et al., 1988). Although more recent studies have reported rates of rape experiences that are closer to 5 to 7 percent, rather than the 27.5 percent reported by Koss (Bridgeland, Duane, & Stewart 1995; Finkelson & Oswalt, 1995), a methodologically sophisticated study in Australia reported results that are very similar to Koss' earlier findings (Patton & Mannison, 1995). In any case, rape is a common and serious problem throughout the world.

In dealing with rape, we are faced with the question of why a man who presumably could find a willing sex partner, even if a prostitute, would violently force himself on an unwilling woman. There seem to be several answers to this question. Some men apparently resort to rape because they cannot find—or feel they cannot find—a willing sex partner. Like the typical voyeur and exhibitionist, this type of rapist is described as a timid, submissive male lacking in empathy who has grave doubts about his masculinity and is so fearful of rejection that he cannot seek sexual gratification through more acceptable channels (Janssen, 1995; Marshall & Hambley, 1996; Marshall, Hudson, Jones, et al., 1995; Ward, Hudson, & Marshall, 1996). Other rapists have clearly antisocial personalities—they simply seize whatever they want and are indifferent to the pain they inflict on others. In still other cases, the element of force may be a necessary prerequisite of sexual arousal for them, much as cruelty is for the sadist (as discussed in the box on pages 498–499, most serial killers are sexual sadists). In some instances, however, the rapist's motivation appears to be more aggressive than sexual (Malamuth, Linz, Heavey, et al., 1995; Marshall & Hambley, 1996). A significant proportion of rapists were victims of child abuse (Haapasalo J. & Kankkkonen, 1997; Hall & Barongan, 1997); for them, hurting and humiliating women is a form of revenge or "identification with the aggressor." But many rapists are no different psychologically from other men. They have adequate sexual relationships and show no pattern of abnormality on tests of psychological functioning (Polaschek, Ward, & Hudson, 1997).

This last finding suggests that many rapes are the result not of psychological disorders but of our cultural emphasis on sex and violence. To some extent, men in our culture are socialized to become sexual predators. A comparison of college undergraduates who admitted that they had forced a date to have intercourse and undergraduates who had never done so found that the former were "sexually very active, successful, and aspiring"; they believed that rape was justified under certain circumstances (if they thought the woman was "loose," a "pickup," or a "tease"); they said their best friends would "definitely approve" of coercive tactics with certain women; and they felt considerable pressure from their peers to engage in sexual exploits (Hall & Barongan, 1997). An integrative theory (Malamuth, Linz, Heavey, et al., 1995) highlights these same cognitive variables but claims that sexual aggression is best explained as a confluence of two factors: hostile masculinity (hostility toward women, attitudes supporting violence toward women, antisocial personality characteristics) and impersonal sex (a strong sexual appetite and a preoccupation with sex without a specific partner in mind).

With rape, as with pedophilia and incest, psychology must concern itself not only with the perpetrator but also with the victim. The psychological damage suffered by rape victims is enormous (see the box on page 506). Rape victims are at risk for a number of psychological disorders—above all, sexual dysfunctions and posttraumatic stress disorder (see Figure 17.2). At the same time, many women who report rape find that the search for justice leads to humiliation. Until recently, the laws in many states were de-

signed to protect men from false accusations of rape, not to protect victims of rape. New York State, for example, required that there be a witness to the crime. (Needless to say, there rarely is.) The vast majority of rape cases reported to the police do not go to trial, either because identification of the rapist is uncertain or the evidence is insufficient. Thus, not only is justice not done, but the woman is left open to retaliation. If the case does go to court, the woman may feel that she, not the rapist, is on trial. Her way of dressing, her sexual history, her "reputation" may all be subject to skeptical scrutiny. If, to save her life, she submitted to the rape without a struggle, this may be used against her. Thus, the trial may be as traumatic as the rape.

Fortunately, these injustices are now receiving some attention. Counseling centers have been set up for rape victims. Police officers are being given special training for handling rape cases. (Some police departments have set up "rape squads" staffed with female officers.) And state laws dealing with rape are being revised. For example, many states no

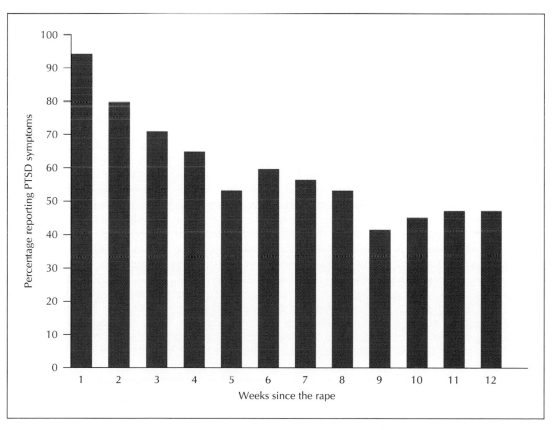

FIGURE 17.2 Almost all women show symptoms of posttraumatic stress disorder severe enough to be diagnosed with PTSD in the first or second week following a rape. Over the 3 months following a rape, the percentage of women continuing to show PTSD declines. However almost 50 percent of women continue to be diagnosed with PTSD 3 months after a rape (Adapted from Foa & Riggs, 1995).

Rape and Its Aftermath

Of all the calamities that people can encounter in ordinary life, one that is especially likely to have lasting psychological consequences is rape. A large study involving 3,132 adults in 2 Los Angeles communities found that those who had been raped at some time in their lives—13.2 percent of the sample—were 2½ times more likely than others to develop major depression, alcoholism, and drug abuse and 4 times more likely to develop phobia, panic disorder, and obsessive-compulsive disorder after the assault (Burnam, Stein, Golding, et al., 1988). Not surprisingly, sexual dysfunction—low desire, low arousal —is also a problem for many rape victims (Becker, Skinner, Abel, et al., 1986). But the psychological disorder most likely to follow upon rape is probably posttraumatic stress disorder. In a study of 95 rape victims by Barbara Rothbaum and her colleagues, two-thirds of the subjects had posttraumatic stress disorder 1 month after the rape, with symptoms including flashbacks, nightmares, insomnia, hyperalertness, blunted emotions, concentration problems, and continuing feelings of fear and guilt (Rothbaum, Foa, Riggs, et al., 1992). Interestingly, rape is more likely than many other serious traumas—robbery, assault, natural disasters, the death of a family member or close friend—to precipitate posttraumatic stress disorder (Norris, 1992). This may be due, in part, to the nature of this assault and to the stigma that is still attached to rape. Robbery victims will tell their friends about their experience; rape victims, out of shame, tend to keep silent and, thus, have less chance to vent their feelings (Koss, Woodruff, & Koss, 1991). They also tend not to seek treatment (Koss, 1988). Until re-

cently, was there was not much treatment available to them. It was not until the 1970s, with the rise of the women's movement, that rape crisis centers came into being. Typically, rape victims simply go back to their normal routines and "try not to think about it."

For many of them, this works. But, for almost as many, apparently, it does not—or not soon. In the study by Rothbaum and her team, as we saw, two-thirds of the rape victims showed posttraumatic stress disorder 1 month postrape. Three months postrape, more than half still had not recovered (Rothbaum, Foa, Riggs, et al., 1992). Are there certain responses to rape that predict how fast a person will get over it? Most studies are in a poor position to answer this question, because they are retrospective studies, with victims being interviewed long after the rape and trying to piece together their reactions from memory. But the study by Rothbaum's team was a longitudinal study, in which the victims were first interviewed soon after the rape (12 days, on average) and then reinterviewed weekly for 3 months. In this way, the researchers were able to pinpoint factors that seemed to affect recovery. What they found was the women least likely to improve spontaneously were those who, at the first interview, reported the most distress and the most "intrusion" symptoms: flashbacks, nightmares, involuntary relivings of the trauma.

Other studies, combining victims of rape and victims of nonsexual assault, have linked three additional factors with the likelihood and severity of posttraumatic stress disorder: feelings of guilt, feelings of threat, and bodily injury during the assault (Kilpatrick, Saunders, Amick-McMullen, et al., 1989; Riggs, Foa, Rothbaum, et al.,

1991). One group of researchers claims that anger, too, can be crucial in slowing the victim's return to normal functioning (Riggs, Dancu, Gershuny, et al., 1992). As many as 25 percent of rape survivors still suffer from posttraumatic disorders four to five years after the rape (Foa & Riggs, 1995). According to Rothbaum's team, rape victims who have not recovered from posttraumatic stress disorders two months after the assault are not likely to recover spontaneously; they need treatment (Rothbaum, Foa, Riggs, et al., 1992).

Rape shatters many of its victims' most fundamental and comforting beliefs: the belief in one's safety, in one's personal efficacy, in the goodness of other human beings. It may also create an intense, easily reactivated fear memory, which then triggers further anxiety. According to many experts, the key to relieving rape-induced posttraumatic stress disorder is to reverse this cognitive process. The victim's fear memory must be confronted and then challenged by new, fear-incompatible information: that she can, in fact, protect herself against future assaults, that this does not require staying home every night, that not all men are potential rapists, and so forth (Foa, Steketee, & Rothbaum, 1989). Most of the treatments that have been effective for rape victims, such as systematic desensitization and cognitive therapy, involve this scenario of activating and then challenging the fear memory. Some experts, however, believe that the best treatment for rape victims is group therapy, on the grounds that women who have survived the same trauma are the best suited to listen, validate feelings, share grief, counteract guilt, and rebuild self-esteem (Koss & Harvey, 1991).

longer require a witness and do not permit the victim's sexual history (even with the defendant) to be brought into evidence unless it relates directly to the alleged crime.

Acquaintance Rape

Acquaintance, or "date" rape was described and documented in the 1950s, but it did not receive wide attention until the 1980s, when it became a pressing issue on American college campuses. Date rape, like other rape, is very common, as even its perpetrators acknowledge, or used to acknowledge. A survey of 3,187 college women found that 54 percent had experienced some form of unwanted sexual contact and 15 percent had been raped by an acquaintance (Koss, Gidycz, & Wisniewski, 1987). More recently, sexual coercion techniques including rape were revealed to be at least as common as in the earlier study by Koss and colleagues (Waldner-Haugrud & Magruder, 1995). Coercive tactics commonly used by men include using their greater physical strength, preventing women from leaving an enclosed space so that they could not escape, continuing to touch them despite the women's saying no, and lying to women about their intentions.

While one might expect date rape to be less traumatic than an assault by a stranger, this is apparently not the case. There are no differences between victims of stranger rape and victims of acquaintance rape on measures of postassault depression, anxiety, relationship quality, or sexual adjustment (Koss, Goodman, Brown, et al., 1994). The psychological consequences for the victim of date rape are similar to those of incest and child molestation. This may be due in part to a factor already mentioned in Chapter 12: the presumption of collusion on the part of the victim. Many studies have shown that rape victims tend to blame themselves for the rape, but victims of acquaintance rape seem to blame themselves more (Finkelson, & Oswalt, 1995), and the public agrees with them. In a survey of undergraduates, both the men and the women blamed the rape victim more if she knew the rapist (Humphreys & Herold, 1996).

This presumption of female responsibility is related to old "boys will be boys" attitudes: the idea that men are by nature sexually uncontrollable and that it is up to women, insofar as they are able (and even when they are not able), to set limits in a sexual encounter. As one might expect, it is the men who hold such attitudes who are most likely to commit date rape. The pattern is as follows: sexually coercive men are more likely to have stereotyped ideas about gender roles, to view male-female relationships as fundamentally adversarial, to believe that women are responsible for preventing rape, and to endorse "rape myths"—for example, that women unconsciously want to be raped or that they set up the circumstances for rape and then blame the man. Coercive men are also more aggressive, more tolerant of aggression (they tend to have histories of family violence), more sexually experienced, less sexually satisfied, and, not surprisingly, more sexually aroused by the use of force (Hall & Barongan, 1997; Marshall & Hambley, 1996; Ward, McCormack, & Hudson, 1997).

The Sociocultural Perspective

The most influential sociocultural views on rape come from feminist thinking (Hall & Barongan, 1997). These theories state that sexual aggression toward women is not only tolerated by the culture, but even accepted and sometimes rewarded by it. Although not all men are rapists, they are all socialized to be potential rapists, according to this view. In fact, when sexual aggression is defined broadly enough, most men admit to having been perpetrators at least once in their lives (Muehlenhard & Linton, 1987).

Sociocultural risk factors are also thought to exist at the community level. For example, subcultures within the larger culture may restrict information on sex, which may lead to the perpetuation of rape myths (e.g., if he forced me to have sex, I must have really wanted it). Some ethnic minority cultures are particularly patriarchal when it comes to sex, and aggression may be seen as part of the male role, with the result that women accept being victimized as part of life. For example, Majors (1992) has argued that some African American men take out their anger at the culture that has oppressed them on African American women through sexual aggression.

However, poverty better predicts sexual aggression than does either race or ethnicity. In fact, the differences in rape incidence among racial and ethnic groups disappear when class is taken into account. Thus, generally speaking, it is the climate of poverty that increases the risk of sexual aggression, not the racial or ethnic characteristics of the group. In short, the same sociocultural variables that predict antisocial and violent behavior predict rape. This is not surprising, because rape is primarily a violent crime.

Psychologists can't entirely explain why the United States is one of the most violent countries in the world (Lore & Schultz, 1993), or why there is more rape in America than in any other industrialized society (Allison & Wrightsman, 1993). But sociocultural factors help to explain the difference: when patriarchal attitudes toward women are combined with poverty and the widespread acceptance of sexual aggression, the remaining question is *which men* will become rapists, not whether there will be high rates of rape.

The Cognitive and Behavioral Perspectives

Cognitive and behavioral theories of rape have generally been subsumed under theories that are applicable to all paraphilias. We discussed these theories in Chapter 12. However, by examining some of the recent developments in the psychological study of rape, we can help to answer the question posed in the section on sociocultural perspectives: given that we live in a culture which has historically sanctioned sexual aggression, how do we identify the types of learning histories which make people more likely to engage in rape?

First, it is clear that there is a connection between alcohol use and rape (Seto & Barbaree, 1995). In experimental laboratory studies, alcohol increases aggression in college students. It is also well established that alcohol use is commonly involved when rape occurs. However, the causal connection remains murky. The research findings are equivocal, and the studies are not always methodologically sound. To the extent that alcohol is related to rape, it probably has to do with the removal of inhibitions that would otherwise make the violence unlikely.

Rapists are also lonely men who have little intimacy in their lives (Marshall & Hambley, 1996). Moreover, they tend to have extremely hostile attitudes toward women and subscribe to the "rape myth": that sexual assault is acceptable because women are second-class citizens and adversaries. Like psychopaths, rapists also tend to lack empathy, especially for their victims or prospective victims (Marshall, Hudson, Jones, et al., 1995).

None of this is surprising, because many rapists are also psychopaths (Brown & Forth, 1997). Thus, one would expect a lack of empathy and a thrill-seeking, hedonistic approach toward all aspects of life, including gratification. However, rapists who are psychopaths differ greatly from those who are not. Psychopaths rape, but it is typically part of a larger pattern of criminal behavior going back to an early age, which includes being a sex offender as an adolescent. Psychopaths are less likely to stalk victims and to see rape as an end in itself; rather, when the opportunity arises, psychopaths commit rape. Thus, with psychopaths, rape is less likely to be associated with a particular set of attitudes toward women and more likely to be part of a general disregard for others, as well as an indifference to society's standards for moral conduct.

Can Rapists Be Treated?

Therapies for rapists have mixed results. Several approaches try to help offenders to unlearn their deviant patterns, to change their sexual arousal patterns, behavior, and beliefs. In one prison program, rape victims were brought into group therapy sessions with their attackers, and the victims told their side of the story—a confrontation that required considerable courage on the part of the victims (Freeman & Leaf, 1989).

Other programs attempt to retrain rapists so that they no longer become aroused by violence, or they teach them how to keep themselves from committing the same offense again. The latter approach, called **relapse prevention**, involves training rapists how to avoid situations that place them at risk for repeating the crime and how to resist the impulse to commit the offense. Reports indicate that these programs successfully prevent relapse among rapists (Furby, Weinrott, & Blackshaw, 1989; Marshall & Pithers, 1994; Pithers & Cumming, 1989).

In general, treatment of sex offenders appears to have some effect, although the effect may be lacking in clinical significance (Hall, 1995). Cognitive and behavioral treatments have had generally disappointing outcomes with rapists (Harris, 1995). Some researchers have moved to alternatives that involve the criminal justice system. For example, in the state of Washington, community supervision and treatment have been com-

Pictured here is one of the lines from The Clothesline Project. Women or friends of women who have been battered, raped, sexually abused, or murdered design the shirts to be hung on the line. The line is then displayed at universities, churches, and women's events to raise awareness about and humanize the statistics of violence against women.

pared with standard criminal justice punishment, an initiative known as the Special Sex Offender Sentencing Alternative (Berliner, Schram, Miller, et al., 1995). The results thus far are equivocal for rapists. However, there are some offenders who do respond to cognitive and behavioral treatments. Those with high levels of education and a normal family life outside of their crimes appear to be the best candidates (Shaw, Herkov, & Greer, 1995).

Unfortunately, rapists are the most likely of all sex offenders to reoffend (Quinsey, Rice, & Harris, 1995). In fact, reoffense is the norm, not the exception. The rate of reoffense is especially likely among psychopaths, especially those who show strong physiological arousal to rape films. In short, psychopaths who "get off" on hurting women will most likely do it again when they get out of prison.

As with other antisocial behaviors, prevention may be the only hope. Most rapists are men, men who rate themselves as less "feminine" in their gender identity than do nonrapists (Lisak & Ivan, 1995). Socialization which produces a more androgynous gender identity may be part of the solution to the problem of rape. For example, men are more attracted than women are to sex outside the context of a relationship (Oliver & Hyde, 1993). Socialization experiences which place sex within the context of a relationship could reduce the appeal of impersonal sex of all kinds, including rape. A more integrated, multicultural socialization experience for men might also discourage sexual aggression—especially to the extent that the mainstream culture is less supportive of sexual aggression than are many subcultures.

Domestic Violence

Domestic violence is really a euphemism for men battering women. Although *DSM-IV* uses the term **partner abuse** to label violence between people who are romantically involved, in both legal marriage and unmarried relationships, women are almost always the victims and men the perpetrators when the violence becomes severe enough to warrant either medical attention or legal action (Jacobson & Gottman, 1998). This point can be confusing to some, because, on superficial inspection, it appears to contradict the results of a widely cited national survey (Straus & Gelles, 1990). In that survey, and others before it (e.g., Straus, Gelles, & Steinmetz, 1980), married men and women reported approximately equal frequencies of physically aggressive acts. Some have interpreted these findings to mean that wives are as violent as husbands. However, this interpretation is inappropriate for a number of reasons. First, the vast majority of physi-

cally aggressive acts reported in national surveys are pushing and shoving, rather than the more serious and potentially lethal levels of violence that bring batterers to the attention of the criminal justice system. Second, when more serious acts of violence are considered, there is a dramatic gender difference: for example, husbands are much more likely to kill their wives than wives are to kill their husbands. Although rates vary from state to state, approximately 50 percent of all women who are murdered in this country are killed by boyfriends, husbands, exboyfriends, or exhusbands. In contrast, only about 6 percent of male homicide victims are killed by intimate female partners; even the vast majority of these are in self-defense (Wilt, Fagan, & Davies, 1997).

Third, frequency counts of assaultive acts do not take into account either the impact or the function of the violence of the act. The typical impact of violent acts perpetrated by men against their female partners is much more severe than the reverse: women are not only more likely to be killed but are also more likely to be injured enough to require medical attention (Stets & Straus, 1990; Vivian & Langhinrichsen-Rohling, 1994). But perhaps the most important evidence that domestic violence in marriage is predominantly a male problem comes from an examination of gender differences in the function of violence. Battering is not just physical aggression; it is physical aggression used to intimidate, subjugate, or control an intimate partner. Generally, battering requires both the physical strength to use violence as a method of control and a learning history which justifies the use of violence against intimate partners. Throughout history, our legacy as a patriarchal culture has provided men, and only men, with such a learning history; in the vast majority of heterosexual relationships, it is only the men who combine physical dominance with the learning history that it takes to produce a batterer. Because it is difficult if not impossible to directly measure the function of violence, behavioral scientists have used indirect markers, such as fear and injury, to distinguish battering from physical aggression without battering. Even in couples in which both the husbands and wives admit to violence, it is rare for men to report fear, whereas it is the norm for women to do so. Even when fear is coded by those trained to read affect in the face, body language, and voice tone of couples during videotaped conversations, women show a great deal of fear, while the men exhibit nary a trace (Jacobson, Gottman, Waltz, et al., 1994).

In short, in heterosexual adult relationships, most batterers are men, and most of those battered are women. How serious a problem is battering? Between 2 and 4 million women are severely assaulted by their male partners per year. About one-third of all married women are physically assaulted by their husbands at least once during the course of their marital relationship. Although homicide occurs in only a small percentage of marriages in which there is battering, battering is so common that the homicides are a serious social problem. As mentioned earlier, the risk of homicide increases dramatically for women who try to leave their abusive husbands (Wilson & Daly, 1993). Following the battered woman's decision to leave, more commonly than murder, there is a period of terrorism, including stalking, threats, rape, and violence, which gradually subsides. Given the twin threats of terrorism and homicide, it is a wonder that as many battered women leave as statistics suggest. Other deterrents to leaving include poverty and a lack of a social support network. But, eventually, most women who stay alive get out of abusive relationships. Then, after a period of terrorism, they are safe, and they begin to rebuild their lives. In the meantime, their lives can only be truly understood by those who have been through the experience. One battered woman likened it to being in a concentration camp, but in a state of solitary confinement. It is not surprising that some battered women suffer from posttraumatic stress disorder or depression once they are out of the abusive relationship. What is surprising is how resilient battered women tend to be.

Leaving is often the only way to make the violence stop. Violence is even more common among dating couples than it is among the married, and, in general, battering is most common among men in their twenties and slowly decreases with age. Part of this decrease is because the women have left. In Leonard's study of newlyweds (Quigley, Leonard, & Senchak, 1966), even one episode of severe violence prior to marriage meant that there was an 87 percent chance of continued violence after marriage. Jacobson and Gottman (1998) found that physical abuse ended in only 7 percent of the married couples over a two-year period. Studies which provide more optimistic appraisals tend to ignore the fact that battering, once established, can still occur, even though it can no longer be detected. Then, it can become emotional abuse.

Throughout history, it was legal for husbands to beat their wives (Dobash & Dobash, 1979). Women have historically been considered the property of men; in the same way that it was legal to beat slaves because they were the property of slaveowners, it was legal for husbands to beat wives. It wasn't until 1870 that two states—Massachusetts and Mississippi—made battering illegal. Now, although battering is illegal in all states, the chances of getting punished for wife-beating are still miniscule. Why? Because values are often slower to change than laws. Most severe

battering episodes never get reported to the police, partly because battered women are afraid that their husbands will simply escalate the violence and partly because many battered women do not even know that battering is against the law. When incidents do get reported, even the police, who are mandated to arrest the batterer, often fail to do so. Most states have mandatory arrest laws now, requiring that a police officer arrest the primary perpetrator in a domestic dispute if he or she believes that an assault has occurred. Although these laws have led to more arrests, the law is unevenly enforced by police officers who, in many cases, still view domestic violence as a family matter. When batterers are arrested, prosecutors have to decide whether or not to indict them. They may decide that the court docket is too full. The wife, because she is afraid of what her husband will do to her once the trial is over, may decide not to press charges. Or the prosecutors themselves may be biased against crimes they view as "family matters." Thus, only some who are arrested are prosecuted. And a conviction is far from automatic: judges tend not to like "domestic disputes," especially in criminal courts. Finally, even when convicted, the batterer usually gets off with little more than a slap on the wrist: probation, a small fine, or a referral to an outpatient rehabilitation program which is unlikely to work (Dutton, 1988).

Police pull a woman through her bathroom window to rescue her from a domestic dispute with her husband, who had a gun. Statistics show that arresting poor or working-class batterers may actually increase the probability of future violence.

Batterers, in short, are seldom punished for assaulting their partners, unless the result is homicide. Because there is no known "cure" for battering, holding batterers accountable through punishment by the criminal justice system is the only real protection battered women have. Arrest by itself has been shown to deter only middle- and upper-middle-class batterers (Holtzworth-Munroe, Markman, O'Leary, et al., 1995). Most batterers earn working-class incomes or are in poverty: statistics show that arrest may actually increase the likelihood of further violent episodes from them, unless it leads to "doing some serious time."

Types of Batterers

Until recently, batterers were discussed as if they were a homogenous group, with all receiving the same treatment. But, over the past decade, that view has changed as increasing evidence has mounted for different types of batterers, each type with a unique family history, its own additional problems, and other characteristics setting it off from other types. Holtzworth-Munroe and Stuart (1994) integrated and summarized this growing literature and concluded that there were three types of batterers: (1) those resembling men with APD, (2) those who combined depression with borderline personality disorder, and (3) men who appear not to have disorders but batter their wives.

Jacobson and associates discovered two types of batterers who fit nicely with those described by Holtzworth-Munroe and Stuart (Gottman, Jacobson, Rushe, et al., 1995; Jacobson & Gottman, 1998; Jacobson, Gottman, & Shortt, 1995). To understand these subtypes, it is important to remember that, when most of us get upset, we become physiologically aroused. Both conflict and stress lead to increases in heart rate, blood pressure, amount of blood rushing from the trunk to the periphery of the body, sweating, and motor activity. Most batterers respond in this typical way. However, Jacobson, Gottman, and their colleagues found that 20 percent of the batterers actually showed decreases in heart rate as they moved from a state of relaxation to marital conflict; in other words, they calmed down as they became more aggressive during arguments. Not only were there two distinct groups of batterers— those who calmed down when they became aggressive (Type I batterers) and those who became physiologically aroused (Type II batterers)—but the two groups differed in a variety of ways.

As Jacobson and Gottman (1998) put it, the Type I batterers were like cobras. Physiological tranquility during stress has been associated by psychophysiologists with focused attention: the cobra type of batterer appears to be calm and focused on his partner, probably in order to maximize the impact of his aggression. Type I batterers are more severely violent than Type IIs, show more verbal and emotional abuse, come from chaotic and violent family backgrounds, tend to be generally violent (not just toward their current partner), have histories of abusing both alcohol and illegal drugs, virtually always meet *DSM-IV* criteria for APD, and are married to women who are (not surprisingly) quite frightened and depressed. The Type II batterers, according to Jacobson and Gottman, are more like pit bulls: they are slower to resort to violence, but, once they "sink their teeth into their partners," they don't let go.

Perhaps the most interesting difference between Type I and Type II batterers is in the long-term stability of their relationships. Women do not stay married to Type IIs very long. The divorce rate in the general population is about 50 percent during the course of one's lifetime: over a two-year period, it is 1–2 percent. However, in the sample studied by Jacobson and Gottman, 38 percent of the women married to Type IIs had left their husbands within two years of their contact with the researchers. This is an extraordinarily high rate of separation or divorce over a two-year period. However, over the same time period, not a single Type I couple stopped living together. Jacobson and Gottman speculate that this difference is primarily a function of Type I batterers' wives' being afraid to leave. Given the severity of the batterers' violence, this fear seems quite warranted. In fact, it is well established that, for all battered women, the most dangerous period for a potential homicide is the time when they are trying to escape from their battering partner.

Role of Alcohol Abuse in Battering

Leonard (1993) has documented that battering episodes are often triggered by alcohol. However, until recently, many have assumed that alcohol intoxication causes battering by removing inhibitions that normally curtail male aggression. In fact, more recent findings suggest that alcohol use probably does not explain battering episodes, even among alcoholics. Men who batter may be more likely to abuse alcohol than nonviolent men, but this does not necessarily mean that alcohol abuse causes battering. It seems more likely that this is an illusory correlation, better explained by one or more third variables that do contribute to battering. For example, both alcohol abusers and batterers are more likely than other men to have APD; APD might mediate the relationship between alcohol abuse and battering.

The counter to this more recent interpretation is that, in fact, many batterers become violent only when they have been drinking. However, rather than causing the violence, intoxication probably provides a handy rationalization for batterers who, in fact, drink because they want to be violent anyway. Batterers often admit as much. Alcohol provides a handy mechanism for batterers to minimize the significance of their battering problem. They deny that they have a problem with violence, instead blaming the problem on alcohol; thus, they avoid having to take responsibility for the violence. Minimization, denial, and distortion are the coping mechanisms that batterers use in order to be able to live with themselves and their violent behavior.

On the other hand, in some cases, alcohol abuse can be one of the causes of a violent episode. Alcohol may be, for some men, part of the immediate social context that contributes to battering episodes. Leonard and Senchak (1996) found, for example, that among newlywed couples alcohol abuse in men was one of the best predictors of subsequent aggression. Although the exact role of alcohol in the causal scheme of battering remains to be determined, it is fair to conclude that it is far from trivial, but, whatever alcohol's role, it is by no means the whole story.

Emotional Abuse

Emotional abuse is sometimes referred to as verbal aggression. The term *emotional abuse* is more generic and defines all forms of power and control which do not involve the use of violence or threats of violence. Emotional abuse can be as frightening and terrifying as physical abuse.

There are many varieties of emotional abuse. First, there is the commission of damage to pets or property, such as throwing and breaking furniture or beating the family dog. Such acts scare both women and children and help to remind the wife that she is also at risk. Another variety of emotional abuse is sexual coercion, which is not the same as such violent acts as rape. Sexual coercion involves belittling the wife's sexual prowess or her physical appearance or taunting her with tales (real or fictional) of sexual relationships with other women. The most common category of emotional abuse, though, is **degradation;** battered women are humiliated, often publicly, and insulted in dehumanizing ways. For example, one batterer announced at a party, "Anyone want to talk about current events? Don't bother with my wife. She can't read, and, even if she could, she wouldn't understand it, she's so stupid." Descriptors such as "whore," "bitch," "cunt," and "slut" roll off the tongue of a batterer when talking or referring to his partner as smoothly as most of us would ask our family members to pass the pepper at the dinner table. Perhaps

the most serious category of emotional abuse is isolation, in which batterers systematically make their wives totally dependent on them. Batterers often bar their partners from having contact with family or friends; one batterer rigged his front door so that he could tell whether or not his wife had left the house. Another checked his wife's grocery store receipts to see by the checkout time on the receipt whether she had come straight home.

Some relationships include a great deal of emotional abuse and never cross the line of physical violence. However, emotional abuse serves a different function when it follows battering. Because of its association with violence, emotional abuse can become as effective a technique for power and control as the battering itself. This may explain why high levels of emotional abuse (especially degradation and isolation) are actually more likely to lead to divorce than are high rates of physical abuse (Jacobson, Gottman, Gortner, et al., 1996). It may also explain the evidence for an inverse relationship between physical and emotional abuse over time: in cases in which the husband's physical abuse declines in frequency and severity, emotional abuse tends to increase (Jacobson & Gottman, 1998). Because physical abuse is against the law and emotional abuse is not, and because both serve similar controlling functions in battering marriages, it is not hard to understand why, over time, batterers are reinforced for emotional abuse more powerfully than they are for physical abuse. Physical abuse can be punished by arrest, which carries with it the stigma associated with being a batterer, criminal proceedings, fines, imprisonment, and loss of the relationship. Emotional abuse, on the other hand, has a different outcome. When emotional abuse increases as physical abuse declines, the batterer maintains power and control, and the battered woman is temporarily reassured that things are changing for the better. Battered women then feel better about the long-term prospects of the marriage. Because it is so effective, emotional abuse is very dangerous to battered women.

How Battered Women Escape

Battered women are no more a homogenous group than batterers are. Though these women are predominantly from lower socioeconomic classes, there are notable exceptions. Nicole Brown Simpson drove a Ferrari, and Darryl Hannah (battered by her former boyfriend, Jackson Browne) is a rich movie star. Highly educated women also are found in battering relationships. Batterers are almost always charming and show no signs of their violent tendencies during the early stages of the relationship. The first episode shocks the woman, and a large percentage of women immediately end the relationship shortly thereafter. Unfortunately, by the time of the first episode, often they are attached, in love, and may even be married, with children. It is easy to explain away that first episode as an isolated, unprecedented experience. The first episode is also often followed by a showering of the partner with love, apologies, and promises, and there may be a long interval between the first and second episodes. By that time, fear, economic dependency, and children can make it almost impossible to leave. The wives of Type I batterers have a harder time escaping. However, the wives of Type IIs appear to find ways to get out, often at great personal risk. There are four factors that seem to drive women married to Type IIs out of the relationship, despite the dangers and deterrents.

First, emotional abuse—especially degradation and isolation—drives battered women away. Even though physical abuse kills, emotional abuse can actually be less tolerable on a day-to-day basis. Type IIs are always "in the faces" of their victims, and there is no relief. For many couples, battering episodes are followed by periods of quiet. It is the relentless and humiliating quality of the emotional abuse that drives women away.

Second, "alarm" on the part of husbands is very effective. Jacobson, Gottman, and colleagues (1996) found that the men who showed a physiological alarm response (a response preparing them to fight or flee) during arguments were more likely to lose their wives within the next two years. The sense of alarm is extremely oppressive. It is a reflection of many batterers' emotional dependency, their morbid preoccupation with the comings and goings of their partners, their jealousy, and their constant vigilance. Battered women are aware of this alarm, and it becomes intolerable.

Third, during an argument, women who are preparing to leave show the signs in their faces, their voices, and in their choices of words: their emotional stance shifts from fear to contempt. During the argument, they assertively defend themselves while skillfully avoiding any kind of response in kind to the husband's emotional abuse. Still, correlation should not be confused with causation. Battered women don't leave because they develop contempt or assertiveness. Rather, showing these emotional expressions and standing one's ground are signs that they are ready to go.

Fourth, the wife's overall level of marital satisfaction is very indicative of how long she will stay in the marriage, hoping that the violence will change. Despite being battered, these women vary considerably in their degree of overall marital satisfaction. At one extreme, there are battered women who love their husbands and want the relationship to succeed, even if they want the abuse to stop. At the other extreme, there are women who are dissatisfied with the marriage across the board and would be unhappy even if there were no abuse. It is the latter who are most likely to leave quickly.

When women do leave, they are saving not only themselves. Frequently, they are also removing their children from a dangerous environment. Many batterers also abuse their children, and stress, a constant feature in many batterers' homes, promotes parental aggression against children (see the box on page 514).

Domestic Violence: Theory and Therapy

The Sociocultural Perspective

Patriarchy is at the root of domestic violence, according to the sociocultural perspective (Dobash & Dobash, 1979). Since the beginning of time, and in most cultures throughout the world, marriage has been an institution created by men, primarily for the benefit of men. Furthermore, marriage has been fundamentally a financial arrangement between families, rather than a union of lovers, as in traditional notions of romantic love. Men have been the heads of households, and their authority over women and children has been absolute. Battering wives, and even murdering them under some circumstances, was legal throughout the Western world until the latter part of the nineteenth century. Because women and children were viewed as the property of men, the absolute authority of men over women followed.

Even though the laws have changed so that it is now illegal for husbands to batter wives, the patriarchal values which spawned such laws continue to make battering acceptable to many men, and even some women. In 1970, two states—Texas and New Mexico—had statutes permitting a man to kill his wife if he found her in bed with another man. Although such killing was considered justifiable homicide, it was murder if the cuckold also killed the other man. Wives had no reciprocal power were they to catch their husbands in the act with another woman.

Although patriarchal values cannot explain why some men are batterers and others are not, they can help us to understand why battering is so common. Evidence supports patriarchy as at least part of the explanation for battering. Battering rates are higher in states with more traditional laws and attitudes toward women, and battering rates are higher in religions and subcultures which support men as having greater power than women.

Child Abuse: Causes and Effects

State child protective services confirm over 1 million cases of child abuse in the United States each year (U.S. Bureau of the Census, 1997). The number of cases that are not reported is probably very high. For many reasons—the abusers' shame, the inability of small children to seek help outside the home, the reluctance of teachers and physicians to interfere with parents—child abuse is probably one of the most underreported of crimes.

Some researchers have emphasized the psychological causes of child abuse, some the social causes, but most agree that the problem is due to multiple, interlocking factors. One thing that is clear is that the majority of child abusers were themselves abused as children (Whipple & Webster-Stratton, 1991; Widom, 1991), so this behavior was modeled for them. Furthermore, many abused children suffer psychological damage and are therefore less able, as adults, to cope with their own children. Other factors that predispose parents to abuse their children are immaturity, rigidity, dependency, a sense of powerlessness, inappropriate expectations for parenthood, and, predictably, psychological disturbance (Azar & Twentyman, 1986; Ney, Fung, & Wickett, 1992). Abusing parents are rarely psychotic, but they are likely to show personality disorders and very likely to abuse alcohol or other drugs.

Apart from personal risk factors, there are obvious social factors, namely poverty and unemployment. "What often separates abusers from nonabusers is a job" (Steinberg & Meyer, 1995, p. 313). Some critics claim that child abuse is better reported among the poor because the poor have more contact with social agencies, but even this cannot account for the vastly increased risk of abuse in impoverished families. Children from families with an income of less than $15,000 are five times more likely to be maltreated than are children from higher-income families (Sedlack, 1989). Poverty is a powerful stressor, and stress promotes aggression. Animal mothers under stress have been observed to attack their offspring, and human parents may do likewise (Williams, 1976). But poverty is not the only stressor that can push parents over the line. Marital discord contributes, too. Families that are socially isolated and that are dominated by a male are also more likely to have abused children (Azar & Perlmutter, 1993).

Beyond socioeconomic pressures, large-scale cultural factors probably help to account for the high rate of child abuse in the United States. Ours is a violent society; it is also one that guards privacy heavily and considers individual family values more privileged than community values. Other societies have much lower rates of child abuse. In China, it is rare for a child to be subjected to physical pun-

ishment (Kessen, 1979); in Sweden, it is illegal (that includes spankings).

Even after it is reported, child abuse tends to be repeated (Williams, 1983), and, the more often it happens, the greater the likelihood of irreversible effects, including death. According to the National Committee for the Prevention of Child Abuse, about 1,300 American children died of abuse in 1993 alone. As for those who survive frequent abuse, they are likely to suffer permanent gastrointestinal, orthopedic, and, above all, neurological injuries. Up to 30 percent of abused children show brain damage, which, by making it harder for them to do what their parents want from them, exposes them to further abuse—a cruel scenario. Repeated blows to the head can lead to mental retardation, cerebral palsy, and other disorders (Williams, 1983).

Those are only the physical effects. The psychological effects can be equally profound. Young children who are abused are also more likely to show aggressiveness, impulsiveness, destructiveness, frequent temper tantrums, and low self-esteem (Alessandri, 1991; Kaufman & Cicchetti, 1989; Vondra, Barnett, & Cicchetti, 1990)—all of which, again, are likely to get on their parents' nerves, with predictable consequences. As teenagers, they are more prone to conduct disorders (Widom, 1989), and, when they become adults, as we saw, they are more likely to abuse their children, thus continuing the cycle.

The Cognitive and Behavioral Perspectives

Because not all men raised in our patriarchal culture become batterers, psychologists need to explain what types of men are at greatest risk. Dutton (1995) has formulated a theory which takes into account the empirical facts that many batterers are exposed to early trauma, including abuse from their own parents. This theory could account for the Type II subtype described by Jacobson and Gottman (1998), or the depressed, borderline subtype described by Holtzworth-Munroe and Stuart (1994). These batterers grow up fearing abandonment and having markedly ambivalent attitudes toward women.

Dutton believes that batterers often experience dissociation during battering episodes. He provides some empirical support for his theory, based on personality test data. However, Jacobson and Gottman (1998) found little evidence for dissociation during battering episodes among either Type Is or Type IIs. At times, the Type IIs in the study denied that they had battered, but this seemed to be a form of **gaslighting,** a term from a 1944 Hollywood film, in which a husband attempts to drive his wife insane. The purpose of gaslighting is to make the battered woman think she is crazy, by denying her perception of reality. In truth, most of the batterers in the study seemed to recall their battering episodes in great detail, and their recollections corresponded quite well with those of their wives.

Cognitive-behavioral theories generally view battering as resulting from social-skill and social information-processing deficits, similar to those described earlier for conduct-disordered teenagers (Dodge & Schwartz, 1997; Hamberger & Lohr, 1989; Holtzworth-Munroe, Markman, O'Leary, et al., 1995). These deficits include poor impulse control and an inability to manage anger, combined with attitudes toward women that justify violence when necessary. It is not clear whether these deficits cause battering, though. In some studies, batterers show deficits. In others, they do not. As we will see, one reason for pessimism is that therapies resulting from these theories have not been very successful (Rosenfeld, 1992).

The Biological Perspective

There are no biological theories to explain why violence is directed toward intimate partners. However, the literature on APD appears to be relevant for Type I batterers, and for some Type IIs. To the extent that batterers have APD, they have a general tendency toward violence. And, to the extent that they also have a learning history that justifies violence against women, a model which takes biological factors into account may help explain battering.

Some theorists have interpreted Jacobson and Gottman's Type I/Type II distinction as evidence for biological causation. Type Is and Type IIs differ in their physiological response to conflict with their wives, which might explain the other differences between Type Is and Type IIs. Still, biological markers do not necessarily imply causality. In this instance, a number of explanations compete with biological theories. For example, Type Is may have learned in childhood that the best way to cope with a stressful family environment is to calm down when situations become tense. Later in life, these men may apply these skills to their adult intimate relationships. Or, perhaps Type Is are reinforced for calming down as arguments ensue, because their aggression is more effective when it is calm, controlled, and calculated.

Is Therapy Effective?

The brutal murder of Nicole Brown Simpson and her friend, Ronald L. Goldman; the subsequent arrest of former football star O. J. Simpson; and the ultimate finding in civil court that he was responsible for their deaths focused national attention on battering in the United States. Nicole Brown Simpson had called the police eight times, claiming her husband had beaten

The murder of Nicole Brown Simpson and the widespread publication of photos like the one here focused national attention on domestic violence.

her. Simpson had been arrested and pleaded "no contest" to charges that he had beaten and threatened to kill his wife on New Year's Day, 1989. He was sentenced to probation, fined $700, and required to perform community service and seek psychological counseling. Simpson's lenient treatment was not due to his celebrity. "It doesn't have to be O. J. Simpson," says Rita Smith, coordinator of the National Coalition Against Domestic Violence. "It could be Joe Jones in Iowa. The system makes all kinds of concessions in these cases" (Lewin, 1994, p. 21).

How should society deal with violent spouses? One strategy is to arrest the batterer. But we have seen that arrest is not typically effective in preventing recurrences of battering or emotional abuse. Studies comparing the impact of different forms of police intervention—separation of the spouses, police counseling, and arrest—found arrest to be the most effective. But a recent review (summarized by Holtzworth-Munroe, Markman, O'Leary, et al., 1995) concluded that arrest usually does not serve as a deterrent to repeat battering.

Another possible answer is shelters for battered women. Each year, more than 300,000 women and children seek emergency help at 1,200 shelters (Reiss & Roth, 1993). In addition to temporary housing, shelters provide a variety of services, including help finding employment and housing, day care, educational training in parenting, budgeting, and support groups. Shelters also offer **safety planning,** an invaluable service to battered women when conducted by a well-trained advocate. In fact, safety planning can reduce the risk of further violence to battered women, although the risk reduction is not always immediately apparent (Sullivan, Campbell, Angelique, et al., 1994). Safety planning is a specialized procedure for helping women handle potentially violent altercation without harm, and can be a useful tool when it comes to planning the ultimate escape. For example, many safety plans involve friends of the victim and ways of signaling those friends that danger is imminent. In one case, when the wife alerted her friend Betty by saying, "Hope it doesn't rain," Betty was supposed to meet her at the bus station with a suitcase full of clothes, a passport, and other relevant documents.

Psychological interventions for batterers usually take the form of group therapy, provided separately for batterers and their victims. Group therapy for victims, nearly all of whom are women, often takes place in shelters and typically focuses on the issues of safety, the effective use of police and legal protection, and practical advice in achieving self-sufficiency. Therapy also addresses such psychological issues as feelings of powerlessness and misplaced responsibility for being abused (Dutton, 1992). Many abused women believe that they provoke abuse from their men. Falling into the "Beauty and the Beast syndrome," they are convinced that, if they had been better wives or lovers, the "monster" who abused them would have become a "prince."

Many women say that the support they receive from other battered women is the most important factor in helping them to achieve self-sufficiency and overcome feelings of isolation and powerlessness (Reiss & Roth, 1993). The problem is that most shelters and support services for battered women are underfunded, and the services often stop once the woman is physically safe. Unfortunately, many battered women still have significant problems—such as substance abuse, depression, and posttraumatic stress disorder even after their exit from abusive relationships. For those who are indigent, the majority of battered women, it is hard to find help once they leave the safety of the shelters.

Group therapy for abusers sometimes emphasizes cognitive restructuring, anger management, and alternatives to violence. Typically, men who batter "blame the victim": they deny that they have done anything wrong and/or claim that they were provoked, says Evan Stark, codirector of the Domestic Violence Training Program (Ingrassia & Beck, 1994). Often, these men have failed to measure up to material and cultural standards of manhood (they may be unemployed or underemployed), and they lack skills in verbal assertiveness and problem solving (Gelles, Lackner, & Wolfner, 1994). In therapy, the men are expected to take responsibility for violence, whether or not there was any provocation or participation by their partners. They are taught to recognize extramarital sources of frustration as well as internal signals of rage and to manage their anger more constructively. The coordination of education groups attempting to change men's attitudes toward women, and criminal justice sanctions, has become the primary method of treatment for batterers. In contrast, couples therapy is generally considered ineffective and unethical when applied to batterers. It seems to place battered women at greater risk for staying in an abusive relationship, and it implies that the wife is at least partially responsible for the violence (Jacobson & Gottman, 1998). Studies that imply that couples therapy is harmless are misleading, because they generally screen out most of the men described as batterers (O'Leary & Heyman, 1997).

Neither education groups nor group therapy for batterers seems to be particularly effective (Dunford, 1996; Holtzworth-Munroe, Markman, O'Leary, et al., 1995; Rosenfeld, 1992). Most abusive men avoid treatment, but those who complete treatment programs are less likely to continue battering than those who drop out or attend irregularly. Only half of the men who are required by the courts to seek treatment ever show up, and only half of those who start therapy complete the program (Ingrassia & Beck, 1994).

Furthermore, it is doubtful that any form of psychotherapy will be useful in changing Type I batterers. These men are calm when expressing hostility. Clearly, anger management would not be therapeutic for them.

Although Type Is may be out of the reach of therapy, it would be premature to give up altogether on psychotherapy for batterers. To date, there have been few studies evaluating the outcome of these treatments, but most suggest that groups for batterers are no better than no treatment at all. Moreover, therapy does not end violence in many cases; neither does it eliminate emotional abuse.

However, studies conducted up until now have treated all batterers uniformly, ignoring the possibility of tailoring the treatment to batterer subtypes. Saunders (1996) has completed one study in which batterers were divided into two subtypes: antisocial and dependent. Then the men were randomly assigned to either cognitive-behavioral treatment or psychodynamic therapy. The antisocial subtype responded favorably to CBT but not to psychodynamic approaches. The opposite was true for the dependent subtype. Thus, when treatments were matched by type of batterer, the results were encouraging. Nevertheless, few of the subjects described by Saunders would have been classified as Type Is. In short, these results suggest that, for batterers without APD, the

Self-help groups such as Parents Anonymous have formed to help families eliminate child abuse in their homes.

more antisocial they are, the more likely it is that they will benefit from CBT; the more dependent they are, the more likely that psychodynamic approaches are indicated.

The entire idea of therapy for spouse abuse has been criticized. Sociologists Richard Gelles and Murray Straus (1988) argue that battering is not primarily an individual problem but is also a social problem. The ideas that a man is "king of his castle" (or that he should be) and that how he treats "his wife" (that is, his property) is his business still run strong in our culture. The sports subculture, in particular, emphasizes that it is a "man's world" and that a woman's place is on the sidelines, cheering men on. Feminist theorists (Walker, 1989) argue that marital violence is a reflection of gender inequality and is better understood as a technique of control and dominance than as an expression of anger.

This brings us back to the ultimate answer to problems related to violence and antisocial behavior: prevention. Although experimental prevention programs are currently underway on college campuses and in high schools, the research on APD suggests that we have to begin much earlier in life, when children are infants or are in preschool. Stopping the transmission of violence from fathers to sons is a major goal. Related to this goal is the recognition that that children are victimized by battering almost as much as women are, and perhaps even more. First of all, battering is child abuse. Children are harmed, sometimes irreparably, by growing up in a home where their fathers beat their mothers. Second, many batterers also abuse their children. All 50 states now prosecute child abusers, but legal measures have not curbed the problem. Studies by the National Center on Child Abuse and Neglect have led to the develop-

ment of educational programs, which in turn have made teachers, physicians, and other professionals more watchful for signs of abuse and more likely to report them. There are now parents' support groups, including the Voluntary Intervention and Treatment Program (VITP) and Parents Anonymous, a self-help group. The courts have shown greater willingness to remove children from homes in which they are likely to go on being victimized. In some cases, removal seems to be the only treatment. Ironically, abused children have fewer treatment opportunities than do child abusers.

The road to eliminating domestic violence seems to end with our gaps in the science of prevention. Chapter 19 will discuss what we can do now to prevent violence in the future. At the present time, the only thing that is known for sure is that, if batterers are in jail, their partners are safe—as long as the batterers stay there. The woman's safety is and has to be the highest priority. Saving the marriage should not be the issue. Rather, the man should be held accountable and punished, and the woman must be safe. As we will see in Chapter 18, there are circumstances in which psychological disturbances affect legal judgments. However, in cases of battering, the issues are clear. Battering must be stopped.

Groups at Risk for Antisocial and Violent Behavior

Antisocial personality disorder, like other violent syndromes, is generally diagnosed in men. Overall, males commit most of the violent crimes, with males between the ages of 15 and 24 at particular risk for engaging in violent crimes (Potter & Mercy, 1997).

After gender, poverty is the single greatest risk factor for violent behavior, especially in combination with other factors. Men who are raised in poor families and who suffered medical problems before or at birth have a higher rate of APD than their wealthier or healthier cohorts (Raine, Brennan, Mednick, et al., 1996). Drug users are also at high risk for violent behavior. At least 50 percent of people meeting the criteria for substance abuse also have antisocial personalities. (Strain, 1995). However, it is not clear whether drug abuse causes aggression or whether both behaviors are caused by a third factor, such as underarousal or cortical immaturity. Underarousal seems to increase the probability of violent behavior. Three-year-olds with low resting heart rates and teenagers who have low levels of physiological arousal have an increased chance of displaying violent behavior. Social factors such as bad parenting and neglect also make violence more likely (Raine, Brennan, & Mednick, in press).

Many of the factors that put men at risk for APD, such as poverty, a history of family violence, and having been a victim of child abuse, also make them more likely to commit rape (Haapasalo, & Kankkkonen, 1997; Hall & Barongan, 1997). Though many rapists are no different psychologically from other men (Polaschek, Ward, & Hudson, 1997), men at risk tend to have hostile attitudes toward women, and they view male-female relationships as adversarial. Some ethnic-minority subcultures may encourage male dominance aggression, but simply living in the United States increases the probability that men will rape; the United States has a higher rate of rape than any other industrialized nation (Allison & Wrightsman, 1993).

Domestic violence is also influenced by poverty as well as location. Furthermore, living in states with more traditional laws and attitudes toward women increases the chance that a man will commit domestic violence. Some batterers resemble men with APD, while others suffer both depression and borderline personality disorder; still another group of batterers is apparently "normal" when not abusing their wives (Holtzworth-Munroe & Stuart, 1994). Many battering episodes are triggered by alcohol (Leonard, 1993), but alcohol abuse serves as an excuse for, not a cause of, battering.

All Americans are at risk for violence. The United States is one of the most violent countries in the world (Lore & Schultz, 1993). Our society encourages male violence, particularly violence against women. To change the rate of assault, rape, and domestic violence, we must change our society. When men are not rewarded for aggressive, violent behavior, both women and men will be better able to live in peace.

KEY TERMS

antisocial behavior, 495	evolutionary psychology, 502	passive avoidance learning, 497	reactive aggression, 497
antisocial personality disorder (APD), 494	gaslighting, 514	prosocial behavior, 501	relapse prevention, 508
degradation, 512	instrumental aggression, 497	rape, 504	safety planning, 515
	partner abuse, 509		

SUMMARY

- The defining trait of antisocial personality disorder (APD) is a predatory attitude toward other people. It is marked by a history of antisocial activity beginning before age 15 and continuing into adulthood, failure to show constancy and responsibility, irritability and aggressiveness, reckless and impulsive behavior, and a disregard for the truth. A subset of people with APD are considered psychopaths. These individuals lack empathy and fail to learn from experience; they are particularly bad at passive avoidance learning.

- Most antisocial adults were delinquents during their adolescent and preadolescent years. Factors that lead to delinquency include poor impulse control, low intelligence, other criminals in the family, poverty, and bad parenting. Certain biological factors seem to protect 15-year-old boys from becoming adult criminals, though. High levels of physiological arousal and other signs of tension may prevent these boys from committing crimes calmly; these boys eventually abandon their delinquent ways.

- The sociocultural perspective traces APD to poverty. According to this view, poor individuals have little access to society's rewards except through antisocial behavior. However, a combination of poverty and prenatal or birth complications dramatically increases the probability that a boy will grow up to have APD.

- The behavioral perspective observes that environmental factors, especially child abuse, have a profound impact on APD. In addition, parents' failure to reinforce prosocial behavior can teach the child that rewards are independent of behavior, so that the child becomes desensitized to social stimuli such as rules and laws. Peers—especially teenage peers—often directly reinforce antisocial behavior.

- The cognitive perspective focuses on social information processing. Antisocial children and adolescents are not good at reading social cues, deciding on appropriate responses, and solving problems in social situations. These habits may be acquired through learning and may be a response to developmental conditions. Individuals with APD also hold rigid, unchanging beliefs, which distort their social interactions.

- Two prominent factors dominate the biological perspective: genetics and physiological signs. Twin and adoption studies have produced evidence that heredity may play a role in criminal behavior, especially among middle-class criminals. Genetic research also suggests that the overlap among APD, alcoholism, and other drug addictions are part of the same heritability factor. Moreover, what seems to be inherited is a general vulnerability toward antisocial behavior, not a specific vulnerability toward violence. Antisocial personalities often have a defect in brain functioning, such as increased activation in the left hemisphere of the frontal lobe. According to one school of thought, this is a sign of "cortical immaturity," an inability to respond normally to fear-inducing stimuli. An alternative theory suggests that people with APD are not fearless but are simply underaroused stimulus-seekers. There is evidence for strong biosocial interactions that increase the probability that teenagers will commit violent crimes.

- There is no effective treatment for APD. These individuals seldom seek therapy, tend not to be motivated to change, and seem to be limited in their capacity to change. Medications may have promise with a subgroup of men with APD: those with mood disorders who also abuse alcohol. Most experts in the field seem to agree that the only way to stop APD is to prevent it from starting. In the absence of an aggression-producing environment, biological variables may be the primary predictors of APD. Stressful environments, though, are best counteracted by prevention programs.

- Rape, or sexual intercourse with a nonconsenting partner, is a common crime. Some men apparently resort to rape because they cannot find—or feel they cannot find—a willing sex partner. Other rapists have antisocial personalities. In still other cases, the element of force may be a necessary prerequisite for sexual arousal. A significant proportion of rapists were victims of child abuse. But many rapists are no different psychologically from "normal" men. Thus, many rapes are the result not of psychological disorders but of our cultural emphasis on sex and violence.

- Rape victims are at risk for a number of psychological disorders, such as sexual dysfunctions and posttraumatic stress disorder. The vast majority of rape cases reported to the police do not go to trial, either because identification of the rapist is uncertain or the evidence is insufficient. However, counseling centers have been set up for victims, and many police officers are being trained to deal with rape victims.

- Acquaintance rape, like other rape, is very common. Coercive tactics commonly used by men include using their greater physical strength, preventing a woman from leaving an enclosed space so that she cannot escape, continuing to touch the woman, despite her saying no, and lying to a woman about their intentions. There are no differences between victims of stranger rape and victims of acquaintance rape on measures of postassault depression, anxiety, relationship quality, and sexual adjustment. Men who believe that men are by nature sexually uncontrollable and who believe that it is up to women to set limits in sexual encounters are most likely to commit date rape. These sexually coercive men are aggressive, tolerant of aggression (they tend to have histories of family violence), sexually experienced, sexually unsatisfied, and, not surprisingly, sexually aroused by the use of force.

- The sociocultural perspective observes that sexual aggression toward women is not only tolerated by the culture, but even accepted and sometimes rewarded by it. At the community level, some subcultures are particularly patriarchal when it comes to sex, and aggression may be seen as part of the male role, with the result that women accept being victimized as part of life. Overall, poverty better predicts sexual aggression than does either race or ethnicity.

- The cognitive and behavioral perspectives examine the connection between alcohol use and rape; alcohol is commonly involved when rape occurs. The causal connection remains murky. Rapists are also lonely men who have extremely hostile attitudes toward women. Like psychopaths, rapists tend to lack empathy. However, rapists who are psychopaths differ greatly from those who are not. With psychopaths, rape is less likely to be associated with a particular set of attitudes toward women and more likely to be part of a general disregard for others.

- Therapies for rapists have mixed results. Several approaches help offenders to unlearn their deviant patterns—to change their sexual arousal patterns, behavior, and beliefs. Reports indicate that these programs successfully prevent relapse among rapists. Cognitive-behavioral treatments have had generally disappointing outcomes with rapists. Rapists are the most likely of all sex offenders to reoffend. As with other antisocial behaviors, prevention may be the only hope. Socialization which produces a more androgynous gender identity, or which places sex within the context of a relationship, could reduce rape.

- Domestic violence almost always involves men battering women. Battering requires both the physical strength to use violence as a method of control and a learning history that explains the use of violence against intimate partners. About one-third of all married women are physically assaulted by their husbands at least once during the course of their marital relations. Leaving is often the only way to make the violence stop. When women decide to leave battering relationships, there is a period of terrorism, including stalking, threats, rape, and violence, following the battered woman's decision to leave, which gradually subsides. Other deterrents to leaving include poverty and the lack of a social support network. Eventually, most women who stay alive get out of abusive relationships.

- There are two basic types of batterers. Twenty percent of batterers show decreases in heart rate as they move from a state of relaxation to marital conflict (Type I), while the rest become physiologically aroused (Type II)—but the two groups differ in a variety of ways. Type Is are more severely violent than are Type IIs, they show more verbal and emotional abuse, they come from chaotic and violent family backgrounds, and they virtually always meet *DSM-IV* criteria for APD. Type IIs are slower to resort to violence. Women do not stay married to Type IIs very long, while women married to Type Is are probably afraid to leave.

- Men who batter may be more likely than nonviolent men to abuse alcohol. However, rather than causing the violence, intoxication probably provides a handy rationalization for batterers who drink because they wanted to be violent anyway.

- Emotional abuse can be as dangerous and terrifying as physical abuse. The commission of damage to pets or property, sexual coercion, degradation, and isolation are common methods of emotional abuse. Because of its association with violence, emotional abuse can become as effective a technique for power and control as the battering itself. When emotional abuse increases as physical abuse declines, the batterer maintains power and control, and the battered woman is temporarily reassured that things are changing for the better.

- By the first episode of abuse, fear, economic dependency, and children can make it almost impossible to leave an abusive relationship. However, emotional abuse and "alarm" on the part of husbands can drive women away. Women who are preparing to leave shift from fear to contempt, defending themselves during arguments. Although no battered women like the violence, they do vary considerably in their degree of overall marital satisfaction. Some want the relationship to succeed, even if they want the abuse to stop. When women do leave, they are not only saving themselves but also removing their children from a dangerous environment.

- Patriarchy is at the root of domestic violence, according to sociocultural perspectives. Even though the laws have changed, so that it is now illegal for husbands to batter wives, the patriarchal values continue to make battering acceptable to many men, and even some women. Battering rates are higher in states with more traditional laws and attitudes toward women, and battering rates are higher in religions and subcultures which support men as having greater power than women.

- Cognitive and behavioral theories take into account the fact that many batterers are exposed to early trauma, including abuse from their own parents. These batterers grow up fearing abandonment and having markedly ambivalent attitudes toward women. Battering may result from social-skill and social information-processing deficits similar to those described earlier for conduct-disordered teenagers, including poor impulse control and inability to manage anger, combined with attitudes toward women that justify violence when necessary. It is not clear whether these deficits cause battering, though.

- The biological perspective has no theories to explain why violence is directed toward intimate partners. To the extent that batterers have APD, they have a general tendency toward violence. And, to the extent that they have a learning history that justifies violence against women, a model which takes biological factors into account may help explain battering. Type Is and Type IIs differ in their physiological response to conflict with their wives. However, learning theories can also account for these differences.

- Treatment for battering is more effective for the victim than for the batterer. Arrest usually does not deter repeat battering. Shelters offering safety planning can reduce the risk of further violence to battered women. Group therapy for victims typically focuses on the issues of safety, the effective use of police and legal protection, and practical advice for achieving self-sufficiency, as well as such psychological issues as feelings of powerlessness and misplaced responsibility for being abused. Group therapy for abusers emphasizes cognitive restructuring, anger management, and alternatives to violence. Most abusive men avoid treatment, but those who complete treatment programs are less likely to continue battering than are those who drop out or attend irregularly. When treatments were matched to types of batterers, though, the results were encouraging. The entire idea of therapy for spouse abuse has been criticized, as abuse is not primarily an individual problem but is also a social problem. Prevention is probably the only effective treatment for domestic violence.

- Like other violent syndromes, APD is generally diagnosed in men. After gender, poverty is the single greatest risk factor for violent behavior. Other social factors, such as bad parenting and neglect, also make violence more likely. Many of the factors that put men at risk for APD also make them more likely to commit rape. Domestic violence is also influenced by location. Within the United States, living in states with more traditional laws and attitudes toward women increases the chance that a man will commit domestic violence.

Chapter 18

According to Lorena Bobbitt, a 24-year-old manicurist living in Manassas, Virginia, she was asleep on the night of June 23, 1993, when her husband, John Bobbitt, came home drunk and raped her. He then passed out, and she went into the kitchen. There, as she later testified, she began having flashbacks of the many instances of rape and other abuse she had suffered at her husband's hands. Her eye lighted on a 12-inch carving knife. That, she said, was the last thing she remembered until she "came to" later in her car, some distance from home. In one hand she was holding the carving knife—in the other, two-thirds of her husband's penis. She threw the severed organ into some underbrush. (It was later retrieved and surgically reattached.) Lorena Bobbitt was arrested on the charge of malicious wounding, a crime for which she could have been imprisoned for 20 years.

It seemed a clear-cut case. No one, not even Lorena Bobbitt, contested that she had cut off her husband's penis. According to the prosecution, she did so out of hatred and revenge, and knew what she was doing. Indeed, a friend of hers testified that, some time before, Lorena Bobbitt had said that she would cut off her husband's penis if she ever caught him cheating on her. But, according to Virginia law, a person accused of a crime may be held blameless if "his mind has become so impaired by disease that he is totally deprived of mental power to control or restrain his act" (Margolick, 1994a). At the trial, three expert witnesses, a psychiatrist and two forensic psychologists, testified that, despite the mental stress Lorena Bobbitt was under, her actions were purposeful and goal-oriented. As one of them put it, "She came to the conclusion that the penis was at fault, and that she was going to remove the source of all her problems" (Margolick, 1994c). At the same time, another psychiatrist claimed that Lorena Bobbitt was not just under mental stress at the time of the crime; after the rape, she suffered a brief reactive psychosis (Chapter 13), during which she could not summon any defense against her wish to retaliate. She succumbed to an "irresistible impulse"—grounds, in Virginia, for acquittal. This was the explanation that the jury eventually accepted. Amid mixed cries of jubilation and disgust from a nation that had watched this trial intently, Lorena Bobbitt was acquitted on the grounds of temporary insanity.

The Lorena Bobbitt case was a notorious example of the kinds of controversies that arise when issues of mental health and the law intersect. Despite the prosecution's contention that she cut off her husband's penis out of anger and a desire for revenge, the jury agreed with Mrs. Bobbitt's defense that she had been temporarily insane.

This case is a typical illustration of the overlap between mental health and the law. By now, the issues generated by that overlap are familiar to the public. When we read newspaper accounts of bizarre crimes, we take it for granted that a psychiatrist or psychologist will be called on to make judgments about the defendant's sanity and possibly to give "expert testimony" at the trial. In other widely publicized court cases—such as the 1975 case of Kenneth Donaldson, who sued officials of the state of Florida for wrongfully keeping him in a mental institution for 14 years—the public saw the mental health system itself on trial.

These court cases are only the most obvious examples of the fact that decisions about people's mental health have important legal implications. For one thing, people who are judged to be insane may be relieved of legal responsibility for crimes that they commit. For another thing, if they are institutionalized for their own or for society's protection, they may also be relieved of many of their constitutional rights.

Mental health law, the branch of law that deals with such matters, has been changing at a rapid pace. Since 1970, nearly all states have substantially revised their laws regarding the commitment and treatment of the psychologically disturbed (La Fond & Durham, 1992), and more changes can be expected. These new laws are attempting to settle what are essentially three issues:

1. *Psychological disturbance and criminal law.* Can psychologically disturbed people be held guilty of breaking the law? Can such people be given a fair trial? If they are not tried or are acquitted by reason of insanity, what should the state then do with them?

2. *Civil commitment.* Under what circumstances can a person who has committed no crime but appears to be severely disturbed be involuntarily institutionalized by the state?

3. *Patients' rights.* Once a person is institutionalized, what are his or her rights concerning living conditions, psychological treatment, and so forth?

Most of this chapter will be devoted to an examination of these three issues. Then, in a final section, we will address the larger issue of the power of the mental health profession—how that power is used and how, in recent years, it has been challenged.

Psychological Disturbance and Criminal Law

Abnormal behavior, as we saw in Chapter 1, can be defined as a violation of the society's norms. Many social norms, however, are not just standards of behavior but legal requirements. Hence, abnormal behavior may also be illegal behavior, ranging from drug abuse to murder. Most people agree that, when deeply disturbed people commit such crimes, they should not be treated in the same way as ordinary lawbreakers. But how they should be treated is a matter of great controversy.

The Insanity Defense

Though psychologists may question the concept of free will, criminal law does not. The business of criminal law is to fix blame for and to penalize socially intolerable conduct. For the law to carry out these functions, it must assume that human beings freely choose their actions. (If they don't, how can we justifiably blame them?) Thus, when a court pronounces someone guilty, it is making both a judgment of fact *and* a moral judgment: the defendant not only committed the crime but is also morally responsible for it and can, therefore, be punished for it.

However, the law does acknowledge that certain people commit crimes not out of free choice but because mental disturbance has somehow deprived them of free choice. For such people, there is what is known in legal terms as the **insanity defense,** whereby the defendant admits to having committed the crime but pleads not guilty, stating that because of mental disturbance he or she was not morally responsible at the time of the crime. Though guilty in fact, the defendant claims to be innocent in moral terms, and, therefore, exempt from punishment.

The insanity defense, then, is intended to protect the mentally disturbed from the penalties that we impose on the mentally sound. At the same time, it serves to protect the moral prestige of the law (Meehl, 1991). By making exceptions of people who cannot be held responsible for their actions, the insanity defense

implies that every other defendant does have the capacity to choose "between good and evil."

Legal Tests of Insanity If the defendant pleads insanity, how is the jury to decide whether that plea is justifiable? In other words, what is the legal test of insanity? This question has haunted the courts for many years and has been answered in a variety of ways.

For the purposes of modern law, the first important ruling on this matter was the so-called irresistible-impulse decision, handed down by an Ohio court in 1834. According to this test, defendants are acquitted if, as a result of mental illness, they could not *resist* the impulse to do wrong. The main problem with this test is obvious: how is the jury to distinguish between resistible and irresistible impulses? (From the point of view of psychoanalytic or behavioral theory, *is* there any difference?) But, as we will see, this distinction may be no more difficult to draw than the distinctions required by other tests of insanity (LaFave & Scott, 1972).

Historically, the second important test is the so-called M'Naghten rule, handed down by an English court in 1843. The defendant in this case, Daniel M'Naghten, claimed that he had been commanded by the voice of God to kill the English prime minister, Sir Robert Peel. He then killed Peel's secretary by mistake. In acquitting M'Naghten, the court ruled that defendants are legally insane and, therefore, not criminally responsible if, as a result of a "disease of the mind" and consequent impairment of reason, they either (1) did not know what they were doing or (2) did not know that what they were doing was wrong (hence, the commonly heard question "Did the defendant know right from wrong?") Thus, while the irresistible-impulse test stresses the whole matter of self-control, the M'Naghten test singles out one aspect of self-control, cognition, and makes the test of insanity rest on that.

Critics of this test (e.g., Bromberg, 1965; Weihofen, 1957) argue that cognitive activity cannot be separated from emotion or from any other mental activity; the mind is an integrated whole, not a collection of separate compartments. Legal scholars have responded that, while the mind may be integrated, it is not an undifferentiated blob; almost all psychological theories recognize the existence of distinguishable mental processes. Furthermore, the M'Naghten rule has the virtue of limiting the insanity defense to those who are perceived by the public as truly insane. All of us have difficulty, in varying degrees, with resisting impulses, but very few of us commit misdeeds because we do not know what we are doing or because we do not know that they are wrong. By reserving the insanity defense for people who are in this extreme situation and who, therefore, cannot reasonably be expected to comply with the law, the M'Naghten test, in the eyes of some legal scholars (e.g., Livermore & Meehl, 1967), serves the purpose of excusing the truly excusable and preserving the moral authority of the law.

A third test, known as the Durham test, states that the defendant is not criminally responsible "if his unlawful act was the product of mental disease or mental defect." As is obvious from the wording, this test forces the jury to rely on expert testimony, for how is a jury of ordinary citizens to determine whether the defendant has a mental disease or defect? But in American courts people are supposed to be tried by their peers, not by the mental health profession. Actually, the rules preceding the Durham test also involve this problem. How can a jury decide whether the defendant was under the sway of an irresistible impulse or knew right from wrong? But the Durham test, because of its wording, more or less *requires* expert judgment, and for this reason it has been replaced in most jurisdictions that had adopted it (Melton, Petrila, Poythress, et al., 1997).

The most recent formulation of the insanity defense is that adopted by the American Law Institute (ALI) in its Model Penal Code of 1962:

1. A person is not responsible for criminal conduct if at the time of such conduct as a result of mental disease or defect he lacks substantial capacity either to appreciate the criminality of his conduct or to conform his conduct to the requirements of law.

2. As used in the Article [of the code], the terms "mental disease or defect" do not include an abnormality manifested only by repeated criminal or otherwise antisocial conduct (sec. 4.01).

Many legal scholars feel that the ALI test is the best that can be hoped for. To a degree, it incorporates the irresistible-impulse criterion ("conform his conduct to the requirements of law") and the M'Naghten criterion ("appreciate the criminality of his conduct") and the Durham criterion ("as a result of mental disease or defect"). At the same time, however, it states these criteria in broader terms and adds the phrase "substantial capacity." The result is a test that *can* be applied without expert knowledge. In effect, the ALI rule asks the jury, "Can the defendant be justly blamed for his or her misbehavior?" In the opinion of many legal scholars, this is the question that should be asked— and of the jury, not of the mental health profession. The ALI test has been adopted by many states. Other states are still using the M'Naghten test, with or without a supplemental irresistible-impulse test. Only New Hampshire uses the Durham test. In 1984, Congress

adopted an insanity test for federal courts that is similar to the M'Naghten test (Steadman, McGreevy, Morrissey, et al., 1993).

After all this discussion, it must be added that the verbal formula used to define legal insanity may have little practical significance. While some studies have shown that the definition may affect the verdict (Melton, Petrila, Poythress, et al., 1997), other research indicates that the verdict will often be the same under any of the insanity test now in use (Steadman, McGreevy, Morrisey, et al., 1993).

A New Verdict—Guilty but Mentally Ill Several scholars have expressed concern that, as the concept of mental illness has expanded from encompassing only the grossly psychotic to embracing what is potentially a very substantial fraction of the population, many defendants may escape responsibility for their crimes. This situation may weaken the deterrent effect of criminal law (Wilson, 1997). The deterrent effect is not compromised when an obviously psychotic person is found not guilty by reason of insanity, but, when someone who appears to be "sane" is found to lack criminal responsibility, the authority of criminal law may seem to be diminished. (See the box on page 527.) A case often cited in this regard is that of John Hinckley, who in 1982 was acquitted on grounds of insanity after he tried to assassinate President Ronald Reagan. Hinckley claimed that he did this in order to "gain [the] love and respect" of movie actress Jodie Foster, whom he had never met.

Hinckley's trial focused not on whether he had committed the assassination attempt—clearly, he had—but on his sanity at the time. The jury was presented with vast amounts of conflicting evidence from expert witnesses called by both sides. The defense witnesses portrayed Hinckley as driven by a delusion of achieving a "magical union" with Jodie Foster and as suffering from a severe form of schizophrenia, as well as numerous other mental problems. The psychiatrists called by the prosecution testified that Hinckley made a conscious choice to shoot Reagan and had no "compelling drive" to do so. They depicted Hinckley as selfish and manipulative and suffering from only some minor personality disorders.

The jury's verdict of not guilty by reason of insanity stunned the courtroom, including the judge and Hinckley himself, who had fully expected conviction. Law professor Charles Nesson (1982) expressed the feelings of many when he wrote, "For anyone who experiences life as a struggle to act responsibly in the face of various temptations to let go, the Hinckley verdict is demoralizing, an example of someone who let himself go and who has been exonerated because of it" (p. A19).

Evolution, Misfortune, and Criminal Responsibility

Wania-6672 was the name given to a neurologically impaired young macaque monkey observed by primatologists among a group of macaques in an enclosed setting in Texas in 1972. He would stumble around, bumping into, among other things, bushes and cacti. Because of his obvious impairment, other monkeys in effect exempted him from the monkey version of the criminal law. Older, stronger monkeys that routinely responded aggressively to other monkeys that bumped into them responded passively when Wania-6672 collided with them. It was as if they knew it wasn't his fault, so there was no point in punishing him (de Waal, 1996). That such a phenomenon can be observed in monkeys suggests that the moral intuitions that underlie the insanity defense may have deep roots in our evolutionary history.

To the extent that such evolutionary origins affect the content of our moral intuitions, they may apply to current problems in mental health law. Because the effectiveness of the criminal law is dependent on its congruence with our moral intuitions (Robinson & Darley, 1997)—in other words, dependent on its making moral sense to people—those who are not conspicuously crazy may undermine the effectiveness of the criminal law.

To sort out those whose condition *should* excuse them from criminal responsibility, psychologist Paul E. Meehl (1991) has proposed that criminal statutes be revised to include a list of specific psychiatric diagnoses that would have to be established in order for an insanity defense to succeed. These include major affective disorders, paranoid and catatonic schizophrenia, coarse brain syndrome, and psychomotor epilepsy. Meehl explains:

> Nothing else goes so you can't plead not guilty by reason of mental illness on the grounds that you had a battle-ax mother or a pick-pocket uncle or a poverty-stricken childhood or whatever. . . .
>
> The point is that mere intensity of motivation, of whatever character and origin, is not an excuse for predatory conduct. (p. 488)

In other words, Meehl would require that an insanity acquittee be as conspicuously impaired in our eyes as Wania-6672 was in the eyes of his fellow monkeys.

This dispute is not limited to the insanity defense. Various "abuse excuse" defenses are increasingly offered either to reduce the severity of the crime charged (e.g., from murder to manslaughter) or to justify a more lenient sentence for the crime. The response of the courts has been mixed. Some courts have given these defenses a sympathetic hearing; others have been far more skeptical (Wilson, 1997).

A recent decision by the United States Court of Appeals for the Seventh Circuit illustrates the more skeptical response. A defendant named Doss Pullen had been convicted of armed robbery and sentenced to over 15 years in prison. He appealed his sentence on the ground that the maltreatment he had suffered as a child warranted a more lenient sentence. Although the court did not deny that he had suffered serious abuse, it did not believe that the abuse should affect the length of his sentence:

> The defendant's father was a drunkard and a gambler. He beat his wife and children and threatened them with guns and knives. When the defendant was five years old, his father abused him sexually over a period of several months. His parents divorced and the defendant lived with his mother, but when he was 15, and drinking, smoking marijuana, and having scrapes with the law, his mother could no longer control him and the juvenile court sent him to live with his father. The two would go out drinking together and once after a bout of drinking, his father raped him. He ran away. His troubles with the law escalated. At the age of nineteen, he committed his first bank robbery. . . .
>
> A psychologist evaluated the defendant and concluded that as a result of the history of abuse that we have sketched, the defendant "has a need to punish himself, hence his illegal acts and the relative ease with which he is caught." The psychologist also found that the defendant suffers from "schizoid disorder" and "borderline personality disorder," and that these conditions too are both "clinically linked to the history of abusive treatment by his father" and causative of his criminal activity because they "reduce impulse and behavioral controls" and impair "his ability to think and act clearly."
>
> In emphasizing the causal history of Pullen's crimes, his lawyer overlooks the gap between cause and responsibility. The existence of the one does not cancel the other. The male violent-crime rate is roughly ten times the female. . . . This means that being male is a predisposing characteristic to violent crime; it is a "cause" of such crime in the same sense in which Pullen's history of being abused as a child may be a cause of his violent crimes. Would anyone argue that men are therefore less responsible for their violent crimes than women and so should be punished less severely? (*United States v. Pullen*, 1996, pp. 369–370, 372)

This concern has led to consideration of a new verdict of "guilty but mentally ill" to serve as an intermediate between "guilty" and "not guilty by reason of insanity." It would be appropriate in cases in which the defendant knew what he or she was doing and that it was wrong but, nonetheless, had some form of mental illness. A defendant convicted by this verdict would serve time within the penal system but would also receive psychological treatment. Michigan was the first state to adopt the "guilty but mentally ill" verdict (in 1975). About a dozen states have since followed suit. It appears, however, that this new

The successful use of the insanity defense by John W. Hinckley, Jr., following his attempt to assassinate President Ronald Reagan set off a storm of controversy. The uproar obscured the fact that very few defendants are found not guilty by reason of insanity.

verdict has not reduced the number of insanity acquittals (Steadman, McGreevy, Morrissey, et al., 1993). Furthermore, some legal scholars find the "guilty but mentally ill" verdict senseless and have called for its repeal. In the words of one expert, "The mental illness component of the verdict adds nothing to a simple guilty verdict except a diagnosis of the defendant at the time of the crime. It's no different than rendering a verdict of guilty, but suffering from influenza" (Morse, 1997, p. A19).

Procedural Aspects of the Insanity Defense   The John Hinckley case stirred interest in two procedural aspects of the insanity defense. First, whose responsibility is it to prove the defendant's insanity (or sanity)? Second, if the defendant is acquitted, how do we determine whether he or she should be committed to a mental hospital or released back into the community?

As a general rule, the prosecution must prove beyond a reasonable doubt all elements of a criminal offense—including both the physical act and the requisite mental state, which in a murder case is the intent to kill (LaFave & Scott, 1972). When defendants raise the insanity defense, must they prove that they were insane at the time of the crime, or must the prosecution instead prove that they were sane?

Before the *Hinckley* verdict, a majority of states placed the burden on the prosecution to prove sanity, and prove it beyond a reasonable doubt, once the defense had presented evidence, such as psychiatric testimony, suggesting insanity. This is the rule under which Hinckley was tried. But, in 1984, partly because of the outcome of that case, the fed-

eral rules were changed to place the burden of proving insanity on the defendant, and about three-quarters of the states now do so as well. This shift has substantially reduced the number of insanity acquittals, which are now more likely to involve people with serious mental illnesses, such as schizophrenia or major mood disorders (Steadman, McGreevy, Morrissey, et al., 1993).

What is to be done with defendants who are acquitted by reason of insanity? Prior to the 1970s, they were usually subjected to long-term confinement in a mental hospital, often a high-security hospital that seemed much like a prison. Then, in the 1970s, the field of mental health law was swept by a wave of reform, drawing on the antiestablishment politics of the 1960s. Law after law was changed, almost always in the direction of protecting civil rights, and this included laws governing defendants acquitted on the grounds of insanity. In many states, such acquittals were no longer automatically followed by commitment. The person might be placed briefly in a mental health facility for evaluation, but prolonged hospitalization was permitted only under standards of ordinary civil commitment ("Commitment Following," 1981). As we will see later, these standards typically require a finding that the person is *currently* mentally ill and dangerous. Because a great deal of time may have elapsed between the commission of the offense and the acquittal, the defendant's mental condition may have changed. Thus, under the new rules of the 1970s, it was entirely possible that a defendant might not meet commitment criteria at the postacquittal commitment hearing.

This possibility alarmed many people, including a majority of U.S. Supreme Court justices, and in *Jones v. United States* (1983) the court ruled that it is permissible to commit insanity acquittees automatically. The acquittees could then be hospitalized until they proved themselves either no longer mentally ill or no longer dangerous. Further, the court ruled that they could be hospitalized for longer than they could have been imprisoned, had they been convicted. The year of this decision is significant: 1983, a year after the *Hinckley* verdict. In the wake of the Hinckley trial, a majority of states also tightened up postacquittal procedures so as to make release more difficult (Steadman, McGreevy, Morrissey, et al., 1993).

Criticism of the Insanity Defense. In the abstract, it seems only fair to provide an insanity defense for people who violate the law as a result of psychological disturbance. In reality, however, the insanity defense poses thorny problems, both practical and moral.

For one thing, how can a jury accurately determine whether the case conforms to the court's definition of insanity? To rule on a person's sanity is to arrive at a subjective judgment that is extremely difficult to make. Furthermore, the jury must make that judgment *retrospectively*. The question is not the defendant's current mental state, which the jury might at least guess at by observing his or her courtroom behavior, but the defendant's mental state at the time of the crime.

In most cases, the jury must rely on testimony of psychological professionals, but this is no solution. Psychiatrists and psychologists have as much difficulty making retrospective diagnoses as other people do. They often produce diametrically opposed diagnoses, thus producing a "battle of the shrinks" in the courtroom (Meehl, 1991). Often, even experts who are called by the same side contradict one another. And, as we have already mentioned, the opinions of expert witnesses are at best only partially relevant in criminal proceedings. The court is there not to make a scientific judgment but to make a legal judgment— whether the defendant should be held legally responsible for the crime. This is a judgment that only the jury, not the mental health profession, is empowered to make. But, because the jury has so little concrete information to go on, that judgment may be wrong.

A second criticism of the insanity defense, based on a totally different point of view, is that of Thomas Szasz (1963). According to Szasz, the problem with the insanity defense is not that it is difficult for the jury to evaluate but that the special circumstance that it attempts to deal with—insanity—does not exist. As we saw in Chapter 1, Szasz claims that mental illness is a myth perpetuated by an arrogant profession.

Lyle (left) *and Erik Menendez enter a courtroom soon after their arrest for killing their parents in 1989. Expert psychological witnesses gave contradictory testimony at their trial, some asserting that the brothers had committed cold-blooded murder to gain a sizable inheritance, others that they had acted in self-defense against their father's abuse. Their first trial ended in a hung jury, but the brothers were convicted of first-degree murder when retried.*

In his opinion, all behavior is of a purposeful and, therefore, responsible nature. If people act in socially offensive or hostile ways, they do so because they *mean* to. To label them "insane" is to deny their behavior any meaning and thus, by extension, to deny that there is any conflict between the individual and society. Szasz proposes that the courts get out of the business of judging people on their intentions and judge them instead on their behavior. If a person has committed hostile and dangerous acts, Szasz (1977) argues, "he should be punished, not treated—in jail, not in a hospital" (p. 135).

Szasz's stance brings us to the third major criticism of the insanity defense: that those who successfully plead it sometimes end up in a worse situation than if they had been convicted of their crimes. As we pointed out earlier, people who are found not guilty by reason of insanity are usually not set free, like others who are acquitted of crimes. Rather, they are often committed to mental hospitals and are kept there until such time as experts testify that they are no longer dangerous. Such testimony is usually long in coming; indeed, it may never come. Thus, while people convicted of crimes are deprived of their liberty for a specific period of time—after which, by law, they are free—many people acquitted by reason of insanity are given **indeterminate sentences,** sentences with no limit. They could languish for the rest of their lives in a mental hospital before a staff member decides that they are no longer dangerous.

These considerations, among others, have led to widespread criticism of the insanity defense, and not just by extremists such as Szasz. Three states—Idaho, Montana, and Utah—actually abolished the insanity defense in the early 1980s. It remains to be seen if the courts will decide that such a defense is, in fact, constitutionally required. It should be added that, statistically speaking, the insanity defense is much less important than other questions linking law and psychology. Because it is sometimes involved in especially notorious cases, such as those of Bobbitt and Hinckley, and because it touches on the elemental question of free will, the insanity defense receives a great deal of public attention, yet it is invoked in less than 1 percent of felony cases, and it is successful in less than one-quarter of the cases in which it is raised (Melton, Petrila, Poythress, et al., 1997).

Competency to Stand Trial

The number of people confined in mental hospitals as a result of successful insanity pleas is small compared with the number who are there because they are judged mentally unfit even to be tried (American Bar Association, 1989). In most states, defendants, in order to stand trial, must understand the nature of the proceedings against them and must be able to assist counsel in their own defense. When a defendant does not meet these requirements, the trial is delayed, and the person is sent to a mental health facility in hope of restoring competency. As with the insanity defense, the purpose is to protect the defendant and at the same time to preserve the court's reputation for justice. The courts would not inspire public trust if they tried people who were obviously out of touch with reality.

Incompetency to stand trial must not be confused with legal insanity. The insanity defense has to do with the defendant's mental state *at the time of the crime;* competency to stand trial has to do with the defendant's mental state *at the time of the trial.* Furthermore, while the insanity defense concerns moral responsibility for crime, competency to stand trial is merely a question of ability to understand the charges

and to confer fairly reasonably with one's attorney. Thus, a person who is judged competent to stand trial can still successfully assert an insanity defense. Even people diagnosed as psychotic may be competent to stand trial. Many are lucid enough to meet the competency requirements (Melton, Petrila, Poythress, et al., 1997).

Incompetency, then, is a limited concept. The rule is often applied in a loose fashion, however. Both prosecutors and defense attorneys have been accused of abusing the competency issue (American Bar Association, 1989). Prosecutors who fear that their cases are too weak can use it to keep the defendant locked up, thus accomplishing the same purpose that would be gained by a conviction. On the other hand, defense attorneys may use the competency proceedings in order to delay the trial, either in the hope that some of the prosecutor's witnesses may become unavailable to testify or simply in order to convince the defendant that they are doing all they can.

For the defendants, the consequences used to be grave. Once ruled incompetent, they were often denied bail; cut off from their jobs, friends, family, and other social supports; and confined in a hospital for the criminally insane, when in fact they might never have committed the crimes they were charged with. They often remained in the hospital for years, because there was often no means of restoring their competency (Morris & Meloy, 1993). However, this particular abuse was ruled unconstitutional by the U.S. Supreme Court in the case of *Jackson v. Indiana* (1972). The defendant in this case was a mentally retarded deaf-mute who had been charged with robbery. Judged incompetent to stand trial, he was being held in a state hospital indefinitely, because there was no way to render him competent to stand trial. The court ruled that, when a person is detained solely on the grounds of incompetency to stand trial, the detention can last only as long as it takes to determine whether the defendant is likely to become competent to stand trial in the foreseeable future. If the likelihood is poor or nil, the defendant must be either released or committed to an institution according to the state's ordinary civil commitment procedures. (Civil commitment will be discussed later.)

One controversy surrounding the competency issue has to do with antipsychotic drugs. If defendants fulfill the competency requirements only when under the influence of antipsychotic drugs, are they competent to stand trial? On the one hand, it seems almost unfair not to try such patients if the drugs render them lucid enough to be tried. On the other hand, these drugs, as we have seen, often render people groggy and passive—an inappropriate state in which to attend one's own trial. Furthermore, antipsychotic medication might well affect the defendant's chances of successfully pleading the insanity defense. The "crazier" the defendant seems during the trial, the more likely it is that the jury will accept the insanity plea. But whatever crazy behavior the defendant normally exhibits may well be reduced by the medication. Should we then allow defendants to undergo trial without medication, so that the jury can see them in their "true" state? But, even if this were the most direct route to justice (which is questionable), many defendants could not be tried, because they would not be competent to stand trial without the medication. This catch-22 has not yet been fully resolved, but in *Riggins v. Nevada* (1992) the Supreme Court ruled that people being tried for a crime could not be forced to take psychotropic (mind-affecting) medication unless the trial court specifically found this necessary to a fair trial.

Civil Commitment

Criminal commitment accounts for only a small percentage of those committed involuntarily to mental hospitals. The remainder are there as a result of **civil commitment.** That is, they have been committed not because they were charged with a crime but because the state decided that they were disturbed enough to require hospitalization. About 55 percent of admissions to public mental hospitals are involuntary (Brakel, 1985). Because it does not involve interesting crimes, civil commitment receives far less public attention than criminal commitment, yet the legal questions it involves are equally difficult and directly affect far more people.

Procedures for Commitment

The U.S. Constitution provides that the government may not deprive a person of life, liberty, or property without "due process of law." Involuntary commitment to a mental hospital is clearly a deprivation of liberty. What in the way of "due process," or legal procedures, is required before a person may be subjected to involuntary commitment? This is a question that the Supreme Court has not fully considered. Many lower courts have addressed it, but the answers they have given vary from jurisdiction to jurisdiction.

A useful way to approach the problem is to consider the rights that a defendant has in a criminal trial and then to ask whether a person faced with the possibility of involuntary civil commitment should have the same rights. Among other things, the following are guaranteed to people accused of serious crimes: (1) a jury trial, (2) the assistance of counsel, (3) a

right not to be compelled to incriminate themselves, and (4) the requirement that guilt be proved "beyond a reasonable doubt." Should these rights also apply to involuntary civil commitment?

The Right to a Jury Trial Today, states typically require a formal judicial hearing before commitment (though the hearing may follow a brief period of emergency commitment). In 15 states, the defendant has a right to have a jury at such a hearing. Other states make no provision for a jury; the decision is rendered by the judge or a lower judicial officer.

The argument against a jury trial is that juries are expensive and time-consuming and, furthermore, that it is not in the best interests of mentally distressed people to have their psychological condition formally debated before a jury. The argument for a jury trial is that, distressed or otherwise, these people stand to lose their liberty and that, in a matter so serious, the judgment must come from the citizenry, just as in a criminal trial, for this is the best protection against oppression. (Keep in mind that many civil libertarians feel that involuntary mental patients are akin to prisoners.) However, because the Supreme Court has ruled that jury trials are not required in juvenile cases, it is unlikely that the court will require them in commitment cases (Brakel, 1985).

The Right to the Assistance of Counsel A central feature of the wave of reform in mental health law in the 1970s was the provision of court-appointed lawyers for people faced with involuntary-commitment proceedings. Prior to the 1970s, commitments were often made on physicians' certifications alone, with little due process (Turkheimer & Parry, 1992). Now, in almost all jurisdictions, people facing involuntary-commitment proceedings are provided with lawyers to protect their rights.

At the same time, there is considerable disagreement about what lawyers are supposed to do for their clients at such hearings (Leavitt & Maykuth, 1989). In criminal trials, defense attorneys have a clear role: they are the adversaries of the prosecutor, and they are supposed to do everything they legally can to get their clients acquitted. It is not their job to worry about the legal question of the defendant's guilt or innocence. Should lawyers at commitment hearings behave in the same way—that is, as advocates for their clients' wishes? Or should they act, instead, as "guardians," pursuing their clients' best interests as they, the lawyers, see them? If we assume that some people are too disturbed to know what their best interests are, then lawyers who take the advocate role run the risk of acting against their clients' best interests. If, on the other hand, they take the guardian role, they may well act in direct opposition to the clients' wishes, deferring instead to the judgment of expert witnesses who claim hospitalization is necessary. Apparently, most lawyers at commitment hearings do precisely that (Turkheimer & Parry, 1992)—a practice that is bitterly criticized by those who feel that clients should be allowed to decide what their best interests are.

The Right Against Self-Incrimination Under the Fifth Amendment to the U.S. Constitution, defendants at criminal trials have the right to remain silent, and their silence may not be used against them. Should the same rule apply at a commitment hearing? Some people would say yes, that people threatened with commitment should have the same protections as those threatened with imprisonment, for they have as much, if not more, to lose. Others would say that, because silence may be a symptom of mental disturbance, it is inappropriate to exclude it from the evidence. Should psychiatrists, for example, be barred from testifying that their diagnosis of psychotic depression is based in part on the patient's muteness? However others decide this question, it seems certain that the Supreme Court would not apply Fifth Amendment rights to civil commitment (Melton, Petrila, Poythress, et al., 1997).

The Standard of Proof Finally, in a criminal trial, a jury can convict only if the prosecution has proved guilt "beyond a reasonable doubt." The degree of certainty is called the **standard of proof.** The *beyond-a-reasonable-doubt* standard is a very high one—perhaps a 90 to 95 percent certainty. Should this requirement also apply to commitment hearings? There are other possibilities. In most civil proceedings (e.g., lawsuits), the standard of proof is the *preponderance of evidence*—in other words, "more likely than not," or at least 51 percent certainty (Stone, 1975). A third possibility is the far lower standard of proof used in medical diagnosis, in which any evidence whatsoever—theoretically, even a 5 to 10 percent certainty—may lead to diagnosis of illness. Which of these standards should apply in the case of involuntary commitment?

To answer this question, we must consider the seriousness of two possible errors: (1) a **false positive,** or an unjustified commitment, and (2) a **false negative,** or a failure to commit when commitment is justified and necessary.* In a criminal trial, a false positive—that is,

---

*These terms are taken from the medical diagnostic vocabulary. A *false positive* is an incorrect diagnosis of illness; a *true positive,* a correct diagnosis of illness; a *false negative,* an incorrect diagnosis of no illness; a *true negative,* a correct diagnosis of no illness.

the conviction of an innocent person—is considered a far more serious error than a false negative—that is, the acquittal of a guilty person. In the famous words of eighteenth-century English jurist William Blackstone, "It is better that ten guilty persons escape than one innocent suffer," hence the extremely high standard of proof in criminal trials: "When in doubt, acquit."

In a civil proceeding, a false positive (the complainant's unjustifiably winning the lawsuit) is considered approximately as serious as a false negative (the complainant's unjustifiably losing the lawsuit). Therefore, the standard of proof falls in the middle: 51 percent certainty. In medical diagnosis, on the other hand, a false positive (a false diagnosis of illness) is considered a negligible error, compared with the extremely serious mistake of a false negative (a false diagnosis of no illness). Imagine, for example, that a person is being tested for cancer and the physician finds only a few slightly suspicious cell changes. If the diagnosis is a false positive, this fact will emerge in the course of further testing, and the diagnosis will be changed, with no harm done except for the patient's suffering a few nights of worry. But a false-negative diagnosis may well eliminate the chance of the cancer's being treated at an early and perhaps curable stage. In other words, a great deal of harm will have been done, hence the extremely low standard of proof in medicine: "When in doubt, diagnose illness."

Which standard we should apply at a commitment hearing depends on what we see as the purpose of commitment. Generally, the law recognizes two justifications for involuntary commitment: the good of the patient and the good of society. At first glance, it would seem that, when commitment is undertaken for the good of society (i.e., to protect people from harm by the patient), the criminal standard of proof should be used because the issue in both cases is the same: public safety versus individual liberty. By the same token, it would seem that, when commitment is sought for the good of the patient (e.g., so that he or she can be treated), the medical standard of proof should be applied.

Critics of civil commitment (e.g., Ennis & Emery, 1978) argue, however, that the medical standard should never be used, because commitment cases, no matter what their stated purpose, are not analogous to medical diagnosis. According to these writers, so-called good-of-the-patient commitments are often undertaken more for the sake of others—usually, the patient's family—than for the sake of the patient. Moreover, unlike medical diagnosis, a diagnosis to commit cannot be disproved, deprives the patient of liberty, stigmatizes the patient, and does not necessarily lead to treatment. For these reasons, among others, critics of commitment insist that, no matter what the

Advances in DNA testing have made possible the correction of a number of "false positives"—the conviction and imprisonment of innocent persons. Kerry Kotler (center, flanked by his attorneys) served eleven years in prison for rape before a comparison of the DNA in his blood with the DNA in a sample of semen used as evidence in his trial showed that he could not have committed the crime.

reason for commitment, the beyond-a-reasonable-doubt standard should be used. It should be added that, in general, civil libertarians are extremely skeptical of procedures that are said to be "for the good of the patient." Their skepticism extends beyond the lowered standard of proof to the nonjury hearing, the "guardian" lawyer, and the lack of protection against self-incrimination. In their opinion, an expressed attitude of concern for patients assumes that they are "guilty" and leads directly to a violation of their civil rights. If these people are threatened with loss of liberty as a result of socially offensive behavior, then they are in the same position as alleged criminals and should be given the same rights.

Unlike the other three procedural questions we have discussed, the standard of proof at commitment hearings *has* been dealt with by the Supreme Court. In the case of *Addington v. Texas* (1979), the defendant was a man whose mother had filed a petition to have him committed. The commitment was approved by a Texas court according to the preponderance-of-evidence standard. The defendant then appealed the decision, arguing that the need for hospitalization should be proved "beyond a reasonable doubt." The Supreme Court quickly rejected the preponderance-of-evidence standard (and by implication any less stringent standard) because of the liberty interest at stake, yet the court also rejected the criminal beyond-a-reasonable-doubt standard, for several reasons. The court observed that, unlike the wrongfully convicted criminal defendant, who would languish in prison until his or her sentence had been served, the wrongfully civilly committed person would probably

be discharged, as doctors would recognize that hospitalization was unwarranted. Thus, the false positive is less serious in the civil context than in the criminal context because of the greater opportunity to correct the error. The consequences of a false-negative error were also seen as different in the two contexts. A truly guilty criminal defendant benefits from a wrongful acquittal, whereas a truly mentally ill person who is not ordered to get treatment suffers from the absence of the needed treatment.

The court, thus, used some of the notions underlying the medical decision rule as grounds for rejecting the beyond-a-reasonable-doubt standard. The Court adopted an intermediate standard of proof, called *clear and convincing evidence,* as the proper standard for commitment hearings. It corresponds to approximately "75 percent sure"—higher than the ordinary civil standard but lower than the criminal one. This decision is, to some extent, a victory for the proponents of the criminal standard in that it at least rules out the civil and medical standards and moves the required degree of certainty that much closer to the criminal standard. But it remains to be seen how jurors and judicial officers will interpret this standard of proof.

Standards for Commitment

So far, we have dealt only with the procedures for commitment; we must now consider the *standards* for commitment. What must be proved in order to justify involuntary commitment?

Until the early 1970s, mental illness alone, or mental illness and "need for treatment," were sufficient grounds for involuntary commitment in many states. Then came the reform movement of the 1970s. Not just the general public but also judges and legislators read Szasz's *Myth of Mental Illness* (1961), as well as Erving Goffman's *Asylums* (1961), which were critical of the concept of mental illness and, above all, of involuntary hospitalization. As a result, there was a trend throughout the 1970s toward changing laws in such a way as to require evidence not just of mental illness but also of dangerousness to self and others as grounds for involuntary commitment (La Fond & Durham, 1992; McHugh, 1992).

The Definition of Dangerousness How do we define dangerousness? Should it be confined to the threat of physical harm to oneself or others? What about emotional harm, such as schizophrenic parents may inflict on their children? What about economic harm, such as people in a manic episode may bring down upon their families by spending their life savings on new Cadillacs? What about harm to property? Various courts and legislatures have taken different positions on this matter, but some states consider a threat of harm to property sufficient for commitment (La Fond & Durham, 1992).

The Determination of Dangerousness Whatever the definition of *dangerousness*, determining it is a difficult matter. To say that someone is dangerous is to predict future behavior. The rarer an event, the harder it is to predict accurately. Hence, if *dangerousness* is defined as homicide or suicide, both of which are rare events, the prediction of dangerousness inevitably involves many unjustified commitments as well as justified ones. Consider, for example, the following hypothetical case:

> A man with classic paranoia exhibits in a clinical interview a fixed belief that his wife is attempting to poison him. He calmly states that on release he will be forced to kill her in self-defense. The experts agree that his condition is untreatable. Assume that statistical data indicate an eighty percent probability that homicide will occur. (Livermore, Malmquist, & Meehl, 1968).

What should the court do? Instinctively, it would seem correct to "play it safe" and commit the patient. (See the box on page 535.) However, as the authors of this case point out, even accepting an 80 percent probability of homicide as sufficient to commit means committing 20 nonhomicidal people for every 80 homicidal ones.

Perhaps society could accept such a ratio. But the fact is that an 80 percent probability is unrealistically high. Despite public alarm over violence, murder is statistically rare: in any year, only 1 person in 10,000

in the United States commits homicide (Department of Justice, 1993), and mental patients without arrest records are no more likely than the general public to commit murder (Monahan, 1981). Further, very few patients threatened with commitment will calmly state in a clinical interview that they intend to commit murder upon release. In many cases, for example, the evidence for possible future homicide is simply a report from a family member that in the past the patient has threatened homicide, perhaps in a moment of extreme anger. In such a case, the probability of homicide would be very low—probably less than 1 percent. Is this a ratio that society can accept? If in criminal law it is better that 10 guilty people go free than that 1 innocent person suffer, how can we say that in cases of civil commitment it is better for 99 harmless people to be locked up than for 1 dangerous person to go free?

In addition to the rarity of dangerous behavior, several other factors tend to make predictions of dangerousness highly speculative (Melton, Petrila, Poythress, et al., 1997). These factors include

1. *Variability in the legal definition.* From state to state, and sometimes from judge to judge, the definition of *dangerousness* may change, so the clinician may be aiming at a moving target.

2. *Complexity of the literature.* The research literature on the prediction of dangerousness is both vast and of uneven quality, making it hard to identify the best methods.

3. *Judgment biases.* Clinicians sometimes rely on unproven assumptions about the relationship between particular diagnoses and the likelihood of dangerousness.

4. *Differential consequences to the predictor.* While false positives suffer in obscurity, false negatives create very bad publicity. When a person who has been spared or released from commitment kills somebody, the names of those who set him or her free are splashed all over the newspapers.

These factors encourage mental health professionals to err in the direction of overpredicting dangerousness. Do they, in fact, do so? Studies of predictions of dangerousness have yielded more false positives than false negatives (Grisso, 1991). But such studies may have limitations, for they are based on predictions from an institutional context applied to a real-world context. In most of these studies, mental health professionals were asked to predict the likelihood of dangerous behavior in patients about to be released from institutions. Because there is considerable evidence that human behavior is situation-specific, changing as we move from classroom to work to home, it is no

The Limits of Confidentiality

On October 27, 1969, a student at the University of California at Berkeley named Prosenjit Poddar killed a young woman named Tatiana Tarasoff. Two months earlier, Poddar had told his therapist that he intended to commit the crime. Although the therapist then notified the police—who detained Poddar briefly but released him upon finding him "rational"—neither Tatiana Tarasoff nor her family was informed of Poddar's threat. After the murder, the young woman's parents brought suit against the therapist and the university that employed him, charging that they should have been warned about the man's intentions. The California Supreme Court agreed, holding that "when a therapist determines ... that a patient presents a serious danger of violence to another, he incurs an obligation to use reasonable care to protect the intended victim against such danger" (*Tarasoff v. Regents of California*, 1976).

In effect, this ruling meant that psychotherapists have obligations to the society at large that override their obligations to their own patients. Traditionally, the relationship between therapist and patient has been considered privileged: information supplied by the patient is held in strict confidence by the therapist. According to this ruling, however, the therapist must divulge such information if the patient is "dangerous"; the police and the family of the threatened victim must be warned. As the court stated in its opinion, "the protective privilege ends where the public peril begins."

But where does the public peril begin? The prediction of dangerousness is an uncertain (if not impossible) task. As a dissenting opinion in this case pointed out, psychotherapists find it difficult enough to diagnose mental illness itself, without also having to predict whether a patient will or will not be dangerous at some time in the future.

The *Tarasoff* decision was widely denounced by mental health professionals. Psychiatrist Alan Stone (1976), for example, wrote that "the imposition of a duty to protect, which may take the form of a duty to warn threatened third parties, will imperil the therapeutic alliance and destroy the patient's expectation of confidentiality, thereby thwarting effective treatment and ultimately reducing the public safety" (p. 368). Under circumstances of reduced confidentiality, a patient who feels a compulsion to do violence might well be reluctant to confide it to a therapist. Potentially dangerous patients might be unwilling to seek therapy at all, for fear that the police would ultimately deal with them. On the other side, therapists, to avoid lawsuits, would be encouraged to report all threats of violence to potential victims and to the police—or even to seek the commitment of "dangerous" patients to avoid possible harm to others and to themselves.

In fact, the impact of the *Tarasoff* decision has not been noticeably negative (Appelbaum, 1994). According to surveys of psychotherapists, it has not seriously affected the way they handle threats, for they were accustomed to taking some protective measures already, simply on ethical grounds (Gouelber, Bowers, & Blitch, 1985). As law professor David Wexler (1981) has pointed out, *Tarasoff* could even have a positive impact on treatment. Because 80 to 90 percent of people threatened by patients in therapy are family members or lovers (MacDonald, 1967), the prospective victim could be encouraged to participate in family or couple therapy with the patient. Direct discussion of the patient's anger and the potential victim's role in precipitating violence might serve to reduce the likelihood of such violence. In any event, the need to breach confidentiality sometimes in order to protect third parties is now so widely accepted that the Supreme Court acknowledged it without discussion in a recent decision establishing psychotherapist-patient privilege in federal courts (*Jaffee v. Redmond*, 1996).

---

surprise that predictions of real-world behavior based on institutional behavior have turned out to have poor validity (Monahan & Steadman, 1994).

Furthermore, this is not actually the kind of prediction that is made at commitment hearings. At such hearings, mental health professionals are called upon to predict real-world behavior on the basis of reports of the patient's prior real-world behavior and of interviews with the patient. But we have little means of determining the validity of such predictions. It is not feasible to have mental health professionals evaluate the dangerousness of a large number of people threatened with commitment and then release all those people and keep track of them to find out whether the predictions have come true. The knowledge to be gained from such an experiment would not justify the hazard to society.

Research has provided clear evidence that there is a connection between mental illness and dangerousness: mental patients experiencing psychotic symptoms commit violent acts at a rate several times higher than that of the general population. But this higher risk exists only during the presence of psychotic symptoms, and in any event it is modest compared with other risk factors such as drug or alcohol abuse (Monahan, 1992). Violent acts associated with mental illness clearly account for only a tiny portion of the violence in our society. Accordingly, some experts seriously question the wisdom of tying commitment criteria to predictions of dangerousness.

The "Thank-You" Proposition   What, then, *should* the courts use as a basis for commitment decisions? In place of dangerousness, Stone (1975) has offered the "thank-you" proposition. If a person is suffering from mental illness, if a treatment is available to relieve that illness, and if the patient refuses treatment on grossly irrational grounds (e.g., "Don't come near me—I'm radioactive"), then the involuntary commitment for the sake of providing that treatment is justified. After the treatment is provided, the patient will be grateful that his or her wishes were disregarded, just as children who are required to go to school are grateful, as adults, that education was forced on them. Not all involuntary patients react this way, of course, but research indicates that a large proportion ultimately agree that they needed the treatment that was forced on them (Hiday, 1996). Furthermore, the thank-you proposition at least has the virtue of stressing the patient's welfare—a matter that is not prominently featured in the dangerousness rule. Critics of involuntary commitment would respond that many wrongs have been inflicted on patients because of someone's judgment of what is in the patient's best interest. A version of Stone's proposition was adopted by the American Psychiatric Association in its model commitment law in 1983 (Stromberg & Stone, 1983).

Expert Testimony in Civil Commitment   Whatever the standard for involuntary commitment—whether dangerousness or the expectation of gratitude—expert testimony will continue to be called for. As we saw earlier, many legal scholars feel that criminal courts rely too much on the opinions of mental health professionals. The same problem exists at commitment hearings. To say what mental health professionals should and should not rule upon in commitment cases requires certain fine distinctions, but they are distinctions that must be made. At commitment hearings, psychologists and psychiatrists may be asked, "How dangerous is this patient?" Though they may have only limited ability to respond to this question, it is not an improper question to put to them. However, expert witnesses are frequently asked not only how dangerous patients are but whether they are *too dangerous to be released*, and this is not a proper question for the expert witness to answer. How dangerous a person must be in order to be deprived of his or her freedom is not a mental health question but a legal and moral question. It involves weighing the person's interest in liberty against the society's interest in public safety, and any judgment about these competing interests is the business not of the mental health profession but of the court (Morse, 1978). Similarly, if involuntary commitment is sought on the basis of the thank-you proposition, the proper ques-

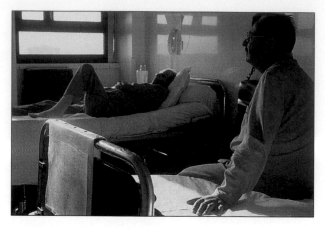

Although states have changed their standards for involuntary commitment, first tightening and then relaxing them, there has been little change in the type or number of people committed.

tion for the expert witness would be "What is the probability that the patient will later be grateful for having been treated involuntarily?" or, at a minimum, "What is the probability that the treatment will be effective?" How high that probability must be in order to justify involuntary treatment is, again, a legal and moral issue that only the courts or the legislatures can decide.

Making Commitment Easier   During the 1970s, as we saw, nearly all states tightened their standards for civil commitment. Then in the 1980s several states decided they had gone too far, and they amended their laws so as to make commitment easier. For example, threats to engage in violent conduct would not have qualified a person for commitment under a typical 1970s statute. But in the 1980s some state legislatures determined that such threats alone did justify commitment. In other states, danger to property was insufficient for commitment in the 1970s but was added to commitment criteria in the 1980s (La Fond and Durham, 1992).

Despite the controversies that commitment criteria often generate, most research reveals little long-term effect of changes in commitment criteria on the type or number of persons committed (Appelbaum, 1994). Here, as in the case with the definition of insanity in the criminal law, decisions seem to be made intuitively, with official definitions and standards having only a small effect.

The Case Against Involuntary Commitment   Just as some people have argued against the insanity plea, some argue that civil commitment itself should be abolished (Morse, 1982; Szasz, 1963). They maintain that people who commit criminal acts should be dealt with by the criminal justice system; those who do not should simply be left alone. "Disturbed" people who truly were dangerous would ultimately find themselves subject to the criminal justice system. This, the proponents argue, would be a benefit—both because of the greater procedural safeguards of the criminal process (trial by jury, etc.) and because of the fixed sentences of the criminal system (in contrast to the indeterminate "sentences" of the mental health system).

Those who want to abolish involuntary commitment are in the minority, however, and their arguments are disputable, particularly in regard to the comparison between commitment and imprisonment. Although the criminal justice system would seem to offer more protection to individual rights, the widespread practice of plea bargaining often negates these legal safeguards. Any procedural protections a defendant has may mean little in a system in which over 90 percent of all defendants plead guilty in exchange for a reduced sentence (Uviller, 1996). The distinction between fixed sentences for criminal defendants and indeterminate "sentences" for those involuntarily committed is also not completely compelling. Modern commitment statutes often put limits on involuntary commitment, though these limits are usually subject to extension through further judicial review (Brakel, 1985).

Nevertheless, the argument against involuntary commitment has gained a certain measure of support, particularly among civil libertarians. In their view, innocent people should never be confined in institutions against their will, no matter how "crazy" their behavior in some eyes or how convincingly it can be argued that they need therapy.

Patients' Rights

Until recently, people who were deprived of their liberty on the grounds that they were mentally ill and dangerous were usually deprived of most of their other civil rights as well. Once institutionalized, they were largely at the mercy of the institution, which decided for them what privileges and duties they should have and what treatments, if any, they should undergo (Appelbaum, 1994). Today there is a strong trend toward guaranteeing patients certain basic rights, especially the right to treatment, the right to refuse certain types of treatment, and the right to decent living conditions.

The Right to Treatment

For decades, the need for treatment has served as a justification, explicit or implicit, for involuntary com-

mitment. However, it was not until the 1960s that the courts suggested that involuntary mental patients had a constitutional *right* to treatment. And it was not until the following decade that this right was spelled out, by an Alabama federal court in the case of *Wyatt v. Stickney* (1972). In this case, the state of Alabama was accused of failure to provide adequate treatment for those confined in its hospitals for mentally disabled and retarded people. As it turned out, treatment was not all that these hospitals failed to provide. In the two institutions where the case originated, the wards were filthy, dark, and chaotic. The food was barely edible. (The state at that time spent less than 50 cents a day on food for each patient.) As for treatment, both of the institutions had well over a thousand patients for every psychologist. Needless to say, no treatment was being given under these conditions. As an expert witness put it, these were neither treatment facilities nor even facilities for "care" or "custody," because these words imply safekeeping. Rather, they were storage facilities.

In deciding the case against the state, the court ruled that it was a violation of due process to deny people their liberty on the grounds that they needed treatment and then to provide no treatment. The court went on to state that all Alabama mental institutions must provide (1) an individualized treatment program for each patient, (2) skilled staff in sufficient numbers to administer such treatment, and (3) a humane psychological and physical environment. This decision, then, established the right to treatment, and although it was binding only in Alabama, it has influenced mental health procedures across the country. Several states have passed revised mental health codes that incorporate most aspects of the *Wyatt* decision.

The next major case to touch upon the right-to-treatment issue was the highly publicized case of *O'Connor v. Donaldson* (1975), mentioned earlier. Kenneth Donaldson had been institutionalized involuntarily in 1957 on the petition of his father. The father claimed that Donaldson had delusions that people were poisoning his food. This testimony, along with the fact that Donaldson had been institutionalized for 3 months 13 years earlier, led the judge to conclude that Donaldson should be committed. He was sent to a Florida state mental hospital, and there he remained for 14 years. During this time, he was given no treatment that could realistically be expected to improve his "condition." He petitioned repeatedly for his release. Finally, under threat of a lawsuit, the hospital authorities discharged him. He then sued them for damages and ultimately settled for $20,000. The Supreme Court ruled that "a finding of mental illness alone cannot justify a State's locking a person up against his will and keeping him indefinitely in simple custodial confinement."

Though it has been hailed as a victory for right-to-treatment advocates, the *Donaldson* ruling, strictly speaking, has to do with the right to liberty rather than the right to treatment. (And even on the right to liberty it is somewhat vague. For example, if a person is found to be dangerous as well as mentally ill, can he or see then be subjected to simple custodial confinement?) However, it does at least lend indirect support to the view that involuntary patients have a constitutional right to treatment (Ennis & Emery, 1978).

The Supreme Court did not directly address the right-to-treatment issue until the case of *Youngberg v. Romeo* (1982). The lawsuit had been initiated on behalf of Nicholas Romeo, a resident of a state institution for the retarded in Pennsylvania. Romeo had been repeatedly injured, both by himself and by other residents. On several occasions, he was placed in physical restraints to prevent harm to himself and others. The Supreme Court held that involuntarily committed mentally retarded people—and presumably mentally ill people as well—have a constitutional right to "conditions of reasonable care and safety, reasonably non-restrictive confinement conditions, and such training as may be required by these interests." The court emphasized, however, that treatment decisions made by professionals are "presumptively valid" and that courts should not second-guess the judgment of professionals responsible for the care of patients. Thus, this decision provided a subtle shift in emphasis from absolute patient right to support for decisions made by mental health professionals.

The court did not decide whether there is a constitutional right to treatment per se, apart from any impact such treatment may have on safety and freedom from restraints. This is a question that remains to be addressed in a future Supreme Court decision.

The Right to Refuse Treatment

If mental patients have a right to treatment, do they also have a right to refuse treatment? This question was addressed in a 1990 case involving a man, Walter Harper, serving a prison sentence for robbery in the state of Washington. Harper was sometimes violent—a condition the prison doctors said was due to manic-depressive illness. At times, Harper took the antipsychotic medication the doctors prescribed for him. At other times, he refused. The prison had a policy whereby medication could be administered over a prisoner's objection if a panel consisting of a psychiatrist, a psychologist, and a prison administrator held a hearing and determined that the prisoner was likely,

without the medication, to do serious harm to himself or others as a result of mental illness. Harper claimed that this procedure was not sufficient to protect his constitutional rights in light of the recognized health risks involved in antipsychotic drugs. He therefore sued the state of Washington, arguing that medication over his objection should not be permitted unless a *judge* determined it was necessary.

Harper's suit ultimately reached the Supreme Court (*Washington v. Harper*, 1990), which upheld the constitutionality of the prison's policy on the grounds that decisions regarding the necessity of medication should be made by doctors, not judges. Thus, again, as in the Romeo case, the court affirmed the "presumptive validity" of treatment decisions made by mental health professionals.

It remains to be seen how this decision will affect lower courts, which generally take a more limited view of the authority of doctors. In any case, the right to refuse treatment is still an open question. We have already discussed one possible solution: Stone's thank-you proposition, which states that, if treatment is refused on irrational grounds, it should be administered involuntarily, for the patient's own good. However, Stone's proposition seems to assume that treatment will be effective and that it will not have harmful side effects—an unsafe assumption. As we have seen in earlier chapters, the history of psychological treatment is replete with unpleasant surprises. When iproniazid was introduced as a treatment for depression, no on knew that it caused liver damage. When chlorpromazine was put on the market, no one knew that it could cause tardive dyskinesia. (In the case of Walter Harper, the risk of tardive dyskinesia was the primary grounds for refusal of treatment.) Thus, there is no reason to assume that, when patients refuse treatment, they are refusing something that will truly work for their good. Furthermore, as civil rights advocates have pointed out, to deprive mental patients of any control over treatment is to make them vulnerable to a wide range of abuses.

But what if a patient's refusal does, in fact, seem grossly irrational? Or what if it is not grossly irrational but nevertheless infringes on the rights of others? Assume that a depressed, suicidal woman, involuntarily hospitalized, refuses electroconvulsive therapy (ECT), insisting instead on antidepressant drugs, which may not be as effective. Should the hospital assign one of its staff members to watch over the patient day and night to make sure she doesn't commit suicide? If so, what about the rights of the other patients, who are then deprived of that staff member's services? One might answer at this point that, because the woman made the choice, she should not be given special treatment; if she commits suicide, that is her decision. But surely the hospital has the duty to prevent suicides on its premises, particularly because it cannot be therapeutic for other patients to watch people kill themselves (Stone, 1975). Should the patient be coerced into receiving a particular treatment because less elaborate security measures would then be required?

State statutes and regulations regarding the right to refuse treatment vary considerably (Reisner, 1985), but the general rule is that involuntary patients may be required to undergo "routine" treatment, which may include psychotropic medication—a rule that will no doubt be strengthened by the Supreme Court's decision in the Harper case. More controversial forms of treatment, such as ECT, are usually regulated more closely, and consent from the patient or next of kin or, in some states, a court order may be required.

The Right to a Humane Environment

As we saw, the decision in the case of *Wyatt v. Stickney* affirmed not only the right to treatment but also the right to a humane environment. What the court meant by a humane environment is spelled out in the decision. The following is only a partial list of the minimum requirements:

1. Patients have a right to privacy and dignity.
2. An opportunity must exist for religious worship on a nondiscriminatory basis.
3. Dietary menus must be satisfying and nutritionally adequate to provide the recommended daily allowances. Nutritionally adequate meals must not be withheld as punishment.
4. Within multipatient sleeping rooms, screens or curtains must be provided to ensure privacy. Each patient must be furnished with a comfortable bed, a closet or locker for personal belongings, a chair, and a bedside table.
5. Toilets must be installed in separate stalls to ensure privacy. If a central bathing area is provided, showers must be separated by curtains to ensure privacy.
6. Patients have a right to wear their own clothes and to keep and use their own personal possessions.*
7. Patients have the same rights to visitation and telephone communications as patients at other public hospitals.*
8. Patients have an unrestricted right to send and receive mail.*

9. Patients have a right to regular physical exercise several times a week, as well as a right to be out of doors at regular and frequent intervals.
10. An opportunity must exist for interaction with members of the opposite sex (*Wyatt v. Stickney*, 1972, pp. 379–393). (Apropos of this last right, see the box on page 540.)

In addition, the *Wyatt* decision addressed the matter of work requirements imposed on institutionalized patients. For years, mental institutions have used patients as a supplementary work force. Throughout the country, mental patients clear tables, wash dishes, scrub floors, feed other patients, and otherwise help to maintain the institutions in which they live. For their work, they often receive some reward—perhaps a small allowance or special privileges—but this reward in no way approximates the compensation they would receive for such work in the outside world. The *Wyatt* ruling declared this practice unconstitutional. The court ruled that patients may not be required to do any work aimed at maintaining the institution in which they live. If, however, they volunteer for such work, they must be given at least minimum-wage compensation for it. The point is that involuntary patients, by definition, do no ask to be committed to an institution. If the society chooses to commit them, and then compels them to work without pay, their position is essentially that of slaves. (Indeed, this practice has been referred to as "institutional peonage.") Subsequent rulings by other courts have reaffirmed the *Wyatt* position on this matter. And, though in some states mental patients are still assigned unpaid jobs in the hospital kitchen or laundry, the practice may be on its way out.

Behavior Therapy and Patients' Rights

Almost every issue raised in this chapter is the subject of intense debate between those concerned primarily with the constitutional rights of mental patients and those concerned primarily with what they consider the "best interests" of such patients. The issue of a humane environment is no exception. On the one hand, it seems indisputable that, if a society confines people to mental hospitals against their will, either to protect itself or to help them, then the people in question should be free from forced labor and should be provided with simple amenities that the rest of us take for granted—a comfortable bed, nourishing meals, privacy in the bathroom, and so forth. To treat

*The asterisks indicate rights that may be abridged if, in the judgment of a mental health professional, their exercise is detrimental to the patient's safety or welfare.

Sex, Lives, and Mental Patients: The Hospital's Dilemma in the Age of AIDS

The federal court's decision in *Wyatt v. Stickney* (1972) stipulates that mental patients have the right to interact with the opposite gender. How far should interaction go? Before the AIDS epidemic, little was said about this question, nor was it felt that anything needed to be said. Now and then, a hospitalized patient was found to be pregnant or to have a sexually transmitted disease—usually curable—and these problems were handled somehow. But, as long as patients conducted their sex lives in private, hospitals had little incentive (or, many thought, legal or ethical justification) to prevent consensual sexual contact between patients. Especially in state mental hospitals, where patients were often shut in for years, sometimes decades, efforts to prevent sexual behavior in private have often been thought cruel.

But that was before AIDS. What now? Are hospitalized mental patients competent to accept the risk of HIV infection? If the hospital knows a particular patient to be HIV-infected, should the staff warn the other patients or just warn them about AIDS and make condoms available?

The problem with these approaches is that they assume that the patients are competent to assess the risks of HIV infection and to act appropriately if properly informed. Recent court cases strongly suggest that, for most patients, this assumption is unfounded. While there are only a few cases that explicitly address the competence of mentally disabled people to consent to sex, two recent decisions, one from Idaho and one from the state of Washington, require a high degree of understanding before the legal standard for competence is satisfied. The Idaho case, *State v. Soura* (1990), involved a mentally retarded woman (IQ of 71) living with her husband. She had sexual relations with another man, who was then charged with and convicted of rape on the grounds that the woman was not competent to consent. The Supreme Court of Idaho upheld the conviction, explaining that, even though the woman was competent to engage in marital sex, she was not competent to engage in extramarital sex, because the former is safe while the latter is dangerous. One of the dangers mentioned was AIDS. The Washington case, *State v. Summers* (1993), involved a mentally ill woman living in a group home. She, too, was found incompetent to consent to sex. The conviction of her sex partner was upheld on the grounds that, although she "had a basic understanding of the mechanical act of sexual intercourse," she did not understand its "nature and consequences," including the risk of AIDS.

The issue of sex between mental patients remains virtually undiscussed (Perlin, 1993–1994), but, in view of these decisions, it will have to be addressed soon. If mental hospitals are to maintain conditions of reasonable safety for their patients, they will probably have to take measures to limit the sexual opportunities of their HIV-positive patients.

---

them otherwise would seem improper. On the other hand, the guarantee of these rights may directly conflict with a mode of therapy that has proved most effective with long-term institutionalized patients: behavior therapy.

As we saw in earlier chapters, behavioral techniques for chronic patients tend to be contingency management techniques, the most widespread and useful being the token economy. The principle on which these techniques work is that patients are given reinforcers as rewards for socially desirable behaviors. In many cases, however, these reinforcers are the same items and activities that such decisions as *Wyatt* have affirmed are absolute rights. If patients have an absolute right to stall showers or to curtains around their beds, you cannot offer them these things in return for completing a reading program, for example. They are entitled to them no matter what they do. A related problem arises with the ban on compulsory labor. Many token economies have used institution-maintaining work as a target response that earns reinforcers. If such work must be compensated by the minimum wage, then institutions may prefer to hire nonpatient labor rather than encourage patients to acquire work skills. In sum, "patients' rights" may make contingency management within institutions more difficult (Wexler, 1981).

Another aspect of behavior therapy that is now being carefully restricted is the use of aversive techniques. As we saw in Chapter 5, aversive techniques are not widely used either inside or outside institutions, but in extreme cases therapists have used hand slapping, and even electric shock to suppress severely self-injurious behavior. Such practices are coming under increasing legal regulation. In the *Wyatt* decision, for example, the court ruled that electric shock could be used only "in extraordinary circumstances to prevent self-mutilation, leading to repeated and possibly permanent physical damage to the resident and only after alternative techniques have failed" (*Wyatt v. Stickney*, 1972, pp. 400–401).

Many behavior therapists feel that their techniques have been unfairly singled out by the courts. To some extent, this may be true. In the past decade, there have been a couple of notorious cases in which mental patients have been cruelly abused in programs masquerading as behavioral aversion therapy. In one case, mentally ill prisoners at the Iowa Security Medical Facility were punished for minor rule violations by injections of apomorphine, a drug that induces continuous vomiting for about 15 minutes (*Knecht v. Gillman*, 1973). The supposed justification for this program was that an aversion to antisocial behavior was being conditioned. However, the rule infractions that resulted in this treatment—failing to get out of bed, giving cigarettes against orders, talking, swearing, lying—are not serious antisocial actions that threaten society. What the hospital administrators were doing, in fact, was using punishment to terrify mental patients into cooperating with rules. Such procedures do not constitute behavior therapy; behaviorists find them as appalling as anyone else would. Nevertheless, because this and other abusive programs have been defended by their administrators as applications of behavioral psychology, the courts have cast an extremely suspicious eye on behavioral techniques in general.

There are other reasons for the emphasis on behavior therapy in patients' rights decisions. First, because many behavioral techniques are still relatively new, they have come under close scrutiny. (Paul & Lentz, 1977). Second, behavior therapy is highly specific and concrete. It is far easier to weigh the dangers of a procedure in which identifiable actions are taken and concrete things are given or withheld than it is to evaluate a process such as insight therapy. Finally, while much less intrusive than medication, electroconvulsive therapy, or psychosurgery, behavior therapy may cause patients distress. They may have to do things that are difficult for them, or in rare cases they may actually experience physical pain. This makes behavior therapy easier to criticize, no matter how positive its results. By contrast, psychodynamic therapy may be of no help to chronic patients, but it is hard to say how such therapy could cause them pain, either.

If in fact the courts severely limit behavior therapy for institutionalized patients, they may be working against these patients' best interests. As we saw in Chapter 13, there is good evidence that, at least with chronic schizophrenics, a token economy in combination with individualized behavioral programs results in a greater increase on adaptive behavior, a greater decrease in bizarre and violent behavior, and a higher rate of release than either of the other two treatments available to such patients, milieu therapy and traditional custodial care (Paul & Lentz, 1977).

Could contingency management procedures be modified in such a way as to conform to decisions such as *Wyatt*? For example, instead of making breakfast contingent upon bedmaking, you might provide a very plain breakfast noncontingently and then offer a fancy breakfast as a reward for bedmaking (Wexler, 1981). It remains to be seen, however,

whether chronic patients would appreciate such gradations. Often it is primary reinforcers—breakfast, not enhancements of breakfast—that are most effective with chronic mental patients.

Another possibility is that the superior effectiveness of behavior therapy, at least with chronic patients, will eventually encourage the courts to ease some restrictions. So far the courts have been concerned primarily with the adequacy of treatment. When they start to focus on the results of treatment—establishing the right to *effective* treatment—the courts may find that previous patients' rights decisions have severely restricted the effective treatments. Should this happen, some of those restrictions may have to be eased.

Power and the Mental Health Profession

The thrust of most of the recent court decisions discussed in this chapter is the same: to limit the power of the mental health profession. However, the power of psychological professionals is still immense. To begin with, it is the mental health profession that declares, in the form of the *DSM*, which among the countless variations of human behavior are abnormal. This is a momentous decision—and one that psychologists and psychiatrists have a questionable right to make. Many homosexuals, for example, find it bitter to recall that in 1973 the American Psychiatric Association voted on the normality of their sexual preference. Presumably, if a condition were severe enough to be labeled abnormal, it should not require a vote.

Whether or not mental health professionals are qualified to make such decisions, they do make them, and today's courts are likely to back them. (For example, the Supreme Court recently granted great sway to mental health professionals in determining when sexual predators should be committed involuntarily [*Kansas v. Hendricks*, 1997].) The very word *abnormal*, as used in psychology, implies a need for change. Thus, included in the right to decide what behavior is abnormal is the right to decide who and what need changing in our society. Again, do mental health professionals have the right to make this decision? Some people feel that the major cause of psychological disturbance in our society is not individual genes or parent-child relationships but poverty. What is the probability that mental health professionals—who are largely middle-class people of middle to high income—will be especially sensitive to this problem?

Finally, as we have seen, psychological professionals are often the ones who determine whether people identified as mentally disturbed should be institutionalized and whether those who are currently institutionalized should be released. It is hard to imagine a one-to-one relationship in our society that involves greater power than this, for what situation in our society involves a greater loss of power than involuntary commitment?

The powers held by the mental health profession are now being disputed. Numerous groups—ethnic minorities, the poor—have asked why a professional class made up largely of affluent white people should be given such broad authority. It has been argued that the mental health profession suffers from a tradition of paternalism that permits a handful of "experts" to determine the fate of a large part of the rest of the population. Just as the consumer movement has demanded of the automobile industry that cars be

equipped with safety devices and of food manufacturers that harmful chemicals be removed from packaged foods, so a "consumer" movement has made demands on the mental health profession. In this case, the demands have been for a sharing of information between professionals and laypeople, so that those who need therapy can give it their *informed consent.* This implies, of course, the right to say no and the right to question the therapist. Patients for whom ECT is recommended should be told that their memory may be impaired by the procedure; those for whom drugs are prescribed should be told about side effects. Alternative treatments—and alternatives to treatment—should be discussed. When information is shared in this way, power is diffused and abuses are less likely.

KEY TERMS

civil commitment, 531
false negative, 532
false positive, 532

indeterminate sentences,
    530
insanity defense, 525

standard of proof, 532

SUMMARY

- Mental health law deals with both the legal responsibility and the constitutional rights of people judged to be mentally disturbed. These rapidly changing laws address three major issues: psychological disturbance and criminal law, involuntary civil commitment, and patients' rights.

- Abnormal behavior may also be illegal behavior. The insanity defense is designed to protect those who are not morally responsible for committing crimes because of mental disturbance. The test of insanity is based on the irresistible-impulse decision of 1834; the M'Naghten rule, handed down by a British court in 1843; and the Durham test. The American Law Institute's formulation of the insanity defense places the burden of deciding a defendant's moral responsibility on the jury rather than on mental health professionals.

- After the Hinckley case, several states adopted a new verdict of "guilty but mentally ill" to serve as an intermediate between "guilty" and "not guilty by reason of insanity." The Hinckley case was also largely responsible for shifting the burden of proof in insanity cases from the prosecution to the defense.

- There are three major criticisms of the insanity defense. First, the jury is asked to make a judgment that is both subjective and retrospective and that often relies on conflicting testimony. A second criticism, based on the views of Thomas Szasz, contends that what a jury is asked to judge—insanity—does not exist and that courts should judge people solely on their behavior, not on their intentions. Third, for those who successfully

plead insanity, commitment to a mental hospital is, in essence, an indeterminate sentence, having no limit.

- Competency is another legal issue in criminal trials. Defendants must be judged mentally competent to stand trial; that is, they must understand the nature of the proceedings against them and be able to assist counsel in their own defense.

- One controversy surrounding competency is whether incompetent defendants should be detained in jail. Another is whether defendants are competent who only fulfill the competency requirement when under the influence of antipsychotic drugs.

- Involuntary civil commitment to a mental hospital raises serious legal questions. The Supreme Court has failed to establish specific legal procedures necessary before a person may be involuntarily committed, and lower courts have differed on the issue. As a result, a person faced with involuntary civil commitment may not have the same legal rights that a criminal defendant has.

- The Supreme Court has held that a person cannot be involuntarily committed to a mental institution without "clear and convincing" evidence that he or she is committable. Typically, statutes require that, to be committable, a person must be found mentally ill and dangerous. The standard of "dangerous" behavior, however, is open to interpretation, and predictions of such behavior are shaky at best.

- Another possible standard for involuntary commitment is the "thank-you" proposition, which states that patients should be involuntarily committed and treated if it is likely that they will benefit from such treatment. Whatever the standard for commitment, distinctions must be made between mental health questions, which psychologists and psychiatrists are qualified to answer, and legal and moral questions, which should be left to the courts.

- Patients' rights include the right to treatment, the right to refuse treatment, and the right to a humane environment. These rights may conflict with some techniques used in behavior therapy: legally guaranteed rights and amenities can no longer be withheld to reinforce desired behavior. Also, it is now questionable whether certain behavioral techniques are legal.

- The mental health profession has the power to determine what is "normal" and whether people judged to be abnormal should be institutionalized. Court decisions limiting this power and challenges from numerous advocate groups indicate that the relationship between the mental health profession and society is in transition.

Chapter 19

Janice cannot remember a time when she did not suffer from hallucinations, delusions, and paranoia. As a teenager, she would spend days lost in her fantasy world. She never told anyone about her strange experiences, though; she was afraid of being labeled "crazy," or being "swallowed" by the illness, or even committing suicide, as her three paternal uncles had done. During college, an entity she called "the Controller" who contained all of Janice's negative feelings would yell at her and punish her constantly. The Controller pervaded her thoughts, until Janice could not tell the difference between reality and the Controller's screams. Still, Janice told no one about her problems. Janice graduated cum laude despite her difficulties, and went on to graduate school. There, a psychology professor told Janice to contact a campus counselor, but the counselor was not helpful, and Janice stopped seeing him. She went on to get a job teaching third graders. After three months on the job, she had deteriorated to the point that she spent most of her time in her fantasy world, listening to the Controller. She was admitted to a psychiatric hospital, where she stayed for four months, and was diagnosed with paranoid schizophrenia. Following the hospitalization, she continued to have psychotic experiences. At one point she looked at her coworkers, and saw that their teeth looked like dangerous fangs that were ready to devour her. Eventually, Janice found a therapist she trusted, and helpful antipsychotic medications, and she has pursued work as a technical editor for twenty years. Her siblings show no sign of psychosis. (Jordan, 1995)

Janice's schizophrenia was not just a "personal problem." Her schizophrenia clearly affected many people around her: her professors, her siblings, her parents, her students, and her coworkers. Janice, in turn, was most likely affected by the mental illness of others in her family, including her three suicidal uncles, who frightened her into silence. Imagine what Janice's life would have been like if her schizophrenia had been prevented: the children could have had a teacher who could concentrate; her coworkers could have had a colleague who was not disoriented and terrified; Janice could have paid full attention to her studies. If mental illness were prevented on a wide scale, perhaps Janice would not have been so scared of being labeled as "crazy" and could have gotten help sooner—just as American women can now receive mammograms without feeling as though they are receiving a death sentence.

Since the 1960s, many people have dreamed of changing American society to allow everyone to lead more mentally healthy lives. At that time, the Civil Rights movement, protests against the war in Vietnam, and the "consciousness raising" that was going on throughout college campuses looked like a political and a cultural revolution. Clinical psychology was touched by these political and social forces. As more and more clinical psychologists became aware of how social, economic, and political circumstances shape mental health, they began to question both the wisdom and the effectiveness of individual therapy for solving mental health problems. The currents of social change that flowed throughout the nation led some psychologists to think in similar terms: perhaps the best way to form a mentally healthy society was to change social institutions for the better.

One aspect of this increased emphasis on social change within psychology was a new focus on **prevention**, the processor of keeping disorders from beginning in the first place by changing the environment, the family, or the individual. For example, an individual might be helped by being taught coping skills for dealing with stress; an entire family could

Many mental health professionals believe that offering classes that teach better parenting techniques, like the one pictured here, is one way to prevent the onset of disorders.

benefit from a class on better parenting techniques; and a community might benefit from an after-school program for children of working parents.

Preventing behavior disorders by changing the environment became popular within the mental health professions in the 1960s. At that time, many of the pioneers of the prevention movement were also progressive advocates of social change, George Albee (1983) perhaps being the most prominent of them. Prevention has continued in the past 20 years. As it becomes more and more apparent that many disorders are almost impossible to cure after their onset, prevention is explored as a viable alternative. Prevention is enjoying a renaissance. It has become a priority for research and treatment in government, as manifested in the funding of large-scale, community-based, public health projects by the National Institutes of Health, Mental Health, Alcohol, Drug Abuse, and Child Development. At the same time, all branches of government have been preoccupied with cutting taxes and balancing the budget, which makes it almost impossible to implement expensive programs designed to bring about social change.

Thus, this chapter carries with it not only the optimistic findings from the prevention movement but also the sobering reminders that we live in an era in which the public is not just skeptical but often is opposed to social change. In this chapter, we will review different types of prevention. After a brief historical review of the prevention movement, we will review some current programs, explore the role of social change, and review prevention as viewed by the theoretical perspectives.

What Is Prevention?

Historically, primary prevention has been distinguished from secondary prevention. Kaplan (1964) included a third type of prevention, called *tertiary prevention*, but it simply involves doing therapy once a disorder has developed.

Primary prevention is preventing mental disorders from developing in the first place by creating environments that are conducive to mental health, by making individuals strong enough to avoid the factors that would put them at risk for mental illness, or by teaching people skills that aid them in coping with risk factors, such as stress. Primary prevention is designed to have an impact on the entire population. One example of an environmental change that would have massive mental health-care benefits would be to ensure that every pregnant woman gets adequate prenatal and postnatal health care. Improving health care for pregnant women, and following it up with postnatal mental health care, would probably have a

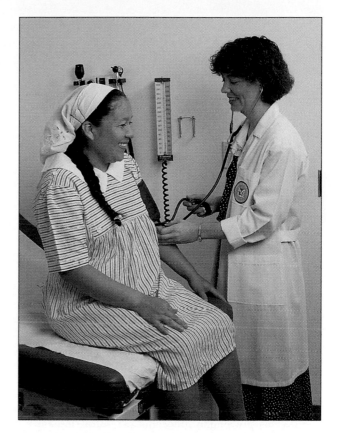

Ensuring that all pregnant women receive adequate prenatal and postnatal health care is one example of primary prevention.

major impact on violence and antisocial behavior, as we saw in Chapters 9, 13, and 17.

Secondary prevention focuses on reducing the risk for a mental disorder in individuals who are most likely to develop that disorder. First, a high-risk population is identified. Then, an intervention is selectively applied to that population in order to reduce the risk of eventually developing the disorder. Thus, secondary prevention requires the ability to identify the population at risk, then target it for an intervention. For example, as we saw in Chapter 15, adolescents with conduct disorders are at high risk for becoming antisocial adults (Farrington, 1995). A program targeted at conduct-disordered adolescents would be an example of secondary prevention if its goal were to prevent antisocial personality disorder. As another example, in Chapter 9 we saw that people who exhibit negative cognitive styles are at high risk for developing depressive disorders (Alloy, Abramson, Murray, et al., 1997). A program called the Penn Optimism Project targets children and adolescents who tend to make maladaptive attributions for stressful events and teaches them to make more benign attributions, which may prevent the later development of depression. (See box on page 548.)

The Penn Optimism Project

If you are more than 18 years old and have not experienced an episode of depression, you have passed one of the important periods of risk for this disorder. A recent longitudinal study of more than 600 people from birth to age 21 (Hankin, Abramson, Moffitt, et al., 1998) revealed that almost 25 percent of the girls and 10 percent of the boys experienced a clinically significant case of depression by the age of 21. As seen in Figure 19.1, the greatest increase in cases occurred during the 15 to 18 age period. Prior to age 15, only about 1 percent of the boys and 4 percent of the girls had experienced a serious case of depression. These findings suggest that, if we are to prevent the majority of adolescent cases of depression, the time to intervene would be prior to age 15. Intervention for girls would be especially important, because of their dramatically greater incidence at this time.

Effective prevention programs for adolescent depression are just being developed. In a very promising effort known as the Penn Optimism Project, researchers at the University of Pennsylvania (Gillham, Reivich, Jaycox, et al., 1995) reported some success in preventing the incidence of depressive symptoms in a group of 69 fifth- and sixth-grade children from a Philadelphia suburban school district. The children were selected because they were above the average in their school on a screening test for childhood depression. A comparison group of 49 children from a different school but with similar screening scores was formed to assess the natural increase in depressive symptoms that were expected to occur in the absence of intervention. Both groups were assessed shortly before the intervention, shortly after the intervention, and at 6-month intervals for a 2-year period.

The intervention took place in small groups (of about 10 children) with a professional leader who conducted exercises and training sessions that lasted about 1½ hours. The sessions occurred once a week for 12 weeks. One component of the training was based on cognitive therapy for depression (see Chapter 9). Children were taught to reconsider negative beliefs about themselves and to think about more realistic and constructive beliefs. They were also taught to identify pessimistic attributions for their successes and failures and to replace them with more optimistic attributions. Another component of the training centered on problem-solving skills that would enable the children to cope more effectively with stressful events, such as conflicts with parents and peers. Training exercises were also conducted to give the children practice in solving problems and in role-playing effective coping behaviors.

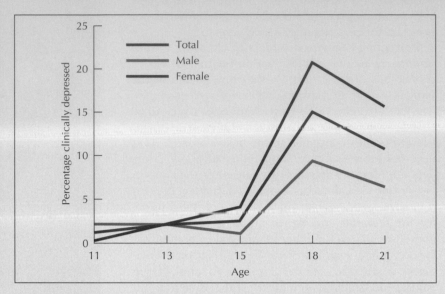

FIGURE 19.1   Development of new cases of clinical depression by age and gender (Hankin, Abramson, Moffitt, et al., 1998).

Public health efforts began 100 years ago, mainly to combat infectious disease (Mrazek & Haggerty, 1994). Between 1900 and 1970, there were dramatic declines in diseases due to vaccines, new standards for cleanliness, and numerous other interventions aimed at the whole society. Since then, prevention has come to be viewed as part of a continuum with treatment. At one extreme, **universal prevention** targets the entire population, as everyone would benefit from the intervention. If high-quality prenatal care were universally available to all socioeconomic classes, it would constitute an excellent example of universal prevention. In contrast, **selective preventive interventions** are aimed at a subgroup whose risk for developing a particular disorder is higher than average. Further along the treatment continuum are **indicated preventive interventions** for individuals who have either early signs of a particular disorder or a biological market indicating a risk for the disorder. These have historically been called "early" interventions, as when aggressive young children are treated because they show early signs of conduct problems.

Another development is that prevention goals have broadened. Although the ideal is still preventing

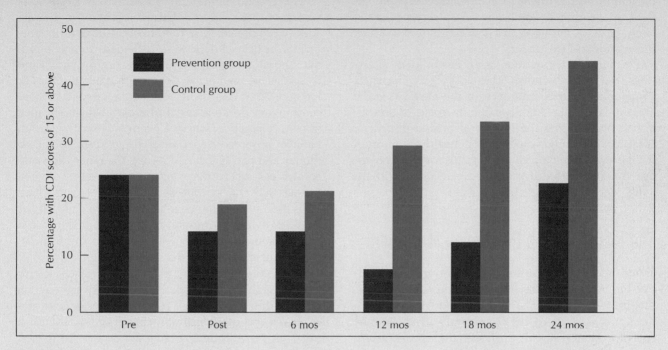

FIGURE 19.2 Depressive symptoms in children (Gillham, Jaycox, & Seligman, 1995).

The results of the program were quite impressive. After 1 year of follow-up, the children in the prevention group began to report less severe symptoms of depression than the children in the comparison group. As seen in Figure 19.2, only about 7 percent of the children in the prevention group reported high levels of depressive symptoms at the 12-month follow-up, while nearly 30 percent of the control group did. This pattern continued through the second year of follow-up. It was also encouraging that the beneficial effects of the program occurred for children who had very few symptoms at the outset of the program as well as for children who had already begun to show symptoms of childhood depression when the program began. In either case, one would expect symptoms of depression to increase, but it was primarily the untreated group that showed the developmentally predicted increases.

It would be interesting to see how well the training received by these children protected them from actual episodes of major depression during the critical 15- to 18-year age period.

The children in this program had not yet entered this period of risk at the time of the 2-year follow-up. Future research will also be needed to determine how well the program works with children from different socioeconomic backgrounds and whether it is equally successful for boys and girls. However, this initial research suggests that it will be possible to prevent early onset of depression by providing children with cognitive and social skills that can be used to cope with stress and other risk factors for depression.

the onset of a particular disorder, other outcomes could still be considered worthwhile from a public health perspective: decreasing the severity of a disorder or delaying the onset of a disorder, as when prevention programs for suicidal adolescents result in depression beginning in one's twenties rather than one's teens. These goals are all worthwhile and can have ramifications for mental health beyond the individual. For example, delaying the onset of depression in new mothers can make a difference in terms of whether or not their children develop a vulnerability to depression.

It is important to distinguish between the prevention and the promotion of mental health. The phrase **mental health promotion** is widely used in the prevention literature, but it means different things to different people. For our purposes, mental health promotion can be thought of as the enhancement of an individual's well-being, including competence, self-esteem, and resilience to stress.

A new classification system for psychological interventions has been proposed by Mrazek & Haggerty (1994) and covers the full range of interventions mental health professionals engage in, from prevention to treatment to maintenance of gains. Indeed, prevention research has cast a very broad net lately, perhaps reflecting this new continuum between prevention and treatment.

Preventive interventions can occur in medical settings, the home, schools, the workplace, churches, community centers, and even in the media (see the box on page 551). And, because the focus of prevention is on reducing the impact of mental disorders, some have distinguished mental health promotion from prevention. Cowen (1991) calls for the recognition that there is a difference between being "without a disorder" and being truly happy.

The History of the Prevention Movement

When people think about how prevention developed in the 1960s, they remember therapeutic communities, day hospitals, an increased focus on children, a sensitivity to environmental causation, new roles for mental health professionals, special attention to mental retardation, and the notion of the community mental health center. For the first time in America, mental health workers looked at public health. There was talk not just of the presence or absence of mental illness but also of "well-being." The ravings of psychotic speech were no longer seen just as evidence for a disease but also as a sign that there is something wrong in the person's moral and social environment.

Also, during the 1960s, professionals began to talk of identifying disorders before they began and offering prevention services to all who needed them, regardless of wealth or social status. Until then, people with mental illnesses received humane treatment if they could afford it, but the poor were hospitalized in squalid and overcrowded facilities. In June 1963, the National Institute of Labor Education issued a report recommending the establishment of community mental health centers, so that low socioeconomic status individuals would have access to humane facilities near their neighborhoods (Hobbs, 1964). Two extremely influential books led to some of these proposed changes. The first was *Social Class and Mental Illness* (Hollingshead & Redlich, 1962). These social scientists examined all the cases in which patients received psychiatric treatment in New Haven, Connecticut, over a period of time. They found that patient care and diagnosis bore little relationship to one another. Rather, socioeconomic status determined the type of treatment received. Poor people received inexpensive, brief therapies, while the rich and middle-class people were much more likely to receive long-term psychotherapy.

The second influential book in the 1960s was George Albee's *Mental Health Manpower Trends*. Albee recommended a fundamental change in how mental health services were provided, to accommodate the short supply of mental health providers and the projected high demand for mental health services. He noted that treatment providers tended to be concentrated in urban areas, and most of them engaged in private practice, where 1 client was seen per hour. He also observed that the services tended to follow money and privilege, abandoning the inner cities and rural areas where poor people lived. Albee argued persuasively that private practice cannot be a sound basis for a national mental health policy, and that the single-patient, 50-minute hour consumed far too many resources, while leaving the most severely disordered people untreated.

Thus, Albee pioneered the idea that mental health professionals should be accessible to all people—rich and poor. But how would psychiatric residencies and clinical psychology training programs accomplish this shift? Given the changing conception of mental illness from a disease to "problems in living," psychologists and psychiatrists needed a broad education which included training in creating a society that maximizes the human potential. This education would induce a sense of responsibility to work for a more just society. Thus, Albee foresaw a number of professions training this new breed of clinician, including public health, education, law, religion, social welfare, and urban planning. This scheme required dramatic changes in clinical training programs which were not interdisciplinary and did not as a rule provide students with skills in collaborating with other professionals from different fields. Albee recommended that psychologists develop programs and train other, less expensive paraprofessionals to do the therapy, both to save money and to reduce the demand for Ph.D.s.

As we will see, in the 1990s, mental illness has once again come to be perceived as a disease, not simply a reflection of "problems in living." However, some of Albee's musings have stood the test of time. Untrained nonprofessionals can, in general, generate outcomes that are comparable to those achieved by fully trained and experienced professional therapists (Christensen & Jacobson, 1994). As prevention received increasing emphasis, psychologists also paid more attention to children. Perhaps this, more than any other recommendation, has produced lasting influence. Prevention programs aimed at children and adolescents are the most lasting legacy of these early articles.

The alternative to Albee's recommendations was to continue to train psychotherapists who would serve an increasingly small percentage of those in

Cigarette smoking remains the single risk behavior most responsible for disease and mortality in the United States (CDC, 1997). The best way to avoid the effects of smoking is never to begin the habit (see Chapter 11). Unfortunately, adolescents between the ages of 10 and 15 are particularly likely to experiment with smoking and to put themselves at risk for dependence on nicotine, the addictive ingredient in tobacco. It would seem that, if adolescents could be persuaded not to begin smoking, the overall prevalence of cigarette smoking would decline.

During the 1970s and 1980s, many educational programs to discourage adolescent smoking were developed and tested in schools. The most successful programs taught children in middle schools (grades 6 to 8) not only about the hazards of smoking and its ill effects but also how to resist pressures from friends and peers that make smoking appear "cool" and adultlike. Although these programs were dramatically effective in preventing smoking in early adolescence, they tended not to last into the later adolescent years. As a result, most teens who were exposed to the programs began to smoke almost as much as teens who had not been exposed to them. This problem raised the question of how else to reach adolescents so that smoking could be prevented throughout the adolescent years.

One solution is to continue to deliver smoking-prevention programs in the schools. This alternative is certainly an option, but it has limitations. Many students do not stay in high school or they attend infrequently, and the school curriculum already has demands from many other sources that require time and teacher commitment. As a result, in recent years attention has turned to the use of the mass media as an additional vehicle to reach teens and persuade them to avoid tobacco. One very successful program combined mass-media prevention messages with school programs to enhance and sustain the effects of the intervention (Flynn, Worden, Secker-Walker, et al., 1994).

In this program, two school districts in Montana and two in New England were chosen to receive a school-based smoking-prevention program in grades 5 to 7. The districts were selected because they had high incidence of adult smoking and were likely to have similarly high levels of smoking in the current middle-school age cohort. In addition to the school-based program, one school district in each region was selected to receive smoking-prevention messages directed to the same age group on television and radio. These messages contained humorous and entertaining vignettes as well as credible testimonials from peer role models attesting to the acceptability of not smoking and to the undesirability of smoking. The two programs continued for four years until the students completed grades 8 to 10. Every year the students in all the participating schools completed a survey of their cigarette use, and surveys were conducted for two years following the completion of the intervention.

The results indicated that, contrary to the typical school-based smoking-prevention program, the addition of media messages enabled the program to maintain effects until the end of high school (two years after the programs ended). About 17 percent of the students in the media-enhanced program reported smoking in the past week, while about 25 percent of the students in the school-only program reported smoking in the past week. This amounts to a 30 percent reduction in cigarette use attributable to the media intervention. Differences between the two treatments were apparent from the beginning of the program (grades 5–7) onward and grew each year. However, the two treatments did not differ at baseline (grades 4–6) before the programs began.

Other findings from the research suggest that the program was especially effective for high-risk youth (Flynn, Worden, Secker-Walker, et al., 1997a) and for girls (Worden, Flynn, Solomon, et al., 1996). Youth in the school-only program who were more likely to initiate smoking at baseline (because of family and peer smoking patterns) were also more likely to smoke two years after the intervention was over than was the average student (36 percent vs. 25 percent). However, high-risk students in the media-enhanced program were less likely to smoke than high-risk students in the school-only program (29 percent vs. 36 percent). In addition, the media program was particularly effective for girls. Although girls in the school-only program were more likely to begin smoking than boys, girls in the media-enhanced program were less likely to smoke in grades 10 to 12 than those in the school-only treatment (17 percent vs. 29 percent).

Analyses of the media program's effects showed that the program operated in part by changing students' perceptions about the acceptability of smoking. As these perceptions were communicated among peers, they created less favorable social norms for smoking that could influence students, even if they were not exposed to the media messages. This is precisely what appeared to happen. The media intervention reduced cigarette use even among students who entered the schools after the program had begun (Flynn, Worden, Secker-Walker, et al., 1997b). As a result, students who may not have been exposed to media messages could still be affected by the altered peer culture that made smoking less popular in the affected communities.

The results of this program suggest that the media can be a useful adjunct to schools in delivering prevention programs to adolescents. Media interventions may change social norms surrounding unhealthy behavior and sustain intervention effects as adolescents age. These characteristics of media interventions make them especially appropriate for reaching out-of-school youth and for encouraging healthier behavior among all adolescents.

need of services. Hospitals would continue to "warehouse" people who had no alternatives and not provide meaningful therapy for most poor patients.

These were the blue prints to create a society that prevented mental illness. However, barriers arose almost immediately, barriers that were political, organizational, and social (Broskowski & Baker, 1974).

The first blow came in 1961, when the Joint Commission on Mental Health and Illness recommended a continued emphasis on treatment and rejected "visionary" primary prevention. The commission felt that the public health model had already been tried and failed. However, a few years later Congress passed the Community Health Centers Act, which gave primary prevention a temporary boost. Beginning in 1963, research and training began to create some specialists at using consultation and education as methods of primary prevention. While it became quite fashionable to discuss prevention, implementation was more difficult in practice than in theory. Major mental health agencies continued to spend most of their money on traditional diagnosis, treatment, and rehabilitation.

Thus, while there was a time when community mental health centers were formed and mental health care included prevention and social change, by the mid-1970s the movement almost disappeared (Rappaport & Chinsky, 1974), but it did leave a lasting legacy: prevention.

Although primary prevention has a less than illustrious track record of implementation, secondary prevention has become dominant in much of the field. Early interventions with high-risk populations have become the most promising methods for treating intractable disorders; some of these programs will be discussed in the next section. Second, the focus on social context produced **community psychology**, a separate area of psychology that examines communities rather than individuals. Community psychology has become a vital field of study, and it has also promoted a much more multiracial and multiethnic perspective within clinical training programs.

However, community and clinical psychologists have had a difficult time finding ways to implement and even define primary prevention programs (Spaulding & Balch, 1983). Since the turn of the century, reformers have aspired to bring mental health services to the community. No road map was ever provided for clinical psychologists to make the transition from scientist-practitioners to social change agents. For example, the original purpose of creating community mental health services was to change the content of service delivery, not just to transport people from state hospitals to community mental health centers. The recipients of mental health care in the community—especially poor, unemployed, or homeless people—had different needs than those fulfilled by traditional therapy provided in a typical state hospital. The idea was to transform the philosophy of care and to create programs which would meet the needs of the community. Instead, all too often the delivery of mental health services in community mental health centers remained the same, despite the good intentions of those who conceived of the idea (Sarason, 1981). Clinical psychology was unable or unwilling to move from a "defect" model of mental illness, one which sees mental illness as resulting from defects within the individual, to a contextual model emphasizing growth and development (Cowen, 1977). A contextual model looks at mental disorders as problems in living, generated by stressful environments. The goal of such a model is not simply to eliminate mental illness but to create mental health. As an example of the "defect" model, severity of depression is measured by the Beck Depression Inventory (BDI), which we discussed in Chapter 9. The least depressed a person can score on the BDI is a "0," indicating no depression at all. The measure stops there. It does not include items about positive growth and development. In short, you can be either depressed or not depressed, but there is no way to be happy on the BDI. Primary prevention has historically been linked to the goal of creating a society oriented toward personal growth. But how does one define the success of a prevention program when the criteria used to measure it are based on a defect model of abnormal behavior (Seligman, 1998)?

More generally, primary prevention was at the heart of the community mental health movement in the 1960s. It was based on a public health model, in which most successes have come not from treating individuals but, rather, from preventing the disorder. The Salk vaccine for polio was an example that advocates in the 1960s could draw upon. The emphasis on primary prevention carried with it the implicit philosophy that both mental health and illness were learned and were caused largely by environmental stress. Like behaviorists, advocates of primary prevention had great faith in the ability to create a better world through environmental change.

In the 1990s, the prevention field has seen a growing emphasis on biological causation. Today's prevention scientists consider mental disorders to be brain diseases. These scientists attempt to reduce the risk in populations vulnerable to the disorder, usually attributable to genetic or brain deficiencies (Mrazek & Haggerty, 1994). New opportunities to prevent biologically based disorders are emerging, ranging from medication administered before symptoms appear to genetic engineering. However, prediction—and, thus, prevention—of disorders from physical signs is far from perfect. It is doubtful that researchers will ever find a single biological or environmental agent that triggers mental illness; prevention must involve both types of factors to be effective.

Risk Reduction vs. Facilitation of Resilience

In theory, reducing the onset of mental disorders seems like a more efficient and cost-effective goal than attempting to eliminate mental disorders once they appear. Even expensive prevention programs would be far less costly to society than a lifetime of mental illness, which affects physical health, lowers work productivity, and creates human suffering that is virtually impossible to quantify. As knowledge grows regarding the factors that predict onset of a mental disorder, more programs are developed for high-risk populations that are subject to those factors. These programs tend to be implemented in the schools, homes, and communities of high-risk individuals, and they typically focus on early intervention; by identifying risk factors early in the lives of potential victims, these programs can focus on high-risk children and adolescents.

Although in the 1960s primary prevention was generally equated with social change, in the 1990s, primary prevention has come to mean strengthening people's resilience, or their ability to cope with stressful environments. Unlike risk reduction, increasing resilience involves working with the population as a whole to help people cope more effectively with such environments. In other words, if you can't get the environment to change, improve the ability of the population to adjust. This solution to unhealthy environments was anathema to progressives in the 1960s, whose motto could have been "Therapy means change, not adjustment" (Steiner, 1972).

In short, prevention science means both risk reduction and facilitating resilience in the general population. We will discuss a third component of preventive science mental health promotion later in the chapter.

Risk Reduction Programs

There are far more risk reduction programs than we can review in a chapter. But in this section we will look at some examples, both to examine how wide a net is cast by these approaches and to highlight those that seem most promising.

Reducing the rate of relapse in schizophrenics is an important concern. One professor used to say, "We know everything there is to know about schizophrenia: except what it is, what causes it, and how to cure it." Although that was 25 years ago, and strides have been made in understanding the nature and causes of schizophrenia, there is still no cure. Once someone has had at least one schizophrenic episode, as we saw in Chapter 13, relapses can be prevented by continuing patients on psychotropic medication even after the episode has subsided. But more importantly for the purposes of the present discussion, there is some evidence that lower doses of medication will do the job if social and psychological interventions accompany medication maintenance (e.g., Fallant & Fadder, 1993). Younger schizophrenics, who have not as yet become chronic, are often better candidates for such psychologically based relapse reduction programs (Hogarty, Kornblith, Greenward, et al., 1995). Generally, it appears that the more far-reaching the service, the better it works. For example, when family education is combined with vocational rehabilitation, social-skills training, and maintenance medication, the probability of relapse is probably lower, or at least delayed. The key to aftercare is continuity, which is best provided by one person who coordinates all the various activities that schizophrenics have a difficult time managing for themselves: efforts are made at increasing the patient's social support network, dealing with life crises, and recognizing the early signs of a relapse or recurrence of schizophrenia (Anthony, Cohen, and Danley, 1988).

Risk Reduction from a Developmental Perspective

Because interventions designed to prevent mental disorders are, by definition, early interventions, many of them involve children and adolescents (see the box on page 554). However, secondary prevention can continue into adulthood, and even during the golden years. There are always opportunities to prevent further suffering due to mental disorder, either before the onset of an episode or after an episode has occurred. In the latter case, the goal would be damage control: preventing recurrence of the disorder, delaying recurrence, and reducing the severity or frequency of subsequent episodes. At each stage of life, the skills needed to prevent new or recurring disorders shift. Let us examine some of the differences in prevention programs throughout the life cycle.

Risk Reduction in Infants   There are numerous ways in which physical health can influence mental health (Rickel & Allen, 1987). As we have seen, high-quality care during pregnancy and postbirth (DHHS, 1991)

Professionals who treat children with psychological disorders often express the wish that more could be done to prevent such problems, yet it is hard to guard children against psychological disturbance as long as they are exposed to social conditions known to breed such problems. The following statistics document something close to an emergency in children's health care:

- One out of every four children under the age of six now lives in poverty, and the rate is increasing (Duncan, Brooks-Gunn, & Klebanov, 1994).

- About one-third of all first births in the United States are to teenage girls, and about half of all teenage mothers—indeed, two-thirds of unmarried teenage mothers—go on welfare within four years of the birth of the child (Carnegie Report, 1994).

- Of the 2.5 million Americans who are homeless, one-third are single mothers and young children (Bassuk & Roseberg, 1990).

- Homeless children have four times more health problems than the average for their age (Alperstein, Rapport, & Flanagan, 1988).

- Approximately 10 million children have no health insurance (Children's Defense Fund, 1991).

- The national commitment to preschool intervention remains precarious. Head Start and other programs must constantly struggle for funding.

- Between 1950 and 1990 the employment rate for American women with children under six rose from 12 to 60 percent (U.S. Department of Commerce, various years), so the majority of preschool children have mothers who work outside the home, yet day care is still woefully inadequate—poorly funded, poorly staffed.

- Between 15 and 22 percent of children and adolescents have diagnosable mental disorders, and between one-quarter and half of them engage in behaviors (drug abuse, unprotected sex, delinquency, early withdrawal from school) that endanger their adjustment as adults (McDermott & Weiss, 1995), yet mental health care for such children is often unavailable. For lack of alternatives, children may be unjustifiably institutionalized, or their problems may be ignored until institutionalization becomes necessary.

In children, as in adults, some measure of psychological disturbance is due to heredity, but environment is also crucial, and, as statistics show, a large percentage of American children are being exposed daily to environmental conditions that foster psychological disorders. To prevent such disorders, those conditions—poverty; parental unemployment; teenage pregnancy; homelessness; inadequate day care, medical care, and mental health care—need to be alleviated. We also need to invest more in genetic counseling, prenatal care, and control of environmental toxins.

and programs aimed at improving parenting (Olds, Henderson, Tatelbaum, et al., 1986) all decrease the risk of violence during adolescence. One program, aimed at poor, single, teenage mothers—a group at high risk for committing child abuse—used visiting nurses as teachers, role models, and informed counselors. Before and after the babies' births, the nurses made regular home visits to the young mothers, teaching them about child development, encouraging them to form close ties to friends and family (thus preventing the social isolation that seems to foster abuse—see Chapter 17). Above all, the nurses bolstered the mothers' self-esteem by emphasizing their capabilities. These measures apparently had an effect. After two years, only 4 percent of the mothers in the program had abused or neglected their children, as opposed to 20 percent of an untreated control group (Olds & Henderson, 1989).

Risk Reduction in Young Children
Two important developmental tasks that reduce young children's risks for later mental health problems are acquiring lan-

guage skills that allow them to read and write along with their peers and learning impulse control (Hawkins & Catalano, 1992). The most famous example of an early childhood education program is one of the few remaining programs from President Lyndon Johnson's War on Poverty: Head Start (Zigler, 1994). All such programs for severely economically deprived preschoolers provides children with an intensive preschool experience to encourage their cognitive development, as well as social services and medical and nutritional intervention. Parents are often taught the skills they needed to keep the momentum going, and many also attained vocational skills and jobs that would enhance their status. Other, more recent programs have been aimed at improving parenting and enhancing child development (e.g., Strayhorn & Wiedman, 1991).

Risk Reduction for Elementary-Age Children
Children who are academically deficient or socially incompetent by fourth grade are at high risk for subsequent depression, substance abuse, and conduct disorder

Head Start, an intervention program for economically deprived preschoolers, is designed to improve children's health and prepare them to learn, thus reducing their risks for future mental health problems.

(Mrazek & Haggerty, 1994). This is especially true if they are either impulsive or aggressive. Family conflict, bad parenting, and neglect through lack of quality interaction can contribute to the risk. Most risk reduction programs have focused on the children, with less attention to the parents. Other programs have also shown promise in increasing social competence in children of divorce, to minimize the otherwise adverse effects of marital conflict followed by divorce (Grynch & Fincham, 1992). Weissberg and his associates (e.g., Weissberg & Bell, 1997) have successfully taught children self-control, communication, problem-solving, and resisting the social influence of behavior disordered classmates. For example, they designed a program for middle school students that has three goals: social competence; communicating more effectively with teachers; preventing antisocial behavior such as fighting, drug use, and premature sex. Instruction occurs in the classroom and therapists also attempt to enlist parental and other environmental support for the teaching of these skills. Students in the program are more likely to generate large numbers of good solutions to typical teenage problems, are less likely to fight and engage in other behaviors that get them into trouble, and think things through before acting. Students also learned to relax and use other techniques to reduce stress; in general, they became more popular with their classmates. It took two years of training to make these changes permanent; one year of intervention produced only short-term benefits. Importantly, teachers almost universally liked the program. Finally, intensive programs in the schools designed to

raise academic achievement have also resulted in lower rates of adolescent depression, delinquency, and alcohol use (Hawkins, Catalano, Morrison, et al., 1992). Many at-risk children are taught cognitive and coping skills in interventions such as the Penn Optimism Program (review the box on page 548).

Risk Reduction in Adults Many types of interventions with adults have shown some promise in reducing the risk of various mental disorders. These include programs designed to enhance the quality of marriage (Markman, 1993), to help minimize the mental health deterioration that typically follows divorce (Bloom, Hodges, Kern, et al., 1985), and to make the transition to parenthood smoother for couples. Markman, for example, developed the PREP program to teach couples communication skills prior to marriage that could serve them when they developed problems later during the difficult years of marriage. The birth of the first child, for example, is typically a stressful time for couples. Markman's program works with engaged couples to help them learn the skills now that will be useful later. It is much easier to prevent marital problems than to treat them once they have developed. Another area of activity has been occupational stress and job loss, including helping people cope with the stress of losing a job (Hearney, 1992) and finding a new job after one is lost (Price, van Ryn, & Vinokur, 1992). Adults who are poor or ethnic minorities are at high risk for depression: this group has been targeted for special preventive interventions, with promising results (Munoz & Ying, 1993). Finally, adults who have to care for aging parents are another group at risk for a variety of mental health problems. Support groups for these adults may be helpful in reducing these risks (Toseland, Rossiter, & Labrecque, 1989).

Risk Reduction in Elderly People   Aging brings with it health problems, a lessened capacity for work, the loss of children who leave home, and the assumption of new roles such as grandparenting. These challenges all generate mental health risks, including the risk of depression. Programs for widows and widowers facing bereavement have received a great deal of attention in recent years; bereavement may be life's most stressful event, especially for the elderly. A variety of programs have been developed, including "Widow to Widow," a mutual self-help program developed by Silverman (1988). This program recruits widowed helpers who have come to terms with their own grief and can help others who are still in mourning. The treatment consists of one-to-one support by another widow, practical advice in locating necessary community resources, and meetings in small groups. The treatment is open-ended. It could last as long as a year, or be as short as one week. The program helps widows find new relationships, more quickly, and with less depression along the way. It has been particularly successful with women who are under tremendous stress immediately following the death of their husbands. It is unknown whether these programs can prevent depression, but the results suggest that women with a strong bereavement reaction are both at high risk for depression and likely to benefit from helpers who have been through the process. More work needs to be done to assess the potential of self-help groups, not just with respect to bereavement but also with other major life transitions, such as decreased ability to work, chronic illness, and loss of particular functions (e.g., memory).

A Model Risk Reduction Program: FAST Track

FAST Track is a multifaceted risk reduction program for conduct disorders that has received a great deal of attention. Women are at high risk for depression at the age when they typically have young children (Brown & Harris, 1979) (see Chapter 9), especially when they also have marital problems or there is no second parent and they have insufficient material resources. We have also seen that children exposed to depressed mothers during the first year of life are at elevated risk for conduct disorders (see Chapter 17). Furthermore, pregnant women with poor prenatal care and subsequent birth complications also produce sons who are at high risk to become delinquents (see Chapter 15) or schizophrenics (see Chapter 13).

Support groups such as "Widow to Widow," pictured here, help older people cope with their grief after the loss of a spouse.

Such women tend to be single and poor. Finally, children with conduct disorders are at high risk for becoming antisocial adults, batterers, sex offenders, and substance abusers (see Chapter 17).

Thus, there is a constellation of risk factors which affects depression, antisocial behavior, battering, depression, and substance abuse. The Conduct Problems Prevention Research Group (1992) comes as close as any group thus far in providing a comprehensive program that targets the schools, families, neighborhoods, and other sources of risk. The program, called "FAST Track," was developed by a group of research psychologists under federal government auspices. This experimental prevention program is being conducted in four cities: Durham, North Carolina; Seattle, Washington; Harrisburg, Pennsylvania; and Nashville, Tennessee. The interventions are aimed at more than 400 families with children identified as being at high risk for conduct disorders. They begin the program in first grade and continue into middle school, 6 years altogether. FAST Track aims to reduce the risk of conduct disorders in several ways. The program gets parents involved in the child's school system from day 1, to preempt the animosity that often develops between the family and the schools; it focuses on reading, making sure that the child doesn't fall behind but, rather, learns to read along with his or her low-risk classmates; it fosters the development of friendships through social skills; it directly teaches children how to express emotions in nonaggressive ways; and it makes sure that every child has a same-sex role model, because so many of the families have high-risk sons and absent or uninvolved fathers.

Thus, FAST Track provides services to families, school systems, and the children themselves. They consider the beginnings of elementary and middle school to be the two crucial periods that determine functioning at home and in school. Therapists work directly with teachers and teach emotional regulation and social skills to children right in the schools. Parents also get help where it is most relevant: in their homes. There, therapists work with them on parenting and help solve problems related to poverty, unemployment, and life stress.

To determine the efficacy of FAST Track, high-risk children were randomly assigned to the experimental program or to a no-treatment control group. The results of this project will not be clear until these children are teenagers, when researchers can tell if the program served its primary purpose: preventing conduct disorders. So far, FAST Track does seem to be successful in keeping families in the program. Because high drop-out rates have been a problem so often in the past, this is an encouraging sign. Also, parents in the FAST Track program are reporting high satisfaction. Although these results are not measures of outcome, they are certainly prerequisites to a positive outcome: the program can't work if families don't stay in it.

Although clinical scientists and officials from the National Institute of Mental Health will be watching the results of this project quite closely, how likely is it that programs such as FAST Track will have a significant impact on antisocial behavior, let alone postpartum depression and substance abuse? In the short run, millions of dollars were required to implement this program in four cities. The cost of implementing similar programs on a nationwide basis may seem prohibitive. Moreover, programs for children even as young as six may be too little too late. Despite the massive nature of these interventions, they follow poverty, unemployment, teenage pregnancy, poor prenatal care, and underfunded public schools. If a social welfare system were in place to eliminate poverty and create jobs, if public education efforts were successful in preventing premature pregnancies,

and if sufficient funds were available to make all public schools successful, there would be few high-risk children to begin with. Thus, we return to the idealistic but ultimately cost-effective goals of the 1960s: social change as the real "ounce" of prevention.

How Effective Are These Programs?

Despite the promise of these risk reduction programs, the only well-replicated positive benefits are for programs with children and adolescents (Durlak & Wells, 1997). Nevertheless, even with these populations, often the findings are preliminary, the samples are small, and the studies are of dubious methodological quality. Much more work needs to be done before we can move from a promising program to a program of proven efficacy. And, even when the efficacy of the program has been proven, the clinical significance of these programs is still an open question (see Chapter 3). Nevertheless, this is an area where a great deal of activity has been generated, and prevention science seems to be one of the most highly emphasized aspects of mental health research and practice.

Mental Health Promotion

Mental health is not just the absence of mental illness. Many have argued that a mentally healthy person functions well physically, socially, and spiritually (Mechanic, 1991). Certainly, functioning effectively at work and in interpersonal relationships and enjoying a sense of well-being and happiness are part of what we mean when we say that someone is doing "well." To draw an analogy to physical health, it is not just the avoidance of disease that determines how long people live; rather, it is whether their health is just "good" or "excellent" (Idler & Kasl, 1991). The purpose of mental health promotion is to enhance competence, self-esteem, resilience, and a sense of well-being rather than to prevent mental disorders (Seligman, 1998). These programs exist in schools, in HMOs, in businesses, and even in local government agencies. Examples can also be found in religion, recreation, and exercise. Although the efficacy of mental health promotion is at present unknown, these programs tend to be expensive. For that reason alone, they deserve some attention. If they don't accomplish their goals, there are many other ways that money could be used.

As summarized by Mrazek & Haggerty (1994), there are many subjective aspects of human experience that are health-promoting, even though they do not fall into the category of prevention: examples are resilience, empowerment, integrity, energy, and a sense of balance in one's life. In addition to reducing the suffering of the mentally ill, mental health promoters would argue that an equally important goal can be accomplished through mental health promotion: the enhancement of self-esteem. Many programs have tried to accomplish these goals. They have not been rigorously evaluated.

Some of these programs may even be harmful. For example, people who are depressed because they live in oppressive environments may join these programs and become convinced that they can overcome their depression through "wellness" programs rather than standard treatment or by working to overcome their oppressive environment. Although it is important to develop alternatives to the "disease model," these programs should be viewed with skepticism until it is shown that they really do enhance mental health.

These concepts of "wellness" have been historically associated with primary prevention (Cowen & Work, 1988). However, they focus their attention on the individual. They assume that, if we can promote mental health successfully, then the individual will be able to withstand stressful environments. In contrast to focusing on changing the individual to better withstand environmental stresses, let's examine eliminating those stresses through social change.

Social Change

Prevention science has created a continuum of interventions that, at one extreme, focuses on environmental change, while the other focuses on changing the individual. Programs at the latter side of the continuum seem at times to resemble traditional therapy more than they do prevention (Coie, Watt, West, et al., 1993; Mrazek & Haggerty, 1994). In two influential documents, an article by Coie and colleagues as well as a handbook published by the Institute of Medicine (Mrazek & Haggerty, 1994), the distinction between primary and secondary prevention was all but obliterated.

The field of prevention science uses the term *universal prevention* to refer to what was originally known as primary prevention. But primary prevention now emphasizes programs based on overcoming risk and bolstering resilience within individuals, not social change. While both individual and social change are laudable goals, the focus on the individual signals a large shift within the prevention movement.

Currently, universal prevention programs have many goals. First, universal prevention programs seek to foster better relations between parent and child, while reducing family violence. Previous chapters showed that secure relationships between parent and child help secure subsequent mental health (see Chapters 9, 13, 15, and 17). Such attachments are often disrupted: either the parents do not naturally bond with their children or the parents are impaired by various mental health problems. Perhaps most important, poverty can make nurturance difficult, either because parents are working long hours and need to leave children with distant relatives or because they are preoccupied with activities to make ends meet. We have discussed the very real problem of child abuse. Because children who are abused or who grow up in homes where fathers hit mothers are at higher risk for becoming antisocial adults (see Chapter 17), stopping child abuse can mean stopping the intergenerational transmission of violence.

Second, universal prevention programs train participants in problem solving, which risk reduction research can do but which may not by itself be applicable to the population as a whole. We have discussed the importance of problem-solving ability in children, from kindergarten through adolescence, in our section on risk reduction research. Now, attempts are being made to teach problem-solving skills to all children. Some data show modest but promising results from teaching skills such as pregnancy avoidance, academic achievement, and social problem solving (Philliber & Allen, 1992).

Third, universal prevention programs teach individuals how to modify their own environments. Historically, this particular approach was seen as consistent with primary prevention. Steiner (1972) and others talked in the 1960s about getting individuals involved in changing their environments. Now the concept has broadened to teaching individuals how to modify their families, school systems, neighborhoods, and legal systems. For example, requiring that a criminal perform community service as an alternative to prison for adolescent criminals could be considered a way to help people change their environment. Community service can improve the neighborhood in which the criminal lives, thus creating a more healthy environment and making further criminal activity less likely. If this concept were applied throughout the United States, it would constitute an example of universal prevention.

Finally, prevention scientists have made use of the term *empowerment,* which means helping traditionally powerless groups—such as racial minorities, women, elderly people, and those who live in poverty—to take control of their lives. To the extent that mental disorders are exacerbated by a sense of learned helplessness (see Chapter 9), gaining a sense of control through actively changing aspects of the environment may promote mental health. For example, battered women can be empowered by seeing the

Rather than being sentenced to serve time in prison for the crimes they committed, these adolescents were required to work with severely handicapped children. Having juvenile offenders perform community service improves the social environment, making further criminal activity less likely.

legal system protect them from their battering partners, especially if they are the ones who initiate use of the legal system.

Some would say that this dissection of primary prevention into focusing on individuals was encouraged by some of the movement's founders, especially Emory Cowen (1977), who proposed taking "baby steps" rather than giant steps that require major changes in the society. By contrast, Albee (1997) calls for "giant steps" but also observes that progressive social change is unlikely to be initiated by groups with a direct interest in preserving the status quo. Albee surveys the conservative forces which have consolidated the status quo in the 1990s, and concludes that economic power, especially corporate power, is directly responsible for the exploitation of women, poor people, minorities, the elderly, and the sexual minorities. Albee clearly has a political agenda. Many have argued that the field of abnormal psychology is inherently political (Halleck, 1970; Jacobson, 1989). Albee (1997) ponders how responsive government would be to findings supporting expensive reforms, such as eliminating poverty, finding jobs for people, creating conditions under which

only babies who are wanted are born, and providing universal, high-quality health care.

The major criticism of prevention programs is not that what they are doing is wrong but that they are not doing enough. Innovative services such as courses for police in how to handle domestic disputes are still the exception rather than the norm. Many community health centers offer only the old, standard services such as psychotherapy and short-term hospitalization. A large percentage of psychiatric emergencies still end up in general hospitals without specialized psychiatric staff or separate psychiatric inpatient facilities, for no such services are available (Hendryx & Bootzin, 1986). The primary reason for the scarcity of innovative services is simply lack of funds. Already in the 1970s, funding for the community mental health centers was being cut back. Then in 1981 the Community Mental Health Centers Act was replaced by block grants to the states, so that community centers were forced to rely on state budgets and third-party reimbursers such as Medicaid. In recent years, this has meant pressure to reduce expenditures—and, ultimately, services.

KEY TERMS

community psychology 552
indicated preventive
  interventions, 548

mental health promotion,
  549
prevention, 546

primary prevention, 547
secondary prevention,
  547

selective preventive
  interventions, 548
universal prevention, 548

SUMMARY

- Since the 1960s, psychologists have investigated prevention, or ways to keep disorders from beginning by changing the environment, the family, and the individual. These efforts have included primary prevention, which is intended to affect the entire population, and secondary prevention, which is aimed at reducing risk among a targeted high-risk population.

- Prevention is part of a continuum with treatment. Universal prevention involves the entire population; selective preventive interventions are aimed at subgroups with a higher-than-average risk for a disorder, and indicated preventive interventions are designed for individuals who either show early signs of a disorder or have a biological marker for that disorder.

- Over time, prevention goals have broadened. Prevention programs not only try to prevent the onset of a disorder but also decrease the severity of or delay the onset of disorders.

- The prevention movement began in the 1960s, with recommendations that community health centers be built. Various researchers observed that poor rural and inner-city residents were underserved by the existing mental health system, which emphasized single-patient therapy sessions by psychologists. The movement demanded access to mental health care for the poor and encouraged psychologists to change society to maximize human potential. The field of community psychology grew out of this movement. Over time, though, the vast programs and recommended social changes grew less popular, and clinical psychologists resisted moving from a "defect" model of mental illness to a contextual model that viewed mental disorders as products of oppressive environments. Current views of mental illness as a biological disease have also discouraged prevention efforts.

- Many modern primary prevention programs attempt to enhance individuals' abilities to cope with stressful environments, otherwise known as resilience. These programs involve working with the population as a whole, not just a high-risk population.

- Risk reduction programs typically involve children and adolescents in early interventions, which are designed to reach high-risk individuals before they develop symptoms of mental illness. However, there are risk reduction programs for people in all stages of life, from infants to the elderly. Head Start and FAST Track are two famous examples of risk reduction programs. The efficacy of these programs is still in question.

- Mental health promotion programs enhance competence, self-esteem, resilience, and a sense of well-being. They do not directly prevent mental disorders. Most of these programs have not been rigorously evaluated. Some may even harm participants by encouraging them to blame themselves, rather than a stressful environment, for their disorders.

- Currently, universal prevention programs have many goals, such as fostering better relations between parents and children and training participants in problem solving. Many of these programs teach participants, including members of traditionally powerless groups, how to change their environment. This process is called empowerment.

Glossary

ABAB design An experimental research design that seeks to confirm a treatment effect by showing that behavior changes systematically with alternate conditions of no treatment (A) and treatment (B). 3

absence seizures Brief generalized epileptic seizures during which patients, usually children, seem to absent themselves from their surroundings. 14

acquired brain injury An injury to a normally developed or developing brain. The injury can result in cognitive, behavioral, and emotional dysfunction. 14

acquired dysfunction A sexual dysfunction that develops after at least one episode of normal functioning. 12

acquired immune deficiency syndrome (AIDS) A disease caused by the human immunodeficiency virus (HIV), which attacks the immune system, making patients susceptible to infection. 8

acrophobia The fear of high places. 6

active phase The second stage of schizophrenia, during which the patient begins showing prominent psychotic symptoms. 13

agitated depression A form of depression characterized by incessant activity and restlessness. 9

agnosia A disturbance in the ability to recognize familiar objects. 14

agoraphobia An anxiety disorder characterized by fear of being in any situation from which escape might be difficult and in which help would be unavailable in the event of panic symptoms. 6

alters In dissociative identity disorder patients, the secondary or multiple identities the person adopts. 7

Alzheimer's disease An organic brain disorder characterized by cognitive deficits such as failure of concentration and memory. The disease can occur as early as age 40, but its prevalence increases with age. 14

amnesia The partial or total forgetting of past experiences. It can be associated with organic brain syndromes or with psychological stress. 7, 14

amniocentesis A clinical procedure that can identify abnormal chromosomes in a developing fetus. 16

amphetamines A group of synthetic stimulants—the most common of which are Benzedrine, Dexedrine, and Methedrine—which reduce feelings of boredom or weariness. 11

anal stage In psychodynamic theory, the second stage of psychosocial development, in which the child's focus is on the pleasurable feelings of retaining and expelling the feces; occurs in the second year of life. 4

analogue experiment An experimental situation that attempts to reproduce, under controlled conditions, the essential features of naturally occurring psychopathology or its treatment. 3

anhedonia A mood abnormality among schizophrenics in which the person's experience of pleasure is reduced. Often experienced by people during major depressive episodes, the inability to enjoy accustomed activities leads to a lack of interest in those activities. 9

anorexia nervosa Chronic failure to eat for fear of gaining weight. Occurring usually among adolescent girls and young women, the disorder results in severe malnutrition, semistarvation, and sometimes death. 15

antidepressant drugs Drugs used to elevate mood in depressed patients. 6

antimanic drugs Drugs, principally lithium, used to prevent and treat manic episodes. 9

antipsychotic drugs Drugs used to relieve symptoms such as confusion, withdrawal, hallucinations, and delusions in psychotic patients. Also called *major tranquilizers* or *neuroleptics*. 13

antisocial behavior Behavior that violates the rights of others; usually associated with antisocial personality. 17

antisocial personality disorder (APD) A disorder marked by chronic indifference to and violation of the rights of others. 17

anxiety A state of fear that affects many areas of functioning and that involves three basic components: subjective reports of tension and dread, behavioral inhibitions and impairments, and certain physiological responses. 4, 6

anxiety disorders Disturbances characterized either by manifest anxiety or by behavior patterns aimed at warding off anxiety. 6

aphasia A language impairment generally attributable to damage in the left hemisphere of the brain. 14

apraxia Impairment of the ability to perform voluntary movements. 14

attention deficit hyperactivity disorder (ADHD) A childhood disorder characterized by incessant restlessness and an extremely poor attention span, leading to impulsive and disorganized behavior. 15

attribution One form of cognitive appraisal concerning beliefs about the causes of life events; how people explain events to themselves will affect their emotional state. 4

autism See **early infantile autism.**

autogynephilia Sexual arousal created by the fantasy of being a female or having a female body. This arousal underlies most transvestism and much cross-dressing. 12

autonomic nervous system (ANS) The part of the nervous system which governs the smooth muscles, the heart muscle, the glands, and the viscera and controls their functions, including physiological responses to emotion. It has two divisions, the sympathetic and parasympathetic. 4

avoidant personality disorder A disorder in which the individual withdraws from social contact out of fear of rejection. 10

barbiturates A group of powerful sedative drugs used to alleviate tension and bring about relaxation and sleep. 11

behavior genetics A subfield of psychology concerned with determining the extent to which behavior, including abnormal behavior, is influenced by genetics. 4

behavior therapy A method of treatment for specific problems that uses the principles of learning theory. 5

behavioral high-risk design A research design in which high-risk subjects are selected on the basis of behavioral traits thought to be associated with the disorder in question. 13

behavioral perspective A theoretical approach which departs from psychodynamic theory in viewing all behavior as a result of learning. 5

benzodiazepines A group of anti-anxiety drugs that reduce anxiety by activating the inhibitory neurotransmitter, GABA. 6

biofeedback training A technique by which subjects, with the help of various machines, can monitor and control their own biological processes such as pulse, blood pressure, and brain waves. 8

biogenic A term used to describe abnormal behavior that results from malfunction within the body. According to biogenic theory, mental disturbance is due to organic disorders. 1

biological perspective A theory of abnormal behavior that concentrates on the physical aspects of a disorder in an effort to understand its characteristics. 1, 4

bipolar disorder A mood disorder involving both manic and depressive episodes. 9

blood alcohol level The amount of alcohol in the bloodstream, expressed in terms of the number of milligrams of alcohol per 100 ml of blood. 11

blunted affect A mood abnormality among schizophrenics in which the person shows little emotion. 13

body dysmorphic disorder A preoccupation with an imagined or a grossly exaggerated defect in one's appearance. 7

borderline personality disorder A disorder marked by an unstable sense of self, distrust, impulsive and self-destructive behavior, and difficulty in controlling anger and other emotions. 10

brain plasticity The brain's ability, during infancy, to be altered by environmental stimulation. 16

brain trauma Injury to brain tissue as a result of jarring, bruising, or cutting. 14

brain tumors Abnormal growths within the brain, classified as either **metastatic** or **primary**. 14

bulimia nervosa Excessive overeating or uncontrolled binge eating followed by self-induced vomiting. 15

case study A research design that focuses on a single individual for description and analysis. 3

case-control design A research design in which *cases*, people diagnosed as having a mental disorder, are compared with *controls*, people who have not been diagnosed as having the disorder. 3

castration anxiety In psychodynamic theory, the male child's fear that his penis will be cut off as punishment for his sexual desire for his mother. 4

catatonic schizophrenia A form of schizophrenia characterized by a marked disturbance in motor behavior: decreases in motion, complete immobility, cessation of speech, or alternating periods of immobility and extreme agitation. 13

catatonic stupor An extreme form of withdrawal in which the individual retreats into a completely immobile state, showing a total lack of responsiveness to stimulation. 13

catecholamine hypothesis The biochemical theory that increased levels of the neurotransmitter norepinephrine produce mania, while decreased levels produce depression. 9

categorical classification The sorting of patients into qualitatively distinct categories, as in the *DSM*. 2

central nervous system (CNS) The part of the nervous system made up of the brain and spinal cord. 4

cerebral abscess A brain infection that becomes encapsulated by connective tissue. 14

cerebrovascular accident (CVA) A blockage of or break in the blood vessels in the brain, resulting in injury to brain tissue. Commonly called *stroke*. 14

childhood depression A disorder of emotional distress with symptoms similar to those of adult depression (sadness, hopelessness, etc.) but expressed differently by children (e.g., by clinging to their parents) and by adolescents (e.g., by engaging in delinquent acts). 15

chromosomes Threadlike structures in all the cells of the body that carry genes in a linear order. 4

circadian rhythm disorders Disruptions in sleep cycles that occur when people try to sleep at times that are inconsistent with circadian rhythms, the cycles dictated by their "biological clocks." 8

civil commitment The commitment of a person to a mental institution because the state has decided that he or she is disturbed enough to require hospitalization. 18

claustrophobia The fear of enclosed places. 6

clinical psychologist A Ph.D. or Psy.D. who spent four to six years in graduate school and completed a one-year clinical internship. Clinical psychology programs emphasize training in psychological assessment and therapeutic intervention, as well as research. 1

clinical significance A statistical effect that has practical value or importance. 3

clinical trials Studies of the effectiveness of treatments, involving randomized comparisons between two or more forms of therapy. 3

clinicians Therapists who work with people with mental health problems. 3

cocaine A natural stimulant, made from the coca plant, that produces feelings of euphoria and omnipotence. 11

coconscious In dissociative identity disorder, the term used to refer to a subordinate personality that is fully aware of the dominant personality's thoughts and actions. 7

cognition The act of knowing, including mental processes such as emotion, thought, expectation, and interpretation. 4

cognitive appraisal According to cognitive behaviorists, the process by which a person evaluates a stimulus in accordance with his or her memories, beliefs, and expectations before responding. It accounts for the wide variation in responses to the same stimulus. 4

cognitive perspective The view of abnormal behavior as the product of mental processing of environmental stimuli (cognition). 4

cognitive restructuring A variety of cognitive therapy techniques that help clients increase coping skills, develop problem-solving skills, and change the way they perceive and interpret their worlds. 4

communication deviance (CD) A measurement of parental deviant or idiosyncratic test responses; used to predict the potential for their children's future schizophrenic behaviors. 13

community mental health centers Facilities designed to provide a variety of psychological services for everyone within a specified area. 1

comorbidity A condition in which a patient meets the criteria for more than one *DSM-IV* Axis I disorders. 2, 9

complex partial seizure A partial epileptic seizure in which cognitive functioning is interrupted. 14

compulsion An action that a person feels compelled to repeat again and again in a stereotyped fashion, though he or she has no conscious desire to do so. 6

computerized tomography (CT) A technique for mapping brain structure in which X rays are passed through cross sections of the brain, measuring the density of the tissue in each section. 4

concussion A head injury caused by a blow to the head that jars the brain and momentarily disrupts its function. 14

conditioned reflex A basic mechanism of learning; if a neutral stimulus is paired with a nonneutral stimulus, the organism will eventually respond to the neutral stimulus as it does to the nonneutral stimulus. 5

conditioned reinforcers Stimuli or needs that one learns to respond to by associating them with primary reinforcers. Also called *secondary reinforcers.* 5

conditioned response A simple response to a neutral stimulus that is the result of repeatedly pairing the neutral stimulus with a nonneutral stimulus that would have naturally elicited the response. 5

conditioned stimulus The neutral stimulus that elicits a particular response as a result of repeated pairings with a nonneutral or unconditioned stimulus that naturally elicits that response 5

conduct disorder A childhood disorder in which a preadolescent or an adolescent persistently violates social norms through aggression against people or animals, destruction of property, deceitfulness or theft, and/or other serious violations of rules. 15

confounding In a research study, a phenomenon that occurs when two or more causal factors are operating on the same thing simultaneously, interfering with accurate measurement of the causal role of either factor. 3

congenital disorders Disorders acquired during prenatal development but not transmitted genetically. 16

contingency In operant conditioning, a perceived association between action and consequence which, once learned, directs behavior: an individual will repeat a behavior or cease it in order to obtain or avoid the consequence. 5

contingency management An operant-conditioning technique in which the consequences of a response are manipulated in order to change the frequency of that response. 5

control techniques The three methods by which the independent variable in an experiment can be controlled: manipulating, holding conditions constant, and balancing. 3

contusion A head injury in which the brain is shifted out of its normal position and pressed against one side of the skull, thus bruising the neural tissue. 14

conversion disorder The loss or impairment of some motor or sensory function for which there is no organic cause; formerly known as "hysteria" or "hysterical neurosis." 7

coronary heart disease A disease brought about by atherosclerosis, the buildup of fatty deposits on the inside walls of the coronary arteries, and manifested as heart attack or sudden cardiac death. 8

correlational research Research studies that seek to find the relationships between subjects' characteristics and their performance. Such studies effectively meet two of the objectives of the scientific method—description and prediction—but the results of correlational studies should not be used to make causal inferences. 3

couple therapy A procedure for approaching relationship problems with both partners seeing a therapist together. 5

covariation of events The first condition to be met before causality can be demonstrated: two events must vary together; when one changes, the other must also change. 3

crack cocaine A cheaper and more powerful and highly addictive form of freebased cocaine, sold in small chunks or "rocks." 11

cyclothymic disorder A chronic mood disorder in which, for years, the person goes no longer than a few months without a phase of hypomanic or depressive behavior. 9

decatastrophizing A strategy used in cognitive therapy whereby clients are helped to realize that their fears are exaggerated by being asked to consider what would actually happen if their worst fears were realized. 4

defense mechanism Any psychic stratagem that reduces anxiety by concealing the source of anxiety from the self and the world 4

degenerative disorders Organic brain syndromes characterized by a general deterioration of intellectual, emotional, and motor functioning as a result of progressive pathological change in the brain. 14

degradation A common form of emotional abuse in which a person is humiliated, often publicly, and insulted in dehumanizing ways.   17

deinstitutionalization The widespread discharge of mental patients from the hospital into the community.   1

delirium A global disorder of cognition and attention that begins suddenly and remits quickly, leaving most patients unharmed. Symptoms include confusion, hallucinations, and emotional lability.   14

delusional disorder A psychosis in which the delusional system is the basic or even the only abnormality, and in all other respects the person seems quite normal   13

demand characteristics A methodological problem in which a subject's response is strongly determined by the expectations of the subject or the researchers.   3

dementia Severe mental deterioration.   14

dependent personality disorder A disorder marked by extreme dependence on others.   10

dependent variable In a research study, the factor (in psychology, a particular behavior) that will be affected by the experimenter's manipulation of the independent variable, and whose changes the researcher wishes to measure.   3

depersonalization disorder A disruption of personal identity that is characterized by a sense of strangeness or unreality in oneself, e.g., feeling that one is viewing oneself from the outside or is functioning like a robot.   7

depressant A drug that acts on the central nervous system to reduce pain, tension, and anxiety, to relax and disinhibit, and to slow intellectual and motor reactivity.   11

depression An emotional state characterized by the exaggeration of negative feelings. The person becomes inactive and dejected and thinks nothing is worthwhile.   9

depth hypothesis Freud's view that almost all mental activity takes place unconsciously.   4

derealization A feeling of strangeness about the world. Other people, and the self, seem robotic, dead, or somehow unreal.   7

description (1) The first objective of the scientific method: the procedure by which events and their relationships are defined, classified, catalogued, or categorized. (2) The first goal of psychological assessment: the rendering of an accurate portrait of personality, cognitive functioning, mood, and behavior.   2

descriptive validity The degree to which an assessment device provides significant information about the current behavior of the people being assessed.   2

detoxification A medical treatment for alcoholism that consists of getting the alcohol out of the alcoholic's system and seeing him or her through the withdrawal symptoms.   11

dexamethasone suppression test (DST) A laboratory test used to identify people suffering from endogenous depression. In depressed individuals, dexamethasone suppresses cortisol secretion for at least 24 hours. Cortisol secretion of individuals with endogenous depression returns to high levels within 24 hours despite administration of dexamethasone.   9

diagnosis The classification and labeling of a patient's problem within one of a set of recognized categories of abnormal behavior.   2

dialectical behavior therapy A form of therapy developed to treat borderline personality disorder, integrating acceptance with change.   10

diathesis-stress model The belief that certain genes or gene combinations may lead to a diathesis, or predisposition, toward a disorder and that, if this is combined with certain kinds of environmental stress, abnormal behavior will result. In schizophrenia research, this is an approach which holds that a predisposition to schizophrenia is inherited but that the disorder must be triggered by environmental stresses.   5

differential deficits Deficits that are specific to the disorder in question (as opposed to other disorders) and that are presumably central to it.   13

dimensional classification The assignment of patients to scores on quantitative dimensions, such as personality, course, and functioning.   2

discrimination The process of learning to distinguish among similar stimuli and to respond only to the appropriate one.   5

disorganized schizophrenia A form of schizophrenia characterized by pronounced incoherence of speech, childlike disturbed affect such as giggling wildly and assuming absurd postures, and disorganized behavior, or lack of goal orientation. Also called hebephrenic schizophrenia.   13

disruptive behavior disorders Childhood disorders characterized by poorly controlled, impulsive, acting-out behavior in situations where self-control is expected.   15

dissociative amnesia Memory loss without any apparent physiological cause, as a response to psychological stress. Dissociative amnesia tends to be anterograde, blotting out a period of time after the precipitating stress.   7

dissociative disorders Disorders resulting from the splitting off of some psychological function—such as identity or memory—from the rest of the conscious mind.   7

dissociative fugue A condition related to amnesia in which a person not only forgets most or all of his or her past but also takes a sudden, unexpected trip away from home.   7

dissociative identity disorder (DID) A condition in which the personality breaks apart into two or more distinct personalities, each well integrated and well developed, which then take turns controlling the person's behavior. Also known as *multiple personality*.   7

dopamine hypothesis The theory that schizophrenia is associated with excess activity of the parts of the brain that use dopamine as a neurotransmitter.   13

double-blind A procedure in scientific research that seeks to minimize the influence of subjects' and experimenters' expectations. Both the subject and the experimenter are unaware of what treatment is being administered, that is, whether they are in the experimental group or the control group.   3

Down syndrome A form of mental retardation caused by an extra chromosome. Individuals with this condition usually have IQs of 50 or less and distinctive physical characteristics, such as an extra fold of skin on the upper eyelid, a flat nose, and poor muscle tone.   16

dream interpretation A psychoanalytic technique in which patients report their dreams as accurately as possible and the therapist explores with the patient the elements of the dreams as symbols of unconscious wishes and conflicts.   4

DSM-IV The most recent revision of the *Diagnostic and Statistical Manual,* the handbook that classifies the symptoms and types of mental disorders.   2

dyspareunia A sexual dysfunction characterized by pain during intercourse.   12

dysthymic disorder A chronic mood disorder involving a mild, persistent depression. Symptoms are similar to those of a major depressive episode, but they are not as severe or as numerous.   9

early infantile autism A disorder in children in which the primary symptom, apparent from infancy, is the inability to relate to anyone outside of oneself.   16

echolalia A speech deficit, characteristic of autistic children and some catatonic schizophrenics, in which the child aimlessly repeats what other people say.   13, 16

ego According to Freud, the psychic component that mediates between the id and the forces that restrict the id's satisfactions.   4

electroconvulsive therapy (ECT) The administering of an electric shock to a patient, thus inducing a convulsion; used in the treatment of serious depression.   9

electroencephalogram (EEG) A brain test in which electrodes, attached to the head with tape, pick up electrical activity within the brain and measure it in oscillating patterns known as brain waves.   2

electromyogram (EMG) A polygraph recording of the changes in the electrical activity of muscles.   2

elimination of plausible alternative causes The third condition to be met before causality can be demonstrated: the proposed causal relationship can

be accepted only after other likely causes have been ruled out.   3

embolism The obstruction of a blood vessel by a ball of a substance such as fat, air, or clotted blood, thus cutting off the blood supply; a common cause of infarction.   14

encephalitis Any acute infection of the brain.   14

encopresis A lack of bowel control past the age when such control is normally achieved.   15

endocrine glands Glands responsible for the production of hormones that, when released into the bloodstream, affect various bodily mechanisms such as physical growth and development.   14

endocrine system The system of endocrine, or ductless, glands—such as the hypothalamus and the pituitary—that is closely integrated with the central nervous system and is responsible for the production of hormones.   4

endogenous In depression, the term used to describe patients whose symptoms are primarily physical.   9

endorphins Brain chemicals, similar to morphine, that may underlie one's natural control of pain and natural experience of pleasure.   11

enuresis A lack of bladder control past the age when such control is normally achieved. Children with *primary enuresis* have never achieved bladder control. Those with *secondary enuresis* have lost the control they once had.   15

epidemiology The study of the frequency and distribution of disorders within specific populations.   3

epilepsy A generic term for a variety of organic disorders characterized by irregularly occurring disturbances in consciousness in the form of seizures or convulsions. The seizures seem to be caused by a disruption in the electrical and physiochemical activity of the discharging cells of the brain.   14

essential hypertension Chronically high blood pressure for which no organic cause can be found.   8

evolutionary psychology A theory that attempts to understand how adaptive psychological mechanisms develop. The theory suggests that the environment may have a greater

influence than genetics on people with antisocial personality disorder.   17

exhibitionism Sexual gratification through displaying one's genitals to an involuntary observer.   12

exorcism The practice of expelling evil spirits from a person believed to be possessed by such demons.   1

experimenter effects A methodological problem in which researchers inadvertently influence the subject's responses or perceive the subjects' behavior in terms of their own biases.   3

explicit memories Memories we are aware of, which may disappear in amnesia. *Cf.* **implicit memories.**   7

exposure A behavioral treatment for anxiety in which the client is confronted (suddenly or gradually) with his or her feared stimulus.   6

expressed emotion (EE) A measurement of key relatives' level of criticism and emotional overinvolvement, used in determining the family type of a hospitalized schizophrenic.   13

external validity The degree to which research results can be generalized, or applied, to different populations, settings, and conditions.   3

extinction A process in which a conditioned response is reduced to its preconditioned level. Previously reinforced responses are no longer reinforced.   5

false negative In commitment hearings, a failure to commit a person when commitment is justified and necessary.   18

false positive In commitment hearings, an unjustified commitment.   18

family systems perspective A theoretical approach by which families are seen as a system in which the whole is more than the sum of its parts.   5

family systems theories Views developed by family therapists that maintain that the causes of abnormal behavior may be found in habitual relationship patterns, usually within the family.   5

family therapy A form of group therapy in which the members of a family are seen together on the assumption that the disturbance lies not only in the symptomatic individual but in the family unit as a whole. Goals include more honest communications and more flexible roles within the family.   5

feedback A process in which information is returned to a system in order to regulate that system.   8

female orgasmic disorder A recurrent, lengthy delay or absence of orgasm in a woman.   12

female sexual arousal disorder In women, the absence or weakness of the physiological changes or feelings of sexual excitement that normally occur in the arousal phase of sexual response.   12

fetal alcohol syndrome (FAS) A complex of physical and behavioral defects found in many children of alcoholic women. The defects include distinctive facial characteristics, retarded physical growth, and, frequently, mental retardation.   16

fetishism Sexual gratification via inanimate objects or some part of the partner's body to the exclusion of the person as a whole.   12

flat affect A mood abnormality among schizophrenics in which the person shows no emotion.   13

fragile X syndrome A condition in which an individual's X chromosome shows a weak spot; the most common genetic cause of mental retardation.   16

free association A psychoanalytic technique in which the patient verbalizes whatever thoughts come to mind, without structuring or censoring the remarks.   1, 4, 6

frotteurism Sexual gratification through touching and rubbing against a nonconsenting person.   12

galvanic skin response (GSR) A polygraphic recording of the changes in the electrical resistance of the skin, an indication of sweat gland activity. There is an intimate relationship between emotion and physiological functioning; when a person's anxiety level rises, so may the activity of the sweat glands.   2

gaslighting A term derived from a 1944 Hollywood film; refers to attempts on the part of male batterers to make the female victim think she is crazy by denying her perception of reality.   17

gender dysphoria The symptom of being unhappy with one's assigned gender. This is one of the components of gender identity disorder.   12

gender identity disorder (GID) A condition in which people identify with the opposite sex so completely that they feel that they belong to that sex and that their own biological gender is simply a mistake. Also called *transsexualism*.   12

gender reassignment The process of changing one's gender to the other gender, usually through adopting the dress, manner, appearance, and physical characteristics of the other gender. This may include hormonal treatment and gender reassignment surgery.   12

general paresis A final stage of syphilis, involving the gradual and irreversible breakdown of physical and mental functioning.   1, 14

generalizability The ability of research results to be applied to different populations, settings, and conditions.   3

generalization The process by which an organism, conditioned to respond in a certain way to a particular stimulus, will respond to other, similar stimuli in the same way.   5

generalized anxiety disorder A chronic state of diffuse anxiety characterized by excessive worry, over a period of at least six months, about several life circumstances (most often family, money, work, and health).   6, 15

generalized dysfunction A sexual dysfunction that occurs in all sexual situations.   12

generalized seizures Epileptic seizures that either involve the entire brain at the outset (primary) or soon spread from one part to the whole brain (secondary). *Cf.* **partial seizure.**   14

genes The units of heredity on a chromosome that carry the instructions, inherited from the parents at conception, about the proteins that the body should produce. The proteins, in turn, determine the hereditary characteristics of the person—height, hair and eye color, and so on.   4

genetic high-risk design A research design in which high-risk subjects are selected on the basis of genetic factors associated with the disorder in question.   13

genital stage According to Freud, the final phase of mature sexuality, by which he meant heterosexual genital mating.   4

genotype The unique combination of genes which represents one's biological inheritance from one's parents.   4

good-poor premorbid dimension A dimension describing a patient's adaptive functioning prior to the onset of a disorder.   13

group therapy Treatment of up to 8 or 10 clients at a time by a single therapist.

hallucinations Sensory perceptions that occur in the absence of any appropriate external stimulus.   13

hallucinogens A class of drugs that acts on the central nervous system in such a way as to cause distortions in sensory perception.   11

hashish A "minor hallucinogen" derived from the resin of cannabis, a hemp plant. It is five times stronger than marijuana, another cannabis derivative.   11

health psychology A research discipline that focuses on the relationship between mental and physical health. Also called *behavioral medicine*.   8

helplessness-hopelessness syndrome A thought process characteristic of deeply depressed persons in which they regard their condition as irreversible, believing that they are both unable to help themselves and unlikely to be helped by external forces.   9

hemorrhage A cerebrovascular accident in which a blood vessel in the brain ruptures, causing blood to spill out into the brain tissue.   14

heroin An addictive opiate derived from morphine.   11

high-risk design A form of longitudinal research that involves the study of people who have a high probability of developing a disorder.   3

histrionic personality disorder A disorder involving the exaggerated display of emotion.   10

hormones Chemical messengers that are released directly into the bloodstream by the endocrine gland and that affect sexual functioning, physical growth and development, and emotional responses.   4

host In dissociative identity disorder patients, the personality corresponding to who the person was before the onset of the disorder.   7

human immunodeficiency virus (HIV) The virus that attacks and breaks down the human immune system and causes AIDS. It is transmitted by blood, semen, vaginal secretions, or breast milk of an infected person through unsafe sex, the sharing of hypodermic needles, a contaminated blood transfusion, or passage to a child in the womb of an infected mother. 8

humors In Hippocrates' view, the four vital fluids possessed by humans: phlegm, blood, black bile, and yellow bile. The balance of these humors in each individual was thought to influence personality. 1

Huntington's chorea A fatal organic brain disorder which is transmitted genetically. Symptoms include spasmodic jerking of the limbs, bizarre behavior, and mental deterioration. 14

hypertension Chronic elevation of blood pressure due to constriction of the arteries; a stress-related physical disorder. Also called *high blood pressure*. 8

hypnosis An artificially induced trance, or sleeplike state, in which the subject is highly susceptible to suggestion. 1

hypnotics Drugs used to induce sleep. Also called *sleeping pills*. 8

hypoactive sexual desire disorder A chronic lack of interest in sex. 12

hypochondriasis A disorder in which a person converts anxiety into a chronic fear of disease. The fear is maintained by the constant misinterpretation of physical signs and sensations as abnormal. 7

hypothesis A tentative explanation for behavior that attempts to answer the questions "How?" and "Why?" Scientific research often begins with a hypothesis. 3

hypothesis testing A strategy used in cognitive therapy whereby clients are urged to test their assumptions in the real world. 4

hysteria A psychogenic disorder that mimics a biogenic disorder. 1,7

iatrogenic A type of symptom brought about as a consequence of therapy or treatment. 7

id According to Freud, the basic psychic structure, consisting of primitive biological drives toward sex and aggression. 4

idiopathic epilepsy A convulsive disorder for which there is no known cause. 14

immune system The body's system of defense against infectious disease and cancer. 8

implicit memories Memories that a person with amnesia cannot call into conscious awareness but that still affect his or her behavior. *Cf.* **explicit memories.** 7

impulse-control disorders Patterns of impulsive behavior that seem to exist not as part of another major syndrome but independently. Their essential feature is the inability to resist the impulse to act in ways harmful to oneself or to others. 10

inappropriate affect A mood abnormality among schizophrenics in which the person's emotional responses seem unsuitable to the situation. 13

incest Sexual relations between family members. 12

incidence The number of new cases of a disorder reported during a specific time period. 3

independent variable In a research study, a factor that has been determined before the experiment and may be manipulated by the experimenters in order to measure its effect. 3

indeterminate sentences Periods of incarceration with no limit, often given to defendants acquitted by reason of insanity. 18

indicated preventive interventions The form of prevention efforts that are aimed at individuals within a particular group who have either early signs of a certain disorder or a biological marker indicating a risk for the disorder. 19

individual response specificity The principle that people seem to have characteristic patterns of autonomic nervous system response which carry over from one kind of stress to another. 8

infarction A cerebrovascular accident in which the supply of blood to the brain is cut off, resulting in the death of brain tissue fed by that source. 14

inpatient A mental patient who is hospitalized. 1

insanity defense A legal plea in which the defendant admits to having committed the crime but pleads not guilty, stating that because of mental disturbance he or she was not morally responsible at the time of the crime. 18

insomnia The chronic inability to sleep. The condition can stem from both physical and psychological factors. 8

instrumental aggression The type of aggression that is considered goal-oriented or hostile. 17

intelligence quotient (IQ) The subject's final score on an adult version of the Stanford-Binet Intelligence scale, a test which measures a child's ability to perform a range of intellectual tasks. IQ tests play an important part in the diagnosis of mental retardation and brain damage. 2

intelligence tests Psychological assessment techniques effective in predicting success in school but questionable as a valid measure of intelligence. 2

interjudge reliability A criterion for judging the reliability of a psychological test: the test should yield the same results when scored or interpreted by different judges. 2

internal consistency A criterion for judging the reliability of a psychological test: different parts of the test should yield the same result. 2

internal validity The extent to which the results of an experiment can be confidently attributed to the effects of the independent variable. 3

interpretation Freud's primary tool for revealing hidden, intrapsychic motives; it involves going beyond observing surface behavior to uncover its latent content. 4

interview An assessment method consisting of a face-to-face conversation between subject and examiner. 2

Korsakoff's psychosis An irreversible nutritional deficiency due to vitamin B_1 deficiency associated with alcoholism; characterized by anterograde amnesia and confabulation. 14

la belle indifférence A response often seen in conversion disorder in which the person does not seem at all disturbed by his or her disability. 7

laceration The most serious form of brain trauma, in which a foreign object, such as a bullet or piece of metal, enters the skull and directly ruptures and destroys brain tissue. 14

latency The dormancy of a particular behavior or response. 4

lateralization The differences in structure and function between the right and the left hemispheres of the brain. 4

law of effect Thorndike's formulation of the importance of reward in the learning process which states that responses that lead to satisfying consequences are strengthened and, therefore, are likely to be repeated, while responses with unsatisfying consequences are weakened and, therefore, unlikely to be repeated. 5

learned helplessness In behavioral theory, the depressive's inability to initiate adaptive responses, possibly due to a helplessness conditioned by earlier, inescapable trauma. 9

learning The process whereby behavior changes in response to the environment. 5

learning disorders Three conditions characterized by reading, writing, or mathematical skills that are substantially below what would be expected for the person's age, education, and intelligence and by a resulting interference with the person's adjustment. The three conditions are reading disorder (dyslexia), disorder of written expression, and mathematics disorder. 15

Lewy body disease A relatively common form of dementia produced by the presence of Lewy bodies in neurons in the brain. The disease may produce Parkinson's symptoms, visual hallucination, and deficits in attention, concentration, and visual-perceptual skills. 14

libido Freud's term for a basic sexual drive, which he saw as the major source of psychic energy. 4

lifelong dysfunction A sexual dysfunction that has existed, without relief, since the person's earliest sexual experiences. 12

lithium A mood-altering drug used to control manic episodes. 9

longitudinal studies Scientific research designs in which a group of subjects is studied several different times over an extended period of time. Also called *prospective studies*. 3

loosening of associations The rambling, disjointed quality that is characteristic of schizophrenic speech. 13

LSD (lysergic acid diethylamide) A hallucinogen derived from a fungus; it interferes with the processing of information in the nervous system, causing perceptual distortions. 11

Mad Cow disease A spongiform brain disease of cows that results in neurological impairment and eventually death. The disease may be related to Cruetzfeld-Jacob disease, which causes similar results in humans. 14

magnetic resonance imagining (MRI) The use of magnetic fields to produce a highly precise picture of the brain. 4

major depressive disorder A condition characterized by one or more major depressive episodes with no intervening periods of mania. 9

major depressive episode An extended period of intense depression that usually begins and ends gradually and causes a radical change in most aspects of the individual's functioning. 9

male erectile disorder In the second phase of sexual arousal, a failure of the tissues in a man's penis to become congested with blood. 12

male orgasmic disorder A recurrent, lengthy delay or absence of ejaculation and orgasm in a man. 12

malingering The conscious faking of disease symptoms in order to avoid responsibility. 7

mania An emotional state characterized by the exaggeration of positive feelings. The person becomes feverishly active and excited and feels capable of accomplishing anything. 9

manic episode An extended period of intense mania that usually begins and ends suddenly and causes a radical change in an individual's social functioning. 9

MAO inhibitors The first important class of antidepressants. Although named on the assumption that they block the action of monoamine oxidase (MAO), their mechanism has not been established. 6, 9

marijuana A "minor hallucinogen" derived from the dried, crushed leaves of cannabis, a hemp plant. 11

masochism Sexual gratification through pain and/or humiliation inflicted on oneself. 12

matching In alcohol treatment, when the patient is directed to a treatment program best suited to his or her personal characteristics. 11

medical model The conceptualization of psychological abnormality as a group of diseases analogous to physical diseases. 1

mental health promotion The enhancement of an individual's well-being, including competence, self-esteem, and resilience to stress. 19

mental retardation A condition that is characterized by subaverage intellectual functioning, by serious deficits in adaptive skills, and by onset before age 18. 16

mental status exam The mental status exam is a set of mental tests used to detect dementia (severe mental deterioration) and other organic brain disorders. The diagnostician evaluates the patient on appearance, speech, mood, perception, thought content, and cognitive processes (e.g., memory). 2

metastatic brain tumors Brain tumors that originate in some other part of the body and then metastasize, or spread, to the brain. 14

methadone A synthetic opiate that satisfies the craving for narcotics but does not produce narcotic euphoria. 11

migraine headache A severe form of chronic headache that is usually localized on one side of the head, is sometimes preceded by perceptual distortion, and is typically accompanied by other symptoms such as nausea or confusion; a stress-related disorder. 8

mind-body problem The issue of the relationship between the psychic and somatic aspects of human functioning. 8

mini mental status exam A shorter version of the mental status exam. 2

Minnesota Multiphasic Personality Inventory-2 (MMPI-2) The most widely used self-report personality inventory, the purpose of which is to simplify differential diagnosis by comparing self-descriptive statements endorsed by new patients to statements endorsed by groups of people already diagnosed with a particular condition.   2

minor tranquilizers Drugs taken to reduce anxiety or tension.   6

mood disorders Emotional conditions in which feelings of depression or mania become so extreme and prolonged that the person's life is completely disrupted. Also called *affective disorders.*   9

moral therapy A nineteenth-century approach to treatment that involved providing an environment in which the mentally ill would be treated humanely and could discuss their difficulties, live in peace, and engage in some useful employment.   1

motivational interviewing In drug and alcohol rehabilitation, a question-and-answer method of interviewing aimed at increasing the patient's motivation to change, leading to discontinuing substance abuse.   11

multiple-baseline design An experimental research design in which treatment is introduced at different intervals across subjects, behaviors, or situations.   3

muscle-contraction headaches Ordinary headaches. Also called *tension headaches.*   8

narcissistic personality disorder A disorder characterized by a grandiose sense of self-importance, often combined with periodic feelings of inferiority.   10

negative feedback Feedback in which the turning on of one component of a system leads to the turning off of another component, in order to regulate the system.   8

negative reinforcement A conditioning procedure in which a response is followed by the removal of an aversive event or stimulus, thereby promoting the response.   5

negative symptoms In schizophrenia, the absence of something that is normally present; poverty of speech, flat affect, withdrawal, apathy, and attentional impairment.   13

nervous system The vast electrochemical conducting network that extends from the brain through the rest of the body and carries information, in the form of electrical impulses, from the brain to the rest of the body and back to the brain.   4

neurons The cells of the nervous system, which connect motor and receptor cells and transmit information throughout the body.   4

neuroses Conditions in which maladaptive behaviors serve as a protection against a source of unconscious anxiety.   4

neurosyphilis The deterioration of brain tissue as a result of syphilis.   14

neurotransmitter One of a group of chemicals that facilitate the transmission of electrical impulses between nerve endings in the brain.   4

night terrors Harrowing dreams experienced by children, who show extreme autonomic arousal and violent movements during the dreams and are confused, disoriented, and upset when awake.   15

nightmares Frightening dreams, which do not cause physiological arousal and do not necessarily awaken the dreamer. During early childhood, nightmares are distinguished from *night terrors*, which are both more physically arousing and more harrowing.   15

norms The rules in any society that define "right" and "wrong." Norms guide most of our actions and are an important standard for defining abnormality.   1

null hypothesis The assumption that the independent variable had no effect on the differences between experimental groups.   3

obesity An excessive amount of fat on the body. Each culture sets its own standard for ideal body weight, so what is considered obese in one culture may be desirable in another.   8

object relations In psychodynamic terminology, "objects" are the people to whom one is attached by strong emotional ties. According to object-relations theorists, the most powerful determinant of psychological development is the child's interaction with the primary caregiver, the child's chief object.   4

obsession A thought or an image that keeps unwillingly intruding into a person's consciousness, though the person may consider it senseless or even unpleasant.   6

obsessive-compulsive disorder Involuntary dwelling on an unwelcome thought (*obsession*) and/or involuntary repetition of an unnecessary action (*compulsion*).   6

obsessive-compulsive personality disorder A disorder marked by excessive preoccupation with trivial details, at the cost of both spontaneity and effectiveness.   10

Oedipus complex According to Freud, the desire that all male children have during the phallic stage to do away with the parent of the same sex in order to take sexual possession of the parent of the opposite sex; a crucial stage of development which determines the child's future sexual adjustment.   4

operant conditioning The process by which an organism learns to associate certain consequences with certain actions it has taken. Also called *instrumental conditioning.*   5

operational definitions The definitions of concepts involved in a hypothesis in terms of operations that can be observed and measured, so that the hypothesis can be tested.   3

opiates A class of drugs that induces relaxation and reverie and provides relief from anxiety and pain.   11

opium A depressant derived from the opium poppy.   11

oral stage In psychodynamic theory, the first stage of psychosocial development, in which the mouth is the primary focus of libidinal impulses and pleasure; occurs in the first year of life.   4

oscillations The rhythmic back-and-forth cycles of the various systems of the body—for example, breathing, heartbeat, blood pressure, temperature, digestion, sleep, menstruation, and the production of hormones, neurotransmitters, and immune cells.   8

outpatient A mental patient who receives treatment outside of the hospital.   1

pain disorder A syndrome characterized by chronic pain that is more severe or persistent than can be explained by medical causes. 7

panic attack An attack of almost unbearable anxiety, beginning suddenly and unexpectedly and usually lasting several minutes, though possibly continuing for hours. 6

panic disorder A disorder characterized by recurrent panic attacks followed by psychological or behavioral problems. 6

paranoid personality disorder A disorder defined by suspiciousness in almost all situations and with almost all people. 10

paranoid schizophrenia A form of schizophrenia characterized by consistent delusions and/or hallucinations, often related to themes of persecution and grandeur. 13

paranoid-nonparanoid dimension The classification of schizophrenics according to the presence (paranoid) or absence (nonparanoid) of delusions of persecution and/or grandeur. 13

paraphilias Sexual patterns—such as fetishism and transvestism—that deviate from the standard of normal sexuality as consisting of a nondestructive interplay between consenting adults. 12

parasympathetic division The division of the autonomic nervous system that decreases physical arousal and is usually dominant under less emotional conditions. It regulates breathing, heart rate, blood pressure, stomach and intestinal activity, and elimination. *Cf.* **sympathetic division.** 4

Parkinson's disease An organic brain disorder involving damage to the basal ganglia. Symptoms include tremors, a masklike countenance, a stiff gait, and psychological disturbances such as a general mental deficit and social withdrawal. 14

partial seizures Epileptic seizures that originate in one part of the brain rather than in the brain as a whole. May be either **simple** or **complex.** *Cf.* **generalized seizures.** 14

passive avoidance learning Learning to stop making certain behavioral responses to stimuli when those responses will result in punishment. 17

PCP (phencyclidine) Also called "angel dust," a hallucinogen widely used in the 1970s that poses the risk for users of harming themselves through burns, falls, or accidents, or harming others as a result of perceptual distortions and paranoia. 11

pedophilia Child molesting—that is, sexual gratification, on the part of an adult, through sexual contact with children. 12

peripheral nervous system The network of nerve fibers that leads from the central nervous system to all parts of the body and carries out the commands of the CNS. It has two branches: the somatic nervous system and the autonomic nervous system. 4

person variables A person's stable traits. Adherents of the psychometric approach hold that personality issues mainly from person variables. 2

personality disorder An enduring pattern of inner experience and behavior that deviates markedly from the expectations of the individual's culture, that is pervasive and inflexible, that has an onset in adolescence or early adulthood, that is stable over time, and that leads to distress or impairment. 10

phallic stage In psychodynamic theory, the third stage of psychosocial development, in which pleasure is derived from masturbation, the stroking and handling of the genitals; occurs from the third to the fifth or sixth year of life. 4

phenothiazines A group of antipsychotic drugs that relieve symptoms such as confusion, withdrawal, hallucinations, and delusions. 13

phenotype The unique combination of observable characteristics that results from the combination of a person's genotype with the environment. 4

phenylketonuria (PKU) A genetic defect caused by a deficiency in a liver enzyme, phenylalanine 4-hydroxylase, which results in severe retardation, hyperactivity, and erratic behavior. 16

placebo An inert substance used in research, which may manifest some effects of the drug it has been substituted for. 3

play therapy A psychodynamic technique in which the therapist provides young patients with drawing materials and toys, rather than asking them questions, on the assumption that whatever is troubling them will be expressed in their drawings and games. 15

polygraph A recording device equipped with sensors, which, when attached to the body, can pick up subtle physiological changes in the form of electrical impulses. The changes are recorded on a moving roll of paper. 2

polysomnography The all-night employment of a variety of measures including EEG, EMG, and respiration invaluable for measuring sleep. 2

positive-negative symptoms dimension A dimension describing a schizophrenic patient's symptoms. *Cf.* **negative symptoms; positive symptoms.** 13

positive reinforcement A situation in which a response is followed by a positive event or stimulus, thereby increasing the probability that the response will be repeated. 5

positive symptoms In schizophrenia, the presence of something that is normally absent, including hallucinations, delusions, bizarre behavior, and incoherent thought patterns. 13

positron emission tomography (PET) A means of examining the brain. The patient is injected with a radioactively labeled sugar solution, and the path of the radioactive particles through the brain is traced. 4

post-synaptic receptors Special proteins on the surface of neurons that bind with neurotransmitters squirted into the synapse from the dendrites of adjoining neurons. Molecules in the neurotransmitter fit into the receptor like a key into a lock. 4

posttraumatic stress disorder A severe psychological reaction to intensely traumatic events, including assault, rape, natural disasters, and wartime combat. Victims may reexperience the traumatic event in recollections or in nightmares, show diminished responsiveness to their present surroundings, and suffer physical symptoms and intense irritability. Generally appearing shortly after the trauma, the symptoms usually disappear within six months, but some may last for years.   6

poverty of content A characteristic of schizophrenic speech in which words are used correctly but communication is poor.   13

prediction (1) The second objective of the scientific method: the ability to predict the relationship between events. (2) The second goal of psychological assessment: the development of hypotheses about future behavior, treatment, and statistical likelihoods.   2

predictive validity The degree to which a test's findings are consistent with the subject's future performance.   2

prefrontal lobotomy A psychosurgical procedure for severely disturbed patients in which some of the connections between the frontal lobe and the lower parts of the brain are severed; very rarely performed today.   1

premature ejaculation A sexual disorder in which the rapidity of ejaculation interferes with the couple's enjoyment.   12

premorbid adjustment The level of functioning that was normal for a person before the onset of a disorder.   9

prevalence The percentage of a population that has a particular disorder at a particular time.   3

prevention The process of keeping psychological disorders from beginning in the first place by changing the environment, the family, or the individual.   19

primary brain tumors Tumors that originate either within the brain or outside the brain but inside the skull.   14

primary gain In conversion disorder, the relief from anxiety that is experienced by the person as a result of the conversion symptom, which blocks the person's awareness of internal conflict.   7

primary prevention The first level of prevention of psychological disorder, the goal of which is to prevent disorders from developing.   19

primary reinforcer A stimulus or need that one responds to instinctively, without learning.   5

process-reactive dimension The classification of schizophrenics according to whether the onset of symptoms is gradual (process) or abrupt and precipitated by a traumatic event (reactive).   13

prodromal phase The initial stage of schizophrenia, during which the person generally becomes withdrawn and socially isolated.   13

prognosis The prediction of the course of a patient's illness.   2

projective personality tests Assessment techniques used to draw out, indirectly, individuals' true conflicts and motives by presenting them with ambiguous stimuli and allowing them to project their private selves into their responses.   2

prophylactic medication An experimental approach by which drugs are given to high-risk people who have not yet developed symptoms of mental illness.   19

prosocial behavior Behavior that encourages social interaction.   17

psychiatric social worker Someone who has earned an M.S.W. (master of social work), with special courses and training in psychological counseling.   1

psychiatrist An M.D. who specializes in diagnosing and treating mental disorders. Because of their medical degree, psychiatrists can also prescribe psychoactive drugs.   1

psychoactive drug A drug that alters one's psychological state.   11

psychoanalysis The psychodynamic therapy method that relies heavily on the techniques of free association, dream interpretation, and analysis of resistance and transference. The aim is to give patients insight into their unconscious conflicts, impulses, and motives.   1, 4

psychoanalyst Someone who has had postgraduate training at a psychoanalytic institute and has undergone psychoanalysis him- or herself. (Most psychoanalysts are psychiatrists, but other mental health professionals may undertake this training.)   1

psychodynamic perspective A school of thought united by a common concern with the dynamics, or interaction, of forces lying deep within the mind. Almost all psychodynamic theorists agree on three basic principles: much human behavior is determined by intrapsychic forces; such forces generally operate unconsciously; and the form taken by these forces is deeply affected by developmental factors, especially by family relationships.   4

psychogenic theory The theory that psychological disturbance is due primarily not to organic dysfunction but to emotional stress.   1

psychological assessment The collection, organization, and interpretation of information about a person and his or her situation.   2

psychological dependence The nonphysiological dimension of drug abuse, characterized by the abuser's growing tendency to center his or her life on the drug.   11

psychological test An assessment technique in which the subject is presented with a series of stimuli to which he or she is asked to respond.   2

psychometric approach A method of psychological testing that aims at locating and measuring stable underlying traits.   2

psychoneuroimmunology (PNI) The subspecialty of health medicine that studies the interaction between psychological factors and the immune system, mediated by the central nervous system.   8

psychopathology Abnormal psychology.   1

psychophysiological disorders Physical disorders that are influenced by emotional factors and that are also scientifically traceable to a clear organic cause. Also called *psychosomatic disorders.*   8

psychoses. *See* **psychosis.**

psychosexual development Freud's theory that personality development takes place in a series of stages, in each of which the child's central motivation is to gratify the drive for pleasure in a different zone of the body.   4

psychosis A condition of ego collapse in which adaptive functioning is drastically curtailed.   4, 13

psychosurgery Surgery aimed at reducing abnormal behavior in the absence of any signs of organic brain pathology.   4

punishment The process in which an organism, in order to avoid (or, less often, obtain) a consequence, stops performing a behavior.   5

radical behaviorism The form of behaviorism developed by B. F. Skinner that proposes that everything a person does, says, or feels constitutes behavior and, even if unobservable, is subject to experimental analysis.   5

random assignment A balancing control technique that involves assigning subjects randomly to the different groups in an experiment.   3

random sample A sample in which every element of a population has an equal likelihood of being included.   3

rape Sexual intercourse with a nonconsenting partner.   17

rational-emotive therapy Ellis' approach to cognitive therapy, which sees emotional disturbances as the result of irrational beliefs that guide people's interpretation of events. Clients are helped to appraise their situations realistically and develop new ways of interpreting experience.   4

reactive In depression, the term used to describe patients whose symptoms are primarily emotional and cognitive.   9

reactive aggression The type of aggression that is considered a response to a perceived provocation.   17

reattribution training A strategy used in cognitive therapy whereby the client is helped to change distorted ideas of cause and effect and to attribute events to their causes in a realistic manner.   4

reinforcement The process by which behavior is increased or maintained by rewarding consequences. Operant conditioning depends on reinforcement: most people would not go to work if it weren't for the paycheck.   5

relapse prevention In alcohol rehabilitation, an approach aimed at reducing the likelihood of "slipping," and preventing an escalation of usage if "slips" do occur; in the treatment of rapists, an approach that trains rapists how to avoid situations that place them at risk for repeating the crime and how to resist the impulse to commit the offense.   11, 17

relaxation training A technique that behaviorists have used in stress-relief programs in which the subject alternately tenses, then relaxes, groups of muscles. The goal is to teach the patient to distinguish between tension and relaxation and ultimately achieve the latter.   8

reliability (1) In the scientific method, the degree to which a description remains stable over time and under different testing conditions. (2) The degree to which a measurement device yields consistent results under varying conditions.   2

replicate To repeat aspects of a research study with some changes in certain variables in order to show whether a previous study's results are found under similar circumstances.   3

representativeness The degree to which a research sample's characteristics match those of the population under study.   3

repression A defense mechanism in which unacceptable id impulses are pushed down into the unconscious, thereby rendered unable to disturb the person consciously.   4

residual phase The third phase of schizophrenia, during which behavior is similar to that seen during the prodromal phase.   13

resistance In psychoanalytic theory, a defense mechanism used by the patient to avoid confronting certain memories and impulses. The patient may argue with the therapist, change the subject, miss appointments, and so on.   4, 6

respondent conditioning The process of learning a conditioned response. Also called *classical conditioning*.   5

response sets Test-taking attitudes that lead subjects to distort their responses, often unconsciously.   2

retarded depression A type of depression in which there is little spontaneous motor activity. Movement is slow and deliberate, with a minimum number of gestures and little verbalization.   9

Rorschach Psychodiagnostic Inkblot Test The most well-known projective personality test, in which subjects are asked to interpret 10 cards, each showing a symmetrical inkblot design.   2

sadism Sexual gratification through infliction of pain and/or humiliation on others.   12

sadomasochistic The term applied to sexual partners in which either a sadist and a masochist pair up to satisfy their complementary needs, or both partners enjoy both sadism and masochism and switch between the two.   12

safety planning An approach offered by battered women's shelters that can reduce the risk of further violence to battered women.   17

savant syndrome A disorder in which a person with greatly diminished mental skill shows extraordinary proficiency in one, isolated skill.   16

schema An organized structure of information about a particular domain in life; it is stored in the mind and helps a person to organize and process newly learned information.   4

schizoid personality disorder A disorder marked by social withdrawal and isolation.   10

schizophrenia A group of psychoses marked by severe distortion of thought, perception, and mood; by bizarre behavior; and by social withdrawal.   13

schizotypal personality disorder A disorder marked by odd speech, behavior, thinking, and/or perception.   10

seasonal affective disorder (SAD) A mood disorder characterized by depression that occurs only during the winter.   9

secondary gain In conversion disorder, the "benefit," of being excused from responsibilities and of attracting sympathy and attention, which accrue to the person as a result of the conversion symptom.   7

secondary prevention The second level of prevention of psychological disorder, the goal of which is to detect and treat disorders at an early stage, so that minor disorders do not develop into major ones.   19

selective attention An adaptive mechanism by which human beings take in and process only some of the information bombarding their senses at any given moment.   4

selective preventive interventions The form of prevention efforts that are aimed at a subgroup whose risk for developing a particular disorder is higher than average.   19

selective serotonin reuptake inhibitors (SSRIs) A class of antidepressants that work by blocking the reuptake of the neurotransmitter serotonin.   6, 9

self-instructional training A cognitive therapy technique that teaches people to control their behavior by controlling what they say to themselves before, during, and after their actions.   15

self-report personality inventories Psychological tests which, unlike projective tests such as the Rorschach and TAT, ask the subjects direct questions about themselves.   2

separation anxiety disorder A childhood disorder characterized by intense fear and distress upon being separated from parents or other caretakers.   15

sexual aversion disorder Active avoidance of sex as a result of feelings of disgust or fear about it.   12

sexual dysfunctions Disorders involving either a disruption of the sexual response cycle or pain during intercourse.   12

sheltered workshops Special work centers designed to meet the needs of the mentally retarded people who are employed in them.   16

simple partial seizure A partial epileptic seizure in which cognitive functioning remains intact.   14

single-case experiment A research design that focuses on behavior change in one person but, unlike the *case study,* methodically varies the conditions surrounding the person's behavior and monitors the behavior under the changing conditions.   3

situational dysfunction A sexual dysfunction that occurs only in certain situations or with certain partners.   12

situational variables The environmental stimuli that precede and follow any given action by a person.   2

sleepwalking A dissociative disorder in which the person walks and performs some complex action while asleep. It is much more common in children than in adults. Also called *somnambulism.*   15

social phobia A phobic disorder in which the person's anxiety is aroused by one or more social situations and is related to the person's fear of being humiliated or criticized. In childhood, this disorder typically takes the form of a paralyzing fear of strangers—peers as well as adults.   6, 15

social-skills training A behavioral therapy that teaches depressed or schizophrenic people basic techniques for engaging in satisfying interactions with others.   9, 13

sociocultural perspective The theory that abnormal behavior is the product of broad social forces and conditions such as poverty, urbanization, and inequality.   5

somatic nervous system The part of the peripheral nervous system that senses and acts on the external world, relaying to the brain information picked up by the sense organs and transmitting the brain's messages to the skeletal muscles, which move the body.   4

somatization disorder A syndrome characterized by numerous and recurrent physical complaints, persisting for several years, for which no medical basis can be found.   7

somatoform disorders Conditions in which psychological conflicts take on a somatic or physical form. These disorders include hypochondriasis, somatization disorder, and conversion disorder.   7

specific phobia A phobic disorder with a particular stimulus, such as heights, enclosed places, injury, or a certain type of animal.   6

spectator role A sexual dysfunction in which a person is constantly watching and judging his or her sexual performance and is not able to relax and experience pleasure. This worry often causes the much-feared failure, because the tension blunts response to sexual stimuli.   12

standard of proof In commitment hearings, the degree of certainty required in order to commit someone to a mental institution. There must be "clear and convincing evidence" that the person is mentally ill and dangerous.   18

statistical inference A technique used by researchers to try to determine whether differences between experimental groups are due to the independent variable. It begins by assuming the *null hypothesis* and then using probability theory to determine the likelihood of having obtained the experimental results if the independent variable had had no effect. If the likelihood is small, the result is judged to be statistically significant, and the independent variable is assumed to have had an effect.   3

stereotypy The act of engaging in purposeless behaviors repetitively for hours, sometimes manifested by schizophrenics.   13

stimulants A class of drugs that provides energy, alertness, and feelings of confidence.   11

stimulus specificity The principle that different kinds of stress produce different kinds of physiological response.   8

strategic approach A program of brief therapy emphasizing paradox and reframing.   5

stress Variously defined as environmental stimulus of the body, as the body's response to the demands of the environment, and as the interaction between an environmental stimulus and the body's appraisal of it.   8

stroke *See* **cerebrovascular accident (CVA).**

structural family therapy A therapeutic approach in which family members are encouraged to fashion more comfortable and flexible roles for themselves within the family unit.   5

structural hypothesis Freud's belief that the mind can be divided into three broad forces: the id, the ego, and the superego.   4

stuttering The interruption of fluent speech through blocked, prolonged, or repeated words, syllables, or sounds.   15

substance abuse A pattern of maladaptive drug use that has not progressed to full-blown dependence. It is determined by the appearance of any one of the following symptoms: recurrent drug-related failure to fulfill major role obligations (e.g., absenteeism from school or work, neglect of children); recurrent drug use in physically dangerous situations (e.g., drunk driving); drug-related legal problems; and continued drug use despite social or interpersonal problems caused by the effects of the drug. *Cf.* **substance dependence.**   11

substance dependence The diagnostic category to which a drug user is assigned who fulfills any three of these seven criteria: preoccupation with the drug; unintentional overuse; tolerance; withdrawal; persistent desire or efforts to control drug use; the abandonment of important social, occupational, or recreational activities for the sake of drug use; and continued drug use despite serious drug-related problems. *Cf.* **substance abuse.**   11

superego According to Freud, the part of the mind that represents the moral standards of the society and parents, as internalized by the child.   4

sympathetic division The division of the autonomic nervous system which becomes dominant in times of stress and which heightens the body's arousal, causing blood pressure, heart rate, perspiration, and adrenaline to increase, pupils to dilate, and salivation and digestive functions to diminish. *Cf.* **parasympathetic division.**   4

symptomatic epilepsy The label applied to convulsions that are a function of brain damage caused by pathologies such as neurosyphilis, alcohol or drug intoxication, tumors, encephalitis, trauma, or strokes.   14

synapse The gap between two neurons across which nerve impulses pass.   4

syndrome The distinct cluster of symptoms that tends to occur in a particular disease.   1

synergistic effect The combined impact of two drugs, which is greater than the effect of either drug when taken alone.   11

systematic desensitization A behavior therapy technique in which the patient, while in a relaxed state, imagines his or her anxiety-provoking stimuli or is presented with the actual stimuli. Progressing from the least to the most feared situations, the patient learns to remain relaxed—a response that should carry over to real-life situations.   5, 6

tardive dyskinesia A muscle disorder that causes uncontrollable grimacing and lip smacking; caused by antipsychotic drugs.   13

Tay-Sachs disease A genetic disorder of lipid metabolism marked by the absence of the enzyme hexosominidase A in brain tissues;

causes mental retardation, muscular deterioration, convulsions, and death before the age of six.   16

test-retest reliability A criterion for judging the reliability of a psychological test: the test should yield the same results when administered to the same person at different times.   2

Thematic Apperception Test (TAT) A frequently used projective personality test in which the subject is presented with a series of pictures showing one, two, or three people doing something. The scenes are ambiguous enough to allow for a variety of interpretations, yet they nudge the subject in the direction of certain kinds of associations, unlike the Rorschach test. For example, a picture of a man in a business suit might tap a subject's feelings about his or her father.   2

theory of the mind The ability, lacking in autistic children, to appreciate the existence of purely mental states, such as beliefs or desires, and to predict or understand behavior based on such states.   16

third-variable problem In scientific research, an alternative factor, not considered by the researchers, that may be causing the covariation of the two factors being investigated.   3

three-term contingency A description including a discriminating stimulus, a response, and the consequence of the response.   5

thrombosis The obstruction of a blood vessel by a buildup of fatty material coating the inside of the vessel, thus blocking the flow of blood; a common cause of infarction.   14

time-order relationship The second condition to be met before causality can be demonstrated: the presumed cause must occur before the presumed effect.   3

token economy A behavior modification procedure, based on operant-conditioning principles, in which patients are given a conditioned reinforcer such as tokens for performing target behaviors. The patients can exchange the tokens for backup reinforcers such as snacks or special privileges.   13

tolerance The physiological condition in which the usual dosage of a drug no longer produces the desired effect.   11

tonic-clonic seizures Generalized epileptic seizures that typically begin with a tonic, or rigid, extension of the arms and legs, followed by a clonic, or jerking, movement throughout the body.   14

traits Stable underlying characteristics that presumably exist in differing degrees in everyone.   2

tranquilizers A group of drugs that produce mild calm and relaxation. They can be addictive and have side effects.   11

transference In psychoanalytic theory, the process by which patients identify the therapist with important people in their lives, usually with their parents, and project onto the therapist their relationship with those people.   4, 6

transsexual *See* **gender identity disorders (GID).**

transvestism Sexual gratification through dressing in the clothes of the opposite sex.   12

traumatic delirium The state of disorientation that a patient suffering from a brain contusion may experience upon awakening from the coma.   14

tricyclics A class of drugs widely used to treat depression, which generally works by blocking the reuptake of the neurotransmitter norepinephrine by the presynaptic neuron.   6, 9

trisomy 21 A condition in which there is an extra chromosome in pair 21 in the human cell; the genetic basis of Down syndrome.   16

Type A A personality characterized by pressure to achieve, impatience, high standards of self-evaluation, and hostility.   8

Type I schizophrenia A dimension of schizophrenia characterized by positive symptoms.   13

Type II schizophrenia A dimension of schizophrenia characterized by negative symptoms.   13

unconditioned response A natural, unlearned response to a stimulus.   5

unconditioned stimulus A stimulus that elicits a natural, or unconditioned, response.   5

unconscious In Freudian theory, the level of consciousness that contains all memories not readily available to the perceptual conscious, because they have been either forgotten or repressed.   4

universal prevention The form of prevention efforts aimed at the entire population of a particular group. 19

vaginismus A sexual dysfunction in which the muscles surrounding the entrance to the vagina undergo involuntary spasmodic contractions, making intercourse either impossible or painfully difficult. 12

validity The degree to which a description or test measures what it is supposed to measure. 2

vascular dementia The impairment of many of the brain's faculties as the cumulative result of many infarctions. 14

voyeurism Sexual gratification through clandestine observation of other people's sexual activities or sexual anatomy. 12

withdrawal Temporary psychological and physiological disturbances resulting from the body's attempt to readjust to the absence of a drug. 6, 11

word salad A schizophrenic speech pattern in which words and phrases are combined in a disorganized fashion, seemingly devoid of logic, meaning, and even associational links. 13

References

Abel, G. G., Becker, J. V., Cunningham-Rathner, J., Mittelman, M., et al. (1988). Multiple paraphilic diagnoses among sex offenders. *Bulletin of the American Academy of Psychiatry and the Law, 16,* 153–168.

Abel, G. G., Gore, D. K., Holland, C. L., Camp, N., Becker, J. V., & Rathner, J. (1989). The measurement of cognitive distortions in child molesters. *Annals of Sex Research, 2,* 135–153.

Abel, G. G., Lawry, A. S., Karlstrom, K., Osborn, C. A., & Gillespie, C. F. (1994). Screening tests for pedophilia. *Criminal Justice and Behavior, 21,* 115–131.

Abel, G. G., Osborn, C., Anthony, D., & Gardos, P. (1992). Current treatment of paraphilias. In J. Bancroft, C. Davis, & H. Ruppel (Eds.), *Annual Review of Sex Research,* 255–290.

Abel, G. G., Rouleau, J., & Cunningham-Rathner, J. (1984). Sexually aggressive behavior. In W. Curran, A. L. McGarry, & S. A. Shah (Eds.), *Modern legal psychiatry and psychology.* Philadelphia: Davis.

Abelson, J. L., Curtis, G. C., & Cameron, O. G. (1996). Hypothalamic-pituitary-adrenal axis activity in panic disorder: Effects of alprazolam on 24 h secretion of adrenocorticotropin and cortisol. *Journal of Psychiatric Research, 30,* 79–93.

Abikoff, H. (1985). Efficacy of cognitive training interventions in hyperactive children: A critical review. Special Issue: Attention deficit disorder: Issues in assessment and intervention. *Clinical Psychology Review, 5,* 479–512.

Abraham, H. D. (1983). Visual phenomenology of the LSD flashback. *Archives of General Psychiatry, 40,* 518–520.

Abraham, H. D., & Wolf, E. (1988). Visual function in past users of LSD: Psychophysical findings. *Journal of Abnormal Psychology, 97,* 443–447.

Abraham, K. (1948a). The first pregenital stage of the libido. In *Selected papers of Karl Abraham, M.D.* (D. Bryan & A. Strachey, Trans.). London: Hogarth Press. Original work published 1916.

Abraham, K. (1948b). Notes on psychoanalytic investigation and treatment of manic-depressive insanity and applied conditions. In *Selected papers of Karl Abraham, M.D.* (D. Bryan & A. Strachey, Trans.). London: Hogarth Press. Original work published 1911.

Abramowitz, S. I. (1986). Psychosocial outcomes of sex reassignment surgery. *Journal of Consulting and Clinical Psychology, 54,* 183–189.

Abrams, R. (1992). *Electroconvulsive therapy* (2nd ed). New York: Oxford University Press.

Abramson, L. Y., Alloy, L. B., & Metalsky, G. I. (1995). Hopelessness depression. In G. Buchanan & M. E. P. Seligman (Eds.), *Explanatory style.* Hillsdale, NJ: Erlbaum.

Abramson, L. Y., Metalsky, G. I., & Alloy, L. B. (1989). Hopelessness depression: A theory-based subtype of depression. *Psychological Review, 96,* 358–372.

Achenbach, T. M., & McConaughy, S. H. (1996). Relations between DSM-IV and empirically based assessment. *School Psychology Review, 25,* 329–341.

Addington v. Texas, 99 S.Ct. 1804 (1979).

Adler, A. (1988). The child's inner life and sense of community. *Individual Psychology, 44,* 417–423. Original work published 1917.

Adler, N. E., Boyce, T., Chesney, M. A., Folkman, S., & Syme, L. (1993). Socioeconomic inequalities in health: No easy solution. *Journal of the American Medical Association, 269,* 3140–3145.

Adler, R. H., Zamboni, P., Hofer, T., Hemmeler, W., Hurny, C., Minder, C., Radvila, A., & Zlot, S. I. (1997). How not to miss a somatic needle in the haystack of chronic pain. *Journal of Psychosomatic Research, 42,* 499–506.

Agency for Health Care Policy and Research. (1993). *Depression in primary care: Treatment of major depression.* Rockville, MD: Author. (DHHS, AHCPR Publication No. 93–0551).

Aggleton, J. P. (1992). *The amygdala: Neurobiological aspects of emotion, memory, and mental dysfunction.* New York: Wiley-Liss.

Agnello, J. G. (1975). Voice onset and voice termination features of stutters. In L. M. Webster & L. C. Furst (Eds.), *Vocal tract dynamics and dysfluency.* New York: Speech and Hearing Institute.

Aichhorn, A. (1935). *Wayward youth.* London: Putnam.

Ainsworth, M. D. S. (1967). *Infancy in Uganda: Infant care and the growth of love.* Baltimore: Johns Hopkins University Press.

Ainsworth, M. D. S. (1982). Attachment: Retrospect and prospect. In C. M. Parkes & J. Stevenson-Hinde (Eds.), *The place of attachment in human behavior* (pp. 3–30). New York: Basic Books.

Ainsworth, M. D. S., & Bowlby, J. (1991). An ethological approach to personality development. *American Psychologist, 46,* 331–341.

Ainsworth, M. D. S., & Wittig, B. A. (1969). Attachment and the exploratory behavior of one-year-olds in a strange situation. In B. M. Foss (Ed.), *Determinants of infant behavior* (Vol. 4, pp. 113–136). London: Methuen.

Akbarian S., Kim, J. J., Potkin, S. G., Hetrick, W. P., Bunney, W. E., Jr., & Jones, E. G. (1996). Maldistribution of interstitial neurons in prefrontal white matter of the brains of schizophrenic patients. *Archives of General Psychiatry, 53,* 425–436.

Akiskal, H. S., & Casano, G. B. (Eds.) (1997). *Dysthymia and the spectrum of chronic depressions.* New York: Guilford Press.

Akiskal, H. S., Judd, L. L., Lemmi, H., & Gillin, J. C. (1997). Subthreshold depressions: Clinical and sleep EEG, validation of dysthymic, residual and masked forms. *Journal of Affective Disorders, 45,* 53–63.

Alarcon, R. D. (1995). Culture and psychiatric diagnosis: Impact on DSM-IV and ICD-10. *Psychiatric Clinics of North America, 18,* 449–465.

Albee, G. W. (1997). Speak no evil? *American Psychologist, October,* 1143–1144.

Albers, G. W. (1997). Rationale for early intervention in acute stroke. *American Journal of Cardiology, 80,* 4D-10D.

Alcoholism Council of Greater New York. (1987). *Some facts of alcoholism in industry.* New York: Author.

Aldrich, M. S. (1989). Cardinal manifestations of sleep disorders. In M. H. Kryger, T. Roth, & W. C. Dement (Eds.), *Principles and practice of sleep medicine* (pp. 351–357). Philadelphia: Saunders.

Alessandri, S. (1991). Play and social behavior in maltreated preschoolers. *Development and Psychopathology, 3,* 191–205.

Alexander, B. K., & Hadaway, P. F. (1982). Opiate addiction: The case for an adaptive orientation. *Psychological Bulletin, 92,* 367–381.

Allderidge, P. (1979). Hospitals, madhouses and asylums: Cycles in the care of the insane. *British Journal of Psychiatry, 134,* 321–334.

Allderidge, P. (1985). Bedlam: Fact or fantasy? In W. F. Bynum, R. Porter, & M. Shepherd (Eds.), *The anatomy of madness: Essays in the history of psychiatry* (Vol. 2). New York: Tavistock.

Allen, J. J., Chapman, L. J., Chapman, J., Vuchetich, J. P., & Frost, L. A. (1987). Prediction of psychoticlike symptoms in hypothetically psychosis-prone college students. *Journal of Abnormal Psychology, 96,* 83–88.

Allen, J. P., Hauser, S. T., & Borman-Spurrell, E. (1996). Attachment theory as a framework for understanding sequelae of severe adolescent psycho-pathology: An 11-year follow-up study. *Journal of Consulting and Clinical Psychology, 64,* 254–263.

Allen, M. G. (1976). Twin studies of affective illness. *Archives of General Psychiatry, 33,* 1476–1478.

Allgood-Merten, B., Lewinsohn, P. M., & Hops, H. (1990). Sex differnces and adolescent depression. *Journal of Abnormal Psychology, 99,* 55–63.

Alloy, L. B., & Abramson, L. Y. (1979). The judgment of contingency in depressed and nondepressed students: Sadder but wiser? *Journal of Experimental Psychology: General, 108,* 441–485.

Alloy, L. B., & Abramson, L. Y. (1988). Depressive realism: Four theoretical perspectives. In L. B. Alloy (Ed.), *Cognitive processes in depression* (pp. 223–265). New York: Guilford Press.

Alloy, L. B., Abramson, L. Y., Murray, L. A., Whitehouse, W. G., & Hogan, M. E. (1997). Self-referent information-processing in individuals at high and low cognitive risk for depression. *Cognition and Emotion, 11,* 539–568.

Alloy, L. B., & Clements, C. M. (1992). Illusion of control: Invulnerability to negative affect and depressive symptoms after laboratory and natural stressors. *Journal of Abnormal Psychology, 101,* 234–245.

Alloy, L. B., & Clements, C .M. (in press). Hopelessness theory of depression: Tests of the symptom component. *Cognitive Therapy and Research.*

Alloy, L. B., Clements, C. M., & Kolden, G. (1985). The cognitive diathesis-stress theories of depression: Therapeutic implications. In S. Reiss & R. R. Bootzin (Eds.), *Theoretical issues in behavior therapy* (pp. 379–410). New York: Academic Press.

Alloy, L. B., Just, N., & Panzarella, C. (1997). Attributional style, daily life events, and hopelessness depression: Subtype validation by prospective variability and specificity of symptoms. *Cognitive Therapy and Research, 21,* 321–344.

Alloy, L. B., Lipman, A. J., & Abramson, L. Y. (1992). Attributional style as a vulnerability factor for depression: Validation by past history of mood disorders. *Cognitive Therapy and Research, 16,* 391–407.

Alperstein, G., Rapport, C., & Flanagan, J. (1988). Health problems of homeless children in New York City. *American Journal of Public Health, 78,* 1231–1233.

Alpert, M., Clark, A., & Pouget, E. R. (1994). The syntactic role of pauses in the speech of schizophrenic patients with alogia. *Journal of Abnormal Psychology, 103,* 750–757.

Alpher, V. S. (1996). Identity and introject in dissociative disorders. *Journal of Consulting and Clinical Psychology, 6,* 1238–1244.

Alterman, A. I., O'Brien, C. P., McLellan, A. T., August, D. S., et al. (1994). Effectiveness and costs of inpatient versus day hospital cocaine rehabilita-tion. *Journal of Nervous and Mental Disease, 182,* 157–163.

Altshuler, L. L., Post, R. M., Leverich, G. S., Mikalauskas, K., Rosoff, A., & Ackerman, L. (1995). Antidepressant-induced mania and cycle acceleration: A controversy revisited. *American Journal of Psychiatry, 152,* 1130–1138.

Amador, X. F., Friedman, J. H., Kasapis, C., Yale, S. A., Flaum, M., & Gorman, J. M. (1996). Suicidal behavior in schizophrenia and its relationship to awareness of illness. *American Journal of Psychiatry, 153,* 1185–1188.

Aman, M. G., & Singh, N. N. (1991). Pharmacological intervention. In J. L. Matson & J. A. Mulick (Eds.), *Handbook of mental retardation* (2nd

ed.) (pp. 347–372). New York: Pergamon Press.

American Bar Association. (1989). *Criminal justice mental health standards.* Washington, DC: American Bar Association.

American Cancer Society. (1994). *Cancer facts and figures—1993.* New York: Author.

American Psychiatric Association. (1987). *Diagnostic and statistical manual of mental disorders (DSM-III-R)* (3rd ed. rev.). Washington, DC: Author.

American Psychiatric Association. (1990). *The practice of electroconvulsive therapy: Recommendations for treatment, training, and privileging.* Washington, DC: Author.

American Psychiatric Association. (1994). *Diagnostic and statistical manual of mental disorders* (4th ed.). Washington, DC: Author.

American Psychiatric Association. (1997). Practice guideline for the treatment of patients with schizophrenia. *Supplement to American Journal of Psychiatry, 154,* 1–63.

American Psychiatric Association membership upholds decision of trustees bid to drop homosexuality from list of mental disorders. (1974, April 9). *The New York Times,* p. 12.

American Sleep Disorders Association. (1990). *The international classification of sleep disorders: Diagnostic and coding manual.* Rochester, MN: Diagnostic Classification Steering Committee.

Amos, P. (Ed.). (1993). *Auditory training as autism therapy: A preliminary review.* Autism Support and Advocacy in Pennsylvania.

Anastasi, A. (1982). *Psychological testing* (5th ed.). New York: Macmillan.

Andersen, S. M. (1992). Toward a psychodynamically relevant empirical science. *Psychological Inquiry, 3,* 14–21.

Andersen, S. M., Reznik, I., & Manzella, L. M. (1996). Eliciting facial affect, motivation, and expectancies in transference: Significant-other representations in social relations. *Journal of Personality and Social Psychology, 71,* 1108–1129.

Anderson, B. L., Kiecolt-Glaser, J. K., & Glaser, R. (1994). A biobehavioral model of cancer stress and disease course. *American Psychologist, 49,* 389–404.

Anderson, E. M., & Lambert, M. J. (1995). Short-term dynamically oriented psychotherapy: A review and meta-analysis. *Clinical Psychology Review, 15,* 503–514.

Anderson, J. C. (1994). Epidemiological issues. In Ollendick, T. H., King, N. J., &

Yule, W. (Eds.), *International handbook of phobic and anxiety disorders in children and adolescents* (pp. 43–65). New York: Plenum Press.

Anderson, N. B. (1989). Racial differences in stress-induced cardiovascular reactivity and hypertension: Current status and substantive issues. *Psychological Bulletin, 105,* 89–105.

Anderson, N. B., & Armstead, C. A. (1995). Toward understanding the association of socioeconomic status and health: A new challenge for the biopsychosocial approach. *Psychosomatic Medicine, 57,* 213–225.

Anderson, V. E., & Hauser, W. A. (1991). Genetics. In M. Dam & L. Gram. (Eds.), *Comprehensive epileptology* (pp. 57–76). New York: Raven Press.

Andreasen, N. C. (1987). Creativity and mental illness: Prevalence rates in writers and their first-degree relatives. *American Journal of Psychiatry, 144,* 1288–1292.

Andreasen, N.C., Arndt, S., Alliger, R., Miller, D., & Flaum, M. (1995). Symptoms of schizophrenia: Methods, meanings, and mechanisms. *Archives of General Psychiatry, 52,* 341–351.

Andreasen, N. C., McDonald-Scott, P., Grove, W. M., Keller, M. B., Shapiro, R. W., & Hirschfeld, R. (1982). Assessment of reliability in multicenter collaborative research with a videotape approach. *American Journal of Psychiatry, 139,* 876–882.

Angst, J., & Merikangus, K. (1997). The depressive spectrum: Diagnostic classification and course. *Journal of Affective Disorders, 45,* 31–40.

Annegers. J. F. (1993). The epidemiology of epilepsy. In E. Wyllie (Ed.), *The treatment of epilepsy: Principles and practice* (pp. 157–164). Philadelphia: Lea & Febiger.

Annis, H. M., Schober, R., & Kelly, E. (1996). Matching addiction outpatient counseling to client readiness to change: The role of structured relapse prevention counseling. *Experimental and Clinical Psychopharmacology, 4,* 37–45.

Antoni, M. H., Baggett, L., Ironson, G., LaPerriere, A., August, S., Klimas, N., Schneiderman, N., & Fletcher, M. A. (1991). Cognitive-behavioral stress management intervention buffers distress responses and immunologic changes following notification of HIV-1 seropositivity. *Journal of Consulting and Clinical Psychology, 59,* 906–915.

Appelbaum, P. A. (1994). *Almost a revolution: Mental health law and the limits of change.* New York: Oxford University Press.

Appelbaum, P. S., & Greer, A. (1994). Who's on trial? Multiple personalities and the insanity defense. *Hospital and Community Psychiatry, 45,* 965–966.

Arango, V., & Underwood, M. D. (1997). Serotonin chemistry in the brain of suicide victims. In R. W. Maris, M. M. Silverman, & S. S. Canetto (Eds.), *Review of suicidology* (pp. 237–250). New York: Guilford Press.

Armour-Thomas, E. (1992). Intellectual assessment of children from culturally diverse backgrounds. *School Psychology Review, 21,* 552–565.

Arndt, S., Andreasen, N.C., Flaum, M., Miller, D., & Nopoulos, P. (1995). A longitudinal study of symptom dimensions in schizophrenia: Prediction and patterns of change. *Archives of General Psychiatry, 52,* 352–360.

Arnold, L. E., Abikoff, H. B., Cantwell, D. P., Connors, C. K., Elliot, G., Greenhill, L. L., Hechtman, I., Hinshaw, S. P., Hoza, B., Jensen, P. S., Kraemer, H. C., March, J. S., Newcorn, J. H., Pelham, W. E., Richters, J. E., Schiller, E., Severe, J., Swanson, J. M. Vereen, D., & Wells, K. C. (1997). National Institute of Mental Health collaborative multimodal treatment study of children with ADHD (the MTA): Design challenges and choices. *Archives of General Psychiatry, 54,* 865–870.

Ashe, J., Rosen, S. A., McArthur, J. C., & Davis, L. E. (1993). Bacterial, fungal and parasitic causes of dementia. In P. J. Whitehouse (Ed.), *Dementia* (pp. 276–306). Philadelphia: F. A. Davis.

Assalian, P., & Margolese, H. C. (1996). Treatment of antidepressant-induced sexual side effects. *Journal of Sex and Marital Therapy, 22,* 218–224.

Asuni, T. (1986). African and western psychiatry: A comparison. In J. L. Cox (Ed.), *Transcultural psychiatry* (pp. 306–321). London: Croom-Helm, Ltd.

Atchison, M., & McFarlane, A. C. (1994). A review of dissociation and dissociative disorders. *Australian and New Zealand Journal of Psychiatry, 28,* 591–599.

Azar, S. T., & Pearlmutter, R. (1993). Physical abuse and neglect. In R. T. Ammermann, C. G. Last, & M. Hersen (Eds.), *Handbook of prescriptive treatments for children and adolescents* (pp. 367–382). Boston: Allyn and Bacon.

Azar, S. T., & Twentyman, C. T. (1986). Cognitive-behavioral perspectives on the assessment and treatment of child abuse. *Advances in cognitive-behavioral research* (Vol. 5, pp. 237–267). New York: Academic Press.

Bachevalier, J. (1994). Medial temporal lobe structures and autism: A review of clinical and experimental findings. *Neuropsychologia, 32,* 627–648.

Baekeland, F., Lundwall, L., Kissin, B., & Shanahan, T. (1971). Correlates of outcome in disulfiram treatment of alcoholism. *Journal of Nervous and Mental Disease, 153*(1), 1–9.

Baer, L. (1995). High-risk drinking across the transition from high school to college. *Alcoholism: Clinical and Experimental Research, 19,* 54–61.

Baer, L., Rauch, S. L., Ballantine, T., Martuza, R., Cosgrove, R., Cassem, E., Giriunas, I., Manzo, P. A., Dimino, C., & Jenike, M. A. (1995). Cingulotomy for intractable obsessive-compulsive disorder: Prospective long-term follow-up of 18 patients. *Archives of General Psychiatry, 52,* 384–392.

Bailey, A., LeCouteur, A., Gottesman, I., Bolton, P., Simonoff, E., Yuzda, E., & Rutter, M. (1995). Autism as a strongly genetic disorder: Evidence from a British twin study. *Psychological Medicine, 25,* 63–78.

Bailey, A., Phillips, W., & Rutter, M. (1996). Autism: Towards an integration of clinical, genetic, neuropsychological, and neurobiological perspectives. *Journal of Child Psychology and Psychiatry, 37,* 89–126.

Baird, T. D., & August, G. J. (1985). Familial heterogeneity in infantile autism. *Journal of Autism and Developmental Disorders, 15,* 315–321.

Baker, B., & Merskey, H. (1982). Parental representations of hypochondriacal patients from a psychiatric hospital. *British Journal of Psychiatry, 141,* 233–238.

Baker, F., & Broskowski, A. (1974). The search for integrality: New organizational forms for human services. In D. Harshbarger & R. F. Maley (Eds.), *Behavior analysis and systems analysis: An integrative approach to mental health programs.* Kalamazoo, MI: Behaviordeli.

Bakwin, H., & Bakwin, R. M. (1972). *Behavior disorders in children.* Philadelphia: Saunders.

Baldessarini, R. J., & Frankenburg, F. R. (1991). Clozapine—a novel antipsychotic agent. *New England Journal of Medicine, 324,* 746.

Ballinger, D., Leviton, A., Waternaux, C., Needleman, H., & Rabinowitz, M. (1987). Longitudinal analyses of prenatal and postnatal lead exposure and early cognitive developpment. *New England Journal of Medicine, 316,* 1037–1043.

Bandura, A. (1977). Self-efficacy: Toward a unifying theory of behavioral change. *Psychological Review, 84,* 191–215.

Bandura, A. (1982). Self-efficacy mechanism in human agency. *American Psychologist, 37,* 122–147.

Bandura, A. (1986). *Social foundations of thought and action.* Englewood Cliffs, NJ: Prentice-Hall.

Bandura, A., Blanchard, E. B., & Ritter, B. (1969). Relative efficacy of desensitization and modeling approaches for inducing behavioral, affective, and attitudinal changes. *Journal of Personality and Social Psychology, 13,* 173–199.

Bandura, A., Taylor, C. B., & Williams, S. L. (1985). Catecholamine secretion as a function of perceived coping self-efficacy. *Journal of Consulting and Clinical Psychology, 53,* 406–414.

Bandura, A., & Walters, R. (1963). *Social learning and personality development.* New York: Holt, Rinehart and Winston.

Barber, J. P., & DeRubeis, R. J. (1989). On second thought: Where the action is in cognitive therapy for depression. *Cognitive Therapy and Research, 13,* 441–457.

Barch, D. M., & Berenbaum, H. (1996). Language production and thought disorder in schizophrenia. *Journal of Abnormal Psychology, 105,* 81–88.

Bargh, J. A. (1989). Conditional automaticity: Varieties of automatic influences in social perception and cognition. In J. S. Uleman & J. A. Bargh (Eds.), *Unintended thought* (pp. 3–51). New York: Guilford Press.

Barkley, R. A. (1989). Attention-deficit hyperactivity disorder. In E. J. Mash & R. A. Barkley (Eds.), *Treatment of childhood disorders.* New York: Guilford Press.

Barkley, R. A. (1990). *Attention-deficit hyperactivity disorder: A handbook for diagnosis and treatment.* New York: Guilford Press.

Barkley, R. A., DuPaul, G. J., & McMurray, M. B. (1990). A comprehensive evaluation of attention-deficit disorder with and without hyperactivity defined by research criteria. *Journal of Consulting and Clinical Psychology, 58,* 775–789.

Barkley, R. A., Fischer, M., Edelbrock, C. S., & Smallish, L. (1990). The adolescent outcome of hyperactive children diagnosed by research criteria: An eight-year prospective follow-up study. *Journal of the American Academy of Child and Adolescent Psychiatry, 29,* 546–557.

Barlow, D. H. (1988). *Anxiety and its disorders.* New York: Guilford Press.

Barlow, D. H. (1993). Covert sensitization for paraphilia. In J. R. Cantela & A. J. Kearney (Eds.), *Covert conditioning casebook* (pp. 187–198). Pacific Grove, CA: Brooks/Cole.

Barnett, P. A., Spence, J. D., Manuck, S. B., Jennings, J. R. (1997). Psychological stress and the progression of carotid artery disease. *Journal of Hypertension, 15,* 49–55.

Barona, A., & Faykus, S. (1992). Differential effects of sociocultural variables on special education eligibility categories. *Psychology in the Schools, 29,* 313–320.

Baron-Cohen, S., Leslie, A. M., & Frith, U. (1985). Does the autistic child have a "theory of mind"? *Cognition, 21,* 37–46.

Barondes, S. H. (1994). Thinking about Prozac. *Science, 263,* 1102–1103.

Barratt, E. S., Standford, M. S., Kent, T.A., & Felthous, A. (1997) Neuropsychological and cognitive psychophysiological substrates of impulsive aggression. *Biological Psychiatry, 41,* 1045–1061.

Barrett, D. E., & Frank, D. A. (1987). *The effects of undernutrition on children's behavior.* New York: Gordon and Breach.

Barrett, J. E., Barrett, J. A., Oxman, T. E., & Gerber, P. D. (1988). The prevalence of psychiatric disorders in a primary care practice. *Archives of General Psychiatry, 45,* 1100–1106.

Barrett, R. P., Walters, A. S., Mercurio, A. F., Klitzke, M., & Feinstein, C. (1992). Mental retardation and psychiatric disorders. In V. B. Van Hasselt & D. J. Kolko (Eds.), *Inpatient behavior therapy for children and adolescents* (pp. 113–149). New York: Plenum Press.

Barrios, B. A., & O'Dell, S. (1997). Fears and anxieties. In E. J. Mash & L. G. Terdal (Eds.), *Behavioral assessment of childhood disorders.* (3rd ed.). New York: Guilford Press.

Barry, M. (1991). The influence of the U.S. tobacco industry on the health, economy, and environment of developing countries. *New England Journal of Medicine, 342,* 917–920.

Barsky, A. J. (1992a). Amplification, somatization, and the somatoform disorders. *Psychosomatics, 33,* 28–34.

Barsky, A. J. (1992b). Hypochondriasis and obsessive compulsive disorder. *Psychiatric Clinics of North America, 15,* 791–801.

Barsky, A. J. (1996). Hypochondriasis: Medical management and psychiatric treatment. *Psychosomatics, 37,* 48–56.

Barsky, A. J., Brener, J., Coeytaux, R. R., & Cleary, P. D. (1995). Accurate awareness of heartbeat in hypochondriacal and non-hypochondriacal patients. *Journal of Psychosomatic Research, 39,* 489–497.

Barsky, A. J., Wool, C., Barnett, M. C., & Cleary, P. D. (1994). Histories of childhood trauma in adult hypochondriacal patients. *American Journal of Psychiatry, 151,* 397–401.

Barsky, A. J., & Wyshak, G. (1989). Hypochondriasis and related health attitudes. *Psychosomatics, 30,* 412–420.

Barsky, A. J., Wyshak, G., & Klerman, G. (1990). The somatosensory amplification scale and its relationship to hypochondriasis. *Journal of Psychiatric Research, 24,* 328–334.

Barta, P. E., Pearlson, G. D., Brill, L. B., II, Royall, R., McGilchrist, I. K., Pulver, A. E., Powers, R. E., Casanova, M. F., Tien, A. Y., Frangou, S., & Petty, R. G. (1997). Planum temporale asymmetry reversal in schizophrenia: Replication and relationship to gray matter abnormalities. *American Journal of Psychiatry, 154,* 661–667.

Bartha, R., Williamson, P. C., Drost, D. J., Malla, A., Carr, T. J., Cortese, L., Canaran, G., Rylett, J., & Neufeld, R. W. J. (1997). Measurement of glutamate and glutamine in the medial prefrontal cortex of never-treated schizophrenic patients and healthy controls by proton magnetic resonance spectroscopy. *Archives of General Psychiatry, 54,* 959–965.

Bartrop, R. W., Luckhurst, E., Lazarus, L., Kiloh, L. G., & Penny, R. (1977). Depressed lymphocyte function after bereavement. *Lancet,* 834–836.

Bass, E., & Davis, L. (1988). *The courage to heal.* New York: Harper & Row.

Bateson, G., Jackson, D., Haley, J., & Weakland, J. (1956). Toward a theory of schizophrenia. *Behavioral Science, 1,* 251–264.

Baucom, D. H., & Epstein, N. (1990). *Cognitive behavioral marital therapy.* New York: Brunner/Mazel.

Bauer, M. S., & Whybrow, P. C. (1990). Rapid cycling bipolar affective disorder: II. Treatment of refractory rapid cycling with high-dose levothyroxine: A preliminary study. *Archives of General Psychiatry, 47,* 435–440.

Bauer, W. D., & Twentyman, C. T. (1985). Abusing, neglectful, and comparison mothers' responses to child-related and non-child stressors. *Journal of Consulting and Clinical Psychology, 53,* 335–343.

Baxter, L. R., Phelps, M. E., Mazziotta, S. C., et al. (1987). Local cerebral glucose metabolic rates in obsessive-compulsive disorder. *Archives of General Psychiatry, 44,* 211–218.

Beach, F. A. (1979). Animal models for human sexuality. In *Sex, hormones and behavior.* Ciba Foundation Symposium 62 (New Series).

Beattie, A. D., Moore, M. R., Goldberg, A., Finlayson, M. J. W., Graham, J. F., Mackie, E. M., Main, J. C., McLaren, D. A., Murdoch, K. M., & Stewart, G. T. (1975). Role of chronic low-level lead exposure in the aetiology of mental retardation. *Lancet, 7907,* 589–592.

Beautrais, A. L., Joyce, P. R., & Mulder, R. T. (1996). Risk factors for serious suicide attempts among youths aged 13 through 24 years. *Journal of the American Academy of Child and Adolescent Psychiatry, 35,* 1174–1182.

Bebbington, P., & Ramana, R. (1995). The epidemiology of bipolar affective disorder. *Social Psychiatry and Psychiatric Epidemiology, 30,* 279–292.

Beck, A. T. (1967). *Depression: Clinical, experimental, and theoretical aspects.* New York: Harper & Row.

Beck, A. T. (1976). *Cognitive therapy and the emotional disorders.* New York: International Universities Press.

Beck, A. T. (1987). Cognitive models of depression. *Journal of Cognitive Psychotherapy, 1,* 5–37.

Beck, A. T., Emery, G., & Greenberg, R. L. (1985). *Anxiety disorders and phobias: A cognitive perspective.* New York: Basic Books.

Beck, A. T., & Freeman, A. (1990). *Cognitive therapy of personality disorders.* New York: Guilford Press.

Beck, A. T., Freeman, A., Pretzer, J., Davis, D., Fleming, B., Ottaviani, R., Beck, J., Simon, K. M., Padesky, C., Meyer, J., & Trexler, L. (1990). *Cognitive therapy of personality disorders.* New York: Guilford Press.

Beck, A. T., Rush, A. J., Shaw, B. F., & Emery, G. (1979). *Cognitive theory of depression.* New York: Guilford Press.

Beck, A. T., Steer, R. A., Kovacs, M., & Garrison, B. (1985). Hopelessness and eventual suicide: A 10-year prospective study of patients hospitalized with suicidal ideation. *American Journal of Psychiatry, 142,* 559–563.

Beck, S. J. (1961). *Rorschach's test: I. Basic processes* (3rd ed.). New York: Grune & Stratton.

Becker, J. V., Skinner, L. J., Abel, G. G., & Cichon, J. (1986). Level of postassault sexual functioning in rape and incest victims. *Archives of Sexual Behavior, 15,* 37–49.

Bedrosian, R. C., & Beck, A. T. (1980). Principles of cognitive therapy. In M. J. Mahoney (Ed.), *Psychotherapy process: Current issues and future directions.* New York: Plenum Press.

Beeder, A. B., & Millman, R. B. (1997). Patients with psychopathology. In J. H. Lowinson, P. Ruiz, R. B. Millman, & J. G. Langrod (Eds.), *Substance abuse: A comprehensive textbook* (pp. 551–563). Baltimore: Williams & Wilkins.

Beitel, A. (1985). The spectrum of gender identity disturbances: An intrapsychic model. In B. W. Steiner (Ed.), *Gender Dysphoria: Development, research, management.* New York: Plenum Press.

Bekker, M. H. J. (1996). Agoraphobia and gender: A review. *Clinical Psychology Review, 16,* 129–146.

Belfer, M. L., & Munir, K. (1997). Acquired immune deficiency syndrome. In J.M. Weiner (Ed.), *Textbook of child and adolescent psychiatry* (pp. 711–725). Washington, DC: American Psychiatric Association.

Bell, D. S. (1973). The experimental reproduction of amphetamine psychosis. *Archives of General Psychiatry, 39*(1), 35–40.

Bellack, A. S., & Mueser, K. T. (1993). Psychosocial treatment for schizophrenia. *Schizophrenia Bulletin, 19,* 317–336.

Bellak, I. (1954). *The Thematic Apperception Test and the Children's Thematic Apperception Test in clinical use.* New York: Grune & Stratton.

Bell-Dolan, D., & Brazeal, T. J. (1993). Separation anxiety disorder, over-anxious disorder, and school refusal. *Child and Adolescent Psychiatric Clinics of North America, 2,* 563–580.

Belluck, P. (1997, November 6). 'Memory' therapy leads to a lawsuit and big settlement. *New York Times,* pp. A1, A13.

Belmont, L., Cohen, P., Dryfoos, J., et al. (1981). Maternal age and children's intelligence. In K. G. Scott, T. Field, & E. G. Robertson (Eds.), *Teenage parents and their offspring* (pp. 177–197). New York: Grune & Stratton.

Belsher, G., & Costello, C. G. (1988). Relapse after recovery from unipolar depression: A critical review. *Psychological Bulletin, 104,* 84–96.

Bemis, K. M. (1978). Current approaches to the etiology and treatment of anorexia nervosa. *Psychological Bulletin, 85,* 593–617.

Benca, R. M., Obermeyer, W. H., Thisted, R. A. & Gillin, J. C. (1992). Sleep and psychiatric disorders: A meta-analysis. *Archives of General Psychiatry, 49,* 651–668.

Bender, L. (1938). A visual motor gestalt test and its clinical use. *Research Monograph of the American Ortho-psychiatric Association, 3,* xi, 176.

Bendich, A., & Cohen, M. (1990). Vitamin B_6 safety issues. *Annals of the New York Academy of Science, 585,* 321–337.

Benioff, L. (1995). What is it like to have schizophrenia? In S. Vinogradov (Ed.), *Treating schizophrenia* (pp. 81–107). San Francisco: Jossey-Bass.

Benjamin, H. (1964). Nature and management of transsexualism: With a report of thirty-one operated cases. *Western Journal of Surgery, Obstetrics and Gynecology,* 105–111.

Benjamin, R. S., Costello, E. J., & Warren, M. (1990). Anxiety disorders in a pediatric sample. *Journal of Anxiety Disorders, 4,* 293–316.

Benson, B. A. (1986). Anger management training. *Psychiatric Aspects of Mental Retardation Reviews, 5*(10), 51–55.

Bentall, R. P., Kinderman, P., & Kaney, S. (1994). The self, attributional processes and abnormal beliefs: Towards a model of persecutory delusions. *Behaviour Research and Therapy, 32,* 331–341.

Bentler, P. M., & Prince, C. (1970). Psychiatric symptomology in transvestites. *Journal of Clinical Psychology, 26*(4), 434–455.

Bentler, P. M., Shearman, R. W., & Prince, C. (1970). Personality characteristics of male transvestites. *Journal of Clinical Psychology, 26,* 287–291.

Berenbaum, H., & Oltmanns, T. F. (1992). Emotional experience and expression in schizophrenia and depression. *Journal of Abnormal Psychology, 101,* 37–44.

Berger, P. A. (1978). Medical treatment of mental illness. *Science, 200,* 974–981.

Bergler, E. (1947). Analysis of an unusual case of fetishism. *Bulletin of the Menninger Clinic, 2,* 67–75.

Berliner, L., Schram, D., Miller, L. L., & Milloy, C. D. (1995). A sentencing alternative for sex offenders: A study of decision making and recidivism. *Journal of Interpersonal Violence, 10,* 487–502.

Berman, A. L. (1988). Fictional depiction of suicide in television films and imitation effects. *American Journal of Psychiatry, 145,* 982–986.

Bernheim, K. F. (1997). *The Lanahan cases and readings in abnormal behavior* (pp. 132–135). Baltimore: Lanahan Publishers, Inc.

Bernstein, A. S. (1987). Orienting response research in schizophrenia: Where we have come and where we might go. *Schizophrenia Bulletin, 13,* 623–641.

Bernston, G. G., Cacioppo, J. T., & Quigley, K. S. (1991). Autonomic determinism: Modes of autonomic control, the doctrine of autonomic space and laws of autonomic constraint. *Psychological Review, 98,* 459–487.

Berrettini, W. H., Ferraro, T. N., Goldin, L. R., Detera-Wadleigh, S. D., Choi, H., Muniec, D., Guroff, J. J., Kazuba, D. M., Nurnberger, J. I., Hsieh, W. T., Hoehe, M. R., & Gershon, E. S. (1997). A linkage study of bipolar illness. *Archives of General Psychiatry, 54,* 27–35.

Berrios, D. C., Hearst, N., Coates, T. J., Stall, R., Hudes, E. S., Turner, H., Eversley, R., & Catania, J. (1993). HIV antibody testing among those at risk for infection: The national AIDS behavioral surveys. *Journal of the American Medical Association, 270*, 1576–1580.

Bettelheim, B. (1967). *The empty fortress.* New York: Free Press.

Beutler, L. E., Kim, E. J., Davison, E., Karno, M., & Fisher, D. (1996). Research contributions to improving managed health care outcomes. *Psychotherapy, 33*, 197–206.

Biederman, J., Newcorn, J., & Sprich, S. (1991). Comorbidity of attention deficit hyperactivity disorder with conduct, depressive, anxiety, and other disorders. *American Journal of Psychiatry, 148*, 564–577.

Biklen, D. (1990). Communication unbound: Autism and praxis. *Harvard Educational Review, 60*, 291–314.

Biklen, D. (1992). Autism orthodoxy versus free speech: A reply to Cummins and Prior. *Harvard Educational Review, 62*, 242–256.

Bini, L. (1938). Experimental researches on epileptic attacks induced by the electric current. *American Journal of Psychiatry* (Suppl. 94), 172–183.

Birmaher, B., Kaufman, J., Brent, D. A., Dahl, R. E., Perel, J. M., Al-Shabbout, M., Nelson, B., Stull, S., Rao, U., Waterman, G. S., Williamson, D. E., & Ryan, N. D. (1997). Neuroendocrine response to 5-Hydroxy-L-Tryptophan in prepubertal children at high risk of major depressive disorder. *Archives of General Psychiatry, 54*, 1113–1119.

Birnbaum, K. (1914). *Die psychopathis-chen verbrecker* (2nd ed.). Leipzig: Thieme.

Birren, J. E. (1974). Translations in gerontology—from lab to life: Psychophysiology and speed of response. *American Psychologist, 29*, 808–815.

Bishop, E. R., Mobley, M. C., & Farr, W. F. (1978). Lateralization of conversion symptoms. *Comprehensive Psychiatry, 19*, 393–396.

Bjorkland, D. F., & Green, B. L. (1992). The adaptive nature of cognitive immaturity. *American Psychologist, 47*, 46–54.

Black, D. W., Noyes, R., Jr., Pfohl, B., Goldstein, R. B., & Blum, N. (1993). Personality disorder in obsessive-compulsive volunteers, well comparison subjects, and their first-degree relatives. *American Journal of Psychiatry, 150*, 1226–1232.

Blair, C. D., & Lanyon, R. I. (1981). Exhibitionism: Etiology and treatment. *Psychological Bulletin, 89*(3), 439–463.

Blanchard, E. B., & Andraski, F. (1985). *Management of chronic headaches: A psychological approach.* New York: Pergamon Press.

Blanchard, J. J., & Neale, J. M. (1992). Medication effects: Conceptual and methodological issues in schizophrenia research. *Clinical Psychology Review, 12*, 345–361.

Blanchard, R. (1989). The concept of autogynephilia and the typology of male gender dysphoria. *Journal of Nervous and Mental Disease, 177*, 616–623.

Blane, L., & Roth, R. H. (1967). Voyeurism and exhibitionism. *Perceptual and Motor Skills, 24*, 391–400.

Blaney, P. H. (1986). Affect and memory: A review. *Psychological Bulletin, 99*, 229–246.

Blashfield, R. K. (1973). An evaluation of the *DSM-II* classification of schizophrenia as a nomenclature. *Journal of Abnormal Psychology, 82*, 382–389.

Blashfield, R. K., & Draguns, J. G. (1976). Evaluative criteria for psychiatric classification. *Journal of Abnormal Psychology, 85*, 140–150.

Blashfield, R. K., & Livesley, W. J. (1991). Metaphorical analysis of psychiatric classification as a psychological test. *Journal of Abnormal Psychology, 100*, 262–270.

Blatt, S. J., & Homann, E. (1992). Parent-child interaction in the etiology of dependent and self-critical depression. *Clinical Psychology Review, 12*, 47–91.

Blazer, D. G., Kessler, R. C., McGonagle, K. A., & Swartz, M. S. (1994). The prevalence and distribution of major depression in a national community sample: The national comorbidity survey. *American Journal of Psychiatry, 151*, 979–986.

Bleuler, E. (1950). *Dementia praecox or the group of schizophrenias* (J. Zinkin, Trans.). New York: International Universities Press. Original work published 1911.

Bleuler, M. E. (1978). The long term course of schizophrenic psychoses. In L. C. Wynne, R. L. Cromwell, & S. Matthyse (Eds.), *The nature of schizophrenia: New approaches to research and treatment.* New York: Wiley.

Bliss, E. L. (1984). A symptom profile of patients with multiple personalities—with MMPI results. *Journal of Nervous and Mental Disease, 172*, 197–202.

Bliss, E. W., & Branch, C. H. (1960). *Anorexia nervosa: Its history, psychology, and biology.* New York: Hoeber Medical Book.

Bliss, R. E., Garvey, A. J., Heinold, J. W., & Hitchcock, J. L. (1989). The influence of situation and coping on relapse crisis outcomes after smoking cessation. *Journal of Consulting and Clinical Psychology, 57*, 443–449.

Blokland, A. (1996). Acetylcholine: A neurotransmitter for learning and memory? *Brain Research Reviews, 21*, 285–300.

Blumer, D., & Walker, A. E. (1975). The neural basis of sexual behavior. In D. F. Benson & D. Blumer (Eds.), *Psychiatric aspects of neurological disease.* New York: Grune & Stratton.

Bockoven, J. S. (1963). *Moral treatment in American psychiatry.* New York: Springer.

Bodlund, O., & Kullgren, G. (1995). *Transsexualism: General outcome and prognostic factors.* Paper presented at the XIVth International Symposium on Gender Dysphoria, Kloster Irsee, Germany.

Bogerts, B. (1993). Recent advances in the neuropathology of schizophrenia. *Schizophrenia Bulletin, 19*, 431–445.

Bogerts, B., & Falkai, P. (1995). Postmortem brain abnormalities in schizophrenia. In C. L. Shrigui & H. A. Nasrallah (Eds.), *Contemporary issues in the treatment of schizophrenia* (pp. 43–59). Washington, DC: American Psychiatric Press.

Bohman, M., Cloninger, C. R., von Knorring, A., & Sigvardsson, S. (1984). An adoption study of somatoform disorders: III. Cross-fostering analysis and genetic relationship to alcoholism and criminality. *Archives of General Psychiatry, 41*, 872–878.

Boll, T. J., Heaton, R., & Reitan, R. M. (1974). Neuropsychological and emotional correlates of Huntington's chorea. *Journal of Nervous and Mental Disease, 158*, 61–69.

Bolton, P., & Rutter, M. (1990). Genetic influences in autism. *International Review of Psychiatry, 2*, 67–80.

Boon, S., & Draijer, N. (1993). Multiple personality disorder in the Netherlands: A clinical investigation of 71 patients. *American Journal of Psychiatry, 150*, 489–494.

Booth, G. K. (1995). Outcome and treatment strategies. In S. Vinogradov (Ed.), *Treating schizophrenia* (pp. 166–169). San Francisco: Jossey-Bass.

Booth-Kewley, S., & Friedman, H. S. (1987). Psychological predictors of heart disease: A quantitative review. *Psychological Bulletin, 101*, 343–362.

Bootzin, R. R., Manber, R., Perlis, M. L., Salvia, M., & Wyatt, J. K. (1993). Sleep disorders. In P. B. Sutker & H. E. Adams (Eds.), *Comprehensive handbook of psychopathology* (2nd ed., pp. 531–561). New York: Plenum Press.

Bootzin, R. R., & Perlis, M. L. (1992). Nonpharmacological treatments for insomnia. *Journal of Clinical Psychiatry.*

Borkovec, T. D., & Costello, E. (1993). Efficacy of applied relaxation and cognitive-behavioral therapy in the treatment of generalized anxiety disorder. *Journal of Consulting and Clinical Psychology, 61,* 611–619.

Borkovec, T. D., Lane, T. W., & VanOot, P. H. (1981). Phenomenology of sleep among insomniacs and good sleepers: Wakefulness experience when cortically asleep. *Journal of Abnormal Psychology, 90,* 607–609.

Borkowski, J. G., Whitman, T. L., Passino, A. W., Rellinger, E. A., Sommer, K., Keogh, D., & Weed, K. (1992). Unraveling the "new morbidity": Adolescent parenting and developmental delays. In N. W. Bray (Ed.), *International review of research in mental retardation* (Vol. 18, pp. 159–196). San Diego, CA: Academic Press.

Bornstein, R. F. (1993a). *The dependent personality.* New York: Guilford Press.

Bornstein, R. F. (1993b). Implicit perception, implicit memory, and the recovery of unconscious material in psychotherapy. *Journal of Nervous and Mental Disease, 181,* 337–344.

Bornstein, R. F., Rossner, S. C., Hill, E. L., & Stepanian, M. L. (1994). Face validity and fakability of objective and projective measures of dependency. *Journal of Personality Assessment, 63,* 363–386.

Bosma, H., Marmot, M. G., Hemingway, H., Nicholson, A. C., Brunner, E., & Stansfield, S. A. (1997). Low job control and risk of coronary heart disease in Whitehall II (prospective cohort) study. *British Medical Journal, 314,* 558–565.

Botzer, M. C., & Vehrs, B. (1997). *Self-integrative traits and pathways to gender transition.* Paper presented at the XVth Harry Benjamin International Gender Dysphoria Association Symposium, Vancouver, Canada.

Bouchard, T. J., Jr., Lykken, D. T., McGue, M., Segal, N.L., et al. (1990). Sources of human psychological differences: The Minnesota study of twins reared apart. *Science, 250,* 223–250.

Bourne, P. G. (1974). *Addiction.* New York: Academic Press.

Bovjberg, D. H., Redd, W. H., Maier, L. A., Holland, J. C., Lesko, L. M., Niedzwiecki, D., Rubin, S. C., & Hakes, T. B. (1990). Anticipatory immune suppression and nausea in women receiving cyclic chemotherapy for ovarian cancer. *Journal of Consulting and Clinical Psychology, 58,* 153–157.

Bower, G. (1994). Temporary emotional states act like multiple personalities. In R. M. Klein & B. K. Doane (Eds.), *Psychological concepts and dissociative disorders* (pp. 207–234). Hillsdale, NJ: Erlbaum.

Bower, G. H. (1981). Mood and memory. *American Psychologist, 36,* 129–148.

Bowers, K. S., & Farvolden, P. (1996). Revisiting a century-old Freudian slip: From suggestion disavowed to the truth repressed. *Psychological Bulletin, 119,* 355–380.

Bowlby, J. (1951). *Maternal care and mental health.* World Health Organization Monograph. (Serial No. 2).

Bowlby, J. (1969). *Attachment and loss, Vol. 1: Attachment.* New York: Basic Books.

Bowlby, J. (1973). *Attachment and loss, Vol. 2: Separation.* New York: Basic Books.

Bowlby, J. (1977). The making and breaking of affectional bonds: I. Aetiology and psychopathology in the light of attachment theory. *British Journal of Psychiatry, 130,* 201–210.

Bowlby, J. (1980). *Attachment and loss, Vol. 3: Loss, sadness and depression.* New York: Basic Books.

Bowlby, J. (1988). Developmental psychiatry comes of age. *American Journal of Psychiatry, 145,* 1–10.

Bowman, E. S., & Markand, O. N. (1996). Psychodynamics and psychiatric diagnoses of pseudoseizure subjects. *American Journal of Psychiatry, 153,* 57–63.

Boyd, J. H., Rae, D. S., Thompson, J. W., Burns, B. J., Bourdon, K., Locke, B. Z., & Regier, D. A. (1990). Phobia: Prevalence and risk factors. *Social Psychiatry and Psychiatric Epidemiology, 25,* 314–323.

Boysen, G. (1993). Prevention of stroke. In J. P. Whisnant (Ed.), *Stroke, populations, cohorts, and clinical trials.* Boston: Butterworth-Heinemann.

Bradford, J. M. W. (1990). The antiandrogen and hormonal treatment of sex offenders. In W. L. Marshall, D. R. Laws, & H. E. Barbaree (Eds.), *Handbook of sexual assault* (pp. 297–310). New York: Plenum Press.

Bradford, J. M. W., & Greenberg, D. M. (1996). Pharmacological treatment of deviant sexual behaviour. *Annual Review of Sex Research, 6,* 283–306.

Bradford, J. M. W., & Pawlak, A. (1993). Double-blind placebo crossover study of cyproterone acetate in the treatment of paraphilias. *Archives of Sexual Behavior, 22,* 383–402.

Brady, J. V. (1958). Ulcers in "executive" monkeys. *Scientific American, 199,* 95–100.

Braff, D. L. (1993). Information processing and attention dysfunctions in schizophrenia. *Schizophrenia Bulletin, 19,* 233–259.

Braff, D. L., & Geyer, M. A. (1990). Sensorimotor gating and schizophrenia: Human and animal model studies. *Archives of General Psychiatry, 47,* 181–188.

Braginsky, B. M., Braginsky, D. D., & Ring, K. (1969). *Methods of madness: The mental hospital as a last resort.* New York: Holt, Rinehart and Winston.

Brakel, S. J. (1985). Involuntary institutionalization. In S. J. Brakel, J. Parry, & B. A. Weiner (Eds.), *The mentally disabled and the law* (3rd ed.). Chicago: American Bar Foundation.

Brandenburg, N. A., Friedman, R. M., & Silver, S. E. (1990). The epidemiology of childhood psychiatric disorders: Prevalence findings from recent studies. *Journal of the American Academy of Child and Adolescent Psychiatry, 29,* 76–83.

Brantley, P. J., & Garrett, V. D. (1993). Psychobiological approaches to health and disease. In P. B. Sutker & H. E. Adams (Eds.), *Comprehensive handbook of psychopathology* (2nd ed., pp. 647–670). New York: Plenum Press.

Brantley, P. J., & Jones, G. N. (1993). Daily stress and stress-related disorders. *Annals of Behavioral Medicine, 15,* 17–25.

Braun, P., et al. (1981). Overview: Deinstitutionalization of psychiatric patients: A critical review of outcome studies. *American Journal of Psychiatry, 138,* 736–749.

Bray, G. A. (1984). The role of weight control in health promotion and disease prevention. In J. D. Matarazzo, S. M. Weiss, J. A. Herd, N. E. Miller (Eds.), *Behavioral health: A handbook of health enhancement and disease prevention* (pp. 632–656). New York: Wiley.

Brebion, G., Smith, M. J., Amador, X., Malaspina, D., & Gorman, J. M. (1997). Clinical correlates of memory in schizophrenia: Differential links between depression, positive and negative symptoms, and two types of memory impairment. *American Journal of Psychiatry, 154,* 1538–1543.

Brebion, G., Smith, M. J., Gorman, J. M., & Amador, X. (1996). Reality monitoring failure in schizophrenia: The role of selective attention. *Schizophrenia Research, 22,* 173–180.

Brehm, N. M., & Khantzian, E. J. (1997). Psychodynamics. In J.H. Lowinson, P. Ruiz, R. B. Millman, & J. G. Langrod (Eds.), *Substance abuse: A comprehensive textbook* (pp. 90–100*).* Baltimore: Williams & Wilkins.

Breier, A., Davis, O. R., Buchanan, R. W., Moricle, L. A., & Munson, R. C. (1993). Effects of metabolic perturbation on plasma homovanillic acid in schizophrenia: Relationship to prefrontal cortex volume. *Archives of General Psychiatry, 50,* 541–550.

Bremner, J. D., Innis, R. B., Salomon, R. M., Staib, L. H., Ng, C. K., Miller, H. L., Bronen, R. A., Krystal, J. H., Duncan, J., Rich, D., Price, L. H., Malison, R., Dey, H., Soufer, R., & Charney, D. S. (1997). Positron emission tomography measurement of cerebral metabolic correlates of tryptophan depletion-induced depressive relapse. *Archives of General Psychiatry, 54,* 364–374.

Bremner, J. D., Krystal, J. H., Charney, D. S., & Southwick, S. M. (1996). Neural mechanisms in dissociative amnesia for childhood abuse: Relevance to the current controversy surrounding the "false memory syndrome." *American Journal of Psychiatry, 153,* 71–82.

Bremner, J. D., Krystal, J. H., Southwick, S. M., & Charney, D. S. (1995). Functional neuroanatomical correlates of the effects of stress on memory. *Journal of Traumatic Stress, 8,* 527–553.

Brenneis, C. B. (1996). Multiple personality: Fantasy proneness, demand characteristics, and indirect communication. *Psychoanalytic Psychology, 13,* 367–387.

Brenner, H. D., Roder, V., Hodel, B., Kienzie, N., Reed, D., & Liberman, R. P. (1995). *Integrated psychological therapy for schizophrenic patients.* Bern, Switzerland: Hogrefe & Huber.

Brenner, I. (1993). The dissociative character: A reconsideration of "multiple personality." *Journal of the American Psychoanalytic Association, 42,* 819–846.

Brenner, I. (1996). The characterological basis of multiple personality. *American Journal of Psychotherapy, 50,* 154–166.

Brent, D. A., Bridge, J., Johnson, B. A., & Connolly, J. (1996). Suicidal behavior runs in families: A controlled family study of adolescent suicide victims. *Archives of General Psychiatry, 53,* 1145–1152.

Bretherton, I. (1992). The origins of attachment theory: John Bowlby and Mary Ainsworth. *Developmental Psychology, 28,* 759–775.

Brewin, C. R., Dagleish, T., & Joseph, S. (1996). *Psychological Review, 103,* 670–686.

Brewin, C. R., MacCarthy, B., Duda, K., & Vaughn, C. E. (1991). Attribution and expressed emotion in the relatives of patients with schizophrenia. *Journal*

of Abnormal Psychology, 100, 546–554.

Bridgeland, W. M., Duane, E. A., & Stewart, C. S. (1995). Sexual victimization among undergraduates. *College Student Journal, 29,* 16–25.

Bridges, P. K., Bartlett, J. R., Hale, A. S., Poynton, A. M., Malizia, A. L., & Hodgkiss, A. D. (1994). Psychosurgery: Stereotactic subcaudate tractotomy: An indispensable treatment. *British Journal of Psychiatry, 165,* 599–611.

Brion, S. (1969). Korsakoff's syndrome: Clinico-anatomical and physiopathological considerations. In G. A. Talland & N. C. Waugh (Eds.), *The pathology of memory.* New York: Academic Press.

Brodaty, H., Peters, K., Boyce, P., Hickie, I., Parker, G., Mitchell, P., & Wilhelm, K. (1991). Age and depression. *Journal of Affective Disorders, 23,* 137–149.

Broman, S., Nichols, P. L., Shaughnessy, P., & Kennedy, W., et al. (1987). *Retardation in young children.* Hillsdale, NJ: Erlbaum.

Bromberg, W. (1965). *Crime and the mind.* New York: Macmillan.

Bron, B., Strack, M., & Rudolph, G. (1991). Childhood experiences of loss and suicide attempts: Significance in depressive states of major depressed and dysthymic or adjustment disordered patients. *Journal of Affective Disorders, 23,* 165–172.

Brookoff, D., O'Brien, K. K., Cook, C. S., Thompson, T. D., & Williams, C. (1997). Characteristics of participants in domestic violence: Assessment at the scene of a domestic assault. *Journal of the American Medical Association, 277,* 1369–1373.

Brooks-Gunn, J. (1988). Antecedents and consequences of variations in girls' maturational timing. *Journal of Adolescent Health Care, 9,* 365–373.

Broskowski, A., & Baker, F. (1974). Professional, organizational, and social barriers to primary prevention. *American Journal of Orthopsychiatry, 44,* 707–719.

Brown, G. P., Hammen, C. L., Craske, M. G., & Wickens, T. D. (1995). Dimensions of dysfunctional attitudes as vulnerabilities to depressive symptoms. *Journal of Abnormal Psychology, 104,* 431–435.

Brown, G. W., Harris, T. O., & Hepworth, C. (1994). Life events and endogenous depression: A puzzle reexamined. *Archives of General Psychiatry, 51,* 525–534.

Brown, H. N., & Vaillant, G. E. (1981). Hypochondriasis. *Archives of Internal Medicine, 141,* 723–726.

Brown, L. S. (1992). A feminist critique of the personality disorders. In L. S. Brown & M. Ballou (Eds.), *Personality and psychopathology: Feminist reappraisals* (pp. 206–228). New York: Guilford Press.

Brown, P. (1997). The risk of bovine spongiform encephalopathy ("Mad Cow Disease") to human health. *Journal of the American Medical Association, 278,* 1008–1011.

Brown, S. A., Goldman, M. S., & Christiansen, B. A. (1985). Do alcohol expectancies mediate drinking patterns of adults? *Journal of Consulting and Clinical Psychology, 53,* 512–519.

Brown, S. A., Goldman, M. S., Inn, A., & Anderson, L. R. (1980). Expectations of reinforcement from alcohol: Their domain and relation to drinking patterns. *Journal of Consulting and Clinical Psychology, 48,* 419–426.

Brown, S. A., Vik, P. W., Patterson, T. L., Grant, I., & Schuckit, M. A. (1995). Stress, vulnerability, and adult alcohol relapse. *Journal of Studies on Alcohol, 56,* 538–545.

Brown, S. L., & Forth, A. E. (1997). Psychopathy and sexual assault: Static risk factors, emotional precursors, and rapist subtypes. *Journal of Consulting and Clinical Psychology, 65,* 848–857.

Browne, A., & Finkelhor, D. (1986). Impact of child sexual abuse: A review of the research. *Psychological Bulletin, 99,* 66–77.

Brownell, K. D. (1986). Public health approaches to obesity and its management. *Annual Review of Public Health, 7,* 521–533.

Brownell, K. D. (1993). Whether obesity should be treated. *Health Psychology, 12,* 339–341.

Brownell, K. D., & Wadden, T. A. (1992). Etiology and treatment of obesity: Understanding a serious, prevalent, and refractory disorder. *Journal of Consulting and Clinical Psychology, 60,* 505–517.

Bruce, M. L., & Kim, K. M. (1992). Differences in the effects of divorce on major depression in men and women. *American Journal of Psychiatry, 149,* 914–917.

Bruch, H. (1978). *The golden cage: The enigma of anorexia nervosa.* Cambridge, MA: Harvard University Press.

Bruch, H. (1985). Four decades of eating disorders. In D. M. Garner & P. E. Garfinkel (Eds.), *Handbook of psychotherapy for anorexia and bulimia.* New York: Guilford Press.

Bruch, M. A., & Heimberg, R. G. (1994). Differences in perceptions of parental and personal characteristics between generalized and nongeneralized social phobics. *Journal of Anxiety Disorders, 8,* 155–168.

Bryan, T., & Bryan, J. (1990). Social factors in learning disabilities. In H. L. Swanson & B. Keogh (Eds.), *Learning disabilities: Theoretical and research issues*. Hillsdale, NJ: Erlbaum.

Bryant, R. A., & Harvey, A. G. (1995). Processing threatening information in posttraumatic stress disorder. *Journal of Abnormal Psychology, 104,* 537–541.

Bryson, S. E. (1997). Epidemiology of autism: Overview and issues outstanding. In D. J. Cohen & F. R. Volkmar (Eds.), *Handbook of autism and pervasive developmental disorders* (2nd ed.). (pp. 41–46). New York: Wiley.

Bryson, S. E., Clark, B. S., & Smith, I. M. (1988). First report of a Canadian epidemiological study of autistic syndromes. *Journal of Child Psychology and Psychiatry, 29,* 433–445.

Buchanan, R. W., Strauss, M. E., Breier, A., Kirkpatrick, B., & Carpenter, W. T. (1997). Attentional impairments in deficit and nondeficit forms of schizophrenia. *American Journal of Psychiatry, 154,* 363–370.

Buchsbaum, M. S., Someya, T., Teng, C. Y., Abel, L., Chin, S., Najafi, A., Haier, R. J., Wu, J., & Bunney, W. E., Jr. (1996). PET and MRI of the thalamus in never-medicated patients with schizophrenia. *American Journal of Psychiatry, 153,* 191–199.

Bullough, V. L., & Bullough, B. (1993). *Cross-dressing, sex and gender.* Philadelphia: University of Pennsylvania Press.

Burgess, A. W., Groth, A. N., & McCausland, M. P. (1981). Child sex initiation rings. *American Journal of Orthopsychiatry, 51,* 110–119.

Burke, J. D., Jr., Burke, K. C., & Rae, D. S. (1994). Increased rates of drug abuse and dependence after onset of mood or anxiety disorders in adolescence. *Hospital and Community Psychiatry, 45,* 451–455.

Burke, K. C., Burke, J. D., Jr., Regier, D. A., & Rae, D. S. (1990). Age at onset of selected mental disorders in five community populations. *Archives of General Psychiatry, 47,* 511–518.

Burke, K. C., Burke, J. D., Roe, D. S., & Regier, D. A. (1991). Comparing age at onset of major depression and other psychiatric disorders by birth cohorts in five U. S. community populations. *Archives of General Psychiatry, 48,* 789–795.

Burnam, M. A., Stein, J. A., Golding, J. M., Siegel, J. M., Sorenson, S. B., Forsythe, A. B., & Telles, C. A. (1988). Sexual assault and mental disorders in a community population. *Journal of Consulting and Clinical Psychology, 56,* 843–850.

Bushman, B. J., & Cooper, H. M. (1990). Effects of alcohol on human aggression: An integrative research review. *Psychological Bulletin, 107,* 341–354.

Butcher, J. N. (1978). Present status of computerized MMPI reporting devices. In O. Buros (Ed.), *Eighth mental measurements yearbook*. Highland Park, NJ: Gryphon Press.

Butcher, J. N. (1990). *MMPI-2 in psychological treatment*. New York: Oxford University Press.

Butler, J., O'Halloran, A., & Leonard, B. E. (1992). The Galway study of panic disorder: II. Changes in some peripheral markers of noradrenergic and serotonergic function in *DSM-III-R* panic disorder. *Journal of Affective Disorders, 26,* 89–100.

Butler, L. D., Duran, R. E. F., Jasiukaitis, P., Koopman, C., & Spiegel, D. (1996). Hypnotizability and traumatic experience: A diathesis-stress model of dissociative symptomatology. *American Journal of Psychiatry, 153,* 42–63.

Butler, R. W., & Braff, D. L. (1991). Delusions: A review and integration. *Schizophrenia Bulletin, 17,* 633–647.

Buvat, J., Buvat-Herbaut, M., Lemaire, A., Marcolin, G., & Quittelier, E. (1990). Recent developments in the clinical assessment and diagnosis of erectile dysfunction. *Annual Review of Sex Research, 2,* 265–308.

Buydens-Branchey, L., Branchey, M. H., & Noumair, D. (1989). Age of alcoholism onset: I. Relationship to psychopathology. *Archives of General Psychiatry, 46,* 225–230.

Buysse, D. J., & Kupfer, D. J. (1993). Sleep disorders in depressive disorders. In J. J. Mann & D. J. Kupfer (Eds.), *Biology of depressive disorders: Part A. A systems perspective* (pp. 123–154). New York: Plenum.

Cain, J. W. (1992). Poor response to fluoxetine: Underlying depression, serotonergic overstimulation, or a "therapeutic window"? *Journal of Clinical Psychiatry, 53,* 272–277.

Cairns, R. B., Cadwallader, T. W., Estell, D., & Neckerman, H. J. (1997). Groups to gangs: Developmental and criminological perspectives and relevance for prevention. In D. M. Stoff, J. Breiling, & J. D. Maser (Eds.), *Handbook of antisocial behavior* (pp. 194–204). New York: Wiley.

Campaigne, B. N., Morrison, J. A., Schumann, B. C., Faulkner, F., Lakatos, E., Sprecher, D., & Schrieber, G. B. (1994). Indexes of obesity and comparisons with previous national survey data in 9- and 10-year-old black and white girls: The National Heart, Lung, and Blood Institute Growth and Health Survey. *Journal of Pediatrics, 124,* 675–680.

Campbell, M. (1988). Annotation: Fenfluramine treatment of autism. *Journal of Child Psychology and Psychiatry, 29,* 1–10.

Campbell, M., Adams, P., Small, A. M., Curren, E. L., Overall, J. E., Anderson, L. T., Lynch, N., & Perry, R. (1988). Efficacy and safety of fenfluramine in autistic children. *Journal of the American Academy of Child and Adolescent Psychiatry, 27,* 434–439.

Campbell, M., Overall, J. E., Small, A. M., Sokol, M. S., Spencer, E. K., Adams, P., Foltz, R. L., Monti, K. M., Perry, R., Nobler, M., & Roberts, E. (1989). Naltrexone in autistic children: An open dose range tolerance trial. *Journal of the American Academy of Child and Adolescent Psychiatry, 28,* 200–206.

Campbell, M., Schopler, E., Cueva, J. E., & Hallin, A. (1996). Treatment of autistic disorder. *Journal of the American Academy of Child and Adolescent Psychiatry, 35,* 134–143.

Cannon, T. D., & Mednick. S. A. (1993). The schizophrenia high-risk project in Copenhagen: Three decades of progress. *Acta Psychiatrica Scandinavica,* (Suppl. 370), 33–47.

Cannon, W. B. (1936). *Bodily changes in pain, hunger, fear, and rage*. New York: Appleton-Century.

Cantwell, D. P. (1982). Childhood depression: A review of current research. In B. B. Lahey & A. E. Kazdin (Eds.), *Advances in clinical child psychology*. New York: Plenum Press.

Carey, G., & Goldman, D. (1997). The genetics of antisocial behavior. In D. M. Stoff, J. Breiling, & J. D. Maser (Eds.), *Handbook of antisocial behavior* (pp. 243–254). New York: Wiley.

Carey, M. P., & Johnson, B. T. (1996). Effectiveness of yohimbine in the treatment of erectile disorder: Four meta-analytic integrations. *Archives of Sexual Behavior, 25,* 341–360.

Carey, G., & Gottesman, I. I. (1981). Twin and family studies of anxiety, phobic and obsessive disorders. In D. F. Klein & J. G. Rabkin (Eds.), *Anxiety: New research and changing concepts*. New York: Raven Press.

Carlson, G. A., & Garber, J. (1986). Developmental issues in the classification of depression in children. In M. Rutter, C. Izard, & P. Read (Eds.), *Depression in young people: Issues and perspectives*. New York: Guilford Press.

Carnegie Corporation of New York. (1994). *Starting points: Meeting the needs of our youngest children* (Report of the Carnegie Task Force on Meeting the Needs of Young Children).

Carnes, P. Sexual addiction: Progress, criticism, challenges. *American Journal of Preventive Psychiatry and Neurology, 2,* 1–8.

Carr, J. (1994). Annotation: Long term outcome for people with Down syndrome. *Journal of Child Psychology and Psychiatry, 35,* 425–439.

Carroll, K. M. (1996). Relapse prevention as a psychosocial treatment. *Experimental and Clinical Psychopharmacology, 4,* 40–54.

Carroll, M. E., & Comer, S. D. (1996). Animal models of relapse. *Experimental and Clinical Pharmacology, 4,* 11–18.

Carroll, R. A. (1997). *The diversity of psychosocial outcomes of treatment of gender dysphoria.* Paper presented at the XVth Harry Benjamin International Gender Dysphoria Association Symposium, Vancouver, Canada.

Carson, R. C. (1996). Aristotle, Galileo, and the DSM taxonomy: The case of schizophrenia. *Journal of Consulting and Clinical Psychology, 64,* 1133–1139.

Carter, C. S., Mintun, M., Nichols, T., & Cohen, J. D. (1997). Anterior cingulate gyrus dysfunction and selective attention deficits in schizophrenia: [^{15}O]H$_2$O PET study during single-trial Stroop task performance. *American Journal of Psychiatry, 154,* 1670–1675.

Carter, M. M., Hollon, S. D., Carson, R., & Shelton, R. C. (1995). Effects of a safe person on induced distress following a biological challenge in panic disorder with agoraphobia. *Journal of Abnormal Psychology, 104,* 156–163.

Cartwright, S. A. (1981). Report on the diseases and physical peculiarities of the Negro race. In A. L. Caplan, H. T., Englehardt, Jr., & J. J. McCartney (Eds.), *Concepts of health and disease: Interdisciplinary perspectives* (pp. 305–326). Reading, MA: Addison-Wesley. Original work published 1851.

Casey, R. J., & Berman, J. S. (1985). The outcome of psychotherapy with children. *Psychological Bulletin, 98,* 388–400.

Casson, I. R., Seigel, O., Sham, R., Campbell, E. A., Tarlau, M., & DiDomenico, A. (1984). Brain damage in modern boxers. *Journal of the American Medical Association, 251,* 2663–2667.

Castelloe, P., & Dawson, G. (1993). Subclassification of children with autism and pervasive developmental disorder: A questionnaire based on Wing's subgrouping scheme. *Journal of Autism and Developmental Disorders, 23.*

Castillo, R. J. (1997a). *Culture & mental illness: A client-centered approach.* Pacific Grove, CA: Brooks/Cole.

Castillo, R. J. (1997b). Dissociation. In W. S. Tseng & J. Streltzer (Eds.), *Culture and psychopathology: A guide to clinical assessment* (pp. 101–123). New York: Brunner/Mazel.

Castle, D. J., Abel, K., Takei, N., & Murray, R. M. (1995). Gender differences in schizophrenia: Hormonal effect or subtypes? *Schizophrenia Bulletin, 21,* 1–12.

Castle, D. J., & Murray, R. M. (1993). The epidemiology of late-onset schizophrenia. *Schizophrenia Bulletin, 19,* 691–700.

Caton, C. L. (1982). Effect of length of inpatient treatment for chronic schizophrenia. *American Journal of Psychiatry, 139,* 856–861.

Catts, S.V., Shelley, A. M., Ward, P. B., Liebert, B., McConaghy, N., Andrews, S., & Michie, P. T. (1995). Brain potential evidence for an auditory sensory memory deficit in schizophrenia. *American Journal of Psychiatry, 152,* 213–219.

Cavallin, H. (1966). Incestuous fathers: A clinical report. *American Journal of Psychiatry, 122*(10), 1132–1138.

Center for Disease Controls. (1997). Smoking-attributable mortality and years of potential life lost—United States, 1984 and Editorial Note. *Morbidity and Mortality Weekly Report, 46,* 444–451.

Cercy, S. P., & Bylsma, F. W. (1997). Lewy bodies and progressive dementia: A critical review and meta-analysis. *Journal of the International Neuropsychological Society, 3,* 179–194.

Chadwick, P. D. J., Lowe, C. F., Horne, P. J., & Higson, P. J. (1994). Modifying delusions: The role of empirical testing. *Behavior Therapy, 25,* 35–49.

Chaplin, S. L. (1997). Somatization. In W. S. Tseng & J. Streltzer (Eds.), *Culture and psychopathology: A guide to clinical assessment* (pp. 67–86). New York: Brunner/Mazel.

Chapman, L. J., & Chapman, J. P. (1973). *Disordered thought in schizophrenia.* New York: Appleton-Century-Crofts.

Chapman, L. J., & Chapman, J. P. (1978). The measurement of differential deficit. *Journal of Psychiatry Research, 14,* 303–311.

Chapman, L. J., & Chapman, J. P. (1985). Psychosis proneness. In M. Alpert (Ed.), *Controversies in schizophrenia* (pp. 157–172). New York: Guilford Press.

Chapman, L. J., & Chapman, J. P. (1987). The search for symptoms predictive of schizophrenia. *Schizophrenia Bulletin, 13,* 497–503.

Chapman, L. J., Chapman, J. P., Kwapil, T. R., Eckblad, M., & Zinser, M. C. (1994). Putatively psychosis-prone subjects 10 years later. *Journal of Abnormal Psychology, 103,* 171–183.

Charcot, J., & Marie, P. (1892). On hystero-epilepsy. In D. H. Tuke (Ed.), *A dictionary of psychological medicine* (Vol. 1). Philadelphia: Blakiston.

Chemtob, C. M., Hamada, R. S., Roitblat, H. L., & Muraoka, M. Y. (1994). Anger, impulsivity, and anger control in combat-related posttraumatic stress disorder. *Journal of Consulting and Clinical Psychology, 62,* 827–832.

Children's Defense Fund. (1991). *The state of America's children.*

Chodorow, N. (1978). *The reproduction of mothering: Psychoanalysis and the sociology of gender.* Berkeley: University of California Press.

Christensen, A., & Jacobson, N. S. (1994). Who (or what) can do psychotherapy: The status and challenge of non-professional therapies. *Psychological Science, 5,* 8–14.

Christenson, G. A., Pyle, R. I., & Mitchell, J. E. (1991). Estimated lifetime prevalence of trichotillomania in college students. *Journal of Clinical Psychology, 52,* 415–417.

Christian, L., & Poling, A. (1997). Drug abuse in persons with mental retardation: A review. *American Journal on Mental Retardation, 102,* 126–136.

Christiansen, B. A., Smith, G. T., Roehling, P. V., & Goldman, M. S. (1989). Using alcohol expectancies to predict adolescent drinking behavior after one year. *Journal of Consulting and Clinical Psychology, 57,* 93–99.

Christoffel, H. (1956). Male genital exhibitionism. In S. Lorand & M. Bolint (Eds.), *Perversions: Psychodynamics and therapy.* New York: Random House.

Christophersen, E. R., & Edwards, K. J. (1992). Treatment of elimination disorders. State of the art. *Applied and Preventive Psychology, 1,* 15–22.

Chugani, H. (1993). Positron emission tomography scanning in newborns. *Clinics in Perinatology, 20*(2), 398.

Chugani, H., Phelps, M. E., & Mazziotta, J. C. (1987). Positron emission tomography study of human brain functional development. *Annals of Neurology, 22*(4), 495.

Clark, D. M. (1991, September 23–25). *Cognitive therapy for panic disorder.* Paper presented at the NIH Consensus Development Conference on the Treatment of Panic Disorders, Bethesda, MD.

Clark, D. M. (1993). Cognitive mediation of panic attacks induced by biological challenge tests. *Advances in Behaviour Research and Therapy, 15,* 75–84.

Clark, D. M., Gelder, M., Salkovskis, P. M., & Anastasiades, P. (1991). *Cognitive mediation of lactate-induced panic.* Paper presented at the annual conference of the American Psychiatric Association, New Orleans.

Clark, D. M., Salkovskis, P. M., & Chalkley, A. J. (1985). Respiratory control as a treatment for panic attacks. *Journal of Behavior Therapy and Experimental Psychiatry, 16,* 23–30.

Clark, D. M., Salkovskis, P. M., Gelder, M., Koehler, C., Martin, M., Anastasiades, P., Hackmann, A., Middleton, H., & Jeavons, A. (1988). Tests of a cognitive theory of panic. In I. Hand & H. V. Wittchen (Eds.), *Panic and phobias 2.* Berlin: Springer-Verlag.

Clark, D. M., Salkovskis, P. M., Hackmann, A., Middleton, H., Pavlos, A., & Gelder, M. (1994). A comparison of cognitive therapy, applied relaxation and imipramine in the treatment of panic disorder. *British Journal of Psychiatry, 164,* 759–769.

Clark, K. B. (1974). *The pathos of power.* New York: Harper & Row, p. 144.

Clarkin, J. F., Marziali, E., & Monroe-Blum, H. (1991). Group and family treatments for borderline personality disorder. *Hospital and Community Psychiatry, 42,* 1038–1043.

Cleckley, H. M. (1976). *The mask of sanity.* St. Louis: Mosby.

Cleghorn, J. M., Franco, S., Szechtman, B., Kaplan, R. D., Szechtman, H., Brown, G. M., Nahmias, C., & Garnett, E. S. (1992). Toward a brain map of auditory hallucinations. *American Journal of Psychiatry, 149,* 1062–1069.

Clementz, B. A., McDowell, J. E., & Zisook, S. (1994). Saccadic system functioning among schizophrenia patients and their first-degree biological relatives. *Journal of Abnormal Psychology, 103,* 277–287.

Clinthorne, J. K., Cisin, I. H., Balter, M. B., Mellinger, G. D., & Uhlenhuth, E. H. (1986). Changes in popular attitudes and beliefs about tranquilizers: 1970–1979. *Archives of General Psychiatry, 43,* 527–532.

Cloninger, C. R., Bayon, C., & Przybeck, T. R. (1997). Epidemiology and axis I comorbidity of antisocial personality. In D. M. Stoff, J. Breiling, & J. D. Maser (Eds.), *Handbook of antisocial behavior* (pp. 12–21). New York: Wiley.

Cloninger, C. R., Sigvardsson, S., von Knorring, A., & Bohman, M. (1984). An adoption study of somatoform disorders: II. Identification of two discrete somatoform disorders. *Archives of General Psychiatry, 41,* 863–871.

Coalition against Misdiagnosis. (1986). *Information packet: The DSM-III-R diagnoses.* Seattle, WA: Author.

Cobb, S. C., & Rose, R. M. (1973). Hypertension, peptic ulcer, and diabetes in air traffic controllers. *Journal of the American Medical Association, 224,* 489–492.

Coccaro, E. F. (1993). Psychopharmologic studies in patients with personality disorders: Review and perspective. *Journal of Personality Disorders, 7,* 181–192.

Cohen, B. D., Nachmani, G., & Rosenberg, S. (1974). Referent communication disturbances in acute schizophrenia. *Journal of Abnormal Psychology, 83*(1), 1–13.

Cohen, B. M., & Cox, C. T. (1995). *Telling without talking: Art as a window into the world of multiple personality.* New York: Norton.

Cohen, K., Auld, F., & Brooker, H. (1994). Is alexithymia related to psychosomatic disorder and somatizing? *Journal of Psychosomatic Research, 38,* 119–127.

Cohen, M., & Seghorn, T. (1969). Sociometric study of the sex offender. *Journal of Abnormal Psychology, 74,* 249–255.

Cohen, P., Cohen, J., Kasen, S., Velez, C. N., Hartmark, C., Johnson, J., Rojas, M., Brook, J., Streuning, E. L. (1993). An epidemiological study of disorders in late childhood and adolescence: I. Age- and gender-specific prevalence. *Journal of Child Psychology and Psychiatry and Allied Disciplines, 34,* 851–867.

Cohen, S., Doyle, W. J., Skoner, D. P., Rabin, B. S., & Gwaltney, J. M. (1997). Social ties and susceptibility to the common cold. *Journal of the American Medical Association, 24,* 1940–1944.

Cohen, S., & Lichtenstein, E. (1990). Partner behaviors that support quitting smoking. *Journal of Consulting and Clinical Psychology, 58,* 304–309.

Cohen, S., Tyrrell, D. A. J., & Smith, A. P. (1991). Psychological stress and susceptibility to the common cold. *New England Journal of Medicine, 325,* 606–612.

Cohen, S., & Williamson, G. M. (1991). Stress and infectious disease in humans. *Psychological Bulletin, 109,* 5–24.

Cohen, S., & Wills, T. A. (1985). Stress, social support, and the buffering hypothesis. *Psychological Bulletin, 98,* 310–357.

Cohen-Kettenis, P., & van Goozen, S. (1995). *Post-operative functioning in adolescent transsexuals.* Paper presented at the XIVth International Symposium on Gender Dysphoria, Kloster Irsee, Germany.

Coie, J. D., Watt, N. F., West, S. G., et al. (1993). The science of prevention: A conceptual framework and some directions for a national research

program. *American Psychologist, 48,* 1013–1022.

Cole, C. M., O'Boyle, M., Emory, L. E., & Meyer, W. (1997). Comorbidity of gender dysphoria and other major psychiatric diagnoses. *Archives of Sexual Behavior, 26,* 13–27.

Cole, D. A., & Turner, J. E., Jr. (1993). Models of cognitive mediation and moderation in child depression. *Journal of Abnormal Psychology, 102,* 271–281.

Cole, S. W., Kemeny, M. E., Taylor, S. E., & Visscher, B. R. (1996). Elevated physical health risk among gay men who conceal their homosexual identity. *Health Psychology, 15,* 243–251.

Coleman, E. The obsessive-compulsive model for describing compulsive sexual behavior. *American Journal of Preventive Psychiatry and Neurology, 2,* 1–8.

Coleman, M. (1989). Medical evaluation of individuals with an autistic disorder. *Forum Medicum.*

Coleman, M. J., Levy, D. L., Lenzenweger, M. F., & Holzman, P. S. (1996). Thought disorder, perceptual aberrations, and schizotypy. *Journal of Abnormal Psychology, 105,* 469–473.

Collier, J. L. (1978). *The making of jazz. A comprehensive history.* New York: Dell.

Combs, B. J., Hales, D. R., & Williams, B. K. (1980). *An invitation to health: Your personal responsibility.* Menlo Park, CA: Benjamin/Cummings.

Commitment following an insanity acquittal. (1981). *Harvard Law Review, 94,* 604–625.

Compas, B. E., Ey, S., & Grant, K. E. (1993). Taxonomy, assessment, and diagnosis of depression during adolescence. *Psychological Bulletin, 114,* 323–344.

Conduct Problems Prevention Research Group. (1992). A developmental and clinical model for the prevention of conduct disorder: The FAST Track Program. Special Issue: Developmental approaches to prevention and intervention. *Development and Psychopathology, 4,* 509–527.

Conger, J. J. (1951). The effects of alcohol on conflict behavior in the albino rat. *Quarterly Journal of Studies on Alcohol, 12,* 1–29.

Conte, J. R., & Berliner, L. (1981). Sexual abuse of children: Implications for practice. *Social Casework, 62,* 601–606.

Cook, M., Mineka, S., Wolkenstein, B., & Laitsch, K. (1985). Observational conditioning of snake fear in unrelated rhesus monkeys. *Journal of Abnormal Psychology, 94,* 591–610.

Cools, J., Schotte, D. E., & McNally, R. J. (1992). Emotional arousal and overeating in restrained eaters. *Journal of Abnormal Psychology, 101,* 348–351.

Coons, P. M. (1986). Treatment progress in 20 patients with multiple personality disorder. *Journal of Nervous and Mental Disease, 174,* 715–721.

Coons, P. M. (1991). Iatrogenesis and malingering of multiple personality disorder in the forensic evaluation of homicide defendants. *Psychiatric Clinics of North America, 14,* 757–768.

Coons, P. M. (1994). Confirmation of childhood abuse in child and adolescent cases of multiple personality disorder and dissociative disorder not otherwise specified. *Journal of Nervous and Mental Disease, 182,* 461–464.

Coons, P. M., & Milstein, V. (1992). Amnesia: A clinical investigation of 25 cases. *Dissociation, 5,* 73–79.

Cooper, J. E., Kendell, R. E., Gurland, B. J., Sharp, L., Copeland, J. R. M., & Simon, R. (1972). *Psychiatric diagnosis in New York and London: A comparative study of mental hospital admissions.* New York: Oxford University Press.

Coplan, J. D., Andrews, M. W., Rosenblum, L. A., Owens, M. J., Friedman, S., Gorman, J. M., & Nemeroff, C. B. (1996). Persistent elevations of cerebrospinal fluid concentrations of corticotropin-releasing factor in adult nonhuman primates exposed to early-life stressors: Implications for the pathophysiology of mood and anxiety disorders. *Proceedings of the National Academy of Science, 93,* 1619–1623.

Corbitt, E. M., and Widiger, T. A. (1995). Sex differences among the personality disorders: An exploration of the data. *Clinical Psychology: Science and Practice, 2,* 225–238.

Corder, E. H., Saunders, A. M., Strittmatter, W. J., Schmechel, D. E., Gaskell, P. C., Small, G. W., Roses, A. D., Haines, J. L., & Pericak-Vance, M. A. (1993). Gene dose of apolipoprotein E type 4 allele and the risk of Alzheimer's disease in late onset families. *Science, 261,* 921–924.

Cornblatt, B. A., & Keilp, J. G. (1994). Impaired attention, genetics, and the pathophysiology of schizophrenia. *Schizophrenia Bulletin, 20,* 31–46.

Cornblatt, B. A., Lenzenweger, M. F., Dworkin, R. H., & Erlenmeyer-Kimling, L. (1985). Positive and negative schizophrenic symptoms, attention, and information processing. *Schizophrenia Bulletin, 11,* 397–408.

Cornell, G., Warren, J., Hawk, G., Stafford, E., Oram, G., & Pine, D. (1996). Psychopathy in instrumental and reactive violent offenders. *Journal of Consulting and Clinical Psychology, 64,* 783–790.

Coryell, W. (1996). Psychotic depression. *Journal of Clinical Psychiatry, 57,* 27–31.

Coryell, W., Akiskal, H. S., Leon, A. C., Winokur, G., Maser, J. D., Mueller, T. I., & Keller, M. B. (1994). The time course of nonchronic major depressive disorder: Uniformity across episodes and samples. *Archives of General Psychiatry, 51,* 405–410.

Coryell, W., Leon, A., Winokur, G., Endicott, J., Keller, M., Akiskal, H., & Solomon, D. (1996). Importance of psychotic features to long-term course in major depressive disorder. *American Journal of Psychiatry, 153,* 483–489.

Coryell, W., Scheftner, W., Keller, M., Endicott, J., Maser, J., & Klerman, G. L. (1993). The enduring psychosocial consequences of mania and depression. *American Journal of Psychiatry, 150,* 720–727.

Costa, E., & Guidotti, A. (1985). Endogenous ligands for benzodiazepine recognition sites. *Biochemical Pharmacology, 34,* 3399–3403.

Costa, P. T., & Widiger, T. A. (Eds.). (1994). *Personality disorders and the five-factor model of personality.* Washington, DC: American Psychological Association.

Cotello, C. G. (1982). Fears and phobias in women: A community study. *Journal of Abnormal Psychology, 91,* 280–286.

Council for Exceptional Children. (1994). Statistical profile of special education in the United States. *Teaching Exceptional Children, 26,* Supplement.

Courchesne, E., Townsend, J., Akshoomoff, N. A., Saitoh, O., Yeung-Courchesne, R., Lincoln, A. J., James, H. E., Haas, R. H., Schreibman, L., & Lau, L. (1994). Impairment in shifting attention in autistic and cerebellar patients. *Behavioral Neuroscience, 108,* 848–865.

Couture, E. G., & Guitar, B. E. (1993). Treatment efficacy research in stuttering. *Journal of Fluency Disorders, 18,* 253–387.

Cowen, E. L., & Work, W. C. (1988). Resilient children, psychological wellness, and primary prevention. *American Journal of Community Psychology, 16,* 591–607.

Cowley, G. (1992a, June 29). Poison at home and at work. *Newsweek,* p. 54.

Cowley, G. (1992b, April 6). A quit-now drive that worked. *Newsweek,* p. 54.

Cox, B. J. (1996). The nature and assessment of catastrophic thoughts in panic disorder. *Behaviour Research and Therapy, 34,* 363–374.

Coyne, J. C. (1976). Toward an interactional description of depression. *Psychiatry, 39,* 14–27.

Coyne, J. C. (1990). Interpersonal processes in depression. In G. I. Keitner (Ed.), *Depression and families* (pp. 31–54). Washington, DC: American Psychiatric Press.

Coyne, J. C., & Whiffen, V. E. (1995). Issues in personality as diathesis for depression: The case of sociotropy-dependency and autonomy-self-criticism. *Psychological Bulletin, 118,* 358–378.

Craighead, L. W., & Agras, W. S. (1991). Mechanisms of action in cognitive-behavioral and pharmacological interventions for obesity and bulimia nervosa. *Journal of Consulting and Clinical Psychology, 59,* 115–125.

Craighead, W. E., Ilardi, S. S., Greenberg, M. D., & Craighead, L. W. (1997). Cognitive psychology: Basic theory and clinical implications. In A. Tasman, J. Kay, & J. A. Lieberman (Eds.), *Psychiatry* (Vol. 1, pp. 350–370). Philadelphia: W. B. Saunders Co.

Craske, M. G. (1991). Phobic fear and panic attacks: The same emotional states triggered by different cues? *Clinical Psychology Review, 11,* 599–620.

Craske, M. G., & Barlow, D. H. (1988). A review of the relationship between panic and avoidance. *Clinical Psychology Review, 8,* 667–685.

Craske, M. G., & Freed, S. (1995). Expectations about arousal and nocturnal panic. *Journal of Abnormal Psychology, 104,* 567–575.

Crino, R. D., & Andrews, G. (1996). Personality disorder in obsessive compulsive disorder: A controlled study. *Journal of Psychiatric Research, 30,* 29–38.

Crisp, A. H. (1984). The psychopathology of anorexia nervosa: Getting the "heat" out of the system. In A. J. Stunkard & E. Stellar (Eds.), *Eating and its disorders.* New York: Raven Press.

Crits-Christoph, P., Siqueland, L., Blaine, J., Frank, A., Luborsky, L., Onken, L. S., Muentz, L., Thase, M. E., Weiss, R. D., Gastfiend, D. R., Woody, G., Barber, J. P., Butler, S. F., Daley, D., Bishop, S., Najavits, L. M., Lis, J., Mercer, D., Griffin, M. L., Moras, K., & Beck, A. T. (1997). The National Institute of Drug Abuse Collaborative Cocaine Treatment Study. *Archives of General Psychiatry, 54,* 721–726.

Cromwell, R. L. (1993). Searching for the origins of schizophrenia. *Psychological Science, 4,* 276–279.

Cronkite, R. C., & Moos, R. H. (1995). Life context, coping processes, and depression. In E. E. Beckham & W. R. Leber (Eds.), *Handbook of depression* (2nd ed., pp. 569–587). New York: Guilford Press.

Crossette, B. (1996, February 29). Agency sees risk in drug to temper child behavior. *New York Times*, p. A14.

Crow, T. J. (1989). A current view of the Type II syndrome: Age of onset, intellectual impairment, and the meaning of structural changes in the brain. *British Journal of Psychiatry, 155*, 15–20.

Crowe, R. R. (1991). Genetic studies of anxiety disorders. In M. T. Tsuang, K. S. Kendler, & M. T. Lyons (Eds.), *Genetic issues in psychosocial epidemiology* (pp. 175–190). New Brunswick, NJ: Rutgers University Press.

Cui, X., & Valliant, G. E. (1996). Antecedents and consequences of negative life events in adulthood: A longitudinal study. *American Journal of Psychiatry, 153*, 21–26.

Cummings, C., Gordon, J. R., & Marlatt, G. A. (1980). Relapse: Prevention and prediction. In W. R. Miller (Ed.), *The addictive disorders: Treatment of alcoholism, drug abuse, smoking, and obesity*. New York: Pergamon Press.

Cummings, J. L. (1985). *Clinical neuropsychiatry*. Orlando, FL: Grune & Stratton.

Cummings, J. L. (1987). Multi-infarct: Diagnosis and management. *Psychosomatics, 28*, 117–126.

Cummings, J. L., & Benson, D. F. (1992). *Dementia: A clinical approach* (2nd ed.). Boston: Butterworths.

Curry, S., Wagner, E. H., & Grothaus, L. C. (1990). Intrinsic and extrinsic motivation for smoking cessation. *Journal of Consulting and Clinical Psychology, 58*, 310–316.

Custer, R. L., & Custer, R. F. (1978). *Characteristics of the recovering compulsive gambler: A survey of 150 members of Gamblers Anonymous*. Paper presented at the fourth annual Conference on Gambling, Reno, NV.

Dain, N. (1964). *Concepts of sanity in the United States, 1789–1895*. New Brunswick, NJ: Rutgers University Press.

Daley, S. E., Hammen, C., Burge, D., Davila, J., Paley, B., Lindberg, N., & Herzberg, D. S. (1997). Predictors of the generation of episodic stress: A longitudinal study of late adolescent women. *Journal of Abnormal Psychology, 106*, 251–259.

Daly, M., & Wilson, M. (1988). *Homicide*. New York: Aldine Books.

Datel, W. E., & Gengerelli, J. A. (1955). Reliability of Rorschach interpretations. *Journal of Projective Techniques, 19*, 372–381.

Davey, G. C. L. (1995). Preparedness and phobias: Specific evolved associations or a generalized expectancy bias? *Behavioral and Brain Sciences, 106*, 289–325.

David, A., Blamire, A., & Breiter, H. (1994). Functional magnetic resonance imaging: A new technique with implications for psychology and psychiatry. *British Journal of Psychiatry, 164*, 2–7.

Davidson, J. R. T., & Foa, E. B. (1991). Diagnostic issues in posttraumatic stress disorder: Considerations for the *DSM-IV. Journal of Abnormal Psychology, 106*, 289–325.

Davidson, J. R. T., Smith, R. D., & Kudler, H. S. (1989). Familial psychiatric illness in chronic posttraumatic stress disorder. *Comprehensive Psychiatry, 30*, 339–345.

Davidson, K., & Tyrer, P. (1996). Cognitive therapy for antisocial and borderline personality disorders: Single case study series. *British Journal of Clinical Psychology, 35*, 413–429.

Davidson, L., & McGlashan, T. H. (1997). The varied outcomes of schizophrenia. *Canadian Journal of Psychiatry, 42*, 34–43.

Davidson, R. J. (1992). Emotion and affective style: Hemispheric substrates. *Psychological Science, 3*, 39–43.

Davidson, R. J. (1993). The neuropsychology of emotion and affective style. In M. Lewis & J. M. Haviland (Eds.), *Handbook of emotions* (pp. 143–154). New York: Guilford Press.

Davidson, R. J., & Fox, N. A. (1989). Frontal brain asymmetry predicts infants' response to maternal separation. *Journal of Abnormal Psychology, 98*, 127–131.

Davis, G. C., & Breslau, N. (1994). Post-traumatic stress disorder in victims of civilian trauma and criminal violence. *Psychiatric Clinics of North America, 17*, 289–299.

Davis, J. O., & Bracha, H. S. (1996). Prenatal growth markers in schizophrenia: A monozygotic co-twin control study. *American Journal of Psychiatry, 153*, 1166–1172.

Davis, J. O., & Phelps, J. A. (1995). Twins with schizophrenia: Genes or germs? *Schizophrenia Bulletin, 21*, 13–18.

Davis, K. L., Kahn, R. S., Ko, G., & Davidson, M. (1991). Dopamine in schizophrenia: Review and reconceptualization. *American Journal of Psychiatry, 148*, 1474–1486.

Dawes, R. M. (1994). *House of cards: Psychology and psychotherapy built on myth*. New York: Free Press.

Dawes, R. M., Faust, D., & Meehl, P. E. (1989). Clinical versus actuarial judgment. *Science, 243*, 1668–1674.

Dawkins, R. (1976). *The selfish gene*. Oxford: Oxford University Press.

Dawson, G., Klinger, L. G., Panagiotides, H., Lewy, A., & Castelloe, P. (1995). Subgroups of autistic children based on social behavior display distinct patterns of brain activity. *Journal of Abnormal Child Psychology, 23*, 569–583.

Dawson, M. E., Nuechterlein, K. H., & Schell, A. M. (1992). Electrodermal anomalies in recent-onset schizophrenia: Relationships to symptoms and prognosis. *Schizophrenia Bulletin, 18*, 295–311.

Dean, M. (1995). Recreational and medicinal cannabis wars. *Lancet, 346*, 761.

Debakey, S. F., Stinson, F. S., Grant, B. F., Dufour, M. C. (1996). Liver cirrhosis mortality in the United States, 1970–1993. *Surveillance Report* No. 41. Washington, DC: CSR, Incorporated.

Deckel, A. W., Hesselbrock, V., & Bauer, L. (1996). Antisocial personality disorder, childhood delinquency, and frontal brain functioning: EEG and neuropsychological findings. *Journal of Clinical Psychology, 52*, 639–650.

Delgado, P. L., Price, L. H., Heninger, G. R., & Charney, D. S. (1992). Neurochemistry. In E. S. Paykel (Ed.), *Handbook of affective disorders* (2nd ed., pp. 219–254). New York: Guilford Press.

DeHart, D. D. & Mahoney, J. M. (1994). The serial murderer's motivations: An interdisciplinary review. *Omega, 29*, 29–45.

DelCastillo, J. (1970). The influence of language upon symptomatology in foreign-born patients. *American Journal of Psychiatry, 127*, 242–244.

Delong, R. G. (1992). Autism, amnesia, hippocampus, and learning. *Neuroscience and Biobehavioral Review, 16*, 63–70.

DeLongis, A. D., Coyne, J. C., Dakof, G., Folkman, S., & Lazarus, R. S. (1982). Relationship of daily hassles, uplifts, and major life events to health status. *Health Psychology, 1*, 119–136.

Denicola, J. & Sandler, J. (1980). Training abusive parents in child management and self-control skills. *Behavior Therapy, 11*, 263–270.

Department of Health and Human Services. (1991). *Healthy people 2000*. Washington, DC: U.S. Government Printing Office; DHHS Pub. no. (PHS) 91–50212.

Department of Justice. (1993). *Uniform crime reports*. Washington, DC: U.S. Government Printing Office.

Destun, L. M., & Kuiper, N. A. (1996). Autobiographical memory and recovered memory therapy: Integrating cognitive, clinical, and individual difference perspectives. *Clinical Psychology Review, 16,* 421–450.

Deutsch, A. (1944). The first U.S. census of the insane (1840) and its use as pro-slavery propaganda. *Bulletin of the History of Medicine, 15,* 469–482.

Deutsch, A. (1949). *The mentally ill in America* (2nd ed.). New York and London: Columbia University Press.

de Waal, F. (1996). *Good natured: The origins of right and wrong in humans and other animals.* Cambridge: Harvard University Press.

Dhawan, S., & Marshall, W. L. (1996). Sexual abuse histories of sexual offenders. *Sexual Abuse: Journal of Research and Treatment, 8,* 7–15.

Di Cara, L., & Miller, N. (1968). Instrumental learning of vasomotor responses by rats: Learning to respond differentially in the two ears. *Science, 159,* 1485–1486.

Didden, R., Duker, P. C., & Korzilius, H. (1997). Meta-analytic study on treatment effectiveness for problem behaviors with individuals who have mental retardation. *American Journal on Mental Retardation, 101,* 387–399.

Dishion, T. J., Spracklen, K. M., Andrews, D. W., & Patterson, G. R. (1996). Deviancy training in male adolescent friendships. *Behavior Therapy, 27,* 373–390.

Dobash, R. E., & Dobash, R. P. (1979). *Violence against wives: A case against patriarchy.* New York: Free Press.

Dobson, K. S. (1989). A meta-analysis of the efficacy of cognitive therapy for depression. *Journal of Consulting and Clinical Psychology, 57,* 414–419.

Docherty, N. M., Hawkins, K. A., Hoffman, R. E., Rakfeldt, J., & Sledge, W. H. (1996). Working memory, attention, and communication disturbances in schizophrenia. *Journal of Abnormal Psychology, 105,* 212–219.

Dodge, K. H., & Schwartz, D. (1997). Social information processing mechanisms in aggressive behavior. In D. M. Stoff, J. Breiling, & J. D. Maser (Eds.), *Handbook of antisocial behavior* (pp. 171–180). New York: Wiley.

Dodrill, C. B. (1992). Neuropsychological aspects of epilepsy. *Psychiatric Clinics of North America, 15,* 383–394.

Dodrill, C. B. (1993). Neuropsychology. In J. Laidlaw, A. Richens, & D. Chadwick (Eds.), *A textbook of epilepsy* (pp. 459–473). Edinburgh: Churchill Livingstone.

Dohrenwend, B. P., & Dohrenwend, B. S. (1987). Social and cultural influences on psychopathology. In B. J. Gallagher (Ed.), *The sociology of mental illness* (p. 437). Englewood Cliffs, NJ: Prentice-Hall.

Dohrenwend, B. S., & Dohrenwend, B. P. (1981). Hypotheses about stress processes linking social class to various types of psychopathology. *American Journal of Community Psychology, 9,* 146–159.

Dolan, B. (1991). Cross-cultural aspects of anorexia nervosa and bulimia: A review. *International Journal of Eating Disorders, 10,* 67–79.

Dolberg, O. T., Iancu, I., Sasson, Y., & Zohar, J. (1996). The pathogenesis and treatment of obsessive-compulsive disorder. *Clinical Neuropharmacology, 19,* 129–147.

Doleys, D. M. (1989). Enuresis and encopresis. In T. H. Ollendick & M. Hersen (Eds.), *Handbook of child psychopathology* (2nd ed.). New York: Plenum Press.

Dorris, M. A. (1989). *The broken cord.* New York: Harper & Row.

Drake, R. E., & Vaillant, G. E. (1985). A validity study of axis II of *DSM-III. American Journal of Psychiatry, 142,* 553–558.

Drukteinis, A. M. (1992) Serial murderer: The heart of darkness. *Psychiatric Annals, 22,* 532–538.

Dubovsky, S. L., & Thomas, M. (1995). Beyond specificity: Effects of serotonin and serotonergic treatments on psychobiological dysfunction. *Journal of Psychosomatic Research, 39,* 429–444.

Duman, R. S., Heninger, G. R., & Nestler, E. J. (1997). A molecular and cellular theory of depression. *Archives of General Psychiatry, 54,* 597–606.

Duncan, G. J., Brooks-Gunn, J., & Klebanov, P. K. (1994). Economic deprivation and early childhood development. *Child Development, 65,* 296–318.

Dunham, H. W. (1965). *Community and schizophrenia: An epidemiological analysis.* Detroit: Wayne State University Press.

Dunn, M. (1994). Neurophysiologic observations in autism. In M. L. Bauman & T. L. Kempner (Eds.), *The neurobiology of autism.* Baltimore: Johns Hopkins University Press.

Dunner, D. L. (1997). *Current psychiatric therapy II.* Philadelphia: W. B. Saunders Co.

Dunst, C. J., Johanson, C., Trivette, C. M., & Hamby, D. (1991, October–November). Family-oriented early intervention policies and practices: Family-centered or not? *Exceptional Children.*

DuPaul, G. J., & Barkley, R. A. (1990). Medication therapy. In R. A. Barkley (Ed.), *Attention-deficit hyperactivity disorder: A handbook for diagnosis and treatment* (pp. 573–612). New York: Guilford Press.

DuPaul, G. J., & Barkley, R. A. (1993). Behavioral contributions to pharmacotherapy: The utility of behavioral methodology in medication treatment of children with attention-deficit hyperactivity disorder. *Behavior Therapy, 24,* 47–65.

Durand, V. M. (1990). *Severe behavior problems: A functional communication training approach.* New York: Guilford Press.

Durkheim, E. (1951). *Suicide* (J. A. Spaulding & G. Simpson, Trans.). Glencoe, IL: Free Press. Original work published 1897.

Durrant, J. E. (1994). A decade of research on learning disabilities: A report card on the state of the literature. *Journal of Learning Disabilities, 27,* 25–33.

Dutton, D. (1988). *The domestic assault of women: Psychological and criminal justice perspectives.* Boston: Allyn and Bacon.

Dutton, D. (1995). *The batterer.* New York: Basic Books.

Dworkin, R. H., & Lenzenweger, M. F. (1984). Symptoms and the genetics of schizophrenia: Implications for diagnosis. *American Journal of Psychiatry, 141,* 1541–1546.

Dyer, K., Christian, W. P., & Luce, S. C. (1982). The role of response delay in improving the discrimination performance of autistic children. *Journal of Applied Behavior Analysis, 15,* 231–240.

Eagly, A. H., Makhijana, M. G., & Klonsky, B. G. (1992). Gender and the evaluation of leaders: A meta-analysis. *Psychological Bulletin, 111,* 3–22.

Eames, P. (1992). Hysteria following brain injury. *Journal of Neurology, Neurosurgery, and Psychiatry, 55,* 1046–1053.

Earnst, K. S., & Kring, A. M. (1997). Construct validity of negative symptoms: An empirical and conceptual review. *Clinical Psychology Review, 17,* 167–189.

Eaton, W. W., Anthony, J. C., Gallo, J., Cai, G., Tien, A., Romanoski, A., Lyketsos, C., & Chen, L. S. (1997). Natural history of diagnostic interview schedule/ *DSM-IV* major depression: The Baltimore Epidemiologic Catchment Area follow-up. *Archives of General Psychiatry, 54,* 993–999.

Eaton, W. W., Kessler, R. C., Wittchen, H. U., & Magee, W. J. (1994). Panic and panic disorder in the United States. *American Journal of Psychiatry, 151,* 413–420.

Eaton, W. W., & Keyl, P. M. (1990). Risk factors for the onset of diagnostic interview schedule/*DSM-III* agoraphobia in a prospective, population-based study. *Archives of General Psychiatry, 47,* 819–824.

Eaton, W. W., Mortensen, P. B., Herrman, H., Freeman, H., Bilder, W., Burgess, P., & Wooff, K. (1992). Long-term course of hospitalization for schizophrenia: Part I. Risk for rehospitalization. *Schizophrenia Bulletin, 18,* 217–228.

Eberlin, M., McConnachie, G., Ibel, S., & Volpe, L. (1993). Facilitated communication: A failure to replicate the phenomenon. *Journal of Autism and Developmental Disorders, 23.*

Edwards, G. (1989). As the years go rolling by: Drinking problems in the time dimension. *British Journal of Psychiatry, 154,* 18–26.

Egeland, J. A., Gerhard, D. S., Pauls, D. L., Sussex, J. N., Kidd, K. K., Allen, C. R., Hostetter, A. M., & Housman, D. E. (1987). Bipolar affective disorders linked to DNA markers on chromosome 11. *Nature, 325,* 783–787.

Egeland, J. A., & Hostetter, A. M. (1983). Amish study: I. Affective disorders among the Amish. *American Journal of Psychiatry, 140,* 56–61.

Eggert, L. L., Thompson, E. A., Herting, J. R., & Nicholas, L. J. (1995). Reducing suicide potential among high-risk youth: Tests of a school-based prevention program. *Suicide and Life-Threatening Behavior, 25,* 276–296.

Ehlers, C. L., Frank, E., & Kupfer, D. J. (1988). Social zeitgebers and biological rhythms. A unified approach to understanding the etiology of depression. *Archives of General Psychiatry, 45,* 948–952.

Eilbracht, A., & Thompson, T. (1977). Behavioral intervention in a sheltered work activity setting for retarded adults. In T. Thompson & J. Grabowski (Eds.), *Behavior modification of the mentally retarded* (2nd ed.). New York: Oxford University Press.

Eisen, A. R., & Engler, L. B. (1995). Chronic anxiety. In A. R. Eisen, C. A. Kearney, & C. E. Schaefer (Eds.), *Clinical handbook of anxiety disorders in children and adolescents.* Northvale, NJ: Aronson.

Eisen, A. R., Kearney, C. A., & Schaefer, C. E. (Eds.) (1995). *Clinical handbook of anxiety disorders in children and adolescents.* Northvale, NJ: Aronson.

Eisen, A. R., & Silverman, W. K. (in press). Treating generalized anxiety disorder in children: A second study showing that it matters if children are taught to relax or change their thoughts depending on their symptoms. *Behavior Therapy.*

Elkin, I., Shea, T., Watkins, J. T., Imber, S. D., Sotsky, S. M., Collins, J. F., Glass, D. R., Pilkonis, P. A., Leber, W. R., Docherty, J. P., Fiester, S. J., & Parloff, M. B. (1989). National Institute of Mental Health treatment of depression collaborative research program. *Archives of General Psychiatry, 46,* 971–982.

Elkins, T. E., & Andersen, H. F. (1992). Sterilization of persons with mental retardation. *Journal of the Association for Persons with Severe Handicaps, 17,* 19–26.

Elkis, H., Friedman, L., Wise, A., & Meltzer, H. Y. (1995). Meta-analyses of studies of ventricular enlargement and cortical sulcal prominence in mood disorders: Comparisons with controls or patients with schizophrenia. *Archives of General Psychiatry, 52,* 735–746.

Ellason, J. W., & Ross, C. A. (1997). Two-year follow-up of inpatients with dissociative identity disorder. *American Journal of Psychiatry, 154,* 832–839.

Elliott, D. M. (1997). Traumatic events: Prevalence and delayed recall in the general population. *Journal of Consulting and Clinical Psychology, 65,* 811–820.

Elliott, D. S., Ageton, S. S., Huizinga, D., Knowles, B. A., & Canter, R. J. (1983). *The prevalence and incidence of delinquent behavior: 1976–1980* (National Youth Survey Report No. 26). Boulder, CO: Behavioral Research Institute.

Ellis, A. (1962). *Reason and emotion in psychotherapy.* New York: Lyle Stuart.

Ellis, A. (1980). An overview of the clinical theory of rational-emotive therapy. In R. Grieger & J. Boyd (Eds.), *Rational-emotive therapy: A skills-based approach.* New York: Van Nostrand Reinhold.

Elmer-De Witt, P. (1994, October 17). Now for the truth about Americans and sex. *Time.*

Emmelkamp, P. M. G. (1994). Behavior therapy with adults. In A. E. Bergin & S. L. Garfield (Eds.), *Handbook of psychotherapy and behavior change* (4th ed., pp. 379–427). New York: Wiley.

Endicott, J., & Spitzer, R. A. (1978). A diagnostic interview: The Schedule for Affective Disorders and Schizophrenia. *Archives of General Psychiatry, 35,* 837–844.

Engel, B. T. (1960). Stimulus-response and individual-response specificity. *Archives of General Psychiatry, 2,* 305–313.

Engel, B. T., & Bickford, A. F. (1961). Response specificity: Stimulus response and individual response specificity in essential hypertension. *Archives of General Psychiatry, 5,* 478–489.

Engel, J., & Liljequist, S. (1983). The involvement of different neurotransmitters in mediating stimulatory and sedative effects of ethanol. In L. A. Pohorecky & J. Brick (Eds.), *Stress and alcohol use* (pp. 153–169). New York: Elsevier.

Engel, J., Van Ness, P. C., Rasmussen, T. B., Ojemann, L. M. (1993). Outcome with respect to epileptic seizures. In J. Engel, Jr. (Ed.), *Surgical treatment of the epilepsies* (2nd ed., pp. 609–621). New York: Raven Press.

Engle-Friedman, M., Baker, E. A., & Bootzin, R. R. (1985). Reports of wakefulness during EEG identified states of sleep. *Sleep Research, 14,* 121.

Ennis, B. J., & Emery, R. D. (1978). *The rights of mental patients.* New York: Avon.

Epstein, S. (1983). The stability of confusion: A reply to Mischel and Peake. *Psychological Review, 90,* 179–184.

Erdelyi, M. H. (1985). *Psychoanalysis: Freud's cognitive view.* New York: Freeman.

Erdelyi, M. H., & Goldberg, B. (1979). Let's not sweep repression under the rug: Toward a cognitive psychology of repression. In J. F. Kihlstrom & F. J. Evans (Eds.), *Functional disorders of memory.* Hillsdale, NJ: Erlbaum.

Erikson, K. T. (1976). *Everything in its path: Destruction of community in the Buffalo Creek flood.* New York: Simon & Schuster.

Erlenmeyer-Kimling, L., Adamo, U. H., Rock, D., Roberts, S. A., Bassett, A. S., Squires-Wheeler, E., Cornblatt, B. A., Endicott, J., Pape, S., & Gottesman, I. I. (1997). The New York High-Risk Project: Prevalence and comorbidity of Axis I disorders in offspring of schizophrenic parents at 25-year follow-up. *Archives of General Psychiatry, 54,* 1096–1102.

Eron, L. D. (1997). The development of antisocial behavior from a learning perspective. In D. M. Stoff, J. Breiling, & J. D. Maser (Eds.), *Handbook of antisocial behavior* (pp. 140–147). New York: Wiley.

Esterling, B., Antoni, M., Kuman, M., & Schneiderman, N. (1990). Emotional repression, stress disclosure responses, and Epstein-Barr viral capsid antigen titers. *Psychosomatic Medicine, 52,* 397–410.

Evans, J. D., Paulsen, J. S., Harris, M. J., Heaton, R. K., & Jeste, D. V. (1996). A clinical and neuropsychological comparison of delusional disorder and schizophrenia. *Journal of Neuropsychiatry and Clinical Neurosciences, 8,* 281–286.

Evans, M. D., Hollon, S. D., DeRubeis, R. J., Piasecki, J. M., Grove, W. M., Garvey, M. J., & Tuason, V. B. (1992). Differential relapse following cognitive therapy and pharmacotherapy for depression. *Archives of General Psychiatry, 49,* 802–808.

Ewen, D. (1956). *Journey to greatness: The life and music of George Gershwin.* New York: Holt, Rinehart and Winston.

Exner, J. E. (1978). *The Rorschach: A comprehensive system* (Vol. 1). New York: Wiley.

Exner, J. E. (1982). *The Rorschach: A comprehensive system* (Vol. 2). New York: Wiley.

Exner, J. E. (1986). *The Rorschach: A comprehensive system* (Vol. 3). New York: Wiley.

Eysenck, H. J. (Ed.). (1967). *The biological basis of personality.* Springfield, IL: Charles C Thomas.

Fabian, W. D., Jr., & Fishkin, S. M. (1981). A replicated study of self-reported changes in psychological absorption with marijuana intoxication. *Journal of Abnormal Psychology, 90,* 546–553.

Falloon, I. R. H., Boyd, J. L., McGill, C. W., et al. (1982). Family management in prevention of exacerbation of schizophrenia: A controlled study. *New England Journal of Medicine, 306*(24), 1437–1440.

Falloon, I. R. H., Boyd, J. L., McGill, C. W., Williamson, M., Razani, J., Moss, H. B., Gilderman, A. M., & Simpson, G. M. (1985). Family management in the prevention of morbidity of schizophrenia. *Archives of General Psychiatry, 42,* 887–896.

Fals-Stewart, W., Birchler, G. R., & O'Farrell, T. J. (1996). Behavioral couples therapy for male substance-abusing patients: Effects on relationship adjustment and drug-using behavior. *Journal of Consulting and Clinical Psychology, 64,* 959–972.

Farberow, N. L., & Litman, R. E. (1970). *A comprehensive suicide prevention program. Suicide Prevention Center of Los Angeles, 1958–1969.* Unpublished final report, DHEW NIMH Grants No. MH 14946 and MH 00128, Los Angeles.

Farlow, M., Gracon, S. I., Hershey, L. A., Lewis, K. W., Sadowsky, C. H., & Dolan-Ureno, J. (1992). A controlled trial of tacrine in Alzheimer's disease. *Journal of the American Medical Association, 268,* 2523–2529.

Farrington, D. P. (1991). Childhood aggression and adult violence: Early precursors and later-life outcomes. In D. J. Pepler & K. H. Rubin (Eds.), *The development of aggression* (pp. 5–29). Hillsdale, NJ: Erlbaum.

Farrington, D. P. (1995a). Crime and physical health: Illnesses, injuries, accidents and offending behavior in the Cambridge study. *Criminal Behavior and Mental Health, 5,* 261–278.

Farrington, D. P. (1995b). The development of offending and antisocial behavior from childhood: Key findings from the Cambridge Study in delinquent development. *Journal of Child Psychology and Psychiatry, 360,* 929–964.

Fauman, M. A. (1994). *Study guide to DSM-IV.* Washington, DC: American Psychiatric Press.

Faustman, W. O. (1995). What causes schizophrenia? In S. Vinogradov (Ed.), *Treating schizophrenia* (pp. 57–79). San Francisco: Jossey-Bass.

Fava, G. A., Grandi, S., Rafanelli, C., & Canestrari, R. (1992). Prodromal symptoms in panic disorder with agoraphobia: A replication study. *Journal of Affective Disorders, 26,* 85–88.

Fava, M., Alpert, J. E., Borus, J. S., Nierenberg, A. A., Pava, J. A., & Rosenbaum, J. F. (1996). Patterns of personality disorder comorbidity in early-onset versus late-onset major depression. *American Journal of Psychiatry, 153,* 1308–1312.

Fawzy, F. L., Fawzy, N. W., Hyun, C. S., Elashoff, R., Guthrie, D., Fahey, J. L., & Morton, D. L. (1993). Malignant melanoma: Effects of an early structured psychiatric intervention, coping, and affective state on recurrence and survival 6 years later. *Archives of General Psychiatry, 50,* 681–689.

Fear, C., Sharp, H., & Healy, D. (1996). Cognitive processes in delusional disorders. *British Journal of Psychiatry, 168,* 61–67.

Federal Bureau of Investigation. (1991) *Uniform crime reports.* Washington, DC: U.S. Department of Justice.

Fein, D., & Waterhouse, L. (1990). Social cognition in infantile autism. *Forum Medicum.*

Feingold, A. (1994). Gender differences in personality: A meta-analysis. *Psychological Bulletin, 116,* 429–456.

Felce, D., & Perry, J. (1995). Quality of life: Its definition and measurement. *Research in Developmental Disabilities, 16,* 51–74.

Felton, R. H., & Wood, F. B. (1989). Cognitive deficits in reading disability and attention deficit disorder. *Journal of Learning Disabilities, 22,* 3–13.

Fenichel, O. (1945). *The psychoanalytic theory of neurosis.* New York: W. W. Norton.

Fenton, W. S., & McGlashan, T. H. (1991). Natural history of schizophrenia subtypes: I. Longitudinal study of paranoid, hebephrenic, and undifferentiated schizophrenia. *Archives of General Psychiatry, 48,* 969–977.

Fenton, W. S., & McGlashan, T. H. (1994). Antecedents, symptom progression, and long-term outcome of the deficit syndrome in schizophrenia. *American Journal of Psychiatry, 151,* 351–356.

Fenton, W. S., McGlashan, T. H., Victor, B. J., & Blyler, C. R. (1997). Symptoms, subtype, and suicidality in patients with schizophrenia spectrum disorders. *American Journal of Psychiatry, 154,* 199–204.

Fergusson, D. M., Horwood, L. J., & Lynskey, M. T. (1995). The stability of disruptive childhood behaviors. *Journal of Abnormal Child Psychology, 23,* 379–396.

Fernando, S. (1991). *Mental health: Race and culture.* New York: St. Martin's Press.

Ferster, C. B. (1973). A functional analysis of depression. *American Psychologist, 28,* 857–870.

Fiester, S. J. (1991). Self-defeating personality disorder: A review of data and recommendations for DSM-IV. *Journal of Personality Disorders, 5,* 194–209.

Finch, J. R., Smith, J. P., & Pokorny, A. D. (1970, May). *Vehicular studies.* Paper presented at meetings of the American Psychiatric Association.

Fine, R. H. (1965). Psychotherapy with the mentally retarded adolescent. *Current Psychiatric Therapies, 5,* 58–66.

Fineman, H., Turque, B., Rosentiel, T., Beals, G., Glick, D., & Carroll, G. (1996, August 26). Bring on the baby boomers. *Newsweek, 128* (9), 19–25.

Fink, C. M., Turner, S. M., & Beidel, D. C. (1996). Culturally relevant factors in the behavioral treatment of social phobia: A case study. *Journal of Anxiety Disorders, 10,* 201–209.

Finkelhor, D. (1984). *Child sexual abuse: New theory and research.* New York: Free Press.

Finkelhor, D. (1994). The international epidemiology of child sexual abuse. *Child Abuse and Neglect, 18,* 409–411.

Finkelhor, D., & Araji, S. (1986). Explanations of pedophilia: A four factor model. *The Journal of Sex Research, 22,* 145–161.

Finkelson, L., & Oswalt, R. (1995). College date rape: Incidence and reporting. *Psychological Reports, 77,* 526.

Finkelstein, J. R. J., Cannon, T. D., Gur, R. E., Gur, R. C., & Moberg, P. (1997). Attentional dysfunctions in neuroleptic-naive and neuroleptic-withdrawn schizophrenic patients and their siblings. *Journal of Abnormal Psychology, 106,* 203–212.

Firoe, M. C., Novotny, T. E., Pierce, J. P., Hatziandreu, E. J., Patel, K. M., & Davis, R. M. (1989). Trends in cigarette smoking in the United States: The changing influence of gender and race. *Journal of the American Medical Association, 261,* 49–55.

First, M. B., Frances, A., Widiger, T. A., Pincus, H. A., & Davis, W. W. (1992). DSM-IV and behavioral assessment. *Behavioral Assessment, 14,* 297–306.

First, M. B., Spitzer, R. L., Gibbon, M., & Williams, J. B. W. (1997). *Structured Clinical Interview for DSM-IV Axis I Disorders (SCID).* Biometrics Research Department, New York Psychiatric Institute, p. A1.

Fishbain, D. A., & Goldberg, M. (1991). The misdiagnosis of conversion disorder in a psychiatric emergency room. *General Hospital Psychiatry, 13,* 177–181.

Fisher, S., & Greenberg, R. P. (1977). *The scientific credibility of Freud's theories and therapy.* New York: Basic Books.

Fiske, S. T., & Taylor, S. E. (1991). *Social cognition* (2nd ed.). New York: McGraw-Hill.

Flaum, M., & Schultz, S. K. (1996). When does amphetamine-induced psychosis become schizophrenia? *American Journal of Psychiatry, 153,* 812–815.

Fletcher, J. M., Shaywitz, S. E., Shankweiler, D., Katz, L., Liberman, I. Y., Steubing, K. K., Francis, D. J., Fowler, A. E., & Shaywitz, B. A. (1994). Cognitive profiles of reading disability. Comparisons of discrepancy and low achievement definitions. *Journal of Educational Psychology, 86,* 6–23.

Flett, G. L., Vredenburg, K., & Krames, L. (1997). The continuity of depression in clinical and nonclinical samples. *Psychological Bulletin, 121,* 395–416.

Flint, A. J., Cook, M. & Rabins, P. V. (1996). Why is panic disorder less frequent in late life? *American Journal of Geriatric Psychiatry, 4,* 96–109.

Flor-Henry, P. (1987). Cerebral aspects of sexual deviation. In G. D. Wilson (Ed.), *Variant sexuality: Research and theory.* Baltimore: Johns Hopkins University Press.

Flor-Henry, P., Fromm-Auch, D., Tapper, M., & Schopflocher, D. (1981). A neuropsychological study of the stable syndrome of hysteria. *Biological Psychiatry, 16,* 601–626.

Flynn, B. S., Worden, J. K., Secker-Walker, R. H., Badger, G., & Carpenter, J. (1997). Cigarette smoking prevention effects of mass media and school interventions on cross-sectional adolescent populations followed into secondary school. (Unpublished manuscript).

Flynn, B. S., Worden, J. K., Secker-Walker, R. H., Pirie, P. L, Badger, G., & Carpenter, J. (1994). Mass media and

school interventions for cigarette smoking prevention: Effects 2 years after completion. *American Journal of Public Health, 84,* 1148–1150.

Flynn, B. S., Worden, J. K., Secker-Walker, R. H., Pirie, P. L, Badger, G., & Carpenter, J. (1997). Long-term responses of higher and lower risk youths to smoking prevention interventions. *Preventive Medicine, 26,* 389–394.

Foa, E. B., Hearst-Ikeda, D., & Perry, K. J. (1995). Evaluation of a brief cognitive-behavioral program for the prevention of chronic PTSD in recent assault victims. *Journal of Consulting and Clinical Psychology, 63,* 948–955.

Foa, E. B., & Liebowitz, M. (1995). *Recent findings on the efficacy of behavior therapy and clomipramine for obsessive-compulsive disorder.* Paper presented at the annual meeting of the Psychiatric Research Society, February 1995, Park City, Utah.

Foa, E. B., Steketee, G., & Rothbaum, B. O. (1989). Behavioral/cognitive conceptualization of post-traumatic stress disorder. *Behavior Therapy, 20,* 155–176.

Foerster, A., Lewis, S. W., Owen, M. J., & Murray, R. M. (1991). Low birth weight and a family history of schizophrenia predict poor premorbid functioning in psychosis. *Schizophrenia Research, 5,* 13–20.

Folkman, S. (1984). Personal control and stress and coping processes: A theoretical analysis. *Journal of Personality and Social Psychology, 46,* 839–852.

Folkman, S., Lazarus, R., Dunkel-Schetter, C., DeLongis, A., & Gruen, R. (1986). The dynamics of a stressful encounter: Cognitive appraisal, coping, and encounter outcomes. *Journal of Personality and Social Psychology, 50,* 992–1003.

Follette, W. C., & Houts, A. C. (1996). Models of scientific progress and the role of theory in taxonomy development: A case study of the DSM. *Journal of Consulting and Clinical Psychology, 64,* 1120–1132.

Folstein, S., & Rutter, M. (1977). Genetic influences and infantile autism. *Nature, 265,* 726–728.

Ford, C. S., & Beach, F. A. (1951). *Patterns of sexual behavior.* New York: Ace.

Ford, C.V. (1995). Dimensions of somatization and hypochondriasis. *Neurologic Clinics, 13,* 241–253.

Foreyt, J. P., & Goodrick, G. K. (1993). Obesity in children. In R. T. Ammerman & M. Hersen (Eds.), *Handbook of behavior therapy with children and adults: A developmental and*

longitudinal perspective. Boston: Allyn & Bacon.

Forsyth, R. P. (1974). Mechanisms of the cardiovascular responses to environmental stressors. In P. A. Obrist, A. H. Black, J. Brener, & L. U. Di Cara (Eds.), *Cardiovascular psychophysiology: Current issues in response mechanisms, biofeedback and methodology.* Hawthorne, NY: Aldine.

Fortmann, S. P., & Killen, J. D. (1995). Nicotine gum and self-help behavioral treatment for smoking relapse prevention: Results from a trial using population-based recruitment. *Journal of Consulting and Clinical Psychology, 63,* 460–468.

Foulks, E. F. (1996). Culture and personality disorders. In J. E. Mezzich, A. Kleinman, H. Fabrega, & D. L. Parron (Eds.), *Culture and psychiatric diagnosis: A DSM-IV perspective* (pp. 243–252). Washington, DC: American Psychiatric Press.

Foy, D. W., Resnick, H. S., Sipprelle, R. C., & Carroll, E. M. (1987). Premilitary, military, and post-military factors in the development of combat-related stress disorders. *Behavior Therapist, 10,* 3–9.

Frances, A., Docherty, J. P., & Kahn, D. A. (1996). The Expert Consensus Guideline Series: Treatment of schizophrenia. *Journal of Clinical Psychiatry, 57,* Supplement 12B, 1–58.

Frances, A., First, M. B., & Pincus, H. A. (1995). *DSM-IV guidebook.* Washington, DC: American Psychiatric Press.

Frank, E., Anderson, B., Reynolds, C. F., III, Ritenour, A., & Kupfer, D. J. (1994). Life events and the research diagnostic criteria endogenous subtype. *Archives of General Psychiatry, 51,* 519–524.

Free, M. J., & Oei, T. P. S. (1989). Biological and psychological processes in the treatment and maintenance of depression. *Clinical Psychology Review, 9,* 653–688.

Freeman, A., & Leaf, R. (1989). Cognitive therapy applied to personality disorders. In A. Freeman, K. Simon, L. Beutler, & H. Arkowitz (Eds.), *Comprehensive handbook of cognitive therapy.* New York: Plenum Press.

Freeman, H. (1989). Relationship of schizophrenia to the environment. *British Journal of Psychiatry, 155,* 90–99.

French, S. A., & Jeffrey, R. W. (1994). Consequences of dieting to lose weight: Effects on physical and mental health. *Health Psychology, 13,* 195–212.

Freud, A. (1946). *The ego and mechanisms of defense.* New York: International Universities Press.

Freud, A. (1958). Adolescence. *Psycho-analytic Study of the Child, 13,* 255–278.

Freud, A. (1965). *Normality and pathology: Assessment of development.* New York: International Universities Press.

Freud, S. (1953a). Three essays on sexuality. In J. Strachey (Ed.), *The standard edition of the complete psychological works of Sigmund Freud* (Vol. 3). London: Hogarth Press. Original work published 1905.

Freud, S. (1953b). The questioning of lay analysis. In J. Strachey (Ed.), *The standard edition of the complete psychological works of Sigmund Freud* (Vol. 20). London: Hogarth Press. Original work published 1926.

Freud, S. (1957). Mourning and melancholia. In J. Rickman (Ed.), *A general selection from the works of Sigmund Freud.* Garden City, NY: Doubleday. Original work published 1917.

Freud, S. (1962a). Analysis of a phobia in a five-year-old boy. In J. Strachey (Ed.), *The standard edition of the complete psychological works of Sigmund Freud* (Vol. 10). London: Hogarth Press. Original work published 1909.

Freud, S. (1962b). Studies on hysteria. In J. Strachey (Ed.), *The standard edition of the complete psychological works of Sigmund Frued* (Vol. 2). London: Hogarth Press. Original work published 1895.

Freud, S. (1974). Femininity. In J. Strachey (Ed.), *The standard edition of the complete psychological works of Sigmund Freud* (Vol. 22). London: Hogarth Press. Original work published 1932.

Freund, K., & Blanchard, R. (1989). Phallometric diagnosis of pedophilia. *Journal of Consulting and Clinical Psychology, 57,* 100–105.

Fried, D., Crits-Christoph, P., & Luborsky, L. (1992). The first empirical demonstration of transference in psychotherapy. *Journal of Nervous and Mental Disease, 180,* 326–331.

Friedman, R., Sandler, J., Hernandez, M., & Wolfe, D. (1981). Child abuse. In E. J. Marsh & L. G. Terdal (Eds.), *Behavioral assessment of childhood disorders* (pp. 221–255). New York: Guilford Press.

Friedman, M., & Rosenman, R. H. (1974). *Type A behavior and your heart.* New York: Knopf.

Frith, C.D. (1992). *The cognitive neuropsychology of schizophrenia.* Hillsdale, NJ: Erlbaum.

Fromm, Erich. (1980). *Greatness and limitations of Freud's thought.* New York: Harper & Row.

Frosch, W. A., Robbins, E. S., & Stern, M. (1965). Untoward reactions to lysergic acid diethylamide (LSD) resulting in hospitalization. *New England Journal of Medicine, 273*(23), 1236.

Furby, L., Weinrott, M. R., & Blackshaw, L. (1989). Sex offender recidivism: A review. *Psychological Bulletin, 105*(1), 3–30.

Fyer, A. J., Liebowitz, M. R., & Klein, D. F. (1990). Treatment trials, comorbidity, and syndromal complexity. In J. D. Maser and C. R. Cloninger (Eds.), *Comorbidity of mood and anxiety disorders.* Washington, DC: American Psychiatric Press.

Fyer, A. J., Mannuzza, S., Chapman, T. F., Martin, L. Y., & Klein, D. F. (1995). Specificity in familial aggregation of phobic disorders. *Archives of General Psychiatry, 52,* 564-573.

Fyer, M. R. (1990). Phobia. In M. E. Thase, B. A. Edelstein, & M. Hersen (Eds.), *Handbook of outpatient treatment of adults: Nonpsychotic mental disorders* (pp. 161–175). New York: Plenum Press.

Gabbard, G. O. (1992). Psychodynamic psychiatry in the "Decade of the Brain." *American Journal of Psychiatry, 149,* 991–998.

Gabbard, G. O. (1994). *Psychodynamic psychiatry in clinical practice. The DSM-IV edition.* Washington, DC: American Psychiatric Press.

Gabriel, S. M., Haroutunian, V., Powchik, P., Honer, W. G., Davidson, M., Davies, P., & Davis, K. L. (1997). Increased concentrations of presynaptic proteins in the cingulate cortex of subjects with schizophrenia. *Archives of General Psychiatry, 54,* 559–566.

Gagnon, J. H., Rosen, R. C., & Leiblum, S. R. (1982). Cognitive and social aspects of sexual dysfunction: Sexual scripts in sex therapy. *Journal of Sex and Marital Therapy, 8,* 44–56.

Galen, L. W., Henderson, M. J., & Whitman, R. D. The utility of novelty seeking, harm avoidance, and expectancy in the prediction of drinking. *Addictive Behaviors, 22,* 93–106.

Gallagher, B. J., III. (1987). *The sociology of mental illness.* Englewood Cliffs, NJ: Prentice-Hall.

Ganellen, R. J. (1994). Attempting to conceal psychological disturbance: MMPI defensive response sets and the Rorschach. *Journal of Personality Assessment, 63,* 423–437.

Garber, H. L., & McInerney, M. (1982). Sociobehavioral factors in mental retardation. In P. T. Legelka & H. G. Prehm (Eds.), *Mental retardation: From categories to people.* Columbus, OH: Charles E. Merrill.

Garcia, M. E., Schmitz, J. M., & Doerfler, L. A. (1990). A fine-grained analysis of the role of self-efficacy in self-initiated attempts to quit smoking. *Journal of Consulting and Clinical Psychology, 58,* 317–322.

Gardner, H., & Hatch, T. (1989). Multiple intelligences go to school: Educational implications of the theory of multiple intelligences. *Educational Research, 18*(8), 6.

Garland, A. F., & Zigler, E. (1993). Adolescent suicide prevention: Current research and social policy implications. *American Psychologist, 48,* 169–182.

Garssen, B., De Beurs, E., Buikhuisen, M., van Balkom, A., Lange, A., & van Dyck, R. (1996). On distinguishing types of panic. *Journal of Anxiety Disorders, 10,* 173–184.

Gatz, M., Bengtson, V. L., & Blum, M. J. (1990). Caregiving families. In J. E. Birren & K. W. Schaie (Eds.), *Handbook of the psychology of aging* (3rd ed., pp. 405–426). New York: Academic Press.

Gatz, M., Lowe, B., Berg, S., Mortimer, J., & Pedersen, N. (1994). Dementia: Not just a search for the gene. *Gerontologist, 34,* 251–255.

Gawin, F. H., & Kleber, H. D. (1986). Abstinence symptomatology and psychiatric diagnosis in cocaine abusers. *Archives of General Psychiatry, 43,* 107–113.

Gay, M. (1989). Personality disorder among child abusers. In R. L. Spitzer (Chair), *Psychiatric diagnosis, victimization, and women.* Symposium conducted at the 142nd Annual Meeting of the American Psychiatric Association, San Francisco, CA.

Geddes, J. R., & Lawrie, S. M. (1995). Obstetric complications and schizophrenia: A meta-analysis. *British Journal of Psychiatry, 167,* 786–793.

Gelder, M. (1991). Psychological treatment for anxiety disorders: Adjustment disorder with anxious mood, generalized anxiety disorders, panic disorder, agoraphobia, and avoidant personality disorder. In W. Coryell & G. Winokur (Eds.), *The clinical management of anxiety disorders* (pp. 10–27). New York: Oxford University Press.

Gelenberg, A. J. (1991). Psychoses. In A. J. Gelenberg, E. L. Bassuk, & S. C. Schoonover (Eds.), *The practitioner's guide to psychoactive drugs* (3rd ed., pp. 125–218). New York: Plenum Press.

Geller, E., Ritvo, E. R., Freeman, B. J., & Yuwiler, A. (1982). Preliminary observations on the effect of fenfluramine on blood serotonin and symptoms in three autistic boys. *New England Journal of Medicine, 307,* 165–167.

Gelles, R. J., Lackner, R., & Wolfner, G. D. (1994). *Violence Update, 4*(12), 1–10 passim.

Gelles, R. J., & Straus, M. (1988). *Intimate violence.* New York: Simon & Schuster.

Gelman, D. (1990, March 26). Drugs vs. the couch. *Newsweek,* pp. 42–43.

Gibbs, N. A. (1996). Nonclinical populations in research on obsessive-compulsive disorder: A critical review. *Clinical Psychology Review, 16,* 729–773.

Giesler, R. B., Josephs, R. A., & Swann, W. B., Jr. (1996). Self-verification in clinical depression: The desire for negative evaluation. *Journal of Abnormal Psychology, 105,* 358–368.

Giles, D. E., Biggs, M. E., Rush, A. J., & Roffwarg, H. P. (1988). Risk factors in families of unipolar depression: I. Psychiatric illness and reduced REM latency. *Journal of Affective Disorders, 14,* 51–59.

Gill, M., McKeon, P., & Humphries, P. (1988). Linkage analysis of manic depression in an Irish family using H-ras 1 and INS DNA markers. *Journal of Medical Genetics, 25,* 634–635.

Gillberg, C. (1991). Outcome in autism and autistic-like conditions. *Journal of the American Academy of Child and Adolescent Psychiatry, 30,* 375–382.

Gillberg, C., Melander, H., Liis von Knorring, A., Lars-Olof, J., Thernlund, G., Hagglof, B., Eidevall, Wallin, L., Gustafsson, P., & Kopp, S. (1997). Long-term stimulant treatment of children with attention-deficit hyperactivity disorder symptoms. *Archives of General Psychiatry, 54,* 857–864.

Gillberg, C., & Steffenburg, S. (1987). Outcome and prognostic factors in infantile autism and similar conditions: A population-based study of 46 cases followed through puberty. *Journal of Autism and Developmental Disorders, 17,* 273–287.

Gillham, J. E., Reivich, K. J., Jaycox, L. H., & Seligman, M. E. P. (1995). Prevention of depressive symptoms in school-children: Two-year follow-up. *Psychological Science, 6,* 343–351.

Gilligan, C. (1982). *In a different voice.* Cambridge, MA: Harvard University Press.

Ginsberg, G. L. (1985). Psychiatric history and mental status examination. In H. I. Kaplan & B. J. Sadock (Eds.), *Comprehensive textbook of psychiatry, IV* (pp. 487–495). Baltimore: William & Wilkins.

Girgus, J. S., Nolen-Hoeksema, S., Paul, G., & Spears, H. (1991, April). *Does participation in feminine or masculine activities predict sex differences in adolescent depression?* Paper presented at the meeting of the Eastern Psychological Association, New York.

Gitlin, M. J., Swendsen, J., Heller, T. L., & Hammen, C. (1995). Relapse and impairment in bipolar disorder. *American Journal of Psychiatry, 152,* 1635–1640.

Glantz, L.A., & Lewis, D.A. (1997). Reduction of synaptophysin immunoreactivity in the prefrontal cortex of subjects with schizophrenia: Regional and diagnostic specificity. *Archives of General Psychiatry, 54,* 943–952.

Glanz, L. M., Haas, G. L., & Sweeney, J. A. (1995). Assessment of hopelessness in suicidal patients. *Clinical Psychology Review, 15,* 49–64.

Glaser, R., Pearson, G. R., Bonneau, R. H., Esterling, B. A., Atkinson, C., & Kiecolt-Glaser, J. K. (1993). Stress and the memory T-cell response to the Epstein-Barr virus in healthy medical students. *Health Psychology, 12,* 435–442.

Gleaves, D. H. (1996). The sociocognitive model of dissociative identity disorder: A reexamination of the evidence. *Psychological Bulletin, 120,* 42–59.

Glucksman, M. L. (1995). Psychodynamics and neurobiology: An integrated approach. *Journal of the American Academy of Psychoanalysis, 23,* 179–195.

Goffman, E. (1959). The moral career of the mental patient. *Psychiatry: Journal for the Study of Interpersonal Processes, 22,* 123–131.

Goffman, E. (1961). *Asylums: Essays on the social situation of mental patients and other inmates.* New York: Doubleday.

Gold, M. S. (1989). *Marijuana.* New York: Plenum Press.

Gold, M. S., & Miller, N. S. (1997). Cocaine (and crack): Neurobiology. In J. H. Lowinson, P. Ruiz, R. B. Millman, & J. G. Langrod (Eds.), *Substance abuse: A comprehensive textbook* (pp. 166–181). Baltimore: Williams & Wilkins.

Goldberg, D. P., & Bridges, K. (1988). Somatic presentations of psychiatric illness in primary care settings. *Journal of Psychosomatic Research, 32,* 137–144.

Goldberg, J. F., Harrow, M., & Grossman, L. S. (1995). Course and outcome in bipolar affective disorder: A longitudinal follow-up study. *American Journal of Psychiatry, 152,* 379–384.

Golden, C. J., Moses, J. A., Jr., & Zelazowski, R. (1980). Cerebral ventricular size and neuropsychological impairment in young chronic schizophrenics. *Archives of General Psychiatry, 37,* 619–626.

Goldman, M. S., Brown, S. A., & Christiansen, B. A. (1987). Expectancy theory: Thinking about drinking. In H. T. Blane & K. E. Leonard (Eds.), *Psychological theories of drinking and alcoholism* (pp. 181–226). New York: Guilford Press.

Goldsmith, S. K., Shapiro, R. M., & Joyce, J. N. (1997). Disrupted pattern of D2 dopamine receptors in the temporal lobe in schizophrenia: A postmortem study. *Archives of General Psychiatry, 54,* 649–658.

Goldstein, A. (1976). Opioid peptides (endorphins) in pituitary and brain. *Science, 193,* 1081–1086.

Goldstein, J. M., Faraone, S. V., Chen, W. J., Tolomiczencko, G. S., & Tsuang, M. T. (1990). Sex differences in the familial transmission of schizophrenia. *British Journal of Psychiatry, 156,* 819–826.

Goldstein, M. J. (1987). Family interaction patterns that antedate the onset of schizophrenia and related disorders: A further analysis of data from a longitudinal prospective study. In K. Hahlweg & M. J. Goldstein (Eds.), *Understanding major mental disorder: The contribution of family interaction research* (pp. 11–32). New York: Family Process Press.

Goldstein, R. B., Black, D. W., Nasrallah, A., & Winokur, G. (1991). The prediction of suicide: Sensitivity, specificity, and predictive value of a multivariate model applied to suicide among 1906 patients with affective disorders. *Archives of General Psychiatry, 48,* 418–422.

Goleman, D. (1986, November 11). For mentally ill on the street, a new approach shines. *The New York Times,* pp. C1, C3.

Gomberg, E. S. (1997). Alcohol abuse: Age and gender differences. In R. W. Wilsnack & S. C. Wilsnack (Eds.), *Gender and alcohol: Individual and social perspectives* (pp. 39–84). New Brunswick, NJ: Alcohol Research Dissemination, Inc.

Goodkin, K., Blaney, N. T., Feasler, D., Fletcher, M. A., Baum, M. K., Mantero-Atienza, E., Klimas, N. G., Millon, C., Szapocznik, J., & Eisdorfer, C. (1992). Active coping style is associated with natural killer cell cytotoxicity in asymptomatic HIV-1 seropositive homosexual men. *Journal of Psychosomatic Research, 36,* 635–650.

Goodsitt, A. (1985). Self-psychology and the treatment of anorexia nervosa. In D. M. Garner & P. E. Garfinkel (Eds.), *Handbook of psychotherapy for anorexia nervosa and bulimia* (pp. 55–82). New York: Guilford Press.

Goodwin, D. W., & Gabrielli, W. F. (1997). Alcohol: Clinical aspects. In J. H. Lowinson, P. Ruiz, R. B. Millman, & J. G. Langrod (Eds.), *Substance abuse: A comprehensive textbook* (pp. 142–148). Baltimore: Williams & Wilkins.

Goodwin, D. W., Schulsinger, F., Hermansen, L., Guze, S. B., & Winokur, G. (1973). Alcohol problems in adoptees raised apart from alcoholic biological parents. *Archives of General Psychiatry, 28,* 238–243.

Goodwin, D. W., Schulsinger, F., Moller, N., Mednick, S., & Guze, S. (1977). Psychopathology in adopted and nonadopted daughters of alcoholics. *Archives of General Psychiatry, 34,* 1005–1009.

Goodyer, I. M. (1992). Depression in childhood and adolescence. In E. S. Paykel (Ed.), *Handbook of affective disorders* (2nd ed., pp. 585–600). New York: Guilford Press.

Gorman, J. M., Liebowitz, M. R., Fyer, A. J., & Stein, J. (1989). A neuroanatomical hypothesis for panic disorder. *American Journal of Psychiatry, 146,* 148–161.

Gorman, J. M., Liebowitz, M. R., & Shear, M. K. (1992). Panic and anxiety disorders. In R. Michels (Ed.), *Psychiatry* (chap. 32). Philadelphia: J. B. Lippincott.

Gortner, E.T., Gollan, J. K., Dobson, K. S., & Jacobson, N. S. (1998). Cognitive-behavioral treatment for depression: relapse prevention. *Journal of Consulting and Clinical Psychology, 66,* 377–378.

Gotlib, I. H., Gilboa, E., & Sommerfield, B. K. (in press). Cognitive functioning in depression: Nature and origins. In R. J. Davidson (Ed.), *Wisconsin symposium on emotion* (Vol. 1). New York: Oxford University Press.

Gottesman, I. I. (1991). *Schizophrenia genesis: The origins of madness.* New York: Freeman.

Gottesman, I. I. (1996). Blind men and elephants: Genetic and other perspectives on schizophrenia. In L. L. Hall (Ed.), *Genetics and mental illness: Evolving issues for research and society* (pp. 51–77). New York: Plenum Press.

Gottesman, I. I., & Bertelsen, A. (1989). Confirming unexpressed genotypes for schizophrenia. *Archives of General Psychiatry, 46,* 867–872.

Gottesman, I. I., & Shields, J. (1982). *Schizophrenia: The epigenetic puzzle.* New York: Cambridge University Press.

Gottman, J. M. (1979). *Marital interaction: Experimental investigations.* New York: Academic Press.

Gottman, J. M. (1994). *What predicts divorce?* Hillsdale, NJ: Erlbaum.

Gottman, J. M., Jacobson, N. S., Rushe, R. H., Short, J. W., Babcock, J., La Taillade, J. J., & Waltz, J. (1995). The relationship between heart rate reactivity, emotionally aggressive behavior and general violence in batterers. *Journal of Family Psychology, 9,* 227–248.

Gould, M. S., Fisher, P., Parides, M., Flory, M., & Shaffer, D. (1996). Psychosocial risk factors of child and adolescent completed suicide. *Archives of General Psychiatry, 53,* 1155–1162.

Gould, M. S., Shaffer, D., Fisher, P., Kleinman, M., & Morishima, A. (1992). The clinical prediction of adolescent suicide. In R. W. Maris, A. L. Berman, J. T. Maltsberger, & R. I. Yufit (Eds.), *Assessment and prediction of suicide* (pp. 130–143). New York: Guilford Press.

Gould, R., Miller, B. L., Goldberg, M. A., & Benson, D. F. (1986). The validity of hysterical signs and symptoms. *Journal of Nervous and Mental Disease, 174,* 593–597.

Gove, W., & Herb, T. (1974). Stress and mental illness among the young: A comparison of the sexes. *Social Forces, 53,* 256–265.

Grabowski, J., & Thompson, T. (1977). Development and maintenance of a behavior modification program for behaviorally retarded institutionalized men. In T. Thompson & J. Grabowski (Eds.), *Behavior modification of the mentally retarded* (2nd ed.). New York: Oxford University Press.

Graham, D. T. (1967). Health, disease, and the mind-body problem: Linguistic parallelism. *Psychosomatic Medicine, 39,* 52–71.

Graham, J. R. (1990). *MMPI-2: Assessing personality and psychopathology.* New York: Oxford University Press.

Granholm, E., Morris, S. K., Sarkin, A. J., Asarnow, R. F., & Jeste, D. V. (1997). Pupillary responses index overload of working memory resources in schizophrenia. *Journal of Abnormal Psychology, 106,* 458–467.

Grant, I., & Martin, A. (1994). *Neuropsychology of HIV infection.* New York: Oxford University Press.

Grant, L. D., & Davis, J. M. (1989). Effects of low-level lead exposure on paediatric neurobehavioural development: Current findings and future directions. In M. A. Smith, L. D. Grant, & A. I. Sors (Eds.), *Lead exposure and child development: An international assessment* (pp.

49–115). Boston: Kluwer Academic Publishers.

Grantham-McGregor, S., Powell, C., Walker, S., Chang, S., & Fletcher, P. (1994). The long-term follow-up of severely malnourished children who participated in an intervention program. *Child Development, 65,* 428–439.

Gräsbeck, A., Rorsman, B., Hagnell, O., & Isberg, P. E. (1996). Mortality of anxiety syndromes in a normal population: The Lundby Study. *Neuropsychobiology, 33,* 118–126.

Graves, A. B., Larson, E. B., White, L. R., Tcng, E. L., & Homma, A. (1994). Opportunities and challenges in international collaborative epidemiologic research of dementia and its subtypes: Studies between Japan and the U.S. *International Psychogeriatrics, 6,* 209–224.

Green, M. F. (1996). What are the functional consequences of neuro-cognitive deficits in schizophrenia? *American Journal of Psychiatry, 153,* 321–330.

Green, M. F., Marshall, B. D., Jr., Wirshing, W. C., Ames, D., Marder, S. R., McGurk, S., Kern, R. S., & Mintz, J. (1997). Does risperidone improve verbal working memory in treatment-resistant schizophrenia? *American Journal of Psychiatry, 154,* 799–804.

Green, M.F., Nuechterlein, K.H., & Breitmeyer, B. (1997). Backward masking performance in unaffected siblings of schizophrenic patients: Evidence for a vulnerability indicator. *Archives of General Psychiatry, 54,* 465–472.

Green, R. (1987). *The "sissy boy syndrome" and the development of homosexuality.* New Haven: Yale University Press.

Greenberg, G. (1977). The family interactional perspective: A study and examination of the work of Don D. Jackson. *Family Process, 16,* 385–412.

Greenfeld, L. A. (1997). *Sex offenses and offenders: An analysis of data on rape and sexual assault.* Bureau of Justice Statistics, U.S. Department of Justice, Office of Justice Programs, #NCJ-16J-163392, 1–39.

Greenwald, E., & Leitenberg, H. (1989). Long-term effects of sexual experiences with siblings and nonsiblings during childhood. *ASB, 18,* 389–400.

Greist, J. H., Jefferson, J. W., Kobak, K. A., Katzelnick, D. J., & Serlin, R. C. (1995). Efficacy and tolerability of serotonin transport inhibitors in obsessive-compulsive disorder: A meta-analysis. *Archives of General Psychiatry, 21,* 53–60.

Grenyer, B. F. S., & Luborsky, L. (1996). Dynamic change in psychotherapy: Mastery of interpersonal conflicts. *Journal of Consulting and Clinical Psychology, 64,* 411–416.

Griffin, M. G., Resick, P. A., & Mechanic, M. B. (1997). Objective assessment of peritraumatic dissociation: Psychophysiological indicators. *American Journal of Psychiatry, 154,* 1081–1088.

Grinspoon, L. (1977). *Marihuana reconsidered* (2nd ed.). Cambridge, MA: Harvard University Press.

Grinspoon, L., & Bakalar, J. B. (1994). The war on drugs—a peace proposal. *New England Journal of Medicine, 330,* 357–360.

Grinspoon, L., & Bakalar, J. B. (1997). Marihuana. In J. H. Lowinson, P. Ruiz, R. B. Millman, & J. G. Langrod (Eds.), *Substance abuse: A comprehensive textbook* (pp. 199–206). Baltimore: Williams & Wilkins.

Grisso, T. (1991). Clinical assessments for legal decision making. In S. A. Shah & B. D. Sales (Eds.), *Law and mental health: Major developments and research needs.* Rockville, MD. National Institute of Mental Health.

Gronwall, D., Wrightson, P., & Waddell, P. (1990). *Head injury: The facts. A guide for families and care-givers.* New York: Oxford University Press.

Groth, N. A. (1978). Guidelines for assessment and management of the offender. In A. Burgess, N. Groth, S. Holmstrom, & S. Sgroi (Eds.), *Sexual assault of children and adolescents* (pp. 25–42). Lexington, MA: Lexington Books.

Group for the Advancement of Psychiatry. (1996). *Alcoholism in the United States: Racial and ethnic considerations.* Formulated by the Committee on Cultural Psychiatry, Report no. 141. Washington, DC: American Psychiatric Press.

Grove, W. M., et al. (1990). Heritability of substance abuse and antisocial behavior: A study of monozygotic twins reared apart. *Biological Psychiatry, 27,* 1293–1304.

Grove, W. M., Lebow, B. S., Clementz, B. A., Cerri, A., Medus, C., & Iacono, W. G. (1991). Familial prevalence and coaggregation of schizotype indicators: A multitrait family study. *Journal of Abnormal Psychology, 100,* 115–121.

Guerra, N. G., Attar, B., & Weissberg, R. P. (1997). Prevention of aggression and violence among inner-city youths. In D. M. Stoff, J. Breiling, & J. D. Maser (Eds.), *Handbook of antisocial behavior* (pp. 375–383). New York: Wiley.

Guggenheim, F. G., & Babigian, H. M. (1974). Catatonic schizophrenia— epidemiology and clinical course— 7-year register study of 798 cases. *Journal of Nervous and Mental Disease, 158*(4), 291–305.

Guilette, E. C. D., Blumenthal, J. A., Babyak, M., Jiang, W., Waugh, R. A., Frid, D. J., O'Connor, C. M., Morris, J. J., & Krantz, D.S. (1997). Effects of mental stress on myocardial ischemia during daily life. *Journal of the American Medical Association, 277,* 1521–1526.

Gunderson, J. G. (1984). *Borderline personality disorder.* Washington, DC: American Psychiatric Press.

Gunderson, J. G. (1992). Diagnostic controversies. In A. Tasman & M. B. Riba (Eds.), *Review of psychiatry* (Vol. 11, pp. 9–24). Washington, DC: American Psychiatric Press.

Gunderson, J. G. (1996). The borderline patient's intolerance of aloneness: Insecure attachments and therapist availability. *American Journal of Psychiatry, 153,* 752–758.

Gunderson, J. G., & Phillips, K. A. (1991). A current view of the interspace between borderline personality disorder and depression. *American Journal of Psychiatry, 148,* 967–975.

Gur, R. E., Mozley, P. D., Shtasel, D. L., Cannon, T. D., Gallacher, F., Turetsky, B., Grossman, R., & Gur, R. C. (1994). Clinical subtypes of schizophrenia: Differences in brain and CSF volume. *American Journal of Psychiatry, 151,* 343–350.

Gur, R. E., Petty, R. G., Turetsky, B. I., & Gur, R. C. (1996). Schizophrenia throughout life: Sex differences in severity and profile of symptoms. *Schizophrenia Research, 21,* 1–12.

Gureje, O., Simon, G. E., Üstün, T. B., & Goldberg, D. P. (1997). Somatization in cross-cultural perspective: A World Health Organization study in primary care. *American Journal of Psychiatry, 154,* 989–995.

Gurevich, E. V., Bordelon, Y., Shapiro, R. M., Arnold, S. E., Gur, R. E., & Joyce, J. N. (1997). Mesolimbic dopamine D_3 receptors and use of antipsychotics in patients with schizophrenia: A post-mortem study. *Archives of General Psychiatry, 54,* 225–232.

Gurland, B., Dean, L., Craw, P., & Golden, R. (1980). The epidemiology of depression and delirium in the elderly: The use of multiple indicators of these conditions. In J. O. Cole & J. E. Barrett (Eds.), *Psychopathology in the aged.* New York: Raven Press.

Gurman, A. S., & Kniskern, D. P. (1978). Research on marital and family therapy: Progress, perspective, and prospect. In S. L. Garfield & A. E. Bergin (Eds.), *Handbook of psychotherapy and behavior change: An empirical analysis* (2nd ed.). New York: Wiley.

Guze, S. B., Cloninger, C. R., Martin, R. L., & Clayton, P. J. (1986). A follow-up and family study of Briquet's syndrome. *British Journal of Psychiatry, 149,* 17–23.

H. B. I. G. D. A. (1990). *Standards of care: The hormonal and surgical sex reassignment of gender dysphoric persons.* Palo Alto, CA: The Harry Benjamin International Gender Dysphoria Association.

Haaga, D. A. F., & Beck, A. T. (1995). Perspectives on depressive realism: Implications for cognitive theory of depression. *Behaviour Research and Therapy, 33,* 41–48.

Haaga, D. A. F., Dyck, M. J., & Ernst, D. (1991). Empirical status of cognitive theory of depression. *Psychological Bulletin, 110,* 215–236.

Haapasalo, J., & Kankkonen, M. (1997). Self-reported childhood abuse among sex and violent offenders. *Archives of Sexual Behavior, 26,* 421–431.

Haas, G. L., & Sweeney, J. A. (1992). Premorbid and onset features of first-episode schizophrenia. *Schizophrenia Bulletin, 18,* 373–386.

Hadeed, A., & Seigel, S. (1989). Maternal cocaine use during pregnancy: Effect on the newborn infant. *Pediatrics, 84,* 205–210.

Hagerman, R. J. (1992). Annotation: Fragile X syndrome: Advances and controversy. *Journal of Child Psychology and Psychiatry, 33,* 1127–1139.

Hagerman, R. J., & McBogg, P. M. (1983). *The fragile X syndrome: Diagnosis, biochemistry, and intervention.* Dillon, CO: Spectra.

Hale, R. (1994). The role of humiliation and embarrassment in serial murder. *Psychology: A Journal of Human Behavior, 31,* 17–23.

Haley, J. (1963). *Strategies of psychotherapy.* New York: Grune & Stratton.

Haley, J. (1976). *Problem-solving therapy.* San Francisco: Jossey-Bass.

Haley, R. W., Kurt, T. L., & Hom, J. (1997). Is there a Gulf War Syndrome? Searching for syndromes by factor analysis of symptoms. *Journal of the American Medical Association, 277,* 215–222.

Halford, W. K., & Hayes, R. (1991). Psychological rehabilitation of chronic schizophrenic patients: Recent findings on social skills training and family psychoeducation. *Clinical Psychology Review, 11,* 23–44.

Hall, E. T. (1976). *Beyond culture: Into the cultural unconscious.* Garden City, NY: Anchor Press.

Hall, G. C. N. (1995). Sexual offender recidivism revisited: A meta-analysis of recent treatment studies. *Journal of Consulting and Clinical Psychology, 63,* 802–809.

Hall, G. C. N., & Barongan, C. (1997). Prevention of sexual aggression: sociocultural risk and protective factors. *American Psychologist, 52,* 5–14.

Hall, S. M., Havassy, B. E., & Wasserman, D. A. (1990). Commitment to abstinence and acute stress in relapse to alcohol, opiates, and nicotine. *Journal of Consulting and Clinical Psychology, 58,* 175–181.

Hall, S. M., Havassy, B. E., & Wasserman, D. A. (1991). Effects of commitment to abstinence, positive moods, stress, and coping on relapse to cocaine use. *Journal of Consulting and Clinical Psychology, 59,* 526–532.

Halleck, S. L. (1970). The changing nature of student psychiatry in an era of political awareness. *American Journal of Psychotherapy, 24,* 566–578.

Halmi, K. A. (1974). Anorexia nervosa: Demographic and clinical features in 94 cases. *Journal of Psychosomatic Medicine, 36,* 18–25.

Halper, J. P., Brown, R. P., Sweeney, J. A., Kocsis, J. H., Peters, A., & Mann, J. J. (1988). Blunted ß-adrenergic responsivity of peripheral blood mononuclear cells in endogenous depression. *Archives of General Psychiatry, 45,* 241–244.

Hamberger, L. K., & Lohr, J. M. (1989). Proximal causes of spouse violence. In P. L. Caesar & L. K. Hamberger (Eds.), *Treating men who batter* (pp. 53–76). New York: Springer.

Hamblin, M. W. (1997). Neuroreceptors and their place in psychiatry. In D. L. Dunner (Ed.), *Current psychiatric therapy II* (pp. 11–27). Philadelphia: W. B. Saunders Co.

Hammen, C., Adrian, C., & Hiroto, D. (1988). A longitudinal test of the attributional vulnerability model in children at risk for depression. *British Journal of Clinical Psychology, 27,* 37–46.

Hankin, B. L., Abramson, L. Y., Moffitt, T. E., et al. (1998). Development of depression from preadolescence to young adulthood: Emerging gender differences in a 10-year longitudinal study. *Journal of Abnormal Psychology, 107,* 128–140.

Hansen, W. B. (1993). School-based alcohol prevention programs. *Alcohol, Health & Research World, 17*(1), 54–60.

Hanson, M. J. (1987). *Teaching the infant with Down syndrome* (pp. 23–30). Austin, TX: Pro-Ed.

Harada, S., Agarwal, D., Goedde, H., Takagi, S., & Ishikawa, B. (1982). Possible protective role against alcoholism for aldehyde dehydrogenase isozyme deficiency in Japan. *Lancet, 2,* 827.

Harburg, E. (1978). Skin color, ethnicity and blood pressure in Detroit blacks. *American Journal of Public Health, 68,* 1177–1183.

Harchik, A. E., Sherman, J. A., Sheldon, J. B., & Bannerman, D. J. (1993). Choice and control: New opportunities for people with developmental disabilities. *Annals of Clinical Psychiatry, 5,* 151–161.

Hardy, J. (1993, November). Genetic mistakes point the way for Alzheimer's disease. *Journal of NIH Research, 5,* 46–49.

Hare, R. D. (1992). *The Hare Psychopathy Checklist-Revised.* Toronto: Multi-Health Systems.

Hare, R. D. (1993). *Without conscience: The disturbing world of the psychopaths among us.* New York: Pocket Books.

Hare, R. D. (1996). Psychopathy: A clinical construct whose time has come. *Criminal Justice and Behavior, 23,* 25–44.

Harlow, J. (1868). Recovery from the passage of an iron bar through the head. *Publication of the Massachusetts Medical Society, 2,* 327–340.

Harrington, R. (1993). Similarities and dissimilarities between child and adult disorders: The case of depression. In C. G. Costello (Ed.), *Basic issues in psychopathology* (pp. 103–124). New York: Guilford Press.

Harrington, R., Fudge, H., Rutter, M., Pickels, A., & Hill, J. (1990). Adult outcomes of childhood and adolescent depression. *Archives of General Psychiatry, 47,* 465–473.

Harris, J. (1996). Physical restraint procedures for managing challenging behaviours presented by mentally retarded adults and children. *Research in Developmental Disabilities, 17,* 99–134.

Harris, J. C. (1995). *Developmental neuropsychiatry* (Vol. 2). New York: Oxford (see pages 97–99).

Harris, P. M. (1995). Prison-based sex offender treatment programs in the post sexual psychopath era. *Journal of Psychiatry and Law, 23,* 555–581.

Harris, S. L., Alessandri, M., & Gill, M. J. (1991). Training parents of developmentally disabled children. In J. L. Matson & J. A. Mulick (Eds.), *Handbook of mental retardation* (2nd ed.) (pp. 373–381). New York: Pergamon Press.

Harris, S. L., & Handleman, J. S. (1997). Helping children with autism enter the mainstream. In D. J. Cohen & F. R. Volkmar (Eds.), *Handbook of autism and pervasive developmental disorders* (2nd ed.) (pp. 665–675). New York: Wiley.

Harris, T. O., Brown, G. W., & Bifulco, A. T. (1990). Depression and situational helplessness/mastery in a sample selected to study childhood parental loss. *Journal of Affective Disorders, 20,* 27–41.

Harrison, P. (1997). Suicidal behavior. In W. S. Tseng & J. Streltzer (Eds.), *Culture & psychopathology: A guide to clinical assessment* (pp. 157–172). New York: Brunner/Mazel.

Harrow, M., Carone, B. J., & Westermeyer, J. (1985). The course of psychosis in early phases of schizophrenia. *American Journal of Psychiatry, 142,* 702–707.

Harrow, M., Rattenbury, F., & Stoll, F. (1988). Schizophrenic delusions: An analysis of their persistence, of related premorbid ideas, and of three major dimensions. In T. F. Oltmanns & B. A. Maher (Eds.), *Delusional beliefs* (pp. 184–211). New York: Wiley.

Hart, S. D., & Hare, R. D. (1989). Discriminant validity of the Psychopathy Checklist in a forensic psychiatric population. *Psychological Assessment: A Journal of Consulting and Clinical Psychology, 1,* 211–218.

Hart, S. D., & Hare, R. D. (1997). Psychopathy: Assessment and association with criminal conduct. In D. M. Stoff, J. Breiling, & J. D. Maser (Eds.), *Handbook of antisocial behavior* (pp. 22–35). New York: Wiley.

Hartlage, S., Alloy, L. B., Vázquez, C., & Dykman, B. (1993). Automatic and effortful processing in depression. *Psychological Bulletin, 113,* 247–278.

Hartlage, S., Howard, K. I., & Ostrov, E. (1984). The mental health professional and the normal adolescent. *New Directions for Mental Health Services, 22,* 29–43.

Hartmann, H. (1939). *Ego psychology and the problem of adaptation.* New York: International Universities Press.

Harvey, A. G., Bryant, R. A., & Rapee, R. M. (1996). Preconscious processing of threat in posttraumatic stress disorder. *Cognitive Therapy and Research, 20,* 613–623.

Harvey, P. D., Lombardi, J., Leibman, M., Parrella, M., White, L., Powchik, P., Mohs, R.C., Davidson, M., & Davis, K. L. (1997). Age-related differences in formal thought disorder in chronically hospitalized schizophrenic patients: A cross-sectional study across nine decades. *American Journal of Psychiatry, 154,* 205–210.

Hathaway, S. R., & McKinley, J. C. (1940). A multiphasic personality schedule (Minnesota): 1. Construction of the schedule. *Journal of Psychology, 10,* 249–254.

Hathaway, S. R., & McKinley, J. C. (1943). *Minnesota Multiphasic Personality Inventory: Manual.* New York: Psychological Corporation.

Hathaway, S. R., & McKinley, J. D. (1989). *Manual for administration and scoring MMPI-2.* Minneapolis: University of Minnesota Press.

Hauser, W. A., & Hesdorfer, D. C. (1990). *Epilepsy: Frequency, causes, and consequences.* New York: Demos.

Hawkins, J. D., Arthur, M. W., & Olson, J. J. (1997). Community interventions to reduce risks and enhance protection against antisocial behavior. In D.M. Stoff, J. Breiling, & J.D. Maser (Eds.), *Handbook of antisocial behavior* (pp. 384–394). New York: Wiley.

Hawkins, J. D., Catalano, R. F., & Miller, J. Y. (1992). Risk and protective factors for alcohol and other drug problems in adolescence and early adulthood: Implications for substance abuse prevention. *Psychological Bulletin, 112,* 64–105.

Hawkins, J. D., Catalano, R. F., Morrison, D. M., O'Donnell, J. Abbott, R. D., & Day, L. E. (1992). The Seattle Social Development Project: Effects of the first four years on protective factors and problem behaviors. In J. McCord & R. Tremblay (Eds.), *The prevention of antisocial behavior in children* (pp. 114–140). New York: Guilford Press.

Hawley, T. L., & Disney, E. R. (1992). Crack's children: The consequences of maternal cocaine abuse. *Social Policy Report of the Society for Research in Child Development, 6,* 1–22.

Hawton, K. (1992). Sex therapy research: has it withered on the vine? *Annual Review of Sex Therapy, vol. 3,* 49–72.

Hay, D. P., & Hay, L. K. (1990). The role of ECT in the treatment of depression. In C. D. McCann & N. S. Endler (Eds.), *Depression: New directions in theory, research, and practice* (pp. 255–272). Toronto: Wall & Emerson.

Hayes, S. C. (1987). A contextual approach to therapeutic change. In N. S. Jacobson (Ed.), *Psychotherapists in clinical practice: Cognitive and behavioral perspectives* (pp. 327–387). New York: Guilford Press.

Hayes, S. C. (1989). *Rule governed behavior: Cognition, contingencies and instructional control.* New York: Plenum Press.

Hayes, S. C., Jacobson, N. S., Follette, V., & Dougher, M. (1994). *Acceptance and change in psychotherapy.* Reno, NV: Context Press.

Hayes, S. C., Wilson, K. G., Gifford, E. V., Follette, V. M., & Strosahl, K. (1996). Experiential avoidance and behavior disorders: A functional dimensional approach to diagnosis and treatment. *Journal of Consulting and Clinical Psychology, 64,* 1152–1168.

Hayman, C. R., Stewart, W. F., Lewis, F. R., & Grant, M. (1968). Sexual assault on women and children in the District of Columbia. *Public Health Reports, 83,* 12–20.

Hays, R. D., Wells, K. B., Sherbourne, C. D., Rogers, W., & Spritzer, K. (1995). Functioning and well-being outcomes of patients with depression compared with chronic general medical illnesses. *Archives of General Psychiatry, 52,* 11–19.

Hazlett, E. A., Dawson, M. E., Filion, D. L., Schell, A. M., & Nuechterlein, K. H. (1997). Autonomic orienting and the allocation of processing resources in schizophrenia patients and putatively at-risk individuals. *Journal of Abnormal Psychology, 106,* 171–181.

Heatherton, T. F., Herman, C. P., & Polivy, J. (1991). Effects of physical threat and ego threat on eating behavior. *Journal of Personality and Social Psychology, 60,* 138–143.

Heavey, C. L., Adelman, H. S., Nelson, P., & Smith, D. C. (1989). Learning problems, anger, perceived control and misbehavior. *Journal of Learning Disabilities, 22,* 46–50.

Hécaen, H., & Albert, M. C. (1978). *Human neuropsychology.* New York: Wiley.

Heckers, S. (1997). Neuropathology of schizophrenia: Cortex, thalamus, basal ganglia, and neurotransmitter-specific projection systems. *Schizophrenia Bulletin, 23,* 403–421.

Hedlund, J. L. (1977). MMPI clinical scale correlates. *Journal of Consulting and Clinical Psychology, 45,* 739–750.

Hedlund, S., & Rude, S. S. (1995). Evidence of latent depressive schemas in formerly depressed individuals. *Journal of Abnormal Psychology, 104,* 517–525.

Hegerl, U., & Herrmann, W. M. (1990). Event-related potentials and the prediction of differential drug response in psychiatry. *Neuropsychobiology, 23,* 99–108.

Heiman, J. R. (1997). *Empirically validated treatments of sexual dysfunction.* Paper presented at the Annual Meeting of the Society for Sex Therapy and Research, Chicago, IL.

Heiman, J. R., & LoPiccolo, L. (1983). Clinical outcome in sex therapy. *Archives of General Psychiatry, 40,* 443–449.

Heiman, J. R., LoPiccolo, L., & LoPiccolo, J. (1981). The treatment of sexual dysfunction. In A. Gurma & D. Kniskern (Eds.), *Handbook of family therapy.* New York: Brunner/Mazel.

Heiman, J. R., & Meston, C. (1997). Empirically validated treatment for sexual dysfunctions. *Annual Review of Sex Research, vol. 8.*

Heimberg, R. G., Salzman, D. G., Holt, C. S., & Blendall (1993). Cognitive-behavioral group treatment for social phobia. *Cognitive Therapy and Research, 4,* 325–339.

Hellige, J. B. (1993). *Hemispheric asymmetry: What's right and what's left.* Cambridge, MA: Harvard University Press.

Helmes, E., & Reddon, J. R. (1993). A perspective on developments in assessing psychopathology: A critical review of the MMPI and MMPI-2. *Psychological Bulletin, 113,* 453–471.

Helzer, J. E., Brockington, I. F., & Kendell, R. E. (1981). Predictive validity of DSM-III and Feigner definitions of schizophrenia. *Archives of General Psychiatry, 38,* 791–797.

Helzer, J. E., Robins, L., & McEvoy, L. (1987). Posttraumatic stress disorder in the general population. *New England Journal of Medicine, 317,* 1630–1634.

Hendryx, M., & Bootzin, R. R. (1986). Psychiatric episodes in general hospitals without psychiatric units. *Hospitals and Community Psychiatry, 37,* 1025–1029.

Henggeler, S. W., Pickrel, S. G., Brondino, M. J., & Crouch, J. L. (1996). Eliminating treatment dropout of substance abusing or depdendent delinquents through home-based multisystemic therapy. *American Journal of Psychiatry, 153,* 427–428.

Heninger, G. R. (1990). A biologic perspective on co-morbidity of major depressive disorder and panic disorder. In J. D. Maser & C. R. Cloninger (Eds.), *Comorbidity of mood and anxiety disorders.* Washington, DC: American Psychiatric Press.

Heninger, G. R., Charney, D. S., & Price, L. H. (1988). α_2-adrenergic receptor sensivity in depression: The plasma MHPG, behavioral, and cardiovascular response to yohimbine. *Archives of General Psychiatry, 45,* 718–726.

Herdt, G., & Stoller, R. J. (1990). *Intimate communications: Erotics and the study of culture.* New York: Columbia University Press.

Herman, C. P., & Mack, D. (1975). Restrained and unrestrained eating, *Journal of Personality, 43,* 647–660.

Herman, J. L. (1981). *Father-daughter incest.* Cambridge, MA: Harvard University Press.

Herman, J. L. (1992). *Trauma and recovery.* New York: Basic Books.

Herman, J. L., Perry, J. C., & van der Kolk, B. A. (1989). Childhood trauma in borderline personality disorder. *American Journal of Psychiatry, 146,* 490–495.

Hernandez-Peon, R., Chavez-Ibarra, G., & Aguilar-Figueroa, E. (1963). Somatic evoked potentials in one case of hysterical anaesthesia *Electroencephalography and Clinical Neurophysiology, 15,* 889–892.

Hersen, M., & Barlow, D. H. (1976). *Single case experimental designs: Strategies for studying behavior change.* New York: Pergamon Press.

Hersen, M., & Turner, S. M. (1984). *DSM-III and behavior therapy.* In S. M. Turner & M. Hersen (Eds.), *Adult psychopathology and diagnosis.* New York: Wiley.

Hesselbrock V., & Hesselbrock, M. (1992). Relationship of family history, antisocial personality disorder, and personality traits in young men at risk for alcoholism. *Journal of Studies of Alcohol, 53,* 619–625.

Heston, L. L. (1966). Psychiatric disorders in foster home reared children of schizophrenic mothers. *British Journal of Psychiatry, 112,* 819–825.

Hewitt, P. L., Flett, G. L., & Ediger, E. (1996). Perfectionism and depression: Longitudinal assessment of a specific vulnerability hypothesis. *Journal of Abnormal Psychology, 105,* 276–281.

Hibbs, E. D. (1993). Psychosocial treatment research with children and adolescents: Methodological issues. *Psychopharmacology Bulletin, 29,* 27–33.

Hiday, V. A. (1996). Outpatient commitment. In D. L. Dennis & J. Monahan (Eds.), *Coercion and aggressive community treatment.* New York: Plenum Press.

Hietala, J., Syvälahti, E., Vuorio, K., Nagren, K., Lehikoinen, P., Ruotsalainen, U., Rakkolainen, V., Lehtinen, V., & Wegelius, U. (1994). Striatal D2 dopamine receptor characteristics in neuroleptic-naive schizophrenic patients studied with positron emission tomography. *Archives of General Psychiatry, 51,* 116–123.

Higgins, S. T., Budney, A. J., Bickel, W. K., Foerg, F. E., Donham, R., & Badger, G. J. (1994). Incentives improve outcome in outpatient behavioral treatment of cocaine dependence. *Archives of General Psychiatry, 51,* 568–576.

Higgins, S. T., Delaney, D. D., Budney, A. J., Bickel, W. K., Hughes, J. R., Foerg, B. A., & Fenwick, J. W. (1991). A behavioral approach to achieving initial cocaine abstinence. *American Journal of Psychiatry, 148,* 1218–1224.

Hildebran, D., & Pithers, W. D. (1989). Enhancing offender empathy for sexual abuse victims. In D. R. Laws (Ed.), *Relapse prevention with sex offenders* (pp. 236–243). New York: Guilford Press.

Hilts, P. J. (1994, April 15). Tobacco chiefs say cigarettes aren't addictive. *The New York Times,* p. A1.

Hiroto, D. J., & Seligman, M. E. P. (1975). Generality of learned helplessness in man. *Journal of Personality and Social Psychology, 31,* 311–327.

Hirsch, B. J., & Rapkin, B. D. (1987). The transition to junior high school: A longitudinal study of self-esteem, psychological symptomatology, school life, and social support. *Child Development, 58,* 1235–1243.

Ho, A. P., Gillin, J. C., Buchsbaum, M. S., Wu, J. C., Abel, L., & Bunney, W. E., Jr. (1996). Brain glucose metabolism during non-rapid eye movement sleep in major depression: A positron emission tomography study. *Archives of General Psychiatry, 53,* 645–652.

Ho, B. T., Richard, D. W., & Chute, D. L. (Eds.). (1978). *Drug discrimination and state dependent learning.* New York: Academic Press.

Hobson, R. P. (1993). *Autism and the development of mind.* Hillsdale, NJ: Erlbaum (see chapter on "The growth of interpersonal learning").

Hodapp, R. M., & Dykens, E. M. (1996). Mental retardation. In E. J. Mash & R. A. Barkley (Eds.), *Child psychopathology* (pp. 362–389). New York: Guilford Press.

Hodges, J., & Tizard, B. (1989). IQ and behavioral adjustment of ex-institutional adolescents. *Journal of Child Psychology and Psychiatry, 30,* 53–75.

Hodgkinson, S., Sherrington, R., Gurling, H., Marchbanks, R., Reeders, S., Mallet, J., McInnis, M., Petursson, H., & Brynjolfsson, J. (1987). Molecular genetic evidence for heterogeneity in manic depression. *Nature, 325,* 805–806.

Hodkinson, H. M. (1976). *Common symptoms of disease in the elderly.* Oxford: Blackwell.

Hoenig, J. (1985). Etiology of transsexualism. In B. W. Steiner (Ed.), *Gender dysphoria: Development, research, management.* New York: Plenum Press.

Hoffman, A. (1971). LSD discoverer disputes "chance" factor in finding. *Psychiatric News, 6*(8), 23–26.

Hogarty, G. E., Anderson, C. M., Reiss, D. J., Kornblith, S. J., Greenwald, D. P., Javna, C. D., & Madonia, M. J. (1986). Family psychoeducation, social skills training, and maintenance chemotherapy in the aftercare treatment of schizophrenia: I. One-year effects of a controlled study on relapse and expressed emotion. *Archives of General Psychiatry, 43,* 633–642.

Hogarty, G. E., Greenwald, D., Ulrich, R. F., Kornblith, S. J., DiBarry, A. L., Cooley, S., Carter, M., & Flesher, S. (1997). Three-year trials of personal therapy among schizophrenic patients living with or independent of family, II: Effects on adjustment of patients. *American Journal of Psychiatry, 154,* 1514–1524.

Hogarty, G. E., Kornblith, S. J., Greenwald, D., DiBarry, A. L., Cooley, S., Ulrich, R. F., Carter, M., & Flesher, S. (1997). Three-year trials of personal therapy among schizophrenic patients living with or independent of family, I: Description of study and effects on relapse rates. *American Journal of Psychiatry, 154,* 1504–1513.

Holcomb, H. H., Cascella, N. G., Thaker, G. K., Medoff, D. R., Dannals, R. F., & Tamminga, C. A. (1996). Functional sites of neuroleptic drug action in the human brain: PET/FDG studies with and without haloperidol. *American Journal of Psychiatry, 153,* 41–49.

Holland, J. G. (1978). Behaviorism: Part of the problem or part of the solution? *Journal of Applied Behavior Analysis, 11,* 163–174.

Holland, J. G., & Tross, S. (1985). The psychosocial and neuropsychiatric sequelae of the acquired immunodeficiency syndrome and related disorders. *Annals of Internal Medicine, 103,* 760–764.

Hollander, E., Liebowitz, M., Winchel, R., & Klumker, A. (1989). Treatment of body-dysmorphic disorder with serotonin reuptake blockers. *American Journal of Psychiatry, 146,* 768–770.

Hollingshead, A. B., & Redlich, F. C. (1958). *Social class and mental illness.* New York: Wiley.

Hollon, S. D., & Beck, A. T. (1994). Cognitive and cognitive-behavioral therapies. In A. E. Bergin & S. L. Garfield (Eds.), *Handbook of psychotherapy and behavior change* (4th ed., pp. 428–466). New York: Wiley.

Hollon, S. D., DeRubeis, R. J., Evans, M. D., Wiemer, M. J., Garvey, M. J., Grove, W. M., & Tuason, V. B. (1992). Cognitive therapy and pharmacotherapy for depression: Singly and in combination. *Archives of General Psychiatry, 49,* 774–781.

Hollon, S. D., Shelton, R. C., & Davis, D. D. (1993). Cognitive therapy for depression: Conceptual issues and clinical efficacy. *Journal of Consulting and Clinical Psychology, 61*, 270–275.

Hollon, S. D., Shelton, R. C., & Loosen, P. T. (1991). Cognitive therapy and psychopharmacotherapy for depression. *Journal of Consulting and Clinical Psychology, 59*, 88–99.

Holmes, D. S. (1978). Projection as a defense mechanism. *Psychological Bulletin, 85*, 677–688.

Holmes, R. M., & DeBurger, J. E. (1985). Profiles in terror: The serial murderer. *Federal Probation, 49*, 29–34.

Holmes, T. H., & Rahe, R. H. (1967). The social readjustment rating scale. *Journal of Psychosomatic Research, 11*, 213–218.

Holsboer, F. (1992). The hypothalamic-pituitary-adrenocortical system. In E. S. Paykel (Ed.), *Handbook of affective disorders* (2nd ed., pp. 267–288). New York: Guilford Press.

Holtzworth-Munroe, A. (1995). The assessment and treatment of marital violence. In N. S. Jacobson & A. S. Gurman (Eds.), *Clinical handbook of couple therapy* (pp. 317–339). New York: Guilford Press.

Holtzworth-Munroe, A., Beatty, S. B., & Anglin, K. (1995). The assessment and treatment of marital violence. In N. S. Jacobson & A. S. Gurman (Eds.), *Clinical handbook of couple therapy* (pp. 317–339). New York: Guilford Press.

Holtzworth-Munroe, A., Markman, H., O'Leary, K. D., Neidig, P., Leber, D., Heyman, R., Hulbert, D., & Smutzler, N. (1995). The need for marital violence prevention efforts: A behavioral-cognitive secondary prevention program for engaged and newly married couples. *Applied and Preventive Psychology: Current Scientific Perspectives, 4*, 77–88.

Holtzworth-Munroe, A., & Stuart, G. (1994a). The relationship standards and assumptions of violent versus nonviolent husbands. *Cognitive Therapy and Research, 18*, 87–103.

Holtzworth-Munroe, A., & Stuart, G. (1994b). Typologies of male batterers: Three subtypes and the differences among them. *Psychological Bulletin, 116*, 476–497.

Holzer, C. E., III., Tischler, G. L., Leaf, P. J., & Myers, J. K. (1984). An epidemiologic assessment of cognitive impairment in a community population. *Research in Community and Mental Health, 4*, 3–32.

Hooker, E. (1957). The adjustment of the male overt homosexual. *Journal of Projective Techniques, 21*(1), 18–31.

Hooley, J. M., & Teasdale, J. D. (1989). Predictors of relapse in unipolar depressives: Expressed emotion, marital distress, and perceived criticism. *Journal of Abnormal Psychology, 98*, 229–235.

Horne, J. (1992). Sleep and its disorders in children. *Journal of Child Psychology and Psychiatry, 33*, 473–487.

Horne, R. L., Pettinati, M. M., Sugerman, A., & Varga, E. (1985). Comparing bilateral to unilateral electroconvulsive therapy in a randomized study of EEG monitoring. *Archives of General Psychiatry, 42*, 1087–1092.

Horney, K. (1937). *The neurotic personality of our time.* New York: W. W. Norton.

Horowitz, L. M., & Vitkus, J. (1986). The interpersonal basis of psychiatric symptoms. *Clinical Psychology Review, 6*, 443–469.

Hough, M. S. (1990). Narrative comprehension in adults with right and left hemisphere brain damage: Theme organization. *Brain and Language, 38*, 253–277.

House, J. S., Landis, K. R., & Umberson, D. (1988). Social relationships and health. *Science, 241*, 540–545.

Houts, A. C. Berman, J. S., & Abramson, H. (1994). Effectiveness of psychological and pharmacological treatments for nocturnal enuresis. *Journal of Consulting and Clinical Psychology, 62*, 737–745.

Howard, K. I. (1962). The convergent and discriminant validation of ipsative ratings from three projective instruments. *Journal of Clinical Psychology, 18*, 183–188.

Howard, K. I., Kopta, S. M., Krause, M. S., & Orlinsky, D. E. (1986). The dose-effect relationship in psychotherapy. *American Psychologist, 41*, 159–164.

Howells, K. (1981). Some meanings of children for pedophiles. In M. Cook & G. Wilson (Eds.), *Love and attraction* (pp. 57–82). London: Pergamon Press.

Hoyer, G., & Lund, E. (1993). Suicide among women related to number of children in marriage. *Archives of General Psychiatry, 50*, 134–137.

Hrubec, Z., & Omenn, G. S. (1981). Evidence of genetic predisposition to alcoholic cirrhosis and psychosis: Twin concordances for alcoholism and its biological end points by zygosity among male veterans. *Alcoholism: Clinical and Experimental Research, 5*, 207–215.

Hudson, S. M., Marshall, W. L., Ward, T., Johnston, D. W., et al. (1995). Kia Marama: A cognitive-behavioral program for incarcerated molesters. *Behaviour Change, 12*, 64–80.

Huesmann, L. R., Moise, J. F., & Podolski, C. (1997). The effects of media violence on the development of antisocial behavior. In D. M. Stoff, J. Breiling, & J. D. Maser (Eds.), *Handbook of antisocial behavior* (pp. 181–193). New York: Wiley.

Hull, J. G., & Bond, C. F., Jr. (1986). Social and behavioral consequences of alcohol consumption and expectancy: A meta-analysis. *Psychological Bulletin, 99*, 347–360.

Hulme, C., & Roodenrys, S. (1995). Practitioner review: Verbal working memory development and its disorders. *Journal of Child Psychology and Psychiatry, 36*, 373–398.

Humphreys, T. P., & Herold, E. (1996). Date rape: a comparative analysis and integration of theory. *Canadian Journal of Human Sexuality, 5*, 69–82.

Iacono, W. G., & Beiser, M. (1992a). Are males more likely than females to develop schizophrenia? *American Journal of Psychiatry, 149*, 1070–1074.

Iacono, W. G., & Beiser, M. (1992b). Where are the women in the first-episode studies of schizophrenia? *Schizophrenia Bulletin, 18*, 471–480.

Iacono, W. G., & Grove, W. M. (1993). Schizophrenia revisited: Toward an integrative genetic model. *Psychological Science, 4*, 273–276.

Ickovics, J. R., Viscoli, C. M., & Horwitz, R. I., Functional recovery after myocardial infarction in men: The independent effects of social class. *Annals of Internal Medicine, 127*, 518–525.

Idler, E. L., & Kasl, S. (1991). Health perceptions and survival: Do global evaluations of health status really predict mortality? *Journal of Gerontology, 46*, S55-S65.

Iezzi, A., & Adams, H. E. (1993). Somatoform and factitious disorders. In P. B. Sutker & H. F. Adams (Eds.), *Comprehensive handbook of psychopathology* (2nd ed.). New York: Plenum Press.

Ilardi, S. S., Craighead, W. E., & Evans, D. D. (1997). Modeling relapse in unipolar depression: The effects of dysfunctional cognitions and personality disorders. *Journal of Consulting and Clinical Psychology, 65*, 381–391.

Ingram, R. E. (1990). Self-focused attention in clinical disorders: Review and a conceptual model. *Psychological Bulletin, 107*, 156–176.

Ingrassia, M., & Beck, M. (1994, July 4). Patterns of abuse. *Newsweek*, p. 26.

Insel, T. R., Zahn, T., & Murphy, D. L. (1985). Obsessive-compulsive disorder: An anxiety disorder? In A. H. Tuma & J. D. Maser (Eds.), *Anxiety and the anxiety disorders*. Hillsdale, NJ: Erlbaum.

Institute of Medicine. (1982). *Marijuana and health*. Washington, DC: National Academy Press.

Institute of Medicine. (1994). *Reducing risks for mental disorders: Frontiers for prevention research*. Washington, DC: National Academy Press.

Ironson, G., Taylor, C. B., Boltwood, M., Bartzokis, T., Dennis, C., Chesney, M., Spitzer, S., & Segall, G. (1992). Effects of anger on left ventricular ejection fraction in coronary artery disease. *American Journal of Cardiology, 70,* 281–285.

Isacsson, G., & Rich, C. L. (1997). Depression, antidepressants, and suicide: Pharmaco-epidemiological evidence. In R. W. Maris, M. M. Silverman, & S. S. Canetto (Eds.), *Review of suicidology* (pp. 168–201). New York: Guilford Press.

Isometsä, E. T., Henriksson, M. E., Aro, H. M., Heikkinen, M. E., Kuoppasalmi, K. I., & Lonnqvist, J. K. (1994). Suicide in major depression. *American Journal of Psychiatry, 151,* 530–536.

Israel, A. C., Silverman, W. K., & Solotar, L. C. (1986). An investigation of family influences on initial weight status, attrition, and treatment outcome in a childhood obesity program. *Behavior Therapy, 17,* 131–143.

Jablensky, A., Sartorius, N., Ernberg, G., Anker, M., Korten, A., Cooper, J. E., Day, R., & Bertelsen, A. (1992). Schizophrenia: Manifestations, incidence and course in different cultures—A World Health Organization ten-country study. *Psychological Medicine, Monograph Supplement 20,* 1–97.

Jackson, v. Indiana, 92 S. Ct. 1845 (1972).

Jackson, D. N., & Messick, S. (1961). Acquiescence and desirability as response determinants on the MMPI. *Education and Psychological Measurement, 21,* 771–790.

Jacobson, E. (1938). *Progressive relaxation*. Chicago: University of Chicago Press.

Jacobson, N. S. (1989). The politics of intimacy. *Behavior Therapist, 12,* 29–32.

Jacobson, N. S. (1995). The overselling of therapy. *Family Therapy Networker, 19,* 41–47.

Jacobson, N. S., & Christensen, A. (1996). Studying the effectiveness of psychotherapy: How well can clinical trials do the job? *American Psychologist, 51,* 1031–1039.

Jacobson, N. S., Christensen, A., Prince, S., Cordova, J., & Eldredge, K. (1998). Integrative behavioral couple therapy: A promising treatment for relationship discord. Manuscript submitted for publication.

Jacobson, N. S., Dobson, K. S., Truax, P. A., Addis, M. E., Koerner, K., Gollan, J. K., Gortner, E., & Prince, S. E. (1996). A component analysis of cognitive behavioral treatment for depression. *Journal of Consulting and Clinical Psychology, 64,* 295–304.

Jacobson, N. S., Follette, W. C., & McDonald, D. W. (1982). Reactivity to positive and negative behavior in distressed and nondistressed married couples. *Journal of Consulting and Clinical Psychology, 50,* 706–714.

Jacobson, N. S., Follette, W. C., & Revenstorf, D. (1984). Psychotherapy outcome research: Methods for reporting variability and evaluating clinical significance. *Behavior Therapy, 15,* 336–452.

Jacobson, N. S., & Gottman, J. M. (1998). *When men batter women: New insights into ending abusive relationships*. New York: Simon & Schuster.

Jacobson, N. S., Gottman, J. M., Gortner, E. T., Berns, S. B., & Shortt, J. W. (1996). Psychological factors in the longitudinal course of battering: When do the couples split up? When does the violence stop? *Violence and Victims, 11,* 371–391.

Jacobson, N. S., Gottman, J. M., & Shortt, J. W. (1995). The distinction between type I and type II batterers—Further considerations: Reply to Ornduff et al. (1995), Margolin et al. (1995), and Walker (1995). *Journal of Family Psychology, 9,* 272–279.

Jacobson, N. S., Gottman, J. M., Waltz, J., Rushe, R. H., Babcock, J. C., & Holtzworth-Munroe, A. (1994). Affect, verbal content, and psychophysiology in the arguments of couples with a violent husband. *Journal of Consulting and Clinical Psychology, 62,* 982–988.

Jacobson, N. S., & Hollon, S. D. (1996). Cognitive-behavior therapy versus pharmacotherapy: Now that the jury's returned its verdict, it's time to present the rest of the evidence. *Journal of Consulting and Clinical Psychology, 64,* 74–80.

Jacobson, N. S., & Holtzworth-Munroe, A. (1986). Marital therapy: A social learning-cognitive perspective. In N. S. Jacobson & A. S. Gurman (Eds.), *Clinical handbook of marital therapy*. New York: Guilford Press.

Jacobson, N. S., & Margolin, G. (1979). *Marital therapy: Strategies based on social learning and behavior-exchange principles*. New York: Brunner/Mazel.

Jacobson, N. S. & Prince, S. (in press). Couple and family therapy. In M. Lambert, S. Garfield, & A. Bergin (Eds.), *Handbook of psychotherapy and behavior change*. New York: Wiley.

Jacobson, N. S., Wilson, L., & Tupper, C. (1988). The clinical significance of treatment gains resulting from exposure-based interventions for agoraphobia: A reanalysis of outcome data. *Behavior Therapy, 19,* 539–552.

Jaffee v. Redmond, 116 S. Ct. 1923 (1996).

Jagger, J., Vernberg, K., & Jones, J. A. (1987). Airbags: Reducing the toll of brain trauma. *Neurosurgery, 20(5),* 815–817.

James, L., Singer, A., Zurynski, Y., Gordon, E., Kraiuhin, C., Harris, A., Howson, A., & Meares, R. (1987). Evoked response potentials and regional cerebral blood flow in somatization disorder. *Psychotherapy and Psychosomatics, 47,* 190–196.

James, W. E., Mefford, R. B., & Kimbell, I. (1969). Early signs of Huntington's chorea. *Diseases of the Nervous System, 30,* 556–559.

Jamison, K. R. (1992). *Touched with fire: Manic-depressive illness and the artistic temperament*. New York: Free Press.

Jampala, V. C., Sierles, F. S., & Taylor, M. A. (1986). Consumers' views of *DSM-III:* Attitudes and practices of U.S. Psychiatrists and 1984 graduating psychiatric residents. *American Journal of Psychiatry, 143,* 148–153.

Janca, A., Isaac, M., Bennett, L.A., & Tacchini, G. (1995). Somatoform disorders in different cultures—a mail questionnaire survey. *Social Psychiatry and Psychiatric Epidemiology, 30,* 44–48.

Janet, P. (1929). *The major symptoms of hysteria*. New York: Macmillan.

Jang, K. L., Lam, R. W., Livesley, W. J., & Vernon, P. A. (1997). Gender differences in the heritability of seasonal mood change. *Psychiatry Research, 70,* 145–154.

Janssen, E. (1995a). Understanding the rity toward women among rapists. *Journal of Interpersonal Violence, 11,* 586–592.

Janssen, E. (1995b). Understanding the rapist's mind. *Perspectives in Psychiatric Care, 31,* 9–13.

Jaspers, J. P. C. (1996). The diagnosis and psychopharmocological treatment of trichotillomania: A review. *Pharmacopsychiatry, 29,* 115–120.

Javitt, D. C., Doneshka, P., Grochowski, S., & Ritter, W. (1995). Impaired mismatch negativity generation reflects widespread dysfunction of working memory in schizophrenia. *Archives of General Psychiatry, 52,* 550–558.

Javitt, D. C., & Silipo, G. S. (1997). Use of electroencephalograms and evoked potentials in psychiatry. In D. L. Dunner (Ed.), *Current psychiatric therapy II* (pp. 28–36). Philadelphia: W. B. Saunders Co.

Jefferson, J. W. (1996). Social phobia: Everyone's disorder? *Journal of Clinical Psychiatry, 57,* 28–32.

Jellinek, E. M. (1946). *Phases in the drinking history of alcoholics.* New Haven, CT: Hillhouse Press.

Jernigan, T. L. (1990). Techniques for imaging brain structure: Neuropsychological applications. In A. A. Boulton, G. R. Baker, & H. Hiscock (Eds.), *Neuromethods* (Vol. 17) Neuropsychology. Clifton, NJ: Humana Press.

Jeste, D. V., Gladsjo, J. A., Lindamer, L. A., & Lacro, J. P. (1996). Medical comorbidity in schizophrenia. *Schizophrenia Bulletin, 22,* 413–430.

Jeste, D. V., Heaton, S. C., Paulsen, J. S., Ercoli, L., Harris, M. J., & Heaton, R. K. (1996). Clinical and neuropsychological comparison of psychotic depression with nonpsychotic depression and schizophrenia. *American Journal of Psychiatry, 153,* 490–496.

Jiang, W., Babyak, M., Krantz, D. S., Waugh, R. A., Coleman, R. E., Hanson, M. M., Frid, D. J., McNulty, S., Morris, J. J., O'Connor, C. M., & Blumenthal, J. A. (1996). Mental stress-induced myocardial ischemia and cardiac events. *Journal of the American Medical Association, 275,* 1651–1656.

Johansson, B., & Zarit, S. H. (1991). Dementia and cognitive impairment in the oldest old: A comparison of two rating methods. *International Psychogeriatrics, 3,* 29–38.

Johansson, B., & Zarit, S. H. (1995). Prevalence and incidence of dementia in the oldest old: A longitudinal study of a population-based sample of 84–90-year-olds in Sweden. *International Journal of Geriatric Psychology, 10.*

Johnson, D., Walker, T., & Rodriguez, G. (1993, March). *Teaching low-income mothers to teach their children.* Paper presented at the biennial meeting of the Society for Research in Child Development, New Orleans.

Johnson, M. R., & Lydiard, R. B. (1995). The neurobiology of anxiety disorders. *Psychiatric Clinics of North America, 18,* 681–725.

Johnson, S. L., & Miller, I. (1997). Negative life events and time to recovery from episodes of bipolar disorder. *Journal of Abnormal Psychology, 106,* 449–457.

Johnson, S. L., & Roberts, J. E. (1995). Life events and bipolar disorder: Implications from biological theories. *Psychological Bulletin, 117,* 434–449.

Johnson, S. M., & Greenberg, L. S. (1995). The emotionally focused approach to problems in adult attachment. In N. S. Jacobson, A. S. Gurman, et al. (Eds.), *Clinical handbook of couple therapy* (pp. 121–141). New York: Guilford Press.

Johnson, W. G., & Hinkle, L. K. (1993). Obesity. In T. H. Ollendick & M.

Hersen (Eds.), *Handbook of child and adolescent asssessment.* Boston: Allyn and Bacon.

Johnston, M. B., Whitman, T. L., & Johnson, M. (1980). Teaching addition and subtraction to mentally retarded children: A self-instruction program. *Applied Research in Mental Retardation, 1,* 141–160.

Joiner, T. E., Jr. (1995). The price of soliciting and receiving negative feedback: Self-verification theory as a vulnerability to depression theory. *Journal of Abnormal Psychology, 104,* 364–372.

Joiner, T. E., Jr., & Metalsky, G. I. (1995). A prospective test of an integrative interpersonal theory of depression: A naturalistic study of college roommates. *Journal of Personality and Social Psychology, 69,* 778–788.

Joiner, T. E., Jr., & Wagner, K. D. (1995). Attributional style and depression in children and adolescents: A meta-analytic review. *Clinical Psychology Review, 15,* 777–798.

Jones v. United States, 103 S. Ct. 3043 (1983).

Jones, M. M. (1980). Conversion reaction: Anachronism or evolutionary form? A review of the neurologic, behavioral, and psychoanalytic literature. *Psychological Bulletin, 87,* 427–441.

Jordan, J. C. (1995). First person account: Schizophrenia—adrift in an anchorless reality. *Schizophrenia Bulletin, 21,* 501–503.

Jorgensen, R. S., Johnson, B. T., Kolodziej, M. E., & Schreer, G. E. (1996). Elevated blood pressure and personality: A meta-analytic review. *Psychological Bulletin, 120,* 293–320.

Joseph, S., Williams, R., & Yule, W. (1995). Psychosocial perspectives on post-traumatic stress. *Clinical Psychology Review, 15,* 515–544.

Judd, L. L. (1997). The clinical course of unipolar major depressive disorders. *Archives of General Psychiatry, 54,* 989–991.

Jung, C. G. (1935). Fundamental psychological conceptions. In M. Barker & M. Game (Eds.), *A report of five lectures.* London: Institute of Medical Psychology.

Junginger, J., Barker, S., & Coe, D. (1992). Mood theme and bizarreness of delusions in schizophrenia and mood psychosis. *Journal of Abnormal Psychology, 101,* 287–292.

Just, N., & Alloy, L. B. (1997). The response styles theory of depression: Tests and an extension of the theory. *Journal of Abnormal Psychology, 106,* 221–229.

Juster, H. R., Heimberg, R. G., Frost, R. O., Holt, C. S., Mattia, J. I., & Faccenda, K.

(1996). Social phobia and perfectionism. *Personality and Individual Differences, 21,* 403–410.

Kafka, M. P., & Pretky, R. (1992). Fluoxetine treatment on nonparaphilic sexual addictions and paraphilias in men. *Journal of Clinical Psychiatry, 53,* 351–358.

Kahn, M. W., Hannah, M., Hinkin, C., Montgomery, C., & Pitz, D. (1987). Psychopathology on the streets: Psychological measurement of the homeless. *Professional Psychology.*

Kalra, S., Bergeron, C., & Lang, A. E. (1996). Lewy body disease and dementia: A review. *Archives of Internal Medicine, 156,* 487–493.

Kamarck, T., & Jennings, J. R. (1991). Biobehavioral factors in sudden cardiac death. *Psychological Bulletin, 109,* 42–75.

Kanfer, F. H., & Hagerman, S. M. (1985). Behavior therapy and the information-processing paradigm. In S. Reiss & R. R. Bootzin (Eds.), *Theoretical issues in behavior therapy.* New York: Academic Press.

Kannel, W. B., & Higgins, M. (1990). Smoking and hypertension as predictors of cardiovascular risk in population studies. *Journal of Hypertension, 8,* S3–S8.

Kansas v. Hendricks, 117 S. Ct. 2072 (1997).

Kaplan, B. (Ed.). (1964). *The inner world of mental illness.* New York: Harper & Row.

Kaplan, G. A., & Keil, J. E. (1993). Socioeconomic factors and cardiovascular disease: A review of the literature. *Circulation, 88,* 1973–1998.

Kaplan, H. I., & Sadock, B. J. (1991). *Synopsis of psychiatry: Behavioral sciences, clinical psychiatry* (6th ed.). Baltimore: Williams & Wilkins.

Kaplan, H. S. (1974). *The new sex therapy: Active treatment of sexual dysfunctions.* New York: Brunner/Mazel, in cooperation with Quadrangle/New York Times Book Co.

Kaplan, H. S. (1979). *Disorder of sexual desire.* New York: Brunner/Mazel.

Kaplan, J. A., Brownell, H. H., Jacobs, J. R., & Gardner, H. (1990). The effects of right hemisphere damage on the pragmatic interpretation of conversational remarks. *Brain and Language, 38,* 315–333.

Kaplan, J. R., Adams, M. R., Clarkson, T. B., & Koritnik, D. R. (1984). Psychosocial influences on female "protection" among cynomologus macaques. *Atherosclerosis, 53,* 283–295.

Kaplan, M. (1993, July). A woman's view of DSM-III. *American Psychologist,* 786–792.

Kaprio, J., Koskenvuo, M., Langinvainio, H., Romanov, K., Sarna, S., & Rose, R. J. (1987). Genetic influences on use and abuse of alcohol: A study of 5638 adult Finnish twin brothers. *Alcoholism: Clinical and Experimental Research, 11,* 349–356.

Kapur, S., & Remington, G. (1996). Serotonin-dopamine interaction and its relevance to schizophrenia. *American Journal of Psychiatry, 153,* 466–476.

Karasek, R., Baker, D., Marxer, F., Ahlbom, A., & Theorell, T. (1981). Job decision latitude, job demands, and cardiovascular disease: A prospective study of Swedish men. *American Journal of Public Health, 71,* 694–705.

Karasek, R., & Theorell, T. (1990). *Healthy work: Stress, productivity and the reconstruction of working life.* New York: Basic Books.

Karno, M., Golding, J. M., Sorenson, S. B., & Burnam, M. A. (1988). The epidemiology of obsessive-compulsive disorder in five U.S. communities. *Archives of General Psychiatry, 45,* 1094–1099.

Karper, L. P., & Krystal, J. H. (1997). Pharmacotherapy of violent behavior. In D. M. Stoff, J. Breiling, & J. D. Maser (Eds.), *Handbook of antisocial behavior* (pp. 436–444). New York: Wiley.

Karpman, (1954). *The sexual offender and his offenses.* New York: Julian Press.

Kashani, J. H., Carlson, G. A., Beck, N. C., et al. (1990). Depression, depressive symptoms, and depressed mood among a community sample of adolescents. *American Journal of Psychiatry, 144,* 931–934.

Kashner, T. M., Rost, K., Cohen, B., Anderson, M., & Smith, G. R. (1995). Enhancing the health of somatization disorder patients: Effectiveness of short-term group therapy. *Psychosomatics, 36,* 462–470.

Kass, D. J., Silver, F. M., & Abrams, G. M. (1972). Behavioral group treatment of hysteria. *Archives of General Psychiatry, 26,* 42–50.

Kassirer, J. P. (1997). Federal foolishness and marijuana. *New England Journal of Medicine, 336,* 366–367.

Kaszniak, A. W., Nussbaum, P. D., Berren, M. R., & Santiago, J. (1988). Amnesia as a consequence of male rape: A case report. *Journal of Abnormal Psychology, 97,* 100–104.

Katerndahl, D. A. (1996). Panic attacks and panic disorder. *Journal of Family Practice, 43,* 275–282.

Katsanis, J., Iacono, W. G., & Beiser, M. (1996). Eye-tracking performance and adaptive functioning over the short-term course of first-episode psychosis. *Psychiatry Research, 64,* 19–26.

Kaufman, J., & Cicchetti, D. (1989). The effects of maltreatment on school-age children's socioemotional development. *Developmental Psychology, 25,* 516–524.

Kaye, W. H., Berrettini, W., Gwirtsman, H., & George, D. T. (1990). Altered cerebrospinal fluid neuropeptide Y and peptide YY immunoreactivity in anorexia and bulimia nervosa. *Archives of General Psychiatry, 47,* 548–556.

Kazdin, A. E. (1978). Methodological and interpretive problems of single-case experimental designs. *Journal of Consulting and Clinical Psychology, 46,* 629–642.

Kazdin, A. E. (1987). Treatment of anti-social behavior in children: Current status and future directions. *Psychological Bulletin, 102,* 187–203.

Kazdin, A. E. (1993a). Psychotherapy for children and adolescents: Current progress and future research directions. *American Psychologist, 48,* 644–657.

Kazdin, A. E. (1993b). Treatment of conduct disorder: Progress and directions in psychotherapy research. *Development and Psychopathology, 5,* 277–310.

Kazdin, A. E., & Rogers, T. (1978). On paradigms and recycled ideologies: Analogue research revisited. *Cognitive Therapy and Research, 2,* 105–117.

Kazdin, A. E., & Wilson, G. T. (1978). *Evaluation of behavior therapy: Issues, evidence and research strategies.* Cambridge, MA: Ballinger.

Kearney, C. A. (in press). *Casebook for childhood behavior disorders.* Pacific Grove, CA: Brooks/Cole.

Kearney, C. A., Durand, V. M., & Mindell, J. A. (1995a). Choice assessment in residential settings. *Journal of Developmental and Physical Disabilities, 7,* 203–213.

Kearney, C. A., Durand, V. M., & Mindell, J. A. (1995b). It's not where but how you live: Choice and adaptive/maladaptive behavior in persons with severe handicaps. *Journal of Developmental and Physical Disabilities, 7,* 203–213.

Kearney, C. A., & McKnight, T. J. (1997). Preference, choice, and persons with disabilities: A synopsis of assessments, interventions, and future directions. *Clinical Psychology Review, 17,* 217–238.

Kearney, C. A., & McKnight, T. J. (in press; anticipated 1998). Mental retardation. In C. Radnitz (Ed.), *Cognitive-behavioral interventions for persons with disabilities.* Northvale, NJ: Aronson.

Kearney, C. A., & Silverman, W. K. (1996). The evolution and reconciliation of taxonomic strategies for school refusal behavior. *Clinical Psychology: Science and Practice, 3,* 339–354.

Keefe, R. S. E., Silverman, J. M., Mohs, R. C., Siever, L. J., Harvey, P. D., Friedman, L., Roitman, S. E. L., DuPre, R. L., Smith, C. J., Schmeidler, J., & Davis, K.L. (1997). Eye tracking, attention, and schizotypal symptoms in nonpsychotic relatives of patients with schizophrenia. *Archives of General Psychiatry, 54,* 169–176.

Keller, M. B., Lavori, P. W., Mueller, T. I., Endicott, J., Coryell, W., Hirschfeld, R. M. A., & Shea, T. (1992). Time to recovery, chronicity, and levels of psychopathology in major depression. *Archives of General Psychiatry, 49,* 809–816.

Kellner, R. (1985). Functional somatic symptoms and hypochondriasis: A survey of empirical studies. *Archives of General Psychiatry, 42,* 821–833.

Kelly, J. A., & Drabman, R. S. (1977). The modification of socially detrimental behavior. *Journal of Behavior Therapy and Experimental Psychiatry, 8,* 101–104.

Kelly, J. A., & Murphy, D. A. (1992). Psychological interventions with AIDS and HIV: Prevention and treatment. *Journal of Consulting and Clinical Psychology, 60,* 576–585.

Kemp, S. (1990). *Medieval psychology,* New York: Greenwood Press.

Kemper, T. L., & Bauman, M. L. (1992). Neuropathology of infantile autism. In H. Nanse & E. Ornitz (Eds.), *Neurobiology of infantile autism* (pp. 43–57). Amsterdam: Elsevier Science Publishers.

Kendall, P. C. (1990). *Coping cat workbook.* Ardmore, PA: Workbook Publishing.

Kendall, P. C. (1992). Healthy thinking. *Behavior Therapy, 23,* 1–11.

Kendall, P. C., Flannery-Schroeder, E., Panichelli-Mindel, S. M., Southam-Gerow, M., Henin, A., & Warman, M. (1997). Therapy for youths with anxiety disorders: A second randomized clinical trial. *Journal of Consulting and Clinical Psychology, 65,* 366–380.

Kendall-Tuckett, K. A., Williams, L. M., & Finkelhor, D. (1993). Impact of sexual abuse on children: A review and synthesis of recent empirical studies. *Psychological Bulletin, 113,* 164–180.

Kendler, K. S. (1996). Major depression and generalised anxiety disorder: Same genes, (partly) different environments–revisited. *British Journal of Psychiatry, 168,* 68–75.

Kendler, K. S., & Davis, K. L. (1981). The genetics and biochemistry of paranoid schizophrenia and other paranoid psychoses. *Schizophrenia Bulletin, 7,* 689–709.

Kendler, K. S., & Diehl, S. R. (1993). The genetics of schizophrenia: A current, genetic-epidemiological perspective. *Schizophrenia Bulletin, 19,* 261–285.

Kendler, K. S., Eaves, L. J., Walters, E. E., Neale, M. C., Heath, A. C., & Kessler, R. C. (1996). The identification and validation of distinct depressive syndromes in a population-based sample of female twins. *Archives of General Psychiatry, 53,* 391–399.

Kendler, K. S., Gallagher, T. J., Abelson, J. M., & Kessler, R. C. (1996). Lifetime prevalence, demographic risk factors, and diagnostic validity of nonaffective psychosis as assessed in a US community sample. *Archives of General Psychiatry, 53,* 1022–1031.

Kendler, K. S., Kessler, R. C., Neale, M. C., Heath, A. C., & Eaves, L. J. (1993). The prediction of major depression in women: Toward an integrated etiologic model. *American Journal of Psychiatry, 150,* 1139–1148.

Kendler, K. S., Kessler, R. C., Walters, E. E., MacLean, C., Neale, M. C., Heath, A. C., & Eaves, L. J. (1995). Stressful life events, genetic liability, and onset of an episode of major depression in women. *American Journal of Psychiatry, 152,* 833–842.

Kendler, K. S., McGuire, M., Gruenberg, A. M., & Walsh, D. (1994). Outcome and family study of the subtypes of schizophrenia in the west of Ireland. *American Journal of Psychiatry, 151,* 849–856.

Kendler, K. S., McGuire, M., Gruenberg, A. M., & Walsh, D. (1995). Examining the validity of DSM-III-R schizoaffective disorder and its putative subtypes in the Roscommon Family Study. *American Journal of Psychiatry, 152,* 755–764.

Kendler, K. S., Neale, M. C., Kessler, R. C., Heath, A. C., & Eaves, L. J. (1992a). Childhood parental loss and adult psychopathology in women: A twin study perspective. *Archives of General Psychiatry, 49,* 109–116.

Kendler, K. S., Neale, M. C., Kessler, R. C., Heath, A. C., & Eaves, L. J. (1992b). Generalized anxiety disorder in women: A population-based twin study. *Archives of General Psychiatry, 49,* 267–272.

Kendler, K. S., Neale, M. C., Kessler, R. C., Heath, A. C., & Eaves, L. J. (1992c). A population-based twin study of major depression in women: The impact of varying definitions of illness. *Archives of General Psychiatry, 49,* 257–266.

Kendler, K. S., Neale, M. C., Kessler, R. C., Heath, A. C., & Eaves, L. J. (1993). A longitudinal twin study of 1-year prevalence of major depression in women. *Archives of General Psychiatry, 50,* 843–852.

Kendler, K. S., & Walsh, D. (1995). Schizotypal personality disorder in parents and the risk for schizophrenia in siblings. *Schizophrenia Bulletin, 21,* 47–52.

Kennedy, B. P., Isaac, N. E., & Graham, J. D. (1996). The role of heavy drinking in the risk of traffic fatalities. *Risk Analysis, 16,* 565–569.

Kenrick, D. T., & Funder, D. C. (1988). Profiting from controversy: Lessons from the person-situation debate. *American Psychologist, 43,* 23–34.

Kent, D. A., Tomasson, K., & Coryell, W. (1995). Course and outcome of conversion and somatization disorders: A four-year follow-up. *Psychosomatics, 36,* 138–144.

Kernberg, O. F. (1975). *Borderline conditions and pathological narcissism.* New York: Aronson.

Kerr, S. H., & Cooper, E. B. (1976). *Phonatory adjustment times in stutterers and nonstutterers.* Unpublished manuscript.

Kessler, J. W. *Psychopathology of childhood.* Englewood Cliffs, NJ: Prentice-Hall.

Kessler, R. C., Foster, C., Joseph, J., Ostrow, D., Wortman, C., Phair, J., & Chmiel, J. (1991). Stressful life events and symptom onset in HIV infection. *American Journal of Psychiatry, 148,* 733–738.

Kessler, R. C., McGonagle, K. A., Zhao, S., Nelson, C. B., Hughes, M., Eshleman, S., Wittchen, H. U., & Kendler, K. S. (1994). Lifetime and 12-month prevalence of *DSM-III-R* psychiatric disorders in the United States: Results from the National Comorbidity Study. *Archives of General Psychiatry, 51,* 8–19.

Kessler, R. C., Sonnega, A., Bromet, E., Hughes, M., & Nelson, C. B. (1995). Posttraumatic stress disorder in the National Comorbidity Survey. *Archives of General Psychiatry, 52,* 1048–1060.

Kessler, R. C., Zhao, S., Blazer, D. G., & Swartz, M. (1997). Prevalence, correlates, and course of minor depression and major depression in the national comorbidity survey. *Journal of Affective Disorders, 45,* 19–30.

Kety, S. S. (1988). Schizophrenic illness in the families of schizophrenic adoptees: Findings from the Danish national sample. *Schizophrenia Bulletin, 14,* 217–222.

Kety, S. S., Rosenthal, D., Wender, P. H., & Schulsinger, F. (1968). The types and prevalence of mental illness in the biological and adoptive families of adopted schizophrenics. In D. Rosenthal & S. S. Kety (Eds.), *The transmission of schizophrenia.* Oxford: Pergamon Press.

Kety, S. S., Rosenthal, D., Wender, P. H., Schulsinger, F., & Jacobsen, B. (1975). Mental illness in the biological and adoptive families of adopted individuals who have become schizophrenic: A preliminary report based upon psychiatric interviews. In R. Fieve, D. Rosenthal, & H. Brill (Eds.), *Genetic research in psychiatry.* Baltimore: Johns Hopkins University Press.

Kety, S. S., Wender, P. H., Jacobsen, B., Ingraham, L. J., Jansson, L., Faber, B., & Kinney, D. K. (1994). Mental illness in the biological and adoptive relatives of schizophrenic adoptees: Replication of the Copenhagen study in the rest of Denmark. *Archives of General Psychiatry, 51,* 442–455.

Khanna, S., & Mukherjee, D. (1992). Checkers and washers: Valid subtypes of obsessive compulsive disorder. *Psychopathology, 25,* 283–288.

Kiecolt-Glaser, J. K., Dura, J. R., Speicher, C. E., Trask, O. J., & Glaser, R. (1991). Spousal caregivers of dementia victims: Longitudinal changes in immunity and health. *Psychosomatic Medicine, 53,* 345–362.

Kiecolt-Glaser, J. K., Fisher, L., Ogrocki, P., Stout, J. C., Speicher, C. E., & Glaser, R. (1987). Marital quality, marital disruption, and immune function. *Psychosomatic Medicine, 46,* 7–14.

Kiecolt-Glaser, J. K., & Glaser, R. (1991). Stress and immune function in humans. In R. Ader, D. Felten, & N. Cohen (Eds.), *Psychoneuroimmunology II* (pp. 849–867). San Diego: Academic Press.

Kiecolt-Glaser, J. K., Glaser, R., Williger, D., Stout, J., Messick, G., Sheppard, S., Ricker, D., Romisher, S. C., Briner, W., Bonnell, G., & Donnerberg, R. (1985). Psychosocial enhancement of immunocompetence in a geriatric population. *Health Psychology, 4,* 25–41.

Kiecolt-Glaser, J. K., Malarkey, W. B., Chee, M., Newton, T., Cacioppo, J. T., Hsiao-Yin, M., & Glaser, R. (1993). Negative behavior during marital conflict is associated with immunological down-regulation. *Psychosomatic Medicine, 55,* 395–409.

Kiecolt-Glaser, J. K., Malarkey, W. B., Chee, M., Newton, T., Cacioppo, J. T., Mao, H., & Glaser, R. (1993). Negative behavior during marital conflict is associated with immunological down-regulation. *Psychosomatic Medicine, 55,* 395–409.

Kiesler, C. A. (1982a). Mental hospitals and alternative care. *American Psychologist, 37,* 349–360.

Kiesler, C. A. (1982b). Public and professional myths about mental hospitalization. *American Psychologist, 37,* 1323–1339.

Kiesler, D. J. (1983). The 1982 interpersonal circle: A taxonomy for complementarity in human transactions. *Psychological Review, 90,* 185–214.

Kihlstrom, J. F. (1987). The cognitive unconscious. *Science, 237,* 1445–1452.

Kihlstrom, J. F., Barnhardt, T. M., & Tataryn, D. J. (1991). Implicit perception. In R. F. Bornstein & T. S. Pittman (Eds.), *Perception without awareness.* New York: Guilford Press.

Kihlstrom, J. F., & Schacter, D. L. (1995). Funtional disorders of autobiographical memory. In A. D. Baddeley, B. A. Wilson, & F. N. Watts (Eds.), *Handbook of memory disorders* (pp. 337–364). New York: Wiley.

Kihlstrom, J. F., Tataryn, D. J., & Hoyt, I. P. (1993). Dissociative disorders. In P. B. Sutker & H. E. Adams (Eds.), *Comprehensive handbook of psychopathology* (2nd ed.). New York: Plenum Press.

Killen, J. D., Hayward, C., Wilson, C. B., Taylor, C. B., Hammer, L. D., Litt, T. N., Simmonds, B., & Haydel, F. (1994). Factors associated with eating disorder symptoms in a community sample of 6th and 7th grade girls. *International Journal of Eating Disorders, 15,* 357–367.

Killen, J. D., Taylor, C. B., Hayward, C., Haydel, K. F., Wilson, D. M., Hammer, L., Kraemer, H., Blair-Greiner, A., & Strachowski, D. (1996). Weight concerns influence the development of eating disorders: A 4-year prospective study. *Journal of Consulting and Clinical Psychology, 64,* 936–940.

Kilpatrick, D. G., Saunders, B., Amick-McMullen, A., Best, C., Veronen, L., & Resnick, H. (1989). Victim and crime factors associated with the development of posttraumatic stress disorder. *Behavior Therapy, 20,* 199–214.

Kinderman, P., & Bentall, R. P. (1996). Self-discrepancies and persecutory delusions: Evidence for a model of paranoid ideation. *Journal of Abnormal Psychology, 105,* 106–113.

King, C. A. (1997). Suicidal behavior in adolescence. In R. W. Maris, M. M. Silverman, & S. S. Canetto (Eds.), *Review of suicidology* (pp. 61–95). New York: Guilford Press.

King, J. A., Campbell, D., & Edwards, E. (1993). Differential development of the stress response in congenital learned helplessness. *International Journal of Developmental Neuroscience, 11,* 435–442.

Kinney, D. K., Holzman, P. S., Jacobsen, B., Jansson, L., Faber, B., Hildebrand, W., Kasell, E., & Zimbalist, M. E. (1997). Thought disorder in schizophrenic and control adoptees and their relatives.

Archives of General Psychiatry, 54, 475–479.

Kinsey, A. C., Pomeroy, W. B., & Martin, C. E. (1948). *Sexual behavior in the human male.* Philadelphia: Saunders.

Kinsey, A. C., Pomeroy, W. B., Martin, C. E., & Gebhard, P. H. (1953). *Sexual behavior in the human female.* Philadelphia: Saunders.

Kirch, D. G. (1993). Infection and autoimmunity as etiologic factors in schizophrenia: A review and reappraisal. *Schizophrenia Bulletin, 19,* 355–370.

Kirmayer, L. J., Young, A., & Hayton, B. C. (1995). The cultural context of anxiety disorders. *Psychiatric Clinics of North America, 18,* 503–521.

Klajner, R., Herman, C. P., Polivy, J., & Chhabra, R. (1981). Human obesity, dieting, and anticipatory salivation. *Physiology and Behavior, 27,* 195–198.

Klatka, L. A., Louis, E. D., & Schiffer, R. B. (1996). Psychiatric features in diffuse Lewy body disease: A clinico-pathologic study using Alzheimer's disease and Parkinson's disease comparison groups. *Neurology, 47,* 1148–1152.

Klein, D. F. (1996a). Panic disorder and agoraphobia: Hypothesis hothouse. *Journal of Clinical Psychiatry, 57,* 21–27.

Klein, D. F. (1996b). Preventing hung juries about therapy studies. *Journal of Consulting and Clinical Psychology, 64,* 81–87.

Klein, D. N., Kocsis, J. H., McCullough, J. P., Holzer, C. E., III, Hirschfeld, R. M. A., & Keller, M. B. (1996). Symptomatology in dysthymic and major depressive disorder. *Psychiatric Clinics of North America, 19,* 41–53.

Klein, D. N., Taylor, E. B., Dickstein, S., & Harding, K. (1988). The early-late onset distinction in *DSM-III-R* dysthymia. *Journal of Affective Disorders, 14,* 25–33.

Klemm, E., Grunwald, F., Kasper, S., Menzel, C., Broich, K., Danos, P., Reichmann, K., Krappel, C., Rieker, O., Briele, B., Hotze, A. L., Moller, H. J., & Biersack, H. J. (1996). [^{123}I]IBZM SPECT for imaging of striatal D_2 dopamine receptors in 56 schizophrenic patients taking various neuroleptics. *American Journal of Psychiatry, 153,* 183–190.

Klerman, G. L. (1988). The current age of youthful melancholia. *British Journal of Psychiatry, 152,* 4–14.

Klerman, G. L. (1990). Approaches to the phenomena of comorbidity. In J. D. Maser & C. R. Cloninger (Eds.), *Cormorbidity of mood and anxiety disorders.* Washington, DC: American Psychiatric Press.

Klerman, G. L., Lavori, P. W., Rice, J., Reich, T., Endicott, J., Andreasen, N. C., Keller, M. B., & Hirschfeld, R. M. A. (1985). Birth cohort trends in rates of major depressive disorder among relatives of patients with affective disorder. *Archives of General Psychiatry, 42,* 689–693.

Klerman, G. L. Weissman, M. M., Rounsaville, B. J., & Chevron, E. S. (1984). *Interpersonal psychotherapy of depression.* New York: Basic Books.

Klin, A., & Volkmar, F. R. (1997). Autism and the pervasive developmental disorders. In J. D. Noshpitz, S. Greenspan, S. Wieder, & J. Osofsky (Eds.), *Handbook of child and adolescent psychiatry* (Vol. 1; pp. 536–560). New York: Wiley.

Kling, M. A., Kellner, C. H., Post, R. M., Cowdry, R. W., Gardner, D. L., Coppola, R., Putnam, F. W., Gold, P. W. (1987). Neuroendocrine effects of limbic activation by electrical, spontaneous, and pharmacological modes: Relevance to the pathophysiology of affective dysregulation in psychiatric disorders. *Progress in Neuropsychopharmacology and Biological Psychiatry, 11,* 459–481.

Klinger, L. G., & Dawson, G. (1996). Autistic disorder. In E. J. Mash & R. A. Barkley (Eds.), *Child psychopathology* (pp. 311–339). New York: Guilford Press.

Kluft, R. P. (1984). Treatment of multiple personality disorder: A study of 33 cases. *Psychiatric Clinics of North America, 7,* 9–29.

Kluft, R. P. (1986). Personality unification in multiple personality disorder: A follow-up study. In B. G. Braun (Ed.), *Treatment of multiple personality disorder.* Washington, DC: American Psychiatric Press.

Kluft, R. P. (1988). Dissociative disorders. In J. A. Talbott, R. E. Hales, & S. C. Yudofsky (Eds.), *The American Psychiatric Press textbook of psychiatry* (pp. 557–586). Washington, DC: American Psychiatric Press.

Kluft, R. P. (1991). Clinical presentations of multiple personality disorder. *Psychiatric Clinics of North America, 14,* 605–629.

Kluft, R. P. (1992). A specialist's perspective on multiple personality disorder. *Psychoanalytic Inquiry, 12,* 139–171.

Kluft, R. P. (1996). Treating the traumatic memories of patients with dissociative identity disorder. *American Journal of Psychiatry, 153,* 103–110.

Knight, R. A., & Roff, J. D. (1985). Affectivity in schizophrenia. In M. Alpert (Ed.), *Controversies of schizophrenia* (pp. 280–313). New York: Guilford Press.

Knopp, F. H. (1976). *Instead of prisons.* Syracuse, NY: Safer Society Press.

Kobayashi, R., Murata, T., & Yoshinaga, K. (1992). A follow-up study of 201 children with autism in Kyushu and Yamaguchi areas, Japan. *Journal of Autism and Developmental Disorders, 22,* 395–411.

Kocsis, J. H., Friedman, R. A., Markowitz, J. C., Leon, A. C., Miller, N. L., Gniwesch, L., & Parides, M. (1996). Maintenance therapy for chronic depression: A controlled clinical trial of desipramine. *Archives of General Psychiatry, 53,* 769–774.

Koegel, R. L., & Rincover, A. (1977). Research on the difference between generalization and maintenance in extra-therapy responding. *Journal of Applied Behavior Analysis, 10,* 1–12.

Kohen-Raz, R. (1968). Mental and motor development of kibbutz, institution- alized, and home-reared infants in Israel. *Child Development, 39,* 489–504.

Kohlenberg, R. J. (1973). Behavioristic approach to multiple personality: A case study. *Behavior Therapy, 4,* 137–140.

Kohlenberg, R. J., & Tsai, M. (1992). *Functional analytic psychotherapy: Creating intense and curative thera- peutic relationships.* New York: Plenum Press.

Kohler, F. W., & Strain, P. S. (1997). Procedures for assessing and increasing social interaction. In N. N. Singh (Ed.), *Prevention and treatment of severe behavior problems: Models and methods in developmental disabilities* (pp. 49–59). Pacific Grove, CA: Brooks/Cole.

Kohut, H. (1966). Forms and transforma- tions of narcissism. *Journal of the American Psychoanalytic Association, 14,* 243–272.

Kohut, H. (1972). Thoughts on narcissism and narcissistic rage. *Psychoanalytic Study of the Child, 27,* 360–400.

Kohut, H. (1977). *The restoration of the self.* New York: International Universities Press.

Kohut, H., & Wolf, E. S. (1978). The disorders of the self and their treatment: An outline. *International Journal of Psychoanalysis, 59,* 413–425.

Kokmen, E., Beard, C. M., O'Brien, P. C, Offord, K. P., & Kurland, L. T. (1993). Is the incidence of dementing illness changing?: A 25-year time trend study in Rochester, Minnesota (1960–1984). *Neurology, 43,* 1887–1892.

Kokmen, K., Beard, C. M., Offord, K. P., & Kurland, L. T. (1989). Prevalence of medically diagnosed dementia in a defined United States population. *Neurology, 39,* 773–776.

Kolb, B. (1989). Brain development, plasticity, and behavior. *American Psychologist, 44,* 1203–1212.

Kolb, L. C. (1982). *Modern clinical psychiatry* (10th ed.). Philadelphia: Saunders.

Kolodny, R. C., Masters, W. H., Kolodner, R. M., & Gelson, T. (1974). Depression of plasma testosterone levels after chronic intensive marihuana use. *New England Journal of Medicine, 290*(16), 872–874.

Koopman, C., Classen, C., Cardena, E., & Spiegel, D. (1995). When disaster strikes, acute stress disorder may follow. *Journal of Traumatic Stress, 8,* 29–46.

Kopelman, M. D., Christensen, H., Puffett, A., & Stanhope, N. (1994). The great escape: A neuropsychological study of psychogenic amnesia. *Neuropsycho- logia, 32,* 675–691.

Koss, M. P. (1988). Hidden rape: Sexual aggression and victimization in a national sample of students in higher education. In A. W. Burgess (Ed.), *Rape and sexual assault* (Vol. 2, pp. 3–26). New York: Garland.

Koss, M. P. (1996). The measurement of rape victimization in crime surveys. *Criminal Justice and Behavior, 23,* 55–69.

Koss, M. P., Dinero, T. E., Seibel, C. A., & Cox, S. L. (1988). Stranger and acquaintance rape: Are there differences in the victim's experience? *Psychology of Women Quarterly, 12,* 1–24.

Koss, M. P., Gidycz, C. A., & Wisniewski, N. (1987). The scope of rape: Incidence and prevalence of sexual aggression and victimization in a national sample of higher education students. *Journal of Consulting and Clinical Psychology, 55,* 162–170.

Koss, M. P., Goodman, L. A., Browne, A., Fitzgerald, L. F., Keitas, G. P., & Russo, N. F. (Eds.). (1994). *No safe haven: Male violence against women at home, at work, and in the community.* Washington, DC: American Psychological Association.

Koss, M. P., & Harvey, M. R. (1991). *The rape victim: Clinical and community interventions.* Newbury Park, CA: Sage.

Koss, M. P., Woodruff, W. J., & Koss, P. (1991). Criminal victimization among primary care medical patients: Prevalence, incidence, and physician usage. *Behavioral Sciences and the Law, 9,* 85–96.

Kotrla, K. J., & Weinberger, D. R. (1995). Brain imaging in schizophrenia. *Annual Reviews of Medicine, 46,* 113–122.

Kovacs, M., Devlin, B., Pollock, M., Richards, C., & Mukerji, P. (1997). A controlled family history study of childhood-onset depressive disorder.

Archives of General Psychiatry, 54, 613–623.

Kraepelin, E. (1923). *Textbook of psychiatry.* New York: Macmillan. Original work published 1883.

Kraepelin, E. (1968). *Lectures on clinical psychiatry* (T. P. Johnstone, Trans.). New York: Hafner. Original work published 1904.

Krafft-Ebing, R. von. (1900). *Textbook of psychiatry.* Original work published 1879.

Krafft-Ebing, R. von. (1965). *Psychopathia sexualis* (F. S. Klaf, Trans.). New York: Bell. Original work published 1886.

Kramer, P. D. (1993). *Listening to Prozac.* New York: Viking.

Krantz, D. S., Contrada, R. J., Hill, D. R., & Friedler, E. (1988). Environmental stress and biobehavioral antecedents of coronary heart disease. *Journal of Consulting and Clinical Psychology, 56,* 333–341.

Krantz, D. S., & Manuck, S. B. (1984). Acute psychophysiologic reactivity and risk of cardiovascular disease: A review and methodologic critique. *Psychological Bulletin, 96,* 435–464.

Kraus, J. F., Black, M., Hessol, N., Ley, P., Rokaw, W., Sullivan, C., Bowers, S., Knowlton, S., & Marshall, L. (1984). The incidence of acute brain injury and serious impairment in a defined population. *American Journal of Epidemiology, 119*(2), 186–201.

Krauss, D. (1983). The physiologic basis of male sexual dysfunction. *Hospital Practice, 2,* 193–222.

Kring, A. M., & Neale, J. M. (1996). Do schizophrenic patients show a disjunctive relationship among expressive, experiential, and psychophysiological components of emotion? *Journal of Abnormal Psychology, 105,* 249–257.

Kringlen, E., & Cramer, G. (1989). Offspring of monozygotic twins discordant for schizophrenia. *Archives of General Psychiatry, 46,* 873–877.

Kristiansson, M. (1995). Incurable psychopaths? *Bulletin of the American Academy of Psychiatry and the Law, 23,* 555–562.

Kroll, J. (1988). *The challenge of the borderline patient.* New York: W. W. Norton.

Kuiper, N. A., Olinger, L. J., & MacDonald, M. R. (1988). Depressive schemata and the processing of personal and social information. In L. B. Alloy (Ed.), *Cognitive processes in depression.* New York: Guilford Press.

Kulkarni, J. (1997). Women and schizophrenia: A review. *Australian and New Zealand Journal of Psychiatry, 31,* 46–56.

Kumanyika, S. (1987). Obesity in black women. *Epidemiological Review, 9,* 31–50.

Kunovac, J. L., & Stahl, S. M. (1995). Future directions in anxiolytic pharmacotherapy. *Psychiatric Clinics of North America, 18,* 895–909.

Kupfer, D. J., Frank, E., Carpenter, L. L., Neiswanger, K. (1989). Family history in recurrent depression. *Journal of Affective Disorders, 17,* 113–119.

Kurland, L. T., Faro, S. N., & Siedler, H. (1960). Minamata disease. The outbreak of neurologic disorder in Minamata, Japan, and its relationship to the ingestion of seafood contaminated by mercuric compounds. *World Neurology, 1,* 370–395.

Lacks, P., & Morin, C. M. (1992). Recent advances in the assessment and treatment of insomnia. *Journal of Consulting and Clinical Psychology, 60,* 586–594.

LaFave, W. F., & Scott, A. (1972). *Criminal law.* St. Paul, MN: West.

La Fond, J. Q., & Durham, M. L. (1992). *Back to the asylum.* New York: Oxford University Press.

La Greca, A. M., & Fetter, M. (1995). Peer relations. In A. R. Eisen, C. A. Kearney, & C. E. Schaefer (Eds.), *Clinical handbook of anxiety disorders in children and adolescents.* Northvale, NJ: Aronson.

La Greca, A. M., Silverman, W. K., Vernberg, E. M., & Prinstein, M. J. (1996). Symptoms of posttraumatic stress in children after Hurricane Andrew: A prospective study. *Journal of Consulting and Clinical Psychology, 64,* 712–723.

Lahey, B. B., & Loeber, R. (1997). Attention deficit/hyperactivity disorder, oppositional defiant disorder, conduct disorder, and adult antisocial behavior: A life span perspective. In D. M. Stoff, J. Breiling, & J. D. Maser (Eds.), *Handbook of antisocial behavior* (pp. 51–59). New York: Wiley.

Lahey, B. B., Loeber, R., Hart, E.L., Frick, P. J., Applegate, B., Zhang, Q., Green, S. M., & Russo, M. F. (1995). Four-year longitudinal study of conduct disorder in boys: Patterns and predictors of persistence. *Journal of Abnormal Psychology, 104,* 83–93.

Lam, R. W., Zis, A. P., Grewal, A., Delgado, P. L., Charney, D. S., & Krystal, J. H. (1996). Effects of rapid tryptophan depletion in patients with seasonal affective disorder in remission after light therapy. *Archives of General Psychiatry, 53,* 41–44.

Lampert, P. W., & Hardman, J. M.(1984). Morphological changes in brains of boxers. *Journal of the American Medical Association,251,* 2676–2679.

Landesman-Dwyer, S. (1981). Drinking during pregnancy: Effects on human development [Monograph]. *Alcohol and Health, 4.*

Landrine, H. (1988). Revising the framework of abnormal psychology. In P. Bronstein & K. Quina (Eds.), *Teaching a psychology of people: Resources for gender and sociocultural awareness* (pp. 37–44). Washington, DC: American Psychological Association.

Lanyon, R. I. (1986). Theory and treatment in child molestation. *Journal of Counseling and Clinical Psychology, 54,* 176–182.

LaPerriere, A. R., Antoni, M. H., Schneiderman, N., Ironson, G., Klimas, N., Caralis, P., & Fletcher, M. A. (1990). Exercise intervention attenuates emotional distress and natural killer cell decrements following notification of positive serologic status for HIV-1. *Biofeedback and Self-Regulation, 15,* 229–242.

Larsson, B., & Melin, L. (1992). Prevalence and short-term stability of depressive symptoms in school children. *Acta Psychiatrica Scandinavica 85,* 17–22.

Latz, T. T., Kramer, S. I., & Hughes, D. L. (1995). Multiple personality disorder among female inpatients in a state hospital. *American Journal of Psychiatry, 152,* 1343–1348.

Laufer, R. S., Brett, E., & Gallops, M. S. (1985). Symptom pattern associated with post-traumatic stress disorder among Vietnam veterans exposed to war trauma. *American Journal of Psychiatry, 142,* 1304–1311.

Laumann, E. O., Gagnon, J. H., Michael, R. T., & Michaels, S. (1994). *The social organization of sexuality: Sexual practices in the United States.* Chicago: The University of Chicago Press.

Lazarus, R. S. (1980). The stress and coping paradigm. In C. Eisdorfer, D. Cohen, & A. Kleinman (Eds.), *Conceptual models for psychopathology.* New York: Spectrum.

Lazarus, R. S., & Folkman, S. (1984). *Stress, appraisal, and coping.* New York: Springer Publishing Company.

Lazarus, R. S., Kanner, A., & Folkman, S. (1980). Emotions: A cognitive-phenomenological approach. In R. Plutchik & H. Kellerman (Eds.), *Theories of emotion.* New York: Academic Press.

Leavitt, N., & Maykuth, P. L. (1989). Conformance to attorney performance standards: Advocacy behavior in a maximum security prison hospital. *Law and Human Behavior, 13,* 217–230.

Leckliter, I. N., & Matarazzo, J. D. (1994). Diagnosis and classification. In V. B.

Van Hasselt & M. Hersen (Eds.), *Advanced abnormal psychology* (pp. 3–18). New York: Plenum Press.

LeDoux, J. E. (1993). Emotional networks in the brain. In M. Lewis & J. M. Haviland (Eds.), *Handbook of emotions* (pp. 109–118). New York: Guilford Press.

Lee, S., & Chiu, H. F. (1989). Anorexia nervosa in Hong Kong—Why not more in Chinese? *British Journal of Psychiatry, 154,* 683–688.

Lee, T. M., Blashko, C. A., Janzen, H. L., Paterson, J. G., & Chan, C. C. H. (1997). Pathophysiological mechanism of seasonal affective disorder. *Journal of Affective Disorders, 46,* 25–38.

Leenaars, A. A., & Wenckstern, S. (1991). The school-age child and adolescent. In A. A. Leenaars (Ed.), *Life span perspectives of suicide: Timeliness in the suicide process.* New York: Plenum Press.

Leibenluft, E. (1996). Women with bipolar illness: Clinical and research issues. *American Journal of Psychiatry, 153,* 163–173.

Leibowitz, S. F. (1991). Brain neuropeptide Y: An integrator of endocrine, metabolic, and behavioral processes. *Brain Research Bulletin, 27,* 333–337.

Leigh, B. C. (1989). In search of the seven dwarves: Issues of measurement and meaning in alcohol expectancy research. *Psychological Bulletin, 105,* 361–373.

Lemere, F., & Voegtlin, W. (1950). An evaluation of the aversion treatment of alcoholism. *Quarterly Journal of Studies on Alcohol, 11,* 199–204.

Lenzenweger, M. F., Cornblatt, B. A., & Putnick, M. (1991). Schizotypy and sustained attention. *Journal of Abnormal Psychology, 100,* 84–89.

Lenzenweger, M. F., Dworkin, R. H., & Wethington, E. (1989). Models of positive and negative symptoms in schizophrenia: An empirical evaluation of latent structures. *Journal of Abnormal Psychology, 98,* 62–70.

Lenzenweger, M. F., & Loranger, A. W. (1989). Detection of familial schizophrenia using a psychometric measure of schizotypy. *Archives of General Psychiatry, 46,* 902–907.

Leon, G. R. (1990). *Case histories of psychopathology.* (4th ed.). Boston: Allyn and Bacon.

Leonard, K. E. (1993). Drinking patterns and intoxication in marital violence. In S. E. Martin (Ed.), *Alcohol and interpersonal violence.* National Institute of Alcohol Abuse, Monograph #24, NIH, Pub. no. 93–3496.

Leonard, K. E., & Senchak, M. (1996). Prospective prediction of husband marital aggression within newlywed couples. *Journal of Abnormal Psychology, 105,* 369–380.

LeShan, L. (1966). An emotional life-history pattern associated with neoplastic disease. *Annals of New York Academy of Sciences, 125,* 780–793.

Lester, D., & Murell, M. E. (1980). The influence of gun control laws on suicidal behavior. *American Journal of Psychiatry, 137,* 121–122.

Levendusky, P. G., & Dooley, C. P. (1985). An inpatient model for the treatment of anorexia nervosa. In S. Emmett (Ed.), *Eating disorders: Research, theory, and treatment* (pp. 211–233). New York: Brunner/Mazel.

Levine, F. M., & Ramirez, R. (1989). Contingent negative practice as a home-based treatment of tics and stuttering. In C. E. Schaefer and J. M. Briesmeister (Eds.), *Handbook of parent training: Parents as co-therapists for children's behavior problems.* New York: Wiley.

Levis, D. J. (1985). Implosive theory: A comprehensive extention of conditioning theory of fear/anxiety to psychology. In S. Reiss & R. R. Bootzin (Eds.), *Theoretical issues in behavior therapy.* New York: Academic Press.

Levitan, R. D., Lesage, A., Parikh, S. V., Goering, P., & Kennedy, S. H. (1997). Reversed neurovegetative symptoms of depression: A community study of Ontario. *American Journal of Psychiatry, 154,* 934–940.

Levy, D., Kimhi, R., Barak, Y., Demmer, M., Harel, M., & Elizur, A. (1996). Brainstem auditory evoked potentials of panic disorder patients. *Neuropsychobiology, 33,* 164–167.

Levy, D. L., Holzman, P. S., Matthysse, S., & Mendell, N. R. (1993). Eye tracking dysfunction and schizophrenia: A critical perspective. *Schizophrenia Bulletin, 19,* 461–536.

Levy, R., & Mushin, J. (1973). The somatosensory evoked response in patients with hysterical anaesthesia. *Journal of Psychosomatic Research, 17,* 81–84.

Lewin, T. (1994, June 19). The Simpson case: The syndrome. *The New York Times,* sec. 1, p. 21.

Lewinsohn, P. M. (1974). Clinical and theoretical aspects of depression. In K. S. Calhoun, H. E. Adams, & K. M. Mitchell (Eds.), *Innovative treatment methods of psychopathology.* New York: Wiley.

Lewinsohn, P. M., & Gotlib, I. H. (1995). Behavioral theory and treatment of depression. In E. E. Becker & W. R. Leber (Eds.), *Handbook of depression* (pp. 352–275). New York: Guilford Press.

Lewinsohn, P. M., Hoberman, H. M., & Rosenbaum, M. (1988). A prospective study of risk factors for unipolar depression. *Journal of Abnormal Psychology, 97,* 251–264.

Lewinsohn, P. M., Hoberman, H., Teri, L., & Hautzinger, M. (1985). An integrative theory of depression. In S. Reiss & R. R. Bootzin (Eds.), *Theoretical issues in behavior therapy* (pp. 331–359). New York: Academic Press.

Lewinsohn, P. M., Hops, H., Roberts, R. E., Seely, J. R., & Andrews, J. A. (1993). Adolescent psychopathology: I. Prevalence and incidence of depression and other *DSM-III-R* disorders in high school students. *Journal of Abnormal Psychology, 102,* 133–144.

Lewinsohn, P. M., Mischel, W., Chaplin, W., & Barton, R. (1980). Social competence and depression: The role of illusory self-perceptions. *Journal of Abnormal Psychology, 89,* 203–212.

Lewinsohn, P. M., Roberts, R. E., Seeley, J. R., Rohde, P., Gotlib, I. H., & Hops, H. (1994). Adolescent psychopathology: II. Psychosocial risk factors for depression. *Journal of Abnormal Psychology, 103,* 302–315.

Lewinsohn, P. M., Rohde, P., Seeley, J. R., & Fischer, S. A. (1993). Age-cohort changes in the lifetime occurrence of depression and other mental disorders. *Journal of Abnormal Psychology, 102,* 110–120.

Lewinsohn, P. M., Rohde, P., Seeley, J. R., & Hops, H. (1991). Comorbidity of unipolar depression: I. Major depression with dysthymia. *Journal of Abnormal Psychology, 100,* 205–213.

Lewinsohn, P. M., Sullivan, J. M., & Grosscup, S. J. (1980). Changing reinforcing events: An approach to the treatment of depression. *Psychotherapy: Theory, Research, and Practice, 17,* 322–334.

Ley, R. (1988a). Panic attacks during relaxation and relaxation-induced anxiety: A hyperventilation interpretation. *Journal of Behavior Therapy and Experimental Psychiatry, 19,* 305–316.

Ley, R. (1988b). Panic attacks during sleep: A hyperventilation-probability model. *Journal of Behavior Therapy and Experimental Psychiatry, 19,* 181–192.

Lezak, M. D. (1995). *Neuropsychological assessment.* New York: Oxford University Press.

Li, T., Lumeng, L., McBride, W. J., & Murphy, J. M. (1987). Alcoholism: Is it a model for the study of mood or consummatory behavior? *Annals of the New York Academy of Science, 499,* 239–249.

Liberman, R. P., & Eckman, T. (1981). Behavior therapy vs. insight-oriented therapy for repeated suicide attemptors. *Archives of General Psychiatry, 38,* 1126–1130.

Lichtenstein, E., & Glasgow, R. E. (1992). Smoking cessation: What have we learned over the past decade? *Journal of Consulting and Clinical Psychology, 60,* 518–527.

Liebenluft, E., & Wehr, T. A. (1992). Is sleep deprivation useful in the treatment of depression? *American Journal of Psychiatry, 149,* 159–168.

Lieberman, J. A., & Koreen, A. R. (1993). Neurochemistry and neuroendocrinology of schizophrenia: A selective review. *Schizophrenia Bulletin, 19,* 371–429.

Liebert, R. M., Neale, J. M., & Davison, E. S. (1973). *The early window.* Elmsford, NY: Pergamon Press.

Liebowitz, M. R. (1992). Diagnostic issues in anxiety disorders. In A. Tasman & M. B. Riba (Eds.), *Review of psychiatry* (Vol. 11, pp. 247–259). Washington, DC: American Psychiatric Press.

Lilienfeld, S. O. (1992). The association between antisocial personality and somatization disorders: A review and integration of theoretical models. *Clinical Psychology Review, 12,* 641–662.

Lim, K. O., Tew, W., Kushner, M., Chow, K., Matsumoto, B., & DeLisi, L. E. (1996). Cortical gray matter volume deficit in patients with first-episode schizophrenia. *American Journal of Psychiatry, 153,* 1548–1553.

Lindemann, J. E., & Matarazzo, J. D. (1990). Assessment of adult intelligence. In G. Goldstein & M. Hersen (Eds.), *Handbook of psychological assessment* (2nd ed.). New York: Pergamon Press.

Linden, W., Stossel C., & Maurice, J. (1996). Psychosocial interventions for patients with coronary artery disease: A meta-analysis. *Archives of Internal Medicine, 156,* 745–752.

Lindsay, D. S., & Read, J. D. (1994). Psychotherapy and memories of childhood sexual abuse: A cognitive perspective. *Applied Cognitive Psychology, 8,* 281–338.

Linehan, M. M. (1987). Dialectical behavior therapy for borderline personality disorder. *Bulletin of the Menninger Clinic, 41(3),* 261–276.

Linehan, M. M. (1992). Behavior therapy, dialectics, and the treatement of borderline personality disorder. In D. Silver, M. Rosenbluth, el al. (Eds.), *Handbook of borderline disorders* (pp. 415–434). Madison, WI: International Universities Press.

Linehan, M. M. (1993). *Cognitive-behavioral treatment of borderline personality disorder.* New York: Guilford Press.

Linehan, M. M., Heard, H. L., & Armstrong, H. E. (1993). Naturalistic follow-up of a behavioral treatment for chronically parasuicidal borderline patients. *Archives of General Psychiatry, 50,* 971–974.

Linszen, D. H., Dingemans, P. M., Nugter, M. A., Van der Does, A. J. W., Scholte, W. F., & Lenior, M. A. (1997). Patient attributes and expressed emotion as risk factors for psychotic relapse. *Schizophrenia Bulletin, 23,* 119–130.

Lion, J. R. (1981). A comparison between *DSM-III* and *DSM-II* personality disorders. In J. R. Lion (Ed.), *disorders: Diagnosis and management* (2nd ed.). Baltimore: Williams & Wilkins.

Lipowolty, Z. J. (1989). Delirium in the elderly patient. *New England Journal of Medicine, 320,* 578–582.

Little, K. B., & Shneidman, E. S. (1959). Congruencies among interpretations of psychological test and anamnestic data. *Psychological Monographs, 73* (6, Whole No. 476).

Littlewood, R., & Lipsedge, M. (1986). The 'culture-bound syndromes' of the dominant culture: Culture, psycho-pathology, and biomedicine. In J. L. Cox (Ed.), *Transcultural psychiatry* (pp. 253–273). London: Croom-Helm, Ltd.

Livermore, J. M., Malmquist, C. P., & Meehl, P. E. (1968). On the justifications for civil commitment. *University of Pennsylvania Law Review, 117,* 75–96.

Livermore, J. M., & Meehl, P. E. (1967). The virtues of M'Naghten. *Minnesota Law Review, 51,* 789–856.

Livingston, R., Witt, A., & Smith, G. R. (1995). Families who somatize. *Developmental and Behavioral Pediatrics, 16,* 42–46.

Lizardi, H., Klein, D. N., Ouimette, P. C., Riso, L. P., Anderson, R. L., & Donaldson, S. K. (1995). Reports of the childhood home environment in early-onset dysthymia and episodic major depression. *Journal of Abnormal Psychology, 104,* 132–139.

Lloyd, J. W., Hallahan, D. P., Kauffman, J. M., & Keller, C. E. (1991). Academic problems. In R. J. Morris & T. R. Kratochwill (Eds.), *The practice of child therapy* (2nd ed.). Elsmford, NY: Pergamon Press.

Loeber, R., & Dishion, T. (1983). Early predictors of male delinquency: A review. *Psychological Bulletin, 94,* 68–99.

Loeber, R., Green, S. M., Keenan, K., & Lahey, B. B. (1995). Which boys will fare worse? Early predictors of the onset of conduct disorder in a six-year longitudinal study. *Journal of the American Academy of Child and Adolescent Psychiatry, 34,* 499–509.

Loewenstein, R. J. (1991). Psychogenic amnesia and psychogenic fugue: A comprehensive review. *Annual Review of Psychiatry, 10,* 223–247.

Loewenstein, R. J. (1994). Diagnosis, epidemiology, clinical course, treatment, and cost effectiveness of treatment for dissociative disorders and MPD: Report submitted to the Clinton administration Task Force on Health Care Financing Reform. *Dissociation, 7,* 3–11.

Loewenstein, R. J., & Ross, D. R. (1992). Multiple personality and psycho-analysis: An introduction. *Psychoanalytic Inquiry, 12,* 3–48.

Loftus, E. F. (1993). The reality of repressed memories. *American Psychologist, 48,* 518–537.

Lopez, S. R. (1988). The empirical basis of ethnocultural and linguistic bias in mental health evaluations of Hispanics. *American Psychologist, 43,* 1095–1097.

Lopez, S. R. (1989). Patient variable biases in clinical judgment: Conceptual overview and methodological considerations. *Psychological Bulletin, 106,* 184–203.

Lopez, S. R., & Hernandez, P. (1986). How culture is considered in evaluations of psychopathology. *Journal of Nervous and Mental Disease, 176,* 598–606.

LoPiccolo, J. (1977). Direct treatment of sexual dysfunction in the couple. In J. Money & H. Musaph (Eds.), *Handbook of sexology.* Amsterdam: Excerpta Medica.

LoPiccolo, J. (1992). Post-modern sex therapy for erectile failure. In R. C. Rosen & S. R. Leiblum (Eds.), *Erectile failure: Assessment and treatment.* New York: Guilford Press.

LoPiccolo, J., & Lobitz, W. C. (1973). Behavior therapy of sexual dysfunction. In L. A. Hammerlynck, L. C. Handy, & E. J. Mash (Eds.), *Behavior change: Methodology, concepts and practice.* Champaign, IL: Research Press.

LoPiccolo, J., & Stock, W. E. (1986). Treatment of sexual dysfunction. *Journal of Consulting and Clinical Psychology, 54,* 158–167.

Loughrey, G. C., Bell, P., Kee, M., Roddy, R. J., et al. (1988). Post-traumatic stress disorder and civil violence in Northern Ireland. *British Journal of Psychiatry, 153,* 554–560.

Lovaas, O. I. (1987). Behavioral treatment and normal educational and intellectual functioning in young autistic children. *Journal of Consulting and Clinical Psychology, 55,* 3–9.

Lovaas, O. I., & Buch, G. (1997). Intensive behavioral intervention with young children with autism. In N. N. Singh (Ed.), *Prevention and treatment of severe behavior problems: Models and methods in developmental disabilities* (pp. 61–76). Pacific Grove, CA: Brooks/Cole.

Lowing, P. A., Mirsky, A. F., Pereira, R. (1983). The inheritance of schizo-phrenia spectrum disorders: A re-analysis of the Danish adoptee study data. *American Journal of Psychiatry, 140,* 1167–1171.

Lubin, B., Larsen, R. M., & Matarazzo, J. D. (1984). Patterns of psychological test usage in the United States: 1935–1982. *American Psychologist, 39,* 451–454.

Luborsky, L. (1984). *Principles of psychoanalytic psychotherapy.* New York: Basic Books.

Lucas, A. R., Beard, C. M., O'Fallon, W. M., & Kurlan, L. T. (1991). Fifty year trends in the incidence of anorexia nervosa in Rochester, Minnesota: A population-based study. *American Journal of Psychiatry, 148,* 917–922.

Luchins, A. S. (1993). Social control doctrines of mental illness and the medical profession in nineteenth-century America. *Journal of the History of the Behavioral Sciences, 29,* 29–47.

Luchins, D. J., Lewine, R. J., & Meltzer, H. Y. (1983). Lateral ventricular size in the psychoses: Relation to psycho-pathology and therapeutic and adverse response to medication. *Schizophrenia Bulletin, 9,* 518–522.

Luckasson, R. R., Coulter, D. L., Polloway, E. A., Reiss, S., Schalock, R. L., Snell, M. E., Spitalnik, D. M., & Stark, J. A. (1992). *Mental retardation: Definition, classification, and systems of support.* Washington, DC: American Association on Mental Retardation.

Ludwig, A. M. (1986). *Principles of clinical psychiatry.* New York: Free Press.

Luepnitz, R. R., Randolph, D. L., & Gutsch, K. W. (1982). Race and socioeconomic status as confounding variables in the accurate diagnosis of alcoholism. *Journal of Clinical Psychology, 38,* 665–669.

Luisada, P. V. (1977, August). *The PCP psychosis: A hidden epidemic.* Paper presented at the Sixth World Congress of Psychiatry, Honolulu, HI.

Lydiard, L. R., Brawman, M. O., & Ballenger, J. C. (1996). Recent developments in the psychopharma-cology of anxiety disorders. *Journal of Consulting and Clinical Psychology, 64,* 660–668.

Lykken, D. T. (1995). *The antisocial personalities.* Hillsdale, NJ: Erlbaum.

Lynam, D. R. (1996). Early identification of chronic offenders: Who is the fledgling psychopath? *Psychological Bulletin, 120,* 209–234.

Lynch, J. J. (1977). *The broken heart: The medical consequences of loneliness.* New York: Basic Books.

Lyon, G. R., Learning disabilities. (1996). In E. J. Mash & R. A. Barkley (Eds.), *Child psychopathology* (pp. 390–435). New York: Guilford Press.

Lytton, H., & Romney, D. (1991). Parents' differential socialization of boys and girls: A meta-analysis. *Psychological Bulletin, 109,* 267–296.

MacDonald, J. (1967). Homicidal threats. *American Journal of Psychiatry, 124,* 475.

MacFarlane, K. (1978). Sexual abuse of children. In J. R. Chapman & M. Gates (Eds.), *The victimization of women* (pp. 81–109). Beverly Hills, CA: Sage.

MacGregor, M. W. (1996). Multiple personality disorder: Etiology, treatment, and treatment techniques from a psychodynamic perspective. *Psycho-analytic Psychology, 13,* 389–402.

Mack, A. H., Forman, L., Brown, R., & Frances, A. (1994). A brief history of psychiatric classification: From the ancients to *DSM-IV*. *Psychiatric Clinics of North America, 17,* 515–523.

MacMahon, S., Peto, R., Cutter, J., Collins, R., Sorlie, P., Neaton, J., Abbott, R., Godwin, J., Dyer, A., & Stamler, J. (1990). Blood pressure, stroke, and coronary heart disease. *Lancet, 335,* 765–774.

MacMillan, D. L. (1982). *Mental retardation in school and society* (2nd ed.). Boston: Little, Brown.

Madden P. A. F., Heath, A. C., Rosenthal, N. E., & Martin, N. G. (1996). Seasonal changes in mood and behavior: The role of genetic factors. *Archives of General Psychiatry, 53,* 47–55.

Maes, M. (1995). Evidence for an immune response in major depression: A review and hypothesis. *Progress in Neuro-Psychopharmacology & Biological Psychiatry, 19,* 11–38.

Magee, W. J., Eaton, W. W., Wittchen, H. U., McGonoagle, K. A., & Kessler, R. C. (1996). Agoraphobia, simple phobia, and social phobia in the National Comorbidity Survey. *Archives of General Psychiatry, 53,* 159–168.

Maher, B. A., & Spitzer, M. (1993). Delusions. In P. B. Sutker & H. E. Adams (Eds.), *Comprehensive handbook of psychopathology* (2nd ed., pp. 263–293). New York: Plenum Press.

Maher, W. B., & Maher, B. A. (1985). Psychopathology: I. From ancient times to the eighteenth century. In G. A. Kimble & K. Schlesinger (Eds.), *Topics in the history of psychology* (Vol. 2). Hillsdale, NJ: Erlbaum.

Mahler, M. S., Pine, F., & Bergman. A. (1975). *The psychological birth of the human infant.* New York: Basic Books.

Mahoney, M. J. (1991). *Human change process: The scientific foundations of psychotherapy.* New York: Basic Books.

Maidenberg, E., Chen, E., Craske, M., Bohn, P., & Bystritsky, A. (1996). Specificity of attentional bias in panic disorder and social phobia. *Journal of Anxiety Disorders, 10,* 529–541.

Maier, S. F., Seligman, M. E. P., & Solomon, R. L. (1969). Pavlovian fear conditioning and learned helplessness. In B. A. Campbell & R. M. Church (Eds.), *Punishment.* New York: Appleton.

Main, M. (1996). Introduction to the special section on attachment and psychopathology: 2. Overview of the field of attachment. *Journal of Consulting and Clinical Psychology, 64,* 237–243.

Malamuth, N. M., Heavey, C. L., & Linz, D. (1993). Predicting men's antisocial behavior against women: The interaction model of sexual aggression. In C. C. Nagayama Hall, R. Hirschman, J. Graham, & M. Zaragoza (Eds.), *Sexual aggression: Issues and etiology, assessment and treatment (pp. 63–97).* Washington, DC: Taylor Francis.

Malamuth, N. M., Linz, D., Heavey, C. L., Barnes, G., et al. (1995). Using the confluence model of sexual aggression to predict men's conflict with women: A 10-year follow-up study. *Journal of Personality and Social Psychology, 69,* 353–369.

Malec, J. F., & Basford, J. S. (1996). Postacute brain injury rehabilitation. *Archives of Physical Medicine and Rehabilitation, 77,* 198–207.

Malmo, R. B., & Shagass, C. (1949). Physiologic study of symptom mechanisms in psychiatric patients under stress. *Psychosomatic Medicine, 11,* 25–29.

Mann, J. J., & Kapur, S. (1994). Elucidation of biochemical basis of the antidepressant action of electroconvulsive therapy by human studies. *Psychopharmacology Bulletin, 30,* 445–453.

Mann, J. J., Malone, K. M., Diehl, D. J., Perel, J., Cooper, T. B., & Mintun, M. A. (1996). Demonstration in vivo of reduced serotonin responsivity in the brain of untreated depressed patients. *American Journal of Psychiatry, 153,* 174–182.

Mann, J. J., McBride, A., Brown, R. P., Linnoila, M., Leon, A. C., DeMeo, M., Mieczkowski, T., Myers, J. E., & Stanley, M. (1992). Relationship between central and peripheral serotonin indexes in depressed and suicidal psychiatric inpatients. *Archives of General Psychiatry, 49,* 442–446.

Manschreck, T. C. (1992). Delusional disorders: Clinical concepts and diagnostic strategies. *Psychiatric Annals, 22,* 241–251.

Mansueto, C. S., Stemberger, R. M. T., Thomas, A. M., & Golomb, R. G. (1997). Trichotillomania: A comprehensive behavioral model. *Clinical Psychology Review, 17,* 567–577.

Manuck, S. B., Marsland, A. L., Kaplan, J. R., & Williams, J. K. (1995). The pathogenicity of behavior and its neuroendocrine mediation: An example from coronary artery disease. *Psychosomatic Medicine, 57,* 275–283.

Manuzza, S., & Klein, R. (1992). Predictors of outcome of children with attention-deficit hyperactivity disorder. In G. Weiss (Ed.), *Child and Adolescent Psychiatric Clinics of North America: Attention-deficit hyperactivity disorder* (pp. 567–578). Philadelphia: Saunders.

Marchese, M. C. (1992). Clinical versus actuarial prediction: A review of the literature. *Perceptual and Motor Skills, 75,* 583–594.

Marcos, L. R., Alpert, M., Urcuyo, L., & Kesselman, M. (1973). The language barrier in evaluating Spanish-American patients. *Archives of General Psychiatry, 29,* 655–659.

Marder, S. R., Wirshing, W. C., Mintz, J., McKenzie, J., Johnston, K., Eckman, T. A., Lebell, M., Zimmerman, K., & Liberman, R. P. (1996). Two-year outcome of social skills training and group psychotherapy for outpatients with schizophrenia. *American Journal of Psychiatry, 153,* 1585–1592.

Margolese, H. C., & Assalian, P. (1996). Sexual side effects of anti-depressants: A review. *Journal of Sex & Marital Therapy, 22,* 209–218.

Margolick, D. (1994a, January 16). Does Mrs. Bobbitt count as another battered wife? *The New York Times,* p. E5.

Margolick, D. (1994b, January 19). Psychiatrist says years of abuse led woman to cut husband. *The New York Times,* p. A9.

Margolies, A. (1977). Behavioral approaches to the treatment of early infantile autism: A review. *Psychological Bulletin, 84,* 249–264.

Maris, R. W. (1992). The relation of nonfatal suicide attempts to completed suicides. In R. W. Maris, A. L. Berman, J. T. Maltsberger, & R. I. Yufit (Eds.), *Assessment and prediction of suicide* (pp. 362–380). New York: Guilford Press.

Mark, V. H., Sweet, W. H., & Ervin, F. R. (1967). Role of brain disease in riots and urban violence. *Journal of the American Medical Association, 201,* 895.

Marks, I. M., & Nesse, R. M. (1994). Fear and fitness: An evolutionary analysis of anxiety disorders. *Ethology and Sociobiology, 15,* 247–261.

Markus, H. (1977). Self-schemata and processing information about the self. *Journal of Personality and Social Psychology, 35,* 63–78.

Marlatt, G. A., Curry, S., & Gordon, J. R. (1988). A longitudinal analysis of unaided smoking cessation. *Journal of Consulting and Clinical Psychology, 56,* 715–720.

Marlatt, G. A., & Gordon, J. R. (1985). *Relapse prevention: Maintenance strategies in addictive behavior change.* New York: Guilford Press.

Marmot, M. G., Bosma, H., Memingway, H., Brunner, E., & Stansfeld, S. (1997). Contribution of job control and other risk factors to social variations in coronary heart disease incidence. *Lancet, 350,* 235–239.

Marrazzi, M. A., & Luby, E. D. (1986). An autoaddiction model of chronic anorexia nervosa. *International Journal of Eating Disorders, 5,* 191–208.

Marsden, C. D. (1986). Hysteria—a neurologist's view. *Psychological Medicine, 16,* 277–288.

Marsh, L., Harris, D., Lim, K. O., Beal, M., Hoff, A. L., Minn, K., Csernansky, J. G., DeMent, S., Faustman, W. O., Sullivan, E. V., & Pfefferbaum, A. (1997). Structural magnetic resonance imaging abnormalities in men with severe chronic schizophrenia and an early age at clinical onset. *Archives of General Psychiatry, 54,* 1104–1112.

Marshall, D. S. (1971). Sexual behavior on Mangaia. In D. S. Marshall & R. C. Suggs (Eds.), *Human sexual behavior.* New York: Basic Books.

Marshall, W. L., & Hambley, L.S. (1996). Intimacy and loneliness, and their relationship to rape myth acceptance and hostility toward women among rapists. *Journal of Interpersonal Violence, 11,* 586–592.

Marshall, W. L., Hudson, S. M., Jones, R., & Fernandez, Y. M. (1995). Empathy in sex offenders. *Clinical Psychology Review, 15,* 99–113.

Marshall, W. L., & Pithers, W. D. (1994). A reconsideration of treatment outcome with sex offenders. *Criminal Justice and Behavior, 21,* 10–27.

Martin, R. L. (1995). DSM-IV changes for the somatoform disorders. *Psychiatric Annals, 25,* 29–39.

Masserman, J. H. (1961). *Principles of dynamic psychiatry* (2nd ed.). Philadelphia: Saunders.

Masters, W. H., & Johnson, V. E. (1966). *Human sexual response.* Boston: Little, Brown.

Masters, W. H., & Johnson, V. E. (1970). *Human sexual inadequacy.* Boston: Little, Brown.

Mathews, A., Richards, A., & Eysenck, M. (1989). Interpretation of homophones related to threat in anxiety states. *Journal of Abnormal Psychology, 98,* 31–34.

Matson, J. L., & Andrasik, F. (1982). *Treatment issues and innovations in mental retardation.* New York: Plenum Press.

Matthews, K. A. (1988). Coronary heart disease and Type A behaviors: Update on and alternative to the Booth-Kewley and Friedman (1987) quantitative review. *Psychological Bulletin, 104,* 373–380.

Matthews, K. A. (1989). Interactive effects of behavior and reproductive hormones on sex differences in risk for coronary heart disease. *Health Psychology, 8,* 373–387.

Maugh, T. H. (1982). Marijuana "justifies serious concern." *Science, 215,* 1488–1489.

Maxmen, J. S., & Ward, N. G. (1995). *Psychotropic drugs: Fast facts* (2nd ed.). New York: W. W. Norton.

Mayes, L. C., Granger, R. H., Bornstein, M. H., & Zuckerman, B. (1992). The problem of prenatal cocaine exposure: A rush to judgment. *Journal of the American Medical Association, 267,* 406–408.

McArdle, P., O'Brien, G., & Kolvin, I. (1995). Hyperactivity: Prevalence and relationship with conduct disorder. *Journal of Child Psychology and Psychiatry, 36,* 279–303.

McArthur, J. C., Cohen, B. A., Seines, O. A., Kumar, A. J., Cooper, K., McArthur, J. H., Soucy, G., Cronblath, D. R., Chmile, J. S., Wang, M. C., Starkleym, D. J., Ginzburg, H., Ostrow, D., Johnson, R. T., Phair, J. P., & Polk, B. F. (1989). Low prevalence of neurological and neuropsychological abnormalities in otherwise healthy HIV-1-infected individuals. Results from the Multicenter AIDS Cohort Study. *Annals of Neurology, 26,* 601–611.

McArthur, J. C., Hoover, D. R., Bacellar, H., Miller, E. N., Cohen, B. A., Becker, J. T., Graham, N. M. H., McArthur, J. H., Selnes, O. A., Jacobson, L. P., Visscher, B. R., Concha, M., & Saah, A. (1993). Dementia in AIDS patients: Incidence and risk factors. *Neurology, 43,* 2245–2252.

McAuliffe, W. E. (1990). A randomized controlled trial of recovery training and self-help for opioid addicts in New England and Hong Kong. *Journal of Psychoactive Drugs, 22,* 197–209.

McCartney, J. R., & Holden, J. C. (1981). Toilet training for the mentally retarded. In J. L. Matson & J. R. McCartney (Eds.), *Handbook of behavior modification with the mentally retarded.* New York: Plenum Press.

McConaghy, N. (1989). Validity and ethics of penile circumference measures of sexual arousal: A critical review. *Archives of Sexual Behavior, 18,* 357–369.

McCord, J. (1979). Some child-rearing antecedents of criminal behavior in adult men. *Journal of Personality and Social Psychology, 37,* 1477–1486.

McDermott, P. A., & Weiss, R. V. (1995). A normative typology of healthy, subclinical, and clinical behavior styles among American children and adolescents. *Psychological Assessment, 7,* 162–170.

McDermott, S. (1994). Explanatory model to describe school district prevalence rates for mental retardation and learning disabilities. *American Journal of Mental Retardation, 99,* 175–185.

McElroy, S. L., Strakowski, S. M., West, S. A., Keck, P. E., Jr., & McConville, B. J. (1997). Phenomenology of adolescent and adult mania in hospitalized patients with bipolar disorder. *American Journal of Psychiatry, 154,* 44–49.

McEwen, B. S. (1992). *Hormones and brain development.* Address to the American Health Foundation, Washington, DC.

McFarlane, A. C. (1988). The aetiology of post-traumatic stress disorders following a natural disaster. *British Journal of Psychiatry, 152,* 116–121.

McFarlane, A. C. (1989). The aetiology of post-traumatic morbidity: Predisposing, precipitating and perpetuating factors. *British Journal of Psychiatry, 154,* 221–228.

McFarlane, W. R., Lukens, E., Link, B., Dushay, R., Deakins, S. A., Newmark, M., Dunne, E. J., Horen, B., & Toran, J. (1995). Multiple-family groups and psychoeducation in the treatment of schizophrenia. *Archives of General Psychiatry, 52,* 679–687.

McGeer, P. L., Eccles, J. C., & McGeer, E. G. (1987). *Molecular neurobiology of the mammalian brain* (2nd ed.). New York: Plenum Press.

McGhie, A., & Chapman, J. (1961). Disorders of attention and perception in early schizophrenia. *British Journal of Medical Psychology, 34,* 103–116.

McGinnis J. M., & Foege, W. H. (1993). Actual causes of death in the United States. *Journal of the American Medical Association, 270,* 2207–2212.

McGorry, P. D. (1995). the clinical boundaries of posttraumatic stress disorder. *Australian and New Zealand Journal of Psychiatry, 29,* 385–393.

McGue, M., Pickens, R. W., & Svikis, D. S. (1992). Sex and age effects on the inheritance of alcohol problems: A twin study. *Journal of Abnormal Psychology, 101,* 3–17.

McGuffin, P., Katz, R., Watkins, S., & Rutherford, J. (1996). A hospital-based twin register of the heritability of DSM-IV unipolar depression. *Archives of General Psychiatry, 53,* 129–136.

McHugh, P. R. (1992). Psychiatric misadventures. *The American Scholar, 61*(4), 497–510.

McKay, J. R., Alterman, A. I., McLellan, T., Snider, E. C., & O'Brien, C. P. (1995). Effects of random versus nonrandom assignment in a comparison of inpatient and day hospital rehabilitation for male alcoholics. *Journal of Consulting and Clinical Psychology, 63,* 70–78.

McKeith, I. G., Galasko, D., Kosaka, K., Perry, E. K., Dickson, D. W., Hansen, L. A., Salmon, D. A., Lowe, J., Mirra, S. S., Byrne, E. J., Lennox, G., Quinn, N. P., Edwardson, J. A., Ince, P. G., Bergeron, C., Burns, A., Miller, B. L., Lovestune, S., Collerton, D., Jansen, E. N. H., Ballard, C., de Vos, R. A. I., Wilcock, G. K., Jellinger, K.A., & Perry, R. H. (1996). Consensus guidelines for the clinical and pathologic diagnosis of dementia with Lewy bodies (DLB): Report of the consortium on DLB international workshop. *Neurology, 47,* 1113–1124.

McLellan, A. T., Alterman, A. I., Metzger, D. S., Grissom, G. R., Woody, G. E., Luborsky, L., & O'Brien, C. P. (1994). Similarity of outcome predictors across opiate, cocaine, and alcohol treatments: Role of treatment services. *Journal of Consulting and Clinical Psychology, 62,* 1141–1158.

McMahan, B. T., & Flowers, S. M. (1986). The high cost of a bump on the head. *Business and Health, 3*(7), 47–48.

McNally, R. J. (1995). Automaticity and the anxiety disorders. *Behaviour Research and Therapy, 33,* 747–754.

McNally, R. J., Riemann, B. C., & Kim, E. (1990). Selective processing of threat cues in panic disorder. *Behavior Research and Therapy, 28,* 407–412.

McReynolds, P. (1975). Historical antecedents of personality assessment. In P. McReynolds (Ed.), *Advances in psychological assessment* (Vol. 3). San Francisco: Jossey-Bass.

McReynolds, P. (1989). Diagnosis and clinical assessment: Current status and major issues. *Annual Review of Psychology, 40,* 83–108.

Meador-Woodruff, J. H., Haroutunian, V., Powchik, P., Davidson, M., Davis, K. L., & Watson, S. J. (1997). Dopamine receptor transcript expression in striatum and prefrontal and occipital cortex: Focal abnormalities in orbitofrontal cortex in schizophrenia. *Archives of General Psychiatry, 54,* 1089–1095.

Mechanic, D. (1962). The concept of illness behavior. *Journal of Chronic Diseases, 15,* 189–194.

Mednick, S. A. (1970). Breakdown in individuals at high risk for schizophrenia: Possible predispositional perinatal factors. *Mental Hygiene, 54,* 50–63.

Mednick, S. A. (1971). Birth defects and schizophrenia. *Psychology Today, 4,* 48–50.

Mednick, S. A., Machon, R. A., Huttunen, M. O., & Bonett, D. (1988). Adult schizophrenia following prenatal exposure to an influenza epidemic. *Archives of General Psychiatry, 45,* 189–192.

Meehl, P. E. (1991). The insanity defense. In C. A. Anderson & K. Gunderson (Eds.), *Paul E. Meehl: Selected philosophical and methodological papers.* Minneapolis: University of Minnesota Press.

Meesters, Y., Jansen, J. H. C., Beersma, D. G. M., Bouhuys, A. L., & van der Hoofdakker, R. H. (1993). Early light treatment can prevent an emerging winter depression from developing into a full-blown depression. *Journal of Affective Disorders, 29,* 41–47.

Meichenbaum, D. H. (1975). Self-instructional methods. In F. H. Kanfer & A. P. Goldstein (Eds.), *Helping people change: A textbook of methods.* New York: Pergamon Press.

Meichenbaum, D. H. (Ed.). (1977). *Cognitive behavior modification: An integrative approach.* New York: Plenum Press.

Meichenbaum, D. H., & Cameron, R. (1973). Training schizophrenics to talk to themselves: A means of developing attentional controls. *Behavior Therapy, 4,* 515–534.

Meichenbaum, D. H., & Goodman, J. (1971). Training impulsive children to talk to themselves: A means of developing self control. *Journal of Abnormal Psychology, 77,* 115–126.

Meichenbaum, D. H., & Jaremko, M. E. (Eds.). (1983). *Stress reduction and prevention.* New York: Plenum Press.

Meinardi, H., & Pachlatko, C. (1991). Special centers for epilepsy. In M. Dam & L. Gram (Eds.), *Comprehensive epileptology* (pp. 769–779). New York: Raven Press.

Mellin, L. M., Irwin, C. E., & Scully, S. (1992). Prevalence of disordered eating in girls: A survey of middle-class children. *Journal of the American Dietetic Association, 92,* 851–853.

Mellsop, G., Varghere, F., Joshua, S., et al. (1982). The reliability of axis II of DSM-III. *American Journal of Psychiatry, 139,* 1360–1361.

Melton, G. B., Petrila, J., Poythress, N. G., & Slobogin, C. (1997). *Psychological evaluation for the courts* (2nd ed.). New York: Guilford Press.

Meltzer, H. Y., Rabinowitz, J., Lee, M. A., Cola, P. A., Ranjan, R., Findling, R. L., & Thompson, P. A. (1997). Age at onset and gender of schizophrenic patients in relation to neuroleptic resistance. *American Journal of Psychiatry, 154,* 475–482.

Melzack, R. (1988). The tragedy of needless pain: A call for social action. In R. Dubner, R. G. F. Gebhart, & M. R. Bond (Eds.), *Proceedings for the Fifth World Congress on Pain.* New York: Elsevier.

Mendel, W. M. (1976). *Schizophrenia: The experience and its treatment.* San Francisco: Jossey-Bass.

Mendlewicz, J., & Rainer, J. D. (1977). Adoption study supporting genetic transmission in manic-depressive illness. *Nature, 168,* 327–329.

Menkes, M. S., Matthews, K. A., Krantz, D. S., Lundberg, U., Mead, L., Qaqish, B., Liang, K. Y., Thomas, C. B., & Pearson, T. A. (1989). Cardiovascular reactivity to the cold pressor test as a predictor of hypertension. *Hypertension, 14,* 524–530.

Mental Health Services Administration, Office of Applied Studies. Preliminary estimates from the 1995 National Household Survey on Drug Abuse (1996, #18).

Merckelbach, H., de Jong, P. J., Muris, P., & van den Hout, M. (1996). The etiology of specific phobias: A review. *Clinical Psychology Review, 16,* 337–361.

Merikangus, K. R. (1990). Comorbidity for anxiety and depression: Review of family and genetic studies. In J. D. Maser & C. R. Cloninger (Eds.), *Comorbidity of mood and anxiety disorders.* Washington, DC: American Psychiatric Press.

Merikangus, K. R., & Angst, J. (1995). Comorbidity and social phobia: Evidence from clinical, epidemiologic, and genetic studies. *European Archives of Psychiatry and Clinical Neuroscience, 244,* 297–303.

Merritt, H. H. (1967). *A textbook of neurology* (4th ed.). Philadelphia: Lea & Febiger.

Merskey, H. (1995). The manufacture of personalities: The production of multiple personality disorder. In L. M. Cohen, J. N. Berzoff, & M. R. Elin (Eds.), *Dissociative identity disorder:*

Theoretical and treatment controversies (pp. 3–32). Northvale, NJ: Aronson.

Metalsky, G. I., Joiner, T. E., Jr., Hardin, T. S., & Abramson, L. Y. (1993). Depressive reactions to failure in a naturalistic setting: A test of the hopelessness and self-esteem theories of depression. *Journal of Abnormal Psychology, 102,* 101–109.

Metz, M. E., Pryor, J. L., Nesvacil, L. J., Abuzzhab, F., & Koznar, J. (1997). Premature ejaculation: A psychophysiological review. *Journal of Sex and Marital Therapy, 23,* 3–23.

Meyer, G. J. (1996). The Rorschach and MMPI: Toward a more scientifically differentiated understanding of cross-method assessment. *Journal of Personality Assessment, 67,* 558–578.

Meyer, G. J. (1997). On the integration of personality assessment methods: The Rorschach and MMPI. *Journal of Personality Assessment, 68,* 297–330.

Meyer, J. M. (1979). The theory of gender identity disorders. *Journal of the American Psychoanalytic Association, 30,* 381–418.

Mezzich, J. E., Fabrega, H., Coffman, G. A., & Haley, R. (1989). DSM-III disorders in a large sample of psychiatric patients: Frequency and specificity of diagnoses. *American Journal of Psychiatry, 146,* 212–219.

Michelson, L. K., & Marchione, K. (1991). Behavioral, cognitive, and pharmacological treatments of panic disorder with agoraphobia: Critique and synthesis. *Journal of Consulting and Clinical Psychology, 59,* 100–114.

Miklowitz, D. J., Goldstein, M. J., Doane, J. A., Neuchterlein, K. H., Strachan, A. M., Snyder, K. S., & Magana-Amato, A. (1989). Is expressed emotion an index of a transactional process? I. Parents' affective style. *Family Process, 22,* 153–167.

Miklowitz, D. J., Goldstein, M. J., & Nuechterlein, K. H. (1995). Verbal interactions in the families of schizophrenic and bipolar affective patients. *Journal of Abnormal Psychology, 104,* 268–276.

Miklowitz, D. J., Strachan, A. M., Goldstein, M. J., Doane, J. A., Snyder, K. S., Hogarty, G. E., & Falloon, I. R. H. (1986). Expressed emotion and communication deviance in the families of schizophrenics. *Journal of Abnormal Psychology, 95,* 60–66.

Miklowitz, D. J., Velligan, D. I., Goldstein, M. J., Nuechterlein, K. H., & Gitlin, M. J. (1991). Communication deviance in families of schizophrenic and manic patients. *Journal of Abnormal Psychology, 100,* 163–173.

Mikulincer, M., & Solomon, Z. (1988). Attributional style and combat-related posttraumatic stress disorder. *Journal of Abnormal Psychology, 97,* 308–313.

Milberg, W. (1996). Issues in the assessment of cognitive function in dementia. *Brain and Cognition, 31,* 114–132.

Miller, G. (1956). The magical number seven, plus or minus two: Some limits of our capacity for processing information. *Psychological Review, 63,* 81–97.

Miller, G. E., & Prinz, R. J. (1990). Enhancement of social learning family interventions for childhood conduct disorder. *Psychological Bulletin, 108,* 291–307.

Miller, H. L., Delgado, P. L., Salomon, R. M., Berman, R., Krystal, J. H., Heninger, G. R., & Charney, D. S. (1996). Clinical and biochemical effects of catecholamine depletion on antidepressant-induced remission of depression. *Archives of General Psychiatry, 53,* 117–128.

Miller, L. J., O'Connor, E., & DiPasquale, T. (1993). Patients' attitudes toward hallucinations. *American Journal of Psychiatry, 150,* 584–588.

Miller, M. B., Chapman, J. P., Chapman, L. J., & Collins, J. (1995). Task difficulty and cognitive deficits in schizophrenia. *Journal of Abnormal Psychology, 104,* 251–258.

Miller, N. E. (1969). Learning of visceral and glandular responses. *Science, 163,* 434–445.

Miller, N. E. (1972). Comments on strategy and tactics of research. In A. E. Bergin & H. H. Strupp (Eds.), *Changing frontiers in the science of psychotherapy.* New York: Aldine-Atherton.

Miller, S. D., & Triggiano, P. J. (1992). The psychophysiological investigation of multiple personality disorder: Review and update. *American Journal of Clinical Hypnosis, 35,* 47–61.

Miller, T. Q., Smith, T. W., Turner, C. W., Guijarro, M. L., & Hallet, A. J. (1996). A meta-analytic review of research on hostility and physical health. *Psychological Bulletin, 119,* 322–348.

Miller, W.R., & Rollnick, S. (1991). *Motivational interviewing: Preparing people to change addictive behavior.* New York: Guilford Press.

Millon, T. (1981). *Disorders of personality.* New York: Wiley.

Millon, T. (1994). *Millon Clinical Multiaxial Inventory—III Manual.* Minneapolis: National Computer Systems.

Millon, T., & Davis, R. D. (1996). *Disorders of personality. DSM-IV and beyond.* New York: Wiley.

Mindell, J. A., & Cashman, L. (1995). Sleep disorders. In A. R. Eisen, C. A. Kearney, & C. E. Schaefer (Eds.),

Clinical handbook of anxiety disorders in children and adolescents. Northvale, NJ: Aronson.

Mindus, P., & Jenike, M. A. (1992). Neurosurgical treatment of malignant obsessive compulsive disorder. *Psychiatric Clinics of North America, 15,* 921–938.

Minshew, N. (1991). Evidence of neural function in autism: Clinical and biological implications. *Pediatrics, 87 (Supplement),* 774–780.

Minshew, N. J., & Dombrowski, S. M. (1994). In vivo neuroanatomy of autism: Neuroimaging studies. In M. L. Bauman & T. L. Kemper (Eds.), *The neurobiology of autism.* Baltimore: Johns Hopkins University Press.

Minuchin, S. (1972). Structural family therapy. In G. Caplan (Ed.), *American handbook of psychiatry* (Vol. 2). New York: Basic Books.

Minuchin, S. (1974). *Families and family therapy.* Cambridge, MA: Harvard University Press.

Minuchin, S., Rosman, B. L., & Baker, L. (1978). *Psychosomatic families: Anorexia nervosa in context.* Cambridge, MA: Harvard University Press.

Mirsky, A. F., & Duncan, C. C. (1986). Etiology and expression of schizophrenia: Neurobiological and psychosocial factors. *Annual Review of Psychology, 37,* 291–319.

Mirsky, A. F., Kugelmass, S., Ingraham, L. J., Frenkel, E., & Nathan, M. (1995). Overview and summary: Twenty-five-year followup of high-risk children. *Schizophrenia Bulletin, 21,* 227–239.

Mischel, W. (1973). Toward a cognitive social learning reconceptualization of personality. *Psychological Review, 80,* 252–283.

Mischel, W. (1979). On the interface of cognition and personality: Beyond the person-situation debate. *American Psychologist, 34,* 740–754.

Mischel, W., & Peake, P. K. (1982). Beyond deja vu in the search for cross-situational consistency. *Psychological Review, 89,* 730–755.

Mitchell, J., McCauley, E., Burke, P. M., & Moss, S. J. (1988). Phenomenology of depression in children and adolescents. *Journal of the American Academy of Child and Adolescent Psychiatry, 27,* 12–20.

Mittelman, M. S., Ferris, S. H., Shulman, E., Steinberg, G., & Levin, B. (1996). A family intervention to delay nursing home placement of patients with Alzheimer's disease. *Journal of the American Medical Association, 276,* 1725–1731.

Mittleman, M., Ferris, S. H., Steinberg, G., Shulman, E., Mackell, J. A., Ambinder,

A., & Cohen, J. (1993). An intervention that delays institutionalization of Alzheimer's disease patients: Treatment of spouse-caregivers. *Gerontologist, 33,* 730–740.

Mittleman, M. A., Maclure, M., Sherwood, J. B., Mulry, R. P., Tofler, G. H., Jabobs, S. C., Friedman, R., Benson, H., & Muller, J. E. (1995). Triggering of acute myocardial infarction onset by episodes of anger. *Circulation, 92,* 1720–1725.

Moffitt, T. E. (1991). *Juvenile delinquency: Seed of a career in violent crime, just sowing wild oats—or both?* Paper presented at the Science and Public Policy Seminars of the Federation of Behavioral, Psychological, and Cognitive Sciences, Washington, DC.

Moffitt, T. E. (1993). Adolescence-limited and life-course-persistent antisocial behavior: A developmental taxonomy. *Psychological Review, 100,* 674–701.

Mogg, K., Bradley, B. P., Millar, N., & White, J. (1995). A follow-up study of cognitive bias in generalized anxiety disorder. *Behaviour Research and Therapy, 33,* 927–935.

Mogg, K., Mathews, A., & Weinman, J. (1989). Selective processing of threat cues in anxiety states: A replication. *Behavior Research and Therapy 27,* 317–320.

Mohr, J. W., Turner, R. E., & Jerry, M. B. (1964). *Pedophilia and exhibitionism.* Toronto: University of Toronto Press.

Mohs, R. C. (1995). Assessing cognitive function in schizophrenics and patients with Alzheimer's disease. *Schizophrenia Research, 17,* 115–121.

Monahan, J. (1981). *The clinical prediction of violent behavior.* Rockville, MD: National Institute of Mental Health.

Monahan, J. (1992). Mental disorder and violent behavior. *American Psychologist, 47,* 511–521.

Monahan, J. (1996). Violence prediction: The past twenty and the next twenty years. *Criminal Justice and Behavior, 23,* 107–120.

Monahan, J., & Steadman, H. (1994). Toward a rejuvenation of risk assessment research. In J. Monahan & H. Steadman (Eds.), *Violence and mental disorder: Developments in risk assessment.* Chicago: University of Chicago Press.

Money, J., Hampson, J. G., & Hampson, J. L. (1957). Imprinting and the establishment of the gender role. *Archives of Neurology and Psychiatry, 77,* 333–336.

Monroe, S. M., & Simons, A. D. (1991). Diathesis-stress theories in the context of life stress research: Implications for the depressive disorders. *Psychological Bulletin, 110,* 406–425.

Moore, J. (1985). *Roads to recovery.* New York: Guilford Press.

Moore, S., Donovan, B., Hudson, A., Dykstra, J., & Lawrence, J. (1993). Brief report: Evaluation of eight case studies of facilitated communication. *Journal of Autism and Developmental Disorders, 23.*

Mora, G. (1980). Mind-body concepts in the Middle Ages: Part II. The Moslem influence, the great theological systems and cultural attitudes toward the mentally ill in the late Middle Ages. *Journal of the History of the Behavioral Sciences, 16,* 58–72.

Moran, E. (1970). Varieties of pathological gambling. *British Journal of Psychiatry, 116,* 593–597.

Morey, L. (1988). The categorical representation of personality disorder: A cluster analysis of *DSM-III-R* personality features. *Journal of American Psychology, 97,* 314–321.

Morey, L. C. (1991). *The Personality Assessment Inventory Professional Manual.* Odessa, FL: Psychological Assessment Resources, Inc.

Morgan, G. D., Ashenberg, Z. S., & Fisher, E. B., Jr. (1988). Abstinence from smoking and the social environment. *Journal of Consulting and Clinical Psychology, 56,* 298–301.

Morgenstern, J., Labouvie, E., McCrady, B. S., Kahler, C. W., & Frey, R. M. (1997). Affiliation with Alcoholics Anonymous after treatment: A study of therapeutic effects and mechanisms of action. *Journal of Consulting and Clinical Psychology, 65,* 768–777.

Morris, G. H., & Meloy, J. R. (1993). Out of mind? Out of sight: The uncivil commitment of permanently incompetent criminal defendants. *University of California Davis Law Review, 27,* 1–23.

Morrison, R. L. (1991). Schizophrenia. In M. Hersen & S. M. Turner (Eds.), *Adult psychopathology and diagnosis* (2nd ed., pp. 149–169). New York: Wiley.

Morse, S. J. (1978). Law and mental health professionals: The limits of expertise. *Professional Psychology, 9,* 389–399.

Morse, S. J. (1982). A preference for liberty: The case against the involuntary commitment of the mentally disordered. *California Law Review, 70,* 55–106.

Morse, S. J. (1997, February 28). A verdict of guilty but mentally ill doesn't work medically or morally. *Philadelphia Inquirer,* p. A19.

Moscicki, E. K. (1995). Epidemiology of suicide. *International Psychogeriatrics, 7,* 137–148.

Moser, C., & Levitt, E. E. (1987). An exploratory-descriptive study of a sadomasochistically oriented sample.

Journal of Sex Research, 23(3), 322–337.

Mosley, T. H., Jr., Penizen, D. B., Johnson, C. A., et al. (1991). Time-series analysis of stress and headache. *Cephalalgia, 11,* 306–307.

Mowrer, O. H. (1948). Learning theory and the neurotic paradox. *American Journal of Orthopsychiatry, 18,* 571–610.

Mowrer, O. H., & Mowrer, W. M. (1938). Enuresis: A method for its study and treatment. *American Journal of Orthopsychiatry, 8,* 436–459.

Moyles, E. W., & Wolins, M. (1971). Group care and intellectual development. *Developmental Psychology, 4,* 370–380.

Mrazek, P. J., & Haggerty, R. J. (1994). *Reducing risk for mental disorders: Frontiers for preventive intervention research.* Washington, DC: National Academy Press.

Muesser, K. T., Valenti-Hein, D., & Yarnold, P. R. (1987). Dating-skills groups for the developmentally disabled. *Behavior Modification, 11*(2), 200–228.

Mulvey, E. P., & Wooland, J. L. (1997). Themes for consideration in future research on prevention and intervention with antisocial behaviors. In D. M. Stoff, J. Breiling, & J. D. Maser (Eds.), *Handbook of antisocial behavior* (pp. 454–462). New York: Wiley.

Murphy, J. M., Gatto, G. J., Waller, M. B., McBride, W. J., Lumeng, L., & Li, T.-K. (1986). Effects of scheduled access on ethanol intake by the alcohol-preferring P line of rats. *Alcohol, 3,* 331–336.

Murphy, W. D. (1990). Assessment and modification of cognitive distortions in sex offenders. In W. L. Marshall, D. R. Laws, & H. E. Barbaree (Eds.), *The handbook of sexual assault: Issues, theories, and treatment of the offender* (pp. 331–342). New York: Plenum Press.

Murray, C. J. L., & Lopez, A. D. (Eds.). (1996). *The global burden of disease.* Geneva, Switzerland: The Harvard School of Public Health on behalf of The World Health Organization and The World Bank.

Myers, J. K., & Bean, L. L. (1968). *A decade later: A follow-up of social class and mental illness.* New York: Wiley.

Myers, P. I., & Hammill, D. D. (1990). *Learning disabilities: Basic concepts, assessment practices, and instructional strategies* (4th ed.). Austin, TX: Pro-Ed.

Nagayama, G. C., & Barongan, C. (1997). Prevention of sexual aggression: Sociocultural risk and protective factors. *American Psychologist, 52,* 5–14.

Nathan, P. E., Marlatt, G. A., & Loberg, T. (Eds.). (1978). *Alcoholism: New directions in behavioral research and treatment.* New York: Plenum Press.

National Center for Education Statistics. (1989). *Digest of education statistics.* Washington, DC: U.S. Department of Education, Office of Education Research and Improvement.

National Center for Health Statistics. (1993). *Advance report of final mortality statistics, 1990* (Monthly Vital Statistics Report, Vol. 41, No. 7, Suppl.). Hyattsville, MD: Public Health Service.

National Institute of Mental Health. (1985). *Electroconvulsive therapy: Consensus development conference statement.* Bethesda, MD: Office of Medical Applications of Research.

National Institute on Drug Abuse. (1989). *1988 National Household Survey on Drug Abuse.* Rockville, MD: NIDA.

National Institute on Drug Abuse. (1997). *National household survey on drug abuse: Population estimates.* Rockville, MD: NIDA.

Needles, D. J., & Abramson, L. Y. (1990). Positive life events, attributional style, and hopefulness: Testing a model of recovery from depression. *Journal of Abnormal Psychology, 99,* 156–165.

Nelson, J. C., & Davis, J. M. (1997). DST studies in psychotic depression: A meta-analysis. *American Journal of Psychiatry, 154,* 1497–1503.

Nemeroff, C. B., Krishnan, R. R., Reed, D., Leder, R., Beam, C., & Dunnick, N. R. (1992). Adrenal gland enlargement in major depression: A computed tomographic study. *Archives of General Psychiatry, 49,* 384–387.

Nesson, C. (1982, July 1). A needed verdict: Guilty but insane. *The New York Times,* p. A19.

Nestor, P. G., Kimble, M. O., O'Donnell, B. F., Smith, L., Niznikiewicz, M., Shenton, M. E., & McCarley, R. W. (1997). Aberrant semantic activation in schizophrenia: A neurophysiological study. *American Journal of Psychiatry, 154,* 640–646.

Neugebauer, R. (1978). Treatment of the mentally ill in medieval and early modern England: A reappraisal. *Journal of the History of the Behavioral Sciences, 14,* 158–169.

Neumeister, A., Praschak-Rieder, N., NeBelmann, B., Rao, M. L., Gluck, J., & Kasper, S. (1997). Effects of tryptophan depletion on drug-free patients with seasonal affective disorder during a stable response to bright light therapy. *Archives of General Psychiatry, 54,* 133–138.

Newberger, C. M., Melnicore, L. H., & Newberger, E. H. (1986). *The American family at crisis: Implications for children*

(Vol. 16, No. 12). Chicago: Year Book Medical.

Newman, J. P. (1997). Conceptual models of the nervous system: Implications for antisocial behavior. In D. M. Stoff, J. Breiling, & J. D. Maser (Eds.), *Handbook of antisocial behavior* (pp. 324–335). New York: Wiley.

Newman, S. C., & Bland, R. C. (1994). Life events and the 1-year prevalence of major depressive episode, generalized anxiety disorder, and panic disorder in a community sample. *Comprehensive Psychiatry, 35,* 76–82.

Ney, P. G., Fung, T., & Wickett, A. R. (1992). Causes of child abuse and neglect. *Canadian Journal of Psychiatry, 37,* 401–405.

Niccols, G. A. (1994). Fetal alcohol syndrome: Implications for psychologists. *Clinical Psychology Review, 14,* 91–111.

Nichols, M. P., & Schwartz, R. C. (1991). *Family therapy: Concepts and methods* (2nd ed.). Boston: Allyn and Bacon.

Nicholson, I. R., & Neufeld, R. W. J. (1993). Classification of the schizophrenias according to symptomatology: A two-factor model. *Journal of Abnormal Psychology, 102,* 259–270.

Nicolosi, A., Molinari, S., Musicco, M., Saracco, A., Ziliani, N., & Lazzarin, A. (1991). Positive modification of injecting behavior among intravenous heroin users from Milan and northern Italy, 1987–1989. *British Journal of Addiction, 86,* 91–102.

Nielson, P. E. (1960). A study in transsexualism. *Psychiatric Quarterly, 34,* 203–235.

Nietupski, J., Hamre-Nietupski, S., VanderHart, N.S., & Fishback, K. (1996). Employer perceptions of the benefits and concerns of supported employment. *Education and Training in Mental Retardation and Developmental Disabilities, 31,* 310–323.

Nietzel, M. T., & Harris, M. J. (1990). Relationship of dependency and achievement/autonomy to depression. *Clinical Psychology Review, 10,* 279–297.

Nigg, J. T., & Goldsmith, H. H. (1994). Genetics of personality disorders: Perspectives from personality and psychopathology research. *Psychological Bulletin, 115,* 346–380.

NIH Technology Assessment Panel (1996). Integration of Behavioral and Relaxation Approaches into the Treatment of Chronic Pain and Insomnia. *Journal of the American Medical Association, 276,* 313–318.

Nisbett, R. E. (1968). Taste, deprivation, and weight determinants of eating behavior. *Journal of Personality and Social Psychology, 10,* 107–116.

Nisbett, R. E., & Ross, L. (1980). *Human inference: Strategies and shortcomings of social judgment.* Englewood Cliffs, NJ: Prentice-Hall.

Nisbett, R. E., & Wilson, T. D. (1977). Telling more than we can know: Verbal reports on mental processes. *Psychological Review, 84,* 231–259.

Niznikiewicz, M. A., O'Donnell, B. F., Nestor, P. G., Smith, L., Law, S., Karapelou, M., Shenton, M. E., & McCarley, R. W. (1997). ERP assessment of visual and auditory language processing in schizophrenia. *Journal of Abnormal Psychology, 106,* 85–94.

Nolen-Hoeksema, S. (1987). Sex differences in unipolar depression: Evidence and theory. *Psychological Bulletin, 101,* 259–282.

Nolen-Hoeksema, S. (1991). Responses to depression and their effects on the duration of depressive episodes. *Journal of Abnormal Psychology, 100,* 569–582.

Nolen-Hoeksema, S., & Girgus, J. S. (1994). The emergence of gender differences in depression during adolescence. *Psychological Bulletin, 115,* 424–443.

Nolen-Hoeksema, S., Girgus, J. S., & Seligman, M. E. P. (1992). Predictors and consequences of childhood depressive symptoms: A 5-year longitudinal study. *Journal of Abnormal Psychology, 101,* 405–422.

Nopoulos, P., Torres, I., Flaum, M., Andreason, N. C., Ehrhardt, J. C., & Yuh, W. T. C. (1995). Brain morphology in first-episode schizophrenia. *American Journal of Psychiatry, 152,* 1721–1723.

Nopoulos, P., Flaum, M., & Andreason, N. C. (1997). Sex differences in brain morphology in schizophrenia. *American Journal of Psychiatry, 154,* 1648–1654.

Nordquist, V. M., & Wahler, R. G. (1973). Naturalistic treatment of an autistic child. *Journal of Applied Behavior Analysis, 6,* 79–87.

Nordstrom, A. L., Farde, L., Nyberg, S., Karlsson, P., Halldin, C., & Sedvall, G. (1995). D_1, D_2, and 5-HT_2 receptor occupancy in relation to clozapine serum concentration: A PET study of schizophrenic patients. *American Journal of Psychiatry, 152,* 1444–1449.

Norman, R. M., & Malla, A. K. (1993a). Stressful life events and schizophrenia: I. A review of the research. *British Journal of Psychiatry, 162,* 161–166.

Norman, R. M., & Malla, A. K. (1993b). Stressful life events and schizophrenia: II. Conceptual and methodological issues. *British Journal of Psychiatry, 162,* 167–174.

Norris, F. H. (1992). Epidemiology of trauma: Frequency and impact of different potentially traumatic events on different demographic groups. *Journal of Consulting and Clinical Psychology, 60,* 409–418.

Novick, D. M., Haverkos, H. W., & Teller, D. W. (1997). The medically ill substance abuser. In J. H. Lowinson, P. Ruiz, R. B. Millman, & J. G. Langrod (Eds.), *Substance abuse: A comprehensive textbook* (pp. 534–551). Baltimore: Williams & Wilkins.

Noyes, R., Jr., Kathol, R. G., Fisher, M. M., Phillips, B. M., Suelzer, M. T., & Woodman, C. L. (1994). Psychiatric comorbidity among patients with hypochondriasis. *General Hospital Psychiatry, 16,* 78–87.

Noyes, R., Jr., Woodman, C., Garvey, M. J., Cook, B. L., Suelzer, M., Clancy, J., & Anderson, D. J. (1992). Generalized anxiety disorder vs. panic disorder: Distinguishing characteristics and patterns of comorbidity. *Journal of Nervous and Mental Disease, 180,* 369–379.

Nuechterlein, K. H., & Dawson, M. E. (1984a). A heuristic vulnerability/stress model of schizophrenic episodes. *Schizophrenia Bulletin, 10,* 300–312.

Nuechterlein, K. H., & Dawson, M. E. (1984b). Information processing and attentional functioning in the developmental course of schizophrenic disorders. *Schizophrenia Bulletin, 10,* 160–203.

Neuchterlein, K. H., Dawson, M. E., Gitlin, M., Ventura, J., Goldstein, M. J., Snyder, K. S., Yee, C. M., & Mintz, J. (1992). Developmental processes in schizophrenic disorders: Longitudinal studies of vulnerability and stress. *Schizophrenia Bulletin, 18,* 387–425.

Nunes, D. (1975, September 15). The anguish behind the three faces of Eve. *New York Post,* pp. 4, 26.

Nunnally, J. (1978). *Psychometric theory* (2nd ed.). New York: McGraw-Hill.

Nutt, D., & Lawson, C. (1992). Panic attacks: A neurochemical overview of models and mechanisms. *British Journal of Psychiatry, 160,* 165–178.

Nyhan, W. L., & Haas, R. (1993). Inborn errors of amino acid metabolism and transport. In R. N. Rosenberg, S. B. Prusiner, S. DiMauro, R. L. Barchi, & L. M. Kunkel (Eds.), *The molecular and genetic basis of neurological disease* (p. 151). Boston: Butterworth-Heinemann.

O'Brien, C. P., Volpicelli, L. A., & Volpicelli, J. R. (1996). Naltrexone in the treatment of alcoholism: A clinical review. *Alcohol, 13,* 35–39.

O'Connor v. Donaldson, 95 S. Ct. 2486 (1975).

O'Donohue, W., & Elliott, A. (1992). The current status of posttraumatic stress disorder as a diagnostic category: Problems and proposals. *Journal of Traumatic Stress, 5,* 421–439.

O'Farrell, T., & Murphy C. M. (1995). Marital violence before and after alcoholism treatment. *Journal of Consulting and Clinical Psychology, 63,* 256–262.

Oesterhed, J. D., McKenna, M. S., & Gould, N. B. (1987). Group psychotherapy for bulimia: A critical review. *International Journal of Group Psychotherapy, 37,* 163–184.

Offord, D. R. (1997). Bridging development, prevention, and policy. In D. M. Stoff, J. Breiling, & J. D. Maser (Eds.), *Handbook of antisocial behavior* (pp. 357–364). New York: Wiley.

Okazaki, S., & Sue, S. (1995). Methodological issues in assessment research with ethnic minorities. *Psychological Assessment, 7,* 367–375.

Olds, D., & Henderson, C. (1989). The prevention of child maltreatment. In D. Cicchetti & V. Carlson (Eds.), *Child maltreatment* (pp. 722–763). New York: Cambridge University Press.

O'Leary, K. D., Heyman, R. E., & Neidig, P. H. (1997). *Treatment of wife abuse: A comparison of gender specific and conjoint treatments.* Paper presented at the Fifth International Conference on Family Violence Research, July 1997, Durham, NH.

O'Leary, K. D., & Wilson, G. T. (1975). *Behavior therapy—application and outcome.* Englewood Cliffs, NJ: Prentice-Hall.

Olfson, M., & Mechanic, D. (1996). Mental disorders in public, private nonprofit, and proprietary general hospitals. *American Journal of Psychiatry, 153,* 1613–1619.

Olin, S. S., & Mednick, S. A. (1996). Risk factors of psychosis: Identifying vulnerable populations premorbidly. *Schizophrenia Bulletin, 22,* 223–240.

Ollendick, T. H., Mattis, S. G., & King, N. J. (1994). Panic in children and adolescents: A review. *Journal of Child Psychology and Psychiatry, 35,* 113–134.

Olney, J. W., & Farber, N. B. (1995). Glutamate receptor dysfunction and schizophrenia. *Archives of General Psychiatry, 52,* 998–1007.

Op den Velde, W., Hovens, J. E., Aarts, P. G. H., Frey-Wouters, E., Falger, P. R. J., Van Duijn, H., & De Groen, J. H. M. (1996). Prevalence and course of posttraumatic stress disorder in Dutch veterans of the civilian resistance during World War II: An overview. *Psychological Reports, 78,* 519–529.

Oren, D. A., & Rosenthal, N. E. (1992). Seasonal affective disorders. In E. S. Paykel (Ed.), *Handbook of affective disorders* (2nd ed., pp. 551–568). New York: Guilford Press.

Osgood, C., Luria, Z., Jeans, R., & Smith, S. (1976). The three faces of Evelyn: A case report. *Journal of Abnormal Psychology, 85,* 247–286.

Otto, M. W., Pollack, M. H., Sachs, G. S., Reiter, S. R., Meltzer-Brody, S., & Rosenbaum, J. F. (1993). Discontinuation of benzodiazepine treatment: Efficacy of cognitive-behavioral therapy for patients with panic disorder. *American Journal of Psychiatry, 150,* 1485–1490.

Ouimette, P. C., Finney, J. W., & Moos, R. H. (1997). Twelve-step and cognitive behavioral treatment for substance abuse: A comparison of treatment effectiveness. *Journal of Consulting and Clinical Psychology, 65,* 220–240.

Overholser, J., Evans, S., & Spirito, A. (1990). Sex differences and their relevance to primary prevention of adolescent suicide. *Death Studies, 14,* 391–402.

Overton, D. A. (1966). State-dependent learning produced by depressant and atropine-like drugs. *Psychopharmacologia, 10,* 6–31.

Overton, D. A. (1984). State dependent learning and drug discriminations. In J. L. Iverson, S. D. Iverson, & S. H. Snyder (Eds.), *Handbook of psychopharmacology* (Vol. 18, pp. 59–127). New York: Plenum Press.

Ozonoff, S. (1995). Executive functions in autism. In E. Schopler & G. Mesibov (Eds.), *Learning and cognition in autism* (pp. 199–219). New York: Plenum Press.

Ozonoff, S., & Miller, J. N. (1995). Teaching theory of mind: A new approach to social skills training for individuals with autism. *Journal of Autism and Developmental Disorders, 25,* 415–433.

Palfai, T. P., Monti, P. M., Colby, S. M., & Rohsennow, D. J. (1997). Effects of suppresing the urge to drink on the accessibility of alcohol outcome expectancies. *Behavior Research and Therapy, 35,* 59–65.

Papero, D.V. (1995). Bowen family systems and marriage. In N. S. Jacobson, A. S. Gurman, et al. (Eds.), *Clinical handbook of couple therapy* (pp. 11–30). New York: Guilford Press.

Pariante, C. M., Nemeroff, C. B., & Miller, A. H. (1997). In D. L. Dunner (Ed.), *Current psychiatric therapy II* (pp. 44–51). Philadelphia: W. B. Saunders Co.

Parker, G., & Lipscombe, P. (1980). The relevance of early parental experiences to adult dependency, hypochondriasis and utilization of primary physicians. *British Journal of Medical Psychology, 53,* 355–363.

Parker, J. G., & Asher, S. R. (1987). Peer relations and later personal adjustment: Are low-accepted children at risk? *Psychological Bulletin, 102,* 357–389.

Parker, K. C. H., Hanson, R. K., & Hunsley, J. (1988). MMPI, Rorschach, and WAIS: A meta-analytic comparison of reliability, stability, and validity. *Psychological Bulletin, 103,* 367–373.

Parnas, J., Cannon, T. D., Jacobsen, B., Schulsinger, H., Schulsinger, F., & Mednick, S. A. (1993). Lifetime *DSM-III-R* diagnostic outcomes in the offspring of schizophrenic mothers: Results from the Copenhagen high-risk study. *Archives of General Psychiatry, 50,* 707–714.

Patterson, G. R. (1982). *A social learning approach: Vol. 3. Coercive family processes.* Eugene, OR: Castilia.

Patterson, G. R. (1993). Orderly change in a stable world: The antisocial trait as a chimera. *Journal of Consulting and Clinical Psychology, 61,* 911–919.

Patterson, G. R., & Hops, H. (1972). Coercion: A game for two: Intervention techniques for marital conflict. In R. Ulrich & P. Mountjoy (Eds.), *The experimental analysis of social behavior.* New York: Appleton-Century-Crofts.

Patton, R. B., & Sheppard, J. A. (1956). Intercranial tumors found at autopsy in mental patients. *American Journal of Psychiatry, 113,* 319–324.

Patton, W., & Mannison, M. (1995). Sexual coercion in dating situations among university students. *Australian Journal of Psychology, 47,* 66–72.

Paul, G. L., & Lentz, R. J. (1977). *Psychosocial treatment of chronic mental patients: Milieu versus social-learning programs.* Cambridge, MA: Harvard University Press.

Paul, W. M., Gonsiorek, J. C., & Hotvedt, M. E. (Eds.). (1982). *Homosexuality.* Beverly Hills, CA: Sage.

Pauls, D. L., Alsobrook, J. P., II, Goodman, W., Rasmussen, S., & Leckman, J. F. (1995). A family study of obsessive-compulsive disorder. *American Journal of Psychiatry, 152,* 76–84.

Paykel, E. S. (1979). Recent life events in the development of the depressive disorders. In R. A. Depue (Ed.), *The psychobiology of the depressive disorders.* New York: Academic Press.

Paykel, E. S., & Cooper, Z. (1992). Life events and social stress. In E. S. Paykel (Ed.), *Handbook of affective disorders.* (2nd ed., pp. 149–170). New York: Guilford Press.

Pearlin, L. I., Mullan, J. T., Semple, S. J., & Skaff, M. M. (1990). Caregiving and the stress process: An overview of concepts and their measures. *Gerontologist, 30,* 583–594.

Pearson, D. A., Doyle, M. D., Pickering, L. K., & Ortegon, J. (1996). Pediatric HIV infection: A review of epidemiology, clinical manifestations, and current intervention. *Journal of Developmental and Physical Disabilities, 8,* 179–210.

Peck, C. P. (1986). A public mental health issue. Risk-taking behavior and compulsive gambling. *American Psychologist, 41,* 461–465.

Pelham, W. E., Gnagy, E. M., Greenslade, K. E., & Milich, R. (1992). Teacher ratings of *DSM-III-R* symptoms for the disruptive behavior disorders. *Journal of the American Academy of Child and Adolescent Psychiatry, 31,* 210–218.

Penick, E. C., Powell, B. J., Campbell, J., Liskow-Barry, I., et al. (1996). Pharmacological treatment for antisocial personality disorder alcoholics: A preliminary study. *Alcoholism: Clinical and Experimental Research 20,* 477–484.

Penn, D. L., Corrigan, P. W., Bentall, R. P., Racenstein, J. M., & Newman, L. (1997). Social cognition in schizophrenia. *Psychological Bulletin, 121,* 114–132.

Penn, D. L., & Mueser, K. T. (1996). Research update on the psychosocial treatment of schizophrenia. *American Journal of Psychiatry, 153,* 607–617.

Pennebaker, J. W. (1990). *Opening up: The healing power of confiding in others.* New York: Morrow.

Pennebaker, J. W. (1993). Putting stress into words: Health, linguistic and therapeutic implications. *Behavior Research and Therapy, 31,* 539–548.

Pennebaker, J. W., Kiecolt-Glaser, J., & Glaser, R. (1988). Disclosure of traumas and immune function: Health implications for psychotherapy. *Journal of Consulting and Clinical Psychology, 56,* 239–245.

Pennebaker, J. W., & Watson, D. (1991). The psychology of somatic symptoms. In L. J. Kirmayer & J. M. Robbins (Eds.), *Current concepts of somatization: Research and clinical perspectives* (pp. 21–35). Washington, DC: American Psychiatric Press.

Perlin, M. L. (1993–1994). Hospitalized patients and the right to sexual interaction: Beyond the last frontier? *NYU Review of Law and Social Change, 20,* 517–547.

Perry, S., Frances, A., & Clarkin, J. (1990). *A DSM-III-R casebook of treatment selection.* New York: Brunner/Mazel.

Perry, W., & Braff, D. L. (1994). Information-processing deficits and thought disorder in schizophrenia. *American Journal of Psychiatry, 151,* 363–367.

Perske, R. (1973). About sexual development. *Mental Retardation, 11,* 6–8.

Peterson, G., & Putnam, F. W. (1994). Preliminary results of the field trial of proposed criteria for Dissociative Disorder of Childhood. *Dissociation, 7,* 212–220.

Pfäfflin, F. (1992). Regrets after sex reassignment surgery. In W. O. Bockting & E. Coleman (Eds.), *Gender dysphoria: Interdisciplinary approaches in clinical management.* Binghamton, NY: Haworth Press.

Phillips, K. A. (1996a). *The broken mirror: Understanding and treating body dysmorphic disorder.* New York: Oxford University Press.

Phillips, K. A. (1996b). Pharmacologic treatment of body dysmorphic disorder. *Psychopharmacology Bulletin, 32,* 597–605.

Phillips, K. A., Atala, K. D., & Albertini, R. S. (1995). Case study: Body dysmorphic disorder in adolescents. *Journal of the American Academy of Child and Adolescent Psychiatry, 34,* 1216–1220.

Phillips, K. A., McElroy, S. L., Hudson, J. I., & Pope, H. G., Jr. (1995). Body dysmorphic disorder: An obsessive-compulsive spectrum disorder, a form of affective spectrum disorder, or both? *Journal of Clinical Psychiatry, 56,* 41–51.

Pickar, D. (1988). Perspectives on a time-dependent model of neuroleptic action. *Schizophrenia Bulletin, 14,* 255–265.

Pickar, D., Su, T. P., Weinberger, D. R., Coppola, R., Malhotra, A. K., Knable, M. B., Lee, K. S., Gorey, J., Bartko, J. J., Breier, A., & Hsiao, J. (1996). Individual variation in D_2 dopamine receptor occupancy in clozapine-treated patients. *American Journal of Psychiatry, 153,* 1571–1578.

Pierce, J. W., & Wardle, J. (1993). Self-esteem, parental appraisal and body size in children. *Journal of Child Psychology and Psychiatry, 34,* 1125–1136.

Pigott, T. A. (1996). OCD: Where the serotonin selectivity story begins. *Journal of Clinical Psychiatry, 57,* 11–20.

Pilowsky, I. (1994). Abnormal illness behaviour: A 25th anniversary review. *Australian and New Zealand Journal of Psychiatry, 28,* 566–573.

Pinel, P. (1967). *A treatise on insanity* (D. D. Davis, Trans.). New York: Hafner. Original work published 1801.

Pines, M. (1982a, June). Infant-stim. It's changing the lives of handicapped kids. *Psychology Today,* pp. 48–52.

Pines, M. (1982b, April 16). Recession is linked to far-reaching psychological harm. *The New York Times*, p. C1.

Pini, S., Cassano, G. B., Simonini, E., Savino, M., Russo, A., & Montgomery, S. A. (1997). Prevalence of anxiety disorders comorbidity in bipolar depression, unipolar depression and dysthymia. *Journal of Affective Disorders, 42*, 145–153.

Piotrowski, C., Keller, J. W., & Ogawa, T. (1993). Projective techniques: An international perspective. *Psychological Reports, 72*, 179–182.

Piper, A., Jr. (1994a). Multiple personality disorder. *British Journal of Psychiatry, 164*, 600–612.

Piper, A., Jr. (1994b). Treatment for multiple personality disorder: At what cost? *American Journal of Psychotherapy, 48*, 392–400.

Pithers, W. D., & Cumming, G. F. (1989). *Can relapse be prevented? Initial outcome data from the Vermont treatment program for sexual aggressors.* New York: Guilford Press.

Pitman, R. K. (1988). Post-traumatic stress disorder, conditioning, and network theory. *Psychiatric Annals, 18*, 182–189.

Pitman, R. K. (1989). Editorial: Post-traumatic stress disorder, hormones, and memory. *Biological Psychiatry, 26*, 221–223.

Pitman, R. K., Orr, S. P., Forgue, D. F., Altman, B., de Jong, J. B., & Herz, L. R. (1990). Pychophysiologic responses to combat imagery of Vietnam veterans with posttraumatic stress disorder versus other anxiety disorders. *Journal of Abnormal Psychology, 99*, 49–54.

Plomin, R., & Daniels, D. (1986). Genetics and shyness. In W. H. Jones, J. M. Cheek, & S. R. Briggs (Eds.), *Shyness: Perspectives on research and treatment* (pp. 63–90). New York: Plenum Press.

Plomin, R., Owen, M. J., & McGuffin, P. (1994). The genetic basis of complex human behaviors. *Science, 264*, 1733–1739.

Plomin, R., & Rende, R. (1991). Human behavioral genetics. *Annual Review of Psychology, 42*, 161–190.

Polaschek, D. L. L., Ward, T., & Hudson, S. M. (1997). Rape and rapists: Theory and treatment. *Clinical Psychology Review, 17*, 117–144.

Polivy, J., & Herman, C. P. (1985). Dieting and binging: A causal analysis. *American Psychologist, 40*, 193–201.

Pollitt, E. (1994). Poverty and child development: Relevance of research in developing countries to the United States. *Child Development, 65*, 283–295.

Pollock, C., & Andrews, G. (1989). Defense styles associated with specific anxiety disorders. *American Journal of Psychiatry, 146*, 1500–1502.

Pope, H. G., & Katz, D. L. (1990). *Journal of Clinical Psychology, 51.*

Portenoy, R. K., & Payne, R. (1997). Acute and chronic pain. In J. H. Lowinson, P. Ruiz, R. B. Millman, & J. G. Langrod (Eds.), *Substance abuse: A comprehensive textbook* (pp. 563–591). Baltimore: Williams & Wilkins.

Portin, P., & Alanen, Y. O. (1997). A critical review of genetic studies of schizophrenia. I. Epidemiological and brain studies. *Acta Psychiatrica Scandinavica, 95*, 1–5.

Potter, L. B., & Mercy, J. A. (1997). Public health perspective on interpersonal violence among youths in the United States. In D. M. Stoff, J. Breiling, & J. D. Maser (Eds.), *Handbook of antisocial behavior* (pp. 3–21). New York: Wiley.

Prasher, V. P., & Chung, M. C. (1996). Causes of age-related decline in adaptive behavior of adults with Down syndrome: Differential diagnoses of dementia. *American Journal on Mental Retardation, 101*, 175–183.

Preu, P. W. (1944). The concept of the psychopathic personality. In J. McV. Hunt (Ed.), *Personality and the behavior disorders* (Vol. 2). New York: Ronald Press.

Pribor, E. F., Yutzy, S. H., Dean, J. T., & Wetzel, R. D. (1993). Briquet's syndrome, dissociation, and abuse. *American Journal of Psychiatry, 150*, 1507–1511.

Price, C., & Cuellar, I. (1981). Effects of language and related variables on the expression of psychopathology of Mexican Americans. *Hispanic Journal of Behavioral Sciences, 3*, 145–160.

Price, J., & Hess, N. C. (1979). *Australian and New Zealand Journal of Psychiatry, 13*, 63–66.

Price, R. H. (1978). *Abnormal behavior: Perspectives in conflict* (2nd ed.). New York: Holt, Rinehart and Winston.

Price, R. H., van Ryn, M., & Vinokur, A. D. (1992). Impact of a preventive job search intervention on likelihood of depression among the unemployed. *Journal of Health and Social Behavior, 33*, 158–167.

Prieto, S. L., Cole, D. A., & Tageson, C. W. (1992). Depressive self-schemas in clinic and nonclinic children. *Cognitive Therapy and Research, 16*, 521–534.

Prince, M. (1905). *The dissociation of personality.* New York: Longman.

Prince, S. E., & Jacobson, N. S. (1995a). Couple and family therapy for depression. In E. E. Beckham & W. R. Leber (Eds.), *Handbook of depression* (pp. 404–424). New York: Guilford Press.

Prince, S. E., & Jacobson, N. S. (1995b). A review and evaluation of marital and family therapies for affective disorders. *Journal of Marital and Family Therapy, 21*, 377–401.

Pring, L., Hermelin, B., & Heavey, L. (1995). Savants, segments, art and autism. *Journal of Child Psychology and Psychiatry, 36*, 1065–1076.

Polloway, E. A., Smith, J. D., Patton, J. R., & Smith, T. E. C. (1996). Historic changes in mental retardation and developmental disabilities. *Education and Training in Mental Retardation and Developmental Disabilities, 31*, 3–12.

Project MATCH Research Group. (1997). Matching alcoholism treatments to client heterogeneity: Project MATCH post-treatment drinking outcomes. *Journal of Studies on Alcohol, 58*, 7–29.

Prouty, G. (1976). Pre-therapy—a method of treating preexpressive psychotic and retarded patients. *Psychotherapy: Theory, Research, and Practice, 13*, 290–294.

Provins, K. A. (1997). Handedness and speech: A critical reappraisal of the role of genetic and environmental factors in the cerebral lateralization of function. *Psychological Review, 104*, 554–571.

Purba, J. S., Hoogendijk, W. J. G., Hofman, M. A., & Swaab, D. F. (1996). Increased number of vasopressin- and oxytocin-expressing neurons in the paraventricular nucleus of the hypothalamus in depression. *Archives of General Psychiatry, 53*, 137–143.

Putnam, F. W. (1989). *Diagnosis and treatment of multiple personality disorder.* New York: Guilford Press.

Putnam, F. W., Guroff, J. J., Silberman, E. K., Barban, L., & Post, R. M. (1986). The clinical phenomenology of multiple personality disorder: Review of 100 recent cases. *Journal of Clinical Psychiatry, 47*, 285–293.

Putnam, F. W., & Loewenstein, R. J. (1993). Treatment of multiple personality disorder: A survey of current practices. *American Journal of Psychiatry, 150*, 1048–1052.

Pykett, I. L. (1982). NMR imaging in medicine. *Scientific American, 246*, 78–88.

Quindlen, A. (1994, April 30). Public and private: Second-stage smoke. *The New York Times*, p. 23.

Quinsey, V. L., Rice, M. E., & Harris, G. T. (1995). Actuarial prediction of sexual recidivism. *Journal of Interpersonal Violence, 10*, 85–105.

Rabinowicz, E. F., Opler L. A., Owen, D. R., & Knight, R. A. (1996). Dot enumeration perceptual organization task (DEPOT): Evidence for a short-term visual memory deficit in schizophrenia. *Journal of Abnormal Psychology, 105,* 336–348.

Rabkin, J. G., Williams, J. B., Remien, R. H., Goetz, R., Kertzner, R., & Gorman. (1991). Depression, distress, lymphocyte subsets, and human immunodeficiency virus symptoms on two occasions in HIV-positive homosexual men. *Archives of General Psychiatry, 48,* 111–119.

Rachman, S. J., & Hodgson, R. J. (1980). *Obsessions and compulsions.* Englewood Cliffs, NJ: Prentice-Hall

Rachman, S., Lopatka, C., & Levitt, K. (1988). Experimental analyses of panic—II. Panic patients. *Behaviour Research and Therapy, 26,* 33–40.

Rack, P. (1982). *Race, culture, and mental disorder.* London: Tavistock Publications.

Rada, R. T. (1978). Psychological factors in rapist behavior. In R. T. Rada (Ed.), *Clinical aspects of the rapist.* New York: Grune & Stratton.

Ragland, D. R., & Brand, R. J. (1988). Type A behavior and mortality from coronary heart disease. *New England Journal of Medicine, 318,* 65–69.

Raguram, R., Weiss, M. G., Channabasavanna, S. M., & Devins, G. M. (1996). Stigma, depression, and somatization in South India. *American Journal of Psychiatry, 153,* 1043–1049.

Raiche, M. E. (1994). Visualizing the mind. *Scientific American, 270*(4), 58–64.

Raine, A. (1997). Antisocial behavior and psychophysiology: A biosocial perspective and a pre-frontal dysfunction hypothesis. In D. M. Stoff, J. Breiling, & J. D. Maser, (Eds.), *Handbook of antisocial behavior* (pp. 289–304). New York: Wiley.

Raine, A., Brennan, P., Mednick, B., & Mednick, S. A. (1996). High rates of violence, crime, academic problems, and behavioral problems in males with both early neuromotor deficits and unstable family environments. *Archives of General Psychiatry, 53,* 544–549.

Raine, A., Brennan, P., & Mednick, S. A. (1997). The interaction between birth complications and early maternal rejection in predisposing to adult violence: Specificity to serious, early onset violence. *American Journal of Psychiatry, 154,* 1265–1271.

Raine, A., & Buchsbaum, M. (1996). Violence, brain imaging, and neuropsychology. In D. M. Stoff & R. B. Cairns (Eds.), *Aggression and violence: Genetic, neurobiological, and biosocial perspectives.* Mahwah, NJ: Erlbaum.

Raine, A., Venables, P., & Mednick, S. A. (1997). Low resting heart rate at age 3 years predisposed to aggression at 11 years: Evidence from the Mauritius child health project. *Journal of the American Academy of Child Adolescent Psychiatry, 36.*

Raine, A., Venables, P., & Williams, M. (1995). High autonomic arousal and electrodermal orienting at age 15 years as protective factors against criminal behavior at age 29 years. *American Journal of Psychiatry, 152,* 1595–1600.

Rapaport, D., Gill, M., & Schaefer, R. (1968). *Diagnostic psychological testing.* New York: International Universities Press.

Rapee, R. M. (1991). Generalized anxiety disorder: A review of clinicial features and theoretical concepts. *Clinical Psychology Review, 11,* 419–440.

Rapee, R. M. (1997). Potential role of childrearing practices in the development of anxiety and depression. *Clinical Psychology Review, 17,* 47–67.

Rapee, R. M., & Barlow, D. H. (Eds.). (1991). *Chronic anxiety: Generalized anxiety disorder and mixed anxiety-depression.* New York: Guilford Press.

Rapee, R. M., & Barlow, D. H. (1993). Generalized anxiety disorder, panic disorder, and the phobias. In P. B. Sutker & H., E. Adams (Eds.), *Comprehensive handbook of psychopathology* (2nd ed., pp. 109–127). New York: Plenum Press.

Rapin, I. (1991). Autistic children: Diagnosis and clinical features. *Pediatrics, 87* (Suppl.), 751–760.

Raskin, N. H., Hosobuchi, Y., & Lamb, S. A. (1987). Headache may arise from perturbation of brain. *Headache, 27,* 416–420.

Rauschenberger, S. L., & Lynn, S. J. (1995). Fantasy proneness, DSM-III-R Axis I psychopathology, and dissociation. *Journal of Abnormal Psychology, 104,* 373–380.

Ray, O. S. (1983). *Drugs, society, and human behavior.* St. Louis, MO: Mosby.

Raz, S. (1993). Structural cerebral pathology in schizophrenia: Regional or diffuse? *Journal of Abnormal Psychology, 102,* 445–452.

Redlich, F. C., & Freedman, D. X. (1966). *The theory and practice of psychiatry.* New York: Basic Books.

Redmond, D. E. (1977). Alterations in the function of the nucleus locus coeruleus: A possible model for studies of anxiety. In I. Hanin & E. Uskin (Eds.), *Animal models in psychiatry and neurology.* New York: Pergamon Press.

Redmond, D. E. (1979). New and old evidence for the involvement of a brain norepinephrine system in anxiety. In W. E. Fann, I. Karacan, A. D. Pokorny, et al. (Eds.), *Phenomenology and treatment of anxiety.* New York: SP Medical & Scientific Books.

Reed, G. (1988). *The psychology of anomalous experience* (rev. ed.). Buffalo, NY: Prometheus.

Regier, D. A., Boyd, J. H., Burke, J. D., Jr., Rae, D. S., Myers, J. K., Kramer, M., Robins, L. N., George, L. K., Karno, M., & Locke, B. Z. (1988). One-month prevalence of mental disorders in the United States. *Archives of General Psychiatry, 45,* 977–986.

Reid, J. B., & Eddy, J. M. (1997). The prevention of antisocial behavior: some considerations in the search for effective interventions. In D. M. Stoff, J. Breiling, & J. D. Maser (Eds.), *Handbook of antisocial behavior* (pp. 343–356). New York: Wiley.

Reisner, R. (1985). *Law and the mental health system.* St. Paul, MN: West.

Reiss, A. J., Jr., & Roth, J. A. (Eds.). (1993). *Understanding and preventing violence.* Washington, DC: National Academy Press.

Reiss, S. (1985). The mentally retarded, emotionally disturbed adult. In M. Sigman (Ed.), *Children with emotional disorders and developmental disabilities.* New York: Grune & Stratton.

Reiss, S. (1992). Assessment of psychopathology in persons with mental retardation. In J. L. Matson & R. P. Barrett (Eds.), *Psychopathology and mental retardation.* New York: Grune & Stratton.

Reiss, S., & Benson, B. A. (1985). Psychosocial correlates of depression in mentally retarded adults: I. Minimal social support and stigmatization. *American Journal of Medical Deficiency, 89,* 331–337.

Reiss, S., Levitan, G. W., & Szysko, J. (1982). Emotional disturbance and mental retardation: Diagnostic overshadowing. *American Journal of Mental Deficiency, 86*(6), 567–574.

Reiss, S., Peterson, R. A., Gursky, D. M., & McNally, R. J. (1986). Anxiety sensitivity, anxiety frequency, and the prediction of fearfulness. *Behaviour Research and Therapy, 24,* 1–8.

Reiss, S., & Valenti-Hein, D. (1990). *Reiss scales for children's dual diagnosis test manual.* Worthington, OH: International Diagnostic Systems.

Reite, M., Sheeder, J., Teale, P., Adams, M., Richardson, D., Simon, J., Jones, R. H., & Rojas, D. C. (1997). Magnetic source imaging evidence of sex differences in cerebral lateralization in schizophrenia. *Archives of General Psychiatry, 54,* 433–440.

Reynolds, D. K. (1981). Naikan psychotherapy. In R. J. Corsini (Ed.), *Handbook of innovative psycho-therapies* (pp. 544–553). New York: Wiley.

Reynolds, D. K. (1993). *Plunging through the clouds: Constructive living currents.* Albany: State University of New York Press.

Reynolds, W. M., & Mazza, J. J. (1994). Suicide and suicidal behaviors in children and adolescents. In W. M. Reynolds & H. F. Johnston (Eds.), *Handbook of depression in children and adolescents* (pp. 525–580). New York: Plenum Press.

Rice, M. (1997). Violent offender research and implications for the criminal justice system. *American Psychologist, 53,* 414–423.

Rich, C. L., Warsradt, M. D., Nemiroff, R. A., Fowler, R. C., & Young, D. (1991). Suicide, stressors, and the life cycle. *American Journal of Psychiatry, 148,* 534–527.

Richards, R. L., Kinney, D. K., Lunde, I., et al. (1988). Creativity in manic-depressives, cyclothymes, their normal relatives and control subjects. *Journal of Abnormal Psychology, 97,* 281–288.

Richens, A., & Perucca, E. (1993). Clinical pharmacology and medical treatment. In J. Laidlaw, A. Richens, & D. Chadwick (Eds.), *A textbook of epilepsy* (pp. 495–559). Edinburgh: Churchill Livingstone.

Richters, J. E., & Martinez, P. E. (1993). Violent communities, family choices, and children's chances: An algorithm for improving the odds. *Development and Psychopathology, 5,* 609–627.

Rickels, K., Schweizer, E., Case, W. G., & Greenblatt, D. J. (1990). Long-term therapeutic use of benzodiazepines: I. Effects of abrupt discontinuation. *Archives of General Psychiatry, 47,* 899–907.

Riether, A. M., & Stoudemire, A. (1988). Psychogenic fugue states: A review. *Southern Medical Journal, 81,* 568–571.

Riggins v. Nevada, 112, S. Ct. 1810 (1992).

Riggs, D. S., Dancu, C. V., Gershuny, B. S., Greenberg, D., & Foa, E. B. (1992). Anger and post-traumatic stress disorder in female crime victims. *Journal of Traumatic Stress, 5,* 613–625.

Riggs, D. S., Foa, E. B., Rothbaum, B. O., & Murdock, T. (1991). *Post-traumatic stress disorder following rape and non-sexual assault: A predictive model.* Unpublished manuscript.

Rihmer, Z. (1996). Strategies of suicide prevention: Focus on health care. *Journal of Affective Disorders, 39,* 83–91.

Robbins, J. M., & Kirmayer, L. J. (1996). Transient and persistent hypochondriacal worry in primary care. *Psychological Medicine, 26,* 575–589.

Roberts, R. E., Kaplan, G. A., Shema, S. J., & Strawbridge, W. J. (1997). Does growing old increase the risk for depression? *American Journal of Psychiatry, 154,* 1384–1390.

Robins, L. N. (1966). *Deviant children grow up.* Baltimore: Williams & Wilkins.

Robins, L. N. (1991). Conduct disorder. *Journal of Child Psychology and Psychiatry and Allied Disciplines, 32,* 193–212.

Robins, L. N., Helzer, J. E., Croughan, J., & Ratcliff, K. S. (1981). National Institute of Mental Health diagnostic interview schedule. *Archives of General Psychiatry, 38,* 381–389.

Robins, L. N., Helzer, J. E., Weissman, M. M., Orvaschel, H., Gruenberg, E., Burke, J. D., & Regier, D. A. (1984). Lifetime prevalence of specific psychiatric disorders in three sites. *Archives of General Psychiatry, 41,* 949–958.

Robins, L. N., & Price, R. K. (1991). Adult disorders predicted by childhood conduct problems: Results from the NIMH epidemiologic catchment area project. *Psychiatry, 54,* 116–132.

Robins, L. N., Tipp, J., & Przybeck, T. (1991). Antisocial personality. In L. N. Robins & D. A. Regier (Eds.), *Psychiatric disorders in America* (pp. 258–290). New York: Free Press.

Robinson, N. S., Garber, J., & Hilsman, R. (1995). Cognitions and stress: Direct and moderating effects on depressive versus externalizing symptoms during the junior high school transition. *Journal of Abnormal Psychology, 104,* 453–463.

Robinson, P. H., & Darley, J. M. (1997). The utility of desert. *Northwestern University Law Review, 91,* 453–499.

Robinson, R. G. (1997). Neuropsychiatric consequences of stroke. *Annual Review of Medicine, 48,* 217–229.

Rodin, G., & Voshort, K. (1986). Depression in the medically ill: An overview. *American Journal of Psychiatry, 143,* 696–705.

Rodin, J. (1977). Bidirectional influences of emotionality, stimulus responsivity and metabolic events in obesity. In J. D. Maser & M. E. P. Seligman (Eds.), *Psychopathology: Experimental models.* San Francisco: Freeman.

Rodin, J. (1981). Current status of the internal-external hypothesis for obesity: What went wrong? *American Psychologist, 36,* 361–372.

Rodin, J., & Salovey, P. (1989). Health psychology. *Annual Review of Psychology, 40,* 533–579.

Rodning, C., Beckwith, L., & Howard, J. (1989). Characteristic of attachment organization and play organization in prenatally drug-exposed toddlers. *Development and Psychopathology, 1,* 277–289.

Rodning, C., Beckwith, L., & Howard, J. (1992). Quality of attachments and home environments in children prenatally exposed to PCP and cocaine. *Development and Psychopathology, 3,* 351–366.

Rodriguez, N., Ryan, S.W., Vande Kemp, H., & Foy, D.W. (1997). Posttraumatic stress disorder in adult female survivors of childhood sexual abuse: A comparison study. *Journal of Consulting and Clinical Psychology, 65,* 53–59.

Rogers, S. L., Friedhoff, L. T., Apter, J. T., et al. (1996). The efficacy and safety of Donepezil in patients with Alzheimer's disease: Results of a US multicentre, randomized, double-blind, placebo-controlled trial. *Dementia, 7,* 293–303.

Rohde, P., Lewinsohn, P. M., & Seeley, J. R. (1990). Are people changed by the experience of having an episode of depression? A further test of the scar hypothesis. *Journal of Abnormal Psychology, 99,* 264–271.

Rohsenow, D. J. (1983). Drinking habits and expectancies about alcohol's effects for self versus others. *Journal of Consulting and Clinical Psychology, 51,* 752–756.

Rojas, D. C., Teale, P., Sheeder, J., Simon, J., & Reite, M. (1997). Sex-specific expression of Heschl's Gyrus functional and structural abnormalities in paranoid schizophrenia. *American Journal of Psychiatry, 154,* 1655–1662.

Rokeach, M. (1964). *The three Christs of Ypsilanti.* New York: Random House.

Rorschach, H. (1942). *Psychodiagnostics: A diagnostic test based on perception.* New York: Grune & Stratton.

Rose, J. E. (1996). Nicotine addiction and treatment. *Annual Review of Medicine, 47,* 493–507.

Rose, R. J., & Chesney, M. A. (1986). Cardiovascular stress reactivity: A behavioral-genetic perspective. *Behavior Therapy, 17,* 314–323.

Rosen, J. C., Reiter, J., & Orosan, P. (1995). Cognitive-behavioral body image therapy for body dysmorphic disorder. *Journal of Consulting and Clinical Psychology, 63,* 263–269.

Rosen, R. C., & Leiblum S. R. (1995). *Disorders of sexual desire.* New York: Guilford Press.

Rosenbaum, J. F., Biederman, J., Pollock, R. A., & Hirshfeld, D. R. (1994). The etiology of social phobia. *Journal of Clinical Psychiatry, 55,* 10–16.

Rosenbaum, J. F., & Gelenberg, A. J. (1991). Anxiety. In A. J. Gelenberg, E. L. Bassuk, & S. C. Schoonover (Eds.),

The practitioner's guide to psychoactive drugs (3rd ed.). New York: Plenum Press.

Rosenberg, D. R., Sweeney, J. A., Squires-Wheeler, E., Keshavan, M. S., Cornblatt, B. A., & Erlenmeyer-Kimling, L. (1997). Eye-tracking dysfunction in offspring from the New York High-Risk Project: Diagnostic specificity and the role of attention. *Psychiatry Research, 66,* 121–130.

Rosenblatt, A. (1984). Concepts of the asylum in the care of the mentally ill. *Hospital and Community Psychiatry, 35,* 244–250.

Rosenfarb, I. S., Goldstein, M. J., Mintz, J., & Nuechterlein, K. H. (1995). Expressed emotion and subclinical psycho-pathology observable within the transactions between schizophrenic patients and their family members. *Journal of Abnormal Psychology, 104,* 259–267.

Rosenfeld, B. D. (1992). Court-ordered treatment of spouse abuse. *Clinical Psychology Review, 12,* 205–226.

Rosenhan, D. L. (1973). On being sane in insane places. *Science, 179,* 250–258.

Rosenman, R. H., Brand, R. J., Jenkins, C. D., Friedman, M., Straus, R., & Wurm, M. (1975). Coronary heart disease in the Western Collaborative Group study: Final follow-up experience in 8½ years. *Journal of the American Medical Association, 8,* 872–877.

Rosenstein, D. S., & Horowitz, H. A. (1996). Adolescent attachment and psychopathology. *Journal of Consulting and Clinical Psychology, 64,* 244–253.

Rosenthal, D. (1970). *Genetic theory and abnormal behavior.* New York: McGraw-Hill.

Rosenthal, D., Wender, P. H., Kety, S. S., Schulsinger, F., Welner, J., & Ostergaard, L. (1968). Schizophrenics' offspring reared in adoptive homes. In D. Rosenthal & S. S. Kety (Eds.), *The transmission of schizophrenia.* Oxford, England: Pergamon Press.

Rosenthal, T., & Bandura, A. (1978). Psychological modeling: Theory and practice. In S. L. Garfield & A. E. Bergin (Eds.), *Handbook of psycho-therapy and behavior change: An empirical analysis* (2nd ed.). New York: Wiley.

Rosewater, L. B. (1986, August). The *DSM-III-R:* Ethical and legal implications for feminist therapists. In R. Garfinkel (Chair), *Politics of diagnosis: Feminist psychology and the DSM-III-R.* Symposium conducted at the 94th Annual Meeting of the American Psychological Association, Washington, DC.

Ross, C. A. (1997). *Dissociative identity disorder: Diagnosis, clinical features,* *and treatment of multiple personality,* 2nd ed. New York: Wiley.

Ross, C. A., Joshi, S., & Currie, R. (1991). Dissociative experiences in the general population: A factor analysis. *Hospital and Community Psychiatry, 42,* 297–301.

Ross, C. A., Miller, S. D., Reagor, P., Bjornson, L., Fraser, G. A., & Anderson, G. (1990). Structured interview data on 102 cases of multiple personality disorder from four centers. *American Journal of Psychiatry, 147,* 596–601.

Ross, D. E., Thaker, G. K., Buchanan, R. W., Lahti, A. C., Medoff, D., Bartko, J. J., Moran, M., & Hartley, J. (1996). Association of abnormal smooth pursuit eye movements with the deficit syndrome in schizophrenic patients. *American Journal of Psychiatry, 153,* 1158–1165.

Ross, H. E., Glaser, F. B., & Germanson, T. (1988). The prevalence of psychiatric disorders in patients with alcohol and other drug problems. *Archives of General Psychiatry, 45,* 1023–1031.

Rosse, R. B., Kendrick, K., Wyatt, R. J., Isaac, A., & Deutsch, S. I. (1994). Gaze discrimination in patients with schizophrenia: Preliminary report. *American Journal of Psychiatry, 151,* 919–921.

Rossi, P. H. (1990). The old homeless and the new homelessness in historical perspective. *American Psychologist, 45,* 945–959.

Rothbaum, B. O., Foa, E. B., Murdock, T., Riggs, D., & Walsh, W. (1990). *Post-traumatic stress disorder following rape.* Unpublished manuscript.

Rothbaum, B. O., Foa, E. B., Riggs, D. S., Murdock, T., & Walsh, W. (1992). A prospective examination of post-traumatic stress disorder in rape victims. *Journal of Traumatic Stress, 5,* 455–475.

Rotheram-Borus, M. J., Koopman, C., & Haignere, C. (1991). Reducing HIV sexual risk behaviors among runaway adolescents. *Journal of the American Medical Association, 266,* 1237–1241.

Roueché, B. (1974, September 9). Annals of medicine: As empty as Eve. *The New Yorker,* pp. 84–100.

Roy, A., DeJong, J., Lamparski, D., Adinoff, B., George, T., Moore, V., Garnett, D., Kerich, M., & Linnoila, M. (1991). Mental disorders among alcoholics: Relationship to age of onset and cerebrospinal fluid neuropeptides. *Archives of General Psychiatry, 48,* 423–427.

Roy, M. A., Neale, M. C., Pedersen, N. L., Mathe, A. A., & Kendler, K. S. (1995). A twin study of generalized anxiety disorder and major depression. *Psychological Medicine, 25,* 1037–1049.

Roy-Byrne, P. P. (1996). Generalized anxiety and mixed anxiety-depression: Association with disability and health care utilization. *Journal of Clinical Psychiatry, 57,* 86–91.

Ruderman, A. J. (1986). Dietary restraint: A theoretical and empirical review. *Psychological Bulletin, 99,* 247–262.

Ruderman, A. J., & Wilson, G. T. (1979). Weight, restraint, cognitions, and counterregulation. *Behaviour Research and Therapy, 17,* 581–590.

Ruedrich, S. L., Chu, C., & Wadle, C. V. (1985). The amytal interview in the treatment of psychogenic amnesia. *Hospital and Community Psychiatry, 36,* 1045–1046.

Rundell, J. R., & Ursano, R. J. (1996). Psychiatric responses to war trauma. In R. J. Ursano & A. E. Norwood (Eds.), *Emotional aftermath of the Persian Gulf War: Veterans, families, communities, and nations* (pp. 43–81). Washington, DC: American Psychiatric Press.

Rusch, F. R., Martin, J. E., & White, D. M. (1985). Competitive employment: Teaching mentally retarded employees to maintian their work behavior. *Education and Training of the Mentally Retarded, 20,* 182–189.

Rusch, F. R., & Mithaug, D. E. (1980). *Vocational training for mentally retarded adults: A behavior analytic approach.* Champaign, IL: Research Press.

Rush, A. J., & Weissenburger, J. E. (1994). Melancholic symptom features and *DSM-IV. American Journal of Psychiatry, 151,* 489–498.

Rushton, J. P. (1995). Race and crime: International data for 1989–1990. *Psychological Reports, 76,* 307–312.

Rutenfanz, J., Haider, M., & Koller, M. (1985). Occupational health measures for nightworkers and shiftworkers. In S. Folkard & T. W. Monk (Eds.), *Hours of work: Temporal factors in work scheduling* (pp. 199–210). New York: Wiley.

Rutter, M. (1983). Cognitive deficits in the pathogenesis of autism. *Journal of Child Psychology and Psychiatry, 24,* 513–531.

Rutter, M., Macdonald, H., LeCouteur, A., Harrington, R., Bolton, P., & Bailey, A. (1990). Genetic factors in child psychiatric disorders: II. Empirical findings. *Journal of Child Psychology and Psychiatry, 31,* 39–83.

Rutter, M., & Bailey, A. (1994). Thinking and relationships: mind and brain (some reflections on theory of mind and autism). In S. Baron-Cohen, H. Tager-

Flusberg, & D. Cohen (Eds.), *Understanding other minds: Perspectives from autism* (pp. 481–504). Oxford: Oxford University Press.

Rutter, M. I. (1997). Nature-nurture integration: The example of antisocial behavior. *American Psychologist, 52,* 390–398.

Saccuzzo, D. S., Cadenhead, K. S., & Braff, D. L. (1996). Backward versus forward masking deficits in schizophrenic patients: Centrally, not peripherally, mediated? *American Journal of Psychiatry, 153,* 1564–1570.

Sackeim, H. A., & Devanand, D. P. (1991). Dissociative disorders. In M. Hersen & S. M. Turner (Eds.), *Adult psychopathology and diagnosis* (2nd ed., pp. 279–322). New York: Wiley.

Sacks, O. (1985). *The man who mistook his wife for a hat and other clinical tales.* New York: Summit Books.

Sadowski, C., & Kelley, M. L. (1993). Social problem solving in suicidal adolescents. *Journal of Consulting and Clinical Psychology, 61,* 121–127.

Saghir, M. T., & Robins, E. (1969). Homosexuality: I. Sexual behavior of the female homosexual. *Archives of General Psychiatry, 20,* 192–201.

Saghir, M. T., Robins, E., & Walbran, B. (1969). Homosexuality: II. Sexual behavior of the male homosexual. *Archives of General Psychiatry, 21,* 219–229.

St. George-Hyslop, P. H., et al. (1987). The genetic defect causing familial Alzheimer's disease maps on chromosome 21. *Science, 235,* 885–889.

Saks, E. R. (1995). The criminal responsibility of people with multiple personality disorder. *Psychiatric Quarterly, 66,* 119–131.

Salkovskis, P. M., & Clark, D. M. (1993). Panic disorder and hypochondriasis. *Advances in Behaviour Research and Therapy, 15,* 23–48.

Salkovskis, P. M., & Clark, D. M. (in press). Cognitive therapy for panic disorder. *Journal of Cognitive Psychotherapy.*

Salkovskis, P. M., Clark, D. M., & Gelder, M. G. (1996). Cognition-behaviour links in the persistence of panic. *Behaviour Research and Therapy, 34,* 453–458.

Salkovskis, P. M., & Warwick, H. M. C. (1986). Morbid preoccupations, health anxiety and reassurance: A cognitive-behavioural approach to hypochondriasis. *Behaviour Research and Therapy, 24,* 597–602.

Salmon, P., & Calderbank, S. (1996). The relationship of childhood physical and sexual abuse to adult illness behavior. *Journal of Psychosomatic Research, 40,* 329–336.

Salo, R., Robertson, L. C., Nordahl, T. E., & Kraft, L. W. (1997). The effects of antipsychotic medication on sequential inhibitory processes. *Journal of Abnormal Psychology, 106,* 639–643.

Salthouse, T. A. (1985). Speed of behavior and its implications for cognition. In J. E. Birren & K. W. Scale (Eds.), *Handbook for the psychology of aging.* Englewood Cliffs, NJ: Prentice-Hall.

Samson, J. A., Mirin, S. M., Hauser, S. T., Fenton, B. T., & Schildkraut, J. J. (1992). Learned helplessness and urinary MHPG levels in unipolar depression. *American Journal of Psychiatry, 149,* 806–809.

Sana, M., Ernesto, C., Thomas, R. G., Klauber, M. R., Schafer, K., Grundman, M., Woodbury, P., Growdon, J., Cotman, C. W., Pfeiffer, E., Schneider, L. S., & Thal, L. J. (1997). A controlled trial of selegiline, alpha-tocopherol, or both as treatment for Alzheimer's disease. *New England Journal of Medicine, 336,* 1216–1247.

Sanders, B. (1992). The imaginary companion experience in multiple personality disorder. *Dissociation: Progress-in-the-Dissociative Disorders, 5,* 159–162.

Sanderson, W. C., Rapee, R. M., & Barlow, D. H. (1989). The influence of an illusion of control on panic attacks induced via inhalation of 5.5% carbon dioxide-enriched air. *Archives of General Psychiatry, 46,* 157–162.

Sapolsky, R. M., Alberts, S. C., & Altmann, J. (1997). Hypercortisolism associated with social subordinance or social isolation among wild baboons. *Archives of General Psychiatry, 54,* 1137–1143.

Sar, V., Yargic, L. I., & Tutkun, H. (1996). Structured interview data on 35 cases of dissociative identity disorder in Turkey. *American Journal of Psychiatry, 153,* 1329–1333.

Sarrel, P. (1977). Biological aspects of sexual functioning. In R. Gemene & C. C. Wheeler (Eds.), *Progress in sexology* (pp. 227–244). New York: Plenum Press.

Sartorius, N., Üstün, B., Korten, A., Cooper, J. E., & van Drimmelen, J. (1995). Progress toward achieving a common language in psychiatry, II: Results from the international field trials of the ICD-10 Diagnostic Criteria for Research for Mental and Behavioral Disorders. *American Journal of Psychiatry, 152,* 1427–1437.

Satel, S. L., & Edell, W. S. (1991). Cocaine-induced paranoia and psychosis proneness. *American Journal of Psychiatry, 148,* 1708–1711.

Satir, V. (1967). *Conjoint family therapy* (rev. ed.). Palo Alto, CA: Science and Behavior Books.

Saunders, D. G. (1996). Feminist-cognitive-behavioral and process-psychodynamic treatments for men who batter. *Violence and Victims, 11,* 393–414.

Saxena, S., & Prasad, K. (1989). *DSM-III* subclassifications of dissociative disorders applied to psychiatric outpatients in India. *American Journal of Psychiatry, 146,* 261–262.

Schachter, S. (1971). Eat, eat. *Psychology Today,* pp. 44–47, 78–79.

Schachter, S. (1982). Recidivism and self-cure of smoking and obesity. *American Psychologist, 37,* 436–444.

Schachter, S., & Gross, L. (1968). Manipulated time and eating behavior. *Journal of Personality and Social Psychology, 10,* 98–106.

Schacter, D. L. (1986a). Amnesia and crime: How much do we really know? *American Psychologist, 41,* 286–295.

Schacter, D. L. (1986b). On the relation between genuine and simulated amnesia. *Behavioral Sciences and the Law, 4,* 47–64.

Schacter, D. L., Wang, P. L., Tulving, E., & Freedman, M. (1982). Functional retrograde amnesia: A quantitative case study. *Neuropsychologia, 20,* 523–532.

Schalock, R. L., Stark, J. A., Snell, M. E., Coulter, D. L., Polloway, E. A., Luckasson, R., Reiss, S., & Spitalnik, D. M. (1994). The changing conception of mental retardation: Implications for the field. *Mental Retardation, 32,* 181–193.

Scharff, D. E., & Scharff, J. S. (1991). *Object relations couple therapy.* Northvale, NJ: Aronson.

Scharff, L. (1997). Recurrent abdominal pain in children: A review of psychological factors and treatment. *Clinical Psychology Review, 17,* 145–166.

Scheele, L. A., Maravilla, K. R., & Dager, S. R. (1997). Neuroimaging of medical disorders in clinical psychiatry. In D. L. Dunner (Ed.), *Current psychiatric therapy II* (pp. 37–44). Philadelphia: W. B. Saunders Co.

Scheerer, M., Rothmann, E., & Goldstein, K. (1945). A case of "idiot savant": An experimental study of personality organization. *Psychology Monograph, 58,* 1–63.

Scheff, T. J. (1966). *Being mentally ill: A sociological theory.* Chicago: Aldine.

Scheff, T. J. (1975). *Labeling madness.* Englewood Cliffs, NJ: Prentice-Hall.

Scheiffelin, E. (1984). *The cultural analysis of depressive affect: An example from New Guinea.* Unpublished manuscript. University of Pennsylvania, Philadelphia.

Schildkraut, J. (1965). The catecholamine hypothesis of affective disorders: A review of supporting evidence. *American Journal of Psychiatry, 122,* 509–522.

Schildkraut, J. J. (1972). Neuropharmacological studies of mood disorders. In J. Zubin & F. A. Freyhan (Eds.), *Disorders of mood*. Baltimore: Johns Hopkins University Press.

Schleifer, S. J., Keller, S. E., Bartlett, J. A., Eckholdt, H. M., & Delaney, B. R. (1996). Immunity in young adults with major depressive disorder. *American Journal of Psychiatry, 153*, 477–482.

Schlenger, W. E., Kulka, R. A., Fairbank, J. A., Hough, R. L., Jordan, B. K., Marmar, C. R., & Weiss, D. S. (1992). The prevalence of post-traumatic stress disorder in the Vietnam generation. A multimethod, multisource assessment of psychiatric disorder. *Journal of Traumatic Stress, 5*, 333–363.

Schlundt, D. G., & Johnson, W. G. (1990). *Eating disorders: Assessment and treatment*. Boston: Allyn and Bacon.

Schmeck, H. M., Jr. (1982, September 7). The biology of fear and anxiety: Evidence points to chemical triggers. *The New York Times*, p. C7.

Schmidt, A. J. M. (1994). Bottlenecks in the diagnosis of hypochondriasis. *Comprehensive Psychiatry, 35*, 306–315.

Schmidt, N. B., Lerew, D. R., & Jackson, R. L. (1997). The role of anxiety sensitivity in the pathogenesis of panic: Prospective evaluation of spontaneous panic attacks during acute stress. *Journal of Abnormal Psychology, 106*, 355–364.

Schmitz, J. M., Schneider, N.G., & Jarvik, M. E. (1997). Nicotine. In J. H. Lowinson, P. Ruiz, R. B. Millman, & J. G. Langrod (Eds.), *Substance abuse: A comprehensive textbook* (pp. 276–294). Baltimore: Williams & Wilkins.

Schneider, F., Gur, R. E., Alavi, A., Seligman, M. E. P., Mozley, L. H., Smith, R. J., Mozley, P. D., & Gur, R. C. (1996). Cerebral blood flow changes in limbic regions induced by unsolvable anagram tasks. *American Journal of Psychiatry, 153*, 206–212.

Schneider, L. S. (1996). Overview of generalized anxiety disorder in the elderly. *Journal of Clinical Psychiatry, 57*, 34–45.

Schneier, F. R. (1991). Social phobia. *Psychiatric Annals, 21*, 349–353.

Schooler, N. R., Keith, S. J., Severe, J. B., Matthews, S. M., Bellack, A. S., Glick, I. D., Hargreaves, W. A., Kane, J. M., Ninan, P. T., Frances, A., Jacobs, M., Lieberman, J. A., Mance, R., Simpson, G. M., & Woerner, M. G. (1997). Relapse and rehospitalization during maintenance treatment of schizophrenia: The effects of dose reduction and family treatment. *Archives of General Psychiatry, 54*, 453–463.

Schou, M. (1997). Forty years of lithium treatment. *Archives of General Psychiatry, 54*, 9–13.

Schover, L. R., & LoPiccolo, J. (1982). Treatment effectiveness for dysfunctions of sexual desire. *Journal of Sex and Marital Therapy, 8*(3), 179–197.

Schreiber, F. (1974). *Sybil*. New York: Warner.

Schreiber, W., Lauer, C. J., Krumrey, K., Holsboer, F., & Krieg, J. C. (1996). Dysregulation of the hypothalamic-pituitary-adrenocortical system in panic disorder. *Neuropsychopharmacology, 15*, 7–15.

Schreibman, L. (1994). Autism. In L.W. Craighead, W. E. Craighead, A.E. Kazdin, & M. J. Mahoney (Eds.), *Cognitive and behavioral interventions: An empirical approach to mental health problems* (pp. 335–358). Boston: Allyn and Bacon.

Schreibman, L., & Koegel, R. L. (1996). Fostering self-management: Parent-delivered pivotal response training for children with autistic disorder. In E. D. Hibbs & P. S. Jensen (Eds.), *Psychosocial treatments for child and adolescent disorders: Empirically based strategies for clinical practice* (pp. 525–552). Washington, DC: American Psychological Association.

Schroder, M. & Carroll, R. A. (1996). *Psychosexual outcome in 19 male-to-female post-operative transsexuals*. Paper presented at the Annual Meeting of the Society for Sex Therapy and Research, Miami Beach, FL.

Schuckit, M. A., & Rayses, V. (1979). Ethanol ingestion: Differences in blood acetaldehyde concentrations in relatives of alcoholics and controls. *Science, 203*, 54–55.

Schulz, S. C., Schulz, P. M., & Wilson, W. H. (1988). Medication treatment of schizotypal personality disorder. *Journal of Personality Disorders, 2*, 1–13.

Schwartz, G. E. (1977). Psychosomatic disorders and biofeedback: A psychobiological model of disregulation. In J. D. Maser & M. E. P. Seligman (Eds.), *Psychopathology: Experimental models*. San Francisco: Freeman.

Schwartz, G. E. (1978). Psychobiological foundations of psychotherapy and behavior change. In S. L. Garfield & A. E. Bergin (Eds.), *Handbook of psychotherapy and behavior change*. New York: Wiley.

Schwartz, G. E., Weinberger, D. A., & Singer, J. A. (1981). Cardiovascular differentiation of happiness, sadness, anger, and fear following imagery and exercise. *Psychosomatic Medicine, 43*, 343–364.

Schwartz, P. J., Brown, C., Wehr, T. A., & Rosenthal, N. E. (1996). Winter seasonal affective disorder: A follow-up study of the first 59 patients of the National Institute of Mental Health seasonal studies program. *American Journal of Psychiatry, 153*, 1028–1036.

Schwartz, S. M., Gramling, S. E., & Mancini, T. (1994). The influence of life stress, personality, and learning history on illness behavior. *Journal of Behavior Therapy and Experimental Psychiatry, 25*, 135–142.

Schwarz, J. R. (1981). *The Hillside strangler: A murderer's mind*. New York: New American Library.

Schweizer, E., Rickels, K., Case, W. G., & Greenblatt, D. J. (1990). Long-term therapeutic use of benzodiazepines: II. Effects of gradual taper. *Archives of General Psychiatry, 47*, 908–916.

Scott, J. (1996). Cognitive therapy of affective disorders: A review. *Journal of Affective Disorders, 37*, 1–11.

Scott, J. E., & Dixon, L. B. (1995). Psychological interventions for schizophrenia. *Schizophrenia Bulletin, 21*, 621–630.

Scotti, J. R., Nangle, D. W., Masia, C. L., Ellis, J. T., Ujcich, K. J., Giacoletti, A. M., Vittimberga, G. L., & Carr, R. (1997). Providing an AIDS education and skills training program to persons with mild developmental disabilties. *Education and Training in Mental Retardation and Developmental Disabilities, 32*, 113–128.

Scull, A. (1993). *The most solitary of afflictions: Madness and society in Britain, 1700–1900*. New Haven, CT: Yale University Press.

Sedlack, A. (1989). *National incidence of child abuse and neglect*. Paper presented at the biennial meeting of the Society for Research in Child Development, Kansas City, MO.

Seeley, S. M. F. (1997). In R. W. Maris, M. M. Silverman, & S. S. Canetto (Eds.), *Review of suicidology* (pp. 251–270). New York: Guilford Press.

Segal, G. (1991). *A primer on brain tumors* (5th ed.). Des Plaines, IL: American Brain Tumor Association.

Segal, N. L. (1984, July–August). The nature vs. nurture laboratory. *Twins*, 56–67.

Segal, Z. V., Gemar, M., Truchon, C., Guirguis, M., & Horowitz, L. M. (1995). A priming methodology for studying self-representation in major depressive disorder. *Journal of Abnormal Psychology, 104*, 205–213.

Segrin, C., & Abramson, L. Y. (1994). Negative reactions to depressive behaviors: A communication theories analysis. *Journal of Abnormal Psychology, 103*, 655–668.

Sekuler, R., & MacArthur, R. D. (1977). Alcohol retards visual recovery from glare by hampering target acquisition. *Nature, 270,* 428–429.

Selfe, L. (1978). *Nadia: A case of extraordinary drawing ability in an autistic child.* New York: Academic Press.

Seligman, M. E. P. (1971). Phobias and preparedness. *Behavior Therapy, 2,* 307–320.

Seligman, M. E. P. (1975). *Helplessness: On depression, development, and death.* San Francisco: Freeman.

Seligman, M. E. P. (1988). Research in clinical psychology: Why is there so much depression today? *G. Stanley Hall Lecture Series, 9,* 79–96.

Seligman, M. E. P., Abramson, L. Y., Semmel, A., & von Baeyer, C. (1979). Depressive attributional style. *Journal of Abnormal Psychology, 88,* 242–247.

Selling, L. S. (1940). *Men against madness.* New York: Greenberg.

Seltzer, A. (1994). Multiple personality: A psychiatric misadventure. *Canadian Journal of Psychiatry, 39,* 442–445.

Selye, H. (1956). *The stress of life.* New York: McGraw-Hill.

Selye, H. (1974). *Stress without distress.* Philadelphia: Lippincott.

Selye, H. (1976). *Stress in health and disease.* Woburn, MA: Butterworths.

Semans, J. H. (1956). Premature ejaculation: A new approach. *Southern Medical Journal, 49,* 353–357.

Servan-Schreiber, D., Cohen, J. D., & Steingard, S. (1996). Schizophrenic deficits in the processing of context: A test of a theoretical model. *Archives of General Psychiatry, 53,* 1105–1112.

Seto, M. C., & Barbaree, H. E. (1995). The role of alcohol in sexual aggression. *Clinical Psychology Review, 15,* 545–566.

Seto, M. C., Khattar, N. A., Lalumiere, M. L., & Quinsey, V. L. (1997). Deception and sexual strategy in psychopathy. *Personality and Individual Differences, 22,* 301–307.

Shader, R. I. (Ed.). (1994). *Manual of psychiatric therapeutics* (2nd ed.). Boston: Little, Brown.

Shader, R. I., & Greenblatt, D. J. (1993). Use of benzodiazepines in anxiety disorders. *New England Journal of Medicine, 328,* 1398–1405.

Shader, R. I., Greenblatt, D. J., & Balter, M. B. (1991). Appropriate use and regulatory control of benzodiazepines. *Journal of Clinical Pharmacology, 31,* 781–784.

Shadish, W. R., Montgomery, L. M., Wilson, P., Wilson, R. R., Bright, I., & Okwumabua, T. (1993). *Journal of Consulting and Clinical Psychology, 61,* 992–1002.

Shaffer, D., Garland, A., Vieland, V., et al. (1991). The impact of curriculum-based suicide prevention programs for teenagers. *Journal of the American Academy of Child and Adolescent Psychiatry, 30,* 588–596.

Shaffer, D., Gould, M. S., Fisher, P., Trautman, P., Moreau, D., Kleinman, M., & Flory, M. (1996). Psychiatric diagnosis in child and adolescent suicide. *Archives of General Psychiatry, 53,* 339–348.

Shah, A., & Frith, U. (1983). An islet of ability in autistic children: A research note. *Journal of Child Psychology and Psychiatry, 24,* 613–620.

Shapiro, D., & Goldstein, I. B. (1982). Biobehavioral perspectives on hypertension. *Journal of Consulting and Clinical Psychology,* 841–858.

Shapiro, T. (1989). Our changing science. *Journal of the American Psychoanalytic Association, 37,* 3–6.

Sharf, R. S. (1996). *Theories of psychotherapy and counseling: Concepts and cases.* Pacific Grove, CA: Brooks/Cole.

Sharff, J. S. (1995). Psychoanalytic marital therapy. In N. S. Jacobson, A.S. Gurman, et al. (Eds.), *Clinical handbook of couple therapy* (pp. 164–193). New York: Guilford Press.

Shaw, D. S., & Winslow, E. B. (1997). Precursors and correlates of antisocial behavior from infancy to preschool. In D. M. Stoff, J. Breiling, & J. D. Maser (Eds.), *Handbook of antisocial behavior* (pp. 148–158). New York: Wiley.

Shaw, T. A., Herkov, M. J., & Greer, R. A. (1995). Examination of treatment completion and predicted outcome among incarcerated sex offenders. *Bulletin of the American Academy of Psychiatry and the Law, 23,* 35–41.

Shea, M. T., Elkin, I., Imber, S. D., Sotsky, S. M., Watkins, J. T., Collins, J. F., Pilkonis, P. A., Beckham, F., Glass, D. R., Dolan, R. T., & Parloff, M. B. (1992). Course of depressive symptoms over follow-up. *Archives of General Psychiatry, 49,* 782–787.

Shear, M. K. (1996). Factors in the etiology and pathogenesis of panic disorder: Revisiting the attachment-separation paradigm. *American Journal of Psychiatry, 153,* 125–136.

Shear, M. K., Cooper, A. M., Klerman, G. L., Busch, F. N., & Shapiro, T. (1993). A psychodynamic model of panic disorder. *American Journal of Psychiatry, 150,* 859–866.

Shear, M. K., Pilkonis, P. A., Clotre, M., & Leon, A. C. (1994). Cognitive behavioral treatment compared with nonprescriptive treatment of panic disorder. *Archives of General Psychiatry, 51,* 395–401.

Sheehan, S. (1982). *Is there no place on earth for me?* Boston: Houghton Mifflin.

Sherman, S. (1996). Epidemiology. In R. J. Hagerman & A. C. Silverman (Eds.), *The fragile X syndrome: Diagnosis, treatment, and research* (2nd. ed., pp. 165–192). Baltimore, MD: Johns Hopkins University Press.

Shiffman, S. (1982). Relapse following smoking cessation: A situational analysis. *Journal of Consulting and Clinical Psychology, 50,* 71–86.

Shiffman, S., Gnys, M., Richards, T. J., Paty, J. A., Hickcox, & Kassel, J. D. (1996). *Health Psychology, 15,* 455–461.

Shiffman, S., Paty, J. A., Gnys, M., Kassel, J. A., & Hickcox, M. (1996). First lapses to smoking: Within-subjects analysis of real-time reports. *Journal of Consulting and Clinical Psychology, 64,* 366–379.

Shilony, E., & Grossman, F. K. (1993). Depersonalization as a defense mechanism in survivors of trauma. *Journal of Traumatic Stress, 6,* 119–128.

Shisslak, C. M., Crago, M., & Estes, L. S. (1995). The spectrum of eating disturbances. *International Journal of Eating Disorders, 18,* 209–219.

Shneidman, E. S. (1992). A conspectus of the suicidal scenario. In R. W. Maris, A. L. Berman, J. T. Maltsberger, & R. I. Yufit (Eds.), *Assessment and prediction of suicide* (pp. 50–64). New York: Guilford Press.

Shneidman, E. S., & Farberow, N. L. (1970). Attempted and completed suicide. In E. S. Shneidman, N. L. Farberow, & R. E. Litman (Eds.), *The psychology of suicide.* New York: Science House.

Shoham-Salomon, V., & Rosenthal, R. (1987). Paradoxical interventions: A meta-analysis. *Journal of Consulting and Clinical Psychology, 55,* 22–28.

Shore, J., Tatum, E., & Vollmer, W. (1986). Psychiatric reactions to disaster: The Mount St. Helens experience. *American Journal of Psychiatry, 143,* 590–595.

Shorter, E. (1995). The borderland between neurology and history: Conversion reactions. *Neurologic Clinics, 13,* 229–239.

Shulman, I. D., Cox, B. J., Swinson, R. P., Kuch, K., & Reichman, J. T. (1994). Precipitating events, locations, and reactions associated with initial unexpected panic attacks. *Behaviour Research and Therapy, 32,* 17–20.

Siegel, B. V., Buchsbaum, M. S., Bunney, W. E., Jr., Gottschalk, L. A., Haier, R. J., Lohr, J. B., Lottenberg, S., Najafi, A., Nuechterlein, K. H., Potkin, S. G., & Wu, J. C. (1993). Cortical-striatal-thalamic circuits and brain glucose metabolic activity in 70 unmedicated male schizophrenic patients. *American Journal of Psychiatry, 150,* 1325–1336.

Siever, L. J. (1992). Schizophrenia spectrum disorders. In A. Tasman & M. B. Riba (Eds.), *Review of psychiatry* (Vol. 11, pp. 25–42). Washington, DC: American Psychiatric Press.

Siever, L. J., & Davis, K. L. (1991). A psychobiological perspective on personality disorders. *American Journal of Psychiatry, 148,* 1647–1658.

Siever, L. J., Friedman, L., Moskowitz, J., Mitropoulou, V., Keefe, R., Roitman, S. L., Merhige, D., Trestman, R., Silverman, J., & Mohs, R. (1994). Eye movement impairment and schizotypal psychopathology. *American Journal of Psychiatry, 151,* 1209–1215.

Sigman, M. (1995). Behavioral research in childhood autism. In M. Lenzenweger & J. Haugaard (Eds.), *Frontiers of developmental psychopathology* (pp. 190–206). New York: Springer/Verlag.

Sigman, M., & Mundy, P. (1989). Social attachments in autistic children. *Journal of the American Academy of Child and Adolescent Psychiatry, 28,* 74–81.

Silove, D., Manicavasagar, V., Curtis, J., & Blaszczynski, A. (1996). Is early separation anxiety a risk factor for adult panic disorder?: A critical review. *Comprehensive Psychiatry, 37,* 167–179.

Silver, L. B. (1991). Developmental learning disorders. In M. Lewis (Ed.), *Child and adolescent psychiatry: A comprehensive textbook.* Baltimore: Williams and Wilkins.

Silverman, M. M. (1997). Introduction: Current controversies in suicidology. In R. W. Maris, M. M. Silverman, & S. S. Canetto (Eds.), *Review of suicidology* (pp. 1–21). New York: Guilford Press.

Silverman, W. K. (1989). *Self-control manual for phobic children.* Unpublished Treatment Protocol. (Available from the author. Department of Psychology, Florida International University, University Park, Miami, FL 33199.)

Sim, J. P., & Romney, D. M. (1990). The relationship between a circumplex model of interpersonal behavior and personality disorders. *Journal of Personality Disorders, 4,* 329–341.

Simeon, D., Gross, S., Guralnik, O., Stein, D. J., Schmeidler, J., & Hollander, E. (1997). Feeling unreal: 30 cases of *DSM-III-R* depersonalization disorder. *American Journal of Psychiatry, 154,* 1107–1113.

Simeon, D., & Hollander, E. (1993). Depersonalization disorder. *Psychiatric Annals, 23,* 382–388.

Simeon, D., Hollander, E., Stein, D. J., Cohen, L., & Aronowitz, B. (1995).

Body dysmorphic disorder in the *DSM-IV* field trial for obsessive-compulsive disorder. *American Journal of Psychiatry, 152,* 1207–1209.

Simeon, D., Stein, D. J., & Hollander, E. (1995). Depersonalization disorder and self-injurious behavior. *Journal of Clinical Psychiatry, 56,* 36–39.

Simola, S. K. (1992). Differences among sexist, nonsexist, and feminist family therapies. *Professional Psychology: Research and Practice, 23,* 397–403.

Simonoff, E., Bolton, P., & Rutter, M. (1996). Mental retardation: Genetic findings, clinical implications and research agenda. *Journal of Child Psychology and Psychiatry, 37,* 259–280.

Singleton, L., & Johnson, K. A. (1993). *The black health library guide to stroke.* New York: Holt.

Sivec, H. J., & Lynn, S. J. (1995). Dissociative and neuropsychological symptoms: The question of differential diagnosis. *Clinical Psychology Review, 15,* 297–316.

Sizemore, C. C., & Pittillo, E. S. (1977). *I'm Eve.* Garden City, NY: Doubleday.

Skeels, H. M., & Dye, H. B. (1938–1939). A study of the effects of differential stimulation on mentally retarded children. *AAMD Proceedings, 44,* 114–136.

Skinner, B. F. (1953). *Science and human behavior.* New York: Macmillan.

Sklar, L. S., & Anisman, H. (1979). Stress and coping factors influence tumor growth. *Science, 205,* 513–515.

Skre, I., Onstad, S., Torgersen, S., Lygren, S., & Kringlen, E. (1993). A twin study of *DSM-III-R* anxiety disorders. *Acta Psychiatrica Scandinavia, 88,* 85–92.

Slaghuis, W. L., & Bakker, V. J. (1995). Forward and backward visual masking of contour by light in positive- and negative-symptom schizophrenia. *Journal of Abnormal Psychology, 104,* 41–54.

Slap, G. B., Vorters, D. F., Khalid, N., Margulies, S. R., et al. (1992). Adolescent suicide attempters: Do physicians recognize them? *Journal of Adolescent Health, 13,* 286–292.

Sloan, H. R. (1991). Metabolic screening methods. In J. L. Matson & J. A. Mulick (Eds.), *Handbook of mental retardation* (2nd. ed.; pp. 292–307). New York: Pergamon.

Sloane, R. B., Staples, F. R., Cristol, A. H., Yorkston, N. J., & Whipple, K. (1975). *Psychoanalysis versus behavior therapy.* Cambridge, MA: Harvard University Press.

Sluzki, C. E. (1991). Foreword. In M. P. Nichols & R. C. Schwartz, *Family therapy: Concepts and methods*

(2nd ed., pp. ix–x). Boston: Allyn and Bacon.

Small, J. G., Klapper, M. H., Milstein, V., Kellams, J. J., Miller, M. J., Marhenke, J. D., & Small, I. F. (1991). Carbamazepine compared with lithium in the treatment of mania. *Archives of General Psychiatry, 48,* 915–921.

Smith, A. L., & Weissman, M. M. (1992). Epidemiology. In E. S. Paykel (Ed.), *Handbook of affective disorders* (pp. 111–129). New York: Guilford Press.

Smith, G. R., Monson, R. A., & Ray, D. C. (1986). Patients with multiple unexplained symptoms. *Archives of Internal Medicine, 146,* 69–72.

Smith, T. E., Bellack, A. S., & Liberman, R. P. (1996). Social skills training for schizophrenia: review and future directions. *Clinical Psychology Review, 16,* 599–617.

Smith, T. W. (1992). Hostility and health: Current status of a psychosomatic hypothesis. *Health Psychology, 11,* 139–150.

Smith, T. W., & Brown, P. C. (1991). Cynical hostility, attempts to exert social control, and cardiovascular reactivity in married couples. *Journal of Behavioral Medicine, 14,* 581–592.

Smith, T. W., & Leon, A. S. (1992). *Coronary heart disease: A behavioral perspective.* Champaign, IL: Research Press.

Smyth, C., Kalsi, G., Brynjolfsson, J., O'Neill, J., Curtis, D., Rifkin, L., Moloney, E., Murphy, P., Sherrington, R., Petursson, H., & Gurling, H. (1996). Further tests for linkage of bipolar affective disorder to the tyrosine hydroxylase gene locus on chromosome 11p15 in a new series of multiplex British affective disorder pedigrees. *American Journal of Psychiatry, 153,* 271–274.

Snyder, C. R. (1958). *Alcohol and the Jews.* New York: Free Press.

Snyder, D., & Fruchtman, L. (1981). Differential patterns of wife abuse: A data-based typology. *Journal of Consulting and Clinical Psychology, 49,* 878–885.

Snyder, S. H. (1979). The true speed trip: Schizophrenia. In D. Goleman & R. J. Davidson (Eds.), *Consciousness: Brain, states of awareness, and mysticism.* New York: Harper & Row.

Soares, J. C., & Mann, J. J. (1997). The anatomy of mood disorders—Review of structural neuroimaging studies. *Biological Psychiatry, 41,* 86–106.

Sobell, L. C., Toneatto, A., & Sobell, M. B. (1990). Behavior therapy (alcohol and other substance abuse). In A. S. Bellack & M. Hersen (Eds.), *Handbook of comparative treatments for adult disorders* (pp. 479–505). New York: Wiley.

Solomon, D. A., Keller, M. B., Leon, A. C., Mueller, T. I., Shea, M. T., Warshaw, M., Maser, J. D., Coryell, W., & Endicott, J. (1997). Recovery from major depression: A 10-year prospective follow-up across multiple episodes. *Archives of General Psychiatry, 54,* 1001–1006.

Solomon, Z., Laor, N., & McFarlane, A. C. (1996). Acute posttraumatic reactions in soldiers and civilians. In B. A. van der Kolk, A. C. McFarlane, & L.Weisaeth (Eds.), *Traumatic stress: The effects of overwhelming experience on mind, body, and society* (pp. 102–114). New York: Guilford Press.

Solomon, Z., Mikulincer, M., & Benbenishty, R. (1989). Locus of control and combat-related posttrauma stress disorder: The intervening role of battle intensity, threat appraisal and coping. *British Journal of Clinical Psychology, 28,* 131–144.

Solomon, Z., Mikulincer, M., & Flum, H. (1988). Negative life events, coping responses, and combat-related psycho-pathology: A prospective study. *Journal of Abnormal Psychology, 97,* 302–307.

Sonnerborg, A. B., Ehrnst, A.C., Bergdahl, S. K., Pehronson, P. O., Skoldenberg, B. R., & Strannegard, O. O. (1988). HIV isolation from cerebrospinal fluid in relation to immunological deficiency and neurological symptoms. *AIDS, 2,* 89–93.

Sorenson, S., & Kraus, J. F. (1991). Occurrence, severity, and outcome of brain injury. *Journal of Head Trauma Rehabilitation, 6,* 1–10.

Sotsky, S. M., Glass, D. R., Shea, M. T., Pilkonis, P. A., Collins, J. F., Watkins, J. T., Imber, S. D., Leber, W. R., Moyer, J., & Oliver, M. E. (1991). Patient predictors of response to psychotherapy and pharmacotherapy: Findings in the NIMH Treatment of Depression Collaborative Research Program. *American Journal of Psychiatry, 148,* 997–1008.

Southern-Gerow, M. A., & Kendall, P. C. (1997). Parent-focused and cognitive-behavioral treatments of antisocial youth. In D. M. Stoff, J. Breiling, & J. D. Maser (Eds.), *Handbook of antisocial behavior* (pp. 384–394). New York: Wiley.

Spanos, N. P. (1978). Witchcraft in histories of psychiatry: A critical analysis and an alternative conceptualization. *Psychological Bulletin, 85,* 417–439.

Spanos, N. P. (1994). Multiple identity enactments and multiple personality disorder: A sociocognitive perspective. *Psychological Bulletin, 116,* 143–165.

Spanos, N. P., Weekes, J. R., & Bertrand, L. D. (1985). Multiple personality: A social psychological perspective. *Journal of Abnormal Psychology, 94,* 362–376.

Spector, I. P., & Carey, M. P. (1990). Incidence and prevalence of the sexual dysfunctions: A critical review of the empirical literature. *Archives of Sexual Behavior, 19,* 389–408.

Spiegel, D., Bloom, J. R., Kraemer, H. C., & Gottheil, E. (1989). Effect of psychosocial treatment on survival of patients with metastatic breast cancer. *Lancet, 888* 891.

Spirito, A., Overholser, J. C., & Stark, L. J. (1989). Common problems and coping strategies: II. Findings with adolescent suicide attempters. *Journal of Abnormal Child Psychology, 17,* 213–221.

Spitz, R. A. (1945). Hospitalism: An inquiry into the genesis of psychiatric conditions in early childhood. *Psychoanalytic Study of the Child, 1,* 53–74.

Spitzer, R. L. (1976). More on pseudoscience in science and the case for psychiatric diagnosis. A critique of D. L. Rosenhan's "On being sane in insane places" and "The contextual nature of psychiatric diagnosis." *Archives of General Psychiatry, 33,* 459–470.

Spitzer, R. L., Fiester, S. J., Gay, M., & Pfohl, B. (1991). Results of a survey of forensic psychiatrists on the validity of the sadistic personality disorder diagnosis. *American Journal of Psychiatry, 146,* 1561–1567.

Spitzer, R. L., Gibbon, M., Skodol, A.E., Williams, J. B. W., & First, M. B. (Eds.). (1994). *DSM-IV casebook: A learning companion to the diagnostic and statistical manual of mental disorders, fourth edition.* Washington, DC: American Psychiatric Press.

Spitzer, R. L., Skodol, A. E., Gibbon, M., & Williams, J. B. W. (1983). *Psychopathology: A case book.* New York: McGraw-Hill.

Squire, L. R., & Slater, P. C. (1978). Bilateral and unilateral ECT: Effects on verbal and nonverbal memory. *American Journal of Psychiatry, 135,* 1316–1320.

Squire, L. R., Slater, P. C., & Miller, P. L. (1981). Retrograde amnesia and bilateral electroconvulsive therapy. *Archives of General Psychiatry, 38,* 89–95.

Stacy, A. W. (1997). Memory activation and expectancy as prospective predictors of alcohol and marijuana use. *Journal of Abnormal Psychology, 106,* 61–73.

Stacy, A. W., Newcomb, M. D., & Bentler, P. M. (1991). Cognitive motivation and drug use: A 9-year longitudinal study. *Journal of Abnormal Psychology, 100,* 502–515.

Stahl, S. M. (1996). *Essential psychopharmacology.* Cambridge: Cambridge University Press.

Stanton, M. D., & Shadish, W. R. (1997). Outcome, attrition, and family-couples treatment for drug abuse. *Psychological Bulletin, 122,* 170–191.

State v. Soura, 796 P.2d 109 (Idaho 1990).

State v. Summers, 853 P.2d 953 (Wash. App. 1993).

Steadman, H., McGreevy, M. A., Morrissey, J. P., et al. (1993). *Before and after Hinckley: Evaluating insanity defense reform.* New York: Guilford Press.

Steege, J. F., Stout, A. L., & Culley, C. C. (1986). Patient satisfaction in Scott and Small-Carrion penile implant recipients: A study of 52 patients. *Archives of Sexual Behavior, 15(5),* 393–399.

Steffenburg, S., & Gillberg, C. (1986). Autism and autistic-like conditions in Swedish rural and urban areas: A population study. *British Journal of Psychiatry, 149,* 81–87.

Steffenburg, S., Gillberg, C., Hellgren, L., Andersson, L., Gillberg, I. C., Jakobssen, G., & Bohman, M. (1989). A twin study of autism in Denmark, Finland, Iceland, Norway, and Sweden. *Journal of Child Psychology and Psychiatry, 30,* 405–416.

Stein, M. A. Szumowski, E., Blondis, T. A., & Roizen, N. (1995). Adaptive skills dysfunction in ADD and ADHD children. *Journal of Child Psychology and Psychiatry, 36,* 663–670.

Stein, M. B., Kirk, P., Prabhu, V., Grott, M., & Terepa, M. (1995). Mixed anxiety-depression in a primary-care clinic. *Journal of Affective Disorders, 34,* 79–84.

Steinberg, L., & Meyer, R. (1995). *Childhood.* New York: McGraw-Hill.

Steinhausen, H. C. (1994). Anorexia and bulimia nervosa. In M. Rutter, E. Taylor, & L. Hersov (Eds.), *Child and adolescent psychiatry.* Oxford, England: Blackwell Scientific Publications.

Stemberger, R. T., Turner, S. M., Beidel, D. C., & Calhoun, K. S. (1995). Social phobia: An analysis of possible developmental factors. *Journal of Abnormal Psychology, 104,* 526–531.

Stern, Y., Gurland, B., Tatemichi, T. K., Tang, M. X., Wilder, D., & Mayeux, R. (1994). Influence of education and occupation on the incidence of Alzheimer's disease. *Journal of the American Medical Association, 271,* 1004–1010.

Stets, J. E., & Straus, M. A. (1990). Gender differences in reporting of marital violence and its medical and psychological consequences. In M. A. Straus & R. J. Gelles (Eds.), *Physical violence in*

American families (pp. 151–165). New Brunswick, NJ: Transaction Press.

Stetson, B. A., Rahn, J. M., Dubbert, P. M., Wilner, B. I., & Mercury, M. G. (1997). Prospective evaluation of the effects of stress on exercise adherence in community-residing women, 16, 515–520.

Stiebel, V. G. (1994). The amytal interview in the treatment of conversion disorder: Three case reports. *Military Medicine, 159,* 350–353.

Stoller, R. J. (1975). *Sex and gender: The transsexual experiment.* London: Hogarth Press.

Stone, A. A. (1975). *Mental health and law: A system in transition.* Rockville, MD: National Institute of Mental Health.

Stone, A. A. (1976). The *Tarasoff* decision: Suing psychotherapists to safeguard society. *Harvard Law Review, 90,* 358.

Stone, A. A., Bovbjerg, D. M., Neale, J. M., & Napoli, A. (1992). Development of cold symptoms following experimental rhinovirus infection is related to prior stressful life events. *Behavioral Medicine, 18,* 115–120.

Stone, A. A., Valdimarsdottir, H. B., Katkin, E. S., Burns, J., & Cox, D. S. (1993). Effects of mental stressors on mitogen-induced lymphocyte responses in the laboratory. *Psychology and Health, 8,* 269–284.

Stone, M. H. (1993). *Abnormalities of personality. Within and beyond the realm of treatment.* New York: W. W. Norton.

Strain, E. C. (1995). Antisocial personality disorder, misbehavior, and drug abuse. *Journal of Nervous and Mental Disease, 183,* 162–165.

Strakowski, S. M., Flaum, M., Amador, X., Bracha, H. S., Pandurangi, A. K., Robinson, D., & Tohen, M. (1996). Racial differences in the diagnosis of psychosis. *Schizophrenia Research, 21,* 117–124.

Straus, M. A., & Gelles, R. J. (1990). *Physical violence in American families: Risk factors and adaptations to violence in 8,145 families.* New Brunswick, NJ: Transaction Press.

Straus, M. A., Gelles, R. J., & Steinmetz, S. K. (1980). *Behind closed doors.* New York: Doubleday Press, 1980.

Strauss, M. E. (1993). Relations of symptoms to cognitive deficits in schizophrenia. *Schizophrenia Bulletin, 19,* 215–231.

Straw, R. B. (1982). *Meta-analysis of deinstitutionalization in mental health.* Unpublished doctoral dissertation, Northwestern University, Evanston, IL.

Strober, M., Morrell, W., Burroughs, J., Lampert, C., Danforth, H., & Freeman, R. (1988). A family study of bipolar I disorder in adolescence: Early onset of symptoms linked to increased familial

loading and lithium resistance. *Journal of Affective Disorders, 15,* 255–268.

Stromberg, C. D., & Stone, A. A. (1983). A model state law on civil commitment of the mentally ill. *Harvard Journal on Legislation, 20,* 275–396.

Stroop, J. R. (1935). Studies of interference in serial verbal reactions. *Journal of Experimental Psychology, 18,* 643–661.

Stunkard, A. J., & Koch, C. (1964). The interpretation of gastric motility: I. Apparent bias in the reports of hunger by obese persons. *Archives of General Psychiatry, 11,* 74–82.

Sturgis, E. T. (1993). Obsessive-compulsive disorders. In P. B. Sutker & H. E. Adams (Eds.), *Comprehensive handbook of psychopathology* (2nd ed., pp. 129–144). New York: Plenum Press.

Substance Abuse and Mental Health Services Administration. (1996). *National household survey on drug abuse: Population estimates 1993.* Rockville, MD: DHHS Publication no. (SMA), 1994:94–3017.

Sullivan, C. M., Campbell, R., Angelique, H., Eby, K. K., & Davidson, W. S., II (1994). An advocacy intervention program for women with abusive partners: Six-month follow-up. *American Journal of Community Psychology, 22,* 101–122.

Suomi, S. J. (1982). Relevance of animal models for clinical psychology. In P. C. Kendall & J. N. Butcher (Eds.), *Handbook of research methods in clinical psychology.* New York: Wiley.

Super, C. M., Herrera, M. G., & Mora, J. O. (1990). Long-term effects of food supplementation and psychosocial intervention on the physical growth of Columbian infants at risk of malnutrition. *Child Development, 61,* 29–49.

Suppes, T., Baldessarini, R. J., Faedda, G. L., & Tohen, M. (1991). Risk of recurrence following discontinuation of lithium treatment in bipolar disorder. *Archives of General Psychiatry, 48,* 1082–1088.

Sushinsky, L. (1970). An illustration of a behavioral therapy intervention with nursing staff in a therapeutic role. *Journal of Psychiatric Nursing and Mental Health Services, 8(5),* 24–26.

Susser, E., Fennig, S., Jandorf, L., Amador, X., & Bromet, E. (1995). Epidemiology, diagnosis, and course of brief psychoses. *American Journal of Psychiatry, 152,* 1743–1748.

Susser, E., Lin, S. P., Brown, A. S., Lumey, L. H., & Erlenmeyer-Kimling, L. (1994). No relation between risk of schizophrenia and prenatal exposure to influenza in Holland. *American Journal of Psychiatry, 151,* 922–924.

Sutker, P. B., & Allain, A. N., Jr. (1996). Assessment of PTSD and other mental disorders in World War II and Korean conflict POW survivors and combat veterans. *Psychological Assessment, 8,* 18–25.

Swados, E. (1991, August 18). The story of a street person. *The New York Times Magazine,* pp. 16–18.

Swann, W. B., Jr., Wenzlaff, R. M., Krull, D. S., & Pelham, B. W. (1992). Allure of negative feedback: Self-verification strivings among depressed persons. *Journal of Abnormal Psychology, 101,* 293–306.

Swedo, S. E., Leonard, H. L., & Rapoport, J. L. (1992). Childhood-onset obsessive compulsive disorder. *Psychiatric Clinics of North America, 15,* 767–775.

Swendsen, J., Heller, T. L., & Hammen, C. (1995). Relapse and impairment in bipolar disorder. *American Journal of Psychiatry, 152,* 1635–1640.

Swerdlow, N. R., Braff, D. L., Taaid, N., & Geyer, M. A. (1994). Assessing the validity of an animal model of deficient sensorimotor gating in schizophrenic patients. *Archives of General Psychiatry, 51,* 139–154.

Szasz, T. S. (1961). *The myth of mental illness.* New York: Harper & Row.

Szasz, T. S. (1963). *Law, liberty, and psychiatry.* New York: Macmillan.

Szasz, T. S. (1977). *Psychiatric slavery.* New York: Free Press.

Szatmari, P., Jones, M. B., Tuff, L., Bartolucci, G., Fisman, S., & Mahoney, W. (1993). Lack of cognitive impairment in first-degree relatives of children with pervasive developmental disorders. *Journal of the American Academy of Child and Adolescent Psychiatry, 32,* 1264–1273.

Szatmari, P., Tuff, L., Finlayson, M. A., & Bartolucci, G. (1989). Asperger's syndrome and autism: Neurocognitive aspects. *Journal of the American Academy of Child and Adolescent Psychiatry, 29,* 130–136.

Szymanski, L. S., & Kaplan, L. C. (1997). Mental retardation. In J. M. Weiner (Ed.), *Textbook of child and adolescent psychiatry* (pp. 183–218). Washington, DC: American Psychiatric Association.

Szymanski, L. S., & Rosefsky, Q. B. (1980). Group psychotherapy with retarded persons. In L. S. Szymanski & P. E. Tanguay (Eds.), *Emotional disorders of mentally retarded persons* (pp. 173–194). Baltimore: University Park Press.

Szymanski, S. (1996). Sex differences in schizophrenia. In M. F. Jensvold, U. Halbreich, & J. A. Hamilton (Eds.), *Psychopharmacology and women: Sex, gender, and hormones* (pp. 287–297).

Washington, DC: American Psychiatric Press.

Szymanski, S., Lieberman, J. A., Alvir, J. M., Mayerhoff, D., Loebel, A., Geisler, S., Chakos, M., Koreen, A., Jody, D., Kane, J., Woerner, M., & Cooper, T. (1995). Gender differences in onset of illness, treatment response, course, and biologic indexes in first-episode schizophrenic patients. *American Journal of Psychiatry, 152,* 698–703.

Szyrynski, V. (1973). Anorexia nervosa and psychotherapy. *American Journal of Psychotherapy, 27,* 492–505.

Takei, N., Lewis, S., Jones, P., Harvey, I., & Murray, R. M. (1996). Prenatal exposure to influenza and increased cerebrospinal fluid spaces in schizophrenia. *Schizophrenia Bulletin, 22,* 521–534.

Takeshita, J. (1997). Psychosis. In W. S. Tseng & J. Streltzer (Eds.), *Culture and psychopathology: A guide to clinical assessment* (pp. 124–138). New York: Brunner/Mazel.

Taller, A. M., Asher, D. M., Pomeroy, K. L., Eldadah, B. A., Godec, M. S., Falkai, P. G., Bogerts, B., Kleinman, J. E., Stevens, J. R., & Torrey, E. F. (1996). Search for viral nucleic acid sequences in brain tissues of patients with schizophrenia using nested polymerase chain reaction. *Archives of General Psychiatry, 53,* 32–40.

Tam, W. C., & Sewell, K. W. (1995). Seasonality of birth in schizophrenia in Taiwan. *Schizophrenia Bulletin, 21,* 117–127.

Tamminga, C. A. (1997). The promise of new drugs for schizophrenia treatment. *Canadian Journal of Psychiatry, 42,* 265–273.

Tancer, M. E. (1993). Neurobiology of social phobia. *Journal of Clinical Psychiatry, 54,* 26–30.

Tanner, J. M. (1990). *Fetus into man: Physical growth from conception to maturity.* Cambridge, MA: Harvard University Press.

Tarasoff v. Regents of California, 17 Cal. 3d 425, 131 Cal. Rptr. 14 (1976).

Tarrier, N., Barrowclough, C., Porceddu, K., et al. (1988). The assessment of psychophysiological reactivity to the expressed emotion of the relatives of schizophrenic patients. *British Journal of Psychiatry, 152,* 618–624.

Tarrier, N., Harwood, S., Yusopoff, L., Beckett, R., & Baker, A. (1990). Coping strategy enhancement (CSE): A method of treating residual schizophrenic symptoms. *Behavioural Psychotherapy, 18,* 283–293.

Tarullo, L. B., Richardson, D. T., Radke-Yarrow, M., & Martinez, P. E. (1995).

Multiple sources in child diagnosis: Parent-child concordance in affectively ill and well families. *Journal of Clinical Child Psychology, 24,* 173–183.

Taylor, C. B., & Arnow, B. (1988). *The nature and treatment of anxiety disorders:* New York: Free Press.

Taylor, H. G. (1989). Learning disabilities. In E. J. Mash & R. A. Barkley (Eds.), *Treatment of childhood disorders.* New York: Guilford Press.

Taylor, S., & McLean, P. (1993). Outcome profiles in the treatment of unipolar depression. *Behaviour Research and Therapy, 31,* 325–330.

Teasdale, J. D., Taylor, M. J., Cooper, Z., Hayhurst, H., & Paykel, E. S. (1995). Depressive thinking: Shifts in construct accessibility or in schematic mental models? *Journal of Abnormal Psychology, 104,* 500–507.

Teicher, M. H., Glod, C. A., Magnus, E., Harper, D., Benson, G., Krueger, K., & McGreenery, C. E. (1997). Circadian rest-activity disturbances in seasonal affective disorder. *Archives of General Psychiatry, 54,* 124–130.

Telch, M. J., Brouillard, M., Telch, C. F., Agras, W. S., & Taylor, C. B. (1989). Role of cognitive appraisal in panic-related avoidance. *Behaviour Research and Therapy, 27,* 373–383.

Tellegen, A., Lykken, D. T., Bouchard, T. J., Wilcox, K. J., Segal, N. L., & Rich, S. (1988). Personality similarity in twins reared apart and together. *Journal of Personality and Social Psychology, 54,* 1031–1039.

Templeton, B. (1997). Alcohol-impaired driving: The family's tragedy and the public's health. *Journal of the American Medical Association, 277,* 1279.

Terént, A. (1993). Stroke mortality. In J. P. Whisnant (Ed.), *Stroke, populations, cohorts, and clinical trials* (pp. 37–58). Boston: Butterworth-Heinemann.

Test, D. W., Hinson, K. B., Solow, J., & Keul, P. (1993). Job satisfaction of persons in supported employment. *Education and Training in Mental Retardation, 28,* 39–46.

Test, M. A., & Stein, L. I. (1978). Training in community living: Research design and results. In L. I. Stein & M. A. Test (Eds.), *Alternatives to mental hospital treatment.* New York: Plenum Press.

Thase, M. E., Dube, S., Bowler, K., Howland, R. H., Myers, J. E., Friedman, E., & Jarrett, D. B. (1996). Hypothalamic-pituitary-adrenocortical activity and response to cognitive-behavior therapy in unmedicated, hospitalized depressed patients. *American Journal of Psychiatry, 153,* 886–891.

Thase, M. E., Fava, M., Halbreich, U., Kocsis, J. H., Koran, L., Davidson, J., Rosenbaum, J., & Harrison, W. (1996). A placebo-controlled, randomized clinical trial comparing sertraline and imipramine for the treatment of dysthymia. *Archives of General Psychiatry, 53,* 777–784.

Thase, M. E., Frank, E., & Kupfer, D. J. (1985). Biological processes in major depression. In E. E. Beckham & W. R. Leber (Eds.), *Handbook of depression* (pp. 816–913). Homewood, IL: Dorsey Press.

Thase, M. E., Greenhouse, J. B., Frank, E., Reynolds, C. F., III., Pilkonis, P. A., Hurley, K., Grochocinski, V., & Kupfer, D. J. (1997). Treatment of major depression with psychotherapy or psychotherapy-pharmacotherapy combinations. *Archives of General Psychiatry, 54,* 1009–1015.

Thase, M. E., & Kupfer, D. J. (1996). Recent developments in the pharmacotherapy of mood disorders. *Journal of Consulting and Clinical Psychology, 64,* 646–659.

Thase, M. E., Simons, A. D., Cahalano, J. F., & McGeary, J. (1991). Cognitive behavior therapy of endogenous depression: I. An outpatient clinical replication series. *Behavior Therapy, 22,* 457–467.

Thase, M. E., Simons, A. D., Cahalano, J., McGoory, J., & Harden, T. (1991). Severity of depression and response to cognitive behavior therapy. *American Journal of Psychiatry, 148,* 784–789.

Thase, M. E., Simons, A. D., & Reynolds, C. F., III. (1996). Abnormal electroencephalographic sleep profiles in major depression: Association with response to cognitive behavior therapy. *Archives of General Psychiatry, 53,* 99–108.

Thayer, J. F., Friedman, B. H., & Borkovec, T. D. (1996). Autonomic characteristics of generalized anxiety disorder and worry. *Biological Psychiatry, 39,* 255–266.

Theodore, W. H. (Ed.) (1988a). *Clinical neuroimaging (Vol. 7) Frontiers in neuroscience.* New York: Alan R. Liss.

Theodore, W. H. (1988b). Introduction. In W. H. Theodore (Ed.), *Clinical neuroimaging (Vol. 7) Frontiers in neuroscience.* New York: Alan R. Liss.

Thigpen, C. H., & Cleckley, H. (1957). *The three faces of Eve.* New York: McGraw-Hill.

Thompson, M. G., McInnes, R. R., & Willard, H. F. (1991). *Genetics in medicine* (5th ed.). Philadelphia: Saunders.

Thomson, N., Fraser, D., & McDougall, A. (1974). The reinstatement of speech in near-mute chronic schizophrenics by instructions, imitative prompts and reinforcement. *Journal of Behavior Therapy and Experimental Psychiatry, 5,* 83–89.

Thornberry, T. P., & Krohn, M. D. (1997). Peers, drug use, and delinquency. In D. M. Stoff, J. Breiling, & J. D. Maser (Eds.), *Handbook of antisocial behavior* (pp. 218–233). New York: Wiley.

Thorpy, M., & Glovinsky, P. (1987). Parasomnias. *Psychiatric Clinics of North America, 10,* 623–639.

Tiefer, L., Pedersen, B., & Melman, A. (1988). Psychosocial follow-up of penile prosthesis implant patients and partners. *Journal of Sex and Marital Therapy, 14,* 184–201.

Tienari, P., Wynne, L. C., Moring, J., Lahti, I., Naarala, M., Sorri, A., Wahlberg, K. E., Saarento, O., Seitamaa, M., Kaleva, M., & Laksy, K. (1994). The Finnish Adoptive Family Study of Schizophrenia: Implications for family research. *British Journal of Psychiatry, 164,* 20–26.

Timio, M., Verdecchia, P., Venanzi, S., Gentili, S., Ronconi, M., Francucci, B., Montanari, M., & Bichisao, E. (1988). Age and blood pressure changes: A 20-year follow-up study in nuns in a secluded order. *Hypertension, 12,* 457–461.

Tinklenberg, J. R. (1971). A clinical view of the amphetamines. *American Family Physician, (5),* 82–86.

Tolan, P. H., & Thomas, P. (1995). The implications of age of onset for delinquency risk II: Longitudinal data. *Journal of Abnormal Child Psychology, 23,* 157–181.

Tolbert, L., Haigler, T., Waits, M. M., & Dennis, T. (1993). Brief report: Lack of response in an autistic population to a low dose clinical trial of pyridoxine plus magnesium. *Journal of Autism and Developmental Disorders, 23.*

Tolman, E. C. (1948). Cognitive maps in rats and men. *Psychological Review, 55,* 189–208.

Tolman, E. C., & Honzig, C. H. (1930). "Insight" in rats. *University of California Publications in Psychology, 4,* 215–232.

Tomarken, A. J. (1995). A psychometric perspective on psychophysiological measures. *Psychological Assessment, 7,* 387–395.

Tomarken, A. J., Sutton, S. K., & Mineka, S. (1995). Fear-relevant illusory correlations: What types of associations promote judgmental bias? *Journal of Abnormal Psychology, 104,* 312–326.

Tonigan, J. S., Toscova, R., & Miller, W. R. (1996). Meta-analysis of the literature on Alcoholics Anonymous: Sample and study characteristics moderate findings.

Journal of Studies on Alcohol, 57, 65–72.

Toomey, R., Kremen, W.S., Simpson, J. C., Samson, J. A., Seidman, L. J., Lyons, M. J., Faraone, S. V., & Tsuang, M. T. (1997). Revisiting the factor structure for positive and negative symptoms: Evidence from a large heterogeneous group of psychiatric patients. *American Journal of Psychiatry, 154,* 371–377.

Torgersen, S. (1983). Genetic factors in anxiety disorders. *Archives of General Psychiatry, 40,* 1085–1089.

Torgersen, S. (1986). Genetics of somatoform disorders. *Archives of General Psychiatry, 43,* 502–505.

Torrey, E. F., Bowler, A. E., Rawlings, R., & Terrazas, A. (1993). Seasonality of schizophrenia and stillbirths. *Schizophrenia Bulletin, 19,* 557–562.

Trenerry, M. R., Jack, C. R., Jr., Cascino, G. D., Sharbrough, F. W., & Ivnik, R. J. (1995). Gender differences in post-temporal lobectomy verbal memory and relationships between MRI hippocamal volumes and preoperative verbal memory. *Epilepsy Research, 20,* 69–76.

Trenerry, M. R., Jack, C. R., Jr., Cascino, G. D., Sharbrough, F. W., & Ivnik, R. J. (1996). Sex differences in the relationship between visual memory and MRI hippocamal volumes. *Neuropsychology, 10,* 343–351.

Trzepacz, P. T., & Baker, R. W. (1993). *The psychiatric mental status examination.* New York: Oxford University Press.

Tsai, L.Y. (1987). Pre-, peri-, and neonatal factors in autism. In E. Schopler & G. B. Mesibov (Eds.), *Neurobiological issues in autism* (pp. 179–189). New York: Plenum Press.

Tsai, L.Y. (1992). Medical treatment in autism. In D.E. Berkell (Ed.), *Autism: Identification, education, and treatment* (pp. 151–184). Hillsdale, NJ: Erlbaum.

Tsai, L.Y., & Ghaziuddin, M. (1997). Autistic disorder. In J. M. Weiner (Ed.), *Textbook of child and adolescent psychiatry* (pp. 219–254). Washington, DC: American Psychiatric Association.

Tucker, J. S., Friedman, H. S., Wingard, D. L., & Schwartz, J. E. (1996). Marital history at midlife as a predictor of longevity: Alternative explanations to the protective effect of marriage. *Health Psychology, 15,* 94–101.

Turkat, I. D., & Levin, R. A. (1984). Formulation of personality disorders. In H. E. Adams & P. B. Sutker (Eds.), *Comprehensive handbook of psychopathology.* New York: Plenum Press.

Turkheimer, E., & Parry, C. D. H. (1992). Why the gap? Practice and policy in civil commitment hearings. *American Psychologist, 47,* 646–655.

Turner, L. A., Althof, S. E., Levine, S. B., Bodner, D. R., Kursh, E. D., & Resnick, M. I. (1991). External vacuum devices in the treatment of erectile dysfunction: A one-year study of sexual and psychosocial impact. *Journal of Sex and Marital Therapy, 17,* 81–93.

Turner, L. A., Althof, S. E., Levine, S. B., Risen, C. B., Bodner, D. R., Kursh, E. D., & Resnick, M. I. (1989). Self-injection of papaverine and phentolamine in the treatment of psychogenic impotence. *Journal of Sex and Marital Therapy, 15,* 163–176.

Turner, S. M., & Beidel, D. C. (1989). Social phobia: Clinical syndrome, diagnosis, and comorbidity. *Clinical Psychology Review, 9,* 3–18.

Turner, S. M., Beidel, D. C., Dancu, C. V., & Keys, D. J. (1986). Psychopathology of social phobia and comparison to avoidant personality disorder. *Journal of Abnormal Psychology, 95,* 389–394.

Turner, S. M., Jacob, R. G., & Morrison, R. (1985). Somatoform and factitious disorders. In H. E. Adams & P. Sutker (Eds.), *Comprehensive handbook of psychopathology* (pp. 307–345). New York: Plenum Press.

Tymchuk, A. J., Andron, L., & Rahbar, B. (1988). Effective decision-making/problem-solving training with mothers who have mental retardation. *American Journal on Mental Retardation, 92*(6), 510–516.

Uchino, B. N., Caccioppo, J. T., & Kiecolt-Glaser, J. K. (1996). The relationship between social support and physiological processes: A review with emphasis on underlying mechanisms and implications for health. *Psychological Bulletin, 119,* 488–531.

Uhde, T. W., Tancer, M. E., Black, B., & Brown, T. M. (1991). Phenomenology and neurobiology of social phobia: Comparison with panic disorder. *Journal of Clinical Psychiatry, 52,* 31–40.

Uhlenhuth, E. H., Balter, M. B., Mellinger, G. D., Cisin, I. H., & Clinthorne, J. (1983). Symptom checklist syndromes in the general population. *Archives of General Psychiatry, 40,* 1167–1173.

Ullmann, L. P., & Krasner, L. (Eds.). (1965). *Case studies in behavior modification.* New York: Holt, Rinehart and Winston.

Ullmann, L. P., & Krasner, L. (1975). *A psychological approach to abnormal behavior* (2nd ed.). Englewood Cliffs, NJ: Prentice-Hall.

United States v. Pullen, 89 F. 3d 368 (7th Cir. 1996).

Unnewehr, S., Schneider, S., Margraf, J., Jenkins, M., & Florin, I. (1996).

Exposure to internal and external stimuli: Reactions in children of patients with panic disorder or animal phobia. *Journal of Anxiety Disorders, 10,* 489–508.

U.S. Bureau of the Census. (1990). *Statistical abstract of the United States* (110th ed.). Washington, DC: U.S. Government Printing Office.

U.S. Department of Health and Human Services. (1991). *Health status of minorities and low-income groups.* Hyattsville, MD.

U.S. Department of Justice, Federal Bureau of Investigation. (1993). *Crime in the United States, 1992.* Washington, DC: U.S. Government Printing Office.

U.S. Public Health Service. (1964). *Smoking and health* (Report of the Advisory Committee to the Surgeon General of the Public Health Service). Washington, DC: Department of Health, Education, and Welfare.

Üstün, T. B., Bertelsen, A., Dilling, H., vanDrimmelen, J., Pull, C., Okasha, A., Sartorius, N., et al. (1996). *ICD-10 casebook: The many faces of mental disorders—adult case histories according to ICD-10* (pp. 67–69). Washington, DC: American Psychiatric Press, Inc.

Uviller, H. R. (1996). *Virtual justice.* New Haven: Yale University Press.

Valenzuela, M. (1990). Attachment in chronically underweight young children. *Child Development, 61,* 1984–1996.

Van Italli, J. B. (1985). Health implications of overweight and obesity in the United States. *Annals of Internal Medicine, 103,* 983–988.

Vasey, M. W. (1995). Social anxiety disorder. In A. R. Eisen, C. A. Kearney, & C. E. Schaefer (Eds.), *Clinical handbook of anxiety disorders in children and adolescents* (pp. 131–168). Northvale, NJ: Aronson.

Vaughan, S. C., & Roose, S. P. (1995). The analytic process: Clinical and research definitions. *International Journal of Psycho-Analysis, 76,* 343–356.

Vaughn, C. E., & Leff, J. P. (1976). The influence of family and social factors on the course of psychiatric illness: A comparison of schizophrenic and depressed neurotic patients. *British Journal of Psychiatry, 129,* 125–137.

Veale, D., Gournay, K., Dryden, W., Boocock, A., Shah, F., Willson, R., & Walburn, J. (1996). Body dysmorphic disorder: A cognitive behavioural model and pilot randomised controlled trial. *Behaviour Research and Therapy, 34,* 717–729.

Velligan, D. I., Mahurin, R. K., Eckert, S. L., Hazleton, B. C., & Miller, A. (1997).

Relationship between specific types of communication deviance and attentional performance in patients with schizophrenia. *Psychiatry Research, 70,* 9 20.

Velting, D. M., & Gould, M. S. (1997). Suicide contagion. In R. W. Maris, M. M. Silverman, & S. S. Canetto (Eds.), *Review of suicidology* (pp. 96–137). New York: Guilford Press.

Venables, P. H. (1996). Schizotypy and maternal exposure to influenza and to cold temperature: The Mauritius Study. *Journal of Abnormal Psychology, 105,* 53–60.

Venter, A., Lord, C., & Schopler, E. (1992). A follow-up study of high-functioning autistic children. *Journal of Child Psychology and Psychiatry, 33,* 489–507.

Vernon, P. (1941). Psychological effects of air raids. *Journal of Abnormal and Social Psychology, 36,* 457–476.

Vinogradov, S., Willis-Shore, J., Poole, J. H., Marten, E., Ober, B. A., & Shenaut, G. K. (1997).Clinical and neurocognitive aspects of source monitoring errors in schizophrenia. *American Journal of Psychiatry, 154,* 1530–1537.

Virkkunen, M., Goldman, D., Nielsen, D., & Linnoila, M. (1995). Low brain serotonin turnover rate (Low CSF5-HIAA) and impulsive violence. *Journal of Psychiatry and Neuroscience, 20,* 271–275.

Visintainer, M. A., Volpicelli, J. R., & Seligman. M. E. P. (1982). Tumor rejection in rats after inescapable or escapable shock. *Science, 216(23),* 437–439.

Vitkus, J., & Horowitz, L. M. (1987). The poor social performance of lonely people: Lacking a skill or adopting a role? *Journal of Personality and Social Psychiatry, 57,* 1266–1273.

Vivian, D., & Langhinrichsen-Rohling, J. (1994). Are bi-directionality violent couples mutually victimized? A gender-sensitive comparison. *Violence and Victims, 9,* 107–123.

Voas, R. B., Holder, H. D., & Gruenewald, P. J. (1997). The effect of drinking and driving interventions on alcohol-involved traffic crashes within a comprehensive community trial. *Addiction, 92,* Supplement 2, S221–S236.

Volkmar, F. R., & Nelson, D. S. (1990). Seizure disorders in autism. *Journal of the American Academy of Child and Adolescent Psychiatry, 29,* 127–129.

Volpicelli, J. R., Rhines, K.C., Rhines, J. S., Volpicelli, L. A., Alterman, A. I., & O'Brien, C. P. (1997). Naltrexone and alcohol dependence. *Archives of General Psychiatry, 54,* 737–742.

Vondra, J., Barnett, D., & Cicchetti, D. (1990). Self-concept, motivation and competence among preschoolers from maltreating and comparison families. *Child Abuse and Neglect, 14,* 525–540.

Voth, E. A., & Schwartz, R. H. (1997). Medicinal applications of delta-9-tetrahydrocannabinol and marijuana. *Annals of Internal Medicine, 1997,* 791–798.

Wachtel, P. L. (1973). Psychodynamics, behavior therapy, and the implacable experimenter: An inquiry into the consistency of personality. *Journal of Abnormal Psychology, 82,* 324–334.

Waggoner, R. W., & Bagchi, B. K. (1954). Initial masking of organic brain changes by psychic symptoms. *American Journal of Psychiatry, 110,* 904–910.

Wagner, B. M. (1997). Family risk factors for child and adolescent suicidal behavior. *Psychological Bulletin, 121,* 246–298.

Wahlberg, K. E., Wynne, L. C., Oja, H., Keskitalo, P., Pykalainen, L., Lahti, I., Moring, J., Naarala, M., Sorri, A., Seitamaa, M., Laksy, K., Kolassa, J., & Tienari, P. (1997). Gene-environment interaction in vulnerability to schizo phrenia: Findings from the Finnish Adoptive Family Study of Schizo-phrenia. *American Journal of Psychiatry, 154,* 355 362.

Wakefield, J. C. (1992). The concept of mental disorder. *American Psychologist, 47,* 373 388.

Waldinger, R. J., & Gunderson, J. G. (1987). *Effective psychotherapy with borderline patients: Case studies.* New York: Macmillan.

Waldner-Haugrud, L. K., & Magruder, B. (1995). Male and female sexual victimization in dating relationships: Gender differences in coercion techniques and outcomes. *Violence and Victims, 10,* 203–215.

Waldron, I., Lye, D., & Brandon, A. (1991). Gender differences in teenage smoking. *Women and Health, 17(2),* 65–90.

Walker, E. F., & Diforio, D. (1997). Schizophrenia: A neural diathesis-stress model. *Psychological Review, 104,* 667–685.

Walker, L. E. A. (1989). Psychology and violence against women. *American Psychologist, 44,* 695–702.

Walker, L. E. A. (1994). Are personality disorders gender biased? In S. A. Kirk & S. D. Einbinder (Eds.), *Controversial issues in mental health* (pp. 22–29). New York: Allyn and Bacon.

Wallace, C. J., & Liberman, R. P. (1985). Social skills training for patients with schizophrenia: A controlled clinical trial. *Psychiatry Research, 15,* 239–247.

Waller, N. G., Putnam, F. W., & Carlson, E. B. (1996). Types of dissociation and dissociative types: A taxometric analysis of dissociative experiences. *Psychological Methods, 1,* 300–321.

Waller, N. G., & Ross, C. A. (1997). The prevalence and biometric structure of pathological dissociation in the general population: Taxometric and behavior genetic findings. *Journal of Abnormal Psychology, 106,* 499–510.

Walsh, R., & Shapiro, D. (Eds.). (1980). *Beyond health and normality: Explorations of extreme psychological well-being.* New York: Van Nostrand.

Ward, K. E., Friedman, L., Wise, A., & Schulz, S. C. (1996). Meta-analysis of brain and cranial size in schizophrenia. *Schizophrenia Research, 22,* 197–213.

Ward, T., Hudson, S. M., Johnston, L., & Marshall, W. I. (1997). Cognitive distortions in sex offenders: An integrative review. *Clinical Psychology Review, 17,* 479–507.

Ward, T., Hudson, S. M., & Marshall, W. L. (1996). Attachment style in sex offenders: A preliminary study. *Journal of Sex Research, 33,* 17–26.

Ward, T., McCormack, J., & Hudson, S. M. (1997). Sexual offenders' perceptions of their intimate relationships. *Sexual Abuse: Journal of Research and Treatment, 9,* 57–74.

Wardle, J. (1980). Dietary restraint and binge eating. *Behavioral Analysis and Modification, 4,* 201–209.

Warren, J. L., Hazelwood, R. R., & Dietz, P. E. (1996). The sexually sadistic serial killer. *Journal of Forensic Sciences, 41,* 970–974.

Warwick, H. M. C., & Marks, I. M. (1988). Behavioural treatment of illness phobia and hypochondriasis: A pilot study of 17 cases. *British Journal of Psychiatry, 152,* 239–241.

Washington v. Harper, 110 S. Ct. 1028 (1990).

Waterhouse, L. (1994). Severity of impairment in autistic spectrum disorders. In S. H. Broman & J. Grafman (Eds.), *Atypical cognitive deficits in developmental disorders: Implications for brain function* (pp. 159–182). Hillsdale, NJ: Erlbaum.

Waterhouse, L., Wing, L., & Fein, D. (1989). Reevaluating the syndrome of autism in the light of empirical research. In G. Dawson & S. Segalowitz (Eds.), *Autism: Perspectives on diagnosis, nature and treatment* (pp. 263–281). New York: Guilford Press.

Watkins, M. J. (1990). Mediationism and the obfuscation of memory. *American Psychologist, 45,* 328–335.

Watson, J. B. (1913). Psychology as the behaviorist views it. *Psychological Review, 20,* 158–177.

Watson, J. B., & Rayner, R. (1920). Conditioning emotional responses. *Journal of Experimental Psychology, 3,* 1–14.

Watson, L. S., & Uzzell, R. (1981). Teaching self-help skills to the mentally retarded. In J. L. Matson & J. R. McCartney (Eds.), *Handbook of behavior modification with the mentally retarded.* New York: Plenum Press.

Watzlawick, P., Beavin, J., & Jackson, D. (1967). *Pragmatics of human communication: A study of interaction patterns, pathologies, and paradoxes.* New York: W. W. Norton.

Webb, L. J., Gold, R. S., Johnstone, E. E., & DiClemente, C. C. (1981). Accuracy of *DSM-III* diagnoses following a training program. *American Journal of Psychiatry, 138,* 376–378.

Wechsler, D. (1958). *The measurement and appraisal of adult intelligence* (4th ed.). Baltimore: Williams & Wilkins.

Wechsler, H., Davenport, A., Dowdall, G., Moeykens, B., & Castillo, S. (1994). Health and behavioral consequences of binge drinking in college: A national survey of students at 140 campuses. *Journal of the American Medical Association, 272,* 1672–1677.

Wehman, P., & Kregel, J. (1995). At the crossroads: Supported employment a decade later. *Journal of the Association for Persons with Severe Handicaps, 20,* 286–299.

Wehr, T. A. (1990). Effects of wakefulness and sleep on depression and mania. In J. Montplaisir & R. Godbout (Eds.), *Sleep and biological rhythms: Basic mechanisms and applications to psychiatry* (pp. 42–86). New York: Oxford University Press.

Weihofen, H. (1957). *The urge to punish.* London: Gollancz.

Weinberger, D. R., Cannon-Spoor, E., Poktin, S. G., & Wyatt, R. J. (1980). Poor premorbid adjustment and CT scan abnormalities in chronic schizophrenia. *American Journal of Psychiatry, 137,* 1410–1413.

Weiner, B., Frieze, L., Kukla, A., Reed, L., Rest, S., & Rosenbaum, R. M. (1971). *Perceiving the causes of success and failure.* New York: General Learning Press.

Weiner, H. (1994). The revolution in stress theory and research. In R. P. Liberman & J. Yager (Eds.), *Stress in psychiatric disorders* (pp. 1–36). New York: Springer.

Weiner, I. B. (1996). Some observations on the validity of the Rorschach Inkblot Method. *Psychological Assessment, 8,* 206–213.

Weisman, A., López, S. R., Karno, M., & Jenkins, J. (1993). An attributional analysis of expressed emotion in Mexican-American families with schizophrenia. *Journal of Abnormal Psychology, 102,* 601–606.

Weiss, D. S., Marmar, C. R., Schlenger, W. E., Fairbank, J. A., Jordan, B. K., Hough, R. L., & Kulka, R. A. (1992). The prevalence of lifetime and partial posttraumatic stress disorder in Vietnam theater veterans. *Journal of Traumatic Stress, 5,* 365–376.

Weiss, G., & Hechtman, L. (1993). *Hyperactive children grown up.* New York. Guilford Press.

Weiss, J. M. (1977). Psychosomatic disorders. In J. D. Maser & M. E. P. Seligman (Eds.), *Psychopathology: Experimental models.* San Francisco: Freeman.

Weiss, J. M. (1982, August). *A model for neurochemical study of depression.* Paper presented at the annual meeting of the American Psychological Association, Washington, DC.

Weissberg, R. P., & Bell, D. N. (1997) A meta-analytic review of primary prevention in programs for children and adolescents: Contributions and caveats. *American Journal of Community Psychology, 25,* 207–214.

Weissman, M. M. (1990). Evidence for comorbidity of anxiety and depression: Family and genetic studies of children. In J. D. Maser & C. R. Cloninger (Eds.), *Comorbidity of mood and anxiety disorders.* Washington, DC: American Psychiatric Press.

Weissman, M. M. (1993). Family genetic studies of panic disorder. *Journal of Psychiatric Research, 27,* 69–78.

Weissman, M. M., Bland, R. C., Canino, G. J., Greenwald, S., Hwu, H. G., Lee, C. K., Newman, S. C., Oakley-Browne, M. A., Rubio-Stipec, M., Wickramaratne, P. J., Wittchen, H. U., & Yeh, E. K. (1994). The cross national epidemiology of obsessive compulsive disorder: The Cross National Collaborative Group. *Journal of Clinical Psychiatry, 55,* 5–10.

Weissman, M. M., Warner, V., Wickramaratne, P., & Prusoff, B. A. (1988). Early-onset major depression in parents and their children. *Journal of Affective Disorders, 15,* 269–277.

Weisz, J. R., Suwanlert, S., Chaiyasit, W., & Walter, B. (1987a). Epidemiology of behavioral and emotional problems among Thai and American children: Parent reports for ages 6–11. *Journal of the American Academy of Child and Adolescent Psychiatry, 26,* 890–897.

Weisz, J. R., Suwanlert, S., Chaiyasit, W., & Walter, B. (1987b). Over- and undercontrolled referral problems among children and adolescents from Thailand and the United States: The *Wat* and *Wai* of cultural differences. *Journal of Consulting and Clinical Psychology, 55,* 719–726.

Weisz, J. R., Suwanlert, S., Chaiyasit, W., Weiss, B., Achenbach, T. M., & Eastman, K. I. (1993). Behavioral and emotional problems among Thai and American adolescents: Parent reports for ages 12–16. *Journal of Abnormal Psychology, 102,* 395–403.

Weisz, J. R., Weiss, B., Alicke, M. D., & Klotz, M. L. (1987). Effectiveness of psychotherapy with children and adolescents: A meta-analysis for clinicians. *Journal of Consulting and Clinical Psychology, 55,* 542–549.

Wekstein, L. (1979). *Handbook of suicidology: Principles, problems, and practice.* New York: Brunner/Mazel.

Welch, M. W., & Gist, J. W. (1974). *The open token economy system: A handbook for a behavioral approach to rehabilitation.* Springfield, IL: Charles C Thomas.

Wells, K. B., Golding, J. M., & Burnam, M. A. (1989). Chronic medical conditions in a sample of the general population with anxiety, affective, and substance use disorders. *American Journal of Psychiatry, 146,* 1440–1446.

Weltzin, T. E., Starzynski, J., Santelli, R., & Kaye, W. H. (1993). Anorexia and bulimia nervosa. In R. T. Ammerman, C. G. Last, & M. Hersen (Eds.), *Handbook of prescriptive treatments for children and adolescents* (pp. 214–239). Boston: Allyn and Bacon.

Wender, P. H., Kety, S. S., Rosenthal, D., Schulsinger, F., Ortmann, J., & Lunde, I. (1986). Psychiatric disorders in the biological and adoptive families of adopted individuals with affective disorders. *Archives of General Psychiatry, 43,* 923–929.

Wesson, D. R., & Smith, D. E. (1971, December 15). *Barbiturate use as an intoxicant: A San Francisco perspective.* Testimony presented at the subcommittee to investigate juvenile delinquency.

Wexler, D. B. (1981). *Mental health law: Major issues.* New York: Plenum Press.

Whipple, E., & Webster-Stratton, C. (1991). The role of parental stress in physically abusive families. *Child Abuse and Neglect, 15,* 279–291.

Whisman, M. A. (1993). Mediators and moderators of change in cognitive therapy of depression. *Psychological Bulletin, 114,* 248–265.

Whisnant, J. P. (1993). Natural history of transient ischemic attack and ischemic stroke. In J. P. Whisnant (Ed.), *Stroke, populations, cohorts, and clinical trials*

(pp. 135–153). Boston: Butterworth-Heinemann.

Whitehouse, M. A., & McCabe, M. P. (1997). Sex education programs for people with intellectual disability: How effective are they? *Education and Training in Mental Retardation and Developmental Disabilities, 32,* 229–240.

Whitlatch, C. J., Zarit, S. H., & von Eye, A. (1991). Efficacy of interventions with caregivers: A reanalysis. *Gerontologist, 31,* 9–14.

Whitman, T. L. (1994). Mental retardation. In L. W. Craighead, W. E. Craighead, A. E. Kazdin, & M. J. Mahoney (Eds.), *Cognitive and behavioral interventions: An empirical approach to mental health problems* (pp. 313–333). Boston: Allyn and Bacon.

Whitman, T. L., Scherzinger, M. F., & Sommer, K. S. (1991). Cognitive instruction and mental retardation. In P.C. Kendall (Ed.), *Child and adolescent therapy: Cognitive-behavioral procedures* (pp. 276–315). New York: Guilford Press.

Whybrow, P. C., Akiskal, H. S., & McKinney, W. T., Jr. (1984). *Mood disorders: Toward a new psychobiology.* New York: Plenum Press.

Widiger, T. A. (in press). Sex biases in the diagnosis of personality disorders. *Journal of Personality Disorders.*

Widiger, T. A. (1995). Detection of self-defeating and sadistic personality disorder diagnoses. In W. J. Livesley (Ed.), *The DSM-IV personality disorders* (pp. 359–373). New York: Guilford Press.

Widiger, T. A., Cadoret, R., Hare, R., Robins, L., Rutherford, M., Zanarini, M., Alterman, A., Apple, M., Corbitt, E., Forth, A., Hart, S., Kultermann, J., Woody, G., & Frances, A. (1996). *DSM-IV* Antisocial Personality Disorder field trial. *Journal of Abnormal Psychology, 105,* 3–16.

Widiger, T. A., & Costa, P. T. (1994). Personality and personality disorders. *Journal of Abnormal Psychology, 103,* 78–91.

Widiger, T. A., Mangine, S., Corbitt, E. M., Ellis, C. G., & Thomas, G. V. (1995). *Personality Disorder Interview-IV. A semistructured interview for the assessment of personality disorders.* Odessa, FL: Psychological Assessment Resources.

Widiger, T. A., & Sanderson, C. J. (1997). Personality disorders. In A. Tasman, J. Kay, & J. A. Lieberman (Eds.), *Psychiatry* (Vol. 2, pp. 1291–1317). Philadelphia: W. B. Saunders.

Widiger, T. A., & Trull, T. J. (1991). Diagnosis and clinical assessment. *Annual Review of Psychology, 41,* 109–135.

Widiger, T. A., & Trull, T. J. (1993). Borderline and narcissistic personality disorders. In P. B. Sutker & H. E. Adams (Eds.), *Comprehensive handbook of psychopathology* (2nd ed.) (pp. 181–201). New York: Plenum Press.

Widom, C.S. (1997). Child abuse, neglect, and witnessing violence. In D. M. Stoff, J. Breiling, & J. D. Maser (Eds.), *Handbook of antisocial behavior* (pp. 159–170). New York: Wiley.

Wielgus, M. S., & Harvey, P. D. (1988). Dichotic listening and recall in schizophrenia and mania. *Schizophrenia Bulletin, 14,* 689–700.

Wile, D. B. (1995). The ego-analytic approach to couple therapy. In N. S. Jacobson, A. S. Gurman, et al. (Eds.), *Clinical handbook of couple therapy* (pp. 91–120). New York: Guilford Press.

Willerman, L., & Cohen, D. B. (1990). *Psychopathology.* New York: McGraw-Hill.

William, F., Birchler, G. R., & O'Farrell, T. J. (1996). Behavioral couples therapy for male substance-abusing patients. *Journal of Consulting and Clinical Psychology, 64,* 959–972.

Williams, G. J. R. (1983). Child abuse. In C. E. Walker & M. C. Roberts (Eds.), *Handbook of clinical child psychology* (pp. 1219–1248). New York: Wiley.

Williams, J. M. G., Mathews, A., & MacLeod, C. (1996). The emotional Stroop task and psychopathology. *Psychological Bulletin, 120,* 3–24.

Williams, L. B., & Pratt, W. F. (1990). *Wanted and unwanted childbearing in the United States: 1973–88* (data from the National Survey of Family Growth; advance data from *Vital and Health Statistics, 189*). Hyattsville, MD: National Center for Health Statistics.

Williams, L. M. (1994). Recall of childhood trauma: A prospective study of women's memories of child sexual abuse. *Journal of Consulting and Clinical Psychology, 62,* 1167–1176.

Williams, L. M. (1995). Recovered memories of abuse in women with documented child sexual victimization histories. *Journal of Traumatic Stress, 8,* 649–673.

Williams, R. B., Barefoot, J. C., Califf, R. M., Haney, T. L., Saunders, W. B., Pryor, D. B., Hlatky, M. A., Siegler, I. C., & Mark, D. B. (1992). Prognostic importance of social and economic resources among medically treated patients with angiographically documented coronary artery disease. *Journal of the American Medical Association, 267,* 520–524.

Williams, R. L., Schaefer, C. A., Shisslak, C. M., Gronwaldt, V. H., Comerci, G. D. (1986). Eating attitudes and behaviors in adolescent women: Discrimination of normals, dieters, and suspected bulimics using the eating attitudes test and eating disorder inventory. *International Journal of Eating Disorders, 5,* 879–894.

Williamson, D. F., Kahn, H. S., Remington, P. L., & Anda, R. F. (1990). The 10-year incidence of overweight and weight gain in U.S. adults. *Archives of Internal Medicine, 150,* 665–672.

Wilson, D. C., & Lantz, E. M. (1957). The effect of cultural change on the Negro race in Virginia as indicated by a study of state hospital admissions. *American Journal of Psychiatry, 114,* 24–32.

Wilson, G. D. (1987). An ethological approach to sexual deviation. In G. D. Wilson (Ed.), *Variant sexuality: Research and theory.* Baltimore: Johns Hopkins University Press.

Wilson, G. T., & Fairburn, C. G. (1993). Cognitive treatments for eating disorders. *Journal of Consulting and Clinical Psychology, 61,* 261–269.

Wilson, J. J., & Gil, K. M. (1996). The efficacy of psychological and pharmacological interventions for the treatment of chronic disease-related and non-disease-related pain. *Clinical Psychology Review, 16,* 573–597.

Wilson, J. Q. (1997). *Moral judgment.* New York: Basic Books.

Wilson, M. (1984). Female homosexuals' need for dominance and endurance. *Psychological Reports, 55,* 79–82.

Wilson, M., & Daly, M. (1993). An evolutionary perspective on male sexual proprietariness and violence against wives. Special issue: Social and cultural aspects of interpersonal violent behaviors. *Violence and Victims, 8,* 271–294.

Wilt, S. A., Fagan, J., & Davies, G. (1997). *Spatial and structural predictors of domestic and nondomestic homicides of women.* Paper presented at the Fifth International Family Violence Research Conference, July, 1997, Durham, NH.

Wincze, J. P. (1989). Assessment and treatment of atypical sexual behavior. In S. R. Leiblum & R. C. Rosen (Eds.), *Principles and practice of sex therapy.* New York: Guilford Press.

Wincze, J. P., Bansal, S., & Malamud, M. (1986). Effects of medroxyprogesterone acetate on subjective arousal, arousal to erotic stimulation, and nocturnal penile tumescence in male sex offenders. *Archives of Sexual Behavior, 15*(4), 293–305.

Wing, L. (1993). The definition and prevalence of autism: A review. *European Child and Adolescent Psychiatry, 2,* 61–74.

Wing, L., & Attwood, A. (1987). Syndromes of autism and atypical development. In D. J. Cohen & A. Donnelan (Eds.), *Handbook of autism* (pp. 3–17). New York: Wiley.

Wing, L., & Gould, J. (1979). Severe impairments of social interaction and associated abnormalities in children: Epidemiology and classification. *Journal of Autism and Developmental Disorders, 9,* 11–29.

Winick, B. J. (1997). *The right to refuse mental health treatment.* Washington, DC: American Psychological Association.

Winokur, G., Coryell, W., Endicott, J., & Akiskal, H. (1993). Further distinctions between manic-depressive illness (bipolar disorder) and primary depressive disorder (unipolar depression). *American Journal of Psychiatry, 150,* 1176–1181.

Winokur, G., Coryell, W., Keller, M., Endicott, J., & Leon, A. (1995). A family study of manic-depressive (Bipolar I) disease: Is it a distinct illness separable from primary unipolar depression? *Archives of General Psychiatry, 52,* 367–373.

Wise, R. A. (1988). The neurobiology of craving: Implications for the understanding and treatment of addiction. *Journal of Abnormal Psychology, 97,* 118–132.

Wittchen, H. U., & Essau, C. A. (1993). Epidemiology of panic disorder: Progress and unresolved issues. *Journal of Psychiatric Research, 27,* 47–68.

Wittchen, H. U., Zhao, S., Kessler, R. C., & Eaton, W. W. (1994). DSM-III-R generalized anxiety disorder in the National Comorbidity Survey. *Archives of General Psychiatry, 51,* 355–364.

Witzig, J. S. (1968). The group treatment of male exhibitionists. *American Journal of Psychiatry, 25,* 75–81.

Wolf, S., & Wolff, H. G. (1947). *Human gastric functions.* New York: Oxford University Press.

Wolpe, J. (1958). *Psychotherapy by reciprocal inhibition.* Stanford, CA: Stanford University Press.

Wolpe, J. (1969). *The practice of behavior therapy.* New York: Pergamon Press.

Wolpe, J. (1973). *The practice of behavior therapy* (2nd ed.). New York: Pergamon Press.

Wolpe, J. (1976). *Theme and variations: A behavior therapy casebook.* Elmsford, NY: Pergamon Press.

Wolpe, J., & Rowan, V. C. (1988). Panic disorder: A product of classical conditioning. *Behaviour Research and Therapy, 26,* 441–450.

Wolpe, J., & Wolpe, D. (1981). *Our useless fears.* Boston: Houghton Mifflin.

Wong, D. F., Gjedde, A., Wagner, H. N., Jr., Tune, L. E., Dannals, R. F., Pearlsson, G. D., Links, J. M., Tamminga, C. A., Broussolle, E. P., Ravert, H. T., Wilson, A. A., Toung, J. K. T., Malat, J., Williams, F. A., O'Touma, L. A., Snyder, S. H., Kuhar, M. J., & Gjedde, A. (1986). Positron emission tomography reveals elevated D2 dopamine receptors in drug-naive schizophrenics. *Science, 234,* 1558–1563.

Woodruff, P. W .R., Wright, I. C., Bullmore, E. T., Brammer, M., Howard, R. J., Williams, S. C. R., Shapleske, J., Rossel, S., David, A. S., McGuire, P. K., & Murray, R. M. (1997). Auditory hallucinations and the temporal cortical response to speech in schizophrenia: A functional magnetic resonance imaging study. *American Journal of Psychiatry, 154,* 1676–1682.

Woods, J. H., Katz, J. L., & Winger, G. (1987). Abuse liability of benzo-diazepines. *Pharmacological Reviews, 39,* 251–413.

Woody, G. E., McLellan, A. T., Luborsky, L., & O'Brien, C. P. (1995). Psychotherapy in community methadone programs. *American Journal of Psychiatry, 152,* 1302–1308.

Woolson, A. M., & Swanson, M. G. (1972). The second time around: Psychotherapy with the "hysterical woman." *Psychotherapy: Theory, Research, and Practice, 9,* 168–173.

Worden, J. K., Flynn, B. S., Secker-Walker, R. H., Soloman, L. J., Badger, G., & Carpenter, J. (1996). Using mass media to prevent cigarette smoking among adolescent girls. *Health Education Quarterly, 23,* 453–468.

Wright, L. (1994). *Remembering Satan.* New York: Knopf.

Wright, P., Takei, N., Rifkin, L., & Murray, R. M. (1995). Maternal influenza, obstetric complications, and schizophrenia. *American Journal of Psychiatry, 152,* 1714–1720.

Wulfert, E., Greenway, D. E., & Dougher, M. J. (1996). A logical functional analysis of reinforcement-based disorders: Alcoholism and pedophilia. *Journal of Consulting and Clinical Psychology, 64,* 1140–1151.

Wyatt v. Stickney, (1972). 1974 AL. 503 Fed 1305. U.S. Court of Appeals, 5th Circuit.

Wylie, K. R. (1997). Treatment outcome of brief couple therapy in psychogenic erectile disorder. *Archives of Sexual Behavior, 26,* 527–545.

Wynne, L. C., & Singer, M. T. (1963). Thought disorder and family relations of schizophrenics: I. A research strategy. *Archives of General Psychiatry, 9,* 191–198.

Wynne, L. C., Singer, M. T., Bartko, J. J., & Toohey, M. L. (1975). Schizophrenics and their families: Recent research on parental communication. In J. M. Tanner (Ed.), *Psychiatric research: The widening perspective.* New York: International Universities Press.

Yang, B., & Clum, G. A. (1996). Effects of early negative life experiences on cognitive functioning and risk for suicide: A review. *Clinical Psychology Review, 16,* 177–195.

Yehuda, R., Levengood, R. A., Schmeidler, J., Wilson, S., Guo, L. S., & Gerber, D. (1996). Increased pituitary activation following metyrapone administration in post-traumatic stress disorder. *Psychoneuroendocrinology, 21,* 1–16.

Yehuda, R., Teicher, M. H., Trestman, R. L., Levengood, R. A., & Siever, L. J. (1996). Cortisol regulation in posttraumatic stress disorder and major depression: A chronobiological analysis. *Biological Psychiatry, 40,* 79–88.

Yetman, N. R. (1994). Race and ethnic inequality. In C. Calhoun & G. Ritzer (Eds.), *Social problems.* New York: McGraw-Hill/Primis.

Yirmiya, N., Solomonica-Levi, D., Schulman, C., & Pilowsky, T. (1996). Theory of mind abilities in individuals with autism, Down syndrome, and mental retardation of unknown etiology: The role of age and intelligence. *Journal of Child Psychology and Psychiatry, 37,* 1003–1014.

Yonkers, K. A., & Gurguis, G. (1995). Gender differences in the prevalence and expression of anxiety disorders. In M.V. Seeman (Ed.), *Gender and psychopathology* (pp. 113–130). Washington, DC: American Psychiatric Press.

Young, D. M. (1997). Depression. In W. S. Tseng & J. Streltzer (Eds.), *Culture & psychopathology: A guide to clinical assessment* (pp. 28–45). New York: Brunner/Mazel.

Young, J. E., Beck, A. T., & Weinberger, A. (1993). Depression. In D. H. Barlow (Ed.), *Clinical handbook of psycho-logical disorders: A step-by-step treatment manual* (pp. 240–277). New York: Guilford Press.

Young, J. G., Kavanagh, M. E., Anderson, G. M., Shaywitz, B. A., & Cohen, D. J. (1982). Clinical neurochemistry of autism and associated disorders. *Journal of Autism and Developmental Disorders, 12,* 147–165.

Young, M. A., Meaden, P. M., Fogg, L. F., Cherin, E. A., & Eastman, C. I. (1997). Which environmental variables are related to the onset of seasonal affective disorder? *Journal of Abnormal Psychology, 106,* 554–562.

Youngbird v. Romeo, 102 S. Ct. 2452, 2462, 2463 (1982).

Zagon, I. K. (1995). Psychopathy: A viable alternative to antisocial personality disorder? *Australian Psychologist, 30,* 11–16.

Zahn-Waxler, C. (1993). Warriors and worriers: Gender and psychopathology. *Development and Psychopathology, 5,* 79–89.

Zaidel, D. W., Esiri, M. M., & Harrison, P. J. (1997). Size, shape, and orientation of neurons in the left and right hippocampus: Investigation of normal asymmetries and alterations in schizophrenia. *American Journal of Psychiatry, 154,* 812–818.

Zarit, S. H. (1992). Concepts and measures in family caregiving research. In B. Bauer (Ed.), *Conceptual and methodological issues in family caregiver research* (pp. 1–19). Toronto, Canada: University of Toronto Press.

Zarit, S. H. (1994). Research perspectives on family caregiving. In M. Cantor (Ed.), *Family caregiving: Agenda for the future* (pp. 9–24). San Francisco: American Society on Aging.

Zarit, S. H., Orr, N. K., & Zarit, J. M. (1985). *The hidden victims of Alzheimer's disease: Families under stress.* New York: New York University Press.

Zax, M., & Stricker, G. (1963). *Patterns of psychopathology: Case studies in behavioral dysfunction.* New York and London: Macmillan.

Zeskind, P. S., & Ramey, C. T. (1981). Preventing intellectual and interactional sequelae of fetal malnutrition: A longitudinal, transactional, and synergistic approach to development. *Child Development, 52,* 213–218.

Zhang-Wong, J., Beiser, M., Bean, G., & Iacono, W. G. (1995). Five-year course of schizophreniform disorder. *Psychiatry Research, 59,* 109–117.

Zigler, E. (1994). Reshaping early childhood intervention to be a more effective weapon against poverty. *American Journal of Community Psychology, 22,* 37–46.

Zigman, W. M., Schupf, N., Zigman, A., et al. (1993). Aging and Alzheimer disease in people with mental retardation. *International Review of Research in Mental Retardation, 19,* 63.

Zinborg, R. E., Barlow, D. H., Liebowitz, M., Street, L., Broadhead, E., Katon, W., Roy-Byrne, P., Lepine, J. P., Teherani, M., Richards, J., Brantley, P. J., & Kraemer, H. (1994). The DSM-IV field trial for mixed anxiety-depression. *American Journal of Psychiatry, 151,* 1153–1162.

Zoccolillo, M. (1993). Gender and the development of conduct disorder. *Development and Psychopathology, 5,* 65–78.

Zoccolillo, M., & Rogers, K. (1991). Characteristics and outcome of hospitalized adolescent girls with conduct disorder. *Journal of the American Academy of Child and Adolescent Psychiatry, 30,* 973–981.

Zucker, K. J., & Bradley, S. J. (1995). *Gender identity disorder and psychosexual problems in children and adolescents.* New York: Guilford Press.

Zuckerman, B., & Frank, D. A. (1992). "Crack kids": Not broken. *Pediatrics, 89,* 337–339.

Credits

PHOTOGRAPHS

Chapter 1
Opener: © Jim Pickerell/The Image Works, 4: © Paul Conklin/PhotoEdit, 6: © Jeff Greenberg/ Photo Researchers, 10: Corbis-Bettmann, 13: Scala/Art Resource, 15: Diputacion de Valencia, 16 top: Corbis-Bettmann, 16 bottom: Belzeaux/ Photo Researchers, 17: Corbis-Bettmann, 22: Corbis-Bettmann, 21: © Eunice Harris/Photo Researchers.

Chapter 2
26: © Will & Deni McIntyre/SPL/ Photo Researchers, 28: © Victor Habbick Visions/ SPL/Photo Researchers, 30: David Frazier PhotoLibrary CD, 37: © Alan Carey/The Image Works, 41: © Dan McCoy/Rainbow, 42 bottom: © Bob Daemmrich/The Image Works, 42 top: Reproduced by permission of The Psychological Corporation, 43: Reproduced by permission of The Psychological Corporation, 44, 50: © Richard Nowitz/Photo Researchers, 51: © Jeff Greenberg/The Picture Cube, 52: © Phil McCarten/PhotoEdit.

Chapter 3
Opener: © Randy Duchaine/The Stock Market, 60: © Chuck Savage/The Stock Market, 64: © Erich Hartmann/Magnum, 65: © Sidney Harris, 68: © Donna DeCesare/Impact Visuals, 70: © John A. Giordano/SABA.

Chapter 4
Opener: © Skjold/The Image Works, 79: © Will McIntyre/Photo Researchers, 80 : © Bob Sacha, 83: © CNRI/SPL/Photo Researchers, 89: © Wellcome Dept. of Cognitive Neurology/SPL/ Photo Researchers, 90: © A. Glauberman/ Photo Researchers, 93: © John Ficara/Woodfin Camp, 95: © Lynne J. Weinstein/Woodfin Camp, 96: Mary Evans Picture Library, 98: © Tom McCarthy/PhotoEdit, 100: Corbis-Bettmann, 101: Corbis-Bettmann, 102: Corbis-Bettmann, 103 left: Corbis-Bettmann, 103 right: © Alan Carey/The Image Works, 104: Manuscript Library, Yale University Library, 105: Freud Museum London, 106: Rousseau, Henri. The Dream. 1910. Oil on canvas, 6'8½" x 9'9½". The Museum of Modern Art, New York. Gift of Nelson A. Rockefeller. Photograph © 1995 The Museum of Modern Art, New York, 111: © James Pickerell/The Image Works, 116: © John Neubauer/PhotoEdit.

Chapter 5
Opener: © SuperStock, 123: Archives of the History of American Psychology, 124: © Joe McNally, 128: © Martha Cooper/Peter Arnold, 130: The Far Side, © 1987 Universal Press Syndicate. Reprinted with permission,

133: © Sidney Harris, 137: © Bob Daemmerich/ Stock, Boston, 138: © Richard T. Nowitz/Photo Researchers, 141: © Kirk Condyles/Impact Visuals.

Chapter 6
Opener: © Jerry Driendl/FPG International, 152: © Arthur Tress/Photo Researchers, 154: © David Grossman/Photo Researchers, 155: © Collins/Monkmeyer, 158: © Jeffrey D. Smith/Woodfin Camp, 160: Corbis-Bettmann, 162 left: © Will & Deni McIntyre/Photo Researchers, 162 right: © Richard T. Nowitz/ Photo Researchers, 164: © Nubar Alexanian/ Stock, Boston, 172: © Damien Lovegrove/ SPL/Photo Researchers.

Chapter 7
Opener: © Jasen Melson, From "Telling Without Talking" by Barry M. Cohen and Carol Thayer Cox, 179: Corbis-Bettmann, 182: The Kobal Collection, 186: AP/Wide World Photos, 185: Courtesy Dr. Bennett Braun, 190: Michael Newman/PhotoEdit, 191: Susan Ragan/Corbis-Bettmann, 193: Corbis-Bettmann, 194: © Robert Brenner/ PhotoEdit, 196: Gerry Goodstein/Hartman Theatre Company, 201: Mary Evans Picture Library/ Photo Researchers, 203: © Terry Vine/Tony Stone Images.

Chapter 8
Opener: © Mark Richards/PhotoEdit, 209: © Brian Brake/Photo Researchers, 213: © David Young-Wolff/PhotoEdit, 215: © SuperStock, 217: © Hank Morgan/Photo Researchers, 220: © Bernstein/Gamma Liaison, 221: © Alon Reininger/Woodfin Camp, 223: Scala/Art Resource, 225: © Oscar Burriel/Latin Stock/ SPL/Photo Researchers, 229: © David Young-Wolff/PhotoEdit.

Chapter 9
Opener: © David Young-Wolff/PhotoEdit, 239: Corbis-Bettmann, 241: © David Young-Wolff/ PhotoEdit, 243: © Jane O'Neal/The Kobal Collection, 245 left: © Sylvia Beach Collection/ Photo Researchers, 245 right: Corbis-Bettmann, 247: © Kathy McLaughlin/The Image Works, 250: © Goldberg/Monkmeyer, 253: © Brian Masck/The Muskegon Chronicle, 257: © Reinstein/The Image Works, 261: © David Strickler/The Picture Cube, 263: © Erik Hill/ Anchorage Daily News, 265: © Wellcome Dept. of Cognitive Neurology/ SPL/Photo Researchers, 268: © Stephen Frisch.

Chapter 10
Opener: © Monkmeyer/Kerbs, 276: © Spencer Grant/PhotoEdit, 278: The Kobal Collection, 279: Superstock, 280: © M. Bridwell/PhotoEdit, 288: © Nancy Richmond/The Image Works,

289: © Sidney Harris, 290: © Gary Conner/ PhotoEdit.

Chapter 11
294: © Michael Newman/PhotoEdit, 297: © Robert Brenner/PhotoEdit, 298: Corbis-Bettmann, 301: © A. Glauberman/Photo Researchers, 303: TL Corbis-Bettmann, 303: TM Corbis-Bettmann, 303: TR Corbis-Bettmann, 303 bottom left: Corbis-Bettmann, 303 bottom middle, 303 bottom right: © Lesley Cohen/Shooting Star, 304: © Bill Aron/ PhotoEdit, 306: © John Boykin/PhotoEdit, 311: © Billy E. Barnes/PhotoEdit, 314: Corbis-Bettmann, 316: © James Prince/Photo Researchers, 323: © Bob Daemmrich/The Image Works, 325: © J. Pickerell/The Image Works, 327: © Rudi Vonbriel/PhotoEdit, 329: © D. Crawford/The Image Works.

Chapter 12
334: © Stephanie Rausser/FPG International, 336: The Metropolitan Museum of Art, Rogers Fund, 1941, 338: © Vanessa Vick/ Photo Researchers, 346: © Rob Goldman/FPG International, 348: © Theo Westenberger/ Gamma-Liaison, 349: Courtesy Imagyn Medical Technologies, Inc., 351: © Monkmeyer/Farley, 353: © Susan Leaviges/Photo Researchers, 354: Corbis-Bettmann, 357A: © Rob Crandall/Stock, Boston, 357B: © Rob Crandall/The Image Works, 361 left: AP/Wide World Photos, 361 right: Corbis-Bettmann.

Chapter 13
Opener: National Library of Medicine, 371: The Granger Collection, 373A: Bert, Print by L. Rosen, Courtesy of the Roger Pryor Dodge Collection, Dance Collection, The New York Public Library for the Performing Arts, Astor, Lenox and Tilden Foundations, 373B: From "The Diary of Vaslav Nijinsky:, edited by Romila Nijinsky, Simon & Schuster, NY, 1936, 379: © Eric Roth/The Picture Cube, 380: National Institute for Health, 381: © Monkmeyer/Grunitus, 386: Courtesy of Camarillo State Hospital, 389: Courtesy Edna A. Morlok, 393 left & right: © Tim Beddow/SPL/ Photo Researchers, 397: © David J. Deluhery, 400: Fine Line Features/Shooting Star, 402: © Monkmeyer/Gelfon, 403: © Joel Gordon.

Chapter 14
Opener: © Mehan Kalyn/SPL/Photo Researchers, 411: Corbis-Bettmann, 414: © Richard Pasley/Gamma Liaison, 415: top & bottom: © Biophoto Associates/SPL/Photo Researchers; © Ralph Eagle Jr./Photo Researchers, 421: © Bob Daemmrich/Stock, Boston, 424: Gamma Liaison, 426: Corbis-Bettmann, 430: © Monkmeyer/Shackman.

Chapter 15

Opener: © Bob Daemmrich/Stock,Boston, 439: © Ken Gaghan/Jeroboam, 441: © Jose Azell/Aurora & Quanta Productions, 446: © Monkmeyer/Brady, 447: Kansas City Star/ Gamma Liaison, 449: © Bob Daemmrich/ Stock, Boston, 451: © Dan McCoy/Rainbow, 455: © Heron/ Monkmeyer, 458: Kendall, P.C. (1990). "Coping cat workbook". Ardmore, PA: Workbook Publishing. Reproduced by permission of Philip C. Kendall and Peter Mikulka.

Chapter 16

Opener: © Monkmeyer/MacPherson, 465: © Bill Lyons/Photo Researchers, 467: © CNRI/ SPL/Photo Researchers, 468: © George Steinmetz/National Geographic Society, 470: © Monkmeyer/Shackman, 473: MGM/ Shooting Star, 480: © Conklin/Monkmeyer, 485: © Bob Daemmrich/The Image Works, 487: © Alan Carey/The Image Works.

Chapter 17

Opener: © R. Lord/The Image Works, 501: Corbis-Bettmann, 508: © Ilene Perlman/Stock, Boston, 510: © Lannis Waters/Palm Beach Post, 575: © Steve Allen/Gamma Liaison, 577: © L. Kolvoord/The Image Works.

Chapter 18

Opener: Seattle Times/Gamma Liaison, 524: Gamma Liaison, 528: AP/Wide World Photos, 529: © John Barr/Gamma Liaison, 533: © Renato Rotolo/Gamma Liaison, 536: © SuperStock.

Chapter 19

Opener: © Frances M. Roberts, 546: © Michael Siluk/The Image Works, 547: © S. Agricola/The Image Works, 555: © Monkmeyer/Conklin, 556: © Bob Daemmrich/The Image Works, 559: © Tony Savino/The Image Works.

EXCERPTS, LINE ART, AND TABLES

Chapter 1

7 (case): From *Culture and Mental Illness* by R. J. Castillo. Copyright © 1997 Brooks/Cole Publishing Company, Pacific Grove, CA 93950, a division of International Thomson Publishing Inc. By permission of the publisher. 7 (table 1.1): From "Epidemiology," by A. L. Smith and M. M. Weissman, in *Handbook of Affective Disorders* (p. 118), by E. S. Paykel (Ed.), 1992, New York: The Guilford Press. Copyright © 1992 by Guilford Publications, Inc. Adapted with permission. 14 (quote): From "Hospitals, Madhouses and Asylums: Cycles in the Care of the Insane," by P. Allderidge, 1979, *British Journal of Psychiatry, 134*, p. 327. Copyright © 1979 by Royal College of Psychiatrists. Reprinted with permission. 17 (quote): From *The Mentally Ill in America*, 2nd ed. (p. 165), by A. Deutsch, 1949, New York: Columbia University Press. Copyright © 1949 by Columbia University Press. 20 (box): From "The Story of a Street Person," by Elizabeth Swados, August 18, 1991, *New York Times Magazine*, p. 18. Copyright © 1991 by The New York Times Co. Reprinted with permission. 23 (case): From "African and Western Psychiatry: A Comparison," by T. Asuni, in *Transcultural Psychiatry* (p. 313), by J. L. Cox (Ed.), 1986, London: Croom-Helm,

Ltd. Copyright © 1986 by Routledge. Adapted with permission.

Chapter 2

31 (box): Abstracted with permission from "On Being Sane in Insane Places," by D. L. Rosenhan, 1973, *Science, 179*, p. 253. Copyright © 1973 American Association for the Advancement of Science. 32 (quote): From "More on Pseudoscience in Science and the Case for Psychiatric Diagnosis: A Critique of D. L. Rosenhan's 'On Being Sane in Insane Places' and 'The Contextual Nature of Psychiatric Diagnosis,'" by R. L. Spitzer, 1976, *Archives of General Psychiatry, 33*, p. 469. Copyright © 1976 by American Medical Association. Reprinted with permission. 33 (quotes). Reprinted with permission from the *Diagnostic and Statistical Manual of Mental Disorders*, Fourth Edition. Copyright © 1994 American Psychiatric Association. 35 (figure 2.1): From "Models of Scientific Progress and the Role of Theory in Taxonomy Development: A Case Study of the DSM," by W. C. Follette and A. C. Houts, 1996, *Journal of Consulting and Clinical Psychology, 64*, pp. 1120–1132. Copyright © 1996 by American Psychological Association. Reprinted with permission. 39 (box): From *Structured Clinical Interview for DSM-IV Axis I Disorders (SCID-I)* (p. A1), by M. B. First, R. L. Spitzer, M. Gibbon and J. B. W. Williams, 1997, New York: Biometrics Research Department. Copyright © 1997 by New York State Psychiatric Institute. Adapted with permission. 40 (box): From "An Epidemiologic Assessment of Cognitive Impairment in a Community Population," by C. E. Holzer, III, G. L. Tischler, P. J. Leaf, and J. K. Myers, 1984, *Research in Community and Mental Health, 4*. Copyright © 1984 by JAI Press Inc. Adapted with permission. 42 (figure 2.2): Simulated items similar to those in the Wechsler Intelligence Scales for Adults and Children. Copyright © 1949, 1974, 1981, 1990 by The Psychological Corporation. Reproduced by permission. All rights reserved. 44 (figure 2.4): Simulated items similar to those in the Thematic Apperception Test (TAT). Copyright © 1971 by Henry A. Murray. Reproduced with permission of Mrs. Caroline C. Murray. 48 (table 2.1): From "On the Integration of Personality Assessment Methods: The Rorschach and MMPI," by G. J. Meyer, 1997, *Journal of Personality Assessment, 68*, p. 299. Copyright © 1997 by Lawrence Erlbaum Associates, Inc. Reprinted with permission. 49 (figure 2.5): From "A Visual Motor Gestalt Test and its Clinical Use," by L. Bender, 1938, *Research Monographs of the American Orthopsychiatric Association 3, xi*, p. 176. Copyright © 1938 by American Orthopsychiatric Association. Reprinted with permission. 52 (case): From "The Influence of Language Upon Symptomatology in Foreign-Born Patients," by J. Del Castillo, 1970, *American Journal of Psychiatry, 127*, p. 161. Copyright © 1970 by American Psychiatric Association. Reprinted with permission.

Chapter 3

60 (quote): From "Comments on Strategy and Tactics of Research," by N. E. Miller, in *Changing Frontiers in the Science of Psychotherapy* (p. 348), by A. E. Bergin and H. H.

Strupp (Eds.), 1972, Aldine-Atherton. Copyright © 1972 by Neal E. Miller. Reprinted with permission. 71 (figure 3.2): Reprinted from *Journal of Behavior Therapy and Experimental Psychiatry, 8*, J. A. Kelly and R. S. Drabman, "The Modification of Socially Detrimental Behavior." Copyright © 1977, with permission from Elsevier Science. 72 (figure 3.3): From "The Role of Response Delay in Improving the Discrimination Performance of Autistic Children," by K. Dyer, W. P. Christian, and S. C. Luce, 1982, *Journal of Applied Behavior Analysis, 15*, p. 233. Copyright © 1982 by Department of Human Development, University of Kansas. Reprinted with permission.

Chapter 4

99 (quote): From *In a Different Voice* by Carol Gilligan. Copyright © 1982, 1993 by Carol Gilligan. Reprinted by permission of Harvard University Press.

Chapter 5

130 (list): From *Our Useless Fears* (p. 54), by J. Wolpe and D. Wolpe, 1981, New York: Houghton Mifflin. Copyright © 1981 by Joseph Wolpe. Reprinted by permission. 134 (quote): From *Science and Human Behavior* by B. F. Skinner, © 1953. Reprinted by permission of Prentice-Hall, Inc., Upper Saddle River, NJ. 136 (list): Reprinted from *Clinical Psychology Review, 6*, L. M. Horowitz and J. Vitkus, "The Interpersonal Basis of Psychiatric Symptoms," 1986, with permission from Elsevier Science.

Chapter 6

150 (case): From *DSM-IV Casebook: A Learning Companion to the DSM-IV* (pp. 298–299), by R. L. Spitzer, M. Gibbon, A. E. Skodol, et al. (Eds.), 1994, Washington, DC: American Psychiatric Press, Inc. Copyright © 1994 by American Psychiatric Association. Reprinted with permission. 154 (cases): Reprinted from *Journal of Anxiety Disorders, 10*, C. M. Fink, S. M. Turner and D. C. Beidel, "Culturally Relevant Factors in the Behavioral Treatment of Social Phobia: A Case Study," 1996, with permission from Elsevier Science. 156 (case): From *Obsessions and Compulsions* (pp. 66–67), by S. J. Rachman and R. J. Hodgson, 1980, Upper Saddle River, New Jersey: Prentice-Hall, Inc. Copyright © 1980 by Stanley J. Rachman and Ray J. Hodgson. Reprinted with permission. 158 (quote): Reprinted with the permission of Simon & Schuster from *Everything in its Path* by Kai T. Erikson. Copyright © 1976 by Kai T. Erikson. 166 (figure 6.1): Reprinted from *Behavior Research and Therapy, 24*, D. M. Clark, "A Cognitive Approach to Panic," p. 463. Copyright © 1986, with permission from Elsevier Science.

Chapter 7

178 (case): Adapted from *Journal of Behavior Therapy and Experimental Psychiatry, 16*, L. S. Lyon, "Facilitating Telephone Number Recall in a Case of Psychogenic Amnesia," pp. 147–149. Copyright © 1985, with permission from Elsevier Science. 181 (box): From "Dissociative Disorders," by J. F. Kihlstrom, D. J. Tataryn and I. P. Hoyt, in *Comprehensive Handbook of Psychopathology*, 2nd ed., by P. B. Sutker and H. E. Adams (Eds.), 1993, New York:

Plenum Publishing Corporation. Copyright © 1993 by Plenum Publishing Corporation. Abstracted with permission. **182** (case): From *Principles of Dynamic Psychiatry*, 2nd ed. (pp. 35–37), by J. H. Masserman, 1961, Philadelphia: W. B. Saunders Company. Copyright © 1961 by W. B. Saunders Company. Adapted with permission. **183** (case): From *The Three Faces of Eve*, by C. H. Thigpen, M.D. and H. M. Cleckley, M.D., 1957, New York: McGraw-Hill, Inc. Copyright © 1957 by Corbett H. Thigpen and H. M. Cleckley. Reprinted with permission of Mrs. Emily S. Cleckley. **183** (quotes): From "The Anguish Behind the Three Faces of Eve," by D. Nunes, (September 15, 1975), *New York Post*, p. 4. Copyright © 1975 by New York Post. **188** (case): From "Feeling Unreal: 30 Cases of DSM-III-R Depersonalization Disorder," by D. Simeon, S. Gross, O. Guralnik, D. J. Stein, J. Schmeidler and E. Hollander, 1997, *American Journal of Psychiatry, 154*, pp.1107–1113. Copyright © 1997 by American Psychiatric Association. Reprinted with permission. **191** (quotes): From *The Hillside Strangler* by J. R. Schwarz. Copyright © 1981 by Ted Schwarz. Used by permission of Doubleday, a division of Bantam Doubleday Dell Publishing Group, Inc. **195** (case): From "Case Study: Body Dysmorphic Disorder in Adolescents," by K. A. Phillips, K. D. Atala and R. S. Albertini, 1995, *Journal of the American Academy of Child and Adolescent Psychiatry, 34*, pp. 1216–1220. Copyright © 1995 by Williams & Wilkins Publishing House. Reprinted with permission. **198** (case): From "Somatization," by S. L. Chaplin, in *Culture and Psychopathology: A Guide to Clinical Assessment* (pp. 69–70), by W. S. Tseng and J. Streltzer (Eds.), 1997, New York: Brunner/Mazel, Inc. Copyright © 1997 by Brunner/Mazel, Inc. Reprinted with permission.

Chapter 8

208 (quotes): Reprinted with permission from the *Diagnostic and Statistical Manual of Mental Disorders*, Fourth Edition. Copyright © 1994 American Psychiatric Association. **228** (figure 8.1): From *Differential Mortality in the United States: A Study in Socioeconomic Epidemiology* by Evelyn M. Kitagawa and Philip M. Hauser. Copyright © 1973 by the President and Fellows of Harvard College. Reprinted by permission of Harvard University Press. **233** (figures 8.2 & 8.3): From "Stress and Infectious Disease in Humans," by S. Cohen and G. M. Williamson, 1991, *Psychological Bulletin, 109*, p. 8. Copyright © 1991 by American Psychological Association. Adapted with permission.

Chapter 9

238, 240 (cases): From *Psychopathology: A Casebook* (pp. 115, 118), by R. L. Spitzer, A. E. Skodol, M. Gibbon and J. B. W. Williams, 1983, New York: McGraw-Hill, Inc. Copyright © 1983 by McGraw-Hill, Inc. Reprinted with permission. **243** (case): From *Modern Clinical Psychiatry*, 10th ed. (pp. 376–377), by L. C. Kolb, 1982, Philadelphia: W. B. Saunders Company. Copyright © 1982 by W. B. Saunders Company. Reprinted with permission. **249** (figure 9.1): From "Epidemiology of Suicide," by E. K. Moscicki, 1995, *International Psychogeriatrics, 7*, p. 140. Copyright © by Springer

Publishing Company, Inc., New York 10012. Adapted with permission. **251** (list): From "A Conspectus of the Suicidal Scenario," by E. S. Shneidman, in *Assessment and Prediction of Suicide* (pp. 51–52), by R. W. Maris, A. L. Berman, J. T. Maltsberger and R. I. Yufit (Eds.), 1992, New York: The Guilford Press. Copyright © 1992 by The Guilford Press. Reprinted with permission. **259** (figure 9.4): From "Depression," by J. E. Young, A. T. Beck and A. Weinberger, in *Clinical Handbook of Psychological Disorders: A Step-by-Step Treatment Manual* (p. 250), by D. H. Barlow (Ed.), 1993, New York: The Guilford Press. Copyright © 1993 by Guilford Publications, Inc. Reprinted with permission.

Chapter 10

274 (case): From "Personality Disorders," by T. A. Widiger and C. J. Sanderson, in *Psychiatry*, vol. 2 (pp. 1291–1317), by A. Tasman, J. Kay, and J. A. Lieberman (Eds.), 1997, Philadelphia: W. B. Saunders Company. Copyright © 1997 by W. B. Saunders Company. Reprinted with permission. **274** (quotes): Reprinted with permission from the *Diagnostic and Statistical Manual of Mental Disorders*, Fourth Edition. Copyright © 1994 American Psychiatric Association. **276** (case): From *DSM-IV Case Studies: A Clinical Guide To Differential Diagnosis*, (pp. 288–289), by A. Frances and R. Ross, 1996, Washington, DC: American Psychiatric Press, Inc. Copyright © 1996 by American Psychiatric Association. Reprinted with permission. **281** (case): From *A DSM III R Casebook of Treatment Selection* (pp. 324–326), by S. Perry, A. Frances and J. Clarkin, 1990, New York: Brunner/Mazel, Inc. Copyright © 1990 by Brunner/Mazel, Inc. Reprinted with permission. **281** (case): From *DSM-IV Casebook: A Learning Companion to the DSM-IV* (pp. 179–180), by R. L. Spitzer, M. Gibbon, A. E. Skodol, et al. (Eds.), 1994, Washington, DC: American Psychiatric Press, Inc. Copyright © 1994 by American Psychiatric Association. Reprinted with permission.

Chapter 11

299 (case): From "Alcohol-Impaired Driving: The Family's Tragedy and the Public's Health," by B. Templeton, 1997, *Journal of the American Medical Association, 277*, p. 1279. Copyright © 1997 by American Medical Association. Adapted with permission. **299, 300** (tables 11.1 and 11.2): From *Drugs, Society and Human Behavior*, 6th ed., by O. S. Ray and C. J. Ksir, 1993, New York: McGraw-Hill, Inc. Copyright © 1993 by McGraw-Hill, Inc. Adapted with permission. **309** (figure 11.1): From "Despite Increasing Hostility, One in Four Americans Still Smokes," by L. Hugick and J. Leonard, 1991, *Gallup Poll Monthly* (December). Copyright © 1991 Gallup Poll News Service. Reprinted with permission. **317** (quote): From "LSD Discoverer Disputes 'Chance' Factor in Finding," by A. Hoffman, 1971, *Psychiatric News, 6 (9)*, p. 23. Copyright © 1971 by American Psychiatric Association. Reprinted with permission. **317** (figure 11.3): From "Abstinence Symptomatology and Psychiatric Diagnosis in Cocaine Abusers," by F. H. Gawin and H. D. Kleber, 1986, *Archives of General Psychiatry, 43*, pp. 107–113. Copyright © 1986 by American Medical Association. Reprinted with permission. **319** (quote): From "What a

Physician Should Know About Marijuana," by J. R. Tinklenberg, 1975, *Rational Drug Therapy, 4*, p. 4. Copyright © 1975 by W. B. Saunders Company. Reprinted with permission. **324** (case): From "Eliminating Treatment Dropout of Substance Abusing or Dependent Delinquents Through Home-Based Multisystemic Therapy," by S. W. Henggeler, S. G. Pickrel, M. J. Brondino and J. L. Crouch, 1996, *American Journal of Psychiatry, 153*, pp. 427–428. Copyright © 1994 by American Psychiatric Association. Adapted with permission.

Chapter 12

336 (case): From *DSM-IV Casebook: A Learning Companion to the DSM-IV* (pp. 266–267), by R. L. Spitzer, M. Gibbon, A. E. Skodol, et al. (Eds.), 1994, Washington, DC: American Psychiatric Press, Inc. Copyright © 1994 by American Psychiatric Association. Reprinted with permission. **341, 342, 363–364** (cases): Unpublished case examples from the clinical files of Dr. Richard Carroll, Northwestern University Medical School, Chicago, Illinois. Reprinted with permission. **343, 344, 345** (tables 12.1 & 12.2, figure 12.1): From *The Social Organization of Sexuality: Sexual Practices in the United States* (pp. 369–371), by E. O. Laumann, J. H. Gagnon, R. T. Michael and S. Michaels, 1994, Chicago: The University of Chicago Press. Copyright © 1994 by The University of Chicago Press. Adapted with permission. **344** (quote): From *The Psychoanalytic Theory of Neurosis* (p. 170), by O. Fenichel, 1945, New York: W. W. Norton & Company, Inc. Copyright © 1945 by W. W. Norton & Company, Inc. Reprinted with permission. **345** (quote): From *Human Sexual Inadequacy* (p. 177), by W. H. Masters and V. E. Johnson, 1970, St. Louis, Missouri: Masters & Johnson Institute. Copyright © 1970 by Dr. W. H. Masters. **352** (case): From *Study Guide to DSM-IV* (p. 295), by M. A. Fauman, 1994, Washington, DC: American Psychiatric Press, Inc. Copyright © 1994 by American Psychiatric Association. Reprinted with permission.

Chapter 13

371 (case): Excerpt from *Is There No Place on Earth for Me?* by Susan Sheehan. Copyright © 1982 by Susan Sheehan. Reprinted by permission of Houghton Mifflin Company. All rights reserved. **374** (letter): From *Dementia Praecox or the Group of Schizophrenia*, trans. J. Zinkin (p. 17), by E. Bleuler, 1911/1950, Madison, Connecticut: International Universities Press, Inc. Copyright © 1911, 1950 by International Universities Press, Inc. Reprinted with permission. **375, 378** (cases): Unpublished case examples from the clinical files of Dr. Richard L. Hagen, Florida State University. Adapted with permission. **376** (case): From "What is it Like to Have Schizophrenia?" by L. Benioff, in *Treating Schizophrenia* (p. 88), by S. Vinogradov (Ed.), 1995, San Francisco: Jossey-Bass, Publishers. Copyright © 1995 by Jossey-Bass, Publishers. Reprinted with permission. **376** (quote): From "Disorders of Attention and Perception in Early Schizophrenia," by A. McGhie and J. Chapman, 1961, *British Journal of Medical Psychology*, pp. 105, 108. Copyright © 1961 by British Psychological Society. Access with permission from *British Journal of Medical Psychology,* The British Psychological Society. **377 (quotes in box):** From "Patients' Attitudes Toward Hallucinations," by L. J. Miller, E. O'Connor and T. DiPasquale, 1993, *American Journal of Psychiatry,* 150, pp. 586-587. Copyright © 1993 by American Psychiatric Association. Reprinted with permission. **380–381 (case):** From "Outcome and Treatment Strategies," by G. K. Booth, in *Treating Schizophrenia* (pp. 166–169), by S. Vinogradov (Ed.), 1995, San Francisco: Jossey-Bass, Publishers. Copyright © 1995 by Jossey-Bass, Publishers. Reprinted with permission. **382 (case):** From *ICD-10 Casebook: The Many Faces of Mental Disorders—Adult Case Histories According to ICD-10* (pp. 67–69), by T. B. Üstün, A. Bertelsen, H. Dilling, J. vanDrimmelen, C. Pull, A. Okasha, N. Sartorius, et al., 1996, Switzerland: World Health Organization. Copyright © 1996 by World Health Organization. Reprinted with permission. **382 (case):** From "When Does Amphetamine-Induced Psychosis Become Schizophrenia?" by M. Flaum and S. K. Schultz, 1996, *American Journal of Psychiatry,* 106, pp. 812–813. Copyright © 1996 by American Psychiatric Association. Reprinted with permission. **385 (case):** Bernheim, Kayla F., *The LANAHAN Cases and Readings in Abnormal Behavior* (Baltimore: LANAHAN, 1997), pp. 132–134. Copyright © 1997 by LANAHAN PUBLISHERS, INC. Adapted by permission of the publisher. **388 (figure 13.1):** From *Schizophrenia Genesis: The Origins of Madness* by Irving I. Gottesman. Copyright © 1991 by Irving I. Gottesman. Used with permission. **390 (list):** From "Birth Defects and Schizophrenia," by S. A. Mednick, 1971, *Psychology Today, 4,* p. 80. Reprinted with permission from Psychology Today Magazine, Copyright © 1971 by Sussex Publishers, Inc. **394 (figure 13.2):** From "Schizophrenia and Season of Birth," by E. Hare, L. Bulusu and A. Adelstein, 1979, *Population Trends, 17.* Adapted with permission of Office for National Statistics, London. © Crown copyright. **400 (quote):** From "Toward a Theory of Schizophrenia," by G. Bateson, D. Jackson, J. Haley and J. Weakland, 1956, *Behavioral Science, 1,* p. 251. Copyright © 1956 by Behavioral Science. Reprinted with permission. **401 (quote):** From "Thought Disorder and Family Relations of Schizophrenics: A Research Strategy," by L. C. Wynne and M. T. Singer, 1963, *Archives of General Psychiatry, 9,* p. 195. Copyright © 1963 by American Medical Association. Reprinted with permission. **402 (case):** From "An Illustration of a Behavioral Therapy Intervention With Nursing Staff in a Therapeutic Role," by L. Sushinsky, 1970, *Journal of Psychiatric Nursing and Mental Health Services, 8(5),* p. 24. Copyright © 1970 by Slack, Inc. Reprinted with permission.

Chapter 14
413 (quotes): Reprinted with the permission of Simon & Schuster from *The Man Who Mistook His Wife for a Hat and Other Clinical Tales* by Oliver Sacks. Copyright © 1970, 1981, 1983, 1984, 1985 by Oliver Sacks. **416 (case):** From *Study Guide to DSM-IV* (p. 63), by M. A. Fauman, 1994, Washington, DC: American Psychiatric Press, Inc. Copyright © 1994 by American Psychiatric Association. Reprinted with permission. **417 (figure 14.1):** From "The Worst Case," by M. Farber, (December 1994), *Sports Illustrated.* Illustration by Paragraphics. Copyright © 1994 by Paragraphics. Adapted by permission. **428 (box):** From "Concepts and Measures in Family Caregiving Research," by S. H. Zarit, in *Conceptual and Methodological Issues in Family Caregiver Research* (pp. 1–5), by B. Bauer (Ed.), 1992, Canada: Faculty of Nursing, University of Toronto. Copyright © 1992 by Faculty of Nursing, University of Toronto. Reprinted with permission.

Chapter 15
438 (case): Unpublished case examples from the clinical files of Dr. Karen L. Bierman, Pennsylvania State University. Adapted with permission. **440, 445 (cases):** Unpublished case examples from the personal files of Dr. Andrew R. Eisen, Fairleigh Dickinson University, Teaneck, New Jersey. Reprinted with permission. **442 (case):** From *Casebook in Child Behavior Disorders* by C. A. Kearney. Copyright © 1999 Brooks/Cole Publishing Company, Pacific Grove, CA 93950, a division of International Thomson Publishing Inc. By permission of the publisher. **448 (case):** From *The Golden Cage: The Enigma of Anorexia Nervosa* by H. Bruch. Copyright © 1978 by the President and Fellows of Harvard College. Reprinted by permission of Harvard University Press.

Chapter 16
464 (case): From "The Mentally Retarded, Emotionally Disturbed Adult," by S. Reiss, in *Children With Emotional Disorders and Developmental Disabilities* (pp. 173–174), by M. Seligman (Ed.), 1985, Needham Heights, Massachusetts: Allyn & Bacon. Copyright © 1985 by Allyn & Bacon. Adapted with permission. **464 (quote):** Reprinted with permission from the *Diagnostic and Statistical Manual of Mental Disorders,* Fourth Edition. Copyright © 1994 American Psychiatric Association. **466 (figure 16.1):** From *The Fragile X Syndrome: Diagnosis, Biochemistry, and Intervention,* by R. J. Hagerman and P. M. McBogg, 1983, Dillon, Colorado: Spectra Publishing. Copyright © 1983 by National Fragile X Foundation, 1441 York Street, Suite 303, Denver, Colorado 80206. Reprinted with permission. **474 (quote):** From *Medical Evaluation of Individuals with an Autistic Disorder,* by M. Coleman, 1989, Forum Medicum, Inc. Copyright © 1989. Reprinted with permission. **476 (case):** From *Casebook in Child Behavior Disorders* by C. A. Kearney. Copyright © 1999 Brooks/Cole Publishing Company, Pacific Grove, CA 93950, a division of International Thomson Publishing Inc. By permission of the publisher. **478 (figure 16.2):** Adapted from H. Naruse and E. M. Ornitz (Eds.), *Neurobiology of Infantile Autism,* 1992, (pp. 43–57) "Neuropathology of Infantile Autism," by T. L. Kemper and M. L. Bauman, with permission from Elsevier Science.

Chapter 17
495 (list): Reprinted with permission from the *Diagnostic and Statistical Manual of Mental Disorders,* Fourth Edition. Copyright © 1994 American Psychiatric Association. **495 (quote):** From *The Mask of Sanity* (p. 342), by H. M. Cleckley, 1976, St. Louis, Missouri: Mosby-Year Book, Inc. Copyright © 1976 by H. M. Cleckley. Reprinted with permission of Mrs. Emily S. Cleckley. **496 (quote):** From *Patterns of Psychopathology: Case Studies in Behavioral Dysfunction* (p. 240), by M. Zax and G. Stricker, 1963, New York: Macmillan/Simon & Schuster, Inc. Copyright © 1963 by Prentice-Hall, Inc. Reprinted with permission. **497 (case):** From "The Extreme Regressive Reaction of a Psychopath," by G. N. Conacher and R. L. Fleming, 1996, *Psychiatric Quarterly,* vol. 67, pp. 1–10. Copyright © 1996 by Plenum Publishing Corporation. Reprinted with permission. **505 (figure 17.2):** From "Current Directions," by E. B. Foa and D. S. Riggs, 1995, *Psychological Science, 4(23),* pp. 61–65. Copyright © 1995 by Blackwell Publishers. Adapted with permission.

Chapter 18
526 (list): From *Model Penal Code, sec. 4.01,* 1962. Copyright © 1985 by The American Law Institute; as adopted at the 1962 Annual Meeting of The American Law Institute. Reprinted with permission. **534 (quote):** From "On the Justifications for Civil Commitment," by J. M. Livermore, C. P. Malmquist and P. E. Meehl, 1968, *University of Pennsylvania Law Review, 117,* pp. 75–96. Copyright © 1968 by University of Pennsylvania Law Review. Reprinted with permission.

Chapter 19
546 (case): From "First Person Account: Schizophrenia—Adrift in an Anchorless Reality," J. C. Jordan, 1995, *Schizophrenia Bulletin, 21 (3),* pp. 501–503. Copyright © 1995 by Janice C. Jordan. Reprinted with permission. **548 (figure 19.1):** From "Development of Depression From Preadolescence to Young Adulthood: Emerging Gender Differences in a 10-Year Longitudinal Study," by B. L. Hankin, L. Y. Abramson, T. E. Moffitt, et al., 1998, *Journal of Abnormal Psychology, 107,* pp. 128–140. Copyright © 1998 by American Psychological Association. Reprinted with permission. **549 (figure 19.2):** From "Prevention of Depressive Symptoms in Schoolchildren: Two-Year Follow-Up," by J. E. Gillham, K. J. Reivich, L. H. Jaycox and M. E. P. Seligman, 1995, *Psychological Science,* 6, pp. 343–351. Copyright © 1995 by Blackwell Publishers. Reprinted with permission.

End papers
Reprinted with permission from the *Diagnostic and Statistical Manual of Mental Disorders,* Fourth Edition. Copyright © 1994 American Psychiatric Association.

Subject Index

Anxiety Disorders

Panic Disorder without Agoraphobia
Panic Disorder with Agoraphobia
Agoraphobia without History of Panic
  Disorder
Specific Phobia
Social Phobia
Obsessive-Compulsive Disorder
Posttraumatic Stress Disorder
Acute Stress Disorder
Generalized Anxiety Disorder
Anxiety Disorders Due to a General Medical
  Condition
Substance-Induced Anxiety Disorder
Anxiety Disorder NOS

Somatoform Disorders

Somatization Disorder
Undifferentiated Somatoform
  Disorder
Conversion Disorder
Pain Disorder
Hypochondriasis
Body Dysmorphic Disorder
Somatoform Disorder NOS

Factitious Disorders

Factitious Disorder
Factitious Disorder NOS

Dissociative Disorders

Dissociative Amnesia
Dissociative Fugue
Dissociative Identity Disorder
Depersonalization Disorder
Dissociative Disorder NOS

Sexual and Gender Identity Disorders

Sexual Dysfunctions
  Sexual Desire Disorders
    Hypoactive Sexual Desire Disorder
    Sexual Aversion Disorder
  Sexual Arousal Disorders
    Female Sexual Arousal Disorder
    Male Erectile Disorder

Orgasmic Disorders
  Female Orgasmic Disorder
  Male Orgasmic Disorder
  Premature Ejaculation
Sexual Pain Disorders
  Dyspareunia
  Vaginismus
Sexual Dysfunction Due to a General
  Medical Condition
Substance-Induced Sexual Dysfunction
Sexual Dysfunction NOS

Paraphilias
  Exhibitionism
  Fetishism
  Frotteurism
  Pedophilia
  Sexual Masochism
  Sexual Sadism
  Transvestic Fetishism
  Voyeurism
  Paraphilia NOS

Gender Identity Disorders
  Gender Identity Disorder in Children
  Gender Identity Disorder in Adolescents
    or Adults
  Gender Identity Disorder NOS

Other Sexual Disorder
  Sexual Disorder NOS

Eating Disorders

Anorexia Nervosa
Bulimia Nervosa
Eating Disorder NOS

Sleep Disorders

Primary Sleep Disorders
  Dyssomnias
    Primary Insomnia
    Primary Hypersomnia
    Narcolepsy
    Breathing-Related Sleep Disorder
    Circadian Rhythm Sleep Disorder
    Dyssomnia NOS
  Parasomnias
    Nightmare Disorder
    Sleep Terror Disorder
    Sleepwalking Disorder
    Parasomnia NOS